This page has been designed to fold out for easy reference, particularly

How to use this book

Explore Australia begins with an introduction giving information on planning a trip, accommodation, driving in outback conditions, breakdowns and travelling with children. From page 37 both text and maps are colour coded on a state-by-state basis.

The text

Each state section has a general introduction, a detailed description of the capital city and suggested tours, followed by an A–Z listing of towns. Each town description includes:

- a population figure (to provide an idea of the size of the town)
- a listing of what is of interest in the town and in the area
- an address for the local tourist information centre
- a guide to accommodation: hotels, motels, caravan/camping parks, bed & breakfast accommodation and hostels (includes backpacker and youth hostels)
- a reference to the map/s on which the town appears

The maps

Every part of Australia is mapped in *Explore Australia*. Heavily-populated areas are mapped in greater detail. Distance is shown by black and red markers on the maps and a scale bar at the top of each map. A ❶ symbol alongside a town name indicates there is a description of the town in the A–Z listing for that state.

Cont... ...up to another there is always some overlap when maps are at the same scale. The symbol on the edges of the map pages indicates the next map page that should be turned to. **283**

Feature maps of holiday regions: Holiday regions are mapped to show tourist highlights in detail.

Inter-city route maps: These maps have been designed to help you plan your route between major cities. Information is given on distances between the towns along each route, roadside rest areas and road conditions where relevant.

Cross-references

Text to maps: Each town described in the A–Z listings includes a reference to the map/s on which the town appears.

Maps to text: The ❶ symbol alongside a town name on the maps indicates there is a description of that town in the text.

The index

To find out about a particular place mentioned in the text or shown on a map, it is essential to use the index. For example:

Sale	Vic.	225 M6,		179, 190,	**194**
Town	State	Sale appears on this map page	Grid reference	Sale is mentioned on these pages	Main text entry about Sale

Symbols used on the maps

Freeway with Freeway Route Number	▰▰ F3 ▰▰	
Freeway under construction	▰▰▰▰▰	
Highway, sealed, with National Route Number	31	
Highway, sealed, with Metroad Route Number	5	
Highway, unsealed, with Tasmania Route Number	A10	
Highway under construction	▰▰▰▰	
Main road, sealed, with State Route Number	156	
Main road, unsealed		
Main road under construction		
Secondary road, with Tourist Route		
Secondary road unsealed		
Other road, with traffic direction arrow	←	
Other road, unsealed		
Vehicle track		
Walking track		
Railway with station	Paratoo	
Underground railway with station	Flagstaff	
Total kilometres between two points	114	
Intermediate kilometres	77	
State border		
Major fence line	Vermin Proof Fence	
Lake		
Intermittent lake		
Aboriginal land		
State capital city	**DARWIN**	
Town, over 50 000 inhabitants	**GEELONG** ○	
Town, 10 000–50 000 inhabitants	**Bairnsdale** ○	
Town, 5 000–10 000 inhabitants	Hamilton ○	
Town, 1 000–5 000 inhabitants	Maffra ○	
Town, 200–1 000 inhabitants	Omeo ○	
Town, under 200 inhabitants	Eskdale ○	
Locality	BUNGALLA	
Suburb	GLENORCHY	
Pastoral station homestead	Alroy Downs ■	
Closed Aboriginal town	Murgenella ○	
Roadhouse	Fortesque ▣	
Commercial airport	✈	
Place of interest	● ■	
Landmark feature	●	
General interest feature	■	
Accommodation		
Hill, mountain	+	
Lighthouse	★	
Route destination	*GOULBURN*	
Adjoining page number	**284**	
National parks		
Prohibited areas		
Other named areas		
Text entry in A-Z listing	❶	

EXPLORE AUSTRALIA

Viking
A division of Penguin Books Australia Ltd
487 Maroondah Highway, PO Box 257
Ringwood, Victoria 3134, Australia
Penguin Books Ltd
Harmondsworth, Middlesex, England
Viking Penguin, A division of Penguin Books USA Inc.
375 Hudson Street, New York, New York 10014, USA
Penguin Books Canada Limited
10 Alcorn Avenue, Toronto, Ontario, Canada M4V 3B2
Penguin Books (N.Z.) Ltd
182-190 Wairau Road, Auckland 10, New Zealand

This fourteenth edition published by Penguin Books Australia Ltd, 1995
First published by George Philip & O'Neil Pty Ltd, 1980

Second edition 1981	Fourth edition 1985
Third edition 1983	Fifth edition 1986
Reprinted 1984	

Sixth edition published by Penguin Books Australia, 1987

Seventh edition 1988	Eleventh edition 1992
Eighth edition 1989	Twelfth edition 1993
Ninth edition 1990	Thirteenth edition 1994
Tenth edition 1991	

Copyright © Penguin Books Australia Ltd, 1995

ISBN 0 670 86316 5

Printed and bound in **China** through Bookbuilders Ltd

Publisher's Note: Every effort has been made to ensure that the
information in this book is accurate at the time of going to press.
The publisher welcomes information and suggestions for corrections
or improvement. A Suggestion Form is provided on page 561.

Disclaimers: The publisher cannot accept responsibility for any
errors or omissions. The representation on the maps of any road
or track is not necessarily evidence of public right of way.
The population figures given in *Explore Australia* have been taken
from the most recent Census result available. They are intended to
provide only an approximate idea of the size of the various cities
and towns. Accommodation listed is a guide to accommodation
available in each town.

HALF-TITLE PAGE: Black Spur, Maroondah Highway, Victoria (Richard I'Anson)
TITLE PAGE: Uluru (Ayers Rock), Northern Territory (Richard I'Anson)

EXPLORE AUSTRALIA

The Complete Touring Companion

VIKING

Acknowledgements

State Cartographic Consultants

Australian Capital Territory: Paul Sjoberg
New South Wales: Bruce Whitehouse (Ass. Dip. Cart.)
Northern Territory: Len Carter, AMAIC
Queensland: David Gooding (Ass. Dip. Cart.), Brenda Gooding (Cert. Cart.)
South Australia: George Ricketts, MAIC
Tasmania: Phil Broughton, FAIC
Victoria: Christopher Cook ARMIT (Cartog.)
Western Australia: Peter Tarwin, AMAIC

Text Design
Guy Mirabella

Copy editor
Jenny Lang

Motoring consultant
Royal Automobile Club of Victoria (RACV)

Photographers
George Bareth, Ross Barnett, Andrew Chapman, G.A. & V. M Crimp, Stuart Grant, Richard I'Anson, Gary Lewis, PD Munchenberg, Nick Rains, Don Skirrow, Robin Smith, Ken Stepnell, Bruce Stewart, Stock Photos: David Austen, Bill Bachman, Benaji, Diana Calder, Roger Du Buisson, Excitations, Ron Gale, Noeline Kelly, James Lauritz, David Marshall, Natfoto, Lance Nelson, Rolf Richardson, Otto Rogge, Paul Steel, Ken Stepnell, Stocktake, Ken Straiton.

Text
For the preparation of this edition, each tourist information centre for the 800 towns described was contacted and the information for each town checked. The revision of this edition could not have occurred without their assistance, many of whom also supplied photographs. As well, assistance was received from the following organisations:

New South Wales
Sydney Convention & Visitors Bureau
National Parks and Wildlife Service

Australian Capital Territory
Canberra Tourism Commission
ACT Parks and Conservation Service

Victoria
Tourism Victoria
Department of Conservation and Natural Resources

South Australia
South Australian Tourism Commission
Adelaide Convention & Tourism Authority
Department of Environment and Natural Resources

Western Australia
Western Australia Tourism Commission
Department of Conservation and Land Management

Northern Territory
Northern Territory Tourism Commission
Darwin Region Tourism Association
Australian Nature Conservation Agency
Conservation Commission of the Northern Territory

Queensland
Queensland Tourist & Travel Corporation
Brisbane Visitors & Convention Bureau
Department of Environment & Heritage

Tasmania
Tasmanian Travel & Information Centre
Parks and Wildlife Service

St John Ambulance Australia

Maps
The publisher acknowledges the assistance to revise and check the maps from the various regional tourism authorities and state cartographic consultants.

Contents

Mount Sonder, Northern Territory

Aboriginal rock art

Opera House and Harbour Bridge, Sydney

Calendar of Events

Note: The information given here was accurate at the time of printing. However, as the timing of events held annually is subject to change and some events may extend into the following month, it is best to check with the local tourism authority or event organisers to confirm the details. The calendar is not exhaustive. Most towns and regions throughout Australia hold sporting competitions, regattas and rodeos, arts, craft, and trade exhibitions, agricultural and flower shows, music festivals and other such events annually. Details of these events are available from tourism outlets in each state.

JANUARY

ALL STATES Public holidays: New Year's Day; Australia Day.

NSW Sydney: Sydney Festival and Carnivalé. **Manly:** Iron Man Gold. **Bermagui:** Blue Water Fishing Classic. **Brunswick Heads:** Fish and Chips (wood chop) Festival. **Byron Bay:** Arts and Music Festival. **Cooma:** Rodeo. **Corowa:** Federation Festival. **Culburra–Orient Point:** Open Fishing Carnival. **Deniliquin:** Sun Festival. **Gunnedah:** National Tomato Competition. **Guyra:** Lamb and Potato Festival; Hydrangea Festival. **Hay:** Australia Day 'Surf' Carnival. **Lake Cargelligo:** Hovercraft Meeting. **Quirindi:** Wallabadah New Year's Day Cup Meeting. **Tamworth:** Australian Country Music Festival. **The Entrance:** Australia Day Family Concert and Fireworks. **Tumbarumba:** New Year's Day Rodeo. **Wentworth Falls:** Australia Day Regatta.

ACT Canberra: Australia Day in the National Capital; Australia Day Cup; Embassies Open Day; Multicultural Festival; Australian Long Track Speedway Motor Cycle Grand Prix.

VIC. Melbourne: Australian Open (grand slam tennis championships); Summer in the City. **Eltham:** Montsalvat Jazz Festival. **Cobram:** 'Peaches and Cream' Festival (biennial, odd-numbered years). **Hanging Rock:** New Year's Day Picnic Race Meeting. **Harrietville:** CAE Music Camp. **Inverloch:** Fun Festival. **Jeparit:** Beach Carnival. **Lakes Entrance:** Australian Wood Design Exhibition. **Lorne:** Pier to Pub Swim, Surf to Mountain Foot Race. **Murtoa:** New Year's Day Race Meeting. **Portland:** Foreshore Carnival, Fishing Competition. **Terang:** Horse Carnival.

SA Adelaide: Sheffield Shield Cricket, Schutzenfest German Festival. **Ardrossan:** Ardrossan Alive (biennial, odd-numbered years). **Glenelg:** Greek Blessing of the Waters. **Goolwa:** Milang to Goolwa Freshwater Classic. **Hahndorf:** Founders Day. **Kingston S.E.:** Yachting Regatta, Lobster Fest. **Loxton:** Apex Fisherama. **Minlaton:** Yacht Race. **Port Germein:** Festival of the Crab. **Port Lincoln:** Lincoln Week Regatta; Tunarama Festival. **Port Vincent:** Gala Day; Birdman Event; Classic Yacht Race. **Riverland:** Wine and Fruit Festival. **Robe:** Beer Can Regatta. **Streaky Bay:** Aquatic Sports Day; Family Fish Day Contest. **Tanunda:** Oom Pah Festival. **Tumby Bay:** Fishing Competition. **Wallaroo:** Regatta. **Whyalla:** Whyalla Gift; National Jet Ski Titles.

WA Perth: Hopman Cup (tennis); Matilda Festival; Perth Cup (horse racing); Vines Golf Classic. **Beverley:** Cross-country gliding Regatta. **Busselton:** Festival of Busselton. **Denmark:** Rainbow Festival. **Geraldton:** Windsurfing Blast. **Guilderton:** Lancelin Ocean Classic. **Harvey:** Australia Day Breakfast. **Mandurah:** Mandurah Festival. **Narrogin:** State Gliding Championships. **Rockingham:** Cockburn Yachting Regatta.

QLD Clermont: Beef 'N Beer Festival. **Caloundra:** Kabi Cook, Aboriginal cultural festival. **Redcliffe:** Blessing of the Fleet.

TAS. Hobart: Summer Festival. **Burnie:** New Year's Day Athletic Carnival. **Cygnet:** Huon Folk Festival. **Triabunna:** Spring Bay Crayfish Derby.

Horseracing in outback WA

FEBRUARY

NSW Sydney: Gay and Lesbian Mardi Gras. **Blue Mountains:** Blue Mountains Summer Classic held at Blackheath, Leura and Katoomba golf courses. **Cessnock:** Hunter Vintage Walkabout. **Kiama:** Jazz Festival. **Lake Macquarie:** Cross the Lake Swim. **Nelson Bay:** Festival of Port Stephens. **Orange:** Banjo Patterson Festival. **Temora:** Golden Gift (foot race). **Tweed Heads:** Tweed Valley Triathlon. **Walcha:** Agricultural Show.

ACT Canberra: Royal Canberra Show; Sri Chinmoy Triathlon and Mini Triathlon.

VIC. Melbourne: Australian Masters

Clown at Melbourne's Moomba Festival

Golf Tournament; Formula 5000 (motor racing); Chinese New Year Festival. **Camperdown:** Leura Festival. **Donald:** Dead Centre Motorbike Rally. **Drouin:** Ficifolia Festival. **Edenhope:** Henley-on-Lake Wallace. **Halls Gap:** Grampians Jazz Festival. **Healesville:** Coldstream Country and Western Festival. **Korumburra:** Coal Creek Twilight Music and Theatre Festival. **Leongatha:** Cycling Carnival. **Warrnambool:** Wunta Fiesta.

SA Adelaide: Adelaide Festival Fringe (biennial, even-numbered years). **Kingscote:** Kangaroo Island Racing Carnival. **Loxton:** Mardi Gras. **Milang:** Goolwa to Milang Freshwater Classic. **Mount Compass:** Compass Cup Cow Race. **Port Lincoln:** Lincoln Week Regatta; Adelaide to Lincoln Yacht Race. **Tailem Bend:** Gumi Racing Festival. **Waikerie:** International Food Fair.

WA Perth: Chinese New Year Festival; Festival of Perth; Kyana Aboriginal Festival; Moon Chow Festival. **Albany:** Great Southern Wine Festival. **Katanning:** Katanning Triathlon. **Margaret River:** Leeuwin Estate Concert; Wine and Food Festival.

QLD Killarney: Two-day Agricultural Show. **Warwick:** Antique and Collectables Fair. **Yeppoon:** Surf Life Saving Championships.

TAS. Public holidays: Hobart Cup Day and Hobart Regatta Day (southern Tas. only); Launceston Cup Day (northern Tas. only). **Hobart:** Hobart Cup; Royal Hobart Regatta. **Devonport:** Food and Wine Festival. **Evandale:** Village Fair, and National Penny Farthing Championships. **Fingal:** World Coal Shovelling and Roof Bolting Championships. **Oatlands:** Rodeo. **Richmond:** Country Music Festival. **Scottsdale:** Golconda: Tasmanian Circus Festival.

MARCH

NSW Sydney: Australian Motor Cycle Grand Prix. **Alstonville:** Tibouchina Festival. **Bega:** Cheese Pro-Am. **Blayney:** Agricultural Show. **Bulahdelah:** Prawn Festival. **Eden:** Amateur Fish Club Competition. **Inverell:** Art Exhibition. **Jamberoo:** Illawarra Folk Festival. **Jindabyne:** Strzelecki Polish Festival. **Moruya:** Music Festival. **Newcastle:** Surfest. **Parkes:** Marbles Tournament. **Picton:** Thirlmere Festival of Steam. **Richmond:** RAAF Open Day. **Wagga Wagga:** Australian Veterans Games. **Wauchope:** Lasiondra Festival. **Wyong:** Festival of Arts.

ACT Public holiday: Canberra Day. **Canberra:** Black Opal Stakes; Canberra Festival.

VIC. Public holiday: Labour Day. **Melbourne:** Australian Formula One Grand Prix (from 1996); Autumn Racing Carnival; International Dragon Boat Festival; Moomba Festival. **Apollo Bay:** Music Festival. **Bairnsdale:** Riviera Festival. **Ballan:** Arcadian Festival. **Ballarat:** Begonia Festival. **Casterton:** Motorcycle Hill Climb. **Colac:** Kana Festival. **Corryong:** High Country Festival. **Geelong:** Weerama Festival. **Healesville:** Australian Car Rally Championship. **Horsham:** Fishing Contest. **Inverloch:** Jazz Festival. **Koo-wee-rup:** Potato Festival. **Korumburra:** Karmai (Giant Worm) Festival. **Kyabram:** Rodeo. **Maffra:** Harvest Festival. **Mildura:** Great Mildura Paddleboat Race. **Moe:** Jazz Festival. **Mount Beauty:** The Conquestathon (foot race). **Myrtleford:** Tobacco, Hops and Timber Festival. **Nagambie:** Goulburn Valley Vintage Festival. **Port Albert:** Fishing Competition. **Port Fairy:** Folk Festival. **Portland:** Dahlia

Festival. **Rutherglen:** Tastes of Rutherglen. **Sale:** Sale Cup. **Seymour:** Rafting Festival. **Walhalla:** Erica King of the Mountains Woodchop. **Warragul:** Gippsland Field Days. **Wodonga:** Show.

SA Adelaide: Adelaide Arts Festival (biennial, even-numbered years); 'Come Out' Youth Arts Festival (odd-numbered years). **Thebarton:** Glendi Greek Festival. **Coonawarra:** Centenary Festival. **Kapunda:** Celtic Festival (weekend before Easter). **Lucindale:** Field Days and Tractor Pull. **Millicent:** Radiata Festival. **Mid-North:** Australian Country Games (including Burra). **Port Pirie:** Street Go-Kart Grand Prix. **Strathalbyn:** Penny Farthing Race. **Streaky Bay:** Streaky Bay Cup Race Meeting. **Tanunda:** Essenfest.

WA Augusta: Dragon Boat Racing. **Bridgetown:** Carnival. **Bunbury:** Aqua Spectacular. **Kalbarri:** Sport Fishing Classic **Mount Barker:** The Field Day Wine Festival. **Pemberton:** King Karri Karnival. **Wagin:** Woolorama.

QLD Stanthorpe: Rodeo.

TAS. Public holiday: Eight Hours Day. **Hobart:** Garden Week. **Cygnet:** Port Cygnet Fishing Carnival. **Devonport:** Harbours Festival. **Kingsborough:** Kingsborough Festival (incl. road cycle race). **Longford:** Targa Tasmania. **New Norfolk:** Hop Festival. **St Helens/Port Arthur:** Tasmanian Sport and Game Fishing Festival. **Westbury:** Maypole Festival.

EASTER

ALL STATES Public holidays: Good Friday; Easter Monday; Easter Tuesday (Tas. only).

NSW Sydney: Royal Easter Show. **Balranald:** Homebush Gymkhana. **Bermagui:** Four Winds Concerts. **Berridale:** Fair. **Brunswick Heads:** Blessing of the Fleet and Fishing Festival. **Byron Bay:** Blues Festival. **Canowindra:** Model Aircraft Championships. **Deniliquin:** Jazz Festival. **Grenfell:** Guinea Pig Races. **Griffith:** Wine and Food Festival. **Holbrook:** Ultra Fly-In. **Huskisson:** White Sands Carnival. **Koondrook:** Rodeo. **Leeton:** Rice Festival (even-numbered years). **Maclean:** Highland Gathering. **Moree:** Carnival of Sport. **Moulamein:** Yabby Races. **Narooma:** Tilba Festival. **Tocumwal:** Craft Festival. **Ulladulla:** Blessing of the Fleet.

VIC. Easterbike (various locations). **Benalla:** Arts Festival. **Bendigo:** Easter Fair. **Echuca–Moama:** Working Horse Fair. **Kerang:** Australian Tractor Pull Championships. **Kyabram:** Antique Aeroplane Fly-in. **Kyneton:** Antique Fair. **Lake Bolac:** Yachting Regatta. **Mallacoota:** Carnival. **Omeo:** Race Day. **Quambatook:** Australian Tractor Pull Championship. **Stawell:** Easter Gift (professional foot race). **Torquay:** Bells Beach Surfing Classic. **Warracknabeal:** Wheatlands Easter Carnival. **Wonthaggi:** Carnival. **Yarram:** Tarra Festival.

SA Andamooka: Easter Family Fun Day and White Dam Walk. **Berri:** Carnival and Rodeo. **Clare:** Clare Valley Easter Festival; Racing Carnival. **Coober Pedy:** Opal Festival; Outback Festival. **Kadina:** Bowling Carnival. **Kapunda:** Celtic Festival: **Oakbank:** Easter Racing Carnival (picnic race meeting). **Port Victoria:** Annual Fishing Competition. **Waikerie:** Horse and Pony Club. **Whyalla:** Sportfishing Convention.

WA Perth: BMX National Championships. **Donnybrook:** Apple Festival (odd-numbered years). **Guilderton:** King of the River. **Karratha:** Pilbara Pursuit Jetboat Classic. **Lancelin:** Beach Buggy Championships. **Nannup:** Music Festival. **Northcliffe:** Forest Festival.

NT Borroloola: Fishing Classic.

QLD Brisbane: Brisbane–Gladstone Yacht Race. **Airlie Beach:** Easter Regatta. **Boulia:** Rodeo/gymkhana. **Bundaberg:** Country Music Roundup. **Beenleigh:** Brisbane to Gladstone Yacht Race. **Burketown:** World Barramundi Handline—Rod Fishing Championships. **Emerald:** Sunflower Festival. **Miles:** Museum Display. **Roma:** Easter in the Country. **Tin Can Bay:** Easter Festival.

TAS. Hobart/Devonport/Pipers River: Tazz Jazz.

APRIL

ALL STATES Heritage Week. Public holiday: Anzac Day.

NSW Sydney: AJC Autumn Racing Carnival; Australian International Dragon Boat Festival; finish of Great NSW Bike Ride; Sydney Cup Week. **Bourke:** Fred Hollows Footrace to Sydney. **Bundanoon**: Brigadoon Festival (Highland Games). **Crookwell:** High Country Gardens Openings. **Gulgong:** Foundation

Day. **Leeton:** Rice Festival (biennial, even-numbered years). **Maitland:** Steamfest; Indoor Equestrian Dressage Championships. **Molong:** Cabonne Country Day. **Murrurundi:** Sheepdog Trials. **Nyngan:** Anzac Day Race Meeting. **Shellharbour:** Sunshine Festival. **Taree:** Taree and District Eisteddfod. **Tumut:** Tumut Valley Festival of the Falling Leaf.

ACT Canberra: Marathon; Anzac Day Service, Australian War Memorial.

VIC: Melbourne: Comedy Festival. **Bright**: Autumn Festival. **Echuca–Moama:** Barmah Muster. **Inglewood:** Blue Eucalyptus Festival (biennial, even-numbered years). **Tallangatta:** Red Breeds Dairy Festival.

SA Aldgate: Autumn Leaves Festival. **Barossa Valley:** Vintage Festival (biennial, odd-numbered years). **Coober Pedy:** Opal Festival. **Crystal Brook:** Folk Fair. **Goolwa:** Boat Rally and Picnic Races. **Kimba:** Yeltana Horse Spectacular. **Laura:** Folk Fair. **Maitland:** Agricultural Show. **Mid North:** Australian Country Games. **Stansbury:** Oyster Festival.

WA Perth: National Trust Heritage Week. **Kununurra:** Dam to Dam Regatta.

NT Darwin: National Dance Week. **Wauchope:** Outback Go Kart Classic. **Alice Springs:** Country Music Festival. **QLD Allora:** 500 Endurance Motor Race. **Comet:** Rodeo. **Ipswich:** Heritage Week. **Kingaroy:** Peanut Festival (biennial, odd-numbered years). **Mount Isa:** Country Music Festival. **Rockhampton:** Good Earth Expo. **Stanthorpe:** Opera at Sunset. **Surfers Paradise**: Gold Coast Cup.

TAS. Hobart: Three Peaks Race (Mounts Strzelecki/Freycinet/Wellington).

MAY

NSW Casino: Beef Reach Festival. **Dubbo:** Agricultural Show. **Glen Innes:** Celtic Festival. **Goulburn:** Woolfest. **Merriwa:** Polocrosse Carnival. **Scone:** Horse Week. **Tathra:** Game-fishing Competition. **Wee Waa:** Cotton Festival (biennial). **White Cliffs:** Gymkhana and Rodeo. **Windsor:** Bridge to Bridge Power Boat Classic. **Yanco:** Murrumbidgee Farm Fair.

VIC. Melbourne: Next Wave Festival. State-wide: Victoria's Garden Scheme closes. **Daylesford:** Hepburn Swiss-

Italian Festival. **Kalorama:** Chestnut Festival. **Warrnambool:** Southern right whales due at Logans Beach; Three-day May Racing Carnival.

SA Public holiday: Adelaide Cup Day. **Adelaide:** Adelaide Cup Carnival. **Burra:** Antique and Decorating Fair. **Ceduna:** Regional 'Come Out' Week. **Clare Valley:** Clare Valley Gourmet Weekend. **Goolwa:** Vintage Steam Festival (odd-numbered years). **Hawker:** Horseracing Carnival. **Mannum:** Houseboat Hirers Open Days. **Nuriootpa:** Hot Air Balloon Regatta (at Seppeltsfield). **Stansbury:** Sheepdog trials. **Yorke Peninsula:** (**Kadina/ Moonta/Wallaroo**): Kernewek Lowender (Cornish Festival, biennial, odd-numbered years). **Yunta:** Races.

WA Carnarvon: Mirari Festival. **Eucla:** Golf Day. **Fremantle:** Fremantle–Carnarvon Yachting Classic. **Gingin:** British Car Day. **Toodyay:** Moondyne (Colonial and Convict) Festival.

NT Public Holiday: May Day. **Darwin:** Arafira Sports Festival (biennial, odd-numbered years); Fred's Pass Rural Show including 'Litchfield Gift' (foot race). **Alice Springs:** Alice Craft Acquisition; Agricultural Show Bangtail Muster.

QLD Public holiday: Labour Day. **Cardwell:** Country and Western Music Festival. **Charters Towers:** Country Music Festival. **Eromanga:** Race Day. **Fraser Island:** Orchid Beach Fishing Expo. **Gatton:** Heavy Horse Day. **Ingham:** Australian-Italian Festival. **Julia Creek:** Campdraft. **Kuranda:** Folk Festival. **Mareeba:** Dimbulah Festival. **Maryborough:** Best of Brass. **Mount Morgan:** Golden Mount Festival. **Normanton:** Show, Rodeo and Gymkhana. **Noosa:** Festival of the Arts. **Port Douglas:** Reef and Rainforest Festival. **Richmond:** Rodeo. **Taroom:** Agricultural Show. **Thursday Island:** Cultural Festival. **Warwick:** Bush Week.

TAS. Carrick: Agfest. **Glenorchy:** City to Casino Fun Run. **Stanley:** Literature Fair.

JUNE

ALL STATES Public holiday: Queen's Birthday (except WA).

NSW Sydney: Sydney Film Festival. **Manly:** Food and Wine Festival. **Blue Mountains:** Yulefest. **Bourke:** Bourke to B—Bash (charity car rally).

Coonamble: Rodeo. **Dubbo:** Eisteddfod. **Gloucester:** Billykart Derby. **Grenfell:** Henry Lawson Festival of Arts. **Gulgong:** Henry Lawson Birthday Celebrations. **Jerilderie:** League of Silent Flight. **Manilla:** Lake Keepit Kool Sailing Regatta. **Merimbula:** Jazz Festival. **Merriwa:** Festival of Fleeces, Fireworks. **Snowy Mtns Region:** Opening of Ski Season (long weekend). **Southern Highlands Region:** Christmas in June. **Tibooburra:** Festival.

ACT Canberra: Embassies Open Day.

VIC. Melbourne: Melbourne International Film Festival. **Echuca–Moama:** Steam, Horse and Vintage Car Rally. **Hamilton:** Eisteddfod. **Rutherglen:** Winery Walkabout Weekend.

SA Barmera: Riverland Country Music Festival and Awards. **Gawler:** Equestrian Event. **Kingscote:** Half Marathon.

WA Public holiday: Foundation Day. West Week (week-long celebration of foundation of state). **Broome:** Fringe Arts Festival. **Cossack:** Cossack Fair and Yachting Regatta. **Kambalda:** Sky Diving Gathering. **Manjimup:** 15 000 Motocross. **Marble Bar:** Cup Race Weekend Gymkhana. **Wagin:** Foundation Day.

NT Darwin: NT Expo; Golf Classic. **Adelaide River:** Bush Race Meeting. **Alice Springs:** World Paddymelon Bowls Championship. **Batchelor:** International Skydiving and Parachuting Championships. **Katherine:** Barunga Sport and Cultural Festival; Katherine Cup; Canoe Marathon.

QLD Brisbane: Eagle Farm: QTC Sires Produce Stakes. **Atherton:** Pro-Rodeo. **Blackall:** Race Meeting. **Cardwell:** Coral Sea Memorial. **Charters Towers:** Annual Vintage Car Restorers Swap Meet. **Cloncurry:** Agricultural Show. **Cooktown:** Discovery Festival. **Coolangatta:** Wintersun. **Croydon:** Rodeo. **Gayndah:** Orange Festival (biennial, odd-numbered years). **Landsborough:** William Landsborough Day. **Longreach:** Hall of Fame Race Meeting. **Monto:** Dairy Festival (biennial, even-numbered years). **Mossman:** Bavarian Festival. **Muttaburra:** Landsborough Flock Ewe Show. **Normanton:** Show, Rodeo and Gymkhana. **Strathpine:** Pine Rivers Heritage Festival. **Taldora Station:** Saxby Roundup. **Whitsunday:** Festival of Sail.

TAS. St Helens: Suncoast Jazz Festival.

JULY

NSW Blue Mountains: Yulefest. **Kyogle:** Rodeo. **Pitt Town:** Fun Run. **Urunga:** Bowling Club Carnival. **White Cliffs:** Royal Flying Doctor Ball.

VIC. Daylesford: Mid-Winter Festival. **Hamilton:** Wool Heritage Week. **Swan Hill:** Italian Festa.

SA Cowell: Jade Marathon (or first weekend in August). **Morgan:** Fun Run, Walk, Cyclathon. **Willunga:** Almond Blossom Festival.

WA Perth: Perth Marathon. **Denmark:** Winter Festival. **Derby:** Boab Festival; Country and Western Music Festival. **Exmouth:** Gala Week; Arts and Crafts Show. **Fitzroy Crossing:** Rodeo. **Onslow:** Bougainvillea Festival. **Roebourne:** Royal Show, Roebourne Cup and Ball. **Wickham:** Cossack–Wickham Fun Run.

NT Darwin: Agricultural Show (regional public holiday); Darwin Cup Carnival. **Alice Springs:** Camel Cup. **Katherine:** Agricultural Show (regional public holiday). **Tennant Creek:** Agricultural Show (regional public holiday).

QLD Brisbane: Jumbo Tennis Day. **Broadbeach:** Gold Coast International Marathon. **Burketown:** Rodeo and Races. **Chinchilla:** Polocrosse Carnival. **Cleveland:** Flinders Day (enactment of landing on Coochiemudlo Island). **Cooktown:** Laura-Cape York Aboriginal Dance Festival. **Emu Park:** Service of Rememberance. **Esk:** Picnic Races. **Hughenden:** Dinosaur Festival (biennial, even-numbered years). **Ipswich:** Mediaeval Fair and Markets. **Karumba:** Karumba Kapers. **Mackay:** Festival of the Arts. **Mareeba:** Rodeo. **Mission**

Beach: Cassowary Festival. **Nebo:** Rodeo. **Pomona:** King of the Mountain Festival. **Rockhampton:** Bauhinia Arts Festival. **Sarina:** Visual Arts Festival. **Townsville:** Australian Festival of Chamber Music.

TAS. Hobart: Brighton Craft Fair.

AUGUST

NSW Public Holiday: Bank Holiday. **Sydney:** Sun City to Surf (fun run to Bondi Beach). **Bellingen:** Jazz Festival. **Blue Mountains:** Yulefest. **Cootamundra:** Wattle Time Festival and Garden Fair. **Dungog:** Canoe Classic. **Evans Head:** Bowling Carnival. **Forster-Tuncurry:** Australian Veteran Cycling Championships. **Lismore:** International Festival of Friendship. **Murwillumbah:** Banana Festival. **Narrandera:** Camellia Show. **Newcastle:** Jazz Festival. **Nundle:** Camp Drafting and Dog Trials. **Quirindi:** Polo Carnival. **Thredbo:** FIS Australian Championships and Continental Cup (snow skiing). **Tweed Heads:** Bowls Tournament. **Wellington:** Eisteddfod. **Wollongong:** South Coast Youth Arts and Skills Festival.

VIC. State-wide: Victoria's Garden Scheme opens. **Harrietville:** International Ski Marathon Kangaroo Hoppet (Falls Creek). **Hopetoun:** Speed Field Days.

SA Barossa Valley: Classic Gourmet Weekend. **Cleve:** Eyre Peninsula Field Days (biennial, even-numbered years). **Crystal Brook:** Agricultural Show; Yacka Sheepdog trials. **Gawler:** Agricultural Show. **Kadina:** Agricultural Show. **Mount Gambier:** Eisteddfod. **Old Noarlunga:** Cobb and Co. Coach Re-enactment. **Strathalbyn:** Collectors,

Face painter at the Warana Festival, Brisbane

Hobbies and Antique Fair.
WA Perth: City to Surf Fun Run.
Broome: Shinju Matsuri (Festival of the Pearl). **Dampier/Karratha:** Fe-NaCLNG Festival, incorporating Dampier Game Fishing Classic. **Halls Creek:** Races. **Mullewa:** Wildflower Show. **Newman:** Fortescue Festival. **Northam:** Avon Descent (white-water raft race) Festival. **Port Hedland:** Spinifex Spree. **Tom Price**: Nameless Festival. **Wyndham:** Top of the West Festival and Race Meeting.
NT Public holiday: Picnic Day. **Darwin:** Beer Can Regatta; Bougainvillea Festival; Darwin Rodeo. **Alice Springs:** Yuendumu Aboriginal Sports Carnival. **Borroloola:** Agricultural Show, Rodeo. **Jabiru:** Arts Council, Wind Festival. **Mataranka:** Rodeo. **Tennant Creek:** Goldrush Folk Festival.
QLD Public holiday: Brisbane Show Day. **Brisbane:** Brisbane International Film Festival; Royal Brisbane National Show (Ekka). **Boulia:** Rodeo and Gymkhana. **Bowen:** Art, Craft and Orchid Expo. **Cloncurry:** Merry Muster Rodeo. **Cunnamulla:** Opal Festival. **Eulo:** World Lizard Racing Championships. **Hervey Bay:** Whale Festival. **Mount Isa:** Rodeo. **Richmond:** Rodeo. **Townsville:** Festival of Peace. **Tully:** Rain Festival.
TAS. New Norfolk: Winter Challenge.

SEPTEMBER

NSW Sydney: Rugby League Grand Final. **Armidale:** Springfest. **Barham:** Pro-Am Golf Tournament. **Bondi:** Festival of the Winds (kite flying). **Bellingen:** Azalea Festival. **Berrima:** District Art Society Exhibition. **Boggabri:** Gum Tree Clay Pigeon Shoot. **Bowral:** Tulip Time Festival. **Broken Hill:** Silver City Show. **Camden:** Open Homestead Weekend; Celebrate Camden Festival. **Canowindra:** Agricultural Show. **Coffs Harbour:** Garden Competition. **Cowra:** World Peace Day (ceremony at Peace Bell). **Crookwell:** High Country Gardens Openings. **Dungog:** Floral Festival. **Glen Innes:** Minerama Gem Festival. **Gloucester:** Mountain Man Triathlon. **Henty:** Machinery Field Days. **Maclean:** Cane Harvest Festival. **Mudgee:** Wine Festival. **Mullumbimby:** Chincogan Fiesta. **Nimbin:** Spring Arts Festival. **Richmond:** Hawkesbury District Orchid Spring Show. **Singleton:** Broke Village Fair. **Stroud:** Rodeo.

Tamworth: Spring Cup. **Toukley:** Azalea Festival. **Wagga Wagga:** National Festival of the Voice. **Woolgoolga:** Lillipilli Festival. **Yamba:** Family Fishing Festival.
ACT Canberra: Floriade Spring Festival.
VIC. Springbike (various locations). **Melbourne:** Antiquarian Book Fair; Australian Football League and Association Finals; Fringe Arts Festival; Royal Melbourne Show. **Anglesea:** Angair Festival. **Bacchus Marsh:** Pioneer Day Festival. **Cowes:** Motor Racing. **Leongatha:** Daffodil and Floral Festival. **Little Desert:** Wildflower Exhibition, Little Desert Lodge. **Maryborough:** Golden Wattle Festival. **Olinda:** Rhododendron Festival (3 months). **Silvan:** Tulip Festival. **Wedderburn:** Wool Expo. **Yarrawonga:** Ice Breaker Yacht Regatta.
SA Adelaide: Royal Adelaide Show. **Adelaide Hills:** Spring Festival; Handmade in the Hills. **Beltana:** Picnic Races and Gymkhana. **Glenelg:** Bay to Birdwood Run (vintage car rally; biennial). **Hawker:** Art Exhibition. **Mannum:** River Festival (Spring). **Paskeville:** Yorke Peninsula Field Days. **Port Pirie:** Blessing of the Fleet. **Robe:** Blessing of the Fleet. **Stirling:** Food and Wine Affair.
WA Perth: Football League Finals; Kings Park Wildflower Festival; Perth Royal Show; Rally Australia. **Augusta:** Spring Flower Show. **Boyup Brook:** Country Music Weekend. **Brookton:** Wildflower Display. **Coolgardie:** Camel Races; Coolgardie Day. **Cossack:** Art Awards, Art Ball. **Cranbrook:** Wildflower Show. **Dumbleyung:** Tracmach Vintage Fair. **Kalgoorlie:** Kalgoorlie Cup; Spring Festival. **Kojonup:** Wildflower and Country Festival. **Mingenew:** Rural Expo, Wildflower Display. **Mount Magnet:** Fun Day. **Nannup:** Discovery Weekend. **Northcliffe:** Mountain Bike Carnival. **Port Hedland:** All Can Regatta. **Ravensthorpe:** Wildflower Display. **Toodyay:** Folk Festival. **York:** Jazz Festival.
NT National Aboriginal Week. **Alice Springs:** Alice Springs Rodeo. **Daly Waters:** Rodeo. **Tennant Creek:** Desert Harmony Festival. **Timber Creek:** Races. **Wauchope:** Two-day Wimbledon at Wauchope.
QLD Brisbane: City of Brisbane Chelsea Flower Show; Spring Hill Festival; Warana Festival. **Airlie Beach:** Fun Race. **Atherton:** Maize Festival. **Big-**

genden: Rose Festival (biennial, odd numbered years). **Biloela:** Thaugool Arts Festival. **Birdsville:** Birdsville Races. **Boonah:** Fassifern German Festival. **Caloundra:** Art and Craft Show. **Charleville:** Booga Woongaroo Festival. **Clermont:** Rodeo. **Dunk Island:** Billfish Classic. **Gympie:** Kilkivan Great Horse Ride. **Herberton:** Tin Festival. **Laidley:** Chelsea Festival Week. **Longreach:** Starlight Stampede (biennial, even-numbered years). **Mackay:** Sugartime Festival. **Maryborough:** Heritage Festival. **Miles:** Wildflower Festival. **Noosa:** Jazz Party. **Port Douglas:** Regatta. **Redland Bay:** Strawberry Festival. **Tambo:** Spring Flower Festival, Ram Racing. **Taroom:** Leichhardt Festival. **Toowoomba:** Carnival of Flowers. **Winton:** Outback Festival (biennial, odd-numbered years). **Yeppoon:** Pineapple Festival.
TAS. Hobart: Film Festival; Tasmanian Football League Grand Final; Tasmanian Tulip Festival. **Burnie:** Burnie Festival. **Sheffield:** Daffodil Festival. **Stanley:** Circular Head Arts Festival.

OCTOBER

NSW Public Holiday: Labour Day. **Bathurst:** 1000 Touring Car Championship. **Broken Hill:** Country Music Festival. **Bundanoon:** Gullies Gallop Fun Run. **Casino:** Agricultural Show. **Cessnock:** Jazz Concerts. **Cobar:** Back to Cobar. **Condobolin:** Art Exhibition. **Coonabarabran:** Sky and Space Astrofest. **Coonamble:** Cup Race Meeting. **Cowra:** Sakura Bonsai and Japanese Cultural Exhibition. **Gilgandra:** Cooee Festival. **Gosford:** Mangrove Mountain District Country Fair, Agricultural Show. **Grafton:** Jacaranda Festival; Bridge to Bridge Ski Race. **Griffith:** Festival of Gardens. **Gundagai:** Spring Flower Show. **Gunnedah:** Dorothea MacKellar Children's Festival. **Inverell:** Sapphire City Floral Festival. **Jerilderie:** Yanco Bush Picnic. **Kiama:** Seaside Festival. **Lake Macquarie:** Children's Festival. **Leura:** Gardens Festival. **Lismore:** Folk Festival. **Lithgow:** National Go-Kart Championships. **Manilla:** Festival of Spring Flowers. **Merimbula:** Veterans Tennis. **Murrurundi:** Bushman's Carnival. **Nambucca Heads:** Show'n'-Shine Hot Rod Exhibition. **Narrabri:** Spring Festival. **Narromine:** Festival of Sport. **Nowra-Bomaderry** Spring Festival. **Raymond Terrace:** Twin Rivers

Festival. **Singleton:** Romance of the Rose Festival. **Tenterfield:** Federation Festival; Spring Wine Festival. **Tibooburra:** Gymkhana and Rodeo. **Toukley:** Cycle Classic. **Ulladulla:** Milton Settlers Fair. **Walgett:** Weekend Extravaganza; raft races, go-karts (biennial). **Wauchope:** Colonial Carnival. **Windsor/Richmond:** Macquarie Towns Festival. **Wyong:** Cycle Classic. **Young:** Cherry Festival.

ACT Canberra: Canberra Cup; Embassies Open Day; Floriade Spring Festival; Oktoberfest.

VIC. Melbourne: Fantastic Entertainment in Public Places (FEIPP) summer program begins; Oktoberfest; Spring Racing Carnival, including Caulfield Cup; Sun Tour of Victoria; International Festival of the Arts. **Chinatown:** Autumn Moon Lantern Festival. **Ararat:** Golden Gateway Festival. **Avoca:** Wool and Wine Festival. **Bright:** Springtime in Bright. **Broadford:** Scottish Festival. **Buchan:** Art and Craft Festival. **Charlton:** Art Show. **Chiltern:** Art Show. **Cowes:** Superbike Championships. **Creswick:** Brackenbury Festival. **Dunolly:** Tamagulla Gold Spectacular. **Echuca–Moama:** Rich River Festival. **Euroa:** Wool Week, Agricultural Show. **Heathcote:** Golden Grape Festival. **Moe:** Moe Cup. **Nhill:** Little Desert Wildflower Exhibition. **Port Fairy:** Spring Classical Music Festival. **Rainbow:** Iris Festival. **Tallangatta:** Arts Festival. **Wangaratta:** Wangaratta Festival. **Warrnambool:** Melbourne–Warrnambool Cycling Classic.

SA Public Holiday: Labour Day.

Camel Cup, Alice Springs

Adelaide: SA Football League Finals. **Andamooka:** Opal Festival. **Balaklava:** Festival of Gardens and Galleries. **Barmera:** Show. **Barossa Valley:** Music Festival. **Bordertown:** Clayton Farm Vintage Field Day. **Ceduna:** Oyster Fest. **Coober Pedy:** Races. **Edithburgh:** State Sailboarding Championships. **Hawker:** Henley-on-Arkaba fun day. **Kapunda:** Agricultural Show and Rodeo. **Kingscote:** Blessing of the Fleet. **Koppio:** Smithy Museum Open Day. **Loxton:** Show. **Marrabel:** Rodeo. **Marree:** Outback Ball (biennial, even-numbered years). **McLaren Vale:** Wine Bushing (One Continuous Picnic). **Naracoorte:** Show. **Penola:** Petticoat Lane Street Party. **Port Pirie:** Festival of Country Music. **Renmark:** Show. **Strathalbyn:** Glenbarr Scottish Festival. **Victor Harbour:** Folk Festival. **Wellington:** Strawberry Fair. **Whyalla:** Australian Amateur Snapper Fishing Championships. **Yorketown:** Picnic races and Gymkhana.

WA Public Holiday: Queen's Birthday. **Perth:** Spring in the (Swan) Valley Festival. **Boyup Brook:** Blackwood River Marathon Relay. **Bridgetown:** Blackwood Classic (powerboat race). **Busselton:** Four-week Cape to Cape Festival. **Donnybrook:** Apple Blossom Festival. **Eucla:** Eucla Shoot. **Geraldton:** Geraldton Festival. **Leonora:** Art Prize Inc. and Ball. **Morawa:** Music Spectacular. **Narrogin:** Spring Festival. **Three Springs:** White Rock Stakes Wheelbarrow Race. **Yallingup:** October Festival.

NT Alice Springs: Henley-on-Todd.

QLD Brisbane: Colonial George Street Festival. **Ayr:** Water Festival. **Bowen:** Coral Coast Festival. **Cairns:** Fun in the Sun Festival. **Crows Nest:** Crows Nest Day; Worm Races. **Dalby:** Harvest Festival. **Emu Park:** Octoberfest. **Goondiwindi:** Spring Festival. **Gympie:** Gold Rush Festival. **Hervey Bay:** Hervey Bay–Fraser Island Sailboard Marathon. **Ingham:** Maraka Festival. **Innisfail:** Harvest Festival. **Jundah:** Two-day Race Carnival. **Laidley:** Festival of Performing Arts. **Logan City:** Street Parade. **Maroochydore:** Mapleton Yarn Festival. **Mission Beach:** Aquatic Festival. **Nanango:** Pioneer Festival. **Noosa:** Beach Car Classic, Triathlon. **Ravenswood:** Halloween Ball. **Yandina:** Spring Flower and Ginger Festival.

TAS. Public holidays: Hobart Show Day (southern Tas. only); Launceston Show Day (northern Tas. only); Flinders Island Show Day (Flinders Island only); Burnie Show Day (Burnie only). **Hobart:** Royal Hobart Agricultural Show. **Burnie:** Rhododendron Festival. **Derby:** River Derby. **Great Lake:** Tasmanian Trout Fishing Championships. **Kingston:** Oliebollen Festival. **Launceston:** Garden Festival; Royal National Show; Tasmanian Poetry Festival. **Richmond:** Village Fair. **Wynyard:** Tulip Festival. **Zeehan:** Octoberfest.

NOVEMBER

NSW Barraba: Fine Music Festival. **Batemans Bay:** Neptune Festival. **Bulahdelah:** Show and Rodeo. **Glen Innes:** Land of the Beardies Bush Festival. **Gundagai:** Dog on the Tuckerbox Festival. **Kyogle:** Festival and Golf Tournament. **Lithgow:** Festival of the Valley (even-numbered years). **Moree:** Golden Grain Festival. **Queanbeyan:** Community Celebrations, Agricultural Show. **Robertson:** Rodeo. **Tenterfield:** Gem Festival. **Tumbarumba:** Heritage Week. **Uralla:** Thunderbolt Picnic Race Meeting. **Warren:** Cotton Cup Carnival. **Wellington:** Festival of Dance. **Wentworth:** Melbourne Cup Day Horseracing. **Windsor:** Bridge to Bridge Water Ski Classic. **Young:** National Cherry Festival.

ACT Canberra: Canberra International Car Rally.

VIC. Public holiday: Melbourne Cup Day. **Melbourne:** Spring Racing Carnival, including Melbourne Cup and Oaks

Day. **Carlton:** Melbourne Lygon Arts Festival. **Benalla:** Rose Festival. **Bendigo:** Swap Meet. **Casterton:** Agricultural Show. **Castlemaine:** State Festival (biennial, odd-numbered years); Spring Garden Festival (even-numbered years). **Dimboola:** Rowing Regatta. **Dunkeld:** Dunkeld Cup. **Lakes Entrance:** World Cup Sport Kiting Championships. **Macedon:** Mount Macedon Festival. **Natimuk:** Harrow National Bush Billycart Championships. **Omeo:** Agricultural Show. **Ouyen:** Farmers Festival. **Shepparton-Mooroopna:** Strawberry Festival. **Skipton:** Lake Goldsmith Steam Rally, Art Show. **Wandin:** Victorian Cherry Festival. **Wangaratta:** Festival of Jazz. **Yarragon:** Dairy Fest.

SA Adelaide: Australian Formula One Grand Prix (until 1996); Christmas Pageant. **Goolway:** Goolwa-Meningie Classic. **Hahndorf:** Blumenfest (Festival of Flowers). **Kapunda:** Antique and Craft Fair. **Kingscote:** Agricultural Show. **Mount Gambier:** Blue Lake Festival. **Murray Bridge:** Big River Challenge Festival. **Streaky Bay:** Snapper Fishing Contest. **Whyalla:** Proclamation Day Concert.

WA Albany: Perth–Albany Ocean Yacht Race. **Bunbury:** Festival. **Corrigin:** Creative Arts Exhibition. **Dongara-Port Denison:** Blessing of the Fleet. **Dunsborough:** Down South Dive Classic. **Exmouth:** Gamex, world class game fishing. **Fitzroy Crossing:** Barra Bash (barramundi fishing competition). **Fremantle:** Fremantle Festival. **Jurien:** Expo and Blessing of the Fleet. **Kalbarri:** Blessing of the Fleet. **Kalgoorlie:** Goldfields Mining Expo. **Kambalda:** Raft Regatta. **Manjimup:** Timber Festival. **Mount Barker:** Vintage Motorbike Hill Climb. **Northam:** Avon Valley Country Music Festival. **Rockingham:** Rocky Spring Festival. **Wyndham:** Hang Gliding Competition.

NT Ross River: Ross Cup.

QLD Atherton: Tablelands Band Festival. **Beaudesert:** Australian Rodeo Championships. **Bribie Island:** Bribie Cup Yacht Race. **Home Hill:** Harvest Festival. **Kynuna:** Rodeo. **Logan City:** River Festival and Raft Race. **Whitsunday Passage and Outer Reef:** Whitsunday Game Fishing Championships.

TAS. Public holiday: Recreation Day (northern Tas. only). **Hobart:** North Hobart Fiesta. **Battery Point:** Salamanca's Writers Weekend. **Campbell Town:** Country Music Muster. **Deloraine:** Tasmanian Cottage Industry Exhibition and Craft Fair. **Ross:** Rodeo. **Stanley:** Tasmania Day. **Zeehan:** King of the Mountain Fun Run.

DECEMBER

ALL STATES Public holidays: Christmas Day; Boxing Day. Carols by Candlelight (various locations).

NSW Sydney: World Series Cricket; Sydney–Hobart Yacht Race. **Abercrombie Caves:** Underground music in caves. **Corowa:** National Skydiving Championships. **Jindabyne:** Lake Jindabyne Sailing Club Hobie Cat Races. **Moulamein:** Horseracing Cup. **The Entrance:** Tuggerah Lakes Mardi Gras Festival and Fireworks. **Tocumwal:** New Year's Eve Carnival. **Wollongong:** Junior Surf Lifesaving Championships. **Yass:** Warrambalulah Festival.

ACT Canberra: Street Machine Summernats (national hot-rod exhibition and races).

VIC. Melbourne: Finish of Great Victorian Bike Ride. **Broadford:** Hells Angels Concert. **Corryong:** Nariel Creek Folk Music Festival. **Horsham:** Kannamaroo Festival. **Lancefield:** Horse Festival. **Nagambie:** Rowing Regatta. **Paynesville:** Speedboat Championships.

SA Public holiday: Proclamation Day. **Barmera:** Christmas Pageant. **Berri:** Rowing Regatta. **Glenelg:** Proclamation Day Celebrations. **Jamestown:** Christmas Pageant. **Loxton:** Christmas Magic. **Naracoorte:** Street Traders Party; Carols by Candlelight. **Renmark:** Christmas Pageant; Rowing Regatta. **Streaky Bay:** Carols by the Sea.

WA Perth: Australian Derby; Christmas Pageant; Hopman Cup (tennis); City Beach Fun Run. **Derby:** Kimberley Boxing Day Sports. **Esperance:** Turf Racing. **Jurien:** Slalom Carnival. **Katanning:** Katanning Caboodle. **Lancelin:** Ledge Point Ocean Race. **Yallingup:** Malubu Competition.

QLD Karumba: Fisherman's Ball. **Pittsworth:** Great Australiana Team Truck Pull. **Tin Can Bay:** Robert Pryde Memorial Surf Classic. **Whitsunday:** Festival of Sail.

TAS. Hobart: Brighton Craft Fair; Christmas Pageant; Summer Festival; Sydney–Hobart/Melbourne–Hobart Yacht Races. **Battery Point:** Salamanca's All Ears World Music Festival. **Latrobe:** Latrobe Wheel Race and Latrobe Gift. **Port Arthur:** Chopping Carnival. **Triabunna:** Tandara Woodchoppers Classic. **Ulverstone:** Christmas Mardi Gras.

Hobart end of the Sydney-Hobart yacht race

Introduction

Exploring Australia by motor vehicle provides the traveller with the opportunity to venture into remote areas, tropical rainforests and inland deserts, and to visit large cosmopolitan cities and tiny outback settlements.

Australia's deserts are as vast as the Sahara; its snowfields are huge and dramatically picturesque; its surfing beaches are among the best in the world. The entire continent is criss-crossed by a combination of bitumen highways and rough bush tracks, almost all navigable in the modern motor car, although some require 4WD vehicles.

Australia comprises an area of some 8.5 million square kilometres; it covers a distance of 3700 kilometres from north to south, and 4000 kilometres east to west. Within these boundaries there is an extraordinary range of flora and fauna, a variety of climatic extremes and a host of geological wonders.

Australia's temperatures vary from an average 30°C in the midsummer of the Red Centre to an average of 6°C in the highlands in winter.

It is a land of extremes. The parched deserts of central Australia may be totally dry for years until flooding rains produce a short-term sea. Sydney has a population of almost 4 million, whereas Innamincka in South Australia, near the Queensland border, has only 14 permanent residents.

Australia has been the home of Aborigines for over 40 000 years and evidence of their occupation abounds. Cave paintings and rock carvings made thousands of years ago are found at Uluru (Ayers Rock), that superb monolith sited almost in the centre of this island continent, and at numerous other locations.

The predominant landscape colours of Australia are red, blue and green. Inland, the stark red of the Simpson Desert sand dunes contrasts dramatically with the deep azure blue of the noonday sky. Dotted here and there are clumps of velvet-green scrub and, after rain, Sturt's desert pea blooms scarlet.

In the Red Centre the moonscapes of sand and rocky tors and hardy bush scrub have a forbidding beauty all their own, even in times of drought. After rain, gardens of brilliant wildflowers are added to the landscape.

Across the Far North, from Cape York Peninsula in the east to the Kimberleys in the west, tropical rainforests are in parts impenetrable, and of a green so luxuriant as to rival the colour from an artist's paintbrush.

Almost all Australia is accessible to the exploring traveller. It is possible to drive from Melbourne in the south of the mainland to Cooktown in the Far North.

The intrepid can plan a trip from the Pacific to the Indian Ocean; from the rainforest in the north to the temperate beaches of the southern coast. And for the traveller seeking peace and tranquillity, there are the green pasturelands and rugged, splendidly scenic mountain areas of Tasmania, the Island State.

Simply put, Australia is a wonderland. And in order to discover what it has to offer, either for a one-day tour or as a full-year once-in-a-lifetime adventure, *Explore Australia* is an invaluable travelling companion. It is designed to be of assistance with every facet of your travel itinerary. It is an encouragement and an almanac; a manual and a tour guide. It is recommended that you read it as part of your travel planning, particularly for long-distance journeys. For experienced road travellers, it will reinforce knowledge acquired in the past; for 'new chums' it can ensure the utmost pleasure from the holiday you have planned, and help to make it trouble-free.

Have a good trip—and drive carefully!

Shark Bay, near Monkey Mia

Planning Ahead

There is so much of Australia to see and so many ways to see it. Today, even the most remote sections of this vast continent are accessible, particularly to 4WD vehicles designed for use on bush tracks and unmade roads.

For some, exploring Australia will mean touring the made highways and staying in motels and hotels. Others will tow their accommodation behind them in the form of a caravan or camper and probably, as a result, stay mainly on made roads. Still others will fit out a commercial van with sleeping and cooking facilities and produce a mobile home, and yet another group, perhaps the true adventurers, will load a tent, a mobile fridge and a barbecue into the back of a 4WD station wagon and go bush. In all cases careful planning will enhance the journey immeasurably.

Obviously a one-, two- or three-day tour will not require the time and effort necessary for a round-Australia jaunt, but in any case, advance planning of the route and of overnight stopping-points, and a careful estimate of travel time, make for safety, comfort and enjoyment. So, indeed, will the roadworthiness of the vehicle. While as a matter of course your travel vehicle will be properly maintained and in reliable condition, some extra attention will not go astray, especially for long journeys. More of that later.

Advance Information

Any journey will benefit from careful **advance planning**. The idea of throwing a bag in the back and taking off is attractive in theory but creates complications in practice. Try to gather as much information as possible as far ahead of your planned departure as you can. Remember, the planning is half the fun. Research will confirm, or perhaps deny, your original choice of destination; it also will reveal ways and means, and problems where they exist. And bear in mind that although information sources are extensive, there is nothing like local knowledge. So remember to re-check everything you have learned as you go.

The first places to obtain information are the relevant **State tourist bureaus** and **motoring organisations** (**see:** Useful Information). They are excellent sources for travel brochures, regional maps and accommodation guides and they usually have up-to-date knowledge of local conditions. For details of specific areas, they can put you in touch with the appropriate tourist authority.

If you are planning a fly/drive holiday, or intend to combine rail and motor travel, the various **travel agencies**, **airline travel centres** and the **main railway booking offices** in each State can provide advice and information.

Also, read this book. The introductions to each State provide information on main tourist areas. Once you have decided on your destination, check it out by consulting the A–Z entries for specific towns and the features articles for other points of interest. Do note that while the capital cities and towns have been covered quite comprehensively in this book, the fine detail will be available locally.

How Far Ahead to Start

It can be a major disappointment to decide on a certain destination and then discover that motels, caravan parks and camping grounds in the area are booked out. In some regions at certain times of the year—Christmas, Easter, school holiday periods—accommodation can be booked out a year in advance. Explore all possibilities and, on long journeys, remember the travel-time factor. When booking accommodation in advance, allow enough time to travel comfortably to your destination. Your trip will lose a great deal of its charm if you have to rush from one point to the next (**see:** Itineraries).

While all popular destinations are likely to be busy at holiday peak times, some will be booked out around the time of special events: Melbourne at Melbourne Cup time; Adelaide at the time of the Adelaide Festival, for example (**see:** Calendar of Events). Check ahead for the timing of local special events.

If you wish to go to a favourite hotel or try a special type of accommodation—a farm homestead, a houseboat or charter boat—book well ahead. Other holidaymakers will have the same interests. And remember, most national parks require advance notice to give permission for camping within their boundaries.

When to Go

With a few exceptions you can travel Australia at any time of the year. The exceptions include parts of the Far North between October and May, that is, in the 'wet' or tropical monsoon season (this applies particularly if you plan to use bush tracks and unmade roads, many of which are impassable for months). Tropical cyclones are random summer hazards between November and March. In the NSW and Victorian high country, from about May to August many roads will be snow-bound. The Red Centre is not especially inviting in midsummer, when daytime temperatures can reach 45°C, while it can be bitterly cold at night.

Otherwise, remember the **holiday peaks.** If you can avoid the dense traffic during the major vacation periods, do so.

Which Way to Go

If you flinch at the thought of driving seemingly endless kilometres, you should consider an alternative: both fly/drive packages and MotoRail facilities

Useful Information

Motoring Organisations

There are motoring organisations in all Australian States and territories. All are affiliated under the Australian Automobile Association and reciprocal rights are available to their members. Membership can consist of service and social membership or service membership only.

When planning a trip it would be advisable for you to take out **service membership** of the motoring organisation in your home State. Not only will this ensure that you receive service in that State, but by producing your membership card you can request assistance from the equivalent organisation in other States.

The advantages of service membership of a motoring organisation are wide-ranging. They include emergency breakdown and towing services, vehicle inspection and 'approved repairer' services; tuition in safe and defensive driving for licensed drivers; legal advice on matters like the procedure to be followed after motor vehicle accidents or traffic charges, and the possible penalties; and motor vehicle insurance cover.

Service membership also makes available touring information and advice for motoring holidays, including guides, maps and reports on road conditions, accommodation and travel bookings; and special tours, package holidays and accommodation at concessional rates, as well as car accessories.

Social or 'club' membership entitles members to the use of club facilities and accommodation, including reciprocal use in some 50 clubs throughout Australia.

New South Wales
National Roads & Motorists'
Association (NRMA)
151 Clarence St, Sydney 2000
(02) 260 9222. Fax: (02) 260 8472

Australian Capital Territory
National Roads & Motorists'
Association (NRMA)
92 Northbourne Ave, Braddon 2601
(06) 243 8805. Fax: (06) 243 8892

Victoria
Royal Automobile Club of Victoria Ltd
(RACV)
422 Little Collins St, Melbourne 3000
(03) 9790 3333. Fax: (03) 9670 8605

South Australia
Royal Automobile Association of
South Australia Inc. (RAA)
41 Hindmarsh Sq, Adelaide 5000
(08) 223 4555. Fax: (08) 202 4520

Western Australia
Royal Automobile Club of Western
Australia Inc. (RAC)
228 Adelaide Tce, Perth 6000
(09) 421 4444. Fax: (09) 221 1887

Northern Territory
Automobile Association of the
Northern Territory Inc. (AANT)
79–81 Smith St, Darwin 0800
(089) 81 3837. Fax: (089) 41 2965

Queensland
Royal Automobile Club of Queensland
(RACQ)
300 St Pauls Tce, Brisbane 4000
(07) 3361 2444. Fax: (07) 3257 1863

Tasmania
Royal Automobile Club of Tasmania
(RACT)
Cnr Patrick and Murray Sts, Hobart 7000
(002) 32 6300. Fax: (002) 34 8784

Tourist Bureaus

New South Wales
NSW Travel Centre
19 Castlereagh St, Sydney 2000
(02) 231 4444. Fax: (02) 232 6080

Australian Capital Territory
Canberra Tourism Commission
Visitor Information Centre
Northbourne Ave, Dickson 2602
(06) 205 0044. Fax: (06) 205 0776

Victoria
RACV Travel Centre
230 Collins St, Melbourne 3000
(03) 9650 1522. Fax: (03) 9650 1212

South Australia
South Australian Travel Centre
1 King William St, Adelaide 5000
(08) 212 1505. Fax: (08) 303 2249

Western Australia
WA Tourist Centre, Albert Facey House
Cnr Forrest Place and Wellington St,
Perth 6000
(09) 483 1111. Fax: (09) 481 0190

Northern Territory
Darwin Region Tourism Association
33 Smith St Mall, Darwin 0800
(089) 81 4300. Fax: (089) 81 7346
Northern Territory Holiday Centre
Phone/Fax enquiries only:
1800 621 336. Fax: (089) 51 8581

Queensland
Queensland Government Travel Centre
Cnr Adelaide and Edward Sts,
Brisbane 4000
(07) 3221 6111. Fax: (07) 3221 5320

Tasmania
Tasmanian Travel and Information
Centre
20 Davey St, Hobart 7000
(002) 30 8233. Fax: (002) 24 0289

Other Accommodation

**Backpackers Resorts of Australia
(head office)**
PO Box 1000, Byron Bay NSW 2481
(018) 66 6888 (9–5 Mon.–Fri.). Fax:
(066) 847 1000

**Bed and Breakfast Australia
(head office)**
PO Box 408, Gordon NSW 2072
(02) 498 5344, (02) 498 1539 (AH). Fax:
(02) 498 6438

Farm holidays
The following is a list of contact addresses in each State if you wish to arrange a farm holiday.

New South Wales
Australian Farm Host Holidays Pty Ltd
PO Box 65, Culcairn 2660
(060) 29 8621. Fax: (060) 29 8770
(Properties available Australia-wide)

Victoria
Host Farms Association Inc.
6th Floor, 230 Collins St, Melbourne
(03) 9650 2922. Fax: (03) 9650 9434

South Australia
SA Host Farms Association Inc.
PO Box 74, Burra North 5417
(088) 8892 2755

Western Australia
WA Farm and Country Holidays
Association
Munaleeun Farm, Jackson Road
Narrikup 6326 (Albany Region)
(098) 53 2091. Fax: (098) 53 2090

Northern Territory
Northern Territory Government Tourist
Bureau in any State

Queensland
Queensland Host Farm Association
c/o RACQ Travel Service
GPO Box 1403, Brisbane 4001
(07) 3361 2390, 1800 77 7888. Fax: (07)
3257 1504

Tasmania
Homehost Tasmania Pty Ltd
PO Box 780, Sandy Bay 7005
(002) 24 1612. Fax: (002) 24 0472

Youth Hostels (head office)
10 Mallett St, Camperdown NSW 2050
(02) 565 1699. Fax (02) 565 1325

Emergency (for all States)

For police, ambulance and fire-brigade services, dial 000.

eliminate time-consuming travel and allow for concentration on areas of interest. Given fuel costs, neither of these is necessarily an extravagance. Cost them out against the expenses involved in using your own car for the entire trip.

MotoRail: For information on this easy way of covering long distances, contact the State tourist bureaus or the main State railway offices. Enquire about **CAPER fares**: a reduction in rail fare is available on some interstate services if travel is booked and paid for in advance. For all Rail-travel reservations and enquiries phone 13 22 32. For the price of a local call you will reach your nearest capital city, where operators will give you Australia-wide information.

Additional details are as follows:

New South Wales
Country Link Travel Centre
Wynyard Station
11–31 York St, Sydney 2000
(02) 224 4744

Victoria
V/Line Reservations and Information
Level 2, Transport House
589 Collins St, Melbourne 3000
(03) 9619 5000

South Australia
Australian National Passenger
Reservations and Enquiries
1 Richmond Rd, Keswick 5035
(08) 217 4111

Western Australia
Westrail Centre
West Pde, East Perth 6000
(09) 326 2222

Queensland
Queensland Rail
305 Edward St, Brisbane 4000
(07) 3235 2222

MotoRail services:
Perth–Sydney–Perth
Indian–Pacific
Two services a week each way: leaves Sydney Mon. and Thurs., leaves Perth Fri. and Mon.; 66 hours.
Perth–Adelaide–Perth
Indian–Pacific
Two services a week each way: leaves Adelaide Tues. and Fri., leaves Perth Mon. and Fri.; 38 hours. This service connects with *The Overland* to Melbourne.
Melbourne–Adelaide–Melbourne
The Overland
Daily, each way (overnight); 12 hours.
Adelaide–Alice Springs–Adelaide
The Ghan

May–October, 2 services a week each way; November– April, 1 service a week each way; 22 hours.
Brisbane–Townsville–Cairns– Townsville–Brisbane
The Queenslander
One service a week each way: leaves Brisbane Sun., leaves Cairns Tues.; 33 hours. An extra service each way a week including Proserpine stop; check frequency.
Brisbane–Longreach
Spirit of the Outback
Two services a week each way: leaves Brisbane Tues. and Fri., leaves Longreach Thurs. and Sun.
Note: No MotoRail services between Melbourne–Sydney and Sydney–Brisbane.

Other Touring Possibilities

The *Spirit of Tasmania* car and passenger ferry makes three return voyages weekly between Melbourne and Devonport, northern Tasmania. Bookings can be made through the TT Line Tasmania at Port Melbourne and Dockside, Devonport, or through your local Tasmanian Travel Centre.

Campervan rental is available in all States and most cities and major towns. Campervans are fully equipped and vary in size and level of luxury. Costs vary accordingly and also with the season. There are often restrictions on where you can take a campervan. Check first.

If you are interested in a full-on

Houseboat, Richmond River, NSW

adventure tour, but are intimidated by the thought of doing it alone, there are motoring organisations and many private tour operators that provide escorted group trips into more remote areas, Cape York for example. These tag-along tours save you the worry of navigation and planning (except for your vehicle) and also provide expert help and backup in case of a mechanical breakdown.

You also could leave your vehicle behind and tour in a 4WD coach, or take a **camel trek** or try a **canoe adventure**— or travel almost any way you choose. Check with your travel agent or tourist bureau (**see:** Useful Information).

For the young at heart, there are over 100 **youth hostels** throughout Australia. For information, contact the main headquarters of the Australian Youth Hostels Association, 10 Mallett St, Camperdown, NSW 2050; (02) 565 1699.

If you are planning a stay in a city or at a resort area for any length of time, a sensible family alternative to motel or hotel accommodation is a **serviced** or **self-service holiday flat**. The relevant tourist bureau (**see:** Useful Information) will provide details.

House swapping is yet another possibility for a lengthy stay. This can be arranged through organisations such as Latitudes Home Exchange, PO Box 436, South Perth WA 6151; (09) 367 9412. In addition, advertisements for those seeking a house-swapping holiday often appear in the classified sections of the newspapers. Make sure you are totally satisfied with the arrangements made concerning your commitments and with the people with whom you are dealing. Also check that your householder's insurance covers you in such circumstances (**see:** Insurance).

A **host farm** can make a refreshing change from the norm. Such accommodation varies from spartan to luxurious and, in some cases, guests are invited to take part in farm life. Associations in each State (**see:** Useful Information) or tourist authorities will provide details.

If you would prefer **bed and breakfast** accommodation only in a homestay or farmstay environment throughout Australia, contact Bed & Breakfast Australia, PO Box 408, Gordon NSW 2072; (02) 498 5344, 498 1539 (AH).

Not to be confused with bushwalking, **backpacking** is a mode of travel using accommodation provided at budget rates in a communal environment. Note, however, that the accommodation offered is not always suitable for children. During the high season, resort hostels may not accept telephone reservations without payment and it is advisable to book well in advance. For information on the range of accommodation available, contact The Secretary, Backpackers Resorts of Australia, PO Box 1000, Byron Bay NSW 2481; (018) 66 6888 (9–5, Mon.–Fri.). A Backpackers VIP Discount Kit $20 (add $2 for postage and handling), valid in 21 countries with an accommodation guide (free) to 122 hostels Australia-wide is available from this organisation.

If you are into **staying afloat**, consider hiring a paddlewheeler on the Murray or a houseboat on the Hawkesbury or Eildon Weir, or even chartering a yacht to cruise in the Whitsundays. Check with your travel agent or Government tourist bureau (**see**: Useful Information).

Dividing Up the Dollars

Very few people can afford the 'money-no-object' approach to holidays, no matter what the length of stay. Your planning should include **budgeting**. You will need principally to consider accommodation, food, fuel and entertainment, although emergency funds should not be forgotten. **Travel insurance** is a wise precaution (**see**: Insurance). Accommodation costs can be estimated when you book, but you might simply average the figure. If you do, estimate high rather than low. **Food** is a matter of personal choice: you may eat out every night or prepare all or some of your meals yourself. Be realistic when budgeting the cost of eating out or preparing meals: allow for the unexpected, and for the higher cost of food and meals in popular holiday destinations or in remote areas. If you are travelling with children, budget for snacks and recreational treats.

Once you know your vehicle's fuel consumption you can work out your **fuel** costs in advance. The usual method is based on litres per 100 kilometres. If your vehicle uses 16 litres per 100 kilometres and your journey distance works out at 5000 kilometres, you will use 50 times 16 litres of fuel, or 800 litres. Allow for rises in the cost of petrol and other vehicle expenses, and also for the fact that fuel is more expensive in remote areas.

When budgeting, allow for such 'budget biters' as admission charges, postcards, camera film, chemist's items, tips, bridge tolls and car repairs. Remember also that accommodation, travel and rental charges rise during peak periods.

Carrying large amounts of **cash** with you is not a good idea, which is why travellers cheques were invented. Use them, or credit cards, but also make arrangements with your bank to enable you to draw from the bank's branches on your route.

Car Maintenance Courses

If you plan to tour in the remoter areas you should acquire basic mechanical knowledge and skills. In general you should have a broad understanding of the technology of your vehicle and know how much roadside repair is possible in the event of a breakdown (**see also**: Breakdowns). You should also have some specific knowledge; for example how to change a tyre on the vehicle you will be using; and whether you can use jumper leads to start your car and if so, how it is done. Car care and basic car-maintenance courses are run by Adult Education centres, TAFE Colleges and automobile clubs in all States. The courses vary widely in content and length. A call to these organisations will ascertain what course is available and appropriate. Test your knowledge by reading through the flow-charts and the list of tools and spare parts (**see**: Trouble Shooting, Tools and Spare Parts).

Insurance

The benefits of a comprehensive insurance policy on your vehicle, caravan or trailer are obvious. As well as cover against loss or damage due to accident, theft and vandalism, your personal effects are covered against loss or damage when they are in the insured vehicle. Additional policies will cover such eventualities as the cost of temporary accommodation should your caravan become uninhabitable, for example. Some companies provide short-term (maximum 6 weeks) travel insurance, for example to cover loss of luggage or the cancellation of accommodation bookings. Information and advice can be obtained from the various motoring organisations and insurance companies.

Itineraries

Some people make itineraries and stick to them; others do not. At the very least, a rough schedule to ensure a mixture of travel and sightseeing time is essential.

Allow some flexibility. You never know what might detain you: the weather, for example (rest breaks are necessary in extreme heat), or children, who have a low tolerance for long stretches of driving without a break (**see**: Child's Play).

Clothing

Be strict with yourself and the family when you are packing and travel as lightly as you can. It is better to spend an hour at a laundromat than overburden your vehicle with clothing you probably will not wear.

Essentials are a warm **jumper** or **jacket**, even in summer; sensible **comfortable shoes**; and a **wide-brimmed hat** to protect yourself from the sun at all times. Non-irons are practical. Carry items like swimwear, towels, spare socks and jumpers in a bag that can be kept within easy reach. **Gumboots** are a handy item also.

First-aid Kit

A first-aid kit is essential. Include band-aids, antiseptic, bandages, headache tablets, extra blockout, sunburn cream, insect repellent and a soothing lotion for bites. Eye drops are a good idea, as is a thermometer and a tourniquet. Such kits are available from various suppliers including St John Ambulance Australia, which also conducts basic courses in first aid. As **car sickness** is often a problem on long journeys, particularly with young children, include medication to counter this. Your chemist or a doctor will advise you.

Useful Extras

Depending on the length and nature of your tour, some items are valuable, some essential (**see**: Tools and Spare Parts). Carry picnic and barbecue equipment, tissues, toilet paper and a container or plastic bag for rubbish—and take it with you rather than leaving it behind, at least until you can find a legitimate rubbish tip. Rugs or blankets are a necessary extra (**see**: Bushfire), as is a large sheet of plastic, which can be used as an emergency windscreen (**see also**: How to Obtain Water). Having a mobile phone may be useful if you are travelling within signal range; check the coverage before you buy. If you are going outback, a necessary item is some type of shade cover, such as a tarpaulin, as sun protection in case of an emergency stop (**see**: Surviving in the Outback).

6

Other Information

Pets

Don't forget: whether you are leaving your pets behind or taking them with you, you will need to make a booking for them also.

Leaving them behind:

- Pet care services (*Yellow Pages*). These provide care of pets in their own environment. They also will care for plants and property, etc.
- Dog boarding kennels and catteries (*Yellow Pages*): provide care and accommodation. Some have pickup and delivery services.
- Animal welfare organisations/veterinary surgeons (*Yellow Pages*): For advice and information.

Taking them with you:

- Make sure, in advance, that the accommodation or mode of travel booked permits animals. Many caravan parks and most national parks do not admit animals.
- During the trip, carry additional water and stop at regular intervals for toileting and exercise.
- Do not leave an animal unattended in a vehicle for any length of time; always provide fresh air.
- Allow sufficient room in the vehicle to comfortably accommodate the animal.
- Do not transport an animal in a moving caravan.

Before Departure

- Cancel newspapers, mail deliveries.
- Make arrangements for the garden to be watered and lawns mowed. Board out your indoor plants or place them in the sink, surround with damp peat, and water thoroughly. Encasing each in a sealed polythene bag also helps.
- If you have a pet, arrange for its safekeeping well in advance (**see:** Pets).
- Arrange for a neighbour to keep an eye on the house. Your local police will cooperate. Alternatively, consult a professional home security service (*Yellow Pages*).
- Valuable items, such as jewellery, are best left for safekeeping at your bank.
- Turn the electricity off at the mains and leave the fridge door open. If you have equipment that must operate in your absence, for example a stocked freezer, leave power on and remove plugs from all other power points. Make sure that everything else that should be turned off is off.
- Check that all windows and doors are locked; then check again.

- Leave a contact address with a friend or neighbour.

Carrying a Camera

You probably will want to preserve the highlights of you trip on film. Check the following points.

- If you have recently bought or hired a camera, take at least one test film so that you know how the equipment reacts to different light conditions.
- As weather conditions may vary, it is a good idea to carry film with a range of speeds. If you are not an expert, talk to your local dealer about the varieties of film available.
- Before you leave, have a good supply of film, batteries and a lens brush. Other useful accessories are a close-up lens, exposure meter, lens hood, filters and a tripod.
- Keep your equipment in a plastic bag inside a camera bag to protect it from water, heat, sand and dust. It can get very hot in a closed car, so always keep the camera in the shade. The best place is on the floor, on the side opposite the exhaust pipe. Make sure, however, that the bag can't rattle around.
- High temperatures and humidity can damage colour film. Store your film in the coolest spot available and do not break the watertight vapour seal until just before use. Once the film is used, remove it from the camera, mark it with an E for 'exposed' and send it for processing as soon as possible.

- Even with automatic exposure, when filming in hot conditions it may be necessary to allow one stop or half of a stop down to compensate for the brilliance of the light. If in doubt, consult the instruction sheet included with the film.
- Check that your personal property insurance covers the loss of cameras and photographic equipment while travelling (**see**: Insurance).

Time Zones

Australia has 3 time zones:

- **Eastern Standard Time** (EST), in Queensland, ACT, New South Wales, Victoria and Tasmania.
- **Central Standard Time** (CST is half an hour behind EST), in South Australia and Northern Territory.
- **Western Standard Time** (WST is 2 hours behind EST), in Western Australia.

Daylight saving is adopted by some States in the summer months. In New South Wales, Victoria, Tasmania, Australian Capital Territory and South Australia, clocks are put forward 1 hour at the beginning of summer. Northern Territory, Western Australia and Queensland do not have daylight saving.

Quarantine Regulations

Throughout Australia, State quarantine regulations prohibit the transport by travellers of certain plants and foods, and even soil, across State borders. Further information is available from offices of agricultural departments in all States.

Yampire Gorge, Hamersley Range National Park, WA

Inter-city Route Maps

The following inter-city route maps will help you plan your route between major cities. As well, you can use the maps during your journey, since they provide information on distances between towns along the route, roadside rest areas and road conditions. The map below provides an overview of the routes mapped, together with a listing of the maps and the pages on which they appear.

Sydney-Melbourne
via Hume Highway/Freeway 〔31〕

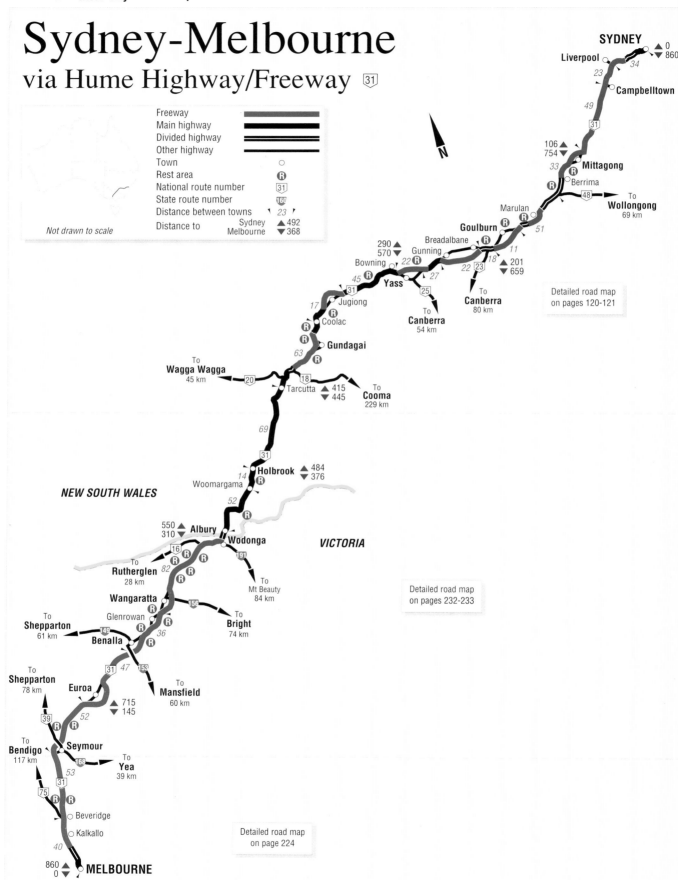

Freeway
Main highway
Divided highway
Other highway
Town ○
Rest area Ⓡ
National route number 〔31〕
State route number 〔160〕
Distance between towns ＼ 23 ＞
Distance to Sydney ▲492
Melbourne ▼368

Not drawn to scale

SYDNEY ▲0 ▼860
Liverpool 34
23
Campbelltown
49
〔31〕
106▲ 754▼
33
Mittagong
Ⓡ Berrima
〔48〕 To **Wollongong** 69 km
Marulan
Ⓡ 51
Goulburn Ⓡ
11
Breadalbane Ⓡ
290▲ Gunning 18
570▼ 22 ⓇⒷ 201▲ 659▼
Bowning 22 〔23〕
45 Ⓡ 27
Yass
〔31〕 25
17 Jugiong To **Canberra** 80 km
Ⓡ Coolac To **Canberra** 54 km
Ⓡ
63 **Gundagai**
Ⓡ
To **Wagga Wagga** 45 km 〔20〕 〔18〕
Tarcutta 415▲ 445▼ To **Cooma** 229 km
69
〔31〕
14 **Holbrook** 484▲ 376▼
Woomargama Ⓡ
NEW SOUTH WALES 52
Ⓡ
550▲ **Albury**
310▼ **Wodonga** **VICTORIA**
〔16〕 Ⓡ 〔191〕
To **Rutherglen** 82 Ⓡ Ⓡ To **Mt Beauty** 84 km
28 km Ⓡ
Wangaratta 〔156〕
Glenrowan Ⓡ To **Bright** 74 km
To **Shepparton** 〔149〕 Ⓡ 36
61 km **Benalla** Ⓡ
〔31〕 47 〔153〕
To **Shepparton** To **Mansfield** 60 km
78 km **Euroa** 715▲ 145▼
〔39〕 52
Ⓡ Ⓡ
To **Bendigo** **Seymour**
117 km 〔168〕 To **Yea** 39 km
53
〔31〕
〔75〕 ⓇⓇ
○ Beveridge
○ Kalkallo
40
860▲ **MELBOURNE**
0▼

Detailed road map on pages 120-121

Detailed road map on pages 232-233

Detailed road map on page 224

Sydney-Melbourne
via Princes Highway ①

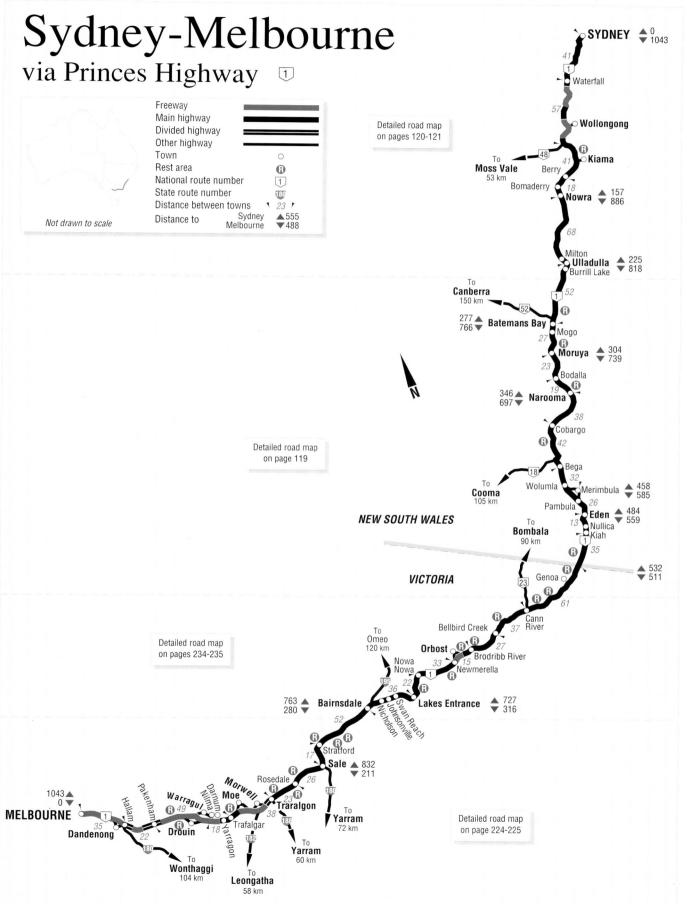

Legend:
- Freeway
- Main highway
- Divided highway
- Other highway
- Town ○
- Rest area ®
- National route number ①
- State route number 180
- Distance between towns ↘ 23 ↙
- Distance to: Sydney ▲555 / Melbourne ▼488

Not drawn to scale

Detailed road map on pages 120-121

Detailed road map on page 119

Detailed road map on pages 234-235

Detailed road map on page 224-225

SYDNEY ▲0 ▼1043
41
Waterfall
57
Wollongong
48 — To Moss Vale 53 km
Kiama ®
41
Berry
Bomaderry 18
Nowra ▲157 ▼886
68
Milton
Ulladulla ▲225 ▼818
Burrill Lake
To **Canberra** 150 km
52 — ① 52
Batemans Bay ▲277 ▼766 ®
Mogo 27
Moruya ® ▲304 ▼739
23
Bodalla ®
19
Narooma ▲346 ▼697
38
Cobargo
® 42
18 — To **Cooma** 105 km
Bega
Wolumla 32
Merimbula ▲458 ▼585
Pambula 26
Eden ▲484 ▼559
To **Bombala** 90 km
Nullica 13
Kiah
① 35
NEW SOUTH WALES

▲532 ▼511

VICTORIA

23 — Genoa ○
® 61
Cann River
Bellbird Creek ® 37
27
Orbost ® ® Brodribb River
To Omeo 120 km
Nowa Nowa 33 15 Newmerella ®
① 22
195 36
Bairnsdale ▲763 ▼280
Swan Reach
Johnsonville
Nicholson
Lakes Entrance ▲727 ▼316
52
® ®
17 Stratford
Sale ® ▲832 ▼211
Rosedale ® 26
180 — To **Yarram** 72 km
Morwell
Moe ® 23 ®
Datnum Nilma **Traralgon**
Warragul ® 49
188
1043▲ 0▼
MELBOURNE
① Hallam Pakenham
35 **Drouin** ® 38
Dandenong 22 Trafalgar Yarragon 18
182 — To **Leongatha** 58 km
180 — To **Wonthaggi** 104 km
To **Yarram** 60 km
N

Sydney-Brisbane
via Pacific Highway ⟨1⟩

QUEENSLAND

Detailed road map
on page 475

NEW SOUTH WALES

BRISBANE ▲ 0 ▼ 964

Loganholme ®
Beenleigh — Yatala
Ormeau — 70
Oxenford
Nerang — Southport
Mudgeeraba — Surfers Paradise
35 — Coolangatta
® — Tweed Heads ▲ 105 ▼ 859
Murwillumbah — 24
16 — Burringbar
16 — Ocean Shores ▲ 161 ▼ 803
20 — Brunswick Heads ®
Bangalow — 25
To — Newrybar
Lismore — 44
35 km — 25 — Ballina ▲ 206 ▼ 758
25 — Wardell
12 — Broadwater
41 — Woodburn
1
To — Chatsworth ®
Glen Innes — Tyndale — Maclean
159 km — 38 — 13 — 39
336 ▲ 628 ▼ — Grafton ← Ulmarra
56 ®
Detailed road map — 25 — Woolgoolga ▲ 392 ▼ 572
on page 123 — Moonee Beach — Emerald Beach
28 — Coffs Harbour ▲ 417 ▼ 547
® — Sawtell
30 — Urunga
Valla Beach
475 ▲ 489 ▼ — Macksville ® — Nambucca Heads
46
Frederickton — 1
7 — Kempsey ▲ 528 ▼ 436
To — Kundabung ® — ®
Walcha — 29
166 km — Telegraph Point
34 — 40 — ® — Port Macquarie
Kew — ®
® —
646 ▲ 318 ▼ — Taree — 49
® — Coopernook
To — 27
Maitland — 47 — Nabiac
12 km — 43 — Bulahdelah ▲ 720 ▼ 244
15 — Karuah ®
26 — ®
Kurri Kurri — Raymond Terrace ▲ 789 ▼ 175
30
1 — To
79 — Newcastle
52 km
® — Gosford
66
Detailed road map
on page 121
SYDNEY ▲ 964 ▼ 0

N

Legend	
Freeway	
Main highway	
Divided highway	
Other highway	
Town	○
Rest area	®
National route number	⟨1⟩
State route number	⟨160⟩
Distance between towns	⟍ *23* ⟋
Distance to	Brisbane ▲ 528
	Sydney ▼ 436

Not drawn to scale

Sydney-Brisbane
via New England Highway 1 82 15

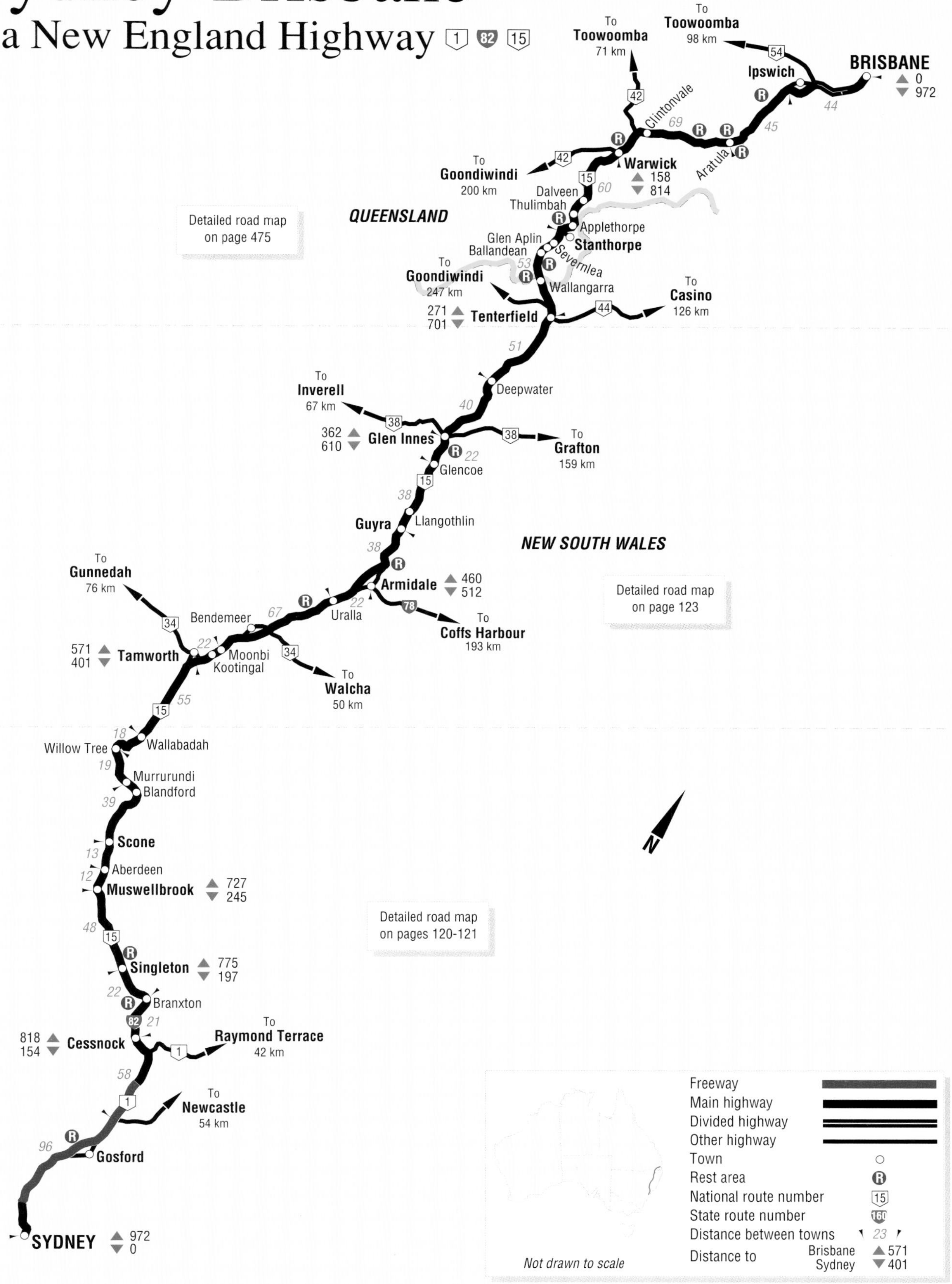

BRISBANE ▲ 0 ▼ 972

To Toowoomba 71 km

To Toowoomba 98 km

54

Ipswich

Clintonvale 69

42

42

Warwick ▲ 158 ▼ 814

45

Aratula 44

To Goondiwindi 200 km

15 60

Dalveen
Thulimbah

Applethorpe

QUEENSLAND

Glen Aplin
Ballandean

Stanthorpe

Severnlea

53

To Goondiwindi 247 km

Wallangarra

To Casino 126 km

271 ▲ 701 ▼ **Tenterfield**

44

51

To Inverell 67 km

Deepwater

40

38

362 ▲ 610 ▼ **Glen Innes**

38

To Grafton 159 km

Glencoe 22

15

38

Guyra Llangothlin

NEW SOUTH WALES

38

Armidale ▲ 460 ▼ 512

22

Uralla

78

To Coffs Harbour 193 km

To Gunnedah 76 km

Bendemeer 67

34

22

571 ▲ 401 ▼ **Tamworth**

Moonbi
Kootingal

34

To Walcha 50 km

55

15

18

Willow Tree Wallabadah

19

Murrurundi
Blandford

39

13

Scone

12

Aberdeen

Muswellbrook ▲ 727 ▼ 245

48

15

Singleton ▲ 775 ▼ 197

22

Branxton

82

21

818 ▲ 154 ▼ **Cessnock**

To Raymond Terrace 42 km

1

58

1

To Newcastle 54 km

96

Gosford

SYDNEY ▲ 972 ▼ 0

Detailed road map on page 475

Detailed road map on page 123

Detailed road map on pages 120-121

Freeway	
Main highway	
Divided highway	
Other highway	
Town	○
Rest area	R
National route number	15
State route number	160
Distance between towns	23
Distance to	Brisbane ▲ 571
	Sydney ▼ 401

Not drawn to scale

Melbourne-Adelaide
via Western & Dukes Highways [8] [1]

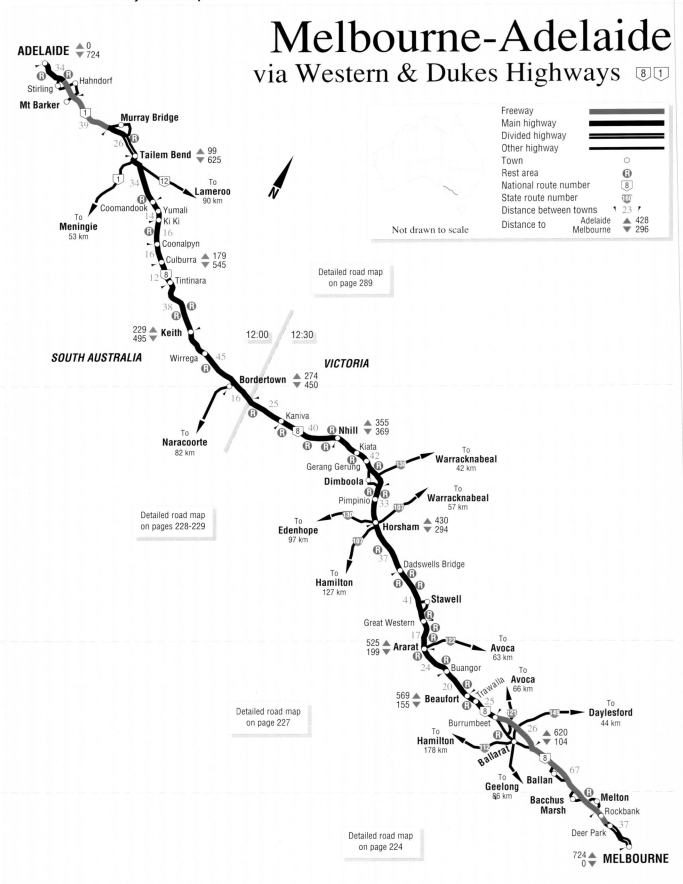

ADELAIDE ▲ 0 ▼ 724

34

Ⓡ Ⓡ Hahndorf

Stirling

Mt Barker ○

[1] 39

Murray Bridge

26 Ⓡ

Tailem Bend ▲ 99 ▼ 625

[1] 34 [12]

To **Lameroo** 90 km

Ⓡ Coomandook

To **Meningie** 53 km

Yumali
Ki Ki 14

16

Coonalpyn

16 Culburra ▲ 179 ▼ 545

12 [8] Tintinara

38 Ⓡ

229 ▲ 495 ▼ **Keith**

SOUTH AUSTRALIA

Wirrega 45 Ⓡ

12:00 | 12:30

VICTORIA

Bordertown ▲ 274 ▼ 450

16

To **Naracoorte** 82 km

25

Kaniva Ⓡ

[8] 40 Ⓡ **Nhill** ▲ 355 ▼ 369

Kiata
42

Gerang Gerung [133] To **Warracknabeal** 42 km

Dimboola

Pimpinio 33 [107] To **Warracknabeal** 57 km

To **Edenhope** 97 km [130]

[107] **Horsham** ▲ 430 ▼ 294

37 Ⓡ

Dadswells Bridge

To **Hamilton** 127 km

Ⓡ Ⓡ

41 **Stawell**

Great Western Ⓡ

17 Ⓡ [22] To **Avoca** 63 km

525 ▲ 199 ▼ **Ararat**

24 Ⓡ Buangor

To **Avoca** 66 km

20 Ⓡ Trawalla

569 ▲ 155 ▼ **Beaufort**

25 [8] [121] [149] To **Daylesford** 44 km

Burrumbeet Ⓡ

26 ▲ 620 ▼ 104

To **Hamilton** 178 km [12]

Ballarat [8]

To **Geelong** 86 km

67 **Ballan**

Ⓡ **Melton**

Bacchus Marsh Rockbank

Deer Park 37

724 ▲ 0 ▼ **MELBOURNE**

Detailed road map on page 289

Detailed road map on pages 228-229

Detailed road map on page 227

Detailed road map on page 224

Freeway
Main highway
Divided highway
Other highway
Town ○
Rest area Ⓡ
National route number [8]
State route number [160]
Distance between towns ↘ 23 ↗
Distance to — Adelaide ▲ 428 — Melbourne ▼ 296

Not drawn to scale

Melbourne-Adelaide
via Princes Highway ①

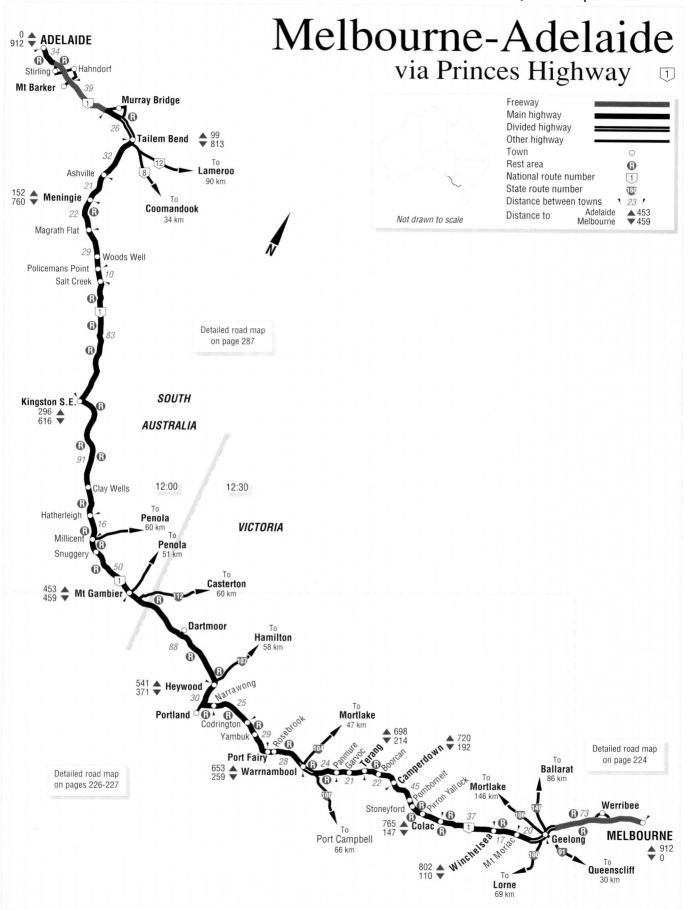

Legend

Freeway	
Main highway	
Divided highway	
Other highway	
Town	○
Rest area	Ⓡ
National route number	①
State route number	160
Distance between towns	↘ 23 ↗
Distance to	Adelaide ▲453
	Melbourne ▼459

Not drawn to scale

ADELAIDE 0 / 912
34
Stirling — Ⓡ — Hahndorf
Mt Barker ①
39
Murray Bridge
Ⓡ
26
Tailem Bend ▲99 ▼813
32
12
Ashville — 8 — **To Lameroo** 90 km
21
Meningie 152 / 760
Ⓡ
22
Magrath Flat — **To Coomandook** 34 km
29
Woods Well
Policemans Point — 10
Salt Creek
Ⓡ
Ⓡ ①
83
Ⓡ

Detailed road map on page 287

SOUTH AUSTRALIA

Kingston S.E. Ⓡ 296 ▲ / 616 ▼
Ⓡ
Ⓡ
91
Clay Wells
Ⓡ
Hatherleigh
16 — **To Penola** 60 km
Millicent — Ⓡ
Snuggery — Ⓡ — **To Penola** 51 km
Ⓡ 50
①
Mt Gambier 453 / 459 — Ⓡ — 12 — **To Casterton** 60 km

12:00 12:30

VICTORIA

Dartmoor
88 — **To Hamilton** 58 km
Ⓡ 107
Heywood 541 / 371 — Ⓡ
30 — Narrawong
Portland — Ⓡ — Ⓡ — 25
Codrington — Ⓡ
Yambuk — 29 — Rosebrook
Port Fairy 28 — 104
Warrnambool 653 / 259 — Ⓡ 24 — Panmure — Garvoc — **To Mortlake** 47 km
100 — 21 — Ⓡ — 22 — Boorcan — **Terang** ▲698 ▼214
Stoneyford — 45 — Pomborneit — **Camperdown** ▲720 ▼192
To Port Campbell 66 km — Ⓡ — Pirron Yallock — **To Mortlake** 146 km
Colac 765 / 147 — Ⓡ — 37 — **To Ballarat** 86 km
Winchelsea 802 / 110 — ① — Mt Moriac — 17 — 106 — 149
20 — Ⓡ — **Geelong** — Ⓡ 73 — **Werribee**
100 — 91 — **MELBOURNE** ▲912 ▼0
To Lorne 69 km — **To Queenscliff** 30 km

Detailed road map on page 224

Detailed road map on pages 226-227

Melbourne-Brisbane
via Newell Highway [31] [39] [42] [15]

QUEENSLAND

Detailed road map on pags 474-475

To Miles 219 km

To Toowoomba 130 km

To Toowoomba 73 km

▲ 0
▼ 1681 **BRISBANE**

[39]

Yelarbon

Karara

54

15 62

Mutdapilly

Warrill View

[42] 51

[42]

Aratula

95

357 ▲
1324 ▼ **Goondiwindi**

R 50

R 58

[42]

[15]

Clintonvale

Inglewood 41

123

Boggabilla

R

Warwick

157 ▲
1524 ▼

To Walgett 217 km

[38]

Moree 480 ▲
1201 ▼

[38]

To Inverell 145 km

To Stanthorpe 60 km

R 100

Detailed road map on pages 122-123

[39]

R

Narrabri 580 ▲
1101 ▼

121

R 37

To Gunnedah 95 km

To Warren 89 km

[34]

To Gunnedah 100 km

94

Coonabarabran 701 ▲
980 ▼

To Narromine 40 km

[34]

R **Gilgandra** 795 ▲
886 ▼

66

Eumungerie

NEW SOUTH WALES

INSET OF VICTORIA/NSW BORDER AREA

NEW SOUTH WALES

Tocumwal

25

[16]

Strathmerton R

[16]

30

VICTORIA

Numurkah

Wunghnu R

[32]

R **Dubbo** 861 ▲
820 ▼

53

[32]

17 Tomingley

25 Peak Hill

To Wellington 50 km

Detailed road map on page 120

24 Alectown

Parkes 980 ▲
701 ▼

33

R

[39] **Forbes**

To Hay 261 km

Marsden

69

[24] 37

1119 ▲
562 ▼ **West Wyalong**

R

[24]

Wyalong

To Cowra 124 km

To Hay 175 km

Ardlethan

70 Mirrool

Beckom

67

Detailed road map on page 127

[20]

Morundah

Narrandera ▲ 1256
▼ 425

Grong Grong

R

To Deniliquin 61 km

Jerilderie

[39]

[20]

To Wagga Wagga 101 km

58 35

Finley

58

To Albury 145 km

To Echuca 92 km

[16] 102 [16]

To Wodonga 131 km

Congupna

Tallygaroopna

Shepparton ▲ 1502
▼ 179

Detailed road map on page 232

R

Nagambie

56 [31]

To Euroa 47 km

N

R

123

Seymour

168

To Yea 39 km

75

R

Bendigo 117 km

[31]

To **VICTORIA**

MELBOURNE ▲ 1681
▼ 0

Detailed road map on page 224

Not drawn to scale

Freeway	
Main highway	
Divided highway	
Other highway	
Town	○
Rest area	R
National route number	[39]
State route number	[160]
Distance between towns	23
Distance to Brisbane / Melbourne	▲ 980 / ▼ 701

Adelaide-Darwin
via Stuart Highway 87 1

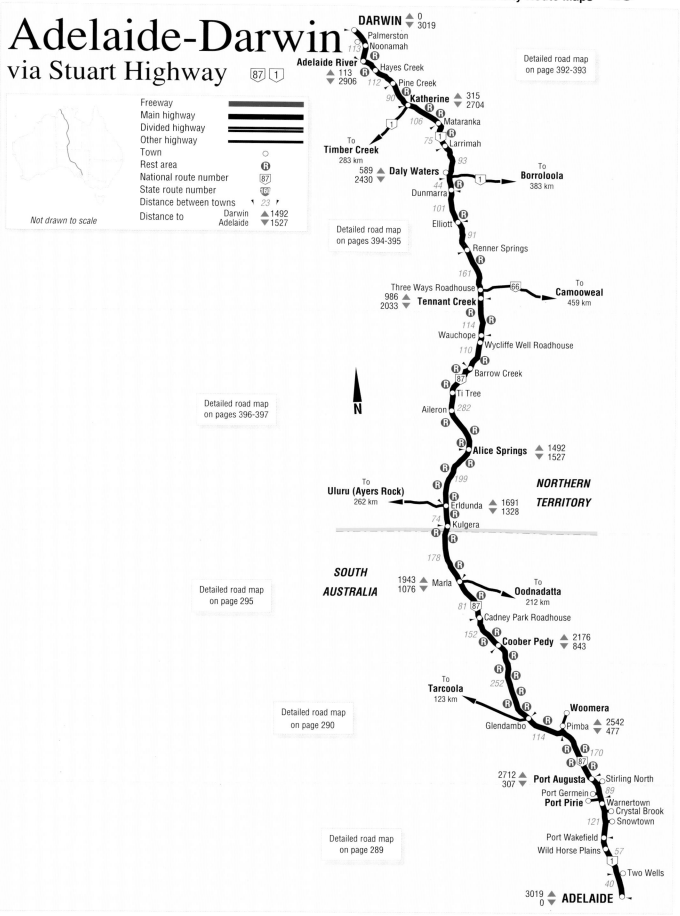

Detailed road map on page 392-393

DARWIN ▲0 / ▼3019
Palmerston
Noonamah
113
Adelaide River
Hayes Creek
▲113 / ▼2906
112
Pine Creek
90
Katherine ▲315 / ▼2704
106
Mataranka
To Timber Creek 283 km
75
Larrimah
93
589 / 2430 Daly Waters
To Borroloola 383 km
44
Dunmarra
101
Elliott
91
Renner Springs
161
Three Ways Roadhouse
66 To Camooweal 459 km
986 / 2033 Tennant Creek
114
Wauchope
110
Wycliffe Well Roadhouse
Barrow Creek 87
Ti Tree
Aileron 282
Alice Springs ▲1492 / ▼1527
199
To Uluru (Ayers Rock) 262 km
Erldunda ▲1691 / ▼1328
74
Kulgera
178
Marla 1943 / 1076
To Oodnadatta 212 km
81 87
Cadney Park Roadhouse
152
Coober Pedy ▲2176 / ▼843
252
To Tarcoola 123 km
Woomera ▲2542 / ▼477
Glendambo Pimba
114
170
2712 / 307 Port Augusta 87 Stirling North
89
Port Germein Warnertown
Port Pirie Crystal Brook
121 Snowtown
Port Wakefield
Wild Horse Plains 57
1 Two Wells
40
3019 / 0 ADELAIDE

Detailed road map on pages 394-395

Detailed road map on pages 396-397

NORTHERN TERRITORY

SOUTH AUSTRALIA

Detailed road map on page 295

Detailed road map on page 290

Detailed road map on page 289

N

Adelaide-Perth
via Eyre & Great Eastern Highways ⏹1 ⏹94

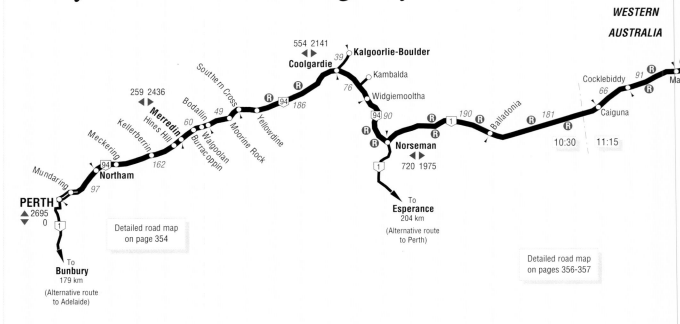

Adelaide-Sydney
via Hume & Sturt Highways ⏹31 ⏹20

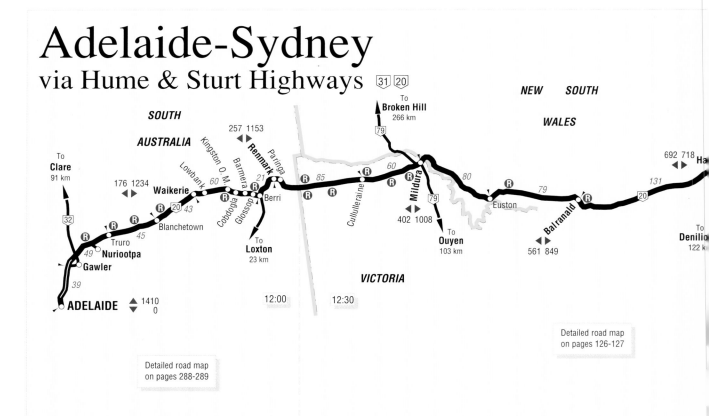

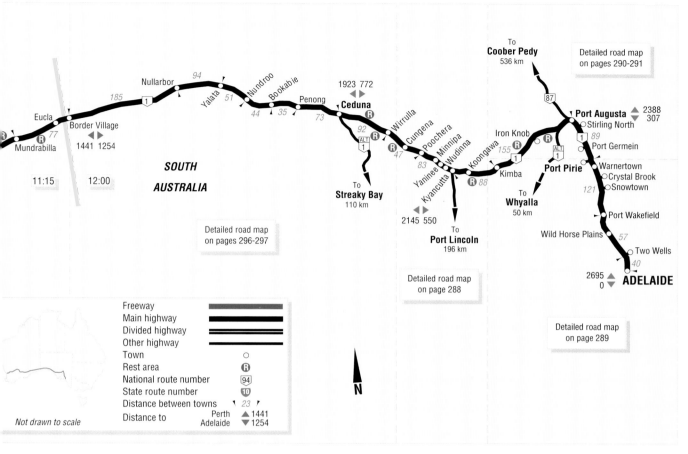

Nullarbor
94
To
Coober Pedy
536 km
Detailed road map
on pages 290-291

185

Eucla
77
Border Village
Yalata
51
Nundroo
44
35
Bookabie
Penong
73
1923 772
Ceduna

1441 1254
Mundrabilla

Iron Knob
155
87
Port Augusta
2388
307
Stirling North

Wirrulla
92
ALT 1
Cungena
Poochera
Minnipa
Wudinna
Koongawa
1
Kimba
ALT 1
89
Port Germein

SOUTH
AUSTRALIA
47
83
Yaninee
Kyancutta
88
Port Pirie
Warnertown
Crystal Brook
Snowtown

11:15
12:00

To
Streaky Bay
110 km
2145 550
To
Port Lincoln
196 km
To
Whyalla
50 km
121
Port Wakefield
57
Wild Horse Plains
Two Wells
40
2695
0
ADELAIDE

Detailed road map
on pages 296-297

Detailed road map
on page 288

Detailed road map
on page 289

Freeway
Main highway
Divided highway
Other highway
Town   ○
Rest area   Ⓡ
National route number   94
State route number   10
Distance between towns 23
Distance to   Perth   ▲1441
               Adelaide ▼1254

Not drawn to scale

N

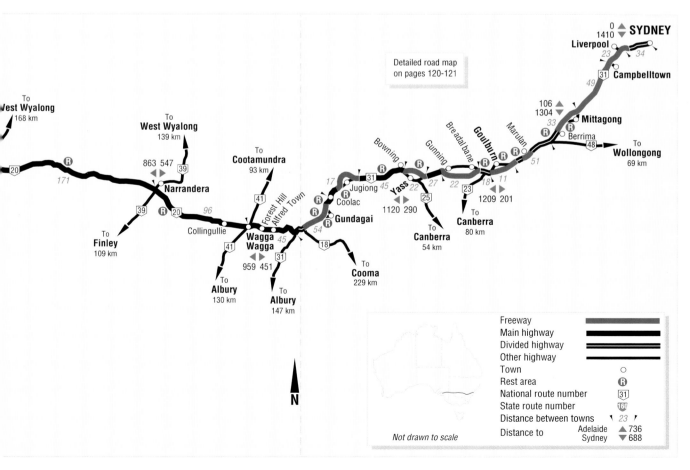

0
SYDNEY
1410
Liverpool
23
34

Detailed road map
on pages 120-121

31
Campbelltown
49

To
West Wyalong
168 km

To
West Wyalong
139 km

106
1304
Mittagong
33

863 547
39
To
Cootamundra
93 km

Bowning
Gunning
Breadalbane
Goulburn
Marulan
Berrima
48
To
Wollongong
69 km

20
171
Ⓡ
Narrandera
41
Forest Hill
Alfred Town
17
31
Jugiong
45
Yass
22
27
22
23
18
11
51

39
20
96
Collingullie
Ⓡ
Coolac
Gundagai
1120 290
25
1209 201
To
Canberra
80 km

To
Finley
109 km
Wagga
Wagga
45
54
18
To
Cooma
229 km
To
Canberra
54 km

41
959 451
To
Albury
130 km
To
Albury
147 km

N

Freeway
Main highway
Divided highway
Other highway
Town   ○
Rest area   Ⓡ
National route number   31
State route number   160
Distance between towns 23
Distance to   Adelaide ▲736
               Sydney   ▼688

Not drawn to scale

Perth-Darwin
via Brand, Northwest Coastal, Great Northern, Victoria & Stuart Highways ⑴

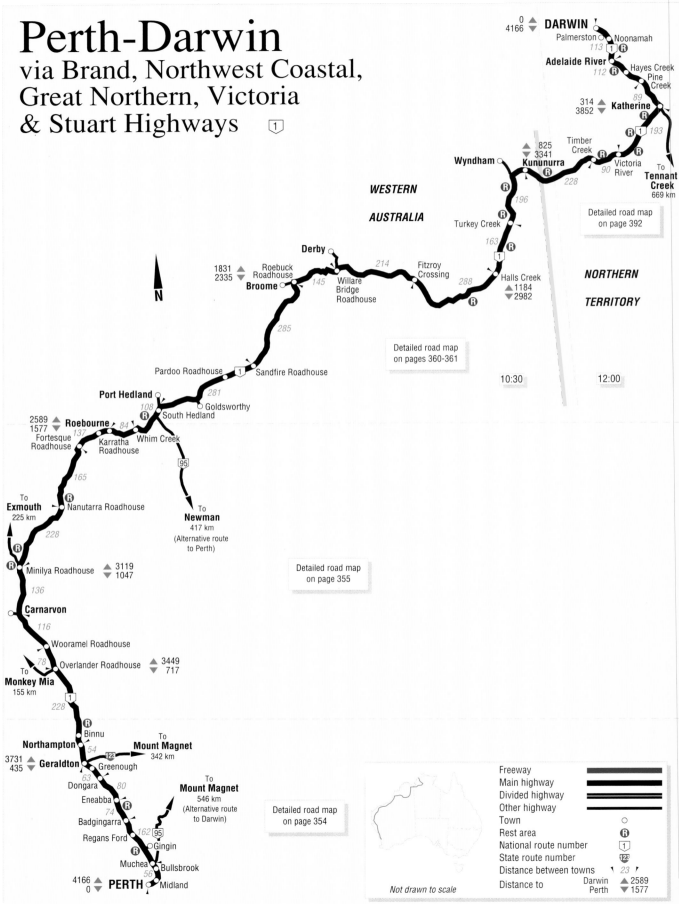

0 DARWIN
4166
Palmerston Noonamah
113 ①Ⓡ
Adelaide River
112 Ⓡ Hayes Creek
Pine Creek
89
314 **Katherine**
3852 Ⓡ
Ⓡ ① 193
Timber Creek
825
3341
Ⓡ
Wyndham **Kununurra** 90 Victoria River
228 To **Tennant Creek**
669 km
Ⓡ
196
WESTERN AUSTRALIA
Ⓡ Turkey Creek
163
Ⓡ
① Detailed road map on page 392
Derby **NORTHERN TERRITORY**
1831 Roebuck 214 Fitzroy Crossing
2335 Roadhouse
145 Willare Bridge Roadhouse 288 Halls Creek
Broome Ⓡ ▲1184 ▼2982
285
Detailed road map on pages 360-361
10:30   12:00
Pardoo Roadhouse ① Sandfire Roadhouse
281
Port Hedland Goldsworthy
108 Ⓡ South Hedland
2589 **Roebourne** 84
1577 137 Whim Creek
Fortesque Karratha Roadhouse ⑼⁵
Roadhouse Roadhouse
165 To **Newman** 417 km (Alternative route to Perth)
To Ⓡ Nanutarra Roadhouse
Exmouth 225 km
228
Ⓡ
Ⓡ Minilya Roadhouse ▲3119 ▼1047
136 Detailed road map on page 355
Carnarvon
116
Wooramel Roadhouse
78 Overlander Roadhouse ▲3449 ▼717
To **Monkey Mia** 155 km
228
①
Ⓡ Binnu
Northampton 54 To **Mount Magnet** 342 km
3731 **Geraldton** ⑴²³
435 Greenough
63 80 To **Mount Magnet** 546 km (Alternative route to Darwin)
Dongara
Eneabba 74 Ⓡ Detailed road map on page 354
Badgingarra
Regans Ford 162 ⑼⁵
Ⓡ Gingin
Muchea Bullsbrook
56
4166 **PERTH** Midland
0

Freeway	━━━
Main highway	━━━
Divided highway	═══
Other highway	━━━
Town	○
Rest area	Ⓡ
National route number	①
State route number	⑴²³
Distance between towns	↘ 23
Distance to	Darwin ▲2589 / Perth ▼1577

Not drawn to scale

Brisbane-Darwin
via Warrego, Landsborough, Barkly & Stuart Highways 54 71 66 87 1

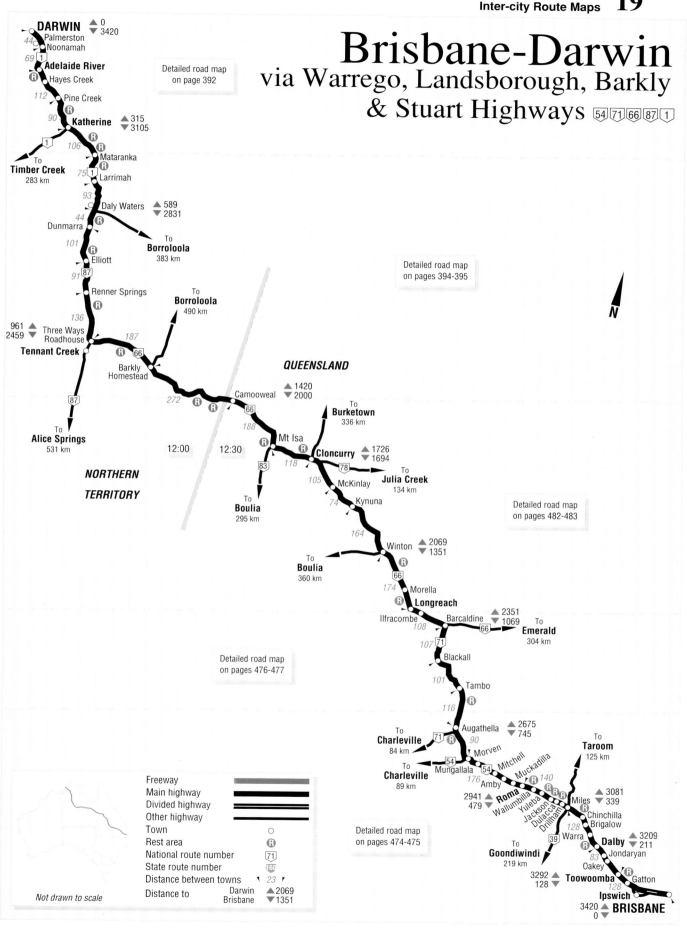

DARWIN ▲ 0 ▼ 3420
Palmerston
44 Noonamah
69 **Adelaide River**
Ⓡ Hayes Creek
112 Pine Creek Ⓡ
90 **Katherine** Ⓡ ▲ 315 ▼ 3105
1 106 Ⓡ Mataranka
To 75 1 Larrimah
Timber Creek 283 km
93
Daly Waters ▲ 589 ▼ 2831
44 Ⓡ
Dunmarra
101 Ⓡ To **Borroloola** 383 km
Elliott
91 87
Ⓡ Renner Springs To **Borroloola** 490 km
136
961 2459 ▲▼ **Three Ways Roadhouse**
Tennant Creek 187
Ⓡ 66
Barkly Homestead
87
To **Alice Springs** 531 km
272 Ⓡ Ⓡ Camooweal
66
QUEENSLAND
▲ 1420 ▼ 2000
188
To **Burketown** 336 km

NORTHERN TERRITORY

12:00 12:30

Ⓡ Mt Isa Ⓡ
83 118 **Cloncurry** ▲ 1726 ▼ 1694
105 78 To **Julia Creek** 134 km
To **Boulia** 295 km McKinlay
74 Kynuna
164
Winton ▲ 2069 ▼ 1351
Ⓡ
To **Boulia** 360 km 66
174 Morella
Ⓡ **Longreach**
Ilfracombe 108 Barcaldine ▲ 2351 ▼ 1069
107 71 66 To **Emerald** 304 km
Blackall
101
Tambo
Ⓡ
116

Detailed road map on page 392

Detailed road map on pages 394-395

Detailed road map on pages 482-483

Detailed road map on pages 476-477

▲ 2675 ▼ 745
To **Charleville** 84 km 71 Ⓡ Augathella
90
To **Charleville** 89 km Mungallala 54 Morven Mitchell Muckadilla
176 Amby Ⓡ 140
2941 479 **Roma** Yuleba ▲ 3081 ▼ 339
Wallumbilla Jackson Dulacca Miles
Drillham 128 Chinchilla
39 Warra Brigalow
To **Goondiwindi** 219 km Ⓡ Dalby ▲ 3209 ▼ 211
83 Jondaryan
Oakey
3292 128 **Toowoomba** Gatton
128
Ipswich
3420 0 **BRISBANE**

To **Taroom** 125 km

Detailed road map on pages 474-475

Freeway	▬▬▬
Main highway	▬▬▬
Divided highway	▬▬▬
Other highway	▬▬▬
Town	○
Rest area	Ⓡ
National route number	71
State route number	160
Distance between towns	‹ 23 ›
Distance to	Darwin ▲ 2069
	Brisbane ▼ 1351

Not drawn to scale

Brisbane-Cairns
via Bruce Highway [1]

Freeway	▬▬▬
Main highway	▬▬▬
Divided highway	═══
Other highway	───
Town	○
Rest area	®
National route number	[1]
State route number	[160]
Distance between towns	＼ *23* ＿
Distance to	Cairns ▲738
	Brisbane ▼972

Not drawn to scale

CAIRNS
0 ▲
1710 ▼

Edmonton
Gordonvale
88
Babinda
Innisfail ▲ 88
▼ 1622
Silkwood ®
El Arish ®
52
Tully
Euramo
44 ®
Cardwell
52 ®
Ingham
Toobanna ®
110 Rollingstone
Bluewater
Townsville ▲ 346
▼ 1364
87
Brandon
[78] [1] ® **Ayr**
Home Hill
To
Charters Towers
135 km
115 Gumlu ®
Guthalungra
Merinda **Bowen** ▲ 548
▼ 1162
®
66
Proserpine
Bloomsbury
Elaroo
Yalboroo Calen
124
Glenella **Mackay** ▲ 738
® ▼ 972
Bakers Creek
36 Sarina
To Koumala *39* ®
Clermont Ilbilbie
274 km Carmila *26*
Flaggy Rock ®
[1] ®
131
Marlborough
102 Glen Geddes
Kunwarara Yaamba The Caves ®
Parkhurst
1072 ▲ **Rockhampton** Midgee
638 ▼ [66] ® Raglan
To [17] *73* Mt Larcom
Emerald ® **Gladstone** ▲1179
270 km *34* ® ▼ 531
To Calliope ®
Biloela *51*
145 km Bororen
13 Miriam Vale
To
Biloela [1] *99* To
98 km ® **Bundaberg**
Gin Gin 47 km
56
Wallaville Childers
Booyal ®
® Howard
Torbanlea
57 **Maryborough** ▲1455
▼ 255
Tiaro Owanyilla
To
Kingaroy Gunalda *89*
135 km ® **Gympie**
®
40 ®
® Cooroy
Nambour ®
To ®
Kingaroy [1] *126*
164 km Caboolture
[ALT 1]
®
1710 ▲ **BRISBANE**
0 ▼

Detailed road map
on page 479

Detailed road map
on pages 476-477

Detailed road map
on page 475

To
Charters Towers
542 km

N

Have A Good Trip

Checking the Car

All the care that you devote to your own comfort can be for nothing if you do not make sure that the car checks out too.

For a one-, two- or three-day tour, you could simply fuel up, check the tyre pressures, clean all the windows and head off; if you maintain your vehicle at all times in reasonable condition—as indeed you should—probably little further preparation is required. However, a vacation of a week or more, or any time involving long-distance driving, will need more thorough preparation. If you intend travelling through remote areas, for example, you should first check that your vehicle is able to handle off-road conditions. The service department of your State motoring organisations (**see:** Motoring Organisations) will give advice and make a preliminary inspection of your vehicle.

Regardless of the length of your tour, you should check the wheelbrace, jack and under-vehicle jacking points, in case you have to change a tyre.

Unless you are able to service your vehicle yourself, this preparation should be left to your mechanic. To avoid breakdowns and to confirm the reliability of safety-related items, ask the mechanic to include a check of the fuel supply, electrics, brakes, tyres and certain ancillary equipment, as follows.

- **Fuel supply** Check fuel pump for flow. Check carburettor for wear and potential blockages or check condition of electronic or mechanical fuel injection. When the tank is almost empty, remove the drain plug and drain the tank, to check that the remaining fuel is perfectly clean. Check fuel-supply lines for cracks and poor connections, and make sure no fuel line is exposed to damage by rocks or low-clearance projections.
- **Electrics** Check battery output and condition (including terminals), alternator/generator output and condition, spark plugs, condenser, coil, distributor and all terminals and cables. If the vehicle is fitted with electronic ignition it should be checked in the prescribed manner. Check all lights, not just to see that they work, but to make sure that they are aligned correctly and are likely to continue to work. It can be very, very dark at night in outback Australia.
- **Brakes** Check wear of pads and/or linings and check discs for runout and drums for scoring. Brake dust should be cleaned off. Check brake lines and hoses for cracks and wear. Make sure brake lines are not liable to be damaged by rocks or low projections. Check parking brake for adjustment and cable stretch.
- **Tyres** Check for uneven or excessive wear. Check walls for cracks and stone or kerb fractures. Check pressures. Include spare (or spares) in all checks. Make sure that the spare wheel matches those on the car, and uses the same kind of wheel nuts.
- **Other items** Check windscreen-wiper blades for wear and proper contact and washers for direction and effectiveness. Include rear wiper and washer, where fitted.
- Check **windscreen glass** for cracks and replace if necessary.
- Check **seat mountings and adjustments.**
- Check **levels** of all **lubricants** (including brake and clutch fluid) and either top up or drain and refill.
- Check **wheel bearings** for play and adjust or replace.
- Check **universal and constant velocity joints,** where appropriate, and replace if necessary.
- Check **dust and water sealing.** (A pre-run test in appropriate conditions will reveal any problems. What you do not need is dust, exhaust fumes or water inside the vehicle.)
- If you carry a **roof rack**, check mounts and welds for weaknesses and cracks.
- Check all **seat belts** for tears or sun-hardening. Replace if necessary. Also check inertia reels.
- Check **radiator water level and condition**. Drain and flush, if necessary. Check radiator for leaks and radiator pressure cap for pressure release accuracy. Check water-pump operation. Check radiator and heater hoses for cracks and general condition, and replace if necessary. Check hose clamps.
- Check **fan belt** for tension and fraying.
- Check anything else you might think is worthwhile.
- This should be done as near as practicable to your departure date. Allow time for unexpected work or part replacement, and for a return to the garage if a particular problem persists. Note: *Nothing should be overlooked*—lives may be at stake.

Packing the Car

First and most important, you should carry only those items that are absolutely necessary with you in the passenger compartment. In a sedan this is not difficult. You have a boot, and that is where most items should be carried; but in a station wagon it is much more difficult. Loose items in the passenger compartment get under your feet (especially a hazard for the driver), interfere with your comfort and will become

Hazards

Flood

In some remote areas, floods can occur without warning. Do not camp in dry river beds or close to the edges of creeks or streams. Always exercise extreme caution when approaching flooded roads or bridges. Floodwaters are deceptive; always check the depth before attempting to cross. If you do find yourself stranded in deep water:

- Do not panic.
- Wind up all the windows, to slow down or prevent water entering. (You should have closed all the windows before you tried to cross.)
- When the car has stabilised, undo the seatbelts.
- Turn the headlights on to help rescuers locate the car.
- If the car does not sink, but drifts (which is often the case with a well-sealed car), wait until it reaches shallow water or is close to the bank, then open the door or windows and climb out.
- Form a human chain and help children to keep their heads above water.
- If the car is sinking, it will be necessary to wait for the water pressure to equalise before you can open the doors or windows. As a last resort, kick out the windscreen or rear window.

Bushfire

If you have to travel on days of critical fire danger (that is, total fire ban days), make sure you carry some woollen blankets and a filled water container. If you are trapped as a bushfire approaches:

- Do not panic.
- Stop the car in the nearest cleared area.
- Wind up all the windows.
- Turn on the hazard lights to warn any other traffic.
- DO NOT GET OUT OF YOUR CAR. The temperature may become unbearably hot, but it is still safer to stay in the car.
- Lie on the car floor, below window level, to avoid radiant heat.
- Cover yourself and your passengers with blankets.
- The car will not explode or catch fire, and a fast-moving wildfire will pass quickly overhead.

Animals

Although some species of Australia's unique wildlife are immensely appealing, some species are extremely dangerous.

Marine life

Box jellyfish (or **sea wasps**) are found in the coastal waters of Queensland and northern Australia in the summer months (end November–end April). A sting from their many long tentacles can be lethal, and for that reason swimming on coastal beaches north of Rockhampton is prohibited at this time. Also, walking barefoot at the water's edge in this region in summer is not advisable.

Among Australia's several species of poisonous stinging fish, the **stonefish**, found all around the northern coastline, is best avoided.

The small **blue-ringed octopus** is common in Australian coastal waters. Its bite can paralyse in 15 minutes. Do not handle in any circumstances.

Sharks are common in Australian waters. Avoid swimming in deep water and do not swim where sharks have been seen.

Freshwater and saltwater crocodiles are found in north and north-western Australia. The saltwater crocodile is particularly dangerous and may be found in both salt water and fresh water. The freshwater crocodile will bite if disturbed. Neither species is easy to see in the water. Heed local warning signs and do not swim or paddle in natural waterways or allow children or animals near the water's edge.

Snakes

Snakes are timid and generally do not attack unless threatened. However, several species are highly venomous.

Spiders

The bite from both the **funnel-web** and **red-back spider** can be deadly. The funnel-web is found in and around Sydney. The red-back is widespread.

Insects

Wasps, **bees**, **ticks**, **ants** (particularly the **bull-ant**), **scorpions** and **centipedes** are found throughout Australia. Their sting or bite normally is not harmful, except to those people who are allergy-prone, but it may cause pain and discomfort. Ticks should be removed promptly.

Study Australia's wildlife and learn to identify dangerous species. Remember also that some plant species are poisonous. When visiting a new area, check with local authorities to ascertain which dangerous species, if any, are found there.

Check depth of floodwaters before crossing

dangerous projectiles if you have a collision. So for your station wagon, buy or rig up a safety net, which can be fitted behind the rear seat to separate you from the objects that could otherwise harm you.

This rule applies also to food and drink. Empty bottles and cartons should be stowed out of the way in a rubbish bag, until you are able to dispose of them.

And if you are short of space, cull some non-essential items.

In order to provide extra space, many drivers fix a **roof rack** to their vehicle. This is not recommended. Laden roof racks upset the balance of the vehicle by changing its centre of gravity, making it top-heavy. They disturb the air flow, which can destabilise the vehicle, and they certainly increase fuel consumption by interfering with the aerodynamics. In some circumstances they can snag on overhanging limbs of trees.

If you must use a roof rack, carry as little on it as possible and keep the maximum loading height as low as you can. Protect the load by wrapping it in a tarpaulin or groundsheet and, if possible, create a sharp (aerofoil) leading edge on the load to improve air flow.

A better alternative to a roof rack is a small, strong, lightweight **trailer,** but there are times when this will be a disadvantage also.

If you are towing a **caravan,** some items can be carried inside the van on the floor, preferably strapped down (anything loose will be flung about) and located over the axle (or axles). In some States, caravans must be fitted with a fire extinguisher. (And remember, no people or animals are to be transported in a towed caravan.)

Once your vehicle is loaded, and preferably with the passengers aboard check the **tyre pressures** (yes, even as you leave home on day one). The additional load will mean higher pressures are needed. The tyre placard or owner's handbook can be used as a guideline, but modern steel radials, fully laden, are best inflated to around 250 kilopascals (36 psi). This is not too high. For a country trip with a heavy load on a hot day 280 kPa (40 psi) is about right. Light vans and 4WD vehicles should have higher pressure: at least 315 kPa (45 psi) for the highway, and as high as 350 kPa (50 psi) for highway travel on a hot day with a heavy load. The tyre will bag if it is under-inflated and destabilise the car. It also will offer a baggy sidewall to rocks and stones, encouraging wall fractures and potential blowouts. Laden-tyre pressure requirements vary with tyre size and design, but the pressure is important. If you are in any doubt, contact the tyre manufacturer (**see also:** Outback Motoring).

When to Set Off

There is evidence to suggest that people drive best during the hours in which they are accustomed to being awake, and probably at work. As drowsiness is deadly in drivers, this is worth noting. Leaving home, for example at 1 a.m., might avoid the heat of the day and beat the traffic to a large extent, but somewhere between 3 and 5 a.m. you may find yourself wanting to doze off again.

Plan to share long-distance driving as much as possible. Depart around or just before sunrise and stop no later than sundown. Allow regular stops, not just to stretch your legs but to take nourishment as well. Food helps keep the energy levels up. You might care to leave later if you are travelling east, to avoid the rising sun, and finish earlier if you are travelling west, for the converse reason.

Leaving Home

Everyone knows the feeling that usually comes when you are a good distance from home: did I lock all the windows, turn off the electricity at the meter...? Usually all is well, but it is reassuring to double-check everything before you leave (**see**: Before Departure).

An early start, Mt Rowland, Tas.

Better Driving

The two most important ingredients in skilful driving are **concentration** and **smoothness.**

For the first, get comfortable and stay comfortable. Discomfort destroys concentration. Lack of concentration is the biggest single cause of road accidents.

Wear the right clothes: loose-fitting, cool or warm as appropriate, but capable of being changed (not while you are driving!) as temperatures change. Lightweight shoes are better than boots. (There are such things as driving shoes, which are excellent.) Wear good quality antiglare sunglasses. Sit comfortably: neither too close to the steering wheel and cramped, nor too far back and stretching; and be sure you can reach the foot controls through the entire length of their movement. Drive with both hands all the time. No one can control a car properly with one hand. Driving gloves are recommended. Make all seat, belt and rear-view mirror adjustments before you drive off. (This is especially relevant if you share the driving with someone not your size.)

Concentration means *no distractions.* It is probably unrealistic to suggest that no conversation takes place while you are driving, but do not allow conversations to interfere with your concentration. Aim to keep the children quiet and amused (**see:** Child's Play). **If an important issue needs to be resolved, first stop the car and then sort it out.**

Smoothness is vital for the vehicle's safe, effective operation, but unfortunately many people are not smooth drivers. A vehicle in motion is a tonne or so of iron, steel and plastic sitting atop a set of springs. It is inherently unstable and prone to influences such as pitch and roll. This is difficult enough to control in normal motion, but worse when the driver exaggerates these instabilities by stabbing at the brakes, jerking the steering wheel and crashing the gears. Two things derive from being a smooth driver. The first is passenger comfort; on a long trip, everyone will arrive much fresher and more relaxed if the driver has provided a smooth and therefore pleasant journey. The second is increased safety; the vehicle will react better to smooth, controlled input than it will to hamfisted driving. Smooth driving brings even further benefits: less wear and tear and lower fuel consumption.

However, to define better driving as a combination of concentration and smoothness only would not be wholly accurate. There are other factors:

- **Know your vehicle.** Understand its breaking capacities, especially in emergencies—some cars move around a lot, or become directionally unstable under harsh braking. Be aware of its usable power and its limitations. And drive well within the cornering and road-holding limits of the vehicle's suspension and tyre combination.
- **Drive defensively.** Assume all other drivers are asleep, inattentive or devoid of skill. It is remarkable how such an attitude will increase driving awareness.
- **Do not be impatient.** Advance planning should have provided you with ample time for the day's journey.
- **Do not drive with an incapacitating illness or injury.** Something as simple as a bruised elbow might restrict rapid arm movement when you most need it.

Emergencies

Of course, the best way to handle emergencies is to avoid them. However, to suggest one problem or another will never occur is unrealistic. (A course in defensive driving is an advantage; **see:** Motoring Organisations.)

The possibility of **skidding** worries most drivers, as well it should. There are a number of causes of a skid, some of them composite. Essentially skidding occurs when the tyres lose their grip on the road. The most common form is a front-wheel (or sometimes all-wheel) skid caused by over-braking. When the wheels stop rolling, the vehicle will no longer react to steering input. If you avoid jumping on the brake pedal, (that is, drive smoothly), you will avoid this type of skid. However if you do skid, quickly ease just sufficient pressure off the brake pedal to allow the wheels to roll again. The steering will come back, which at least will allow you to take avoiding action as well as to slow down. A rear-wheel skid also may occur as a result of harsh braking, usually while turning at the same time (for example corner entry speed too high, braking too harsh). In slippery conditions the tail of the car may also fishtail because you have entered a corner too fast or, in rear-wheel drive vehicles, because too much power has been applied too soon, causing the rear tyres to break traction. A rear-wheel skid of any kind requires some reverse steering, often only briefly. It is not enough to advise turning the steering in the direction of the skid: the question is, by how much? Turn the steering wheels to point them in the direction you wish to travel and, at the same time, try to recognise what you did to cause the skid in the first place. If it was because of excessive acceleration, back off a little and re-apply the accelerator more gently. If it was because you entered the corner too fast or because of your braking (or both at the same time), ease the brakes and let your corrective steering realign

Safe Driving

Basic Traffic Laws

There are variations in road traffic laws from State to State throughout Australia. Some affect the traveller, some do not. Drivers are expected to know and observe those rules that apply to a vehicle's operation; however, specific State laws that affect the registration of vehicles, trailers or caravans, for example, are not enforced between States.

The city of Melbourne, which is the last stronghold of the tram, has its unique hook turn, where at some inner-city intersections a vehicle making a righthand turn must move to the far left of the intersection and wait until the traffic clears and the traffic lights change before completing the turn. Overtaking on the right of a tram is forbidden and no vehicle may pass a stationary tram at a recognised tram stop.

Drink-driving laws are extremely strict in all States and drivers can be pulled up at random and be required to take a blood alcohol test.

Speed regulations vary in each State. In some States, the use of cameras to catch speeding drivers, both in the city and country, is widespread; as well, cameras are positioned at traffic lights on many intersections to record drivers who do not stop at the red light.

In most other respects, the road traffic laws are essentially the same from State to State. However, legislation is subject to change and the cautious driver will check first with the relevant State motoring organisation (**see**: Motoring Organisations) for answers to any questions raised on specific regulations.

Positioning

Positioning is vital on any road.

• Try to stagger the position of your car in the line of traffic so that you can see well ahead.

• When turning right on a two-lane highway, do not angle the car; keep it square to the other traffic so that cars can pass on the left.

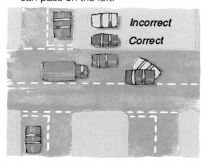

In Case of Accident

In all States of Australia, any accident in which someone is injured or killed *must* be reported to police at once, or within 24 hours. In Western Australia, any accident involving a car must be reported.

It is highly advisable to report to police any accident that involves substantial property damage. Police may or may not decide to attend the scene, but they at least will have your report on record, which may well be useful should there be legal proceedings or insurance claims.

When involved in an accident and if required by police, you *must* give your name and address and produce your driver's licence. If you do not have it with you, you may be liable for an on-the-spot fine. It is advisable to obtain the insurance details of the other parties involved.

All parties involved in the accident should exchange names and addresses and insurance details. **Do not volunteer any other information**. In particular, do not discuss the accident. Should court action result, you may find something said in the stress of the aftermath of the accident used against you. Above all, **do not admit you are at fault in any way**.

You are not obliged to make a statement to police. If you are disturbed and upset, wait until you can think clearly.

An accident that involves damage to persons or property should be reported to your insurance company as soon as possible (**see also**: Accident Action, inside back cover).

the car and then, smoothly, increase the power again.

Skids can be complex and difficult to control. Over-correction is common, with the result that the vehicle swings into another skid in the opposite direction. Do not panic, and be smooth in your reaction. Easy to say—not so easy to do.

Aquaplaning is a form of skidding where the tyres roll a layer of water up in front of the vehicle and then ride on to it, breaking contact with the road surface. What you sense is a sudden loss of driving 'feel'. Slow down, very smoothly, until the tyres come off the layer of water and then proceed more carefully. Watch out for deep puddles: they are the danger.

Driving in snow, ice and mud also produces adhesion problems. Once again, smooth, steady progress, while 'feeling' the vehicle and staying on top of its movements, is the only answer.

For a visit to the **snow,** your vehicle should be fitted with chains. If it is not and the car's back wheels begin to spin wildly on packed and rutted snow or ice:

• Stop the car.
• Look for and remove any obstructions under the car.
• Pack loose gravel, sticks or vegetation under the driving wheels.
• Remember that on a level surface a gentle push sometimes will get the car going.

• Because it cannot be seen, ice can be more dangerous than snow.
  When driving in **fog:**
• Switch on dipped headlights, or foglights if your car is fitted with them.
• Use front and back demisters.
• If visibility is reduced to such an extent that driving becomes an ordeal, pull as far off the road as you can and wait until you feel able to continue.

The advice in this section applies equally to driving in the cities and in the outback. The techniques are the same; only the conditions vary (**see**: Outback Motoring for more detail on bush driving).

Towing

Towing your accommodation behind you will provide the advantage of low-budget touring and flexibility with stopovers. It can be a disadvantage also, in that it may restrict access to some areas. You can, however, use the caravan for most sections of your journey and park it somewhere while you go off and explore the more difficult tracks.

If you are new to towing, the first thing you must do is to get expert advice on your **towing hitch** (**see:** Motoring Organisations). It is very important that **the rig** (that is, car and caravan, boat or trailer) is balanced and the weight over the tow ball is not excessive. An adjustable height hitch with spring bars is best.

Once you have decided on the hitch and you have learned how to hook up and unhook, you must learn to **reverse** the rig. Find a wide open area, an empty car park for example, and practise. Get the feel of the rig and aim to be proficient before you depart.

On the road, remember to make allowances for the added overall length and give yourself extra space for turning and extra distance for overtaking. The added weight will obviously affect the towing vehicle's performance in acceleration and braking.

In most States there are **speed limits** on articulated vehicles and you should know what they are and abide by them (**see**: Basic Traffic Laws). High-speed towing of vans and trailers can cause major difficulties, magnifying driving problems substantially.

Cross-winds can be a problem when towing a caravan, the van's slab sides acting like sails. The combination of high speed and cross-winds can cause **trailer sway,** a dangerous characteristic that dramatically destabilises both towing vehicle and caravan. You probably will feel it happening before you see it, but checking in the rear-view mirrors will confirm it. Should the trailer begin to move about, ease back on your speed, braking if necessary, but very gently. Harsh or sudden braking will compound the problem. When the caravan stabilises, resume speed, perhaps very gradually if you are continuing in a cross-wind area.

Fit good-quality towing mirrors on your vehicle. It is very important that your rear view down both sides of the trailer or caravan is not obscured.

If, because of the relative slowness of your progress, you find a line of vehicles banking up behind you, be courteous and pull over when and where you can, to allow vehicles to overtake.

The carrying of goods and equipment in a caravan has been mentioned, but it is worth repeating that such items should be located as much as possible over and just to the front of the caravan axle (or axles); never behind, which will lift the front of the caravan and the tow ball.

Before setting off and every day of the trip, whatever the vehicle, always **check and double-check that the hitch is secure**, that the **safety chains are correctly fitted**, and that the **electrical connections are working** so that indicator lights function at the rear of the towed vehicle.

Finally when towing, remember to allow extra time for each day's travel, and remain alert.

Checklist

When towing anything:

- Check the hitch for security. The law in most States demands that tow bars are fitted with safety chains.
- Check that the tail and stop lights, marker lights and signal lights are working.
- Remember to check the air in the caravan or trailer tyres.
- If towing a boat, check the lashings.
- Check that caravan doors, windows and roof vents are closed before departure.
- If the caravan or trailer is fitted with separate brakes, check these as soon as you start to move.

Towing your accommodation requires extra care

Outback Motoring

Australia's size and remoteness deter many people from exploring it. However, properly set up and equipped, and armed with common sense and a little background knowledge, every intending traveller can explore the country's huge open spaces.

If you intend travelling in the outback, planning ahead is vital, for it is possible to travel in some sections of the Australian outback and not see another vehicle or person for several days. (The Canning Stock Route is a good example.)

It is possible to travel in some areas of the outback in a 2WD vehicle, but it is safer and much more practical to do so in a 4WD vehicle suited to off-road conditions (**see:** Checking the Car).

Remember that if you rent a vehicle, there may be restrictions on insurance if you drive on unclassified roads; seek advice before you make plans.

Your vehicle should be fitted with **air conditioning** to counteract high inland daytime temperatures and make it possible to drive with all the windows closed through dusty areas. You should be able to carry out **small running repairs** and must carry a workshop manual for the vehicle, tools and spare parts (**see:** Tools and Spare Parts).

Outback **driving conditions** vary greatly. The deserts are usually dry; conditions change after rain. Much of the tropics is accessible only in the 'dry' season, and even then there are streams to ford and, washaways to contend with.

Pre-reading **road conditions** is vital. Recognising that a patch of different colour may represent a change in surface is an example. Sand can give way to rock; rock may lead to mud; hard surfaces become bulldust with little warning.

Soft sand, bulldust and mud are best negotiated at the highest reasonable speed and in the highest possible gear

and in 4WD. However, examine the road surface first. Do not enter deep mud or mud covered with water without first establishing the depth of either or both.

Deep **sand** requires low tyre pressures. Carry a tyre pressure gauge and drop pressures to about 10 psi. Reinflate when on gravel or bitumen roads again, because the soft tyres will perform very badly and may blow out as a result of stone fractures on hard surfaces.

When **crossing a creek or stream,** stop to check the track across for clear passage and water depth. If the water is deep but fordable, cover the front of the vehicle with a tarpaulin and remove the fan belt to stop water being sprayed over the engine electrics. Drive through in low range second gear or high range first gear, and clear the opposite embankment before stopping again. If it has rained, beware of flash flooding.

Dips are common on outback roads and can break suspension components if you enter too fast. To cross a dip, brake on entry to drop the vehicle's nose, and hold the brake on until just before the bottom of the depression. Then accelerate again to lift the nose and therefore the suspension, as you exit. This will prevent the springs from bottoming out and will give maximum clearance.

Cattle grids are also a potential hazard. They are often neglected, with broken approaches and exits. If a grid appears to be in disrepair, stop and check first, before attempting to cross.

Road trains operate in many parts of outback Australia. These long, multi-trailered trucks are difficult and often dangerous to overtake, particularly on dusty roads. Wait for a chance to get the front of your vehicle out to a position where the road train driver can see you in the rear-view mirror, but even then do not try to overtake until he has signalled

that he knows you are there. Sometimes it is prudent to stop and take a break, rather than try to overtake a road train. If you meet an oncoming road train, pull over and stop until it has passed.

Animals present hazards on outback roads. There are vast areas of unfenced property where stock roam free. A bullock or a large kangaroo can seriously damage your vehicle. Be especially wary around sunrise and sunset when animals are more active. A bull-bar or roo-bar gives limited protection at low speeds only, especially against larger animals.

Driver concentration should be at as high a level as in city peak hours.

Surviving in the Outback

You might be stranded in a remote area with a major mechanical breakdown, or if your vehicle becomes bogged. For this eventuality you should be equipped to wait at that spot until you are found. Always carry a week's supply of spare water, minimum 20 litres per head. **Keep it for an emergency.**

Iron rations of dry biscuits and canned food will keep hunger at bay, but body evaporation and thirst is the vital factor. **Do not drink radiator coolant.** Often it is not water but a chemical compound, and even if it is water, usually it has been treated with chemicals.

Do not try to walk out of a remote area. You are going to survive only if you wait by the car. Before entering a remote area, check with police or a local authority, and tell them where and when you are going, and when you expect to arrive. When you reach your destination, telephone and advise of your arrival.

If stranded, set up some type of shelter and, in the heat of the day, remain in its shade as motionless as possible. Movement accelerates fluid loss (**see also:** How to Obtain Water).

Outback Advice

Critical Rules for Outback Motoring

- Check intended routes carefully.
- Check the best time of year to travel.
- Check that your vehicle is suited to the conditions.
- Check your load; keep it to a minimum.
- Check ahead for local road conditions, weather forecasts and fuel availability.
- Check that you have advised someone of your route, destination and arrival time.
- Check that you have essential supplies: water, food, fuel, spare parts.
- Carry detailed maps.
- Carry one week's extra supply of food and water in case of emergency.
- **Always remain with your vehicle if it breaks down.**

Warning: When Driving on Desert Roads Remember:
- There is no water, except after rains.
- Unmade roads can be extremely hazardous, especially when wet.
- Traffic is almost non-existent, except on main roads.

Outback Advice Service

The Royal Flying Doctor Service of Australia offers a service to tourists who plan to tour the outback. Royal Flying Doctor Service bases and Visitors Centres provide advice on outback touring and on proper emergency procedures. Bases at Broken Hill (NSW), Charleville (Qld) and Jandakot (WA) also hire out transceiver sets with a fixed

Road sign beside Eyre Highway, SA

emergency call button in case of accident or sickness, at a very reasonable cost. Those bases that do not hire out sets, can suggest local outlets for them.

New South Wales
*Broken Hill: Broken Hill Airport 2880; (080) 88 0777. Open: Mon.–Fri. 10.30 a.m. and 3.30 p.m.; Sat.–Sun. 10.30 a.m.

South Australia
*Port Augusta: 4 Vincent St 5700; (086) 42 2044. Open: Mon.–Fri. 10 a.m., 11 a.m. and 2 p.m.

Western Australia
Carnarvon: 29 Douglas St 6701; (099) 41 1758
*Derby: Clarendon St 6728; (091) 91 1211. Open: Mon.–. 8 a.m.–12 noon, 2.30–3.30 p.m.
*Jandakot: 3 Eagle Dr, Jandakot Airport 6164; (09) 332 7733. Open Mon. and Thurs. 10.00 a.m.; bookings essential.
*Kalgoorlie: St Albans Rd 6430; (090) 21 2211. Open Mon.–Fri. 2.30 p.m.
*Meekatharra: Main St 6642; (099) 81 1107. Open Mon.–Fri. 7 a.m.–5 p.m., Sat., Sun, and holidays 9–10 a.m.
*Port Hedland: The Esplanade 6721; (091) 73 1386. Open Mon.–Fri. 11 a.m.–11.30 a.m.

Northern Territory
*Alice Springs: Stuart Tce 0870; (089) 52 1033. Open Mon.–Sat. 9 a.m.–4 p.m., Sun. 1–4 p.m.

Queensland
*Cairns: 1 Junction St 4870;

(070) 53 1952. Open daily 8.30 a.m.–5 p.m.
*Charleville: Town Hall Bldg, Wills St 4470;
(076) 54 3057. Telephone for details of service.
*Mount Isa: Barkly Highway 4825;
(077) 43 2800. Open Mon.–Fri. 9 a.m.–5 p.m., Sat. 9 a.m.–1 p.m.; subject to change in off-season.

Tasmania
Launceston: 17 Adelaide St 7250;
(003) 31 2228
*These bases have Visitors Centres; check opening times.

For general information relating to the services offered by the Royal Flying Doctor Service, contact: The Australian Council of the Royal Flying Doctor Service of Australia, Level 5, 15–17 Young St, Sydney 2000; (02) 241 2411, fax (02) 247 3351.

Sharing the Outback

As you travel through the outback, remember: You are sharing the land with its traditional Aboriginal owners, pastoralists, other tourists—and even nature itself. In order to protect and preserve the outback for future visitors:

- Respect Aboriginal sacred and cultural sites, and heritage buildings and pioneer relics.
- Protect native flora and fauna: take photographs not specimens.
- Follow restrictions on the use of firearms and shooting. These restrictions protect wildlife and stock.
- Carry your own fuel source (for example portable gas stove), to avoid lighting fires in fire-sensitive areas.
- When lighting a campfire (if you must), keep it small and use any fallen wood sparingly. Never leave a fire unattended; and extinguish completely before you move on.
- Do not drive off-road.
- Do not camp immediately adjacent to water sources (for example on riverbanks or by dams). Allow access for stock and native animals.
- Do not bury your rubbish; carry out everything you take in.
- Dispose of faecal waste by burial.
- Leave gates as you find them: open or shut.
- Do not ignore signs warning of dangers or entry restrictions. These are there for your protection.

Direction Finding

Clever electronic hand-held navigation devices, using the Global Positioning System (GPS), are now available from bushwalking shops and outdoor centres. These can be used with or without a map and are much more sophisticated and accurate than a magnetic compass.

If you cannot read a map or use a compass—or if you have no navigational device with you—it is vital to have some means of orientating yourself if you are lost.

A simple method of finding north is to use a conventional wristwatch.

Place the 12 on the watch in line with the sun and bisect the angle between it and the hour hand. This will give a fairly accurate indication of north.

At night, the Southern Cross can be used to determine south.

When exploring a side track off the main road, make a rough sketch of the route you are following, noting all turnoffs, and distances between them, using the speedometer, together with any prominent landmarks. When you return, reconcile your return route with the sketch, point by point.

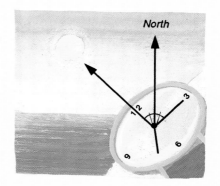

How to Obtain Water

Less than 24 hours without water can be fatal in outback heat.

It is essential to conserve body moisture. Take advantage of any shade that can be found.

Do not leave your vehicle. It may be the only effective shade available.

Ration your drinking water. **Do not drink radiator coolant**.

Although a river or creek bed may be dry, there is often an underground source of water. A hole dug about a metre deep may produce a useful soak.

Where there is vegetation, it is possible to extract water from it using an **Arizona still**.

- Dig a hole about one metre across and a little more than half a metre deep. Put a vessel of some kind in the hole's centre to collect the water.
- Surround the vessel with cut vegetation. (Fleshy plants, such as succulents, will hold more moisture than drier saltbush.)
- Cover the hole with a plastic sheet held down by closely packed rocks, so that the hole is sealed off. Put a small stone in the centre of the sheet, directly above the collection vessel.

The sun's heat will evaporate moisture from the plants. This moisture will condense on the inside of the plastic, run down the cone formed by the weight of the stone and drip off into the vessel.

In uninterrupted sunlight, with suitable plants, about one litre of water should be collected about every six hours.

The Arizona still takes about three hours to start producing and it will become less efficient as the ground moisture dries out. A new hole will need to be dug at intervals.

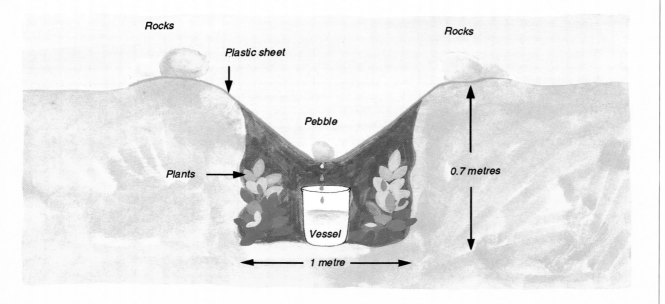

Breakdowns

There are many causes of motor vehicle breakdown, but fortunately modern vehicle technology has vastly reduced the possibility of being stuck by the roadside. Breakdowns that do occur can sometimes be cured with a roadside 'fix'; but this is less often possible with today's computer-driven vehicles. Inexpert or makeshift repairs may lead to further complications and a bigger repair bill.

Proper **vehicle preparation and maintenance** should reduce the possibility of roadside breakdowns and, on long journeys, the regular vehicle-service schedule should be maintained.

In areas where you have access to service through a motoring organisation, it is better to leave even slightly complicated repairs to the specialist. (Remember to carry your membership card, which entitles you to assistance in other States; **see**: Motoring Organisations.)

If you are driving a **rental car**, most rental companies list their recognised repair organisations in the manual supplied. (Before you drive the car you should check that these details are provided.) If your rental vehicle cannot be repaired immediately, you should request an exchange vehicle.

If you plan to journey into remote areas, it is a good idea to first take a basic course in vehicle maintenance (**see:** Car Maintenance Courses). As well, you should carry a range of tools and spare parts (**see:** Tools and Spare Parts).

Most **modern vehicles** are fitted with electronic engine-management systems, or with electronic ignition and fuel injection. Generally these are more reliable than older systems and usually, in case of partial failure of the system, they have a 'limp home' mode, which enables travelling a limited distance at limited speed. However, total failure of such a system is difficult or impossible to remedy at the roadside without expert knowledge and equipment. This means that travel into remote areas is rendered much safer by travelling with at least one other vehicle, and by installing or hiring an appropriate long-range radio transmitter, receiver and aerial (**see**: Outback Advice Service).

For those who drive **earlier-model vehicles** with less complex electrics and fuel systems, the trouble-shooting flow-charts are designed to be of assistance (**see**: Trouble Shooting). But first, always remember to:

- **Watch warning gauges:** These have been installed to warn that things *may* be going wrong. A flickering battery warning light will suggest all is not well with the generator/alternator charge rate and should be attended to. A fluctuating temperature gauge *may* suggest the onset of a problem with the cooling system. Act on the warning at the earliest opportunity.
- **Make a daily check** of levels of fuel, water and oil (including spare supplies). Also check tyre pressures and fan-belt tension and condition.
- **Make a regular check** of brake-fluid and battery-acid levels, and pressure of spare tyre.
- **Strange sounds:** If the vehicle develops an unexplained sound, move to the side of the road as soon as possible. Park on flat ground if you can. You may have to spend some time under the bonnet, so look for shade or shelter. A loud, 'serious' sound usually indicates a major problem. Try to locate the source of the sound. If it is coming from the engine, do nothing and seek help.

When the Engine Stops

When the engine either splutters to a stop, constantly misfires or stops suddenly but was otherwise running smoothly, the problem is probably in one of two areas: fuel supply or electrics. Use the flow-charts to establish where the problem lies. If the problem is within the drive-train—gearbox, drive-shaft or differential—once again, seek help.

Roadside repairs, north Qld

Tools and Spare Parts

Remote-area travelling requires that someone in the vehicle knows, at least, the basics of breakdown repairs (**see**: Breakdowns). This means carrying emergency tools, spare parts and spare fuel. The following is a guide to what may be appropriate for your vehicle:

Tools

- Set of screwdrivers
- Small set of socket spanners
- Set of open-end/ring combination spanners
- Small ball pein (engineer's) hammer
- Pliers and wire-cutters
- Small and medium adjustable wrenches
- Hand drill and bits
- Workshop scissors
- Tyre-pressure gauge
- Wheel brace

- Jack with supplementary wide base for sand or mud (block of wood, slightly bigger than a brick but not as thick)
- Battery-operated soldering-iron
- Jumper leads
- Hydrometer
- Small backpackers shovel
- Pair of vice grips
- Small bolt-cutters
- Good quality tow-rope
- Heavy duty torch, spare batteries

Spare Parts

- Epoxy resin bonding 'goo'
- Plastic insulating tape
- Roll of cloth adhesive tape
- 1 metre fuel line (reinforced plastic)
- Spare electrical connections (range)
- Spare hose-clips (range)
- Distributor cap
- Set of high tension leads

- Condenser (where appropriate)
- Rotor
- Set of spark plugs
- Set of points
- Coil
- Spare fuel filters (replace daily in areas of constant dust)
- Fuel pump kit, water pump kit
- Small-diameter plastic tubing
- Nuts, bolts, washers, split pins
- At least one spare tyre, mounted, in good condition and over-inflated (to allow for some air loss)
- Tube of hand cleaner, clean rags

Fuel

- Spare fuel (40 litres minimum) in steel jerry cans. (Do *not* use plastic containers; some plastics react with fuel.) Check fuel range, and distance between refuelling points.

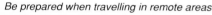

Be prepared when travelling in remote areas

Trouble Shooting (for earlier-model vehicles)

Engine will not turn over

Check battery for charge.

If flat...
recharge or replace, or tow-start (if manual transmission vehicle) until next service opportunity. (If automatic, check handbook. Most autos cannot be tow- or clutch-started.)

If battery OK...
check if battery terminals and straps are loose, broken or dirty. If so, clean, repair or replace.

If terminals OK...
check for jammed starter motor. For manual vehicle, put in top gear and rock back and forth to try to free pinion. An indication that starter may be jammed is an audible click when you try to start the engine and it will not turn over. With an automatic vehicle, try to turn engine back and forth with a spanner on crankshaft pulley to free pinion. Put gearbox into 'N' first.

If the starter motor is free...
it is possible a solenoid has failed. Unless you are an auto electrician and carry a spare, seek help.

Starter motor whirrs but will not turn engine

Very likely, you have stripped a starter ring-gear, which means major repair work. But check to see that the starter motor is fully bolted to its mounting bracket, and tighten if not.

Engine turns over but will not fire, or fires but will not run cleanly, or misfires regularly, or runs and stops

Problem may be electrics or fuel supply. If unsure, begin with electrics.

Electrics

1   Check that spark is getting to spark plugs. Remove high tension (HT) lead from No. 1 plug and remove No. 1 plug. Reattach HT lead to plug and hold plug body with insulated pliers 1 mm from cylinder-head bolt or similar and turn engine over. Plug should produce strong blue spark at regular intervals.

2   **If not...**
the simplest and fastest way to deal with an electrical problem is to replace parts, either at once or progressively, with spares (see: Tools and Spare Parts). Replace coil and all HT leads and try engine. If problem persists, remove distributor cap and replace condenser and points. Re-set points and fit new rotor and distributor cap. Engine should start and run cleanly.

3   If you carry no spare parts, you can still confirm electrics as the problem by a process of elimination. If there is no spark at the spark plugs, the problem has to be between battery and plug. Check that low tension lead at side of distributor is connected properly and tightly mounted. If so, remove distributor cap and check for cracks. If there is a crack, repair with an epoxy glue/filler until it can be replaced. Check that condenser is tightly mounted and its LT wire is connected. Check that points open and close properly by turning engine over by hand slowly and watching for a spark between points. Points may be burned or deeply pitted. If so, remove points and use nail-file to clean up faces, then replace and re-set. If, however, you have established an electrical problem and you have no spares, seek assistance.

4   If you have a spark at the plugs, most likely you have a fuel-supply problem.

Fuel supply

Check fuel tank for fuel, despite gauge reading. (It may be faulty.)

1   **If fuel OK...**
Check accelerator cable connection and for free operation and check choke cable and operation. For vehicle with automatic choke, remove air-cleaner carrier and element and look down choke tube. If choke butterfly is not fully open, open it and check to see if it stays open. If it closes again, engine is flooding, and may not run for that reason. A faulty auto choke cannot be repaired at the roadside.

2   **If accelerator and choke cables are operating correctly...**
do not replace air cleaner; remove fuel line to carburettor and turn engine over. Fuel should flow freely. If so, check it is not contaminated by pumping small amount into clear glass or plastic container and examine for water and/or dirt.

3   **If water or dirt are apparent...**
check and replace fuel filter and remove and check fuel pump. Examine glass for contamination. If none or very little, replace fuel line to carburettor and try engine again.

4   **If there is substantial contamination...**
it may be coming from fuel tank. Tank will need to be drained and perhaps flushed. Drained fuel should be saved and strained back. If you are travelling a long way before next fuel stop, be careful not to waste fuel.

5   **If no fuel at fuel line and no apparent blockage...**
fuel pump has failed for some reason. If you are carrying a spare, replace pump. If not, seek assistance.

6   **If fuel is clean and running freely...**
blockage may be inside carburettor. Carefully remove top and then main jet and float. Clear main jet and clean out float bowl. Be careful not to interfere with float level. Replace parts and try engine again.

Overheating in a water-cooled engine

(Occurs when coolant level falls or circulation is interrupted. Dash gauge gives warning, but vehicle also will lose power.)

1 Stop vehicle. Do not remove radiator cap. Check hoses and hose connections for signs of leakage—steam if system is boiling. Any identified leak can be cured temporarily with spare hoses or binding with cloth tape.

2 If no sign of leakage...
After about 10 minutes and holding radiator cap with a thick cloth, slowly remove cap, letting out steam under pressure at same time. Top up radiator and fill with engine running and car's heater on hot setting. Do not add cold water until engine is running and then mix cold with hot water.

3 Check again for leaks.

4 If there is a slow drip from radiator core itself...
fix with an internal chemical sealant or externally with an epoxy filler or adhesive.

5 If no leak is apparent...
check fanbelt for tension. It may be slipping and not driving water pump. If so, tighten by releasing bolts on generator/alternator and increasing tension and re-tightening.

6 If you cannot account for overheating by any of the preceding, you may have a failed water-pump, a blocked system, a failed pressure cap or a combination of all three. Seek help as soon as possible, but you may drive on if you can continue topping up.

top: Great Ocean Road, Vic.
bottom: Touring near the Hamersley Range, WA

Child's Play

Everyone in the family looks forward to a holiday, but most parents dread a long car trip, when children travelling in the back seat can become bored and irritable passengers.

Most children are good travellers, but there are some car journeys that are inappropriate for small children (say, under the age of 10). Usually, however, children will consider every trip an adventure, looking forward to it for weeks ahead. A little thought and planning by parents will avoid the boredom of a long drive and ease the strain on all concerned, and particularly the driver, who needs to be able to apply total concentration.

Dos and Donts

Several days before setting out, make a list of 'dos' and 'donts' for the children and explain, seriously, why their cooperation is necessary. Make it quite clear that you expect them to observe the rules because they are safety measures, and reinforce this message at the time of departure. For example:

- DO NOT fight or yell while the car is in motion. This distracts the driver and can cause a collision or a serious mishap, which might bring the holiday to an abrupt end.
- DO NOT play with door handles or locks. (Set the child-proof locks on rear doors before departure.)
- DO keep head, arms and hands inside the car. DO NOT lean out of the windows, ever.
- DO NOT unbuckle seat belts or restraints while the car is in motion.

Handy Hints

- Any long car trip, even with frequent stops, can be tiring. Make sure the children are as cool and comfortable as possible. Curtains (or substitutes, for example a towel) or sun screens on rear windows are advisable. Babies and pre-school children may need their security blankets or favourite soft toy. These items can save the day if the children are upset or sleepy.
- Pack a small bag—a cosmetic bag is ideal—with packets of moist towelettes or a damp face cloth.
- Make sure your first-aid kit contains some junior aspirin and supplies of any other medication taken by the children. It is important to carry some insect repellent and sunblock, since children tend to get bitten easily, and their skin must be protected from the sun. Also bring a mosquito net to cover your baby's bassinette when you are outdoors.
- Make up a 'busy box' for the children to take on the trip. Use a small box—a shoe box is best—and keep it on the back seat where the children can reach it easily. Fill the box with small note-pads, crayons or felt-tipped pens (pencils break and need to be sharpened) and activity books. Choose activity books for each child's age group. Do not forget to include your children's favourite storybooks.
- If your car has a radio and cassette player, include some tapes of stories and children's songs for 'quiet times'. Music soothes and lulls children to sleep.
- Although your main concern will be to keep the children happy and occupied during the car trip, it is also important to take along some games, such as Snakes and Ladders or Monopoly, or a pack of cards, to keep them amused in the evenings and on rainy days. Encourage older children to keep a diary. A rubber ball and skipping rope will be welcomed by young children who like to play outdoors.
- If you have room, breakfast trays can be used as book supports for colouring-in or drawing. If not, a clipboard will serve as well.
- When travelling with young children, make sure that you stop the car every hour or so, so that they can stretch their legs and let off steam. Try to stop at a park or an area with some play equipment. If it is raining, stop at a newsagent or bookshop where the children can browse and perhaps buy something to read.
- If children complain of feeling sick, stop the car as soon as possible and let them out for some fresh air. Sit with them for a while and persuade them to take a sip of water before continuing the trip.
- When approaching a rest area or a small town, offer the children a toilet stop. Do not delay until they get desperate and cannot wait.
- Even though you plan to stop for meals and snacks on your journey, you should still pack some food and drink. Children become very hungry and thirsty when travelling and it is important that they eat little but often. Pack small snacks in their own lunch boxes. Avoid chocolate, which is messy and can make children feel sick, and potato chips which are almost as messy and encourage thirst. Avoid greasy foods. Good for snacks are sultanas, nuts (for older children only), bananas, grapes, cheese cubes, celery and carrot sticks, boiled sweets. For lunches, pack easy-to-eat meals like chicken drumsticks or bite-size rolled-up pieces of cold meat with ready-spread bread on the side. Children can find large sandwiches difficult to handle, so remember to cut their sandwiches small. Sandwich fillings require some thought: avoid anything moist or runny.

Safety

Note the following safety hints:

Safe Swimming, Surfing

- Swim or surf only at those beaches patrolled by lifesavers.
- Swim or surf within the area indicated by the red and yellow flags.
- An amber flag indicates that the surf is dangerous.
- A red flag and sign 'Danger—closed to bathing' indicates the beach is unsafe. Do not swim or surf in this area.
- Do not enter the water directly after a meal or under the influence of alcohol.
- If you are caught in a rip or strong current, swim diagonally across it. If you tire or cannot avoid the current, do not panic. Straighten and raise one arm as a distress signal and float until help arrives.

- If seized with a cramp, keep the affected part perfectly still, raise one arm as before and float until help arrives.

Safe Skiing

Skiing is fun, but like any other sport, there is the risk of injury. It is also strenuous. If possible, train beforehand, and avoid overdoing it on the slopes. All ski resorts have instructors if you need to take lessons. Choose slopes that suit your ability. Wear clothing suited to the conditions. Check equipment before setting out. Avoid skiing alone; if you must, then tell someone where you are going. If lost, stay where you are, or retrace your tracks if they are very clear. **Cross-country skiing** requires careful planning. Tell someone in authority of your intended route; travel in a group; take plenty of food and adequate equipment for your survival; protect yourself against sunburn; and watch the weather. Be alert for signs of exposure (hypothermia)—tiredness, reluctance to carry on, clumsiness, loss of judgement, collapse.

Safe Boating

- Tell someone where you are going.
- Carry adequate equipment.
- Carry effective life jackets.
- Carry enough fuel and water.
- Ensure engine reliability.
- Guard against fire.
- Do not overload the craft.
- Know the boating rules and local regulations; also distress signals.
- Watch the weather.
- Do not drink alcohol while boating.

- Avoid spills and breakages by buying milk or fruit juice in small cartons and making sure you have a good supply of drinking straws. If you carry drinks in a flask, take training cups for younger children. For older children use paper or styrofoam cups with tight-fitting lids and straws, and recycle as much as possible.
- Have plastic bags for waste paper and empty drink cartons in the cars.
- When eating out, choose places that have fast service—or have meals sent to your room.

Games

To while away the long hours you will spend in the car with your children, here are some games for them to play.

For younger children

Colour contest: Each child selects one colour, then tries to spot cars of that colour. The first with ten cars wins.

Spot the mistake in the story: Either you or an older child tells a story with obvious mistakes. For example, 'Once upon a time, there was a boy called Goldilocks, and he visited the house of the seven dwarfs.'

Scavenger: Make a list of 10 things you are likely to come across during your trip,

for example farmhouse, bus stop, cow, lamb, chemist shop, woman with a hat. Ask the children to spot them, one at a time. Older children cross the objects off the list as they are seen.

Alphabet game: Select a letter and ask the children to spot as many things as possible beginning with that particular initial.

For older children

Rhyme stories: One child starts a story, and the next has to take up the story with a line that rhymes. The second child also continues the story with a line of new rhyme. For example:

1st child: 'I know a man called Sam.'
2nd child: 'He loves to eat ham.
   The more he eats the more he wants.'

Cliff-hangers: One child begins a story and stops at the most exciting part, leaving the next child to continue.

I packed my bag...(a good memory game): Each player has to name one object she or he puts into a bag. As each child takes a turn, she or he lists all the objects in order and adds a new item to the list. For example:

1st child: 'I packed my bag and put an apple in it.'
2nd child: 'I packed my bag and put an apple and a comb in it.'

3rd child: 'I packed my bag and put an apple, a comb and a key in it.'
4th child: 'I packed my bag and put an apple, a comb, a key and a ball in it.'

What am I? This is an old favourite. One player thinks of an object or an animal and keeps it secret. The others take turns to ask questions, which must be answered only by 'Yes' or 'No', for clues to the player's identity.

Number-plate messages: Take the letters of a number plate on a nearby car and ask the children to make up a message or conversation from them. For example:
WFL: 'What's for lunch?'
EYH: 'Eat your hat.'

Navigation: Older children enjoy this game very much. All you need is a spare road-map covering the route you are taking. The children can follow your progress with a coloured marker.

The following games take only a few minutes to prepare:

Word scramble: Prepare a list of words with jumbled letters and get the children to unscramble them.

Crossword: Draw crossword squares on several note-pads. During the trip, play the crossword game by calling out letters at random. The children write the letters in any square they wish and try to make up words.

New South Wales

Founding State

In 1770 Captain Cook took possession for the British of all Australian territories east of the 135th meridian of east longitude and named them New South Wales. Today the founding State has shrunk somewhat and occupies just ten per cent of the continent. It is a State of contrasts, covering an area of 801 428 square kilometres, with extremes of country ranging from subtropical to alpine.

The State's capital, Sydney, is Australia's largest city. Established as the site of a penal colony in 1788, the settlement at Sydney Cove was developed under the guiding hand of Governor Arthur Phillip. Following his departure in 1792, however, much of Arthur's initial planning was negated, owing to the influence of the infamous NSW Corps, until 1810 heralded the arrival of the redoubtable Governor Macquarie.

In 1813 Blaxland, Lawson and Wentworth discovered the lands to the west of the Blue Mountains. Further exploration quickly followed and settlement fanned out from Sydney. Sydney itself thrived and its citizens agitated against the stigma of the penal presence, with the result that transportation of convicts ended in 1840. The goldrushes of the 1850s swelled the population and led to much development throughout the State. With the granting of responsible government in 1856, the founding State was well on its way.

Today New South Wales is the most populous State and its central region, around Sydney, Newcastle and Wollongong–Port Kembla, has been described as 'the heart of industrial Australia'. New South Wales produces two-thirds of the nation's black coal from huge deposits in the Hunter Valley, the Blue Mountains and the Illawarra Region. Its other main source of mineral wealth is the silver–lead–zinc mines of Broken Hill. Primary production is diversified and thriving—New South Wales is the nation's main wheat producer and has more than one-third of the nation's sheep population.

The State is divided naturally into four regions: the sparsely populated western plains, which take up two-thirds of the state; the high tablelands and peaks of the Great Dividing Range; the pastoral and farming country of the Range's western slopes; and the fertile coastal region.

The climate varies with the landscape: subtropical along the north coast; temperate all year round on the south coast. The north-west has dry summers, and the high country has brisk winters with extremes of cold in the highest alpine areas. Sydney has a midsummer average of 25.7°C, a midwinter average of 15.8°C and boasts sunshine for an average of 342 days a year.

Lively and sophisticated, Sydney offers the shopping, restaurants and nightlife expected of a great cosmopolitan city, yet within a 200-kilometre radius is much of the best country in New South Wales: superb beaches, the myriad of intricate bays and inlets of Pittwater, the Hawkesbury and Tuggerah Lakes and the breathtaking Illawarra coastline. The scenic Blue Mountains and the Jenolan Caves can be reached in a day trip. Most of the State's highways lead out from the capital. The Pacific Highway runs north to Port Macquarie and the industrial city of Newcastle. Inland, you can sample the products of the rich Hunter Valley vineyards. Further north, the country becomes hilly and subtropical, with irresistible golden beaches, and the New England tablelands inland—high mountain and grazing country, at its best in autumn.

The State's extreme north and west is still frontier territory, with limited tourist facilities. If you enjoy getting off the beaten track, and if you and your car are well prepared, the region can be very rewarding. Highlights include the spectacular Nandewar and Warrumbungle Ranges, Lightning Ridge, and the green oasis of Broken Hill, the State's storehouse of mineral wealth. The best time for touring is between March and November when the temperature is relatively cool and the winter days are clear and dry, but remember, if you break down in the 'outback' areas, stay with your vehicle.

Many relics of the early goldmining and agricultural history of the rich central tablelands and plains region can be seen in and around such towns as Bathurst, Dubbo, Wellington, Griffith and Wagga Wagga. Towards the Victorian border, where the Murray River forms a natural State boundary, irrigation greens the countryside and supports many vineyards and citrus groves. The Murray River towns retain much of the history of the riverboat era when the Murray was a major transport route.

The Princes Highway leads south from Sydney down the Illawarra Coast, famous for its panoramic views, excellent beaches and numerous national parks. Good fishing of all kinds can be enjoyed and there is splendid bushwalking and climbing in the nearby foothills of the Southern Highlands.

The Snowy Mountains area includes the natural grandeur of the Kosciusko National Park and the wonder of the Snowy Mountains hydro-electric scheme.

Linked by a network of freeways, highways and roads, New South Wales offers a wide variety of regions to explore.

Sydney, host city for the 2000 Olympic Games

Sydney

Australia's First City

Sydney, a thriving harbourside metropolis populated by almost 4 million people, is Australia's largest and probably best-known city. It was the first site of European settlement on the Australian continent, a settlement vastly different from today's cosmopolitan showcase.

As Captain Cook sailed up the east coast of Australia in 1770, he noted the entrance to what is now Sydney Harbour and named the craggy headland Port Jackson, in honour of the then Secretary of the British Admiralty, Sir George Jackson.

New Holland, as the continent was known, was deemed a perfect spot for a penal colony, providing also a reason for a British presence in the South Pacific. Command of the first colonial expedition was entrusted to Captain Arthur Phillip. On his arrival at Botany Bay in 1788, Phillip was not impressed with this proposed settlement site. Looking further afield, on January 26 he sailed into a beautiful natural harbour, where he dropped anchor, named the area Sydney Cove, hoisted the flag and proclaimed the colony of New South Wales.

Sydney Cove, now Circular Quay, saw those First Fleet convicts toiling to clear a site for the settlement that was to become the city of Sydney. Testament to their endeavours is **The Rocks**, an area of winding lanes and sandstone buildings situated near the **Harbour Bridge**. An integral part of Sydney's history, providing rich memories of how the city was forged, today The Rocks features outdoor cafes, art and craft centres, museums, curio shops and rollicking pubs. The **Sydney Observatory**, a group of colonial buildings, houses a museum of astronomy with some hands-on displays. Another attraction with interactive exhibits at The Rocks is the **Earth Exchange** (formerly the Geological and Mining Museum), 18 Hickson Road, where visitors can journey across millions of years from the creation of our Earth to the present.

In the sandstone building alongside the Sydney Cove Passenger Terminal is the **Museum of Contemporary Art**, which houses the J.W. Power Collection of some 4500 works of art, including Australian and Aboriginal art. It is Australia's first major museum dedicated to the contemporary visual arts.

Sydney Cove has remained the gateway to Australia, situated in calm waters some eleven kilometres from the towering bluffs that flank the harbour mouth: **North Head** and **South Head**. Both headlands command a breathtaking view back along the harbour to the city, automatically drawing the focus to the shimmering city skyline that highlights the **Harbour Bridge**, the **Opera House** and **Sydney Tower**.

While these three structures may be the city's best known landmarks, it is the harbour itself that is Sydney's pride and

The Rocks from Observatory Hill

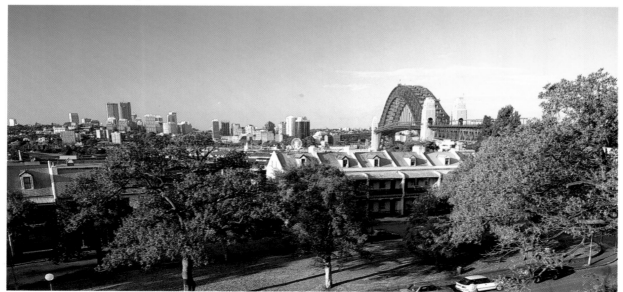

City skyline as seen from McMahons Point

Hotels
Hotel Nikko Darling Harbour
161 Sussex St, Sydney
(02) 299 1231
Park Grand
161 Elizabeth St, Sydney
(02) 286 6000
Quay West Apartments
98 Gloucester St, The Rocks
(02) 240 6000
Regent, Sydney
199 George St, Sydney
(02) 238 0000
Ritz Carlton
93 Macquarie St, Sydney
(02) 252 4600
Sebel Town House
23 Elizabeth Bay Rd, Elizabeth Bay
(02) 358 3244
Sydney Hilton
259 Pitt St, Sydney
(02) 266 0610
Sydney Renaissance
30 Pitt St, Sydney
(02) 259 7000

The Observatory
89-113 Kent St, The Rocks
(02) 256 2222

Family and Budget
Russell
143a George St, Sydney
(02) 241 3543
The York
5 York St, Sydney
(02) 210 5000
YWCA
5–11 Wentworth Ave, Darlinghurst
(02) 264 2451

Motel Groups: Bookings
Best Western 1800 22 2166
Golden Chain 1800 02 3966
Flag 13 2400
Travelodge 1800 22 2446

This list is for information only; inclusion is not necessarily a recommendation.

joy. Its innumerable waterways extend in all directions, the product of a drowned valley system that finds bottom in the depths of the Pacific. Its surface is a glistening blue aquatic playground for Sydneysiders.

With the harbour as its heart, the city proper is bounded by water to the north and west and fringed to the east by the extensive green parklands of the Botanic Gardens and the Domain. **Hyde Park**, in the middle of the city, provides areas of tranquil, verdant delight in a bustling central business district.

Within these boundaries, Sydney is an exciting and rewarding city to explore—elegant, lively, relaxed, solemn, Georgian, Edwardian, Victorian and dazzlingly contemporary; a perfect blend of historic bedrock and futuristic planning.

In line with Sydney's boundaries, the city's bus services terminate at three main points: **Circular Quay** in the north, **Wynyard Square** in the west and, in the south, **Central Railway Station**, the grand, domed building that is the outlet for all country and interstate train services. An underground train service goes above ground outside the central business area and connects the city with outlying suburbs. The **Sydney Explorer** tourist bus loops around 28 km of the city daily, stopping at 27 leading attractions and allowing passengers to alight and rejoin following buses at will.

Where Phillip's First Fleet dropped anchor, the shoreline has become a neat U-shaped area, with major wharves on either arm and harbour ferry terminals at its base. **Circular Quay** is the hub of Sydney's water traffic and a bright, colourful part of town where buskers play for the entertainment of strolling lunchtime shoppers.

The Quay was built in the nineteenth century to handle overseas shipping and, in the final great era of sail, the days of the superb clipper ships, Sydney Cove was a forest of majestic masts. Today it boasts a huge international shipping terminal with anchorage for ships of 40 000 tonnes. Several five-star restaurants where patrons dine while overlooking the harbour lights and the luxurious **Park Hyatt** hotel are nearby.

Across the water from the Quay, the Harbour Bridge disgorges its congested traffic into Sydney's mini-twin—**North Sydney**, a high-rise, high-density satellite of the 1960s. The **Harbour Tunnel**, which runs beneath the harbour, links both business districts.

Under the shadow of the Bridge to the west of the harbour is **Pier One**, a complex of shops, restaurants (specialising in seafood) and a tavern decorated in Old Sydney style. Once a disembarkation point for immigrants, Pier One has been remodelled to reflect its original purpose.

In keeping with the maritime atmosphere is nearby **Pier Four**, which has been converted into a permanent home for the Sydney Theatre Company. The Wharf Theatre is a modern, yet moody, venue for the Sydney Theatre Company's year-round calendar, while the Wharf Restaurant, with award-winning cuisine, commands one of Sydney's best views.

Standing sentinel at the eastern end of Sydney Cove is the **Sydney Opera House**, a building whose aspect is breathtaking against the blue of the harbour. Its white arches seem to flow out of the water, just as designer Joern Utzon intended, like sails scudding up from the waves. At weekends, the Opera House promenade is alive with audiences listening to free outdoor concerts.

The Quay is typically waterfront. **Circular Quay Plaza** and the Rocks area are the home of some of the city's oldest pubs, many of which are early openers, catering for night-shift workers from 6 a.m.

Detached from these, and from its high-rise neighbours, in the centre of the Plaza the old **Customs House** continues to preside over the scene, a monument in sandstone to nineteenth-century Sydney. Its time-honoured clock is surrounded by tridents and dolphins, and the coat of arms above the entrance is one of the best stone carvings in Australia.

Immediately behind Circular Quay Plaza, a series of maritime-flavoured laneways and narrow streets culminates in **Macquarie Place** and its sheltering canopies of giant Moreton Bay fig trees. An anchor and a cannon from Phillip's flagship HMS *Sirius* are preserved in the park, which they share with gas lamps, an 1857 drinking fountain, an ornate Victorian 'gents' (classified by the National Trust) and a weathered obelisk from which distances to all points in the colony used to be measured.

In the surrounding laneways look for one of the world's smallest churches, the tiny **Marist Chapel** at 5 Young Street, run by the Marist Fathers.

Government House is an imposing neo-Gothic sandstone mansion of the 1840s, not open to the public but easily admired from the adjacent Botanic Gardens. Between the entrances to both, the fortress-like lines of the **NSW Conservatorium of Music** successfully conceal the building's origin as stables, designed in 1816 by the renowned convict architect Francis Greenway, and completed in 1821 as part of an earlier Government House on the site.

The **Royal Botanic Gardens**, more than twenty-four hectares of formal landscaping, were originally dedicated in 1816. Today they are a perennial landscape of colour where more than 17 000 native and exotic plants bloom throughout the year. In one small corner there is a stone wall, over 200 years old, marking the original plot of the colony's first vegetable garden, planted at the direction of Governor Phillip. The Pyramid greenhouse contains Australian tropical plants, and nearby is the elegant glass Ark, a major tropical-plant centre housing some of the world's rarest plants.

An imposing sandstone building on the western side of **Macquarie Street**, the **State Library of New South Wales**, overlooks the Botanic Gardens. In the library's Mitchell and Dixson wings is one of the world's great repositories of national archives and memorabilia, a priceless collection of Australiana and historical records. The new wing of the State Library is sited between the old building and Parliament House. This high-tech building features the latest technology, including study aids for the disabled. A brochure for a self-guide tour of the library is available.

Adjacent to the Library are two of Sydney's oldest buildings, the **New South Wales Parliament** and the **Colonial Mint** (now a museum). Between them, in all its dour Victorian splendour,

Circular Quay

City on the Water

In the arid continent of Australia, Sydney is a cosmopolitan subtropical oasis, set around the bays and inlets of Port Jackson. The unspoiled foreshore stretching over 250 kilometres is scalloped with white sandy beaches, while the southern Pacific Ocean caresses the shores in sheltered coves and thunders in on some of the best surf beaches in the country. The climate is mild, the water warm enough for swimming most of the year.

Australia's best-known city sits majestically on the shores of its beautiful natural harbour—a harbour bustling with commuter ferries and jetcats, small tugs and massive container ships, and visiting luxury liners. Sydneysiders are rightly proud of their city. It is the cradle of Australian history and, industrially and commercially, the focal point of the South Pacific. The people are relaxed yet sophisticated. The water that surrounds them has a major impact on their lifestyle; many office workers commute by ferry and spend their lunch hours by the foreshore, enjoying the cool sea breeze in hot summer months. At weekends Sydneysiders collectively stretch out on the beaches, set sail, swim or surf. Year-round, Sydneysiders ensure their harbour is a hub of activity.

Sydney owes a lot to its harbour, first discovered in 1770 by Captain James Cook, who named it Port Jackson. In 1788 Captain Arthur Phillip declared it 'the finest harbour in the world'. Today, due to its vast size, its protection from storms, its uniform depth, small tides, freedom from silting, and lack of navigational hazards, together with its wharves conveniently situated close to the city's business centre, it is arguably the world's best natural harbour. It embraces more than fifty-five square kilometres of water and caters for more than 6000 vessels each year.

Sydneysiders take delight in the water and at weekends sailing boats, speedboats, yachts and launches join the busy harbour traffic. Sydney Harbour is also the venue for many boating classics, including the Festival of Sydney's Ferry Boat Race in January and the classic Sydney to Hobart Yacht Race, which sets out from Sydney on Boxing Day, escorted to the Heads by a colourful fleet of pleasure boats.

Between Sydney's two most famous landmarks, the Opera House and the Harbour Bridge, is Sydney Cove—the birthplace of city, State and nation. In 1788, Captain Arthur Phillip chose this inlet for the first colony because of its deep bay and running stream of fresh water. Its

Yachts on Sydney Harbour

foreshore, now Circular Quay, in the heart of the city, is dwarfed by skyscrapers, with the City Circle Railway passing immediately overhead and the Cahill Expressway forming a canopy over the railway.

Circular Quay is the nucleus of a network of ferry services that links the city to its suburbs (Manly, Mosman, Neutral Bay, Balmain and Parramatta), beaches, Darling Harbour and Taronga Zoo. Most ferry routes pass close to Fort Denison, also known as Pinchgut, where convicts were once imprisoned on a diet of bread and water. Today this fortress island can be hired as a perfect festive location for special functions. It is possible also to hire an aqua cab (water taxi) to take you to any point around the harbour, while special cruises go to Middle Harbour, the Lane Cove and Parramatta Rivers, and up the coast to Broken Bay and the Hawkesbury River.

The ferry service to Manly dates back to 1854. This resort suburb took as its slogan around the turn of the century: 'seven miles from Sydney and a thousand miles from care', and it stands as true today. Named by Captain Phillip after 'manly' behaviour of the Aborigines, this suburb can be reached by a 35-minute ferry ride, a 15-minute journey in a jetcat or an even quicker trip in a UTA catamaran. Manly stands at the gateway to Sydney Harbour, and each summer its population doubles, thanks to the mild climate and the popularity of the eighteen harbour and ocean beaches nearby. Manly Oceanarium enables visitors to 'walk under the ocean' to view the amazing marine life.

Between Grotto Point and Middle Head is the fishing and boating haven of Middle Harbour. Here the Spit Bridge opens for vessels visiting the area's many channels and bays, which are rich in small coves and beaches.

Along the northern shore of Port Jackson are several well-known beaches: Chowder Bay, where American whalers concocted their famous dish using Sydney rock oysters; Neutral Bay, where ships from foreign countries once anchored; and the picturesque Mosman Bay and Chinamans Beach, a favourite haunt of artists.

On the southern foreshore, almost 100 hectares of parkland in the Domain and Royal Botanic Gardens beckons office workers, who flock to the gardens for a quiet lunch break, a stroll or jog along the foreshore, or a quick game of cricket.

Sydney is also renowned for its fine surf beaches. The scenic northern beaches stretch from Manly to Palm Beach. To the south, Bondi, just seven kilometres from the General Post Office, is the most popular and most famous metropolitan beach. Coogee and Cronulla are also popular. The smaller beaches at Clovelly, Tamarama and Bronte offer quiet seclusion from crowds. Sydney's thirty-four surfing beaches are patrolled by volunteer lifesavers, who stage colourful large-scale carnivals throughout the summer months to test their mettle against other clubs. Lady Jane and Reef beaches on the harbour cater for nude sunbathers.

Surfers should take heed of warning flags placed on the sand, which mark the areas safe for surfing on that day. Rock pools are abundant and are ideal for children. It is not advisable to swim in the harbour.

St Mary's Cathedral dwarfed by the Sydney Tower and MLC Building

is **Sydney Hospital**, a city institution, which opened in 1879.

Parliament House and the former Mint were once a part of the original colonial hospital, which was known as the Rum Hospital. When there was a shortage of coinage in the colony and rum was the currency, the builders were paid in casks of the spirit. Behind the buildings, the **Domain**—a forum for soap-box orators—separates the rear of Macquarie Street from the **Art Gallery of New South Wales**.

During January, when the annual **Sydney Festival and Carnivalé** is in full swing, the Domain becomes a giant outdoor concert hall where hundreds of thousands of Sydneysiders flock to hear jazz, opera and symphonies in the park.

Macquarie Street finally leads into **Queens Square**, arguably one of Sydney's most elegant precincts. The square is encircled by Hyde Park, the towering **Law Courts** building and Francis Greenway's pre-1820 master-

pieces, **St James's Church** and **Hyde Park Barracks** (now a social history museum with unique relics from Sydney's convict origins). Flowing harmoniously on from the old barracks are two great neo-Gothic triumphs of the nineteenth century: the **Registrar-General's Building** and **St Mary's Roman Catholic Cathedral**.

Hyde Park is divided in two by **Park Street**. One half is dominated by the **Archibald Fountain**—a legacy to the city from the first publisher of the *Bulletin*—and the other by a **Pool of Remembrance** and the **Anzac War Memorial**. At night, Hyde Park's avenues of trees are lit with thousands of fairy lights. On the park's eastern boundary, in College Street, stand the **Australian Museum**; one of Sydney's oldest colleges, **Sydney Grammar School**; and two high-rise neighbours, the **Returned Servicemen's League** headquarters and the **NSW Police Department** administration building.

On the city side of Hyde Park runs **Elizabeth Street.** No longer the major city artery it once was, it now serves as a vital, almost continuous, bus feeder route, particularly where two underground railway stations, **St James** and **Museum**, disgorge. It is still, however, noteworthy for one of Sydney's historic buildings, the **Great Synagogue**, and for the headquarters of one of Australia's great retailing empires, **David Jones**.

David Jones, with its marble floors, liveried doormen and title of 'the most beautiful store in the world', stands on the corner of Elizabeth Street and Market Street and is a Sydney landmark. 'I'll see you on DJ's corner' was, and still is, a regular Sydney rendezvous. From here, Elizabeth Street continues north to the spacious semicircle of Chifley Square, named in honour of former Prime Minister J.B. Chifley.

In a wedge-shaped sector of blocks made by Bent, Bridge, Young, Phillip and Loftus Streets stand the office buildings of colonial New South Wales, elaborately constructed from Sydney's superb Hawkesbury sandstone, on which the city is built. Mostly late Victorian, the buildings still serve their original purpose as housing for State departments, such as Education and Agriculture.

All are massively solid and ornamented with either statues, gargoyles, handsomely worked stone, or all three. Inside, cedar-lined offices open on to marbled corridors, staircases with wrought-iron balustrades, and ceilings so high and arched as to be almost vault-like. The ministerial offices further within are treasure troves of priceless colonial artefacts, from grandfather clocks to richly panelled fireplaces.

The disordered pattern of the surrounding streets is a product of the complete lack of planning in the period after Governor Phillip's recall from Sydney. Bullock tracks and cow paths determined the town plan until Governor Macquarie attempted to impose order some twenty years later. Today the result contributes to Sydney's charm.

Castlereagh Street, parallel to Elizabeth Street, also loses itself in the tangle of colonial office blocks above the Quay. In **Martin Place**, a traffic-free plaza running from Elizabeth Street through Castlereagh and Pitt Streets and finishing at George Street, lunchtime office workers attend outdoor concerts in the amphitheatre, flower sellers hawk their wares from colourful barrows, and cut-price theatre and concert tickets are on sale at a Halftix booth. The **GPO** sits in Martin Place, between Pitt and George Streets. South of Martin Place the character of the area changes from a merchant belt to a shopping mecca. The **MLC Centre** dominates almost a whole block and contains suites of luxurious offices above, and at ground level, some exclusive shops, mostly jewellers and fashionable boutiques. The complex also houses a convenient fast-food area, the Australia Tavern, a cinema (the Dendy) and, for the theatre-goer, Sydney's prestigious **Theatre Royal**. The King and Castlereagh Streets crossroads, with its collection of elite retail traders such as Chanel and Gucci, has been compared to New York's Fifth Avenue and London's Bond Street.

There are more cinemas nearby and a less expensive shopping complex, **Centrepoint.** Here you can visit the 270-metre golden **Sydney Tower**, with its two revolving restaurants. From the observation decks at the summit, high-powered binoculars and a video television camera offer spectacular views of Sydney landmarks.

Only two of Sydney's north–south arteries actually make a complete journey from Circular Quay to Central Railway Station: Pitt Street and George Street. As Pitt Street between King and Market Streets is a pedestrian mall, traffic must make this journey using George Street only.

Sydney has several shopping arcades that run off Pitt and George Streets. One of these, **The Strand**, is particularly noteworthy, having been restored to its 1892 splendour and housing some of Australia's leading fashion designers, jewellers and craftspeople.

In both Pitt and George Streets there is little trace of colonial Sydney, although handsome turn-of-the-century commercial buildings are carefully watched over by devoted citizens and the National Trust, lest developers' ambitions exceed their sense of history and good taste.

Of the two streets, Pitt Street is probably the more exciting in terms of shops, cafes and street hawkers.

The monorail beside Pitt Street winds through the city above street level, linking it to the **Darling Harbour Complex**.

Between King and Park Streets, Pitt Street comes into its own: department

Monorail links the city and Darling Harbour

stores, including Grace Bros and Centrepoint; another popular sporting club, **City Tattersalls**; the Pitt Street side of the Methodist Church's Wesley headquarters; cinemas, one a complex of several choices; and, dominating the two blocks, the sumptuous **Sydney Hilton Hotel**, now outstripped by its soaring neighbour Sydney Tower, the tallest building in Sydney.

Pitt Street becomes rather nondescript as it heads south towards Central Railway Station, with some secondhand stores, places offering cheap accommodation, and a laneway that leads to a nineteenth-century police headquarters building, now more a city watchhouse and serving as cells for the grim **Central Criminal Court** building on one of the cross-streets, Liverpool Street.

On carnival-thronged evenings along George Street's entertainment section, cinema complexes, fast-food houses, pin-ball alleys, all-night bookshops and erotic movie houses all compete for the jostling crowd's attention.

Apart from its entertainment area that makes its nights so boisterous, George Street boasts a number of Sydney's most important and interesting buildings, both old and new. Until a few years ago, Sydney's and Australia's tallest building was the **Australia Square Tower**. Tall and circular in shape, it has an observation platform on the forty-eighth floor

and a revolving restaurant, the Summit. These days the tower is dwarfed by the AMP and MLC buildings on Sydney's rocketing skyline, and by the **Sheraton Wentworth Hotel**, situated opposite on Phillip Street.

South from here are Wynyard underground railway station, the GPO, Sydney's Victorian massif, and the remarkable **Queen Victoria Building** (QVB), which monopolises an entire block. The QVB has been restored by the Sydney City Council, in conjunction with an Asian consortium; the restoration includes the refurbishing of its enormous copper dome, which once loomed over the older city skyline. The building now houses many restaurants and over 160 shops. A landmark of the city's earlier days is to be found opposite the Queen Victoria building, through the George Street entrance to the Hilton Hotel. In the hotel's basement, restored to its original ornate detail, is the superb **Marble Bar** of the old Adams Hotel, which once stood on the site of the Hilton. On the next corner stands the spiralling blue **Coopers and Lybrand tower**. With its art deco design, it has been dubbed the Superman Building because of its similarity to the fictitious *Daily Planet* of comic-strip fame.

The **Town Hall**, now dwarfed but not overshadowed by a modern council administration block, is Italian Renaissance

A Colonial Past

At the first settlement at Sydney Cove, Captain Watkin Tench of the Marines wrote: 'to proceed on a narrow, confined scale in a country of the extensive limits we possess, would be unpardonable . . . (the) extent of Empire demands grandeur of design'.

Such grand design began in 1810, when the vision of the new Governor, Lachlan Macquarie, was put into practice by the convict architect Francis Greenway, giving us a heritage of splendid buildings, many of which are landmarks today. It continued through nearly a century of growth and lofty ideals to create a prosperous and busy metropolis—a great symbol of colonial aspirations.

As it developed, Sydney was both 'mean and princely', a mixture of broad, tree-lined avenues and narrow streets and alleys, grand buildings and crowded cottages and terraces. Its switchback, craggy hills around the indented harbour made orderly Georgian-style planning impossible, and the grand outlines of earlier days soon became blurred by the city's growth from first settlement to colonial seat, to State capital to modern city.

In modern Sydney, however, with its gleaming towers, its crowds and its traffic, substantial remnants of old Sydney can still be seen. Some parts of the city, like the Rocks area adjacent to Circular Quay, are almost pure history. The old pubs and bandstands, sandstone cottages and terrace houses, the Argyle Cut and Agar Steps, the Garrison Church and the village green form an oasis separated from the bustling city by Flagstaff Hill, where the old Observatory stands, and the approaches to the Harbour Bridge are seen.

There are many other inner suburban areas that are reminiscent of the feeling of old Sydney. Paddington is the showplace historic suburb, with its picturesque terraces and cottages, many superbly restored by proud owners. The narrow streets of this once working-class suburb provide an intimate, neighbourly feeling. Balmain, Leichhardt and Redfern are becoming popular as the advantages of inner-suburban living attract owners who are conscious of the aesthetic quality of the old sandstone cottages.

In the city itself, the street that best reflects the past is probably Macquarie

Street, which overlooks both the Botanic Gardens and the Domain, where Government House, the Conservatorium of Music, the State Library and Art Gallery of NSW are situated. Governor Macquarie planned for the east side of the street to be occupied by official buildings and for the west to contain the town houses of wealthy citizens, now occupied mainly by medical practitioners.

Other interesting buildings in Macquarie Street are: Parliament House (1816), a verandahed sandstone building, originally one wing of the Rum Hospital; the adjoining Mint Building, restored from the other wing of the original Rum Hospital; Sydney Hospital, whose buildings replaced the central block of the Rum Hospital; the Royal College of Physicians; and the Hyde Park Barracks (1819), now a museum. In nearby Queens Square is the classical St James's Church.

At the harbour end of Mrs Macquarie's Road is a reminder of the Macquarie era—a sandstone shell known as Mrs Macquarie's Chair. The Governor's wife is said to have sat here and gazed out upon the great harbour, now one of the world's busiest and most picturesque waterways.

There are a number of other major buildings in or near the city: such buildings as Elizabeth Bay House, in Regency style, now restored and a showplace for the rich furnishings of the time when it looked out over a harbour backed by cliff and woodland; the General Post Office in Martin Place, completed in 1887 in classic Renaissance style; the Great Hall of Sydney University, and St Andrew's Cathedral, both designed by Edmund Blacket; St Mary's Cathedral, designed by William Wardell; the Greek Revival courthouse in Taylor Square, designed by Mortimer Lewis; and Vaucluse House, the former home of William Charles Wentworth, father of the NSW Constitution. Perhaps the most striking example of colonial architecture in Sydney is Victoria Barracks in Darlinghurst. This two-storeyed building of severe Georgian style, 74 metres long, with white-painted upper and lower verandahs, is a model of elegance. (Visit on Thursday at 10 a.m., watch the changing of the guard and entertainment provided by the Australian Army Band, Sydney, and follow with a guided tour of this historic group of buildings.)

As settlement extended from the harbourside colony, villages were established, first in the upper **Hawkesbury region** to the north-west, then to the south and finally, as the Blue Mountains were

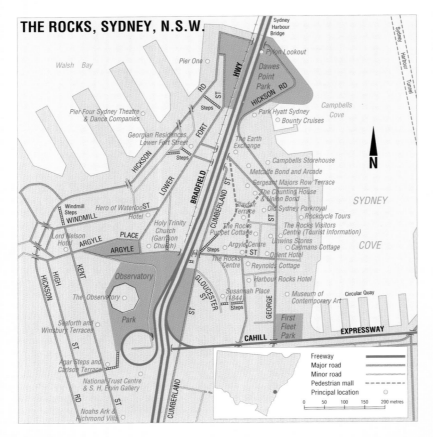

THE ROCKS, SYDNEY, N.S.W.

breached, out to the western plains and throughout New South Wales.

In the upper Hawkesbury valley are the sister towns of Windsor and Richmond, two of the Macquarie Towns, beautifully sited on the river and retaining the peaceful charm and many of the buildings of earlier days. Windsor has a number of fine buildings: Claremont Cottage, St Matthew's Anglican Church, the Macquarie Arms, Tebbutt's Observatory, the Doctor's House and the Toll House, to name a few. At Richmond are Belmont, Hobartville, Toxana House, the School of Arts and St Peter's Anglican Church.

In the **Southern Highlands**, the settlements of Mittagong, Moss Vale, Berrima and Bowral are full of historic interest. The Berrima Village Trust is responsible for the preservation of the village as it was in the 19th century. Sited in a valley, Berrima contains a number of fine sandstone buildings grouped around a central common, among them the gaol and courthouse, the Surveyor-General Inn, the Church of the Holy Trinity, Harper's Mansion and Allington. Throughout New South Wales there are many other historic towns and properties bearing the hallmarks of the nation's foundation.

For further information on colonial towns and buildings, contact the National Trust of Australia office in your State. **See also:** Individual A–Z town listings.

Lord Nelson Hotel, The Rocks

Moss Vale, Southern Highlands

in style. Built of mellow brown sandstone, it was completed in 1874. A graceful, shaded pedestrian plaza, **Sydney Square,** is located around the Town Hall and separates it from Sydney's Anglican Cathedral, **St Andrew's.** Erected in stages from 1839 onwards, it was not until the final additions and alterations to the Cathedral were completed that the present main entrance on George Street was finally opened in 1919. This area is also the proposed site of the new Sydney Casino, scheduled to open in 1997.

Further west is **Darling Harbour**, an ambitious public centre, opened on Australia Day 1988, which has become an entertainment centre for Sydneysiders. This impressive complex includes: the **Chinese Garden of Friendship**, an exhibition and convention centre; waterside walks; a variety of eating places; seven-day-a-week shopping; and splendid parklands around a busy harbour inlet that was once a dull industrial port. At the western end of the National Trust-classified Pyrmont Bridge is the National **Maritime Museum** and near the eastern end of this one-time traffic carrier, now used as a walkway, is the **Sydney Aquarium**.

The Powerhouse Museum on the southern edge of the Darling Harbour Complex is also well worth a visit. Its size is such that it can exhibit aeroplanes, trams, boats and steam engines, plus many equally fascinating smaller exhibits. Opposite is the **Sydney Entertainment Centre,** a major venue for concerts and conventions. Nearby lies **Dixon Street**, the pedestrianised heart of **Sydney's China Town**, a traditional area of restaurants, warehouses, specialty stores and Chinese grocers, where even banks and service stations are labelled in Chinese script. At its southern end the visitor will find the Paddy's Markets, which reopened in 1994.

Not far from Darling Harbour is Australia's largest fish market, the **Sydney Fish Market** at **Pyrmont;** it has retail stores, coffee shops, souvenir outlets and Australia's first seafood school. Walking tours are available.

Of the city's cross-streets, two handsome boulevards are noteworthy: Park Street and **Martin Place**. The authentic heart of the city, Martin Place, with its memorial **Cenotaph** to Australia's war dead, is the annual stage for the city's Anzac Day March on April 25. It is also a stage for a variety of lunchtime entertainment.

Park Street ambles east, its footpaths splitting Hyde Park in two and providing a pleasant walk before turning into William Street, which inevitably leads to **Kings Cross,** Sydney's version of Soho and Greenwich Village. The Cross, though, has its own unique flavour: the breath of a Sydney Harbour breeze and a glimpse of blue water are a delight. Whatever the Cross has borrowed from other cities in its strip joints, gaudy nightspots and colourful characters, it has its own bohemian traditions. In its backyard are **Garden Island** dockyard, where the Fleet is nearly always in, and the encircling apartment houses of select **Elizabeth Bay**. On its boundaries are the lively suburbs of Darlinghurst and Woolloomooloo.

The once notorious **Darlinghurst,** a long-time haunt of pimps, prostitutes and gangsters, boasts the historic Darlinghurst Gaol (where bushrangers were hanged) as one of its attractions. Today, however, the face of Darlinghurst has changed dramatically and it is now the home of artists, musicians and poets. Its main artery, **Oxford Street**, with its adult bookshops, pubs, clothing stores and restaurants, is the gay capital of Australia.

Woolloomooloo (the famous Loo) has seen its cramped houses and narrow streets skyrocket in price as the desire for trendy inner-city living escalates. Individual restaurants and bars are many and various—too numerous to list. Trendy brasseries compete amid the leftovers of 'sleaze' on Bayswater Road and Kellett Street, where the gentrification of the Cross is most apparent. But, even so, there are a great number of erotic movie houses and specialty bookshops—with the red-light-district flavour that seems to go with them—still left in the Cross. A less controversial landmark is the dandelion-shaped **El Alamein Fountain** commemorating the World War II battle.

In the other direction, Darlinghurst Road and Bayswater Road lead to Sydney's trendiest area, **Paddington**, a suburb of steep hills, unplanned streets and picturesque terrace houses, hardly one without ornate Victorian wrought-iron railings and fences and lots of trees. The old-fashioned pubs are now terribly chic; well-spoken children and large dogs exercise on streets once the domain of street urchins, before Paddington underwent its fashionable revival back in the late fifties. Next door to 'Paddo' is **Centennial Park**, Sydney's equivalent to New York's Central and London's Regent Park, where horseriding, cycling and picnicking are weekend activities.

Paddington's counterpart on the other side of Sydney, **Glebe** (bordering historic **Sydney University**) is not quite so leafy or picturesque, and certainly not as expensive, but is seeing a revival. Nearby **Balmain** with its harbour frontage has also undergone a fashionable revival.

At every turn these three suburbs reveal something old and handsome in weathered sandstone: a church, a cottage, a school from Sydney's past. They have also given rise to a Sydney phenomenon: the advent of the Church Bazaar. These village markets, usually held on Saturdays, feature colourful identities plying their wares at open-air stalls in the grounds of schools or churches. For this reason alone, the suburbs are worth a visit.

So is the rest of Australia's first city: from Paddington's neighbours, **Woollahra** and **Rushcutters Bay**, through the harbourside suburbs of exclusive **Double Bay**, **Rose Bay** and **Vaucluse**, to **The Gap** and **South Head**; or across the harbour by the ferry, jetcat or Harbour Bridge to **Manly** and the long line of beaches stretching north to **Palm Beach**, competing in terms of wealth and privilege with the precipitous bush gorges and superior heights of the elegant **North Shore** suburbs. Beyond all that again lies the metropolitan heartland of Sydney's great urban sprawl—75 km from the harbour across the vast, flat western suburbs to the foothills of the **Blue Mountains**.

A floatplane service at **Rose Bay** has flights between Sydney and Palm Beach, Gosford and Newcastle; and the Manly Ferry *Collaroy* offers cruises from Circular Quay up the coast into Broken Bay and the Hawkesbury River. Near the Hawkesbury at **Berowra** is the famous Berowra Waters Inn, ranked as one of the best restaurants in Australia.

It is not possible to list all Sydney's restaurants. In Sydney one can dine out on the cuisines of virtually every nation in the world. (However, it should be mentioned that Sydney is famous for its rock oyster and the Balmain Bug—an odd-looking but tasty crustacean.) The choice of cinema, live theatre and live-theatre restaurants is just as comprehensive.

For further information, contact the NSW Travel Centre, 19 Castlereagh St, Sydney 2000; (02) 231 4444.

Tours from Sydney

Sydney's range of available day tours out and about is almost unrivalled for the variety of scenic and recreational attractions on offer.

In the frantic rush to get out of the city, however, it is easy to overlook two of Sydney's greatest assets: **Royal National Park**, little more than an hour's drive south from the GPO, and **Ku-Ring-Gai Chase National Park**, 40 km N.

Harbour Cruises from Circular Quay

An ideal way to view Sydney and its harbour is by boat. Several cruises are available. State Transit run three daily: a two-and-a-half hour harbour sights or harbour history cruise, and a one-and-a-half hour harbour lights cruise. The Harbour lights cruise does not run on Sun. evening. Bookings not necessary; for further information: (02) 9956 4790.

Coffee cruises, operated by Captain Cook Cruises, run twice daily through Main and Middle Harbours and the same company's luncheon cruises travel up the Parramatta and Lane Cove Rivers daily. The *John Cadman* makes a dinner cruise daily. The 38-m cruise ship *Proud Sydney* offers overnight harbour cruises. Experience the thrill of sailing on a harbour luncheon cruise aboard the *Solway Lass,* a restored sailing-ship.

Captain Cook Cruises also conducts tours to Fort Denison, one of the most historic relics in Australia, Tues.– Sun.

Taronga Zoo, 12 minutes by ferry from Circular Quay, Wharf 5

Taronga is set in 30 ha of harbourside bushland, giving it a magnificent and unique setting: the views back to the city are splendid. Of particular interest are the displays of Australian native animals and the nocturnal house. Children will enjoy meeting the tame animals at the Friendship Farm (open daily).

Palm Beach, 48 km from Sydney via Pittwater Rd

This beautiful beach in bush surroundings offers swimming and boating facilities and a choice of ocean or Pittwater beaches. The drive from Sydney reveals many of Sydney's lovely northern beaches and it is tempting to stop at every one. The Mona Vale road provides a shorter route if you are based in the northern suburbs; allow time to visit the fauna reserve Waratah Park at Terrey Hills.

Captain Cook's Landing Place, Kurnell, 35 km from Sydney via Princes Hwy and Captain Cook Bridge

The site of the first recorded landing by Europeans on the east coast of Australia in 1770 is set aside as an historic site on a pleasant reserve. An excellent museum displays items related to Captain James Cook's life and discoveries. A short

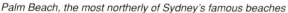
Palm Beach, the most northerly of Sydney's famous beaches

The Blue Mountains

For more than a century, the Blue Mountains have been a favourite holiday resort for Sydneysiders. Rising from the coastal plain 65 kilometres west of Sydney, they combine a unique blend of superb mountain scenery, outstanding geographical features and highly developed tourist attractions. Although the January 1994 bushfires affected large areas of bushland and destroyed property; the process of recovery and rebuilding is evident.

The towering cliffs of the Blue Mountains presented a seemingly impassable barrier to the early European settlers until Blaxland, Lawson and Wentworth made their historic crossing in 1813—thus opening up much-needed pasture-land beyond.

In the late 1870s the well-to-do of Sydney discovered the area's charms as a resort, and started to build elaborate holiday houses to escape the summer heat of the coast. At first they travelled by Cobb & Co. coach, later by train. Now the mountains are less than two hours from Sydney by road or rail. One-day round-trip coach tours run daily between Sydney and Katoomba.

The Blue Mountains are justly famous for their spectacular scenery of high precipices rising from densely wooded valleys. Their highest point is about 1100 metres above sea level. Although the area has been developed for tourism, deep gorges and high rocks make much of the terrain inaccessible except to skilled bushwalkers and mountaineers. Climbing schools offer rock-climbing weekends for beginners, and there are day courses in beginners' abseiling.

The panoramic **Blue Mountains National Park**, which covers an area of 216 000 hectares, is the fourth largest national park in the state.

The City of Blue Mountains incorporates over 20 towns and villages, including the main towns of **Katoomba**, **Blackheath**, **Wentworth Falls**, **Springwood** and **Glenbrook**. All these towns depend on tourism and are geared for the holiday trade. They offer a wide range of accommodation, from bed and breakfast at old-style guest houses to luxury living at modern resorts.

The Blue Mountains' reputation for natural wonders is rapidly being rivalled by its popularity as a gastronomic centre. Wining and dining to suit all tastes and budgets, combined with an overnight or weekend stay, is attracting further visitors to the area.

For further information, contact the Blue Mountains Tourism Authority, PO Box 8, Glenbrook 2773; (047) 39 6266, or visit the Information Centres at Echo Point, Katoomba or Glenbrook on the Great Western Hwy. A *Holiday Book*, produced by the BMTA, also details activities and accommodation in the area. **See also:** Katoomba–Wentworth Falls in A–Z listing. **Note** detailed map of Blue Mountains on page 106.

Why are the Blue Mountains so blue?
The whole area is heavily timbered with eucalypts, which constantly disperse fine droplets of oil into the atmosphere. These droplets cause the blue light-rays of the sun to be scattered more effectively, thus intensifying the usual light refraction phenomenon (Rayleigh Scattering), which causes distant objects to appear blue.

The Three Sisters

historical walk takes visitors past several points of interest. There are picnic/barbecue facilities in the grounds.

Parramatta, 22 km from Sydney via Great Western Hwy

Although it has now become a city within Sydney, Parramatta retains its individuality and has some interesting buildings. Pick up an Historic Houses self-guide leaflet from the tourist centre in Prince Alfred Park; (02) 630 3703. Elizabeth Farm (1793), in Alice St, contains part of the oldest surviving building in Australia and, as the home of Elizabeth and John Macarthur, was for the first 40 years of the colony the social, political and agricultural centre. Don't miss the audiovisual and period gardens (1830s). Experiment Farm Cottage in Ruse St was the site of James Ruse's 'experiment' to support himself from the land in the early years of the colony. Closer to the centre of the city are two historic sites. Old Government House, in attractive Parramatta Park, has been beautifully restored from its 1799 beginnings (enlarged 1815) and is maintained by the National Trust. Take the guided tour to learn more. The guide will also explain the significance of St John's Church (1850s), in the heart of the shopping district. St John's cemetery is a block away from the church itself and contains the oldest headstone in the colony, dated January 1791. A ferry runs between Parramatta and Circular Quay.

Windsor and Richmond, 60 km from Sydney via Great Western Hwy and Windsor Rd

These two towns on the Hawkesbury River are reminders of the earliest days of settlement in New South Wales. In Windsor there are many historic buildings in George Street and Thompson Square. The Doctor's House, Thompson Square, built in 1844, is one of the most impressive, but the courthouse and the many churches and hotels in both towns are all of interest. The Hawkesbury Museum at 7 Thompson Square, Windsor is housed in an old colonial building. It contains various items of historic interest relating to pioneer days. **See also:** Entries in A–Z listing.

Historic Camden and Campbelltown, 60 km from Sydney via Liverpool, on Hume Hwy

Liverpool, situated 32 km from Sydney and a major retail and commercial centre, has many buildings of historic interest: St Luke's Church (1818); Liverpool Hospital (1825–30), designed by Francis Greenway and now the Liverpool College of TAFE; and Glenfield Farm (1817). The ultra-modern Liverpool Museum, built as a bicentennial project, fronts Collingwood Cottage, built in 1810 for a whaling captain. A good stopping-point is Chipping Norton Lakes, a reclaimed area with picnic and barbecue facilities, and walking tracks. Further down the highway, lovers of history can enjoy a relaxed stroll around the streets of two early towns of New South Wales, Camden and Campbelltown. Although most of the historic buildings are not open to the public, a pleasant day can be spent just taking in the atmosphere. A self-guide walking-tour booklet is available from the Macarthur Country Tourist Association, Liverpool. Between Camden and Campbelltown, off Narellan Road, is the 400-hectare Mt Annan Botanic Garden, the native plant garden of the Royal Botanic Gardens, Sydney. **See also:** Entries in A–Z listing.

Katoomba and the Blue Mountains via Penrith, 104 km from Sydney via Great Western Highway (or by minifare excursion, State Rail)

The historic town of Penrith, 57 km from Sydney, dates back to the opening of the Blue Mountains road in 1815, when a courthouse and a small gaol were built there. Today it makes a pleasant stopover en route to the Blue Mountains. Penrith's attractions include the Museum of Fire in Castlereagh St, the Nepean Belle paddle-boat, which cruises the Nepean Gorge, Vicary's Winery, south of the town, and the Lewers Regional Art Gallery at Emu Plains. **See also:** The Blue Mountains; and Katoomba entry in A–Z listing.

The Hunter Valley Vineyards, 160 km from Sydney via Pacific Hwy

Although it is possible to do this trip in a day, this certainly would not do the area justice—and it is definitely not a good idea if you plan to do any wine-tasting!

The best time to visit the Hunter Valley is at vintage time, when you can see the grapes being fermented in great open vats. Picking starts any time from the end of January, but this can vary considerably, and sometimes does not start until well into February.

Most of the wineries welcome visitors. It is well worth while visiting a few of the smaller wineries. Tyrrell's and Drayton's wineries were established within a few years of each other in the 1850s and at Tyrrell's you can still see the classic hand-presses being used during vintage and fermentation.

Most of the wineries are open daily. Visits can be arranged with the wineries direct or at the Tourist Information Centre, cnr Mt View and Wollombi Rds, Cessnock; (049) 90 4477. **See also:** Vineyards and Wineries.

Rhododendron Gardens, Blackheath, Blue Mountains

New South Wales from A to Z

Adaminaby
Pop. 375

This small town on the Snowy Mountains Hwy is well known as a base for cross-country skiers, and the ski area of Mt Selwyn is nearby. It is the stepping-off point for Lake Eucumbene, where there are a range of lakeside holiday resorts. Excellent fishing, boat hire. At Providence Portal water can be seen gushing from one of the giant Snowy Mountains tunnels into the lake. Feb.: Race meetings. **In the area:** Cruiser hire at Buckenderra, 44 km S. Yarrangobilly Caves and thermal pool, off Snowy Mountains Hwy, 53 km NW. Horseriding and alpine horseback safaris. **Tourist information:** Snowy River Information Centre, Petamin Plaza, Jindabyne; (064) 56 2444. **Accommodation:** 1 hotel/motel, 3 motels, 1 cara./camp. park.
MAP REF. 118 H5, 119 D8, 140 E9, 235 K1

Adelong
Pop. 795

Both fossickers and goldfields historians are attracted to this picturesque tablelands town on the Snowy Mountains Hwy. In the mid-1850s it produced 200 tonnes of gold and drew many thousands of hopeful miners. **Of interest:** Tumut St, from Campbell to Neil Sts, National Trust-classified; some buildings, such as old Bank of NSW, of great historical interest. Also in Tumut St: Gold Fields Galleries, art and craft; restored Old Pharmacy with Old Prison Clock (over 125 years old) originally from Kiandra courthouse; accommodation and restaurant. **In the area:** Adelong Falls, 2 km N, on Tumblong–Gundagai Rd: scenic picnic area, gold fossicking. Oasis, coloured-sheep farm, 8 km along same road: spinning, shearing, sales of wool and garments. **Tourist information:** York's Newsagency, Tumut St; (069) 46 2051. **Accommodation:** 2 hotels, 1 camping/caravan park.
MAP REF. 119 B6, 120 C13

Albury
Pop. 39 975

Albury–Wodonga is situated on the Murray River, 572 km SW from Sydney. Once the meeting-place for local Aboriginal tribes, today the Albury region makes a convenient stopover for motorists driving via the Hume Hwy between Sydney and Melbourne. The building of the Hume Weir in 1936 created Lake Hume, one of the most extensive and beautiful artificial lakes in Australia, a paradise for anglers, canoeists, swimmers, sailors, water-skiers, speedboat enthusiasts and wind-surfers. **Of interest:** Albury Regional Museum, in former Turk's Head Hotel, Wodonga Pl. Botanical Gardens (1871), cnr Wogonga Pl. and Dean St. The Parklands, comprising Noreuil and Australia Parks and Hovell Tree Reserve, on western side of Wodonga Pl at town entrance: riverside walks, river swimming, kiosk, picnic areas. PS *Cumberoona* offers Murray River cruises; embarkation points within parks. Albury Regional Art Centre, Dean St. Performing Arts Centre, Civic Centre, Swift St. 360° views from Albury Monument Hill at end of Dean St. Frog Hollow Leisure Park, Olive St: maze, theatre, mini-golf. Haberfield's Milk Dairy Shop, Hovell St: sales of local dairy products, tours business hours. Feb.–March: Festival of Sport. **In the area:** Ettamogah Wildlife Sanctuary, 12 km NE on Hume Hwy. Hume and Hovell Walking Track from Albury to Gunning, over 300 km NE. Cartoonist Ken Maynard's Ettamogah Pub, worth photographing. Cooper's Ettamogah Winery, 3 km further along hwy. Australian Newsprint Mill, 15 km N, tours by appt. Jindera Pioneer Museum, 14 km NW, former general store. Day trips to wineries of Rutherglen, 47 km W, and into Mad Dan Morgan country, 200 km round trip N. Bogong Mountains, gateway to Victorian snowfields and high country, 130 km S. Hume Weir Trout Farm, 14 km E, trout feeding,

Lake Eucumbene, near Adaminaby

fishing, tastings. **Tourist information:** Gateway Tourist Information Centre, Lincoln Causeway, Wodonga (060) 41 3875; accommodation booking line 1800 80 6939. **Accommodation:** Albury–Wodonga, 2 hotels, 55 motels, 13 cara./camp. parks.
MAP REF. 127 P13, 233 P4

Alstonville Pop. 3678
The village of Alstonville nestles in lush surroundings at the top of the Ballina Cutting between Ballina and Lismore. Famous for the beautiful purple Tibouchina tree, the town holds a Tibouchina Festival during blossom time in March. Surrounding properties produce potatoes, sugarcane, tropical fruits, macadamia nuts and avocados. **Of interest:** Prize-winning town in 'Tidy Towns' competition since 1986. Lumley Park, Bruxner Hwy, open-air pioneer transport museum. Kolinda Gallery, Budgen Ave and Granny's Love, Wardell St: local art and craft. Elizabeth Ann Brown Park, Main St, rainforest park; picnic facilities. March: Tibouchina Festival. **In the area:** House With No Steps, 10 km s; nursery, crafts, fruit sales and tearooms run by disabled. Victoria Park, 10 km s; boardwalks and picnic area. John Cook Studio Gallery, Forest Rd (off Uralba Rd), 6 km E; art and craft. **Tourist information:** Ballina Tourist Information Centre, Las Balsas Plaza, Ballina; (066) 86 3484. **Accommodation:** 1 hotel, 1 motel.
MAP REF. 123 P3, 475 O9

Armidale Pop. 21 605
Situated midway between Sydney and Brisbane in the New England Ranges (altitude 900 m), this university city is the centre of the New England district and an attractive tourist centre, with over 30 National Trust buildings. **Of interest:** New England Regional Art Museum, Kentucky St, contains Hinton Collection, most valuable provincial art collection in Australia. Also in Kentucky St, Aboriginal Centre and Keeping Place: museum and education centre. Folk Museum with display of pioneer relics, in National Trust-classified building, cnr Faulkner and Rusden Sts. In Dangar St: St Mary's Roman Catholic Cathedral (1912), magnificent Gothic revival structure; St Peter's Anglican Cathedral (1875), built of 'Armidale blues' bricks. The Stables (1872), Moore St, now craft shop. Courthouse (1860) and Imperial Hotel (1889), Beardy St. Central Park, Dangar St,

pleasant city park with useful relief map of area. Markets in Mall, last Sun. in month. Sept.–Nov.: Springfest. **In the area:** University of New England, 5 km NW, historic Booloominbah homestead now administration building, Antiquities Museum, Zoology Museum, kangaroo and deer park. National Trust-owned Saumarez Homestead (1888), 6 km s. Rural Life and Industry Museum at ghost town of Hillgrove, 27 km E: exhibits of goldmining equipment. Oxley Wild Rivers National Park, 39 km E, incl. Wollomombi Falls, highest falls in Australia, plunging 220 m. Fine views from Point Lookout (1500 m) in New England National Park, 80 km E. Self-guide leaflets available for National Parks. Mt Yarrowyck Aboriginal rock-art site and cultural walk, 23 km NW off Bundarra Rd. **Tourist information:** Visitors Centre & Coach Station, 82 Marsh St, (067) 73 8527, Freecall (1800) 62 7736. **Accommodation:** 5 hotels, 22 motels, 3 B&B, 2 cara./camp. parks. **See also:** New England.
MAP REF. 123 L8, 475 K12

Ashford Pop. 567
This small New England town is the centre of a tobacco-growing district. **In the area:** Network of limestone caves and spectacular Macintyre Falls, 36 km NW. Pindari Dam, 20 km s; bushwalking, swimming, fishing, camping, picnic/barbecue facilities. **Tourist information:** Shire Tourism Committee, Water Towers Complex, Campbell St, Inverell; (067) 22 1693. **Accommodation:** 1 hotel, 1 cara./camp. park. **See also:** New England.
MAP REF. 123 J4, 475 J10

Ballina Pop. 14 554
A fishing town at the mouth of the Richmond River in northern NSW, Ballina's ideal year-round temperatures, golden beaches, picturesque farmlands and friendly rural atmosphere make the area a popular family holiday destination. Cedar cutters were among the first white settlers, attracted by the red cedar trees along the shores of the river. Farmers followed and by 1900 the dairy-farming industry was established alongside sugarcane plantations. **Of interest:** Naval Museum, adj. to Tourist Information; restored Las Balsas Expedition rafts that sailed from South America in 1973. B Framed Gallery, River St. Opal and Gem Museum, Pine St. Quilts and Collectables, Martin

St. Ballina Outdoor Entertainment Reserve, Canal Rd. The Big Prawn, Pacific Hwy: fresh seafood, antiques, arts and crafts. *Richmond Princess* river cruises. **In the area:** MacKay Harrison Galleries, 2 km N on Lennox Head Rd. Freshwater Lake Ainsworth, 12 km N, at Lennox Head. Macadamia Land, 17 km N at Knockrow, entertainment park. Thursday Plantation Tea Tree Oil, 3 km W, guided tours. Macadamia Magic at Alphadale, 25 km W, processing and packaging of nuts. Broadwater Sugar Mill, on Pacific Hwy at Broadwater, 19 km s: tours during sugar season; covered shoes must be worn. **Tourist information:** Las Balsas Plaza; (066) 86 3484. **Accommodation:** 18 motels, 3 B&B, 1 hostel, 8 cara./camp. parks.
MAP REF. 123 P3, 475 O9

Balranald Pop. 1327
On the Murrumbidgee River, 438 km NW of Melbourne, in a wool, cattle, wheat, fruit and timber area. **Of interest:** Historical Museum and Heritage Park, Market St. Old Police Station, River St; open to public. Lions Park picnic/barbecue facilities and playground. Easter: Homebush Gymkhana. **In the area:** Balranald (low-level) Weir for picnics, barbecues and fishing. Yanga Lake, 7 km SE, good fishing and water sports. Historic Homebush Hotel (1878), 25 km N. Mungo National Park, 150 km NW: Walls of China; Willandra Lakes preserve record of 40 000 years of Aboriginal life. **Tourist information:** Market St; (050) 20 1599. **Accommodation:** 1 hotel/motel, 5 motels, 1 cara./camp. park.
MAP REF. 126 H9, 231 N7

Bangalow Pop. 819
Discover the rustic charm of this delightful village, set amid magnificent scenery. **Of interest:** Art, craft and antique shops. Colourful market, every 4th Sun. **In the area:** Byron Creek walking track, through splendid rainforest to picnic area. Beaches at Byron Bay, 12 km E. **Tourist information:** Byron Tourist Information Office, 80 Jonson St, Byron Bay; (066) 85 8050. **Accommodation:** 1 hotel, 1 motel.
MAP REF. 123 P2, 475 J10

Barham–Koondrook
Pop. 1217
These twin towns, on either side of the Murray River, are centres for the timber,

The Hawkesbury

The Hawkesbury River, north of Sydney is one of the most attractive rivers in Australia and also played an important role in Sydney's early colonial history. The first European settlers arrived in 1794 to establish farming settlements to help feed the starving colony. In 1810 Governor Macquarie founded the towns of **Windsor**, **Richmond**, **Castlereagh**, **Wilberforce** and **Pitt Town** in the upper Hawkesbury valley. Today much of this land is still used for agriculture and there are many oyster leases on the lower river.

Although farming has been pursued since the late 18th century, the charm of the Hawkesbury lies mainly in the fact that the river is still surrounded by large areas of untouched bushland. Large tracts were burnt in the terrible bushfires that swept through the area in January 1994. Two major national parks front the river: upstream the Dharug National Park, noted for its Aboriginal rock carvings, and downstream the Ku-Ring-Gai Chase National Park.

The Hawkesbury River is a popular recreational waterway, particularly at its

Berowra Waters

lower and wider reaches between Brooklyn and Pittwater.

One of the best ways of exploring the Hawkesbury is by boat. Craft of all types, from small rowing dinghies to cruisers and houseboats, are available for hire at **Brooklyn**, a small town near the Hawkesbury River Bridge, and also at **Bobbin Head**, **Berowra Waters** and **Wisemans Ferry**. A delightful way to see the river is to join the mailboat run, which leaves Brooklyn on weekdays and takes 3 hours. Cruises on the river are also available, from 2 hours to a full day, on the *Deerubbin*.

If you are travelling north from Sydney by road, the Newcastle–Sydney Freeway crosses the Hawkesbury and its tributary, Mooney Mooney Creek. This section of the freeway cuts through magnificent sandstone cliffs and offers spectacular views.

For further information, contact the Hawkesbury Visitors Centre, Ham Common Bicentenary Park, Richmond Rd, Clarendon; (045) 88 5895. **See also:** Individual town entries in A–Z listing. **Note** detailed map of Hawkesbury and Central Coast on page 108.

Southern Highlands

When Governor Lachlan Macquarie visited the area to the south of Sydney that came to be known as the Southern Highlands, he recorded in his diary for that year, 1820: 'the situation of the New Settlers, four miles south-west of Throsby Park, is particularly beautiful and rich, resembling a fine extensive pleasure ground in England.'

Located within the Sydney–Canberra–Melbourne transport corridor formed by the Hume Highway and the main railway between Sydney and Melbourne, the Southern Highlands is easily accessible, with Canberra to the south (170 kilometres from Bowral), Wollongong and the coast to the east (50 kilometres from Bowral) and Sydney to the north.

The thriving towns of Mittagong, Bowral, Berrima, Moss Vale, Robertson and Bundanoon are surrounded by the gentle softness of a rural landscape varied by the changing colours of the seasons.

The crisp mountain air has long attracted visitors. The area offers colourful gardens, and in the towns and villages the visitor will find galleries, antiques, arts and crafts. There are also rugged mountain ranges, rolling green hillsides, plunging waterfalls and marvellous bushwalks.

The landscape ranges from gently undulating to rugged, at 650–860 metres above sea level. The eastern parts of the Shire are bounded by the cliffs and ravines of the Illawarra escarpment and Morton National Park. There are small sections of remnant rainforest in the vicinity of Robertson.

Picturesque Fitzroy Falls are part of Morton National Park. Wombeyan Caves, 60 kilometres north-west of Mittagong, are remarkable for their limestone formations. Budderoo National Park is small, but noted for its views and excellent walking tracks. Also popular are the Alpaca Centre at Berrima, the Butterfly House at Mittagong, the Equestrian Centre at Sutton Farm (14 kilometres south-west of Moss Vale) and the Tulip Festival, held in early October at Bowral.

For further information, contact the Southern Highlands Visitor Information Centre, Winifred West Park, Old Hume Hwy, Mittagong; (048) 71 2888. **See also:** Individual town entries in A–Z listing. **Note** detailed map of Southern Highlands on page 116.

fat-lamb, cattle, dairying and tourism industries. **Of interest:** Barham Lakes Complex, Murray St; artificial lakes, walking track, picnic/barbecue facilities, swimming, paddle-boats and canoe hire. Bonum Red Gum Saw Mill, Moulamein Rd. Easter: Koondrook Rodeo. Sept.: Barham Pro-Am Golf Tournament. **In the area:** Kerang Ibis Rookery, 28 km SW from Koondrook on Murray Valley Hwy. Shannkirst Park Zoo, Koondrook. Gannawarra Wetlander Cruises, 15 km S via Koondrook. Koondrook State Forest, East Barham Rd. Brady's Burls, 2½ km N of Koondrook on Murrabit Rd, red-gum woodcraft. **Tourist information:** 25 Murray St, Barham; (054) 53 3100. **Accommodation:** 3 hotels, 6 motels, 3 cara./camp. parks.
MAP REF. 126 I12, 229 Q3, 231 Q13, 232 B1

Barooga   Pop. 843

A small but rapidly growing town near the Victorian town of Cobram, Barooga's beautiful setting and abundant wildlife make it a popular holiday resort. **Of interest:** Sandy beaches along Murray River. In Burkinshaw Rd: Barooga Sports Club, poker machines, bistro; Club Barooga, Olympic-size heated indoor pool, spa, sauna, gym, creche. Cobram—Barooga Golf Club. Binghi Boomerang Factory, Tocumwal Rd. Jan., Easter, June, Aug.: major golf events. **In the area:** Brentwood Fruit Juices, 6 km E. Dropirrigation junction at bridge on Berrigan Rd, 20 km N. Citrus- and grape-growing. **Tourist information:** The Old Grain Shed, cnr Station St and Punt Rd, Cobram; (058) 72 2132. **Accommodation:** 1 hotel, 6 motels, 3 cara./camp. parks.
MAP REF. 127 M13, 233 J3

Barraba   Pop. 1427

Surrounded by magnificent mountain scenery on the Manilla River in the Nandewar Ranges, Barraba is an agricultural and pastoral centre and an ideal base for exploring the eastern part of the Nandewar Mountains. **Of interest:** Nandewar Historical Museum, Queen St; open by appt. Clay Pan Fuller Gallery, Queen St. St Laurence's Anglican Church, Fitzroy St, beautiful old organ recently restored. Nov.: Fine Music Festival. **In the area:** Adam's Lookout, 4 km N. Elembee Fine Fibre Farm, Houghton Falls Rd, 32 km W: goat stud in 500 ha of bushland; walks, fossicking, wildlife. Horton River Falls and Horton Valley, 38

Mogo, a recreated goldmining town near Bateman's Bay

km W towards Mt Kaputar National Park; picnic/barbecue facilities. **Tourist information:** 116 Queen St; (067) 82 1255. **Accommodation:** 3 hotels, 1 motel, 2 cara./camp. parks. **See also:** New England.
MAP REF. 122 I7, 474 I12

Batemans Bay   Pop. 8320

Crayfish and oysters are the specialty of this attractive resort town on the Princes Hwy. The charming site, at the estuary of the Clyde River, 294 km S of Sydney, makes it an ideal picnic and bushwalking spot. **Of interest:** Birdland Animal Park, Beach Rd; rainforest trail. Excellent swimming, diving, surfing, fishing, bowling club and 27-hole golf course. Nov.: Neptune Festival. **In the area:** Shell Museum, Batehaven, 1 km E, shells from around the world. Murramarang National Park, 10 km E, rainforest, swimming beaches. Durras Lake, 10 km NE, fishing, swimming, varied wildlife, houseboat hire. Nelligen, 10 km NW, on Clyde River, picnics, water-skiing, cruises. Araluen, old goldmining town, 82 km NW. Mogo Goldfields Park, Mogo, 8 km S, features working goldmine. Old Mogo Town, 19th-century goldmining town recreated. Mogo Zoo, native and exotic animals. Surfing at Malua Bay, 10 km SE. **Tourist information:** Eurobodalla Coast Visitors Centre, cnr Princes Hwy and Beach Rd; (044) 72 6900. **Accommodation:** 16 motels, 2 B&B, 4 cara./camp. parks. **See also:** The South Coast.
MAP REF. 119 G7, 141 N7

Bathurst   Pop. 24 682

This sedate city, 209 km W of Sydney on the Macquarie River, and the centre of a pastoral and fruit- and grain-growing district, has many historic connections. The birthplace of former Prime Minister, J.B. Chifley, it is better known today for its famous motor racing circuit, Mount Panorama. **Of interest:** Self-guide historic walking tour; leaflets at Tourist Information. Ben Chifley's Cottage, Busby St. Historical Society Museum in East Wing of courthouse, Russell St. Miss Traill's house (c. 1845), 321 Russell St: contents, collected by one family over 100 years, record history of town and reflect family's passion for horse-breeding and racing. Bathurst Regional Art Gallery, Keppel St. Easter: car racing. Oct.: Bathurst 1000 car races. **In the area:** Fossicker's self-drive tour of Bathurst (1-1½ hrs); leaflets at Tourist Information. South of town, on Panorama Ave: Mt Panorama; Bathurst Gold Diggings, Karingal Village, reconstruction of goldmining era. Bathurst Motor Racing Museum, Mt Panorama Circuit. Magnificent views from summit of Mt Panorama; picnic area in McPhillamy Park. Sir Joseph Banks Nature Reserve in park. Abercrombie Caves, 72 km S, via Trunkey, on Bathurst–Goulburn Rd: limestone cave system containing Arch Cave, considered one of finest natural arches in world and larger than Grand Arch at Jenolan Caves. Kanangra–Boyd National Park: major access off Oberon–Jenolan Caves Rd, 5 km S of Jenolan Caves. Abercrombie House (1870s), 6

Port Stephens

The white volcanic sand and aquamarine waters of the beaches of Port Stephens have a distinctly tropical look, and the annual average temperature is within about 2°C of that of the Gold Coast. This large deep-water port, less than an hour's drive from Newcastle, is one of the most unspoiled and attractive seaside holiday areas on the New South Wales coast. Two-and-a-half times the size of Sydney Harbour, and almost enclosed by two volcanic headlands, the harbour is fringed by sheltered white sandy beaches backed by stretches of natural bushland. In spring, wildflowers grow in profusion.

The deep, calm waters of the harbour are ideal for boating and offer excellent fishing. You can hire a wide range of boats, from aquascooters and catamarans to sailing and power boats. Various cruises are available, including the popular Dolphin Watch and the Myall River cruise. Big-game fishing waters are within reach outside the harbour, but local fishing clubs warn against going outside the heads unless you are an experienced sailor with a two-motor boat. The best way to reach these waters is aboard one of the many charter boats licensed to take

fishermen and sightseers outside the heads. Early in the afternoon you can watch the local fishing fleet coming into **Nelson Bay**, the main anchorage of the port.

Restaurants in the area—not surprisingly—offer fresh seafood as a specialty. Sample a superb lobster supreme, washed down by a fine Hunter Valley or Port Stephens wine. What more could you ask? For dedicated oyster lovers, a trip to Moffat's Oyster Barn, Swan Bay, is a must. As well as seeing oysters under cultivation and learning about their four-year life cycle, you can enjoy a delicious meal of oysters. If you go by boat, make sure you do not run aground on an oyster lease!

You can hire almost anything in the area: bicycles (how about a tandem?), beach umbrellas, fishing tackle. There are also golf courses, bowling greens and all the other usual sporting facilities.

For surfing, you can visit the spectacular ocean beaches that stretch in both directions outside the harbour. Within about 6 kilometres of Nelson Bay are Zenith, Wreck and Box Beaches, Fingal Bay and One Mile Beach. Always popular is the Coastal Explorer 4WD tour along Newcastle Bight, the largest sand-dune expanse on the east coast. An experienced guide will take you along the beach

to discover Aboriginal shell middens, the *Sygna* wreck and World War II lines of defence.

Other local attractions include: art galleries; craft markets on the first and third Sunday of the month; Aussie Ewe and Lamb Centre, Anna Bay; the toboggan run at Toboggan Hill Park, Salamander Bay; Oakvale Farm and Fauna World; and Fighter World, RAAF Base Williamtown. Accommodation, including hotels, motels and modern holiday flats, is available in the area and there are caravan and camping parks. The main towns, apart from Nelson Bay, are **Shoal Bay**, **Fingal Bay**, **Anna Bay**, **Tanilba Bay**, **Salamander Bay**, **Soldiers Point**, **Corlette** and **Lemon Tree Passage** on the south shore, and **Tea Gardens** and **Hawks Nest** on the north shore.

For further information about the area, including such nearby attractions as the Myall Lakes National Park, contact the Port Stephens Visitors Centre, Victoria Pde, Nelson Bay; (049) 81 1579. **See also:** Individual town entries in A–Z listing. **Note** detailed map of Newcastle Region on page 112.

The Illawarra Coast

Magnificent panoramic views along the rugged Illawarra coast more than compensate for the often winding route of the Princes Highway, which runs the length of it. 'Illawarra' is a corruption of an Aboriginal word appropriately meaning 'high and pleasant place by the sea'. Stretching from Sydney south to Batemans Bay, the Illawarra coast is bounded on the west by the Southern Highlands.

Fine surf beaches stretch along Illawarra's craggy coast, which is liberally dotted with mountain streams, waterfalls, inlets and lakes—ideal for prawning and water sports. Wildflowers and fauna abound in the many reserves along the coast, and the distinctive vegetation includes cabbage palms, tree ferns and giant fig trees. Some of these reserves were burnt out

Lookout near Wollongong

during the devastating bushfires in January 1994. This is the setting for the State's third largest city, **Wollongong**, which has many tourist attractions, scenic lookouts and beautiful beaches.

The other main towns on the coast are **Shellharbour**, a popular holiday resort and residential town south of Lake Illawarra; **Kiama**, the centre of a prosperous dairying and mixed-farming district;

Nowra, the main town of the fascinating Shoalhaven River district; and **Ulladulla**, a picturesque little fishing town and popular summer holiday resort.

For further information, contact Tourism Wollongong, 93 Crown St, Wollongong; (042) 28 0300. **See also:** Individual town entries in A–Z listing. **Note** detailed map of Southern Highlands on page 116.

The South Coast

The southern coast of New South Wales, from Batemans Bay down to the Victorian border, is an angler's paradise. Hemmed by the Great Dividing Range, it is one of the finest areas for fishing in southern Australia. It is also a haven for anyone who enjoys swimming, surfing or bushwalking in an unspoiled setting.

One of the attractions of this stretch of coast is the variety of country: superb white surf beaches and crystal-clear blue sea against a backdrop of craggy mountains, gentle hills, lakes, inlets and forests. The coast is dotted with quaint little fishing and holiday resorts, with a wide range of hotel, motel and holiday-flat accommodation, as well as many caravan parks. These towns are not highly commercialised, although many of them triple their population in the peak summer months. Boats of all kinds can be hired at the major resorts.

Peaceful **Batemans Bay**, at the estuary of the Clyde River, has become very popular with Canberra people since the road linking the Monaro and Princes Highways was updated. **Narooma**, **Montague Island** and **Bermagui** are well known for their big-game fishing. Black marlin, blue fin and hammerhead sharks are the main catch. Narooma also boasts an 18-hole cliff-side golf course where you tee off from the third hole across a narrow canyon.

Bega, to the south, is the unofficial capital of the area and is an important dairying and cheese-making centre. As Bega is about 10 minutes inland from the coast and 2 hours from the snow fields, the town's proud boast is that you can ski in the Snowies and surf in the Pacific on the same day. Further south is the popular holiday resort of **Merimbula** and its sister village of **Pambula**.

The southernmost town of the region is the quaint old fishing village of **Eden**, and its former rival settlement, **Boydtown**,

both reminders of the colourful whaling days of the last century. Whale-watching is popular in Eden in October and November.

Fishing is excellent all along the coast. You can catch a variety of fish, including rock cod, bream and jewfish, from the beach or net crayfish off the rockier parts of the coast. Prawning is good in the scattered inlets; and trout and perch can be caught in the many rivers draining from the mountains.

Because of its position, the South Coast attracts tourists from Victoria and Canberra, as well as from other parts of New South Wales. The region's all-year-round mild climate has made it a favourite with visitors, but you must book well ahead in the peak holiday period.

For further information, contact the Sapphire Coast Tourism Association, Zingel Pl., Pacific Hwy (PO Box 424), Bega; (064) 92 3313. **See also:** Individual town entries in A–Z listing. **Note** detailed map of South Coast on page 117.

Coast near Merimbula

km W, on Ophir Rd, baronial-style Gothic mansion. Hill End Historic Site, 86 km NW: former goldfield, many original buildings, some restored. Visitor Centre in old Hill End Hospital. Equipment for panning and fossicking for hire in village. Other old gold towns nearby incl. Rockley, O'Connell, Trunkey Creek and Sofala. Bathurst Sheep and Cattle Drome at Rossmore Park, 6 km NE on Limekilns Rd, Kelso, performing sheep and cattle; milking, shearing, sheepdog demonstrations. **Tourist information:** 28 William St; (063) 32 1444. **Accommodation:** 7 hotels, 12 motels, 20 B&B, 1 cara./camp. park.
MAP REF. 104 A3, 120 F7

Batlow   Pop. 1143

This timber-milling and former goldmining town in the Great Dividing Range 33 km S of Tumut is situated in a district renowned for its apples, pears and berry fruits. **Of interest:** Historical Society Museum, Mayday Rd. Mountain Maid Cannery, off Kurrajong Ave. Batlow Fruit Packing Complex, Forest Rd. Superb town views from Weemala Lookout Flora and Fauna Reserve, H.V. Smith Dr. **In the area:** Hume and Hovell's Lookout, 6 km E, views over Lake Blowering, picnic area at site where explorers paused in 1824. Lake Blowering, 20 km E, picnic/barbecue facilities. Springfield Orchard, Tumut Rd, 6 km N; 16 apple varieties, picnic/barbecue facilities. Pick- your-own berry fruits and cherries at farms on Tumut Rd. Access points to 370-km Hume and Hovell Walking Trail, which runs from Yass to Albury. Bushwalks and drives through scenic areas on south-west slopes of Bago State Forest, 11 km SW. Spectacular Buddong Falls, 25 km S; picnic/barbecue facilities, fine-weather road only. **Tourist information:** Springfield Orchard, Tumut Rd; (069) 49 1021. **Accommodation:** 1 hotel, 1 motel, 1 camp./cara park.
MAP REF. 119 B6, 120 C13, 140 A4

Bega   Pop. 4202

It is possible to surf and ski on the same day from Bega, set as it is between the beach and the Kosciusko snow resorts. The town is at the junction of the Princes and Snowy Mountains Hwys, which link Sydney, Melbourne and Canberra. **Of interest:** Bega Family Historical Museum, cnr Bega and Auckland Sts. Grevillea Estate Winery, Buckajo Rd. Bega Cheese Factory, North Bega (well signposted);

open to public. March: Cheese Pro-Am. Oct., Bega Valley Art Awards. **In the area:** Dr George Lookout (8 km NE) and Bega Valley Lookout (2 km N), fine views. Brogo Valley Rotolactor, 18 km N, see cows being milked. Historic village of Candelo, 23 km SW, untouched by time; art gallery, monthly market. Tathra, 18 km SE, beautiful beaches, historic wharf. Mimosa Rocks National Park, 17 km N of Tathra: swimming, fishing and bushwalking. Wallagoot Lake, 10 km S of Tathra, water sports. Bournda National Park, 20 km SE, bushwalking, fishing, canoeing. **Tourist information:** Gipps St; (064) 92 2045. **Accommodation:** 5 hotels, 5 motels, 2 cara./camp. parks. **See also:** The South Coast.
MAP REF. 117 F7, 119 F10, 235 P6

Bellingen   Pop. 2298

Attractive tree-lined town on the banks of the Bellinger River in the rich dairylands of the Bellinger Valley. In pioneer days it was a timber-getting and shipbuilding centre. **Of interest:** Much of town classified by Heritage Commission. Restored Hammond and Wheatley Emporium, Hyde St; houses Sweetwater Gallery. Yellow Shed, cnr Hyde and Prince Sts, and Butter Factory Complex, Dopel Lane; local art and craft. Aug.: Jazz Festival. Sept.: Azalea Fair. **In the area:** River walks. Scenic island in river, with flying fox colony. Picnicking at Thora, 14 km NW, at foot of Mt Dorrigo. State forests for bushwalking and horseriding. Trout fishing in streams on Dorrigo Plateau. **Tourist information:** Yellow Shed, cnr High and Prince Sts; (066) 55 1189. **Accommodation:** 1 hotel, 1 motel, 8 B&B, 1 hostel, 1 cara./camp. park.
MAP REF. 123 O8, 475 M12

Bermagui   Pop. 1166

Fishing in all forms—lake, estuary, deep-sea and big-game—is excellent in this delightful small port, 13 km from the Princes Hwy. It was much publicised for its fishing by American novelist-sportsman Zane Grey in the 1930s. Jan.: Blue Water Fishing Classic. Easter: Four Winds Concerts. **Of interest:** Beautiful rock pools, rugged coastline and unspoiled countryside. **In the area:** Mimosa Rocks National Park, 20 km S, spectacular coast, mountain scenery, Mumbulla Mountain. Wallaga Lake National Park, 8 km N, boating, fishing,

swimming, bushwalking, picnicking. Montague Island, 23 km N, mecca for big-game fishermen. Cobargo, on Princes Hwy, 19 km W: unspoiled old working village, several art galleries, wood and leather crafts, pottery, tearooms. **Tourist information:** BP Bermagui, 8 Coluga St; (064) 93 4174. **Accommodation:** Bermagui: 1 hotel, 4 motels, 5 cara./camp. parks. Cobargo: 1 hotel/motel. **See also:** The South Coast.
MAP REF. 117 H4, 119 G9, 141 M13, 235 Q4

Berridale   Pop. 949

A rural town near Lake Eucumbene, Lake Jindabyne and the southern ski fields. **Of interest:** St Marys Church (1860), off Kosciusko Rd. Berridale School (1883), Oliver St. Berridale Inn (1863), in Exchange Sq. Easter: Fair. **In the area:** On Old Dalgety Rd: Snowy River Winery, 12 km S, and Snowy River Ag Barn and Fibre Centre, 15 km S. Llama farm on Snowy Mountains Hwy, 43 km NE. Eucumbene Trout Farm, 30 km N, fishing sales, horseriding, animals, farm tours. **Tourist information:** Snowy River Information Centre, Petamin Plaza, Jindabyne; (064) 56 2444. **Accommodation:** 1 hotel, 5 motels, 1 cara./camp. park.
MAP REF. 118 I10, 119 D9, 140 E12, 235 K4

Berrigan   Pop. 949

A traditional country town with many old buildings reflecting a bygone era, Berrigan is the headquarters of the Berrigan Shire Council and is best known for its connections with horseracing. **Of interest:** Historic buildings. Berrigan Racecourse and Kilfenora Racing Stables. Sojourn Station Art Studio. Golf course and other sports amenities. Oct.: Agricultural Show. **Tourist information:** River Foreshore, Tocumwal; (058) 74 2131. **Accommodation:** 3 hotels, 1 hotel/motel, 1 motel, 1 cara./camp. park.
MAP REF. 127 M12, 233 J1

Berrima   Pop. 723

A superbly preserved 1830s Australian town. **Of interest:** Many old buildings restored as craft and antique shops, restaurants and galleries. White Horse Inn (1832). Australia's oldest licensed hotel, the Surveyor General (1835), still operating. Harper's Mansion (1830s). Historical Museum. Gaol (1839), still in use. Courthouse, display and excellent

video of early Berrima. Australian Alpaca Centre, Market Pl, knitwear, chat to alpacas at weekends. Sept.: District Art Society Exhibition. **Tourist information:** Southern Highlands Visitor Information Centre, Winifred West Park, Old Hume Hwy, Mittagong; (048) 71 2888. **Accommodation:** 1 hotel, 2 motels, 6 B&B.
MAP REF. 116 B7, 119 H3, 120 H10

Berry   Pop. 1570
Old English trees add to the charm of this town on the Princes Hwy, 18 km NE of Nowra. In rich dairying country, it was founded by David Berry, whose brother Alexander was the first European settler in the Shoalhaven area. **Of interest:** Many National Trust-classified buildings incl. Historical Museum, Queen St. Antique shops, art and craft centres. Market at Showgrounds, first Sun. in month. Feb.: Agricultural Show. **In the area:** Cambewarra Lookout, 14 km SW. Coolangatta, 11 km SE, on site of first European settlement in area in 1822; group of convict-built cottages, restored to historic village and resort. Wineries. **Tourist information:** Princes Hwy, Bomaderry; (044) 21 0778. **Accommodation:** 1 hotel, 1 hotel/motel, 1 motel.
MAP REF. 116 F11, 119 H4, 120 I11

Bingara   Pop. 1231
Diamonds, sapphires, tourmalines and gold may be found in the creeks and rivers of this fascinating town. **Of interest:** All Nations Gold Mine, top of Hill St. Historical Society Museum (1860), in slab building thought to be town's first hotel, National Trust-classified; furniture and photographs from last-century settlement; gems, minerals, working smithy. Murray Cod Hatchery, Bandalong St; open by appt. Good fishing in town's rivers and creeks. Gwydir River Rides, Main St. Oct.: Country Music Talent Quest. **In the area:** Glacial area at Rocky Creek, 37 km SW, scenic, good spot for gold-panning. Sawn Rocks, 70 km SW, pipe-shaped volcanic rock formations. At Upper Bingara 24 km S, remains of old gold and copper mines; Chinese cemetery; Three Creeks Tourist Goldmine, working mine, panning and fossicking. Copeton Dam, 42 km E, fishing and boating, excellent camping and accommodation. **Tourist information:**

Bingara Museum, Maitland St; (067) 24 1726. **Accommodation:** 2 hotels, 1 motel, 1 cara./camp. park. **See also:** New England.
MAP REF. 122 I6, 474 I11

Blayney   Pop. 2652
A progressive country town on the Mid Western Hwy between Cowra and Bathurst and close to the historic villages of Carcoar and Millthorpe. **Of interest:** Many National Trust-classified buildings. Avenues of deciduous trees, autumn colour. Forever Country, Adelaide St, local crafts. Heritage and Carrington Parks, picnic/barbecue facilities. March: Agricultural Show. **In the area:** Carcoar Dam, 12 km SW, boating, camping, picnic/barbecue facilities. Carcoar, 14 km SW, National Trust-classified village, scene of NSW's first bank hold-up in 1863; beautifully preserved buildings, shops, tearooms. Newbridge, 20 km E, historic buildings, craft. Taroona Wool Pack, 5 km and Cottesbrook Gallery 15 km, both NE on Mid Western Hwy. Millthorpe, 11 km NW, National Trust-classified village, Golden Memories Museum, craft shops. **Tourist information:** Mid West Mini Market, 20 Adelaide St; (063) 68 2570. **Accommodation:** 4 hotels, 2 motels, 1 B&B, 1 cara./camp. park.
MAP REF. 120 F7

Boggabri   Pop. 751
Situated 115 km NW of Tamworth, this town is the centre of a wool, wheat and cotton area. **Of interest:** Historical Museum, Brent St. Honey factory, Lynn St; open by appt. May: Wean Picnic Races. Oct.: Gum Tree Clay Pigeon Shoot. **In the area:** Dripping Rock waterfall, Manilla Rd, 35 km E. Gemstone fossicking, farm visits. Fishing. Gin's Leap, 4 km N, rock formation. **Tourist information:** Newell Hwy, Narrabri; (067) 92 3583. **Accommodation:** 3 hotels, 1 motel, 1 cara./camp. park.
MAP REF. 122 G8, 474 H13

Bombala   Pop. 1404
This small town on the Monaro Hwy, 89 km S of Cooma, supports wool, beef cattle, sheep, vegetables and timber-milling and is a rich trout-fishing area. **Of interest:** Self-guide historical walk (1 hr) includes Old Mechanics Institute and courthouse; leaflet from Tourist Information. Toorallie Knitting Mill, Maybe St; tours. White House Gallery (c.1835), Caveat St. Endeavour Reserve, Caveat St, walking track, 2 km return. Folk Museum, Mahratta St, local artefacts, farm implements. Bicentennial Park, Mahratta St, river walk. **In the area:** Burnima historic homestead, 6 km N on Monaro Hwy; open by appt. Goldmines at Craigie, 33 km SW. Early Settlers Hut,

Fishing boat, Bermagui

National Parks

The national parks of New South Wales encompass areas ranging from World Heritage-listed rainforests to unspoiled beaches. Tourists return time and time again to these popular scenic retreats, which offer a wide range of activities for holidaymakers. Many of the parks, particularly those on the eastern edge of the State, suffered damage during the devastating bushfires in January 1994 and are gradually regenerating. Some facilities may be affected; visitors planning to visit national parks along the central and south coasts should check first with the National Parks and Wildlife Service; (02) 585 6333.

Many of the State's parks are found along the coast, their rugged headlands, quiet inlets and sweeping beaches pounded by the crashing surf. The easy accessibility of these coastal parks accounts for their popularity. **Sydney Harbour National Park** is made up of pockets of bushland encircling Sydney Harbour and is the closest National Park to the city.

Among the 76 parks proclaimed in New South Wales is Australia's first, the Royal National Park, just 32 kilometres south of Sydney. **Royal National Park** established in 1879, has over 16 000 hectares of sandstone plateau country, broken here and there by fine surf beaches, including Wattamolla and Garie. Over 90 per cent of the Park was affected by the 1994

bushfires. The Hacking River runs almost the entire length of the park. Boats may be hired at Audley and visitors can row in leisurely fashion up the river, following its twisting course.

Also south of Sydney is **Botany Bay National Park** in two sections: the northern section contains the sandy beaches of La Perouse and a maritime museum (guided tours available) while the southern section at Kurnell protects the site of Captain Cook's first Australian landing in 1770. Here a staffed Discovery Centre has exhibitions of the history of the area.

Just north of Sydney are two prominent national parks, on the southern and northern shores of the Hawkesbury River: **Ku-Ring-Gai Chase** and **Brisbane Water National Parks,** which offer sheltered creeks and inlets, ideal for boating, and bushland walking tracks adorned with wildflowers. Both were affected by the 1994 bushfires.

Ku-Ring-Gai Chase, established in 1894 and only 24 kilometres from Sydney, hugs the shores of Cowan Creek, Broken Bay and Pitt Water. Comprising 15 000 hectares of open rainforest, eucalypt forest, scrub and heath, it is the home of a wide range of animal life, including the shy swamp wallaby, the elusive lyrebird, and honeyeaters, waterbirds, colourful parrots and lorikeets. A small colony of koalas lives in the eucalypt forest. A network of walking

tracks leads to Aboriginal hand stencils and rock engravings.

Brisbane Water also has sandstone landscapes rich in Aboriginal art. There are scenic views from Warrah Trig and Staples Lookout, while Somersby Falls and Girakool picnic areas mark the beginning of rainforest walks.

Nearby is **Dharug National Park,** its sandstone cliffs rising high above the meandering Hawkesbury River; damage from the 1994 fires is also evident here. A network of walking tracks includes a section of the convict-built Old Great North Road.

Further inland, to the west of Sydney, are splendid parks nestling in the mountains that overawed the early explorers. Year after year, innumerable visitors return to the **Blue Mountains National Park**, where mysterious blue mists shroud the immense valleys of the Grose and Coxs Rivers, creating ever-changing patterns of green, blue and purple. Large sections were burnt out during the 1994 fires.

At Katoomba, pillars of weathered sandstone rise abruptly like isolated church spires: these are the Three Sisters, the most popular tourist attraction in the Blue Mountains.

The World Heritage **New England National Park**, which preserves one of the largest remaining areas of rainforest in New South Wales, is 576 kilometres

Kinchega National Park

north-east of Sydney. Its 29 985 hectares cover three distinct zones: subalpine with tall snow gums; temperate forests of ancient moss-covered Antarctic beeches; and true subtropical rainforests, rich in ferns, vines and orchids. The park has a diverse range of flora and fauna, including the rare rufous scrub-bird. Some 20 kilometres of walking tracks reveal to visitors the charm of the rainforest, while the trackless wilderness attracts more experienced bushwalkers. The World Heritage **Dorrigo National Park** protects the rainforests of northern NSW. At the Rainforest Centre, visitors can experience the sights, sounds and smells of rainforests. The Skywalk provides magnificent views over the rainforest canopy to the Bellinger Valley and Pacific Ocean beyond. **Yuraygir** and **Bundjalung National Parks**, to the north and south respectively of the Clarence River on the far north coast, are a water wonderland with isolated beaches, quiet lakes and striking scenery. The parks deserve their reputation as prime areas for fishing. Surfing is also popular; waterways invite exploration by canoe; and the estuaries offer safe swimming. Heathwalking offers opportunities for birdwatching and nature photography, particularly in spring when both parks explode in a spectacle of colour.

In the far north of the State, **Border Ranges**, **Mount Warning** and **Nightcap National Parks** offer the visitor vistas of World Heritage-listed rainforest. The 31 508-hectare Border Ranges include the rim of the ancient volcano once centred on Mt Warning to the east. The best access is via the spectacular Tweed Scenic Drive. Stunning escarpments, waterfalls, and walking tracks from picnic areas abound in the eastern part.

Known to the Aborigines as 'Wollumbin', the cloud-catcher, Mt Warning (1157 metres) dominates the landscape and catches the first rays of the rising sun on the continent. A walk through Breakfast Creek rainforest leads to a steep climb and the summit viewing platform. Nightcap National Park is part of the volcanic remnants of Mt Warning and includes the popular summit viewing platform and Protector Falls.

One park frequently visited throughout the year is **Warrumbungle National Park**, on the western slopes of the Great Divide, 491 kilometres north-west of Sydney. Here is some of the most spectacular scenery in the nation: sheltered gorges, rocky spires, permanent freshwater springs.

At Warrumbungle, east meets west: the dry western plains and moist eastern coast combine to give high peaks covered with gums and lower forests filled with fragrant native trees and shrubs. Walking trails lead to lookout points where hikers are rewarded with the fascinating colours of sunrise and sunset. In the spring and summer months the colourful displays of wildflowers and the calls of brightly plumaged birds lure many visitors. There are also easy access tracks for families and the disabled.

Mount Kaputar National Park, near Narrabri, is one of Australia's most accessible wilderness areas. Its vegetation ranges from rainforest to subalpine, and the park is rich in flora and fauna. One of the highlights of the park is Sawn Rocks, a 40-metre-high rock formation resembling a series of organ pipes. This is some of the finest columnar jointing in the country and represents one of the various volcanic formations found in the park.

The largest coastal lake system in New South Wales is protected by the **Myall Lakes National Park**, an important waterbird habitat. Water is the focus of tourist activities: you can enjoy sailing and canoeing on the quiet lake waters, or surfing and beach fishing off the shores of the Pacific Ocean.

The largest national park in New South Wales is **Kosciusko**. Its 690 000 hectares include mainland Australia's only glacial lakes, as well as limestone caves, grasslands, heaths and woodlands. Situated 450 kilometres south-west of Sydney, this park is of particular significance because it embraces a large area of the continent's largest alpine region and contains Australia's highest mountains as well as the sources of the important Murray, Snowy and Murrumbidgee Rivers. Here are the most extensive snowfields of the nation, ski resorts including Thredbo, Perisher, Smiggins, Blue Cow Mountain, Mt Selwyn and Charlotte Pass. There are easy grades for beginners and slopes for expert skiers. Although Kosciusko is associated with winter sports, it is also a superb summer retreat with its crisp, clean air, crystal-clear lakes and a wonderful display of alpine wildflowers. This is a popular venue for those who enjoy camping, fishing, boating and bushwalking. Yarrangobilly Caves, perhaps the first site within the park to be developed for tourism, is open all-year round subject to winter road conditions. Yarrangobilly boasts 5 tourist caves—one with wheelchair access—a naturally heated thermal pool, nature trails, facilities for BYO picnics and historic grounds.

There are a number of national parks in the southern part of the State, some of which suffered bushfire damage, including **Morton National Park**, particularly known for the Fitzroy, Belmore and Carrington Falls, and **Budderoo National Park**, which includes the award-winning Minnamurra Rainforest Centre.

Over 9000 hectares of rocky but beautiful coastline flanking Twofold Bay make up **Ben Boyd National Park**. Flowering heaths and colourful banksias add to the area's attraction. Boyd's Tower, constructed in the 1840s, is a prominent feature of the park.

In the far west of New South Wales are four outstanding national parks. **Kinchega**, 110 kilometres south-east of Broken Hill, contains the beautiful saucer-shaped overflow lakes of the Darling River. The lakes provide a most important breeding ground for a wide variety of waterbirds, including herons, ibises, spoonbills and black swans. Walking tracks pass through forests of river red gums, and scenic drives follow the course of the river and the lake shores.

North-east of Wentworth is the World Heritage-listed **Mungo National Park**, part of the Willandra Lakes World Heritage Area. The shores of the now dry lake hold a continuous record of Aboriginal life dating back more than 40 000 years. The remarkable Walls of China, a great crescent-shaped dune, stretches along the eastern shore of the lake bed. Visitors can enjoy the park on a day trip or take advantage of the shearers' quarters accommodation or camping facilities. A 60-km, self-guide drive tour and self-guide walking tracks provide visitors with the opportunity to see and learn about the many attractions of the parks.

Mootwingee National Park, covering an area of 68 912 hectares and 130 kilometres north-east of Broken Hill, offers breathtaking scenery and a rich heritage of Aboriginal art.

The most remote national park in the State is **Sturt**, 1400 kilometres from Sydney and 330 kilometres north of Broken Hill. This is an ideal place for those who want to get away from it all and experience the real Australian outback. The park's 310 634 hectares comprise scenic red sand dunes, rocky ridges, ephemeral lakes and billabongs, and Mitchell grass plains. Visitors must come well prepared but may camp in the park and enjoy bushwalking over the sandplains. Wildflowers, which include the scarlet and black Sturt's desert pea, are abundant in good seasons. Fort Grey, where Sturt and his party built a stockade to protect their supplies, will repay a visit, even though there is little evidence of his occupation today.

For further information about the national parks of New South Wales, contact the National Parks and Wildlife Service, 43 Bridge St (PO Box 1967), Hurstville, NSW 2220; (02) 585 6333.

Lighthouse at Cape Byron, Byron Bay

Delegate, 36 km SW. Scenic drive to Bendoc Mines, Vic., 57 km SW; gold fossicking along route, with landowners' permission. Errinundra bushwalk, Bonang, Vic., 72 km SW; 20 min. return. Coolumbooka Nature Reserve, 15 km NE. **Tourist information:** Mobil Service Station, 125 Maybe St; (064) 58 3047. **Accommodation:** 3 hotels, 1 motel, 1 cara./camp. park.
MAP REF. 117 A9, 119 E11, 235 M7

Bourke   Pop. 2976

Anything 'Back o' Bourke' is the real outback. Bourke itself is the service centre of a vast area of sheep country that produces up to 55 000 bales of wool a year. It is claimed to be the largest centre for wool shipment in the world. **Of interest:** Tourist Centre in Old Railway Station, Anson St, Aboriginal artefacts, products of local industries, historic displays. Colonial buildings. Fred Hollows' grave and Memorial in cemetery, Cobar Rd. Cotton Gin, Cobar Rd; open for tours. Fishing for cod, Darling River. First lift-up bridge on Darling (1883). Only lock on Darling. Historic wharf and paddle-steamers. April: Fred Hollows Footrace, to Sydney. June: Bourke to B-Bash (charity car rally, different destination each year, always starting with 'B'). **In the area:** Fort Bourke Stockade, 20 km SW, testament to early explorer Major Thomas Mitchell. Mt Gunderbooka, 74 km S, caves with Aboriginal art. Mt Oxley, 40 km E, views of plains. **Tourist information:** Old Railway Station, 45

Anson Street; (068) 72 2280. **Accommodation:** 6 hotels, 5 motels, 1 hostel, 2 cara./camp. parks.
MAP REF. 125 N6, 474 A12, 485 P12

Bowral   Pop. 7929

The friendly township of Bowral nestles below Mount Gibraltar, 114 km S of Sydney. Originally a popular summer retreat for wealthy Sydney residents, who left a legacy of stately mansions and beautiful gardens, Bowral today is a thriving town with a harmonious blending of modern and colonial architecture. **Of interest:** Corbett Gardens, Merrigang St, showpiece of Tulip Time Festival (Sept.–Oct.) as are Milton Park Gardens, Horderns Rd. Bradman Oval, near house where cricketer Sir Donald Bradman spent his youth, and Bradman Museum, St Jude St. Specialty shopping in antiques, especially Bong Bong St. Alpaca Haven, Bong Bong St, knitwear and fleeces, pat alpacas at weekends. Many restaurants. **In the area:** Lookout on Mt Gibraltar, 2 km N. **Tourist information:** Southern Highlands Visitor Information Centre, Winifred West Park, Old Hume Hwy, Mittagong; (048) 71 2888. **Accommodation:** 3 hotels, 7 motels, 4 B&B.
MAP REF. 116 C7, 119 H3, 120 I10

Braidwood   Pop. 976

This old town, 84 km S of Goulburn, has been declared an historic village by the National Trust. Gold was discovered in the area in 1852 and Braidwood developed as the principal town of the

southern goldfields. Much of the architecture from this period has survived. **Of interest:** *Ned Kelly* (1969) and *The Year My Voice Broke* both filmed here. Museum, Wallace St, history of Aborigines, Chinese settlement, goldmining artefacts, period rooms. Churches, old hotels, restaurants, galleries, craft and antique shops. Self-guide tour of historic buildings; leaflet from Tourist Information. **In the area:** Scenic drive; leaflet from Tourist Information. **Tourist information:** Museum, Wallace St; (048) 42 2310. **Accommodation:** 1 hotel, 3 motels, 3 B&B, 1 hostel.
MAP REF. 119 F6, 120 G13, 141 L4

Brewarrina   Pop. 1168

Located 95 km E of Bourke, this town takes its name from an Aboriginal word meaning 'good fishing', which is still appropriate. Pastoral activities include grazing and wheat production. **Of interest:** Aboriginal fisheries in bed of Darling River. Aboriginal Cultural Museum, Bathurst St, aspects of Aboriginal life from Dreamtime to present. Wildlife park, Doyle St. April: Agricultural Show. **In the area:** Narran Lake, 40 km E, native birdlife and other fauna. **Tourist information:** Shire Offices, Bathurst St; (068) 39 2106. **Accommodation:** 2 hotels, 1 motel, 1 cara./camp. park.
MAP REF. 125 P5, 474 C11, 485 R12

Broken Hill   Pop. 23 263

This artificial oasis in the vast arid lands of far western NSW was created to serve the miners working in the rich silver–lead–zinc mines of the Barrier Range. The green parks and colourful gardens, 1170 km NW of Sydney, seem unreal in the semi-desert setting. The city's water supply comes from local storage schemes and the Menindee Lakes on the Darling River. The mines produce 2 million tonnes of ore annually. Note that Broken Hill operates on Central Standard Time, half an hour behind the rest of NSW. **Of interest:** Self-guide heritage trails. Historic streetscape (Argent St), National Trust-classified. Railway, Mineral and Train Museum, cnr Blende and Bromide Sts. Geo Centre Museum, cnr Crystal and Bromide Sts. White's Mineral Art and Mining Museum, Allendale St. Many art galleries, incl. Entertainment Centre, cnr Blende and Chloride Sts, featuring Silver Tree, commissioned by Charles Rasp, discoverer of Broken Hill ore-body in 1883. Broken

Hill is home of Brushmen of the Bush, group of artists that includes Pro Hart and Jack Absalom. Inspection of School of the Air, cnr McCulloch and Lane Sts. Mine tours to Delprat's Mine, off Crystal St. Moslem Mosque (1891), Buck St; built by Afghan community then living in town. Sept.: Silver City Show. Oct.: Country Music Festival. **In the area:** Zinc Twin Lakes, off Wentworth Rd, South Broken Hill. Inspection of Royal Flying Doctor Service, 10 km s, at airport. Water sports, fishing and camping at Menindee Lakes, 110 km SE. Mootwingee National Park, 130 km NE, magnificent scenery and rich in Aboriginal rock art and stencils; visitors are advised to be fully self-sufficient in food, water and fuel. Fred Hollows Sculpture Symposium and The Living Desert, 6 km N on Nine Mile Rd; leaflet from Tourist Information. Sundown Nature Trail, 9 km N on Tibooburra Rd. Silverton, 24 km NW, where silver chlorides were discovered in 1883; location for *Wake in Fright*, *Mad Max 2* and *A Town Like Alice*. At Silverton: tours of Day Dream Mine; heritage walking trail; several galleries; Silverton Hotel; Silverton Gaol Museum; camel rides. Mundi Mundi Plains Lookout, 4 km further N, and Umberumberka Reservoir Lookout, 39 km NW. **Tourist information:** Cnr Blende and Bromide Sts; (080) 87 6077. **Accommodation:** 12 hotels, 13 motels, 2 hostels, 3 cara./camp. parks. MAP REF. 124 C12

Brunswick Heads   Pop. 1662

This town at the mouth of the Brunswick River is well known for its outstanding fishing, and a large commercial fishing fleet is based here. **Of interest:** Canoe hire, good surfing and swimming. First Sat. of month: Brunswick Heads Market. Jan.: Fish and Chips (wood chop) Festival. Easter: Blessing of the Fleet and Fishing Festival. **In the area:** New Brighton Hotel, old pub with character, at Billinudgel, 7 km N. Pioneer Plantation at Mooball, 14 km N, tours of banana farm, walk-through wildlife habitat. Crystal Castle, outside Mullumbimby, 10 km W, collection of crystal. Minyon Falls, 50 km SW, picnic area in Rummery Park, with walking tracks. Cape Byron lighthouse at Byron Bay, 19 km s. **Tourist information:** 80 Jonson St, Byron Bay; (066) 85 8050. **Accommodation:** 1 hotel, 4 motels, 4 cara./camp. parks. MAP REF. 123 P2, 475 O8

Bulahdelah   Pop. 1097

Situated on the Pacific Hwy at the foot of Alum Mountain, Bulahdelah is a good base for a bushwalking or houseboating holiday. **Of interest:** Alum Mountain, huge alonite rock deposits, rare rock orchids. March: Prawn Festival. Nov.: Show and Rodeo. **In the area:** Bulahdelah Logging Railway, 19 km N, full-size steam tourist train, runs Fri., Sat. and school holidays. Myall Lakes National Park, 12 km E, one of State's largest networks (10 000 ha) of coastal lakes; water activities, bushwalking and camping in rainforest. **Tourist information:** Little St, Forster; (065) 54 8799. **Accommodation:** 4 motels, 2 cara./camp. parks. MAP REF. 121 M3

Bundanoon   Pop. 1513

This charming town is 32 km SW of Mittagong. The area is well known for its deep gullies and magnificent views over the rugged mountains and gorges of Morton National Park. Lookouts can be reached by car or on foot. Bundanoon was once well known as a honeymoon resort; today it boasts an English-style pub, delightful guest houses and a health resort. The train stops in the heart of town. April: Brigadoon Festival; highland games. Oct.: Gullies Gallop Fun Run. **Tourist information:** Southern Highlands Visitor Information Centre, Winifred West Park, Old Hume Hwy, Mittagong; (048) 71 2888. **Accommodation:** 1 hotel, 2 motels, 1 cara./camp. park, 1 camping ground. MAP REF. 116 A9, 119 H3, 120 H11

Byron Bay   Pop. 5001

Surfers from near and far gravitate to Wategos Beach, on Cape Byron. Its northerly aspect makes it one of the best beaches for surfboard riding on the east coast. Dairy products, bacon, beef and tropical fruits are produced locally. Visitors can go bushwalking, horseriding, fishing, swimming, scuba diving or trike-flying, or just enjoy the delightful climate and relaxing lifestyle of this idyllic spot. Market, first Sun. of month. Jan.: Arts and Music Festival. Easter: Blues Festival. **In the area:** Award-winning Wheel Resort, 3 km s; caters especially for disabled visitors. Australia's most powerful lighthouse, 3 km SE at Cape Byron, most easterly point on Australian mainland; walking trail and lookout. Ocean Shores Golf Course; 1½ km N, is considered to be best in State. **Tourist**

information: 80 Jonson St; (066) 85 8050. **Accommodation:** 2 hotels, 23 motels, 6 hostels, 7 cara./camp. parks. MAP REF. 123 Q2, 475 O8

Camden   Pop. 8440

In 1805 John Macarthur was granted 5000 acres at what was known as the Cowpastures, where he began his famous sheep-breeding experiments. The town of Camden dates from 1840, and is 60 km SW of Sydney on Camden Valley Way. **Of interest:** Many historic buildings, incl. Belgenny Farm (1819) and Camden Park House (1834), both part of Macarthur's Camden Estate, Elizabeth Macarthur Dr; Church of St John the Evangelist (1840–49), John St; Camelot, designed by J. Horbury Hunt, and Kirkham Stables (1816), both in Kirkham Lane. Camden History Museum, John St. Sept.: Open Homestead Weekend; Celebrate Camden Festival. **In the area:** Museum of Aviation, Narellan, 3 km NE. Mt Annan Botanic Garden, Narellan Rd. Struggletown Fine Arts Complex, 3 km N. El Caballo Blanco, featuring famous dancing Andalusian horses; also horse-drawn carriage museum, large wildlife reserve and fun park. Historic Gledswood Homestead and winery, next door to El Caballo Blanco; both at Catherine Field, 10 km N. Camden Aerodrome, 3 km NW, ballooning, gliding, vintage aircraft. Oran Park Raceway, 4 km W, bike, car and truck racing. **Tourist information:** Macarthur Country Tourist Assocn, Oxley Cottage, Camden Valley Way, Elderslie; (046) 58 1370. **Accommodation:** 4 motels, 1 hotel, 1 cara./camp. park. **See also:** Vineyards and Wineries. MAP REF. 104 I11, 116 F1, 119 I2, 120 I9

Camden Haven   Pop. 4384

A fisherman's dream, consisting of the villages Laurieton, North Haven and Dunbogan, less than 3 km apart, 44 km s of Port Macquarie; Camden Haven has a tidal inlet for estuary fishing. **Of interest:** Historical Museum, in old Laurieton Post Office, Laurie St; open by appt. Oysters, lobsters, crabs, bream and flathead, in local rivers and lakes. Seafront well-known fishing spot. Delightful bushwalks along seafront and around lakes. River cruises. Panoramic views from North Brother Mountain. **In the area:** Timbertown, 34 km NW at Wauchope, re-creation of 1880s town;

The Snowy Mountains

The Snowy Mountains are a magnet to tourists all year round. The combination of easily accessible mountains, alpine heathlands, forests, lakes, streams and dams is hard to beat. In winter, skiers flock to the snug, well-equipped snow resorts in the area. When the snow melts it's time for fishing, bushwalking, cycling, horseriding, waterskiing and boating.

The creation of the Snowy Mountains Hydro-electric Scheme was indirectly responsible for boosting tourism. The roads built for the Scheme through the previously difficult and sometimes inaccessible mountain country helped to open up the area, which is now used for a range of recreational activities year-round.

All the ski resorts of the Snowy Mountains are within Kosciusko National Park, which is the largest national park in the State and includes the highest plateau in the Australian continent. Mount Kosciusko (2228 m) is its highest peak.

The major ski areas are: Thredbo, Perisher, Smiggin Holes, Blue Cow Mountain and Charlotte Pass in the southern part of the Kosciusko National Park; and Mt Selwyn in the northern part.

The resorts are easily accessible and the major centres have first-class amenities such as motels, hotels, restaurants, lodges, apres-ski entertainment, chairlifts, ski-tows and expert instruction. The snow sports season officially begins on the long weekend in June and continues until mid- or late October.

Thredbo Village, 96 kilometres from Cooma at the foot of the Crackenback Range. Thredbo hosted the World Cup ski race in 1989, and has facilities for skiers at all levels, including ski hire and instruction. The chairlift to the summit of Mt Crackenback operates year-round. The village has a wide range of amenities, restaurants, cultural entertainment and outdoor recreation for every season.

Charlotte Pass, 98 kilometres from Cooma and 8 kilometres from the summit of Mt Kosciusko. A convenient base for ski tours to some of Australia's highest peaks and most spectacular ski runs.

Perisher, 90 kilometres from Cooma. One of the highest and most popular ski resorts in the area; all the facilities of a small town. Caters for both downhill and cross-country skiers. Ski hire and instruction.

Smiggin Holes, 89 kilometres from Cooma. Linked to Perisher by ski-lifts and a free shuttle bus service. Essentially for beginners and intermediate skiers. Ski hire and instruction.

Mt Selwyn, at the northern end of Kosciusko National Park, has been designed for beginners, families and school groups. Mt Selwyn is one of the main centres for cross-country skiing. No overnight accommodation. Accommodation is available in nearby towns like Adaminaby. Ski hire and instruction.

Blue Cow Mountain can be reached by skitube underground railway which runs from Bullocks Flat Terminal near Jindabyne up to Perisher and on to Blue Cow Mountain or by road to Guthega. Limited overnight accommodation at Guthega. No overnight accommodation at Blue Cow Mountain. Ski hire and instruction available at Blue Cow Mountain Resort Centre and Guthega Nordic Centre.

A wide variety of accommodation is available at Perisher and Smiggins. However, overnight parking is limited; overnight visitors are advised to use Skitube from Bullocks Flat on the Alpine Way.

For further information on the Snowy Mountains, contact the National Parks and Wildlife Service Visitors Centre at Sawpit Creek; (064) 56 1700 or the Snowy Region Information Centre in Jindabyne; (064) 56 2444. **See also:** Safe Skiing. **Note** detailed map of Snowy Mountains on page 118.

Snow scene alongside Kiandra–Cabramurra road

open daily. Rainforest with waterfalls, 60 km W at Comboyne Plateau. **Tourist information**: Pacific Hwy, Kew; (065) 59 4400. **Accommodation**: Laurieton: 1 hotel, 3 motels, 2 cara./camp. parks; North Haven: 2 motels, 3 cara./camp. parks; Dunbogan: 2 cara./camp. parks. MAP REF. 109 G10

Campbelltown   Pop. 10 004
Named by Governor Macquarie in 1820 after his wife's maiden name, Campbelltown is now a rapidly growing city. It is also the location for the legend of Fisher's ghost. The ghost of a murdered convict is alleged to have pointed to the place where his body was subsequently found and as a result the murderer was brought to justice. **Of interest:** Campbelltown City Bicentennial Art Gallery and Japanese Gardens, Art Gallery Rd, cnr Camden and Appin Rds. Historic buildings incl.: Glenalvon (1840) and Richmond Villa (1830–40), Lithgow St; Colonial Houses, 284–298 Queen St; St Peter's Church (1823), Cordeaux St; Old St John's Church, cnr Broughton and George Sts, with grave of James Ruse; Emily Cottage (1840), cnr Menangle and Camden Rds; and Campbelltown Art and Craft Society (licensed as Farrier's Arms Inn in 1843) and Fisher's Ghost Restaurant, formerly Kendall's Millhouse (1844), both in Queen St. April: Campbelltown Show. Nov.: Annual Festival of Fisher's Ghost. **In the area:** Eschol Park House (1820), 15 km N. Mount Annan Botanic Garden, 10 km W, on Narellan Rd. Menangle House (1839) and St James's Church at Menangle, 9 km SW. Steam and Machinery Museum, 5 km S on Menangle Rd. Horseriding. **Tourist information:** Campbelltown Council, 91 Queen St; (046) 20 1510 **Accommodation:** 4 motels.
MAP REF. 105 J11, 116 G1, 119 I2, 121 J9

Canowindra   Pop. 1721
Bushranger Ben Hall and his gang commandeered this township in 1863. Canowindra today is known as the 'Balloon Capital of Australia'; hot-air balloons fly daily, March–Nov, weather permitting. Situated on the Belubula River, Canowindra is noted for its curving main street and notable buildings; the entire commercial section has been classified by the National Trust as a Heritage Conservation Area. Easter: Model Aircraft Championship. Sept.: Agricultural Show. **Of interest:** Fish fossils of world significance, 360 million years old; discovered 1956. Antique shops, Museum. **Tourist information:** Canowindra Bakery, Gaskill St; (063) 44 1399. **Accommodation:** 3 hotels, 1 motel, 1 cara./ camp. park.
MAP REF. 120 D7

Casino   Pop. 10 850
This important commercial centre on the Richmond River could be dubbed the city of parks. There are about 20 in all, most with picnic/barbecue facilities. **Of interest:** Casino Folk Museum, Walker St. Freshwater fishing on Cooke's Weir and Richmond River. May: Beef Reach Festival, tours of meat works. Oct.: Agricultural Show. **In the area:** Aboriginal rock carvings, 20 km W on Tenterfield Rd; take Dyrabba turnoff. **Tourist information:** Memorial Baths Centre, Centre St; (066) 62 3566. **Accommodation:** 4 hotels, 5 motels, 2 cara./camp. parks.
MAP REF. 123 O3, 475 N9

Cessnock   Pop. 17 506
Many excellent Hunter River table wines are produced in the Cessnock district. The economy of the city, formerly based on coal mining, is now centred on wine and tourism. **Of interest:** Galleries, antique and craft shops. Feb.: Hunter Vintage Walkabout. Oct.: Jazz concerts. **In the area:** Hot-air ballooning at Rothbury, 11 km N. Rusa Zoo, exotic wildlife park, at Nulkaba, 7 km NW. Peppers, guest house resort at Pokolbin, 14 km NW. Over 50 quality wineries in Pokolbin area. Picturesque village of Wollombi, 29 km SW, wealth of historic buildings, incl. beautiful St John's Anglican Church; courthouse (now Endeavour Museum); old-style combined general store and post office; Aboriginal cave paintings; tours. Watagan Mountains and State Forest, 33 km SE; picnic/barbecue facilities at Heaton, Hunter's and McLean's Lookouts. Horseriding. At Pelaw Main, 17 km E, Richmond Main Mining Museum, steam train rides. **Tourist information:** Turner Park, Aberdare Rd; (049) 90 4477. **Accommodation:** 9 hotels, 66 motels, 2 cara./camp. parks.
MAP REF. 112 B10, 113 E11, 121 K5

Cobar   Pop. 4138
A progressive copper, gold, silver, lead and zinc mining town with wide tree-lined streets, Cobar is 723 km NW of Sydney. The town is on the Barrier Hwy, used by travellers to visit outback areas of NSW, Qld and NT. Since the opening of the CSA Copper Mine in the mid-1960s, and the introduction of a channel water supply, the town has been transformed from an arid landscape to a green oasis. There is an abundance of native flora and fauna in the area. The CSA Mine has an annual output of 600 000 tonnes of copper and copper–zinc ores. The Elura silver–lead–zinc mine opened in 1983 and the Peak goldmine in 1992. Wool is the main local primary industry. **Of interest:** Regional Museum, Barrier Hwy, pastoral, mining and technological displays; open daily. Fine early architecture, incl.: courthouse and police station, Barton St; St Laurence O'Toole Catholic Church, Prince St; Great Western Hotel, Marshall St, with longest iron-lace verandah in State. Commonwealth Meteorological Station, Louth Rd; open by appt. May: Agricultural Show: Oct.: Back to Cobar. **In the area:** Mt Grenfell Aboriginal cave paintings, turn-off 40 km W on Barrier Hwy, near Mt Grenfell homestead; human and animal figures densely cover walls of rock shelters; picnic area nearby. **Tourist information:** Cobar Regional Museum, Barrier Hwy. Telephone information; (068) 36 1452. **Accommodation:** 2 hotels, 1 hotel/ motel, 6 motels, 1 cara./camp. park.
MAP REF. 125 N10

Coffs Harbour   Pop. 20 326
One of the larger centres on the Holiday Coast, this subtropical resort town is 580 km N of Sydney on the Pacific Hwy. The surrounding districts produce timber, bananas, vegetables, dairy products and fish. Coffs Harbour is really two towns—one on the highway and the other near the harbour and railway station. **Of interest:** Historic buildings incl. Pier Hotel (rebuilt 1920s) and jetty (1892). Coffs Harbour Museum, High St. Pet Porpoise Pool, Orlando St, sea circus with performing porpoises and seals, also research and nursery facilities. Aquajet Waterslide, Park Beach Rd. Mutton Bird Island National Park, 1-km walk on sea wall. North Coast Regional Botanical Gardens complex, Hardacre St. Sept.: Garden Competition. **In the area:** Clog-making and Dutch village at Clog Barn on Pacific Hwy, 2 km N. The Big Banana, 4 km N along Pacific Hwy; unusual concrete landmark in form of huge banana has

displays illustrating banana industry; Big Banana Theme Park incl. Aboriginal Dreamtime Cave experience and 'realistic' bunyip; World of Horticulture, with monorail, is nearby. Coastline views from surrounding area. Nude bathing at Little Digger Beach, 4 km N. Coffs Harbour Zoo, 14 km N, koalas, kangaroos, deer and wombats; also Devonshire teas. Bruxner Park Flora Reserve, Korora, 9 km NW, dense tropical jungle area of vines, ferns and orchids; bushwalking tracks and picnic area at Park Creek. Georges Gold Mine tours, 38 km W. Hot-air ballooning, white-water rafting, canoeing, game-fishing, scuba diving, horseriding, golf and 4WD tours. Self-guide tours through Wedding Bells State Forest and the Dorrigo Region; 4WD only. **Tourist information:** Visitors and Convention Bureau, cnr Ross Ave and Marcia St; (066) 52 8824. **Accommodation:** 9 hotels, 35 motels, 6 cara./camp. parks.
MAP REF. 123 O7, 475 N12

Coleambally   Pop. 580

This, the State's newest town, officially opened in June 1968 and the centre of the Coleambally Irrigation Area, is south of the Murrumbidgee River. Rice is the main crop of the 87 600 ha under irrigation; vegetables, grain, sorghum, safflower and soya beans also are grown. The town has a modern shopping centre and a rice mill. **Of interest:** Wineglass Water Tower. **Tourist information:** Cnr Banna and Jondaryan Aves, Griffith; (069) 62 4145. **Accommodation:** 1 hotel, 1 motel.
MAP REF. 127 N9

Condobolin   Pop. 3163

On the Lachlan River, 475 km W of Sydney, Condobolin is the centre of a red-soil plains district producing wool, beef cattle, fat lambs, fruit and mixed farm products. The town is the southernmost point to which road trains operate from Northern Territory and Queensland. **Of interest:** Community Centre, in old hotel, cnr Bathurst and Dennison Sts. Gum Bend Lake and Olympic swimming pool. Aug.: Agricultural Show. Oct.: Art Exhibition. **In the area:** Aboriginal relics, 40 km W, incl. monument marking burial place of one of last Lachlan tribal elders. Agricultural research station, 10 km E. Mt Tilga, 8 km N, said to be geographic centre of NSW; stiff climb to summit but view is worth

it. **Accommodation:** 3 hotels, 1 hotel/motel, 2 motels, 1 cara./camp. park.
MAP REF. 127 Q4

Cooma   Pop. 7385

This lively, modern tourist centre at the junction of the Monaro and Snowy Mountains Hwys, on the Southern Tablelands of NSW, was once dubbed Australia's most cosmopolitan town. Thousands of migrants from many different countries worked here on the Snowy Mountains Scheme. It is a busy tourist centre year-round, and the jumping-off point for the Snowies. Motorists are advised to check their tyres and stock up on petrol and provisions before setting off for the snow country. **Of interest:** Self-guide Lambie St walk; National Trust-classified buildings. Old Gaol Museum, Vale St. International Avenue of Flags, Centennial Park, Sharp St; flags of 27 countries, unfurled 1959 to commemorate 10th anniversary of Snowy Mountains Hydro-electric Authority and in recognition of nationalities of people who worked on project. The Time Walk, also in park; Bicentennial project presenting district history in 40 ceramic mosaics. Snowy Mountains Authority Information Centre, Monaro Hwy, displays, films. Jan.: Rodeo. **In the area:** Cloyne Rose Gardens, 4 km N. Southern Cloud Park, on Snowy Mountains Hwy, 1 km W, display (with audiotape) of remains of *Southern Cloud* aircraft, which crashed here in 1931, found 1958. Clog Maker, 2.5 km W on Snowy Mountains Hwy, clog-making demonstration by Dutch craftsman. Llama Farm, 13 km W on Snowy Mountains Hwy. **Tourist information:** 119 Sharp St; (064) 50 1742. **Accommodation:** 7 hotels, 19 motels, 2 hostels, 3 cara./camp. parks.
MAP REF. 117 A2, 119 E9, 140 G11, 235 L3

Coonabarabran   Pop. 2959

A tourist-conscious town in the Warrumbungle Mountains on the Castlereagh River, 465 km NW of Sydney, near Warrumbungle National Park. **Of interest:** Woollen Yarn and Exhibition, Dalgarno St; shearing demonstrations during school holidays. Crystal Kingdom, Oxley Hwy, with unique collection of minerals from Warrumbungle Range. Oct.: Sky and Space Astrofest. **In the area:** Skywatch Night'n'Day Observatory, 2 km NW on National Park road, planetarium, star-gazing; open daily.

Pilliga Pottery, 34 km NW, off Newell Hwy, workshop in bushland setting, German-style tearooms. Pilliga Scrub at Baradine, 44 km NW, 450 000-ha forest (biggest in NSW) mainly white cypress pine and broom plains of dense heath and scrub; location of picnic areas and walking tracks from Baradine Forestry Office. Miniland, 8 km W, life-size models of prehistoric animals displayed in bushland setting; historical museum, children's fun park and water-slide, kiosk, picnic/barbecue facilities. Siding Spring Observatory set atop an extinct volcano, 24 km W, has largest optical telescope (3.9 m) in Australia, and permanent hands-on exhibition, Exploring the Universe. Warrumbungle National Park, 35 km W, bushwalking, rock climbing, nature study, photography, camping facilities. **Tourist information:** Bicentennial Centre, Newell Hwy; (068) 42 1441. **Accommodation:** 3 hotels, 12 motels, 2 B&B, 2 hostels, 2 cara./camp. parks. **See also:** The Newell.
MAP REF. 122 F10

Coonamble   Pop. 2886

This town on the Castlereagh Hwy is situated on the Western Plains, 518 km NW of Sydney. It serves a district that produces wheat, wool, lamb, beef, cypress pine and hardwood timber. **Of interest:** Historical Museum, former police station and stables, Aberford St. Warrana Creek Weir; boating and swimming. June: Rodeo. Oct.: Cup Race Meeting. **In the area:** Youie Bore, 20 km N on Castlereagh Hwy; water from bore is hot and supplies 5 properties with stock water. Macquarie Marshes, 80 km NW; breeding-ground for waterbirds. Warrumbungle National Park and Siding Springs Observatory, 80 km SE. **Tourist information:** Castlereagh Centre, 84 Castlereagh St; (068) 22 3040. **Accommodation:** 5 hotels, 3 motels, 1 cara./camp. park.
MAP REF. 122 C9

Cootamundra   Pop. 6386

This town on the Olympic Way, 427 km SW of Sydney, is less than 2 hours' drive from Canberra, and is well known for the Cootamundra wattle (*Acacia baileyana*). It has a strong retail sector and is a large stock-selling centre for the surrounding pastoral and agricultural rural holdings. **Of interest:** Self-guide 'Two Foot Tour' around town, taking in historic buildings, many restored. Birthplace of Sir Donald

Bradman, town's most famous son, at 89 Adams St; open weekends. Cootamundra Public School Museum, Cooper St; check opening times. Aug.: Wattle Time Festival and Garden Fair. **In the area:** Wineries in the Harden area, 78 km E; picnic/barbecue facilities. Inglenook Deer Farm at Wallendbeen, 19 km NE; bus tours by appt. Yandilla Mustard Seed Oil, 26 km N; tours by appt. **Tourist information:** Railway station, Hovell St; (069) 42 4212. **Accommodation:** 7 hotels, 4 motels, 1 cara./camp. park. MAP REF. 119 B3, 120 C11

Corowa
Pop. 5064

Birthplace of Australia's Federation, Corowa took its name from *Currawa*, an Aboriginal word describing the pine trees that once grew there in profusion. A typical Australian country town, Corowa's wide main street, Sanger St, lined with turn-of-the-century verandahed buildings, runs down to the banks of the Murray River. The town offers visitors opportunities for tennis, golf, bowls, swimming, water-skiing, skydiving, birdwatching and bushwalking. Tom Roberts' painting *Shearing of the Rams*, in the National Gallery of Victoria, was completed nearby at Brocklesby Station in 1889. **Of interest:** Federation Museum, Queen St. Jan.: Federation Festival. Dec.: National Skydiving Championships. **In the area:** Rutherglen wineries, only a short drive or bicycle ride away. Scenic drives from the town. **Tourist information:** Railway Station Building, John St; (060) 33 3221. **Accommodation:** 6 hotels, 20 motels, 4 cara./camp. parks. MAP REF. 127 O13, 233 M4

Cowra
Pop. 8422

The peaceful air of this busy country town on the Lachlan River belies its dramatic recent history. On 5 August 1944, over 1000 Japanese prisoners attempted to escape from a nearby POW camp. Four Australian soldiers and 231 Japanese prisoners were killed in the ensuing struggle. **Of interest:** Australia's World Peace Bell, Darling St. Army Vehicle Museum, River Park Rd. Cowra Rose Garden, adjacent to Tourist Information Centre. Lachlan Valley Railway and Steam Museum, Campbell St, train rides; check times. Sept.: World Peace Day (ceremony at Peace Bell). Oct.: Sakura Matsuri and Japanese Cultural Exhibitions. **In the area:** Australian and

Japanese Garden, Cowra

Japanese War Cemeteries, 5 km N, beside Cowra–Canowindra Rd. Australian soldiers who died are buried in Australian War Cemetery. Japanese soldiers who died during escape, and Japanese internees who died elsewhere in Australia, are buried in Japanese War Cemetery. Sakura Ave, 5 km of flowering cherry trees, links site with POW camp, Breakout Walking Track, and Japanese Garden and Cultural Centre. Gardens cover 5 ha; Cultural Centre incl. traditional teahouse, bonsai house, pottery and display of Japanese artefacts. Historic Croote Cottage, Gooloogong, 25 km NW, built by convicts and raided by bushrangers; by appt. Conimbla National Park, 27 km W. Quarry Cellars winery, 4 km S, on Boorowa Rd. Wyangala Waters State Recreation Area, 40 km SE, mecca for water sports and fishing enthusiasts. Mid State Pioneer Rail Museum, 5 km E on Sydney Road. **Tourist information:** Olympic Park, junct. Boorowa, Grenfell and Young Rds; (063) 42 4333. **Accommodation:** 4 hotels, 2 hotel/motels, 8 motels, 12 B&B, 3 cara./camp. parks. MAP REF. 119 C1, 120 D8

Crookwell
Pop. 1966

Located 45 km NW of Goulburn, Crookwell is the centre of a rich agricultural and pastoral district, producing apples, pears and cherries, and is the State's

major supplier of certified seed potatoes. **Of interest:** Stevensons Mill, Spring St, flour mill restored by local historians; open Wed. or by appt. Crookwell Memorial Park, Spring St. April, Sept.–Nov.: High Country Gardens openings. **In the area:** Many quaint historic villages associated with gold and copper mining and bushranging incl. Tuena, Peelwood, Laggan, Bigga, Binda (all north of town) and Roslyn (south, and birthplace of poet Dame Mary Gilmore). Redground Lookout, 8 km NE. Willow Vale Mill at Laggan, 9 km N, restored flour mill with restaurant, accommodation. Abercrombie Caves, 64 km N along Bathurst Rd, tours. Upper reaches of Lake Wyangala and Grabine State Recreation Area, 65 km NW, water-skiing, picnicking, fishing, sailing, bushwalking and camping. **Tourist information:** Crookwell Promotion Centre, 44 Goulburn St; (048) 32 1988. **Accommodation:** 2 hotels, 2 motels, 1 cara./camp. park. MAP REF. 119 E3, 120 F10

Culburra–Orient Point
Pop. 3145

Famous for its prawning and fishing, this unspoiled resort is situated 23 km SE of Nowra on an ocean beach near Wollumboola Lake. **Of interest:** Surfing, swimming, lake, shore and rock fishing. Beach is patrolled in summer holidays.

Jan.: Open Fishing Carnival. **Tourist information:** Shoalhaven Tourist Centre, 254 Princes Hwy, Bomaderry; (044) 21 0778. **Accommodation:** 1 motel, 2 cara./camp. parks.
MAP REF. 116 G13, 119 I4, 120 I11

Culcairn   Pop. 1175
Dating back to 1880 and planned to service the railway between Sydney and Melbourne, Culcairn today reflects the district's rural prosperity. Bushranger Dan Morgan began his life of crime at Round Hill Station, with a hold-up on 19 June 1864. Once known as the oasis of the Riverina because of its unlimited underground water supply (discovered in 1926), the town owes its picturesque tree-lined streets and parks to this artesian water. **Of interest:** Historic Culcairn Hotel (1891), Railway Pde. Many buildings National Trust-classified in Railway Pde and on Olympic Way. Centenary Mural, Main St. Artesian pumping station, Gordon St. **In the area:** John McLean's Grave, 3 km E; a price was put on Morgan's head after he shot McLean. Round Hill Station, on Holbrook Rd. At Walla Walla, 18 km W, Old Schoolhouse (1875) Museum and largest Lutheran church in NSW (1924); and 4 km N, Morgan's Lookout. Premier Yabbies, 7 km S of Culcairn, farm and catch-out. Pioneer Museum at Jindera, 42 km S. **Tourist information:** Billabong Craft Shop, Railway Pde. **Accommodation:** 1 hotel, 1 motel, 1 cara./camp. park.
MAP REF. 127 P12, 233 P2

Deniliquin   Pop. 7895
At the centre of the largest irrigation complex in Australia, on the Edward River, 750 km SW of Sydney, Deniliquin has the largest rice mill in the southern hemisphere. The northern part of the district is famed for merino sheep studs, such as Wanganella and Boonoke. **Of interest:** Sunrice Visitors Centre, Saleyard Rd. Peppin Heritage Centre (1879), former school, George St. Waring Gardens, in town centre. Island Sanctuary, off Cressy St footbridge, free-ranging animals and birds. River beaches, including McLean and Willoughby's Beaches. 18-hole competition golf course. Jan.: Sun Festival. Easter: Jazz Festival. **In the area:** Pioneer Tourist Resort and Garden Centre, 6 km N, antique steam and pump display. Bird Observatory Tower at Mathoura, 34 km S. Lawsons Syphon, 6 km E and Stevens Weir, 26 km W, irrigation works. **Tourist information:** Peppin Heritage Centre, George St; (058) 81 2878, (058) 81 5555. **Accommodation:** 4 hotels, 3 hotel/motels, 9 motels, 1 B&B, 1 hostel, 5 cara./camp. parks.
MAP REF. 127 K11, 232 F1

Dorrigo   Pop. 1135
Magnificent river, mountain and forest scenery is a feature of this important timber town. **Of interest:** Steam Railway Museum, old railway station, Tallowood St; large collection of locomotive and rolling stock. Calico Cottage, Hickory St, crafts. **In the area:** Dangar Falls, 2 km N. Dorrigo Pottery, Tyringham Rd, 8 km W. Trout Farm, Tyringham Rd, Bostobrick, 14 km W. Dutton Trout Hatchery at Ebor, 49 km W. Excellent trout fishing in district. Dorrigo National Park, 5 km E, birds' eye views over canopy of World Heritage-listed rainforest from Skywalk, beginning at Rainforest Centre. **Tourist information:** Dorrigo Hotel, Hickory St; (066) 57 2016. **Accommodation:** 2 hotel/motels, 1 motel, 1 cara./camp. park.
MAP REF. 123 N7, 475 M12

Dubbo   Pop. 28 064
This pleasant city lies on the banks of the Macquarie River, 420 km NW of Sydney, is recognised as the regional capital of western NSW, and supports many agricultural and secondary industries. **Of interest:** Old Dubbo Gaol, Macquarie St, original gallows and solitary confinement cells, animatronic robots tell story of convicts. Dubbo Museum, Macquarie St. Dubbo Regional Art Gallery, Darling St. Indoor Kart Centre, Mountbatten Dr. May: Agricultural Show. June: Eisteddfod. **In the area:** Western Plains Zoo, 5 km S, Australia's first open-range zoo with over 300 ha of landscaped park; animals from 6 continents, some roaming in natural surroundings. Military Museum, 8 km S, open-air exhibits. Yarrabar Pottery, 4 km further S. Golfworld, Fitzroy St, 3 km N, driving range, mini-golf course. Jinchilla Gardens and Gallery, 12 km N, off Gilgandra Rd. Restored Dundullimal Homestead (1840s), 7 km SE, on Obley Rd. **Tourist information:** cnr Erskine and Macquarie Sts; (068) 84 1422. **Accommodation:** 6 hotels, 33 motels, 1 B&B, 1 hostel, 5 cara./camp. parks. **See also:** The Newell.
MAP REF. 120 D3, 122 D13

Dungog   Pop. 2187
These days an ideal base for bushwalking enthusiasts, Dungog was established in 1838 as a military post to prevent bushranging in the area. Situated on the upper reaches of the Williams River, it is on one of the main access routes to Barrington Tops National Park. Aug.: Canoe Classic. Sept.: Floral Festival. **In the area:** Chichester Dam, 23 km N, in picturesque mountain setting; Duncan Park within is ideal spot for picnic/barbecue. Telegherry Forest Park, 30 km N, walking trails to waterfalls along Telegherry River; picnic, swimming and camping spots. Barrington Tops National Park, 40 km N; Barrington Brush noted for its unusual native flora and rich variety of wildlife. Superb views from Mt Allyn (1100 m), 40 km NW. Clarence Town historic village, 25 km S. **Tourist information:** Shire Offices, cnr Brown and Dowling Sts; (049) 92 1224. **Accommodation:** 3 hotels, 1 motel.
MAP REF. 121 L3

Eden   Pop. 3277
Quiet former whaling town on Twofold Bay, 512 km S of Sydney, with an outstanding natural harbour. Fishing and timber-getting are the main industries. **Of interest:** Eden Killer Whale Museum, Imlay St, exhibits include skeleton of notorious 'Tom the killer whale'. Whale-watching Oct.–Nov. Bay cruises. March: Amateur Fish Club Competition. **In the area:** Ben Boyd National Park, extending 8 km N and 19 km S of Eden, outstanding scenery, ideal for fishing, swimming, camping, bushwalking. Prominent park feature, Boyd's Tower (1840s), at Red Point. On perimeter of park, at Nullica Bay, 9 km S, former rival settlement of Boydtown, incl. convict-built Sea Horse Inn, still licensed; safe beach, excellent fishing. Davidson Whaling Station Historic Site on Kiah Inlet, 14 km S. Harris Daishowa Chipmill Visitors Centre, Jews Head, 26 km S, video and static display on logging and milling operations; tour Thurs. 10.30 a.m. Good fishing at Wonboyn Lake Resort, 40 km S, surrounded by Ben Boyd National Park and Nadgee Nature Reserve. **Tourist information:** Princes Hwy; (064) 96 1953. **Accommodation:** 2 hotels, 10 motels, 6 B&B, 1 hostel, 6 cara./camp. parks. **See also:** The South Coast.
MAP REF. 117 F11, 119 F11, 235 P8

Eugowra
Pop. 572

'The great gold-escort robbery' occurred near this small town on the Orange–Forbes road in 1862. **Of interest:** Eugowra Museum, Aboriginal skeleton and artefacts, gemstones, early farm equipment and wagons. Nangar Gems, Norton St, sapphires, opals, emeralds, garnets. **In the area:** Escort Rock, 3 km E, where bushranger Frank Gardiner and gang hid before ambush of Forbes gold escort. Rock is on private property, but plaque on road gives details, unlocked gate allows entry. Picnic area. **Tourist information:** Visitors Centre, Civic Gardens, Byng St, Orange; (063) 61 5226, or Molong Railway Station Complex, Mitchell Hwy, Molong. **Accommodation:** 2 hotels.
MAP REF. 120 C7

Evans Head
Pop. 2375

This holiday and fishing resort, and centre of the NSW prawning industry, is situated off the Pacific Hwy via Woodburn. It has safe surf beaches and sandy river flats. **Of interest:** Rock, beach and ocean fishing, boating, windsurfing. Aug.: Bowling Carnival. **In the area:** Broadwater National Park, 5 km N, between Evans Head and Broadwater; bushwalking, bird-watching, fishing, swimming. Bundjalung National Park, on southern edge of Evans Head, Aboriginal relics, varied wildlife. **Tourist information:** The Professionals Real Estate, 9 Oak St; (066) 82 4611. **Accommodation:** 1 hotel, 1 motel, 1 cara./camp. park.
MAP REF. 123 P4, 475 N9

Finley
Pop. 2220

This town on the Newell Hwy, 20 km from the Victorian border, is the centre of the Berriquin irrigation scheme. **Of interest:** Log Cabin (replica) and Museum, Mary Lawson Wayside Rest, Newell Hwy, display of rural heritage; open daily. Finley Lake, Newell Hwy, boating, sailing, picnic areas on lake banks. Sept.: Agricultural Show. **Tourist information:** River Foreshore, Tocumwal; (058) 74 2131. **Accommodation:** 3 hotels, 5 motels, 1 cara./camp. park.
MAP REF. 127 M12, 232 I1

Forbes
Pop. 7552

Noted bushranger Ben Hall is buried in this former goldmining town, 386 km w of Sydney on the Lachlan River. He was shot by police just outside the town in 1865. Today the town's industries include an abattoir, feed lots, and export of beef and hay. **Of interest:** Many historic buildings, especially in Camp and Lachlan Sts. Historical museum, Cross St, relics associated with Ben Hall. Forbes Cemetery, Bogan Gate Rd, graves of Ben Hall, Ned Kelly's sister, Kate Foster, and Captain Cook's niece, Rebecca Shields. Historical sites incl. memorial in King George V Park, where 'German Harry' discovered gold in 1861. In small park in Dowling St, memorial marks spot where explorer John Oxley first passed through Forbes. Sept.: Show Day. **In the area:** Sandhills Vineyard, 6 km E on Eugowra Rd, picnic/barbecue facilities. Lachlan Vintage Village, 1 km S, re-creation of gold-rush era, 73-ha site, restaurant, picnic areas. **Tourist information:** Old Railway Station, Union St; (068) 52 4155. **Accommodation:** 9 hotels, 6 motels, 4 cara./camp. parks. **See also:** The Newell.
MAP REF. 120 C7

Forster–Tuncurry
Pop. 14 578

Twin towns on opposite sides of Wallis Lake, a holiday area in the Great Lakes district, Forster and Tuncurry are connected by a bridge. Launches and boats may be hired for lake and deep-sea fishing, and tours are available. The area is well known for its fishing. **Of interest:** Forster Art and Craft Centre, Breese Pde. Aug.: Australian Veteran Cycling Championships. **In the area:** Curtis Collection, 3 km S, vintage cars. The

Ben Boyd National Park, near Eden

New England

Despite the scenery, it is worth keeping your eyes on the ground if you pull over for a rest in the New England area. Some of the best fossicking specimens in the district have been found by the roadside. All kinds of quartz, jaspers, serpentine, crystal and chalcedony are found right throughout this area—not to mention sapphires, diamonds and gold, though these require a little more effort to find.

The round trip from Nundle, through Tamworth, Manilla, Barraba, Bingara, Warialda, then on to the New England towns of **Inverell** and **Glen Innes** and back, is known as 'The Fossickers' Way' and tourist signs have been placed at intervals to guide the motorist. Nearby is the Copeton Dam, which holds two-and-

a-half times as much water as Sydney Harbour, with part of its foreshores forming Copeton State Recreational Area.

Glen Innes and Inverell have nearby sapphire reserves where fossickers may hire tools and try their luck. Anything you find is yours; but remember, you must have a fossicker's licence, available from all New South Wales courthouses, tourist centres, and some sporting stores. The largest find to date in the Nullamanna Fossicking Reserve, near Inverell, is a 70-carat blue, valued at $3000.

The New England district is the largest area of highlands in Australia, and has plenty to offer besides gemstones. The countryside is varied and lovely, with magnificent mountains, and streams cascading into spectacular gorges, contrasting with the rich blacksoil plains of wheat and cotton to the west. Some of the

State's most outstanding national parks and World Heritage features are found in New England, and the southern hemisphere's largest granite monolith, Bald Rock, is near **Tenterfield**.

Fishing is excellent, with trout in the streams of the tablelands, and cod and yellow-belly in the lower New England rivers to the west. You can also fish, picnic, swim, sail or water-ski at Pindari and Copeton Dam.

Other towns in New England, **Ashford**, **Delungra**, **Guyra**, **Tingha**, **Walcha**, **Uralla** and **Deepwater**, and the city of **Armidale**, have much to offer.

For further information, contact the Visitors Centre and Coach Station, 82 Marsh St, Armidale; (067) 73 8527, Freecall (1800) 62 7736. **See also:** Individual town entries in A–Z listing.

The Newell

With its excellent bitumen surface and long, straight stretches, the Newell provides fast and easy driving right across New South Wales. Driving time between Melbourne and Brisbane is up to 6 hours quicker by this route. The time you save could be put to good use enjoying the many interesting towns and attractions along the way.

From the Murray River town of **Tocumwal** to the Queensland border town of **Goondiwindi**, the highway runs through a wide range of scenery and is well served with motels, roadside cafes and service stations.

Tocumwal, with sandy beaches on the Murray, offers swimming and fishing as well as boating. At **Jerilderie**, 57 kilometres further north, visit the tiny restored post office held up by the Kelly gang in 1879. At **Narrandera** there is an excellent caravan park on the shore of Lake Talbot, a popular water sports centre. Beyond **West Wyalong** to the north is Lake Cowal, the largest natural lake in New South Wales and an important bird sanctuary; further north out of **Forbes**

is a major tourist attraction—the Lachlan Vintage Village, a re-creation of a 19th-century goldmining town.

There is plenty to see in **Parkes**, including a vintage car museum and the Henry Parkes Museum. The famous radio telescope is on the highway, north of the town. **Dubbo** boasts what is probably the most popular tourist attraction on the Newell—the Western Plains Zoo, claimed to be the best open-range wildlife park in Australia.

From Dubbo, the highway passes through the spectacular volcanic Warrumbungle National Park, which is ideal for bushwalking. If you have children aboard, do not miss the award-winning fantasy park, Miniland, with its life-size prehistoric animals, just west of **Coonabarabran**. Once you get beyond the Warrumbungle Ranges, the scenery changes dramatically to the vast Pilliga scrub country. **Narrabri**, in the heart of Cotton Country, offers a diversity of attractions, including Mt Kaputar National Park, Sawn Rocks, the CSIRO Telescope Complex, and gemstone fossicking. The northern town of **Moree**, not far from the Queensland border, is well known for its artesian spa baths and pecan nut farm.

Western Plains Zoo, Dubbo

For further information, contact the Tourist Information Office, Kelly Reserve, Newell Highway, Parkes 2870; (068) 62 4365. A booklet on the Newell is available at tourist information centres. **See also:** Individual town entries in A–Z listing.

Green Cathedral, at Tiona on shores of Wallis Lake, 13 km s, unusual 'open-air cathedral'. Booti Booti National Park, 17 km s. Sugar Creek Toymakers at Bungwahl, 22 km s. Wallingat State Forest, 25 km s. Myall Lakes National Park, 35 km s; houseboat hire. Camping and beaches at Seal Rocks, 40 km s. The Grandis, via The Lakes Way, 48 km s in Bulahdelah State Forest, tallest tree in NSW. **Tourist information:** Great Lakes Tourist Board, Little St; (065) 54 8799. **Accommodation:** 2 hotels, 19 motels, 1 hostel, 12 cara./camp. parks.
MAP REF. 121 N3, 123 N13

Gerringong   Pop. 2478

Spectacular views of white sand and rolling breakers can be seen from this resort, 11 km s of Kiama on the Illawarra coast. **Of interest:** Surfing, fishing and swimming at local beaches. Gerroa and Seven Mile are world-famous as windsurfing locations. Memorial to pioneer aviator Sir Charles Kingsford Smith at northern end of Seven Mile Beach, site of his takeoff to New Zealand in the Southern Cross in 1933. **In the area:** Wild Country Park at Fox Ground, 6 km s. Bushwalks through Seven Mile Beach National Park, 13 km s; camping, picnic areas. **Tourist information:** Visitors Centre, Blowhole Pt, Kiama; (042) 32 3322. **Accommodation:** 1 hotel, 3 motels, 3 cara./camp. parks.
MAP REF. 116 G10, 119 I4, 121 J11

Gilgandra   Pop. 2890

An historic town at the junction of three highways, in timber, wool and farming country. Home of the famous Coo-ee March, which left from Gilgandra for Sydney in 1915 in a drive to recruit more soldiers for World War I. Also known for its windmills, which once provided sub-artesian water. **Of interest:** Australian Collection, Miller St, Aboriginal artefacts, display of minerals, fossils, marine specimens, Gwen Collison watercolours. The Observatory and Display Centre, cnr Wamboin and Willie Sts, 31-cm telescope. Museum, Newell Hwy, memorabilia from Coo-ee March. Film *The Chant of Jimmy Blacksmith* was based on Breelong Massacre, which took place near Gilgandra; related items in museum. Orana Cactus World, Newell Hwy. Oct.: Coo-ee Festival. May: Agricultural Show. **In the area:** Warrumbungle National Park, 82 km NE. Gilgandra Flora Reserve, 14.5 km N,

wildflowers in spring. **Tourist information:** Coo-ee March Memorial Park, Newell Hwy; (068) 47 2045. **Accommodation:** 3 hotels, 8 motels, 4 cara./camp. parks.
MAP REF. 120 D1, 122 D12

Glen Innes   Pop. 6140

Gazetted in 1852, this mountain town was the scene of many bushranging exploits. In a beautiful setting, at an altitude of 1073 m, it is now the centre of a lush farming district where sapphire mining is an important industry. **Of interest:** Many original public buildings, particularly in Grey St; self-guide walks. Centennial Parklands with Martin's Lookout, now site of Australian Standing Stones, Celtic monument. Land of the Beardies History House, cnr Ferguson St and West Ave, folk museum housed in town's first hospital and set in extensive grounds; reconstructed slab hut, period room settings, pioneer relics. Local art and craft. May: Celtic Festival. Nov.: Land of the Beardies Bush Festival. **In the area:** Gibraltar Range National Park, 70 km NE, impressive falls, and The Needles and Anvil Rock, granite formations. World Heritage-listed Washpool National Park 75 km NE, rainforest wilderness area. Convict-carved tunnel, halfway between Glen Innes and Grafton, on Old Grafton Rd; also scenic mountain and riverside country. Fishing; trout, perch and cod. Fossicking for sapphire, topaz and quartz, within 45-km radius of town. Horse treks, with accommodation at historic bush pubs. At Deepwater, 25 km N, unique rock formations. Old mining towns, Emmaville, 38 km NW and Torrington, 66 km NW; fossicking. Guy Fawkes River National Park, 77 km SE, wild river area for bushwalking, canoeing, fishing. **Tourist information:** Church St (New England Hwy); (067) 32 2397. **Accommodation:** 4 hotels, 10 motels, 5 cara./camp. parks. **See also:** New England.
MAP REF. 123 L5, 475 K11

Gloucester   Pop. 2465

This quiet town lies at the foot of a range of monolithic hills, The Bucketts. It is at the junction of three tributaries of the Manning River, the upper reaches of which are excellent for trout and perch fishing. **Of interest:** Folk Museum in Church St. The Bucketts Walk, immediately west of town. Gloucester District Park, outstanding sporting complex.

June: Billykart Derby. Sept.: Mountain Man Triathlon; mountain-biking, kayaking, running. **In the area:** Views from Mograni Lookout (5 km E), Kia-ora Lookout (4 km N) and Berrico Trig Station (14 km W). Mountain Maid Gold Mine at Copeland, 16 km W. Altamira Holiday Ranch, 18 km E. **Tourist information:** Gloucester Shire Council, 89 King St; (065) 58 1601. **Accommodation:** 1 hotel, 1 hotel/motel, 2 motels, 2 cara./camp. parks.
MAP REF. 121 L2, 123 L13

Gosford   Pop. 38 205

Gosford is 85 km N of Sydney on beautiful Brisbane Water. **Of interest:** Henry Kendall Cottage (1838), Henry Kendall St, where poet lived 1874–5; picnic/barbecue facilities in pleasant grounds. Oct.: Agricultural Show; Mangrove Mountain District Country Fair. **In the area:** Australian Reptile Park and Wildlife Sanctuary, Pacific Hwy north, taipans, pythons, goannas, a platypus. Old Sydney Town, 9 km W, reconstruction of early pioneer settlement, re-created from carefully researched pre-1810 material. Somersby Falls, near Old Sydney Town, ideal picnic spot. Brisbane Water National Park, 10 km SW, spectacular waratahs in spring. Bouddi National Park, 17 km SE, bushwalking, camping, fishing, swimming. Central Park Family Fun Centre, Forresters Beach, 31 km E. The Ferneries, Oak Rd, Matcham, 11 km NE; rainforest area, children's playground, picnic/barbecue facilities, paddle-boats, Devonshire teas. **Tourist information:** 200 Mann St; (043) 25 2835. **Accommodation:** 3 hotels, 10 motels, 1 cara./camp. parks.
MAP REF. 105 O5, 108 F6, 121 K7

Goulburn   Pop. 21 451

This provincial city, steeped in history (proclaimed a city in 1833), can be accessed from the Hume Hwy bypass some 209 km SW of Sydney. It is the centre of a wealthy farming district at the junction of the Wollondilly and Mulwarry Rivers beyond the Southern Highlands. **Of interest:** Riversdale (1840), Maud St; National Trust-classified coaching-house. St Clair History House (c.1843), Sloane St, 20-room mansion, restored by local historical society. Regional Art Gallery, Bourke St. Garroorigang and Hume Dairy, South Goulburn (1857), in almost original condition; private home, open by appt. Old Goulburn Brewery Hotel, Bungonia Rd. Goulburn Courthouse, Montague St. Cathedral of St Saviour, Bourke St. Cathedral of St Peter and St Paul, cnr Bourke and Verner Sts. Gulfon's Craft Village, Common St, housed in old brickworks (1884), working displays, sales. Goulburn Yurt Works, Copford Rd, tours (by appt) of factory making prefabricated round houses. Fibre Designs Gallery, Montague St, make-your-own fabrics. Woodturning Gallery, Grafton St. Sock Factory, Cathcart St, see process; sock sales. The Big Merino, a 15-m sculptured relief, Hume Hwy, displays of wool products, Australiana. Goulburn Steam Museum, Fitzroy St, rides on Leisureland Express; check times. South Hill, Garooigang Rd, woollen art, accommodation. Picnic/barbecue facilities on Wollondilly River at Marsden Weir. Rocky Hill War Memorial, Memorial Dr, city's best-known landmark, built in memory of local World War I soldiers. May: Woolfest. **In the area:** Pelican Sheep Station, 10 km S, shearing and sheepdog demonstrations by appt. Bungonia State Recreation Area, 35 km E, range of walks, incl. through Bungonia Canyon. **Tourist information:** 6 Montague St; (048) 21 5343. **Accommodation:** 7 hotels, 1 hotel /motel, 13 motels, 3 cara./camp. parks. MAP REF. 119 F4, 120 G11

Grafton   Pop. 16 642
A garden city, famous for its riverbank parks and the jacaranda, wheel and flame trees lining its wide streets, Grafton is situated at the junction of Pacific Hwy and Gwydir Hwy, 665 km N of Sydney. **Of interest:** Numerous National Trust buildings. Schaeffer House (1900), Fitzroy St, now district historical museum. Stately Prentice House, Fitzroy St, one of Australia's finest regional art galleries. Susan Island in Clarence River, recreation reserve covered with rainforest, large fruit bat colony. Passenger ferry services, river cruises, houseboat hire. Oct.: Bridge to Bridge Ski Race. Oct.– Nov.: Jacaranda Festival. **In the area:** Four major national parks within hour's drive: Yuraygir, 50 km E and Bundjalung, 70 km N, coastal parks, Washpool, 88 km and Gibraltar Range, 92 km NW. World Heritage-listed rainforest in Washpool National Park and at Iluka; walking tracks, wildlife. Ulmarra village, 12 km NE, National Trust-classified, fine example of turn-of-the-century river

port; art, craft and antique shops. Riverboat hire at Brushgrove, 20 km NE. Weekend gliding at Eatonsville, 18 km NW. Canoeing and rafting on wild-river systems in surrounding shires such as Nymboida; also many scenic drives. **Tourist information:** Cnr Spring St and Pacific Hwy, South Grafton; (066) 42 4677. **Accommodation:** 17 hotels, 12 motels, 3 cara./camp. parks. MAP REF. 123 O5, 475 N11

Grenfell   Pop. 2037
The birthplace of poet and short-story writer Henry Lawson, this small town is 377 km W of Sydney, on the Mid Western Hwy. **Of interest:** Grenfell Museum, Camp St. O'Brien's Lookout, where gold was discovered; walkway, picnic facilities. Henry Lawson Obelisk, next to Lawson Park, on site of house where poet is believed to have been born, in 1867. Easter: Guinea Pig Races. June: Henry Lawson Festival of Arts. **In the area:** Weddin Mountains National Park, 18 km SW, bushwalking, camping, picnicking; used as hideout by bushrangers Ben Hall, Frank Gardiner, Johnnie Gilbert and others. Easy walk to Ben Hall's Cave. **Tourist information:** CWA Craft Centre, 68 Main St; (063) 43 1612. **Accommodation:** 5 hotels, 1 motel, 1 hostel, 1 cara./camp. park. MAP REF. 119 B1, 120 C8

Griffith   Pop. 13 296
A thriving city developed as a result of the introduction of irrigation, Griffith was designed by Walter Burley Griffin, architect of Canberra, and named after Sir Arthur Griffith, the first Minister for Public Works in the NSW government. Of a diversity of industries, rice is the most profitable, followed by citrus fruits, grapes, vegetables, eggs and poultry. Griffith is well known as a wine-producing area; there are over a dozen wineries in the district. The Murrumbidgee Irrigation Area produces 80 per cent of the State's wines. **Of interest:** Koala Gourmet Foods, Whybrow St; tours. Regional Theatre, Banna Ave, stage curtain designed and created by efforts of 300 residents to reflect city, surrounding villages and industries. Regional Art Gallery, Banna Ave, monthly exhibitions. Griffith Cottage Gallery, Bridge Rd. Crafty Spot, Benerembah St. Easter: Wine and Food Festival. Oct.: Festival of Gardens. **In the area:** Pioneer Park Museum, 2 km N, set in 18 ha of bushland,

drop-log buildings, memorabilia from early 20th century. Bagtown village recreated to give insight into development of area. Lake Wyangan, 10 km NW, water sports, picnic areas. Bagtown Cemetery, 5 km S, reminder of pioneering days. Catania Fruit Salad Farm, Cox Rd, Hanwood, 6 km S, horticultural farm, demonstrates processes; open weekdays p.m., weekends by appt. Cocoparra National Park, 25 km NE. Many wineries; tours. **Tourist information:** Cnr Banna and Jondaryan Aves; (069) 62 4145. **Accommodation:** 2 hotels, 1 hotel/motel, 8 motels, 1 hostel, 2 cara./camp. parks. **See also:** Vineyards and Wineries. MAP REF. 127 N7

Gulgong   Pop. 2042
This old goldmining town, 29 km NW of Mudgee, is known as 'the town on the (original) $10 note'. In its heyday in the 1870s it was packed with fortune hunters from all over the world. Some of its glory remains in the many restored buildings; the town's narrow streets are lined with clapboard and iron buildings decorated in their original iron lace. **Of interest:** Henry Lawson Centre, Mayne St, largest collection of Lawson memorabilia outside Sydney's Mitchell Library. Historic buildings on self-guide Town Trail incl. Prince of Wales Opera House, Mayne St, Ten Dollar Town Motel (formerly Royal Hotel), cnr Mayne and Medley Sts; American Tobacco Warehouse and Fancy Goods Emporium, Mayne St; Gulgong Pioneers Museum, cnr Herbert and Bayly Sts. April: Gulgong Foundation Day. June: Henry Lawson Birthday Celebrations. **Tourist information:** 109 Herbert St; (063) 74 1202. **Accommodation:** 4 hotels, 3 motels. MAP REF. 120 F3

Gundagai   Pop. 2069
Much celebrated in song and verse, this town on the Murrumbidgee River at the foot of Mt Parnassus, 398 km SW of Sydney, has become part of Australian folklore. Its history includes Australia's worst flood disaster in 1852 when 89 people drowned, nearby gold rushes, and many bushranging attacks. Today it is the centre of a rich pastoral and agricultural district that produces wool, wheat, fruit and vegetables, and is a convenient overnight stop for motorists using the Hume Hwy. **Of interest:** Marble carving of cathedral, comprising over 20 000 pieces, by Frank Rusconi

(sculptor of tuckerbox dog) on display in Tourist Information Centre, Sheridan St. Gabriel Gallery, Sheridan St, outstanding collection of early photographs, letters and possessions of poet Henry Lawson. Historical museum, Homer St. Courthouse (1859), building classified by National Trust; scene of many historic trials, incl. that of notorious bushranger Captain Moonlite. St John's Anglican Church (1861), cnr Otway and Punch Sts, and Prince Alfred Bridge (1866), longest timber viaduct in Australia, both National Trust-classified. Excellent views from Mt Parnassus Lookout, Hanley St, and Rotary Lookout, South Gundagai. Oct.: Spring Flower Show. Nov.: Dog on the Tuckerbox Festival. **In the area:** Dog on the Tuckerbox, Caltex service station, 'five miles from' or 8 km N, monument to pioneer teamsters and their dogs, celebrated in song by Jack O'Hagan; larger-than-life copper statues of Dad and Dave characters. Nearby kiosk, fern-house, and ruins of Five Mile Pub. **Tourist information:** Sheridan St; (069) 44 1341. **Accommodation:** 4 hotels, 5 motels, 1 B&B, 2 cara./camp. parks.
MAP REF. 119 B5, 120 C12

Gunnedah
Pop. 8874
A prosperous town on the banks of the Namoi River, Gunnedah is the centre of rich pastoral and agricultural country, and is one of the largest stock-marketing and killing centres in NSW. Other industries include a brickworks, a tannery, flour mills and open-cut and underground coal mining. **Of interest:** Water Tower Museum, Anzac Park. Dorothea MacKellar Memorial statue in park. Rural Museum, Mullaley Rd. Red Chief Memorial, State Office building, Abbott St. Old Bank Gallery, Conadilly St. Creative Arts Centre, Chandos St. 8th Division Memorial Avenue of flowering gums. Self-drive town tour, self-guide Bindea Town Walk. Jan.: National Tomato Competition. Oct.: Dorothea MacKellar Children's Festival. **In the area:** Porcupine Lookout, 3 km SE, picnic spot. Lake Keepit Dam and State Recreation Centre, 34 km NE, water sports, bushwalking, gliding club, picnicking, camping, caravan park. 150° East Time Meridian, 28 km W. **Tourist information:** Anzac Park; (067) 42 1564. **Accommodation:** 6 hotels, 7 motels, 1 B&B, 1 cara./camp. park.
MAP REF. 122 H9

Gunning
Pop. 497
This town, on the Hume Hwy between Goulburn and Yass, is in the centre of lush pastoral country. **Of interest:** On Hume Hwy: Pye Cottage, a slab-style pioneer cottage; post office; Royal Hotel, old courthouse (now church); Do Duck Inn; Caxton House and Cottage. Feb.: Agricultural Show. **In the area:** Greendale Pioneer Cemetery, Gunning–Boorowa Rd. Hume and Hovell Walking Track extends from Gunning to Albury. Tourist information: Visitor Centre, Coronation Park, Cooma St, Yass; (06) 226 2557. **Accommodation:** 1 hotel, 1 motel, 2 B&B.
MAP REF. 119 E4, 120 F11

Guyra
Pop. 1942
Guyra is Aboriginal for 'fish may be caught', and the local streams are excellent for fishing. At 1300 m, this small town in the Great Dividing Range is one of the highest in NSW. Guyra is the centre of a highly productive area known for fat lambs, beef, wool and potatoes. **Of interest:** Historical Society Museum,

Courthouse, Grafton

Bradley St; open Sun. or by appt. Railway Station, Bradley St, large display of antique machinery. Waterbirds at Mother of Ducks Lagoon. Jan.: Hydrangea Festival; Lamb and Potato Festival. **In the area:** Chandler's Peak, spectacular views, 20 km E. Unusual balancing rock formation and gem fossicking at Backwater, 34 km NE. Llangothlin Handcraft Hall on Hwy, 13 km N. Copeton Dam, 90 km NW, fishing, boating, camping. Thunderbolt's Cave, 10 km S. Ebor Falls and picnic reserve, 75 km SE. **Tourist information:** Guyra Nursery, Nincoola St; (067) 79 1420. **Accommodation:** 2 hotels, 2 motels, 1 caravan park. **See also:** New England.
MAP REF. 123 L7, 475 K12

Harden–Murrumburrah
Pop. 2016
Twin towns, 357 km SW of Sydney. Settled in 1830, the area is rich grain and stock country. **Of interest:** Harden–Murrumburrah Historical Museum, Which Craft and Coffee Cottage, both in Albury St. Newson Park, in Harden,

Witcombe Memorial Fountain, Lachlan St, Hay

picnic/barbecue facilities. Sept.: Agricultural Show. **In the area:** Barwang Vineyard, 20 km N. Asparagus plantation at Jugiong, 30 km S. **Tourist information:** Which Craft Cottage, Albury St; (063) 86 2343. **Accommodation:** 4 hotels, 1 motel, 1 B&B, 1 cara./camp. park. MAP REF. 119 C3, 120 D10

Hartley   Pop. 5
This historic village just off the Great Western Hwy, 134 km NW of Sydney, was an important stopover for travellers in the early colonial days. Situated in the Hartley Valley, it is now administered by the National Parks and Wildlife Service. **Of interest:** Self-guide leaflet introduces historic buildings, incl. convict-built courthouse (1837), designed by colonial architect Mortimer Lewis; Royal Hotel (early 1840s); Old Trahlee Cottage; post office (1846); St Bernard's Church and Presbytery (1842); Farmer's Inn; Ivy Cottage; Shamrock Inn. **Tourist information:** 285 Main St, Lithgow; (063) 51 2307. **Accommodation:** 1 cara./camp. park.
MAP REF. 104 F5

Hay   Pop. 2817
Hay serves as the commercial centre for the huge area of semi-arid grazing country on the Murrumbidgee River at the junction of the Cobb, Mid Western and Sturt Hwys. Increasing irrigation from the Murrumbidgee has led to an expansion in vegetable- and fruit-growing. Many world-famous sheep studs are in the area. **Of interest:** Historic buildings in Lachlan St. Witcombe Memorial Fountain (1883) and plaque in Lachlan St commemorate journey of explorer Charles Sturt along Murrumbidgee and Murray rivers in 1829–30. Hay Gaol Museum, Church St, pioneer relics. Restored courthouse, Moppett St. Coachhouse in main shopping area, original Cobb & Co. coach that plied Deniliquin–Hay–Wilcannia run until 1901. Hay Park, children's playgrounds picnic/barbecue facilities. Signposted scenic drive around town. Sandy river beaches along Murrumbidgee for swimming, boating, fishing; Sandy Point Beach venue for Australia Day 'Surf' Carnival. Birdwatching area close to town; breeding ground for inland species. Bishop's Lodge, South Hay (1888), restored as museum, exhibition gallery, conference centre. Jan.: Australia Day 'Surf' Carnival. **In the area:** Ruberto's Winery, Sturt Hwy, South Hay. Sunset viewing area, 16 km N on Booligal Rd. Weir on Murrumbidgee River, 12 km W. Famous sheep studs: Mungadal, Uardry and Cedar Grove. **Tourist information:** 407 Moppett St; (069) 93 1003. **Accommodation:** 7 hotels, 6 motels, 2 cara./camp. parks.
MAP REF. 127 K8

Henty   Pop. 840
The historic pastoral township of Henty, the 'home of the header', is in the heart of Morgan Country, so called because of the infamous but ill-fated bushranger Dan Morgan. Almost midway between Albury–Wodonga and Wagga Wagga, Henty can be reached by the Olympic Way or by the Hume Hwy and Boomerang Way. **Of interest:** Headlie Taylor Header Memorial, Henty Park, off Allen St, tribute to machine (invented 1914) that revolutionised grain industry. Sept.: Machinery Field Days. **In the area:** Sergeant Smith Memorial Stone, 2 km W on Pleasant Hills Rd, marks site where Dan Morgan fatally wounded a policeman. Doodle Cooma Swamp (2000 ha), breeding area for waterbirds, visible from memorial stone. Built of chocks and logs (no nails), Buckarginga Woolshed, on Cookardinia Rd, 11 km E. Squatters Arms Inn (1848), Cookardinia, 24 km E. **Tourist information:** Billabong Craft Shop, Railway Pde, Culcairn. **Accommodation:** 2 hotels.
MAP REF. 127 P11, 233 P1

Holbrook   Pop. 1369
This small town is a noted stock-breeding centre, 521 km SW of Sydney, on the Hume Hwy. **Of interest:** Commander Holbrook submarine in Holbrook Park, Hume Hwy, replica of submarine in which Commander N. D. Holbrook won VC in World War I. Town (formerly Germanton) was renamed in his honour. Woolpack Inn Museum, in former hotel built in 1860, exhibits incl. complete plant of old cordial factory, bakery, horse-drawn vehicles, farm equipment; open daily. Easter: Ultra Fly-in. Nov.: Agricultural Show. **In the area:** Ultralight Centre, Holbrook airport. **Tourist information:** Woolpack Inn Museum, 83 Albury St (Hume Hwy); (060) 36 2131. **Accommodation:** 2 hotels, 6 motels, 1 cara./camp. park.
MAP REF. 127 Q12, 233 Q2

Huskisson   Pop. 900
A thriving town with comprehensive shopping, sporting and entertainment facilities, Huskisson is 24 km SE of Nowra, in Jervis Bay. **Of interest:** Lady Denman Heritage Complex, Dent St, history of wooden shipbuilding at Huskisson; check times. Also in Complex, Laddie Timbery's Aboriginal Art and Craft Centre, artefacts made on site by Aboriginal craftspersons; Museum of

Vineyards and Wineries

A vineyard holiday takes you through peaceful, ordered countryside and gives you the chance to learn more about wine and its making at first hand. It also gives you a perfect excuse for wine-tasting and, later, sampling the local wines with a meal in a first-class restaurant in the area. The obvious place to head for in New South Wales is the famous **Hunter Valley**. It is not far from Sydney (2 hours' drive each way) and, with some 70 wineries, must rate as one of the most important wine-growing districts in Australia. Although it can be a pleasant day trip from Sydney to the Hunter, it is well worth booking into a motel in the area for at least one night, to do it justice. Mid-week with lower tariffs and fewer crowds, is the best time to visit.

The Hunter is Australia's oldest commercial wine-producing area, wine having first been made there in the 1830s. The Hunter's table wines, both red and white, still rank among the best in Australia.

Most of the early colonial vineyards have vanished. Some family concerns have been taken over by the larger companies such as Lindemans and McWilliams.

The high reputation of the district is maintained by such well-known properties as Mount Pleasant, Oakvale, Drayton's, Tyrrell's, Tulloch's Glen Elgin, Wyndham and Rothbury.

Most wineries welcome visitors and are open for inspection and wine-tastings daily. Facilities include picnic grounds, barbecues and excellent restaurants.

Pokolbin Cellars at McGuigan Hunter Village, Blaxland's at Pokolbin and the Casuarina at North Pokolbin are among the restaurants in the area.

The McGuigan Hunter Village at Pokolbin has wine tastings, wine sales, a gallery, accommodation at the Vineyard Resort, specialty shops, a restaurant, kiosk, picnic facilities, an adventure playground for children, an aquagolf driving range, and clay pigeon shooting with laser beams.

It is best to go at vintage time—usually around February in the Hunter—if you want to see a vineyard in full swing. However, this is the most hectic time of year for vignerons, so do not expect their undivided attention. For an idea of the range of wineries in the district, try Tyrrell's and Drayton's wineries for a glimpse of the more traditional family approach, and Lindeman or Hunter Estate for the modern 'big company' style.

South of Sydney at **Camden** is Gledswood, birthplace of Australia's wine

Lindemans Winery, Pokolbin

Vineyard, Mudgee

industry. The first vines were planted in 1827 and the winery was re-established as Gledswood Cellars in 1970. The winery offers wine tastings and sales, an art gallery, shearing demonstrations and picnic facilities. Hayrides and candle-lit dinners for parties can be arranged.

You could have an equally enjoyable wine-tasting holiday in the Riverina towns of **Griffith** and **Leeton**, in the other main winegrowing area of the State. Griffith, Leeton and **Narrandera** are the main towns in the **Murrumbidgee Irrigation Area**, which grows 80 per cent of the State's wine-producing grapes. Well known wineries such as McWilliam's, de Bortoli and Rosetto & Sons are open to visitors who wish to taste the wines of the Riverina. In Leeton, visitors are welcome to sample the vintages at Toorak Winery and Lillypilly Estate. **Mudgee**, 261 kilometres north-west of Sydney, is also in an area where fine wines are produced from some dozen wineries. Other smaller vineyards are scattered throughout the State—some of them quite close to Sydney.

For further information, contact Lower Hunter Tourism Authority. **See also:** Individual town entries in A–Z listing. **Note** detailed map of Lower Hunter Vineyards on page 113.

Jervis Bay Science and the Sea, fine maritime and surveying collections. Antique and craft shops. Diving and dolphin watch. Market Day, White Sands Park, 2nd Sun. in month. Easter: White Sands Carnival. **In the area:** Barry's Bushtucker Tours, Wreck Bay, 23 km SE. **Tourist information:** Shoalhaven Tourist Centre, 254 Princes Hwy, Bomaderry; (044) 21 0778. **Accommodation:** 4 motels, 2 cara./ camp. parks.
119 H5, 120 I12, 141 R1

Iluka   Pop. 1795
A coastal resort on the Clarence River, well known for its fishing. A deep-sea fishing fleet operates from the harbour. **Of interest**: Daily passenger ferry services to Yamba. River cruises. July: Iluka Amateur Fishing Classic. **In the area:** Bundjalung National Park and World Heritage-listed Iluka Rainforest, at northern edge of town. Woombah Coffee Plantation, 14 km W; world's southernmost coffee plantation, tours. Houseboat hire at Brushgrove, 33 km W. **Tourist information:** Lower Clarence Visitors Centre, Ferry Park, Pacific Hwy, Maclean; (066) 45 4121. **Accommodation:** 1 motel, 3 caravan parks.
MAP REF. 123 P4, 475 N10

Inverell   Pop. 9736
Known as 'Sapphire City', this town, 69 km W of Glen Innes, is in fertile farming land also rich in minerals. Industrial diamonds, zircons, tin and 75% of the world's sapphires are mined in the area. **Of interest:** Courthouse, Otho St, National Trust-classified. Pioneer Village, Tingha Rd, buildings dating from 1840, moved from their original sites, incl. Grove Homestead, Paddy's Pub, Mt Drummond Woolshed. Tour Centre and Mining Museum in Water Towers Complex, Campbell St. Art Society Gallery, Evans St. Gem Centre, Byron St. March: Art Exhibition. Oct.: Sapphire City Floral Festival. **In the area:** Lake Inverell Reserve, 3 km E. Draught Horse Centre, Fishers Rd, 4 km E, 6 breeds, display of harness and memorabilia. DeJon Sapphire Centre, 19 km E on Glen Innis Rd; see working sapphire mine. Honey Farm and Bottle Museum, 8 km W. Gwydir Ranch 4WD Park, 28 km W. Popular fossicking area. Copeton Dam State Recreation Area, 40 km SW, boating, water-skiing, swimming, fishing, bushwalking, rock climbing, adventure playgrounds, picnic/barbecue facilities.

Goonoowigall Bushland Reserve, 5 km S. Gilgai Winery, 12 km S. Green Valley Farm, 35 km S, with museum. **Tourist information:** Water Towers Complex, Campbell St; (067) 22 1693. **Accommodation:** 4 hotels, 6 motels, 2 B&B, 3 cara./camp. parks. **See also:** New England.
MAP REF. 123 J6, 475 J11

Jamberoo   Pop. 704
Jamberoo, 13 km W of Kiama, is one of the most picturesque areas of the NSW coast, with lush pastures surrounded by towering escarpments. The district has been well-known for the quality of its dairy products since early white-settlement days. **Of interest:** Jamberoo Hotel, Allowrie St, bush bands Sun. p.m. March: Illawarra Folk Festival. **In the area:** Jamberoo Recreation Park, 3 km N. Breathtaking, State-award-winning Minnamurra Rainforest, 4 km W. **Tourist information:** Kiama Visitors Centre, Blowhole Point, Kiama; (042) 32 3322. **Accommodation:** 1 hotel, 1 motel/ lodge.
MAP REF. 116 F9, 119 I3, 120 I11

Jerilderie   Pop. 898
This town on the Newell Hwy was held by the Kelly gang for two days in 1879 when they captured the police station, cut the telegraph wires and robbed the bank. Today it is the centre of the largest merino stud area in NSW and also supports an expanding vegetable industry. **Of interest:** Telegraph Office Museum, Powell St; next door The Willows historic home, crafts, Devonshire teas, light lunches. Courthouse, Newell Hwy. Lake Jerilderie for water sports; adj. Luke Park features Steel Wings, one of largest windmills in southern hemisphere, also shady picnic areas. June: League of Silent Flight. Oct.: Yanco Bush Picnic. **In the area:** Tomato and onion factory, 2 km E; tours by appt. **Tourist information:** The Willows, Powell St; (058) 86 1666. **Accommodation:** 1 hotel/motel, 3 motels, 1 cara./camp. park. **See also:** The Newell.
MAP REF. 127 M11

Jindabyne   Pop. 4601
Now on the shores of Lake Jindabyne at the foothills of the Snowy Mountains, the original township was on the banks of the Snowy River. From 1962, residents of the old town moved up to the new site chosen by the Snowy Mountains Hydro-electric

Authority. This made way for the damming of the Snowy River to form a water storage as part of the Snowy Mountains Scheme. At an altitude of 930 m and situated in the heart of the Snowy Mountains, Jindabyne attracts skiers in winter and anglers, water-sports enthusiasts and bushwalkers in summer. **Of interest:** Lake Jindabyne, well stocked with trout, ideal for boating, water-skiing and other water sports. March: Strzelecki Polish Festival. Dec.: Lake Jindabyne Sailing Club Hobie Cat Races. **In the area:** Kosciusko National Park Headquarters and Information Centre, Sawpit Creek, 20 km NW, on Kosciusko Rd. Winter shuttle-bus service to Perisher, Smiggins and Thredbo. After snow has melted, 50-min. drive south west from Jindabyne leads to Charlotte Pass, 300-m boardwalk to view main range; 16-km round trip to summit of Mt Kosciusko. At Thredbo, 37 km W, chairlift operates all year, in summer provides easy access over steel-mesh track to summit of Mt Kosciusko, 13-km round trip. **Tourist information:** Snowy River Information Centre, Petamin Plaza; (064) 56 2444. **Accommodation:** 2 hotel/motels, 5 motels, 2 cara./camp. parks.
MAP REF. 118 G11, 119 C9, 140 C12, 235 J4

Junee   Pop. 3673
An important railhead town and commercial centre 482 km SW of Sydney on the Olympic Way. **Of interest:** Monte Cristo Homestead, overlooking town, restored colonial mansion, carriage collection. 47-bay Rail Round House, Railway Pde. Endeavour Park, Olympic Way. Memorial Park, Main St. Hobbin Pond, Peel St. **In the area:** McWilliam's vineyard and winery (not open to the public). Historic Hotel Shirley, Bethungra, 30 km NE. Bethungra Dam, turnoff at Bethungra, canoeing, sailing, picnic facilities. Bethungra Rail Spiral 33 km NE, unique engineering feat. **Tourist information:** Tarcutta St, Wagga Wagga; (069) 23 5402 or Junee Council, Belmore St; (069) 24 1277. **Accommodation:** 4 hotels, 1 motel, 1 cara./camp. park.
MAP REF. 119 A4, 120 B11, 127 R9

Katoomba–Wentworth Falls   Pop. 16 927
Katoomba is the highly developed tourism centre of the Blue Mountains area which attracts 3 million people each year. The smaller towns of Leura and

Wentworth Falls have many interesting features as well as superb mountain scenery. Originally developed as a coal mine last century, it was not long before Katoomba was attracting wealthy Sydney holidaymakers. The coal mine foundered, but Katoomba continued to develop as a tourist resort. Natural and created attractions abound in the Blue Mountains region. **Of interest:** Scenic Skyway and Railway Complex, Violet St/Cliff Dr; first horizontal passenger-carrying ropeway in Australia, Skyway travels 350 m across mountain gorge above Cooks Crossing, giving magnificent views of Katoomba Falls, Orphan Rock, Jamison Valley. Built in late 1800s by founder of Katoomba coal mine to bring out coal and transport miners. The Scenic Railway is reputed to be world's steepest railway. It descends into Jamison Valley at an average incline of 45°, through a sunlit, tree-clad gorge approximately 445 m in length. Famous rock formations (The Three Sisters, Orphan Rock) and Katoomba Falls, floodlit at night. At Wentworth Falls, Yester Grange (1870s), colonial homestead-museum on 4.7-ha site; restored, furnished to late-Victorian splendour. Horse-drawn carriage rides through Leura's tree-lined streets. Everglades Garden, Everglades Ave, Leura, one of Australia's great gardens. Leuralla, Olympian Pde in Leura, historic art deco mansion; major collection of 19th-century Australian art; one of Australia's largest collections of toys, dolls, trains and railway memorabilia; memorial museum to Dr H. V. Evatt. Cliff Drive follows cliff tops around Katoomba–Leura; spectacular views at many lookouts and picnic spots. Walking tracks along cliff tops and descending into Jamison Valley; heathland and rainforest. Wide selection of accommodation. Horseriding, 4WD routes, cycling, scenic flights. **In the area:** Dramatic views from Sublime Point (on Blue Mountains Scenic Drive from Leura) and Hanging Rock (N of Blackheath on 4WD track). Jemby-Rinjah Lodge at Blackheath, 8 km N, incl. environmental studies centre on edge of Blue Mountains National Park. Govett's Leap and Evans Point Lookouts in park. Hydro Majestic Hotel at Medlow Bath, 5 km NW; once a health resort. Mount Victoria, 16 km NW of Katoomba, National Trust-classified village with craft shops, museum; nearby, waterfalls, Pulpit Rock reserve, Mount York Historic Site. Jenolan Caves, some

Rice harvesting, near Jerilderie

of the most splendid underground caves and above-ground arches in Australia, in recreation reserve 76 km SW of Katoomba. Yerranderie, silver-mining ghost town, 200 km S of Katoomba, historic buildings incl. museum and quaint hostel-style accommodation; surrounded by 2430-ha wildlife reserve. Norman Lindsay Gallery and Museum near Faulconbridge, 32 km E; picnic area. Jan.: Australia Day Regatta at Wentworth Falls Lake. Oct.: Leura Gardens Festival. **Tourist information:** Echo Point, Katoomba; or Tourist Information Centre, Gt Western Hwy, Glenbrook; (047) 39 6266. **Accommodation:** In Katoomba: 2 hotels, 7 motels, 1 cara./camp. park. **See also:** The Blue Mountains.
MAP REF. 104 G7, 106 E9, 106 G8, 120 H8

Kempsey   Pop. 9049

Kempsey, situated in the Macleay River Valley, 428 km N of Sydney, is the commercial centre of a growing district of dairying, tourism and light industry, including the Akubra hat factory. The town celebrated its sesquicentenary in 1986.

Of interest: Macleay River Historical Society Museum, Pacific Hwy, South Kempsey. Number of 19th-century buildings in Kemp, Elbow, Sea and Belgrave Sts, West Kempsey. April: Agricultural Show. **In the area:** Bellbrook, 47 km W, National Trust-classified village. Crescent Head, 20 km SE. Limeburners Creek Nature Reserve, 34 km SE. Hat Head National Park, 32 km E. Fish Rock Cave, noted for scuba diving, just off Smoky Cape. South West Rocks, 35 km NE, beach resort; river cruises. Trial Bay Gaol, 40 km NE, built by prisoners in 1880s. **Tourist information:** Information Centre, Ocean St, South West Rocks; (065) 66 7099. **Accommodation:** 6 hotels, 10 motels, 5 cara./camp. parks.
MAP REF. 109 G3, 123 O10

Khancoban   Pop. 416

Set in the lush green Murray Valley at the western end of the Alpine Way, 109 km NW of Jindabyne, this small modern town was built by the Snowy Mountains Authority. Khancoban offers a variety of accommodation from a luxurious alpine retreat to a caravan park. National Parks

and Wildlife Service have videos of the Snowy Mountains Scheme and Kosciusko National Park. **In the area:** Permit required for vehicles entering National Park; contact Tourist Information. Murray 1 Power Station 10 km SE on Alpine Way; guided tours daily. Trout fishing, water sports, whitewater rafting. Excellent picnic and rest areas along Alpine Way. Spectacular mountain views from Scammel's Spur Lookout, 20 km SE. Brilliant roadside displays of wildflowers in spring and autumn. Fishing tours. **Tourist information:** National Parks and Wildlife Service, Scott St; (060) 76 9373. **Accommodation:** 1 hotel/motel, 1 cara./camp. park.
MAP REF. 118 A9, 119 B8, 234 H3

Kiama   Pop. 10 631
The spectacular Blowhole is the best known attraction of this resort town. Discovered by explorer George Bass in 1797, it sprays water up to heights of 60 m and is floodlit each evening. Kiama is the centre of a prosperous dairying and mixed farming district. **Of interest:** Kiama Beach for surfing, swimming, fishing. Pilots Cottage Historical Museum, adj. Kiama Visitors Centre and restaurant at Blowhole Point. Terrace houses, specialty and craft shops in Collins St. Family History Centre, Railway Pde, world-wide collection of records for tracing family history. Feb.: Jazz Festival. Oct.: Seaside Festival. **In the area:** Little Blowhole, 2 km S, off Tingira Cres. Cathedral Rocks, 3 km N, at Jones Beach, scenic rocky outcrop, best at dawn. **Tourist information:** Blowhole Point; (042) 32 3322. **Accommodation:** 2 hotels, 6 motels, 4 cara./camp. parks. **See also:** The Illawarra Coast.
MAP REF. 116 G9, 119 I4, 121 J11

Kyogle   Pop. 2912
Kyogle makes a good base for exploring the mountains nearby. It is also the centre of a lush dairy and mixed-farming area on the upper reaches of the Richmond River near the Qld border. July: Rodeo. Nov.: Festival and Golf Tournament. **In the area:** World Heritage-listed Border Ranges National Park, 27 km N, walking tracks, forestry road access. Views of Mt Warning and Tweed Valley from park lookouts. Tweed Range Scenic Drive, 64 km, through eastern section; pristine rainforest, deep gorges, waterfalls plunging into crystal-clear creeks. Wiangaree State Forest, 30 km N, elevated coastal

views, rainforest. Magnificent views from Mt Lindesay, 45 km NW, on NSW-Qld border. Toonumbar Dam, 31 km W, conference centre, bushwalking, picnic/barbecue facilities; freshwater fishing and camping at Bell's Bay. Picnic spots incl. Roseberry Nursery and Moore Park, 23 km and 27 km N; Tooloom Falls, 95 km NW; scenic area at Nimbin Rocks, 32 km E. **Tourist information:** Old 66 Caltex Garage, Summerland Way; (066) 32 1042. **Accommodation:** 2 hotels, 1 motel, 3 cara./camp. parks.
MAP REF. 123 O2, 475 N8

Lake Cargelligo   Pop. 1256
A small township, 586 km W of Sydney, of the same name as the lake that serves the surrounding agricultural and pastoral district. **Of interest:** Fishing, boating, sailing, water-skiing and swimming on lake, picnic/barbecue facilities. The lake, 8 km long and 3.5 km wide, is home to many species of bird, including at times, the rare black cockatoo. Jan.: Hovercraft Meeting. Sept.: Lake Show. **Tourist information:** Kelly Reserve, Newell Hwy, Parkes; (068) 62 4365. **Accommodation:** 3 hotels, 2 motels, 1 cara./camp. park.
MAP REF. 127 O4

Lake Macquarie
Pop. 158 300
Lake Macquarie is a city without a town centre, but boasts the largest saltwater coastal lake in Australia as its hub. The northern shore townships of Lake Macquarie such as Toronto, Speers Point, Belmont and Boolaroo have many restaurants and sailing clubs. The lake is excellent for water sports. **Of interest:** Lake cruises on *Nambucca Princess* and MV *Macquarie Lady*, both leaving from Toronto Wharf and Belmont Public Wharf. Dobell House, 47 Dobell Dr., Wangi Wangi, home of Australian artist Sir William Dobell, collection of his work and memorabilia. Eraring Power Station; tours. Feb.: Cross the Lake Swim. Oct.: Children's Festival. **In the area:** Bahtabah Land Council Visitors Centre, Lakeview Pde, Blacksmiths, Aboriginal art and crafts; open daily. **Tourist information:** 72 Pacific Hwy, Blacksmiths; (049) 72 1172. **Accommodation:** Belmont: 2 hotels, 10 motels, 9 cara./camp. parks. Charlestown: 2 hotels, 5 motels. Toronto: 1 hotel/motel, 1 cara./camp. park.
MAP REF. 105 Q2, 112 G11

Leeton   Pop. 6245
Located 560 km SW of Sydney, Leeton is the first of the planned towns in the Murrumbidgee Irrigation Area and was designed by American architect Walter Burley Griffin. The town is an important administrative and processing centre for this intensive fruit-, rice- and wine-grape-growing area. **Of interest:** Historic Hydro Hotel (1919), Chelmsford Pl; Sunrice Country Visitors Centre at rice mill, Calrose St and Quelch Juice Factory, Brady Way; tours weekdays. Easter: 11-day Rice Festival (even-numbered years). **In the area:** Toorak and Lillypilly Estate Wineries, both close to town. Fivebough Swamp, 2 km N, waterbird sanctuary. Whitton Court House Museum, 23 km W. Gliding, hot-air ballooning. Gogeldrie Weir, 23 km SW. Yanco Agricultural High School, 10 km S. Murrumbidgee State Forests, 12 km S. Aquatic Park at Yanco, 7 km SE; Yanco Weir, 25 km SE. **Tourist information:** Chelmsford Pl.; (069) 53 2832. **Accommodation:** 2 hotels, 4 motels, 2 caravan parks. **See also:** Vineyards and Wineries.
MAP REF. 127 O8

Lennox Head   Pop. 3036
Just north of Ballina, Lennox Head has a charming seaside village atmosphere. The area is famous for its surfing beaches. **Of interest:** Freshwater Lake Ainsworth, 50 m from surfing beach; popular with windsurfers. Market, second Sun. of month. **In the area:** Pat Morton Lookout, 1 km S, whale-watching July–Aug., Dec. Swimming, surfing, snorkelling. Many scenic walks and rainforests a short drive away. **Tourist information:** Ballina Tourist Information Centre, Las Balsas Plaza, Ballina; (066) 86 3484. **Accommodation:** 3 motels, 1 hostel, 1 cara./camp. park.
MAP REF. 123 Q3, 475 O9

Lightning Ridge   Pop. 1522
Small opal-mining town in the famous Lightning Ridge opal fields, 74 km N of Walgett, via the Castlereagh Hwy. The valuable black opal found in the area attracts gem enthusiasts world-wide. **Of interest:** Bowling Club and Diggers Rest Hotel, Morilla St, share town's social life. Underground mine tours, opal-cutting demonstrations, museums, potteries, and displays of art and craft, including opal jewellery and gem opals. **In the area:** Cactus Nursery, 2 km N, off Bald

Hill Rd. Fauna Orphanage, Opal St, 3 km s. Hot Artesian Bore Baths (free), 2 km NE. Nature reserves, fossicking. **Tourist information:** 77 Fox St, Walgett; (068) 28 1399. **Accommodation:** 3 motels, 5 cara./camp. parks.
MAP REF. 122 B5, 474 E10

Lismore   Pop. 27 246
Regional centre of the Northern Rivers district of NSW, a closely settled and intensively cultivated rural area producing dairy products, tropical fruits, beef, timber and fodder crops, Lismore is situated on Wilsons River (formerly the north arm of the Richmond River), 821 km N of Sydney. It is best known for its rainforest heritage, including the Rotary Rainforest Reserve in the residential area of the city. **Of interest:** Lismore Tourist Information Centre; Rainforest Exhibition, Cultural Gallery and other displays. Surrounding Heritage Park, cnr Ballina and Molesworth Sts, picnic areas. Cedar Log Memorial, Ballina St. Richmond River Historical Museum and Lismore Regional Art Gallery, both in Molesworth St. Robinson's Lookout, Robinson Ave. Claude Riley Memorial Lookout, New Ballina Rd. Wilsons Park and Boatharbour Reserve. River cruises on MV *Bennelong*, The Wharf, Magellan St. Heritage Park market, fifth Sun. of month. Aug.: International Festival of Friendship. Oct.: Folk Festival. **In the area:** Macadamia Magic at Alphadale, 11 km E, macadamia processing plant, tourist complex. Rocky Creek Dam, 25 km N. Minyon Falls and Peates Mountain Lookout, in Whian Whian State Forest, 25 km N. Spectacular volcanic Nimbin Rocks, 3 km s of Nimbin (29 km N). Tucki Tucki Koala Reserve, 15 km s, adj. to Lismore–Woodburn Rd; Aboriginal ceremonial ground nearby. Among six World Heritage-listed areas in vicinity, Border Ranges National Park, 25 km N of Nimbin, and Nightcap National Park, 25 km N of Lismore. Lismore Lake, 3 km s, picnic/barbecue facilities, adventure park, pleasant lagoon for swimming. **Tourist information:** Cnr Ballina and Molesworth Sts; (066) 22 0122. **Accommodation:** 9 hotels, 12 motels, 8 B&B, 2 hostels, 6 cara./camp. parks.
MAP REF. 123 P3, 475 N9

Lithgow   Pop. 11 968
This important coal-mining city on the north-west fringes of the Blue Mountains is a must for railway enthusiasts.

The city itself is highly industrialised with two power stations and several large factories, but the surrounding countryside is beautiful. **Of interest:** Eskbank House, Bennett St, built 1841 by Thomas Brown, who discovered Lithgow coal seam; now museum, fine collection of 19th-century furniture and vehicles, and displays depicting industrial history of area; open Sat.–Sun. Blast Furnace Park, off Inch St, ruins of Australia's first blast furnace complex. Oct.: National Go-Kart Championships. Nov.: Festival of the Valley (even-numbered years). **In the area:** Zig Zag Steam Railway, 10 km E, via Bells Line of Road; breathtaking stretch of railway, built in 1869, restored by enthusiasts; train trips, picnic/barbecue facilities. Mt Piper Power Station, 21 km NW, picnic/barbecue facilities; open daily 9–4, admission free. Lake Lyell, 9 km W, power boating, water-skiing, trout fishing. Lake Wallace, Wallerawang, 11 km W, sailing, trout fishing. Sweeping views from Hassan Walls Lookout, 5 km s, via Hassans Wall Rd. Hartley historic village, 12 km SE, off Great Western Hwy, convict-built courthouse (1837), outstanding architectural and historic interest. Jenolan Caves, 60 km SE. **Tourist information:** 285 Main Street; (063) 51 2307. **Accommodation:** 8 hotels, 5 motels, 1 hostel, 1 cara./camp. park.
MAP REF. 104 F4, 120 H7

Lockhart   Pop. 887
This pleasant historic town, situated 65 km SW of Wagga, was originally known as Green's Gunyah and was renamed Lockhart in 1897. **Of interest:** Fine example of turn-of-the-century streetscape, with wide, shady shop front verandahs, now classified by National Trust. **In the area:** Galore Hill, 3 km s, incl. caves where Mad Dog Morgan hid; also walking tracks, lookouts, picnic/barbecue facilities. **Tourist information:** Tarcutta St, Wagga Wagga; (069) 23 5402. **Accommodation:** 1 hotel, 1 motel, 1 caravan park.
MAP REF. 127 P10

Macksville   Pop. 2869
An attractive town on the Nambucca River, south of Nambucca Heads. **Of interest:** Mary Boulton Pioneer Cottage, River St; replica of pioneer home, incl. furniture, costumes, museum of horse-drawn vehicles. Star Hotel (1885), River St. Craft markets on riverbank, 4th Sat. of month. **In the area:** Joseph and Eliza Newman Folk Museum at unspoiled Bowraville (the 'verandah post town'), 16 km NW. Cosmopolitan Hotel (1903), the 'pub with no beer', made famous by song, at Taylors Arm, 26 km W. **Tourist information:** Ridge St, Nambucca Heads; (065) 68 6954. **Accommodation:** 2 hotels, 3 motels, 2 caravan parks.
MAP REF. 123 O9, 475 M13

View from Mt Pleasant, south of Kiama

Maclean
Pop. 2890

Fishing and river prawning fleets are based at Maclean, on the Clarence River, about 740 km N of Sydney. Fishermen from this pretty town and from the nearby towns of Yamba and Iluka catch about 20% of the State's seafood. Sugarcane, maize and mixed farm crops are grown in the area. **Of interest:** Scottish Corner, River St. Arts and crafts, Ferry Park. Bicentennial Museum and adj. Stone Cottage (1879), Wharf St. Maclean Lookout and Pinnacle Rocks. Rainforest walking track from High School. Easter: Highland Gathering. Sept.: Cane Harvest Festival. **In the area:** Houseboat hire at Brushgrove, 21 km SW. Yuraygir National Park, 24 km SE. **Tourist information:** Lower Clarence Visitors Centre, Ferry Park, Pacific Hwy; (066) 45 4121. **Accommodation:** 3 hotels, 2 motels, 2 cara./camp. parks.
MAP REF. 123 P5, 475 N10

Maitland
Pop. 45 209

On the Hunter River, 28 km NW of Newcastle, Maitland dates back to early colonial days. The flourishing city's winding High St has been recorded by the National Trust as a Conservation Area and over 90% of the buildings date back to the 1800s. First settled in 1818, when convicts were put to work as cedar-cutters, it was a flourishing township by the 1840s. **Of interest:** National Trust properties Grossmann House, Georgian-style folk museum (being restored after earthquake damage), and Brough House (1870), containing city's art collection, both in Church St, are mirror images. Cintra, Regent St, Victorian mansion, weekend B&B. Self-guide heritage walk of East Maitland and Morpeth. Poetry in the Pub, Queens Arms, High St, last Mon. in month. April: Steamfest; Indoor Equestrian Dressage Championships. **In the area:** At Morpeth, 5 km NE, historic buildings with superb iron lace, craft shops. Walka Waterworks, 3 km N, former pumping station, excellent bushwalking and picnic site. At Lochinvar, 13 km W, Windermere Colonial Homestead; built of sandstone brick by convict labour in 1820s, favourite residence of William Charles Wentworth, museum in dungeons where convicts were housed. Also at Lochinvar, NSW Equestrian Centre. **Tourist information:** Maitland Visitor Centre, cnr Banks St and New England Hwy; (049) 33 2611. **Accommodation:** 4 hotels, 6 motels, 2 B&B, 1 cara./camp. park.
MAP REF. 112 C7, 121 K4

Manilla
Pop. 2110

This small town boasts Dutton's Meadery, one of only two meaderys in the State. Visitors can sample and buy fresh honey and mead. **Of interest:** Picturesque street setting with antique and coffee shops. Royce Cottage Historical Museum, Manilla St. June: Lake Keepit Kool Sailing Regatta. Oct.: Festival of Spring Flowers. **In the area:** Manilla Ski Gardens on Lake Keepit, 20 km SW. Warrabah National Park, 40 km NE, peaceful riverside retreat, swimming, fishing and canoeing on Namoi and Manilla Rivers. Split Rock Dam Recreation Area, 40 km N. **Tourist information:** Cnr New England Hwy and Kable Ave, Tamworth; (067) 68 4462. **Accommodation:** 4 hotels, 1 motel, 1 cara./camp. park. **See also:** New England.
MAP REF. 122 I9

Menindee
Pop. 467

It was at this small town, 110 km SE of Broken Hill, that the ill-fated Burke and Wills stayed in 1860 on their journey north. **Of interest:** Maiden's Hotel (where they lodged). Ah Chung's Bakehouse Gallery, Menindee St. Menindee Lakes Lookout. **In the area:** Menindee Lake, 1 km NW, water-storage scheme that guarantees an unfailing water supply to Broken Hill. Yachting, fishing and swimming on lakes in area; nearby Copi Hollow, 12 km E, attracts water-skiers and power boat enthusiasts. Kinchega National Park, 1 km W; emus, red kangaroos, waterbirds; shearers' quarters accommodation. **Tourist information:** Broken Hill Tourist Information Centre, cnr Blende and Bromide Sts, Broken Hill; (080) 87 6077. **Accommodation:** 2 hotels, 1 motel, 3 cara./camp. parks.
MAP REF. 124 E13, 126 E1

Merimbula
Pop. 4259

Excellent surfing, fishing and prawning make this small sea and lake town a popular holiday resort. Its sister village of Pambula also offers fine fishing and surfing. **Of interest:** Aquarium at Merimbula Wharf, Lake St. Old School Museum, Main St. Magic Mountain Family Recreation Park, Sapphire Coast Dr. June: Jazz Festival. Oct.: Veterans Tennis. **In the area:** Lake cruises, boat hire. Tura Beach, 5 km NE. Pambula Beach, 10 km S, walking track and lookout. Ben Boyd National Park, 13 km S. **Tourist information:** Beach St; (064) 95 1129. **Accommodation:** 16 motels, 1 hostel, 4 cara./camp. parks. **See also:** The South Coast.
MAP REF. 117 F9, 119 F11, 235 P7

Merriwa
Pop. 962

This small town in the western Hunter region is noted for its many historic buildings. **Of interest:** Self-guide historic walks; buildings of note in Vennacher and McCartney Sts. Historical Museum in stone cottage (1857), Bettington St. Bottle Museum, Vennacher St. May: Polocrosse Carnival. June: Festival of Fleeces. **In the area:** The Drip picnic area, at Goulburn River National Park, 35 km S. Convict-built Flags Rd, runs from town to Gungal, 25 km SE. Cassilis, 45 km NW, historic sandstone buildings. Aboriginal paintings of hands, on rocks in caves just off Mudgee Rd, 32 km SW of Cassilis. Ulan coal mine, further 8 km SW; largest open-cut mine in southern hemisphere; viewing area. Official gem-fossicking area 27 km SW. **Tourist information:** Community Information Centre, Bettington St; (065) 48 2505. **Accommodation:** 2 hotels, 1 motel, 1 B&B, 1 cara./camp. park.
MAP REF. 120 H3, 122 H13

Mittagong
Pop. 5666

The gateway to the Southern Highlands, Mittagong is 110 km S of Sydney. **Of interest:** Historic cemeteries and many gracious old buildings. Butterfly House, Bessemer St. Natural wonders of Lake Alexandra, Queen St, walking tracks. Mt Gibraltar, once volcanic, via Oxley Dr, picnic facilities, walking tracks, views. **In the area:** Well-planned walk through nearby hills at Box Vale, turnoff 4 km SW. Loopline Scenic Drive incl. Thirlmere Lakes National Park, Thirlmere Railway Museum, potteries, orchards. **Tourist information:** Southern Highlands Visitor Information Centre, Winifred West Park, Main St; (048) 71 2888. **Accommodation:** 2 hotels, 6 motels, 1 B&B, 2 cara./camp. parks.
MAP REF. 116 C6, 119 H3, 120 I10

Moama–Echuca
Pop. 9438

Moama and its twin city Echuca, on the Victorian side of the Murray River,

embody the age of the paddle-steamer, when the port of Echuca was a major outlet for agricultural products. **Of interest:** Restored port at Echuca; Coach House Carriage Museum, Historical Museum, National Holden Museum, Gem Club, Gumnutland Model Village, Port Antique Photographics and Penny Arcade. June: Steam, Horse and Vintage Car Rally. Oct.: Rich River Festival. **In the area:** Murray River tours; cruisers, boats or paddle-steamers. Moira and Barmah red-gum forests, 35 km SE. Go-karts, poker-machine clubs, houseboat hire. **Tourist information:** 2 Leslie St, Echuca; (054) 80 7555. **Accommodation:** 4 hotels, 1 hotel/motel, 28 motels, 11 cara./camp. parks.
MAP REF. 127 K13, 232 E4

Molong   Pop. 1563
The grave of Yuranigh, the Aboriginal guide of explorer Sir Thomas Mitchell, is 2 km E of this Mitchell Hwy town. Yuranigh was buried there in 1850, according to the rites of his tribe. The grave is marked by a headstone that pays tribute to his courage and fidelity. Four trees, one dead but preserved for its Aboriginal carvings, mark the four corners of the burial ground. **Of interest:** Yarn Market, Craft Cottage and Coach House Gallery, Bank St. Molong Country Markets, Railway Station, 2nd Sun. in month (not winter). April: Cabonne Country Day. **In the area:** Mitchell's Monument, 21 km S, marks site of explorer's base camp. **Tourist information:** Visitors Centre, Civic Gardens, Byng St, Orange; (063) 61 5226 or Railway Station Complex, Mitchell Hwy, Molong. **Accommodation:** 2 hotels, 1 motel, 1 B&B, 1 cara./camp. park.
MAP REF. 120 E6

Moree   Pop. 10 062
Situated on the Mehi River, 640 km NW of Sydney, this town is the nucleus of a large cotton and wheat region. It is best known for its artesian spa baths, said to relieve arthritis and rheumatism. **Of interest:** Spa complex, Anne St, with Olympic swimming pool. Mary Brand Park, Gwydir St. Moree Lands Office (1894), National Trust-classified, cnr Frome and Heber Sts. Moree Plains Regional Gallery, Heber St. Yurundiali Aboriginal Corporation, Endeavour Lane, screen-print clothing factory. Easter: Carnival of Sport. Nov.: Golden Grain Festival. **In the area:** Pecan Nut

Menindee Lakes

Farm, 35 km E; tours. Inspection of cotton gins during harvesting season. **Tourist information:** Lyle Houlihan Park, Newell Hwy; (067) 52 7479. **Accommodation:** 6 hotels, 1 hotel/motel, 20 motels, 3 cara./camp. parks. **See also:** The Newell.
MAP REF. 122 G5, 474 H10

Moruya   Pop. 2520
Many well known old dairying estates were founded near this town, which was once a gateway to the Araluen and Braidwood goldfields. Situated on the Moruya River, 322 km S of Sydney, it is now a dairying, timber and oyster-farming centre. Granite used in the pylons of the Sydney Harbour Bridge was quarried in the district. **Of interest:** Eurobodalla Historic Museum, in town centre, depicts discovery of gold at Mogo and general history of district. Courthouse (1880), on Princes Hwy. Catholic Church (1889), Queen St, built in blue granite, by local builder Joseph Ziegler. Moruya River; black swan and sea eagle colonies up-river at Yarragee. March: Music Festival. **In the area:** Mort Memorial Church and historic

cemetery at Moruya Heads, 7 km E. Deua National Park, 20 km W; Hanging Mountain and Mt Wanderer Lookouts. Fishing, surfing and water sports. Nerrigundah, 44 km SW, former goldmining town. Coomerang House at Bodalla, 24 km S, home of 19th-century industrialist and dairy farmer Thomas Sutcliffe Mort. **Tourist information:** Cnr Princes Hwy and Beach Rd, Batemans Bay; (044) 72 6900, and Narooma; (044) 76 2881. **Accommodation:** 3 hotels, 2 motels, 1 B&B, 2 cara./camp. parks.
MAP REF. 119 G8, 141 M18, 235 Q1

Moss Vale   Pop. 5690
The industrial and agricultural centre of the Southern Highlands, this town stands on part of the 1000-acre parcel of land granted to Charles Throsby in 1819. **Of interest:** Leighton Gardens. Cecil Hoskins Reserve with abundance of birdlife. Historic Throsby Park, on northern edge of town; open on special occasions. March: Agricultural Show. **In the area:** A Little Piece of Scotland, Sutton Forest, 6 km SW on Illawarra Hwy, items ranging from shortbread to antiques. Exeter, 4 km further S. Fitzroy Falls, Morton National

Park, 20 km SE. **Tourist information:** Southern Highlands Visitor Information Centre, Winifred West Park, Main St, Mittagong; (048) 71 2888. **Accommodation:** 2 hotels, 2 motels, 1 B&B, 2 cara./camp. parks.
MAP REF. 116 B8, 119 H3, 120 H10

Moulamein   Pop. 459
This is the oldest town in the Riverina, already well established in the 1870s as a prosperous inland port on the Edward River. Today the town is noted for its fishing. **Of interest:** Old wharf, Main St. Restored courthouse. Riverside picnic areas. Lake Moulamein and nearby State Forests. Easter: Yabby Races. Dec.: Horseracing Cup. **Tourist information:** Moulamein Business Centre, Morago St; (058) 87 5007. **Accommodation:** 1 hotel, 1 cara./camp. park.
MAP REF. 126 I10, 231 P10

Mudgee   Pop. 7447
This attractively designed town is the centre of a productive agricultural area on the Cudgegong River, 264 km NW of Sydney. Wine grapes, fine wool, sheep, cattle and honey are among the local produce. There are horse studs in the area. **Of interest:** Many fine buildings in town centre, incl. St John's Church of England (1860), St Mary's Roman Catholic Church, railway station, town hall and Colonial Inn Museum, all in Market St. Mt Vincent Meadery, Common Rd. Honey Haven, cnr Hill End and Gulgong Rds, and Mudgee Honey, Robertson St. Mudgee Creative Yarns, Sydney Rd, tours of working mill, sales. Sept.: Wine Festival. **In the area:** Henry Lawson's boyhood home memorial, plaque on remains of demolished cottage, 6 km N. Cudgegong River Park, 14 km W, on eastern foreshores of Burrendong Dam, water sports, excellent fishing. Langton's Roses, 5 km S, tours, sales. Pick-Your-Own Farm, 12 km S, variety of fruit and vegetables Oct.–May. Windamere Dam, 24 km SE, camping facilities. Eighteen local wineries, incl. Craigmoor, Montrose, Huntington Estate, Botobolar. **Tourist information:** 84 Market St; (063) 72 5875. **Accommodation:** 5 hotels, 9 motels, 22 B&B, 3 cara./camp. parks. **See also:** Vineyards and Wineries.
MAP REF. 120 F4

Mullumbimby   Pop. 2612
Situated in lush subtropical country, Mullumbimby is some 850 km NE of Sydney. **Of interest:** Art Gallery, cnr Burringbar and Stuart Sts. Restored Cedar House, Dalley St, National Trust-classified, with antiques gallery. Brunswick Valley Historical Museum, in old post office (1907), Stuart St. Brunswick Valley Heritage Park, Tyagarah St. Market every 3rd Sat. Sept.: Chincogan Fiesta. **In the area:** Nightcap National Park to east, and Tuntable Falls to south. Sakura Farm, 15 km W, in hills at Mullum; run by Buddhist monk, offers unique retreat-style holidays. Wanganui Gorge and rainforest walking track, 20 km W. Skydiving and paragliding at airstrip at Tyagarah, on Pacific Hwy, 13 km SE. Crystal Castle, 7 km N, large display of natural quartz. **Tourist information:** 80 Jonson St, Byron Bay; (066) 85 8050. **Accommodation:** 2 hotels, 2 motels, 1 camping park.
MAP REF. 123 P2, 475 N8

Mulwala   Pop. 1330
On the foreshores of Lake Mulwala, the town is a major aquatic centre. Lake Mulwala is an artificial lake of over 6000 ha, formed by the damming of the Murray River at Yarrawonga Weir in 1939 to provide water for irrigation. **Of interest:** Yachting, water-skiing, sailboarding, swimming, canoeing, fishing. Linley Animal Park, Corowa Rd; native and exotic animals, horse and pony rides. Tunzafun Amusement Park, Melbourne St, mini-golf, mini-train, dodgem cars; open daily. Bowlers and golfers well catered for in area; excellent facilities, licensed clubs. Cruises on Lake Mulwala. **Tourist information:** Irvine Pde, Yarrawonga; (057) 44 1989. **Accommodation:** 2 hotels, 10 motels, 6 cara./camp. parks.
MAP REF. 127 N13, 233 K3

Murrurundi   Pop. 983
This picturesque town on the New England Hwy, set in a lush valley on the Pages River, is overshadowed by the Liverpool Ranges. **Of interest:** St Joseph's Catholic Church, Polding St, contains 1000 pieces of Italian marble. Murrurundi Museum, Main St. Paradise Park, Paradise Rd, horseshoe-shaped, surrounded by mountains, visits by wildlife in evening. April: Sheepdog Trials. Oct.: Bushman's Carnival. **In the area:** Chilcott's Creek, 15 km N, where huge diprotodon remains, now in Sydney Museum, were found. Burning Mountain at Wingen, 20 km S, deep coal seam that has been smouldering at least 1000 years. Timor Limestone Caves, 43 km E. Horse studs. **Tourist information:** Council Offices, 47 Mayne St; (065) 46 6205. **Accommodation:** 3 hotels, 2 motels, 1 cara./camp. park.
MAP REF. 120 I1, 122 I12

Murwillumbah   Pop. 8003
Situated on the banks of the Tweed River, 31 km S of the Qld border in the beautiful Tweed Valley, Murwillumbah's local industries include cattle-raising and the growing of sugarcane, tropical fruits, tea and coffee. **Of interest:** Tweed River Regional Art Gallery, Tumbulgum Rd. Aug.: Banana Festival. **In the area:** Tweed River houseboat hire, on Pacific Hwy, 1 km N of Tourist Information. Condong sugar mill, 5 km N; open July–Dec. Avocado Adventureland, 15 km N. Hare Krishna Community Farm, Eungella, 10 km W, visitors welcome. Pioneer Plantation, 25 km SE, banana plantation, farm animals, native gardens, tours; open daily. World Heritage-listed areas within radius of 50 km incl. Mt Warning, Nightcap and Border Ranges National Parks. Treetops Environment Centre, 8 km NE. Madura Tea Estates, 12 km NE. **Tourist information:** Cnr Pacific Hwy and Alma St; (066) 72 1340. **Accommodation:** 6 hotels, 4 motels, 2 cara./camp. parks.
MAP REF. 123 P1, 475 N8

Muswellbrook   Pop. 10 140
In the Upper Hunter Valley, Muswellbrook is the centre of pastoral enterprises, including fodder crops, stud cattle and horses, wineries and dairy products. There is also a large open-cut coal-mining industry. **Of interest:** Muswellbrook Art Gallery in old town hall. Historical town walk. April: Agricultural Show. **In the area:** Wollemi National Park, 30 km SW, major Aboriginal carvings and paintings. Bayswater Power Station, 16 km S; tours. Seven local wineries open daily. **Tourist information:** Old Teahouse and Gift Shoppe, 208 Bridge St; (065) 43 3599. **Accommodation:** 3 hotel/motels, 8 motels, 1 cara./camp. park.
MAP REF. 121 J3, 122 I13

Nambucca Heads   Pop. 5683
At the mouth of the Nambucca River, 552 km N of Sydney, this beautifully sited town is ideal for boating, fishing and swimming. **Of interest:** Nambucca Historical Museum, Headland Reserve,

Mystery Bay, Narooma

many old photographs. Model Train Museum, Pelican Cres. April: River Show. Oct.: Show'n'Shine Hot Rod Exhibition. **In the area:** Breathtaking views from several local lookouts. Bakers Creek Station, 40 km SW, horseriding, fishing, canoes, rainforest walks, picnic/barbecue facilities, cabins. **Tourist information:** Ridge St; (065) 68 6954. **Accommodation:** 1 hotel, 9 motels, 6 cara./camp. parks.
MAP REF. 123 O8, 475 N13

Narooma Pop. 3443
This popular fishing resort situated at the mouth of the Wagonga River on the Princes Hwy, 360 km S of Sydney, is well known for its rock oysters. **Of interest:** Excellent golf course on scenic cliff top. Mystery Bay near Lake Corunna, haunt of lapidary collectors, coloured sands, strange rock formations. Other inlets and lakes north and south of town. Cruises on Wagonga Princess. Easter: Tilba Festival. **In the area:** Lake Tuross 34 km N, and other nearby lakes and inlets. Central Tilba, a heritage area, 17 km SW, just off Princes Hwy, classified as 'unusual mountain village' by National Trust; founded in 1894; old buildings in original 19th-century condition, new buildings to National Trust specifications. Montague Island, wildlife sanctuary 5.7 nautical miles offshore; large colony of little

(fairy) penguins and Australian fur seals, year-round tours, bookings necessary. **Tourist information:** Narooma Visitor Centre, Princes Hwy; (044) 76 2881. **Accommodation:** 1 hotel, 13 motels, 4 cara./camp. parks. **See also:** The South Coast.
MAP REF. 117 I2, 119 G8, 141 N11, 235 Q3

Narrabri Pop. 6694
Situated between the Nandewar Range, including Mt Kaputar National Park and the extensive Pilliga scrub country, Narrabri is a phenomenally successful cotton-producing centre. **Of interest:** Historic buildings incl. courthouse (1886), Maitland St. Self-guide town tour. Riverside picnic area, Tibbereena St. April: Agricultural Show. Oct.: Spring Festival. **In the area:** Tours of cotton fields and gins, April–June. Plant Breeding Institute, 9 km N, on Newell Hwy. CSIRO Telescope Complex, 25 km W, 6 giant radio telescopes, Visitors Centre; open daily. Yarrie Lake, 32 km W. Pilliga State Forest, 23 km SW. Mt Kaputar National Park, 53 km E; 360° views from peak take in one-tenth of NSW; dramatic volcanic blue mountain country. Sawn Rocks, 35 km NE, within park (via Bingara Rd), spectacular basaltic formation. **Tourist information:** Newell Hwy; (067) 92 3583. **Accommodation:** 6 hotels, 2 hotel/motels, 8

motels, 4 cara./camp. parks. **See also:** National Parks; The Newell.
MAP REF. 122 G7, 474 H12

Narrandera Pop. 4649
This historic town on the Murrumbidgee River, at the junction of the Newell and Sturt Hwys, has been declared an urban conservation area with buildings classified or listed by the National Trust. Located 580 km SW of Sydney, it is the gateway to the Murrumbidgee Irrigation Area. **Of interest:** Lake Talbot Aquatic Playground, cara./camp. complex; 100-m water-slide, 3 pools, ski area, fishing, bushwalking tracks, koala reserve. Antique Corner, Larmer St. NSW Forestry Tree Nursery, Broad St. Tiger Moth Memorial, Narrandera Park, Newell Hwy. Parkside Cottage Museum, Narrandera Park and Miniature Zoo, Newell Hwy. Aug.: Camellia Show. **In the area:** Inland Fisheries Research Station (with murray cod) and John Lake Centre, 6 km SE. Berembed Weir, 40 km SE. Pine Hill Nursery, 5 km NE. Alabama Ostrich Farm, 30 km N; group tours by appt. Sheep Dairy, 5 km NW; milking-time tours. Craig Top Deer Farm, 6 km NW; tours daily. Citrus Orchard, 6 km NW, group bookings. Robertson Gladioli Farm, 8 km W; group tours by appt. **Tourist information:** Narrandera Park, Newell Hwy; (069) 59 1766. **Accommodation:** 5 hotels, 10 motels, 1 B&B, 1

hostel, 2 cara./camp. parks. **See also:** The Newell; Vineyards and Wineries. MAP REF. 127 O9

Narromine   Pop. 3378

On the Macquarie River, 457 km NW of Sydney, this town is well-known for quality agricultural products, including citrus fruit, tomatoes, corn, sheep, cattle and cotton. Oct.: Festival of Sport. **In the area:** Water-slide and Rural Museum, Mitchell Hwy. Gin Gin Weir. Gliding and ultralight flying at airport. Trangie Agricultural and Yates Research Stations. Narromine Transplants, 2 km N, seedlings grown; open by appt. Swane's Rose Production Nursery, 5 km W. **Tourist information:** Council Chambers, 124 Dandaloo St; (068) 89 1322. **Accommodation:** 4 hotels, 3 motels, 3 cara./camp. parks. MAP REF. 120 C3, 122 C13

Nelson Bay   Pop. 6766

The beautiful bay on which this town is sited is the main anchorage of Port Stephens, about 60 km N of Newcastle. **Of interest:** Restored Inner Lighthouse, Nelson Head. Self-guide heritage walk, from Dutchmans Bay to Little Beach. Native Flora Reserve at Little Beach. Cruises: Dolphin Watch; on harbour; on Myall River. Boat hire. Feb.: Festival of Port Stephens. **In the area:** Gan Gan Lookout, 2 km SW on Nelson Bay Rd. Toboggan Hill Park at Salamander Bay, 5 km SW, toboggan runs, mini-golf course, fun shed. Port Stephens Wines, on Nelson Rd, 10 km SW. Oakvale Farm and Fauna World, 16 km SW on Nelson Bay Rd at Salt Ash. Fighter World, displays of modern and historic aircraft, at RAAF base, Williamtown, 35 km SW. Tomaree National Park, along coastline from Shoal Bay, 3 km NE, to Anna Bay, 10 km SW. Convict-built Tanilba House (1831), 37 km W. **Tourist information:** Port Stephens Visitors Centre, Victoria Pde, Nelson Bay; (049) 81 1579. **Accommodation:** 12 motels, 1 cara./camp. park. **See also:** Port Stephens. MAP REF. 112 H2, 121 M4

Newcastle   Pop. 262 331

Australia's largest industrial city is encircled by some of the finest surfing beaches in the world. Overlooking a huge, spectacular harbour, Newcastle, just 158 km N of Sydney, was always uniquely positioned to claim the image of an aquatic playground. Rebuilding in some areas has followed the 1989 earthquake. Newcastle is experiencing a boom in tourism as visitors are attracted to the wineries and vineyards and picturesque villages of the surrounding Hunter Valley region. **Of interest:** Queens Wharf, centrepoint of foreshore redevelopment, indoor and outdoor restaurants; 'boutique' brewery, brewing range of specialty beers; observation tower; linked by walkway to City Mall, part of Hunter St. Scenic walks along foreshore. Sydney-style terrace houses along nearby city streets. City parks and gardens. Art gallery, King St. Maritime and military museums, Fort Scratchley, Nobbys Rd. City Hall, Laman St. Many fine surf beaches. River and harbour cruises. March: Surfest. Aug.: Jazz Festival. **In the area:** Shortland Wetlands, 15 km W, bird habitat, other wildlife, canoe trail. Lake Macquarie, 20 km S, huge aquatic playground with well-maintained parks lining foreshore; picnic/barbecue facilities. Fighter Aviation Museum and high-tech exhibition at Williamtown RAAF base, 20 km N. About 50 km NW is Australia's famous wine region, the Hunter Valley. Yuelarbah Track, part of Great North Walk from Sydney to Newcastle, covers 25 km from Lake Macquarie to Newcastle harbour. **Tourist information:** 92 Scott St; (049) 29 9299. **Accommodation:** 27 hotels, 30 motels, 13 cara./camp. parks. MAP REF. 110, 112 G8, 121 L5

Nimbin   Pop. 274

The Aquarius Softlicks festival in 1973 established Nimbin as the alternative culture capital of Australia. Today Nimbin's peaceful, friendly atmosphere, and the buildings designed and decorated to reflect the community's ideas and beliefs, attract visitors wishing to experience an alternative lifestyle. **Of interest:** In Cullen St: shops painted in psychedelic colours, feature home-made products, local art and craft. Dancing Dervish Restaurant, 'food from the fourth dimension'. Original Rainbow Cafe, fresh local organic produce. Nimbin Museum, dedicated to hippy culture and history of St Aquarius. Town Hall, mural featuring Aboriginal art. Rainbow Power Company, Alternative Way, alternative power supplier, now exporting; tours. Nimbin Country Market, Showgrounds, 4th Sun. of month; outlet for local craftspeople. Sept.–Oct.: Spring Arts Festival. **In the area:** Spectacular volcanic Nimbin Rocks, 3 km S, on Lismore Rd. Nimbin Rocks Gallery nearby; high-quality art in all mediums. Channon Craft Market, 15 km SE, 2nd Sun. of month at Coronation Park. World Heritage-listed Nightcap National Park, 10 km NE, walking track (1.4 km through rainforest) to Protestors Falls. Calurla Tea Gardens, 10 km N, on Lillian Rock Rd, spectacular views, farmhouse cooking, live music. **Tourist information:** Lismore Visitor Information Centre, cnr Ballina and Molesworth Sts; (066) 22 0122. **Accommodation:** 1 cara./camp. park, 1 hostel. MAP REF. 123 P2, 475 N8

Nowra–Bomaderry

Pop. 21 942

Rapidly becoming a popular tourist centre, Nowra is the principal town of the Shoalhaven district. Bomaderry is directly opposite on the northern side of the river. **Of interest:** Meroogal (1885), cnr Worrigee and West Sts; Historic Houses Trust property; open to public. Shoalhaven Historical Museum, cnr Plunkett and Kinghorn Sts, in old police station. Fishing, water-skiing, canoeing and sailing on Shoalhaven River. Hanging Rock, via Junction St, fine views. Nowra Animal Park, Rockhill Rd, native fauna and peacocks, in rainforest setting. Oct.: Spring Festival. **In the area:** Australian Naval Aviation Museum, South Nowra. Cambewarra Lookout, 12 km NW. Kangaroo Valley, 23 km NW; old buildings, incl. Friendly Inn (National Trust-classified) and Pioneer Farm Museum, reconstruction of dairy farm of 1880s. Fitzroy Falls in Morton National Park, 38 km NW. Camping, cabin/bunkhouse accommodation at Coolendel, 30 km W near Albatross, picnic/barbecue facilities, free-ranging wildlife, canoeing and bushwalks. Many beautiful beaches within 30 km radius of town. **Tourist information:** Shoalhaven Tourist Centre, 254 Princes Hwy, Bomaderry; (044) 21 0778. **Accommodation:** Nowra: 9 motels, 5 cara./camp. parks. Bomaderry: 1 hotel, 4 motels, 1 cara./camp. park. **See also:** The Illawarra Coast. MAP REF. 116 E12, 119 H4, 120 I11

Nundle   Pop. 261

The history of this small town began in the early gold-rush era during the 1850s. Well known for its fishing, Nundle is

situated 60 km SE of Tamworth, at the foot of the Great Dividing Range, in a district that produces sheep, cattle, wheat and timber. **Of interest:** Courthouse, antique shop, old bakery store, historic Peel Inn (1860s), all in Jenkins St. Goldmining display in restored coffin factory, Gill St. Aug.–Sept., Dec.: Camp Drafting and Dog Trials. **In the area:** Hanging Rock and Sheba Dams, 11 km E, picnic, camping. Chaffey Dam, 11 km N. Fossicking at Hanging Rock, gold panning on Peel River. **Tourist information:** Cnr New England Hwy and Kable Ave, Tamworth; (067) 68 4462. **Accommodation:** 1 hotel, 1 motel, 1 cara./camp. park.
MAP REF. 123 J11

Nyngan
Pop. 2311
The centre of a wool-growing district on the Bogan River, 603 km NW of Sydney. **Of interest:** Historic buildings, especially in Cobar and Bogan Sts. April: Anzac Day Race Meeting. May: Agricultural Show. **In the area:** Cairn marking geographic centre of NSW, 65 km S. Grave of Richard Cunningham, botanist with Major Mitchell's party, speared by Aborigines in 1835, on private property, 70 km S. Bird sanctuary in Macquarie Marshes, 64 km N. **Tourist information:** Burns Video, Pangee St; (068) 32 1155. **Accommodation:** 3 hotels, 2 hotel/motels, 3 motels, 2 cara./camp. parks.
MAP REF. 125 Q11

Orange
Pop. 29 635
A prosperous city set in rich red volcanic soil and famous for its apples, parks and gardens, Orange is 264 km NW of Sydney on the slopes of Mt Canobolas. An obelisk marks the birthplace of the city's most famous citizen, poet A. B. (Banjo) Paterson; his birthday is celebrated with the Banjo Paterson Festival, Feb.–March. **Of interest:** Historic Cook Park, Summer St, begonia conservatory (flowers Feb.–May), duck ponds, fernery, picnic area. Museum, McNamara St. Orange Civic Centre, Byng St, comprises a theatre, Regional Art Gallery, City Library, Visitors Centre and exhibition rooms. **In the area:** Campbell's Corner, 8 km S on Pinnacle Rd, roadside picnic/barbecue spot. Apple Stop Antiques, Lucknow Village, 10 km SE. Golden Memories Museum, Millthorpe, 22 km SE, over 5000 exhibits, incl. grandma's kitchen, blacksmith's shop, art and craft

centre. Gallery of Minerals, 1 km E, mineral and fossil collection. Agriculture Research Centre, 5 km N, field days held Nov. Ophir goldfields, 27 km N, site of first discovery of payable gold in Australia in 1851, fossicking centre, picnic area, walking trails to historic gold tunnels, tours of working goldmine and Ophir Reserve. Lake Canobolas Park, 8 km SW via Cargo Rd, recreation and camping area, deer park, children's playground, picnic/barbecue facilities; also trout-fishing. Mt Canobolas Park, 1500-ha bird and animal sanctuary, 14 km SW. Wineries: 3 km NW, Molong Rd; 12 and 15 km W Cargo Rd; 3 km E, Bathurst Rd. **Tourist information:** Civic Gardens, Byng St; (063) 61 5226. **Accommodation:** 9 hotels, 9 motels, 7 B&B, 2 cara./camp. parks.
MAP REF. 120 E6

Parkes
Pop. 8784
Situated 364 km NW of Sydney on the Newell Hwy, Parkes is the commercial and industrial centre of an important agricultural area. **Of interest:** Motor Museum cnr Bogan and Dalton Sts, vintage and veteran vehicles, local art and craft. Henry Parkes Museum, Clarinda St, memorabilia, library of 1000 volumes. Pioneer Park Museum, Pioneer

St, in historic school and church, displays of early farm machinery and transport. Kelly Reserve, on northern outskirts of town, picnics and barbecues in bush setting. Imposing views from Shrine of Remembrance at eastern end of Bushman St. March: Marbles Tournament at Parkes Golf Club. **In the area:** Mugincoble Wheat Sub-terminal, 8 km SE. CSIRO Radio Telescope Visitors Centre, 23 km N; educational aids explain use of giant saucer-shaped telescope. Peak Hill, 48 km N, open-cut goldmine, camel park, accommodation. **Tourist information:** Kelly Reserve, Newell Hwy; (068) 62 4365. **Accommodation:** 8 hotels, 11 motels, 4 cara./camp. parks. **See also:** The Newell.
MAP REF. 120 C6

Picton
Pop. 2116
Picton, named after Sir Thomas Picton, hero of Waterloo, is 80 km SW of Sydney on Remembrance Drive (former Hume Hwy). The old buildings and quiet hills of this small town seem to echo the past. **Of interest:** Historic buildings incl.: old railway viaduct (1862) over Stone quarry Creek, seen from Showgrounds, off Menangle St; St Mark's Church (1848), Menangle St; George IV Inn, which incorporates Scharer's Little Brewery,

Hampden Bridge, Kangaroo Valley, near Nowra

Caves and Caverns

Magical underground limestone caves are one of the wonders of New South Wales. Glittering limestone stalactites and stalagmites, caused by the ceaseless dripping of limestone-impregnated water over tens of thousands of years, glow eerily in cathedral-like caves. These delicate formations of ribbed columns, frozen cascades, 'tapestries' and 'shawls' look like part of a subterranean fairyland.

The most famous are the **Jenolan Caves.** Since being opened in 1866, several million people have visited them. Situated on a spur of the Great Dividing Range, a few kilometres to the south-west of the Blue Mountains, they are open daily for guided tours. The caves are surrounded by a 2430-hectare flora and fauna reserve with walking trails, kiosk, cafe and picnic/barbecue facilities. Accommodation includes the charming Tudor-style guest house, Jenolan Caves House; and Binda Bush Cabins, 8 kilometres from the caves precinct, on the road into the reserve.

The **Wombeyan Caves** are set in a pleasant valley in the Southern Highlands, 193 kilometres south-west of Sydney. They can be reached from the Wombeyan turn-off, 60 kilometres north-west of Mittagong. From here a well-surfaced but narrow road winds through spectacular mountain scenery. The alternative route (recommended for caravanners) is via Goulburn, Taralga and Richlands. Five of the caves are easily accessible by graded paths. They are fully developed for visitors, with steps and handrails, and are open daily or on demand for self-guide, historical and adventure caving tours. There is a Visitors Centre and facilities exist for camping and family or group accommodation. Three walking tracks lead from the reserve to attractions in the area.

The **Yarrangobilly Caves**, 6.5 kilometres off the Snowy Mountains Highway, 109 kilometres north of Cooma, are open daily (subject to winter road conditions) for self-guide or guided tours. On weekends, school and public holidays, additional tours are available, subject to demand. Among some 250 caves in the area only 5 have been developed and are open for inspection (one with wheelchair access). An added attraction here is a thermal pool. Originally a mineral spring, the pool is heated to a constant temperature of 27°C all the year round, and the water is slightly mineralised. Tours include the Adventure Cave Walk during school holidays. The caves are part of Kosciusko National Park and are surrounded by some of the most beautiful unspoiled country in the State. But bring your own food and drink; there is no kiosk in the area.

For further information, contact Jenolan Caves Reserve Trust; (063) 59 3311; Wombeyan Caves; (048) 43 5976; and Yarrangobilly Caves; (064) 54 9597. **See also**: Individual town entries in A–Z listing.

Jenolan Caves House

Argyle St. March: Thirlmere Festival of Steam. **In the area:** Sydney Skydiving Centre, 5 km E. Jarvisfield (1865), 2 km N, on Remembrance Dr, family home of pioneer landholders, now clubhouse of Antill Park Golf Club. Woolaway Woolshed, 3 km N on Remembrance Dr, bush dances nightly, special fixtures. Wollondilly Heritage Centre and slab-built St Matthew's Church (1838) at The Oaks, 21 km N. Burragorang Lookout, 15 km NW of The Oaks. Thirlmere Lakes National Park, 8 km SW. Railway Museum, Thirlmere, 5 km S. Wirrimbirra Sanctuary, 13 km S, National Trust sanctuary; native flora and fauna; overnight cabins. **Tourist information:** Macarthur Country Tourist Assocn, Oxley Cottage, Camden Valley Way, Elderslie; (046) 58 1370. **Accommodation:** 2 hotels, 1 motel, 1 B&B, 1 caravan park. MAP REF. 104 I12, 116 E3, 119 H2, 120 I9

Pitt Town   Pop. 632
One of the 5 Macquarie Towns, Pitt Town was named after William Pitt the elder, and marked out on a site to the east of the present village in January 1811. The surrounding rich alluvial river flats provided early Sydney with almost 50% of its food supply, which was transported by boat down the Hawkesbury River and around to Sydney Town. A 20th-century town centre did not develop at Pitt Town and so it is more modest in architectural style than Windsor. July: Fun Run. **Of interest:** Curious reminder of importance of river, at end of Bathurst St, overlooking Pitt Town Bottoms. Old Manse, belonging to oldest Presbyterian (now Uniting) Church in Australia, 8 km N at Ebenezer. **Tourist information:** Ham Common Bicentenary Park, Richmond Rd, Clarendon; (045) 88 5895. **Accommodation:** None. **See also:** The Hawkesbury. MAP REF. 105 K6

Port Macquarie   Pop. 26 798
Founded as a convict settlement in 1821, and one of the oldest towns in the State, Port Macquarie (known locally as 'Port') is now a major holiday resort, situated at the mouth of the Hastings River, 423 km N of Sydney. **Of interest:** Award-winning Hastings Historical Museum, Clarence St, in 15 rooms of commercial building, built 1835–40; convict and pioneer relics. St Thomas's (1824), Church St, convict-built church designed by convict architect Thomas

Owen. Historic cemetery, Horton St, graves dating from 1842. Roto House and Macquarie Nature Reserve, Lord St, koala hospital and study centre. Port Macquarie Observatory, William St. Fantasy Glades, Pacific Dr, rainforest gardens, picnic/barbecue facilities. Billabong Koala Park and Kingfisher Park; close-up look at Australian animals. World of Models, Clarence St. Town Beach; surf at one end, sheltered coves at other. Kooloonbung Creek Nature Reserve, 50 ha of natural bushland, walking trails. Peppermint Park, slides, roller-skating. River cruises daily. Orchid World, Ocean Dr., Australian and exotic plants, camel rides, safaris. Old World Timber Art, Hastings River Dr. **In the area:** Exceptionally good fishing and all water sports. Charter fishing, incl. reef fishing. Shelly Beach Resort, 3 km SE on Pacific Dr. Cassegrain Winery, 12 km W. Harley Davidson motor bike tours, horseriding, abseiling. Big Bull, Redbank Rd, 20 km W via Wauchope, animal nursery, farm tour, hay rides. Sea Acres Rainforest Centre, Pacific Drive, 5 km S, 30 ha of rainforest, multi-level boardwalk allows viewing of flora and fauna. **Tourist information:** Port Macquarie Visitors Services, cnr Clarence and Hay Sts; (065) 83 1293. **Accommodation:** 1 hotel/motel, 53 motels, 21 cara./camp. parks. MAP REF. 109 G7, 123 O11

Queanbeyan   Pop. 19 383
Adjoining Canberra, Queanbeyan has a special relationship with the Australian capital. The town, proclaimed in 1838, is named from a squattage held by an ex-convict innkeeper, Timothy Beard, on the Molonglo River and called 'Quinbean' ('clear waters'). **Of interest:** Queanbeyan History Museum, Farrer Pl. Byrne's Mill (1883) and restuarant, Collett St. Mill House Gallery, cnr Collett and Morrisset Sts. Design Plus Gallery, Monaro St, pottery, silk, leatherwork. Art Centre, Trinculo Pl. Michelago Steam Train rides; first Sun. in month and special trips. Nov.: Community Celebrations, Agricultural Show. **In the area:** At Bungendore, 26 km NE, historic village square and exhibition depicting story of Jacky Jacky, Aboriginal bushranger; wood-turning, antiques, herbal farm. Bywong Mining Town, 31 km NE. Rehwinkel's Animal Farm, Mac's Reef Rd, off Federal Hwy, 23 km N. **Tourist information:** Cnr

Farrer Place and Lowe St; (06) 298 0241. **Accommodation:** 4 hotels, 18 motels, 2 cara./camp. parks. MAP REF. 119 E6, 120 F13, 137 G4, 140 H3

Quirindi   Pop. 2830
Appropriately named after an Aboriginal word meaning 'nest in the hills', this town in the Liverpool Ranges was proclaimed in 1856. One of the first towns in Australia to organise the game of polo. **Of interest:** Historical Cottage and Museum, Station St. New Year's Day: Wallabadah Cup Meeting. Aug.: Polo Carnival. **In the area:** Who'd-A-Thought-It Lookout, 2 km NE. **Tourist information:** Sports Centre, 248 George St; (067) 46 2128. **Accommodation:** 5 hotels, 2 motels, 1 cara./camp. park. MAP REF. 120 I1, 122 I11

Raymond Terrace   Pop. 11 159
An important wool-shipping centre in the 1840s, several historic buildings remain in this town, set on the banks of the Hunter and William Rivers. **Of interest:** Self-guide Heritage Town Walk takes in significant buildings, incl. courthouse (1838), still in use; Church of England and rectory, built of hand-hewn sandstone in 1830s; and numerous buildings in historic King St, along waterfront. Sketchley Cottage, once sited at Seaham, 8 km N; museum of memorabilia. Oct.: Twin Rivers Festival; water-skiing and motorboat racing. **In the area:** Hunter Region Botanic Gardens, on Pacific Hwy at Motto Farm, 2 km S. Fighter World, RAAF Base Williamtown, 16 km E. **Tourist information:** Council Chambers, 116 Pacific Hwy; (049) 83 1333. **Accommodation:** 5 motels, 2 cara./camp. parks. MAP REF. 112 E6, 121 L4

Richmond   Pop. 18 766
One of the 5 Macquarie towns and sister town to Windsor, 5 km E, Richmond was proclaimed a town in 1810. **Of interest:** Hobartville, Castlereagh Rd. Toxana (1841), Windsor St. St Peter's Church (1841), Windsor St; graveyard where notable pioneers, including William Cox and Australia's convict chronicler Margaret Catchpole, are buried. March: RAAF Open Day. Sept.: Hawkesbury District Orchid Spring Show. **In the area:** RAAF base, 3 km E on Windsor–Richmond Rd, oldest Air Force

establishment in Australia; used for civilian flying from 1915. University of Western Sydney, 3 km S, foundation stone laid in 1895. **Tourist information:** Ham Common Bicentenary Park, Richmond Rd, Clarendon; (045) 88 5895. **Accommodation:** 1 hotel, 1 hotel/motel, 2 motels. **See also:** The Hawkesbury. MAP REF. 105 J6, 120 I7

Robertson   Pop. 252

The link between the Southern Highlands and the coast, Robertson sits at the top of the Macquarie Pass and vantage points offer spectacular views of the coast. It is the centre of the largest potato-growing district in NSW. March: Agricultural Show. Nov.: Rodeo. **In the area:** Fitzroy and Belmore Falls, Morton National Park, 10 km SW, Carrington Falls, Budderoo National Park, 10 km SE. **Tourist information:** Southern Highlands Visitor Information Centre, Winifred West Park, Old Hume Hwy, Mittagong; (048) 71 2888. **Accommodation:** 1 hotel, 1 motel. MAP REF. 116 D8, 119 H3, 120 I10

Rylstone–Kandos   Pop. 721

Aboriginal hand-paintings on a sandstone rock overhang are a feature of the region, which is west of the Great Dividing Range on the Cudgegong River, north-east of Bathurst. **Of interest:** Many historic buildings in Rylstone, especially in Lovee St incl. The Bridge Restaurant (formerly bank), and operating post office. Industrial Museum at Kandos. **In the area:** Fern Tree Gully, 16 km N, tree ferns in subtropical forest. Cudgegong Waters Park, on Lake Windemere, 19 km W, camping, picnic/barbecue facilities. Glen Davis, 56 km SE on Capertee River, surrounded by sheer cliff faces. Many camping spots and fishing areas on Capertee, Cudgegong and Turon rivers. **Tourist information:** Shire Council, Lovee St, Rylstone; (063) 79 1205. **Accommodation:** 4 hotels, 1 motel, 1 cara./camp. park. MAP REF. 120 G5

Sawtell   Pop. 10 809

This peaceful family holiday resort, 8 km S of Coffs Harbour, has safe beaches and tidal creeks for fishing, swimming and surfing. Playground and picnic/barbecue facilities at Boambee Creek Reserve, Sawtell Rd. Enchanting walks and drives in the surrounding bush and mountains, including Sawtell Reserve. **In the area:**

White-water rafting on Nymboida, Gwydir and Murray Rivers. **Tourist information:** Coffs Harbour Visitors and Convention Centre, cnr Ross Ave and Marcia St, Coffs Harbour; (066) 52 8824. **Accommodation:** 2 hotels, 2 motels, 1 cara./camp. park. MAP REF. 123 O7, 475 N12

Scone   Pop. 3329

This pleasant town set in beautiful country on the New England Hwy, 280 km N of Sydney, is the second largest thoroughbred and horse-breeding centre in the world. **Of interest:** Historical Society Museum, Kingdon St. Hungry Horse Gallery and Restaurant, part of well-equipped tourist information centre opp. Elizabeth Park, near mare and foal sculpture. May: Horse Week Festival. **In the area:** Lake Glenbawn, 15 km E, water sports, picnic/barbecue facilities. Hunter Valley Museum of Rural Life, 2 km W of dam. Barrington Tops National Park, 80 km E, scenic drives, walks. Burning Mountain at Wingen, 20 km N, deep coal seam that has been smouldering at least 1000 years. **Tourist information:** Cnr Susan and Kelly Sts; (065) 45 1526. **Accommodation:** 1 hotel, 5 motels, 5 B&B, 1 hostel, 1 cara./camp. park. MAP REF. 121 J2, 122 I13

Shellharbour   Pop. 1754

This attractive holiday resort 7 km S of Lake Illawarra is one of the oldest settlements on the south coast. A thriving port in the 1830s, its importance declined once the south coast railway opened. April: Sunshine Festival. **In the area:** Blackbutt Forest Reserve and Killalea Recreation Park. Bass Point Headland and Marine Reserve, 3 km S, picnic area with views. Scuba diving and snorkelling at Bass Point. Lake Illawarra, 7 km N; boat hire. Fine beaches for fishing, surfing and boating on Windang Peninsula, 10 km N. Jamberoo Valley and Minnamurra Rainforest Centre, 20 km SW. Bike paths and bike hire. BMX circuit at Croom Regional Sporting Complex. **Tourist information:** Addeson St, Wollongong; (042) 21 6038. **Accommodation:** 4 hotels, 1 motel, 3 cara./camp. parks. **See also:** The Illawarra Coast. MAP REF. 116 G8, 120 I3, 121 J10

Singleton   Pop. 11 861

Set beside the Hunter River in rich grazing land, Singleton is the geographical

heart of the Hunter Valley. New wealth in the form of huge open-cut coal mines has joined the traditional rural industry and transformed Singleton into one of the most progressive country centres in the State. **Of interest:** Built as Bicentennial project, monolithic sundial, largest in southern hemisphere; on riverbank, in James Cook Park. Gardens of historic home, Townhead; sales of herbs. Sept.: Broke Village Fair. Oct.: Romance of the Rose Festival. **In the area:** Wollemi National Park, 15 km SW, and Yengo National Park, 15 km S; extensive Aboriginal carvings and paintings. Lake St Clair, 30 km N, magnificent views of Mt Royal Range; extensive recreational and waterway facilities, incl. camping. On New England Hwy between Singleton and Muswellbrook, 26 km NW, Bayswater Power Station, biggest thermal power station in southern hemisphere. Town is home of Singleton Army Camp, whose Royal Australian Infantry Corps Museum of Small Arms, 5 km S, traces development of firearms from 15th century. Singleton is centre for visits to Broke winery area of upper and lower Hunter Valley; 56 vineyards. **Tourist information:** Shire Offices; (065) 72 1866. **Accommodation:** 6 hotels, 2 hotel/motels, 5 motels, 2 cara./camp. parks. MAP REF. 121 J4, 346 C7

Stroud   Pop. 556

There are many historic buildings in this small country town, 75 km N of Newcastle. The convict-built Anglican Church of St John, built in 1833 of local clay bricks, with beautiful stained glass windows and cedar furnishings is one of the finest buildings. Sept.–Oct.: Rodeo. **Of interest:** Rectory of St John's (1836), Stroud House (1832), Parish House (1837), courthouse, post office and Quambi House. Underground silo (one of 8 built in 1841) at Silo Hill Reserve. Self-guide Heritage Tour. **Tourist information:** Great Lakes Tourist Board, Little St, Forster; (065) 54 8799. **Accommodation:** 1 hotel, 1 hostel, 1 camping reserve. MAP REF. 121 L3

Tamworth   Pop. 31 716

This prosperous city at the junction of the New England and Oxley Hwys is the country music capital of Australia, as well as being the heart of many other cultural and musical activities. Thousands of fans flock here for the 10-day Australasia

Bridge over Manning River, Taree

Country Music Festival, held each Jan. since 1973. Tamworth, with its attractive public buildings and parks and gardens, is also the commercial capital of northern NSW. **Of interest:** Country Music Hands of Fame cornerstone at Hands of Fame Park, Kable Ave, has hand imprints of country music stars, including Tex Morton, Slim Dusty and Smoky Dawson. Country music Roll of Renown at Radio Centre, Calala, dedicated to country music artists who have contributed to Australia's heritage. Calala Cottage, Denison St, home of Tamworth's first mayor, National Trust-classified, restored by Tamworth Historical Society. Tamworth City Gallery, Marius St, works by Turner, Hans Heysen and Will Ashton; home of National Fibre Collection. Weswal Gallery, Brisbane St. Tininburra Gallery, Moore Creek Rd. Country Collection, New England Hwy, fascinating gemstone collection, Gallery of Stars Wax Museum, Great Australian Icecreamery, famous Longyard Hotel. Oxley Park Wildlife Sanctuary, north off Brisbane St, bushwalks, picnic/barbecue facilities. Oxley Lookout, views of city and rich Peel Valley. Powerstation Museum traces Tamworth's history as first city in southern hemisphere to have electric street lighting. Sept.: Spring Cup (horseracing). **In the area:** Lake Keepit State Recreation Area, 57 km NW, water sports, visitor facilities. Historic goldmining township of Nundle nestled

in 'Hills of Gold', a 63-km scenic drive SE. Chaffey Dam, 45 km SE, sailing, Dulegal Arboretum on foreshore. Warrabah National Park, 75 km N. **Tourist information:** Cnr Murray and Peel Sts; (067) 68 9422. **Accommodation:** 7 hotels, 2 hotel/motels, 29 motels, 4 cara./camp. parks.
MAP REF. 123 J10

Taree   Pop. 16 303
Taree serves as the manufacturing and commercial centre of the Manning River district, on the Pacific Hwy, 320 km N of Sydney. **Of interest:** Manning River cruises. Houseboats. The Big Oyster. April–May: Taree and District Eisteddfod. **In the area:** Easy car access to top of Ellenborough Falls (160-m drop) on Bulga Plateau, 50 km NW. Taree–Forster Grass Ski Park, Tuncurry Rd, Rainbow Flat, 17.5 km S of Taree. Good surfing beaches on coast 16 km E. Forest drives and walking trails in Manning Valley. Manning River; 150 km navigable waterway, beaches, fishing and holiday spots. Crowdy Bay National Park, 40 km NE, wildflowers in spring, fishing, swimming, bushwalking. Coopernook Forest Drive, 28 km N; Big Nellie (large volcanic plug), 560 m above sea level. Railway Crossing Family Fun Park at Harrington, 30 km N. Middle Brother State Forest, 50 km N. **Tourist information:** Manning Valley Tourist Information Centre, Pacific Hwy, Taree

North; (065) 52 1900 or 1800 80 1522. **Accommodation:** 6 hotels, 21 motels, 3 cara./camp. parks.
MAP REF. 109 C13, 121 N2, 123 N12

Tathra   Pop. 1571
Tathra is a relaxed seaside town, centrally located on the south coast of NSW, 18 km SE of Bega and midway between Merimbula and Bermagui. Tathra is an ideal place for a family holiday, with its patrolled 3-km long surf beach, safe swimming for small children at Mogareka Inlet (the sandy mouth of the Bega River), and good fishing spots. Diving and deep-sea fishing charters at Kianniny Bay. **Of interest:** Sea Wharf, National Trust-classified. Above wharf, Maritime Museum; memorabilia of visiting ships. May: Game-fishing competition. **In the area:** Fishing, water sports on Lake Wallagoot, 9.5 km S. Bournda State Recreation Area, 11 km S of town; camping and bushwalking. Mimosa Rocks National Park, 17 km N. **Tourist information:** Tathra Wharf; (064) 94 4062. **Accommodation:** 1 motel, 1 hotel/motel, 4 cara./camp. parks.
MAP REF. 117 G7, 119 G10, 235 P6

Temora   Pop. 4279
Commercial centre for the rich wheat district of the northern and western Riverina, which also produces oats, barley,

Historic wharf and Maritime Museum, Tathra

fat lambs, pigs and cattle. **Of interest:** Temora Rural Museum, working displays, rock and mineral collection, Wagga Road. Feb.: Golden Gift (foot race). **In the area:** Lake Centenary, 3 km N. Paragon Gold Mine at Gidginbung, 15 km N. **Tourist information:** Temora Community Centre, Hoskins St; (069) 78 0500. **Accommodation:** 2 hotels, 3 motels, 1 cara./camp. park.
MAP REF. 120 A10, 127 R8

Tenterfield Pop. 3310

Tenterfield, astride the Great Dividing Range at the northern end of the New England Highlands in northern NSW, offers a contrast of rugged mountains and serene rural landscapes. Autumn in Tenterfield (April) is spectacular. Primarily a sheep- and cattle-grazing area, other industries include orchards, logging and sawmilling, various farm crops and tourism. **Of interest:** Centenary Cottage (1871), Logan St, local history collection. Self-guide Logan St Historic Walk. Sir Henry Parkes Library and Museum in School of Arts (1876), Rouse St; relics relating to Sir Henry Parkes, who made his famous Federation speech there in 1889. Tenterfield Saddler (1860s), High St. Oct.: Federation Festival, Spring Wine Festival. Nov.: Gem Festival. **In the area:** Mt McKenzie Granite Drive,

30-km circular route incl. Ghost Gully. Silica mine at Torrington, 70 km SW. Bluff Rock, 10 km S on New England Hwy, unusual granite outcrop. Thunderbolt's Hideout, 11 km NE. Boonoo Boonoo Falls (210-m drop), within Boonoo Boonoo National Park, 32 km NE. Goldmine at Drake, 81 km NE. Bald Rock National Park, 35 km N; good views from summit of Bald Rock, largest granite monolith in Australia. **Tourist information:** 157 Rouse St; (067) 36 1082. **Accommodation:** 3 hotels, 2 hotel/motels, 6 motels, 3 caravan parks. **See also:** New England.
MAP REF. 123 L3, 475 L9

Terrigal–Wamberal

Pop. 7453
Excellent surfing is one of the main attractions of this popular holiday resort on the Central Coast. **In the area:** Bouddi National Park, 17 km S, bushwalking, camping, fishing, swimming. **Tourist information:** Rotary Park, Terrigal Dr, Terrigal; (043) 85 4430. **Accommodation:** 1 hotel, 5 motels, 1 hostel, 1 cara./camp. park.
MAP REF. 105 P5, 108 H5, 121 K7

The Entrance Pop. 37 831

Blessed with clear, clean beaches, this beautiful lakeside and ocean resort

between Sydney and Newcastle is the family holiday playground of these two cities. **Of interest:** Daily pelican feeding in the Amphitheatre, Memorial Park, 3.30 p.m. Concerts by the Sea, Jan. weekends. Jan.: Australia Day family concert and fireworks. Dec.: Tuggerah Lakes Mardi Gras Festival and fireworks. **In the area:** Fishing on lakes—Tuggerah, Budgewoi and Munmorah—and ocean beach. During summer months, prawning on lakes. Water sports, Lake Tuggerah. Lake cruises depart from The Entrance public wharf. **Tourist information:** Tuggerah Lakes Tourist Assocn, in Memorial Pk, Marine Pde; (043) 32 9282. **Accommodation:** 3 hotels, 10 motels, 12 caravan parks.
MAP REF. 105 P4, 108 H2, 121 K6

The Rock Pop. 809

This small town, 32 km SW of Wagga Wagga, is noted for its unusual scenery. Walking trails through a flora and fauna reserve lead to the summit of The Rock (about 365 m). One species, the groundsel plant, is believed to be unique to the area. **Of interest:** Fantasia Dolls, Olympic Way, hand-made porcelain dolls. **Tourist information:** Tourism Wagga Wagga, Tarcutta St, Wagga Wagga; (069)235402. **Accommodation:** 1 hotel/motel.
MAP REF. 127 Q11

Tibooburra Pop. 150

The name of this former gold town, 337 km N of Broken Hill, comes from an Aboriginal word meaning 'heaps of rocks'. The town is surrounded by granite outcrops and was previously known as The Granites. **Of interest:** Buildings of local stone, including courthouse (1888), Family Hotel (1888) and Tibooburra Hotel (1890). School of the Air buildings, Briscow St; tours during term time. June: Tibooburra Festival. Oct.: Gymkhana and rodeo, NSW Labour Day weekend. **In the area:** Self-guide Golden Gully Scenic Walk, 3 km N. Nearby goldfields. Sturt National Park, 20 km N, semi-desert area, noted for its wildlife and geological features. Cameron Corner, 140 km NW, where three States meet. Former gold township of Milparinka, 42 km S; restored courthouse, remains of old police station, bank, general store and post office, but Albert Hotel is town's only active concern. Further 11 km NW of Milparinka

are Mt Poole Homestead and Mt Poole, where cairn commemorates Charles Sturt's expedition (marooned there 1845). Pastoralists display at Mt Wood, 27 km E, within park. **Tourist information:** National Parks and Wildlife Service, Tibooburra; (080) 91 3308. **Accommodation:** 2 hotels, 1 motel/cara./ camp. park.
MAP REF. 124 D4, 484 I10

Tingha
Pop. 831

This small tin-mining town is 28 km SE of Inverell. **Of interest:** Campbells Honey Farm, Swimming Pool Rd. Nucoorilma Aboriginal Arts and Crafts. **In the area:** Smith's Mining and Natural History Museum at Green Valley Farm, 10 km S; Aboriginal artefacts, antiques, mineral and gemstone collection, cabin accommodation. Fossicking for gems. Water sports on Copeton Dam, 15 km W. **Tourist information:** New England Hwy, Guyra; (067) 79 1420. **Accommodation:** 1 hotel, 1 caravan park. **See also:** New England.
MAP REF. 123 J6, 475 J11

Tocumwal
Pop. 1587

This peaceful Murray River town on the Newell Hwy is ideal for boating, fishing and swimming. **Of interest:** Huge fibreglass codfish in town square represents Aboriginal legend about giant Murray cod that lived in nearby blowhole. Old Railway Store, Deniliquin St, scale models of Australian trains. Picnic area with lawns and sandy river beach, 200 m from town square. Easter: Craft Festival. New Year's Eve: Carnival. **In the area:** River Murray Heritage Centre, 3 km N. Nallama, 14 km W on Tuppal Rd, historic farm settlement, grave site, giant gum. Several golf courses. Ulupna Island flora and fauna reserve. Binghi Boomerang Factory at Barooga, 19 km E. Aerodrome, 5 km NE, largest RAAF base in Australia during World War II, now houses world-renowned Sportavia Soaring Centre; gliding joy flights and tuition packages. Flights and tuition at Ultralight Aviation, Tocumwal Aerodrome. The Rocks and Blowhole, 11 km NE on Rocks Rd, once stone quarry, now good picnic spot. **Tourist information:** Tocumwal River Foreshore; (058) 74 2131. **Accommodation:** 3 hotels, 1 hotel/motel, 10 motels, 6 cara./camp. parks. **See also:** The Newell.
MAP REF. 127 M12, 206 I2

Tooleybuc
Pop. 300

A quiet, tranquil, riverside town with a village atmosphere, Tooleybuc's social centre is its Sporting Club, Lockhart Rd. The town boasts a range of recreational facilities, incl. fishing, a 9-hole golf course, bowls, picnicking and riverside walks. **Of interest:** River Retreat craft shop, Lea St. **Tourist information:** 25 Murray St, Barham; (054) 53 3100. **Accommodation:** 1 hotel, 3 motels, 1 cara./ camp. park.
MAP REF. 126 H10, 231 M9

Toukley
Pop. 6520

Situated on the peninsula between Tuggerah and Budgewoi Lakes, this delightful coastal hamlet offers pollution-free beaches and breathtaking scenery. **Of interest:** Open-air markets, Sun., Shopping Centre carpark. Shark-free lakes provide venue for all water sports. During summer months prawning from lake foreshores. Sept.: Azalea Festival. Oct.: Cycle Classic. **In the area:** Rock pool at Cabbage Tree Bay, 5 km E. Norah Head Lighthouse, 5 km E; by appt, contact Tourist Information. Many bushwalking trails in magnificent Munmorah State Recreation Area, 10 km N, or Red Gum Forest in Wyrrabalong National Park, 4 km S. **Tourist information:** Tuggerah Lakes Tourist Assocn, Wallarah Point Park, Gorokan; (043) 92 4666. **Accommodation:** 1 hotel, 6 motels, 4 cara./ camp. parks.
MAP REF. 105 P3, 121 K6

Tumbarumba
Pop. 1548

A former goldmining town in the western foothills of the Snowy Mountains, 504 km SW of Sydney, Tumbarumba has much to offer the visitor who prefers to get off the beaten track. It is an ideal base for day trips to the Snowy Mountains. **Of interest:** Bicentennial Botanic Gardens, Prince St. Historical Society Museum, Bridge St, working model of water-powered timber mill. Castanea Orchards, Adelong Rd, hazelnuts, honey, chestnuts, cherries; open daily. New Year's Day: Rodeo. Nov.: Heritage Week. **In the area:** Henry Angel Trackhead on Hume and Hovell Walking Track, facilities for campers and picnickers; starting point for bushwalks. Site of old Union Jack Mine, 3 km N. Pioneer Women's Hut, 8 km NW on Wagga Rd, domestic rural history museum; check times. William's mini hydro-electric scheme and Lake

Mannus, 7 km S. Paddy's River Falls, 16 km S, cascades drop 60 m; walking track, picnic area. Tooma, 34 km S, historic hotel, tearooms, store. Mt Selwyn Ski Resort, 70 km SE. Murray 1 Power Station, 10 km SE of Khancoban on Alpine Way; guided tours daily. Whitewater rafting, fly fishing, paragliding, trail rides. **Tourist information:** Tumbarumba Wool and Craft Centre, 10 Bridge St; (069) 48 2805. **Accommodation:** 2 hotels, 1 motel, 2 cara./camp. parks.
MAP REF. 119 B7

Tumut
Pop. 5955

Situated on the Snowy Mountains Hwy, 424 km SW of Sydney, Tumut attracts visitors all year. Close to ski resorts and the great dams of the Snowy Mountains Hydro-electric Scheme, it is also well known for spectacular mountain scenery. **Of interest:** CSR Woodpanels and Softwood, Adelong Rd; open by appt, contact Tourist Information. Inspections of local power station, marble and millet broom factories. April–May: Festival of the Falling Leaf. **In the area:** Two access points for Hume and Hovell Walking Track. At Batlow, 33 km SW, Cascade Fuschia Nursery; Food Co-op Packhouse, largest in NSW, tours, purchases. Largest African violet farm in Australia, 7 km S on Tumut Plains Rd. Blowering Lake, 10 km S, major centre for water sports; fishing for rainbow trout, brown trout and perch. Talbingo Dam and Reservoir, 40 km S, second tallest rock-filled dam in Australia; set in steep wooded country; renowned for large trout. Excellent fishing in Tumut and Goobraganda Rivers. Whitewater rafting, canoeing, horseriding, abseiling, powered hang-gliding, scenic flights. Local art, craft, pottery. **Tourist information:** Fitzroy St (Snowy Mountains Hwy); (069) 47 1849. **Accommodation:** 6 hotels, 6 motels, 1 B&B, 2 cara./camp. parks.
MAP REF. 119 B6, 120 C13, 140 A2

Tweed Heads
Pop. 5360

This exciting town on the NSW–Qld border combines the attraction of being a comprehensive shopping venue with the pleasurable entertainment provided by its licensed clubs. **Of interest:** World's first laser-beam lighthouse sits atop Point Danger, one half in NSW and the other in Qld. Feb.: Tweed Valley Triathlon. Aug.: Bowls Tournament. **In the area:** Tweed Endeavour cruise boats,

operating from River Tce, visit locations along Tweed River. Minjungbal Museum and Resource Centre, just over Boyds Bay Bridge, Aboriginal ceremonial bora ring; museum and nature walk through sections of mangroves and rainforest. Avocado Adventureland, 15 km S on Pacific Hwy. Cabarita Gardens Lake Resort, 20 km S on Tweed Coast Rd. **Tourist information:** Cnr Pacific Hwy and Alma St, Murwillumbah; (075) 36 4244 or (066) 72 1340. **Accommodation:** 2 hotels, 22 motels, 9 cara./camp. parks.
MAP REF. 123 P1, 475 O7

Ulladulla   Pop. 7381
Ulladulla, a fishing town, and nearby Milton are at the northern end of a stretch of beautiful coastal lakes and lagoons with white sandy beaches. **Of interest:** Town's oldest building (c. 1868) houses Millard's Cottage Restaurant, Princes Hwy, harbour views. Funland, Princes Hwy, large indoor family fun park. Lighthouse, Wardens Head, views, walking tracks. South Pacific Heathland Reserve, Dowling St, native plants, birdlife, walks. Ulladulla Wildflower Reserve, cnr Green and Warden Sts. Easter: Blessing of the Fleet. Oct.: Milton Settlers Fair. **In the area:** Mollymook, 2 km N, surfing, excellent fishing, golf. Narrawallee Beach, 4 km N, surfing. Nearby Narrawallee Inlet has calm shallow water ideal for children. Bendalong, 36 km N, surfing, swimming. Sussex Inlet, 47 km N, fishing carnival in May. Lakes Conjola (23 km NW) and Burrill (5 km SW); swimming, fishing, water-skiing. Views from summit of Pigeon House Mountain in Morton National Park, 25 km NW. **Tourist information:** Princes Hwy; (044) 55 1269. **Accommodation:** 1 hotel, 19 motels, 1 B&B, 1 hostel, 5 cara./camp. parks. **See also:** The Illawarra Coast.
MAP REF. 119 H6, 120 I3, 141 Q3

Uralla   Pop. 2324
'Gentleman' bushranger Thunderbolt was shot dead by a local policeman in 1870, at Kentucky Creek, south-east of this New England town. Rich gold discoveries were made in the vicinity in the 1850s. **Of interest:** Self-guide Heritage Walking Tour introduces town's historic buildings. Hassett's Military Museum, Bridge St, local and national military history, memorabilia. McCrossin's Mill (1870), Salisbury St; museum incl. goldfields history, joss house, local

Aboriginal tribe and Thunderbolt exhibits. Statue of Thunderbolt in Bridge St, grave in old Uralla Cemetery. March: Book Fair. Nov.: Thunderbolt Picnic Race Meeting. **In the area:** Mt Yarrowyck Aboriginal rock-art site, 23 km NW off Bundarra Rd. Fossicking at Old Rocky River diggings, 5 km W; pleasant picnic spot. Gostwyck, 11 km SE, one of oldest properties in area; private chapel open to groups, by appt. **Tourist information:** Bridge St; (067) 78 4496. **Accommodation:** 1 hotel, 1 hotel/motel, 2 motels, 1 B&B, 2 cara./camp. parks. **See also:** New England.
MAP REF. 123 K8

Urunga   Pop. 2666
One of the best fishing spots on the north coast, 32 km S of Coffs Harbour at the mouth of the Bellinger River, Urunga is separated from the ocean by a broad lagoon. **Of interest:** Sailing, water-skiing, bowls, golf. Safe river swimming pool for children, with picnic reserve. July: Bowling Club Carnival. **In the area:** At Raleigh, 4 km north, wingery, horseriding, go-kart complex. **Tourist information:** The Honey Place, Pacific Hwy; (066) 55 6160. **Accommodation:** 1 hotel, 4 motels, 4 cara./camp. parks.
MAP REF. 123 O8, 475 N12

Wagga Wagga   Pop. 40 875
This prosperous city—the largest inland city in NSW—is 478 km SW of Sydney just off the Hume Hwy. Wagga is a major centre for industry, commerce, education, agriculture and the home of two important military bases. The town is renowned for its cultural pursuits and performing arts. **Of interest:** Botanic Gardens and Zoo on Willans Hill; miniature railway runs through gardens. Historical Museum, adj. to gardens, indoor and outdoor exhibits. City Art Gallery, Gurwood St, with National Art Glass collection and Riverina Galleries on The Esplanade. March: Australian Veterans Games. Sept.: National Festival of the Voice. **In the area:** Lake Albert, 7 km S, water sports. Murray Cod Hatcheries and Fauna Park, 5 km E. Wagga Wagga Winery, 15 km NE, early Australiana theme, restaurant, Eunonyhareenyha Cottage. Charles Sturt University (Riverina Campus), 6 km NW, incl. Charles Sturt Winery on campus. Aurora Clydesdale Stud and Pioneer Farm, 9 km W of Collingullie on Sturt Hwy, towards Narrandera. Tours of

military base at Kapooka, 9 km SW. **Tourist information:** Tourism Wagga Wagga, Tarcutta Street; (069) 23 5402. **Accommodation:** 12 hotels, 24 motels, 2 B&B, 6 cara./camp. parks.
MAP REF. 120 A12, 127 Q10

Walcha   Pop. 1782
This town on the eastern slopes of the Great Dividing Range was first settled in 1832. **Of interest:** Pioneer Cottage and Museum, Derby St; incl. Tiger Moth plane, first to be used for crop-dusting in Australia, and replica of blacksmith's shop. Fenwicke House, 19th-century terrace in Fitzroy St, art gallery, B&B accommodation. Australia Day: Breakfast in the Park. Feb.: Agricultural Show. **In the area:** Ohio Homestead (1842), 4 km E; open by appt. Oxley Wild Rivers National Park, 20 km E; areas around Oxley, Tia and Wollomombi Falls developed for picnicking and camping. Trout fishing (with access to private property by appt.). **Tourist information:** Craft Centre, Fitzroy St (Oxley Hwy); (067) 77 2802 or (067) 77 1075. **Accommodation:** 4 hotels, 2 motels, 1 cara./camp. park. **See also:** New England.
MAP REF. 123 K9

Walgett   Pop. 2091
A small rural community situated at the junction of the Barwon and Namoi Rivers, 300 km NW of Dubbo. **Of interest:** Barwon Aboriginal Community, Fox St. First European settler's grave. Good fishing all year. Oct.: Weekend Extravaganza; raft races, go-karts. **In the area:** Grawin, Glengarry and Sheepyard opal fields, 70 km W. (Motorists are warned water is scarce; adequate supply should be carried.) Narran Lake, 96 km W, via Cumborah Rd, one of largest inland lakes in Australia; wildlife sanctuary; no facilities for private visits, but light aircraft tours can be arranged through Walgett Aero Club; (068) 28 1344. **Tourist information:** 77 Fox St; (068) 28 1399. **Accommodation:** 2 hotel/motels, 3 motels, 1 cara./camp. park.
MAP REF. 122 C6, 474 E11

Warialda   Pop. 1285
The first administrative centre in the north-west of the State, this town on Gwydir Hwy, 63 km NW of Inverell, is in a stud farm district. **Of interest:** Historical buildings, especially on Stephen and Hope Sts. Carinda House, Stephen St, historic house, crafts. Pioneer Cemetery,

Bawley Beach, near Ulladulla

Queen and Stephen Sts, graves date from 1850s. Well's Family Gem and Mineral Collection in Heritage Centre, Hope St; also Aboriginal artefacts, bottle display. Self-guide walk around town. May: Agricultural Show. **In the area:** Fossicking, bushwalking, wildflowers. Picnic spots and free-ranging native animals at Cranky Rock Nature Reserve, 8 km E. **Tourist information:** Shire Offices, Hope St; (067) 29 1016. **Accommodation:** 1 hotel, 1 motel, 1 cara./camp. park. MAP REF. 122 I5, 474 I10

Warren
Pop. 2036

In a wool, cattle and cotton district on the Macquarie River, this Oxley Hwy town, 134 km NW of Dubbo, offers excellent fishing. **Of interest:** Macquarie Park, on banks of river, and Tiger Bay Wildlife Park. **In the area:** Excellent racecourse, 3 km W; Cotton Cup carnival Nov. Austcott Cotton Farm, 10 km SW, tours late April to June. Warren Weir, 5 km SE. Visits to merino studs. **Tourist information:** Shire Offices, Dubbo St; (068) 47 4606; Craft Shop, Burton St; (068) 47 3181. **Accommodation:** 2 hotels, 2 motels, 1 cara./camp. park. MAP REF. 120 B1, 122 B12

Wauchope
Pop. 4297

Nearby Timbertown, a major re-creation of a typical timber town of the 1880s, has put Wauchope on the tourist map. The town is the centre of a timber-getting, dairying, beef-cattle and mixed-farming area on the Oxley Hwy, 19 km W of Port Macquarie. **Of interest:** Train Meadows, King Creek Rd, model train display. March: Lasiandra Festival. Oct.: Colonial Carnival. **In the area:** Timbertown, re-created village with shops and school, on edge of Broken Bago State Forest, 3 km W; working bullock team, horse-drawn wagons, smithy, steam-powered train, sleeper-cutting demonstrations. Adjacent small weatherboard church houses Historical Society Museum. The Big Bull, 2 km E off Oxley Hwy; dairy farming display, hay rides, animal nursery. **Tourist information:** Cnr Hay and Clarence Sts, Port Macquarie; (065) 83 1293. **Accommodation:** 2 hotels, 2 motels, 1 cara./camp. park. MAP REF. 109 E8, 123 N11

Wee Waa
Pop. 2030

This small town near the Namoi River is the centre of a cotton-growing district producing the highest cotton yield in Australia. **Of interest:** Guided tours from Namoi Cotton Co-op, Short St, to Merah North Cotton Gin (9 km), April–Aug. April: Agricultural Show. May: Cotton Festival (biennial). **In the area:** Cubbaroo Winery, 45 km W, tour groups welcome. Cuttabri Wine Shanty, 25 km SW, original Cobb & Co. coaching stop between Wee Waa and Pilliga. Yarrie Lake, 24 km S, boating, birdwatching. **Tourist information:** Newell Hwy, Narrabri; (067) 92 3583. **Accommodation:** 1 hotel, 2 motels, 2 caravan parks. MAP REF. 122 F7, 474 G12

Wellington
Pop. 5433

Limestone caves are one of the interesting features of this town at the junction of the Macquarie and Bell Rivers, 362 km NW of Sydney. **Of interest:** Historical Museum in old bank (1883), cnr Percy and Warne Sts. From Mt Arthur Reserve, 3 km W of town, walking trails to Mt Binjang, lookout at summit. Maps from Visitors Centre in Cameron Park, attractive area on western side of main street (Mitchell Hwy). Aug.: Eisteddfod. Nov.: Festival of Dance. **In the area:** Wellington Caves, 9 km S, tours of Cathedral Cave, and smaller Gaden Cave with its rare cave coral; aviary, animal enclosure; fossil and clock museum, picnic/barbecue facilities; kiosk. Wellington Golf Club (18-hole) next to caves; open to public. Markeita Cellars, 16 km S in village of Neurea. Rabbit Farm 20 km S; alpacas, shearing of angora rabbits; coach and group tours, by appt. Lake Burrendong, 32 km E; panoramic views from spillway; Arboretum, native flora reserve open daily. Areas for water-skiing, sailing, power boating and fishing nearby; camping facilities, cabin accommodation. Glenfinlass Wines, 8 km SW on Parkes Rd. Nangara Gallery, 26 km SW, Australia-wide collection of Aboriginal artefacts. **Tourist information:** Cameron Park, Nanima Cr.; (068) 45 2001. **Accommodation:** 7 hotels, 4 motels, 1 B&B, 4 cara./camp. parks. MAP REF. 120 E4

Wentworth   Pop. 1447

Wentworth is an historic town at the junction of the Murray and Darling Rivers. At one time a busy riverboat and customs port, today it is a quiet holiday town. **Of interest:** Rotary Folk Museum and Old Wentworth Gaol (1881), both in Beverly St. Courthouse (1870s), Darling St. Apphara Art Gallery, Adams St. Historic PS *Ruby*, Fotherby Park, Wentworth St. Riverboat cruises on MV *Loyalty*. Lock 10, weir and park, for picnics. Poker machines in town service clubs. Melbourne Cup Day: Horseracing. **In the area:** Houseboat hire. Championship golf courses. Model aircraft display at Yelta, 12 km E. At Buronga, 26 km E, Oasis Botanical Gardens, River Road; Orange World and Stanley Wine Co. both on Silver City Hwy. Mungo National Park, 157 km NE, via Pooncarie. **Tourist information:** Shop 4, Wentworth Pl, Adams St; (050) 27 3624. **Accommodation:** 1 hotel, 6 motels, 2 caravan parks. MAP REF. 126 D7, 230 F3

West Wyalong   Pop. 3458

This former goldmining town, at the junction of the Mid Western and Newell Hwys, celebrated its centenary in 1994. It is now the business centre of a prosperous wheat, wool and mixed-farming area. **Of interest:** Aboriginal Artefacts Gallery, Newell Hwy. Bland District Historical Museum, Newell Hwy, scale model of goldmine, historical displays, archives. Sept.: Agricultural Show. Oct.: Highways Festival. **In the area:** Lake Cowal, 48 km NE, via Clear Ridge, largest natural lake in NSW; bird sanctuary, popular fishing spot. Weethalle Whistlestop, 65 km W, on Hay Rd, Devonshire teas, art and craft. At Barmedman, 32 km SE, Mineral Water Pool, believed to provide relief from arthritis and rheumatism. **Tourist information:** McCann Park, Newell Hwy; (069) 72 3645. **Accommodation:** 7 hotels, 11 motels, 2 cara./camp. parks. **See also:** The Newell. MAP REF. 120 A8, 127 Q6

White Cliffs   Pop. 219

White Cliffs Pioneer Opal Fields, 97 km NW of Wilcannia, is a town where pioneering is a way of life. The opal fields were the first commercial fields in NSW; the first lease was granted in 1890, and in the turn-of-the-century boom years the fields were supporting 4500 people. Precious opal is still mined today. Jewelled opal 'pineapples' are found only in this area. **Of interest:** Underground Art Gallery; Eagles Gallery Pottery; Rosavilla, with antique, rock and mineral collections; Jock's Dugout Museum. Historic buildings incl. the now restored police station (1897), post office (1900), public school (1900). Pioneer children's cemetery. Unique underground motel and dugout homes. Underground guest house in Turley's Hill. Many opal showrooms where opal cutting and polishing can be seen. Stubby Bottle Showroom, built from glass stubbies. Fossicking for opal in old field. Experimental solar power station. Camping, picnic/barbecue facilities, swimming-pool, in Town Reserve. May: Gymkhana and Rodeo. July: Royal Flying Doctor Ball. **In the area:** Mootwingee National Park, 90 km SW,

Opal fields, White Cliffs

guided tours of Aboriginal rock-art sites in cooler months (extremely hot in summer). **Tourist information:** Association Secretary; (080) 91 6611. **Accommodation:** 1 hotel, 1 motel, 1 cara./camp. reserve. MAP REF. 124 G8, 485 K13

Whitton   Pop. 340

Whitton, 24 km W of Leeton, is the oldest town in the Murrumbidgee Irrigation Area and has large rice and grain storage facilities. **Of interest:** Whitton Courthouse and Gaol Museum. **In the area:** Gogeldrie Weir, 14 km SE. **Tourist information:** Chelmsford Pl, Leeton; (069) 53 2832. **Accommodation:** 1 hotel. MAP REF. 127 N8

Wilcannia   Pop. 942

Once the 'queen city of the west', this quaint township still has many impressive sandstone buildings. It was proclaimed a town in 1864 and was once a key inland port in the days of paddle-steamers. Declining in the early 1920s with the advent of the car, today it is the service centre for a far-flung rural population. **Of interest:** Self-guide Historic Town Tour introduces several fine stone buildings, incl. post office, prison and courthouse (1880), and Athenaeum Chambers (1890), which houses Tourist Information Centre; also opening bridge (1895) across Darling River and paddle-steamer wharf upstream. **In the area:** Opal fields at White Cliffs, 97 km NW. **Tourist information:** Central Darling Shire, Athenaeum Chambers, Reid St; (080) 91 5909. **Accommodation:** 2 hotels, 2 motels, 1 cara./camp. park. MAP REF. 124 G11

Windsor Pop. 1869

A town for lovers of history and early architecture, Windsor is one of the oldest towns in Australia, situated 56 km NW of Sydney. **Of interest:** St Matthew's Church, Moses St, oldest Anglican Church in Australia, designed by Francis Greenway and convict-built in 1817. Nearby graveyard is even older. Courthouse, Court St, is another Greenway building. The Doctor's House (1844), Thompson Sq., privately owned. Many other fine buildings in historic George St and Thompson Sq. Hawkesbury Museum, Thompson Sq.; formerly Daniel O'Connell Inn, built in 1843. May: Bridge to Bridge Power Boat Classic. Nov.: Bridge to Bridge Water Ski Classic. **In the area:** Cattai National Park, 14 km NE, historic homestead, friendship farm, horse and pony rides, canoe hire, picnic/barbecue facilities; camping area. Australian Pioneer Village, 6 km N, Rose Cottage, oldest timber dwelling in Australia; wagon and buggy collection; picnic/barbecue facilities; lake with paddle-boats. Tizzana Winery, 14 km N at Ebenezer, fortified wines, picnic/barbecue facilities. Ebenezer Uniting Church (1809), claimed to be oldest church in Australia still holding regular services. Nearby, old cemetery and schoolhouse (1817). **Tourist information:** Ham Common Bicentenary Park, Clarendon; (045) 88 5895. **Accommodation:** 2 hotels, 3 motels. **See also:** The Hawkesbury. MAP REF. 105 K6, 121 J7

Wingham Pop. 4407

The oldest town on the Manning River, 13 km NW of Taree, Wingham was established in 1836. **Of interest:** Manning Valley Historical Society Museum, part of attractive village square with several prominent historic buildings, bounded by Isabella, Bent, Farquhar and Wynter Sts; 10–4 daily. The Wingham Brush, close to town centre, is one of the few remaining subtropical flood-plain rainforests in NSW, with orchids, ferns, Moreton Bay fig trees, grey-headed flying foxes and 100 species of birds. March: Agricultural Show. **In the area:** Fine bush scenery. **Tourist information:** Pacific Hwy, Taree North; (065) 52 1900 or 1800 80 1522. **Accommodation:** 2 hotels, 1 motel. MAP REF. 109 B13, 121 M2, 123 M12

Wisemans Ferry Pop. 400

Situated on the Hawkesbury River, 66 km NW of Sydney, Wisemans Ferry is an important recreational area for those interested in water sports. Two vehicular ferries provide transport across the river. **Of interest:** Wisemans Ferry Inn, named after founder of original ferry service and innkeeper; said to be haunted by his wife, whom he allegedly pushed down front steps of inn to her death. Dharug National Park, on northern side of river, named after local Aboriginal tribe; important for wealth of Aboriginal rock engravings. Convict-built Old Great North Road in park, one of great engineering feats of early colony; walk or cycle along lower section (closed to vehicles) from ferry. **Tourist information:** Ham Common Bicentenary Park, Richmond Rd, Clarendon; (045) 88 5895. **Accommodation:** 1 hotel, 1 motel, 4 cara./camp. parks. **See also:** The Hawkesbury. MAP REF. 105 L4, 121 J6

Wollongong Pop. 211 417

Wollongong is the third largest city in NSW. Clustered around Port Kembla Harbour is the highly automated steel mill operated by BHP, an export coal loader and the largest grain-handling facility in NSW. The area surrounding the city contains some of the South Coast's most spectacular scenery. **Of interest:** Illawarra Historical Society Museum, Market St, incl. handicraft room, Victorian parlour. Wollongong City Gallery, cnr Burrelli and Kembla Sts. Spectacular mall with soaring steel arches, water displays. Botanic Gardens and Rhododendron Park. Surfing beaches and rock pools, to north and south. Foreshore parks for picnicking. Wollongong Harbour, fishing fleet and fish market. Historic lighthouse (1872). Aug.: South Coast Youth Arts and Skills Festival.

Dec.: Junior Surf Lifesaving Championships. **In the area:** Lake Illawarra, 5 km S, stretching from South Pacific Ocean to foothills of Illawarra Range: prawning, fishing, sailing; boat hire. Seaside village of Shellharbour, 22 km S, walking trails in nearby Blackbutt Reserve. Lookouts with superb views of coast, including Bald Hill Lookout, 36 km N, site of aviator Lawrence Hargrave's first attempt at flight in early 1900s; now favourite spot for hang-gliding. Symbio Animal Gardens, 44 km N at Helensburgh, kangaroos, free-roaming wombats, donkeys, other animals. Mt Kembla Village, 15 km W, scene of tragic mining disaster in 1902, features: monument in church; original miners' huts; several historic buildings, incl. Historical Museum in former post office, pioneer kitchen, blacksmith's shop; and reconstruction of Mt Kembla disaster. **Tourist information:** 93 Crown St; (042) 28 0300. **Accommodation:** 4 hotels, 8 motels, 1 B&B, 1 hostel. **See also:** The Illawarra Coast. MAP REF. 114, 116 H6, 119 I3, 121 J10

Woodburn Pop. 592

Woodburn is a pleasant town on the Pacific Hwy, astride the Richmond River. **Of interest:** Riverside Park. Monument and remains of settlement at New Italy, result of ill-fated Marquis de Rays' expedition in 1880. Houseboat hire. **Tourist information:** Cnr Ballina and Molesworth Sts, Lismore; (066) 22 0122. **Accommodation:** 1 motel, 1 hostel. MAP REF. 123 P3, 475 N9

Woolgoolga Pop. 3660

This charming seaside town on the Pacific Hwy, 26 km N of Coffs Harbour, is excellent for crabbing, prawning and whiting fishing. Good surf beaches. **Of interest:** Guru Nanak Sikh Temple, River St, place of worship for town's Indian population. Raj Mahal Indian Cultural Centre. Woolgoolga Art Gallery on Turon Parade, paintings, pottery, workshops. Sept.: Lillipilli Festival. **In the area:** Yuraygir National Park, 10 km N; bushwalking, canoeing, fishing, surfing, swimming, and picnic and camping areas on beautiful stretch of unspoiled coastline. Wedding Bells State Forest 14 km NW. **Tourist information:** Mobil Service Station, Pacific Hwy; (066) 54 1603. **Accommodation:** 7 motels, 3 cara./camp. parks. MAP REF. 123 O7, 475 N12

Yuraygir National Park, near Yamba

Woy Woy
Pop. 12 206

Situated 90 km N of Sydney and 6 km S of Gosford. **Of interest:** Boating, fishing and swimming on Brisbane Water, Broken Bay and Hawkesbury River. Centre for Brisbane Water National Park, 3 km SW, noted for spring wildflowers, bushwalking, birdwatching, Aboriginal rock-art sites. **Tourist information:** Visitors Centre and Tea Rooms, cnr Bullion and West Sts, Umina; (043) 43 2200. **Accommodation:** On peninsula: 3 hotels, 2 motels, 3 cara./camp. parks.
MAP REF. 105 O6, 108 F8, 121 K7

Wyong
Pop. 3902

Wyong is situated on the Pacific Hwy between Tuggerah Lakes and the State Forests of Watagan, Olney and Ourimbah. **Of interest:** Wyong District Museum, Cape Rd, recalls early ferry services across lakes, and forest logging. Many sports catered for, including golf, swimming, most water sports, horse and greyhound racing. March: Festival of Arts. Oct.: Cycle Classic. **In the area:** Hinterland popular for bushwalking and camping. Burbank Nursery, at Tuggerah, 3 km S, 20 ha of azaleas; open daily; flowering time Sept. Award-winning Forest of Tranquillity at Ourimbah, 12 km S. **Tourist information:** Tuggerah Lakes Tourist Assocn, Caltex Twin Service Centre, F3 Freeway; (043) 52 2944. **Accommodation:** 2 hotels, 1 motel, 2 cara./camp. parks.
MAP REF. 105 P4, 108 F1, 121 K6

Yamba
Pop. 3707

This prawning and fishing town at the mouth of the Clarence River offers sea, lake and river fishing. It is the largest coastal resort in the Clarence Valley. **Of interest:** Story House Museum, River St, historical records of early Yamba. Views from base of lighthouse, reached via steep Pilot St. Sept.–Oct.: Family Fishing Festival. **In the area:** Daily passenger ferry services to Iluka. River cruises. Houseboat hire at Brushgrove, 35 km SW. Lake Wooloweyah, 4 km S, fishing and prawning. Yuraygir National Park, 5 km S; swimming, fishing and bushwalking in area dominated by sand ridges and banksia heath. The Blue Pool at Angourie, 5 km S, only 50 m from ocean, freshwater pool of unknown depth and origin; popular swimming and picnic spot. **Tourist information:** Lower Clarence Visitors Centre, Ferry Park, Pacific Hwy, Maclean; (066) 45 4121. **Accommodation:** 1 hotel, 8 motels, 3 caravan parks.
MAP REF. 123 P5, 475 N10

Yanco
Pop. 651

Located 8 km S of Leeton, this town is where Sir Samuel McCaughey developed his own irrigation scheme, which led to the establishment of the Murrumbidgee Irrigation Area. **Of interest:** McCaughey's mansion is now an agricultural high school; with nearby Yanco Agricultural Institute, open to public. Yanco Powerhouse Museum. Nearby, Yanco Aquatic Park. May: Murrumbidgee Farm Fair. **In the area:** extensive red gum forests along the Murrumbidgee River. Well-marked forest drives lead to sandy beaches and fishing spots. **Tourist information:** Chelmsford Pl, Leeton; (069) 53 2832. **Accommodation:** 1 hotel.
MAP REF. 127 O8

Yass
Pop. 4828

Close to the junction of two major highways (the Hume and the Barton), this interesting old town is on the Yass River, surrounded by beautiful, rich, rolling country, 280 km SW of Sydney and 55 km from Canberra. **Of interest:** Grave of Hamilton Hume, who discovered Yass Plains in 1824, in Yass Cemetery; signposted from Ross St. Hume lived at Cooma Cottage (1830), 3 km E, for 40 years; cottage classified by National Trust; open 10–4, closed Tues. Hamilton Hume Museum, Comur St. Self-guide walk introduces many old buildings in town that relate to Australia's heritage. March: Agricultural Show. **In the area:** Crisp Art Glass and Crisp-Grow Lavender Nursery, 19 km NW, on Hume Hwy. At Wee Jasper, 53 km SW, Goodradigbee River for trout fishing; Micalong Creek; Carey's Cave, with superb limestone formations; Hume and Hovell Walking Track. Burrinjuck State Recreation Area, 54 km SW off Hume Hwy; bushwalking, water sports and fishing. Numerous wineries in Murrumbateman area, 19 km S, on Barton Hwy. Quamba Emu Farm 10 km NE on Wargeila Rd. **Tourist information:** Coronation Park, Cooma St; (06) 226 2557. **Accommodation:** 4 hotels, 8 motels, 1 cara./camp. park.
MAP REF. 119 D4, 120 E11

Young
Pop. 6666

Attractive former goldmining town in the western foothills of the Great Dividing Range, 395 km SW of Sydney. Today there is mining and a range of agriculture in the area. Cherries and prunes are the area's best-known exports, as well as flour, and fabricated steel. **Of interest:** Lambing Flat Historic Museum, Campbell St, fascinating reminders of town's colourful history, incl. 'roll-up' flag carried by miners during infamous anti-Chinese Lambing Flat riots of 1861. Art Gallery, Olympic Way. Backguard Gully with historic Pug-mill, on Boorowa Rd, reconstruction showing early goldmining methods. Nov.: National Cherry Festival. **In the area:** Chinaman's Dam, 4 km SE, recreation area with picnic/barbecue facilities, children's playground, scenic walks. At Murringo Village, 24 km E, several historic buildings, home of glass blower and engraver Helmut Heibel. Four wineries. **Tourist information:** Olympic Way; (063) 82 3394. **Accommodation:** 6 hotels, 6 motels, 1 hotel/ motel, 4 B&B, 1 cara./camp. park.
MAP REF. 119 B2, 120 C10

New South Wales

Location Map

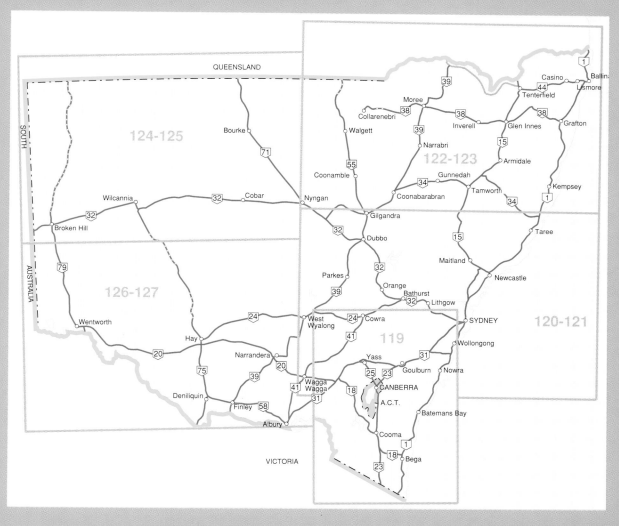

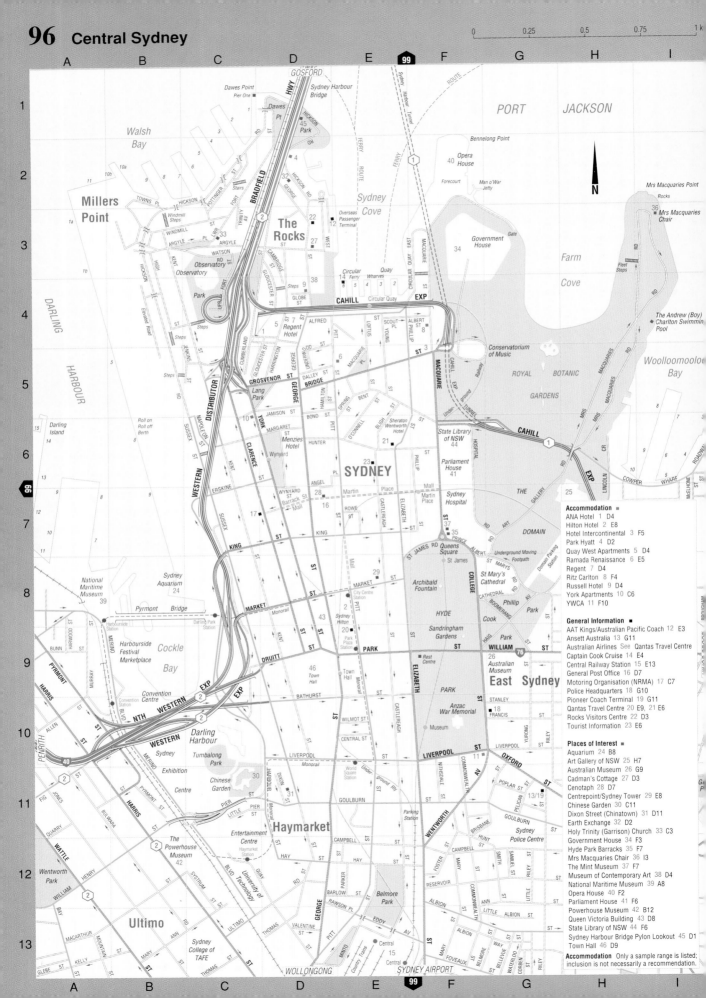

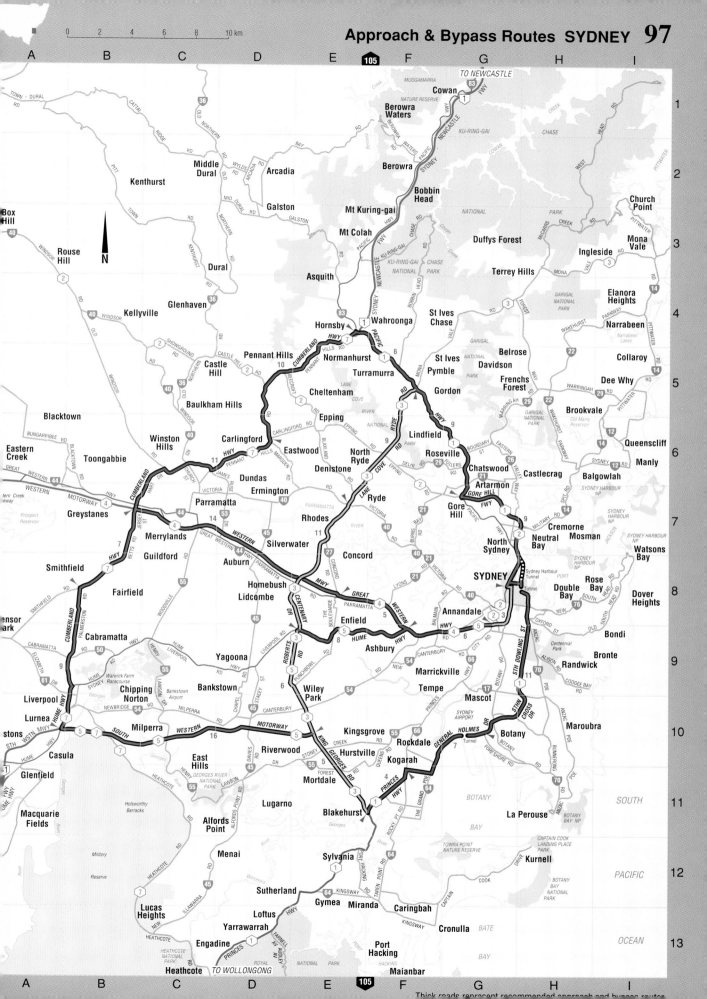

100

A B C D E F G H

1

WINDSOR RD
SHOWGROUND RD
Rogans Hill
Castle Hill
Thornleigh
Pennant Hills
Normanhurst
HILLS
PENNANT
Duffy AV
GOODLANDS AV
NEPEAN
FOX
VALLEY
COMENARRA PKWY
ROLAND AV

2
CUMBERLAND STATE FOREST
Koala Park
Baulkham Hills
Excelsior Park
Beecroft
Cheltenham
South Turramurra
Pennant Hills Park
CUMBERLAND HWY
BEECROFT
MALTON RD
Lane Cove
Devlins Ck

3
Darling Mills State Forest
Muirfield Golf Course
Macquarie Park
West Pymble
LANE COVE RIVER NATIONAL PARK
Macquarie University
EPPING

4
Winston Hills
North Rocks
Carlingford
CARLINGFORD RD
Epping
Eastwood
North Ryde
WINDSOR RD
HILLS
MARSDEN RD
BLAXLAND RD

5
Old Toongabbie
Lake Parramatta Reserve
Telopea
Oatlands Golf Course
Dundas Valley
Denistone
West Ryde
PENNANT
BRIENS
Northmead
CHURCH ST
JAMES RD
Dundas
Ryde-Parramatta Golf Course
Ryde

6
Pendle Hill
Wentworthville
Westmead
Parramatta
Rydalmere
Meadowbank
Melrose Park
GREAT WESTERN HWY
VICTORIA RD
HART DR

105
7
Mays Hill
Harris Park
Camellia
Rosehill Racecourse
Ermington
Rhodes
Putney
Royal Rehab Centre
CONCORD RD
JERSEY ST

8
Granville
Merrylands
Guildford
Rosehill Showground
Silverwater
Silverwater Corrective Services Complex
Olympics Site
Bi-Centennial Park
Homebush Bay
Concord
Mortlake
Cabarita
GREAT WESTERN HWY
PARRAMATTA RD
CUMBERLAND RD

9
Fairfield
Yennora
Auburn
Auburn Golf Course
Lidcombe
Flemington
Homebush
Strathfield
Burwood
Canada Bay
State Sports Centre
Main Venue for Olympic Games
Concord Golf Course
OLYMPIC DR

10
Villawood
Leightonfield
Chester Hill
Berala
Rookwood Cemetery
Hudson Park Golf Course
Strathfield Golf Course
Enfield
Croydon
Strathfield
Burwood
THE BOULEVARDE

11
Carramar
Lansvale
Sefton
Regents Park
Chullora
Carnarvon Golf Course
Rookwood
Ashfield
Croydon Park
Ashbury
LIVERPOOL RD

12
HUME HWY
Lansdowne
Bass Hill
Birrong
Yagoona
Greenacre
Belfield
Mirambeena Regional Park
Lansdowne Park
Potts Hill Reservoirs
HUME HWY
LIVERPOOL RD

13
Warwick Farm Racecourse
Shipping Norton
Condell Park
Bankstown
Mt Lewis
Punchbowl
Lakemba
Campsie
Clemton Park
Belmore
Georges Hall
Crest Of Bankstown
Bankstown Airport
Motor Racing Circuit
Liverpool Golf Course

A B C D E F G H

0 1 2 3 4 5 km

101

J K L M N O P Q R

1
Killeaton St · Douglas · St Ives · Pymble Golf Course · Belrose · Davidson · Wheeler Heights · Cromer Golf Course · Toronto Av · Cromer · Collaroy Plateau · Parkes · Collaroy · The Basin

2
Pymble · Gordon · Killara · Frenchs Forest · Oxford Falls · Beacon Hill · Narraweena · Dee Why · Long Reef Golf Course · Long Reef Beach · Dee Why Beach

3
Pacific Hwy · Forestville · Garigal National Park · Allambie Heights · Brookvale · Wingala · Dee Why Head · Harbord

4
Lindfield · Roseville Golf Course · Killarney Heights · Bantry Bay · Garigal National Park · Old Manly Reservoir · Manly Vale · Queenscliff · Warringah Golf Course · Curl Curl · Harbord · Harbord Beach · Curl Curl Head · Queenscliff Beach · North Steyne Beach

5
Roseville · Chatswood · Middle Cove · Castle Cove · Willoughby · Seaforth · Balgowlah · Fairlight · Manly · Manly Beach · Underwater World · Manly Cove

6
Lane Cove · Artarmon · Northbridge · Middle Harbour · Beauty Point · The Spit · Clontarf · North Harbour · Dobroyd Head · Sydney Harbour National Park · Military Reserve · North Head · Outer North Head

7
Gore Hill · Naremburn · Crows Nest · Cammeray · Spit Junction · Cremorne · Balmoral · Georges Heights · Mosman · Middle Head · Inner North Head · Sydney Harbour National Park

8
Linley Point · Riverview · Northwood · St Leonards · Wollstonecraft · Waverton · Neutral Bay · Cremorne Point · Clifton Gardens · Chowder Bay · Georges Head · Watsons Bay · Inner South Head · Military Reserve · Outer South Head

Hunters Hill · Longueville · Greenwich · Woolwich · North Sydney · Birchgrove · Taronga Zoological Park · Bradleys Head · Sydney Harbour NP

9
Drummoyne · Russell Lea · Balmain · Sydney Harbour Bridge · Opera House · Port Jackson · Garden Island · Shark Island · Vaucluse · South · Pacific

10
Rodd Pt · Lilyfield · Rozelle · Pyrmont · Sydney · Potts Point · Elizabeth Bay · Darling Point · Double Bay · Rose Bay · Point Piper · Dover Heights · Pacific

11
Leichhardt · Glebe · Ultimo · Surry Hills · Darlinghurst · Paddington · Kings Cross · Rushcutters Bay · Edgecliff · Woollahra · Bellevue Hill · North Bondi · Ocean · Annandale · University of Sydney

12
Petersham · Stanmore · Camperdown · Redfern · Alexandria · Moore Park · Centennial Park · Sydney Cricket Ground · Waverley · Bronte · Bondi · Bondi Junction · Tamarama · Enmore · Newtown · Erskineville

13
Marrickville · Sydenham · St Peters · Zetland · Beaconsfield · Rosebery · Kensington · Randwick · Clovelly · Coogee · Kingsford · Mascot · Tempe · The Australian Golf Course · University of NSW · Coogee Bay

For more detail of Central Sydney see page 96

J K L M N O P Q R

0 1 2 3 4 5 km

108

KU-RING-GAI CHASE NATIONAL PARK

Lookout

Barrenjoey Head

Great Mackerel Beach

Palm Beach Golf Course

Palm Beach

PACIFIC RD

WHALE

BARRENJOEY

CYNTHEA RD

BYNYA RD

Whale Beach

JERUSALEM BAY

CREEK

Refuge Bay

Cowan Pt

CHASE

HEAD

WEST

Towlers Bay

Scotland Island

Taylors Pt

Careel Bay

PITTWATER

Careel Bay

GEORGE ST

PATRICK ST

RIVIERA

CENTRAL RD

RIVERVIEW RD

PDE

Avalon

AVALON PDE

TASMAN

14

St Michaels Cave

Clareville

HUDSON

PLATEAU RD

Avalon Golf Course

Hole In the Wall

Bilgola

RD

Newport

IRRUBEL RD

GLADSTONE ST

14

Newport Beach

MYOLA RD

Bungan Head

KU-RING-GAI

Cottage Pt

COTTAGE

COAL and CANDLE

COWAN

Smiths Creek

POINT

COAL

COAL & CANDLE DR

CANDLE DR

CREEK

RD

PARK

NATIONAL

Church Point

MIN KARA

NARLA RD

LENTARA

PITTWATER

CABBAGE TREE RD

Bayview

MONA

BASSETT ST

CRESCENT

BARREN JOEY

Smiths Creek

McCARRS

Mc Carrs Creek

Wirreanda Creek

CREEK

RD

CICADA GLEN RD

WALTER RD

SAMUEL ST

MAXWELL PARK ST

DARLEY ST

EMMA ST

ST

Duffys Forest

BOORALIE RD

Terrey Hills Country Club (Golf Course)

Waratah Park

THUDDUNGRA

TOORONGA RD

CHILTERN RD

LANE COVE RD

Ingleside

VINEYARD ST

3

RD

WARRIEWOOD RD

MACPHERSON RD

ST

Mona Vale

Mona Vale Golf Course

BARREN

ST

COOYONG RD

3

MONA

VALE

Baha'i Temple

POWDER WORKS RD

Monash Golf Course

INGLESIDE RD

GARDEN ST

MULLET Creek

Warriewood

PITTWATER RD

14

JACKSONS RD

North Narrabeen Reserve

Turimetta Head

Terrey Hills

MYOORA RD

Elanora Golf Course

ANANA RD

RICKARD RD

Elanora Heights

PITTWATER

OCEAN ST

Narrabeen Head

SOUTH

Ring-Gai dflower arden

St Ives Showground

3

MONA VALE RD

FOREST

GARIGAL NATIONAL PARK

Deep Creek

Narrabeen Lakes

22

PARKWAY

Narrabeen Beach

Narrabeen

PACIFIC

Middle

Bare

Harbour

Creek

WAKEHURST

22

Narrabeen Lakes Sport and Recreation Centre

JAMIESON PARK

EDGECLIFFE AV

PITTWATER BLVD

OCEAN

MORGAN RD

Cromer Golf Course

ROSE AV

VETERANS PDE

Collaroy Plateau

Collaroy

RD

ACRON RD

ST

GARIGAL NATIONAL PARK

COTTERIN RD

RALSTON AV

ELM AV

Wheeler Heights

OXFORD FALLS RD

Middle

Belrose

TORONTO AV

HUDSON

Creek

PARKES RD

ANZAC AV

WESTMORELAND RD

RD

Long Reef Golf Course

Long Reef Point

Davidson

KAMBORA AV

BLACKBUTTS RD

PRINGLE AV

GRACE AV

WEARDEN RD

Oxford Falls

Cromer

CARAWA RD

South Creek

ST

PRESCOTT AV

RD

Dee Why

14

Dee Why Lagoon

Harbord Lagoon

PRAHRAN AV

Frenchs Forest

WAY

FRENCHS FOREST RD

IRIS ST

22

Beacon Hill

WILLANDRA RD

McINTOSH RD

ALFRED ST

VICTOR RD

FISHER RD

HOWARD AV

PACIFIC PDE

KOOLA AV

SAIALA RD

DEAKIN

BROWN ST

MAXWELL PDE

WARRINGAH

29

WAKEHURST

GOVERNMENT RD

Narraweena

29

PITTWATER RD

BEACON HILL RD

HEADLAND RD

12

GRIFFIN RD

Forestville

29

CURRIE RD

COOK ST

BANTRY BAY RD

ALLAMBIE RD

Allambie Heights

ABBOTT RD

PITT RD

CHURCHILL

ARTERIAL

TRYON RD

WELLINGTON RD

MELWOOD AV

DARLEY

ST

GARIGAL NATIONAL PARK

22

Manly-Warringah (Manly Dam Reserve) War Memorial Park

Brookvale

14

HARBORD RD

WYADRA AV

Wingala

Curl Curl

Dee Why Head

Roseville Golf Course

99

WARRINGAH

N

1

83

Creek

NATIONAL

A B C D E F G H I

1 2 3 4 5 6 7 8 9 10 11 12 13

St Johns Park
Canley Heights
Canley Vale
Cabramatta
Mt Pritchard
Hargrave Park
Ashcroft
Liverpool
Lurnea
Casula
Chatham Village
Anzac Village
Wattle Grove
Warwick Farm
Moorebank
Holsworthy Village
Hammondville
Carramar
Lansvale
Villawood
Leightonfield
Chipping Norton
Milperra
New Brighton Golf Course
Riverlands Golf Course
Deepwater Park
Pleasure Point
Sandy Point
Lucas Heights
Heathcote
Military Reserve
Holsworthy Barracks
Chester Hill
Sefton
Bass Hill
Birrong
Lansdowne
Georges Hall
Bankstown Airport
Bankstown Golf Course
Kelso Park
Panania
East Hills
Picnic Point
Sandy Point
Engadine
Berala
Regents Park
Rookwood
Chullora
Greenacre
Yagoona
Condell Park
Mt Lewis
Bankstown
Revesby
Padstow
Alfords Point
Menai
Bangor
Woronora
Woronora Heights
Yarrawarrah
Punchbowl
Wiley Park
Roselands
Narwee
Riverwood
Peakhurst
Lugarno
Illawong
Como
Bonnet Bay
Jannali
Sutherland
Loftus
Oyster Bay
Penshurst
Kirrawee
Royal National Park
Heathcote National Park
Georges River National Park
Australian Nuclear Science and Technology Organisation
Prince Edward Park
Tramway Museum
Hurstville Golf Course
Oatley Park
Rookwood Cemetery
Strathfield Golf Course
Potts Hill Reservoirs
Sydney Water Supply
Cabramatta Golf Course
Cabramatta Sports Ground
Warwick Farm Racecourse
Motor Racing Circuit
Liverpool Golf Course
Mirambeena Regional Park
Lansdowne Park
Riverwood Golf Course
Crest of Bankstown
Lieutenant Cantello Reserve
Sewage Treatment Works

0 1 2 3 4 5 km

J K L M N 99 O P Q R

Enfield
Croydon
Haberfield
Leichhardt
Annandale
Glebe
Ultimo
Surry Hills
Paddington
Edgecliff
Bellevue Hill
Woollahra
Bondi
Ashfield
Camperdown
University Of Sydney
Victoria Barracks
Sydney Cricket Ground
Show Grounds
Centennial Park
Bondi Junction
Croydon Park
Petersham
Stanmore
Newtown
Redfern
Summer Hill
Salisbury
Macdonaldtown
Waverley
Ashbury
Lewisham
Enmore
Erskineville
Alexandria
Zetland
Bronte
Canterbury Racecourse
Dulwich Hill
Sydenham
St Peters
Beaconsfield
Rosebery
Kensington
Randwick
Clovelly
Marrickville
Sydney Park
Epsom
Randwick Racecourse
Coogee
Campsie
Hurlstone Park
The Australian Golf Course
University of NSW
Coogee Bay
Earlwood
Tempe
Mascot
Kingsford
Clemton Park
Undercliffe
Eastlakes
Daceyville
Commonwealth Property
Turrella
Arncliffe
Sydney Airport Drive
The Lakes Golf Course
Pagewood
Maroubra Junction
Maroubra
Bardwell Park
Kogarah Golf Course
International Terminal
Domestic Terminal
SYDNEY AIRPORT DRIVE
Bonnie Doon Golf Course
Kingsgrove
Bexley
Banksia
Barton Park
Botany
Banksmeadow
Hillsdale
Matraville
Rockdale
Kyeemagh
Eastlakes Golf Course
Botany Bay Golf Course
Malabar
Hurstville
Kogarah
Brighton-le-Sands
Chifley
Bexley Golf Course
Carlton
Monterey
Container Terminal
Long Bay Gaol
Phillip Bay
Allawah
Beverley Park
Ramsgate
Prince Henry Hospital
Connells Point
Carss Park
La Perouse
Little Bay
Blakehurst
Bare Island
NSW Golf Course
Sans Souci
Dolls Point
Sandringham
Kurnell
Sylvania
Captain Cook Bridge
TOWRA POINT NATURE RESERVE
BOTANY BAY NATIONAL PARK
Sylvania Waters
Taren Point
BOTANY BAY
Sylvania Heights
Miranda
SOUTH
Caringbah
Woolooware
PACIFIC
Yowie Bay
Dolans Bay
Woolooware
OCEAN
Lilli Pilli
Port Hacking
Burraneer
Cronulla
BATE
N
BAY
Maianbar

J K L M N 105 O P Q R

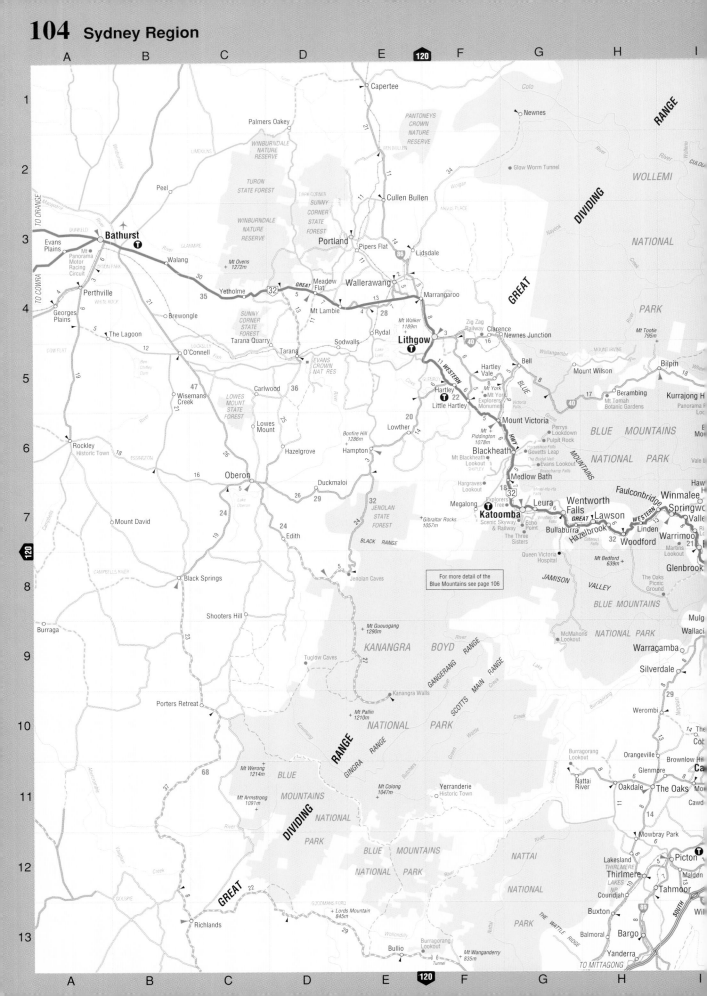

0   5   10   15   20 km

TO NEWCASTLE

For more detail of the Hawkesbury
& Central Coast see page 108

For more detail of Sydney
Suburbs see pages 98 - 103

SOUTH

PACIFIC

OCEAN

N

Major places:

SYDNEY
CAMPBELLTOWN
Richmond
Windsor
Pitt Town
Wilberforce
Gosford
Wyong
Woy Woy
Umina
Belmont
Swansea
Toukley
Norah Head
The Entrance
Bateau Bay
Terrigal
Kincumber
Avoca Beach
Erina
Wamberal

YENGO NATIONAL PARK
HOWES RANGE
BULGALABEN RANGE
BALA RANGE
JUDGE DOWINGS RANGE
WOMERAH RANGE
PARR STATE RECREATION AREA
DHARUG NATIONAL PARK
MARRAMARRA NATIONAL PARK
MUOGAMARRA NATURE RESERVE
KU-RING-GAI CHASE NATIONAL PARK
GARIGAL NP
LANE COVE NP
BOUDDI NATIONAL PARK
WYRRABALONG NP
BRISBANE WATER
ROYAL NATIONAL PARK
HEATHCOTE NP
SYDNEY HARBOUR NP
BOTANY BAY NP

Yallambie
Watagan
Flat Rock Lookout
Mt Warrawolong 641m
Wishing Well
Bucketty
Avondale
Cooranbong
Rathmines
Wangi Wangi
Blacksmiths
MOON ISLAND NAT RES
Morisset
Dora Creek
Bonnells Bay
Brightwaters
Nords Wharf
Muirs Lookout
Mandalong Lookout
Mandalong
Gwandalan
Wyee
Mannering Park
Catherine Hill Bay
Cedar Brush
CEDAR BRUSH CREEK
Ravensdale
Brush Creek
Dooralong
Frazer Park
Kulnura
Yarramalong
LITTLE JILLIBY
Jilliby
Lake Munmorah
Gorokan
Budgewoi
Upper Mangrove Creek
Central Mangrove
Wyong Creek
Norahville
Norah Head
Mangrove Mountain
Peats Ridge
Palm Dale
Wyong
Toukley
Tuggerah
Tuggerah Lake
St Albans
Ten Mile Hollow
Somersby
Palm Grove
Fowlers Lookout
Long Jetty
The Entrance
Webbs Creek
Lower Mangrove
Glenworth Valley
Gunderman
Spencer
Mount White
Calga
Narara
Ourimbah
Tumbi Umbi
Bateau Bay
Wamberal
Old Sydney Town
Lisarow
Reptile Park
Holgate
WYRRABALONG NP
Upper Colo
Colo
Colo Heights
Leets Vale
Laughtondale
Maroota
Sackville North
Cattai
Gosford
Erina
Terrigal
The Skillion
Koolewong
Pt Clare
Kincumber
Avoca Beach
WAMBERAL LAGOON NAT RES
Blaxlands Ridge
East Kurrajong
Glossodia
Freemans Reach
Wilberforce
Richmond
Pitt Town
PITT TOWN NAT RES
SCHEYVILLE
Maraylya
Woy Woy
Ettalong
McMasters Beach
Windsor
McGraths Hill
Hawkesbury Museum
Glenorie
Brooklyn
Umina
Wagstaff
Killcare Heights
Warrah Lookout
Patonga
Broken Bay
Agnes Banks
Mulgrave
Marsden Park
Nelson
Annangrove
Riverstone
Schofields
Glenhaven
Galston
Vineyard
Quakers Hill
Hornsby
Terrey Hills
Mona Vale
Newport
Avalon
Palm Beach
Whale Beach
PENRITH
Mt Druitt
Rooty Hill
Blacktown
Castle Hill
Baulkham Hills
Pymble
Gordon
Narrabeen
Collaroy
Frenchs Forest
WESTERN HWY
Australia's Wonderland and Wildlife Park
HOXLEY PARK
Radio Astronomy Centre
Prospect Reservoir
Parramatta
Lane Cove
Gladesville
Chatswood
Deewhy
Manly
Balgowlah Heights
SYDNEY HARBOUR NP
Outer North Head
Quarantine Station
Cecil Park
Merrylands
Cabramatta
Flemington
Balmain
Mosman
Watsons Bay
Dover Heights
SYDNEY
Liverpool
Bankstown
Belfield
Paddington
North Bondi
Bondi
Kingsford
Clovelly
Coogee
Milperra
Revesby
Marrickville
Bexley
SYDNEY AIRPORT
Botany
Maroubra
Macquarie Fields
Minto
Hurstville
Blakehurst
Brighton-le-Sands
Military
Sylvania
La Perouse
Cape Banks Inscription Point
Botany Bay
Leumeah
Sutherland
Kurnell
CAMPBELLTOWN
RESERVE
Audley
Bate Bay
Port Hacking Point
BUNDEENA
Wedderburn
Waterfall
Helensburgh
WATTAMOLLA
Appin
Otford
Lawrence Hargrave Memorial & Lookout
Stanwell Park
Coalcliff
Clifton
Scarborough
Wombarra
Coledale
Austinmer
Sublime Point Lookout
TO WOLLONGONG

J K L M N O P Q R

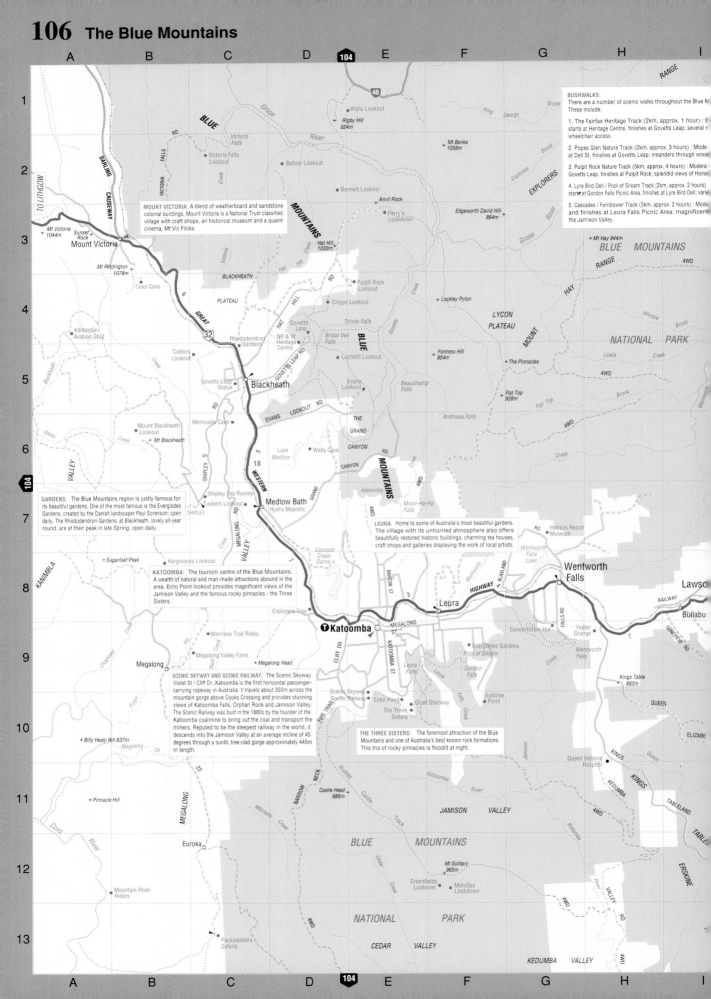

BUSHWALKS:
There are a number of scenic walks throughout the Blue M
These include:

1. The Fairfax Heritage Track (2km, approx. 1 hour) : E
starts at Heritage Centre, finishes at Govetts Leap; several r
wheelchair access.

2. Popes Glen Nature Track (2km, approx. 3 hours) : Mode
at Dell St, finishes at Govetts Leap; meanders through woo

3. Pulpit Rock Nature Track (5km, approx. 4 hours) : Modera
Govetts Leap, finishes at Pulpit Rock; splendid views of Horse

4. Lyre Bird Dell / Pool of Siloam Track (2km, approx. 2 hours)
starts at Gordon Falls Picnic Area, finishes at Lyre Bird Dell; varie

5. Cascades / Fernbower Track (3km, approx. 2 hours) : Mode
and finishes at Leura Falls Picnic Area; magnificen
the Jamison Valley.

MOUNT VICTORIA: A blend of weatherboard and sandstone colonial buildings, Mount Victoria is a National Trust classified village with craft shops, an historical museum and a quaint cinema, Mt Vic Flicks.

GARDENS: The Blue Mountains region is justly famous for its beautiful gardens. One of the most famous is the Everglades Gardens, created by the Danish landscaper Paul Sorenson; open daily. The Rhododendron Gardens, at Blackheath, lovely all-year round, are at their peak in late Spring; open daily.

KATOOMBA: The tourism centre of the Blue Mountains. A wealth of natural and man-made attractions abound in the area. Echo Point lookout provides magnificent views of the Jamison Valley and the famous rocky pinnacles - the Three Sisters.

LEURA: Home to some of Australia's most beautiful gardens. The village with its unhurried atmosphere also offers beautifully restored historic buildings, charming tea houses, craft shops and galleries displaying the work of local artists.

SCENIC SKYWAY AND SCENIC RAILWAY: The Scenic Skyway, Violet St / Cliff Dr.,Katoomba is the first horizontal passenger-carrying ropeway in Australia. It travels about 350m across the mountain gorge above Cooks Crossing and provides stunning views of Katoomba Falls, Orphan Rock and Jamison Valley. The Scenic Railway was built in the 1880s by the founder of the Katoomba coalmine to bring out the coal and transport the miners. Reputed to be the steepest railway in the world, it descends into the Jamison Valley at an average incline of 45 degrees through a sunlit, tree-clad gorge approximately 445m in length.

THE THREE SISTERS: The foremost attraction of the Blue Mountains and one of Australia's best known rock formations. This trio of rocky pinnacles is floodlit at night.

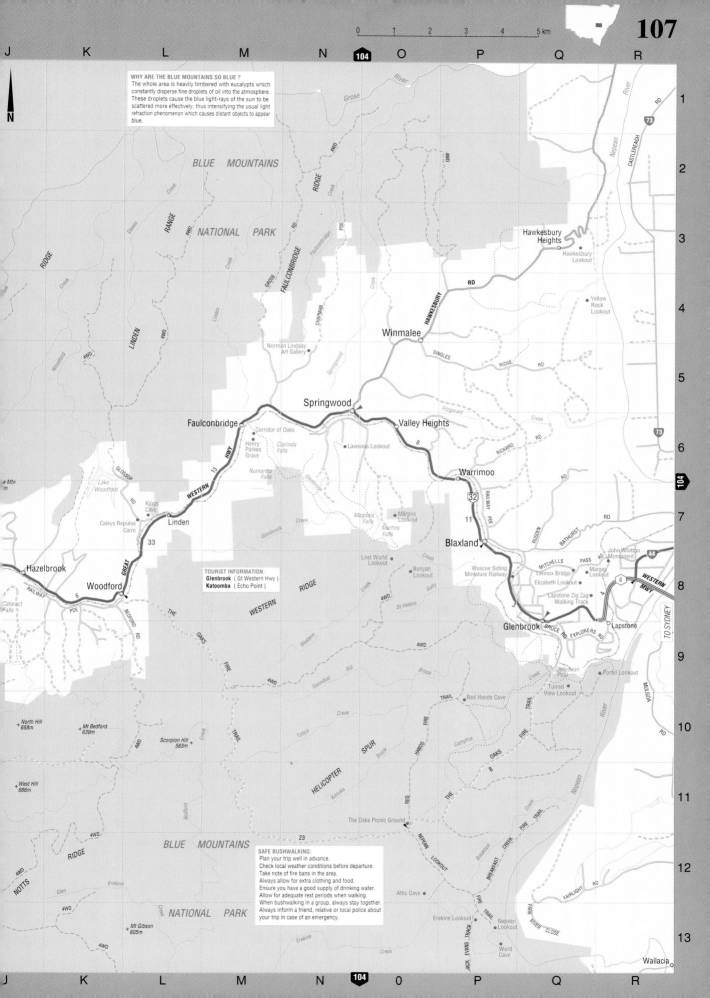

0 1 2 3 4 5 km

WHY ARE THE BLUE MOUNTAINS SO BLUE ?
The whole area is heavily timbered with eucalypts which constantly disperse fine droplets of oil into the atmosphere. These droplets cause the blue light-rays of the sun to be scattered more effectively, thus intensifying the usual light refraction phenomenon which causes distant objects to appear blue.

BLUE MOUNTAINS

RANGE   NATIONAL PARK

LINDEN   RIDGE

GROSE   FAULCONBRIDGE   RIDGE

Grose   River

Hawkesbury Heights
Hawkesbury Lookout

HAWKESBURY   RD

Yellow Rock Lookout

Winmalee

SINGLES   RIDGE   RD

Norman Lindsay Art Gallery

Springwood

Faulconbridge
Corridor of Oaks
Henry Parkes Grave
Clarinda Falls

Valley Heights

Fitzgerald   Creek

RICKARD   RD

WESTERN   HWY

13

Numantia Falls

Lawsons Lookout

8

Warrimoo

32   RAILWAY   PDE

RUSSEN

BATHURST

RD

104

Lake Woodford
Kings Cave
GLOSSOP   RD

Linden

Caleys Repulse Cairn

33

Magdala Falls
Martins Lookout
Martins Falls

11

Blaxland

John Whitton Monument

44

Lost World Lookout

Bunyan Lookout

Wascoe Siding Miniature Railway

MITCHELLS
Lennox Bridge
Elizabeth Lookout

PASS   Marges Lookout

4   WESTERN   MWY

Hazelbrook

GREAT   BEDFORD RD

Woodford

6   RAILWAY   PDE

Cataract Falls

Glenbrook   Creek

St Helens

4WD

WESTERN   RIDGE

Lapstone Zig Zag Walking Track

3

Glenbrook   BRUCE RD   EXPLORERS RD   Lapstone

TO SYDNEY

TOURIST INFORMATION:
Glenbrook (Gt Western Hwy)
Katoomba (Echo Point)

THE   OAKS   FIRE   TRAIL

4WD

Goondral   Rill

Brook

Jellybean Pool
Tunnel View Lookout

Portal Lookout

MULGOA   RD

North Hill
658m

Mt Bedford
639m

Scorpion Hill
563m

4WD

Bedford   Creek

HELICOPTER   SPUR

Tobys   Creek

Kanuka   Brook

TRAIL   Red Hands Cave

RED   HANDS   FIRE   TRAIL

THE   OAKS   FIRE   TRAIL

8

Campfire

Creek

Nepean   River

West Hill
686m

RIDGE

NOTTS   4WD

Glen

Erskine   Creek

NATIONAL PARK

Mt Gibson
605m

4WD

23

The Oaks Picnic Ground

Attic Cave

NEPEAN   LOOKOUT

BREAKFAST   CREEK   FIRE   TRAIL

FAIRLIGHT   RD

PARK   RIVER   CLOSE

SAFE BUSHWALKING:
Plan your trip well in advance.
Check local weather conditions before departure.
Take note of fire bans in the area.
Always allow for extra clothing and food.
Ensure you have a good supply of drinking water.
Allow for adequate rest periods when walking.
When bushwalking in a group, always stay together.
Always inform a friend, relative or local police about your trip in case of an emergency.

JACK   EVANS   TRACK
Erskine Lookout
Nepean Lookout

Word Cave

Wallacia

Erskine   Creek

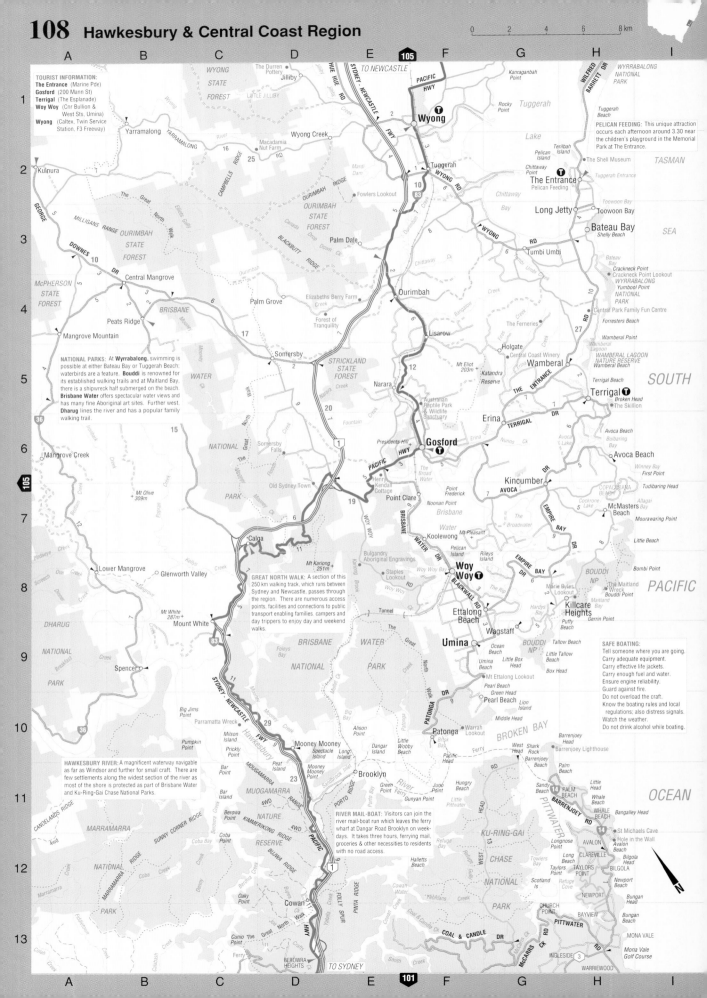

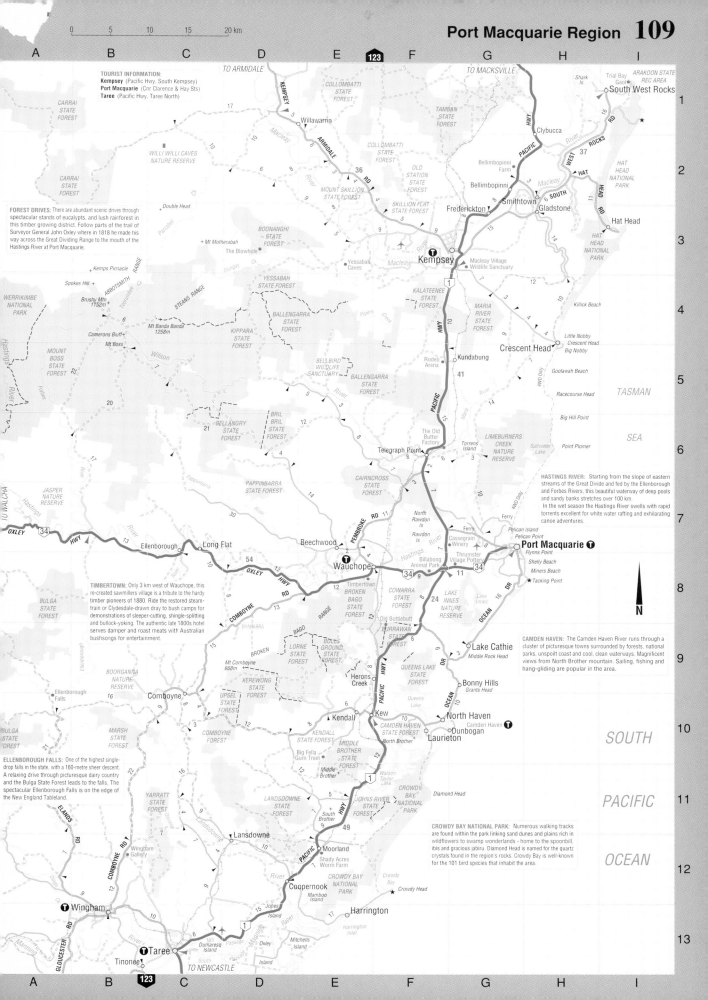

TOURIST INFORMATION:
Kempsey (Pacific Hwy, South Kempsey)
Port Macquarie (Cnr Clarence & Hay Sts)
Taree (Pacific Hwy, Taree North)

FOREST DRIVES: There are abundant scenic drives through spectacular stands of eucalypts, and lush rainforest in this timber growing district. Follow parts of the trail of Surveyor General John Oxley where in 1818 he made his way across the Great Dividing Range to the mouth of the Hastings River at Port Macquarie.

TIMBERTOWN: Only 3 km west of Wauchope, this re-created sawmillers village is a tribute to the hardy timber pioneers of 1880. Ride the restored steam-train or Clydesdale-drawn dray to bush camps for demonstrations of sleeper-cutting, shingle-splitting and bullock-yoking. The authentic late 1800s hotel serves damper and roast meats with Australian bushsongs for entertainment.

ELLENBOROUGH FALLS: One of the highest single-drop falls in the state, with a 160-metre sheer descent. A relaxing drive through picturesque dairy country and the Bulga State Forest leads to the falls. The spectacular Ellenborough Falls is on the edge of the New England Tableland.

HASTINGS RIVER: Starting from the slope of eastern streams of the Great Divide and fed by the Ellenborough and Forbes Rivers, this beautiful waterway of deep pools and sandy banks stretches over 100 km.
In the wet season the Hastings River swells with rapid torrents excellent for white water rafting and exhilarating canoe adventures.

CAMDEN HAVEN: The Camden Haven River runs through a cluster of picturesque towns surrounded by forests, national parks, unspoilt coast and cool, clean waterways. Magnificent views from North Brother mountain. Sailing, fishing and hang-gliding are popular in the area.

CROWDY BAY NATIONAL PARK: Numerous walking tracks are found within the park linking sand dunes and plains rich in wildflowers to swamp wonderlands - home to the spoonbill, ibis and gracious jabiru. Diamond Head is named for the quartz crystals found in the region's rocks. Crowdy Bay is well-known for the 101 bird species that inhabit the area.

TASMAN SEA

SOUTH PACIFIC OCEAN

0   0.5   1   1.5   2 k

Accommodation ■
Aloha Motor Inn 1 B10
City Motel 2 F7
Lucky Lil's 3 E7
Newcastle Backpackers 4 C7
Newcastle Star Hotel 5 E7
Noahs on the Beach 6 I7
Novocastrian Motor Inn 7 I7
Radisson Hotel 8 D7
The Esplanade Motor Inn 9 I7

General Information ■
Ansett Australia 10 F7
City Hall 11 F7
Ferry Terminal 12 G6
Motoring Organisation (NRMA) 13 F7
Newcastle Railway Station 14 H6
Police 15 H7
Post Office 16 H7
Qantas Travel Centre 17 F7
Royal Newcastle Hospital 18 H7
Tourist Information 19 H7
Water Police 20 F6

Places of Interest ■
Bogie Hole 21 H8
Christ Church Cathedral 22 G7
Convict Stockade 23 H7
Cooks Hill Gallery 24 E8
Fort Scratchley 25 I6
Historical Navigation Tower 26 G7
Hunter Street Mall 27 G7
King Edward Park 28 G8
Maritime & Military Museum 29 I6
Newcastle Workers Club 30 E7
Obelisk 31 G8
Queens Wharf 32 G6
Regional Art Gallery 33 F7
Regional Museum 34 C7
Supernova 35 C7
Sydney Harbour Seaplanes 36 G6
von Bertouch Galleries 37 E8
War Memorial Cultural Centre 38 F7
Wharf Road Markets 39 F7
William IV Steamship 40 G6

Accommodation Only a sample range
is listed; inclusion is not necessarily
a recommendation.

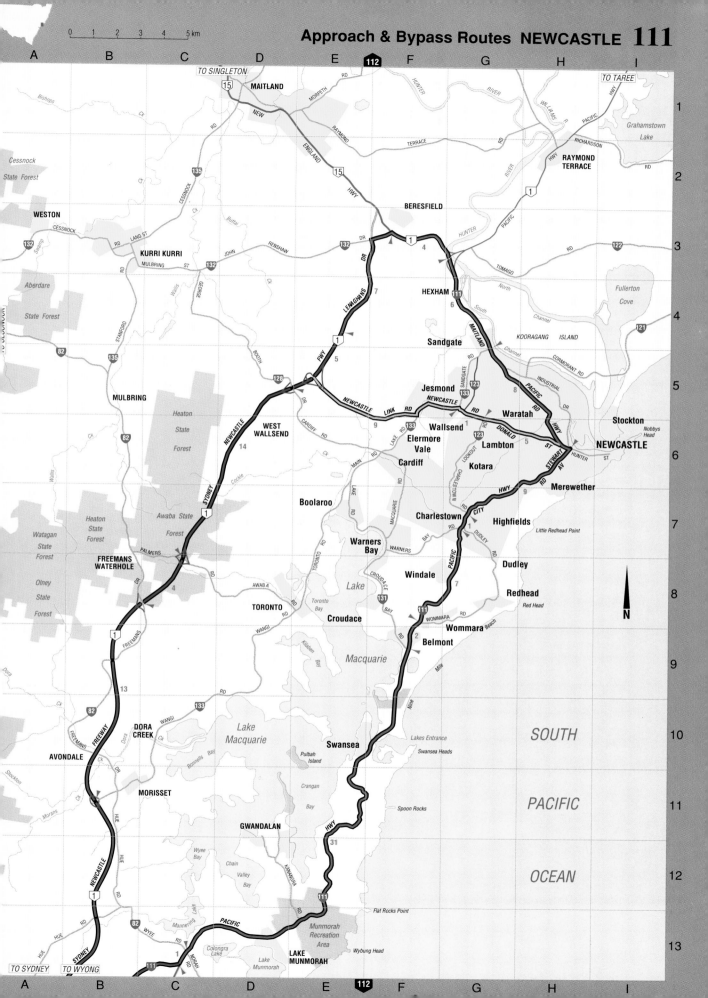

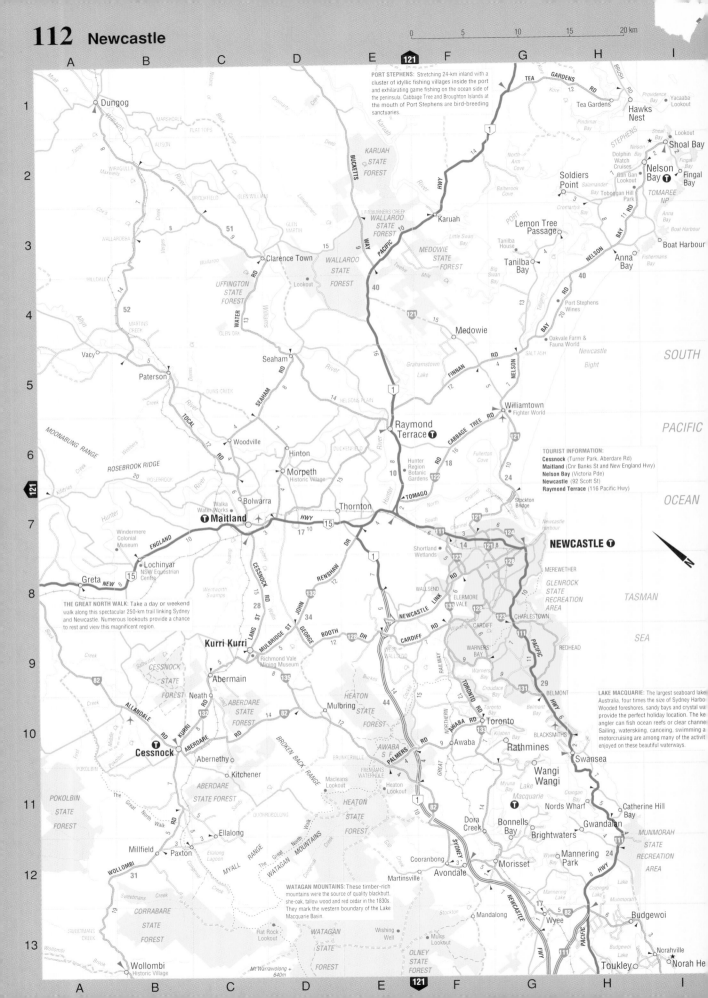

0   5   10   15   20 km

PORT STEPHENS: Stretching 24-km inland with a cluster of idyllic fishing villages inside the port and exhilarating game fishing on the ocean side of the peninsula. Cabbage Tree and Broughton Islands at the mouth of Port Stephens are bird-breeding sanctuaries.

TOURIST INFORMATION:
Cessnock (Turner Park, Aberdare Rd)
Maitland (Cnr Banks St and New England Hwy)
Nelson Bay (Victoria Pde)
Newcastle (92 Scott St)
Raymond Terrace (116 Pacific Hwy)

THE GREAT NORTH WALK: Take a day or weekend walk along this spectacular 250-km trail linking Sydney and Newcastle. Numerous lookouts provide a chance to rest and view this magnificent region.

LAKE MACQUARIE: The largest seaboard lake Australia, four times the size of Sydney Harbo Wooded foreshores, sandy bays and crystal wa provide the perfect holiday location. The ke angler can fish ocean reefs or clear channe Sailing, waterskiing, canoeing, swimming a motorcruising are among many of the activit enjoyed on these beautiful waterways.

WATAGAN MOUNTAINS: These timber-rich mountains were the source of quality blackbutt, she-oak, tallow wood and red cedar in the 1830s. They mark the western boundary of the Lake Macquarie Basin.

Dungog
Tea Gardens
Hawks Nest
Shoal Bay
Nelson Bay
Fingal Bay
Soldiers Point
Boat Harbour
Karuah
Lemon Tree Passage
Tanilba Bay
Anna Bay
Clarence Town
Medowie
Seaham
Williamtown
Vacy
Paterson
Woodville
Hinton
Morpeth
Raymond Terrace
Bolwarra
Thornton
Tomago
Maitland
Greta
Lochinvar
NEWCASTLE
Kurri Kurri
Abermain
Neath
Mulbring
Toronto
Cessnock
Abernethy
Awaba
Rathmines
Kitchener
Wangi Wangi
Swansea
Nords Wharf
Catherine Hill Bay
Ellalong
Bonnells Bay
Gwandalan
Millfield
Paxton
Brightwaters
Mannering Park
Dora Creek
Wollombi
Cooranbong
Morisset
Avondale
Budgewoi
Martinsville
Wyee
Mandalong
Toukley
Norahville
Norah He

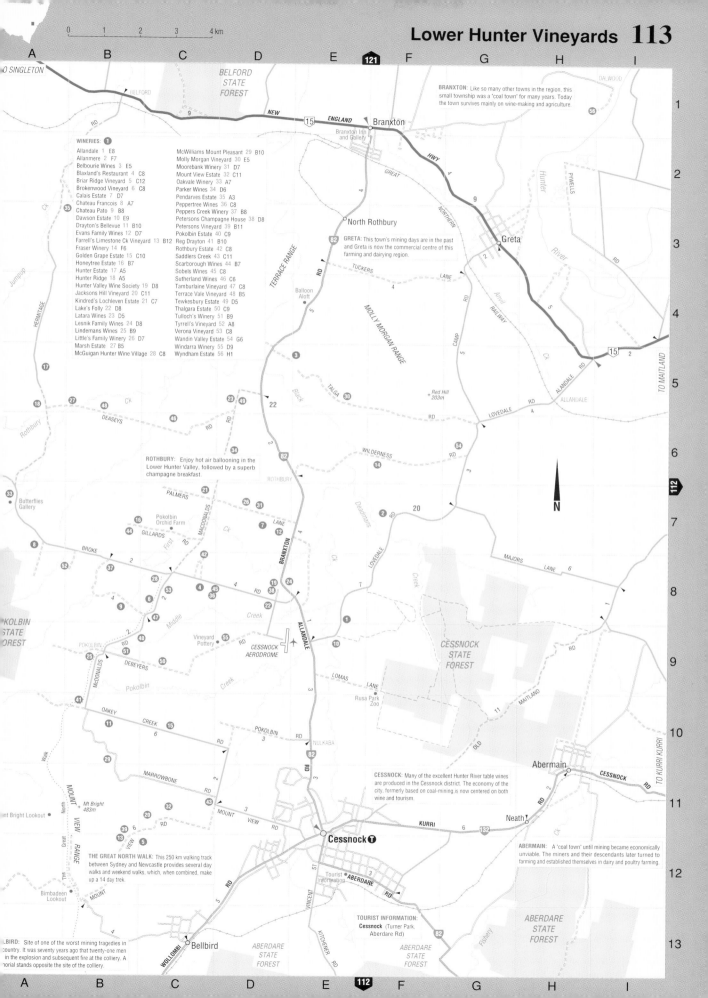

0 1 2 3 4 km

WINERIES:

Allandale 1 E8
Allanmere 2 F7
Belbourie Wines 3 E5
Blaxland's Restaurant 4 C8
Briar Ridge Vineyard 5 C12
Brokenwood Vineyard 6 C8
Calais Estate 7 D7
Chateau Francois 8 A7
Chateau Pato 9 B8
Dawson Estate 10 E9
Drayton's Bellevue 11 B10
Evans Family Wines 12 D7
Farrell's Limestone Ck Vineyard 13 B12
Fraser Winery 14 F6
Golden Grape Estate 15 C10
Honeytree Estate 16 B7
Hunter Estate 17 A5
Hunter Ridge 18 A5
Hunter Valley Wine Society 19 D8
Jacksons Hill Vineyard 20 C11
Kindred's Lochleven Estate 21 C7
Lake's Folly 22 D8
Latara Wines 23 D8
Lesnik Family Wines 24 D8
Lindemans Wines 25 B9
Little's Family Winery 26 D7
Marsh Estate 27 B5
McGuigan Hunter Wine Village 28 C8
McWilliams Mount Pleasant 29 B10
Molly Morgan Vineyard 30 E5
Moorebank Winery 31 D7
Mount View Estate 32 C11
Oakvale Winery 33 A7
Parker Wines 34 D6
Pendarves Estate 35 A3
Peppertree Wines 36 C8
Peppers Creek Winery 37 B8
Petersons Champagne House 38 D8
Petersons Vineyard 39 B11
Pokolbin Estate 40 C9
Reg Drayton 41 B10
Rothbury Estate 42 C8
Saddlers Creek 43 C11
Scarborough Wines 44 B7
Sobels Wines 45 C8
Sutherland Wines 46 C6
Tamburlaine Vineyard 47 C8
Terrace Vale Vineyard 48 B5
Tewkasbury Estate 49 D5
Thalgara Estate 50 C9
Tulloch's Winery 51 B9
Tyrrell's Vineyard 52 A8
Verona Vineyard 53 C8
Wandin Valley Estate 54 G6
Windarra Winery 55 D9
Wyndham Estate 56 H1

BRANXTON: Like so many other towns in the region, this small township was a "coal town" for many years. Today the town survives mainly on wine-making and agriculture.

GRETA: This town's mining days are in the past and Greta is now the commercial centre of this farming and dairying region.

ROTHBURY: Enjoy hot air ballooning in the Lower Hunter Valley, followed by a superb champagne breakfast.

CESSNOCK: Many of the excellent Hunter River table wines are produced in the Cessnock district. The economy of the city, formerly based on coal-mining, is now centered on both wine and tourism.

ABERMAIN: A "coal town" until mining became economically unviable. The miners and their descendants later turned to farming and established themselves in dairy and poultry farming.

THE GREAT NORTH WALK: This 250 km walking track between Sydney and Newcastle provides several day walks and weekend walks, which, when combined, make up a 14 day trek.

TOURIST INFORMATION:
Cessnock (Turner Park, Aberdare Rd)

BELLBIRD: Site of one of the worst mining tragedies in country. It was seventy years ago that twenty-one men in the explosion and subsequent fire at the colliery. morial stands opposite the site of the colliery.

TO SINGLETON

BELFORD STATE FOREST

Branxton
Branxton Inn and Gallery

North Rothbury

Greta

Balloon Aloft

MOLLY MORGAN RANGE

Red Hill 203m

TERRACE RANGE

Butterflies Gallery

Pokolbin Orchid Farm

Vineyard Pottery

CESSNOCK AERODROME

POKOLBIN STATE FOREST

Rusa Park Zoo

CESSNOCK STATE FOREST

Abermain

Neath

Mt Bright 483m

Bright Lookout

Cessnock

Tourist Information

ABERDARE

Bimbadeen Lookout

Bellbird

ABERDARE STATE FOREST

ABERDARE STATE FOREST

ABERDARE STATE FOREST

TO MAITLAND

TO KURRI KURRI

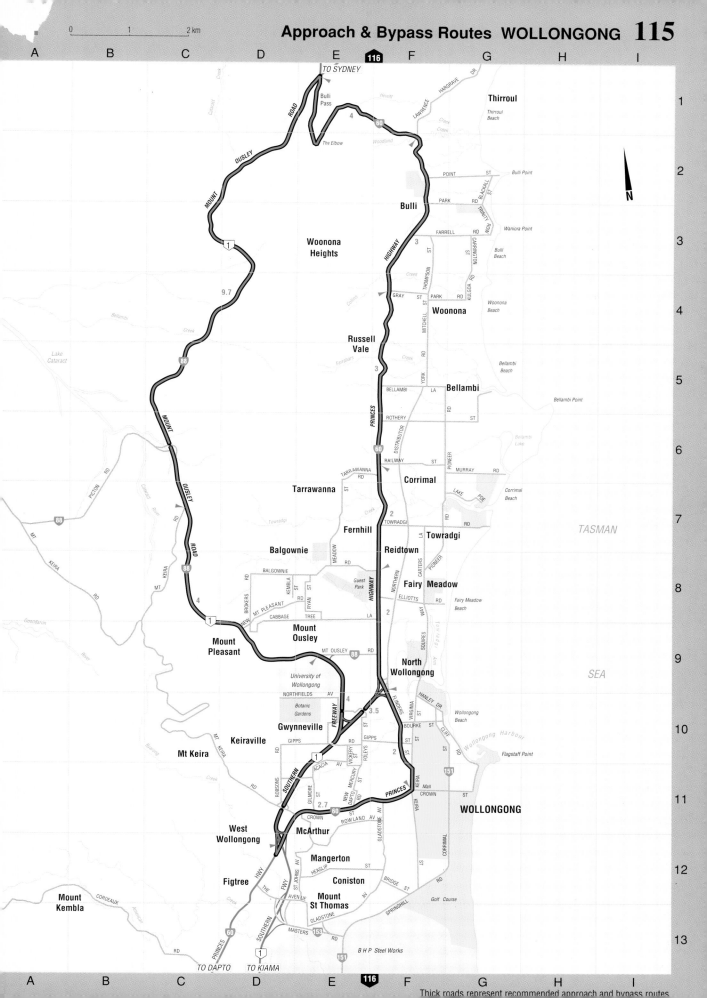

0 1 2 km

A B C D E F G H I

116

TO SYDNEY

Bulli
Pass

Hewitt

4

60

Thirroul

*Thirroul
Beach*

MOUNT

OUSLEY

The Elbow

Woodland

LAWRENCE
DR

HARGRAVE
DR

Creek

1

POINT
ST

Bulli Point

ROAD

Bulli

PARK
ST

BLACKALL
ST

TRINITY
ROW

2

**Woonona
Heights**

FARRELL
RD

*Bulli
Beach*

CARRINGTON
RD

KULGOA
RD

3

1

9.7

HIGHWAY

Creek

Collins

GRAY
ST

THOMPSON
ST

PARK
RD

Woonona

*Woonona
Beach*

4

**Russell
Vale**

MITCHELL
RD

Farrahars

Creek

YORK
ST

Bellambi

*Bellambi
Beach*

5

88

3

BELLAMBI
LA

LA

ROTHERY
ST

RD

ST

*Bellambi
Lake*

Bellambi Point

PRINCES

DISTRIBUTOR

60

RAILWAY

ST

PIONEER
ST

MURRAY
RD

*Corrimal
Beach*

6

MOUNT

TARRAWANNA
RD

Corrimal

Tarrawanna

ST

TOWRADGI
RD

LAKE
PDE

7

OUSLEY

Towradgi

Creek

2

LA

ST

RD

TASMAN

88

Fernhill

MEADOW
RD

Towradgi

CARTERS
LA

PIONEER

8

ROAD

Balgownie

BALGOWNIE
RD

*Guest
Park*

Reidtown

NORTHERN

SQUIRES
WAY

Towradgi Arm

KEMBLA
ST

ST

HIGHWAY

Fairy Meadow

4

NEW

MT PLEASANT
RD

RYAN
ST

ELLIOTTS
RD

RD

*Fairy Meadow
Beach*

BROKERS
RD

CABBAGE

TREE

LA

1

**Mount
Pleasant**

MT OUSLEY
RD

2

9

**Mount
Ousley**

88

**North
Wollongong**

SEA

MT KEIRA
RD

*University of
Wollongong*

FLINDERS
ST

HANLEY
DR

PICTON
RD

NORTHFIELDS
AV

4

VIRGINIA
ST

*Wollongong
Beach*

MT KEIRA
RD

*Botanic
Gardens*

3.5

BOURKE
ST

CLIFF
RD

10

88

Gwynneville

FREEWAY

GIPPS
ST

GIPPS
ST

Wollongong Harbour

MT

Keiraville

GIPPS
RD

Flagstaff Point

Mt Keira

1

VICKERY
ST

FOLEYS
ST

2

ST

ROBSONS
RD

151

ACACIA
AV

SOUTHERN

MERCURY
ST

PRINCES

KEIRA
ST

Mall
CROWN

11

60

GILMORE
ST

2.7

NEW
DAPTO
RD

ROW LAND
AV

WOLLONGONG

Creek

**West
Wollongong**

CROWN

McArthur

GLADSTONE
AV

KEIRA
ST

ST

Mangerton

HEASLIP
ST

CORRIMAL
ST

12

THE

Figtree

HWY

FWY

ST JOHNS
AV

AVENUE

Coniston

BRIDGE
ST

RD

Golf Course

**Mount
Kembla**

CORDEAUX
RD

Creek

**Mount
St Thomas**

GLADSTONE

SPRINGHILL
RD

60

PRINCES

SOUTHERN

MASTERS
RD

153

B H P Steel Works

13

RD

TO DAPTO

1

TO KIAMA

151

N

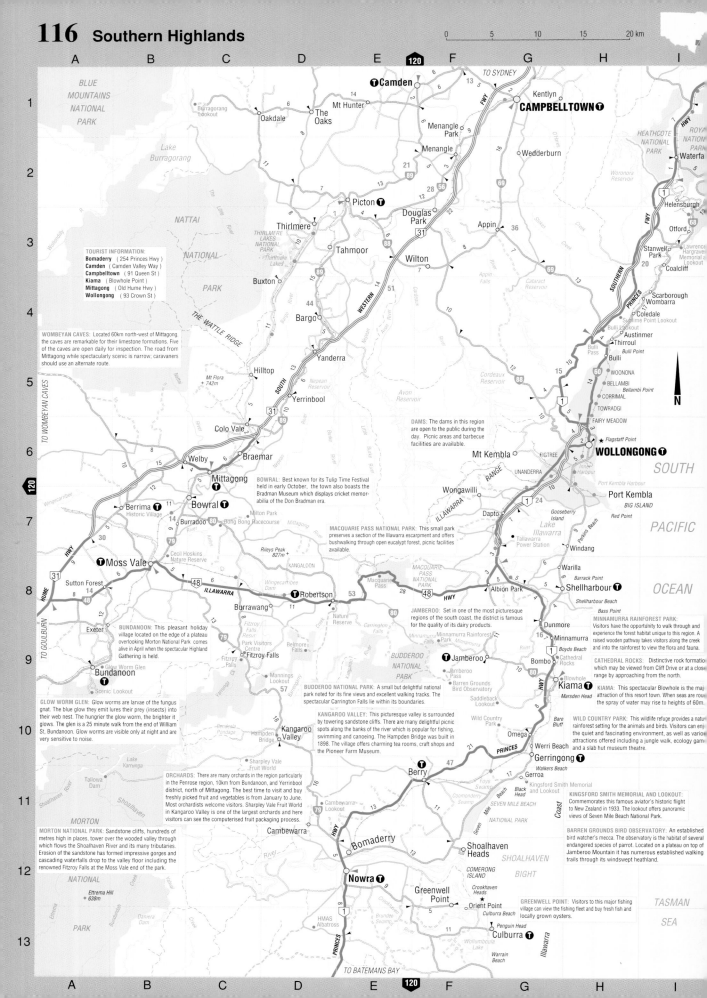

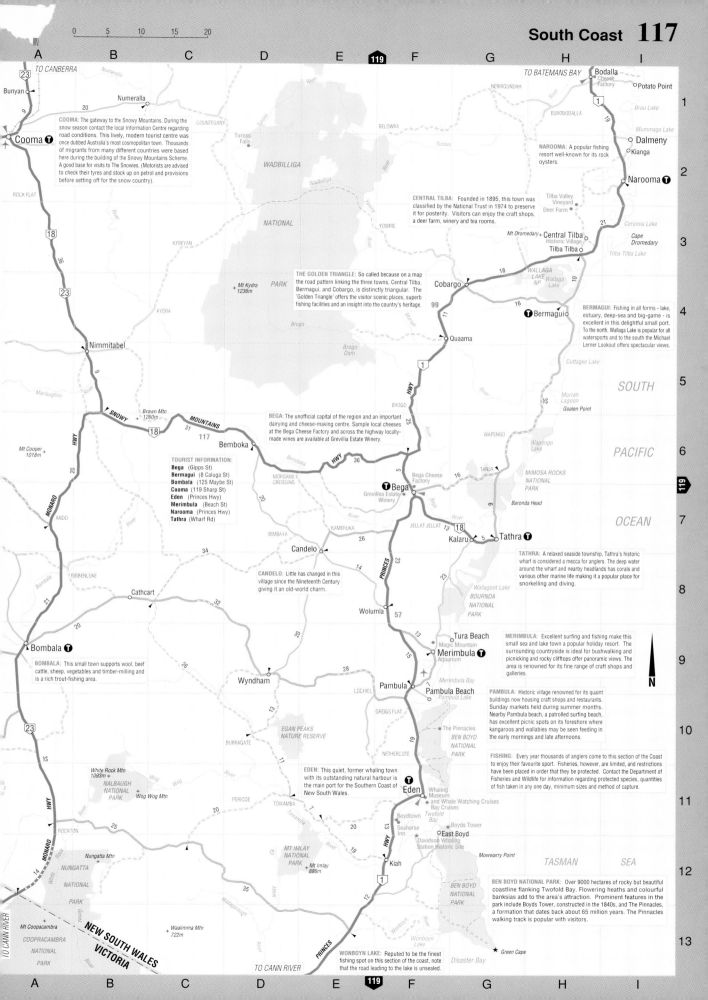

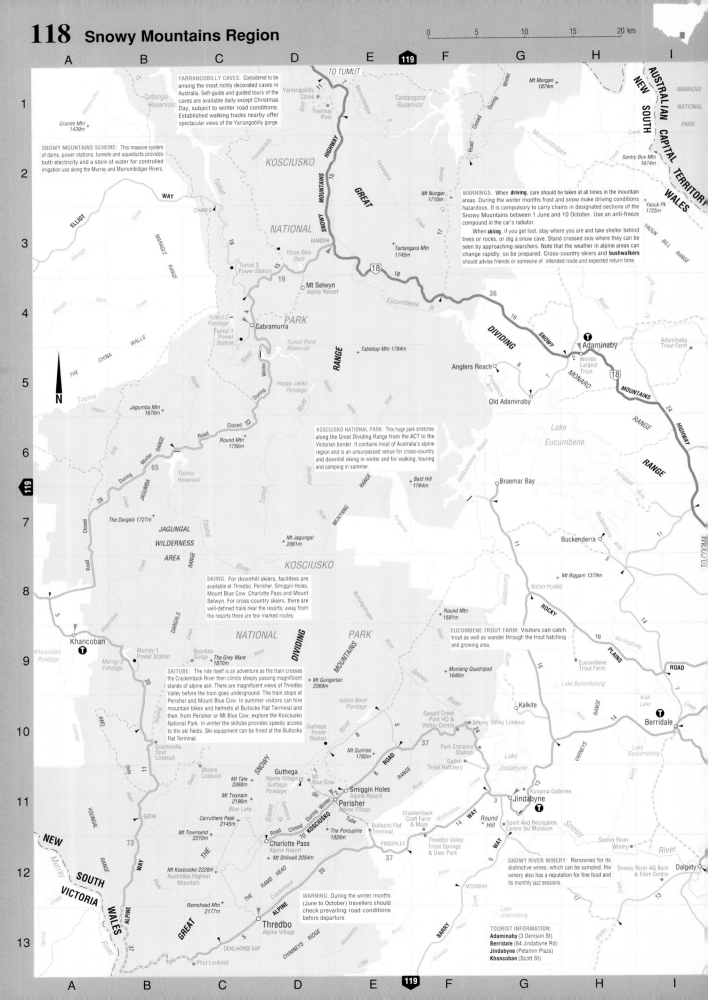

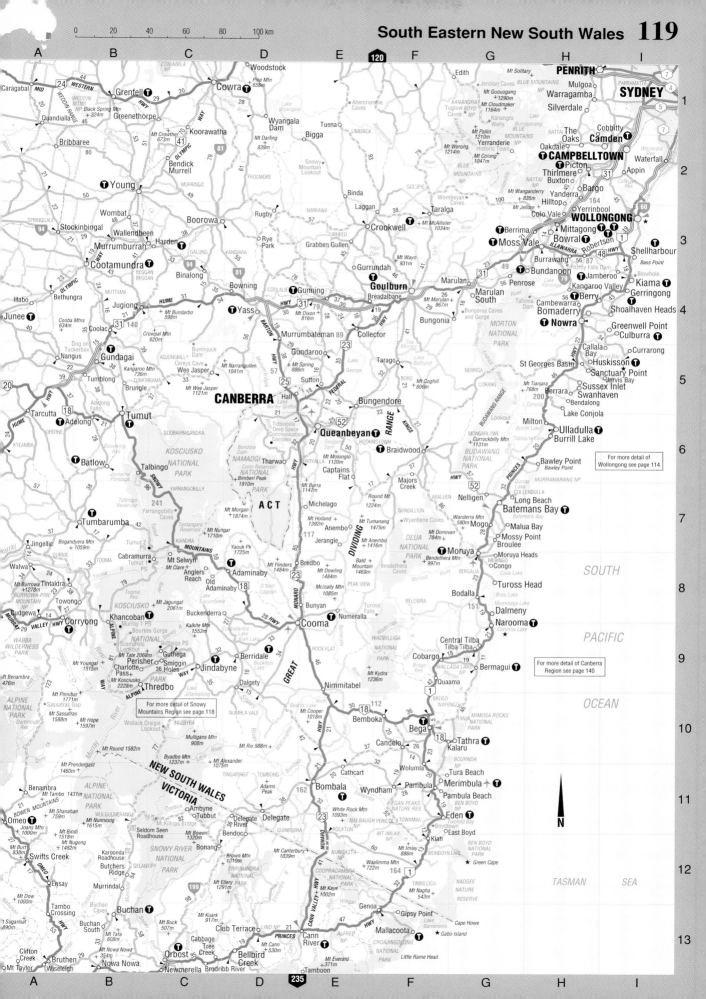

A B C D 122 HWY E F G H I

1 MITCHELL · Reedy Corner · Belaringar · 34 Warren · 20 · OXLEY 49 HWY · Collie · 36 · 55 · OXLEY · Binnaway · Blackville · 44 · Willow · 19 · Quirindi

2 · Nevertire · 33 HIGHWAY · Marthaguy · Dragon Cowal · CA · 65 · 65 · 39 · 74 · Eumungerie · Old Harbor Lagoon · Mendooran · Merrygoen · 39 · Dunedoo · Coolah · 37 · Leadville · 69 · 48 · Tabragar · Cassilis · GOULBURN RIVER NATIONAL PARK · Merriwa · Bunr · M

3 · Trangie · 32 · 33 · Buddah Lake · Minore Falls · 40 · Dubbo 38 · 84 · Ballimore · 80 · 33 · 43 · Goolma · 31 · Gulgong · 41 · Munghorn Gap · 70 · GREAT · Ulan · 53 · 58 · Sandy Hollow · Denm

· Tottenham · 20 · Narromine · 38 · 44 · NEWELL · Wongarbon · Geurie · 55 · 22 · 46 · Mt Emiguyley 686m · Wellington · Mudgee · 86 · 47 · Lue · WOLLEMI NATIONAL PARK · Windamere Dam · DIVIDING · Mt Nullo Mtn 1189m · Mt Coriaday 1257m · Rylstone

· Albert · 37 · Tullamore · 43 · Tomingley · HERVEY'S RANGE · 18 · 37 · Little · 50 · 71 · CATOMBAL RANGE · Wellington Caves · Yeoval · 43 · 65 · 150 · Lake Burrendong · Mumbil · Stuart Town · Mt Boiga 1058m · Kandos · Ilford · RANGE · Mt Coorongooba · Gospers Mtn 843m

5 · Fifield · 35 · Trundle · 78 · Peak Hill · 120 · Open Cut Gold Mine · 32 · MITCHELL · 26 · Cumnock · 22 · Mt Golding · Hill End Historic Site · Turon · Sofala Historic Town · 86 · Capertee · BEN BULLEN · Mt Wagdon 1015m · Mt Davidson 1081m · Cullen Bullen · WOLLEMI NATIONAL PARK

6 · Derriwong Mtn 414m · 90 · Bogan Gate · 38 · Parkes · Alectown · CK Radio Telescope · CURUMBENYA NATURE RESERVE · 56 · Molong · Manildra · 81 · 90 · 35 · Orange · Lucknow · LEWIS PONDS · 56 · Peel · Portland · 22 · Wallerawang · ANGUS PLACE · Mt Tootie · Lidsdale · Bilpin

127 · 24 · Forbes · Manna Mtn 552m · 39 · HWY · DAROOBALGIE · 39 · Cudal · Cargo · BOREE CAVES · BOWAN PARK · Mt Canobolas 1397m · Columbine Mtn 866m · GUYONG · 56 · Bathurst · DUNKELD · Yetholme · 30 · Rydal · Zig Zag Railway · Hartley · LOCKSLEY · Lithgow · 89 · 40 · Freeman · Richm

7 · Burcher · Wamboyne Mtn 412m · NERANG COWAL · BIRD AND ANIMAL SANCTUARY · 138 · Eugowra · 37 · BUNDABURRAH · Nangar Mtn 778m · NANGAR NP · Gooloogong · 34 · BANDON · Canowindra · CANOMODINE · FOREST REEFS · Sugarloaf · Millthorpe · 38 · Blayney · Perthville · 45 · Newbridge · Georges Plains · O'Connell · 47 · Mount Victoria · Blackheath · 32 · Springwood · MOUNTAINS · Lawson

· West Wyalong · WESTERN · Marsden · CLEAR RIDGE · 23 · Caragabal · 24 · WEDDIN MTNS · Black Spring Mtn 324m · 44 · Grenfell · 29 · HWY · 262 · Cowra · Mandurama · 24 · Carcoar · Lyndhurst · Hobbys Yards · Rockley · Oberon · Edith · Mt Solitary 965m · Katoomba · BLUE MOUNTAINS NP · Warragamba

8 · Wyalong · 85 · WIRRINYA WEST · PULLABOOKA · CONIMBLA NATIONAL PARK · Woodstock · Pine Mtn 656m · 40 · Lake Wyangala · WALLI · Trunkey · Abercrombie Caves · KANANGRA BOYD NP · Mt Pallin 1210m · Mt Colong 1047m · Yerranderie · THE BLUE

9 · Barmedman · REEFTON · Pinnacle Mtn 447m · Bribbaree · 80 · Greenethorpe · Mt Crowther 673m · Koorawatha · 81 · Bendick Murrell · 41 · Wyangala Dam · Mt Darling 839m · Bigga · Snowy Mountain Lookout · FROGMORE · GOLSPIE · WOMBEYAN CAVES NP · Mt Wanganderry 835m · Oakdale · Thirlmere · Buxton · Bargo

· Ariah Park · Young · MURRINGO · Wombat · Boorowa · Rugby · NARRAWA · Binda · Laggan · Taralga · Mt McAllister 1034m · Colo Vale · Berrima · Moss Vale · Bowral

10 · Temora · 94 · 55 · Stockinbingal · Wallendbeen · Murrumburrah · GALONG · KANGIARA · Rye Park · WHEEO · Crookwell · Grabben Gullen · Gurrundah · TARLO RIVER NP · Marulan · 31 · Burrawang · Bundanoon · Penrose · 79 · Kang

11 · Coolamon · Marrar · MIMOSA · SEBASTOPOL · 85 · Illabo · Bethungra · Cootamundra · OLYMPIC · Harden · BEGGAN BEGGAN · 94 · Binalong · Bookham · Bowning · 81 · 31 · Gunning · 37 · Breadalbane · Goulburn · Bungonia · Marulan South · BUNGONIA CAVES · Cambewarra · Bomaderry · Nowra

12 · Wagga Wagga · Junee · Dhulura · 41 · Nangus · Jugiong · Coolac · 140 · Cooba Mtns 634m · Crowpal Mtn 620m · Yass · BARTON · Murrumbateman · Mt Dixon 816m · 89 · Collector · Gundaroo · FEDERAL · 23 · Tarago · THE MORASS · Lake George · Mt Coghill 806m · BORO · St Georges Basin · Sussex Inlet · Berrara

· Forest Hill · Uranquinty · Alfred Town · 20 · HUME · Gundagai · Tumblong · Kangaroo Mtn 738m · TUMORRAMA · ADJUNGBILLY · Careys Cave · Wee Jasper · Mt Narrangullen 1041m · 57 · Mt Spring 886m · Sutton · CANBERRA · 25 · Bungendore · KINGS · Mt Gillamatong 907m · Milton · Ulladu

13 · Mangoplah · BURRANDANA · Mt Flakney 536m · Tarcutta · 18 · Adelong · Adelong Falls · Tumut · GOOBARRAGANDRA · KOSCIUSKO NATIONAL PARK · Blowering Res · Bendora Dam · ACT · Tidbinbilla Deep Space Communication Complex · NAMADGI NP · Royalla · Mt Molonglo 1120m · Queanbeyan · HOSKINSTOWN · Braidwood · BUDAWANG RANGE · Bawley Point

For more detail of Canberra Region see page 140

· Batlow · KYEAMBA · 119

0 20 40 60 80 100 km

J K L **123** M N O P Q R

1

Nowendoc

GREAT DIVIDING RANGE

Combyne
Ellenborough Falls
Lake Cathie
Bonny Hills
Kendall
Kew
North Haven
Laurieton

WOKO NP

Rawley's River

Manning River

CROWDY BAY NP

2

Gundy
Lake Glenbawn

BARRINGTON TOPS NATIONAL PARK
Mt McKenzie

Barrington
Gloucester
Stratford

RANGE

Lansdowne
Wingham
Tinonee
Coopernook
Harrington

Taree
Old Bar

Nabiac
Diamond Beach
Hallidays Point

wellbrook

Lake Liddell
Lake St Clair
Lake Chichester

Dungog
Gresford
Vacy

Wards River

Tuncurry
Forster

Elizabeth Bay
BOOTI BOOTI NP
Wallis Lake

3

ENGLAND

Stroud
Booral

Bulahdelah
Seal Rocks

MYALL LAKES NATIONAL PARK

Singleton

Paterson
Branxton

Clarence Town

Karuah
Tea Gardens
Hawks Nest
Port Stephens

PACIFIC

TAMBOY
Myall Lake

4

Maitland
Morpeth
Raymond Terrace
Williamtown

Nelson Bay
Anna Bay

TOMAREE NP
TOMAREE NP

Kurri Kurri
Cessnock
Millfield
Abernethy
Paxton
Ellalong

Wollombi

HWY

NEWCASTLE

5

Rathmines
Avondale
Belmont
Wangi Wangi
Mannering Park
Catherine Hill Bay

Jilliby
Budgewoi
Toukley

For more detail of Newcastle Region see page 112

6

Mangrove
Kulnura
St Albans
Peats Ridge

Wyong
The Entrance
Bateau Bay

DHARUG NP
Old Sydney Town

Gosford
Terrigal
Kincumber
Killcare Heights

7

SOUTH

Woy Woy
Umina

Mount White

PACIFIC

KURING-GAI CHASE NP
Broken Bay

HORNSBY

8

SYDNEY

POOL

Cape Banks

PACIFIC

9

PBELLTOWN
Waterfall

ROYAL NATIONAL PARK

For more detail of Sydney Suburbs see pages 98 - 103

OCEAN

10

LLONGONG
ongong Harbour

lharbour

11

a
jong

Coast

12

13

J K L M N O P Q R

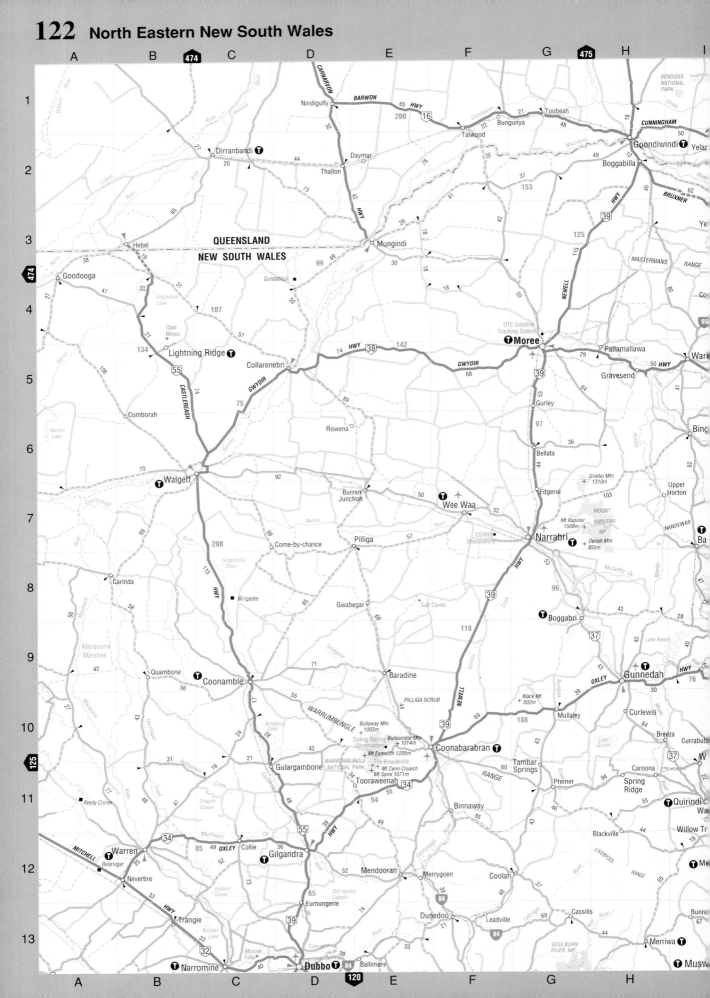

0   20   40   60   80   100 km

J   K   L   M   N   475 O   P   Q   R

QUEENSLAND

NEW SOUTH WALES

GREAT DIVIDING

Karara
200
Mt Burrabaranga 794m
20
Coolmunda Dam
21
55
24
Mt Bullaganang 629m
247
Texas
Glenlyon Dam

Warwick
Tannymorel
Killarney
Legume
HWY 15
Dalveen
Pozieres
Thulimbah
Amiens 113 Appletthorpe
Stanthorpe 142
Severnlea
Glen Aplin
Ballandean
Wallangarra
Tenterfield
HWY 44
Torrington
England 91
Emmaville
Deepwater
12
26
GWYDIR 38

Rathdowney
MAIN RANGE NP
MT BARNEY NP
Woodenbong
Urbenville
Bonalbo
Mummulgum
Tabulam Mallanganee
Drake
Mt Belmore 650m
Baryulgil
Mt Bajimba 1446m
WASHPOOL NP
GIBRALTAR RANGE NATIONAL PARK
162
NYMBOIDA NP

Hillview
Springbrook
Tumbulgum
LAMINGTON NP
Murwillumbah
Tyalgum
MT WARNING NP
Uki
Burringbar
Mullumbimby
Nimbin
Kyogle
Coraki
Woodburn
Evans Head
Iluka
Yamba
Angourie
Lawrence
Brooms Head

Tweed Heads
Banora Point
Chinderah
Kingscliff
Bogangar
Pottsville
Ocean Shores
Brunswick Heads
Cape Byron
Byron Bay
Newrybar
Lennox Head
Ballina
Wardell
Broadwater

Lismore
Alstonville
Casino
190
Woodburn

Inverell
Glen Innes
Gilgai
Tingha
Ben Lomond
Glencoe
Red Range
Balancing Rock
The Black Mtn 591m

Grafton
Coutts Crossing
Nymboida
Glenreagh
Arrawarra
Woolgoolga
Emerald Beach
Moonee Beach
Coramba

Minnie Water
Wooli
Red Rock
North Solitary Island
North West Solitary Island
Groper Island
South Solitary Island
Split Solitary Island

SOUTH

Bundarra
Guyra
Llangothlin 98
Thunderbolt's Cave
Armidale 78
Hillgrove
Uralla
Dangars Falls

Dorrigo
Bellingen
Urunga
Valla Beach
Nambucca Heads

Coffs Harbour
Sawtell
Mylestom

PACIFIC

Walcha Road
Walcha
OXLEY HWY
264
Niangala
Nundle
Tuggolo Falls
Nowendoc

Bowraville
Macksville
Scotts Head
Stuarts Point
South West Rocks
Frederickton
Smithtown
Gladstone
Hat Head
Kempsey
Crescent Head
Kundabung

OCEAN

Wingham
Tinonee
Barrington
Gloucester
Stratford
Wards River

Lansdowne
Coopernook
Harrington
Taree
Old Bar
Diamond Beach
Hallidays Point
Tuncurry
Forster

Telegraph Point
Beechwood
Port Macquarie
Wauchope
Lake Cathie
Bonny Hills
North Haven
Dunbogan
Laurieton
CROWDY BAY NP

For more detail of the Port Macquarie Region see page 109

J   K   L   M   N   O   P   Q   R

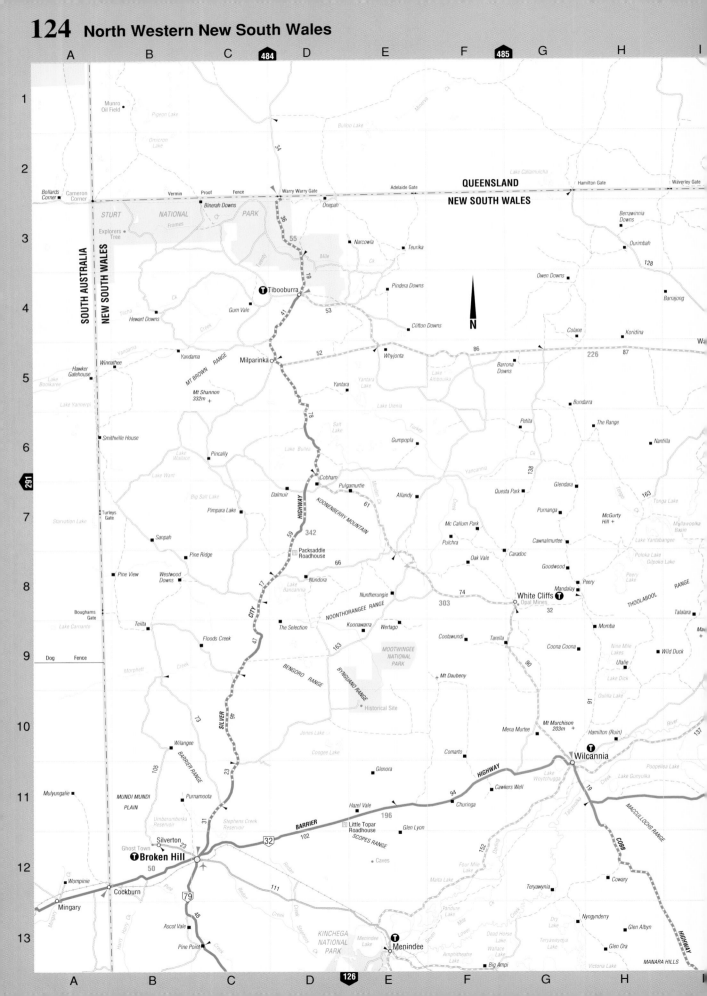

484 **485**

291

126

Map labels

SOUTH AUSTRALIA

NEW SOUTH WALES

QUEENSLAND

NEW SOUTH WALES

Bollards Corner
Cameron Corner
Munro Oil Field
Pigeon Lake
Omicron Lake
Lake Callamulcha
Bulloo Lake
Minerva
Hamilton Gate
Waverley Gate
Vermin
Proof
Fence
Warry Warry Gate
Adelaide Gate
Berrawinnia Downs
STURT NATIONAL PARK
Binerah Downs
Onepah
Ourimbah
Fromes
Explorers Tree
Narcowla
Teurika
Owen Downs
128
Twelve Mile Ck
Pindera Downs
Barrajong
Tibooburra
Gum Vale
53
Clifton Downs
Colane
Koridina
Hewart Downs
Yandama Range
41
Whyjonta
Barrona Downs
86
87
226
Winnathee
Yandama
Milparinka
52
Yantara
Yantara Lake
Lake Altiboulka
Bundarra
Hawker Gatehouse
MT BROWN RANGE
Mt Shannon 332m
Lake Boolkaree
Lake Yannerpi
Salt Lake
Lake Ulema
Turkey Ck
Petita
The Range
Gumpopla
Nantilla
Smithville House
Lake Wallace
78
Pincally
Lake Bulleo
Yancannia Ck
138
Big Salt Lake
Lake Want
Cobham
Pulgamurtie
Allandy
Questa Park
Glendara
163
Tonga Lake
Starvation Lake
Turleys Gate
Dalmuir
342
61
Purnanga
McGurty Hill
Mullawoolka Basin
Pimpara Lake
HIGHWAY
KOONENBERRY MOUNTAIN
59
Mc Callum Park
Cawnalmurtee
Lake Yantabangee
Sanpah
Packsaddle Roadhouse
66
Pulchra
Oak Vale
Caradoc
Goodwood
Poloka Lake Gilpoko Lake
Pine Ridge
Nundora
74
Peery
Peery Lake
Pine View
Westwood Downs
Boughams Gate
Teilta
CITY
17
Nuntherungie
303
White Cliffs
Mandalay
THOOLABOOL RANGE
Lake Carnanto
The Selection
Koonawarra
Wertago
Opal Mines
32
Talalara
Dog Fence
Floods Creek
163
NOONTHORANGEE RANGE
Cootawundi
Tarella
Momba
Nine Mile Lakes
Wild Duck
Morphett Ck
47
BENGORO RANGE
BYNGUANO RANGE
MOOTWINGEE NATIONAL PARK
Mt Daubeny
Coona Coona
Ulalie
Lake Dick
Jones Lake
Historical Site
91
Oulilla Lake
137
Coogee Lake
Mena Murtee
Mt Murchison 203m
Hamilton (Ruin)
River
Wilangee
73
23
Comarto
HIGHWAY
Wilcannia
Poopelloa Lake
105
BARRIER RANGE
Glenora
94
Cawkers Well
19
Lake Gunyulka
Mulyungalie
MUNDI MUNDI PLAIN
Purnamoota
31
Hazel Vale
196
Churinga
MACCULLOCHS RANGE
Stephens Creek Reservoir
Little Topar Roadhouse
Glen Lyon
COBB
Umberumberka Reservoir
BARRIER
102
SCOPES RANGE
152
Teryawynia
Cowary
Silverton
23
32
Caves
Four Mile Lake
Ghost Town
Broken Hill
50
111
Malta Lake
Dry Lake
Nyngynderry
Glen Albyn
Wompinie
Cockburn
79
Redan Ck
Fowlers Ck
Pandurra Lake
Teryaweynia Lake
Glen Ora
Mingary
48
KINCHEGA NATIONAL PARK
Menindee Lake
Dead Horse Lake Wallace Lake
HIGHWAY
Ascot Vale
Menindee
Amphitheatre Lake
Victoria Lake
MANARA HILLS
Pine Point
Big Ampi

J K L M N O P Q R

485   474

0   20   40   60   80   100 km

71
MITCHELL

1

CURRAWINYA NP

Noorama Sports Centre

Kungie Lake

Lake Thonlindah

Paroo

2

Hungerford

Lake Wombah

Vermin   Proof   Fence

QUEENSLAND

Jobs Gate

NEW SOUTH WALES

Parragundy Gate

Barringun

Goodooga

3

Sharoon

Cuttaburra Basin

Yantabulla

Beulah

27

River

Maureen Joy

145

Enngonia

213

142

River

Bullaroon

94

4

HIGHWAY

42

Lake Coonany

Lake Denman

52

Bone

Culgoa

5

Lake Burkanoko

Fords Bridge

62

68

Narran

Lake Nichebulka

134

Murphys Lake

Narran Lake

191

97

Barwon

Brewarrina

64

6

85

Bogan

Bourke

71

Mt Bendemeer 149m

70

Utah Lake

Warrego

River

OXLEYS   TABLELAND

41

28

50

122

Mt Burragurry

101

River

28

Darling

76

32

56

7

Talowla Mtn

Louth

Mulga

Creek

62

Carinda

Mulyah Mtn 162m

Ben Lomond

90

Mt Gunderbooka 497m

43

34

8

Jinki Lake

River

328

Mt Wammiga 380m

76

Wilga Downs

Colossal

32

25

Lake

104

159

Dijou Mountain 317m

Coronga Pk 415m

50

202

27

9

RANKINS RANGE

MT DEERINA

RANGE

Mt Merrere 297m

Mt Booroondara 441m

131

Mt Billagoe 336m

55

Mulga Dam

27

MITCHELL

71

Girilambone

The Brothers 287m

76

41

Mickwilly Lake

96

Mt Buckwaroon 441m

Aboriginal Cave Paintings

Reedy Corner

10

urtabunna Lake

Ck

C.S.A. Copper Mines

River

16

Nyngan

260   BARRIER

84

Cobar

HIGHWAY

44

132

45

32

HIGHWAY

59

ndale dhouse

Barnato Lake

Buckaroon

43

65

Belaringar

11

103

Mt Nurri 421m

Sandy

75

47

55

Nevertire

The Rookery

65

Buckambool Mtn 407m

Sandy

Buddabaddah

39

12

00   RANGE

Creek

JACKERMAROO   RANGE

31

Nymagee 519m

THE BALD HILLS

Bogan

Bibblewindi

WARNING: In outback Australia, long distances separate some towns. Travellers should familiarise themselves with prevailing conditions before departure, and take care to ensure their vehicle is roadworthy and that they carry adequate supplies of petrol, water and food.

In northern Australia, rainfall during the 'wet' season (Oct-March) can make some roads impassable. Full information on road conditions should be obtained before departure.

If visitors intend diverting off public roads within Aboriginal Land areas, a permit is required from the relevant Aboriginal authority.

Nymagee

41

47

Creek

TARRAN HILLS

Moore

Tottenham

20

13

Albert

K L M N 127 O P Q R

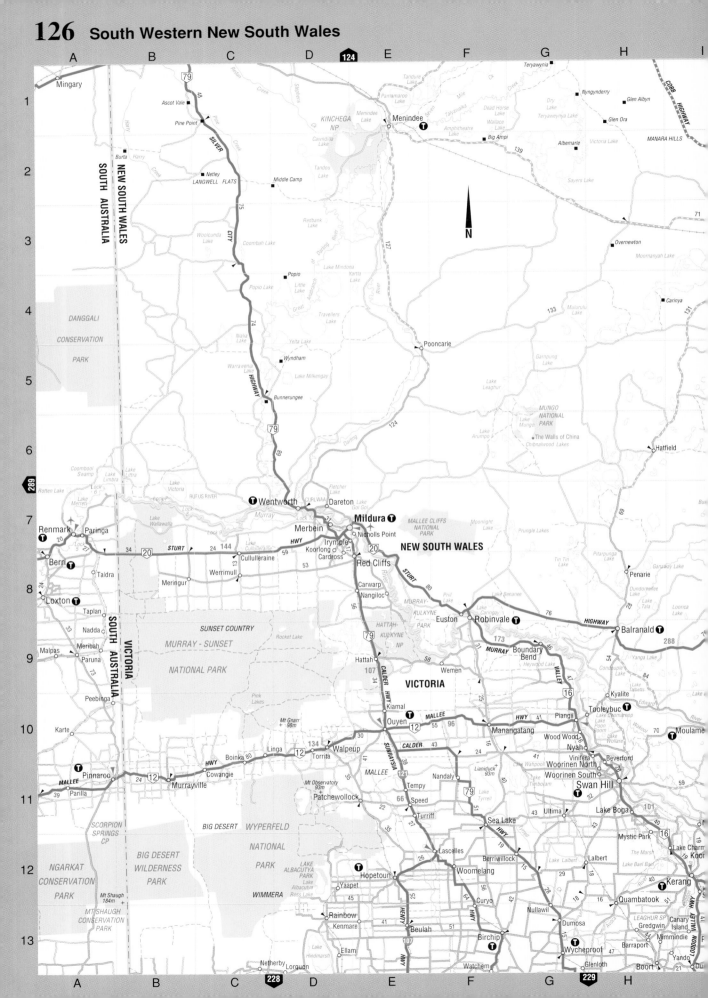

K L M N 125 O 233 P Q R

0 20 40 60 80 100 km

1

Tottenham
Albert
2
Tullamore
Fifield
Trundle
3
Condobolin
Bogan Gate
90
4
Mt Tilga 329m Derriwong Mtn 414m
Euabalong West
Euabalong
Kilparney 294m
Mt Allen 518m Mt Urambie 371m
Mt Tallebung 458m
Mt Nobby 325m
Mt Susannah 483m
Yellow Mtn 574m

KEGINNI RANGE
MERRIMERRIWA RANGE
YABABINGARA RANGE
MAROOBA RANGE
BROKEN RANGE
MOONEE RANGE
WALTERS RANGE
TARRAN HILLS
MARIBEE RANGE
CREAMY HILLS
GOOBOTHERY RANGE

Conoble Lake
Warranary Hill 309m
Warraway Mtn 272m
WILLANDRA NATIONAL PARK
Purcells Lake
Waverley
Restick Lake

Lake Cargelligo
Lake Cargelligo
Tullibigeal
5
Burcher
Ungarie
Mt Bygalore 422m
Manna Mtn 552m
Wamboyne Mtn 412m
Lake Cowal
Bird and Animal Sanctuary
WIRRINYA WEST
NEWELL HWY
Caragabal
6
Rankins Springs
Weethalle
Narriah Mtn 487m
West Wyalong
Wyalong
Quandialla
120
ERIGOLIA
YALGOGRIN
Hillston
Merriwagga
Goolgowi
COCOPARRA RANGE
COCOPARRA NP
Brogden Mtn 390m
Bingar Mtn 455m
Mt Ariah 421m
Tallimba
Barmedman
7
Pinnacle Mtn 447m
REEFTON
Beelbangera
Bilbul
Tenda
Barellan
Bolero Mt 399m
MOOMBOOLDOOL
Beckom
Mirrool
Ariah Park
8
Griffith
Hanwood
Carrathool
Murrumbidgee Irrigation Area
Ardlethan
Mt Beckham 374m
Temora
SPRINGDALE
94
Hay
Darlington Point
Whitton
Leeton
Yanco
KAMARAH
9
Narrandera
Grong Grong
Matong
Ganmain
Marrar
Bethungra
Illabo
Coleambally
Coleambally Irrigation Area
Mt Arthur 240m
Coolamon
Junee
Booroorban
Morundah
Dhulura
10
Currawarna
Collingullie
Wagga Wagga
Nangus
Boree Creek
Alfred Town
Forest Hill
Uranquinty
Wanganella
Lockhart
Milbrulong
The Rock
Mt Flakney 536m
Mangoplah
Tarcutta
11
Conargo
Urana
Rand
Yerong Creek
Henty
Morven
Jerilderie
Oaklands
Coreen
Walbundrie
Walla Walla
Culcairn
Holbrook
12
Deniliquin
Blighty
Finley
Berrigan
Rennie
Lowesdale
Brocklesby
Gerogery
Woomargama
Mathoura
Tocumwal
Barooga
Balldale
Burrumbuttock
Gerogery West
Jingellic
NEW SOUTH WALES
Strathmerton
Cobram
Katunga
Mulwala
Corowa
Rutherglen
Wahgunyah
Jindera
Table Top
Albury
Talgarno
Walwa
13
Moama
Echuca
Nathalia
Waaia
Yarrawonga
Numurkah
Katamatite
Bundalong
Barnawatha
Chiltern
Wodonga
Bonegilla
Bethanga
VICTORIA
Wunghnu
Wilby

232 233

Australian Capital Territory

The Capital State

The ACT is a 2400 square-kilometre area with an air of spaciousness and grace, typical of eastern rural Australia and enhanced by the beautiful valley of the Molonglo River and the surrounding hills, mountains and pastureland. The capital State is surrounded by New South Wales and lies roughly halfway between Sydney and Melbourne. The Australian Capital Territory was created by the Commonwealth Constitution Act of 1901 when the Commonwealth of Australia was inaugurated: a nation was formed from the six colonies. One of the provisions of the Act was that the seat of government should be on land vested in the Commonwealth. Nine years of prolonged wrangling followed, as two Royal Commissions and parliamentary committees considered the various claims of established towns and cities to be the federal capital, before the location of the new territory and the site for the new city was decided. In addition the area of Jervis Bay was ceded to the Commonwealth to provide a seaport for the nation's capital. Melbourne was the provisional seat of government until 1927 when a temporary building was erected in Canberra. This building was used until 1988 when the new House of Parliament was completed.

Canberra, Australia's modern capital city, was built on an undulating plain in an amphitheatre of the Australian Alps. The Molonglo River, a tributary of the Murrumbidgee, runs through the city and was dammed in 1964 to create Lake Burley Griffin, around which Canberra has been developed.

It is one of the world's best-known fully-planned cities and has become an increasing source of pride and interest for Australians and for overseas visitors. Its public buildings, its areas of parkland and bush reserves, its leafy suburbs and broad tree-lined streets have resulted from brilliant planning by its architect, Walter Burley Griffin, and from care taken in its development over the years. Its architecture and its atmosphere are unique and stimulating considering there is little over 50 years old. Although the city has an air of being contrived, it contains so much that educates, absorbs and stimulates the visitor, this somewhat sterile quality is soon forgotten.

The land on which the city is sited was discovered in 1820 by Charles Throsby Smith and his party of explorers. The area became known as Limestone Plains and was destined for settlement as grazing property. The first white settler, Joshua Moore, took up a thousand acres (2500 hectares) of land on the Murrumbidgee River in 1824 and named his property Canberry, an Aboriginal word meaning 'meeting place'. A year later Robert Campbell, a wealthy Sydney merchant, took up 4000 acres (10 000 hectares) of land, which formed the first part of the Duntroon estate.

When the land on which the city is now built was acquired by the Commonwealth Government in 1911 it contained only two small villages.

Construction of the first public buildings started in 1913, and in 1914 a rail service was opened between Sydney and the new capital. The Depression and World War II slowed building construction, but the rate of development has been spectacular since the mid-1950s and the population is now over 285 000.

There are four distinct seasons: a warm spring, a hot dry summer, a brilliant cool autumn, and a cold winter with occasional snow. Perhaps the best time to visit the ACT is in the autumn, when there is a magnificent display of golden foliage. Over two million Australian and overseas visitors come to the ACT each year.

Spring in Canberra

Australia's Coat of Arms, Parliament House

Canberra

The Nation's Capital

As well as being Australia's capital, Canberra is a model city. Its unique concentric circular streets, planted with more than 10 million trees and shrubs, are set graciously on the shores of the constructed Lake Burley Griffin. Driving in Canberra can be confusing; it is wise to study a map before beginning to tour.

The old Parliament House, completed in 1927, and a number of government department buildings and hostels for public servants were among the first buildings in the national capital. They are now dwarfed by the grand buildings of later development, which have turned Canberra into a showpiece.

A number of lookouts on the surrounding hills give superb views of the city. The 195-metre **Telecom Tower** on Black Mountain is the highest. **Mount Ainslie** offers fine views of central Canberra and Lake Burley Griffin. **Red Hill** overlooks Parliament House, South Canberra and the Woden Valley. **Mount Pleasant** has memorials to the Royal Regiment of Australian Artillery and the Royal Australian Armoured Corps at its summit.

The city took on a new character in 1964 when Lake Burley Griffin was created. The shoreline totals 35 kilometres and the lake has become popular for swimming, sailboarding, rowing, sailing and fishing, while ferries operating from Acton Jetty offer day and dinner cruises.

In recent years Canberra has spread outwards into the plains, with satellite towns at Belconnen, Woden, Tuggeranong, Weston Creek and Gungahlin, but the focus is still the city centre and the modern architectural development around Lake Burley Griffin.

Black Mountain, close to the city centre and the lakeshore, is topped by a telecommunications tower with public viewing galleries and a revolving restaurant. On the lower slopes of Black Mountain are Canberra's **Botanic Gardens**. They follow Walter Burley Griffin's original plan for an Australian native garden. The superb gardens have arrowed walks, which allow for varying degrees of stamina, and take visitors through areas of foliage indigenous to various Australian regions. In the rainforest area a misting system simulates rainforest conditions. The **Australian Institute of Sport** is on the edge of Black Mountain Reserve in Bruce. Tours of training facilities and stadiums are conducted daily.

Most of Canberra's major buildings lie within a triangle formed by **Kings, Commonwealth** and **Constitution** Avenues, with Capital Hill at the apex and the central business district on the northern corner. On Capital Hill is the new **Parliament House**, topped by its massive flagpole. A grassed walkway forms the roof of Parliament House and provides visitors with splendid views of Canberra. In front is the **old Parliament House**, open to the public.

A new attraction off Binara Street in Glebe Park is the **Canberra Casino**, now at its permanent site.

On the southern foreshore of Lake

Parliament House

The imposing Anzac Parade

Burley Griffin is the **Australian National Gallery**, which houses an outstanding collection of modern and post-modern art, including a wide representation of Australian painters. In the grounds, works by Australian and international sculptors are placed in a landscape setting. The gallery has a restaurant which overlooks the lake. A footbridge connects the National Gallery and the **High Court of Australia**, the nation's final court of appeal. The court's lofty public gallery is encircled by open ramps that lead off to the courts, and it features Jan Senbergs' murals reflecting the history, functions and operations of the High Court.

Further along the foreshore is the **National Library**, which contains over 5 million books, as well as newspapers, periodicals, films, documents and photographs. The foyer features three magnificent tapestries woven from Australian wool in Aubusson, France, and superb stained glass windows, the work of the Australian artist Leonard French.

Also on the foreshore of the lake between the National Library and the High Court is **Questacon**, the **National Science and Technology Centre** in King Edward Terrace. The Centre features hands-on science displays where simple do-it-yourself experiments and explanations make the understanding of everyday scientific principles easy. Adults and children alike are enthralled for hours by the hundreds of exhibits in the five galleries (Waves, Microcosm, Forces, Visions, and 0011–OTC). Further south of the lake is the **Canberra Railway Museum**, which has Australia's oldest working steam locomotive (built in 1878), as well as four other engines and 40 carriages.

Lake Burley Griffin is the centre piece of Canberra. On the lake are three places of interest: the **Carillon**, a three-column belltower that was a gift from the British Government to mark Canberra's Jubilee; the **Captain Cook Memorial**, a 150-metre water jet and terrestrial globe on the foreshore; and the **National Capital Planning Exhibition** at Regatta Point, which has a pavilion with exhibits showing Canberra's development. Overlooking the lake is the Australian–American Memorial, which celebrates America's contribution to Australia's defence during World War II.

The lake is surrounded by parklands, most with picnic facilities. One of the largest is **Commonwealth Park** on the northern foreshore, with its wading pools and cherry-tree grove. Another lakeside park is **Weston Park**, which features superb conifer trees, a miniature train, a maze and a playground for able and disabled children. Cycling is popular in Canberra; there are more than 200 kilometres of cycle paths. It is possible to cycle right round the lake. Bikes can be hired near the ferry terminal. Sightseeing cruises of the lake are available, and also occasional inspections of the Murray paddlesteamer *Enterprise*. Paddle-boats, windsurfers and sailing boats also can be hired. Hot-air ballooning is popular throughout the year, and during the **Canberra Festival** in March and the **Floriade**, Canberra's Spring Festival, a fleet of balloons takes off each morning. Although the **National Museum of Australia** (which will include the Gallery of Aboriginal Australia) is still in the planning stage, its Yarramundi Visitor Centre off Lady Denman Drive on the shores of the lake features objects from the museum's extensive collections, a viewing platform and a theatrette. The **National Aquarium**, further along Lady Denman Drive near Scrivener Dam, has over 60 display tanks containing marine life from giant sharks to tiny reef fish.

Imposing **Anzac Parade** stretches from the northern side of the lake to the **Australian War Memorial,** one of Australia's most frequently visited attractions. The War Memorial houses a huge collection of relics, models and

Hotels
Capital Parkroyal
1 Binara St, Canberra City
(06) 247 8999
The Hyatt
Commonwealth Ave, Yarralumla
(06) 270 1234
Lakeside Hotel
London Circuit, Canberra
(06) 247 6244
The Pavilion
Cnr Canberra Ave and National Circuit, Forrest
(06) 295 3144

Family and Budget
Bruce Hall/Burton
Daley Rd, Aust. Nat. University, Acton
(06) 267 4700

Eagle Hawk Hill Resort
Federal Hwy, Sutton
(06) 241 6033
Heritage Motor Inn
203 Goyder St, Narrabundah
(06) 295 2944
Macquarie Private Hotel
18 National Circuit, Barton
(06) 273 2325

Motel Groups: Bookings
Best Western 1800 22 2166
Flag 1800 01 1177
Travelodge 1800 22 2446

This list is for information only; inclusion is not necessarily a recommendation.

paintings from all theatres of war. Its cloisters, pool of reflection, hall of memory and many galleries of war relics provide an unforgettable experience. An interesting walk to the summit of **Mount Ainslie** starts from the picnic grounds behind the War Memorial.

Another distinctive landmark in Canberra is the **Academy of Science**, situated in Gordon Street, Acton. Its copper-covered dome rests on arches set in a circular pool. Nearby, the **National Film and Sound Archive** in McCoy Circuit displays movie memorabilia and has public screenings from its collection of historic films, radio and television programs. Also at Acton is the **Australian National University**, set in 145 hectares of landscaped gardens.

Diplomatic missions bring an international flavour to the city's architecture. It is well worth driving around the suburb of Yarralumla to see the many embassy buildings. The official residence of Australia's Governor-General is on Dunrossil Drive at Yarralumla. In Deakin, on the corner of Adelaide Avenue and National Circuit, is the **Prime Minister's Lodge**, the official residence of the Australian Prime Minister. The **Royal Australian Mint** in Denison Street, Deakin, has plate-glass windows in its visitors' gallery, allowing excellent views of the process of making coins.

Despite the gleaming modern style of the city of Canberra, there are still interesting vestiges of the old Limestone Plains settlement. In Campbell the sandstone homestead of the **Duntroon estate**, now the Officer's Mess at Duntroon Royal Military College, is the finest old house in the ACT. The single-storey part of the house was built in 1833 and the two-storey extension was completed in 1856. Tours of the **Australian Defence Force Academy** and the **Royal Military College** are available.

The **Church of St John the Baptist** off Anzac Park dates back to 1841 and its tombstones and other memorials provide a record of much of the area's early history. The adjacent schoolhouse containing relics of this history is regularly open to visitors. Many of the stained glass windows of St John's Church commemorate members of the pioneer families, including Robert Campbell, the founder of Duntroon estate. **Blundell's farmhouse** on the northern shore of the lake was built in 1858 by Campbell for his ploughman and has been furnished

by the Canberra and District Historical Society with pieces contemporary to the district's early history.

The **Central Business District** for Canberra surrounds London Circuit at the end of Commonwealth Avenue. **Civic Centre** is the major retail area. At the head of the **Civic Square** is the **Canberra Theatre Centre** and nearby in **Petrie Plaza** is the old St Kilda merry-go-round, a favourite with children. The **General Post Office** in Alinga Street displays Australia's largest and most valuable collection of stamps. For touring the city's attractions, the **Canberra Explorer** bus service runs every hour, 7 days a week, around a 25-kilometre route with 19 stops. Leave the bus any time and reboard, or take the full hour tour.

Around Canberra too there are many attractions. **Cockington Green** on the Barton Highway, 9 kilometres north of the city, is a miniature English village (named after Cockington in Devon, UK). Adjacent is the historic village of **Ginninderra**, featuring craft studios, an art gallery, shops and a restaurant. Adjacent is a new shopping area, Federation Square, with a number of craft and specialty shops, and children's play areas. Directly opposite Ginninderra on the Barton Highway is the 300-exhibit **National Dinosaur Museum**, between Gold Creek Road and Northbourne Avenue.

Telecom Tower

The **Australian Heritage Village**, on the corner of Federal Highway and Antill Street, features shops, eating-houses and amusements in a parkland setting, and is open daily, admission free. Further north off the Federal Highway is **Rehwinkel's Animal Park**, popular for its Australian fauna collection displayed in a natural bushland setting. The **Bywong Mining Town** at Geary's Gap NSW (off the Gundaroo Road), is a recreation of the mining settlement that prospered in the late 1800s. Tourists can see working machinery and enjoy panning for gold. Bywong is open daily. Guided tours and special programs are available.

At the **Tidbinbilla Nature Reserve**, 40 kilometres south-west of the city, an area of more than 5000 hectares has been developed to enable visitors to see Australian flora and fauna in natural surroundings. Nearby is the **Corin Forest Recreation Area**, with a 1-kilometre alpine slide, bushwalking, and skiing in winter. Another favourite spot is the **Cotter Dam** and Reserve, 22 km west of the city, where there are pleasant picnic and camping areas, a restaurant, river swimming and a children's playground. Nearby is the **Mount Stromlo Observatory**, its large silver domes and buildings housing the huge telescope of the Department of Astronomy of the Australian National University. Further south at Tidbinbilla, the **Canberra Space Centre**, a deep-space tracking station, features spacecraft models and audiovisual presentations. It is operated by the Department of Science for the US National Aeronautics and Space Administration.

The historic homestead **Lanyon**, 30 kilometres south of the city, enjoys the National Trust's highest classification. Set in landscaped gardens and picturesque parklands on the banks of the Murrumbidgee River, Lanyon serves as a reminder of nineteenth-century rural living and houses a collection of Sidney Nolan paintings. Further south and also on the Murrumbidgee River is the historic **Cuppacumbalong** homestead with its cottages, outbuildings, private cemetery, craft centre, restaurant, picnic areas and river swimming.

For further information on Canberra and the ACT, contact the Canberra Tourism Commission, Visitors Information Centre, Northbourne Ave, Dickson; (06) 205 0044, or 1800 02 6166.

Early morning, Lake Burley Griffin

The Carillon

Cockington Green

Tours from Canberra

Forty per cent of the city of Canberra is national park and about a third is native bush. The city is unique in that bushland is an easy drive from the city centre. A longer leisurely drive takes the visitor to the heart of the Snowy Mountains in the south or to the picturesque coastal resorts in the east.

Bungendore and Braidwood, 35 km and 90 km from Canberra via the Kings Highway

This popular route passes Lake George, which mysteriously empties periodically. At Bungendore, the Village Square features a historic re-creation from the 1850s telling the story of a local bushranger. The entire town of Braidwood is classified by the National Trust. Antique and art and craft shops, museums and restaurants are found in many of the town's lovely old sandstone buildings.

Batemans Bay, 150 km from Canberra via the Kings Highway

This popular resort is at the mouth of the Clyde River. Of particular interest are the penguins and other birds at Tollgate Island Wildlife Reserve. In the area are many picturesque coastal resorts and the old gold mining towns of Mogo and Araluen.

The Snowy Mountains, 228 km from Canberra via the Monaro and Snowy Mountains Highways

The Snowy Mountains, centre of the world-famous hydro-electric scheme, is an all-year-round resort and tourist area. Thredbo is the centre of activity during the ski season. Lake Eucumbene is popular for water sports and trout fishing.

Jervis Bay, 285 km from Canberra via the Kings and Princes Highways

This fine natural port was the site of the Royal Australian Navy Training College, established in 1915. In that year its jurisdiction was transferred from New South Wales to the ACT, to give the federal capital sea access. Popular Aboriginal-owned Jervis Bay National Park is jointly managed by the Wreck Bay Aboriginal Community Council and the Commonwealth Department of the Environment. Of particular interest in the area are several holiday resorts, ideal for swimming, fishing, boating and bushwalking.

Namadgi National Park, 30 km from Canberra via the Tuggeranong Parkway and Tharwa Drive to Tharwa

This park, the most northerly alpine environment in Australia, covers some 40 per cent of the ACT. The special qualities of remoteness and rugged beauty that make up a wilderness are evident in the area surrounding the park's highest point, Bimberi Peak (1911 m).

Public access roads in the park pass through majestic mountain scenery. Picnic areas, some with barbecues and toilets, are sited along most roads. The pleasant bushland settings at Mt Clear and Orroral are ideal for low-key camping. Much of Namadgi's attractions lie beyond its main roads and picnic areas. Over 150 kilometres of marked walking tracks allow further exploration. Bushwalkers who venture into Namadgi's more remote parts reap some of the park's greatest rewards. Namadgi's streams attract trout fishermen. Horse-riding is permitted in certain areas and cross-country skiing is possible when snow conditions permit.

Batemans Bay, south-east of Canberra

Australian Capital Territory

Location Map

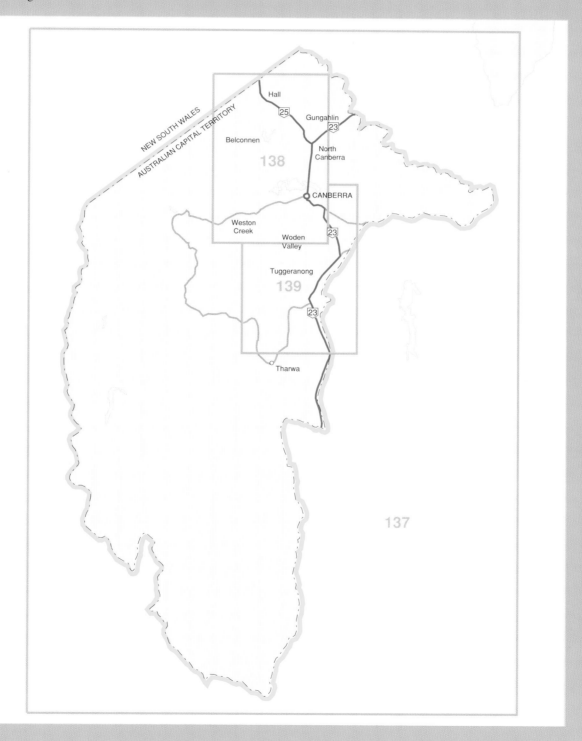

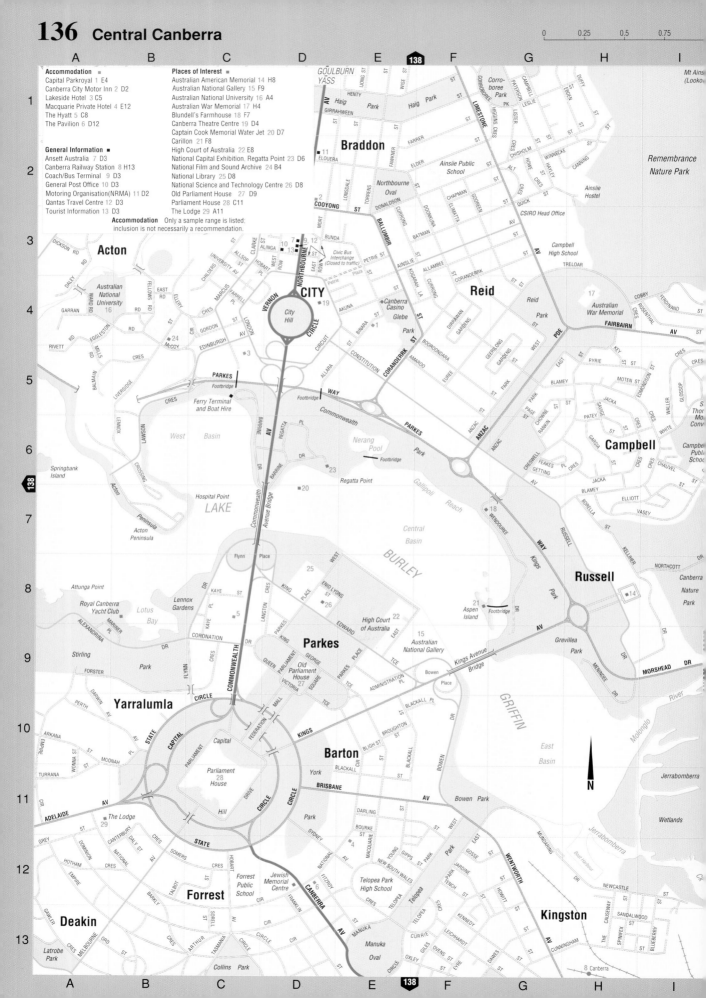

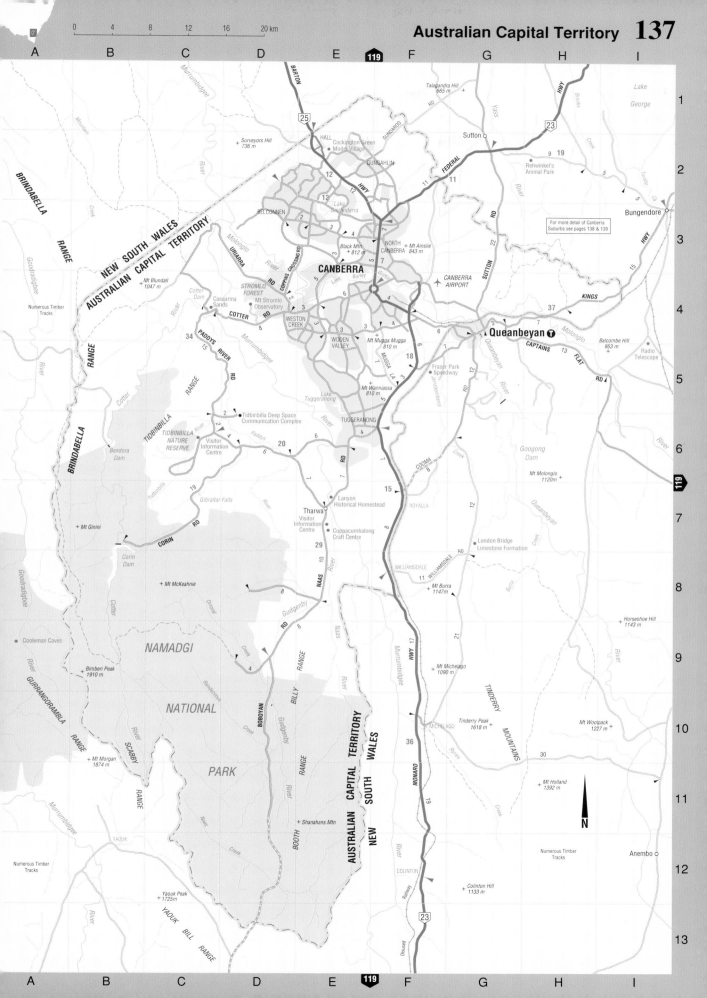

0   4   8   12   16   20 km

A   B   C   D   E   119   F   G   H   I

1   2   3   4   5   119   6   7   8   9   10   11   12   13

BRINDABELLA RANGE

NEW SOUTH WALES

AUSTRALIAN CAPITAL TERRITORY

Goodradigbee River

Numerous Timber Tracks

BRINDABELLA RANGE

Murrumbidgee River

Cotter River

+ Mt Blundall 1047 m

Cotter Dam

Casuarina Sands

COTTER RD

PADDYS RIVER

34

15

RANGE

Tidbinbilla River

TIDBINBILLA NATURE RESERVE

Bendora Dam

2

2   4

+ Tidbinbilla Deep Space Communication Complex

Visitor Information Centre

6

19

Gibraltar Falls

RD

URIARRA RD

Molonglo River

Murrumbidgee

STROMLO FOREST

Mt Stromlo Observatory

8

3

3

COPPINS CROSSING RD

WESTON CREEK

WODEN VALLEY

HALL

Cockington Green Model Village

GUNGAHLIN

12

12

12

BELCONNEN

2

4

5

Black Mtn + 812 m

2

3

Lake Ginninderra

Lake Burley Griffin

CANBERRA

6

NORTH CANBERRA

+ Mt Ainslie 843 m

7

5

+ Mt Mugga Mugga 810 m

3

4

MUGGA LA

18

BARTON

25

HWY

GUNDAROO

Surveyors Hill + 736 m

GUNGADERRA RD

Talagandra Hill 665 m +

Sutton

FEDERAL HWY

11

11

Yass River

23

9   19

Rehwinkel's Animal Park

5

5

Bungendore

HWY

15

For more detail of Canberra Suburbs see pages 138 & 139

CANBERRA AIRPORT

SUTTON RD

22

KINGS

37

7

3

Queanbeyan

CAPTAINS

13

FLAT

RD

Balcombe Hill 953 m +

Radio Telescope

Molonglo

Queanbeyan River

6

Fraser Park Speedway

12

Jerrabomberra Creek

Googong Dam

Mt Wanniassa 810 m +

TUGGERANONG

4

20

6

6

RD

Paddys River

Lake Tuggeranong

7

COOMA

8

Creek

15

ROYALLA

9

Mt Molonglo 1120m +

Queanbeyan River

Murrumbidgee

Mt McKeahnie +

Cooleman Caves

+ Mt Ginini

CORIN RD

Corin Dam

NAMADGI

NATIONAL

PARK

Bimberi Peak 1910 m +

GURRAMGORAMBLA RANGE

+ Mt Morgan 1874 m

SCABBY RANGE

Cotter River

NAAS RD

Gudgenby

29

10

8

8

4

BOBOYAN

BILLY RANGE

Gudgenby

BOOTH RANGE

Naas River

+ Shanahans Mtn

Tharwa

Visitor Information Centre

Lanyon Historical Homestead

Cuppacumbalong Craft Centre

WILLIAMSDALE

WILLIAMSDALE RD

11

London Bridge Limestone Formation

+ Mt Burra 1147m

HWY

17

Murrumbidgee River

AUSTRALIAN CAPITAL TERRITORY

NEW SOUTH WALES

36

MONARO

19

21

Rynes

+ Mt Michelago 1090 m

MICHELAGO

TINDERRY MOUNTAINS

Tinderry Peak 1618 m +

30

Horseshoe Hill 1143 m +

Buria

+ Mt Woolpack 1227 m

+ Mt Holland 1392 m

Anembo

Numerous Timber Tracks

NEW SOUTH WALES

COLINTON

+ Colinton Hill 1133 m

N

Goodradigbee River

Numerous Timber Tracks

YAOUK

Naas Creek

YAOUK BILL RANGE

Yaouk Peak + 1725 m

Murrumbidgee River

Railway

Disused

23

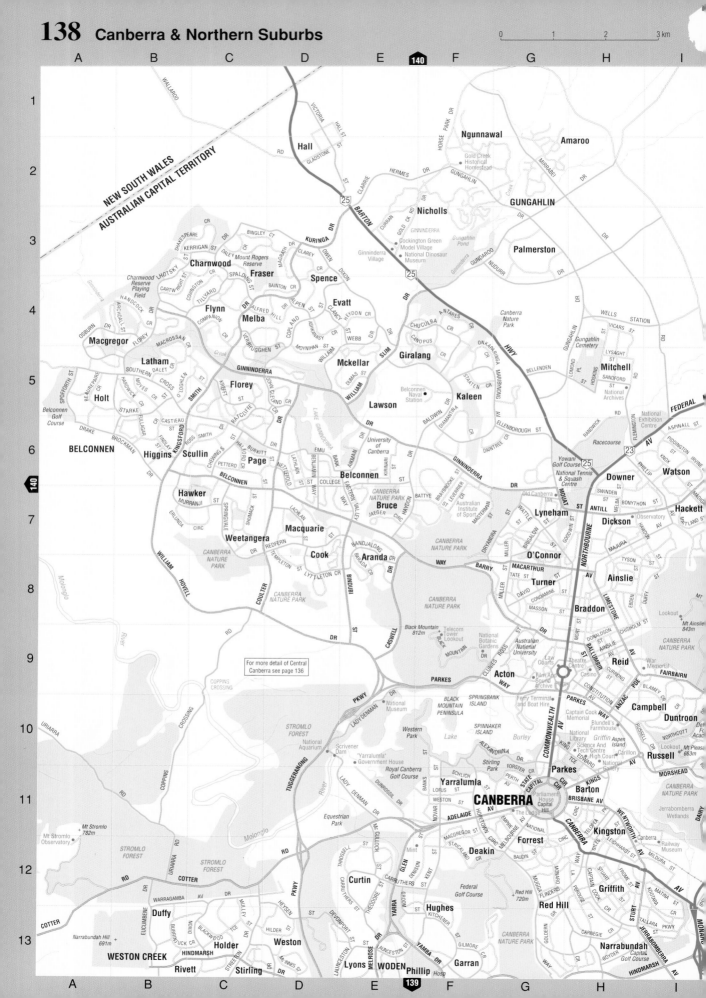

0   1   2   3 km

A   B   C   D   E   140   F   G   H   I

NEW SOUTH WALES
AUSTRALIAN CAPITAL TERRITORY

1

Hall

Ngunnawal

Amaroo

2

Nicholls

GUNGAHLIN

Cockington Green
Model Village
National Dinosaur
Museum

Palmerston

3

Charnwood

Fraser

Spence

Charnwood
Reserve
Playing
Field

Mount Rogers
Reserve

Flynn

Melba

Evatt

Canberra
Nature
Park

Gungahlin
Cemetery

Mitchell

4

Macgregor

Latham

Mckellar

Giralang

National
Archives

5

Holt

Florey

Lawson

Kaleen

Belconnen
Golf
Course

Belconnen
Naval
Station

National
Exhibition
Centre

FEDERAL

6

BELCONNEN

Higgins   Scullin

Page

Belconnen

University
of
Canberra

Ginninderra

Yowani
Golf Course
National Tennis
& Squash
Centre

Racecourse

Downer

Watson

7

Hawker

Weetangera

Macquarie

Cook

Bruce

Canberra
Nature
Park

Australian
Institute
of Sport

Lyneham

O'Connor

Dickson

Hackett

Ainslie

8

Aranda

Canberra
Nature
Park

Canberra
Nature
Park

Turner

Braddon

Lookout

Mt Ainslie
843m

CANBERRA
NATURE
PARK

9

For more detail of Central
Canberra see page 136

Black Mountain
812m

Telecom
Tower
Lookout

National
Botanic
Gardens

Australian
National
University

Acton

Reid

FAIRBAIRN

War
Memorial

10

COPPINGS
CROSSING

URIARRA

National
Museum

Western
Park

Black
Mountain
Peninsula

SPRINGBANK
ISLAND

SPINNAKER
ISLAND

Lake

Burley

Acton

Campbell

Duntroon

Russell

National
Aquarium

Scrivener
Dam

'Yarralumla'
Government House
Royal Canberra
Golf Course

Captain Cook
Memorial
Blundell's
Farmhouse
National
Science And
Tech Centre

Griffin

Aspen
Island

National
Gallery

11

Mt Stromlo
Observatory

Mt Stromlo
782m

STROMLO
FOREST

Equestrian
Park

Yarralumla

CANBERRA

Parkes

Barton

Kingston

Canberra
Railway
Museum

CANBERRA
NATURE
PARK

Jerrabomberra
Wetlands

12

STROMLO
FOREST

Curtin

Deakin

Forrest

Federal
Golf Course

Red Hill
720m

Red Hill

Griffith

13

Narrabundah Hill
691m

Duffy

Holder

Weston

Hughes

Garran

Canberra
Nature
Park

Narrabundah

Canberra
Golf Course

WESTON CREEK

Rivett

Stirling

Lyons

WODEN

Phillip
Hosp

A   B   C   D   E   139   F   G   H   I

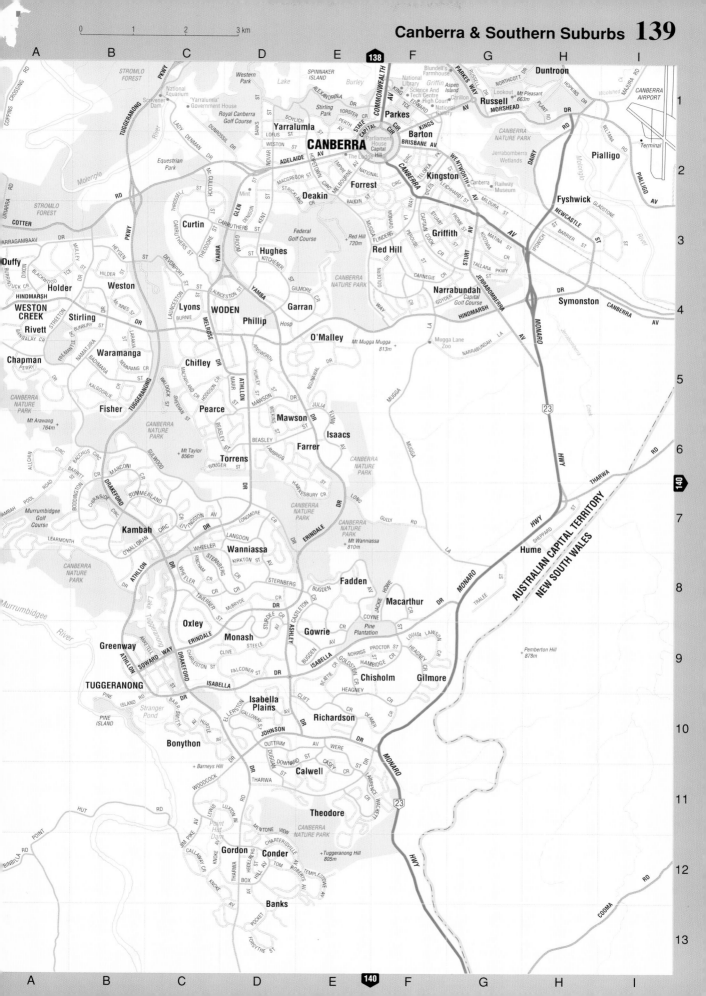

0   1   2   3 km

138

A B C D E F G H I

STROMLO FOREST

TUGGERANONG PKWY

National Aquarium
Scrivener Dam
"Yarralumla" Government House

Western Park
Lake Burley
Griffin

SPINNAKER ISLAND

COMMONWEALTH AV

Blundell's Farmhouse
National Library
Science And Tech Centre
High Court
National Gallery

PARKES WAY
RUSSELL DR
NORTHCOTT DR

Duntroon

KING

Molonglo River

Equestrian Park

Royal Canberra Golf Course

ALEXANDRINA
STIRLING Park
SCHLICH ST
FORSTER ST
PERTH ST

FORSTER
STATE CIR
CAPITAL CIR

Parkes
KINGS AV

EDWARD

Russell
MORSHEAD

Lookout Mt Pleasant 663m
PLANT DR

HOPKINS DR

CANBERRA AIRPORT

Woolshed
MAJURA RD
BELTANA RD

Yarralumla

LADY DENMAN DR
DUNROSSIL DR

BANKS
LOFUS ST
WESTON ST
NOVAR ST

CANBERRA
ADELAIDE AV

HOPETOWN CIRC
MELBOURNE AV
CAPITHE

The Lodge
Parliament House Capital Hill

CANBERRA AV
Brisbane AV

Barton
KINGS
National Gallery

WENTWORTH AV

Canberra Railway Museum

DAIRY RD

Jerrabomberra Wetlands

Molonglo River

Pialligo

Terminal

PIALLIGO AV

STROMLO FOREST

TUGGERANONG PKWY RD

COTTER RD

CARRUTHERS ST

MCCULLOCH ST
THEODORE ST
DEVONPORT ST

HEYSEN ST

Curtin

YARRA GLEN

Hughes

GROOM

KENT ST

DENISON ST

CARRUTHERS ST

STRICKLAND
Deakin
BAUDIN

Forrest
National CIRC

Federal Golf Course

Red Hill 720m
GILMORE

Red Hill

MUGGA WAY
FLINDERS WAY

LA PEROUSE ST

MONARO

CAPTAIN COOK CR

STUART ST

CANBERRA AV

Kingston

LEICHHARDT ST
GILES ST
TELOPEA

Griffith

MILDURA ST

NEWCASTLE ST

IPSWICH ST
BARRIER ST

Fyshwick
GLADSTONE ST

Canberra River

URIARRA RD
COTTER RD
ARRAGAMBAAV DR

Duffy
BURRINJUCK TCE
DIXON
BLACKWOOD
HINDMARSH

Holder

HILDER ST
McINNES ST

Weston

STREETON DR

HEYSEN ST

WESTON CREEK

Stirling

Rivett
BANGALAY CR

MULEY ST

LARMER

NAMATJIRA DR

Waramanga
BADIMARA ST

KALGOORLIE ST

Fisher

CARRUTHERS ST

THEODORE ST

Lyons
LAUNCESTON ST
BURNIE ST

YARRA GLEN
YAMBA

WODEN

MELROSE DR

Phillip
Hosp

Garran

CANBERRA NATURE PARK

GOLDEN GR
MUGGA WAY

Narrabundah
Capital Golf Course

GOYDER ST

HINDMARSH DR

Symonston

MONARO HWY

Canberra Nature Park

Chapman
PERRY DR

ALLCHIN

Chifley

MACFARLAND CR
WALDOCK
HODGSON CR
MARR ST
ATHLON DR
AINSWORTH ST

HURLEY ST
MAWSON

O'Malley

Mt Mugga Mugga 813m

Mugga Lane Zoo

NARRABUNDAH LA

MONARO HWY

23

Mt Arawang 764m

CANBERRA NATURE PARK

TUGGERANONG DR

BACCHUS CIRC
BARRITT CR

Pearce
BEASLEY ST
SULWOOD DR

BEASLEY ST

Torrens
GOUGER ST

WILKINS ST

Mawson
CAMBRIDGE

Farrer

Isaacs

JULIA FLYNN

NGUNAWAL DR

HAWKESBURY CR

Mt Taylor 856m

LONG GULLY RD

CANBERRA NATURE PARK

MUGGA LA

TRALEE ST

MONARO HWY
SHEPPARD ST
THARWA HWY

AUSTRALIAN CAPITAL TERRITORY
NEW SOUTH WALES

110

Murrumbidgee Golf Course

BODDINGTON CR
DRAKEFORD DR
CHURNSIDE CR
MARCONI CR
SUMMERLAND CR

LIVINGSTON AV

Kambah
O'MALLORAN CIRC

LEARMONTH

CANBERRA NATURE PARK

ATHLON DR

LANGDON AV

Wanniassa
STERNBERG CR
KIRKTON

WHEELER CR
FINCHAM

STERNBERG CR

Fadden

BUGDEN

HOME
JACKIE

Macarthur

COYNE
Pine Plantation

HUME

Pemberton Hill 878m

Murrumbidgee River

PINE ISLAND RD

Stranger Pond

Greenway
ATHLON DR
SOWARD WAY
DRAKEFORD DR

TUGGERANONG

CHARLESTON ST
DRAKEFORD DR

BARR SMITH

Oxley
ERINDALE DR
CLIVE

Monash
STEELE
FALCONER ST

ISABELLA DR

TAVERNER ST
McBRYDE
STURDEE CR
ASHLEY DR

CASTLETON CR
BUGDEN
Gowrie

Isabella
BEATTIE

NORRIS
PROCTOR ST
HAMBIDGE
GOLDSTEIN CR

LOUISA ST
LAWSON ST
HEAGNEY

Gilmore

Chisholm
HEAGNEY CR

PINE ISLAND

Isabella Plains
ELLERSTON AV
GALLOWAY
HURTLE AV

JOHNSON DR

CLIFT

Richardson
DEAMER

LAWRENCE WACKETT

MONARO HWY

Bonython
WOODCOCK DR

OUTTRIM AV
DUGGAN ST
DOWNARD ST
WERE ST
CASEY CR

Barneys Hill
THARWA DR

Calwell

LEWIS
LUXTON AV

MM PIKE AV

Point Hut Dam

MENTONE VIEW
CHARTERSVILLE AV

Theodore

CANBERRA NATURE PARK

Tuggeranong Hill 805m

23
MONARO HWY

HUT RD
BINBILLA RD
POINT
CALLAWAY CR
KNOKE AV
THARWA

Gordon
HEDLEY
BOX

Conder
HILL
TOM

ROBERTS AV
TEMPLESTOWE AV

COOMA RD

KNOKE AV

Banks

POCKET

FORSYTHE ST

A B C D E 140 F G H I

1 2 3 4 5 6 7 8 9 10 11 12 13

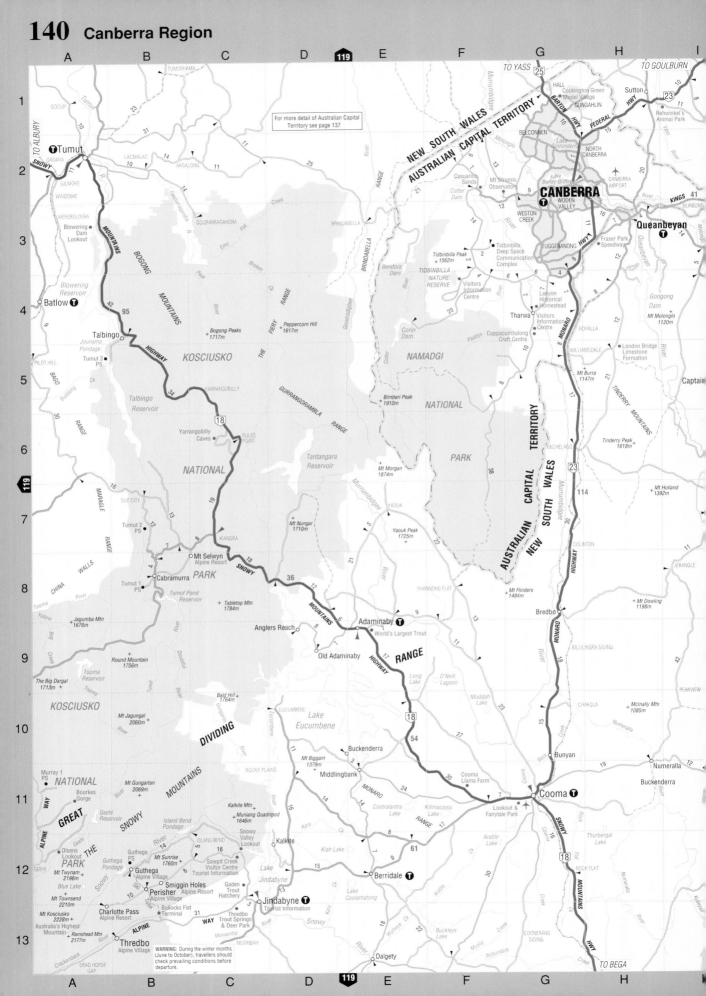

For more detail of Australian Capital Territory see page 137

WARNING: During the winter months (June to October), travellers should check prevailing conditions before departure.

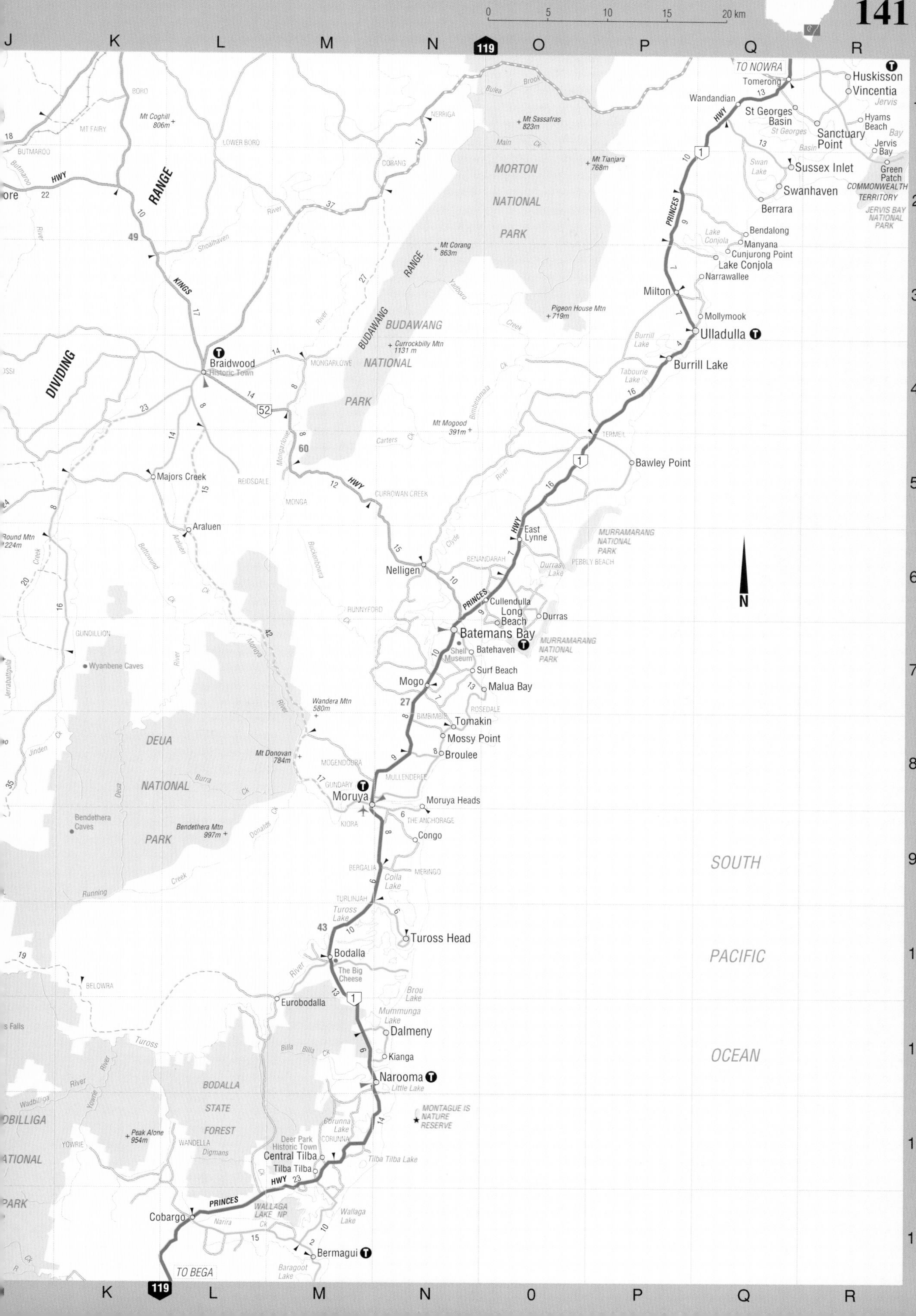

0 5 10 15 20 km

J K L 119 M N O P Q R

TO NOWRA
Tomerong
Huskisson
Vincentia
Wandandian
St Georges Basin
Hyams Beach
Sanctuary Point
Jervis Bay
Green Patch
COMMONWEALTH TERRITORY
Sussex Inlet
Swanhaven
Berrara
JERVIS BAY NATIONAL PARK
Bendalong
Manyana
Cunjurong Point
Lake Conjola
Narrawallee
Milton
Mollymook
Ulladulla
Burrill Lake
Bawley Point

Mt Coghill 806m
BORO
RANGE
MT FAIRY
HWY
KINGS
49
DIVIDING
Braidwood Historic Town
52
60
Majors Creek
Araluen
Round Mtn 224m
Wyanbene Caves
DEUA NATIONAL PARK
Mt Donovan 784m
Bendethera Caves
Bendethera Mtn 997m
43
Bodalla
Eurobodalla
BODALLA STATE FOREST
Peak Alone 954m
Central Tilba
Tilba Tilba
PRINCES HWY
Cobargo
WALLAGA LAKE NP
TO BEGA
119

NERRIGA
MORTON NATIONAL PARK
Mt Sassafras 823m
Mt Tianjara 768m
Mt Corang 863m
BUDAWANG RANGE
BUDAWANG NATIONAL PARK
Currockbilly Mtn 1131 m
Pigeon House Mtn 719m
Mt Mogood 391m
TERMEIL
East Lynne
MURRAMARANG NATIONAL PARK
PEBBLY BEACH
Nelligen
PRINCES HWY
Cullendulla
Long Beach
Durras
Batemans Bay
Batehaven
Shell Museum
Surf Beach
Mogo
Malua Bay
Tomakin
Mossy Point
Broulee
ROSEDALE
27
Moruya
Moruya Heads
THE ANCHORAGE
Congo
Coila Lake
Tuross Head
Tuross Lake
The Big Cheese
Brou Lake
Mummunga Lake
Dalmeny
Kianga
Narooma
Little Lake
MONTAGUE IS NATURE RESERVE
Deer Park Historic Town
Corunna Lake
Tilba Tilba Lake
Wallaga Lake
Bermagui

SOUTH PACIFIC OCEAN

N

Victoria

Garden State

Victoria is an ideal State for the motoring tourist. In one day's drive, explore mountain country, pastoral landscape and spectacular coastline, yet still arrive at your destination in time to watch the sunset.

Victoria's earliest explorers, of course, were from a pre-motor age. What they saw did little to arouse their enthusiasm. After an unsuccessful attempt at settlement in the Port Phillip area in 1803, it was not until 1834 that parties from Van Diemen's Land, searching for more arable land, settled along the southwest coast of Victoria. Their glowing reports prompted John Batman and John Fawkner to investigate the Port Phillip area and then purchase land on opposite sides of the Yarra from Aboriginal tribes. The Colonial Office in London expressed disapproval of these transactions, but in those times possession was nine tenths of the law. A squatting colony grew up rapidly in the district and the new town was named Melbourne after the British prime minister of the day.

Nervous of inheriting the penal system of settlement, Victoria sought separation from New South Wales; it was granted in 1851. At about that time, gold was discovered near Ballarat and the State's population more than doubled within a year. Apart from a serious but short-lived setback caused by land speculation in the early 1890s, Victoria has gone from strength to strength ever since.

Today Victoria is the most closely settled and industrialised part of the nation, responsible for about one-third of the gross national product. Melbourne has been traditionally regarded as the financial capital of the country.

Melbourne's inner areas are graced by spacious parks and street upon street of elegant and well-preserved Victorian and Edwardian architecture, contrasting strongly with modern tower blocks. Other attractions include the city's parks and gardens and its renowned retail shopping, theatres, restaurants and unusual theatre restaurants.

Beyond the city, the Dandenong Ranges, fifty kilometres to the east, are noted for their forests of eucalyptus and graceful tree ferns, their many established gardens and an increasing number of good restaurants and galleries. Phillip Island, less than two hours' drive away, is famed for its unique little (fairy) penguin parade as well as for its good surfing. To the south-west, the Mornington and Bellarine Peninsulas provide Melbourne with its seaside playgrounds, extremely popular during the summer months.

The weather can be unpredictable in Victoria, particularly along the coastal regions. Despite its rather volatile weather, however, the State enjoys a generally temperate climate. Spring, late summer and autumn provide the most settled and pleasant touring weather. The road system is good and penetrates most areas; much of the State can be reached easily in a day's driving.

Each of Victoria's five main geographical regions has its own special attraction. The central and western districts, due north and west of Melbourne, offer highlights such as the historic goldrush areas, with well-preserved, attractive towns such as Bendigo, Castlemaine and Ballarat—the last always popular during its March Begonia Festival—and the Grampians, Victoria's most beautiful national park, particularly noted for its spring wildflowers. Travelling south from these impressive ranges brings you into the Western District, where rich grazing land is dotted with splendid old properties. No exploration of this region would be complete without a drive along the Great Ocean Road, which runs for 320 kilometres along the dramatic south-west coast. The spectacular rock formations in the Port Campbell National Park are without doubt its most imposing sights, but along its length there are excellent beaches and pleasant small resort towns.

The north-east high-country region has equally magnificent scenery and is dotted with well-patronised winter ski resorts. Popular in spring and summer, this region would hardly ever be described as crowded, and the wildflowers, sweeping views and clear air can be enjoyed with a fair degree of solitude. Fishing, bushwalking and climbing are well provided for. Down in the foothills the Eildon Reservoir and Fraser National Park area are good for water sports.

Gippsland stretches to the south-east; it contains some of the State's most beautiful and varied country. Rolling pastures lead to densely wooded hill country, still relatively unpopulated and peaceful. National parks such as the Tarra-Bulga and Wilsons Promontory Park are all well worth visiting. The coastal region includes the Ninety Mile Beach bordering the Gippsland Lakes system, Australia's largest inland waterway network, and Croajingolong National Park, a wilderness area.

Following the Murray can be an interesting way of exploring Victoria's north. The river begins as a narrow, rapidly flowing alpine stream near Mt Kosciusko, and changes to a broad expanse near the aquatic playgrounds of Lakes Hume and Mulwala; it has waterbird and wildlife reserves and sandy river beaches and offers fascinating glimpses of life in the riverboat era at cities such as Echuca, Swan Hill and Mildura.

The Twelve Apostles, near Port Campbell

Melbourne The Shopping City

At first glance Melbourne may look like any other modern city with its skyline crammed with concrete and glass. However, if you look a little closer you'll find the real Melbourne: clanging trams, swanky boutiques, friendly taxi drivers, Australian football, fickle weather, and BYOs (restaurants to which you bring your own liquor) by the hundred. Add to this Melbourne's traditional virtues of tree-lined boulevards, glorious parks, elegant buildings and imposing Victorian churches and banks—and the Melbourne Cricket Ground—and you'll have some idea of the city.

In recent years it has become a polyglot society with a huge influx of migrants from many countries, particularly from Asia and Greece; the city has one of the largest Greek-speaking populations in the world. This cosmopolitan influence is reflected in Melbourne's bustling markets, delicatessens and restaurants. Eating out has become one of the great Melbourne pastimes and the city and suburban restaurants give an opportunity to eat your way around the food cultures of the world; the food of almost every nation imaginable is available.

Situated at the head of Port Phillip Bay and centred on the north bank of the Yarra River, Melbourne has a population of over three million. Suburbs stretch in all directions, particularly round the east coast of the bay right out to the Dandenongs, a picturesque mountain range.

Both John Batman and John Pascoe Fawkner were associated in the founding of Melbourne in 1835, and Melbourne soon entered a boom period with the discovery of gold in the State in 1851.

The goldfields of Bendigo, Ballarat and Castlemaine attracted fortune-hunters from all over the world, and by 1861 Melbourne had become Australia's largest city. By the end of the century it was firmly established as the business and cultural centre of the colony.

Today Melbourne's position as a financial and cultural centre of the nation is shared with Sydney, but it has an elegance and style all its own. Melbourne has been the only Australian capital to retain its network of pollution-free electric trams, and the clang of the old green thunderers adds a special flavour to the city. Many of these have been given a new lease of life after being decorated by leading artists, while others have been replaced by new trams and the light rail. The World Health Organisation has rated Melbourne as one of the least polluted

The Southgate riverside development

Building facades in Collins St

cities of its size; Melbourne has also been acclaimed the world's most livable city by the internationally renowned Population Crises Centre, based in Washington D.C., USA.

Melbourne has a huge range of retail stores, and one of the joys is shopping in the city area, at **Southgate** across the Yarra, and in such suburbs as fashionable **South Yarra**. Several other suburbs such as **Carlton, Camberwell, Prahran, Armadale**, and **Toorak** rival the city centre with their retail stores and restaurants.

Melburnians are also great sports lovers and this is reflected in the huge crowds that attend cricket and Australian Rules football matches. A peculiarly Melbourne phenomenon is the football fever that grips the city each year, with enthusiasm building up to mass hysteria on Grand Final day in late September.

The **Melbourne Cricket Ground** is the venue for many sporting and entertainment fixtures. Just outside the Members' entrance, the **Australian Gallery of Sport** celebrates Australian sporting history. The **Olympic Museum**, located in the Gallery of Sport, houses memorabilia dating back to the first modern Olympics, held in Olympia in 1896.

Horseracing is another popular Melbourne spectator sport and the **Melbourne Cup** at Flemington Racecourse brings Australia to a halt for three minutes on the first Tuesday of each November. Melbourne's other main racecourses are at Caulfield, Moonee Valley and Sandown Park; the **Victorian Racing Museum** is at Caulfield Racecourse. The city's 3½-week **Spring Racing Carnival** runs from early October to early November. **Moomba** in March, **Comedy Festival** in April and **Melbourne International Festival of the Arts** in October are other outstanding events on the Melbourne calendar.

The **National Tennis Centre** at Flinders Park hosts the **Australian Open**, one of the world's four grand slam events, in January each year. The Centre Court with its unique retractable roof seats 16 000 people and is used also as a venue for entertainment extravaganzas. Tours of the city's top sporting venues are available through the Melbourne Sports Network.

For cyclists, there is a comprehensive network of trails throughout the city and suburbs. Skiers can practise all year round on a dry ski slope conveniently located at Ski Haus in the north-eastern suburb of **Ivanhoe**.

Hotels

Grand Hyatt
123 Collins St, Melbourne
(03) 9657 1234

Le Meridien
495 Collins St, Melbourne
(03) 9620 9111

Novotel Melbourne
270 Collins St, Melbourne
(03) 9650 650 5800

Rockmans Regency
Cnr Exhibition and Lonsdale Sts, Melbourne
(03) 9662 3900

Sheraton Towers Southgate
1 Brown St, South Melbourne
(03) 9696 3100

The Hotel Como
630 Chapel St, South Yarra
(03) 9824 0400

The Regent
25 Collins St, Melbourne
(03) 9653 0000

The Windsor
103 Spring St, Melbourne
(03) 9653 0653

Family and Budget

City Limits
20 Little Bourke St, Melbourne
(03) 9662 2544

Lygon Lodge
220 Lygon St, Carlton
(03) 9663 6633

The Victoria
215 Little Collins St, Melbourne
(03) 9653 0441

YWCA Family Accommodation
489 Elizabeth St, Melbourne
(03) 9329 5188

Motel Groups: Bookings
Flag 13 2400
Best Western 1800 22 2166
Travelex 1800 22 2446

This list is for information only; inclusion is not necessarily a recommendation.

Yarra River and city skyline

The **World Congress Centre** is on the corner of Flinders and Spencer Streets and houses the temporary **Crown Casino**. Next door are the **Centra on the Yarra** hotel, and the **World Trade Centre** which hosts international trade displays. Further along Flinders Street past the Banana Alley Vaults is the **Flinders Street Station** complex with its restaurants and shops. It is the main terminus for the suburban rail system. Melbourne's **Underground Rail Loop** has three stations located on the edge of the central business district. Above ground, the distinctive burgundy-and-cream City Circle tram, which is free, offers a daily 10-minute service (between 10 a.m. and 6 p.m.) around the central city area. The circuit, along Flinders, Spring and Nicholson Streets, Victoria Parade and LaTrobe and Spencer Streets, takes 30 minutes. The **City Explorer** tourist bus departs Flinders Street Station hourly between 10 a.m. and 4 p.m., stopping at some major attractions.

To get a different view of Melbourne, take a river cruise on the Yarra, departing from the **Princes Walk Terminal**, or a Yarra Yarra Water Taxi trip from Southgate, on the opposite bank of the river. The new and exciting Southgate development includes restaurants, wine bars, a licensed food court, shops and the **Sheraton Towers Southgate**. As well, **Experience Australia**, a sensor vision theatre, is a thrilling way to experience the historical, natural and cultural aspects of the country.

The city centre is compact, its wide streets laid out in a grid system. Take a tram to the top of **Collins Street** and wander down—the street somehow epitomises Melbourne. At night, hundreds of small bud lights in the trees lining the street create a spectacular effect.

Looking down on Collins street, in Spring Street, is the elegant **Old Treasury Building**, built in 1853, now refurbished and open as a museum of Melbourne's early history. Just down from Spring Street is the august **Melbourne Club**, mecca of Melbourne's Establishment. On the opposite side of the street on the Exhibition Street corner is **Collins Place**, a multistorey complex that houses **The Regent Melbourne** hotel in one of its high towers. Described as 'the city within the city', this complex has many shops and boutiques open all weekend. Another tall building, **Nauru House**, is diagonally opposite.

Continuing down the hill you will see fashionable boutiques and two old churches, the **Uniting Church** and **Scots Church**. Across the road the **Grand Hyatt** hotel complex has an interesting food hall and shopping plaza. Between Russell and Swanston Streets there are pavement tables shaded by colourful sunshades. Opposite these is a unique Melbourne institution—**Georges**, Australia's most elegant department store. Just down the hill is the graceful porti-

coed **Baptist Church**, built in 1845. Melbourne's imposing **Town Hall** and soaring **St Paul's Cathedral** in Swanston Walk provide an attractive contrast to the modern **City Square** on the corner of Collins Street and Swanston Walk; with its huge glass canopy, shady trees and fountains it is an ideal place for relaxing or meeting a friend. Other popular meeting places are the Sportsgirl complex in Collins Street, the stylish Australia-on-Collins complex and the Centreway Arcade nearby.

Further down Collins Street is the elegant old **Block Arcade** with its mosaic floor, glass and iron-lace roof and stylish shops. The small lane at the back of this arcade (Block Place) leads through to Little Collins Street and to another gracious old arcade. This is the **Royal Arcade** where, every hour, the huge statues of mythical figures, Gog and Magog, strike the hour. This arcade leads through to the **Bourke Street Mall**, between Elizabeth and Swanston Streets. Several department stores and fashion chains, including **Myer**, Australia's largest department store, and **David Jones**, front on to the mall. David Jones has another store on the opposite side and its food hall is worth a visit to see the beautifully presented displays. Nearby, the shopping complex **Centre Point** is a handy place to browse under shelter or to stop for a snack in one of its many coffee bars. You can sit and watch city buskers from the seats provided in the mall, but be aware of the trams—the only traffic, apart from delivery and emergency vehicles, allowed in this block. The **Half-Tix** booth in the mall offers the opportunity to purchase theatre tickets for the day's performances at reduced prices.

Swanston Street Walk, a recently developed and innovative pedestrian mall, encourages a stroll between Flinders and Latrobe Streets. Window-shop at your leisure or take time for coffee at one of the many sidewalk cafes. An appealing combination of bookshops and bistros has sprung up in the uppermost block of **Bourke Street**. The front coffee bar at Pellegrini's, a bustling Italian restaurant, is a great favourite, and the BYO restaurant at the rear is an Italian-style cafeteria where you make your selection from mouth-watering hot and cold dishes. On the Spring Street corner is one of the last of Melbourne' grand old hotels, the elegant **Windsor** (1883), which looks over the peaceful **Treasury Gardens**.

Proudly surveying the city from Spring Street is the classical-style **State Parliament House**. The Corinthian style of the Legislative Council Chamber is legacy of Melbourne's golden era. The massive bluestone of **St Patrick's Cathedral** can be seen from the gardens that surround Parliament House. Melbourne's elegant and beautifully restored **Princess Theatre**, is also in Spring Street.

At the top of Little Bourke Street is **Gordon Place**, a unique old building designed by the colonial architect William Pitt in 1883. The building is now an attractive tourist apartment complex.

If you like Chinese food don't miss Melbourne's **Chinatown** in Little Bourke Street, between Exhibition and Swanston Streets. Dozens of fascinating restaurants, quaint grocery shops and mixed stores date back to Melbourne's post-gold-rush days, when it became the city's Chinese quarter. The standard of the restaurants is good and prices vary from fairly cheap to very expensive. Among the outstanding eating-houses are the Bamboo House, the Flower Drum and the Mask of China. Located in the heart of Chinatown at Cohen Place, the **Museum of Chinese Australian History** is worth a visit.

Further down Little Bourke Street is the **Information Victoria Centre**, which provides the public with access to Victorian Government information resources, including public record research facilities.

Just half a block away in Lonsdale Street is the huge retail complex **Melbourne Central** and department store **Daimaru**, which together occupy most of the block bounded by Lonsdale, Swanston, Latrobe and Elizabeth Streets and are well serviced by Museum station on the underground rail loop. There is a direct walk-through access between Melbourne Central and the Myer department store. Further east along Lonsdale Street, Greek music cafes and flaky pastry shops make Melbourne a mini-Athens.

The **Museum of Victoria** in Swanston Street has many interesting exhibits; examples are a large collection of Australiana; natural history exhibits, including the legendary racehorse Phar Lap; and the **Children's Museum**, a first in Australia. This imposing old building also houses the **Planetarium** (where slides are projected on the ceiling); the magnificent domed **State Library** and the **La Trobe Library**.

Shot tower and dome at Melbourne Central

A block away, opposite the Russell Street Police Station, is the grim **Old Melbourne Gaol** and **Penal Museum** with its chillingly macabre exhibits, including the gallows where folk-hero and bushranger Ned Kelly swung.

More cheerful sights such as clothing, souvenirs, plants, cheeses, sausages and decoratively arranged vegetables can be seen at Melbourne's bustling **Queen Victoria Market**, bounded by Peel, Victoria and Elizabeth Streets, and open Tuesdays, Thursdays, Fridays, Saturdays and Sundays. Near the market on the corner of Queen and Franklin Streets is the fascinating **Queen Victoria Arts and Craft Centre**, open daily. From here it's only a short stroll to the beautiful **Flagstaff Gardens**, once used as a pioneer graveyard and later a signalling station. Today this is a pleasant place to relax, with shady old trees, a children's playground, tennis courts and barbecues. Facing the park in King Street you can see **St James' Old Cathedral**, built in 1839.

The lower part of the city is the sedate legal and financial sector. Back towards the city centre along William Street are the former **Royal Mint** and the **Supreme Court** and **Law Courts**, which were built between 1877 and 1884. At the bottom end of Collins Street is the luxury hotel **Le Meridien at the Rialto**. The elaborate Rialto building and its neighbours, erected between 1889 and 1893, have been retained as a facade to this

towering hotel and office complex, the tallest building in the southern hemisphere. An observation deck on level 55 gives 360-degree views from large internal and external viewing areas.

In contrast, two of Melbourne's finest city parks, the quiet old **Treasury Gardens** and the beautiful **Fitzroy Gardens**, lie to the eastern boundary of the central city grid. The John F. Kennedy Memorial is located beside the lake in the Treasury Gardens. The Fitzroy Gardens have superb avenues of huge English elms planted along gently contoured lawns, giving them a serene beauty all year round. Attractions within the gardens include **Cook's Cottage**, the **Fairy Tree**, a model Tudor village, a restaurant and kiosk, and a children's playground. In summer the Fitzroy Gardens and other city parks have a programme of entertainment called Fantastic Entertainment in Public Places (FEIPP), including the Melbourne Symphony Orchestra's Prom Concerts, art shows, children's plays, jazz and ballet.

The **Carlton Gardens**, north-east of the city, flank the **Exhibition Buildings** —a grandiose domed hall originally built for the Great Exhibition in 1880 and still used for trade fairs. The southern side of the gardens has an ornamental pond and ornate fountain and the northern section an adventure playground and mini-traffic circuit popular with junior cyclists.

The **Victorian Arts Centre** is just over Princes Bridge on St Kilda Road, south of the central business area, and comprises the **National Gallery of Victoria**, the **Melbourne Concert Hall**, three theatres, other performance spaces, several gallery areas, and a variety of restaurants and bars. The National Gallery features a fine collection of Australian and overseas masterpieces. The intricate stained glass ceiling of the Great Hall was designed by Australian artist Leonard French. The Concert Hall is used for classical music and large concerts. It also contains the **Performing Arts Museum**, which offers a programme of regularly changing exhibitions covering the whole spectrum of the performing arts. The theatres include the **State Theatre** for opera, ballet and large musicals, the **Playhouse** for drama and the **George Fairfax Studio** for experimental theatre. Not far away at the **Malthouse**, 117 Sturt Street, South Melbourne, the Playbox Theatre Company has two theatres.

The **Kings Domain**, across St Kilda Road, is a huge stretch of shady parkland where you will see the **Myer Music Bowl**, used in the summer months as the venue for outdoor concerts and in the winter months as an ice-skating rink; the tower of **Government House** (house is open to the public second-last Sunday in October); the majestic, pyramid-style **Shrine of Remembrance,** which dominates St Kilda Road and is open to the public; the **Old Observatory** in Birdwood Avenue and, just past this, **La Trobe's Cottage**, Victoria's first Government House. This quaint cottage with many original furnishings—a reminder of Melbourne's humble beginnings— was brought out from England by the first Governor (La Trobe) in prefabricated sections. It is now a National Trust property, furnished in the original style with many of La Trobe's personal belongings, and open daily. The main entrance to the **Royal Botanic Gardens** is nearby. These lush, beautifully landscaped gardens with gently sloping lawns, attractively grouped trees and shrubs, shady ferneries and ornamental lakes, are a peaceful retreat for city dwellers. Many of the majestic old oaks in the western end of the garden are over 100 years old. The tearooms, open daily, serves morning and afternoon teas and lunch. Guided walks operate at 10 a.m. and 11 a.m. daily (not Mondays,

Saturdays and public holidays) departing from the Visitor Centre; there is no charge.

If you walk through the gardens you will come to shady **Alexandra Avenue**, which runs beside the Yarra River. Barbecues are dotted along the Yarra's grassy banks. At weekends, hire bicycles and ride the scenic **Yarra River Cycle Path**, or take a ferry trip from Princes Bridge downriver to Morrell Bridge, or past historic **Como House**.

Nearby **Albert Park**, just south of St Kilda Road, is another good place for families—and sports enthusiasts. There are barbecues on the edge of the huge Albert Park Lake and boats are available for hire. You can jog or cycle around the lake, or play golf on the adjoining public golf course. This park is also the proposed venue for the annual Australian Formula One Grand Prix car race, scheduled for 1996.

Albert Park and its neighbouring suburbs, **South Melbourne** and **Port Melbourne**, are popular places with their trendy restaurants, bookshops, pubs and markets leading down to Melbourne's bayside beaches. **Albert Park Beach** has a brightly equipped playground with a tunnel slide on to the sand. In summer you can hire windsurfers on the beach near Fraser Street, in West St Kilda.

Cosmopolitan **St Kilda** is a combination of London's Soho and an old-fashioned fun resort. **Luna Park** and the enormous **Palais Theatre** are relics of the days when St Kilda was Melbourne's leading seaside playground. St Kilda is worth a visit, particularly on Sundays, when a collection of art and craft stalls appears on the **Esplanade**, and **Acland Street** offers bookshops, restaurants and luscious continental cakes. For a delightful fish meal, visit Jean Jacques restaurant or take-away on the Lower Esplanade. The **Jewish Museum** is now at its now St Kilda site, 26 Alma Road.

Just outside St Kilda at 192 Hotham Street, Elsternwick, is **Rippon Lea**, a National Trust property open daily. This huge Romanesque mansion is famed for its beautiful English-style landscaped gardens and strutting peacocks.

Two of Melbourne's wealthiest suburbs are **South Yarra** and **Toorak**. **Como**, another magnificent National Trust mansion, is in Como Avenue, off Toorak Road. Set in pleasant gardens, which once spread right down to the

river, charmingly balconied Como is a perfectly preserved example of nineteenth-century colonial grandeur.

Although many of Toorak's and South Yarra's grand old estates have been subdivided, there is no shortage of imposing gates and high walls screening huge mansions. You could easily spend the best part of a day strolling down **Toorak Road**. This is a place to see and be seen—where there are probably more boutiques, expensive restaurants and gourmet food shops per metre than in any other part of Melbourne.

Another of Melbourne's great shopping streets, **Chapel Street**, crosses Toorak Road in South Yarra. Here yet more fashion boutiques and antique and jewellery shops abound, but the air is not quite so rarefied, nor are the price tags quite as high. The **Jam Factory** is a huge redbrick building that still looks like a factory from the outside, but inside there are shops, an attractive glass-topped courtyard and restaurants. Further on towards Malvern Road, Chapel Street becomes more cosmopolitan and the emphasis shifts from fashion to food. The **Prahran Market** is just around the corner in Commercial Road. This market springs to life on Tuesdays, Thursdays, Fridays and Saturdays. Catch a tram down nearby **High Street** to Armadale and you will come to Melbourne's antique area. Art and craft galleries, antique shops and designer-clothes shops stretch along High Street for several blocks.

Melbourne's city centre has been revitalised by Sunday trading, Swanston Walk, and the popularity of the various shopping complexes. Once-depressed inner suburbs north of the Yarra have also been recharged with life. Theatres, theatre restaurants, antique shops, fashion boutiques and dozens of BYOs have bloomed in the suburbs of **Carlton**, **North Fitzroy** and **Richmond**. Most of the elegant iron-lace terrace houses in the more fashionable inner suburbs have been lovingly restored, but these areas still have a lively mixture of migrants and Australian old-timers. Carlton, the site of **Melbourne University**, has one of the largest concentrations of beautiful Victorian houses in Melbourne. Its shady wide streets and squares of restored terraces can make you forget you are within walking distance of a modern city.

Lygon Street, known locally as 'little Italy', has three blocks of Italian restaurants, delicatessens, bookshops, boutiques and 'arty' shops. Have lunch and take in the Carlton scene at Jimmy Watson's, Melbourne's oldest wine bar, at 333 Lygon Street. The wine is good but cheap, the food self-service and the atmosphere frenetic.

Walk through the Melbourne University grounds—a mixture of original ivy-clad buildings and modern blocks—and you come to **Parkville**, another little pocket of gracious Victorian terraces and shady streets. And at the **Melbourne Zoo**, just across nearby **Royal Park**, you can see a magnificent collection of butterflies in the unique walk-through Butterfly House, and families of lions at play from the safety of a 'people cage', an enclosed bridge that takes you right through the lions' large, natural-looking enclosure. This innovation is typical of the zoo's policy of making enclosures for animals as large and as natural as possible, with a minimum of bars. There is also an amusement park and kiosk.

Melbourne's old metropolitan meat market at 42 Courtney Street, North Melbourne has been converted to a large craft gallery and workshop complex. The **Meat Market Craft Centre** features changing exhibitions, demonstrations and sales of high-quality crafts. For more information on craft shops and galleries, contact Craft Victoria on (03) 9417 3111.

Another old inner suburb worth exploring is **Fitzroy**, which is similar in character to Carlton. Raffish Brunswick Street, Fitzroy, has an interesting mixture of antique shops, bookshops, clothes boutiques, pubs and first-class BYOs. In the suburb of **Fairfield**, a few kilometres east of Fitzroy, are the Fairfield Park Boathouse and Tea Gardens, with rowing skiffs and canoes for hire.

East Melbourne, another extremely well-preserved area of beautiful terrace houses, has such 'grand old ladies' as **Clarendon Terrace** (in Clarendon Street) with its graceful, colonnaded central portico, and **Tasma Terrace** in Parliament Place, which now houses the National Trust Preservation Bookshop. The **Fire Services Museum of Victoria** is at 48 Gisborne Street, East Melbourne.

Swan Street, Richmond has one of the best selections of Greek restaurants in Melbourne. Most are cheap and unpretentious with excellent food enhanced by a lively atmosphere. **Victoria Street** is the Vietnamese heartland of the city. Restored Victorian shops in **Bridge Road** house both boutiques and bargain

St Kilda pier

'seconds' outlets. As well as Bridge Road, factory outlets and seconds shops can be found in Swan Street and Church Street, making Richmond the bargain shopping district of Melbourne.

It is possible in Melbourne to dine and see the sights at the same time. The Colonial Tramcar Company runs a restaurant aboard a 1927 tram, thus allowing patrons to enjoy a meal in elegant style while travelling through Melbourne and some of its suburbs. This has proved so popular that three old-style trams are now in use. Another novel way to wine and dine is aboard The Showboat Cruising restaurant, which leaves from North Wharf, West Melbourne or hire a Bar-B-Boat, a novel way to enjoy a barbecue while cruising on the Yarra.

South-west of the city is Melbourne's oldest suburb, **Williamstown**, founded in the 1830s. This fascinating former maritime village has many quaint old seafront pubs, historic churches, fishermen's cottages and relics of its days as an important seaport. Because it was shielded from modern development until the completion of the **West Gate Bridge** to the city centre, much of Williamstown has changed little, and retains a strong seafaring character. At weekends you can see over HMAS *Castlemaine*—a World War II minesweeper restored by the Maritime Trust—and picnic along the grassy foreshore. You can also see model ships, early costumes and relics at the Williamstown **Historical Museum** in Electra Street and look over a superb exhibition of old steam locomotives at the **Railway Museum** in Champion Road, North Williamstown. Williamstown Bay and river cruises are available.

The award-winning science and technology museum, **Scienceworks**, is located in a former pumping station in the suburb of **Spotswood**, close to Williamstown and only a ten-minute drive from the city. Australia's first plane and car are exhibited here.

Closer to the city is the **Living Museum of the West** at Pipemakers Park, Van Ness Avenue, in the suburb of **Maribyrnong**; Australia's first ecomuseum, it presents the environment and heritage of the total community, the focus being on the people of the region. Cruises on the Maribyrnong River visit some of the attractions to the west and north-west of Melbourne. At the **Craigieburn** noteprinting branch of the Reserve Bank of Australia, visitors can observe the printing of Australian currency notes; appointment required (03) 303 0444.

The *Polly Woodside*, a square-rigged commercial sailing ship built in 1885, is moored at the old Duke and Orr's Dry Dock at the corner of Phayer Street and Normanby Road, **South Melbourne** (near Spencer Street Bridge), and is the focal point of the **Melbourne Maritime Museum**. In Coventry Street South Melbourne are three portable houses, assembled in the 1850s, of the kind popular in Victoria during the gold-rush era.

For detailed information on Melbourne there are a number of guidebooks available. **RACV** offices, 230 Collins Street; (03) 790 3333, or 422 Little Collins Street; (03) 790 3333, provide maps, brochures and other information. As well as the Zone 1 Daily Ticket, **The Met**, Melbourne's public transport system, offers an Explorers Pack consisting of three adult Met passes, a map, and a 92-page booklet of tourist attractions in and around Melbourne and suggested day trips on public transport. Contact (03) 617 0900 or visit the Met shop at 103 Elizabeth Street.

Parks and Gardens

Rhododendron Gardens at Olinda, the Dandenongs

Melbourne is a city that has grown to become a place of dignity and beauty, designed as it was with wide, tree-shaded streets and magnificent public gardens. The feeling for greenery and open space has been maintained by individual residents, many of whom take great pride in their gardens, whether they be planted with exotic species or with Australian native trees and shrubs.

The jewel of Victoria is the **Royal Botanic Gardens**, situated beside the Yarra River, only two kilometres from the city. Here there are 36 hectares of plantations, flower-beds, lawns and ornamental lakes, so superbly laid out and cared for that they are considered to be among the best in the world.

The site was selected in 1845 but the main work of their development was carried out by Baron Ferdinand von Mueller, who was appointed Government Botanist in 1852. He was succeeded by W. R. Guilfoyle, a landscape artist, who further remodelled and expanded the gardens. The gardens and the riverside are now a favourite place for Melburnians on Sundays. Families flock to picnic, feed the swans and waterbirds on the lakes or simply take a pleasant stroll.

Adjoining the gardens and flanking St Kilda Road is another large area of parkland, the **Kings Domain**, comprising 43 hectares of tree-shaded lawns and containing the Shrine of Remembrance, La Trobe's Cottage, which was the first

Government House, and the Sidney Myer Music Bowl, an unconventional aluminium and steel structure that creates a perfect amphitheatre for outdoor concerts in the summer months, and is converted into an ice-skating rink during winter. This vast garden area is completed by the adjoining **Alexandra and Queen Victoria Gardens**, a further 52 hectares of parkland.

The city's first public gardens were the **Flagstaff Gardens** at William Street, West Melbourne. A monument in the gardens bears a plaque describing how the site was used as a signalling station to inform settlers of the arrival and departure of ships at Williamstown. On the other side of the city, not far from the centre, in East Melbourne are the **Treasury and Fitzroy Gardens** close by the State government offices. In the Fitzroy Gardens is Captain Cook's cottage, which was transported in 1934 from the village of Great Ayton, Yorkshire, where Cook was born, and which was re-erected to commemorate Melbourne's centenary. Also in these gardens is a model Tudor village, laid out near an ancient tree trunk, a fairy tree carved with tiny figures by the late Ola Cohn. Another garden close to the city is the **Carlton Gardens**, in which the domed Exhibition Buildings are situated. They were erected for the Great Exhibition of 1880. The building was for 27 years the meeting-place of the Victorian Parliament; Federal Parliament met in

the State Parliament buildings while awaiting the building of Canberra.

Apart from these formal gardens, Melbourne also has large recreational areas around the city and throughout the urban regions, and these meet the demands of a sport-loving populace. The most notable is Albert Park, where there are golf courses, indoor sports centres, two major cricket and football grounds and many other ovals, and a lake for sailing and rowing; the park is also the proposed venue for the annual Australian Formula One Grand Prix car race, scheduled for 1996. Another large sporting area in East Melbourne contains the famous **Melbourne Cricket Ground**, which has been established for more than 100 years as a venue for test cricket and football and which now has stands that can accommodate 100 000 people. Nearby is the award-winning **National Tennis Centre**, the venue for international tennis tournaments, including the Australian Open each January. Courts are available for public hire. The Melbourne metropolitan area has eighty golf courses, many of which are accessible to the public. The **Royal Melbourne Golf Club** ranks sixth in world ratings, and hosts many world-class tournaments.

The created beauty of Melbourne is surpassed by nature in the Dandenong Ranges, about 49 kilometres from the city. The heavily forested ranges have such trees as mountain ash, grey gums, messmate, peppermint and box euca-lypts, and spectacular fern gullies. A network of good roads connects the many small towns in the Dandenongs, most of which blend into their bushland surround-ings. The private gardens in the district are beautifully maintained and a drive through the hills is delightful at any time of the year, but particularly in spring when fruit trees and ornamentals are in blos-som, or in autumn when the exotic trees are at their most colourful.

There are a number of natural forests in the Dandenongs with tracks for bush-walkers. The best known is **Sherbrooke Forest**, which seems beautifully un-spoiled despite the fact that it is visited by tens of thousands of people every year. It is a bird sanctuary and a home of the famous but shy lyrebird. A rare delight is to see the elaborate mating dance and display of these birds and to hear their brilliant mimicking calls.

A good way to see the Dandenongs is to take a trip on Puffing Billy, a delightful narrow-gauge steam railway maintained by a preservation society. It runs from Belgrave to Emerald Lake through bush-land and flower farms. Visits to art galleries, antique shops, restaurants, sanctuaries or plant nurseries can add to the pleasure of a visit to the Dande-nongs.

There are many other spectacular natural areas throughout Victoria and over the years the Government has been active in preserving many of these for the people—places such as the **Wilsons Promontory National Park** with its se-cluded beaches and superb coastal scenery; the **Tarra-Bulga National Park** in the Strzelecki Ranges, with its moun-tain ash trees and rainforest vegetation; the **Wyperfeld National Park** in the north-west, with its spring wildflowers and dry-country birdlife; and the **Alpine Na-tional Park**, which stretches across 642 000 hectares of the State's high country.

The quality of Victoria's public and pri-vate gardens is exceptional wherever you go. Each year, Australia's Open Garden Scheme publishes a guidebook to numerous private gardens open through-out spring, summer and autumn, right across Victoria as well as in five other States. Most major towns have large, me-ticulously maintained garden areas, each with its own special quality. The **Ararat** Botanical Gardens are noted for orchid glasshouse displays. The gardens at **Bal-larat** are the centre of the notable annual Begonia Festival held in March. **Benalla** has a Rose Festival every November. In autumn, visitors are attracted to the col-ours of autumn foliage on the trees in and around the small town of Bright.

For further information on various garden festivals and displays, contact the RACV, 230 Collins St, Melbourne; (03) 9790 3333. **See also:** National Parks.

Sherbrooke Forest

Tours from Melbourne

Some of Australia's most beautiful and interesting tours start from Melbourne and include historic towns and stunning scenery. Many require an overnight stop to do them justice and in such cases booking ahead is recommended.

Ballarat and Sovereign Hill, 110 km from Melbourne via the Western Freeway

A must for the tourist if only to visit Sovereign Hill, arguably the most authentic reconstruction of a nineteenth-century goldmining township in the world. Ballarat is one of Victoria's most attractive old cities with many splendid colonial buildings, parks and gardens. Other attractions in Ballarat include the Eureka Stockade and the Begonia Festival held in March. Allow plenty of time for your Sovereign Hill visit. At Sovereign Hill you can stay overnight in the re-creation of Government Camp. **See also:** The Golden Age and Ballarat entry in A–Z listing.

Geelong, Queenscliff and Point Lonsdale, 107 km from Melbourne via the Princes Highway and Bellarine Highway

Allow two days for this tour. Spend some time in Geelong, especially around the historic waterfront and at the National Wool Museum, before continuing to Queenscliff, Melbourne's favourite summer resort of the late nineteenth century and still a popular weekend spot. Look for the lost treasure of Pirate Benito reputedly buried here and visit Fort Queenscliff, Melbourne's first defence establishment, before continuing on to William Buckley's cave at Point Lonsdale. Stay overnight at a classic nineteenth-century hotel; try the Vue Grand, Ozone or the Queenscliff, each

located in Queenscliff. **See also:** Individual entries in A–Z listing.

Werribee Park, 35 km from Melbourne via the Princes Highway

Just outside the township of Werribee, now almost a suburb of Melbourne, Werribee Park is a large estate with a magnificent Italianate mansion of some sixty rooms, built in the 1870s for the Chirnside brothers, who had established a pastoral empire in the Western District. Now owned by the Victorian Government, Werribee Park is open daily. There are extensive formal gardens, including the Victorian State Rose Garden, an open-range zoo, an equestrian centre, restaurant, kiosk, picnic and barbecue facilities, a golf course and tennis courts.

Fort Queenscliff

Nearby Point Cook RAAF Museum (open Sun.–Fri.) has adjacent picnic and barbecue facilities. There is nude bathing at Campbell's Cove.

The Great Ocean Road and the Otway Range, 200 km from Melbourne along the south-west coast

See: The Great Ocean Road.

Port Phillip Bay Cruises from Station Pier, Port Melbourne

The steam tug *Wattle*, a beautifully restored 1933 tugboat, makes day trips to Portarlington on the Bellarine Peninsula on Saturdays, and fascinating 90-minute round trips from Station Pier to Gem Pier, Williamstown on Sundays and public holidays. These cruises operate from

Bridge between San Remo and Newhaven, Phillip Island

October to June. In January the *Wattle* runs daily seal-colony cruises from Rye. The *Wattle* is also available for charter. Bookings are essential; contact (03) 328 2739.

Healesville Sanctuary, 60 km from Melbourne via the Maroondah Highway

To see all of Australia's distinctive fauna in one huge natural enclosure, take a one-day tour to Healesville Sanctuary. Many of the animals roam freely; there are 'walk-through' aviaries, excellent nocturnal displays and viewing of the extraordinary platypus. The highlight, however, is the 'Where Eagles Fly' exhibit, for which rangers and birds of prey combine in an awe-inspiring display. Open daily, with self-service restaurant, picnic and barbecue facilities. Mt Saint Leonard, north of Healesville, offers a fine 360-degree view, but requires a one-kilometre uphill walk. **See also:** Healesville entry in A–Z listing.

The Dandenong Ranges, 49 km from Melbourne via the Burwood Highway

See: The Dandenongs.

Phillip Island, 140 km from Melbourne via the Mulgrave Freeway and the South Gippsland and Bass Highways

Famous for the nightly parade at dusk of little (fairy) penguins up to their burrows at Summerland Beach, Phillip Island attracts thousands of visitors annually. Other wildlife attractions include fur seals all year, but especially in November–December, and mutton-birds in spring and summer. The island is situated in Western Port and also offers excellent surfing and fishing. There is usually some activity at the Phillip Island Motor Racing Circuit, venue for the first 500 cc motorcycle Australian Grand Prix. **See also:** Phillip Island; and Cowes entry in A–Z listing.

South Gippsland and Wilsons Promontory, 180 km from Melbourne via the South Gippsland Highway

Leaving Melbourne behind, this tour takes you through the towns of Cranbourne, Korumburra and Leongatha and through the lush, rolling hills and the spectacular countryside of South Gippsland to Foster, where you turn right for the southernmost point on the Australian mainland at Wilsons Promontory National Park. See kangaroos and koalas and take some short (or long) bushwalks to tiny coves and sandy beaches. This tour deserves at least two days. Return along the coast road through Inverloch and Wonthaggi. **See also:** Individual entries in A–Z listing.

Warburton and the Upper Yarra Dam, 120 km via the Maroondah and Warburton Highways

On the way to some of Victoria's high country, visit wineries in the Yarra Valley region. Some of the Warburton–Upper Yarra Dam area may be snow-covered in mid-winter. If you visit in the warmer months, picnic by the Upper Yarra Dam and go trout fishing at Tommy Finn's Trout Farm at Millgrove. Hot-air balloon flights are available at Yarra Glen. Warburton has giant waterslides and an art gallery; the Lal Lal Falls are just out of town. You can cross the range to Noojee (but take care, as the road is unsealed), and return via Warragul and the Princes Highway. The Gippsland region produces some of the world's great cheeses. **See also:** Warburton entry in A–Z listing; Yarra Valley wineries tour, below.

Yarra Valley wineries, 40–60 km from Melbourne via the Maroondah and Melba Highways, or via Heidelberg, Greensborough and the Diamond Valley

Throughout the Yarra Valley, 37 wineries and 82 vineyards, from Cottlesbridge in the north to Warburton in the south (centred on Coldstream/Yarra Glen), produce premium and quality reds and whites that are acclaimed world-wide. Of these, 20 have cellar-door facilities, many are open daily, while others open on weekends and public holidays. Some offer picnic facilities and several—such as Fergusson's, De Bortoli, Kellybrook and Yarra Burn—have restaurants on the premises. Further information and a listing of cellar-door details from the Yarra Valley Wine Growers Association; (059) 64 2016.

Mornington Peninsula, 100 km from Melbourne via the Nepean Highway

See: The Mornington Peninsula.

154

The Mornington Peninsula

This boot-shaped promontory separates Port Phillip Bay and Western Port and provides Melburnians with a beachside playground. It is a mixture of resort towns, varying in size and tourist development, and inland rural countryside. As well as safe bayside beaches, there are excellent surf beaches, particularly along the stretch of rugged coast between Portsea and Cape Schanck at the end of the Peninsula. The Point Nepean National Park includes the key beaches in this area— **Portsea**, **Sorrento**, **Diamond Bay**, **Koonya** and **Gunnamatta**. A number of walking tracks have been established. Swimming is considered safe only in those areas controlled by the Surf Lifesaving Association.

The Western Port side of the Peninsula is less developed, much of its foreshore having remained relatively unspoiled and being still devoted to farming and grazing land. **French Island**, which is set in the centre of this bay, was a Victorian penal settlement for forty years and is now administered by the Victorian government as a State park. The island is notable for its fauna.

Port Phillip Bay is linked for vehicle access by the Peninsula Searoad Transport ferry, which operates between Sorrento and Queenscliff. A passenger ferry links Sorrento, Portsea and Queenscliff in the summer season as well.

Frankston, now mainly a residential area for Melbourne commuters, could also be considered the gateway to the Peninsula. It is a thriving town within easy reach of good beaches on Port Phillip Bay at Daveys Bay, Canadian Bay and Mount Eliza. McClelland Art Gallery at Langwarrin is open Tuesday to Sunday, and public holidays except Christmas Day and Good Friday. Sage's Cottage (1850), at nearby Baxter, is now a colonial-style restaurant.

The Peninsula itself is well developed for tourists, with good sporting facilities and many art galleries, craft shops, restaurants and take-away food shops. Because of its popularity it is advisable to book accommodation, whatever your choice, well ahead during the summer and Easter seasons. The Port Phillip Bay foreshore from **Dromana** to **Blairgowrie** is almost entirely devoted to campers and caravans during these peak seasons.

Mornington was established in 1864. The deep safe harbour at Point Schnapper first attracted settlers to this area and it has been a popular resort town ever

Point Nepean National Park, near Portsea

since. Today it is a pleasant commercial, farming and recreational centre. Street Market operates on Wednesday mornings and the second Sunday in each month. Between the town and nearby Mount Martha stretches a fine coastline with sheltered sandy bays separated by rocky bluffs and backed by steep wooded slopes. A self-guide walk introduces the town's historic buildings, including the gaol and courthouse on the Esplanade, and the old post office on the Esplanade corner, which is now an historic museum. The Australian Museum of Modern Media, 1140 Nepean Highway, has film, television, radio and pop music memorabilia. The Mornington Peninsula Arts Centre is in the Civic Reserve, Duns Road. Fossil Beach, between Mount Martha and Mornington, is one of only two exposed fossil plains in the world. Located at Mount Martha, The Briars, an old homestead (1866) and property, incorporates old gardens and buildings, wetland areas, bird hides, a Woodland Walk and the Briars Wine Centre in the Josephine Restaurant.

Dromana rests at the foot of Arthurs Seat, the 305-metre mountain that provides the Peninsula with panoramic views over both bays. Safety Beach has boat-launching ramps and trailer facilities. A good road leads to the summit and a chairlift operates at weekends and school and public holidays May to mid-September, but daily from then until to the end of April. At the summit there are a lookout tower, picnic reserve and licensed restaurant. Seawinds, a section of the Arthurs Seat State Park, which has beautiful gardens complete with sculptures, picnic facilities and splendid views is also nearby.

Main Ridge and **Red Hill**, in the hinterland behind Arthurs Seat, are known for wineries. At Main Ridge attractions include Kings Waterfall, also in Arthurs Seat State Park; the Drum Drum wildflower farm; Seaview Nursery and tearooms; Sunny Ridge Strawberry Farm; Arthurs Seat Riding School; and the Pine Ridge Car Museum. Red Hill is particularly well known for its Community Market, held on the first Saturday of the months September to May.

McCrae is a small resort centre, noted for the McCrae Homestead, built in 1844, now a National Trust property, open daily. It was the first homestead on the Peninsula.

Rosebud is a busy commercial centre with wide foreshore camping areas.

Rye has extensive camping, picnicking and recreational foreshore areas, and boat-launching and parasailing facilities.

Sorrento was the site of Victoria's first settlement in 1803, when Colonel Collins landed in this area. The early settlers'

graves and a memorial to Collins can be found in the cliff-top cemetery overlooking Sullivans Bay. Sorrento was energetically developed as a watering place by George Coppin in the 1870s; the Sorrento, Koonya and Continental Hotels have been restored as fine examples of early Victorian architecture. At nearby Point King, the Union Jack was raised for the first time in Australia. South Channel Fort, a constructed island that is now a bird habitat, lies 6 kilometres off Sorrento and is open to visitors.

Portsea, situated at the end of the Nepean Highway, is an attractive resort with excellent deepwater bayside beaches and first-class surfing at its Back Beach. Victoria's first Quarantine Station (now an Army training camp) was built here in 1856 after 82 deaths from smallpox on the vessel *Ticonderoga* anchored in Weroona Bay. Off-limits to the public until recently, this area is now incorporated into the Point Nepean National Park; open daily. Panoramic views of the impressive rocky coastline abound and near Back Beach is London Bridge, a spectacular rock formation created by sea erosion.

Flinders is the most southerly Peninsula township, on Western Port. It is a fishing and holiday resort, with good surfing, swimming and fishing. Cape Schanck lighthouse (1859) with its museum, the Blowhole and Elephant Rock are worth visiting.

Hastings, also fronting Western Port, is an attractive fishing port and holiday centre with a seawater swimming pool, yacht club, marina and boat-launching ramps south of the pier. There is a fauna park next to the high school in High St, and a 52 000-hectare coastal area of designated wetlands north of town.

Other towns in Western Port include

Shoreham, a sprawling holiday settlement on Stony Creek, close to the sea. On Red Hill Road is Ashcombe Maze, which features hedge mazes surrounded by gardens. Five kilometres from Shoreham is **Point Leo**, which has one of the safest surf beaches on the Peninsula. Between Point Leo and **Balnarring**, short access roads from the main Flinders–Frankston road lead to very pleasant beaches at Merricks, Coles, Point Sumner and Balnarring.

Somers, a quiet village with many holiday homes, has good beaches, excellent fishing, tennis and yacht clubs. Coolart mansion, a National Trust-classified homestead dating from the 1890s, is set on 87 hectares. Now a bird sanctuary, it has developed wetlands, bird hides and walking trails as well as landscaped gardens. Between Somers and Crib Point is HMAS *Cerberus*, a Royal Australian Navy training establishment.

The Mornington Peninsula is a rapidly growing wine-producing area. From the hinterland of Mount Martha to the shores of Western Port, 17 vineyards open regularly for cellar-door tastings and sales; 13 more open by appointment. For further detailed information, contact the Mornington Peninsula Vignerons Association; PO Box 400, Mornington 3931; (059) 74 4200.

For further information on the area contact Peninsula Tourism, Nepean Hwy, Dromana; (059) 87 3078, or the Frankston Information Centre, 54 Playne St, Frankston; (03) 9781 5244, or the Mornington Information Centre, cnr Main and Elizabeth Sts, Mornington; (059) 75 1644. **Note** detailed map of Mornington Peninsula on page 212.

Ashcombe Maze, near Shoreham

The Dandenongs

These ranges, 50 kilometres from the centre of Melbourne, are a tourist attraction renowned for their beauty. Heavy rainfall and rich volcanic soil have created a lush vegetation with spectacular hills and gullies crowded with creepers, tree ferns and soaring mountain ash. The area is fairly closely settled and there are a number of pretty townships dotted about the hills.

It has long been a traditional summer retreat for people from Melbourne and many of the gracious old homes have now been converted into guest houses and restaurants.

The entire area is famous for its beautiful gardens and for its great variety of European trees, particularly attractive in spring and autumn. Many excellent restaurants, art and craft galleries, antique shops and well-stocked plant nurseries add to the charm of these hills, ideally placed for a relaxed day's outing from Melbourne. At 633 metres, Mount Dandenong is the highest point of the ranges, and at its summit there are excellent views, picnic facilities and the Skyhigh Restaurant from which a magnificent night-time view of Melbourne can be seen.

Ferntree Gully National Park, Doongalla and Sherbrooke Forest are now the 1920-hectare Dandenong Ranges National Park, where you can see lush trees and ferns and a wide variety of flora and fauna. The lyrebird and eastern whipbird can be heard here. Sherbrooke Forest, on the road from **Belgrave** to **Kallista**, is unspoiled bushland with a population of many lyrebirds. A tourist road runs through the park area from **Ferntree Gully** to **Montrose**. William Ricketts Sanctuary (open daily), on Mount Dandenong Tourist Road, is a natural forest area in which Ricketts, a musician and naturalist who died in 1993, sculpted in clay a number of Aboriginal figures and symbolic scenes. Near **Sherbrooke** the Nicholas Memorial Gardens, 13 hectares of a formerly private garden, are open daily.

The Puffing Billy narrow-gauge steam train, one of the Dandenongs' most famous attractions, leaves from **Belgrave** and travels 13.5 kilometres to **Emerald Lake**. The Puffing Billy Steam Museum at **Menzies Creek**, open Saturday, Sunday and public holidays, displays some restored locomotives and rolling-stock. This small train runs daily except on Christmas Day and fire-ban days. A timetable is available from the RACV, 230 Collins St, Melbourne, (03) 9790 3333; or telephone (03) 9870 8411 for recorded information. Each April, the Great Train Race is held: runners attempt to race Puffing Billy from Belgrave to Emerald Lake Park.

Emerald was the first settlement in the area and is situated on a high ridge. It has a number of interesting galleries and in the surrounding countryside there are lavender farms and attractive picnic spots. **Olinda** is a pretty township with some good restaurants. The home of one of Victoria's first settlers, Edward Henty, is now sited here on Ridge Road. Constructed from prefabricated sections brought from England, the house has a number of historic domestic items and original furnishings; open daily except Friday. Also of interest is the National Rhododendron Garden, especially in spring, when the annual show is held. Another spring flower festival is held at **Silvan**, where tulip bulbs are cultivated. **Ferntree Gully**, at the foot of the ranges, is now virtually an outer suburb of Melbourne.

For further information on the Dandenongs, contact the RACV, 230 Collins St, Melbourne; (03) 9790 3333. **See also:** Individual town entries in A–Z listings. **Note** detailed map of Yarra Valley Region on page 214.

Nicholas Memorial Gardens, near Sherbrooke

Victoria from A to Z

Alexandra   Pop. 1965

Alexandra is a farming and holiday centre, 24 km W of Lake Eildon. **Of interest:** Timber and Tramway Museum in former railway station, Station St. Historic buildings incl. National Trust-classified Post Office and adj. Law Courts, Downey St (Goulburn Valley Hwy). Community Market, usually last Sat. of month. Easter: Art Show. **In the area:** Fraser National Park, 12 km E, excellent walks. Bonnie Doon, 37 km NE, on Lake Eildon; base for trail-riding, bushwalking, water sports, scenic drives. Starglen Lodge, Bonnie Doon, accommodation, horseriding, 4WD tours. Southern edge of town, McKenzie Nature Reserve, virgin bushland with abundance of winter and spring orchids. Stonelea Country Retreat at Acheron, 8 km S. Taggerty, 18 km S in the Acheron Valley, good trout fishing in all rivers. Taggerty Pioneer Education Centre; farm holidays. Cathedral Range State Park, 3 km further S from Taggerty, camping, bushwalking, rock climbing, fishing. **Tourist information:** Redgate Nursery and Craft Cottage, 73 Downey St; (057) 72 2169. **Accommodation:** 4 hotels, 2 motels, 8 B&B, 2 cara./camp. parks.
MAP REF. 211 O2, 233 J11

Anglesea   Pop. 1965

This attractive seaside town on the Great Ocean Road has excellent swimming and surfing. The golf course has tame kangaroos, and Taberet facilities at the clubhouse. Behind the town in Coalmine Rd there is an open-cut brown-coal mine and power station with a viewing platform and information. **Of interest:** Melaleuca Gallery, Gt Ocean Rd. Coogoorah Park, on Anglesea River, bushland reserve, waterways, islands, boardwalks, bridges, picnic areas. Sept.:

Angair Festival. **In the area:** J.E. Loveridge Lookout, 1 km W. Point Roadknight beach, 2 km W. Angahook–Lorne State Park, attractive reserve, many walking tracks; access from behind Anglesea or from Aireys Inlet, 10 km SW, on Great Ocean Rd; features incl. Ironbark Basin, Currawong Falls, Treefern Grove, Melaleuca Swamp. **Tourist information:** Christmas–Easter from caravan, Anglesea Riverbank; other months from Shire Offices, Grossmans Rd, Torquay; (052) 61 4202. **Accommodation**: 3 motels, 4 cara./camp. parks. **See also:** The Great Ocean Road; The Western District.
MAP REF. 210 E11, 217 C11, 227 Q9

Apollo Bay   Pop. 894

The Great Ocean Road leads to this attractive coastal town, the centre of a rich dairying and fishing area and the base for a huge fish-freezing plant. The wooded mountainous hinterland offers memorable scenery and there is excellent sea and river fishing in the area. The rugged and beautiful coastline has been the scene of many shipwrecks in the past. **Of interest:** Bass Strait Shell Museum, Noel St. Old Cable Station Museum, Gt Ocean Rd. March: Music Festival. **In the area:** Self-guide walks; leaflet from Tourist Information. Carisbrook Falls, 14 km NE on Great Ocean Road, walking tracks to spectacular views. Grey River Scenic Reserve, 24 km NE. Elliot River, 6 km SW, and adj. Shelly Beach Viewpoint. Otway National Park, 13 km SW, excellent bushwalking through park to sea, through forest to waterfalls. Follow signs to Barham Paradise Scenic Reserve, 10 km NW, in beautiful Barham River Valley. Maits Rest, 17 km W, in Otway National Park, walking tracks, 300-yr-old National Trust-registered native beech tree. Melba

Gully State Park, 3 km W of Lavers Hill, 49 ha, self-guide rainforest walk, glow-worm habitat. Hang-gliding and horseriding. Lavers Hill, 53 km W; tiny now in comparison with the booming timber centre of its heyday. Scenic touring roads, Turton's Track, 25 km N, Wild Dog Road, 3 km E. **Tourist information:** 155 Great Ocean Rd; (052) 37 6529. **Accommodation:** 2 hotels, 20 motels, 6 cara./camp. parks. **See also:** The Great Ocean Road.
MAP REF. 215 G12, 227 N11

Ararat   Pop. 7633

The Ararat area gold boom came in 1857. It was short-lived and sheep farming became the basis of the town's economy. Today the town is the commercial centre of a prosperous farming and winegrowing region. The area also produces fine merino wool. The first vines in the district were planted by French settlers in 1863 and the little town of Great Western, 16 km NW of Ararat, gave its name to some of Australia's most famous wines. **Of interest:** Beautiful bluestone buildings in Barkly St incl. Post Office, splendid Town Hall, Civic Square, War Memorial. Chinese Gold Discovery Memorial, Lambert St. Langi Morgala Folk Museum, Queen St, incl. Aboriginal weapons and artefacts. Ararat Art Gallery, regional gallery specialising in wool and fibre pieces by leading artists. Alexandra Park and Botanical Gardens, orchid glasshouse display, walk-in fernery, herb garden. J-Ward, Old Ararat Gaol, off Lowe St; open Sun., guided tours, groups by appt. Oct.: 10-day Golden Gateway festival. **In the area:** Green Hill Lake, 4 km E off Western Hwy, constructed lake, fishing, water sports. Buangor, 23 km SE, century-old Buangor Hotel; old Cobb & Co. changing station

(c. 1860). Mt Buangor State Park and Fern Tree Waterfalls, with picnic facilities, 18 km further on. Langi Ghiran State Park, 13½ km E off Western Hwy, scenic walks to nearby reservoir, picnic/barbecue facilities, children's playground. Several wineries: Seppelt's Great Western Vineyards (est. 1865), 17 km NW, specialises in dry red wines and sparkling wines, underground cellars National Trust-classified; Best's Wines, 2 km NW on Western Hwy; Mt Langi Ghiran Wines, 20 km E on Western Hwy; Montara Winery, 3 km S on Chalambar Rd; Cathcart Ridge Winery at Cathcart, 6 km W. Cathcart, and Mafeking 20 km further west, historic gold areas. Mafeking, once a bustling settlement with 10 000 people, has picnic facilities. Care must be taken when walking in these areas, watch for many deep mine shafts. **Tourist information:** Barkly St; (053) 52 2096. **Accommodation:** 5 hotels, 6 motels, 4 B&B, 2 cara./camp. parks. **See also:** Wine Regions.
MAP REF. 220 D8, 227 K2, 229 K13

Avoca   Pop. 1004
In the Central Highlands region, Avoca was established with the discovery of gold in the area in 1852. Located at the junction of the Sunraysia and Pyrenees Hwys, the surrounding Pyrenees Range foothills offer attractive bushwalking and are the home of numbers of kangaroos, wallabies and koalas. **Of interest:** Early National Trust-classified bluestone buildings incl. old gaol and powder magazine, Camp St; courthouse and one of State's earliest pharmacies, Lalor's, in High St. Rock and Gem Museum, High

St. Oct.: Wool and Wine Festival. **In the area:** Fishing: Avoca River, through town; Wimmera River 42 km W; Bet Bet Creek, 11 km E. Several wineries incl. Mt Avoca vineyard, 7 km W; Chateau Remy Vineyards, 8 km W on Vinoca Rd; Redbank Winery, Redbank, 20 km NW; Summerfield Winery, Moonambel Village, 20 km N; Warrenmang Vineyard, 1 km E of Moonambel, and Taltarni Dalwhinnie wines, 5 km W. **Tourist information:** High St; (054) 65 3767. **Accommodation:** 2 hotels, 2 motels, 1 cara./camp. park. **See also:** Wine Regions.
MAP REF. 210 A1, 220 I5, 227 M1, 229 M12

Bacchus Marsh   Pop. 13 000
The trees of the Avenue of Honour provide an impressive entrance to Bacchus Marsh, 49 km from Melbourne on the Western Hwy. This long-established town is in a fertile valley, once marshland, between the Werribee and Lerderderg Rivers. **Of interest:** Manor House, Manor St, home of town's founder, Captain Bacchus; privately owned. In Main St: original blacksmith's shop and cottage; courthouse, lockup and National Bank; all National Trust-classified; and Border Inn (1850), thought to have been first coaching service stop in Victoria when Bacchus Marsh was staging post for Cobb & Co. coaches travelling to goldfields. Holy Trinity Anglican Church (1877), Gisborne Rd. Gallery 22, Maddingley Blvd. Express Building Art Gallery, Gisborne Rd. Ra Ceramics and Crafts, Station St. Big Apple Tourist Orchard, Avenue of

Honour. Sept.: Pioneer day Festivals. **In the area:** At Blackwood, 26 km NW, Mineral Springs Reserve; Garden of St Erth. Maddingley open-cut coal mine, 3 km S. Werribee and Lerderderg Gorges, 10 km W and 10 km N, picnics, bushwalking, swimming. Popular with anglers and bushwalkers: Merrimu Reservoir and Wombat State Forest, both about 10 km N; Brisbane Ranges National Park, 16 km SW; Anakie Gorge, 26 km SW; Long Forest Fauna Reserve, 2 km NE, bull mallee, some specimens centuries old. Willows Historic Homestead, Melton, 14 km E. Wineries and vineyards: St Anne's Vineyard on the Western Fwy, 6 km W, old bluestone cellar, built from remains of old Ballarat gaol; Craiglee Winery and Goonawarra Vineyard, Sunbury, 47 km NE; Wildwood Vineyard, Bulla, 9 km SE. **Tourist information:** Shire Offices, Main Street; (053) 67 2111. **Accommodation:** 4 hotels, 1 motel, 1 cara./camp. park. **See also:** The Golden Age.
MAP REF. 210 G5, 221 R13, 224 A3, 227 R5

Bairnsdale   Pop. 10 770
This Gippsland trade centre and holiday town is at the junction of the Princes Hwy, the Omeo Hwy and the road east to Lakes Entrance, which makes it an excellent touring base. It is a pleasant town with good sporting facilities and attractive gardens. **Of interest:** Historical Museum, Macarthur St, building (1891) houses furnishing and memorabilia; grounds display photographs, family histories, publications. St Mary's Church, Main St, wall and ceiling murals by Italian artist. Bairnsdale Recreation Centre, McKeen St, incl. sports hall. Port of Bairnsdale site and river walk, below post office; picnic facilities. March: Riviera Festival. **In the area:** Lindenow, 19 km W, small town close to Mitchell River National Park. In park: good bushwalking tracks; in gorge on Mitchell River, Den of Nargun, Aboriginal cultural site. River empties into Lake King at Eagle Point Bluff, world's second longest silt jetty. About 2 km S of Bairnsdale, a boardwalk (closed during duck season) leads across part of McLeod's Morass, bird wetland habitat; main access about 10 km S. Jolly Jumbuk Country Craft Centre; 5 km E on Princes Hwy, woollen products for sale, workshops. Adjacent, Archery and Mini Golf Park, family fun centre. Metung, 30 km E, picturesque fishing village on shores of Lake King,

Bacchus Marsh

some solid pioneer holiday homes still standing. Scenic drive north along Omeo Hwy through Tambo River valley; stunning in spring when wattles bloom. Nicholson River Winery, 10 km E, and Golvinda winery, 5 km N. **Tourist information:** 240 Main Street; (051) 52 3444. **Accommodation:** 3 hotels, 8 motels, 3 cara./camp. parks. **See also:** Gippsland Lakes.
MAP REF. 225 P4, 234 E13

Ballan   Pop. 1053
A small town on the Werribee River, noted for its mineral springs. **Of interest:** Caledonian Park, eastern edge of town, picnic areas, swimming. March: Arcadian Festival. **In the area:** Pikes Creek Reservoir, 12 km E, good trout fishing. **Tourist information:** Shire Offices, cnr Stead and Steiglitz Sts; (053) 68 1001. **Accommodation:** 3 hotels, 2 caravan parks.
MAP REF. 210 F4, 221 P12, 227 Q4

Ballarat   Pop. 64 980
Ballarat is Victoria's largest inland city, situated in the Central Highlands. Its inner areas retain much of the charm of its gold-boom era, with many splendid original buildings still standing. Ballarat was just a small rural township in 1851, when its enormously rich alluvial goldfields were discovered. Within two years it had a population of nearly 40 000. Australia's only civil battle occurred here in 1854, when miners refused to pay Government licence fees and fought with police and troops at the Eureka Stockade. Today Ballarat is a bustling city with the added attraction of many galleries, museums, antique and craft shops. It has excellent recreational facilities and beautiful garden areas and parks, making it most attractive to visitors. The begonia is the city's floral emblem. Bridge Street Mall in the centre of the city has many shops set in a relaxed atmosphere. **Of interest:** Constructed Lake Wendouree, via Hamilton Ave; water sports. Paddle-steamer tours, commentary on history of city. Adjoining the lake area, Botanic Gardens (40 ha), splendid begonia conservatories; Prime Ministers' Avenue, displaying busts of Australian prime ministers. Elegant statuary pavilion nearby. Vintage Tramway, via Wendouree Pde; rides weekends, public and school holidays. Fine Art Gallery, Lydiard St Nth, comprehensive collection of Australian art,

Main street, Ballarat

incl. works by Lindsay family. Award-winning Montrose Cottage (1856), Eureka St, first masonry cottage built on the goldfields. Adjacent, Eureka Museum, large collection of gold-era relics. Eureka Exhibition and Orpheus Radio Museum, cnr Stawell and Eureka Sts, historical information on Eureka Rebellion, comprehensive exhibition of radios. The Old Curiosity Shop, Queen St, pioneer relics. In Stawell St Sth: Eureka Stockade Park, with life-size replica of the famous battle; self-guide Eureka Trail. Ballarat Wildlife and Reptile Park, cnr of York and Fussell Sts. In Lydiard St: Craig's Royal Hotel, George Hotel, and Ballarat Terrace (1889); dining and accommodation in old-world surroundings. March: Begonia Festival. Aug.–Oct.: Royal South Street Eisteddfod. **In the area:** Sovereign Hill, major tourist attraction 2 km S, reconstruction of goldmining settlement, with orientation centre and working displays. Blood on the Southern Cross, night sight-and-sound exhibition. During Begonia Festival in March, guided lamplight tours of Sovereign Hill. Excellent barbecue facilities. Kiosk, restaurant and licensed hotel. Government Camp, comfortable family-type accommodation. Adjoining Sovereign Hill, Gold Museum, exhibits of gold history; large collection of gold coins; display of the uses of gold 'today and tomorrow'. Enfield State Park, near Enfield, 16 km S of Ballarat. Lal Lal Falls (30 m) on Moorabool River, 25 km SE of city. Lal Lal Blast Furnace, beautiful archaeological remains from 19th century. Kryal Castle, 8 km E on Western Hwy, reconstruction of a medieval castle, family entertainment. On western edge of city, Avenue of Honour (22 km) and Arch

of Victory, honouring those who fought in World War I. White Swan Reservoir, 8 km NE off Daylesford Rd, attractive picnic spot, lawns, water views, picnic/barbecue facilities. Ballarat Aviation Museum, 4 km NW on Learmonth Rd. Lake Burrumbeet, 22 km NW, water sports, picnic spots, excellent trout fishing. 8 wineries, in Avoca area, 70 km W. Yellowglen Winery, Smythesdale, 24 km SW. Berringa Mines Historic Reserve, 8 km from Smythesdale. Mooramong Homestead, National Trust property, Skipton, 53 km SW; by appt. Mt Widderin Caves, 6 km S of Skipton. **Tourist information:** Cnr Sturt and Albert Sts; (053) 32 2694. **Accommodation:** 11 hotels, 23 motels, 22 B&B, 1 hostel, 8 cara./camp. parks. **See also:** The Golden Age; Wine Regions.
MAP REF. 210 C4, 219, 221 M12, 227 O4

Beaufort   Pop. 1171
This small town on the Western Hwy, midway between Ballarat and Ararat, has a gold-rush history, like so many of the other towns in this area. The discovery of gold at Fiery Creek swelled its population in the late 1850s to nearly 100 000. Today Beaufort is primarily a centre for the surrounding pastoral and agricultural district. **Of interest:** Historic courthouse, Livingstone St. Turn-of-century band rotunda. May: Steam Rally. **In the area:** Mt Cole State Forest, part of Great Dividing Range, 16 km NW, via Raglan, peaceful natural area, bushwalks, native flora and fauna, picnics, camping facilities. Lake Goldsmith, 14 km S. Hang-gliding and paragliding. **Tourist information:** Shire Offices, 5 Lawrence St; (053) 49 2000, or The Cooperative

The Golden Age

The cities and towns of the goldfields region of Victoria came to a peak of style and affluence in the 1880s, an affluence built on the first gold discoveries in the 1850s. The towns display all the frivolity and grandeur of Victorian architecture, having grown up in an age when it was believed that gold and wealth would be a permanent benefit in Victoria.

The two major cities of the region are Ballarat and Bendigo, but there are many other towns, large and small, in the area. They all have beautiful historic houses and public buildings, and many have other trappings of the past—statues, public gardens (some with lakes), ornamental bandstands and grand avenues of English trees. Spring and autumn are the best seasons to visit this region, because then there are not the extremes of summer and winter temperatures and the flowers and foliage are at their best.

It is a quiet region now. The remaining small towns serve the rich pastoral district, and secondary industries and services centre on the two cities.

It was once, however, an area of frantic activity. Gold was found at Clunes in 1851 and within three months 8000 people were on the diggings in the area between Buninyong and Ballarat. Nine months later 30 000 men were on the goldfields and four years later 100 000. The population of the city of Melbourne dwindled alarmingly and immigrants rushed to the diggings from Great Britain, America and many other countries. Ships' crews, and sometimes even their captains, abandoned their vessels and trekked to the diggings to try their luck. Tent cities sprang up on the plains as men dug and panned for gold. There were remarkable finds of huge nuggets in the early days, but finally the amount of gold obtained by panning in the rivers and by digging grew less and less. The communities were remarkable: there were shanty towns, the streets crowded day and night with hawkers and traders; there were pubs and dancing-rooms and continuous sounds of music and revelry.

As time went on, the surface gold was worked out and expensive company-backed operations followed: mining in deep shafts, stamping and crushing the ore in steam-powered plants on the surface.

Botanic Gardens, Ballarat

The success of these methods heralded a new era, that of the company mines, outside investors and stock-exchange speculation. It led to a more stable workforce and to the well-established communities that slowly evolved into towns of the region today. As the pastoral potential began to be fully exploited, it was the perfect scene for expansion and optimism.

The years between 1870 and 1890 saw the towns embellished with fine civic buildings, mansions, solid town houses, churches, hotels and all the trappings of affluence. Thus Ballarat, Bendigo, Castlemaine and to a lesser extent Clunes, Creswick, Daylesford and Maldon became extraordinary *nouveau riche* visions of the current British taste.

The Western Highway between Melbourne and Ballarat is at its most scenic as it rises into the Pentland Hills. Rounded volcanic hills encircle **Bacchus Marsh**, which is approached by a magnificent avenue of North American elms commemorating soldiers who died in the Great War. Bacchus Marsh is adjacent to the Lerderderg and Werribee Rivers, which enter dramatic gorges close to the town. Just off the highway are the small rural towns of Myrniong and Ballan, Gordon and Bungaree. South of the highway near Bungaree is Dunnstown, dominated by its bluestone distillery and the bulk of Mount Warrenheip, where an excellent view of the district can be had from the summit.

A turnoff to the south near Ballarat leads to **Buninyong**, the scene of one of the first gold strikes in Victoria. This impressive township with a grand tree-lined main street has a number of striking buildings—the Crown Hotel and white-walled Uniting Church are of the 1860s, while the combined council chambers

and courthouse of 1886 are in rich Italianate design, unified by a central clock tower.

The city of **Ballarat** was laid out to the west of the diggings within twelve months of the first discovery of gold. The design included a magnificent chief thoroughfare, Sturt Street, wide enough for future plantations and monuments. The primitive buildings of early settlement were gradually replaced by boom-style architecture in the 1880s. Italianate, Romanesque, Gothic and French Renaissance styles are mingled; porticoes, colonnades and ornamental stone facades vie with verandahs of lavish cast-iron decoration. There are many superb buildings, the most notable being the post office, the railway station, the town hall, the stock exchange, the former Ballarat gaol, the Wesley Church, the George Hotel, Reids Coffee Palace, the Bailey Mansion, the Roman Catholic bishop's residence, Loreto Abbey and the art gallery. It is a city of many beautiful gardens, particularly the Botanical Gardens adjacent to Lake Wendouree, famous for the annual begonia display in March.

Without doubt Ballarat's major attraction is **Sovereign Hill**. This re-created goldmining township is a fascinating place for a day's outing to interest all the family. Begin your outing by visiting the excellent Voyage to Discovery orientation centre, near the main entrance.

Gold was discovered in Ballarat in 1851, and a visit to the Red Hill Gully Diggings at Sovereign Hill will show you something of the life of those early days. Your visit will not be complete without the chance to pan for 'colour'. A friendly digger will give you a lesson, but you must be sure to purchase your licence first or you may find yourself being arrested by the watchful trooper!

Panning for gold at Sovereign Hill, Ballarat

Main Street is lined with faithfully re-created shops and businesses of the 1851–1861 period. These are based on actual shops and businesses that were operating in Ballarat at that time. Perhaps you will be tempted by the aroma of freshly-baked bread from the wood-fire brick oven of the Hope Bakery. Next door you may dress in topcoat or crinoline and be photographed in true Victorian pose. Across the road, mid-nineteenth-century printing-presses in the Ballarat *Times* office can be used to print your name on a WANTED poster, similar to that issued for Lalor and Black after the uprising at the Eureka Stockade in 1854.

Few can even pass the well-stocked grocery without a surge of nostalgia for days gone by. The tiny sweet shop nearby sells all manner of sweets made to Victorian recipes at Brown's confectionery factory, further up the street.

Those with larger appetites may wine and dine at the United States Hotel or enjoy a digger's lunch of soup, roast meat and apple pie at the New York Bakery. For some energetic relaxation, try your hand at ninepin bowling on the 40-metre-long alley in the Empire Bowling Saloon. The accommodation complex, Government Camp, provides comfortable and inexpensive lodging ranging from tents to self-contained units.

During school terms you will be enchanted to watch a 'class of 1856' at the Red Hill National School. Here children dress in period costume, learn from actual 1850s texts, and are totally involved in living the life of a mid-nineteenth-century goldfields child.

The towering poppet-head, the hiss of steam and the thunder of the stamper battery will draw you to the Sovereign Quartz Mine. Take a guided tour of the underground area; here you will see examples of early mining techniques and even some original workings of the 1880s.

As you wander through the streets you will meet costumed diggers and business-folk, and ladies in bell-shaped crinolines and bonnets. Stop and talk to them and you will learn more about life in the days of the 'rush'.

Sovereign Hill is open daily, except on Christmas Day. There are admission charges, and ample parking is available. Enquiries to the Marketing Department, Sovereign Hill Post Office, Ballarat 3350.

The Gold Museum, opposite Sovereign Hill, has a collection of nuggets, alluvial gold and coins, as well as a Eureka Exhibition outlining the Eureka rebellion.

Beyond Ballarat, on the Midland Highway is **Creswick**, a picturesque valley town with a wonderfully ornate town hall. The bluestone tower of St John's Church dominates the town's western hill and on the hilltop across the valley is a Tudor-style hospital building which is now a school of forestry.

To make a turn off the highway to **Clunes** is well worth while. Gold was first discovered here in July 1851, but it proved difficult to get supplies to this remote township, so the rush was limited and the later discoveries at Buninyong and Ballarat quickly diverted attention from the area. Of particular interest in Clunes are the rich verandahed facades in the shopping area of Fraser Street and the elegant

architectural style of the banks, hotels, post office and town hall.

On the Western Highway, 133 kilometres north-west of Ballarat, past **Ararat** (where a gold rush began in 1857), is **Stawell**. Gold was discovered at the present site of Stawell in 1853; by 1857 there was a population of 30 000, and the township was proclaimed the following year. Goldmining continued in the area until 1920. Today visitors can recapture some of the atmosphere of the gold-rush era at the Mount Pleasant Diggings and Alluvial Gold Memorial.

North-east of Ballarat up the Midland Highway is **Daylesford**, another former goldmining town set in picturesque wooded hills around Wombat Hill Gardens and Lake Daylesford. The town has a number of churches in the Gothic Revival style and an imposing town hall, post office and school. On the hill are groves of rhododendrons, exotic trees and a lookout tower that provides a view of Mount Franklin (a perfectly preserved volcanic crater) and Mount Tarrengower. Several kilometres north of Daylesford are natural springs containing lime, iron, magnesia and other minerals. This is the famed Hepburn Spa, which attracted visitors in the nineteenth century for its medicinal properties. Bottling mineral water is still the town's main industry.

Further north on the road to Bendigo is **Castlemaine**, a larger town and one of the most picturesque in the region. The streetscape in the centre of the town has remained virtually unaltered since the early days, for the prosperity of the 1860s diminished and the town settled down to a quieter rural life. One of the most notable buildings is the Town Market, an unusual Palladian-inspired building which was restored in 1974 and which now contains a museum portraying the history of the town and the Mount Alexander goldfields. The town boasts some other fine buildings, including the great post office in Italianate style with a central clock tower, the former telegraph office, the mechanics' institute, the Imperial Hotel and the Commercial Banking Company building. High on a hill above the town are the stone and redbrick gaol and the obelisk built in 1862 to commemorate the ill-fated Burke and Wills expedition.

Nearby **Maldon** was declared a notable town by the National Trust in 1962. The winding streets are flanked by low buildings, with deep verandahs shading the bluestone pavements laid in 1866.

The city of **Bendigo** is the jewel of the region and is Victoria's most outstanding example of a boom town. Gothic- and classical-style buildings have been designed in vast proportions, richly ornamented and combined with the materials of the age, cast iron and cast cement.

The post office and law courts are among the most impressive high-Victorian public buildings in Australia. Opposite the post office is the Shamrock Hotel—a massive, verandahed structure that once boasted an electric bell to ring for service in each of its 100 rooms. Many of Bendigo's important buildings were designed by the German architect William Charles Vahland. His work included the Benevolent Asylum and Hospital, the school of mines, the mechanics' institute, the town hall, the Masonic hall, the Capital Theatre, four banks and the handsome Alexandra fountain at Charing Cross, the centre of Bendigo.

Bendigo Art Gallery houses a large collection of 19th-century British and European artworks and decorative arts, which complements its outstanding collection of Australian paintings.

Central Deborah Goldmine was the last deep-reef goldmine in Bendigo. Sunk in 1909 and closed in 1954, it has been restored and is open for inspection. The mine is 411 metres deep with seventeen levels, and the visitor level at 61 metres has a 350-metre circuit illustrating the geological features of the Bendigo region and the machinery used in the gold-retrieval process. At ground level are the 21-metre poppet head, the engine room, installations and other exhibits, all of which can be inspected. The mine is also the point of departure for the 8-kilometre (1-hour) tour through Bendigo by the city's famous Vintage Talking Trams, with their taped commentary on attractions and historic points of interest.

Sandhurst Town, off the Loddon Valley Highway, 12 kilometres from Bendigo, represents a typical country town of 1929 with all the glamour of the gold-rush days. Its attractions include the Fair Dinkum Eucalyptus Distillery, the Honey Pavilion and various fascinating shops. The Red Rattler train leaves the town regularly to travel through the Whipstick Forest to the Goldrush Gully diggings with its entertaining street theatre involving colourful characters. In the third week in September every year, Sandhurst Town stages a re-enactment of Bendigo's gold-digger uprising of 1854, in which more than 80 actors replay the struggle against the injustice of the Gold Licence.

The goldfields region can be enjoyed in three days or three weeks, according to time and taste. Bendigo Goldseeker Tours organise gold-fossicking excursions and include instruction in the use of metal detectors. Reasonably priced accommodation is available throughout the region. An excellent way to see the region is via the **Goldfields Tourist Route**, a 450-kilometre triangle road route linking Ballarat, Ararat, Stawell, Bendigo and Castlemaine. Free maps marking the route are available at the Victorian Information Centre, RACV offices and various tourist information centres throughout the goldfields.

More detailed information can be obtained also from the Bendigo Tourist Information Centre, 26 High St, Kangaroo Flat; (054) 47 1383. **See also:** Individual town entries in A–Z listing. **Note** detailed map of Goldfields Region on page 220.

Conservatory Gardens, Bendigo

Crafts, Lawrence St. **Accommodation:** 3 hotels, 1 motel, 2 cara./camp. parks. MAP REF. 220 H10, 227 M3

Beechworth   Pop. 3136

Once the centre of the great Ovens goldmining region, Beechworth lies 24 km off the Ovens Hwy, between Wangaratta and Wodonga on 'The Kelly Way' (Old Sydney Rd). This is one of Victoria's best-preserved and most beautiful gold towns, magnificently sited in the foothills of the Alps. Its public buildings are of architectural merit and the whole town has been classified as historically important by the National Trust. The rich alluvial goldfield at Woolshed Creek was discovered by a local shepherd during the 1850s. A total of 1 121 918 ounces of gold was mined in 14 years. A story is told of Daniel Cameron, campaigning to represent the Ovens Valley community; he rode through the town at the head of a procession of miners from Woolshed, on a horse shod with golden shoes. Sceptics claim they were merely gilded, but the tale is an indication of what Beechworth was like during the boom, when its population was 42 000 and it boasted 61 hotels and a theatre at which international celebrities performed. **Of interest:** Fine 1850s government buildings built of local honey-coloured granite, all still in use; especially in Camp and Ford Sts. Daily historic town tour from Tourist Information Centre; bookings essential. In Albert Rd: Harness and Carriage Museum, run by National Trust; Tanswell's Hotel, privately restored lacework building; under Shire Offices, Ned Kelly's cell; Beechworth Gaol (1859), still used as a prison. Bank of Victoria building, cnr Camp and Ford Sts, Rock Cavern, gemstone collection. Historic former Bank of Australasia, Ford St, fine dining in elegant surroundings. Country Rustica and Buckland Gallery, Ford St. Beechworth Galleries, Camp St. Robert O'Hara Burke Memorial Museum, Loch St, relics of gold rush; 16 mini-shops depicting town's main street as it was more than 100 years ago. Feb.: Drive Back in Time (rally of vintage, veteran and classic vehicles). Easter: Golden Horseshoes Festival. **In the area:** Beechworth Historic Park, surrounds Beechworth area; Woolshed Falls historic walk; Gorge Scenic Drive (5 km); gold fossicking in limited areas. Lake Sambell, fishing, swimming, sailing, boating, canoeing. Golden Hills Trout Farm, 2 km S. Stan-ley, historic village, 4 km S, in hills above Beechworth, among apple orchards, berry farms, nut plantations and tall forests. Fletcher Dam, Beechworth Forest Drive, 2½ km SE towards Stanley; picnic facilities. Kelly's lookout, Woolshed Creek, about 4 km N. Waterfalls: Reids, Woolshed and Clear Creeks. On road north to Chiltern, Beechworth Cemetery, Chinese burning towers, Chinese cemetery. At Chiltern, 26 km NW, Lake View, home of Henry Handel Richardson, restored and landscaped by National Trust; open daily. **Tourist information:** The Rock Cavern, cnr Ford and Camp Sts; (057) 28 1374. **Accommodation:** 2 hotels, 5 motels, 11 B&B, 2 cara./camp. parks.
MAP REF. 233 N6, 234 A4

Benalla   Pop. 8334

This small city, just off the Hume Freeway, is 40 km SW of Wangaratta. Lake Benalla, created in the Broken River, which runs through the city, has recreation and picnic facilities and a bird sanctuary. During the late 1870s Benalla experienced the activities of the notorious Kelly Gang, who were eventually captured at nearby Glenrowan in 1880. It is also the birthplace of Sir Edward ('Weary') Dunlop, and Michael J. Savage, NZ Prime Minister in the 1940s. **Of interest:** Botanical Gardens, Bridge St, incl. splendid rose gardens. Benalla Art Gallery, Bridge St, on shores of lake, important Ledger Collection of Australian paintings; open daily. In Mair St: Pots 'n' More, paintings, pottery, craft; Costume and Pioneer Museum, Ned Kelly's cummerbund on display; Three-dimensional ceramic mural. At aerodrome on the outskirts of town: Gliding Club of Victoria; hot-air ballooning; ultra-light planes. Nov.: Rose Festival. **In the area:** Reef Hills State Park, 4 km S on Midland Hwy, 2040 ha of forest and wide variety of native flora and fauna. Pleasant day trip south east to King Valley and spectacular Paradise Falls. Winton Motor Raceway, 10 km NE. **Tourist information:** Pots 'n' More, 14 Mair St; (057) 62 1749. **Accommodation:** 5 hotels, 7 motels, 1 cara./camp. park.
MAP REF. 222 A2, 233 K7

Bendigo   Pop. 57 427

This is one of Victoria's most famous goldmining towns. Sited at the junction of 5 highways, it is central for trips to many other gold towns nearby. The gold rush began here in 1851 and gold production continued for 100 years. The affluence of the period can still be seen today in many splendid public and commercial buildings. Built in 1897, the Shamrock Hotel has been restored to its original charm. **Of interest:** Many attractive buildings with lacework-verandahs. Sacred Heart Cathedral, Wattle St, largest outside Melbourne, 92-m spire. Alexandra Fountain at Charing Cross. Renaissance-style Post Office (1887) and Law Courts (1896), Pall Mall. Self-guide Heritage Walk. Bendigo Art Gallery (1890), View St. Central Deborah Gold Mine, Violet St, working order, vivid reminder of Bendigo's history; open daily. Vintage Talking Trams, run daily from mine on 8-km city trip; taped commentary; incl. stop at Tram Depot Museum, 30 vintage trams on display. Golden Dragon Museum, Bridge St, Chinese history of the goldfields; largest display of Chinese processional regalia in the world, incl. world's oldest imperial dragon 'Loong' and largest imperial dragon, 'Sun Loong', more than 300 m long. Dudley House (1859), View St, National Trust-classified; gracious old home in lovely gardens; historical display. Lookout tower in Rosalind Park. Easter: Fair (first held 1871, features Chinese dragon). Nov.: National Swap Meet (Australia's largest for vintage car and bike enthusiasts). **In the area:** Fortuna Villa mansion (1871), Chum St, 2 km S; open Sun. Pratts Park Pottery, Harcourt Valley, 29 km S, surrounded by apple and pear orchards. Vineyards and wineries, incl.: Chateau Le Amon winery, 10 km S; Balgownie Vineyard, Maiden Gully, 10 km W. Lake Eppalock, 26 km SE; camping, fishing, water sports, picnic/barbecue facilities. In Mandurang Valley, 8 km E, Adventure Park and Water Playland, pick-your-own berries, water sports, trout fishing, Thunder Cave rapid-river ride, picnicking; historic Chateau Dore winery; Orchid Nursery; Tannery Lane Pottery. Epsom Market, 6 km NE, Sun. Chinese Joss House, Emu Point, 1 km N, built by Chinese miners; National Trust-classified, open daily. Hartland's Eucalyptus Factory and Historic Farm, Whipstick Forest, off Neilborough Rd, 12 km N; built 1890 to process eucalyptus oil obtained from surrounding scrub. At Myers Flat, 12 km NW, Sandhurst Town, re-creation of colonial town; gold diggings, eucalyptus distillery, antique vehicles, working 2-ft-gauge railway. Horsedrawn caravan hire at Bridgewater on Loddon, 37 km NW. Bendigo Mohair Farm, Lockwood, 11 km SW; open weekends 10–3, guided tours, admission free. **Tourist information:** Bendigo Tourism, 26 High St, Kangaroo Flat; (054) 47 7788, (054) 41 5244. **Accommodation:** 10 hotels, 25 motels, 11 B&B, 9 cara./camp. parks. **See also:** The Golden Age; Wine Regions. MAP REF. 218, 221 Q2, 229 Q10, 232 C8

Birchip   Pop. 827
On the main rail link between Melbourne and Mildura, Birchip gets its water supply from the Wimmera–Mallee stock and domestic channel system. **Of interest:** In Cumming Ave: Big Red (Mallee bull); Historical Society Museum, in old courthouse; by appt. **In the area:** Junction of two major irrigation channels constructed in early 1900s, 1 km N of town. Sections of original Dog Fence, 20 km N, vermin-proof barrier constructed in 1883 between Murray River near Swan Hill and South Australian border. Tchum Lake, 8 km E, facilities for motor boats, caravan park. Sites of historic interest within Shire are indicated by markers; leaflet from Tourist Information. **Tourist information:** Council Chambers, 22 Cumming Ave; (054) 92 2200. **Accommodation:** 2 hotels, 1 motel, 1 cara./camp. park. MAP REF. 126 F13, 229 K5

Boort   Pop. 801
A pleasant rural and holiday town on the shores of Lake Boort, with excellent sporting facilities. The lake is popular for water sports, has good picnic facilities and beaches, and offers trout and redfin fishing. There is prolific native birdlife in the area. **Tourist information:** Boort Lake Caravan Park, Durham Ox Rd; (054) 55 2064. **Accommodation:** 1 motel, 1 cara./camp. park. MAP REF. 126 H13, 229 O6

Bright   Pop. 1881
In the heart of the beautiful Ovens Valley and at the foothills of the Victorian Alps, Bright is an attractive tourist centre and a base for winter sports enthusiasts. The town offers easy access to the resorts of Mt Hotham, Mt Buffalo and Falls Creek, and a number of ski-hire shops in the town stay open late during the winter

season. The area is excellent for bushwalking and trout fishing, and is very photogenic, particularly in autumn. The discovery of gold was responsible for the town's beginnings. Tensions between European and Chinese miners led to the notorious Buckland Valley riots of 1857 in which the Chinese were driven from their claims with some brutality. The remains of alluvial goldfields can still be seen. There is a good variety of restaurants, counter meals, cafes and take-away food shops. **Of interest:** Deciduous trees, spectacular autumnal colours. In Main St: Gallery 90, Country Collectables. Bright Art Gallery and Cultural Centre, Mountbatten Ave. Historical Museum, old railway station, Station Ave. Lotsafun Amusement Park adj., entrance Mill Rd. Ovens River flows through town, picnic and camping spots, walk to Riverside Canyon. Excellent summer swimming in deep weir next to Memorial Park, Main St; coin-operated barbecues, children's playground, shallow pool. April–May: Autumn Festival. Oct.: Springtime in Bright. **In the area:** Walking tracks: Clearspot Lookout, from Bakers Gully Rd; Huggins Lookout, from Deacon Ave. Wandiligong, National Trust-classified hamlet in scenic valley, 6 km S; linked to Bright by walking and cycle track. At Harrietville, tiny tranquil town 25 km SE of Bright, Pioneer Park open-air museum; two trout farms, 4 km N. Porepunkah, 6 km NW of Bright, at junction of Ovens and Buckland Rivers, convenient access to Mt Buffalo; Boyntons of Bright Winery; open daily. From Alpine Road south-east to Mt Hotham, superb views of Mt Feathertop, the Razor Back, Mt Bogong. Horseriding. **Tourist information:** Delany Ave, opposite Centennial Park; (057) 55 2275, Sports Centre, Gavan St; (057) 55 1339. **Accommodation:** 2 hotel/motels, 9 motels, 6 B&B, 2 hostels, 7 cara./camp. parks. MAP REF. 223 L5, 233 P8, 234 B6

Broadford   Pop. 2215
A small town off the Hume Freeway near Mt Piper. Picnic facilities at Anderson's Gardens, at the entrance to the State Forest. **Of interest:** Display of old printing equipment in *Broadford Courier* building, High St. Picnic/barbecue facilities in park in town centre, also replica of drop-slab pioneer cottage. Oct.: Scottish Festival. Dec.: Hells Angels Concert. **In the area:** Turnoff 20 km E to Strath

Creek for scenic drive through Valley of a Thousand Hills. At Kilmore, 14 km SW, fine old buildings, incl. Whitburgh Cottage (1857); cable tram rides in Hudson Park. **Tourist information:** Shire Offices, 113 High St; (057) 84 1204. **Accommodation:** 2 hotels, 1 motel. MAP REF. 211 K2, 232 F11

Buchan   Pop. 220
This small town, in the heart of Gippsland mountain country north-east of Bairnsdale, is famous for its remarkable series of limestone caves. Tours of two main caves, Royal and Fairy, are conducted daily. A park and a spring-fed swimming pool are located in the hills behind the caves. **Of interest:** Conorville Heritage Model Village, Main St, display of Australian building to 1900. Oct.: Art and Craft Festival. **In the area:** Suggan Buggan schoolhouse (1865), 64 km N. Cobberas–Tingaringy National Park, 10 km NW of Suggan Buggan; spectacular mountain scenery. Spectacular views from lookout over Little River Gorge, 70 km N on road to McKillops Bridge. Litte River Falls near Gorge. Stonehenge Rockhounds Museum, Buchan South, 7 km SW. **Tourist information:** General Store, Main St; (051) 55 9202. **Accommodation:** 1 hotel, 1 motel, 1 hostel, 2 cara./camp. parks. MAP REF. 119 B13, 225 R2, 234 H11

Camperdown   Pop. 3315
This south-western town on the Princes Hwy has the English-style charm of gracious buildings and avenues of elms. Over 50 buildings are of historical significance and can be seen by following the Heritage Trail; brochure from Tourist Information. The centre for a rich pastoral district, Camperdown is also noted for the fishing in the volcanic crater lakes in the area. **Of interest:** Clock tower (1896), cnr Manifold and Pike Sts. Also in Manifold St: Historical Society Museum; courthouse; post office. Old Mill, Curdie St, gallery, plant nursery, restored buggies, tearooms, in 120-yr-old restored building. Elm Avenue Tearooms. Craft Market, Finlay Ave or Theatre Royal, 1st Sun. in month. Feb.: Leura Festival. **In the area:** At Mt Noorat, near Noorat, 21 km NW, Alan Marshall Memorial Walking Track, off Glenormiston Rd, 3-km summit and return (1 hr) or crater-rim 1.5-km circuit (30 mins); perfect volcanic cone provides excellent views over Western District.

Phillip Island

Situated at the entrance to Western Port, 120 kilometres south-east of Melbourne, Phillip Island (10 300 hectares) is a year-round destination for those who want to get away from it all.

Once over the bridge between **San Remo** and **Newhaven**, the visitor is greeted by wide open spaces of farming land with panoramic views of ocean and bay. Most of the native bush has been cleared, although there are remnant pockets of native vegetation.

The greatest attraction for visitors is the fascinating little (fairy) penguin parade on Summerland Beach. The penguins spend the day out at sea, catching whitebait for their young. Each evening at sunset they return in small groups and waddle up the beach to their sand-dune burrows. Visitors watch the parade under subdued flood-lights from elevated stands and walkways. No flashlight photography is permitted. The Phillip Island Penguin Reserve is open daily. Enquiries (059) 56 8300; bookings for parade (059) 56 8691.

Seal Rocks at the south-west tip of the island is the home of colonies of fur seals. A ferry service from Cowes allows close-up views of the seals sunbathing on the rocks. Coin-operated telescopes give landlubbers a view of the seals from The Nobbies kiosk.

Take the road down to the surf beach at Cape Woolamai, a rugged granite headland. A two-hour walk leads to the highest point on the island, from where there are breathtaking views of the coastline. The sand dunes all along the Cape are the home of many short-tailed shearwaters. Arriving from Siberia on their annual migration, the birds nest in the rookeries here in spring and summer. Koalas also make their home on this island and can be seen at the Koala Conservation Centre.

Visit nearby historic Churchill Island, reached by bridge near Newhaven. A pamphlet available at the island shop outlines the Homestead Walk and there are several walking trails.

Everyone will enjoy hand-feeding the tame emus, kangaroos and wallabies at the Phillip Island Wildlife Park, which is set in 32 hectares of bushland. Other fauna to be seen there include wombats, venomous and non-venomous snakes, eagles and pelicans. Nearly 7 hectares is wetlands, consisting of ponds and waterways that are breeding grounds for rare and endangered birds.

Some unusual bird species make their homes in The Nits at **Rhyll**, a fishing resort on the northern side of the island. Pelicans, ibis, royal spoonbills, swans and gulls inhabit the swamplands there.

Also on the north coast is **Cowes**, the most popular summer resort on Phillip Island. Its unspoilt beaches are sheltered for safe swimming, yachting and other water sports.

For further information, ticket sales for penguins and other attractions, free map and visitors guide as well as interesting displays, contact the Phillip Island Information Centre, Phillip Island Rd, Newhaven; (059) 56 7447. **See also:** Individual town entries in A–Z listing. **Note** detailed map of Mornington Peninsula on page 212.

Little (fairy) penguins

Lookout at Mt Leura, 1 km W, extinct volcano next to the perfect cone shape of Mt Sugarloaf; views over numerous crater lakes and volcanoes north across plains to the Grampians. Cobden, 13 km S, peaceful dairying town. Timboon, 27 km further S, pretty timbered township also centred on dairying. Just south, Timboon Farmhouse Cheese tastings, sales. Old Timboon Railway Line Walk (10 km), 3–4 hours, requires 14-km car shuttle. Picturesque road leads 18 km S from Timboon to tiny seaside village of Port Campbell; good rock fishing, close to spectacular stretch of scenery along Great Ocean Road. Adjacent, Port Campbell National Park, camping and caravan facilities. Otway Ranges Deer and Wildlife Park, 20 km E of Port Campbell. Lake Corangamite, salt lake 13 km E, is Victoria's largest. Excellent fishing lakes incl. Bullen Merri, 3 km W; Purrumbete, 4 km SE, well stocked with Quinnat salmon, excellent water sports facilities, picnic spots, caravan park. **Tourist information:** Fragrant Cottage, Old Courthouse building, Manifold St; (055) 93 2288. **Accommodation:** 3 hotels, 3 motels, 1 cara./camp. park. **See also:** The Western District.
MAP REF. 215 C5, 227 L8

Cann River   Pop. 336

A popular stop for Sydney–Melbourne motorists using the Princes Hwy. Excellent fishing and bushwalking in the rugged hinterland. **Of interest:** Croajingolong National Park, main access 50 km S, stretches from Sydenham Inlet to NSW border; incorporates Captain James Cook Lighthouse Reserve at Point Hicks, Wingan, Tamboon and Mallacoota Inlets. **Tourist information:** Conservation and Natural Resources Information Centre, Princes Hwy; (051) 58 6351. **Accommodation:** 1 hotel, 3 motels, 1 cara./camp. park.
MAP REF. 119 E13, 235 M11

Casterton   Pop. 1808

Given the Roman name meaning 'walled city' because of lush hills surrounding the valley, Casterton is on the Glenelg Hwy, 42 km E of the South Australian border. The Glenelg River flows through the town and provides excellent fishing and mineral and gem fossicking along its banks near the town, as well as water-skiing at Nelson, some 70 km SW. Launch trips go from Nelson to the river's mouth, on the coast at Discovery Bay. **Of interest:** Casterton Historical Museum, Old Railway Buildings, cnr Jackson and Clarke Sts; by appt. Bryan Park, Henty St, children's playground. David Geschke Fine Porcelain Gallery, Casterton Racecourse Rd. Alma and Judith Zaadstra Fine Art Gallery, Henty St. Long Lead Swamp, Penola Rd, excellent sporting facilities, swimming pool, trail-bike facilities. Tourist Information Centre, displays of local art and craft, picnic/barbecue facilities. March: Motorcycle Hill Climb. Nov.: Agricultural Show. **In the area:** Mainly grazing land with rolling hills and areas of natural forest; excellent bushwalks, variety of fauna and flora. Baileys Rocks, 50 km N, giant granite boulders, unique green colour. Other interesting geological formations at the Hummocks, 12 km NE, and Bahgalah Bluff, 20 km SW. Camel treks. Angling Club Reserve, Roseneath, 24 km NW, picnic and camping facilities. Warrock Homestead (1843), 26 km NE, National Trust-classified, unique collection of buildings; open daily. **Tourist information:** Shiels Tce; (055) 81 2070. **Accommodation:** 2 hotel/motels, 1 motel, 1 B&B, 1 cara./camp. park. **See also:** The Western District.
MAP REF. 226 D4

Castlemaine   Pop. 6812

Along with Kyneton and Maldon, Castlemaine epitomises the goldmining towns of north-western Victoria. An attractive and interesting town, it is built on low hills at the foot of Mt Alexander, on the Calder Hwy, 119 km from Melbourne. In the 1850s and 1860s enormous quantities of gold were found in its surface fields. This gold boom saw Castlemaine grow rapidly and many of its fine old buildings were built during this period. **Of interest:** Town Market (1862), Mostyn St: Palladian style building, National Trust-operated, audiovisual displays, photographic collection, relics of district; open weekends. Midland and Imperial Hotels, in Templeton and Lyttleton Sts, splendid iron lacework verandahs. Also in Lyttleton St: courthouse; town hall and library; art gallery and museum. Buda, Urquhart St, home from late 1850s of silversmith and jeweller Ernest Leviny and his family; beautifully preserved gardens of the era, delightful house. Botanic Gardens, Parker St. Nov.: Spring Garden Festival (odd-numbered years); Castlemaine State Festival (even-numbered years). **In the area:** Excellent restaurants, antique shops, B&B accommodation. Burnett Gallery and Garden, Burnett Road, North Castlemaine; open weekends. At Harcourt, 10 km N, Skydances, walk-through butterfly house; good fishing; picnic spots; Harcourt Valley Estate and Mt Alexander wineries. Nearby on Mt Alexander, koala reserve. Big Tree at Guildford, 11 km SW. Pottery at Newstead, 16 km SW. Chinese cemetery, mineral springs, Vaughan, 12 km S. Wattle Gully goldmine, Chewton, 4 km SE. Duke of Cornwall mine buildings, Fryerstown, 10 km SE. **Tourist information:** Duke St; (054) 72 3222. **Accommodation:** 5 hotels, 3 motels, 2 cara./camp. parks. **See also:** The Golden Age.
MAP REF. 210 F1, 221 P5, 227 Q1, 229 Q12, 232 C10

Charlton   Pop. 1182

A supply centre for a rich wheat district, Charlton is set on the banks of the Avoca River, at the intersection of the Calder and Borung Hwys in north-central Victoria. **Of interest:** Fishing in Avoca River. Walking track along river, about 2 km one way, from town to weir. Oct.: Art Show. **In the area:** Wooroonook Lake, 12 km W, swimming, boating. Bish Deer Farm, further 18 km W. Wychitella State Forest, 27 km E, interesting native flora and fauna, incl. the lowan (mallee fowl). **Tourist information:** Shire Offices, 1 High St; (054) 91 1755. **Accommodation:** 2 hotels, 2 motels, 1 cara./camp. park.
MAP REF. 229 M7

Chiltern   Pop. 1157

Halfway between Wangaratta and Wodonga, Chiltern is 1 km off the Hume Freeway. It was once a goldmining boom town with 14 suburbs. Many of its attractive buildings have been classified by the National Trust; Historic Walk leaflet available. **Of interest:** In Conness St: Athenaeum Museum (1866), Goldfields Library collection; The Pharmacy (1868), National Trust-owned, chemist shop with all original features; Stephen's Motor Museum, motoring memorabilia. Famous Grapevine Attraction, formerly Grape Vine Hotel, cnr Conness and Main Sts; boasts the largest grapevine in Australia (in Guinness Book of Records, planted 1867). Federal Standard newspaper office, Main St, dates from goldmining era (1860-61),

National Trust-classified; by appt for groups. Picnic spots with barbecues at Lake Anderson, via Main St. Walking track from lakeshore over bridge to 'Lake View', Victoria St, home of author Henry Handel Richardson, National Trust-classified; open weekends, public and school holidays. Oct.: Annual Art Show. **In the area:** Chiltern State Park, surrounds town, historic drive, bushwalking, nature observation, picnicking. Magenta open-cut mine, 2 km E. Pioneer Cemetery, 2 km N. Black Dog Creek Pottery, 3 km NW on Chiltern Valley Rd. **Tourist information:** Famous Grapevine Attraction, Main St; (057) 26 1395. **Accommodation:** 1 hotel, 1 motel, 2 B&B, 1 cara./camp. park. **See also:** Wine Regions.
MAP REF. 127 O13, 233 N5

Clunes   Pop. 846

The first reported gold find in the State was made at Clunes on 7 July 1851 when James Esmond announced his discovery of 'pay dirt'. The town, some 40 km N of Ballarat, has several bluestone buildings classified by the National Trust, and the verandahed elegance of Fraser St is worth noting. Surrounding the town are a number of rounded hills (extinct volcanoes) and a good view of them can be obtained about 3 km S, on the road to Ballarat. **Of interest:** Old Post Office (1873), cnr Bailey and Service Sts, second-hand books. In Bailey St: town hall and courthouse (1870); Bottle Museum, in former South Clunes State School; Keebles of Clunes guest house. Queens Park, maintained as garden, established over 100 years ago on banks of Creswick Creek; picnic/barbecue facilities, playground. Butter Factory Gallery, Cameron St, sculpture and art gallery. Jindalee Arts and Crafts Centre, Talbot Rd, handmade pottery. In Fraser St: the Weavery, handwoven fabrics; Museum, open weekends, public and school holidays. Nov.: Agricultural Show. **In the area:** Clunes Homestead Furniture, 1 km N on Talbot Rd. Possum Road Gallery, 20 km N, sculpture and paintings, major and local artists. At Talbot, historic town 18 km NW, many 1860–1870 buildings, particularly in Camp St and Scandinavian Cres; Arts and Historical Museum, Camp St, in former Primitive Methodist Church (1870); Bull and Mouth restaurant, bluestone building (1860s) housed former hotel of same name. Mt Beckworth, 8 km W, scenic reserve, variety of native flora and fauna, picnic/barbecue facilities. **Tourist information:** (053) 45 3020, or Clunes Museum, Fraser St; (053) 45 3592, or (053) 45 3185. **Accommodation:** 1 hotel, 1 motel, 1 cara./camp. park. **See also:** The Golden Age.
MAP REF. 210 C2, 221 L8, 227 O2, 229 O13, 232 A12

Cobram   Pop. 3797

Magnificent wide sandy beaches are a feature of the stretch of the Murray River at Cobram, so picnicking and water sports are popular. This is also fruit-growing country. **Of interest:** Rotary dairy, 200 cows, on outskirts of town; open at milking time, 3–4 daily. Houseboat hire. Jan.: Peaches and Cream Festival (odd-numbered years). **In the area:** Matata Deer Farm on Tocumwal road, 5 km NW. Sportavia Soaring Centre at Tocumwal airport, 20 km NW. Tyrrell's Heritage Farm Winery, on Murray Valley Hwy, 5 km W, 116-m woodcarving depicting scenes of early River Murray life. At Strathmerton, 16 km W, Spikes and Blooms cactus farm, Coonanga Homestead. Monichino Wineries, 15 km S towards Numurkah. Binghi Boomerang Factory, Barooga, 4 km NE. **Tourist information:** The Old Grain Shed, cnr Station St and Punt Rd; (058) 72 2132. **Accommodation:** 3 hotels, 4 motels, 3 cara./camp. parks. **See also:** The Mighty Murray.
MAP REF. 127 M13, 232 I3

Cohuna   Pop. 2071

Between Kerang and Echuca on the Murray Valley Hwy, Cohuna is beside Gunbower Island, formed by the Murray on the far side and Gunbower Creek just across the highway from the town. This island is covered in red gum and box forest, which provides a home for abundant waterfowl and other birdlife, as well as kangaroos and emus. The central zone of the forest is a sanctuary. The forest is subject to flooding and a large part of the island has breeding rookeries during the flood periods. Picnic/barbecue facilities can be found on the island, and forest tracks give access for driving and riding. Maps are available from the Forests Officer or from stores in Cohuna. **Of interest:** Two-hr cruises in the Wetlander, along Gunbower Creek. Cohuna swimming pool with 45-m water-slide; open daily, from Nov.–Easter. **In the area:** Two potteries open to the public. Box Bridge, at Kow Swamp, 23 km S, in sanctuary, picnic spots, good fishing. Mount Hope (110 m), about 28 km S, easy rock climbing, good views from summit, beautiful wildflowers in spring, picnic facilities. Craft Cottage, 4 km SE; antiques, nursery, gifts, tearoom. Torrumbarry Lock, 40 km SE; during winter, entire weir structure is removed from the river; in summer, water-skiing above the weir. **Tourist information:** Golden River Tourism, 25 Murray St, Barham; (054) 53 3100.

Shopfront, Conness St, Chiltern

National Parks

Coastal scene, Otway National Park

Although it is Australia's smallest mainland State, Victoria houses over 100 national, state, wilderness and regional parks; among them there is something for everyone in every season.

Victoria's parks protect representative samples of a wide range of the State's land and vegetation types: from alps, open grasslands and desert mallee to rainforests, tall forests, coasts, volcanic plains and heathlands. Spring and summer are the best seasons to visit those parks noted for their wildflowers. In summer, sun lovers can head for parks along the coast to swim, surf, canoe, boat or fish. Autumn, with its mild weather, beckons the bushwalker, and winter means skiing at alpine parks.

The **Alpine National Park**, created in December 1989 and currently covering approximately 642 000 hectares, is the State's largest national park. Stretching along the Great Dividing Range, the park links with the Kosciusko National Park in New South Wales and its neighbour Namadgi National Park in the Australian Capital Territory. The park protects the habitats of a variety of flora and fauna, including the rare mountain pygmy possum (the world's only exclusively sub-alpine marsupial). The Alps are renowned for their sublime landscapes, features characterised by Mount Bogong and Mount Feathertop (Victoria's highest mountains) and the unique Bogong High Plains. During spring and summer the high plains are carpeted with wildflowers; more than 1100 native plant species are found in the park, including 12 found nowhere else in the world. The park is ideal for bushwalking, horseriding and cross-country skiing. In the summer months most roads provide easy access for conventional vehicles, allowing a range of

scenic drives with short walks to lookouts and other points of interest. Some huts in the park, popular places for walkers to visit, are being restored for their historic value.

Murray Sunset National Park in the north-west is the State's most recent, and at 633 000 hectares, the second largest national park. It contains a diversity of semi-arid environments from riverine floodplains to heathlands, salt lakes and woodlands, which support a tremendous variety of wildlife, particularly birdlife. This park is best visited in the cooler months of the year. **Wyperfeld National Park** nearby, also contains hundreds of species of plants and birdlife and is also a great park to visit in the spring, autumn and winter. In good rainfall years there are colourful spring wildflower displays, and in the autumn the visitor will enjoy crisp, clear days—perfect for bushwalking and birdwatching.

Another park in the north west of the State is the smaller **Hattah-Kulkyne National Park**. Typically, summers here are long, hot and dry: rainfall is usually under 300 mm per year. The animals of this area have evolved strategies for avoiding or tolerating heat and dryness: some burrow, others just rest during the heat of the day; some birds catch thermals to cooler air. After rainfall and flooding from the Murray River, the serenely beautiful Hattah Lakes system transforms the park into a bird haven and a wonderful wildflower landscape.

The 167 000-hectare **Grampians National Park** offers marvellous scenery, wildlife and tourist facilities. The park is famous for its rugged sandstone ranges, waterfalls, wildflowers, wide variety of birds and mammals, as well as its Aboriginal rock-art sites. The peaks rise to

heights of over 1000 metres and form the western edge of the Great Dividing Range. The Grampians is no doubt best seen by foot and there are many interesting walking tracks, such as the easy-graded, well-marked Wonderland Track, through to the more challenging walks across the Major Mitchell Plateau.

The main thing most visitors to the **Little Desert National Park** discover is that it is neither little nor a desert. It is best known for its amazing displays of wildflowers in spring; more than 600 flowering-plant species are found here, including more than 40 ground orchids. Another special thing about the Little Desert is that it is one of the homes of the mallee fowl. These birds build mounds for eggs that can be as much as 5 metres in diameter and 1.5 metres high.

Several parks contain rock formations of great geological interest. At **Mount Eccles**, an extinct volcano in south-west Victoria, a lava canal, lava cave and the formation called the Stony Rises are exceptional features, while the crater contains the tranquil Lake Surprise.

Better known are the unusual rock structures found at **Port Campbell National Park**: The Twelve Apostles, The Arch and Loch Ard Gorge are majestic formations sculpted out of soft limestone cliffs by the relentless sea.

Obviously it is the spectacular coastal scenery that makes this park so popular. However, this is also an interesting linear park for birds, with around 100 species being recorded. It was a popular place with Aboriginal people too, if the number of shell middens along the coast is an indication. And it is especially notorious for being part of the 'Shipwreck Coast'.

Closer to Melbourne are the beautiful lush tree fern gullies and towering mountain ash forests of the **Otway National Park** and the special **Melba Gully State Park** to the north-west of the national park near Lavers Hill. Because of the treacherous nature of the waters, a lighthouse was the first piece of 'civilisation', opened at Cape Otway in 1848 after two years in the building. Activities to be enjoyed include sightseeing all year (even in winter storms), while camping, surfing, fishing and walking are most enjoyable in spring and summer. There are guided walks in summer to see the glow-worms at Melba Gully.

Eastern Victoria, with its mild and fairly wet climate, has vast areas of dense forest. These are especially attractive to bushwalkers and campers, who will find here a wide range of trees—mainly eucalypts, but also native pines, banksias and paperbarks. Many bushwalkers prefer to explore a coastal park in summer; **Wilsons Promontory National Park** is the best known in Gippsland and one of the most popular in Victoria. The Prom, as it is known, really does have something for everyone. There is the concentration of amenities and accommodation, including camping and caravan sites, at Tidal River, as well as the visitor information centre and park office. Leaflets for 80 kilometres of walking tracks are available here, and visitors should also enquire about the long but rewarding lighthouse walk. Other natural attractions include secluded bays and magnificent stretches of beaches, granite outcrops, and wildflowers that begin blooming in late winter and keep spring colourful. The Prom is very popular in summer, with campsites available only by ballot over the Christmas holiday period.

At **Organ Pipes National Park**, only 20 kilometres north-west of Melbourne, there are more interesting rock formations: a series of hexagonal basalt columns rising more than 20 metres above Jacksons Creek. These 'organ pipes' were formed when lava cooled in an ancient river bed. While this is the best known feature of the small, 85-hectare park, it is also excellent for picnics, walks and bird-observing. Another favourite haunt of bushwalkers 50 kilometres north-east of Melbourne is **Kinglake National Park**, where wooded valleys, fern gullies and timbered ridges provide a perfect setting for two beautiful waterfalls, Masons and Wombelano Falls. From a lookout, visitors can take in a panoramic view of the Yarra Valley, Port Phillip Bay and the You Yangs Range.

Just 35 kilometres east of Melbourne is the green wonderland of the 1920-hectare **Dandenong Ranges National Park**. This park includes tree fern gullies in which huge fronds of ferns form a canopy overhead, screening the sun and creating a cool, moist environment in which mosses, delicate ferns and flowers, including over 30 orchid species, all thrive. There are more than 20 species of native animals in the park, including echidnas, platypuses, ringtail possums and sugar gliders; kookaburras, rosellas and cockatoos often visit picnic areas. The spectacular rufous fantail can be seen in the summer months. There are over 100 bird species, but make sure you identify them by sight and not by sound only, because the lyrebird can mimic their calls.

Point Nepean National Park is probably the most interesting park close to Melbourne, mainly because for more than 100 years the area at the Point has been out of bounds to most people. It has associations with early settlement, shipping, quarantine and defence. As one of Victoria's major Bicentennial projects, an information centre, walking tracks, displays and other facilities were provided during 1988–9. Today the total area of the park, including former Cape Schanck Coastal Park, is 2680 hectares.

To prevent overcrowding and damage to the environment, no more than 600 people are permitted in the Point Nepean area at one time; so bookings for day visits (with a park-use fee) are required, especially during summer. Vehicles are not permitted beyond the orientation centre, so walking or taking the transporter are the ways to get around. Highlights of the park are Fort Nepean itself, the cemetery with burials dating from the 1850s, and the Cheviot Hill walk.

Canoeists will find excitement shooting the rapids or exploring the gorges of **Snowy River National Park** or **Mitchell River National Park**, both in East Gippsland, while bushwalkers can hike through forests of native pine, alpine ash and messmate.

Some of the most attractive coastal scenery close to any major regional centre can be found in and around **The Lakes National Park**. The park is surrounded by the waters of the Gippsland Lakes, ideal for sailing and boating. The 2390 hectares is based on Sperm Whale Head and harbours a large population of kangaroos and more than 140 bird species. Camping, picnicking and an excellent network of walking tracks provide distractions for those who are land-based.

Croajingolong National Park has 87 500 hectares of coastline and hinterland stretching from Sydenham Inlet to the New South Wales border. The area contains remote rainforest, woodland, ocean beaches, rocky promontories, inlets and coves. Several rare species of wildlife can be found here, such as the smoky mouse and the ground parrot, and in the spring the visitor will see an array of wildflowers. There is a wide range of activities for visitors at Croajingolong, with a resort centre at Mallacoota and other towns along the Princes Highway offering accommodation and fine food.

For more information, contact the Department of Conservation and Natural Resources at 240 Victoria Pde, East Melbourne; (03) 9412 4795.

Tidal River, Wilsons Promontory National Park

Accommodation: 1 hotel/motel, 1 cara./camp. park.
MAP REF. 127 J12, 229 Q4, 232 B2

Colac   Pop. 10 241

Colac is situated on the eastern edge of the volcanic plain that covers much of the Western District of Victoria. It is the centre of a prosperous, closely settled agricultural area and is sited on the shores of Lake Colac, which has good fishing and a variety of water sports. **Of interest:** Historical Centre, Gellibrand St; open Thurs., Fri., Sun. 2–4. Sculpture Park on Princes Hwy, permanent and special exhibitions. Historic homes, not open to the public: Balnagowan in Balnagowan Ave; The Parsonage, 81 Wallace St; The Elms, 16 Gellibrand St. Self-guide town walk leaflet and information on full-day mountain scenic drive available from Tourist Information. Botanic Gardens (18 ha), Queen St, picnic/barbecue facilities. Barongarook Creek, walking track to sculpture park, also birdwatcher's haven. March: Kana Festival. **In the area:** Alvie Red Rock Lookout, 22 km N, from which 30 volcanic lakes can be seen, incl. Lake Corangamite, Victoria's largest saltwater lake. Floating Island Reserve, 17 km W, lagoon with islands that change position. Gellibrand Pottery, 10 km S, open daily; cottage accommodation. Barongavale Winery, 15 km S, also sells berry fruits; check times. Otway Ranges, about 30 km S, beautiful winding roads, lush mountain scenery, en route to the coast. Birregurra, 20 km E, interesting old buildings. **Tourist information:** Cnr Murray and Queen Sts; (052) 31 3730. **Accommodation:** 1 hotel/motel, 4 motels, 3 cara./camp. parks.
MAP REF. 210 A10, 215 F7, 227 N9

Coleraine   Pop. 1089

Situated in the attractive Wannon River valley, 35 km NW of Hamilton, the Coleraine area was first settled by the Henty and Whyte brothers in 1838 for pastoral grazing. The primary products are finewool sheep and beef cattle. **In the area:** Historic homesteads incl. Warrock Homestead (1843), National Trust-classified, some 30 buildings to explore, 20 km W towards Casterton; Glendinning Homestead, near Balmoral, 50 km N, wildlife sanctuary, farm holidays. Rocklands Reservoir, 12 km E of Balmoral, excellent fishing and boating, caravan park nearby. Black Range State Park,

northern shores of reservoir, walking tracks, picnic areas. Point's Reserve, lookout on western edge of town, unique planting over 700 native tree and shrub species. Gardens of Nareen, property of Malcolm and Tamie Fraser, 31 km NW; open weekdays by appt and through Australia's Open Garden Scheme (closed Christmas, Easter and May–Aug). Wannon Falls, 14 km SE, and Nigretta Falls, 24 km SE. **Tourist information:** Cobb & Co. Cafe, 75 Whyte St; (055) 75 2386, or Old Railway Station, Pilleau St. **Accommodation:** 2 hotels, 1 cara./camp. park. **See also:** The Western District.
MAP REF. 226 E4

Corryong   Pop. 1226

Situated in alpine country, Corryong is at the gateway to the Snowy Mountains. The district offers superb mountain scenery and excellent trout fishing. The Murray near Corryong is a brisk and gurgling stream running through forested hills. **Of interest:** Jack Riley, reputedly 'The Man from Snowy River', came from these parts and his grave is in Corryong cemetery. The Man from Snowy River Folk Museum, Hanson St, antique ski collection, replica of Riley's original shack. March: High Country Festival. Dec.: Nariel Creek Folk Music Festival. **In the area:** Scenic drive west from Corryong. Scenic views: Mt Mittamatite and Emberys Lookout, 10 km N, and Sassafras Gap, 66 km S. At Upper Nariel, 43 km S, Upper Murray Fish Farm; Upper Murray Historical Society. Players Hill Lookout, 1 km SE. At Khancoban, 27 km E, horse-trekking, whitewater rafting. At Towong, 12 km NE, lookout with views over Kosciusko National Park. Trout fishing, Tintaldra, 23 km N. Canoeing and mountain-bike excursions from Walwa, 47 km NW. Cudgewa Bluff Falls, 27 km W in Burrowa–Pine Mountain National Park, excellent scenery, bushwalking tracks. **Tourist information:** Corryong Newsagency, 43–49 Hanson St; (060) 76 1381; or Mt Mittamatite Caravan Park, Tallangatta Rd; (060) 76 1152. **Accommodation:** 2 hotel/motels, 2 motels, 2 cara./camp. parks.
MAP REF. 119 A8, 234 F3

Cowes   Pop. 2658

This is the main town on Phillip Island, a popular resort area in Western Port linked to the mainland by a bridge at San

Remo. Cowes is on the northern side of the island and is the centre for hotel and motel accommodation. It has pleasant beaches, safe for children, and the jetty is popular for fishing and swimming. The town has a number of art and craft shops, an amusement centre and a variety of restaurants. **Of interest:** Clock Museum and Gallery, Findlay St. Sept.: Motor Racing. Oct.: Superbike Championships. **In the area:** Summerland Beach, on southern shore, about 13 km SW, famous for its nightly penguin parade. Colonies of fur seals can be seen year-round on Seal Rocks, off southern shores, and short-tailed shearwaters Oct.–April. Australian Dairy Centre at Newhaven, 16 km SE, museum, cheese factory. Phillip Island Wildlife Park, Main Tourist Rd, koalas, wombats, kangaroos in natural environment. Churchill Island, 2 km from Newhaven, historic homestead, walking tracks. **Tourist information:** Phillip Island Rd, Newhaven; (059) 56 7447 (incl. tickets for Phillip Island attractions). **Accommodation:** 17 hotel/motels, 22 B&B, 1 hostel, 13 cara./camp. parks. **See also:** Phillip Island.
MAP REF. 211 L12, 213 O11, 224 D8

Creswick   Pop. 2387

This picturesque town, 18 km N of Ballarat, nestles at the foot of the State Forest. One of the richest alluvial goldfields in the world was discovered here. **Of interest:** Mullock heaps on Lawrence Rd. Gold panning. Surrounding volcanic bushland and forest areas attract field naturalists and bushwalking enthusiasts. Creswick Historical Museum, Albert St, early history of area. Gold Battery, Battery Cres. Cemetery, Clunes Rd, early miners' graves, Chinese section. In Melbourne Rd, Koala Park and St Georges Lake, picnic facilities. Olympic pool at Calembeen Park, Cushing Ave. Oct.: Brackenbury Festival. **In the area:** Creswick Forest Nursery, 1 km E. World of Dinosaurs, 1.5 km E off Midland Hwy, life-size models in bushland setting. At Smeaton, 16 km N, Smeaton House (1850s); Anderson's Mill (1860s); Tuki Trout Farm. Tumblers Green Nursery, 1 km W. **Tourist information:** Booth, cnr Raglan and Cambridge Sts; or Shire Offices, 68 Albert St; (053) 45 2000. **Accommodation:** 1 motel, 2 B&B, 1 cara./camp. park. **See also:** The Golden Age.
MAP REF. 210 C3, 221 M10, 227 O3, 232 A13

Convent Gallery, Daylesford

Daylesford Pop. 3347

Daylesford and Hepburn Springs, 4 km N, together constitute a spa town, with 65 documented mineral springs, many with hand pumps. Hepburn Springs Spa Complex, in the Mineral Springs Reserve, Forest Ave, offers public and private baths, flotation tanks, massage and a sauna; open daily. Daylesford rambles up the side of Wombat Hill, at the top of which are the Botanical Gardens in Central Springs Rd, with a lookout tower from which there are views in all directions. **Of interest:** Convent Gallery, in former girls' school, Daly St, seven galleries, meals; open daily. In Vincent St: Alpha Hall Galleria, in former movie house, closed Tues.-Wed; historical museum in former School of Mines. For picnics: Jubilee Lake, Lake Rd; Daylesford Lake, Leggatt St; and Central Springs Spa Reserve, Central Springs Rd. Market near railway station, Sun. During market, Central Highlands Tourist Railway runs rail-motor services between Daylesford and Musk 1st and 3rd Sun. in month, and ganger's trolleys operate to Wombat Forest alternate Sundays. May: Hepburn Swiss–Italian Festival. July: Mid-winter Festival. **In the area:** Breakneck Gorge, 5 km N. Mt Franklin, an extinct volcano, 13 km N. Trentham Falls, 15 km N. At Yandoit, settlement of Swiss–Italian heritage, 18 km NW, Jajarawong Holiday Park, bushwalking, water sports, wildlife. Horseriding, Boomerang Holiday Ranch, 2 km SW. Bin Billa Winery, 6 km S, open daily. Sailors Falls, 10 km S. Newstead Winery, 25 km N, open weekends. **Tourist information:** Information Centre, Vincent St; (053) 48

1339. **Accommodation:** 8 hotels, 3 motels, 3 cara./camp. parks. **See also:** The Golden Age.
MAP REF. 210 E2, 221 P9, 227 Q2, 229 Q13, 232 B12

Derrinallum Pop. 280

Small rural town servicing the local pastoral farming community and surrounded by volcanic plains typical of the Western District of Victoria. **In the area:** Mt Elephant, 2 km SW, scoria cone of volcanic origin rising high above surrounding plains. Significant dry-stone walls, immediately west of town. Elephant Bridge Hotel, at Darlington, 15 km SW, 2-storey bluestone building, National Trust-classified. Rockbank Farmstay, Bass Rd; 5 km SW, splendid views of Mt Elephant. Lake Tooliorook, 6 km SE, fishing, swimming. Deep Lake, 5 km NW, fishing, water sports. **Tourist information:** Fragrant Cottage, Old Courthouse building, Manifold St, Camperdown; (055) 93 2288. **Accommodation:** 1 hotel/motel.
MAP REF. 215 C2, 227 L6

Dimboola Pop. 1581

This is a peaceful town on the tree-lined Wimmera River, 35 km NW of Horsham. **Of interest:** Walking track along Wimmera River. Oct.: Agricultural Show. Nov.: Rowing Regatta. **In the area:** Little Desert National Park, 6 km SW, self-guide walks, incl. Pomponderoo Hill Nature Walk (1 km) from Horseshoe Bend picnic and camping area at river's edge. Wail, 11 km S, well-stocked Department of Conservation and Natural Resources forest nursery. Ebenezer Mission Station (founded 1858), on Jeparit Rd, 15 km N,

restored by National Trust. Pink Lake, coloured salt lake, 9 km NW. At Kiata, 26 km W, mallee fowl can be seen in Lowan Sanctuary all year. **Tourist information:** Shire of Dimboola, 10 Roy St, Jeparit; (053) 97 2070. **Accommodation:** 2 hotels, 1 motel, 1 B&B, 1 cara./camp. park. **See also:** The Wimmera.
MAP REF. 228 G8

Donald Pop. 1505

At the junction of the Sunraysia and Borung Hwys, Donald is situated on the Richardson River and in a Wimmera district known for fine wheat, sheep and fat lambs. **Of interest:** Historic police station (1874), Wood St. Railway steam engine, Steam Loco Park, cnr Hammill and Walker Sts. Agricultural museum, Hammill St. Historic water pump by lake in caravan park. Bullocks Head Lookout, Byrne St. Large, unusual growth on box tree beside Richardson River. Industrial area, Kooka's Country Cookies, Sunraysia Hwy, tours and sales. Feb.: Dead Centre Motorbike Rally. **In the area:** Angora Goat Farm, 1 km E on Racecourse Rd. Deer farm, 10 km E on Charlton Rd. Mt Jeffcott, 20 km NE, flora, fauna, views of Lake Buloke. Richardson River, fishing. Quail-shooting in season. Lake Buloke, 10 km N; wetlands area, limited duck-shooting in season. Watchem Lake, 30 km N, fishing, water sports, picnic/barbecue facilities. **Tourist information:** Shire Offices, McCulloch St; (054) 97 1300, or Caravan Park, Hammill St; (054) 97 1764. **Accommodation:** 3 hotels, 2 motels, 2 B&B, 1 cara./camp. park.
MAP REF. 229 K7

Drouin
Pop. 4455

Drouin, 97km S of Melbourne, is on the Princes Hwy not far from Warragul and the Latrobe Valley. Feb.: Ficifolia Festival. **In the area:** Camping and picnic spots: on Tarago River at Glen Cromie, 8 km N; Picnic Point on Princes Hwy, 10 km W. At Neerim South, 31 km N, Tarago River Cheese Company; picnic/barbecue area at Tarago Reservoir; Woodlyn Park, horseriding into adjacent State Forest. At Nayook, 38 km N, Nayook Fruit and Berry Farm; Country Farm Perennials Nursery and Gardens. At Noojee, 40 km N, Alpine Trout Farm, Noojee Trestle Bridge. At Drouin West, 3 km W, Fruit and Berry Farm; Hilston Lodge Deer Farm. Victoria's Farm Shed, Princes Hwy, Tynong, 22 km W, farm animal and agricultural displays, incl. shearing, sheepdog workouts, milking; open daily. Gumbaya Park, 25 km W on Princes Hwy, wildlife, family fun park. Many of the food attractions are featured on the Gourmet Deli Trail; brochure fromTourist Information. **Tourist information:** Latrobe Valley Tourism, Old Gippstown, Lloyd St, Moe; (051) 27 6928. **Accommodation:** 2 motels, 1 B&B, 3 cara./camp. parks.
MAP REF. 211 P9, 224 G6

Drysdale
Pop. 1166

This is primarily a service centre for the local farming community on the Bellarine Peninsula. **Of interest:** In High St: Old Courthouse Museum; Drysdale Community Crafts. Community Market, Recreation Reserve, Duke St, every 3rd Sun. Sept.–April. **In the area:** Lake Lorne picnic area, 1 km SW. Nearby Bellarine Peninsula Railway offers steam-train rides between Drysdale and Queenscliff; locomotives and carriages dating back to1870s on display. Adjoining township of Clifton Springs had a brief burst of fame in the 1870s when the therapeutic value of its mineral-spring water was discovered; today it offers sporting facilities and a restaurant. **Tourist information:** A Maze'N Things, 1570 Bellarine Hwy, cnr Grubb Rd, Wallington; (052) 50 2669. **Accommodation:** 1 hotel.
MAP REF. 210 H9, 217 H7, 224 A6

Dunkeld
Pop. 440

On the Glenelg Hwy, 31 km NE from Hamilton, Dunkeld is the southern gateway to the Grampians and is convenient for trips to the Victoria Valley (world-famous fine-wool district), the Chimney Pots and Billywing Plantation in Grampians National Park, 25 km N. **Of interest:** Historical museum, Templeton St, history of area's Aborigines, and explorer Major Mitchell's journeys. Detailed map of historic sites and buildings available. Skin Inn, Parker St, sheepskin products and crafts. Nov.: Dunkeld Cup (horseracing). **In the area:** Walking tracks to top of Mt Sturgeon and Mt Abrupt; both climbs steep , but views rewarding. Freshwater Lake Reserve, 8 km N, picnic spots. **Tourist information:** Visitors Centre, Glenelg Hwy; (055) 77 2558. **Accommodation:** 1 hotel/motel, 5 B&B, 2 cara./camp. parks. **See also:** The Western District.
MAP REF. 226 H4

Dunolly
Pop. 686

A small town in north-central Victoria, in the heart of the gold country and on the Goldfields Tourist Route. 'Welcome Stranger', claimed to be the largest nugget ever discovered, was found 15 km NW at Moliagul. The district has produced more nuggets than any other goldfield in Australia; 126 were unearthed in the town itself. Ninety per cent of alluvial gold mined world-wide comes from this area. **Of interest:** In Broadway: handsome original buildings; Bonsai Shop; Goldfields Historical and Arts Museum, replicas of some of town's most spectacular nuggets, weekends or by arrangement. Restored Dunolly Courthouse, Market St, display relating to historic gold discoveries in area. Next door: original lockup (1859), stables. Oct.: Tamagulla Gold Spectacular. **In the area:** Melville Caves (incl. Crystal Mine), 30 km N, haunt of bushranger Captain Melville (1850s). Laanecoorie Reservoir, 16 km E, picnic spot. Countryside around Dunolly abounds with spring wildflowers and native fauna. Gold panning in local creeks. Monuments at Moliagul mark spot where Welcome Stranger nugget was found 1869, and birthplace of Rev. John Flynn, founder of Royal Flying Doctor Service. **Tourist information:** Courthouse, Market St; (054) 68 1205. **Accommodation:** 2 hotels, 1 motel, 6 B&B, 1 cara./camp. park.
MAP REF. 221 L3, 229 O10

Echuca–Moama
Pop. 9438

These twin towns are at the junction of the Murray, Campaspe and Goulburn Rivers. Echuca, now a city and once Australia's largest inland port, took its name from an Aboriginal word meaning 'meeting of the waters', while Moama (NSW) means 'place of the dead'. An iron bridge joins the two. **Of interest:** Along the Murray Esplanade, Port of Echuca, massive red gum wharf restored to the period of its heyday, incl. paddle steamer *Pevensey* (renamed *Philadelphia* for TV mini-series *All the Rivers Run*, filmed here), cruises during peak periods; D26 logging barge, PS *Alexander Arbuthnot* (being restored) and PS *Adelaide*; Star Hotel, underground bar and escape tunnel; and Bridge Hotel, built by Henry Hopwood, founder of Echuca, who ran original punt service. Also part of the Port's attractions, all in Murray Esplanade: Red Gum Works; award-winning Sharp's Magic Movie House and Penny Arcade; Echuca Wharf Pottery; Tisdall Wines and Cellar Door Restaurant; Wistaria Tearooms; and the Coach House Carriage Collection. In High St: Echuca Historical Society Museum (1867) in former police station, National Trust-classified; Gumnutland; and World in Wax Museum. National Holden Museum, Warren St. One-hr cruises on paddlewheelers *Canberra* and *Pride of the Murray*. Accommodation and 1-hr cruises on paddle-steamer *Emmylou*. MV *Mary Ann* and PB *Captain Proud*, cruising restaurants. Gem Club, in old pump station near bridge to Moama; also Oz Maze. Houseboat hire. Feb.: Southern 80 Ski Race from Torrumbarry Weir to Echuca. Easter: Working Horse Fair. April: Barmah Muster. **In the area:** Camping, fishing, kayaking, canoeing, swimming, bushwalking, water-skiing. Excellent sporting facilities incl. golf, tennis, bowls, croquet. Harness and horse races 18–20 times annually. On Cornelia Creek Rd, 4 km S, Joalah Fauna Park, Rich River Yabbie Farm; Raverty's Auto Museum. In Moama: Silverstone Go Kart Track; Aqua Farms Yabbie Farm; 4 clubs with poker machines. Barmah Red Gum Forest and Moira Forest, 41 km NE, cover some 100 000 ha. At Barmah Lakes, wetlands cruise in the *Kingfisher*. Golden Cow Educational Centre, Tongala, 27 km SE. Kyabram Fauna Park, 35 km SE; one of Victoria's best. Upside Down Pub, 15 km E on Murray Valley Hwy. Dharnya Centre, 36 km N in Barmah Forest, illustrates traditions and lifestyle of area's Aboriginal inhabitants. **Tourist information:** 2 Leslie St,

Alpine Country

To the east and northeast of Melbourne, the gently rounded peaks of the Victorian Alps stretch, seemingly endlessly, under clear skies. They are much lower than alpine ranges in other parts of the world, lacking sheer escarpments and jagged peaks, but they still stand majestic, especially when covered in snow. These blue ranges are not high enough to have a permanent cover of snow, but the expanses of the rolling mountains are ideal for cross-country skiing as well as for the downhill variety.

The skiing season officially opens on the Queen's Birthday long weekend each June and closes in October, but it often actually extends beyond these dates. Each year, thousands of people flock to the snow: for the enjoyment of downhill skiing, for leisurely cross-country skiing, for snowboarding or just to enjoy the beauty of nature. Children can have a great time throwing snowballs and building snowmen.

There is bountiful fishing in the lakes and trout streams. Tennis, rock climbing, sailing, swimming, canoeing and water-skiing are popular sports in the summer. Many riding schools in the valleys provide a leisurely pastime for those who want to explore the countryside on horseback. For the more energetic, bushwalking in this beautiful rugged country is a must. Despite their summer beauty, however, the Alps can still claim the life of an ill-prepared bushwalker. Make sure you have the necessary equipment and knowledge to tackle this recreational activity and always tell someone where you are going and when you expect to be back.

Victoria has nine ski resorts, all within easy reach of Melbourne.

Falls Creek, 356 km from Melbourne, via the Snow Road through Oxley. Protected ski runs for novices, intermediate and advanced skiers; good cross-country skiing. Ski hire and instruction.

Lake Mountain, 120 km from Melbourne, via Healesville. Sightseeing and cross-country skiing.

Mount Baw Baw, 177 km from Melbourne, via Drouin. Beginners, novices and cross-country skiing.

Mount Buffalo, 331 km from Melbourne, via Myrtleford. Includes Dingo Dell and Cresta. Beginners, families and cross-country skiing. Ski hire and instruction.

Mount Buller, 221 km from Melbourne, via Mansfield. For beginners to advanced skiers. Ski hire and instruction.

Mount Stirling, 250 km from Melbourne, near Mount Buller. Cross-country skiing. Most trails start at Telephone Box Junction, which has a visitor centre with public shelter, ski hire and trail maps.

Mount Donna Buang, 95 km from Melbourne, via Warburton. Sightseeing and novice skiing.

Mount Hotham, 367 km from Melbourne, via Wangaratta. The 'powder snow capital' of Australia. For experienced downhill skiers; unlimited cross-country skiing. Ski hire and instruction.

Dinner Plain, a 10-minute ski-shuttle ride from Mount Hotham. Offers ski hire, cross-country skiing and horseriding.

For further information on all resorts, contact the Alpine Resorts Commission, Amev House, Whitehorse Road, Box Hill; (03) 9895 6900, or the Falls Creek Information Centre, Bogong High Plains Tourist Rd, Falls Creek; (057) 58 3224. **See also:** Safe Skiing. **Note** detailed map of Alpine Region on page 222.

Snow gums, Mount Baw Baw

Puffing Billy runs between Belgrave and Emerald

Echuca; (054) 80 7555. **Accommodation:** 42 motels, hotels, homesteads and holiday units, 5 B&B, 11 cara. parks. **See also:** The Mighty Murray; Wine Regions.
MAP REF. 127 K13, 232 E4

Edenhope
Pop. 821
On the Wimmera Hwy, just 30 km from the border with South Australia, Edenhope is situated on the shores of Lake Wallace, a haven for waterbirds. When full, the lake is popular for a variety of water sports and has a boat ramp; golf course and tennis courts nearby, and sports centre with squash courts and swimming pool off Lake St. **Of interest:** Cairn beside the lake in Lake St, commemorating visit of first all-Aboriginal cricket team to England. Team was coached by T.W. Willis, who was also the founder of Australian Rules football. Feb.: Henley-on-Lake Wallace (show day with floats). **In the area:** Harrow, 32 km SE, one of Victoria's oldest inland towns, with many interesting historic buildings, including Hermitage Hotel (1851) and log gaol (1862). Rocklands Reservoir, 65 km E of Edenhope, part of Wimmera–Mallee irrigation system, fishing, boating. About 50 km W, over SA border, Naracoorte Caves Conservation Park. **Tourist information:** Shire Offices, 49 Elizabeth St; (055) 85 1011. **Accommodation:** 1 hotel, 1 motel, 1 cara./camp. park.
MAP REF. 228 C11

Eildon
Pop. 740
Built to irrigate a vast stretch of northern Victoria and to provide hydro-electric power, Lake Eildon is the State's largest man-made lake and is a popular resort area, surrounded by the beautiful foothills of the Alps within Eildon State Park. There are excellent recreational facilities around the foreshores, two major boat harbours, launching ramps, picnic grounds and many lookout points. The towns of Eildon and Bonnie Doon, 42 km N, are holiday centres. Power boat and houseboat hire at boat harbours. **In the area:** Signposted Lake Eildon Wall lookout. Lake cruises from Eildon Boat Harbour. Mt Pinninger (503 m), 3 km E, panoramic views of Mt Buller, the Alps and lake. Snobs Creek Fish Hatchery, 6 km S, millions of trout bred, used to stock lakes and rivers; visitors welcome. Eildon Deer Park nearby, on Goulburn Valley Hwy; open weekends and public holidays. Just past the hatchery, Snobs Creek Falls, Rubicon Falls, 18 km SW, via Thornton. Jamieson, 57 km SE, old mining town at junct. of Goulburn and Jamieson Rivers, surrounded by dense, bush-clad mountain countryside. Mt Skene, 48 km SE of Jamieson; wildflowers Dec.–Feb. (road closed in winter). Eildon Pondage and Goulburn River, excellent fishing. There is no closed season for trout in Eildon Lake, which is also stocked with Murray cod; redfin abound naturally. Inland fishing licence required for anglers over 16.

Fraser National Park, 13 km NW, and Eildon State Park surrounding town; bushwalking, camping, boating, fishing. Candlebark Gully Nature Walk, popular walk in Fraser National Park. **Tourist information:** Redgate Nursery and Craft Cottage, 73 Downey St, Alexandra; (057) 72 2169. **Accommodation:** 4 motels, 12 B&B, 6 cara./camp. parks.
MAP REF. 211 Q2, 222 A12, 233 K11

Emerald
Pop. 4693
The Puffing Billy steam railway runs between Belgrave and this pretty town, the first European settlement in the Dandenong Ranges. **Of interest:** Galleries and craft shops. Restaurants incl. Choo Choos, Monbulk Rd, restored Victorian 'red rattler' train with gallery and model railway. Emerald Lake Park, Emerald Lake Rd, once part of famous Nobelius Nursery. Environmental Centre, open daily; walking tracks; free barbecues. Emerald Lake, one of hills' most attractive and best-equipped picnic and swimming sites; water-slides, paddle-boats, model railway, kiosk, tearooms. Lake sited on Dandenongs Walk Track, 40-km trail from Cockatoo and Gembrook to Sassafras. **In the area:** At Menzies Creek, 5 km W, Cotswold House, fine food, views; Lake Aura Vale, sailing, picnics. Sherbrooke Art Gallery, Monbulk Rd, Belgrave, 11 km W. Bimbimbie Wildlife Park, Paternoster Rd, Mount Burnett, 12 km SE. Australian Rainbow Trout Farm, Macclesfield, 8 km N. Monbulk Animal Kingdom, Swales Rd, Monbulk, 11 km N. Tulip farms at Silvan, 14 km N. Olinda, 18 km N, picturesque town; antique gallery; National Rhododendron Garden and nursery; good restaurants; home of settler Edward Henty on Ridge Rd. **Tourist information:** Puffing Billy, Belgrave–Emerald Rd, Belgrave; (059) 754 6800. **Accommodation:** 1 resort. **See also:** The Dandenongs.
MAP REF. 211 M8, 224 E5

Euroa
Pop. 2772
A small town 151 km NE of Melbourne, just off the Hume Freeway, Euroa is a good base for exploring the Strathbogie Ranges and tablelands. The town name originated from the Aboriginal *yerao*, meaning 'joyful'. The district was traversed by Hume and Hovell in 1824 and Major Mitchell in 1836, and in 1879 was proclaimed a municipality. The Kelly gang staged a daring robbery here,

The Great Ocean Road

Very few roads can offer a continuous stretch of more than 300 kilometres of breathtaking scenery, but the Great Ocean Road, along Victoria's south-west coast, does exactly that.

Built to honour the servicemen of World War I and completed in 1932, the road has dramatic stretches of precipitous cliffs, idyllic coves and wide beaches.

The Great Ocean Road begins at **Torquay**, not far from Geelong. This is a popular surfing spot and the Road leads past a collection of famous surfing and safe swimming beaches and resorts. **Lorne** is one of the most charming of these. Despite offering modern holiday amenities and plenty of seaside entertainment for families, its gracious old hotels and guest houses remain as a reminder of days gone by. Behind the town, the

Otway Ranges, which stretch from **Anglesea** to **Cape Otway**, offer beautiful hills, waterfalls, excellent walking tracks and lovely picnic spots. At **Apollo Bay**, the Road leaves the coast and winds through the ferny slopes of Cape Otway. This is rainforest country, silent and untouched, and well worth exploring. Many of the roads are unsealed but quite adequate for standard cars. Try to visit the Melba Gully State Park to the west of the tiny town of **Lavers Hill**. Shipwreck trail signs begin on the eastern side of Lavers Hill. This point marks the beginning of the 'Shipwreck Coast', which stretches through **Port Campbell** and **Warrnambool** to **Port Fairy**. Photographers can be seen risking life and limb to take advantage of the dramatic coastal scenery; it is advisable, however, for drivers to keep their eyes firmly on the road. The coastline takes on tortured, twisted shapes, with amazing rock formations like The Twelve

Apostles—huge stone pillars looming out of the surf, carved over time by the incessant sea. A one-and-a-half-hour nature trail runs between Port Campbell and Two Mile Bay to the west; self-guide leaflets are available from the Port Campbell and Warrnambool information centres.

At **Princetown**, the Great Ocean Road returns to hug the coastline along the entire length of **Port Campbell National Park** and follows the coast to the Bay of Islands, 8 kilometres east of the small seaside town of **Peterborough**, where four shipwrecks are located along the coast. Here the Curdies River enters the sea in a wide, sandy inlet beloved of fishermen.

For further information, contact the Tourist Information Centre for Apollo Bay and the Otways, 155 Great Ocean Rd, Apollo Bay; (052) 37 6529. **See also:** Individual town entries in A–Z listing.

The Prom

Wilsons Promontory, at the southernmost tip of the mainland, is one of Victoria's largest and most spectacular national parks. 'The Prom', as it is affectionately known to Victorians, has an impressive range of landscapes, including tall forested ranges, luxuriant tree fern valleys, open heaths, salt marshes and long drifts of sand dunes. Its wide, white sandy beaches are magnificent, some dominated by spectacular granite tors and washed by spectacular rolling surf. There are also very safe swimming beaches, particularly at Norman Bay near the main camping area at Tidal River and also the aptly named Squeaky Beach, where the sands squeak underfoot.

Birds and other wildlife abound on the Prom: flocks of lorikeets, rosellas and flame robins, kookaburras and blue wrens are in evidence, even in the main general store area at Tidal River village; and for the more dedicated and patient birdwatcher, sightings of treecreepers, herons and lyrebirds can be the reward.

Emus feed unperturbed on the open heath by the side of the main road at the

Refuge Cove

park entry area at Yanakie Isthmus, and kangaroos and wallabies seem unimpressed by their human observers. At night, wombat-spotting by torchlight is a favourite pastime with children staying in the Tidal River area.

There are more than 100 kilometres of walking tracks in the Wilsons Promontory National Park. Some cover short walks, such as the nature trail in Lilly Pilly Gully, where the vegetation varies from bushland inhabited by koalas, to rainforest with ancient tree ferns and trickling streams. Other longer walks can be taken to such places as Sealers Cove or to the tip of the Prom, where there is a lighthouse dating from 1859. Hikers

should consider tide times to make creek crossing easier.

At the visitor information centre and park office at **Tidal River**, leaflets are available detailing walking tracks and the flora and fauna of the park, and an education officer provides a program for school groups. During summer and Easter, rangers give talks and spotlight tours as well as leading children's nature activities. Permits are required for all overnight hikes.

For further information contact the Wilsons Promontory National Park, Park Office, Tidal River; (056) 80 9555, or for bookings (056) 80 9500.

rounding up some 50 hostages at the nearby Faithfull Creek station and then making off with £2200. **Of interest:** Farmers Arms historical museum, Kirkland Ave. Parachuting School, Drysdale Rd; open weekends. Oct.: Agricultural Show, Wool Week. **In the area:** Seven Creeks Run Woolshed complex, 1 km N, sheepdog and shearing demonstrations, bush market, pottery. Balloon Flights Victoria, 10 km S. Forlonge Memorial, off Euroa–Strathbogie road, 10 km SE, commemorates Eliza Forlonge, who with her sister imported first merino sheep into Victoria. Scenic drive to Gooram Falls and around Strathbogie Ranges to SE. Wildflower walks in spring. Faithfull Creek homestead, 9 km NE near Balmattum, ruins remain from 1939 bushfires. Nearby, Faithfull Creek Waterfall, picnic facilities. At Violet Town, 20 km NE, parachuting centre; Dorset Hill Wildlife Park. **Tourist information:** Mon.–Fri., Community Centre, Binney St; weekends and public holidays, Tourist Information Centre, Kirkland Ave. **Accommodation:** 3 motels, 1 cara./camp. park.
MAP REF. 232 I8

Foster   Pop. 1078

A picturesque small town within easy reach of Corner Inlet, Waratah Bay and Wilsons Promontory on the south-east coast of Victoria, and about 170 km from Melbourne. **Of interest:** In Main St: Historical Museum, in old post office; Stockyard Gallery. Feb.: Agricultural Show. **In the area:** Scenic drive to Fish Creek, 11 km SW; Fish Creek Potters. Pleasant beach resorts: Waratah Bay, 34 km SW, Walkerville, 36 km SW, Port Franklin, 12 km SE. Cape Liptrap, 46 km SW, excellent views of rugged coastline and Bass Strait. Good surf beach at Sandy Point, 22 km S; surrounding protected waters of Shallow Inlet popular for fishing, windsurfing, swimming. Toora, 12 km E, proposed SECV windfarm, in experimental stage; Bonlac milk products. Turtons Creek, 18 km N, old gold-rich village; lyrebirds can sometimes be seen in tree fern gullies nearby. Near Turtons Creek, horse-drawn wagons, trail riding. Foster North Lookout, 6 km NW. **Tourist information:** Stockyard Gallery, Main St; (056) 82 1125. **Accommodation:** 2 motels, 10 B&B, 1 hostel, 1 cara./camp. park.
MAP REF. 224 I9

Geelong   Pop. 126 306

Geelong, on Corio Bay, is the largest provincial city in Victoria. A major manufacturing and processing centre, Geelong also has a large petroleum refinery. It is also a traditional wool-selling centre. The Corio Bay area was first settled in the 1830s and, apart from a rush to the diggings during the gold boom, Geelong has grown and prospered steadily. It is a pleasant and well-laid-out city with more than 14% of its area reserved for parks and sports grounds. **Of interest:** National Wool Centre, cnr Moorabool and Brougham Sts, incl. museum, 3 galleries. Geelong Otway Tourist Information Centre in foyer. Swimming at Eastern Beach and Park. Geelong Beachfront Scenic Drive. Botanic Gardens in Eastern Park, Garden St, overlooking Corio Bay. Johnstone Park, cnr Mercer and Gheringhap Sts, art gallery, war memorial, library and city hall; Geelong Historical Records Centre. Queens Park, Queens Park Rd, Newtown, golf course, sports oval, walks to Buckley's Falls. Geelong boasts many interesting buildings, more than 100 with National Trust classifications. They include: Merchiston Hall (1856), Garden St, East Geelong, 8-roomed stone house; in Swinburne St, North Geelong, Osborne House (1858), bluestone mansion, houses Maritime Museum; at Eastern Beach, beautiful Corio Villa (1856), prefabricated cast-iron house; The Heights (1855), Aphrasia St, Newtown, 14-roomed prefabricated timber mansion, open to public. Also open: Barwon Grange (1855), Fernleigh St, Newtown. Christ Church, Moorabool St, oldest Anglican church in Victoria still in continuous use. Customs House and Maritime Museum, Brougham St. Performing Arts Centre, Little Malop St. Pegasus Antiques, 560a Latrobe Tce. Wintergarden Gallery, 51 McKillop St. Pottage Crafts, 189 Moorabool St. Deb's Cottage Collections Crafts, 178 Swanston St, South Geelong. Balyang Bird Sanctuary, Shannon Ave, Newtown. Boat ramps on Corio Bay beaches. Good river and bay fishing. March: Weerama Festival. Oct: Racing Carnival, incl. Geelong Cup. **In the area:** Eleven wineries in Greater Geelong; details from Tourist Information. Norlane Water World, 7 km N. Lara (pop. 6318), 19 km N, swept by bushfires in 1969, but some historic buildings remain at foot of You Yangs, a range of granite hills in You Yangs

Regional Park. Serendip Sanctuary, between Lara and You Yangs, once purely a wildlife research station now open to the public; visitors centre, walking tracks, bird hides, picnic area. Anakie, 31 km N, via Batesford, township at foot of Brisbane Ranges, national park area; many species of ferns and flowering plants in park; walking tracks lead to Anakie Gorge and adjoining wildlife sanctuary. Nearby Fairy Park, miniature houses, scenes from fairytales. Mt Anakie Winemakers, 4 km N of Anakie on Staughton Vale Rd; open Sat. Steiglitz, 10 km NW of Anakie, popular camping ground, courthouse (1875). Batesford, 10 km NW, now a picturesque market garden township, with a history of winemaking. Sandstone Travellers Rest Inn (1849) across Moorabool River from present hotel. At Meredith, 46 km NW, one of the oldest towns in Victoria, once an important stopping-place for diggers on their way to the goldfields, Happy Hens Egg World; shire hall, railway station and bluestone State school. Fyansford, 5 km W, on outskirts of city, one of oldest settlements in region; Monash Bridge across Moorabool River thought to be one of first reinforced-concrete bridges in Victoria. Also at Fyansford, historic buildings incl.: Swan Inn; Balmoral Hotel (1854), now an art gallery; Fyansford Hotel. Brownhill Observation Tower, Ceres, 10 km SW, excellent view of surrounding areas. Deakin University's Institute of the Arts, Waurn Ponds, 13 km SW. Alden Lodge Museum and Coral Gardens, Grovedale, 6 km S; shell and coral displays, flower gardens. Bellarine Peninsula begins about 16 km E, incl. Queenscliff, Portarlington, Ocean Grove and Barwon Heads. At Wallington, 16 km SE, Koombahla Park, horseriding; A Maze'N Things. Lake Connewarre Wildlife Reserve, 2 km S of Leopold on Bellarine Hwy. Bellarine Peninsula Railway, steam and diesel trains on 16-km track between Drysdale and Queenscliff. Great Ocean Rd to Torquay and Lorne provides spectacular coastal scenery. At Moriac, 20 km SW, horse-drawn caravan hire. Vineyards in Moriac area incl. Rebenberg, Tarcoola, Scotchmans Hill, Kilgour Estate. **Tourist information:** National Wool Centre, 26–32 Moorabool St; (052) 22 2900. **Accommodation:** 2 hotels, 24 motels, 9 cara./camp. parks. **See also:** The Great Ocean Road; Wine Regions.
MAP REF. 210 F9, 216, 217 E6, 227 Q7

Grampians National Park, near Halls Gap

Gisborne
Pop. 2819

Once a stopping-place for coaches and foot travellers on their way to the Castlemaine and Bendigo goldfields, Gisborne is an attractive township (now bypassed by the Calder Hwy) on the way to Woodend and Kyneton. Market, cnr Aitken and Hamilton Sts, 1st. Sun. of month, Oct.–May. Dec.: Festival. **In the area:** Mount Macedon, 15 km N, memorial cross at summit. Mt Aitken Estates Winery, 6 km S of Gisborne. **Tourist information:** Ampol Road Pantry; (054) 282 541. **Accommodation:** 2 motels, 1 cara./camp. park (at Macedon). **See also:** Wine Regions.
MAP REF. 210 H4, 224 A2, 232 D13

Glenrowan
Pop. 345

Glenrowan is the famous site of the defeat of Ned Kelly and his gang by the police in 1880. Today the village, set in picturesque country, has craft and souvenir shops, nurseries and tea and coffee shops. **Of interest:** All along Old Hume Hwy: Ned Kelly Memorial Museum and Homestead; Kate's Cottage Gifts and Souvenirs behind huge statue of Ned Kelly; Tourist Centre, with engrossing computer-animated show of capture of Ned Kelly. **In the area:** Warby Ranges and State Park, 12 km N; historic villages, scenic drives, walking tracks, picnic spots. Wineries incl. Booth's Taminick Cellars, Auldstone Cellars, H.J.T. Vineyards, Bailey's Bundarra Vineyards. Milawa–Oxley wineries, 16

km E. **Tourist information:** Wangaratta and Region Visitors Information Centre, cnr Tone Rd and Handley St, Wangaratta; (057) 21 5711. **Accommodation:** 1 motel, 1 caravan park. **See also:** Wine Regions.
MAP REF. 222 D1, 233 L6

Halls Gap
Pop. 334

Beautifully sited in the heart of the Grampians, this little village is adjacent to Lake Bellfield and surrounded by the Grampians National Park and a network of scenic roads. **Of interest:** Tearooms, restaurants, an art gallery, potteries, good shopping. The area is noted for its wildflowers. Feb.: Grampians Jazz Festival. Sept.–Oct.: Wildflower Exhibition. **In the area:** Bushwalking, camping, rock climbing and abseiling in national park, one of largest in State; Visitors Centre, 2 km from town, open daily. Brambuk Aboriginal Living Cultural Centre, 2 km S. Wallaroo Wildlife Park, 5 km SE; open daily. Boroka Vineyards, 2 km E; open daily. Lake Fyans, 17 km E, swimming, fishing, yachting, water-skiing. Roses Gap Recreation Park, Roses Gap Rd, 21 km N, in Northern Grampians section of park; fitness track; base for scenic walks; accommodation, camping. Reids Lookout and The Balconies, 12 km NW. McKenzie Falls, 17 km NW. Wartook Pottery and Restaurant, 20 km NW. **Tourist information:** Halls Gap Newsagency, Grampians Rd; (053) 56 4247. **Accommodation:** 8 motels, 4 cara./camp. parks.

See also: The Grampians; National Parks.
MAP REF. 226 I1, 228 I12

Hamilton
Pop. 10 200

Known as the 'Wool Capital of the World', Hamilton is a prosperous and pleasant city less than an hour's drive from the coastal centres of Portland, Port Fairy and Warrnambool to the south and the Grampian Ranges to the north. **Of interest:** Big Woolbales Complex, Henty Hwy, focuses on wool industry; shearing demonstrations; woolshed memorabilia; craft centre; cafeteria. HIRL (Hamilton Institute of Rural Learning), North Boundary Rd, nature trail, breeding area for eastern barred bandicoots. HEAL (Hamilton Environmental Awareness and Learning) conducts land-care tours; bookings essential. Hamilton Art Gallery, Brown St, varied collections, incl. decorative arts. Lake Hamilton, Ballarat Rd, sandy beach, water sports, trout fishing, picnic facilities. On banks of lake, Sir Reginald Ansett Transport Museum, history and memorabilia of Sir Reginald's life and transport industry begun in Hamilton in 1931. Small zoo at Botanical Gardens (established 1870), French St, free-flight aviary, playground, picnic facilities. Hamilton Pastoral Museum, Glenelg Hwy, in former St Luke's Lutheran Church; by appt. Hamilton History Centre and Aboriginal Keeping Place, Gray St, aspects of local Aboriginal culture. Hamilton is the starting point for Mary McKillop Pilgrims Drive in the Green Triangle region. Grave of Mary's father in cemetery. June: Eisteddfod. July–Aug.: Wool Heritage Week. **In the area:** Summit Park, Nigretta Rd, 15 km NW, specialises in raising Saxon-Merino sheep for superfine wool production; open daily. Wannon and Nigretta Falls, 15 km NW. Points Arboretum at Coleraine, 35 km W, official State collection of eucalypts. Mt Eccles National Park, near Macarthur, 35 km S. Mt Eccles, incl. crater Lake Surprise, one of 3 extinct volcanoes. Grampians Tour to Dunkeld, Halls Gap, Ararat and back via Glenthompson, good day trip from Hamilton. Several historic homes and gardens of note. **Tourist information:** Visitor Information Centre, Lonsdale St; (055) 72 3746 and 1800 80 7056. **Accommodation:** 6 hotels, 7 motels, 2 cara./camp. parks. **See also:** The Western District.
MAP REF. 226 G5

Harrietville   Pop. 250

Tucked into the foothills of Mt Hotham and Mt Feathertop, Harrietville is a convenient accommodation centre for skiers at Mt Hotham or holidaymakers in northeast Victoria. Gold was discovered here in 1862, and the gold-rush village was proclaimed a township in 1879. **Of interest:** Bicycles, fishing rods and gold panning dishes for hire. Horse-riding, golfing. Pioneer Park, open-air museum and picnic area, Alpine Rd. Audrey's Dolls and Crafts, Cobungra Court; handmade porcelain dolls. Jan.: CAE Music Camp. Aug.: International Ski Marathon Kangaroo Hoppet (Falls Creek). **In the area:** Walking tracks: Mt Feathertop (1922 m), 20 km return; Mt Hotham (1859 m), about 32 km one way. Bushwalking in high mountain country of Bogong National Park, which surrounds town (weather conditions can be harsh and change suddenly). Crystal Waters Trout Farm and Mountain Fresh Trout Farm, 4 km N, fishing, educational facilities. **Tourist information:** Old General Store, Alpine Rd; (057) 59 2553. **Accommodation:** 1 hotel/motel, 1 lodge, 1 cara./camp. park.
MAP REF. 223 M7, 233 P9, 234 C7

Healesville   Pop. 6264

Surrounded by mountain forest country, Healesville is about a one and a half hour's drive from Melbourne along the Maroondah Hwy. It has been a popular resort town since the turn of the century, as the climate is cool and pleasant in summer and the area offers excellent bushwalks and scenic drives. **Of interest:** Trolley rides, Healesville railway station to Yarra Glen, Sun. Bicentennial

Koala, Healesville Sanctuary

National Trail, Healesville–Cooktown, 5000 km, for horseriders and walkers. Yarra Valley Winery Tours, Birdwood Ave. Feb.: Coldstream Country and Western Festival. March: Australian Car Rally Championship. **In the area:** Hedgend Maze, 2 km S. Pottery, lapidary and art gallery at Nigel Court, off Badger Creek Rd, 2 km S; open daily. Corranderrk Aboriginal Cemetery, 3 km S. World-famous Healesville Sanctuary, 4 km S, on Badger Creek Rd; open daily. This 32-ha reserve houses a variety of native animals and birds in largely natural bushland setting. Key attractions are close-up displays, see animals in close proximity; check times. Picnic/barbecue facilities, kiosk, self-service restaurant. Badger Weir Park and Dalry Park Deer Farm, 7 km S. Tuscany Gallery, 5 km E. Mt St Leonard, 14 km N. All at Toolangi, 16 km N: Forest Discovery Centre; Singing Gardens of C.J. Dennis; Toolangi Pottery. Grand Hotel, historic hotel at Yarra Glen, 14 km W: meals, accommodation. Drives from Healesville: Toolangi State Forest, criss-crossed with logging roads, 14 km N; Donnelly's Weir Reserve, 37 km NE via the Black Spur, passing Maroondah Reservoir (picnic/barbecue facilities) and towering stands of mountain ash and lush tree fern glades. Ballooning, horseriding, Eco-Adventure Tours. A large number of wineries in the area. Gulf Station Homestead (1854), 2 km N of Yarra Glen. **Tourist information:** Yarra Valley Healesville Visitor Information Centre, 127 Maroondah Hwy; (059) 62 2600. **Accommodation:** 2 hotels, 5 motels, 20 B&B, 1 hostel, 3 cara./camp. parks. **See also:** Wine Regions.
MAP REF. 211 N5, 214 E7, 224 F3

Heathcote   Pop. 1507

In attractive countryside on the McIvor Hwy, Heathcote is set along the McIvor Creek, 47 km SE of Bendigo. **Of interest:** McIvor Cottage Industry Co-op, High St, in old courthouse, historical display, craft marketing, tourist information. Pink Cliffs, Pink Cliffs Rd, off Hospital Rd: created by eroded spoil from gold sluices, brilliant mineral staining. Old Heathcote Hospital (1859), Hospital Rd, listed for preservation by National Trust. Oct.: Golden Grape Festival. **In the area:** Lake Eppalock, 10 km W, one of the State's largest lakes, speedboat racing. Central Victorian Yabbie Farm, on Northern Hwy at South Heathcote. Mount Ida Lookout, 4 km N, excellent views. McIvor Range Reserve, off Barrack St. Wineries incl. Wild Duck Creek Estate, Heathcote Winery and Zuber Estate, within town; Jasper Hill and Huntleigh Vineyards, 6 km N; McIvor Creek Wines and Eppalock Ridge vineyards, 10 km and 22 km SW. **Tourist information:** Shire Offices, 125 High St; (054) 33 3211. **Accommodation:** 1 hotel, 1 hotel/motel, 1 motel, 1 cara./camp. park.
MAP REF. 232 E9

Hopetoun   Pop. 704

This small Mallee town, southeast of Wyperfeld National Park, was named after the seventh Earl of Hopetoun, first Governor-General of Australia. Hopetoun was a frequent visitor to the home of Edward Lascelles, who was largely responsible for opening up the Mallee area. **Of interest:** Hopetoun House, built for Lascelles; National Trust-classified. Mallee Mural, and leadlight window in Shire Office, Lascelles St, depict history of the Mallee. Coorong Homestead (1846), Evelyn St, National Trust-classified, home of first European settler in area, Peter McGinnis. Lake Lascelles, boating, swimming, picnics. Aug.: Speed Field Days. Oct.: Agricultural Show. **In the area:** Wyperfeld National Park, 50 km W; information centre in park. Swamp Tank Museum, Turriff, 45 km NE. **Tourist information:** Shire of Karkarooc, 95 Lascelles St; (050) 83 3001. **Accommodation:** 2 hotels, 1 motel, 1 cara./camp. park.
MAP REF. 126 E12, 228 H3

Horsham   Pop. 12 552

At the junction of the Western, Wimmera and Henty Hwys, Horsham is generally

Gippsland Lakes

Many people regard the Gippsland Lakes as Victoria's most outstanding holiday area. Dominated as it is by Australia's largest system of inland waterways, it certainly does live up to all the superlatives accorded it. With the foothills of the high country just to the north and the amazing stretch of the Ninety Mile Beach separating the lakes from the ocean, the region offers a variety of natural beauty and recreation activities. Here the choice really is yours—lake, river or ocean fishing, boating, cruising, surfing, birdwatching or just sitting by the water.

Within easy reach of the Lakes area the high country begins, so it is possible to vary a waterside trip with days exploring the alpine reaches and some of the fascinating little old townships such as **Omeo, Briagolong** and **Dargo**. The road across

the Dargo High Plains and the Omeo Highway leading to Hotham Heights pass through some stunning country. Check your car thoroughly before you set off—service stations are scarce along the way. Wellington, King, Victoria, Tyers, Reeve and Coleman—these 6 lakes cover more than 400 square kilometres and stretch parallel to the Ninety Mile Beach for almost its entire length. **Sale**, at the western edge of the region, is the local base for the development of the Bass Strait oil and gas fields. Both Sale and **Bairnsdale**, further east on the banks of the Mitchell River, make excellent bases for holidays on the Lakes or for alpine trips. The main resort towns are **Lakes Entrance**, at the mouth of the Lakes, **Paynesville**, a mecca for boating and fishing enthusiasts, and **Metung**, a departure point for cruising

holidays on the Lakes, and **Loch Sport**, nestled between Ninety Mile Beach, Lake Victoria and the national park.

The **Lakes National Park**, the **Mitchell River National Park** and the hills and valleys of the alpine foothills to the north all provide plenty of opportunities for bushwalking or for simply enjoying the peace.

For further information on the Gippsland Lakes, contact the local tourist information centres: cnr Esplanade and Marine Pde, Lakes Entrance; (051) 55 1966, or 240 Main St, Bairnsdale; (051) 52 3444, or Princes Hwy, Sale; (051) 44 1108. **See also:** Individual town entries in A–Z listing.

Lakes Entrance and Ninety Mile Beach

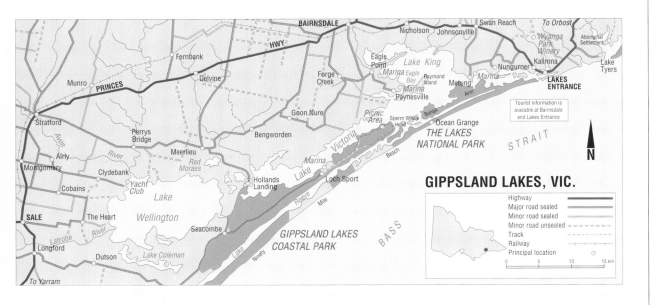

GIPPSLAND LAKES, VIC.

regarded as the capital of the Wimmera region. It is a good base for tours of the region, particularly to the Little Desert National Park, 40 km NW, and to the Grampians, some 50 km SE. **Of interest:** Botanic Gardens, cnr Baker and Firebrace Sts. Horsham Art Gallery, Dimboola Rd, photography and Mack Jost collection of Australian art. Wimmera River flows through town; attractive picnic spots, good fishing. Cottage Delights, Dooen Rd; plants and crafts. March: Fishing Contest. Dec.: Kannamaroo Festival. **In the area:** Wool Factory, Golf Course Rd, 3 km SW, produces top-quality, extra-fine wool from Saxon-Merino sheep; tours daily. Black Range Cashmere and Thryptomene Farm, 40 km S, incl. 4WD tours; bookings essential, through Tourist Information. Many fishing lakes: redfin, trout, Murray cod. Toolondo Reservoir, 44 km S, home of the fighting brown trout; caravan park. Rocklands Reservoir, 90 km S on Glenelg River, built to supplement Wimmera–Mallee irrigation scheme; water sports; picnics, caravan and camping at lake's western edge, 14 km from Balmoral. Olde Horsham Village, 3 km SE; historic buildings, art, craft, antique market, fauna park; open daily. Victorian Institute of Dry Land Agriculture, Natimuk Rd, and cereal research centre at Victorian College of Agriculture and Horticulture, 13 km NE at Longerenong; by appt. Green Lake, 13 km SE, and Natimuk Lake, 24 km NW, picnic/barbecue facilities. Mt Arapiles, 32 km W, popular climbing rock, 360-degree views from lookout. **Tourist information:** 20 O' Callaghan's Pde; (053) 82 1832. **Accommodation:** 6 hotels, 15 motels, 2 cara./camp. parks. **See also:** The Wimmera.
MAP REF. 228 G9

Inglewood   Pop. 740
North along the Calder Hwy from Bendigo are the 'Golden Triangle' towns of Inglewood and Bridgewater on Loddon. Sizeable gold nuggets have been found in this area: 'Welcome Stranger', the largest, weighing 65 kg; and two at Kingower in the last decade. **Of interest:** Old eucalyptus oil distillery. Inglewood Gipsy Tours, Grant St, wagons drawn by Clydesdales. April: Blue Eucalyptus Festival (even-numbered years). **In the area:** Several wineries. Kooyoora State Park, 16 km W; in park, Melville Caves, once haunt of notorious bushranger

Captain Melville. At Bridgewater, 8 km SE, Loddon River, fishing, water-skiing, picnic/barbecue facilities; parachute jumping. Horsedrawn caravan hire at Inglewood and Bridgewater. **Tourist information:** Development and Tourist Information Centre, Old Railway Centre, 1 Thompson St; (054) 38 3175. **Accommodation:** 1 motel, 1 cara./camp. park. **See also:** Wine Regions.
MAP REF. 229 O9, 232 A7

Inverleigh   Pop. 282
On the Leigh River, this little town 29 km W of Geelong has a number of historic buildings. **Of interest:** On Hamilton Hwy: former Horseshoe Inn; 2-storey hotel opposite; Church of England, Presbyterian Church; State School; Whistler's Cottage Art Gallery. **In the area:** Fishing in Leigh and Barwon Rivers. Inverleigh Common, 2 km N, bushland, fauna reserve. Barunah Plains homestead, 17 km W, by appt. **Tourist information:** Geelong Otway Tourist Information Centre, in Wool Centre, 26–32 Moorabool St, Geelong; (052) 22 2900. **Accommodation:** Limited.
MAP REF. 210 D9, 217 B6, 227 P7

Inverloch   Pop. 2195
This is a small seaside resort on Anderson Inlet, east of Wonthaggi. It has good surf and long stretches of excellent beach, and is very popular in summer. **Of interest:** South Gippsland Conservation Society, Environment Centre and Shell Museum, in Information Centre building, The Esplanade. Jan.: Fun Festival. March: Jazz Festival. **In the area:** Adjacent to town, Anderson's Inlet, most southerly habitat of mangroves. Townsend Bluff and Maher's Landing, birdwatching. Inverloch–Cape Paterson Scenic Road, through Bunurong Cliff Coastal Reserve, 15 km SW; views equal those on Great Ocean Rd. Spear fishing and surfing at Cape Paterson Tarwin River, 20 km SE, good fishing. Nearby, Venus Bay, beaches, natural bushland, wildlife, sporting facilities. **Tourist information:** Cnr Ramsay Blvd and The Esplanade; (056) 74 2706. **Accommodation:** 1 motel, 4 B&B, 4 cara./camp. parks.
MAP REF. 224 G9

Jeparit   Pop. 440
This little town in the Wimmera, 37 km N of Dimboola, is 5 km from Lake Hindmarsh, the largest natural freshwater lake in Victoria, with many safe,

sandy beaches, fishing, and good camping facilities. **Of interest:** Spire, illuminated at night, commemorates the fact that the town is the birthplace of Sir Robert Menzies. Menzies Square, cnr Charles and Roy Sts, site of dwelling where Menzies was born. Wimmera–Mallee Pioneer Museum, 4-ha complex of colonial buildings at southern entrance to town, furnished in period, displays of restored farm machinery. Jan.: Beach Carnival. Oct.: Agricultural Show. **In the area:** Near Antwerp, 20 km S, Ebenezer Mission, founded 1859 by Moravian missionaries, restored by National Trust. Wyperfeld National Park, 44 km N and Little Desert National Park, 40 km SW; wildflowers, native fauna, walking. **Tourist information:** Shire Offices, 10 Roy St; (053) 97 2070. **Accommodation:** 2 hotels, 1 cara. park.
MAP REF. 228 G6

Kaniva   Pop. 762
Kaniva in the west Wimmera, 43 km from Bordertown, SA, is just north of the Little Desert, which is noted for its wildflowers in spring. **Of interest:** Historical museum, Commercial St, large collection of items of local history. In Progress St: Mayfare Cement Works; Iris Farm. Eastwoods Herb farm, Western Hwy. Old Kaniva railway station. **In the area:** Billy-Ho Bush Walk begins some 10 km S, 3-km self-guide walk in Little Desert National Park; numbered pegs allow identification of various species of desert flora. Big Desert, just north of town, walking trails, wildflowers, wildlife. Waterbird farm 20 km NW, breeding of black swans and many other varieties; by appt. Railway station (1889) at Serviceton, 23 km W, National Trust-classified. Mooree Reserve, 20 km SW of town, picnic spot. **Tourist information:** 41 Commercial St; (053) 92 2418. **Accommodation:** 1 hotel, 2 motels, 1 cara./camp. park.
MAP REF. 228 C7

Kerang   Pop. 4024
Some 30 km from the Murray and 60 km from Swan Hill, Kerang is the centre of a productive rural area and lies at the southern end of a chain of lakes and marshes. Some of the largest breeding-grounds in the world for ibis and other waterfowl are found in these marshes. The ibis is closely protected because of its value in controlling locusts and other pests. **Of interest:** Old water tower, cnr

of Murray Valley Hwy and Shadforth St, Gem Club, tourist information. Museum, Riverwood Drive, cars, farm machinery. Apex Park recreation area is sited by the first of the three Reedy Lakes; the second has a large ibis rookery. Most lakes in the Kerang area are used for duckshooting. Those suitable for watersports are Lakes Meran, Reedy, Kangaroo and Charm. Excellent year-round bowling, tennis and fishing. **Easter:** Australian Tractor Pull Championships, at Quambatook, 42 km SW. **In the area:** Sharnnkirst Cashmere Stud Farm and Riverside Crafts, Barham, 24 km NE. Murrabit, 29 km N, on the Murray and surrounded by picturesque river forests; country market on 1st Sat. of month. Lake Boga, 44 km NW, good sandy beaches. **Tourist information:** Borough Offices, 71 Wellington St, Barham; (054) 52 1799. **Accommodation:** 4 hotels, 1 hotel/motel, 3 motels, 2 cara./camp. parks. **See also:** The Mighty Murray.
MAP REF. 126 I12, 229 P3, 232 A2

Koo-wee-rup Pop. 1106

Well known for its March Potato Festival, this town is in the middle of a rich market-garden area near Western Port, and is the biggest asparagus-growing area in the Southern Hemisphere. **Of interest:** Historical Society Museum, Rossiter Rd; open Sun. **In the area:** Bayles Flora and Fauna Park, 8 km NE. At Tynong, 20 km NE, Victoria's Farm Shed, displays; Gumbaya Fun Park, in landscaped native bushland. Berwick–Pakenham Historical Society Museum, John St, Pakenham, 21 km N. Military Vehicle Museum, Army Rd, Pakenham. Royal Botanic Gardens Cranbourne Garden, 28 km NW. At Cardinia, 6 km W, Australian Pioneer Farm, re-created farm buildings, opportunities to shear sheep and milk cows. Tooradin, 10 km W, on Sawtell's Inlet; fishing, boating. Between Tooradin and Koo-wee-rup, on Sth Gippsland Hwy, Harewood House (1850s), original furnishings; open weekends. **Tourist information:** Newsagency, 277 Rossiter Rd; (059) 97 1456. **Accommodation:** 1 motel.
MAP REF. 211 N10, 224 F7

Koroit Pop. 968

Koroit is 18 km NW of the coastal resort of Warrnambool in the south-west of Victoria. It is an agricultural town with historic botanic gardens. The commercial and church precincts of the town,

both with historic buildings, have been classified by the National Trust. **In the area:** Tower Hill State Game Reserve, 3 km S, volcanic area, walking tracks, Natural History Centre, bird hides. Coast between Port Fairy and Warrnambool offers delightful scenery. Mahogany Walking Track, 22-km walking track between Port Fairy and Warrnambool. **Tourist information:** Warrnambool Tourist Information Centre, 600 Raglan St, Warrnambool; (055) 64 7837. **Accommodation:** 1 hotel, 2 B&B, 1 cara./ camp. park.
MAP REF. 226 H8

Korumburra Pop. 2906

The giant Gippsland earthworm, sought by fishermen and geologists alike, is found near this town, situated on the South Gippsland Hwy, 116 km SE of Melbourne. The area surrounding the town is given to dairying and agriculture, and the countryside is hilly. **Of interest:** Coal Creek Historical Village, cnr Sth Gippsland Hwy and Silkstone Rd, re-creation of 19th-century coal-mining village; on original site of Coal Creek mine, begun in 1890s; orientation centre in Mechanics' Institute, inside village near

Lake Boga, near Kerang

entrance; open daily. **Feb.:** Coal Creek Twilight Music and Theatre Festival. **March:** Karmai (Giant Worm) Festival. **In the area:** Gooseneck Pottery, Ruby, 4 km SE. Old School Tea Room, 6 km SE, on Sages & Logans Rd, 1916 primary-school building, home cooking. Leongatha, 14 km SE, Murray Goulburn Dairy Factory. Beaches and excellent fishing at Corner Inlet, 58 km SE, and Waratah Bay, 66 km SE. Loch, 16 km NW, antiques, art and craft. At Poowong, 18 km NW, Poowong Pioneer Chapel, fine example of German architecture; Mudlark Pottery. Top Paddock Cheeses, Bena, 4 km SW, tastings and sales of traditional, curd and soft cheeses. **Tourist information:** South Gippsland Tourism, Coal Creek Historical Village, cnr Sth Gippsland Hwy and Silkstone Rd; (056) 55 2233. **Accommodation:** 2 hotels, 1 motel, 2 B&B, 1 cara./camp. park.
MAP REF. 211 P12, 224 G8

Kyabram Pop. 5540

A prosperous town in the Murray–Goulburn area, just 40 km NW of Shepparton, Kyabram is in a rich dairying and fruit-growing district. **Of interest:**

Community-owned waterfowl and fauna park on Lake Rd incl. 5 lakes with duck, ibis, swans and pelicans; 16-ha enclosure for emus and kangaroos; huge flight aviary; a reptile house; open daily. The Stables, adj. to fauna park, pottery and crafts. Mr Ilzyn's Cottages, Breen Ave, mansions, pubs, farmhouses from around the world, all in miniature. Easter: Antique Aeroplane Fly-in. March: Rodeo. **Tourist information:** Fauna park, 75 Lake Rd; (058) 52 2883. **Accommodation:** 3 hotels, 2 motels, 2 cara./camp. parks. **See also:** The Mighty Murray. MAP REF. 232 F6

Kyneton   Pop. 3940

Little more than an hour's drive from Melbourne, along the Calder Hwy, Kyneton is an attractive and well-preserved town with several interesting bluestone buildings. Farms around the town prospered during the gold rushes, supplying large quantities of fresh food to the Ballarat and Bendigo diggings. **Of interest:** Kyneton Museum, Piper St, in former bank (c.1865), drop-log cottage in grounds. Botanic Gardens, Clowes St, 8-ha area above river; 500 specimen trees. Historic buildings: town's churches; mechanics institute; old police depot. In Piper St: Steam Mill; restored to operational condition, open weekends; Meskills Woolstore, wool spinning mill, yarn and garments for sale; Alpaca Shop, tours, demonstrations, sales. Magnolia Cottage Nursery, Fiddlers Green Rd. Easter: Antique fair. **In the area:** Two-storey bluestone mills on either side of town. Upper Coliban, Lauriston and Malmsbury Reservoirs, all 8 km W. At Malmsbury, 10 km NW, historic bluestone railway viaduct; Bleak House (1850s) with rose garden; The Mill (1861), National Trust-classified, gallery, restaurant, accommodation. At Trentham, 22 km SW, historic foundry; Jargon crafts; Minifie's Berry Farm, pick-your-own in season. At Blackwood, further 14 km S, Garden of St Erth. Trentham Falls, 20 km S. Carlsruhe Gallery and Campaspe Art Gallery at Carlsruhe, 5 km SE. Burke and Wills Camel farm, 7 km N on Calder Hwy. Turpins Falls, Metcalfe, 22 km N. Cottage Maze Gardens, Drummond, 12 km N. **Tourist information:** Dapples and Darrell Lea, 6 High St; (054) 22 6075. **Accommodation:** 1 hotel, 2 motels, 3 B&B, 1 cara./camp. park. MAP REF. 210 G2, 224 A1, 227 R2, 229 R13, 232 D12

Lake Bolac   Pop. 266

In the Western District plains area, this small town on the Glenelg Hwy is by a 1460-ha freshwater lake that has sandy beaches around a 20-km shoreline and is good for fishing (eels, trout, perch and yellow-belly), boating and swimming. There are several boat-launching ramps and an aquatic club. A sporting complex is located between town and lake. Easter: 4-day yachting regatta. **Tourist information:** Lake Bolac Motel, Glenelg Hwy; (053) 50 2218. **Accommodation:** 1 motel, 1 B&B, 1 cara./camp. park. MAP REF. 220 C13, 227 J5

Lakes Entrance   Pop. 4622

This extremely popular holiday town is at the eastern end of the Gippsland Lakes, which form the largest inland network of waterways in Australia. They cover an area of more than 400 sq km and are separated from the ocean by a thin sliver of sand dunes forming a large part of the Ninety Mile Beach, which stretches south to Seaspray. A bridge across the Cunningham Arm gives access to the surf beach from Lakes Entrance. The town is well developed for the holidaymaker, catering for both seaside recreation and exploration of the mountain country to the north. It is the home port for a large fishing fleet and many pleasure craft. Large cruise vessels conduct regular sightseeing tours of the lakes throughout the year. Boats can also be hired. Fishing, both ocean and beach, is popular, as are swimming and surfing on a variety of good beaches. **Of interest:** Fisherman's

Buchan Caves, near Lakes Entrance

Co-operative, Bullock Island; viewing platform and fish for sale. Shell Museum, the Esplanade. Potteries and galleries. Jan: Australian Wood Design Exhibition. Nov.: World Cup Sport Kiting Championship. **In the area:** Lake Bunga, 3 km E, nature trail. Kinkuna Country fauna park and family entertainment centre, Princes Hwy, 3.5 km E. Lake Tyers (6–23 km E, depending on access point), sheltered waters; fishing, swimming, boating; cruises depart from Fishermans Landing. Braeburne Park Orchards and tearooms, 6 km N. Woodsedge, 8 km N on Baades Rd, gallery, furniture workshop, glass-blowing demonstrations, refreshments. Wyanga Park Vineyard and Winery, 10 km N reached by boat trip from town. Buchan Caves, 55 km N, well worth a visit. Day trips to old mining areas around Omeo, 126 km N. Blue Gum Ostriches, 6 km NW on Hoggs Lane; tours, display of painted eggs; closed Tues. Good views: Jemmy's Point, 1 km W, and Nyerimilang Park, 10 km NW. In park, original homestead, is open (north wing 1892). Boat hire at Metung, 15 km W by road. Nicholson River, 24 km W, and Golvinda wineries, 50 km NW, via Bairnsdale. **Tourist information:** Visitors Information Centre, cnr Esplanade and Marine Pde; (051) 55 1966. **Accommodation:** 2 hotel/motels, 20 motels, 15 cara./camp. parks. **See also:** Gippsland Lakes; Wine Regions. MAP REF. 225 Q4, 234 G13

Lancefield   Pop. 1063

This historic township with its wide streets and Victorian buildings is located

Wine Regions

Viticulture developed in Victoria following the 1850s gold rush. Unsuccessful diggers began planting vines as a source of income. Later, Edward Henty and William Rye brought cuttings to the new colony and by 1868 more than 1200 hectares of vines had been established.

The light, dry wines produced in these vineyards won wide acclaim, but the event of phylloxera saw a promising industry decline until the early 1960s, when it started to re-emerge and develop into what it is today. One of the oldest regions is in the north-east of the State, 270 kilometres from Melbourne. **Rutherglen** and the other nearby wine-making towns of **Wahgunyah**, **Glenrowan** and **Milawa** produce wine unique to each of the region's environmental subcultures. Many of the wineries are still managed by the descendants of the founders. The wines of the region are famed for their rich flavoursome red, and for the exotic range of fortified wines such as Rutherglen Muscat, Rutherglen Tokay and their famous Port-style wine. On the June long weekend a winery walkabout is organised so that wine lovers can visit the vineyards and sample some of the fine wines of the north-east. It is advisable to book accommodation in advance if planning a visit at this time.

West along the Murray, the towns of **Echuca**, **Swan Hill** and **Mildura** are part of the Murray Valley and north-west region known for the production of wines for everyday drinking.

About 200 kilometres west of Melbourne, between Stawell and Ararat, is the little town of **Great Western**, where the Seppelt and Best wineries developed in the 1860s. Since then they have consistently produced fine wines, including the renowned champagne-style Great Western Special Reserve from the Seppelt winery. The vineyards of Great Western are also noted for their rich red and full-flavoured white table wines.

At **Ararat**, Trevor Mast's Mt Langi Ghiran Wines, and the Montara Winery both produce excellent wine with their own individual character.

To the north-east of Great Western is the region of the Pyrenees with the towns of **Avoca**, **Redbank** and **Moonambel**. Here are the Taltarni, Mt Avoca, Redbank, Chateau Remy, Summerfield, Dalwhinnie and Warrenmang wineries.

Stretching from **Shepparton** along to **Nagambie**, **Seymour** and **Mansfield** is the picturesque region of the Goulburn Valley with a contrast in wineries from the

Yarra Valley vineyard

historic, classified buildings of Chateau Tahbilk to the modern wineries of Delatite and Mitchelton. One grape variety from the region to win acclaim is the Marsanne, a distinct and rather unusual white wine.

One of the two oldest regions near Melbourne is the Yarra Valley region, which is centred round **Cottles Bridge** and **St Andrews** (at the northern end), **Yarra Glen**, **Lilydale**, **Coldstream** and **Healesville** (in the central part of the region), and **Seville** and **Warburton** (to the south). This region's premium wine has had a rebirth after starting in the early 1850s and petering out as late as the 1920s. There is a wide range of wines produced in the area, from sparkling wine to quality reds and white table wines. Wineries of particular interest include Domaine Chandon for its sparkling wines and Fergusson's, Kellybrook, Yarra Burn and De Bortoli for an enjoyable restaurant lunch in the Valley. There are many other wineries worth visiting, including Bianchet for the merlot and verduzzo wines, and St Huberts because it was one of the first wineries in the re-birth of the district.

Another wine-producing area close to Melbourne is the burgeoning Mornington Peninsula area. A cool-climate winegrowing district, its 83 vineyards nestle between farming and coastal hamlets. The main spread covers the area from **Dromana**, through **Red Hill** and across the Peninsula to **Merricks** and **Balnarring**, with **Mornington, Main Ridge** and **Mt Martha** offering isolated vineyards. Of these, 17 vineyards are open, usually on weekends and public holidays, for cellar-door tastings and sales. Another 13 cellar doors are open for sales and visits by appointment.

North of Melbourne's Tullamarine Airport, wineries dot the landscape with pockets of vines stretching into the Macedon Ranges; some were established in the 1860s, others more recently. They include Knight's Granite Hills, Wildwood, Hanging Rock, Virgin Hills, Craiglee, Goonawarra, Cleveland, Cope-Williams, Flynn and Williams—each with its own distinct quality and character.

The Heathcote–Bendigo region is, like so many of Victoria's wine regions, goldmining country that gave up much hidden wealth in the period 1850–1900. Today there are many wineries scattered throughout the region, around the townships of **Heathcote**, **Kingower**, **Bendigo** and **Bridgewater on Loddon**. Wineries include Passing Clouds, Jasper Hill, Osicka's, Zuber Estate, Water Wheel, Le Amon and Mildara's Balgownie.

In the last 30 years Victoria's wine industry has changed from an industry in decline, with about 25 commercial vineyards, to a flourishing concern with about 300 commercial vineyards and 100 smaller ones.

Most larger wineries are open daily for tastings and sales; some of the small wineries have restricted opening times, so it is worth checking before visiting.

For more information contact: the Victorian Wine Centre; (03) 9699 6082; Mornington Peninsula Vignerons Association; (059) 74 4200; or Yarra Valley Wine Growers Association; (059) 64 2016. For tourist information, contact the Victorian Information Centre; (03) 9790 3333. See also: Individual town entries in A–Z listing. **Note** detailed map of Yarra Valley Region on page 214.

67 km NW of Melbourne. **Of interest:** Old Macedonia House, Main Rd, now Antique Centre of Victoria (1889); incl.: Crafts cottage, local crafts. Cleveland, an historic home and winery, 2 km E on Shannons Rd. In High St: paintings, ceramics and glass at The Gallery; Mechanics Hall (1868). Dec.: Horse Festival. **In the area:** A number of wineries and nurseries. Monument Creek Herb Farm, Monument Rd, 5 km W. Horseriding and golf. **Tourist information:** Centre Vic Motor Inn, Main Rd; (054) 29 1777. **Accommodation:** 1 motel.
MAP REF. 210 I2, 224 B1, 232 E12

Leongatha   Pop. 3968

Near the foothills of the Strzelecki Ranges, Leongatha is a large dairying area and a good base for trips to Wilsons Promontory and the seaside and fishing resorts on the coast. **Of interest:** Murray Goulburn Dairy Factory, Yarragon Rd. Historic Society Museum and Art and Craft Gallery, McCartin St. Feb.: Cycling Carnival. Sept.: Daffodil Festival. **In the area:** Firelight Museum, 9 km N, antique lamps, firearms. About 21 km N, Grand Ridge Rd, excellent scenic driving, leads to Tarra–Bulga National Park. Gooseneck Pottery, Ruby, 9 km W. Korumburra, 14 km W along South Gippsland Hwy, Coal Creek Historical Park. Brackenhurst Rotary Dairy, Christoffersens Rd, Nerrena, 5 km E, 350 cows, museum, bottle collection; from 3.30 daily. Mossvale Park, 16 km NE, impressive plantation of exotic trees, picnic/barbecue facilities. At Mirboo North,

Erskine Falls, near Lorne

23 km NE, Grand Ridge Brewing Company, beer-brewing process; Erimae Lavender Farm; Colonial Bank Antiques. **Tourist information:** CAB, Michael Place Complex; (056) 62 2111. **Accommodation:** 5 motels, 1 cara./camp. park.
MAP REF. 211 P12, 224 H8

Lorne   Pop. 1143

The approaches to Lorne along the Great Ocean Road, whether from east or west, are quite spectacular. The town is one of Victoria's most attractive coastal resorts, with the superb mountain scenery of the Otways behind, and a year-round mild climate. Captain Loutit gave the district the name of Loutitt Bay. The village of Lorne was established in 1871, became popular with pastoralists from inland areas, and developed rather in the style of an English seaside resort. When the Great Ocean Road opened in 1932 Lorne grew more popular; however, the town itself has remained relatively unspoiled, with good beaches, surfing, and excellent bushwalking in the hills. **Of interest:** Teddy's Lookout, at edge of George St behind town, excellent bay views. Foreshore reserve incl. children's playground, pool, trampolines, tennis courts, picnic ground. Shipwreck Walk along beach. Pedal boats available for hire. Qdos Contemporary Art Gallery, Mountjoy Pde. Lorne Fisheries on pier; daily supplies from local fleet. Shell Shop and Museum, William St. Cumberland Resort, Mountjoy Pde. Jan: Pier to Pub Swim; Surf to Mountain Foot Race. **In the area:** Angahook–Lorne State

Park, surrounding town; many walking tracks, including one to Kalimna and Phantom waterfalls from Sheoak Picnic area, about 4 km from town. Scenic drives, west in the Otway Ranges; to south-west along Great Ocean Rd. Allenvale, 2 km W, walking. Mt Defiance, 10 km SW. Wye River, 17 km SW, fishing, surfing, limited accommodation. Cumberland River Valley, 4 km S, walking tracks, camping ground. Erskine falls and rapids, 8 km N. Gentle Annie Berry Gardens, 26 km NW, via Deans Marsh. **Tourist information:** 144 Mountjoy Pde; (052) 89 1036. **Accommodation:** 2 hotels, 5 motels, 1 B&B, 1 hostel, 5 cara./camp. parks. **See also:** The Great Ocean Road.
MAP REF. 210 D12, 217 A13, 227 P10

Macedon   Pop. 1137

The town of Macedon is situated off the Calder Hwy, an hour from Melbourne. Large sections of the area were destroyed by bushfires in 1983. Today it is difficult to imagine this devastation, as the residents have rebuilt homes and re-established the beautiful gardens for which the area is renowned. Mount Macedon, formed by volcanic activity, is 1011 m high. At its summit is the memorial cross, erected in honour of those who died in World War I. The small town of Mount Macedon is 3 km NE. **Of interest:** Lavender Place, Mt Macedon Rd, Mount Macedon; art and craft. New Years Day: Hanging Rock Picnic Race Meeting. Nov.: Mt Macedon Festival. **In the area:** Several gardens open spring and autumn. Wineries incl.: Hanging Rock near Hanging Rock, 8 km NW; Cope–Williams Vineyards, Romsey, 21 km NE, and Lancefield; Cleveland Winery, 30 km NE. Woodend, 10 km N, is an attractive old town at the safe 'wood's end' of the dangerous 'Black Forest' where more than a century ago, brigands lurked! Hanging Rock, made famous by Joan Lindsay's story, and the subsequent film, 7 km NE of Woodend; massive rock formation, ideal for climbing, koalas, picnic reserve at base. Trentham, potato-growing area and former goldmining town, 25 km W of Woodend, historic foundry; crafts at Jargon; Minifie's Berry Farm, pick your own in season. **Tourist information:** Woodend Information Centre; (054) 27 2033. **Accommodation:** 3 hotels, 2 motels, 6 B&B, 1 cara. park.
MAP REF. 210 H3, 224 A2, 232 D13

The Grampians

The massive sandstone ranges of the Grampians in Western Victoria provide some of the State's most spectacular scenery. Rising in peaks to heights of over 1000 metres, they form the western extremity of the Great Dividing Range. Major Mitchell climbed and named the highest peak, Mt William, in July 1836 and gave the name 'The Grampians' to the ranges because they reminded him of the Grampians in his native Scotland.

On 1 July 1984 these rugged mountain ranges became a national park. It is a superb area for scenic drives on good roads; bushwalking and rock climbing are also popular. The Western and Northern Grampians have Aboriginal rock-art sites. Lake Bellfield provides for sailing and rowing, and there is trout fishing in the lake and in Fyans Creek.

There is plenty of wildlife to be seen: koalas and kangaroos are numerous, and echidnas, possums and platypuses can be found, while more than 100 bird species have been identified.

Apart from their scenic grandeur, the Grampians are best known for the beauty and variety of their wildflowers. There are more than 1000 species of ferns and flowering plants native to the region and they are at their most colourful from August to November. The Halls Gap Wildflower Exhibition is held annually in October.

Halls Gap, which takes its name from a pioneer pastoralist who settled in the eastern Grampians in the early 1840s, is the focal point of the area; its wide variety of accommodation includes motels, guest houses, bed-and-breakfast, holiday flats, cottages and cabins, a youth hostel and caravan and camping parks.

For further information, contact Stawell and Grampians Tourism Information Centre, 54 Western Hwy, West Stawell; (053) 58 2314, or the Halls Gap Tourist Information Centre, Grampians Rd, Halls Gap; (053) 58 2823, or the Grampians National Park Visitors Centre, Grampians Rd, Halls Gap; (053) 56 4381. **See also:** Entry for Halls Gap in A–Z listing.

Maffra–Heyfield
Pop. 3879, 1614
The Shire of Maffra includes both these towns and extends from the farming lands of the Macalister Irrigation Area north to the mountain scenery of the Great Dividing Range. **Of interest:** Maffra Sugar Beet Museum, River St. All Seasons Herb Gardens, Foster St. Jan.: Heyfield Timber Festival. March: Harvest Festival. **In the area:** Lake Glenmaggie, 11 km N of Heyfield, popular water sports venue, camping facilities. Forest road north (closed in winter), follows Macalister Valley to Licola (49 km from Heyfield), or to Jamieson, (147 km); spectacular scenery; leads to Mt Tamboritha (20 km N of Licola) and Mt Howitt (50 km); access to alpine country and snowfields. Road north from Maffra, via Briagalong (14 km), leads over Dargo High Plains, follows Freestone Creek; Blue Pool and Quarries for swimming. Lake Tarli Karng, in Alpine National Park, 60 km NE of Licola, major focus for bushwalking in the park. Trail-riding and horseback tours from Valencia Creek, 17 km N of Maffra, and from Licola. Historic hotel, art and craft shops and Avonlea Gardens at Briagalong. **Tourist information:** Princes Hwy, Sale; (051) 44 1108. **Accommodation:** Maffra: 3 hotels, 1 motel, 1 B&B, 1 cara./camp. park. Heyfield: 2 hotels, 1 motel. MAP REF. 225 L5, 225 M5

Maldon
Pop. 1174
The National Trust has declared Maldon the 'First Notable Town' in Australia, on the basis that no other town has such an interesting collection of 19th-century buildings, nor such a collection of European trees. Situated 20 km NW of Castlemaine in central Victoria, Maldon is very popular with tourists, especially during the Maldon Easter Fair, and in spring when the wildflowers are in bloom. The deep reef goldmines were among Victoria's richest, and at one stage 20 000 men worked on the nearby Tarrangower diggings. Enthusiasts still search for gold in the area. **Of interest:** Anzac Hill, southern end of High St, good view of town. Many notable buildings, mostly constructed of local stone: Maldon Hospital (1860), cnr Adair and Chapel Sts; Post Office (1870), High St; old council offices, High St (now folk museum); Dabb's General Store in Main St, old storefront faithfully restored. National Trust properties: former Denominational (Penny) School, Welsh Congregational Church, cnr Camp and Church Sts; Cumquat Tea Rooms, High St. The Beehive Chimney (1862), south end of Church St. Castlemaine and Maldon Preservation Society runs steam trains from railway station, Hornsby St, Sun. Town walking tour leaflet available. Feb.: Camp Draft. Oct.: Vintage Car Hill Climb. **In the area:** Delightful bushwalks and intriguing rock formations. Panoramic views from Mt Tarrangower Lookout Tower, 2 km W. Carmen's Tunnel, 2 km SW, vivid reminder of hardships of goldmining days. Cairn Curran Reservoir, 10 km SW, water sports, fishing, picnics, sailing club near spillway. To north-east, goldmining dredge beside road to Bendigo. Nuggetty Ranges and Mt Moorol, 2 km N. To northwest, Tarnagulla (38 km), Dunolly (37 km) and Bealiba (58 km), all former gold settlements. **Tourist information:** High St; (054) 75 2569. **Accommodation:** 2 motels, 2 cara./ camp. parks. **See also:** The Golden Age.
MAP REF. 221 O4, 229 P11, 232 B10

Mallacoota
Pop. 961
On the Gippsland coast, at the mouth of a deep inlet of the same name, Mallacoota is a seaside and fishing township and a popular holiday centre. It offers the Croajingolong National Park, which surrounds the town, as well as beaches and fishing (Mallacoota's specialties are oysters and abalone). Bushwalking and birdwatching are also popular. Easter: Carnival. **In the area:** Lake and river cruises. Gipsy Point, 16 km N, set in attractive countryside. Genoa, 24 km NW, on Princes Hwy, last town before entering NSW. Nearby Genoa Peak, magnificent views. Bastion Point and Betka surfing beaches. **Tourist information:** 57 Maurice Ave; (051) 58 0788. **Accommodation:** Mallacoota: 3 motels, 4 cara./camp. parks. Genoa: 1

motel, 2 cara./camp. parks. **See also:** National Parks.
MAP REF. 119 F13, 235 O11

Mansfield
Pop. 2178

A popular inland resort at the junction of the Midland and Maroondah Hwys, Mansfield is 3 km E of the northern arm of Eildon Weir. It is the nearest sizeable town to Mt Buller Alpine Village and Mt Stirling. **Of interest:** At junct. of High St and Midland Hwy, monument to three police officers shot by Ned Kelly at Stringybark Creek, near Tolmie, 1878; graves in Mansfield cemetery. Highton Manor (1896), Highton Lane. Nov.: Mountain Country Festival. **In the area:** Horse trail-riding. Road north-east over mountains to Whitfield in the King River Valley (62 km) passes through spectacular scenery. Lake William Hovell, 85 km NE, picnic/barbecue facilities, children's playground, boating, canoeing, fishing. Mt Samaria State Park, 14 km N, scenic drives, picnics, camping, bushwalking. Nearby at Lake Nillahcootie, boating, fishing, canoeing, sailing, children's adventure camp. To south, Goulburn and Jamieson Rivers; trout fishing and gold fossicking. Howqua Dale Gourmet Retreat, at Howqua, 29 km S, food weekends, sporting facilities. Historic buildings at old goldmining town of Jamieson, 37 km S, on Jamieson River. Delatite Winery, on Stoneys Rd, 7 km SE. Merrijig, 18 km SE, and Craig's Hut, at Clear Hills, 50 km E, used for filming *The Man from Snowy River*; no vehicle access to Craig's Hut in winter. Hot-air balloon flights. Alpine National Park, 60 km E, less accessible than other Victorian national parks but offers bushwalks through remote terrain. Houseboat hire on Lake Eildon. **Tourist information:** Legendary Country Tourism, 11 High St; (057) 75 1464. **Accommodation:** 3 hotels, 4 motels, 5 B&B, 2 cara./camp. parks. **See also:** Wine Regions.
MAP REF. 211 R1, 222 C10, 233 K10

Maryborough
Pop. 7623

First sheep farming, then the gold rush, contributed to the development of this small city on the northern slopes of the Great Dividing Range, 70 km N of Ballarat. Maryborough is in the centre of an agricultural and forest area and is highly industrialised. **Of interest:** Pioneer Memorial Tower, Bristol Hill. Worsley Cottage (1894), Palmerston St, historical museum. Maryborough railway station,

Victoria St, houses Maryborough Development Promotions, displays. Imposing Civic Square buildings, Clarendon St. Princes Park, Park Rd, good sports facilities. Maryborough Highland Gathering on New Year's Day. Sept.: Golden Wattle Festival. Nov.: 3-day Energy Breakthrough, energy expo, machine races, team competitions, music, food, entertainment. **In the area:** Aboriginal wells, 4 km S. Once-thriving gold towns of Bowenvale–Timor (6 km), Dunolly (23 km) and Tarnagulla (37 km) are to the north. **Tourist information:** Cnr Tuaggra and Alma Sts; (054) 60 4509. **Accommodation:** 1 hotel/motel, 6 motels, 2 B&B, 1 cara./camp. park, 1 cara. park.
MAP REF. 221 L5, 229 O12

Marysville
Pop. 662

The peaceful and attractive sub-alpine town of Marysville, which owes its existence first to gold as it was on the route to the Woods Point goldfields, and later to timber milling, is 37 km NE of Healesville, off the Maroondah Hwy. The town is surrounded by attractive forest-clad mountain country and is a popular resort all year. **Of interest:** Hidden Talents, Murchison St. Goulds Sawmill, Racecourse Rd, open. Nicholl's Lookout, Cumberland Rd, excellent views. Gallipoli Park, Murchison St, historic display within park. Golf. **In the area:** Numerous bushwalking tracks lead to beauty spots, incl. 4-km loop walk in Cumberland Memorial Scenic Reserve, 16 km E; 2-hr walk to Keppel's Lookout; 90-min. walk to Mt Gordon; 2-hr walk to Steavenson Falls (illuminated at night). Lake Mountain, 19 km E, accessible walking and cross-country skiing trails, tobogganing. Big River State Forest, 30 km E, camping, fishing, hunting, trail-bike riding, gold fossicking. Lake Eildon, 46 km NE, and Fraser National Park, 59 km NE, easy driving distance. Buxton Camel Farm, Buxton Trout Farm and Australian Bush Pioneer's Farm, at foot of Mt Cathedral, 10 km N. **Tourist information:** The Old Yarra Track Shoppe, 18 Murchison St; (059) 63 3453. **Accommodation:** 1 hotel, 1 hotel/motel, 3 motels, 3 B&B, 1 cara./camp. park.
MAP REF. 211 P4, 214 I4, 224 G2, 233 J13

Milawa–Oxley
Pop. 120

On what is known as the Snow Road, Milawa, 16 km SE of Wangaratta, is the

home of Brown Brothers Vineyard. John Gehrig's and Read's wineries are to be found at Oxley, 4 km W, and the Markwood Estate Vineyard is 6 km E. Bogong Jack Adventures runs a range of bicycle tours from Oxley. The Snow Road links Oxley, Milawa and Markwood with Wangaratta to the west and the Ovens Hwy to the east. **Of interest:** In Snow Rd: Milawa Royal general store, light meals; Old Emu Restaurant. Milawa Mustards, off Snow Rd, specialist mustards, cottage garden. Milawa Cheese Company, Factory Rd, specialist cheeses, ploughman's lunches. **Tourist information:** Wangaratta and Region Visitors Information Centre, cnr Handley St and Tone Rd, Wangaratta; (057) 21 5711. **Accommodation:** 1 motel, 1 cara./camp. park. **See also:** Wine Regions.
MAP REF. 222 F1, 233 M6

Mildura
Pop. 23 176

Sunny mild winters and picturesque locations on the banks of the Murray make Mildura and neighbouring towns popular tourist areas. Mildura, on the Sunraysia Hwy, 557 km N of Melbourne, is a small and pleasant city that developed along with the irrigation of the area. Alfred Deakin, statesman and advocate of irrigation, persuaded the Chaffey brothers, Canadian-born irrigation experts, to visit this region. They recognised its potential and selected Mildura as the first site for development. The early days of the project were fraught with setbacks, but by 1900 the citrus-growing industry was well established and, with the locking of the Murray completed in 1928, Mildura soon became a city. **Of interest:** W.B. Chaffey, Mildura's first mayor; statue in Deakin Ave. Mildura Arts Centre, Cureton Ave; Rio Vista, original Chaffey home, now museum, colonial household items. Paddle-steamers leave from Mildura Wharf, end of Madden Ave, for trips on Murray and Darling Rivers: PS Melbourne, 2-hr round trips; PS Avoca, luncheon and dinner cruises; PS Coonawarra, 5- and 6-day cruises. Humpty Dumpty Tourist Farm, Cureton Ave. Snakes and Ladders, 17th St, popular with children. Mildura Lock Island and Weir. Other attractions incl.: Aquacoaster waterslide, cnr Seventh St and Orange Ave; Dolls on the Avenue, Benetook Ave; Pioneer Cottage, Hunter St. The Citrus Shop, Deakin Ave, educational aids, sales. March: Great Mildura

Paddleboat Race. **In the area:** Many vineyards, incl. Lindemans (largest winery in southern hemisphere), Mildura Vineyards, Stanley, Trentham Estate, Mildara Blass. Capogreco Wines, Riverside Ave, open Mon.–Sat. River Road Pottery, 10 km w. Woodsie's Gem Shop, 6 km sw. At Irymple, 6 km s, Sunbeam Dried Fruits; tours. Red Cliffs, 15 km s: important area for citrus and dried fruit industries. 'Big Lizzie' steam traction engine at Red Cliffs. Hattah–Kulkyne National Park, 70 km s, bushwalking. Yabbies at Gol Gol Fisheries, 2 km in NSW; open daily. Orange World, 6 km N in NSW, tours of citrus-growing areas. Golden River Zoo, 3 km NW, native and exotic species in natural surroundings. PS *Rothbury*, day cruises. **Tourist information:** 41 Deakin Ave; (050) 21 4424. **Accommodation:** 3 hotels, 45 motels, 25 cara./camp. parks. **See also:** The Mighty Murray; Wine Regions.
MAP REF. 126 E7, 230 G4

Moe   Pop. 17 000

Situated on the Princes Hwy, 134 km SE of Melbourne, Moe is a rapidly growing residential city in the Latrobe Valley and gateway to the alpine region. **Of interest:** Old Gippstown Pioneer Township, Lloyd St, re-creation of 19th-century community; over 30 restored buildings brought from surrounding areas; fine collection of fully restored horse-drawn vehicles; picnic/barbecue facilities, adventure playground; open daily. Cinderella Dolls, display centre, Andrew St. Trout fishing, Narracan Creek.

Picturesque race track, Waterloo Rd. March: Jazz Festival. Oct.: Moe Cup (horse racing). **In the area:** Mair's Coalville Vineyard, Moe South Road; by appt. Edward Hunter Heritage Bush reserve, 3 km s via Coalville St, 57 ha, bushland, walking tracks. Scenic road leads north-east 46 km to picturesque old mining township of Walhalla, Thomson Dam nearby, and through mountains to Jamieson, 147 km further north. Blue Rock Dam, 20 km N; fishing, swimming, sailing, picnic facilities. The Baw Baw plateau, Mt Baw Baw and Mt Saint Gwinear (for cross country and downhill skiing) are accessed 47 km N via Willow Grove. The plateau is the highest alpine point in central Gippsland and has abundant wildflowers in summer, excellent for bushwalking. **Tourist information:** Old Gippstown Pioneer Heritage Park, Lloyd St; (051) 27 6928. **Accommodation:** 3 motels, 1 hostel, 2 cara./camp. parks.
MAP REF. 211 R10, 224 I6

Morwell   Pop. 15 423

Morwell, 150 km SE of Melbourne, is situated in the heart of the Latrobe Valley. This valley contains one of the world's largest deposits of brown coal. Morwell is an industrial town with a number of secondary industries. **Of interest:** State Electricity Commission's Visitors Centre; open daily, guided tours. La Trobe Regional Gallery, Commercial Rd. **In the area:** Scenic day tours can be made from the three main cities in the Latrobe Valley: Morwell; Moe, 20 km

NW; and Traralgon, 12 km NE. Lake Narracan and the Hazelwood pondage, 5 km s; warm waters, year-round water sports, picnics. At Churchill, 10 km s, 84-ha Monash University Gippsland Campus. Morwell National Park, walking tracks, picnic facilities, 12 km s. Tarra–Bulga National Park, 47 km SE, renowned for fern glades, waterfalls, rosellas, lyrebirds, koalas. To the north, 66 km through dense mountain country, old mining township of Walhalla. Further on, Moondarra Reservoir, the beautiful Tanjil and Thomson River valleys. Views of Moe, Yallourn North and valley between Strzelecki Ranges and Baw Baw mountains at Narracan Falls, about 27 km w. **Tourist information:** Power Works Visitors Centre, Commercial Rd; (051) 35 3415. **Accommodation:** 2 hotels, 9 motels, 2 cara./camp. parks.
MAP REF. 225 J7

Mount Beauty   Pop. 1837

Situated in the Upper Kiewa Valley, 344 km NE of Melbourne, Mount Beauty was originally an accommodation town for workers on the Kiewa Hydro-electric Scheme in the 1940s. An ideal holiday centre, the town lies at the foot of Mount Bogong, Victoria's highest mountain (1986 m). **Of interest:** At Tourist Information: Heritage Museum, local craft, woodworker in action. Leaflets outlining walks, excursions and other activities, from various tourist information centres and National Parks Office. McKay Creek power station, access from Lakeside Ave, 80 m underground, tours, bookings

PS Melbourne, *Murray River, Mildura*

preferred; video at Information Centre. March: Conquestathon Footraces. Aug.: 4-day Kangaroo Hoppet, cross-country ski event. **In the area:** Scenic road, 32 km SE to Falls Creek and the Bogong High Plains. Mountain-bike hire, horse-riding and 4WD tours. Excellent hang-gliding. Mount Beauty Pondage, Falls Creek Rd, 26 km S; water sports, fishing. Bogong Village, 16 km SE; walks around Lake Guy. Skiing holidays to suit both cross-country and downhill skiers available at Mount Beauty and Falls Creek. **Tourist information:** Australian High Country Visitors Centre, Kiewa Valley Hwy; (057) 54 3172. **Accommodation:** 2 hotels, 6 motels, 1 hostel, 2 cara./camp. parks.
MAP REF. 223 N5, 233 Q8, 234 C6

Murtoa   Pop. 878

Murtoa is situated on the edge of picturesque Lake Marma, 30 km E of Horsham on the Wimmera Hwy. It is in the centre of Victoria's wheat belt and with two other old wheat towns, Minyip and Rupanyup, makes up the Shire of Borung. **Of interest:** Huge wheat-storage silo. Many buildings c. 1880. Original shopping centre, c. 1900. Four-storey railway water-tower (1886), now a museum, incl. James Hill's taxidermy collection of some 500 birds, prepared between 1885 and 1930; open Sun. p.m. Lake Marma, trout and redfin fishing, caravan park on eastern side. Lake also offers birdwatching and spectacular sunsets. New Years Day: Race Meeting; 6 other meetings annually. **In the area:** Rupanyup, 16 km E; attractive old town. Barrabool Forest Reserve, 7 km S, spring wildflowers. **Tourist information:** Marma Gully Antiques, 50 Marma St; (053) 85 2422. **Accommodation:** 2 hotels, 1 cara./camp. park.
MAP REF. 228 I9

Myrtleford   Pop. 2862

On the Ovens Hwy, 45 km SE of Wangaratta, the town of Myrtleford is surrounded by an area that produces hops, tobacco, chestnuts, vegetables and wine. It also has some of the largest walnut groves in the southern hemisphere. The Ovens Valley was opened up by graziers. Later gold was discovered, and creeks there are still popular for gold panning and gem fossicking. **Of interest:** The Phoenix Tree, sculptured butt of a red gum, crafted by Hans Knorr, on highway at town entrance. Reform Hill

Snow slopes, Falls Creek

Lookout, end of Halls Rd. Jaycees Historic Park and Swing Bridge, Standish St. Many other delightful picnic spots and rest areas. March: Tobacco, Hops and Timber Festival. **In the area:** Swinburne Reserve, 5 km S on road to Bright, starting point for self-guide forest walks and fitness track; picnic facilities. Nug Nug Quarter Horse Stud and Dingo Breeding, 16 km S; coaches only, except school holidays. Red Deer and Emu Farm at Eurobin, 20 km SE off Ovens Hwy. Lake Buffalo, 25 km S, Ovens River and Buffalo River, 31 km S, good fishing. Mt Buffalo National Park and historic towns of Beechworth, Yackandandah and Bright, easy driving distance. Four-wheel-drive vehicle hire. Guided tours to hop and tobacco farms. **Tourist information:** Ponderosa Cabin, 29–31 Clyde St; (057) 52 1727. **Accommodation:** 1 hotel, 1 hotel/motel, 2 motels, 1 hostel, 2 cara./camp. parks.
MAP REF. 223 J2, 233 N7, 234 A5

Nagambie   Pop. 1215

Between Seymour and Shepparton on the Goulburn Valley Hwy, Nagambie is on the shores of Lake Nagambie, which was created by the construction of the Goulburn Weir in 1891. Rowing and yachting regattas, speedboat and water-ski tournaments are held here throughout the year. There is a 65-m water-slide at one of the swimming areas. **Of interest:** Several National Trust-classified buildings. Historical Society display of colonial Victoriana and

early horsedrawn vehicles, in old Shire Offices, High St. Pottery, art and craft shops. The Nut House, High St, Australian nuts, Australian-made products. March: Goulburn Valley Vintage Festival. Boxing Day: Rowing Regatta. **In the area:** Chateau Tahbilk Winery, 6 km SW, National Trust-classified buildings. Mitchelton Winery, 10 km SW, off Goulburn Valley Hwy, 60-m observation tower, licensed restaurant, open daily. Scenic river cruises on the Goulburn River from Mitchelton's; check times. Osicka's Vineyard, Graytown, 24 km W. David Traeger Wines, on Goulburn Valley Hwy, northern end of town. Longleat Winery, 23 km N, near Murchison Also at Murchison: Italian War Memorial and chapel. Meteorite Park, site of 1969 meteorite fall. Days Mill, flour mill with buildings dating from 1865, 5 km S of Murchison. **Tourist information:** 145 High St; (057) 94 2647. **Accommodation:** 5 motels, 1 B&B, 2 cara./camp. parks. **See also:** Wine Regions.
MAP REF. 232 G9

Natimuk   Pop. 464

This Wimmera town, 27 km W of Horsham, is close to the striking Mt Arapiles, a 356-m sandstone monolith that has been described as 'Victoria's Ayers Rock'. This monolith is in the Mount Arapiles–Tooan State Park. A drive to the summit reveals a scenic lookout and a telecommunications relay station. The mountain was first climbed by Major Mitchell in 1836 and is popular with rock-climbing enthusiasts. **Of interest:** Arapiles Historical Society museum in old courthouse, Main St. Nov.: Harrow national Bush Billycart Championships. **In the area:** Lake Natimuk, 2 km N, water sports. Duffholme Cabins and Museum, 21 km W. Mount Arapiles–Tooan State Park, 12 km SW. **Tourist information:** Natimuk Hotel, Main St; (053) 87 1300. **Accommodation:** 1 hotel, 1 cara./camp. park.
MAP REF. 228 F10

Nhill   Pop. 1891

The name of this town is possibly derived from the Aboriginal word *nyell*, meaning 'white mist on water'. A small wheat town on the Western Hwy, exactly halfway between Melbourne and Adelaide, it claims to have the largest single-bin silo in the southern hemisphere. **Of interest:** Historical Society Museum, McPherson St, open weekends, by appt.

Cottage of John Shaw Neilson, lyric poet, Shaw Neilson Park, Western Hwy. Draught Horse Memorial, Goldsworthy Park, to famous Clydesdales, indispensable in opening up Wimmera region. Nhill's Post Office, (1888), National Trust-classified. The Wagan Inn, information display, farming relics. Lowana Craft Shop, local craft, refreshments. **In the area:** Self-guide car-tour; leaflets from Tourist Information. Little Desert National Park and Little Desert Lodge, via Kiata, 23 km S. Little Desert Wildflower Exhibition in Oct. Lake Hindmarsh, 45 km NE, largest freshwater lake in Victoria. Big Desert Wilderness, via Yanac, 32 km NE, on track north to Murrayville; exploration of this remote area by walking tracks only. **Tourist information:** Victoria St; (053) 91 3086 or (053) 91 1811. **Accommodation:** 3 hotels, 5 motels, 1 cara./camp. park.
MAP REF. 228 E7

Numurkah
Pop. 3128

Numurkah, 35 km N of Shepparton on the Goulburn Valley Hwy, is only half an hour from some sandy beaches and excellent fishing spots on the Murray River. The town is in an irrigation area concentrating on dairying, and was originally developed through the Murray Valley Soldier Settlement Scheme. **Of interest:** Steam and Vintage Machinery Display, Melville St. **In the area:** Glen Arran, 4 km N, tourist farm, dairy. Monichino's Winery, Katunga, 11 km N. Ulupna Island flora and fauna reserve, near Strathmerton, 21 km N, large koala population. Red Gum Wildlife Tours of Ulupna Island. At Strathmerton: Kraft cheese factory; Spikes and Blooms cactus garden (2 ha); Coonanga Historic Homestead, blacksmith shop. Barmah Red Gum Forest, largest red gum forest in Southern Hemisphere, 40 km NW. Morgan's Beach Caravan Park, at edge of forest on bank of Murray, bushwalking, horseriding, kangaroos. Historic buildings set on banks of Broken Creek, at Nathalia, 20 km W. Wunghnu Institute Tavern 5 km S, on Goulburn Valley Hwy, restored Mechanics Institute (c. 1880). Brookfield Historic Holiday Farm and Museum, 6 km SE. **Tourist information:** Log Cabin, Saxton St; or Spikes and Blooms, Murray Valley Hwy; (058) 74 5271. **Accommodation:** 2 hotels, 2 motels, 1 cara./camp. park.
MAP REF. 127 M13, 232 H4

Ocean Grove–Barwon Heads
Pop. 10 069

At the mouth of the Barwon River, the resort of Ocean Grove offers fishing and surfing, while nearby Barwon Heads offers safe family relaxation along the shores of its protected river. Both resorts are popular in the summer months as they are the closest ocean beaches to Geelong, 22 km to the NW. **Of interest:** Ocean Grove Nature Reserve, Grubb Rd. **In the area:** Jirrahlinga Koala and Wildlife Sanctuary, Taits Rd, Barwon Heads; open daily. At Lake Connewarre, 7 km N: mangrove swamps; Lake Connewarre State Game Reserve. At Wallington, 8 km N: A Maze'N Things; Koombahla Park Equestrian Centre; Country Connection Adventure Park. **Tourist information:** A Maze'N Things, 1570 Bellarine Hwy (at Grubb Rd), Wallington; (052) 50 2669. **Accommodation:** Ocean Grove: 3 motels, 1 hotel/motel, 5 cara./camp. parks. Barwon Heads: 1 hotel, 1 motel, 2 cara./camp. parks.
MAP REF. 210 G10, 217 G8, 217 G9, 224 A7, 227 R8, 227 R9

Omeo
Pop. 274

The high plains around Omeo were opened up in 1835 when overlanders from the Monaro region moved their stock south to these lush summer pastures. Its name is an Aboriginal word meaning 'mountains', and the township is set in the heart of the Victorian Alps at an altitude of 643 m. It is used as a base for winter traffic approaching Mt Hotham from Bairnsdale, 120 km S, and for bushwalking and fishing expeditions to the Bogong High Plains in summer and autumn. **Of interest:** Omeo has suffered

several natural disasters. It was damaged by earthquakes in 1885 and 1892 and was half destroyed by the Black Friday bushfires of 1939. Nevertheless, several old buildings remaining in the area are of historic interest, some in the A.M. Pearson Historical Park, Main St, incl. old courthouse (1892), at rear of present courthouse. Also in park, log gaol (1858); stables; blacksmith's shop. Petersens Gallery, Day Ave; closed Tues. Gold panning popular along Livingstone Creek, which flows through town; pans for hire from Shire Offices. March: Race Day (horse racing). Nov.: Agricultural Show. **In the area:** Tambo River valley to south; especially beautiful in autumn. Mt Markey Winery, Cassilis Rd, Cassilis, 15 km S; open daily. Scenic road to Corryong, 148 km NE, passes Dartmouth Reservoir; difficult to negotiate in bad weather; motorists should be alert for timber trucks and wandering cattle. Alpine Aviation Joy Flights, Corryong Rd, Benarubra, 20 km N. Blue Duck Inn (1890s) is a base for fishing at Anglers Rest, 29 km NW. Omeo has a gold-rush history; high cliffs left after sluicing for gold can be seen at the Oriental Diggings, 1.5 km W on Alpine Rd. High-country horseback and 4WD tours, walking, skiing, rafting and abseiling. **Tourist information:** Octagon Bookshop, Day Ave; (051) 59 1411. **Accommodation:** 2 hotels, 1 motel, 2 B&B, 1 cara./camp. park.
MAP REF. 119 A11, 234 E8

Orbost
Pop. 2515

Situated on the banks of the Snowy River, this Gippsland timber town is on the Princes Hwy, surrounded by spectacular coastal and mountain territory. **Of**

Big Desert Wilderness, near Nhill

interest: Historical Museum, Nicholson St. Old Pump House, behind Slab Hut Information Centre (1872), hut relocated from its original site 40 km from Orbost. Rainforest Interpretation Centre, Lockiel St, audiovisual display explaining complex nature of rainforest ecology. Croajingolong Mohair Farm, Nicholson St, garments, yarns, fleeces, fabrics, leathergoods. Netherbyre Gemstone and Art Gallery, cnr Browning and Carlyle Sts. **In the area:** Beautiful Bonang Hwy, unsealed in parts, leads north through mountains to Delegate in NSW. At Bonang, 97 km NE, Aurora Mine, working goldmine, open daily; fishing; walking in Snowy River National Park (west) and Errinundra National Park (north-east), incl. rainforest boardwalk at Errinundra, 30 km SE. Tranquil Valley Tavern, on banks of Delegate River near NSW border, about 18 km N of Bonang, cabin accommodation, licensed restaurant. Spectacular road to Buchan, 58 km NW, leads to Little River Falls and McKillop's Bridge on the Snowy River. Scenic coastal drive to Marlo and Cape Conran starts just west of Orbost, returns to Princes Hwy at Cabbage Tree Creek. Cape Conran Reserve, cabin accommodation. Cabbage Tree Palms Flora Reserve, 27 km E. Coopracambra National Park, 136 km NE, near NSW border. Bemm River, on Sydenham Inlet, 57 km E, popular centre for bream anglers. Baldwin Spencer Trail, 262-km driving circuit. Croajingolong National Park, east along coast, from Sydenham Inlet to border. **Tourist information:** The Slab Hut, cnr Nicholson and Clarke Sts; (051) 54 2424. **Accommodation:** 2 hotels, 3 motels, 2 B&B, 1 cara./camp. park.
MAP REF. 119 C13, 234 I12

Ouyen   Pop. 1337
At the junction of the Calder and Mallee Hwys, Ouyen is about 100 km S of Mildura, north-east of the Big Desert area. **Of interest:** Nov.: Farmers Festival. **In the area:** Hattah–Kulkyne National Park, 34 km N, abundant wildlife, birdwatching, bushwalking, canoeing, wildflowers in spring. Murray-Sunset National Park, 60 km W; pink lakes are outstanding subjects for photography. Tag-along and 4WD tours. **Tourist information:** Resource Centre, Oke St; (050) 92 1763. **Accommodation:** 1 hotel, 2 motels, 1 cara./camp. park. **See also:** The Mallee.
MAP REF. 126 E10, 230 H9

Paynesville   Pop. 2444
A popular tourist resort 18 km from Bairnsdale on the McMillan Straits, Paynesville is a mecca for fishing and boating enthusiasts, and is noted for yachting and speedboat racing as well as water-skiing. It is also the headquarters of the Gippsland Lakes Yacht Club. **Of interest:** St Peter-by-the-Lake (1961), church incorporates seafaring symbols. Community Craft Centre, Esplanade. Captain Petries, Wellington St, mini-golf, bike hire. Market Gilsenan Reserve, 2nd Sun. in month. Easter and Christmas: Speedboat Championships. **In the area:** Rotomah Island Bird Observatory, 8 km S by boat. Ninety Mile Beach, 10 km S by boat; free punt crosses Straits to Raymond Island. Koala Reserve on Raymond Island. The Lakes National Park, to the east, 5 km by boat to Sperm Whale Head; otherwise via Loch Sport. Cruises on MV *Lakes Odyssey*. Organised scenic tours of lakes. Boat charter and hire. Dolphins in bay. **Tourist information:** Paynesville Marine Service, Esplanade; (051) 56 6554. **Accommodation:** 1 motel, 2 B&B, 5 cara./camp. parks. **See also:** Gippsland Lakes.
MAP REF. 225 P5, 234 F13

Port Albert   Pop. 307
This tiny historic town on the south-east coast, 120 km SE from Morwell, was the first established port in Victoria. Sailing boats from Europe and America once docked at the large timber jetty here. Boats from China brought thousands of Chinese to the Gippsland goldfields. Originally established for trade with Tasmania, Port Albert was the supply port for Gippsland pioneers until the railway from Melbourne to Sale was completed 1878. The timber jetty is still crowded, as it is a commercial fishing port and its sheltered waters are popular with anglers and boat owners. Some of the original stone buildings are still in use and are National Trust-classified. **Of interest:** Historic buildings in Tarraville Rd incl. original government offices and stores; Bank of Victoria (1861), housing Maritime Museum, photographs and relics of the area. Port Albert Hotel, Wharf St, first licensed in 1842, possibly the oldest hotel still operating in State. Warren Curry Art Gallery, Tarraville Rd, Australian country-town streetscapes. March: Seabank Fishing Competition. **In the area:** Christ Church at Tarraville (1856),

5 km NE, first church in Gippsland. Surfing at Woodside on Ninety Mile Beach, 34 km NE. Alberton, 8 km N, once the administrative centre of Central Gippsland. Tarra–Bulga National Park, 41 km NW. Swimming at Mann's Beach, 10 km E. Wildlife sanctuary on St Margaret Island, 12 km E. **Tourist information:** South Gippsland Tourism, Coal Creek Historical Village, cnr Sth Gippsland Hwy and Silkstone Rd, Korumburra; (056) 552233. **Accommodation:** 1 hotel/motel, 2 cara./camp. parks.
MAP REF. 225 K10

Port Campbell   Pop. 234
This small crayfishing village and seaside resort is situated in the centre of Port Campbell National Park and on a spectacular stretch of the Great Ocean Road. **Of interest:** Historical Museum, Lord St, open school holidays. Loch Ard Shipwreck Museum, Lord St. Self-guide Discovery Walk. Good fishing from rocks and pier. **In the area:** Port Campbell National Park, surrounding town, incl. world-famous Twelve Apostles and Loch Ard Gorge, 10 km SE, and London Bridge (now fallen down), 5 km W. Glenample, 12 km E on Great Ocean Rd, first homestead in area; base for salvage of Loch Ard, survivors recuperated there; check opening times. Walking tracks and historic shipwreck sites; Historic Shipwreck Trail links sites along 'Shipwreck Coast', from Princetown to Port Fairy. Otway Deer and Wildlife Park, 20 km E. **Tourist information:** National Parks Office, Morris St; (055) 98 6382. **Accommodation:** 1 hotel, 4 motels, 1 hostel, 1 cara./camp. park. **See also:** The Great Ocean Road.
MAP REF. 215 A10, 227 K10

Port Fairy   Pop. 2467
The home port for a large fishing fleet and an attractive, rambling holiday resort, Port Fairy is 29 km W of Warrnambool with both ocean and river as its borders. The town's history goes back to whaling days. At one time it was one of the largest ports in Australia. Over 50 of its small cottages and bluestone buildings have been classified by the National Trust. This charming old-world fishing village is popular with heritage lovers and holidaymakers. **Of interest:** History Centre, Gipps St, in old courthouse; several display rooms, booklet and map for Town Walk and Port Fairy Shipwreck Walk available. Battery Hill,

end Griffith St, old fort and signal station at mouth of river. National Trust classifications incl. splendid timber home of Captain Mills, Gipps St and Mott's Cottage, 5 Sackville St. Other attractive buildings: Old Caledonian Inn, Bank St; Seacombe House and ANZ Bank building, Cox St; St John's Church of England (1856), Regent St; *Gazette* Office (1849), Sackville St. Ornamental Shoe and Boot, display, Princes Hwy. Hot Glass Studio, Regent St. March: Award-winning Folk Festival. Oct.: Music Festival. **In the area:** Griffiths Island, connected to east of town by causeway, lighthouse and muttonbird rookeries; spectacular nightly return of the muttonbirds to island during Sept.–April. Other rookeries at Pea Soup Beach and South Beach, on southern edge of town; Australia's only mainland colony of muttonbirds. Lady Julia Percy Island, 10 km off coast, home for fur seals; only accessible by experienced boat operators in calm weather. Tower Hill, 14 km E, fascinating area with an extinct volcano, crater lake, islands. Mt Eccles National Park, 56 km NW. Yambuk and Lake Yambuk, 17 km W. **Tourist information:** 22 Bank St; (055) 68 2682. **Accommodation:** 7 motels, 8 cara./camp. parks. **See also:** The Great Ocean Road.
MAP REF. 226 H9

Portarlington   Pop. 2553

Named after an Irish village and with a history of Irish settlement in the area, Portarlington is a popular seaside resort on the Bellarine Peninsula, 31 km E of Geelong. It has a safe bay for children to swim, good fishing and a variety of water sports. **Of interest:** Historic flour mill (1857), Turner Crt; restored by National Trust, historical and educational display. Isadora's Coffee and Collectables, Geelong Rd. Lavender Cottage Gallery, Fenwick St. Public Reserve, Sprout St, picnic facilities. **Tourist information:** A Maze'N Things, 1570 Bellarine Hwy (at Grubb Rd), Wallington; (052) 50 2669. **Accommodation:** 1 motel, 3 cara./camp. parks.
MAP REF. 210 H9, 217 I6, 224 B6

Portland   Pop. 10 115

Portland, situated about 75 km E of the South Australian border, is the most western of Victoria's major coastal towns and is the only deep-water port between Melbourne and Adelaide. It was the first permanent settlement in

Pyramid Hill

Victoria, founded by the Henty family in 1834. Today it is an important industrial and commercial centre and a popular summer resort with beaches, surfing, fishing and outstanding coastal and forest scenery. There are a number of short walks in and around Portland; self-guide brochures at Tourist Information. For the more energetic, the 250-km Great South West Walk, a scenic circular track that begins and ends at the Centre and travels through a number of national parks and State forests to Discovery Bay and Cape Nelson, can be covered in easy stages. **Of interest:** Botanical Gardens (1857), Cliff St. More than 200 early buildings, some National Trust-classified: incl. customs house and courthouse in Cliff St; Steam Packet Hotel (1842) and Mac's Hotel in Bentinck St. History House, Charles St, historical museum in old town hall (1863); open daily. Fawthrop Lagoon, Glenelg St, 156 recorded bird species. Powerhouse Car Museum, Percy St; open daily. Portland Battery, Battery Hill, good views, picnic facilities. Portland Aluminium Smelter, guided 2-hr tours, check times. Award-winning wineries: Kingsley Winery, Bancroft St; Barrett's Gorae West Wines, Gorae Rd. Jan.: Foreshore Carnival, Fishing Competition. March: Dahlia Festival. **In the area:** Alcoa reclamation and revegetation projects. Historic homesteads: incl. Maretimo, 3

km N; Burswood, Cape Nelson Rd. Cape Nelson State Park, 11 km SW, spectacular coastal scenery and National Trust-classified lighthouse. At Cape Bridgewater, 21 km SW: petrified forest, blowholes, freshwater springs, seal caves, the Watering Place; walks to Discovery Bay and Cape Duquesne, both further west. Narrawong State Forest, 18 km NE. Caledonian Inn, Henty Hwy, 8 km N, historical displays. At Heywood, 22 km N: Cave Hill Gardens, picnic facilities; Bower Birds Nest Museum. Safe swimming and surfing. Mt Richmond National Park, 25 km NW, spring wildflowers. Lower Glenelg National Park, 44 km NW via Kentbruck: spectacular gorges, colourful wildflowers, native birds, excellent fishing, limited accommodation. Along coastal road is charming hamlet of Nelson, 70 km NW. Nearby Princess Margaret Rose Caves, tours. Tours up Glenelg River. **Tourist information:** Cliff St; (055) 23 2671 or 1800 03 5567. **Accommodation:** 10 motels, 4 B&B, 4 hostels, 7 cara./camp. parks.
MAP REF. 226 E9

Pyramid Hill   Pop. 546

A small country town some 40 km SW of Cohuna and 100 km N of Bendigo, Pyramid Hill was named for its unusually shaped hill, 187 m high. **Of interest:** Historical museum, McKay St. A climb to the top of Pyramid Hill itself (also Braille walking trail) allows scenic views of the surrounding irrigation and wheat district. **In the area:** Terrick Terrick State Forest, 11 km SE, 2833-ha Murray Pine forest reserve; numerous granite outcrops, southernmost outcrop Mitiamo Rock; picnic ground, walks, variety of birdlife, other fauna. Mt Hope, 10 km NE, named by Major Mitchell. **Tourist information:** Newsagency; (054) 55 7036. **Accommodation:** 1 hotel, 1 cara./ camp. park.
MAP REF. 126 I13, 229 P5, 232 B4

Queenscliff–Point Lonsdale
Pop. 3681

Queenscliff, 31 km E of Geelong on the Bellarine Peninsula, was established as a commercial fishing centre in the 1850s and still has a large fishing fleet based in its harbour. The town looks out across the famous and treacherous Rip at the entrance to Port Phillip Bay. **Of interest:** Queenscliff Maritime Centre, Weeroona Pde, explores town's long association

with sea, and days of sailing ships. Adjacent Marine Studies Centre, summer holiday programme for visitors. Queenscliff Fine Arts Gallery, in old Wesleyan Church, Hesse St. Hobson's Choice Gallery, Hobson St. Seaview Gallery in Seaview House, Hesse St. Many old buildings, incl. Fort Queenscliff (1882), built during the Crimean War; Black Lighthouse (1861), King St; Vue Grand Hotel, in Hesse St; Ozone and Queenscliff Hotels, Gellibrand St. Queenscliff Historical Tours leave from Queenscliff Pier. Steam train operates between Queenscliff (station in Symonds St) and Drysdale; weekends, daily in summer holidays. Regular passenger ferry service operates between Queenscliff and Portsea across bay; summer and school holidays. Vehicle and passenger ferry service between Queenscliff and Sorrento (about 45 min.); daily. 'Snorkelling with the seals'; arrange through Tourist Information. Point Lonsdale extensively developed as holiday and tourist resort; good swimming, surfing. Queenscliff Market, Symonds St, last Sun. of month, Aug.–April. Pt Lonsdale Market, Bowen Rd, 2nd Sun. in month. **In the area:** Marine life viewing at Harold Holt Marine Reserve, which includes Mud Island and coastal reserves. Lake Victoria, 1 km w of Point Lonsdale. **Tourist information:** A Maze'N Things, 1570 Bellarine Hwy (at Grubb Rd), Wallington; (052) 50 2669. **Accommodation:** Queenscliff: 3 hotels, 4 cara./camp. parks. Point Lonsdale: 2 motels, 2 cara./ camp. parks.
MAP REF. 210 H10, 212 A5, 217 I9, 224 B7

Rainbow   Pop. 587
This Wimmera township, 70 km n of Dimboola, is near Lake Hindmarsh, popular for fishing, boating and water-skiing. **Of interest:** Pascos Cash Store (1928), Federal St; original country general store. Yurunga homestead (1910), on northern edge of town, National Trust-classified, large selection of antiques, original fittings. Oct.: Iris Festival. **In the area:** Lutheran church (1901), Pella, 10 km w, old pipe organ, only 1 other of its kind in State. Lake Albacutya Park, 12 km n, camping facilities. Wyperfeld National Park, 30 km n, via sealed road north from Yaapeet. **Tourist information:** Shire of Dimboola, 10 Roy St, Jeparit; (053) 97 2070.

Accommodation: 2 hotels, 1 motel, 1 cara./camp. park.
MAP REF. 126 D13, 228 F4

Robinvale   Pop. 1795
This small, well-laid-out town on the NSW border, 80 km se of Mildura, is almost entirely surrounded by bends in the Murray River, and the surrounding area is ideal for the production of citrus, dried fruit and wine grapes. It is a picturesque town, and water sports and fishing are popular along the river. **Of interest:** In Moore St: McWilliams Wines; Lexia Room, historical exhibits. **In the area:** Euston weir and lock on Murray, 2.5 km downstream. Robinvale Wines, Greek-style winery, 5 km s on Sea Lake road. Kyndalyn Park almond farm, 23 km se of Robinvale. Hattah–Kulkyne National Park, 66 km sw. **Tourist information:** Tourist Information Centre, Bromley Rd, Robinvale; (050) 26 1388. **Accommodation:** 1 hotel, 3 motels, 2 cara./camp. parks. **See also:** Wine Regions.
MAP REF. 126 F8, 231 J6

Rochester   Pop. 2527
On the Campaspe River, 28 km s of Echuca, Rochester is the centre for a rich dairying and tomato-growing area. A small, busy town, it has some attractive older buildings and boasts the largest dairy factory in Australia. **Of interest:** Museum, Moore St; open Sun., public holidays. Opposite, statue of Sir Hubert Opperman, champion cyclist. Historical Plaque Trail. **In the area:** Random House homestead, amid 4 ha of gardens beside river in Bridge Rd, on eastern edge of town. Campaspe Siphon, 3 km n, engineering achievement, where the Waranga–Mallee irrigation channel runs under the Campaspe River. District channels are popular with anglers; plentiful cod and bream. Field's Cactus Farm near Tennyson, 18 km nw. Pleasant lakes in district, popular for fishing and water sports; incl. Greens Lake and Lake Cooper, 14 km se. Scenic Mt Camel Range 20 km se, attracts gem fossickers. **Tourist information:** Railway Station, Moore St; (054) 84 1860. **Accommodation:** 3 hotels, 1 motel, 1 cara./camp. park.
MAP REF. 232 E6

Romsey   Pop. 2033
Romsey, 7 km s of Lancefield, was settled in the mid 1850s and possesses some

excellent Victorian architecture. **Of interest:** Historic Glenfern Horse Stud, Glenfern Rd. **In the area:** Cope-Williams Romsey Vineyard, Glenfern Rd. Mintaro (1882), at nearby Monegeetta: built by Captain Gardiner; smaller replica of Melbourne's Government House. Huntingdon, just north of Romsey township. The Chase at Monegeetta North. Tourist information: Centre Vic Motor Inn, Main Rd, Lancefield; (054) 29 1777. **Accommodation:** 1 hotel.
MAP REF. 210 I3, 224 B1, 232 E12

Rushworth   Pop. 1012
Rushworth, 20 km west of Murchison, off the Goulburn Valley Hwy, still shows traces of its gold-rush days. **Of interest:** Many of the town's attractive original buildings still stand, witnesses to the days when Rushworth was the commercial centre for the surrounding mining district. Nearly all the buildings in High St are National Trust-classified: St Pauls Church of England, band rotunda, former Imperial Hotel (now a private residence), Glasgow Buildings and the Whistle Stop. History Museum in Mechanics Institute (1913), High St; by appt. **In the area:** Rushworth State Forest, 3 km s. 24 300 ha of ironbark forest, largest natural ironbark forest in world. Whroo Historic Area, 7 km s, Balaclava Hill Open Cut Goldmine, Whroo Cemetery, Aboriginal Waterhole, all with visitor access; walking tracks. Further south, remnants of deserted goldmining towns Bailieston, Angustown and Graytown. Longleat Winery and Campbell's Bend picnic reserve, 20 km e. At Murchison, 21 km e, Meteorite Park, site of meteorite fall 1969. Waranga Basin, 6 km ne, water sports, fishing, camping, excellent picnic facilities. **Tourist information:** Guided Tours of Victoria, 31 High St; (058) 56 1612. **Accommodation:** 1 hotel, 1 hotel/ motel, 2 cara./camp. parks.
MAP REF. 232 F7

Rutherglen   Pop. 1876
Rutherglen is the centre of one of the most important winegrowing areas in Victoria. There is a cluster of vineyards surrounding the town, with winegrowing country stretching south to the Milawa area. Most wineries reflect their history; of particular interest is the National Trust-classified winery building at All Saints, 10 km nw. Other wineries include Anderson's, Bullers, Campbells, Chambers, Cofield, Fairfield, Gehrig Brothers,

The Mighty Murray

As a present-day explorer, a trip following the course of the Murray gives you a chance to discover a rich cross-section of Australian country and history, as well as the infinite variety of natural beauty and wildlife the river itself supports.

The Source

The Murray has its source on the slopes of Mount Pilot, high in the Alps. Here it is just a gurgling mountain stream, rushing through some breathtaking mountain scenery. This is the area of the Snowy Mountains Scheme and the great Australian snowfields.

The Upper Murray

The upper reaches of the river flows through the scenic area around **Jingellic** and **Walwa** and on to the beautiful Lake Hume near **Albury** and **Wodonga** before continuing past **Corowa**, the birthplace of Federation, and into Lake Mulwala.

Lakes, Beaches and Red Gums

As it flows from the aquatic playgrounds of Lakes Hume and Mulwala, the Murray becomes a wide and splendid river. Lined with magnificent red gums, in the region around **Cobram**, the riverbanks are transformed into wide sandy beaches. This is ideal holiday country with pleasant resort towns: **Yarrawonga–Mulwala, Barooga** and **Tocumwal**.

Wine Country

Victoria's main winegrowing area is centred around **Rutherglen** and extends to the wineries of Cobram and the Ovens and Goulburn Valleys. The wineries welcome visitors and many offer conducted tours.

The Heyday of the Riverboats

Famous river towns like **Echuca, Swan Hill** and **Wentworth** have carefully preserved much of the history of the colourful riverboat era. The Port of Echuca, the Swan Hill Pioneer Settlement and the historic Murray Downs homestead are a must if you are in the area. Children especially will delight in the 'living museum', where original buildings, paddle-steamers and old wharves have been restored.

Wildlife

The Murray's abundant bird and animal life is protected in a number of sanctuaries and reserves stretching from the banks of the river. Spoonbills, herons, eagles, harriers and kites are plentiful. Near Picnic Point in the Moira State Forest, near **Mathoura**, waterbirds and wildlife abound and can be seen from the observatory in this beautiful red gum forest. At **Kerang**, which lies at the beginning of a chain of lakes and marshes, you can see huge breeding grounds for the splendid ibis. **Kyabram** has a famous community-owned fauna and waterfowl park which is open daily, and almost all of Gunbower Island is a protected sanctuary for wildlife.

Sunraysia

The beautiful climate of **Mildura** supports flourishing citrus and winegrowing industries as well as attracting countless holidaymakers to the Sunraysia area during both the summer and winter seasons.

Upstream is **Red Cliffs**, a town founded after World War I by returned soldiers, who turned it into a model irrigation town, and the surrounding areas into prosperous winelands. At the junction of the Murray and the Darling lies **Wentworth**, one of the oldest of the river towns, with an historic gaol and the beautifully preserved paddle-steamer *Ruby*. From Wentworth, holidaymakers can cruise along the Darling River in MV *Loyalty*.

Riverland

The Murray crosses into South Australia and at **Renmark** begins its splendid flow down to its mouth at Lake Alexandrina. The banks are lined with such historic river towns as **Renmark, Morgan** and **Murray Bridge. Goolwa** at its mouth has a strong tradition of shipbuilding, originating from the busy riverboat days. Renmark, like Mildura, is famous for its year-round sunshine. All these towns make the Riverland an attractive and interesting place for a holiday. This South Australian stretch of the Murray offers splendid river scenery and birdlife, excellent fishing and water sports and the chance to enjoy the many wineries in the area.

Further information is available from the tourist information centres in the various towns along the river, including Swan Hill; (050) 32 3033, Mildura; (050) 21 4424, Cobram; (058) 72 2132, Echuca–Moama; (054) 80 7555, or Yarrawonga–Mulwala; (057) 44 1989. **See also**: Individual town entries in A–Z listing.

Red gums, Murray River

Jones, Morris's, Mount Prior, Pfeiffers, Stanton and Killeen, and St Leonards. March: 3-day Tastes of Rutherglen. June: 3-day Winery Walkabout Weekend **Of interest:** Walkabout Cellars, Main St; open daily. **In the area:** The House (1882) at Mount Prior Vineyard, 14 km NE, now a guest house. Old Customs House at Wahgunyah, 10 km NW, relic of days when duty was payable on goods coming from NSW. History walk at Wahgunyah traces area's beginnings. Rutherglen is base for day trips to Albury–Wodonga, Yarrawonga, Lake Mulwala, Corowa, Beechworth, Bright, Mt Buffalo. Lake Moodemere, 8 km W, water sports, fauna sanctuary nearby. **Tourist information:** Walkabout Cellar, 84 Main St; (060) 32 9784. **Accommodation:** 2 hotels, 4 motels, 3 B&B, 1 cara./camp. park. **See also:** The Mighty Murray; Wine Regions.
MAP REF. 127 O13, 233 M4

St Arnaud   Pop. 2741
This old goldmining town is on the Sunraysia Hwy between Donald and Avoca and is surrounded by forest and hill country. Many of the town's historic iron-lacework decorated buildings are National Trust-classified. **Of interest:** Josephine Coppens Gallery, Napier St. Squash, basketball, badminton, table tennis and indoor tennis facilities at sports stadium. Queen Mary Gardens, Kings Ave, pleasant site for picnics. Worm Farm, Millet St. Oct.: Agricultural Show. **In the area:** Good fishing in Avoca River and at Teddington Reservoir, 28 km S. St Peter's Church (1869), Carapooee, 11 km SE, made of pebbles. Melville Caves, 38 km E, between St Arnaud and Inglewood, famous as haunt of bushranger Captain Melville, picnic facilities nearby. At Lake Batyo Catyo, 35 km NW, fishing, water sports, camping. **Tourist information:** Josephine Coppens Gallery, 2 Napier St; (054) 95 2313. **Accommodation:** 4 hotels, 3 motels, 1 B&B, 1 cara./camp. park.
MAP REF. 229 L9

St Leonards   Pop. 1206
A small beach resort, 11 km SE of Portarlington on the Bellarine Peninsula, St Leonards has excellent coastal fishing, calm waters for boating and yachting, and is popular for family summer holidays. **Of interest:** Edwards Point Wildlife Reserve, Beach Rd, varied birdlife, picnic facilities. Memorial on The Esplanade commemorates landing by Matthew Flinders in 1802 and John Batman and his party in 1835. **Tourist information:** A Maze'N Things, 1570 Bellarine Hwy (at Grubb Rd), Wallington; (052) 50 2669. **Accommodation:** 1 hotel, 2 cara./camp. parks.
MAP REF. 210 I9, 212 B2, 217 I7, 224 B6

Sale   Pop. 13 858
Sale is the main administrative city in Gippsland. In nearby Bass Strait, there is a concentration of offshore oil development. Just over 200 km E of Melbourne on the Princes Hwy, Sale is convenient for exploration of the whole Gippsland Lakes area, which extends from Wilsons Promontory to Lakes Entrance, and is bordered to the north by the foothills and mountains of the Great Divide and most of the way along the coast by the famous Ninety Mile Beach. **Of interest:** Unique art of Annemieke Mein, wildlife-in-textiles artist, at Central Gippsland Tourism, on Princes Hwy at western approach to city. Port of Sale, thriving during the days of the paddle-steamers, picnic facilities, boat-launching ramps. Cruises from here through 400-sq-km lakes system. Lake Guthridge, on Foster St in city centre, popular picnic spot, fauna park, adventure playground. Historical Museum, Foster St. Attractive buildings: Our Lady of Sion Convent; clock tower; Victoria Hall; Criterion Hotel, beautiful lacework verandahs. RAAF base, Raglan St, home of the famous Roulettes aerobatic team. Sale Regional Arts Centre, Foster St. Pedestrian Mall, cnr Cunningham and Raymond Sts; local art, incl. Annemieke Mein bronzes. Sale Common and State Game Refuge, on southern edge of town; protected wetlands area, boardwalk. March: Sale Cup (horse racing). Nov.: Agricultural Show. **In the area:** To north west, towns of Maffra and Heyfield (18 km), in intensively cultivated country, and Lake Glenmaggie, 6 km N of Heyfield. Road from Stratford, 18 km N, leads across Dargo High Plains to Mt Hotham; scenic drive through high country. Australian Wildlife Gallery, 15 km W of Stratford; paintings and sculptures of artists Dawn and Chris Stubbs. Further on, Black Cockatoo Pottery. Seaspray, on Ninety Mile Beach, 32 km S; excellent surfing and fishing; also Golden and Paradise Beaches, 35 km from Sale, and Loch Sport, another 30 km. Nearby, The Lakes National Park and Rotamah Island Bird Observatory, 15 km from Loch Sport. Marlay Point, on shores of Lake Wellington, 25 km E; extensive launching facilities. Yacht club here sponsors overnight yacht race to Paynesville each March. Popular fishing rivers include the Avon, close to Marlay Point, and the Macalister, Thomson and Latrobe, especially at Swing Bridge (1883), 5 km S of Sale. Holey Plains State Park, 14 km SW, wildlife, wildflowers. **Tourist information:** Central Gippsland Tourism, Princes Hwy; (051) 44 1108. **Accommodation:** 9 motels, 2 B&B, 2 cara./ camp. parks. **See also:** Gippsland Lakes.
MAP REF. 225 M6

Seymour   Pop. 6558
On the Goulburn River, at the junction of the Goulburn Valley Hwy and Hume Fwy, Seymour is a busy commercial, industrial and agricultural town. The area was recommended by Lord Kitchener during his visit in 1909 as being suitable for a military base. Nearby Puckapunyal was an important training place for troops during World War II and is still a major army base. **Of interest:** In Emily St: Royal Hotel, featured in Russell Drysdale's famous 1941 painting, Moody's Pub; Studio Roest Gallery, fine art, restaurant; Somerset Crossing Vineyard and restaurant; Old Court House Craft Shop. Goulburn Park, cnr Progress and Guild Sts, picnic and swimming areas, caravan park adj. Old Goulburn Bridge (1891), at end of Emily St, preserved as historic relic. Steam Train Preservation Society; rides Sun. by appt. Feb.: Alternative Farming Expo. March: Rafting Festival. **In the area:** Mitchelton and Chateau Tahbilk Vineyards, near Nagambie, 23 km N. Other wineries incl.: Somerset Crossing Vineyards, 2 km S, Hankin's Wines, 5 km NW on Northwood Rd, Hayward's Winery, 12 km SE near Trawool. Army Tank and Transport Museum at Puckapunyal, 10 km W. Trawool Valley Angora Stud and Tearooms, 11 km SE. Spotted Jumbuk, Highland Rd, 5 km E; spotted sheep. Capalba Park Alpacas, on Kobyboyne Rd, 11 km E. **Tourist information:** Somerset Winery, Emily St; (057) 92 2445, or Nagambie Tourist Centre, 320 High St, Nagambie; (057) 94 2647. **Accommodation:** 5 motels, 3 cara./camp. parks. **See also:** Wine Regions.
MAP REF. 211 L1, 232 G10

Shepparton–Mooroopna

Pop. 30 511

The 'capital' of the rich Goulburn Valley, this thriving, well-developed city, now known as The Solar City, 175 km N of Melbourne, has 4000 ha of orchards within a 10-km radius and 4000 ha of market gardens along the river valley nearby. The area is irrigated by the Goulburn Irrigation Scheme and is on the junction of the Goulburn and Broken Rivers. The central shopping area of Shepparton is surrounded by 68 ha of parkland, incl. an open-air music bowl and a Civic Centre housing an art gallery, town hall, theatre and municipal centre. **Of interest:** Solar display, Visitors Centre, Wyndham St. Art gallery, Civic Centre, Welsford St, Australian paintings, large range Australian ceramics. On Parkside Dr, International Village and Aboriginal Keeping Place, tourist, educational and cultural centre. Historical Museum, in Historical Precinct, High St, open Sun. p.m. and by appt for coaches. Redbyrne Pottery, Old Dookie Rd, variety of local pottery, ceramics made on premises. Victoria Park Lake, Tom Collins Dr, yachting, water sports, playground, caravan park. SPC, Andrew Fairley Ave, largest cannery in southern hemisphere; guided tours during fruit season, Jan.–April. Lemnos–Campbells soup cannery and Ardmona fruit cannery at Mooroopna. All 3 have direct sales. Driver Education Centre of Australia, Wanganui Rd. Reedy Swamp Walk, at end of Wanganui Rd, wetland area, abundant and varied birdlife. Fruit Connection, at rest stop on causeway between towns, crafts, wines, walks. Nov.: Strawberry Festival. **In the area:** Mud Factory Pottery, 6 km S on Goulburn Valley Hwy. At Kialla, 5 km SE: Boxwood Pottery, Elm Vale Nursery. Several vineyards, incl. Chateau Tahbilk (1860), 36 km S on Goulburn Valley Hwy, near Nagambie; recorded by National Trust. Historic Brookfield Homestead, 20 km N on Goulburn Valley Hwy, old farm machinery, shearing sheds; by appt. Victoria's Irrigation Research Institute, east of Tatura, 16 km W of Shepparton. **Tourist information:** 534 Wyndham St, Shepparton; (058) 31 4400 or 1800 80 8839. **Accommodation:** Shepparton: 4 hotels, 18 motels, 1 B&B, 6 cara./camp. parks. Mooroopna: 4 motels, 5 cara./camp. parks. **See also:** Wine Regions.
MAP REF. 232 H6

Museum, Shepparton

Skipton
Pop. 462

This township on the Glenelg Hwy, south-west of Ballarat, lies in an important pastoral and agricultural district. The town was a major centre for merino sheep sales in the 1850s. Former Premier of Victoria, Sir Henry Bolte, was born in the area. **Of interest:** Eel factory: eels netted in region, snap-frozen and exported, mainly to Germany. Adjacent to eel factory, Gibson's Doll Display. Bluestone Presbyterian Church, National Trust-classified. Nov.: Lake Goldsmith Steam Rally, Art Show. **In the area:** Mooromong, 11 km NW, notable historic homestead, property donated to National Trust by D.J.S. and C. Mackinnon (formerly Claire Adams, silent movie star); open by appt and on National Trust open days; accommodation available in converted shearers' quarters. Mt Widderin Cave, 6 km S, volcanic cave with large underground chamber; tours by appt. Kaolin Mine, 10 km E. **Tourist information:** Skipton Hotel, Glenelg Hwy; (053) 40 2111, or Roadhouse, Glenelg Hwy; (053) 40 2131. **Accommodation:** 1 hotel.
MAP REF. 220 H13, 227 M4

Stawell
Pop. 6339

North-east of Halls Gap and 123 km NW of Ballarat on the Western Hwy, Stawell is well sited for tours to the northern Grampians. It is the home of the Stawell Easter Gift, Australia's most famous professional foot race. **Of interest:** Stawell Gift Hall of Fame Museum, in Athletic Club, Central Park, cnr Seaby and Napier Sts, history of foot race. Leisure Centre, heated indoor pool, Haston St. Big Hill, local landmark and goldmining site, Pioneers Lookout at summit, indicates positions of famous mines. Casper's World in Miniature Tourist Park, London Rd: re-creation of scenes in Australia and Pacific countries, scale working models, dioramas, commentaries; open daily. Doll and Toy Museum, Main St, private collection; open Wed.–Sun. p.m. Pleasant Creek Courthouse Museum, Western Hwy. Easter: Easter Gift (professional foot race), Grampians Highland and National Dancing Club Championships. **In the area:** Joyflights and balloon flights. Bunjil's Shelter, Aboriginal rock paintings in ochre, off Pomonal Rd, 11 km S. The Sisters Rocks: huge granite tors beside Western Hwy, 3 km SE; saved from destruction in 1867 by a local resident, who bought and fenced off land. Wineries at Great Western, Ararat and Halls Gap. Great Western, 14 km SE, picturesque wine village, hotel. Goldmining at Stawell Gold Mine, 2.5 km E; viewing areas off Reefs Rd. Overdale Station, Landsborough Rd, 10 km E, guided tours during school holidays, farm holidays available. Tottington Woolshed, National Trust property, rare example of 19th-century woolshed, 55 km NE on road to St Arnaud. Deep Lead Flora and Fauna Reserve, 6 km W, off Western Hwy. Excellent lakes for all water sports incl. Lake Fyans, 17 km SW, picnic and camping facilities; Lake Lonsdale, 12 km NW; Lake Wartook, in National Park, 60 km W. **Tourist information:** 54 Western Hwy; (053) 58 2314, (053) 58 2823. **Accommodation:** 1 hotel, 8 motels, 3 B&B, 2 cara./camp.

parks. **See also:** The Grampians; The Golden Age; Wine Regions.
MAP REF. 220 C5, 229 J12

Swan Hill   Pop. 9357
In 1836 when the explorer Thomas Mitchell camped on the banks of the Murray, he named the spot Swan Hill because the black swans had kept him awake all night. The township became a busy 19th-century river port and today it is a pleasant city and major holiday centre on the Murray Valley Hwy, 350 km NW of Melbourne. The climate is mild and sunny and the river offers good fishing, boating and water-sports. Swan Hill is a well-laid-out city with a unique garden-like main street. **Of interest:** Australia's first Folk Museum, the Pioneer Settlement, at end of Gray St on Little Murray River features local Aboriginal culture and life in the last century; staff in period costume; old-fashioned transport; Sound and Light tour, nightly theatrical performance of music, lighting and dialogue, bookings essential. In Gray St: Swan Hill Regional Gallery of Contemporary Art; Dowling House Art and Craft Centre. Llanvair Gallery, Beveridge St. Military Museum, Campbell St, fine collection of militaria dating from 1800. Riverboats: PS *Pyap*, daily Murray cruises; stationary PS *Gem* has restaurant. Burke and Wills Fig Tree, Curlewis St: believed largest in Australia, commemorates explorers' visit. July: Italian Festa. Heritage Walk; brochure from Tourist Information. **In the area:** Buller's winery, Beverford, 11 km N. Horseriding, Mulberry Farm, Vinifera, 20 km N. Historic Tyntyndyer Homestead (c. 1846), National Trust-classified, 20 km N on Murray Valley Hwy. Tooleybuc, 45 km NW, pleasant spot for fishing, birdwatching, picnics. Piambie State Forest, 70 km N. Murray Downs Homestead, 2 km NW over bridge into NSW on Moulamein Rd, historic sheep, cattle and irrigation property; animal park, children's playground. Murray Downs Golf and Country Club, 5 km NW over bridge into NSW. Pheasant farm and aviaries, Nowie North, 32 km NW. Lake Boga, 15 km SE, water sports, picnics. Best's St Andrew's Vineyard near Lake Boga, 16 km S. Amboc Mohair Farm, Mystic Park, 29 km S. Daily river cruises, from Murray Downs River Cruises wharf on MV *Kookaburra*, incl. lunch cruise. **Tourist information:** 306 Campbell St; (050) 32 3033. **Accommodation:** 3 hotels, 16

motels, 4 cara./camp. parks. **See also:** The Mighty Murray; Wine Regions.
MAP REF. 126 H11, 229 N1, 231 N11

Tallangatta   Pop. 1021
When the old town of Tallangatta was submerged for the construction of the Hume Weir, many of its buildings were moved to a location above the shoreline. Today, situated 42 km SE from Wodonga on the Murray Valley Hwy, the town has the benefit of this large lake and boasts an attractive inland beach. It is the easternmost main Murray River town and is directly north of the beautiful alpine region of Victoria. The centre of a productive dairying area since early settlement, Tallangatta is the home of the Australian Red Breed Society, established to recognise red dairy cattle breeds throughout the world as a single breeding population. **Of interest:** The Hub, Tallangatta's Community Centre, Towong St; art and craft. April: Red Breeds Dairy Festival. Oct.: Arts Festival. **In the area:** Self-guide walks and drives; leaflets from Tourist Information. Laurel Hill Trout Farm at Eskdale, 33 km S, buy or catch-your-own, picnic/barbecue facilities. Forest drives recommended by the Forests Commission: extend from Mitta Mitta along Omeo Hwy; incl. trips to Cravensville, Mt Benambra, Tawonga and Omeo via Snowy Creek Rd. Alpine Walking Track passes over Mt Wills, 48 km S of Mitta Mitta. Lake Dartmouth, 58 km SE, has good trout fishing, boating, picnic/barbecue facilities. Traron Alpacas at Bullioh, 15 km E; alpacas, other animals, yarns, garments, Paulownia trees. **Tourist information:** The Hub 35–37, Towong St; (060) 71 2695. **Accommodation:** 2 hotels, 1 motel, 1 cara./camp. park. **See also:** The Mighty Murray.
MAP REF. 233 Q5, 234 C3

Terang   Pop. 1937
Terang, located on the Princes Hwy in a predominantly dairy farming area, is a well-laid-out town with grand avenues of deciduous trees, recognised by the National Trust. The town has excellent sporting facilities, with a particular emphasis on horse sports and a good polo field. **Of interest:** Early 20th-century commercial architecture. In High St: Gothic-style sandstone Presbyterian church; cottage crafts shop in century-old cottage, originally police station. Self-guide Historic Town Walk. Walking track, 3

km, beside lake beds and National Trust-classified trees; entrance behind Civic Centre, High St. Jan.: Horse carnival. **In the area:** Noorat, 6 km N, birthplace of Alan Marshall, author of *I Can Jump Puddles*: Alan Marshall Walking Track, gentle climb to summit of extinct volcano; excellent views of crater, surrounding district and across to Grampians. Glenormiston Agricultural College, 4 km further N, tastefully developed around an historic mansion. **Tourist information:** Clarke Saddlery, 105 High St; (055) 92 1164. **Accommodation:** 4 hotels, 2 motels, 1 cara./camp. park.
MAP REF. 215 A6, 227 K8

Torquay   Pop. 4887
The popularity of this resort, 22 km S of Geelong, is well known. Close to the town, the excellent surfing beaches, Bells and Jan Juc, attract surfers from all over the world. The Torquay Surf Lifesaving Club is the largest in the State. Torquay also marks the eastern end of the Great Ocean Road, offering spectacular drives west to Anglesea and beyond. **Of interest:** Surf Coast Plaza, Geelong Rd: surfing products; Surfworld, national surfing exhibition. Mary Elliott Pottery, Geelong Rd. Craft Cottage, Anderson St. Barbara Peake's Studio, Sarabande Cr. Redwood Gallery, Geelong Rd. Torqair Vintage Aeroplane Flights, Blackgate Rd, joyflights, playground, tearooms. Easter: Bells Beach Surfing Classic. **In the area:** Southern Rose, 1 km S on Great Ocean Rd; rose gardens, tearooms, restaurant. Experimental wind-power generator at Breamlea, 10 km NE. Bicycle track along Surfcoast Hwy, Grovedale to Anglesea. Rebenberg Winery (open weekends) and Downunda Weaving Studio at Mt Duneed, 11 km N. Sea Mist, Wensleydale Station Rd, Moriac, 22 km NW, horse rides, lunches. Museum of early Australian horse-drawn carriages near Bellbrae, 6 km W. Pottery Studios in Moores Rd, Bellbrae. **Tourist information:** Shire Offices, Grossmans Rd; (052) 61 4202, and Mary Elliott Pottery, Geelong Rd; (052) 61 3310. **Accommodation:** 3 motels, 1 B&B, 4 cara./camp. parks. **See also:** The Great Ocean Road.
MAP REF. 210 F11, 217 E10, 227 Q9

Traralgon   Pop. 19 699
Situated on the Princes Hwy, 164 km SE of Melbourne, Traralgon is one of the Latrobe Valley's main cities, the others

The Western District

Some famous Australians have been born and bred in this south-western part of Victoria. Many have been members of the land-owning families whose gracious homesteads are dotted about this beautiful pastoral area. The Western District supports one-third of Victoria's best sheep and cattle, and the region's merino wool is acknowledged to be the finest in the land.

Many of the Western District towns boast splendid pioneer buildings. Of special interest are **Hamilton**—recognised as the 'Wool Capital of the World'—and the attractive little towns of **Coleraine** and **Casterton**. Several of the district's historic homesteads are open for inspection, including Warrock (near Casterton), which has 33 original farm buildings still in operation. Of particular interest to nature lovers are the remaining colonies of the eastern barred bandicoot.

Warrnambool, situated on the south coast, is the commercial capital of the Western District and a gateway to the Great Ocean Road. The winter visits of southern right whales are a popular attraction.

The heart of the Western District is fairly flat grazing land. To the east, the volcanic lake area around **Camperdown** offers great fishing and water sports. To the south, a rugged coastline stretches from **Anglesea** to the tiny hamlet of **Nelson**, at the mouth of the Glenelg River. To the north, the high rocky ranges of the Grampians break through the gently rolling countryside. An excellent scenic route to Halls Gap is along the Mt Abrupt Road from **Dunkeld**.

Further information can be obtained from local tourist information centres, especially the Hamilton and District Tourist Information Centre, Lonsdale St, Hamilton; (055) 72 3746, and the Warrnambool Tourist Information Centre, 600 Raglan Pde, Warrnambool; (055) 64 7837. **See also:** Individual town entries in A–Z listing.

The Grampians, near Dunkeld

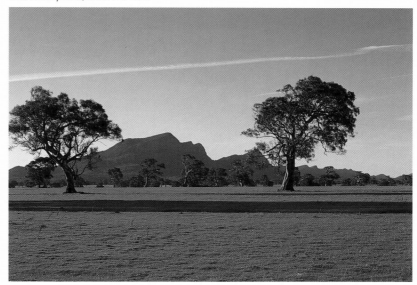

The Wimmera

Travelling through the Wimmera on a hot summer day is an unforgettable experience. The Wimmera is the granary of the State; the wheat fields stretch as far as the eye can see, an endless golden plain broken only occasionally by a gentle ripple in the terrain. In the south-east corner, however, are the Grampians, surrounded by a network of lakes, understandably popular with anglers and water-sports lovers.

The region takes its name from an Aboriginal word meaning 'throwing stick'. Evidence of occupation by the original inhabitants, the Wotjobaluk and Jardwa tribes, can still be seen: canoe trees are common and there are many rock-art sites in the Grampians area. The Ebenezer Mission Station at **Antwerp**, near **Dimboola**, founded by Moravian missionaries to Christianise the Aboriginal population, has been restored by the National Trust and local inhabitants.

Horsham, with its delightful private, public and Botanical gardens, intriguing Olde Horsham Village and an excellent regional art gallery, makes a good base from which to explore the whole region. If you are visiting in March, do not miss the annual Wimmera Machinery Field Days, held at the Victorian College of Agriculture and Horticulture, at Longerenong, and the Labour Day weekend Fishing Contest on the Wimmera River. **Natimuk**, 27 km west of Horsham, is the centre for visitors drawn to climb Mt Arapiles, a 356-metre sandstone monolith.

The agricultural life of the last century has been remembered at **Warracknabeal**, the largest wheat-receiving centre in the State, where an agricultural machinery museum houses huge steam-powered chaff-cutters, headers and tractors and depicts the history of the wheat industry. Near Dimboola, set along the banks of the Wimmera River, is one entrance to the Little Desert National Park. 'Little Desert' is something of a misnomer because the park is not little, and it does not look like a desert. There is a proliferation of plant and animal life, particularly in spring when the scrub and heathlands come into bloom.

For further information, contact the Horsham Tourist Information Centre, 20 O'Callaghan's Pde, Horsham; (053) 82 1832. **See also:** Individual town entries in A–Z listing.

being Moe and Morwell. It is a residential area based on an industrial core. **Of interest:** Walking tours, heritage drive. Old Post Office and Courthouse, cnr Franklin and Kay Sts. Band rotunda and miniature railway at Victory Park. Feb.–March: Music in the Park. **In the area:** Loy Yang power station, 5 km S. Giant mountain ash trees and ferns at Tarra–Bulga National Park, about 40 km S; picnics, walks, scenic drives, native fauna. Tarra–Bulga Visitor Centre at Balook, Grand Ridge Road, interpretive displays. Tambo Cheese Factory, 3 km E of town, cheese, local craft sales, see cheese-making. **Tourist information:** Tambo Cheese Factory, Princes Hwy, Traralgon East; (051) 74 0829. **Accommodation:** 9 motels, 5 cara./camp. parks. MAP REF. 225 K7

Walhalla   Pop. 15
The tiny goldmining town of Walhalla is tucked away in dense mountain country in south-east Gippsland. The drive, 46 km N from Moe, passes through some spectacular scenery. Walhalla is set in a narrow, steep valley, with sides so sheer that its cemetery has graves that have been dug lengthways into the hillside. **Of interest:** Historic buildings and relics of gold-boom days have been preserved. Long Tunnel Extended Goldmine, named after the most successful in the State; guided tours, check times. Old Fire Station, hand-operated fire engine, fire memorabilia. Spett's Cottage (1871), furnished in the period. Museum, opposite Rotunda; craft shop adj. Post Office, crafts. Old bakery (1865), oldest

Tarra-Bulga National Park, near Traralgon

surviving building in town, near rebuilt hotel. Museum, Spett's Cottage, Band Rotunda and Windsor House (1890), all National Trust-classified. Walhalla Coach Company, drives along main road. March: Erica King of the Mountain Woodchop. **In the area:** Alpine Walking Track, and Baw Baw National Park, which edges western side of town. Rawson, 8 km W, 487 000-ha catchment of Thomson Dam, picnic facilities. At Erica, 12 km SW: timber industry display at Erica Hotel; Erica Craftworks and Tea Rooms, resident wood turner. Mountain Saddle Safaris. Thomson River, 4 km S; fishing, picnicking, canoe trail, whitewater rafting. Moondarra State Park, 30 km S. Scenic road between Walhalla and Jamieson, 140 km N. **Tourist information:** Erica General Store, Henty St, Erica; (051) 65 3209. **Accommodation:** Limited. **See also:** Gippsland Lakes. MAP REF. 225 J5

Wangaratta   Pop. 15 984
The Ovens Hwy to Bright and the Victorian Alps, through the Ovens Valley, branches off the Hume Fwy at Wangaratta, 66 km SW of Wodonga. The surrounding fertile area produces wool, wheat, tobacco, kiwifruit, walnuts, chestnuts, hops and table-wine grapes. The city is well planned with good areas of parkland. **Of interest:** In cemetery, grave of Daniel 'Mad Dog' Morgan, the bushranger. His headless body was buried here, the head having been sent to Melbourne for examination. Kooringa Native Plants, Warby Range Rd. Wangaratta Woollen Mills, Textile Ave. At

Visitor Information Centre, cnr Tone Rd and Handley St, Mrs Stell's House in Miniature; history of Kelly Gang. IBM plant, Shanley St, opened 1984, supplies all IBM personal computer requirements for Australia, New Zealand and Southeast Asia. Nov.: Festival of Jazz. **In the area:** Airworld Aviation Museum, 7 km S: world's largest collection of flying antique civil aircraft; antique bicycles, cars, motor cycles and trucks; restaurant; adventure playground. Road 27 km S to Moyhu leads to beautiful King Valley and Paradise Falls; area incl. tiny townships of Whitfield, 54 km S, Cheshunt and Carboor; network of minor roads allows exploration of unspoiled area. King Valley Scenic Drive beside river to Whitfield and Powers Lookout. Newton's Prickle Berry Farm, Whitfield. Many vineyards in area, incl. John Gehrig Winery; Brown Brothers Milawa Vineyards, 16 km SE, family winery since 1889; Baileys Bundarra Vineyards (1870), 7 km N of Glenrowan, vineyard antiques; Auldstone Winery; Booth's Taminick Cellars, 4 km N of Baileys. Warby Range State Park, 12 km W; good vantage points, picnic spots, variety of bird and plant life. 'Carinya' Ladson Store (1860), Tarrawingee, 11 km SE, historic homestead and old goldfields store, property owned by same family for 110 years, all furnishings original; check times. Brookfield Pottery, Everton, 22 km SE. Wombi Toys, Whorouly, 25 km SE. Eldorado, 20 km E, interesting old gold township; largest gold dredge in the southern hemisphere, built in 1936; historical museum, general store, pottery.

Nearby Reedy Creek; popular with gold-panners and gem-fossickers. Glenrowan, 16 km SW, famed for its Kelly history; Ned captured here after gunfight at local hotel, subsequently condemned and hanged in Melbourne. **Tourist information:** Cnr Tone Rd and Handley St; (057) 21 5711. **Accommodation:** 2 hotels, 1 hotel/motel, 11 motels, 3 cara./ camp. parks. **See also:** Wine Regions. MAP REF. 233 M6

Warburton   Pop. 2504

Warburton was established with the gold finds of the 1880s; however, by the turn of the century it had found its niche as a popular tourist town with fine guest houses. It is surrounded by the foothills of the Great Dividing Range and is only about 90 minutes' drive from Melbourne. **Of interest:** Swingbridge Gallery and Crafts, Main St. **In the area:** The Acheron Way begins 2 km E of Warburton, giving access to views of Mt Donna Buang, Mt Victoria and Ben Cairn, on the scenic 37-km drive to St Fillans. Upper Yarra Dam, 23 km NE, picnic facilities. South of town along Warburton Hwy, an attractive area of vineyards: Yarra Burn, Lillydale and Oak Ridge Estate. Countryside around Warburton: bush-walking, riding, birdwatching. Mt Donna Buang, 7 km NW, popular day-trip destination from Melbourne, sometimes snow-covered in winter. Tommy Finn's Trout Farm, Millgrove, 3 km W. Yarra Junction Historical Museum, 10 km W. Yellingbo State Fauna Reserve, 25 km SW. Walk from Powelltown, 27 km S, to East Warburton: leaflet from Tourist Information; this is one branch of the Centenary Trail (the other branch leads from Warburton to Baw Baw National Park). Between Powelltown and Noojee: rainforest gully walk to Ada Tree, giant mountain ash. **Tourist information:** Yarra Valley healesville Visitor Information Centre, 127 Maroondah Hwy, Healesville; (059) 62 2600. **Accommodation:** 1 hotel, 3 motels, 1 cara./camp. park. MAP REF. 211 O6, 214 H9, 224 G4

Warracknabeal   Pop. 2687

On the Henty Hwy, 350 km NW of Melbourne, Warracknabeal is in the centre of a rich grain-growing area. The Aboriginal name means 'the place of the big red gums shading the watercourse'. **Of interest:** Historical Centre, 81 Scott St. Self-guide leaflets available for tour of

Flagstaff Hill, Warrnambool

historic buildings; some National Trust-classified, incl. Warracknabeal Hotel (1872), with iron lacework, and original log lockup (1872) built when Warracknabeal acquired its first permanent policeman. Wheatlands Agricultural Machinery Museum, farm machinery from last 100 yrs, picnic/barbecue facilities. Lions Park, on Yarriambiack Creek, picnic spots, fauna park. Easter: Vintage Machinery and Vehicle Rally, Wheatlands Carnival. **In the area:** Sections of dog fence, some 30 km N, vermin-proof barrier erected in 1883 from the Murray near Swan Hill to the border. Argip Lane Antiques, in old church, 18 km NW on road to Jeparit. Lake Hindmarsh, 60 km NW. Jeparit, 45 km W, Wimmera–Mallee Pioneer Museum. Lake Buloke, 56 km E, limited duck-shooting in season. **Tourist information:** 119 Scott St; (053) 98 1632. **Accommodation:** 4 hotels, 3 motels, 1 cara./camp. park. **See also:** The Wimmera. MAP REF. 228 H6

Warragul   Pop. 8910

Most of Melbourne's milk comes from this prosperous dairy-farming area 103 km south-east of Melbourne. It is also an important commercial centre. **Of interest:** West Gippsland Arts Centre, Civic Place. Lillico Garden Railway, Copelands Rd. Wild Dog Winery, Smith Rd; daily by appt. March: Gippsland Field Days. **In the area:** Mountain country

near Neerim South, 19 km N. Gippsland cheeses at: Neerim South (Gippsland Blue, Jindi Brie); Yarragon, 13 km E (Gippsland Food and Wine); Trafalgar, 21 km E; and Traralgon, 60 km E (Tambo Cheese Factory). Gourmet Deli Trail (brochure available), for a further food trip. Wildflower sanctuary at Labertouche, 16 km W. Darnum Musical Village, 8 km E. Nature reserves and picnic spots: Glen Cromie (Drouin West), Glen Nayook (south of Nayook) and Toorongo Falls (just north of Noogee). **Tourist information:** Latrobe Valley Tourism, Lloyd St, Moe; (051) 27 6928. **Accommodation:** 3 motels, 1 cara./ camp. park. MAP REF. 211 P10, 224 H6

Warrnambool   Pop. 25 500

A beautiful seaside city located 263 km SW of Melbourne on Lady Bay, where the Princes Hwy meets the Great Ocean Road, Warrnambool combines history and thriving progress. First-class sporting, cultural and entertainment facilities and beautifully developed and maintained parks and gardens have resulted in Warrnambool being awarded Victoria's Premier Town title a record 3 times. **Of interest:** Flagstaff Hill Maritime Museum, Merri St, unique 19th-century Maritime Village; Entrance Gallery orientation centre introduces visitors to Maritime Village experience; incl. Flagstaff Hill tapestry, with themes of Aboriginal history, sealing, whaling, exploration, immigration and settlement. Over 100 ships were wrecked on the coast near Warrnambool; famous earthenware Loch Ard Peacock, recovered from Loch Ard wreck in 1878, is on permanent display at Flagstaff Hill Maritime Museum. Annual visit of rare southern right whales; usually May–Oct. (viewing platform east of town at Logans Beach). The Kid's Country Treasure Map (available at Tourist Information); informative way for whole family to enjoy Warrnambool. Performing Arts Centre, Art Gallery, Timor St. Botanic Gardens (designed by Guilfoyle in 1879), Botanic Rd. Fletcher Jones Gardens, Raglan Pde. Lake Pertobe Adventure Playground, Pertobe Rd. The Potter's Wheel, Liebig St. Thunder Point Reserve, end Macdonald St. Middle Island, off Pickering Point, colony of little (fairy) penguins. Wollaston Bridge, over 100 years old, unusual design, on northern outskirts of town. Heritage Trail Walk and arrow

Street scene, Wodonga

tour of city start at Tourist Information Centre (self-guide leaflets available). Feb.: Wunta Festival. Oct.: Melbourne–Warrnambool Cycling Classic. **In the area:** Tower Hill State Game Reserve, 14 km W, incl. one of Victoria's largest and most recently active volcanoes; nature walk starts at the National History Centre. Port Campbell National Park, 54 km SE, 32-km stretch of scenic and historic coastline; incorporates magnificent series of sheer cliffs, deep caverns, great archways, grottos, island gorges, blowholes, spectacular offshore rock stacks. World-famous Twelve Apostles, 77 km SE. Robert Ulmann Studio, 4 km E, paintings of Australian flora and fauna. Allansford Cheese World, 10 km E: dairy promotion store; cheese tasting and sales; viewing of cheese production. Ralph Illidge Sanctuary, 32 km E, wildlife, picnic area, nature walks. Timboon Farmhouse and Cheese and Berry World, Timboon, 53 km E. Historic Shipwreck Trail, highlighting wrecks along the coast from Moonlight Head (↲12 km E) to Port Fairy (29 km W), allows visitors to explore Victoria's 'Shipwreck Coast'. Mahogany Walking Track, 22 km, Warrnambool–Port Fairy, along beach dunes. Helicopter and joy flights along coast. **Tourist information:** 600 Raglan Pde; (055) 64 7837. **Accommodation:** 10 hotels, 23 motels, 6 B&B, 8 cara./camp. parks. **See also:** The Great Ocean Road. MAP REF. 226 I9

Wedderburn   Pop. 764

Once one of Victoria's richest goldmining towns in the 'Golden Triangle', Wedderburn is on the Calder Hwy, 74 km NW of Bendigo. Gold can still be found around the town—nuggets worth over $20 000 were discovered in a local backyard in the 1950s. **Of interest:** Government Battery on northern edge of town. Hard Hill area, former gold diggings and Christmas Reef Mine. In High St: Museum and General

Store (1910), restored building furnished and stocked as it was at turn of century; coach-building factory; old bakery, converted into a kiln for a group of potters using local clay. Sept.: Wool Expo. **In the area:** Wychitella Forest Reserve, 16 km N, wildlife sanctuary. Mount Korong, 16 km SE, picnics, some rock scrambling, bushwalking. **Tourist information:** Shire Offices, High St; (054) 94 3200. **Accommodation:** 1 hotel, 1 motel, 1 cara./camp. park. MAP REF. 229 N8

Welshpool–Port Welshpool
Pop. 241

Welshpool is a small dairying town and Port Welshpool is a deep-sea port servicing fishing and oil industries. Barry Beach Marine Terminal, 8 km S of the South Gippsland Hwy, services the offshore oil rigs in Bass Strait. **In the area:** Excellent fishing and boating. At Port Welshpool, Maritime Museum. Tarra–Bulga National Park, 56 km NE. Agnes Falls, 19 km NW, State's highest. At Toora, 11 km W, panoramic views from Mt Fatigue, off South Gippsland Hwy; scenic drive; accommodation at historic Ambleside guest house or Gumnuts Weaving Gallery; Franklin River Reserve, picnic facilities, nature walk. **Tourist information:** South Gippsland Tourism, Silkstone Rd, Korumburra; (056) 552233. **Accommodation:** 1 motel, 2 cara./camp. parks. MAP REF. 225 J10

Winchelsea   Pop. 969

This town, in the centre of a farming area, is on the Barwon River, 37 km W of Geelong. It originated as a watering-place and shelter for travellers on the road to Colac from Geelong. **Of interest:** Barwon Bridge, graceful stone arches, opened 1867 to handle increasing westward traffic. Alexandra's Antiques and Art Gallery, Main St. Barwon Hotel

(1842), houses museum of Australiana. **In the area:** Barwon Park Homestead, National Trust property, 3 km N on Inverleigh Rd; check times. **Tourist information:** Shire Offices, Hesse St; (052) 67 2104. **Accommodation:** 1 motel, 1 cara./camp. park. MAP REF. 210 D10, 217 A8, 227 P8

Wodonga   Pop. 39 975

Wodonga is the Victorian city in a twin-city complex astride the Murray in north-east Victoria. Albury–Wodonga is a fast-growing city being developed as a decentralised region by the Federal, Victorian and NSW State Governments and, with the attractions of the Murray and nearby Lake Hume, it makes a good base for a holiday. **Of interest:** Wodonga has a number of historic buildings still in use. The city has about 30 km of bicycle paths. The Linc Inn, Lincoln Hwy, teas. Miniature steam railway, Diamond Park, off Lincoln Causeway, runs on 3rd Sun. of month. Sumsion Gardens, Church St, beautiful lakeside park. In Melrose Dr, largest outdoor tennis centre in Australia. Craft markets, Jack Hore Pl., alternate Sundays. Jan.–Feb.: Sports festival. March: Wodonga Show. **In the area:** Military Museum, Bandiana, 4 km SE. Hume Weir, 15 km E; picnic facilities, Hume Weir Trout Farm open. Wodonga is close to 4 areas of interest: Upper Murray, mountain valleys of north-east Victoria; Murray Valley; Riverina district. Short drive 36 km S leads to picturesque township of Yackandandah. Towns worth visiting: Beechworth (47 km), Wangaratta (68 km), both south-west, and Rutherglen, 42 km W. **Tourist information:** Information Centre, Lincoln Causeway; (060) 41 3875. **Accommodation:** 4 hotels, 12 motels, 1 hostel, 2 cara./camp. parks. **See also:** The Mighty Murray. MAP REF. 127 P13, 233 O4, 234 B2

Wonthaggi   Pop. 5751

Once the main supplier of coal to the Victorian Railways, Wonthaggi, situated 8 km from Cape Paterson in Gippsland, is South Gippsland's largest town, and has many original buildings. Wonthaggi began as a tent town in 1909 when the coal mines were opened up by the State Government following industrial unrest in the coalfields in NSW. The mines operated until 1968. Easter: Carnival. **In the area:** State Coal Mine, 1.5 km S on Cape Patterson Rd: tours of re-opened Eastern

Area Mine; museum of mining activities, with experienced ex-coalminer as guide; picnic facilities. Cape Paterson, 8 km s, in Bunurong Marine Park; surfing, swimming, snorkelling, scuba diving, fishing. Scenic drives: beaches at Inverloch, 13 km SE, and Tarwin Lower, 35 km SE. Self-guide 25-km tour links places of interest in area. **Tourist information:** Watts St; (056) 72 2484. **Accommodation:** 2 hotels, 2 motels, 1 hostel, 1 cara./camp. park, 1 cara. park.
MAP REF. 211 N13, 224 F9

Wycheproof   Pop. 777
A railway line runs down the middle of the main street of this town on the edge of the Mallee, 140 km from Bendigo. **Of interest:** Centenary Park, Broadway, picnic/barbecue facilities, children's playground, historic log cabin. Willandra Historical Museum, Broadway. 'Mt Wycheproof', a mere 43 m high and the smallest mountain in the world. Craft Shops. **In the area:** Peppercorn Drive, 5 km NW, country crafts, antique kitchenware. **Tourist information:** Shire Offices, 367 Broadway; (054) 93 7400. . **Accommodation:** 2 hotels, 1 motel, 1 cara./camp. park.
MAP REF. 126 G13, 229 L5

Yackandandah   Pop. 601
About 27 km s of Wodonga, this exceptionally attractive town, with avenues of English trees and traditional verandahed buildings, has been classified by the National Trust. Yackandandah is in the heart of the north-east goldfields country (gold was discovered here in 1852), but today it is better known for its historic buildings. **Of interest:** Number of original buildings in High St, incl. Post Office; several banks and general stores; Bank of Victoria (1865), now historical museum. Self-guide walking tour brochure from Tourist Information. Ray Riddington's Premier Store and Gallery, High St. Art and craft: from Yackandandah Workshop, cnr Kars and Hammond Sts; Haldane Artist Studio, High St. Wildon Thyme, High St, local art and craft, tearooms, restaurant. Vintage Sounds Restorations, Wyndham St, old and antique gramophones, telephones, radios. Yackandandah Trail and Coach Rides, horse or coach rides, 2 hr to full day. Yack Track Tours, 4WD tours for wine tasting, gold panning and bushwalking, booking essential. Market, 2nd Sat. of month, Memorial Gardens, High St. **In the area:** Creeks and old diggings in Yackandandah area still yield specimens of alluvial gold to amateur prospectors. Lavender Patch Plant Farm, 4 km W on Beechworth Rd. Picturesque Indigo Valley, 6 km W, National Trust-classified. Road leads through rolling hills along valley floor to Barnawatha. Koendidda Historic Homestead, Pooleys Rd, near Barnawartha; accommodation. At Dederang, 25 km SE, art, craft and plants. At Allans Flat, 10 km NE, Mr Red's Farm, nursery, native fauna park; Schmidt's Strawberry Winery. At Leneva, 16 km NE, Wombat Valley Tramways; small-gauge railway operates at Easter or by appt. for groups. **Tourist information:** Finders Bric-a-Brac and Old Wares, 28 High St; (060) 27 1222. **Accommodation:** 2 hotels, 1 cara./ camp. park.
MAP REF. 233 O6, 234 A3

Yarram   Pop. 2006
This old-established South Gippsland town, 225 km by road from Melbourne, has some interesting original buildings, and a pleasant golf course inhabited by relatively tame kangaroos. It is situated between the Strzelecki Ranges and Bass Strait. **Of interest:** Tarra Spinning Wheels, Alberton Rd, spinning wheels, boat wheels, beds, general wood turning. Easter: Tarra Festival. Nov.: Seabank Fishing Contest. **In the area:** To south, historic towns of Alberton, 6 km; Tarraville, 11 km; and Port Albert, 14 km. Christ Church (1856) in Tarraville is oldest church in Gippsland. Ninety Mile Beach, very popular with surfers and anglers, begins just north of Port Albert. Woodside, 29 km E; and Seaspray, 68 km NE), beaches patrolled in summer. Fishing beaches: Mann's, 16 km E; or McLoughlin's, 29 km E. To the north; Australian Omega Navigation Facility with 427-m-high steel tower. In the Strzelecki Ranges, 27 km NW, Tarra–Bulga National Park; hilly country, densely forested with mountain ash, myrtle and sassafras, spectacular fern

Yackandandah

glades, splendid river and mountain views, rosellas, lyrebirds, the occasional koala. Walking tracks in both parks, two caravan parks at Tarra Valley. Horseriding nearby. Eilean Donan Gardens and Riverbank Nursery, Tarra Valley: architectural charm, splendid gardens. At Hiawatha, 46-km circuit drive from Yarram; Minnie Ha Ha Falls, on Albert River, picnic facilities. Horses for hire at Hiawatha. Won Wron Forest, on Hyland Hwy, 16 km N, wildflowers in spring. **Tourist information:** Ooly Dooly Motors, Commercial Rd; (051) 82 5119. **Accommodation:** 2 hotels, 3 motels, 2 cara./camp. parks.
MAP REF. 225 K9

Yarragon   Pop. 708

This small town in the Latrobe Valley is situated 116 km E of Melbourne in an agricultural and dairying district. It is a ideal base for exploring the Upper Latrobe and Tanjil River valleys in the mountainous area to the north and for scenic drives along the Grand Ridge Road to the south. **Of interest:** Antiques, crafts, gallery, specialty shops, gourmet food, boutique wines. March: Thorpdale Potato Festival. Nov.: Dairy Fest. **In the area:** Mt Worth State Park, 10 km S. At Childers, 16 km SE, Sunny Creek Fruit and Berry Farm; Windrush Cottage, teas. Thorpdale, 22 km SE, known for its potatoes; potato bread from bakery. Trafalgar Lookout, Narracan Falls and Henderson's Gully near Trafalgar, 8 km E. At Darnum, 7 km W, musical village housing hundreds of musical instruments. Grand Ridge Rd, spectacular 140-km drive traversing top of Strzelecki Ranges. **Tourist information:** Gippsland Food and Wine, Princes Hwy; (056) 34 2451. **Accommodation:** 1 motel.
MAP REF. 211 Q10, 224 H7

Yarrawonga–Mulwala
Pop. 3603

A pleasant stretch of the Murray and the attractive Lake Mulwala have made these border towns an extremely popular holiday resort. The 6000-ha lake was created in 1939 during the building of the Yarrawonga Weir, which controls the irrigation waters in the Murray Valley. **Of interest:** Around the lake and along the river, sandy beaches and still waters provide an ideal environment for all kinds of water sports, picnicking and general relaxation. The towns have excellent sports facilities, including a 45-hole golf

Kinglake National Park, near Yea

course. The islands and backwaters of the lake have abundant birdlife. The Yarrawonga and Mulwala foreshore areas have green lawns and shady willows, and facilities incl. children's playgrounds, giant water-slides, kiosk, barbecues, boat ramps. Old Yarra Mine Shaft, in Tourist Centre, Irvine Pde, Yarrawonga, houses a large collection of gems, minerals and fossils. Carinya Pottery and Hallworth House Gallery, Woods Rd. Tudor House Clock Museum, Lynch St. Daily cruises: *Paradise Queen, Lady Murray*. Ski club conducts exhibitions and lessons. Tunzafun Amusement Park, Melbourne St. Robb & Co., horse-drawn coach rides. Linley Park Animal Farm and Gardens, Corowa Rd, Mulwala, native and exotic animals. Canoe and boat hire, horseriding. Sept.: IceBreaker Yacht Regatta. **In the area:** Byramine Homestead and Country Gardens, 16 km W. Opposite, Fyffe Field Winery. Matata Deer Farm, Cobram, 42 km W. Historical Museum, Katamatite, 35 km SW of Yarrawonga. Fishing in Murray River (no licence required). **Tourist information:** Irvine Pde, Yarrawonga; (057) 44 1989. **Accommodation:** 4 hotels, 2 hotel/motels, 16 motels, 10 cara./camp. parks. **See also:** The Mighty Murray.
MAP REF. 127 N13, 233 K3, 233 K4

Yea   Pop. 995

This town, 58 km N of Yarra Glen, stands beside the Yea River, a tributary of the Goulburn. Set in attractive pastoral and dairy-farming land, it is well situated for touring to Mansfield, Eildon and the mountains, and to the gorge country between Yea and Tallarook, as well as south-east to Marysville. There are some beautiful gorges and fern gullies close to the Yea–Tallarook road, and the area provides easy access to the mountain country south of Eildon Weir. **Of interest:** Beaufort Manor (1870s), High St, restaurant, tearoom, gardens. General Store (1887), High St. **In the area:** Kinglake National Park, 30 km SW, beautiful waterfalls, tall eucalypts, fern gullies, impressive views. Pick-your-own fruit at Berry King Farm, Two Hills Rd, Glenburn, 30 km S. Spectacular Wilhelmina Falls, 32 km S via Melba Hwy. Murrindindi Cascades 11 km away in Murrindindi Reserve, wildlife includes wombats, platypuses, lyrebirds. Grotto at Caveat, 27 km N. Mineral springs, Dropmore, 47 km N, off back road to Euroa. Ibis rookery at Kerrisdale, 17 km W. Several good campsites along Goulburn River. Flowerdale Winery, 23 km SW on Whittlesea–Yea Rd, Flowerdale. **Tourist information:** Shire Offices; (057) 97 2209; Legendary Country Tourism, 11 High St, Mansfield; (057) 75 1464. **Accommodation:** 2 motels, 1 cara./camp. park.
MAP REF. 211 N2, 232 H11

Victoria

Other Map Coverage

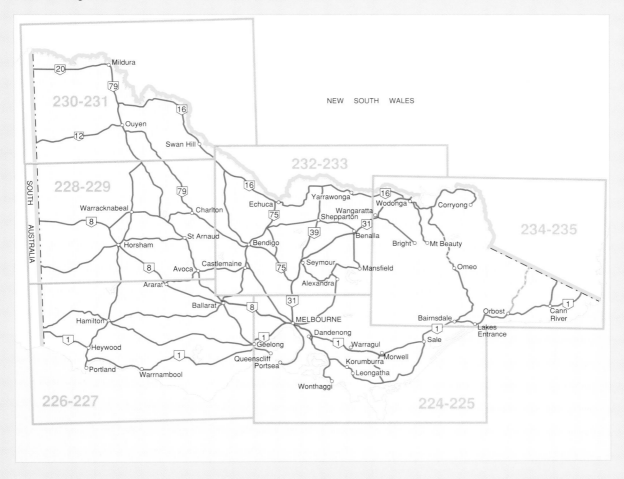

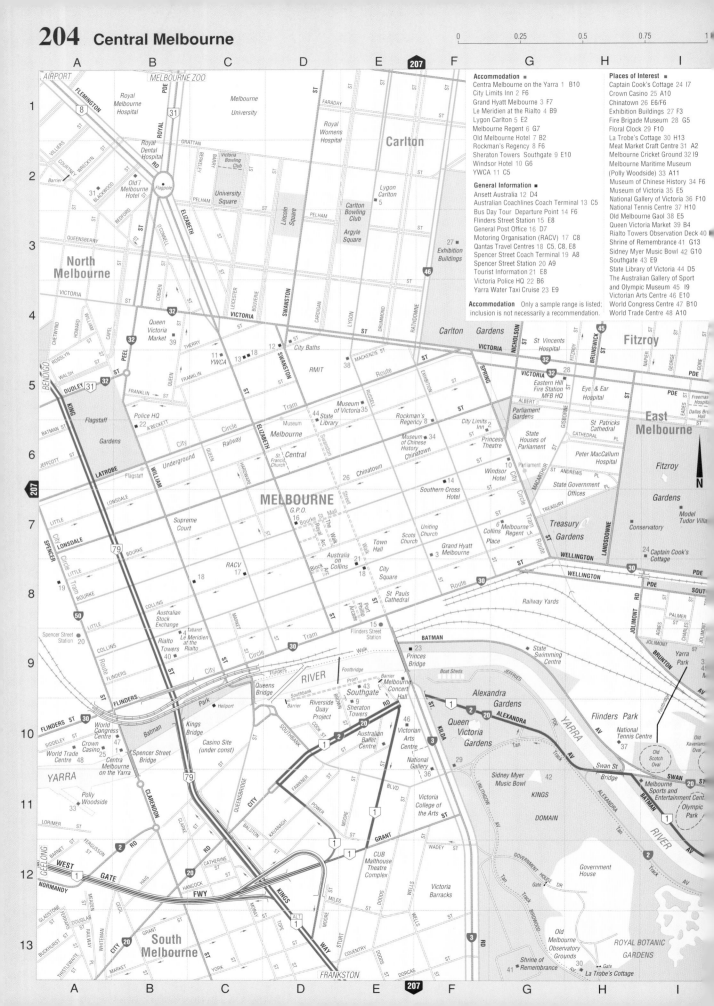

Accommodation ■
Centra Melbourne on the Yarra 1 B10
City Limits Inn 2 F6
Grand Hyatt Melbourne 3 F7
Le Meridien at the Rialto 4 B9
Lygon Carlton 5 E2
Melbourne Regent 6 G7
Old Melbourne Hotel 7 B2
Rockman's Regency 8 G7
Sheraton Towers Southgate 9 E10
Windsor Hotel 10 G6
YWCA 11 C5

General Information ■
Ansett Australia 12 D4
Australian Coachlines Coach Terminal 13 C5
Bus Day Tour Departure Point 14 F6
Flinders Street Station 15 E8
General Post Office 16 D7
Motoring Organisation (RACV) 17 C8
Qantas Travel Centres 18 C5, C8, E8
Spencer Street Coach Terminal 19 A8
Spencer Street Station 20 A9
Tourist Information 21 E8
Victoria Police HQ 22 B6
Yarra Water Taxi Cruise 23 E9

Accommodation Only a sample range is listed;
inclusion is not necessarily a recommendation.

Places of Interest ■
Captain Cook's Cottage 24 I7
Crown Casino 25 A10
Chinatown 26 E6/F6
Exhibition Buildings 27 F3
Fire Brigade Museum 28 G5
Floral Clock 29 F10
La Trobe's Cottage 30 H13
Meat Market Craft Centre 31 A2
Melbourne Cricket Ground 32 I9
Melbourne Maritime Museum
(Polly Woodside) 33 A11
Museum of Chinese History 34 F6
Museum of Victoria 35 E5
National Gallery of Victoria 36 F10
National Tennis Centre 37 H10
Old Melbourne Gaol 38 E5
Queen Victoria Market 39 B4
Rialto Towers Observation Deck 40 B9
Shrine of Remembrance 41 G13
Sidney Myer Music Bowl 42 G10
Southgate 43 E9
State Library of Victoria 44 D5
The Australian Gallery of Sport
and Olympic Museum 45 I9
Victorian Arts Centre 46 E10
World Congress Centre 47 B10
World Trade Centre 48 A10

Thick roads represent recommended approach and bypass routes.

A B C D 210 E F G H

1 2 3 4 5 6 7 8 9 10 11 12 13

HOLDEN RD

CALDER 79

ORGAN PIPES NATIONAL PARK

Calder Park Thunderdome

Keilor Public Golf Course

MELBOURNE AIRPORT

Greenvale Centre

Gellibrand Hill Park

Victoria Police

Domestic & International Terminals

TULLAMARINE FWY

MELTON 54 HIGHWAY

Sydenham

Taylors Lakes

Keilor North

Tullamarine Country Club

Keilor

Tullamarine

OLD CALDER FWY 79

Keilor Park Recreation Reserve

Keilor Park

Westfield Shopping Town

Airport We

WESTERN BALLARAT FREEWAY 8

Department of Defence

Rockbank

BEATTYS RD

PLUMPTON RD

TAYLORS RD

Department of Communications Radio 3RN 3LO

Keilor Downs

TAYLORS RD

GREEN GULLY RD

Green Gully Reserve

Kealba

Brimbank Park

Keilor Cemetery

Keilor SEC Terminal Station

PARK DR

Keilor East

Nid

GREIGS

LEAKES RD

TROUPS RD

WESTERN HIGHWAY 8

GILLESPIE

KINGS RD

MAIN

St Albans

Deer Park Central Shopping Centre

NEALE

Deer Park

Commonwealth of Australia Office of Defence Production

Ginifer

ARTHUR

MAIN

WEST

EAST

SUNSHINE AV

ST ALBANS RD

RING RD 41

MILLERA

Avondale Heights

Ma

Commonwealth of Australia Department of Defence

BOUNDARY

DRY

TROUPS RD

DOHERTYS

Tarneit

HOPKINS RD

ROBINSONS RD

MT DERRIMUT RD

Commonwealth of Australia Office of Defence Production

Deer Park

TILBURN RD

FORREST

Albion

Selwyn Park ST

DEVONSHIRE

WESTERN

Braybrook 8

HAMPSTEAD

MITCHELL

BALLARAT

Glengala

Ardeer

Sunshine Golf Course

ANDERSON RD

FAIRBAIRN RD

WRIGHT

Hill Reserve

Sunshine SOUTH

Skinner Reserve 38 RD 39

Dobson Reserve

RAAF Depot

BARKLY

Footscray West

SUNSHINE RD

SOMERVILLE RD

MARKET RD

Tottenham

Hansen Reserve

Derrimut Grasslands

BOUNDARY 32

FITZGERALD RD

FAIRBAIRN RD

SOMERVILLE RD

Brooklyn

SOMERVILLE

Footscray Cemetery

83

ST

Spotswood

PRINCES FWY

DOHERTYS RD

Truganina

FITZGERALD RD

GEELONG RD

PIPE RD

PRINCES 33

WEST GATE 41

GEELONG RD

FRANCIS

HWY

1 FWY

Mc Ivor Reserve

We

Newport

Altona Gate Shopping Centre

Crematorium and Lawn Cemetery

Crofts Reserve

PDE

39

GRIEVE

BLACKSHAWS

MASON

MILLS ST

Newport Lakes Parkland

37

KOROROIT

CREEK

MILLERS RD

Altona Lakes Public Golf Course

Newport Railway Workshops

Palmers

Laverton Lake Recreation Reserve

FORSYTH RD

OLD GEELONG RD

Victorian Baseball and Softball Park

MAIDSTONE

39

Altona

Grant Reserve

Cherry Lake

35

Altona Sports Park

Cemetery

35

Hogans Road Reserve

HOGANS RD

Laverton RAAF Base

Aircraft

Laverton

AB Shaw Reserve

CIVIC

Westona

Altona

Seaholme

Hoppers Crossing

DERRIMUT RD

MORRIS RD

OLD GEELONG RD

1

CENTRAL AV

QUEEN ST

Kooringal Golf Course 11

ESPLANADE

Werribee Plaza Shopping Centre

HEATHS

Mossfiel Reserve

Laverton

VICTORIA

MERTON

BLYTH

Wyndham Vale

Galvin Park

BALLAN RD

SHAWS

TARNEIT RD

MARKET RD

RAILWAY AV

HOPPERS LA

HIGHWAY

Department of Agriculture

SNEYDES RD

Altona Meadows

Wyndham Centre

Werribee Racecourse

Werribee

DUNCANS RD

FREEWAY

State Research Farm

HOPPERS LA

POINT COOK RD

Point Cook

N

PRINCES

1 MALTBY

BYPASS

Zoological Park

State Equestrian Centre

Werribee Park

DIGGERS RD

AVIATION RD

Drainage Channel

Swamp

Point Cook Metropolitan Park

Point Cook

Point Cook

PORT PH

Melbourne Water Werribee Treatment Complex

Werribee Mansion

Point Cook RAAF Base

210

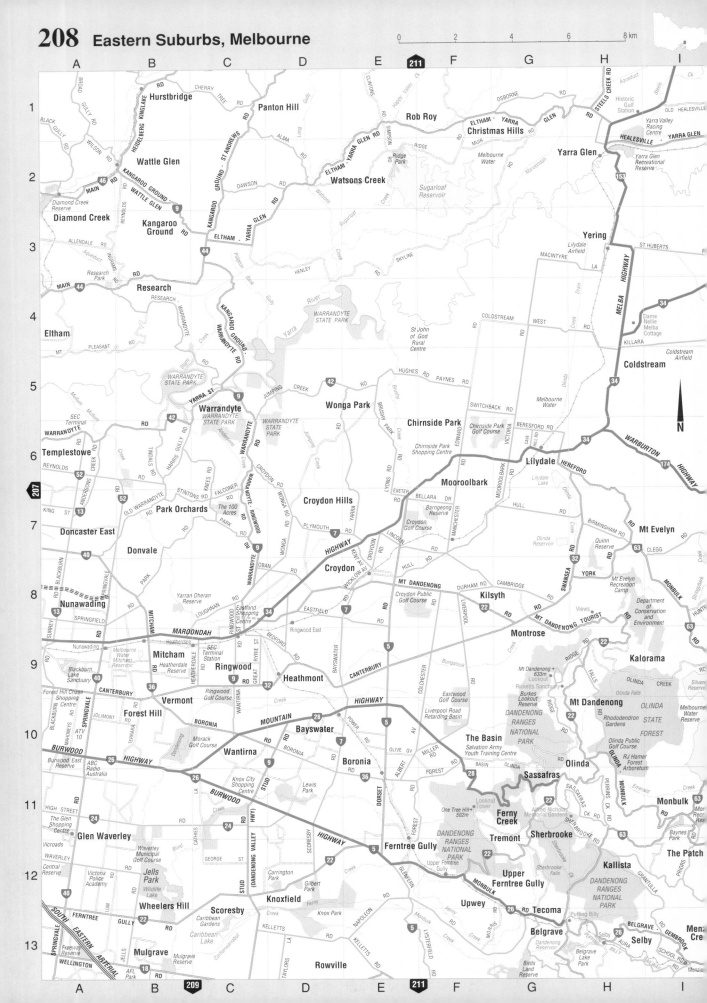

0   2   4   6   8 km

PORT   PHILLIP

N

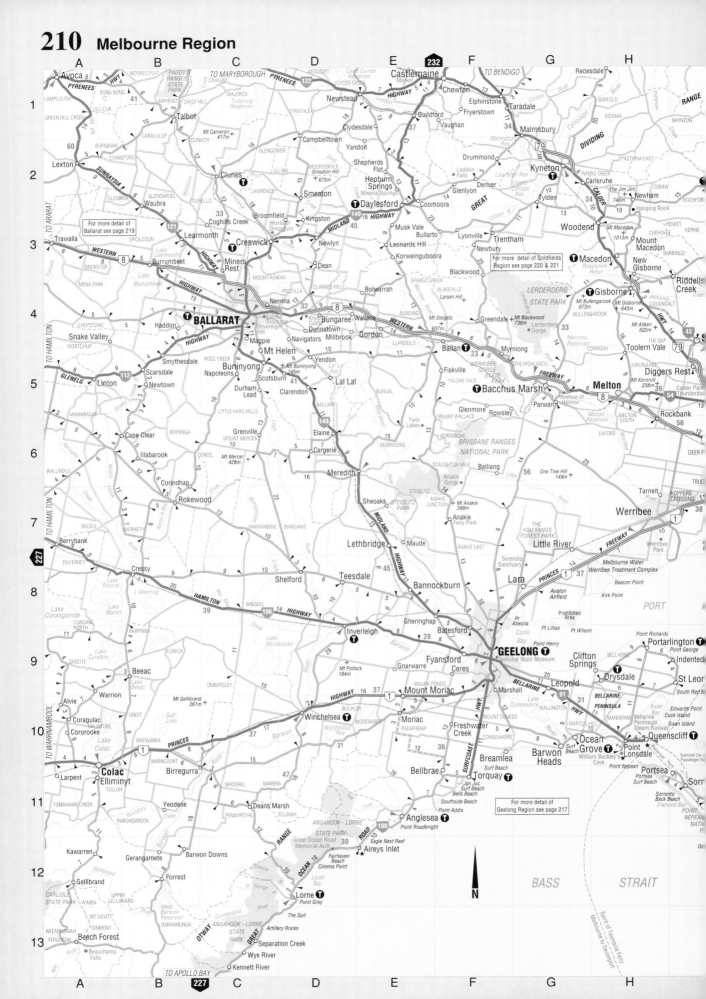

Scale: 0   10   20   30 km

Column/row grid labels: J K L M N O P Q R (top and bottom) — 1 2 3 4 5 6 7 8 9 10 11 12 13 (sides)

Highway markers: 232, 233, 153, 168, 173, 172, 174, 180, 181, 182, 186, 224, 225, 27, 31, 34, 58, 60, 62, 64, 65, 69, 71, 73, 75, 8, 1

TO BENALLA, TO BENALLA, MIDLAND HIGHWAY, MIDLAND HWY

Towns and localities:

Puckapunyal, Seymour, Tallarook, Ruffy, Strathbogie, Merton, Barjarg, Mansfield, Whiteheads Creek, Terip Terip, Bonnie Doon, Nillahcootie, Bridge Creek

Broadford, Tyaak, Strath Creek, Yea, Molesworth, Yarck, Kanumbra, Alexandra, Eildon, Goughs Bay, Macs Cove, Howqua

Kilmore, Wandong, Heathcote Junction, Reedy Creek, Flowerdale, Limestone, Acheron, Thornton, Taggerty, Jamieson

Wallan, Upper Plenty, Beveridge, Glenvale, Murrindindi, Buxton, Marysville

Kalkallo, Whittlesea, Humevale, Kinglake, Toolangi, Narbethong, Gaffneys Creek

Craigieburn, Yan Yean, Strathewen, Pheasant Creek, Steels Creek, Dixons Creek

Mernda, Doreen, Yarrambat, Cottles Bridge, St Andrews, Smiths Gully, Watsons Creek, Healesville, Warburton

Hurstbridge, Panton Hill, Christmas Hills, Yarra Glen, Don Valley, Millgrove, Big Pats Creek

Greensborough, Coldstream, Seville, Wandin, Yallock, Woori Yallock, Yarra Junction

MELBOURNE, Croydon, Silvan, Yellingbo

Box Hill, Ringwood, Mitcham, Olinda, Monbulk, Sherbrooke, Menzies Creek, Avonsleigh, Clematis, Emerald, Cockatoo, Gembrook

Glen Waverley, Upwey, Belgrave, Lysterfield, Upper Ferntree Gully, Narre Warren, Berwick, Beaconsfield, Officer, Pakenham, Nar Nar Goon, Tynong, Garfield, Bunyip, Longwarry, Drouin, Neerim, Hill End, Willow Grove

Caulfield, Brighton, Springvale, Dandenong, Lyndhurst, Cranbourne, Upper Beaconsfield, Rokeby, Buln Buln, Nilma, Warragul, Darnum, Yarragon, Moe, Westbury

Sandringham, Mentone, Mordialloc, Chelsea, Seaford, Frankston, Pearcedale, Tooradin, Koo-wee-rup, Ellinbank, Trafalgar, Narracan

Mornington, Somerville, Moorooduc, Tyabb, Warneet, Cannons Creek, Lang Lang, Nyora, Poowong, Thorpdale, Narracan

Hastings, Crib Point, Stony Point, Tankerton, Lang Lang, Loch, Korumburra, Mirboo North, Strzelecki

Red Hill, Balnarring, Bittern, Corinella, Grantville, Bena, Mirboo

Somers, Merricks, Cowes, Ventnor, Rhyll, Glen Forbes, Kernot, Kongwak, Outtrim, Leongatha

Flinders, The Nobbies, Newhaven, San Remo, Archies Creek, Kilcunda, Dalyston, Wonthaggi, Kilcunda, Koonwarra, Dumbalk, Meeniyan

TO INVERLOCH, TO INVERLOCH, TO MORWELL, TO FOSTER

Parks / features:
FRASER NP, EILDON STATE PARK, CATHEDRAL RANGE STATE PARK, KINGLAKE NATIONAL PARK, WARRANDYTE STATE PARK, DANDENONG RANGES NP, OLINDA STATE FOREST, BUNYIP STATE PARK, GEMBROOK PARK, MT WORTH STATE PARK, FRENCH ISLAND STATE PARK, WESTERN PORT, PHILLIP ISLAND

Rivers / ranges:
GOULBURN VALLEY HIGHWAY, GOULBURN VALLEY HIGHWAY, MAROONDAH HIGHWAY, MELBA HIGHWAY, WARBURTON HWY, PRINCES HIGHWAY, SOUTH GIPPSLAND HWY, BASS HIGHWAY, GREAT DIVIDING RANGE, KINGLAKE RANGE, TORBRECK RANGE, BLUE RANGE, POLEY RANGE, SNAKE RIDGE, STRZELECKI RANGES

Mountains/heights (m):
Mt Piper +442m, Mt Eaglehawk +533m, Mt Tallarook 806m, Mt Marianne +486m, Mt Broughton 677m, Mt Concord 649m, Mt Strathbogie 1007m, Mt Tickatory 604m, Mt Prospect 476m, Mt Bullamite +677m, Mt Caroline 515m, Spion Kopje 486m, Mt Disappointment 793m, Mt Klondyke +869m, Mt Mitchell +957m, Mt Margaret +1573m, Mt Torbreck 1514m, Mt Duffy +1028m, Mt Terrible 1335m, Mt Kitchener 960m, Mt Arnold 1311m, Mt Matlock 1372m, Mt Strickland 1219m, Mt Dom Dom 732m, Mt Juliet +1105m, Mt Donna Buang 1250m, Ben Cairn 1071m, Mt Toole-Be-Wong 792m, Mt Horsfall 1134m, Mt Beenak 743m, Mt Toorongo 1248m, Spion Kopje 898m, Gentle Annie 686m, Mt Towt 353m, Mt Tanjil 456m, Mt Worth 518m

Lake Eildon, Lake Mountain +1470m, Maroondah Reservoir, Sugarloaf Reservoir, Silvan Reservoir, Cardinia Reservoir, Tarago Reservoir, Upper Yarra Reservoir, Blue Rock Dam

For more detail of Yarra Valley Region see page 214

For more detail of Melbourne & suburbs see pages 206 & 207

For more detail of Mornington area see pages 212 & 213

Puffing Billy, Healesville Sanctuary, Tarrawarra, Koala Conservation Centre, Churchill Is., Wildlife Wonderland, Penguin Parade, State Coal Mine, Coal Creek Historical Park, Grand Ridge Brewery, Alpine Trout Farm, Cape Woolamai, Cape Schanck Lighthouse

A B C D E F G H

1

Indented Head
Indented Head

BELLARINE
PENINSULA

St Leonards 🆃
South Red Bluff

2

MURRADOC RD

217

EDWARDS
POINT
WILDLIFE
RESERVE

3

PORT   PHILLIP

Edwards Point

Swan

Bay

Duck Island

HISTORICAL HOMES: The Mornington Peni
array of magnificently preserved historical
Visit Coolart at Somers, a century-old man
in landscaped gardens, or the simple 1844 drop
McCrae Homestead. Sages Cottage at Bax
rural home set in large grounds with an anim
provides an excellent day tour destination.

4

Queenscliff
Golf
Course

Swan Island

Bellarine
Peninsula
Steam Railway

Queenscliff 🆃

Black
Lighthouse
Fort
Queenscliff
Queenscliff
Lighthouse

5

The Rip

Car and Passenger Ferry

Mud
Islands

Mount M
Balcombe Poin

DOLPHIN SWIMS: Join professional divers and swim with
the friendly bottlenose dolphins that inhabit the bay. Tours
depart Sorrento Pier on weekends from September to May.

Mour
Publi
Mt Ma
160

Martha Point

6

Point
Nepean
Nepean
Bay
Observatory Point
Ticonderoga
Bay
Fort
Nepean
POINT NEPEAN
NP
Weeroona
Bay
Cheviot Beach
COMMONWEALTH
LAND
Portsea
POINT
NEPEAN
NP
Portsea Golf
Course
Gollins
Bay
London Bridge
Portsea
Surf Beach
Point King
Sorrento
Golf
Course

Dromana
Bay
Safety Beach

ARTHURS SEAT STATE PARK: Originally named after a similar
mountain near Edinburgh, Scotland during the first exploration
of Port Phillip Bay. Take a ride on the 72-seat chairlift for
spectacular views of the Peninsula and Bay. Visit Arthurs Seat
Fauna Park or enjoy a short walk to scenic Flinders Lookout.

Dromana

MARINE DR
PENINSULA

7

Sorrento

Capel   Sound

McCrae Homestead
Eastern Lighthouse
McCrae
Mornington RD
Arthurs Seat
Chairlift
Arthurs Seat
309m
ARTHURS
SEAT
SP

PENINSULA

Sorrento
Back Beach
Jubilee Point
Diamond Bay
Sorrento
Downs
Golf
Course
Collins Settlement
Historic Site
The Sisters

Rosebud
West
Rosebud

ARTHURS SEAT RD

Sheetwash

BOUNDARY

8

POINT NEPEAN NATIONAL PARK: This magnificent park
extends from the tip of Point Nepean to Cape Schanck.
An unusual transporter service operates, taking visitors
to Cheviot Beach, Observatory Point and the historical
Fort Nepean. Numerous walking tracks provide easy
access to London Bridge, Cape Schanck Lighthouse
and endless spectacular coastal scenery.

Koonya Beach
Spray Point
Koreen Point
Pearces Beach

MELBOURNE
NEPEAN
POINT
CANTEBURY RD
JETTY RD
DUNDAS ST
White
Cliffs
Rye
Tootgarook
Observation
Hill
Tootgarook
Market
NATIONAL
Rosebud
Golf
Course
NEPEAN RD
Rosebud
Country
Club

ARTHURS
SEAT
SP

JETTY RD

12

MAIN CREEK RD

20

9

The Divide
Rye
Ocean Beach

PARK
BROWNS RD
TRUEMANS RD
BROWNS RD
Drum Drum Alloc Ck
Boneo
Market
RD
3

MAIN
RIDGE

PURVES RD

SHANDS

17

BALDRY'S

27

71

10

Capri
Beach

Boneo

MORNINGTON

PENINSULA

25

POINT
NEPEAN
NATIONAL
PARK

School Hill
184m

MORNINGTON RD

Main RD

Musk

71

Boags Rocks
Gunnamatta
Surf Beach

National
Golf
Course

Cape
Schanck
Golf Course

67 ROSEBUD

MEAKINS RD

Stockyard Ck

Spring Ck

Double

11

TOURIST INFORMATION:
Phillip Island (Phillip Island Rd, Newhaven)
Mornington (cnr Main & Elizabeth Sts)
Queenscliff (cnr Bellarine Hwy & Grubb Rd)

FLINDERS RD

The Pinna
77m

Tea Tree
Burrabong Ck

The
Blowhole

12

BASS   STRAIT

WINERIES: 1
Balnarring Vineyard 1 L8
Boonooke Estate 2 K8
Coolart Valley Vineyard 3 J8
Craig Avon Vineyard 4 J7
Darling Park Vineyards 5 J8
Dromana Estate 6 I7
Elan Vineyard 7 L6
Ermes Estate 8 L5
Hanns Creek Estate 9 K8
Karina Vineyard 10 I7
Kings Creek Vineyard 11 L7
Main Ridge Estate 12 I8
Merricks Estate 13 K9
Moorooduc Estate 14 K5
Paringa Estate 15 J9
Peninsula Estate 16 I8
Poplar Bend 17 H9
Port Phillip Estate 18 J8
Red Hill Estate 19 I9
Ryland River 20 H9
Stonier's Winery 21 K9
Stumpy Gully Vineyard 22 L4
Tanglewood Downs 23 K6
T'Gallant 24 J8
The Briars Vineyard 25 J5
Tucks Ridge 26 J9
Tuerong Estate 27 I9
Vintina Estate 28 K3
Willow Creek 29 K7

Cape Schanck Lighthouse

Bushranger
Bay

Cape
Schanck

Picnic
Point
The
Arch

Simmons
Bay

Cairns
Bay

FLINDERS RD

N

13

A B C D E F G H

0   2   4   6   8   10 km

FRANKSTON

TO MELBOURNE

CRANBOURNE RD.

CRANBOURNE RD.

FRANKSTON

TO DANDENONG

SOUTH

CLYDE - FIVEWAYS RD.

Five Ways

BROWNS

211

Pelican Point

Daveys Bay

Ballam Park Homestead

Langwarrin

WESTERNPORT

HWY

Langwarrin Reserve

ROBINSONS

DEVON MEADOWS

GIPPSLAND

HWY

211

TO KORUMBURRA

Mt Eliza

HUMPHRIES

Frankston Reservoir

GOLF

LINKS

RD

WARRANDYTE

HASTINGS

PEARCEDALE

FISHERIES

Sunnyside Beach

Mornington Golf Course

Mt Eliza 160m

Baxter Park

Baxter

BAXTER - TOORADIN RD.

Pearcedale

BAXTER - TOORADIN

Cannons Creek

Tooradin

NEPEAN

Mornington

HWY

Sages Cottage

Railway

Tourist

ERAMOSA

ROAD WEST

FRANKSTON

GRANT

WATSON

QUEENS

RD

DANDENONG

WARNEET

Blind Bight

Bungower

Mornington Racecourse

12

Somerville

ERAMOSA ROAD EAST

FLINDERS

Ck

HWY

TOORADIN

Warneet

Watson Inlet

Quail Island

MORNINGTON

Civic Reserve

TYABB RD

DERRIL

BUNGOWER

JONES

TYABB

WESTERN   PORT

BENTONS

Moorooduc

Moorooduc Airfield

GULLY

FRENCH ISLAND: Named in 1802 by Captain Bauclin, leader of a French scientific expedition, this naturally protected island of state parkland provides the perfect habitat for rare white-breasted sea eagles, potoroos and koalas.

CRAIGIE

MORNINGTON RD

STUMPY

(WESTERNPORT

RD

Tyabb

Western Port Airfield

the Briars Homestead

FREEWAY

Devilbend Golf Course & Rec Res

GRADYENS

RD

BHP Steel Western Port Works

Scrub Point

23

MOOROODUC

Devilbend Reservoir

HODGINS

BOES

BAYVIEW RD

FRENCH   ISLAND

STATE   PARK

BALNARRING

Bittern Reservoir

COOLART

HENDERSONS

RD

Hastings

Long Point

Long Island

FAIRHAVEN

FRENCH

Bulldog Ck

Tubbarubba

23

69

MYERS

Warringine Ck

Hastings Bight

Sandstone Island

ISLAND

Mt Wellington 98m

12

STUMPY

11

Balnarring Racecourse

FLINDERS

RD

Bittern

WOOLLEYS

Crib Point

Passenger

The Pinnacles 66m

RD

29

FRANKSTON

DISNEY

ST

BITTERN

DROMANA

64

67

SOUTH

BEACH

Crib Point

RD

Warrawee Homestead

SANDY POINT RD

Hanns Inlet

Stony Point

Ferry

Tankerton Jetty

Tankerton

MERRICKS NORTH

Coolart Reserve

Coolart Ck

Somers

Flinders Naval Depot

24

18

STANLEYS

Coolart Ck

Balnarring Beach

Somers Beach

South Beach

(Prohibited Area)

Western Park Beach

Sandy Point

Tortoise Head

Long Point

21

13

Merricks

Merricks

Merricks Beach

Point Summer

Point Leo

Point Leo

LEO RD

ASHCOMBE MAZE: Wander through the large green hedge maze with one kilometre of pathways, or wind your way through the beautiful rose maze of over 1200 colourful and fragrant roses. The tea room and extensive gardens provide perfect places for relaxation.

Passenger

17

FLINDERS

shcombe aze

Shoreham

Shoreham Beach

Seal Rocks

Ferry

WESTERN

Penguin Rock

CHURCH ST

Cowes

COWES RD

Cowes Golf Course

Reserve

Observation Point

Rhyll Inlet

PORT

McHaffie Point

VENTNOR RD

ISLAND RD

COWES - RHYLL RD

Rhyll

Fishermans Point

Maritime & Shell Museum

Ventnor

VENTNOR RD

Ventnor Reserve

Mini Europe

Wildlife Park

PHILLIP

6

Bird Sanctuary

NEWHAVEN

Koala Res

BEACH

THE GAP RD

Koala Reserve

RHYLL

PHILLIP

VENTNOR RD

BACK BEACH

RD

A Maze Things

Swan Bay

CHURCHILL IS NP

Churchill Island

ISLAND

12

Racing Circuit

PHILLIP

ISLAND

186

RD

Australian Dairy Centre

Woody Point

Newhaven

Narrows

Cat Bay

Swan Lake

Penguin Parade

The Woolshed

Cunningham Bay

Phillip Is Airport

San Remo

Point Grant

Phillip Is Penguin Reserve

Berrys Beach

Storm Bay

Pyramid Rock

The Nobbies

Seal Rocks

AND: This year-round tourist destination with astline is an excellent weekend getaway. Visit rrain of the Nobbies and view the seal colonies Wander through one of Phillip Island's wild Koala Reserve. Every evening the little (fairy) ade up Summerland Beach providing a delightful e spectacular.

0 2 4 6 8 10 km

WINERIES ①
Bianchet Winery 1 B8
Brahams Creek Winery 2 I9
Chum Creek Winery 3 D6
Coldstream Hills 4 D8
De Bortoli Winery and
  Restaurant 5 C5
Domaine Chandon Australia 6 C7
Fergusson Winery and
  Restaurant 7 C6
Kellybrook Winery and
  Restaurant 8 A8
Lillydale Vineyards 9 D10
Lirralirra Estate 10 A8
Long Gully Estate 11 D6
Lovey's Estate 12 C6
Monbulk Winery 13 C11
Mount Delancy 14 C10
Oakridge Estate 15 D10
St Huberts Vineyard 16 C8
Shantell Vineyard 17 D5
Tarrawarra Vineyard 18 D7
Warramate Vineyard 19 D8
Yarra Burn Winery and
  Restaurant 20 G9
Yarra Edge Vineyard 21 A8
Yarra Ridge Vineyard 22 B7
Yering Station Vineyard 23 B7
Yarra Yering Vineyard 24 D8

KINGLAKE NATIONAL PARK: Home to numerous lyrebirds and wombats, the Kinglake National Park areas were established to protect the wet eucalypt forests on the Great Dividing Range. Tranquil walks through fern gullies and forested spurs take you to the Wombelano and Mason's Falls.

TOOLANGI-BLACK RANGES: Toolangi (once) home of C.J. Dennis, author of 'The Sentimental Bloke' is a mountainous berry producing area nestled in the Black Ranges State Forest. Picturesque roadways provide easy access to the spectacular Wilhelmina Falls and Murrindindi Cascades. There are excellent riding tours available in the area, taking you along rugged mountain tracks and tranquil river paths. Trout and Blackfish can be caught in the Murrindindi River.

GULF STATION: Now owned by the National Trust, Gulf Station at Yarra Glen is one of Victoria's oldest pastoral properties dating back to the 1850s. Visitors can step back in time, explore the original timber buildings, cottage gardens and participate in farm activities.

HEALESVILLE SANCTUARY: Home to over 200 of Australia's unique birds, animals and reptiles, including some endangered species. Healesville Sanctuary, open every day of the year, is recognised as Australia's top wildlife park. Spend the day venturing among friendly kangaroos, emus and wombats in naturally designed enclosures.

SILVAN RESERVOIR: Located on the edge of beautiful Olinda State Forest, Stonyford picnic ground at the magnificent Silvan Reservoir provides excellent BBQ facilities for the perfect break on a day trip to the area. Visit the Tulip Farm or simply stop along the Monbulk Road for breathtaking views of the region.

PUFFING BILLY: This superbly restored vintage steam train ambles its way from the ferny stands of Belgrave through the cool rainforest to Emerald Lake.

TOURIST INFORMATION:
Yarra Valley & Healesville
(127 Maroondah Hwy)
Marysville (18 Murchison S

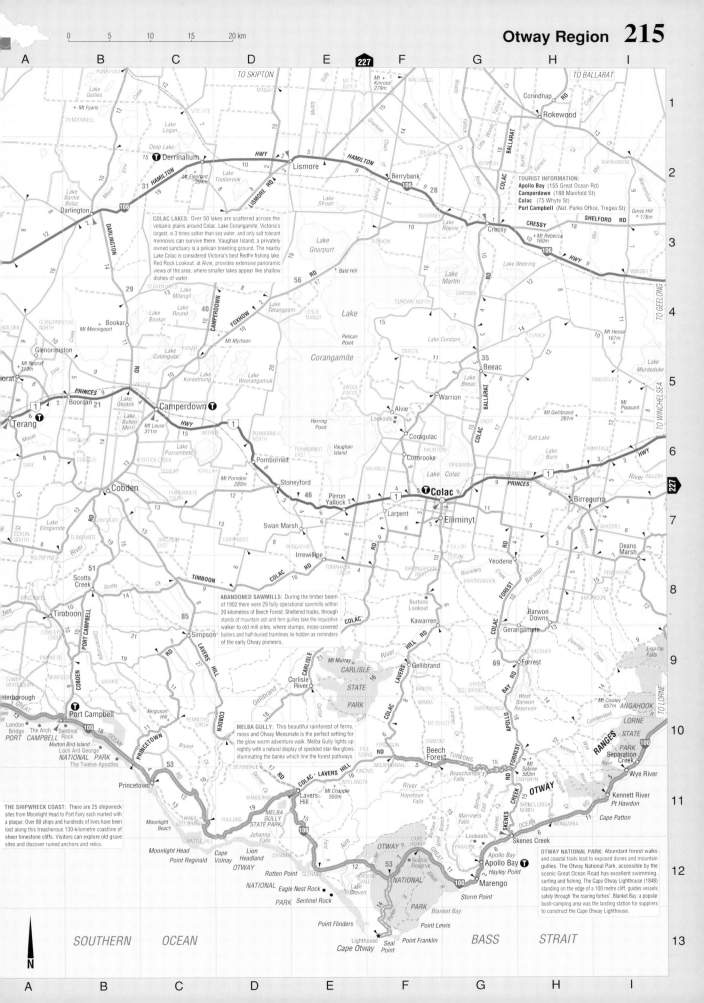

COLAC LAKES: Over 50 lakes are scattered across the volcanic plains around Colac. Lake Corangamite, Victoria's largest, is 3 times saltier than sea water, and only salt tolerant minnows can survive there. Vaughan Island, a privately owned sanctuary is a pelican breeding ground. The nearby Lake Colac is considered Victoria's best Redfin fishing lake. Red Rock Lookout, at Alvie, provides extensive panoramic views of the area, where smaller lakes appear like shallow dishes of water.

TOURIST INFORMATION:
Apollo Bay (155 Great Ocean Rd)
Camperdown (188 Manifold St)
Colac (75 Whyte St)
Port Campbell (Nat. Parks Office, Tregea St)

ABANDONED SAWMILLS: During the timber boom of 1902 there were 29 fully operational sawmills within 20 kilometres of Beech Forest. Sheltered tracks, through stands of mountain ash and fern gullies take the inquisitive walker to old mill sites, where stumps, moss-covered boilers and half-buried tramlines lie hidden as reminders of the early Otway pioneers.

MELBA GULLY: This beautiful rainforest of ferns, moss and Otway Messmate is the perfect setting for the glow worm adventure walk. Melba Gully lights up nightly with a natural display of speckled star-like glows illuminating the banks which line the forest pathways.

THE SHIPWRECK COAST: There are 25 shipwreck sites from Moonlight Head to Port Fairy each marked with a plaque. Over 80 ships and hundreds of lives have been lost along this treacherous 130-kilometre coastline of sheer limestone cliffs. Visitors can explore old grave sites and discover ruined anchors and relics.

OTWAY NATIONAL PARK: Abundant forest walks and coastal trails lead to exposed dunes and mountain gullies. The Otway National Park, accessible by the scenic Great Ocean Road has excellent swimming, surfing and fishing. The Cape Otway Lighthouse (1848) standing on the edge of a 100 metre cliff, guides vessels safely through 'the roaring forties'. Blanket Bay, a popular bush-camping area was the landing station for suppliers to construct the Cape Otway Lighthouse.

SOUTHERN OCEAN

BASS STRAIT

N

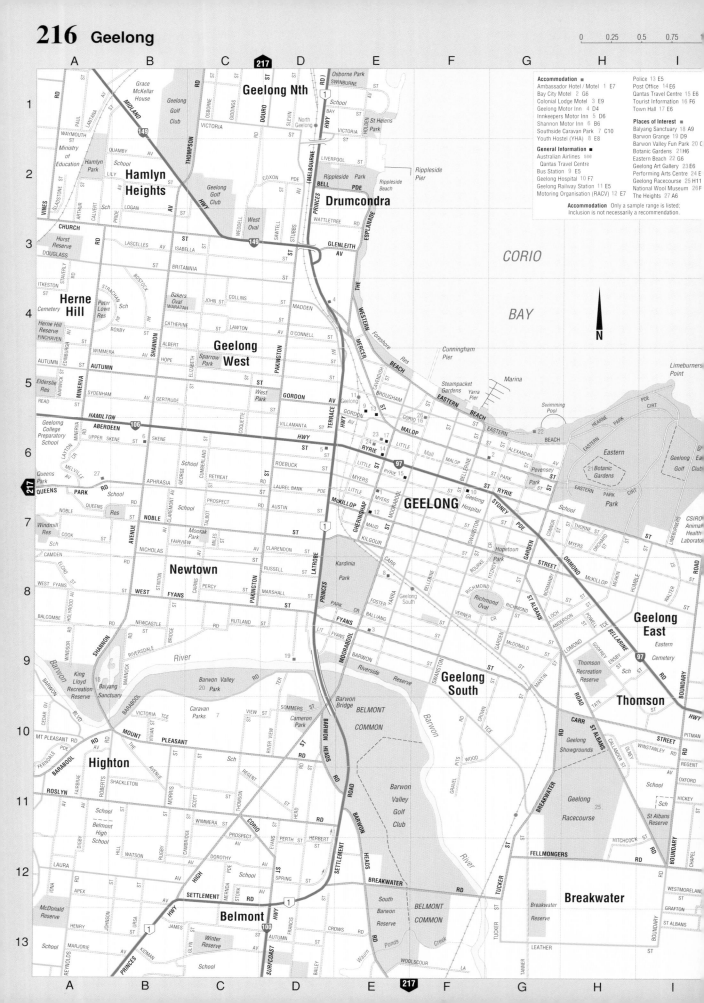

Accommodation ■
Ambassador Hotel / Motel 1 E7
Bay City Motel 2 G6
Colonial Lodge Motel 3 E9
Geelong Motor Inn 4 D4
Innkeepers Motor Inn 5 D6
Shannon Motor Inn 6 B6
Southside Caravan Park 7 C10
Youth Hostel (YHA) 8 E8

General Information ■
Australian Airlines see
  Qantas Travel Centre
Bus Station 9 E5
Geelong Hospital 10 F7
Geelong Railway Station 11 E5
Motoring Organisation (RACV) 12 E7

Police 13 E5
Post Office 14 E6
Qantas Travel Centre 15 E6
Tourist Information 16 F6
Town Hall 17 E6

Places of Interest ■
Balyang Sanctuary 18 A9
Barwon Grange 19 D9
Barwon Valley Fun Park 20 C
Botanic Gardens 21 H6
Eastern Beach 22 G6
Geelong Art Gallery 23 E6
Performing Arts Centre 24 E
Geelong Racecourse 25 H11
National Wool Museum 26 E
The Heights 27 A6

Accommodation Only a sample range is listed;
Inclusion is not necessarily a recommendation.

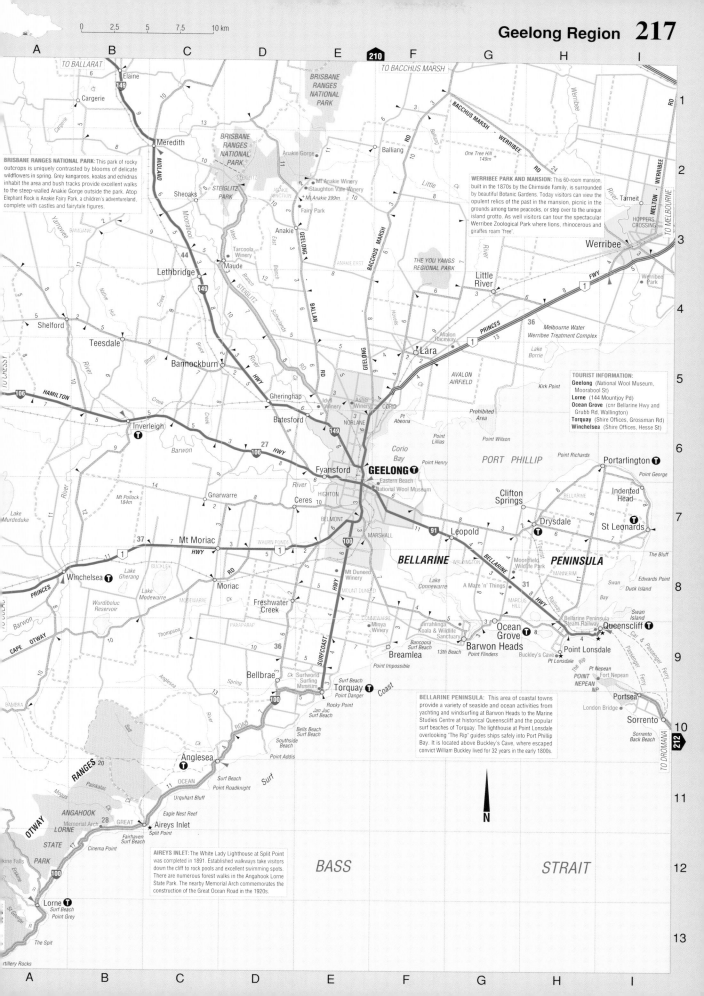

BRISBANE RANGES NATIONAL PARK: This park of rocky outcrops is uniquely contrasted by blooms of delicate wildflowers in spring. Grey kangaroos, koalas and echidnas inhabit the area and bush tracks provide excellent walks to the steep-walled Anakie Gorge outside the park. Atop Elephant Rock is Anakie Fairy Park, a children's adventureland, complete with castles and fairytale figures.

WERRIBEE PARK AND MANSION: This 60-room mansion, built in the 1870s by the Chirnside Family, is surrounded by beautiful Botanic Gardens. Today visitors can view the opulent relics of the past in the mansion, picnic in the grounds among tame peacocks, or step over to the unique island grotto. As well visitors can tour the spectacular Werribee Zoological Park where lions, rhinoceros and giraffes roam 'free'.

TOURIST INFORMATION:
Geelong (National Wool Museum, Moorabool St)
Lorne (144 Mountjoy Pd)
Ocean Grove (cnr Bellarine Hwy and Grubb Rd, Wallington)
Torquay (Shire Offices, Grossman Rd)
Winchelsea (Shire Offices, Hesse St)

BELLARINE PENINSULA: This area of coastal towns provide a variety of seaside and ocean activities from yachting and windsurfing at Barwon Heads to the Marine Studies Centre at historical Queenscliff and the popular surf beaches of Torquay. The lighthouse at Point Lonsdale overlooking "The Rip" guides ships safely into Port Phillip Bay. It is located above Buckley's Cave, where escaped convict William Buckley lived for 32 years in the early 1800s.

AIREYS INLET: The White Lady Lighthouse at Split Point was completed in 1891. Established walkways take visitors down the cliff to rock pools and excellent swimming spots. There are numerous forest walks in the Angahook Lorne State Park. The nearby Memorial Arch commemorates the construction of the Great Ocean Road in the 1920s.

BASS STRAIT

PORT PHILLIP

218 Bendigo

North Bendigo

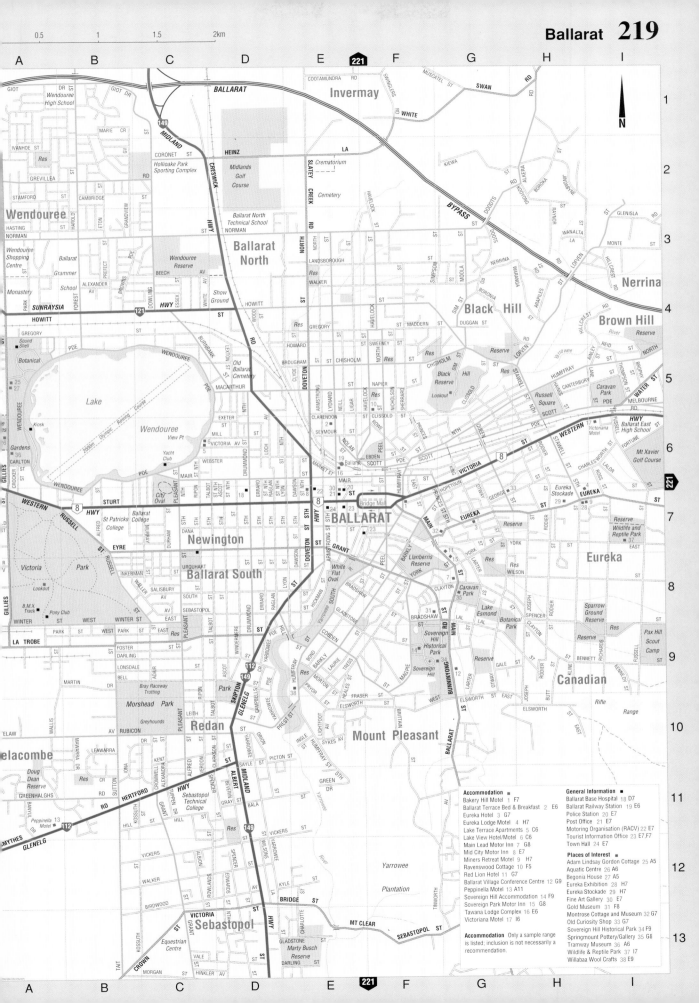

0.5   1   1.5   2km

A   B   C   D   E   221   F   G   H   I

N

1

COOTAMUNDRA   RD   SWAN   RD
GIOT   DR   ST   MUSCATEL   ST
Wendouree   GIOT   DR   SWINGLERS   RD
High School   MARIE   CR   WHITE   ST   KIEWA   ST

Invermay

Wendouree

Ballarat
North

Ballarat North
Technical School

Black Hill

Nerrina

Brown Hill

Lake
Wendouree

Newington

Ballarat South

BALLARAT

Eureka

Redan

Victoria
Park

Mount Pleasant

Canadian

Sebastopol

Accommodation
Bakery Hill Motel   1   F7
Ballarat Terrace Bed & Breakfast   2   E6
Eureka Hotel   3   G7
Eureka Lodge Motel   4   H7
Lake Terrace Apartments   5   C6
Lake View Hotel/Motel   6   C6
Main Lead Motor Inn   7   G8
Mid City Motor Inn   8   E7
Miners Retreat Motel   9   H7
Ravenswood Cottage   10   F5
Red Lion Hotel   11   G7
Ballarat Village Conference Centre   12   G9
Peppinella Motel   13   A11
Sovereign Hill Accommodation   14   F9
Sovereign Park Motor Inn   15   G8
Tawana Lodge Complex   16   E6
Victoriana Motel   17   I6

Accommodation Only a sample range
is listed; inclusion is not necessarily a
recommendation.

General Information
Ballarat Base Hospital   18   D7
Ballarat Railway Station   19   E6
Police Station   20   E7
Post Office   21   E7
Motoring Organisation (RACV)   22   E7
Tourist Information Office   23   E7,F7
Town Hall   24   E7

Places of Interest
Adam Lindsay Gordon Cottage   25   A5
Aquatic Centre   26   A6
Begonia House   27   A5
Eureka Exhibition   28   H7
Eureka Stockade   29   H7
Fine Art Gallery   30   E7
Gold Museum   31   F8
Montrose Cottage and Museum   32   G7
Old Curiosity Shop   33   G7
Sovereign Hill Historical Park   34   F9
Springmount Pottery/Gallery   35   G8
Tramway Museum   36   A6
Wildlife & Reptile Park   37   I7
Willabaa Wool Crafts   38   E9

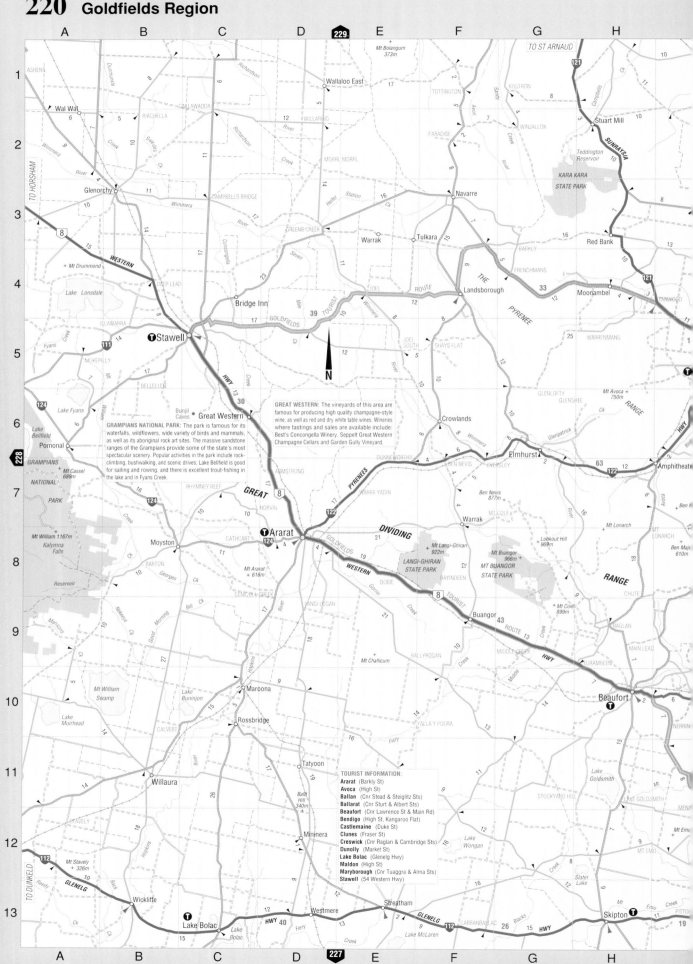

GRAMPIANS NATIONAL PARK: The park is famous for its waterfalls, wildflowers, wide variety of birds and mammals, as well as its aboriginal rock art sites. The massive sandstone ranges of the Grampians provide some of the state's most spectacular scenery. Popular activities in the park include rock-climbing, bushwalking, and scenic drives; Lake Bellfield is good for sailing and rowing, and there is excellent trout-fishing in the lake and in Fyans Creek.

GREAT WESTERN: The vineyards of this area are famous for producing high quality champagne-style wine, as well as red and dry white table wines. Wineries where tastings and sales are available include: Best's Concongella Winery, Seppelt Great Western Champagne Cellars and Garden Gully Vineyard.

TOURIST INFORMATION:
Ararat (Barkly St)
Avoca (High St)
Ballan (Cnr Stead & Steiglitz Sts)
Ballarat (Cnr Sturt & Albert Sts)
Beaufort (Cnr Lawrence St & Main Rd)
Bendigo (High St, Kangaroo Flat)
Castlemaine (Duke St)
Clunes (Fraser St)
Creswick (Cnr Raglan & Cambridge Sts)
Dunolly (Market St)
Lake Bolac (Glenelg Hwy)
Maldon (High St)
Maryborough (Cnr Tuaggra & Alma Sts)
Stawell (54 Western Hwy)

0 5 10 15 20 25 km

K   L   M   N   O   P   Q   R

TO INGLEWOOD
TO KERANG
TO ROCHESTER
TO HEATHCOTE

GOLDFIELDS TOURIST ROUTE

Mt Moliagul 527m
John Flynn Memorial
MURPHYS CREEK
Moliagul
Llanelly
Newbridge
Marong
Sandhurst Town
Eaglehawk
Myers Flat
Epsom
Bendigo Pottery
WHITE HILLS
MIDLAND
McIVOR HWY

Welcome Stranger Monument
Tarnagulla
Gold 'n' Rocks Museum
MAIDEN GULLY
Central Deborah Mine
BENDIGO
Golden Dragon Museum
Junortoun

Bealiba
Mt Bealiba 488m
Goldsborough
PAINSWICK
Laanecoorie
WOODSTOCK
Lockwood
KANGAROO FLAT
Mandurang
Strathfieldsaye

Goldfields and Historical Museum
Dunolly
Eddington
Laanecoorie Reservoir
EASTVILLE
SHELBOURNE
Ravenswood
Sedgwick
Sedgwick Camel Farm
PILCHERS BRIDGE

GARDENS: There are many fine historic and public gardens scattered throughout the region. Public gardens of particular note include the Botanic Gardens of Castlemaine, Daylesford and Malmsbury, and the Queen Mary Gardens at St Arnaud. Many of the cities and towns of the region have spectacular seasonal displays. Ballarat is famous for its begonias; Bendigo has special plantings for its famous Easter Fair and for the Spring racing season. One of the most famous private gardens, open to the public, is Buda Historic Home and garden at Castlemaine.

BENDIGO'S TALKING TRAM: Visitors can take a tram ride through the historic centre of Bendigo and enjoy a potted history provided by a recorded commentary.

FIELDS REGION: The cities and towns of this region to a peak of style and affluence in the 1880s, a built on the first gold discoveries in the 1850s. owns display all the frivolity and grandeur of rian architecture.

MALDON: The National Trust has declared Maldon the "first notable town" in Victoria; interesting collections of 19th-century buildings, and collection of European trees.

PORCUPINE FLAT
Baringhup
Historic Town
WALMER
Harcourt North
Harcourt
Mt Alexander 741m

Bowenvale
Timor
Cornish Pumphouse Ruins
Lookout
Mt Tarrengower 570m
Maldon
Steam Train Rides
PERKINS REEF
Castlemaine Market
Buda House

Maryborough
Carisbrook
PYRENEES
Cairn Curran Resvr
MUCKLEFORD
Welshmans Reef
Castlemaine
Chewton
Golden Point
FARADAY

PADDYS RANGES STATE PARK
Craigie
MOOLORT
JOYCES CREEK
Newstead
Campbells Creek
Elphinstone
Metcalfe

Talbot
MAJORCA
Tullaroop Reservoir
STRATHLEA
Guildford
Vaughan
Fryerstown
Taradale

Mt Cameron 417m
SANDON
Clydesdale
IRISHTOWN
TARILTA
Botanic Gardens
Malmsbury

Campbelltown
GLENOWER
Yandoit
FRANKLINFORD
GLENLUCE
Malmsbury Reservoir

Clunes
Mt Beckworth 635m
ULLINA
WERONA
MOOROOKYLE
SHEPHERDS FLAT
Mt Franklin
Porcupine Ridge
Loddon Falls
Denver
Drummond
Lauriston
Lauriston Reservoir
TO KYNETON

Smeaton
LAWRENCE
Smeaton Hill 675m
KOOROOCHEANG
Mt Franklin
Glenlyon
SPRING HILL
Upper Coliban Resvr
Tylden

Waubra
GLENDARUEL
Hepburn Springs
Convent Gallery Botanic Gardens
Daylesford
Wheatsheaf
Coomoora
RANGE
Fern Hill

Mt Misery 724m
Broomfield
Kingston
BLAMPIED
Eganstown
Musk
Lyonville
Trentham

Coghills Creek
World of Dinosaurs
Newlyn Resvr
Musk Vale
Bullarto
Newbury

Learmonth
ASCOT
Newlyn
Creswick
ROCKLYN
Leonards Hill
Korweinguboora
Blue Mountain
BARRYS REEF

DIVIDING
Dean
Barkstead
SPARGO CREEK
Korweinguboora Reservoir
Garden of St Erth
Green Hill 705m
Blackwood
LERDERDERG STATE PARK

GREAT
MOLLONGGHIP
Moorabool Reservoir
Mt Hops 779m
BLAKEVILLE
Mt Blackwood 736m

Burrumbeet
Lake Burrumbeet
Miners Rest
White Swan Resvr
CLARKES HILL
ROOTILLA
Bolwarrah
Cleevers Hill 665m
BUNDING
Greendale
Lerderderg Gorge

BALLARAT
Eureka Stockade
Sovereign Hill
Nerrina
WESTERN
Wallace
Mt Steiglitz 638m
Pykes Ck Resvr
KORORBIT

Haddon
Lake Wendouree
Bungaree
Gordon
Ballan
Myrniong
TO MELBOURNE

Smythesdale
Magpie
Millbrook
LLANDEILO
Bastock Reservoir
WERRIBEE GORGE STATE PARK

Scarsdale
Mount Helen
Navigators
Dunnstown
Bungal Dam
INGLISTON
THE HIGHLANDS
Bacchus Marsh

GLENELG
SOVEREIGN HILL: This re-created gold-mining township is one of Victoria's major tourist attractions and should not be missed.
Buninyong
Napoleons
Scotsburn
Mt Buninyong 745m
Yendon
Lal Lal Falls
Mt Egerton

MT BUNINYONG: An extinct volcanic crater that rises 750 metres above sea level. A sealed road leads up to the lookout which offers stunning 360° views.

SPA TOWNS: Daylesford and nearby Hepburn Springs are popular holiday centres, set in attractive hill country. They are both "spa" towns, with 65 documented mineral springs, many with hand pumps.

Lal Lal
TO GEELONG
Fiskville

K   L   M   N   O   P   Q   R

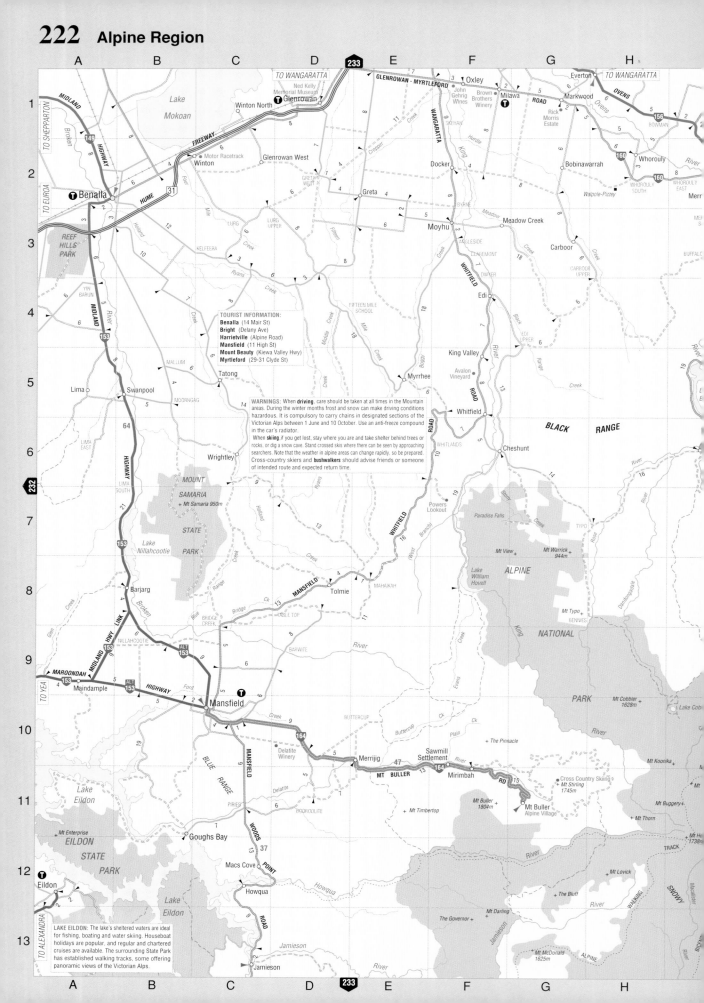

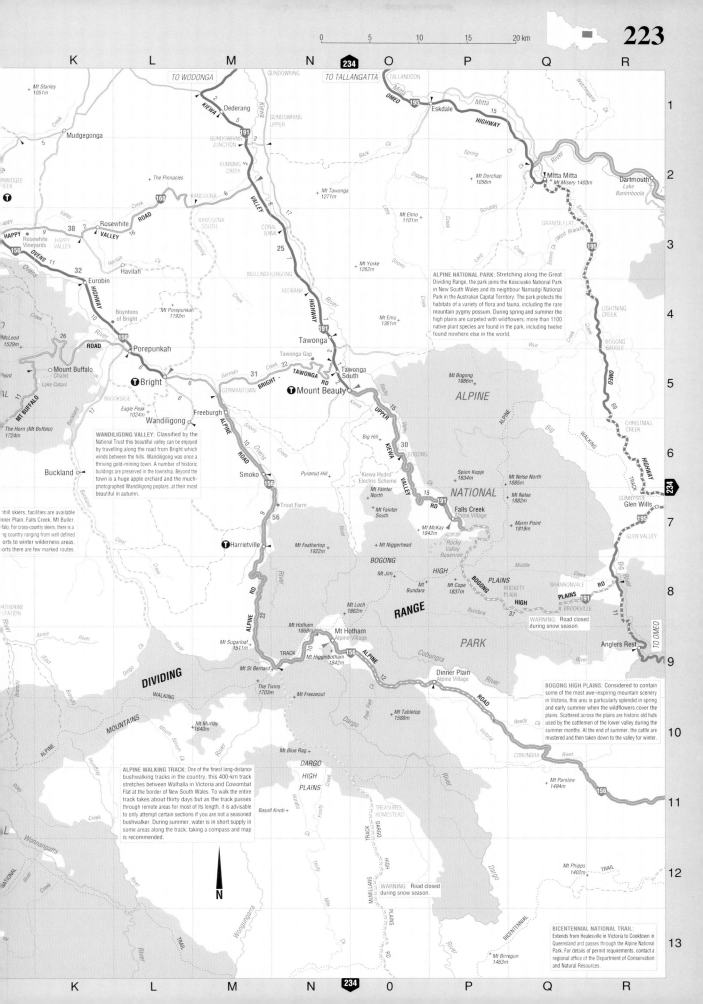

0   5   10   15   20 km

K   L   M   N   O   P   Q   R

1

TO WODONGA
TO TALLANGATTA

Mt Stanley
1051m

Mudgegonga

GUNDOWRING
KIEWA   Dederang
GUNDOWRING
UPPER
Kiewa
GUNDOWRING
JUNCTION

TALLANDOON
OMEO   Mitta
HIGHWAY   Eskdale   15
River

The Pinnacles
KANCOONA
ROAD
ROSEWHITE

RUNNING
CREEK

VALLEY

Mt Tawonga
1271m

Mt Dorchap
1056m

Mt Misery 1403m
Mitta Mitta

Dartmouth
Lake
Banimboola

2

HAPPY
VALLEY
Rosewhite
Vineyards
Happy
Valley
OVENS
38
156
9
16
11

HAVILAH

KANCOONA
SOUTH

CORAL
BANK

MULLINDOLINGONG

REDBANK

Mt Yorke
1262m

Mt Elmo
1101m

Scrubby

GRANITE FLAT

195

LIGHTNING
CREEK

3

Eurobin
32
HIGHWAY
10
Boyntons
of Bright
156
Porepunkah

Mt Porepunkah
1193m

HIGHWAY

Mt Emu
1361m

Tawonga

ALPINE NATIONAL PARK: Stretching along the Great
Dividing Range, the park joins the Kosciusko National Park
in New South Wales and its neighbour Namadgi National
Park in the Australian Capital Territory. The park protects the
habitats of a variety of flora and fauna, including the rare
mountain pygmy possum. During spring and summer the
high plains are carpeted with wildflowers; more than 1100
native plant species are found in the park, including twelve
found nowhere else in the world.

BOGONG
SADDLE

OMEO

4

McLeod
1529m

Mount Buffalo
Chalet
Lake Catani

Bright

26
ROAD

Tawonga Gap
German
Creek
TAWONGA   RD
BRIGHT
GERMANTOWN   Mount Beauty
Tawonga
South

Mt Bogong
1986m

ALPINE

HIGHWAY
69

CHRISTMAS
CREEK

5

MT BUFFALO
The Horn (Mt Buffalo)
1724m
11
17

Buckland

Eagle Peak
1024m
Wandiligong
Freeburgh
ALPINE

WANDILIGONG VALLEY: Classified by the
National Trust this beautiful valley can be enjoyed
by travelling along the road from Bright which
winds between the hills. Wandiligong was once a
thriving gold-mining town. A number of historic
buildings are preserved in the township. Beyond the
town is a huge apple orchard and the much-
photographed Wandiligong poplars, at their most
beautiful in autumn.

BROOKSIDE
Smoko
156
Trout Farm

Pyramid Hill

UPPER
15
KIEWA
VALLEY
Big Hill
30
BOGONG
RD
15
191

Kiewa Hydro-
Electric Scheme
Mt Fainter
North
Mt Fainter
South

Spion Kopje
1834m

Falls Creek
Alpine Village

Mt Nelse North
1885m

Mt Nelse
1882m

Marm Point
1819m

WALKING

SUNNYSIDE
234
Glen Wills
195
GLEN VALLEY

6

7

hill skiers, facilities are available
nner Plain, Falls Creek, Mt Buller,
alo. For cross-country skiers, there is a
g country ranging from well defined
rts to winter wilderness areas.
orts there are few marked routes.

Harrietville
ALPINE
RD
9
56
22

Mt Feathertop
1922m

Mt McKay
1842m

Mt Niggerhead

Mt Jim

Rocky
Valley
Reservoir

BOGONG   Mt
Bundara
Mt Cope
1837m

HIGH

BOGONG

PLAINS

PLAINS

Middle
BUCKETY
PLAIN
SHANNONVALE
RD
191
37

Big   River

Creek

8

DIVIDING

MOUNTAINS

ALPINE

WALKING

Mt Sugarloaf
1511m
Mt Hotham
1868m
Mt Hotham
Alpine Village
Mt St Bernard
TRACK
Mt Higginbotham
1842m
156
ALPINE

The Twins
1703m
Mt Freezeout

Mt Murray
1640m

Mt Blue Rag

DARGO

HIGH

PLAINS

Mt Loch
1862m

RANGE

12

Cobungra
River

Dinner Plain
Alpine Village

ROAD

PARK

Cobungra

HIGH
BROOKVILLE
11

WARNING: Road closed
during snow season.

Anglers Rest

TO OMEO

9

10

BOGONG HIGH PLAINS: Considered to contain
some of the most awe-inspiring mountain scenery
in Victoria, this area is particularly splendid in spring
and early summer when the wildflowers cover the
plains. Scattered across the plains are historic old huts
used by the cattlemen of the lower valley during the
summer months. At the end of summer, the cattle are
mustered and then taken down to the valley for winter.

ALPINE WALKING TRACK: One of the finest long-distance
bushwalking tracks in the country, this 400-km track
stretches between Walhalla in Victoria and Cowombat
Flat at the border of New South Wales. To walk the entire
track takes about thirty days but as the track passes
through remote areas for most of its length, it is advisable
to only attempt certain sections if you are not a seasoned
bushwalker. During summer, water is in short supply in
some areas along the track; taking a compass and map
is recommended.

River

TREASURES
HOMESTEAD

Mt Tabletop
1588m

Victoria

River

156

Mt Parslow
1494m

11

N

McMILLANS
TRACK

DARGO
HIGH
PLAINS
RD

BICENTENNIAL

Mt Phipps
1402m
TRAIL

12

WARNING: Road closed
during snow season.

Basalt Knob

Mt Birregun
1463m

BICENTENNIAL NATIONAL TRAIL:
Extends from Healesville in Victoria to Cooktown in
Queensland and passes through the Alpine National
Park. For details of permit requirements, contact a
regional office of the Department of Conservation
and Natural Resources.

13

K   L   M   N   O   P   Q   R

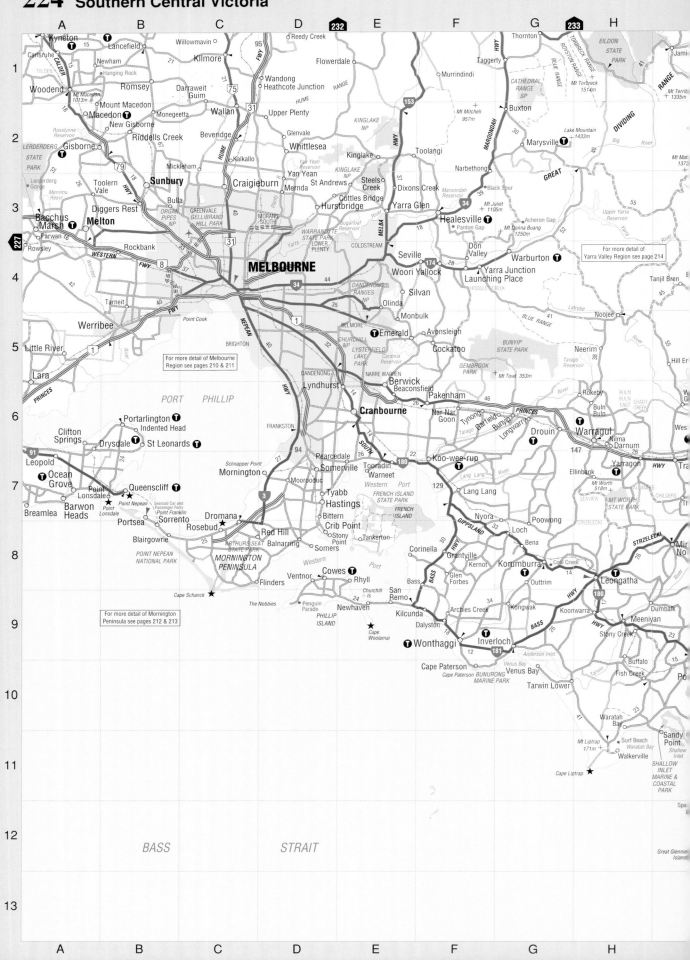

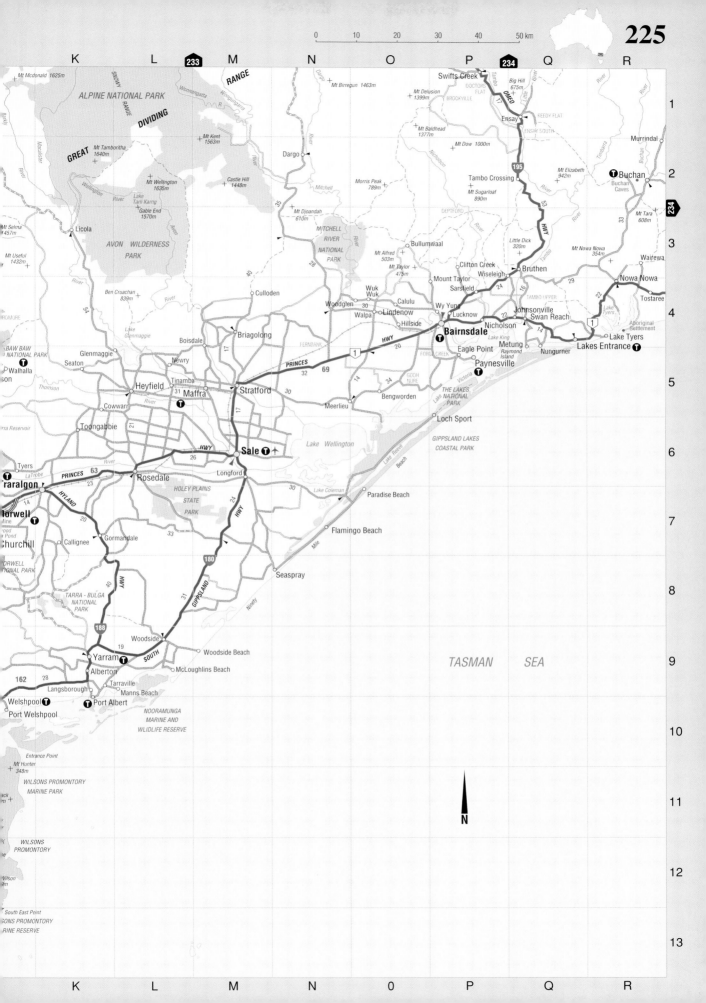

0 10 20 30 40 50 km

J K L M N O P Q R

1

8 Great Western
31
Crowlands
Elmhurst 29
122 HWY
ARMSTRONG
Winneap
Avoca
For more detail of Goldfields Region see page 220 & 221
PADDYS RANGES SP
SUNRAYSIA
26
229
122
Newstead
Castlemaine
Loddon
Elphinstone
15
CALDER
Malmsbury
Malmsbury Reservoir
37 HWY

2

Ararat 124
Moyston
PYRENEES
WESTERN
18
LANGI GHIRAN SP
LANGI LOGAN
Buangor 44
MIDDLE CREEK
Mt Buangor 966m
Amphitheatre
Ben Nevis 877m
Lexton
121
23
Waubra
Mt Beckworth 635m
Clunes
19
Smeaton
Hepburn Springs
Kingston 28
MIDLAND
Newlyn
Daylesford 48
Trentham
Upper Coliban Reservoir
149
Kyneton
Carlsruhe
Tylden
79
Woodend
Rosslynne Reservoir

3

Maroona
Rossbridge
Tatyoon
Mininera
Beaufort
91
Trawalla
25 HWY
Burrumbeet
Learmonth
Miners Rest
Creswick
Dean
Coghills Creek
Broomfield
Newlyn
Blackwood
Greendale
LERDERDERG STATE PARK
Lerderderg Gorge
112
Merrimu Reservoir

4

Lake Bolac
Westmere
Nerrin Nerrin
Mt Hamilton 319m
Lake Gellie
Streatham 175
112
Lake McLaren
26
Skipton
29
Linton
Snake Valley
Haddon
Scarsdale
Smythesdale
Newtown
Durham Lead
BALLARAT
Mt Helen
Buninyong
Napoleons
Clarendon
Lal Lal
For more detail of Ballarat see page 219
Nerrina
Dunnstown
Bungaree
Wallace
Gordon
Ballan
Myrniong
8
Bacchus Marsh
Parwan
Rowsley
Glenmore
WERRIBEE GORGE STATE PARK
BRISBANE RANGES NATIONAL PARK
224

5

GLENELG
Lake Bolac
Lake Eyang
Widgen 360m
Mt Erin 421m
Cape Clear
Dereel Lake
Grenville
Cargerie
Elaine
149
Meredith
Sheoaks
STEIGLITZ PARK
Maude
Anakie
Little River
Balliang

6

rndoo
Deep Lake
VITE VITE
Lismore 146
Derrinallum
Mt Elephant 394m
Lake Tooliorook
Berrybank
Rokewood
Corindhap
HAMILTON
Shelford
Lethbridge
Teesdale
86
Lara
PRINCES
1

7

lake
Darlington
23
Mt Shadwell 292m
Bookaar
Lake Bookaar
Lake Colongulac
Cressy
L Weering
Lake Martin
38
HWY 106
Inverleigh
Lake Murdeduke
Bannockburn
Batesford
Fyansford
GEELONG
Clifton Springs
MIDLAND

8

slie
Mt Noorat 313m
Lake Keilambete
Glenormiston
Noorat
Boorcan
Terang
PRINCES
Camperdown
46
Alvie
Coragulac
Cororooke
Warrion
Beeac
Salt Lake
Winchelsea
37 HWY
Moriac
Mount Moriac
Gnarwarre
Ceres
Freshwater Creek
Leopold
Ocean Grove
Barwon Heads
Breamlea
Bellbrae
Torquay
91

9

HWY
Garvoc
Cobden
187
Pomborneit
Stoneyford
Pirron Yallock
Larpent
Colac
Elliminyt
Swan Marsh
Birregurra
Yeodene
Deans Marsh
Anglesea
5

10

Nullawarre
Timboon
Simpson
Irrewillipe
Kawarren
Gerangamete
Forrest
Barwon Downs
ANGAHOOK-LORNE STATE PARK
100
Aireys Inlet
Lorne
For more detail of Geelong Region see page 217

11

rborough
100
Port Campbell
London Bridge
The Arch
Sentinel Rock
Loch Ard Gorge
PORT CAMPBELL
The Twelve Apostles
NATIONAL PARK
Curdies Inlet
CARLISLE STATE PARK
Carlisle River
Mt Chapple 550m
GELLIBRAND
Beech Forest
Mt Sabine 583m
OTWAY RANGES
OCEAN
Separation Creek
Wye River
Kennett River
Cape Patton
Pizzey Point
Skenes Creek
GREAT
Princetown
MELBA GULLY STATE PARK
Lavers Hill
47
Apollo Bay
Marengo
N

12

Moonlight Head
Point Reginald
OTWAY NATIONAL PARK
For more detail of Otway Region see page 215
Cape Otway

13

BASS STRAIT

J K L M N O P Q R

A B C D **230** E F G H

1 2 3 4 5 6 7 8 9 10 11 12 13

Mt Observatory 93m

Tempy

Patchewollock

Speed

22

Turri

SUNRAYSIA

SCORPION SPRINGS CONSERVATION PARK

BIG DESERT

WYPERFELD

35

La

26

BIG DESERT

NATIONAL

WILDERNESS PARK

Hopetoun

Lake Coorong

Mt Shaugh 184m

PARK

LAKE ALBACUTYA PARK

Lake Albacutya

Yaapeet

45

25

HWY

MT SHAUGH CONSERVATION PARK

WIMMERA

Ross Lake

Rainbow

Kenmare

41

Beulah

GALAQUIL

SOUTH AUSTRALIA

VICTORIA

Lake Hindmarsh

32

Ellam

HENTY

107

Yanac 21

Netherby

Lorquon

42

45

Jeparit

45

143

287

SANDS MERE

31

32

45

37

Antwerp

KATYIL

HWY

Warrackna

Bordertown

Diapur

Nhill

Kiata

Gerang Gerung

39

Borung

138

8

Wolseley

43

WESTERN

HWY

8

River

Serviceton

Kaniva

Miram

40

158

Dimboola

19

Wail

KALKEE

57

24

HWY

48

LITTLE DESERT NATIONAL PARK

Wimmera

Pimpinio

25

17

Jung

HENTY

46

BANGHAM

BANGHAM CP

45

Lake Wyn Wyn

Murtoa

31

Frances

Lake Cadnite

Minimay

34

Goroke

Gymbowen

Mitre

Mitre Lake

Natimuk

Horsham

Mt Arapiles 370m

27

Binnum

31

18

MT ARAPILES-TOOAN STATE PARK

32

HWY

Haven

Taylors Lake

Kybybolite

32

35

99

130

Noradjuha

40

Pine Lake

Mackenzie

41

WESTERN

Hynam

40

Clear Lake

Dadswells Bridge

124

Flat Rocks Caves

Naracoorte

32

Apsley

Lake Wallace

WIMMERA

North Lake

Wombelano

64

River

DIFFICULT RANGE

Mt Difficult 810m

Naracoorte Caves

30

14

21

Edenhope

Douglas

32

Toolondo Reservoir

Mt Talbot 320m

HENTY

Wartook Reservoir

61

Mackenzie Falls

Wrattonbully

32

34

White Lake

Lake Kanagulk

THE BLACK RANGE

BLACK RANGE STATE PARK

Aboriginal Paintings

GRAMPIANS

Bool Lagoon

Poolaijelo

21

River

29

Balmoral

107

NATIONAL

Cave of Fishes

Comaum

DERGHOLM STATE PARK

Glenelg

Chetwynd River

ENGLEFIELD

VASEY

Rocklands Reservoir

VICTORIA RANGE

Cave of Hands

PARK

Coonawarra

GLENROY

A B C **226** D E F G H

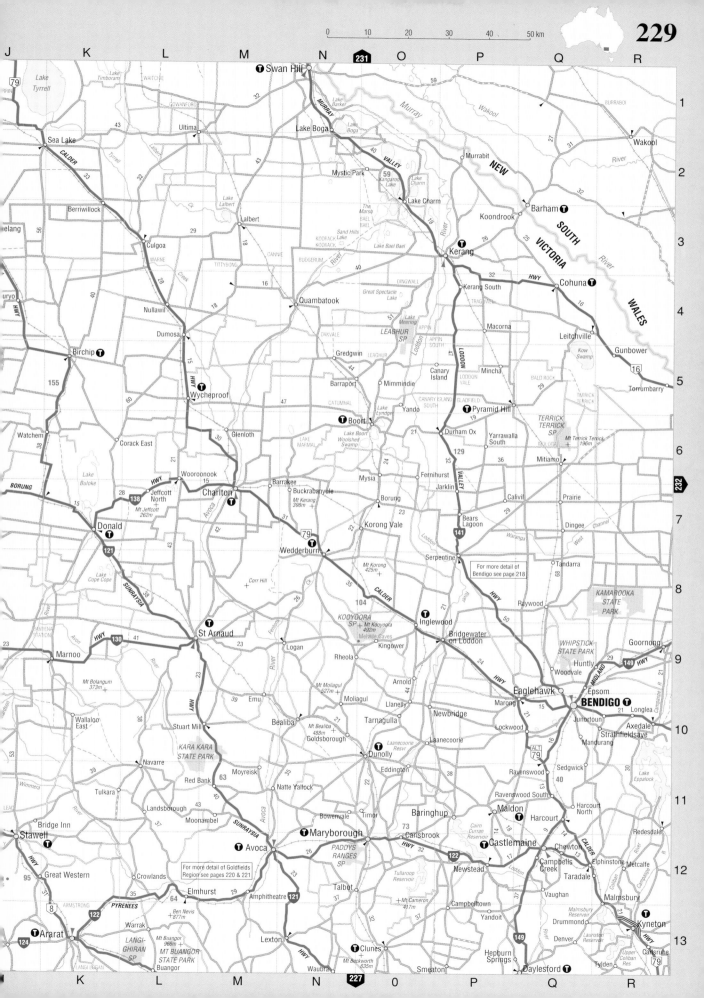

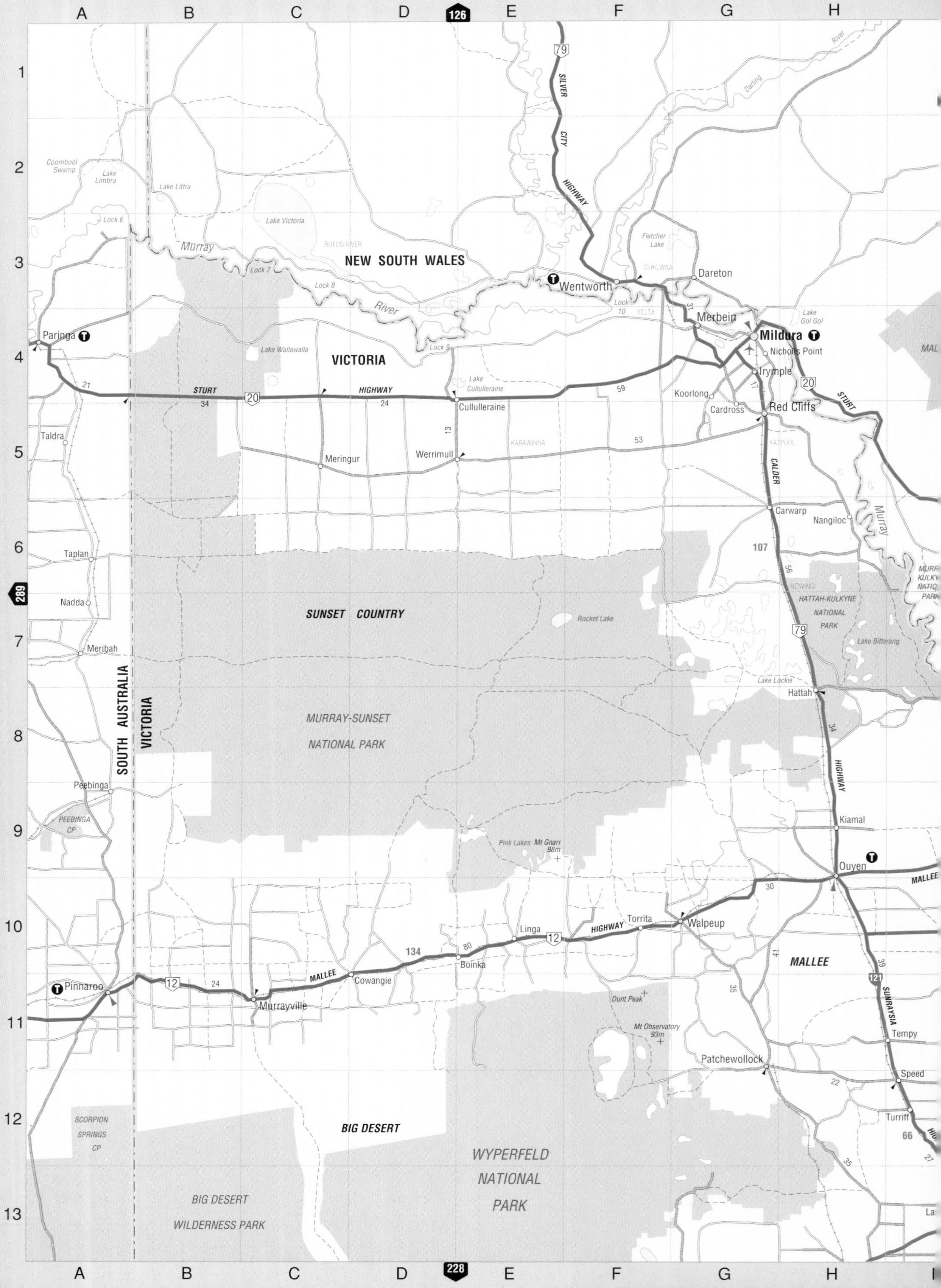

A B C D 126 E F G H

1

2

Coombool Swamp
Lake Limbra
Lake Littra
Lock 6

79
SILVER CITY HIGHWAY
Darling River

3

Murray
Lock 7
Lake Victoria
RUFUS RIVER
NEW SOUTH WALES
Lock 8
River
Lock 10
Wentworth
CURLWAA
YELTA
Dareton
Merbein
31
Fletcher Lake

VICTORIA
Paringa
Lock 9
Lake Wallawalla
Lake Cullulleraine
Mildura
Nicholls Point
Lake Gol Gol
MAL

4

21
STURT 34
20
HIGHWAY 24
13
Cullulleraine
59
Koorlong
Cardross
Irymple
Red Cliffs
11
20
STURT

Taldra
Meringur
Werrimull
KARAWINNA
53
CALDER
YATPOOL

5

SOUTH AUSTRALIA
VICTORIA

Taplan
289

6

SUNSET COUNTRY
Rocket Lake
107
56
NOWINGI
HATTAH-KULKYNE NATIONAL PARK
MURRAY-KULKY NATIO PARK

Nadda

Meribah

7

79
Lake Bitterang
Lake Lockie
Hattah

8

MURRAY-SUNSET
NATIONAL PARK
34
HIGHWAY

Peebinga
Peebinga CP

9

Pink Lakes Mt Gnarr 98m
Kiamal
Ouyen
MALLEE

10

Linga
Torrita
HIGHWAY 12
Walpeup
30
41
MALLEE
39
SURAYSIA

134
80
Boinka
Cowangie
MALLEE
35
121

Pinnaroo
12 24
Murrayville
Dunt Peak
Tempy

11

Mt Observatory 93m
Patchewollock
Speed
22

12

SCORPION SPRINGS CP
BIG DESERT
WYPERFELD
NATIONAL
Turriff
66
HI

13

BIG DESERT
WILDERNESS PARK
PARK
La

A B C D 228 E F G H

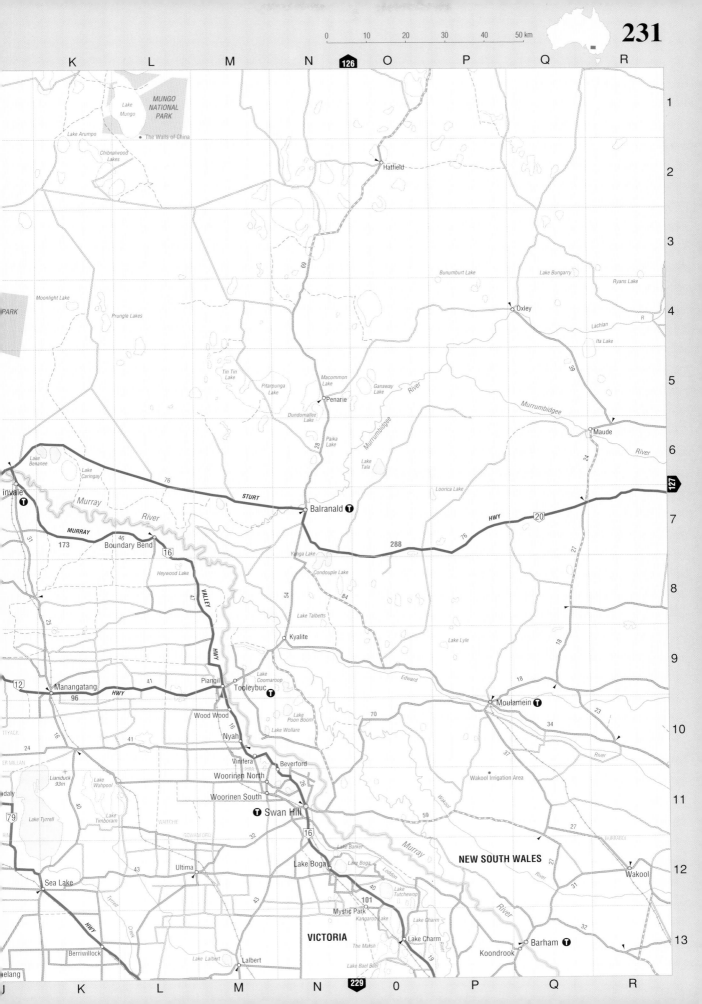

0 10 20 30 40 50 km

K L M N O P Q R

1

2

3

4

5

6

7

8

9

10

11

12

13

MUNGO
NATIONAL
PARK

Lake
Mungo

Lake Arumpa

The Walls of China

Chibnalwood
Lakes

Hatfield

Bunumburt Lake

Lake Bungarry

Ryans Lake

PARK

Moonlight Lake

Oxley

Lachlan

R

Ita Lake

39

Prungle Lakes

Tin Tin
Lake

Macommon
Lake

Ganaway
Lake

River

Murrumbidgee

Pitarpunga
Lake

Penarie

Murrumbidgee

Maude

River

Dundomallee
Lake

28

Paika
Lake

Lake
Tala

24

6

Lake Benanee

Lake
Caringay

76

STURT

Balranald

Loorica Lake

127

invale

Murray

River

HWY

20

7

MURRAY

173

46

Boundary Bend

16

Yanga Lake

288

76

27

31

Heywood Lake

Condouple Lake

8

VALLEY

47

54

84

18

25

Lake Talbetts

HWY

Kyalite

Lake Lyle

9

12

Manangatang

41

Piangil

Lake
Coomaroop

Edward

18

96

HWY

Tooleybuc

Lake
Poon Boom

Moulamein

23

Wood Wood

16

70

34

Nyah

Lake Wollare

37

River

41

Vinifera

Beverford

26

Wakool Irrigation Area

Woorinen North

Woorinen South

NEW SOUTH WALES

Lianiduck
93m

Lake
Wahpool

Swan Hill

Wakool

59

27

79

Lake Tyrrell

Lake
Timboram

16

32

Lake Barker

Murray

27

BURRABOI

31

Wakool

daly

24

WAITCHIE

GOSWAM CREK

Lake Boga

Lake Boga

Loddon

River

Sea Lake

43

Ultima

43

40

Lake
Tutchewop

Lake Charm

32

40

101

River

Koondrook

Barham

Berriwillock

HWY

Mystic Park

Kangaroo Lake

Lake Charm

Tyrrell

Creek

Lalbert

Lake Lalbert

The Marsh

Lake Charm

VICTORIA

Lake Bael Bael

19

J K L M N O P Q R

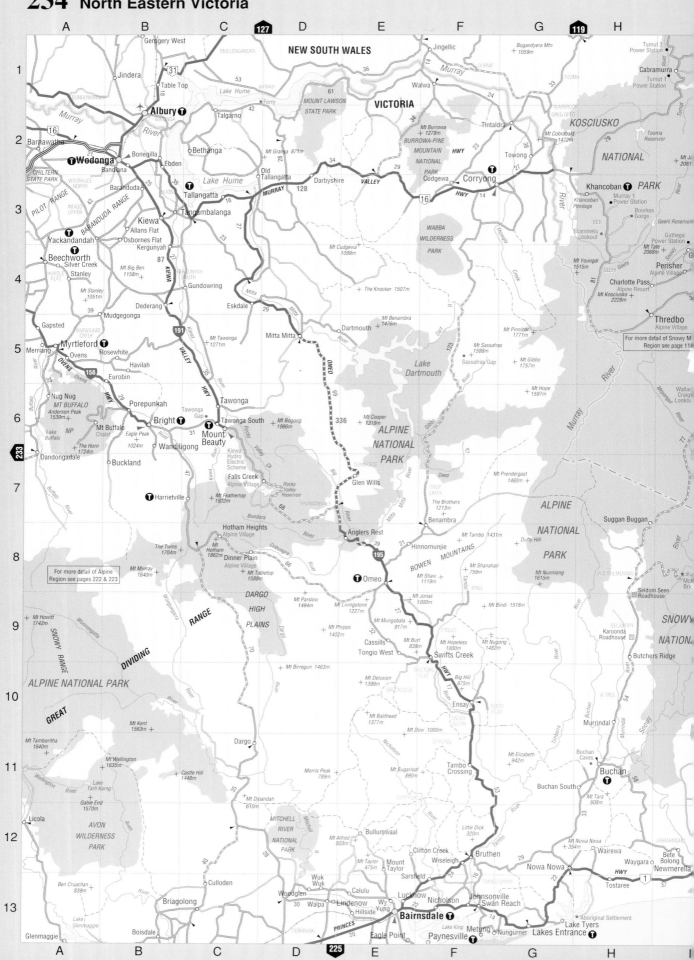

0 10 20 30 40 50 km

119

J K L M N O P Q R

SNOWY

ACT

Mt Anembo 1416m

DEUA

NATIONAL

Moruya

Moruya Heads
Moruya Heads
Congo

Anglers Reach

Adaminaby

Mt Flinders 1484m

Bredbo

Bald Mountain 1469m

Bendethera Caves

Bendethera Mtn 997m

MERINGO

Coila Lake

BERGALIA

TURLINJAH

Old Adaminaby

O'Neill Lagoon

PEAK VIEW

Tuross Head
Tuross Lake

Bodalla

Brou Lake

Lake Eucumbene

EUCUMBENE

McInally Mtn 1085m

CHAKOLA

Mt Dowling 1198 m

Numeralla

Bunyan

SNOWY MOUNTAINS

MONARO HWY

COUNTEGANY

Tuross Falls

BELOWRA

Eurobodalla

Eurobodalla

Dalmeny

Buckenderra

27

28

MOUNTAINS

HWY

23

Cooma

DIVIDING

WADBILLIGA

Kianga

Narooma

Cootralantra Lake

33

RIVER

GREAT

NATIONAL

Montague Island

Berridale

34

18

ROCK FLAT

Mt Dromedary 806m

Central Tilba

Peak Alone 954m

WANDELLA

Lake Jindabyne

Kiah Lake

32

Buckleys Lake

46

Tilba Tilba

CORUNNA

ROCKY PLAINS

Snowy

35

Dalgety

15

Nimmitabel

KYDRA

Mt Kydra 1236m

Cobargo

18

19

Wallaga Lake

WALLAGA LAKE NATIONAL PARK

Bermagui

NUMBLA VALE

Beards Lake

Mt Cooper 1018m

Brown Mtn 1260m

MOUNTAINS

18

30

Bemboka

36

Quaama

1

Brogo Reservoir

BROGO

RIVER

WAPENGO

For more detail of South Coast see page 117

For more detail of Snowy Region see page 118

112

MONARO HWY

SNOWY

22

ANDO

NUMBUGGA

MORANS CROSSING

Bega

18 HWY

ANGLEDALE

MIMOSA ROCKS NATIONAL PARK

SOUTH

Mt Alexander 1075m

Mt Rix 988m

19

KAMERUKA

26

Kalaru

Tathra

TINGARINGY

CURROWONG

37

BIBBENLUKE

Candelo

TOOTHDALE

14

23

Wallagoot Lake

TOMBONG

Adams Pk

21

20

Cathcart

32

19

Wolumla

20

BOURNDA NATIONAL PARK

PACIFIC

Bombala

162

32

Wyndham

28

Tura Beach

Merimbula

OCEAN

Delegate River

Haydens Bog

Mt Delegate 1308m

NEW SOUTH WALES

VICTORIA

36

Boon

MILA

CRAIGIE

White Rock Mtn 1093m

NALBAUGH NATIONAL PARK

PERICOE

52

TOWAMBA

BURRAGATE

EGAN PEAK NATIONAL PARK

NETHERCOTE

Pambula

Pambula Beach

19

BEN BOYD NATIONAL PARK

Bendoc

EDINBURGH

ROCKTON

Mt Canterbury 1039m

Nullica

Eden

Bonang

38

Delegate

Mt Poole 775m

60

KIAH

Mt Imlay 886m

11

Kiah

12

Twofold Bay

Boydtown

East Boyd

BEN BOYD NATIONAL PARK

Green Cape

Brown Mtn 1010m

Mt Eliery 1291m

ERRINUNDRA NATIONAL PARK

58

HWY

Mt Coopracambra 1000m

Waalimma Mtn 722m

164

HWY

Mt Nagha 543m

WONBOYN LAKE

NADGEE NATURE RESERVE

Goongerah

KIWAT

CHANDLERS CREEK

COOPRACAMBRA NATIONAL PARK

32

TIMBILLICA

Noorinbee North

Mt Kaye 1002m

VALLEY

Wangarabell

COMBIENBAR

Genoa

1

Gipsy Point

Cape Howe

Lake Barracoota

N

23

CANN

PRINCES

Noorinbee

47

KARLO CREEK

23

Mallacoota

Mallacoota Inlet

FAIRHAVEN

Club Terrace

21

ALFRED NATIONAL PARK

Gabo Island

Mt Kuark 917m

LIND NATIONAL PARK

Cann River

Mt Cann 530m

CROAJINGOLONG NATIONAL PARK

Cabbage Tree Creek

19

35

Bellbird Creek

23

Mt Everard 371m

Little Rame Head

Bemm River

Sydenham Inlet

Tamboon

Wingan Inlet

Cape Conran

Pearl Point

Point Hicks (Cape Everard)

Rame Head

TASMAN SEA

South Australia

Festival State

The festivals of South Australia provide an excellent chance to discover a community at its liveliest. Given the number and variety of festivals held each year, it seems South Australians enjoy making the most of life. Choose from The Adelaide Festival and the Barossa Valley Vintage Festival (both biennial), *Schutzenfest*, Australian Formula One Grand Prix, the Greek Glendi Festival, and the Cornish Kernewek Lowender.

This energetic spirit also seems to indicate that South Australians have triumphed over what might seem to be rather depressing statistics: it is the driest State in the driest continent, two-thirds is near-desert and eighty-three per cent receives an annual rainfall of less than 250 millimetres. But these facts are easily forgotten when you visit the lush green Barossa Valley or explore the beauty of the Flinders Ranges.

As a result of innovative social changes in the 1960s, today the State's conservative image has virtually disappeared. Appropriately its initial settlement began as the result of one man's idea for creating a model colony. Edward Gibbon Wakefield believed that the difficulties of other Australian colonies were caused by the ease with which anyone could obtain land. He claimed that if land were sold at two pounds an acre, only men of capital could buy; those who could not would provide a supply of labour, and the money generated would encourage investment and the development of resources. In 1834 he tested his ideas in the Gulf St Vincent area. Lieutenant-Colonel Light was dispatched as Surveyor-General to select a site.

Today, although South Australia's economy remains traditionally agrarian, secondary industry provides nine out of ten jobs. Olympic Dam is one of the world's biggest copper mines and probably the biggest uranium mine. The Leigh Creek coalfields supply the fuel for the State's power needs.

South Australia also mines most of the world's opals. Coober Pedy, the main opal-mining town, produces eighty-five per cent of Australia's opals.

The gulf lands of South Australia enjoy a Mediterranean climate while the further north you go, the hotter and more inhospitable the temperatures become. Adelaide, with its average annual rainfall of 585 millimetres, enjoys a midsummer average maximum temperature of about 28°C and a midwinter average maximum of 15°C. Seventy-two per cent of the population lives here, making South Australia the most urbanised of all the States. Adelaide inherited its orderly and pleasant layout from its first Surveyor-General, Colonel Light, and many of its attractive original stone buildings have survived. The Mount Lofty Ranges make a picturesque backdrop. With the Stuart Highway now completely sealed, it is possible to drive from Port Augusta to central Australia on an all-weather road. Certain precautions should be taken before negotiating other roads in the north and west desert regions. (**See:** Outback Motoring.) If you feel intrepid, the opal towns of Coober Pedy and Andamooka are fascinating. Temperatures climb to more than 40°C in Coober Pedy during summer (hence much of the town was built underground), so choose a cool period for your trip.

The spectacular Flinders Ranges have passable roads, although some are unsealed. Wilpena Pound and Arkaroola are the main resort bases. The Heysen Trail (commemorating South Australian painter Sir Hans Heysen) is a well-defined hiking trail that reaches from Cape Jervis almost to Quorn, with extensions into the Flinders Ranges.

Both the Yorke and Eyre Peninsulas have attractive, unspoilt coastlines. Port Lincoln, on the Eyre Peninsula, is a popular base for big-game fishing and on the Yorke Peninsula the three little towns of Wallaroo, Moonta and Kadina, collectively known as Little Cornwall, with their history of copper mining, are well worth a visit.

South of Adelaide is Victor Harbor, the south coast's largest town. A little further on is the Coorong National Park, near the mouth of the Murray at Lake Alexandrina. Here the river completes its 2600-kilometre course. A trip along the Riverland section of the Murray reveals historic river towns, bountiful citrus orchards and extensive vegetable crops, all maintained by irrigation from the Murray. The lakes and lagoons at the river's mouth abound with birdlife and offer excellent fishing and seasonal duck-shooting. Mount Gambier, near the southern Victorian border, is the commercial centre of the south-east, which has Australia's largest pine forest and the beautiful Blue Lake.

The fame of South Australia's wine regions now extends well beyond Australian shores. McLaren Vale on the Fleurieu Peninsula produces excellent wines, and the Riverland region is responsible for much of the national vintage. The Clare Valley, Adelaide Hills and Coonawarra wine regions all have distinct specialities determined by soil and climate. In the famed Barossa Valley region there are more than forty wineries. The valley was originally settled by German Lutherans who planted orchards, olive groves and vineyards and built charming towns and wineries very much in native European style. To explore this area, particularly during the Vintage Festival (every odd-numbered year), is to discover a region and lifestyle unique in Australia.

Brachina Gorge, Flinders Ranges

Adelaide

An Elegant City

Adelaide is a gracious, well-planned city set on a narrow coastal plain between the rolling hills of the Mount Lofty Ranges and the blue waters of Gulf St Vincent. Surrounded by parkland, Adelaide combines the vitality of a large modern city (population nearly one million) with an easy-going Australian lifestyle.

Thanks to Colonel Light's excellent planning and foresight, Adelaide is laid out on a square-mile grid pattern, its wide streets allow easy access for locals and visitors alike. Adelaide is the only major world city completely surrounded by parklands. Known as the Green Belt, these parklands feature children's playgrounds and sports fields, barbecues, and tables and chairs under shady trees. At **Rymill Park** there is a children's boating lake with rowing boats for hire. Flanagan's Riverfront Restaurant is set in parkland and overlooks the waters of the **River Torrens** near the Weir, north of North Terrace. At **Veale Gardens** to the south of the city there are fountains, rockeries and formal rose gardens. Further east along South Terrace is the **Adelaide-Himeji Garden**, a blend of traditional Japanese lake, mountain and dry gardens. The gate is modelled on that of a temple, and a water bowl is provided for visitors to purify themselves by washing their hands and mouths. The beautiful, formal **Botanic Gardens** have sixteen hectares of Australian and imported plants and artificial lakes where children can feed ducks and swans; guided tours are available. While there, don't miss the Palm House, an extensive glasshouse brought out from Germany in 1871. In the north-east corner is the **Bicentennial Conservatory**, considered the largest in the southern hemisphere, housing exotic tropical plants from all over the world. Two serpentine viewing paths on upper and lower levels have wheelchair access.

Near the tree-lined boulevard of **North Terrace** on the edge of the city centre there are some fine colonial buildings. These include Holy Trinity Church, the oldest church in South Australia. The foundation stone was laid by Governor Hindmarsh in 1838, and the clock was made by Vulliamy, clockmaker to King William IV. Near this western end of North Terrace is the **Adelaide Gaol**, last used in 1988. The gaol is now open for inspection each Sunday. Also on North Terrace are the grand **Newmarket Hotel**, built 1884, and the **Lion Centre**, home to the Mercury Cinema, the Jam Factory Craft and Design Centre, and the biennial Fringe Festival.

Adelaide's skyline from across the River Torrens

Hotels
Adelaide Hilton International
233 Victoria Sq., Adelaide
(08) 217 0711
Hindley Parkroyal
65 Hindley St, Adelaide
(08) 231 5552
Hyatt Regency
North Tce, Adelaide
(08) 231 1234
Terrace Intercontinental
150 North Tce, Adelaide
(08) 217 7552

Family and Budget
Adelaide Paringa Motel
15 Hindley St, Adelaide
(08) 231 1000

Austral Hotel
205 Rundle St, Adelaide
(08) 223 4660
YMCA
76 Flinders St, Adelaide
(08) 223 1611

Motel Groups: Bookings
Flag 13 2400
Best Western 1800 22 2166
Travelodge 1800 22 2446

This list is for information only; inclusion is not necessarily a recommendation.

The historic Adelaide Railway Station building, also in North Terrace, has been magnificently restored and now houses the elegant award-winning **Adelaide Casino**. The casino is part of the Adelaide Plaza, which includes the **Adelaide Convention Centre**, and **Exhibition Hall** and the luxurious **Hyatt Regency Adelaide Hotel**.

Further along is the **Old Parliament House**, which today houses Australia's only museum of political history and has an excellent audiovisual display and delightful restaurant. On the corner of King William Road is the present **Parliament House**. Nearby is the oldest building in Adelaide—**Government House**, which is set in a beautiful garden.

The **State Library**, on the corner of Kintore Avenue, holds many major collections. In the Mortlock Wing, volumes on South Australia share space with Donald Bradman's trophies in a beautifully restored Victorian building. Behind the Library is the **Migration Museum**, the first museum to tell the stories of Australia's migrants. Close by, in the former armoury, is the **Police Museum**. Back on North Terrace, the **South Australian Museum** and the **Art Gallery of South Australia** rub shoulders. The museum holds the world's largest collection of Aboriginal artefacts and features this in a range of exhibits. The museum shops offer a wide range of books, posters and souvenirs. The collections of the Art Gallery give one of the best overviews of Australian art available. It also houses important collections of sculptures, paintings and decorative arts from around the world.

The **University of Adelaide** is also on North Terrace. Walk through the landscaped grounds to see the blend of classic and contemporary architecture, and visit the **Museum of Classical Archaeology** in the grounds to view some 500 objects, many dating back to the third millennium BC. **Elder Hall**, with its spectacular pipe organ, is a fine concert venue.

Ayers House, headquarters for the National Trust of South Australia, is at the eastern end of North Terrace. Sir Henry Ayers bought the property in 1855; the house was extended and became one of the major venues for social functions during Ayers' seven terms as Premier of the State. A charming nineteenth-century residence with slate roof and shuttered bay windows, Ayers House has an elegant formal restaurant and a more relaxed bistro extending into the courtyard, enabling visitors to enjoy the historic surroundings while dining. The National Aboriginal Cultural Institute **Tandanya** is on the corner of Grenfell Street and East Terrace.

Back in the heart of the city on King William Street is **Edmund Wright House,** another important reminder of Adelaide's heritage. Built in 1878, the building with its elaborate Renaissance facade is used for civil weddings. Other historic buildings in the city include the **Adelaide Town Hall** in King William Street, with formal portico entrance and graceful tower, the **General Post Office**, and the **Treasury Buildings** on the corner of Victoria Square.

In North Adelaide there are fine old colonial buildings, from delightful stone cottages to stately homes and grand old hotels with lacework balconies and verandahs. **St Peter's Cathedral** in King William Road is one of Australia's finest cathedrals and is a fitting backdrop to the beautiful **Pennington Gardens**. There is an excellent view from **Light's Vision** on Montefiore Hill. A bronze statue of Colonel Light overlooks the city with its broad streets and spacious parks.

The **River Torrens** flows through many of Adelaide's parks. The banks are landscaped, lined with gums and willows, and perfect for a lazy picnic lunch. Walking and cycling trails wind through some of the city's scenic parklands and along the riverbanks. A delightfully different way of travelling to the Adelaide Zoological Gardens is provided by a fleet of *Popeye* motor launches which cruise the river. The zoo has an enormous collection of animals and reptiles and is noted for its variety of Australian birdlife. There is a walk-through aviary sheltering many types of unusual land and water birds, and a nocturnal house designed to display those animals and birds that are most active at night. The zoo grounds are in a perfect setting with magnificent trees (including exotic species), rock beds and rose gardens.

Also situated on the curving banks of the Torrens is the world-renowned **Festival Centre**, hub of the biennial Adelaide Festival, held every even-numbered year. This streamlined, modern building contains a 2000-seat lyric theatre, drama and experimental theatres and an imposing amphitheatre,which is ideal for outdoor entertainment. The building has been acclaimed as one of the finest performing venues in the world. The Southern Plaza incorporates a spectacular environmental sculpture by German artist O. H. Hajek. There are also some fine contemporary tapestries and paintings hung inside the building. Group tours can be arranged, and restaurant and bar facilities are available. The Centre has walkways linking it to King William Road, Parliament House, Adelaide Railway Station, the Casino and Hyatt Regency Adelaide. Nearby is an attractive old band rotunda in **Elder Park**.

Adelaide has a bustling shopping complex centred around **Rundle Mall**. With over 820 shops, Rundle Mall is the largest pedestrian mall in the Southern Hemisphere. The paved area has trees and a fountain, modern sculpture, colourful fruit and flower stalls and seats where you can sit and watch the passing parade.

St Peter's Cathedral

Buskers and outdoor cafes create a European atmosphere. Surrounding arcades and streets have everything ranging from major department stores to tiny specialist boutiques. **King William Street** is lined with impressive bank and insurance buildings, while **Hindley Street** has clusters of restaurants, cafes, and continental food shops, nightclubs and Aussie pubs. A bonus for shoppers is the free Bee-line bus service which operates in the inner-city area.

Make a trip to **Melbourne Street** in North Adelaide for some of the city's most exclusive shops; **Unley Road** for exclusive boutiques and **Magill Road** for antiques and second-hand treasures; the **Parade** at Norwood combines all of the above with great delis, coffee shops, home design stores and bookshops. **King William Road** at Hyde Park has several stylish specialty shops and boutiques. **Glen Osmond Road** at Eastwood offers a wide variety of top label fashions at reduced prices.

A real shopping experience is a visit to the **Central Market** behind the Hilton Hotel, with its stalls packed high with fresh produce (open Tuesday to Saturday). Nearby arcades sell clothing, wine

and spirits; this area is also home to Adelaide's **Chinatown**. The east end of the city around **Rundle Street** has experienced a rebirth, with busy coffee houses, pubs, restaurants and a host of absorbing craft shops and boutiques. The **East End Market** has become the street's focus on Friday, Saturday and Sunday, selling everything from fresh fish, meat and vegetables to clothing and jewellery. In Norwood, the **Orange Lane Markets** (Saturday and Sunday) feature second-hand goods, home-made produce, local crafts and stalls. The **Brickworks Market** at Thebarton (open Friday, Saturday and public holiday Mondays) sells produce and bric-a-brac, and is part of a six-hectare complex featuring an amusement park and international restaurants. Other popular markets featuring fresh foodstuffs and a variety of other goods are the **Junction Market** in Prospect Road, Kilburn (open Saturday, Sunday and public holiday Mondays), and the **Reynella Markets** at 255 Old South Road, Reynella (open Friday to Sunday, and public holiday Mondays).

Adelaide is renowned for its restaurants. The city is credited with being the birthplace of modern Australian cuisine.

Some of the best restaurants are tiny and crowded, with fast service and super-cheap prices. Others are set in historic buildings, serving international-class cuisine in gracious surroundings. **Hindley Street** offers a wide range of cosmopolitan eating. **Gouger Street**, near the Central Market, is known as $10 street—if you can't get a good meal for less than $10, you're in the wrong street—it is particularly noted for its seafood cafes, and South Australian seafood is something special.

Adelaide also has some fine old pubs. Some are friendly 'locals', others incorporate restaurants, wine bars and dance floors. The **Old Lion Hotel** in North Adelaide is a handsome 1880s bluestone building with a first-class restaurant, a sheltered courtyard and popular disco. It is typical of the new boutique-style hotel where beer is brewed on the premises; there are a number of these hotels within the inner-city area.

Not to be missed in Adelaide are the marvellous beaches, stretching right along the coastline with wide sandy shores and clear blue waters. Most are only a short drive from the city centre and perhaps the most famous is **Glenelg**. The best way to see it is by taking the famous 1929 **Bay Tram** from Victoria Square to the foreshore in Glenelg. Spoil yourself by dining at the **Ramada Grand Hotel**, or stroll down Jetty Road to the shopping centre. The **Magic Mountain Waterslide and Amusement Centre** provides entertainment. Restaurants abound, and Greek food here is a specialty. Grand old homes and guest houses along the foreshore are a reminder of Glenelg's days as a seaside resort for the wealthy. The first settlers came ashore here in 1836 and proclaimed the colony of South Australia under a gum tree. The **Old Gum Tree** remains, with a commemorative plaque. HMS *Buffalo* played a significant part in South Australia's early settlement and replica of the vessel at Glenelg is the appropriately, a setting for a maritime museum and restaurant.

Other beaches include **Brighton, West Beach, Henley, Grange** and **Semaphore. Fort Glanville,** at Semaphore is the oldest fortress in South Australia. The Semaphore to Fort Glanville Tourist Railway runs south along the seafront for more than 2 kilometres, from the Semaphore Jetty to Fort Glanville and the nearby caravan park, and operates daily during school holidays and on all public holidays and Sundays during the summer months. Further south, near Hallett Cove, is the **Hallett Cove Conservation Park**, established to preserve the remnants of glacial features that probably occurred 270 million years ago. Many beaches have sailboards and catamarans for hire, while the jetties are used for promenading, swimming and fishing.

Adelaide's suburbs have much to offer the visitor. A short drive west towards the suburb of **Grange** is **Sturt's Cottage** (built 1840), home of Captain Charles Sturt, the famous pioneer and explorer. Managed by the Charles Sturt Memorial Museum Trust, its period furniture and many of Sturt's belongings recall the early days of South Australia.

In **Wayville**, just south-west of the city, is **The Investigator Science and Technology Centre** with hands-on 'gizmos' and fun for the family; it's located in the International Pavilion, Wayville Showgrounds (enter from Rose Tce). Also at the showgrounds in early September, the **Royal Adelaide Show** brings the country to the city.

Port Adelaide has many imposing buildings, a reminder of the port's heyday in the 1880s. Noteworthy are the

Bay Tram

police station and court house, town hall, shipping and transport building, and Ferguson's bond store. Visitors to the **Port Dock Station Railway Museum** can ride miniature steam trains. The Lipson St museum contains a large collection of locomotives and rolling stock, platform displays, a theatrette and an operating HO-gauge model railway. Also located in Lipson St is the **South Australian Maritime Museum**, complete with lighthouses and ships. A few blocks away is the **South Australian Historical Aviation Museum** in Mundy St. There are cruises and fishing trips available from Port Adelaide.

At **St Kilda**, further north, there is an **Electric Transport Museum** where you can take trips on restored trams. A guided walk along the 1.7 km boardwalk of the **Mangrove Walking Trail** is an experience not to be missed.

Near the suburb of **Rostrevor**, east of the city, the **Morialta Conservation Park** has a ruggedly beautiful gorge and many walking tracks. **Brownhill Creek Recreation Park** has giant pine and gum trees in a quiet valley setting. There are barbecue facilities and pretty picnic spots. **Belair National Park** has picnic grounds, bushland, a children's playground and the former summer residence of the Governor. **Cleland Conservation Park** has kangaroos, koalas, wombats and other native fauna in their natural surroundings.

Take a leisurely tour around the city's attractions in the only replica of a road-registered tram. The tram has on-board

commentary. Board or alight the **Explorer Tram** as many times as you wish at any of the stopping points; the tram returns to any given point approximately every 2¼ hours.

The longest guided busway system in the world, **The O-Bahn**, runs north-east from the city centre. It travels beside the River Torrens in its own landscaped park from Adelaide to a major shopping centre at **Tea Tree Plaza**, and has a station at **Paradise**, a suburb named by early settlers. Walking paths and cycling tracks follow the busway track to Tea Tree Plaza, with views over reservoirs, foothills and the city.

Cowell Jade, at **Unley**, sells jewellery and carvings made from local jade. The **South Australian Society of Model and Experimental Engineers** headquarters, in the nearby suburb of **Millswood**, has field days (open to visitors) twice a month. For magnificent views of Adelaide, take a trip to **Windy Point Lookout** or to the summit of **Mount Lofty**. At night, the lights of the city look particularly impressive. Adelaide is the home of the **Australian Formula One Grand Prix** until 1995. This exciting race in November is through city streets, open parklands and the racecourse; the course is regarded by many as the best street circuit in the world. Adelaide also offers sports enthusiasts horseracing at **Victoria Park**, **Morphettville** and **Cheltenham**; greyhound-racing at **Angle Park**; tennis, squash, swimming and golf. Pools, water-slides, fountains, river rapids, waterfalls, and gym, spa and sauna facilities are a feature of the **Adelaide Aquatic Centre** in North Adelaide. The **Municipal Golf Course** in North Adelaide commands splendid views of the city. **Adelaide Oval**, on King William Road, is a venue for interstate and international cricket matches, while the **Memorial Drive Tennis Courts** have played host to international players since 1929. Memorial Drive is also used for outdoor concerts and performances by visiting entertainers. The Ice Arena at 23 East Terrace in the suburb of Thebarton has skating and the world's first indoor artificial ski slope.

For further information on Adelaide and South Australia, contact South Australian Tourism Commission Travel Centre, 1 King William St, Adelaide; (08) 212 1505, Freecall 1800 882 092, fax (08) 303 2231.

Tours from Adelaide

One of Adelaide's greatest assets is its proximity to a number of fascinating regions. Vineyards and wineries, rolling hills and quaint villages, seaside resorts and beautiful wildlife reserves are all within an easy drive of South Australia's capital.

Barossa Valley, 50 km from Adelaide via the Sturt Highway

A must for visitors to Adelaide is the Barossa Valley, Australia's premier wine-producing region. In this area to the north-east of Adelaide there are more than forty wineries and a multitude of historic buildings and galleries. Cafes and restaurants serve top-class cuisine. In August the Barossa Classic Gourmet Weekend offers visitors the opportunity to sample and enjoy fine wines and gourmet food. The award-winning Barossa Music Festival is held in October. Visit Gawler, Lyndoch, Tanunda, Nuriootpa and Angaston, detouring at will to the smaller villages and visiting the tasting facilities at the wineries; make sure the driver is happy to forgo this pleasure! Alternatively, extend your visit and stay overnight at the many and varied accommodation outlets in the area. (**See also**: Festival Fun; Vineyards and Wineries; individual entries in A–Z listing.)

Clare Valley, 135 km from Adelaide via the Sturt Highway and Highway 32 (Highway 83 optional north of Tarlee)

The Clare Valley produces superb wines and the region is known internationally for its riesling. Driving north through Kapunda, Australia's first mining town, you will pass some of the State's richest pastoral country, noted for its stud sheep. The wine towns begin at Auburn and continue to Watervale, Sevenhill and to Clare. The area is also noted for its prize-winning red and white table wines. Sevenhill Cellars winery was started by two Jesuit priests in 1851 and still operates today. Slightly further afield, there are several fine colonial buildings, such as the magnificent Martindale Hall at Mintaro (open daily except Christmas Day and Good Friday), which was used in the film *Picnic at Hanging Rock*. The area also has many charming parks and picturesque picnic spots. (See also: Vineyards and Wineries; individual entries in A–Z listing.)

Southern Vales, 42 km from Adelaide via the South Road

Another trip for wine-lovers is to the vineyards of the Fleurieu Peninsula. There are more than fifty wineries in the area, often in picturesque bush settings. Most are well signposted and have wine tastings and cellar-door sales. Hardy's, D'Arenberg, Seaview and Coriole are some of the names to recognise. Stop for lunch in McLaren Vale at The Barn, a gallery–restaurant complex in an historic coach station, or enjoy a light snack at Pipkins. Your return trip could include a visit to the nearby beaches Moana, Port Noarlunga and Christies Beach. (**See also:** Vineyards and Wineries; The Fleurieu Peninsula; individual entries in A–Z listing.)

Seppeltsfield, Barossa Valley

Adelaide Hills and Hahndorf, 28 km from Adelaide via the South Eastern Freeway

The Adelaide Hills are only half an hour's drive from the city. Stop on the way at Cleland Wildlife Park (open daily) in the Cleland Conservation Park, to see native birds and animals in a bush setting. The Gorge Wildlife Park at Cudlee Creek is also open daily. The hills are a blend of gently rolling mountains, market gardens and orchards with farm buildings nestled in valleys off winding roads. Go off the main highway to visit Stirling (the nearby Mount Lofty Botanic Gardens offers views of Piccadilly Valley) and Aldgate, then Bridgewater with its historic water wheel (1860), now part of the restored mill that houses the wine-making and maturation plant for Petaluma's premium sparkling wines. Mount Lofty (726 m) offers views of Adelaide.

Hahndorf is probably the best known town in the area. Settled by Silesian and Prussian refugees in 1839, its main street is lined with magnificent old elms and chestnut trees. Most of the buildings have been restored and the town has a leisurely, old-world feel about it. The Hahndorf Academy and Art Gallery has a permanent exhibition of paintings by Sir Hans Heysen, who lived in the town for many years and depicted the area's beauty so well. A local German heritage museum is upstairs from the art gallery, and both are open daily. The bakeries here sell delicious *apfelstrudel*, cheesecake and Black Forest cake, and small shops offer interesting local handicrafts and home-made preserves. Other attractions include a model train village, a clock museum and a strawberry farm. The heritage of the town is celebrated with several festivals: **Schutzenfest**, held in Bonython Park, Adelaide each January; Handorf **German Fest** also in January; and **Blumenfest**, the festival of flowers held in November. Two of South Australia's oldest townships, Nairne and Mount Barker, lie to the east and southeast of Hahndorf.

In the town of Oakbank, the Great Eastern Steeplechase, Australia's biggest picnic race meeting, is held with great fanfare every Easter. North of Oakbank are Apple World at Forest Range (open daily) and an archive and historical museum at Lobethal (open Sundays and public holidays). Gardens and plant nurseries throughout the Adelaide Hills are open to the public. At Woodside, Melba's

Horse-drawn carriage, Hahndorf

Chocolates offer daily tours and tastings. From Hahndorf take the back road through winding hills and farmland to the old goldmining town of Echunga, and return to Adelaide via Mylor, where Warrawong Sanctuary, a leader in the preservation of rare and endangered animals, is open daily and offers guided tours, including dawn, day and sunset walks (bookings essential). Stop at the Belair National Park on your return trip to Adelaide. There are walks, a wildlife park, Old Government House, a native plant nursery, tennis courts for hire, and gas barbecues for picnics.

Stay in one of the many home-style accommodation houses dotted throughout the Adelaide Hills and experience inexpensive, quality bed-and-breakfast accommodation or rent a self-contained historic cottage. Aboriginal rock art and environmental tours through the Hills are available. For more information, contact the Adelaide Hills Tourist Information Centre, 64 Main St, Hahndorf; (08) 388 1185. (**See also:** Vineyards and Wineries; Festival Fun; individual entries in A–Z listing.)

Fleurieu Peninsula, 112 km from Adelaide to its furthest point via the South Road

The Fleurieu Peninsula extends south of Adelaide and has much to offer. Down the length of the west coast there are idyllic sandy beaches, such as Maslin (Australia's first official nudist beach), Sellicks and Christies Beach, right to the tip at wild but beautiful Cape Jervis. Some beaches have sheltered coves, some have excellent surf, still others are

ideal for fishing. Inland there are historic buildings, particularly at Willunga, where public buildings vie with small cottages for the visitor's attention. The almond orchards around here are a marvellous sight, especially when they bloom at the end of winter. Late July to early August is Almond Blossom Festival time. Ideal for keen walkers as well as those looking for a quiet picnic spot are a number of conservation parks. There is a scenic drive around Myponga Conservation Park. Only 84 km from Adelaide is Victor Harbor, a popular seaside resorts. The sandy beach is perfect for swimming. Across the causeway is rugged Granite Island, and The Bluff (Rosetta Head) has a licensed restaurant at Whalers Inn. The SA Whale Information Centre has recently opened at Victor Harbour. Further around is Port Elliot on splendid Horseshoe Bay. Goolwa, the historic river port at the mouth of the Murray River is further east; here one of the focal points is the Signal Point Visitor Centre. A ferry takes you across to Hindmarsh Island for views of the area. On the way back to Adelaide, do not miss historic Strathalbyn, first settled in 1839, on the banks of the River Angas. Milang, 20 km to the south-east, is on the shores of Lake Alexandrina. Take your camera—the birdlife is fascinating. (**See also:** The Fleurieu Peninsula; individual entries in A–Z listing.)

National Motor Museum, Birdwood, 46 km from Adelaide via the North-East Road

The National Motor Museum (open daily) houses the most important motor vehicle collection in Australia. Veteran vintage and classic cars and motorcycles number over 300 and the grounds are a perfect venue for a picnic. At Gumeracha, on Torrens Gorge Ring Route en route from Adelaide, is the Toy Factory, where one can climb the largest wooden rocking horse in the world. Drive back to Adelaide through Mount Torrens to the small town of Lobethal, which was founded in the 1840s. The Archives and Historical Museum houses a remarkable exhibit: the old Lobethal College, complete with shingled roof, which was built in 1845; open Sunday afternoons. Fairyland Village at Lobethal has fourteen chalets, each depicting a fairytale or a nursery rhyme; open daily. There is a scenic route through Basket Range and Norton Summit back to Adelaide.

Festival Fun

Because good food and wine go hand in hand with festivities, it seems appropriate that South Australia is both the nation's wine capital and the Festival State. During the year, a wide variety of festivals is held throughout South Australia, ranging from the cultural extravaganza of the Adelaide Festival to carnivals in several country-towns. In November the city is galvanised by the roar of the **Australian Formula One Grand Prix**, which will be held in Adelaide until 1995.

For three weeks in March of each even-numbered year, Adelaide becomes the cultural centre of Australia as it hosts the **Adelaide Festival**. During this time the city is like a giant magnet, drawing throngs of people from interstate and overseas. Hotels are often booked months ahead; restaurants, taxi services and retailers do a roaring trade.

Since it started in 1960, the Adelaide Festival has grown from a modest 51

performances to over 300, with as many as 30 competing for attention in one day. It includes concerts, street-theatre and carnivals. The cosmopolitan atmosphere and the world-renowned guest artists have made this festival an outstanding international event.

Although performances in theatre, dance, musical recitals, opera and ballet are emphasised, the Festival is not confined solely to the performing arts. There are exhibitions, lectures, a writers' week, an artists' week celebrating the visual arts, poetry readings, and outdoor activities to coincide with this three-week-long cultural feast.

The focal point is the Adelaide Festival Centre, which stands on 1.5 hectares on the banks of the River Torrens, just 2 minutes' walk from the commercial heart of the city. The Festival Centre is the permanent home of the South Australia Theatre Company, which presents at

least 10 major productions annually.

When the Festival is not on, Adelaide visitors and residents still use the parks and gardens surrounding the centre, and the two restaurants and terrace-style cafe, which are open 6 days a week are very popular.

Each odd-numbered year, in March–April, the Festival Centre organises a youth arts festival, *Come Out*, which focuses its attention on the arts for children and young people.

The **Barossa Valley Vintage Festival**, in Australia's premier wine-producing district, just one hour's drive from Adelaide, is also held in odd-numbered years. The mellow autumn weather and picturesque towns of the Barossa Valley draw large crowds to this event, which is traditionally a thanksgiving celebration for a successful harvest. The seven-day festival, which starts on Easter Monday, is strictly *gemüt-lichkeit*—happy and friendly. There is

Performances, Adelaide Festival

music and dancing, good food, wine-tasting, a vintage fair, float processions and traditional dinners like the *weingarten*—a big feast featuring German folk songs. The grand finale takes the form of a spectacular fair held at the oval in Tanunda Park, where dancers in colourful national costumes dance around an 18-metre-high maypole, while food and wine are served in the marquees surrounding the oval. The **Barossa Classic Gourmet Weekend** in August combines the pleasures of wine, food and good music over two days.

During the long weekend in May the Clare Valley wineries host the **Gourmet Weekend**, which includes tastings and a progressive Sunday luncheon around the wineries.

McLaren Vale is the venue for **One Continuous Picnic**, held on the October long weekend, when wineries and restaurants provide opportunities to sample the vintages of the Southern Vales. The **McLaren Vale Wine Bushing Festival** follows at the end of October, a time of fun and festivity, with craft exhibitions, parades, picnics and formal balls to celebrate the new vintage.

South Australia is a State of many cultures, which accounts for the many ethnic festivals held throughout the year. The largest of these is *Schutzenfest*, held in Adelaide. Traditionally a shooting festival to raise funds for various charities, it has grown into the biggest German-style beer festival held outside Germany. Bonython Park is transformed into a bustling carnival with 'oompah' music, imported German beer, German folk dancers in national costume, and restaurants serving platters of *sauerbraten* and *apfelstrudel*. The hot, thirsty month of January is ideal for drinking steins of ice-cold beer while listening to brass bands and waiting for a variety of *würst* (cold sausage meats) to be served at your table.

In March, the Greek community organises the Glendi Festival to coincide with the Greek National Day. In May, every odd-numbered year, the colourful **Kernewek Lowender** (Cornish family festival) is held, centred around Kadina, Moonta and Wallaroo on the scenic Yorke Peninsula. Quaint old miners' cottages, abandoned mining installations and many museums remind visitors of the heyday of copper mining. There is music and Cornish dancing, a pasty-making competition and a hilarious wheelbarrow race.

For two weeks in June, Barmera is the country music capital of the state, when visitors from all over Australia attend the **Country Music Festival**.

Other South Australian festivals include the **Tunarama Festival** at the fishing port and resort of Port Lincoln, held every Australia Day holiday in January. Australia's only festival dedicated to a fish, it features competitions, displays, a street procession, sports, a fireworks spectacular and the famous tuna-tossing event; there is fun for the whole family in a gala atmosphere on the beautiful Tasman Terrace foreshore. In April the people of Laura, a small town in the lower Flinders Ranges, organise a **Folk Fair** that attracts thousands of visitors.

Each Easter Monday, the **Great Eastern Steeplechase** is raced at Oakbank racecourse. This event is billed as the largest picnic meeting in the southern hemisphere and is a carnival that leads up to the running of the **Adelaide Cup** in May at Morphettville racecourse.

One special event for children and adults is the November **Christmas Pageant** in the city streets of Adelaide. Floats depicting nursery rhymes and fairytale characters thrill all those who line the streets to welcome Father Christmas to South Australia.

Information on all the SA festivals can be obtained from the South Australian Tourism Commission Travel Centre, 1 King William St, Adelaide; (08) 212 1505. **See also:** Individual town entries in A–Z listing.

The Great Eastern Steeplechase, Oakbank racecourse

South Australia from A to Z

Aldinga
Pop. 3541

This small town 45 km S of Adelaide is 4 km from the west coast of the Fleurieu Peninsula. **Of interest:** St Ann's Anglican Church (1866) and Uniting Church (1863). **In the area:** Aldinga Beach, 4 km SW, good swimming, surfing, diving and fishing, and bush trails through Aldinga Scrub Conservation Park (leaflets available). Off Aldinga Beach: Aldinga Aquatic Reserve, rare reef formation, good diving. At Port Willunga Beach, 3 km N, ruins of *Star of Greece* (1888) visible at low tide. Maslin, 6 km N, Australia's first nude bathing beach. McLaren Vale, 12 km NE, centre of wine-growing region with over 50 wineries. **Tourist information:** Aldinga Bay Holiday Village, Esplanade, Aldinga Beach; (085) 56 5019. **Accommodation:** 3 B&B, 1 cara./camp. park. **See also:** The Fleurieu Peninsula.
MAP REF. 283 K10, 284 B7, 287 B3, 289 K9

Andamooka
Pop. 471

Andamooka is an outback opal field about 600 km N of Adelaide, to the west of the saltpan Lake Torrens. It is off the beaten track, conditions are harsh in summer, the weather is severe and water is precious. There are rough shacks along the dirt road, with many people living in dugouts to protect themselves from the extreme heat. Visitors who have obtained a precious-stone prospecting permit from the Mines Department in Adelaide can stake out a claim and try their luck. Looking for opals on mullock dumps left by miners requires permission from the owners of a claim. There are tours of the area, including underground mine tours and showrooms with opals for sale. The road to Andamooka is fair, but quickly affected by rain. **Of interest:** Duke's

Bottle Home, made entirely of empty beer bottles. In Main St: Andamooka Press, working printing museum, underground house, open daily; Andamooka Gems and Trains, mineral specimens and model railway; quaint 1930s miners' cottages, next to creek bed. Easter: Family Fun Day and White Dam Walk. Oct: Opal Festival. **In the area:** Roxby Downs, 30 km W, service town for nearby Olympic Dam mining operations. Copper, gold, silver and uranium are mined at Olympic Dam; tours of mining operations available. At Woomera, 120 km S, Heritage Centre and Missile Park with displays of rockets and aircraft. **Tourist information:** Opal Creek Showroom, Main St; (086) 72 7193. **Accommodation:** 1 hotel/motel, 1 B&B, 1 cara. park, 1 camp. ground.
MAP REF. 290 G4

Angaston
Pop. 1819

Angaston is in the highest part of the Barossa Valley; within 79 km of the coast, it is 361 m above sea level. The town is named after prominent 1830s Barossa Valley settler, George Fife Angas. **Of interest:** Angas Park Fruit Co., Murray St, produces dried fruit and nuts; open daily. Angaston Galleria, Murray St and Bethany Arts and Crafts, Washington St, for home-made goods, local art and craft. A Clothes Revival, Murray St, clothes of yesteryear and collectables. **In the area:** Saltram Wine Estates, 2 km W. Yalumba Winery, 2 km S. Collingrove Homestead (1850), 7 km SE, National Trust property once owned by Angas pioneering family; viewing, accommodation and meals by prior arrangement. Henschke's Wines 10 km SE. Mountaddin Winery at Eden Valley, 19 km SE. Springton Gallery, Grand Cru Estate, Herbig Tree, Robert Hamilton & Son Winery and Merindah Mohair

Farm, (open daily), at Springton, 27 km SE. Magnificent view of Barossa Valley from Mengler's Hill Lookout, 8 km SW. Yookamurra Sanctuary, 54 km NE, reintroduced local wildlife and plant species, guided walks and tours; check opening times, accommodation, bookings essential. **Tourist information:** Angaston Galleria, 18 Murray St; (085) 64 2648. **Accommodation:** 2 hotels, 1 motel, 3 B&B. **See also:** Vineyards and Wineries.
MAP REF. 283 O4, 286 I4, 287 D1, 289 M7

Ardrossan
Pop. 1008

Ardrossan, 148 km NW of Adelaide, is the largest port on the Yorke Peninsula east coast. An important outlet for wheat and barley, it is an attractive town with excellent crabbing and fishing from the jetty. **Of interest:** Ardrossan and District Historical Museum, Fifth St. The stump jump plough was invented here in the late 1800s; restored plough on display on cliffs at end of First St in East Tce. Jan.: Ardrossan Alive, outdoor music festival (odd-numbered years). **In the area:** Salt and dolomite mines. BHP Lookout, 2 km S. For keen divers, *Zanoni* wreck off coast, 20 km SE; permission required to dive. Clinton Conservation Park, 40 km N. Walks, wildlife tours, campfires, as package, 4 km W. **Tourist information:** Galwey's Servwell Store, First St; (08) 8837 3209. **Accommodation:** 2 hotel/motels, 2 cara./camp. parks.
MAP REF. 282 H4, 289 J6

Arkaroola
Pop. 10

Arkaroola is a remote village settlement, founded in 1968, in the northern Flinders Ranges, about 660 km N of Adelaide. This privately-owned property of 61 000 ha has been opened as a flora and fauna sanctuary. The rugged outback country is

The Yorke Peninsula

Settled as agricultural country, Yorke Peninsula was put on the map by the discovery of rich copper-ore deposits in 1861 and the influx of thousands of miners, including so many from Cornwall that the **Wallaroo– Moonta–Kadina** area became known as Little Cornwall.

The drive down the highway on the east coast is mainly within sight of the sea.

Many of the east-coast towns have excellent fishing from long jetties once used for loading grain ships. Beach, surf and rock fishing are excellent, as is crabbing.

The west coast of Yorke Peninsula is lined with safe swimming beaches and excellent coastal scenery. **Port Victoria**, the last of the windjammer ports, was once the main port of call for sailing ships transporting grain. Further north, Moonta's old stone buildings give it a sense of history and the Moonta mines tell of its mining heyday.

Innes National Park with its diverse hinterland birdlife and impressive coastal scenery is on the southern tip of the Peninsula. Visit the site of a once-flourishing township, **Inneston. Pondalowie Bay** is a must for surfers. Rocky cliff tops and windswept headlands offer views across Investigator Strait.

For further information, contact the Yorke Peninsula Visitor Information Centre, 51 Taylor St, Kadina; (08) 8821 2093. **See also:** Individual entries in A–Z listing.

The Eyre Peninsula

The Eyre Peninsula is a vast region stretching from Whyalla in the east to the Western Australian border in the west, and, in a north– south direction, from the Gawler Ranges to Port Lincoln. Spencer Gulf borders the eastern edge of the Peninsula, along which are located a number of small coastal towns featuring sheltered waters, safe swimming, white sandy beaches and excellent fishing from either shore or boat. The charm of the peaceful resort towns of **Cowell, Arno Bay** and **Port Neill** has a natural appeal. Cowell has the added attraction of being one of the world's major sources of jade.

Whyalla is the second largest city in South Australia and acts as an important gateway to Eyre Peninsula. Located near the top of Spencer Gulf, this bustling, industrially based city also offers a wide range of attractions for the visitor.

The southern Eyre Peninsula includes the tourist resort towns of **Tumby Bay**, famous for fishing and beautiful offshore islands; **Coffin Bay**, with magnificent sheltered waters; and the jewel in the crown, the city of **Port Lincoln**, nestled on blue Boston Bay.

In stark contrast to the sheltered waters of Spencer Gulf, the west coast is exposed to the full force of the Southern Ocean and offers some of the most spectacular coastal scenery to be found in Australia. This coast is punctuated by a

The western side of Eyre Peninsula

number of bays and inlets and, not surprisingly, several resort towns have flourished where shelter can be found from precipitous cliffs and pounding surf. **Elliston, Venus Bay, Streaky Bay, Smoky Bay** and **Ceduna** all offer the visitor a diverse range of coastal scenery, good fishing and other water-related activities.

Ceduna provides a vital service and accommodation facility for traffic across Australia, and acts as a gateway information centre for visitors approaching the region from the west.

The hinterland of the Eyre Peninsula encompasses the picturesque Koppio Hills in the south, the vast grain-growing tracts of the central region and the eternal

beauty of the Gawler Ranges in the far north of the peninsula.

The Nullarbor, the western corridor into the region, is a vast treeless plain, bordered in the south by towering limestone cliffs that drop sheer to the pounding Southern Ocean. Here schools of southern right whales can be seen along the coastline between June and October on their annual breeding migration. Sightings of these beautiful creatures occur regularly and are on the increase.

For more information on the area, contact the Eyre Peninsula Tourism Association, Jobomi House, Liverpool St, Port Lincoln; (086) 82 4688. **See also:** Individual entries in A–Z listing.

crossed by incredible quartzite ridges, deep gorges and rich mineral deposits, and is a haven for birdlife and rare marsupials. **Of interest:** Mineral and Fossil Museum; Outdoor Pastoral and Mining Museum; Astronomical Observatory (check viewing times); pioneer cottage. **In the area:** Marked walking trails; self-guide pamphlets from Information Centre. Old Cornish-style smelters (1861) and scenic waterholes at Bolla Bollana, 12 km NW. About 18 km further west, old log cabin (1856) at Yankaninna Homestead. Famous Mt Painter, 10 km N; further 20 km N, breathtaking views from Freeling Heights, overlooking Yudnamutana Gorge; Siller's Lookout, over Lake Frome (a salt lake). Radioactive Paralana Hot Springs, 27 km N. Gammon Ranges National Park, 20 km SW, extensive wilderness areas; recommended for experienced bushwalkers only. Balcanoona Homestead, 34 km S; Big Moro Gorge (with rock pools), 59 km S; and Chambers Gorge (with Aboriginal rock carvings) 98 km S. Ridgetop Tour, spectacular 4WD trip across Australia's most rugged mountains. Scenic flights and guided tours available. **Tourist information:** Visitors Information Centre; (086) 48 4848. **Accommodation:** 4 motels, 1 hostel, 1 cara./camp. park. **See also:** The Flinders Ranges; National Parks.
MAP REF. 285 G2, 291 M4, 484 D12

Balaklava   Pop. 1439
Balaklava, in a picturesque setting on the banks of the River Wakefield, 91 km N of Adelaide, was named after a famous battle in the Crimean War. **Of interest:** National Trust Museum, May Tce, has relics of district's early days of European settlement; check opening times. Country Crafters, 30 George St, local craft. Courthouse Gallery and Shop, Edith Tce, community art gallery. Urlwin Park Agricultural Museum, Short Tce. Lions Club Walking Trail, along Wakefield River and through town; brochure available at Council offices or Country Crafters. Sept: Agricultural Show. Oct.: Festival of Gardens and Galleries. **In the area:** Devils Gardens, 7 km NE on Auburn Rd, and The Rocks Reserve, 10 km E, both with picnic facilities. Beachside town of Port Wakefield, 26 km W at head of Gulf St Vincent. **Tourist information:** Country Crafters, 30 George St; (088 62 2070. **Accommodation:** 2 hotels, 1 B&B, 1 cara./camp. park.
MAP REF. 283 K1, 289 K5

Barmera   Pop. 1859
The sloping shores of Lake Bonney make a delightful setting for the Riverland town of Barmera, 214 km NE of Adelaide. Lake Bonney is ideal for swimming, water-skiing, sailing, boating and fishing. The irrigated land is given over mainly to vineyards, but there are also apricot and peach orchards and citrus groves. Soldier settlement after World War I marked the beginning of today's community-oriented town. **Of interest**: Donald Campbell Obelisk, Queen Elizabeth Dr, commemorates Campbell's attempt on world water speed record in 1964. Bonneyview Wines, Sturt Hwy, gallery, restaurant and picnic facilities; open daily. Highway Fern Haven, Sturt Hwy, rare ferns in tropical setting; open daily. June: South Australian Country Music Festival and Awards. Oct.: Agricultural Show. **In the area:** At North Lake, 10 km NW, ruins of Napper's Old Accommodation House (1850) preserved by National Trust. Loch Luna Game Reserve, 16 km NW. At Overland Corner, 19 km NW on Morgan Rd: hotel (1859), now also National Trust museum; self-guide historical walking trail. Rocky's Country Hall of Fame, 5 km NE on Renmark Bypass. At Monash, 8 km NE, Wein Valley Estate. At Cobdogla, 5 km W, Irrigation Museum with the only working Humphrey Pump in the world, as well as steam rides, historic displays and picnic areas; check opening times. Cobdogla Coloured Wool, spinning demonstrations, lamb-feeding, coloured fleeces. Moorook Game Reserve, 16 km SW, includes Wachtels Lagoon with birdlife and walking trail; wetlands cruise. Nearby, Yatco Lagoon abounds with birdlife. **Tourist information:** Barmera Travel Centre, Barwell Ave; (085) 88 2289. **Accommodation:** 2 motels, 1 hotel/motel, 1 B&B, 3 cara./camp. parks. **See also:** Festival Fun.
MAP REF. 289 Q6

Beachport   Pop. 443
The site of the south-east's first whaling station, in the 1830s, Beachport is a quiet little town 51 km S of Robe. Rivoli Bay nearby provides safe swimming beaches as well as shelter for lobster boats. **Of interest:** Old Wool and Grain Store, Railway Tce; National Trust Museum with whaling, shipping and local history exhibits. Military Museum, Beach Rd; open daily. Artifacts museum, McCourt St, Aboriginal heritage. Jubilee Lagoon

Park in town centre, barbecues, tennis, playgrounds and skateboard track. **In the area:** Lake George, 4 km N, waterbirds, windsurfing and fishing. Beachport Conservation Park, between Lake George and the Southern Ocean: Aboriginal shell middens; walking trails (self-guide leaflets available). Bowman Scenic Drive off McArthur Pl., spectacular views the Southern Ocean. On Scenic Drive, swimming in Pool of Siloam, a lake with high salt content and reputed therapeutic benefits. Woakwine Cutting, 10 km N on Robe Rd, extraordinary drainage project, with observation platform and machinery exhibit. Canunda National Park, 20 km S, 40-km stretch of spectacular sand dunes and virgin bushland, with fascinating flora and fauna. Seaspray walk along cliff top, self-guide leaflet from ranger at Southend. **Tourist information:** District Council, McCourt St; (087) 35 8029. **Accommodation:** 1 hotel, 1 motel, 2 cara./camp. parks.
MAP REF. 287 F11

Berri   Pop. 3733
The commercial centre of the Riverland region, Berri is 227 km NE of Adelaide. Once a wood-refuelling stop for paddlesteamers and barges which plied the Murray, the town was first proclaimed in 1911. This is fruit- and vine-growing country, dotted with peaceful picnic and fishing areas. **Of interest:** Water Tower Lookout (17 m), Fiedler St, panoramic views of river and town. River crossings on Riverland's only twin ferries crossing Murray River; vehicular, 24-hr service, free of charge. Nearby, sculpture and cave memorial to Jimmy James, Aboriginal tracker. Houseboats, canoes for hire. Feb.: Speedboat Spectacular. Easter: Carnival and rodeo. Nov.: Art, Craft and Fine Food Fair. **In the area:** Large range of dried fruit and confectionery at Angas Park Kiosk, 3 km W on Sturt Hwy. Berri Estates winery and distillery, 13 km W on Sturt Hwy, near town of Glossop, largest wine-making facility in Australia. Katarapko Game Reserve, 10 km SW, Kia Kia Nature Trail for bushwalkers. Martin's Bend, 2 km E, popular for water-skiing and picnicking. Berrivale Orchards, 4 km N on Sturt Hwy, educational audiovisual on Riverland's history and various stages in processing of fruit; open Mon.–Fri., Sat. a.m. Wilabalangaloo flora and fauna reserve, 5 km N, off Sturt Hwy, walking trails, spectacular scenery, museum and paddlewheeler; check opening times.

Rollerama roller-skating centre nearby. On Morgan Rd, art and craft exhibits at the Parlour Australiana Gallery. Township of Monash, 12 km NW on Morgan Rd. Wein Valley Estate, off Morgan Rd. **Tourist information:** 24 Vaughan Tce; (085) 82 1655. **Accommodation:** 1 hotel/motel, 3 motels, 1 hostel, 1 cara./camp. park.
MAP REF. 126 A8, 289 Q6

Blinman   Pop. 30
Blinman, 478 km N of Adelaide and 30 km from the magnificent Flinders Ranges National Park, was a thriving copper-mining centre from 1860 to 1890. **Of interest:** Several historic buildings, incl. hotel (1869), post office (1862) and police station (1874), all in main street. **In the area:** Great Wall of China, ironstone-capped ridge, 10 km S on Wilpena Rd. Further south, beautiful Aroona Valley, with ruins of old Aroona Homestead; nearby Mt Hayward and Brachina Gorge. 'Almost ghost' town of Beltana, 60 km N, declared an historic reserve. Midway between Blinman and Parachilna is Angorichina, located 15 km W in scenic Parachilna Gorge; nearby, the Blinman Pools, fed by a permanent spring. Scenic drive east through Eregunda Valley then north east to Chambers Gorge with rock pools and Aboriginal carvings; then north west, to view spectacular Big Moro Gorge off Arkaroola Rd. **Tourist information:** Hawker Motors, cnr Wilpena and Cradock Rds, Hawker; (086) 48 4014. **Accommodation:** 1 hotel/motel, 1 cara./camp. park.
MAP REF. 285 E6, 291 K6

Bordertown   Pop. 2235
Bordertown is a quiet town on the Dukes Hwy, 274 km SE of Adelaide. Growth was stimulated after 1852 when it became an important supply centre for the goldfields of western Victoria. Today the area is noted for wool, cereals, meat and vegetable production. **Of interest:** Robert J.L. Hawke, former Australian Prime Minister, was born here and his childhood home, in Farquhar St, has been renovated and includes memorabilia; open Mon.–Fri. Town parks offer picnic facilities. Bordertown Wildlife Park, Dukes Hwy; native birds and animals, including pure white kangaroos. **In the area:** Historic Clayton Farm, 3 km S, vintage farm machinery and thatched buildings; open Sun.–Fri. Clayton Farm Vintage Field Day , Oct. long weekend.

At Mundulla, 10 km SW: Mundulla Hotel (1884), now a National Trust Museum, and Wirrega Council Chambers. At Padthaway, 42 km SW, 1882 homestead houses Padthaway Estate winery; meals and accommodation available. Picnic areas among magnificent red gums and stringybarks at Padthaway Conservation Park nearby. Bangham Conservation Park, 30 km SE, near Frances. **Tourist information:** Council Chambers, 43 Woolshed St; (087) 52 1044. **Accommodation:** 2 hotels, 3 motels, 1 cara./camp. park.
MAP REF. 228 A7, 287 I7, 289 R13

Burra   Pop. 1191
Nestled in Bald Hills Range, 154 km N of Adelaide, Burra is a former copper-mining centre. The district of Burra Burra (Hindi for 'great great') is now famous for stud merino sheep, and Burra is the market town for surrounding farms. *Breaker Morant* was filmed here. Copper was discovered in 1845 and extracted to the value of almost $10 million before the mine closed in 1877. **Of interest:** Passport system allows visitors to walk or drive around 11 km of heritage buildings, museums, mine shafts and lookout points (details from Tourist Information). Daily 2-hr bus tours of town and its mining history; bookings essential. Burra Creek miners' dugouts, alongside Blyth St, where over 1 500 people lived during the boom; 2 dugouts preserved. Cemetery, off Spring St. Heritage and cemetery walks; daily, details from Tourist Information Burra Mine Open Air Museum,

off Market St, includes ore dressing tower, powder magazine; spectacular views of open-cut mine and town. Nearby Enginehouse Museum, built 1858, reconstructed 1986, near archaeological excavation of 30-m entry tunnel to Morphett's Shaft. Market Square Museum, opposite Tourist Office. Malowen Lowarth Museum, Kingston St, in old miner's cottage. Underground cellars of old Unicorn Brewery, Bridge Tce. Also in Bridge Tce: Paxton Square Cottages (1850), 33 two-, three- and four-roomed cottages built for Cornish miners, now restored as visitor accommodation. In Burra North: police lockup and stables (1849), Tregony St; Redruth Gaol (1857), off Tregony St; and Bon Accord Mine buildings (1846), Railway Tce, now a museum complex. Picturesque spots alongside creek for swimming, canoeing and picnicking. **In the area:** Chatswood Farm Gallery, 14 km S at Hanson. Wineries in the Clare Valley, about 30 km SW. Scenic 90 km drive, Dares Hill Drive, begins 30 km N on Broken Hill Rd. Picturesque Burra Gorge, 27 km E. **Tourist information:** 2 Market Sq.; (08) 8892 2154. **Accommodation:** 4 hotels, 1 motel, 12 B&B, 1 cara./camp. park.
MAP REF. 289 M4

Ceduna   Pop. 2753
Near the junction of the Flinders and Eyre Hwys, Ceduna is the last major town before you cross the Nullarbor from east to west. It is the ideal place to check your car and stock up with food and water

Brachina Gorge, near Blinman

National Parks

Nowhere else in Australia can wildlife be seen in such close proximity and in such profusion as in the parks of South Australia. To protect its valuable native animals and plants and to conserve the natural features of the landscape, this State has set aside 17 per cent of its total area as national, conservation and recreation parks, and regional and game reserves.

In addition to 16 national parks, the SA Department of Environment and Natural Resources also manages 212 conservation parks, 13 recreation parks, 10 game reserves and 7 regional reserves. The main criteria for each category, as stated in the National Parks and Wildlife Act of 1972, were as follows:

- **National parks** Areas with wildlife or natural features of national significance.
- **Conservation parks** Areas for the preservation and conservation of native flora and fauna representative of South Australia's natural heritage, although historical features may also be included in these parks.
- **Recreation parks** Areas for outdoor recreation in a natural setting.
- **Game reserves** Areas suitable for the management and conservation of native game species, usually duck and quail. Hunting of some species during restricted open seasons.
- **Regional reserves** A new category established in 1988 which protects, at present, 4 large areas within South Australia considered to contain important wildlife and natural features, but where natural resources, such as minerals, may be needed in the future.

The range of climatic zones in South Australia enables visitors to enjoy these parks throughout the year; coastal parks are cool in summer and autumn, while mountain areas are ideal to visit in winter and spring.

The Flinders Ranges, which extend for 430 kilometres, contain the **Flinders Ranges National Park**, which, with its total area of 94 908 hectares, is one of the major national parks in Australia. The Wilpena section, in the south of the park, comprises the famed Wilpena Pound and the Wilpena Pound Range, covering an area of 10 000 hectares. The Pound is one of the most extraordinary geological formations in Australia. Developed in the Cambrian period, it is a vast oval rock bowl, ringed with sheer cliffs and jagged rocks and with a flat floor covered with trees and grass. A homestead dating back

The Cazneaux Tree, Flinders Ranges National Park

to 1889 still stands. Native rock paintings at Arkaroo Rock indicate that this was a significant area in Aboriginal mythology.

Twenty-five kilometres north of Wilpena is the Oraparinna section of the park. The 68 500 hectares of this section were a sheep station last century, at one time maintaining more than 20 000 sheep. Further north, near the **Gammon Ranges National Park**, Arkaroola offers motel accommodation and a serviced camping ground. The park, an arid, isolated region of rugged ranges and deep gorges, provides visitors with the experience of an extensive wilderness area. The mountains sparkle with exposed formations of quartz, fluorspar, hematites and ochres, making the region a gem-hunter's paradise. The Gammon Ranges (camping permitted) are a sanctuary for native birds and animals, including the western grey kangaroo, the big red kangaroo, the grey euro or hill kangaroo and the yellow-footed rock wallaby.

Further north, in the State's arid lands, over 8 million hectares have been set aside to protect the unique desert environment. These desert parks include the **Lake Eyre National Park**, **Witjira National Park, Innamincka Regional Reserve** and the **Simpson Desert Conservation Park**. Lake Eyre, the central feature of the park of the same name, is one of the world's greatest salinas or salt lakes, found 16 metres below sea level. Contrarily, it is both the hub of a huge internal drainage system while being located in the driest part of the Australian continent. In this area vegetation is

sparse, but after heavy rains when the area floods, the ground is carpeted with colourful wildflowers and the animal and bird populations, attracted by the plant rejuvenation, rise accordingly. Care needs to be taken when visiting this area; only 4WD vehicles can access the park and campers must be fully self-sufficient.

Witjira National Park, 120 km north of Oodnadatta, is an area of vast desert landscapes; gibber plains, sand dunes, salt pans and mound springs, upwellings of the Great Artesian Basin. Visitors may explore this extremely arid environment from the park's oasis, Dalhousie Springs.

The **Innamincka Regional Reserve** covers much of the flood prone country around the Cooper and Strzelecki Creeks up to the Queensland border. These arid wetlands, which comprise a series of semi-permanent overflow lakes, hold many surprises for birdwatchers.

The **Simpson Desert Conservation Park**, for the more adventurous park visitor, consists of spectacular red sand dunes, which in places can run parallel for hundreds of kilometres, as well as salt lakes, flood-out plains, hummock grasslands, gibber desert, gidgee woodland, tablelands and mesas.

Visitors who wish to enjoy the attractions of the parks and reserves in this vast desert area must obtain a Desert Parks Pass (included in the **Desert Parks South Australia Handbook** and maps kit), from the SA Department of Environmental and Natural Resources, 60 Elder Terrace, Hawker, 5434; telephone (086) 48 4244. The pass is valid from the date of purchase; it allows twelve months' bush camping in Lake Eyre National Park, Witjira National Park, Innamincka Regional Reserve and the Simpson Desert Conservation Park and Regional Reserve, and also Flinders Ranges and Gammon Ranges National Parks. Information and maps on each park and reserve are included, along with a vehicle-identification sticker and three renewal forms.

The Coorong, one of the State's finest national parks and of international importance, is 185 kilometres from Adelaide, south of the mouth of the mighty Murray River. From the Aboriginal word *karangh,* meaning 'narrow neck', Coorong is a series of saltwater lagoons fed by the Murray and separated from the sea by Younghusband Peninsula.

Cape du Couedic lighthouse, Flinders Chase Nat. Park

In the park are six island bird sanctuaries, prohibited to the public, but which can be viewed through binoculars. These islands house rookeries of pelicans, crested terns and silver gulls. More than 280 species of birds have been recorded in the Coorong. The ocean beach is a favourite haunt of fishermen, but you can take the pleasant drive along the coast road beside the waterway, stopping to camp or picnic. At dusk, kangaroos and wombats come out to feed on the grassed open areas.

Bool Lagoon Game Reserve is on the southern flat plains of South Australia, near Naracoorte. The lagoon's natural cycle of flooding and drying out is perfect for breeding of waterbirds. In spring, when the water is deepest, the thousands of black swans that crowd the lagoon are spectacular. In summer and autumn, when the water is shallow, waterfowl and waders flock to feed on the rich plant life. Bool Lagoon is also the largest permanent ibis rookery in Australia. Dense thickets of paperbark and banks of reeds in its central reaches provide a safe breeding ground. A network of boardwalks provides access to wildlife without disturbing the natural environment.

The **Naracoorte Caves** are preserved in a small conservation park in the south-east of the State. These impressive caves enclose a wonderland of stalagmites, stalactites, shawls, straws and other calcite formations. Four of the limestone caves, including Blanche Cave, the first to be discovered (1845), are open for inspection through guided or adventure tours. A tour through the museum set up in Victoria Fossil Cave shows visitors skeletons of such extinct animals as giant browsing kangaroos, a hippopotamus-sized wombat, the marsupial lion and the Tasmanian tiger.

Flinders Chase National Park, encompassing most of the western end of Kangaroo Island, protects pristine natural vegetation including forests, mallee, and stunted coastal plants. Bushwalkers can enjoy trails along rivers to secluded beaches, or follow the rugged coastline to observe the full force of the Southern Ocean. Lighthouses and keepers' cottages provide cultural interest; visitors may see kangaroos, koalas, fur seals, echidnas and platypus.

Seal Bay Conservation Park, also on Kangaroo Island, allows visitors the unique opportunity to see Australian sea lion breeding colonies. The adjoining **Cape Gantheaume Conservation Park** is a wilderness area attracting experienced bushwalkers.

A twelve-month Kangaroo Island Pass, available from the Department of Environment and Natural Resources office at 37 Dauncy St, Kingscote (PO Box 39, Kingscote 5223); telephone (0848) 22 381, enables access to all parks on the island where an entrance fee is charged.

On the south-west tip of Yorke Peninsula is the 10 000 hectare **Innes National Park**, where wildflowers blanket the park in spring and birdwatching is a favourite pastime. As well as native bushland and magnificent coastal scenery, there is good fishing at the beaches. Walking trails lead to the coast and to the historic ruins of Inneston (1913). This small settlement once housed miners who dug for gypsum, used for plaster and chalk; for many years nearly every schoolchild in Australia was taught with the aid of blackboard chalk mined here and shipped from Stenhouse Bay. Camping and accommodation are available.

The Eyre Peninsula, bordered to the north by the Eyre Highway, contains a number of parks. **Coffin Bay National Park** and **Lincoln National Park** feature wilderness areas and spectacular coastal scenery. Both these National Parks provide excellent opportunities for bush camping, birdwatching and bushwalking. Coffin Bay National Park is 50 kilometres west of Port Lincoln and takes in all of Coffin Bay Peninsula. The western coastline faces the Great Australian Bight while the eastern part has the calming influence of sheltered sandy beaches and islands. Enquire locally about safe swimming.

Lincoln National Park, a 15-kilometre drive south of Port Lincoln, occupies a large part of Jussieu Peninsula and is surrounded by small islands. At its northern tip, on Stamford Hill, the Flinders Monument commemorates exploration by Matthew Flinders in 1802. From this hill visitors can enjoy spectacular views of the surrounding area.

Diverse bird habitats are provided at **Lake Gilles Conservation Park**, also on Eyre Peninsula, by the salt lakes and the dry mallee and western myall vegetation.

A unique and successful experiment of familiarising people with native fauna is evidenced at Cleland Wildlife Park in the centre of the larger **Cleland Conservation Park**, located on the slopes of Mount Lofty overlooking Adelaide. Here visitors are able to walk freely among the animals, which are housed in conditions similar to their native habitat.

Within Adelaide's southern suburbs is **Belair National Park**, which offers self-guide walks, forested hills, spectacular views, parrots, wildflowers, an adventure playground, tennis courts, picnic facilities, and the opportunity to tour Old Government House.

Many of South Australia's national parks charge camping and entrance fees.

For further information on camping restrictions, entry permits and fees, and general advice on visiting the State's national parks, contact the South Australian Department of Environment and Natural Resources Information Centre, 77 Grenfell St, Adelaide 5000 (GPO Box 1047, Adelaide 5001); (08) 204 1910.

before the long drive. The port at Thevenard, 3 km SW, handles bulk grain, gypsum and salt. The fishing fleet is noted for its large whiting hauls. Snapper, salmon, tommy ruff and crab are other catches. Ceduna is set on Murat Bay; sand coves, sheltered bays and offshore islands make the bay an ideal base for a beach holiday, offering swimming, fishing, water-skiing, windsurfing and boating. There was a whaling station on St Peter Island in the 1850s. According to map references in Swift's Gulliver's Travels, the tiny people of Lilliput might well have lived on St Peter Is. (visible from Thevenard) or St Francis Is. **Of interest:** Old Schoolhouse National Trust Museum, Park Tce, pioneering items, artefacts from atomic testing at Maralinga and historic medical room; open Mon.–Sat. Half and full day tours of town, incl. oyster tours, available; contact Tourist Centre. Sept.: Agricultural Show. Oct.: Oyster Fest. **In the area:** Oestmann's Fish Factory at Thevenard Boat Haven, tours available; open daily. At Denial Bay, 13 km W: McKenzie Ruins, site of original settlement; oyster farm. Denial Bay and Davenport Creek, west, and Decres Bay, Laura Bay and Smoky Bay, all south-east, picnicking and safe fishing (boat charter for diving and fishing available at Ceduna); all day trips from town. Amazing sand dunes and excellent surf at Cactus Beach, 54 km W, near Penong. At Penong, 75 km W, restored woolshed, museum, local crafts; 10–4 daily. Gaanywea camel day rides and safaris from Penong; May–Oct. Southern right whales can be seen June–Oct. along coast west of Ceduna; tours available. Spectacular coastline includes prominent headland at Point Brown, 56 km S. **Tourist information:** Gateway Tourist Centre, 58 Poynton St; (086) 25 2780. **Accommodation:** 1 hotel/motel, 4 motels, 5 cara./camp. parks. **See also:** The Eyre Peninsula.
MAP REF. 297 N10

Clare   Pop. 2575
Set in rich agricultural and pastoral country, this charming town was first settled by Europeans in 1842; it was named after County Clare in Ireland. The area is renowned for its prize-winning table wines. Wheat, barley, fruit, honey, stud sheep and wool are other important regional industries. The first vines were planted by Jesuit priests at Sevenhill in 1848; Jesuit priests are still producing table and sacramental wines from Sevenhill Cellars. **Of interest:** National Trust museum, housed in old police station (1850), cnr Victoria Rd and West Tce; open Sat., Sun. and holidays. Inchiquin Lake, White Hut Rd. Lookouts at Billy Goat Hill, from Wright St, and Neagles Rock, Neagles Rock Rd. Maynard Memorial Park, Pioneer Ave, picnic/barbecue facilities. Historic town walk; self-guide leaflets available. Clare Fine Art, Main North Rd, work of prominent Australian craftspersons, paintings. Easter: Festival. May: Gourmet Weekend (long weekend). **In the area:** Stately Wolta Wolta Homestead, West Tce, on western edge of town, built by pastoralist John Hope (1846), and still owned by Hope family. Homestead rebuilt after Ash Wednesday fires; open Sun. 10–1. Over 20 wineries in the area (some not open for inspection and cellar-door sales; check opening times). Around Clare: Tim Adams' Wines, Jim Barry Wines, Tim Knappstein Wines, Leasingham Wines, Wendouree Cellars, Duncan Estate Winery. Sevenhill Cellars, 7 km S, established 1851, monastery buildings, including St Aloysius Church (1864). Wineries in Polish Hill River district (12 km S) include: Pike's Polish Hill River Estate, Paulett Wines, The Wilson Vineyard. Around Penwortham, 10 km S: Skillogalee Wines, Waninga Wines, Penwortham Cellars, Mitchell's Winery. At Mintaro, 19 km SE: Mintaro Cellars. Around Watervale, 12 km S: Clos Clare, Crabtree Watervale Wines, Eaglehawk Estate (also wine museum), Rosenberg Cellars, Horrocks Winery. Around Auburn, 26 km S: Taylors Wines, Grosset Wines. Also at Mintaro: historic Martindale Hall (featured in the film *Picnic at Hanging Rock*); accommodation, dining, and tours afternoons daily (closed Christmas Day and Good Friday); slate quarry, operational since 1856 (not open for tours). Also at Auburn, many historic buildings maintained by National Trust; self-guide walking-tour leaflets available. Birthplace of poet C.J. Dennis in 1876. Accommodation available in historic buildings. Scenic drive to Blyth, 13 km W; flora and fauna in Padnainda Reserve; Medika Gallery, originally a Lutheran church (1886), specialising in Australian bird and flower paintings; open daily. Scenic drive 12 km S to Spring Gully Conservation Park; rare red stringybarks. Springfarm Galleries, Springfarm Rd, 6 km SE. Bungaree Station Homestead (1841), 12 km N, historic merino sheep station, knitting yarns, original patterns and hand-knitted Bungaree jumpers available for sale from Station Store; tours and accommodation. Geralka Rural Farm, 25 km N of Clare, working farm, tours and activities. **Tourist information:** Main North Rd; (08) 8842 2131. **Accommodation:** 2 hotels, 1 hotel/motel, 3 motels, 2 B&B, 2 cara./camp. parks. **See also:** Festival Fun.
MAP REF. 289 L4

Cleve   Pop. 738
Surrounded by rich farming country, this inland town on the Eyre Peninsula was settled in 1853 by Europeans. **Of interest:** Cleve Fauna Park, Fourth St. Old Council Chambers Museum, Third St; contact District Council for appt. Aug.: Eyre Peninsula Field Days (every even-numbered year). Oct.: Agricultural Show. **In the area:** Hincks and Bascombe Well Conservation Parks (35 and 90 km W respectively). Scenic drive along escarpment of Cleve–Cowell Hills. Arno Bay, 26 km SE, and Cowell, 43 km E, both have swimming beaches and fishing jetties. **Tourist information:** District Council, 13 Main St; (086) 28 2004. **Accommodation:** 1 hotel/motel, limited cara./camp. facilities.
MAP REF. 288 F4

Coffin Bay   Pop. 343
A picturesque holiday town and fishing village in a sheltered bay, 51 km NW of Port Lincoln; sailing, water-skiing and swimming are popular here. The coastal scenery in this area is magnificent and fishing is excellent. Oysters cultivated in Coffin Bay are among the best in the country. The bay's unusual name was bestowed by Matthew Flinders in 1802 to honour his friend Sir Isaac Coffin. **Of interest:** Oyster Farm, The Esplanade; also renowned for its lobster. Oyster Walk, a 3-km foreshore walkway from the caravan park to beyond Crinolin Point. **In the area:** Coffin Bay National Park and Kellidie Bay Conservation Park surround township, wildflowers in spring. Camping in national park areas; permit required. Farm Beach and nearby 'Anzac Cove' location for film *Gallipoli*. Yangie Trail drive, 10 km S, through bush to Point Avoid and Yangie Lookout for coastal views and surf beaches. Old stone buildings in Wangary, 29 km N. Further 50 km N, scenic stretch of Flinders Hwy between Mount Hope and Sheringa.

The Breakaways, near Coober Pedy

Blacksmith's museum at Koppio, 45 km NW. **Tourist information:** Beachcomber Agencies, The Esplanade; (086) 85 4057. **Accommodation:** 1 motel, 1 cara./camp. park. **See also:** The Eyre Peninsula. MAP REF. 288 C7

Coober Pedy   Pop. 2491
In the heart of South Australia's outback, 848 km N of Adelaide on the Stuart Hwy, is the opal-mining town of Coober Pedy. This is the last stop for petrol between Cadney Park (155 km N) and Glendambo (253 km S) on the Stuart Hwy. The name Coober Pedy is Aboriginal for 'white fellows in a hole'—most of the population live in dugouts (at a constant 24°C underground) as protection from the severe summer temperatures, often reaching 45°C, and the cold winter nights. There is also a complete lack of timber for building. The countryside is desolate and harsh, and the town has reticulated water provided from a bore 23 km N, and treated by reverse osmosis. Opals were discovered here in 1915; today there are thousands of mines in the area. **Of interest:** Guided tours of working mines and demonstrations of opals being cut and polished. Jewellery and polished stones for sale. On eastern edge of town: Big Winch Lookout, Italian Club Road and Old Timers Mine, Crowders Gully Road, mine museum and interpretive centre with self-guide walks. On Hutchison St: Umoona underground mine, museum and motel; underground churches, including St Peter and St Pauls; Desert Cave, underground pictorial mining display, premier

building and 4-star international motel, underground shopping gallery. Underground Catacomb Church also east of town. Underground Pottery, west of town, features local pottery. April: Opal Festival. Oct.: (long weekend) Coober Pedy races. **In the area:** Opal fields are pocked with diggings; beware of unprotected mine shafts. Avoid entering any field area unless escorted by someone who knows the area. For safety reasons, visitors to the mines are advised to join a tour. Trespassers on claims can be fined a minimum of $1,000. The Breakaways, 30 km N, colourful 40-sq.-km reserve containing unique landscape, ancient seabed. **Tourist information:** Council Offices, Hutchison St; (086) 72 5298. **Accommodation:** 1 hotel/motel, 9 motels, 3 cara./ camp. parks. **See also:** The Outback. MAP REF. 295 R11

Coonalpyn   Pop. 266
This tiny town on the Dukes Hwy, 180 km SE of Adelaide, makes a good base to explore the Mt Boothby (30 km SW) and Carcuma (20 km NE) Conservation Parks, to see grey kangaroos, echidnas, emus and mallee fowl in their natural environment. **Of interest:** Melaleuca Crafts, Dukes Hwy, locally made pottery and clothing. Oct.: Agricultural and Horticultural Show. **In the area:** Farmstay at Bayree Farm, 5 km E. **Tourist information:** Bakery and Craft Shop, Dukes Hwy; (085) 71 1200. **Accommodation:** 1 hotel, 1 cara./camp. park. MAP REF. 287 F5, 289 O11

Coonawarra   Pop. 40
The European settlement of Coonawarra goes back to 1890, when John Riddoch subdivided 2 000 acres of his vast landholding for the development of orchards and vineyards. Although the vines flourished and excellent wines were made, demand was not high until a resurgence of interest in the 1950s and 1960s, when the region became recognised as an important winegrowing area. The terra rossa soil and dedicated viticulturalists and winemakers combine to produce award-winning white and red table wines. **Of interest:** Chardonnay Lodge, Penola Rd, motel, restaurant, art gallery and wine information centre. **In the area:** 23 wineries, incl. Bowen Estate, Brands Laira, Hollick Wines, James Haselgrove, Katnook Estate, Ladbroke Grove Wines, Leconfield Coonawarra, Mildara Wines, Redman Winery, Rouge Homme, St Mary's Vineyard, The Ridge Wines, Wynns Coonawarra Estate, Zema Estate. **Tourist information:** Arthur St, Penola; (087) 37 2855. **Accommodation:** 2 hotels, 1 motel. **See also:** Vineyards and Wineries. MAP REF. 226 A2, 228 A13, 287 I11

Cowell   Pop. 695
A small, pleasant township 108 km S of Whyalla, Cowell is on the almost landlocked Franklin Harbour. One of the world's major jade deposits is in the district, and Cowell is the processing centre for Australia's only commercial jademining operation. The sandy beach is safe for swimming; fishing is excellent.

Oyster farming is a new local industry and fresh oysters can be purchased year round from various outlets. **Of interest:** Old post office and attached residence (1888), Main St, now Franklin Harbour National Trust Historical Museum. Open-air Agricultural Museum, Lincoln Hwy. Jade Workshop, Lincoln Hwy, to view the grading of the stone; opposite, at the Cowell Jade Motel, displays of local jewellery and sales; open daily. Smithy's Shell House, Warnes St. July: Jade Marathon. **In the area:** Entrance Island, in Franklin Harbour. Franklin Harbour Conservation Park, south of Cowell, good fishing spots. Swimming and excellent fishing locations abound, incl. Port Gibbon, 15 km S, and Point Price Sandhills, 5 km further on. Arno Bay, 48 km S, popular holiday resort, sandy beaches, jetty for fishing. **Tourist information:** Council Offices, Main St; (086) 29 2019. **Accommodation:** 2 hotels, 1 motel, 2 cara./camp. parks. **See also:** The Eyre Peninsula.
MAP REF. 288 G4

Crystal Brook   Pop. 1282
Once part of a vast sheep station, this town, 25 km SE of Port Pirie, is now a major centre for the sheep, beef and cereal industries of the region. **Of interest:** National Trust Museum, Brandis St: local history collection in first two-storeyed building in town, original butcher's shop and bakery; underground bakehouse. Crystal Crafts, Bowman St, local craft. Picnicking and swimming in creekside parks. Aug.: Agricultural Show. **In the area:** Bowman Park, 5 km E, surrounds ruins of Bowman family property, Crystal Brook Run (1847); excellent Native Fauna, including reptile collection; (open daily). Heysen Walking Trail runs through Bowman Park. Gladstone, 21 km NE, set in rich rural country in Rocky River Valley: railway yards contain one of world's few junction points of 3 different gauges—narrow, standard and broad—interlaid in one siding; tours of Gladstone gaol (1881); Trend Drinks Factory, home of Old Style Ginger Beer (tours available). Laura, 32 km N: boyhood town of C.J. Dennis, author of *The Songs of a Sentimental Bloke*; Folk Fair (April); cottage craft industry; art galleries; historic buildings (self-guide walking tour leaflet available). Beetaloo Valley and Reservoir, west of Laura. Near Wirrabara, 50 km N, scenic walks through pine forests. Redhill, 25 km S,

riverside walk, museum, craft shop. Koolunga, 10 km E of Redhill, cottage industries and picnic areas. Salt lakes around Snowtown, 50 km S, Lochiel–Ninnes Road lookout for superb view of inland lakes and countryside. Yacka, 40 km SE, sheepdog trials in Aug. **Tourist information**: District Council Offices, Bowman St; (086) 36 2150. **Accommodation:** Crystal Brook, 2 hotels, 1 cara./camp. park. Bowman Park, 1 hostel. Gladstone, 1 cara./camp. park. Laura, 1 cara./camp. park.
MAP REF. 289 K2

Edithburgh   Pop. 453
Located on the cliff top at the southern tip of Yorke Peninsula, Edithburgh overlooks Gulf St Vincent and Troubridge Shoals, a chain of tiny islands. **Of interest:** Native Flora Park (17½ ha), Ansley Tce. Edithburgh Museum, Edith St; historical maritime collection. Town jetty, end of Edith St, built in 1873. Rockpool at cliff base is excellent for swimming. Offshore skindiving is popular and nearby Sultana Bay is good for boating, fishing, swimming and sailboarding. Oct.: State Sailboarding Championships. **In the area:** Coobowie, 5 km N, popular coastal resort with caravan park. Tours to Troubridge Island Conservation Park; ½ hour by boat. Scenic drive along coast passes wreck of *Clan Ranald*. **Tourist information:** Henry's Place, Blanche St; (08) 8852 6009. **Accommodation:** 2 hotels, 1 cara./camp. park.
MAP REF. 282 G9, 288 I9

Elliston   Pop. 242
Nestled in a small range of hills on the shore of Waterloo Bay, Elliston is a pleasant coastal town and the centre for a cereal-growing, mixed-farming and fishing community. Known for its rugged and scenic coastline, excellent fishing and safe swimming beaches, Elliston is a popular holiday destination. **Of interest:** Town hall mural, Main St, an art history of town and district. **In the area:** Clifftop walk at Waterloo Bay; fossilised weevil cocoons (shaped like Dutch clogs), believed to be over 100 000 years old, can be found. Talia Caves, 40 km N. Good surfing just north of town near Anxious Bay. Lock's Well and Sheringa Beach to south, for surf fishing. Scenic drives north and south of town offer superb views of magnificent coastline; good views also from Cummings

Monument Lookout, just off hwy near Kiana, 52 km S. Day trip to summit of Mt Wedge and return via Bramfield. Flinders Is., 35 km offshore; limited accommodation. **Tourist information:** Rally's Roadhouse, Flinders Hwy; (086) 87 9170. **Accommodation:** 1 hotel/motel, 2 cara./camp. parks. **See also:** The Eyre Peninsula.
MAP REF. 288 B4

Gawler   Pop. 13 835
Settled by Europeans in 1839, Gawler, 40 km NE of Adelaide, is the centre for a thriving agricultural district and also the gateway to the Barossa Valley. **Of interest:** Historic buildings, including Gawler Mill and old post office, west of Murray St. Old Eagle Foundry, King St; where local iron lace made. Walking tour of Church Hill district, a State Heritage Area. Self-guide walking, driving and cycling tours; leaflets from Tourist Information. Para Para (1862), Penrith Ave, historic residence open Sat.–Sun. or by appt during renovation. Anglican Church, interesting pipe organ, bellringing Thurs. or by appt. Dead Man's Pass Reserve, end Murray St; picnic facilities and walking trails. June: Equestrian Event. Aug.: Agricultural Show. **In the area:** Restored Willaston post office, 2 km N. Astronomical Society of SA's observatory at Stockport, 30 km N, public viewing nights; check at Tourist Information. Scholz Park Museum at Riverton, 54 km N. Wellington Hotel at Waterloo, 76 km N, near Manoora, once Cobb & Co. staging point. **Tourist information:** 2 Lyndoch Rd; (085) 22 6814. **Accommodation:** 1 hotel, 1 motel, 3 B&B, 1 hostel, 2 cara./camp. parks.
MAP REF. 283 M5, 287 C1, 289 L7

Goolwa   Pop. 3018
Goolwa is a rapidly growing holiday town 12 km from the mouth of the Murray near Lake Alexandrina. Once a key port in the golden days of the riverboats, the area has a strong tradition of shipbuilding, trade and fishing; today, the lakes area is ideal for boating, fishing and aquatic sports and popular with birdwatchers and photographers. Southern right whales visit the bay July–Sept. **Of interest:** Historic buildings, including distinctive railway superintendent's house (1852), known as 'the round-roofed house', and RSL Club, in former stables of Goolwa Railway (1853), both

Kangaroo Island

Only 120 kilometres south-west of Adelaide, Kangaroo Island, the third largest Australian island, shows nature in its wildest and purest form. A walk through bush or along coastal cliffs may provide glimpses of koalas, echidnas or, of course, kangaroos; there are also many species of birds and wildflowers.

Visitors may fly to the island from Adelaide (Air Kangaroo Island, Emu Airways, Albatross Airlines and Kendell Airlines) or go by ferry. The ferry *Super Flyte* takes passengers from Glenelg to Kingscote. The vehicular ferry *Island Seaway* journeys from Port Adelaide to Kingscote. The *Philanderer III* and The *Navigator* operate from Cape Jervis to Penneshaw. Tours are available and hire vehicles include cars, mopeds and bicycles. A bus service operates between Kingscote and the airport. A shuttle bus operates twice daily between Penneshaw and Kingscote. Kangaroo Island's waters—surf, rocks freshwater, and ocean—offer good fishing; big-game-fishing charters are available and fishing equipment can be hired.

At the three main towns, **Kingscote**, American River and **Penneshaw**, there is a range of accommodation from hotels and motels, through flats and cottages to camping and cabins. Many farms provide bed and breakfast accommodation.

American River, a resort nestled in a pine-fringed bay, is ideal for fishing, scuba

Sea Lion, Seal Bay

diving and canoeing. **Pelican Lagoon** is a sanctuary for birds and fish. Penneshaw overlooks the passage separating the island from the mainland. Fairy penguins promenade on the rocks here at night.

The coastline of the island varies from the several kilometres of safe swimming beach at **Emu Bay** in the north to the rugged cliffs and roaring surf of the south. However, in the south, **D'Estrees Bay**'s wide deserted beach is ideal for fishing, shell-collecting and exploring—there is an old whaling station at Point Tinline. **Cape Gantheaume** and **Seal Bay Conservation Parks** are located on this exposed

southern coast. Seal Bay has a permanent colony of sea lions. Fur seal colonies are found at Cape Gantheaume and Cape du Couedic, and leopard seals are occasional visitors. Also on the south coast are limestone formations in the caves at **Kelly Hill Conservation Park**. At **Cape Borda**, on the north-west tip of the island, is one of the most picturesque of Australia's old lighthouses; there are guided tours daily, arranged through the Department of Environment and Natural Resources at Cape Borda. Other attractive spots along the northern coast include the rugged rocks at **Harveys Return**; **Western River Cove** with its idyllic white beach; a superb protected bay at **Snelling Beach**; and **Stokes Bay**, where a secret tunnel leads to the beach. On the west coast, which is dominated by the soaring eucalypt forests of the **Flinders Chase National Park**, are two of the island's natural wonders: **Admirals Arch**, a huge arch where on sunny afternoons stalactites can be seen in silhouette; and the **Remarkable Rocks**, huge, unusually shaped granite boulders.

For further information and for a pass that covers all DENR entry fees and tours, contact the Kangaroo Island Tourist Information Centre, Department of Environment and Natural Resources, 37 Dauncey St, Kingscote, (0848) 2 2381. **See also:** Entry for Kingscote in A–Z listing.

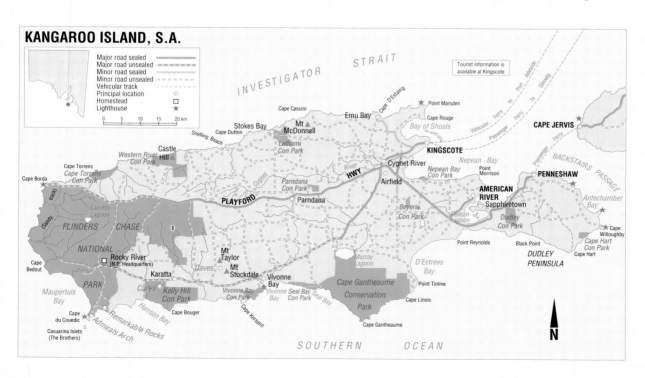

KANGAROO ISLAND, S.A.

Major road sealed
Major road unsealed
Minor road sealed
Minor road unsealed
Vehicular track
Principal location
Homestead
Lighthouse

0   5   10   15   20 km

Tourist information is available at Kingscote

INVESTIGATOR STRAIT

Cape Cassini
Emu Bay
Cape D'Estang
Point Marsden
Cape Rouge
Bay of Shoals
CAPE JERVIS

Stokes Bay
Cape Dutton
Mt McDonnell
Snelling Beach
Lathami Con Park
KINGSCOTE
Nepean Bay
BACKSTAIRS PASSAGE

Castle Hill
Western River Con Park
Cygnet River
Nepean Bay Con Park
Point Morrison
PENNESHAW

Cape Torrens
Cape Torrens Con Park
Parndana Con Park
Airfield
AMERICAN RIVER

Cape Borda
Larrikin Lagoon
PLAYFORD
Parndana
Beyeria Con Park
Sapphiretown
Antechamber Bay

Sandy Track
FLINDERS CHASE
Cygnet River HWY
Pelican Lagoon
Dudley Con Park
Cape Willoughby

NATIONAL
Mt Taylor
Murray Lagoon
Point Reynolds
Black Point
Cape Hart Con Park
Cape Hart

Cape Bedout
Rocky River (N.P. Headquarters)
Mt Stockdale
D'Estrees Bay
DUDLEY PENINSULA

PARK
Karatta
Caves
Vivonne Bay
Point Tinline

Maupertuis Bay
Kelly Hill Con Park
Vivonne Bay Con Park
Vivonne Bay
Seal Bay Con Park
Seal Bay
Cape Gantheaume Conservation Park
Cape Linois

Cape du Couedic
Cape Bouger
Hanson Bay
Cape Kersaint
Cape Gantheaume

Casuarina Islets (The Brothers)
Remarkable Rocks
Admirals Arch

SOUTHERN OCEAN

N

in B.F. Laurie Lane, off Cadell St. In Cadell St, display of first railway carriage used in South Australia, horse-drawn between Goolwa and Port Elliot from 1854. Steam train rides between Goolwa and Victor Harbor; check at Tourist Office. National Trust Museum, Porter St, housed in former blacksmith's shop dating from 1870s. Next door, in original but rebuilt cottage, Goolwa Print Room. Both Goolwa hotels, the Goolwa in Cadell St and the Corio in Railway Pl, date from 1850s. Signal Point Visitor Centre, The Wharf, computerised display of river and district before European settlement, and the impact of local development. Feb.: Wooden Boat Festival (odd-numbered years). **In the area:** Excellent fishing. Bird sanctuary east of Goolwa, swans, pelicans and other waterfowl, also bird hide. Nearby, the Barrages, desalination points that prevent salt water from reaching the Murray. MV *Aroona*, PS *Mundoo* and MV *Coorong Pirate* cruise to mouth of the Murray, the Coorong, the Barrages and the Lower Murray. Hindmarsh Is., via ferry, for view of Murray mouth, and freshwater marina. Malleebrae Woolshed, 2 km N, wool displays, shearing videos, art and craft (open by appt). Scenic flights available; airport 5 km N. Currency Creek, 8 km N: Canoe Tree; Tonkin's Currency Creek Winery (with restaurant and fauna park); creekside park and walking trail. Tooperang Trout Farm, 20 km NW. **Tourist information:** Old Library Bldg, cnr Cadell St and Goolwa Tce; (085) 55 1144. **Accommodation:** 4 motels, 3 cara./camp. parks. **See also:** The Fleurieu Peninsula.
MAP REF. 283 M12, 284 G12, 287 C4, 289 L10

Hawker   Pop. 345
This outback town in the centre of the northern Flinders Ranges is 400 km N of Adelaide. Once a railway town, it is now the centre of a unique area that attracts visitors from both Australia and overseas, who marvel at the colouring and grandeur of the many ranges that make up the Flinders. **Of interest:** Museum at Hawker Motors, cnr Wilpena and Cradock Rds. Historic buildings incl.: post office (1882), Hawker Hotel (1882), old railway-station complex (1885). May: Horseracing carnival. Sept./Oct.: Art exhibition. Oct.: Henley-on-Arkaba fun day. **In the area:** Moralana Scenic Drive, 42 km N, joins roads to Wilpena and

Leigh Creek. Further north, Arkaroo Rock, with paintings by Adnajamathana tribe; nearby Rawnsley Bluff, majestic southern rampart of Wilpena Pound. Scenic flights and 4WD tours available. Merna Mora Station, 46 km N; station holidays available. Walking trail and scenic lookout at Jarvis Hill, 5 km SW. Rock paintings at Yourambulla Caves, 11 km S. Historic Kanyaka ruins, south off main road to Quorn. From Hawker, ruins at Wilson, Hookina, Wonoka and Willow Waters; check directions before departure. **Tourist information:** Hawker Motors, cnr Wilpena and Cradock Rds; (086) 48 4014. **Accommodation:** 1 hotel/motel, 1 motel, 2 cara./camp. parks. **See also:** The Flinders Ranges; National Parks.
MAP REF. 285 D9, 291 K9

Innamincka   Pop. 14
This tiny settlement, 1 027 km NE of Adelaide, is built around a hotel and trading post on the Strzelecki Track, and is on the banks of Cooper Creek in wet periods. Motorists intending to travel along the Track should read the section on Outback Motoring before attempting the journey. There are no supplies or petrol between Lyndhurst and Innamincka. **Of interest:** Cullyamurra Waterhole on Cooper Creek, picturesque spot, Aboriginal carvings, and excellent fishing. Rebuilt Australian Inland Mission hostel, now houses National Parks office. **In the area:** Memorials to explorers Burke and Wills near Innamincka; famous 'Dig Tree' 40 km over border in Qld. Coongie Lakes, 103 km NW (road conditions can vary considerably; 4WD recommended); freshwater lakes are a haven for wildlife. **Tourist information:** Hawker Motors, cnr Wilpena and Cradock Rds, Hawker; (086) 48 4014. **Accommodation:** 1 hotel/motel. **See also:** The Outback.
MAP REF. 293 Q7, 484 G6

Jamestown   Pop. 1359
Jamestown is a well-planned country town 205 km N of Adelaide. The surrounding country produces stud sheep and cattle, cereals, dairy produce and timber. **Of interest:** In Main St: 6 heritage murals. Railway Station Museum; open daily. Parks ideal for picnicking along banks of Belalie Ck; banks floodlit at night. Oct: Agricultural Show. Christmas: Annual pageant. **In the area:**

Scenic drive through Bundaleer Forest Reserve, 9 km S, towards New Campbell Hill for panoramic views of plains towards Mt Remarkable and The Bluff. Around Spalding, 34 km S: series of open waterways with picnic areas and trout fishing opportunities; Geralka Rural Farm, 49 km S, working commercial farm with tours and activities. At Gladstone, 29 km SW: railway yards for train enthusiasts; tours of gaol (1881), and tours of Trend Drinks Factory, home of Old Style Ginger Beer. Appila Springs, scenic picnic spot 8 km from Appila, 24 km NW. **Tourist information:** Jamestown Country Retreat Caravan Park; (086) 64 0077. **Accommodation:** 3 hotels, 1 hotel/motel, 1 cara./camp. park.
MAP REF. 289 L2

Kadina   Pop. 3536
The largest town on Yorke Peninsula, Kadina is the chief commercial centre of the region. The town's history includes the boom copper-mining era during the 1800s and early 1900s, when thousands of Cornish miners flocked to the area; the community is still proud of its ancestry. **Of interest:** Historic hotels, including the Wombat, Taylor St, and Royal Exchange, Digby St, with iron lace balconies and shady verandahs. National Trust Kadina Museum complex includes Matta House (1863), home of manager of Matta Matta Copper Mine; agricultural machinery, blacksmith's shop, printing museum and old Matta mine. Banking and Currency Museum, unique private museum, Graves St; check opening times. Wallaroo Mines site; open for signposted self-guide walking tour. Leaflets for self-guide walking tours of town available from Tourist Information. Easter: Bowling Carnival. May: Prize-winning Kernewek Lowender, Cornish festival, in conjunction with Wallaroo and Moonta (odd-numbered years). Aug.: Agricultural Show. **In the area:** Moonta, 18 km SW and Wallaroo, 10 km W, both of interest. Creative Activities network; expert tutoring in arts and crafts. Yorke Peninsula Field Days at Paskeville (19 km SE) Sept. every odd-numbered year. **Tourist information:** Yorke Peninsula Visitor Information Centre, 51 Taylor St; (08) 8821 2093. **Accommodation:** 2 hotels, 2 motels, 1 B&B, 1 cara./camp. park. **See also:** Festival Fun; The Yorke Peninsula.
MAP REF. 288 I5

The Flinders Ranges

Moralana Scenic Drive, south of Wilpena Pound

The Flinders Ranges are part of a mountain chain which extends for 430 kilometres from its southern end (between Crystal Brook and Peterborough) to a point 160 kilometres east of Marree. The most spectacular peaks and valleys are in two areas: the first north-east of Port Augusta and the second east of Leigh Creek. The Flinders, while similar in scale to many of Australia's mountain ranges, are totally different in both colouration and atmosphere. There is something unique in the contrast of the dry, stony land and richly lined rock faces—the characteristics of a desert range—with the rich vegetation of the river red gums, casuarinas, native pines and wattles that clothe the valleys and cling to hillsides and rock crevices. In spring, after rain, the display of wildflowers is breathtaking, carpeting the whole region with masses of reds, pinks, yellows, purples and white. The wildflowers, together with the natural beauty of the rock shapes, pools, caves and twisted trees, make the Flinders Ranges a favourite haunt of photographers and artists. Many paintings by Sir Hans Heysen embody the shape and spirit of the ranges.

The Flinders is served by reasonably good roads. A pleasant trip, which will take in the best of the scenery, is the drive north-east from Port Augusta through the Pichi Richi Pass to **Quorn** and **Hawker**, and from there on the loop road to **Parachilna**, circling the Wilpena Pound area.

But it is better to stay and explore, preferably on foot or by 4WD. There are kilometres of signposted tracks in the ranges, but as it is still only too easy to lose your way, it is important to be equipped with a good map and to follow a planned route. Drivers should avoid using the secondary roads after rain; they can be treacherous when wet.

The best-known feature of the Flinders Ranges is **Wilpena Pound**, an elevated basin covering about 50 square kilometres and encircled by sheer cliffs, which are set in a foundation of purple shale and rise through red stone to white-topped peaks. The only entrance is a narrow gorge, through which a creek sometimes flows. The external cliffs rise to over 1000 metres, but inside is a gentle slope to the floor of the plain. The highest point in the Pound is **St Mary's Peak**, at 1165 metres, which dominates the northern wall and provides a magnificent view over the mountains. Within the Pound are low, rounded hills and folded ridges, grasslands and pine-clad slopes that descend to the gums along Wilpena Creek. It is a wonderland of birdlife: rosellas, galahs, red-capped robins, budgerigars and wedgetailed eagles are common here. Bushland possums and endangered yellow-footed wallabies can also be seen.

There is a resort at **Wilpena**, catering for levels of accommodation from camping to modern motel. Near the Pound in this central section of the ranges are **Warren Gorge**, **Buckaringa Gorge**, **Brachina Gorge**, **Yourambulla Cave** with its Aboriginal drawings, the **Hills of Arkaba**,

considered the most beautiful spur in this region, **Bunyeroo** and **Aroona Valleys** and the **Flinders Ranges National Park**.

Some features in the northern section of the Flinders are spectacular: **Stokes Hill Lookout**, the **Great Wall of China**, a long rocky escarpment, and **Mount Chambers** and **Chambers Gorge**, which can be reached by vehicle or on foot.

Another region of the Flinders, **Arkaroola** in the far north of the ranges, also invites exploration. The 61 000-hectare privately run **Arkaroola–Mt Painter Sanctuary** is situated in rugged outback country featuring quartzite razorback ridges over elongated valleys, once the sea bed of a great continental shelf, the legacy that remains is rippled rock with embedded marine fossils. There is a profusion of wildlife: emus, ducks, parrots, cockatoos and galahs, marsupial mice possums, and yellow-footed rock wallabies all abound in large numbers.

From the heavily timbered slopes in the southern ranges, through picturesque gorges and rolling plains to the arid ranges of the north, the Flinders offers a variety of experiences. In addition to its unique flora and fauna, its rugged beauty and scenic views, the region contains an important Aboriginal heritage and traces of early pioneering days.

For further information on the area, contact Flinders Ranges and Outback of South Australia Regional Tourism, PO Box 666, Adelaide 5001; (08) 373 3430. **See also:** National Parks; and individual entries in A–Z listing. **Note** detailed map of Flinders Ranges on page 285.

Kapunda
Pop. 1979

Situated 80 km N of Adelaide on the edge of the Barossa Valley, Kapunda is a market town for the surrounding farm country. Copper was discovered here in 1842 and Kapunda became Australia's first mining town. At one stage the population rose to 5 000 and there were 16 hotels in town. A million pounds' ($2m) worth of copper was dug out before the mines closed in 1878. **Of interest:** Historic buildings, incl. Ford House, 1860s general store with unusual vaulted iron roof; heritage trail and historic mine walking trail (maps from Tourist Information). 'Map Kernow' (Son of Cornwall), 8-m-tall bronze statue at southern entrance to town, end of Main St. Historical Museum (1870s), Hill St. High School's main building on South Tce, off Clare Rd, formerly residence of famous cattle king Sir Sidney Kidman. Easter: Celtic Festival. Oct.: Agricultural Show. Nov.: Antique and Craft Fair. **In the area:** Scenic drive 26 km NE through sheep, wheat and dairy country to Eudunda; walks and scenic lookouts. Scholz Park Museum and Heritage-listed railway station at Riverton, 30 km NW. At Marrabel, 25 km N, South Australia's biggest rodeo, held Oct. Historic local stone buildings at Tarlee, 16 km NW. **Tourist information:** 5 Hill St; (085) 66 2902. **Accommodation:** 1 hotel, 1 cara./camp. park.
MAP REF. 283 N3, 289 M6

Keith
Pop. 1176

Keith is a farming town on the Dukes Hwy, 241 km SE of Adelaide. In the centre of the former Ninety Mile Desert, now called Coonalpyn Downs, the area has been transformed from infertile pasture to productive farming by the use of plant nutrition and modern farming methods. **Of interest:** Buildings in Heritage St: former Congregational Church (1910), with 11 locally made leadlight windows depicting the town's life and pioneering history, and The Old Manse, both National Trust; and Penny Farthing Coffee and Crafts. **In the area:** Mount Rescue Conservation Park, 16 km N, vast expanse of sandplain with heath, pink gums and an abundance of native wildlife. Old Settlers Cottage (1894), 2 km NE on Emu Flat Rd. Ngarkat Conservation Park, 25 km NE. Mt Monster Conservation Park, 10 km S, scenic views and diverse wildlife. **Tourist information:** Council Chambers, 43 Woolshed St, Bordertown; (087) 52

1044. **Accommodation:** 1 hotel/motel, 1 motel, 1 cara./camp. park.
MAP REF. 287 G6, 289 P12

Kimba
Pop. 682

A small town on the Eyre Hwy, Kimba is at the edge of SA's Outback. This is sheep- and wheat-growing country. **Of interest:** Historical museum, Eyre Hwy, features Pioneer House (1908), school and blacksmith's shop. The Big Galah, Eyre Hwy. Locally mined and crafted jade, including rare black jade, at adjacent Gem Shop. April: Yaltana Horse Spectacular. Sept.: Agricultural Show. **In the area:** Sturt pea garden on Eyre Hwy, 1 km W. Caralue Bluff, 20 km SW, rock climbing and diverse flora and fauna. Pinkawillinie Conservation Park, 45 km W. Gawler Ranges, north-west, vast wilderness area; check road conditions. Walking trail 1 km NE of town, goes 2½ km through bushland to White's Knob lookout. Lake Gilles Conservation Park, 20 km NE. **Tourist information:** Kimba Halfway Across Australia Gem Shop, Eyre Hwy; (086) 27 2112. **Accommodation:** 1 hotel/motel, 1 motel, 1 cara./camp. park.
MAP REF. 288 F2

Kingscote
Pop. 1443

The largest town and principal port of Kangaroo Island, 120 km SW of Adelaide, Kingscote was the first official white settlement in SA (1836). There is a vehicular ferry from Port Adelaide, a passenger ferry from Glenelg and an air service from Adelaide. **Of interest:** Cairn on foreshore marks State's first post office. Hope Cottage, Centenary Ave, National Trust Folk Museum. St Alban's Church, stained-glass windows, pioneer memorials. Town's cemetery is oldest in State. Rock pool and Brownlow Beach for swimming. Fishing from jetty for squid, tommy ruffs, trevally, garfish and snook. Chriso's Wagon Rides, from The Esplanade; Clydesdale-drawn wagon rides in summer. Feb: Racing Carnival. Oct.: Kingscote Show. **In the area:** Jumbuk Shearing demonstrations, Birchmore Rd, 17 km S. Eucalyptus oil distillery, Wilsons Rd, 20 km S, off South Coast Rd. The town of American River, a fishing village, about 50 km E, and, on the north-east coast of Dudley Peninsula, the village of Penneshaw, where the vehicular ferry arrives from Cape Jervis (1 hour). Folk Museum in former Old Penneshaw School. Dudley,

Cape Hart and Pelican Lagoon Conservation Parks on peninsula. Antechamber Bay, about 20 km SE of Penneshaw, excellent bushwalking, fishing and swimming. On western end of island, Flinders Chase National Park, one of South Australia's important parks and sanctuary for some of Australia's rarest wildlife; Cape Borda Lighthouse, northwest, Remarkable Rocks and Admiral's Arch, south-west. Guided tours available for Seal Bay, Kelly Hill Caves, Cape Borda and Cape Willoughby Lighthouses. Penguin tours at Kingscote and Penneshaw. **Tourist information:** Dept of Environment and Natural Resources, 37 Dauncey St; (0848) 2 2381. **Accommodation:** 2 hotels, 4 motels, 1 hostel, 2 cara./camp. parks. **See also:** Kangaroo Island.
MAP REF. 288 I11

Kingston S.E.
Pop. 1425

At the southern end of the Coorong National Park in Lacepede Bay, Kingston S.E. is a farming and fishing town and seaside resort. The multitude of shallow lakes and lagoons in the area are a haven for birdlife and a delight for naturalists and photographers. **Of interest:** Unusual analemmatic sundial, adjacent to Apex Park, in East Tce. Post office (1867), Hanson St, selected for special Commonwealth Stamp Issue in 1982. National Trust Pioneer Museum (1872), Cooke St. Cape Jaffa Lighthouse (1860s; dismantled and re-erected in 1970s), Marine Pde. Maria Memorial, granite cairn, commemorates massacre of 27 shipwrecked Europeans by Aborigines in 1840. Giant 'Larry Lobster' at entrance to town, Princes Hwy. Jan.: Lobster Fest; Yachting Regatta. **In the area:** Mt Scott Conservation Park, 20 km E. Jip Jip Conservation Park, 50 km NE. **Tourist information:** The Big Lobster, Princes Hwy; (087) 67 2555. **Accommodation:** 3 motels, 1 hostel, 1 cara./camp. park. **See also:** The Coorong.
MAP REF. 287 F9

Lameroo
Pop. 567

A quiet little settlement 212 km E of Adelaide on the Mallee Hwy. **Of interest:** 18-hole golf course, Mallee Hwy. Railway Museum, Railway Tce North; open by appt (contact Tourist Information). **In the area:** Baan Hill Reserve, 20 km SW, a natural soakage area surrounded by sandhills and scrub; picnic facilities. Ngarkat Conservation Park, 25 km s. Byrne Homestead (1898), built of pug and pine, 3 km along old Yappara road. Billiat Conservation Park, 37 km N. **Tourist information:** Council Offices, Railway Tce North; (085) 76 3002. **Accommodation:** 1 hotel/motel. MAP REF. 287 H4, 289 Q10

Leigh Creek   Pop. 1378
Located in the Flinders Ranges, Leigh Creek is the second-largest town north of Port Augusta. The economy is based on the large open-cut coalfield. The open-cut eventually consumed the original Leigh Creek township, about 13 km N, and in 1982 residents moved to the new township. An extensive development and tree-planting scheme has transformed the new site into an attractive oasis. **In the area:** Viewing area for coal workings, 3 km from turnoff to coalfields, on Hawker–Marree Hwy; free tours on Sat. (Mar.–Oct.) and school holidays. Aroona Dam, 4 km w, in steep-sided valley with richly coloured walls, scenic picnic area near gorge. Gammon Ranges National Park, 64 km E, wilderness area, recommended for experienced bushwalkers only. Lakes Eyre, Frome and Torrens, all dry salt pans, which occasionally fill with water. Copley Hotel, 6 km N. Lyndhurst and Marree, 38 km and 119 km N, respective end points of Strzelecki and Birdsville Tracks. At Lyndhurst, unique gallery of sculptures by well-known talc-stone artist 'Talc Alf'; open to visitors. **Tourist information:** The Town Centre, Electricty Trust of SA; (086) 75 4216. **Accommodation:** 1 motel, 1 cara./camp. park. MAP REF. 285 D3, 291 K5, 484 C13

Loxton   Pop. 3322
Known as the Garden City of the Riverland region, Loxton is 251 km NE of Adelaide. The surrounding irrigated land supports thriving citrus, wine, dried-fruit, wool and wheat industries. The area was first named Loxtons Hut, after a boundary rider from the Bookpurnong Station built a primitive pine and pug hut here. Like all towns in the region, Loxton has a strong sense of community and civic pride. There are many landscaped parks and gardens, a modern shopping centre and sporting facilities. The largest war-service settlement scheme in SA was carried out here. **Of interest:** Loxton District Historical Village on riverfront with 28 re-created buildings, as well as

Sand dunes, Coorong National Park, near Kingston S.E.

machinery and implements from late 1880s to mid-1900s; open daily except Christmas Day. Nearby, pepper tree planted by Loxton over 110 years ago. River cruises available. Art galleries and craft shops, local paintings and handcrafts. Jan.: Fisherama. Feb.: Mardi Gras. Oct.: Agricultural Show. Dec.: Christmas Display. **In the area:** Excellent wines at Australian Vintage, Bookpurnong Road (to Berri) in Loxton North. Nearby, Medea Cottage Fruit Train, herbs and unusual perennials; open daily. Picnics at Habels Bend, 3 km NW, on shores of river. Kia Kia Nature Trail, for bushwalkers, in Katarapko Game Reserve, 10 km NW; canoes for hire. Lock 4 and Moore's Woodlot (60 000 trees watered and fertilised by factory waste), 14 km N. Houseboats for hire at Kingston O.M., 40 km N. Unique wood sculpture display, SE on Paruna Rd; open by appt (contact Tourist Information). **Tourist information:** East Tce; (085) 84 7919. **Accommodation:** 1 hotel/motel, 1 hostel, 1 cara./camp. park. MAP REF. 126 A8, 289 Q6

Lyndoch   Pop. 956
At the southern end of the Barossa Valley and a 40-minute drive from Adelaide, Lyndoch is one of the oldest towns in SA. Early industry was farm-oriented, and 4 flour mills operated in the area. The Para River was used to operate a water mill in 1853. Vineyards were established early,

but the first winery was not set up until 1896. Some 8 wineries in the area are family-owned, and range from very small to one of the largest in the Barossa. **Of interest:** SA Museum of Mechanical Music, Barossa Valley Hwy; open daily. **In the area:** Wineries: Wards Gateway Cellar, Chateau Yaldara Winery, Charles Cimicky Wines, Burge Family Winemakers, Redgum Twin Valley, Orlando Wines, Kies Estate Cellars, Kellermeister Wines, Barossa Settlers. At Rowland Flat, 5 km SE: Rovalley Wines, Lieblichwein, Jenke Vineyards. Barossa Reservoir and Whispering Wall, 8 km sw. Kersbrook, 22 km s, historic buildings and trout farm. **Tourist information:** Barossa Valley Visitors Centre, 68 Murray St, Tanunda; 1800 81 2662 or (085) 63 0600. **Accommodation:** 1 motel, 5 B&B, 1 cara./camp. park. MAP REF. 283 N5, 286 C8, 287 C1, 289 M7

McLaren Vale   Pop. 1469
Centre of the Southern Vales winegrowing region, in which about 50 wineries flourish, McLaren Vale is 45 km s of Adelaide. Wine-making really began in 1853 when Thomas Hardy bought Tintara Vineyards. Today, Hardy's Tintara is the largest winery in the area; note huge Moreton Bay fig in grounds. **Of interest:** Historic buildings incl. Hotel McLaren, Main Rd, Congregational Church and Salopian Inn, Willunga Rd. Almond Train,

Main Rd; variety of local almond produce housed in restored railway carriage. Oct.: One Continuous Picnic; Wine Bushing Festival. **In the area:** Many historic buildings are now restaurants, wineries, tearooms and galleries. Wineries often in bushland settings; more details at tourist information centre. **Tourist information:** The Cottage, Main Rd; (08) 323 8537. **Accommodation:** 2 motels, 7 B&B, 1 cara./camp. park. **See also:** Festival Fun; Vineyards and Wineries.
MAP REF. 283 L10, 284 C6, 287 B3, 289 L9

Maitland   Pop. 1066

Maitland, a modern, well-planned town in the centre of the Yorke Peninsula, is the supply centre for the surrounding rich farmland. Wheat, barley, wool and beef cattle are the main primary industries. Parks surround the town centre. **Of interest:** Self-guide nature and history trail; information from District Council, Elizabeth St. St John's Anglican Church (1876), cnr Alice and Caroline Sts, stained-glass depicting Biblical stories in Australian settings. Lions Bicycle Adventure Park, off Elizabeth St. Maitland National Trust Museum, in former school, cnr Gardiner and Kilkerran Tces. The Artist's Window, Robert St, local art and craft for sale. April: Agricultural Show. **In the area:** Paradean Gardens and teas, 10 km SE; check opening times. **Tourist information:** Yorke Peninsula Visitor Information Centre, 51 Taylor St, Kadina; (08) 8821 2093. **Accommodation:** 2 hotels.
MAP REF. 282 F3, 288 I6

Mannum   Pop. 2025

Mannum, 82 km E of Adelaide, is one of the oldest towns on the Murray, with a lively past. Picturesque terraced banks overlook the river. Wool, beef and cereals are produced in the region and the town is the starting point for the Adelaide water-supply pipeline. The first paddle-steamer on the Murray, the *Mary Ann*, left Mannum in 1853 and the first steam car was built in town in 1894 by David Shearer. **Of interest:** Popular recreation Reserve, on banks of Murray; lookout tower and picnic/barbecue facilities; also PS *River Murray Princess*. Historic 'Leonaville' (1883), River Lane, built by town's first private developer, Gottlieb Schuetze. At Arnold Park, Randell St, PS *Marion*, built 1898. Twin ferries to

eastern side of river and scenic upriver drive. Lookout off Purnong Rd to east offers sweeping views. May: Houseboat Hirers Open Days. Sept.: River Festival. **In the area:** Excellent scenic drive from Wongulla to Cambrai; begins 20 km N. Award-winning Choni Leather, 10 km NW on Palmer Rd. Scenic drive along Purnong Rd runs parallel to bird sanctuary for 15 km. Mannum Waterfalls Reserve, 10 km S, picnics, swimming and scenic walks. Boats and houseboats for hire. River cruises available weekends in summer. Water sports at Walker Flat. **Tourist information:** PS *Marion*, Arnold Park, Randell St; (085) 69 1303. **Accommodation:** 1 motel, 3 B&B, 2 cara./camp. parks.
MAP REF. 283 P7, 287 E2, 289 N8

Marree   Pop. 85

Marree is a tiny outback town 645 km N of Adelaide at the junction of the Birdsville Track and the rugged road to Oodnadatta, which leads to the Kingoonya–Alice Springs road. There are remnants of date palms planted by the Afghan traders who drove their camel trains into the Outback in the 1800s. Desolate saltbush country surrounds the town, now a service centre for the vast properties of the north-east of the State and for travellers. Oct. Outback Ball: (even numbered years). **In the area:** The Frome, 6 km N, sandy watercourse that floods the Birdsville Track after heavy rains, can leave travellers stranded for weeks. Lake Eyre, 90 km N, accessible via Marree and Muloorina Station. Mungerannie Roadhouse, 204 km N on the Birdsville Track, fuel, food, accommodation, emergency repairs and camping. Oodnadatta Track, southern section (check track conditions with Marree police before departing; read section on Outback Motoring; fuel available only at Marree and William Creek, 210 km NW). Ruins of railway sidings from original Ghan line to Alice Springs, at Curdimurka Siding and Bore, about 90 km W. Bubbler Mound Springs and Blanche Cup Mound Springs, 6 km S of Oodnadatta Track, near Coward Springs, 136 km W. At Coward Springs: extensive pond formed by warm water bubbling to the surface; old date palms, remnants of old plantation. **Tourist information:** Hawker Motors, cnr Wilpena and Cradock Rds, Hawker; (086) 48 4014. **Accommodation:** 1 hotel. **See also:** The Outback.
MAP REF. 291 J1, 484 B11

Melrose   Pop. 205

Melrose is the oldest town in the Flinders Ranges, a quiet settlement at the foot of Mt Remarkable, 268 km N of Adelaide. **Of interest:** Historic buildings: old police station and courthouse (1862), Stuart St, now a National Trust Museum; ruins of Jacka's Brewery (former flour mill, 1877), Lambert St; North Star Hotel (1881), Nott St; Mt Remarkable Hotel (1857), Stuart St. Melrose Inn, Nott St; National Trust property, not open to the public. Heritage Walk available. Serendipity Gallery, Stuart St. Pleasant walks and picnic spots along creek. Scenic views from War Memorial and Lookout Hill, Joe's Rd. Further on, Cathedral Rock. **In the area:** Walking trail (allow 5 hrs return) from town to top of Mt Remarkable (956 m); superb views. Mt Remarkable National Park, 2 km W. Murraytown sheep property, 3 km SW; visitors welcome. Near Murray Town, 14 km S: scenic lookouts at Box Hill, Magnus Hill and Baroota Nob; scenic drive west through Germein Gorge. Booleroo Steam and Traction Preservation Society's Museum, Booleroo Centre, 15 km E; open by appt. **Tourist information:** Council Offices, Stuart St; (086) 66 2014. **Accommodation:** 1 hotel, 1 cara./camp. park.
MAP REF. 289 K1, 291 J12

Meningie   Pop. 818

Meningie is set on the edge of the freshwater Lake Albert and the northern tip of the vast saltpans of the Coorong National Park, 159 km from Adelaide. It is a farming area, and more than 40 professional fishermen are employed on the lakes and the Coorong; fishing is a major industry in the town. The area abounds with a variety of birdlife including ibis, pelicans, cormorants, ducks and swans. Sailing, boating, water-skiing and swimming are popular. Nov.: Goolwa to Meningie Classic, longest freshwater sailing race in Australia. **In the area:** Camp Coorong, 12 km S, Aboriginal museum and cultural centre. The Coorong, south and west, inland water, islands, ocean beach and wildlife. Scenic drive west following Lake Albert, adjacent to Lake Alexandrina, the largest permanent freshwater lake in the country (50 000 ha). Channel between lakes is crossed by free ferry service at Narrung, 39 km NW. **Tourist information:** Melaleuca Centre, 76 Princes Hwy; (085) 75 1259.

Accommodation: 1 hotel, 2 motels, 3 B&B, 1 cara./camp. park. **See also:** The Coorong.
MAP REF. 283 P13, 287 E5, 289 N11

Millicent   Pop. 5118

A thriving commercial and industrial town 50 km from Mt Gambier, Millicent is in the middle of a huge tract of land reclaimed in the 1870s. Today rural and fishing industries contribute to the area's prosperity, with pine forests supporting two paper mills and a sawmill. **Of interest:** On northern edge of town, gum trees surround a fine swimming lake and picnic area. Award-winning National Trust Museum and Admella Gallery, Mt Gambier Rd, housed in original primary school (1873); several theme rooms, a variety of farming equipment, 19 horse-drawn carriages, T-Class locomotive. Shell Garden, Williams Rd, unusual display surrounded by fuchsias, ferns and begonias. March: Radiata Festival Week. **In the area:** Tantanoola, 21 km SE, home of famous 'Tantanoola Tiger' (a Syrian wolf shot by Tom Donovan in 1890s); 'tiger' now stuffed and displayed in the Tantanoola Tiger Hotel. Underground caves in Tantanoola Caves Conservation Park, fascinating limestone formations; open daily. Also at Caves, Trevor Peters' 4-acre garden and restored National Trust cottage; open Sept.–April (check

times). Scenic pine-forest drive to Mount Burr, 10 km NE. National Trust Woolshed (1863) at Glencoe, 29 km SE; tours available. Massive sand dune system in Canunda National Park, accessed from Millicent and Southend, 27 km W; leaflet for self-guide walk available. **Tourist information:** 1 Mt Gambier Rd; (087) 33 3205. **Accommodation:** 1 hotel/motel, 2 motels, 2 cara./camp. parks.
MAP REF. 287 G12

Minlaton   Pop. 796

Minlaton is a prosperous town serving the nearby coastal resorts of Yorke Peninsula. The town, 209 km W of Adelaide, was originally called Gum Flat because of the giant eucalypts in the area. Pioneer aviator Harry Butler, pilot of the Red Devil, a 1916 Bristol monoplane, was born here. The plane is displayed at the Harry Butler Museum in Main St. **Of interest:** Fauna park, Main St; adjacent to Harry Butler Memorial. National Trust Museum, Main St. **In the area:** Ostrich farm at Curramulka, 15 km NE. Gum Flat Homestead Gallery, 1 km E, pioneer homestead with local artists' work. At Port Vincent, 25 km E: good swimming, yachting and water-skiing; yacht race in Jan. Gipsy Waggon holidays at Brentwood, 14 km SW. Port Rickaby and Bluff Beach, 16 km NW, unique bay with abundant birdlife. **Tourist information:**

Council Offices, Main St; (08) 8853 2102. **Accommodation:** 1 hotel/motel, 1 cara./camp. park.
MAP REF. 282 F7, 288 I7

Mintaro   Pop. 80

The township nestles among rolling hills and rich pastoral land, 19 km SE of Clare. Classified as a Heritage Town, Mintaro is a timepiece of early colonial architecture. Many of the buildings display the fine slate for which the district is world-renowned; the quarry opened in 1854. **Of interest:** Early colonial buildings, incl. 18 with Heritage listings and 2 historic cemeteries. **In the area:** Magnificent classical architecture of Martindale Hall (1880), 3 km SE; location for film *Picnic at Hanging Rock*; tours daily except Christmas Day and Good Friday (check times); overnight accommodation and dining available. Self-contained accommodation at some historic cottages. **Tourist information** Town Hall, 229 Main North Road, Clare; (08) 8842 2131. **Accommodation:** 1 hotel
MAP REF. 289 L4

Moonta   Pop. 2723

The towns of Moonta, Kadina and Wallaroo form the corners of the area known as the 'Copper Triangle' or 'Little Cornwall'. Moonta is a popular seaside resort 163 km NW of Adelaide, with pleasant

Outback town of Marree

beaches and good fishing at Moonta Bay. A rich copper-ore deposit was discovered here in 1861 and soon thousands of miners, including many from Cornwall, flocked to the area. The mines were abandoned in the 1920s with the slump in copper prices and rising labour costs. **Of interest:** Many stone buildings, charming Queen Square, and picturesque town hall opposite the Square in George St. All Saints Church (1873), cnr Blanche and Milne Tces. Galleries include the Pug 'n' Dabble, George St. The prize-winning Kernewek Lowender, a Cornish festival, is held in conjunction with Kadina and Wallaroo in May, odd-numbered years. Oct.: Agricultural Show. **In the area:** Moonta Mines, a State Heritage Area, on Arthurton Rd, about 2 km SE; booklet available. Highlights incl.: Moonta Mines National Trust Museum (old primary school); Cornish miner's cottage (1870) furnished in period style; pump house; shafts and tailings heaps; mines offices. On weekends, public and school holidays, Moonta Mines Railway takes visitors from old railway station, Blanche Tce, through mines area. **Tourist information:** Town Hall, George St; (08) 8825 2622. **Accommodation:** 2 hotels, 1 motel, 4 B&B, 2 cara./camp. parks. **See also:** Festival Fun; The Yorke Peninsula. MAP REF. 282 F1, 288 I5

Morgan
Pop. 446

Once one of the busiest river ports in SA, Morgan is a quiet little township 164 km NE of Adelaide. **Of interest:** Self-guide Heritage Trail leaflets cover all historic sites, including the impressive wharves (1877), standing 12 m high, constructed for the riverboat industry. Customs house and courthouse near railway station, reminders of town's thriving past. Picnic/barbecue facilities, with children's play area, near customs house. Mo's Pottery, Eighth St. Glass Space Studio and Gallery, cnr Second and Ninth Sts. Dockyards on Oval Rd; tours by appt. Port of Morgan Historic Museum in old railway buildings on riverfront, off High St. PS Mayflower (1884), still operating; enquiries to Museum's caretaker. Nor-West Bend private museum, Renmark Rd; open by appt. Overnight horse trail rides; book at Nor-West Bend. Houseboats for hire. July: Fun Run, Walk Cyclathon. **In the area:** Morgan Conservation Park, across river. Fossicking for fossils near township. White Dam Conservation Park, 9 km NW. Engineering

and Water Supply Pumping Station 2 km N on Renmark Rd; tours by appt. Riverland Camel Farm and Trail Ride, 13 km N on Renmark Rd; day and overnight trips. **Tourist information:** Morgan Roadhouse, Fourth St; (085) 40 2205, and Council Offices, Fourth St; (085) 40 2013. **Accommodation:** 1 hotel, 1 hotel/ motel, 1 motel, 1 cara./camp. park. MAP REF. 283 R1, 289 O5

Mount Gambier
Pop. 21 153

In 1800 Lieutenant James Grant, sighted an extinct volcano and named it Mount Gambier. The city is on the slopes of the volcano, in the centre of the largest softwood pine plantations in the country. Surrounded by rich farming, horticulture, viticulture and dairy country, the city is 460 km SE of Adelaide on National Hwy 1. The Hentys built the first dwelling in the area in 1841 and by 1850 there was a weekly postal service to Adelaide. The white Mount Gambier stone used in most of the buildings, together with many fine parks and gardens, make an attractive environment. The city hosts many sporting events annually. **Of interest:** Historic buildings incl. town hall (1862) and post office (1865), in Bay Rd, and many old hotels; Heritage Walk leaflet from Tourist Information Centre. Open caves at Cave Gardens, Bay Rd, adjacent to town hall, and Umpherston Cave, Jubilee Hwy East. Engelbrecht Cave, Jubilee Hwy, water-filled cave or sinkhole. Old Court House Law and Heritage Centre, Bay Rd, National Trust Museum, open daily. Lewis' Museum, Pick Ave; open daily. The *Lady Nelson* Tourist and Interpretive Centre, Jubilee Hwy East, full-scale replica of *Lady Nelson* forms part of Centre's structure. Dimjalla Park, Jubilee Hwy East, fun park, barbecue areas. Riddoch Art Gallery, Commercial St East, in complex of 19th century buildings. Yoey's Cheese and Gourmet Shop, Commercial St West, local and imported cheeses. Nov.: Blue Lake Festival. **In the area:** Mount Gambier's 4 crater lakes, particularly Blue Lake (197 m at its deepest), which provides city's water, and changes from dull grey to brilliant blue each Nov. then reverts at end of summer; scenic 5 km drive offers lookouts, wildlife, picnic areas and walks. Pumping Station on Blue Lake, 2 km S; daily tours down through pumping station to lake level. Tours of timber mills; inspection of treatment process, including pines being felled, trimmed

and sawn ready for loading; contact the *Lady Nelson* Centre for details. Haig's Vineyard, 4 km S. Mount Schank, 12 km S; views of surrounding district. Animal and Reptile Park, 10 km N, off Penola Rd, animal nursery, native gardens, train carriage. Tarpeena Fairy Tale Park, 22 km N on Penola Rd. Glencoe Woolshed (1863), 23 km NW, National Trust building; open Sun. p.m. or by appt. Chant's Place flora and fauna park at Kongorong, 25 km SW. Tours of splendid Tantanoola Caves, 20 km W. Glenelg River cruises from Nelson (Vic.), 36 km SE; tours of spectacular Princess Margaret Rose Caves. **Tourist information:** *Lady Nelson* Tourist Centre, Jubilee Hwy East; (087) 24 1730. **Accommodation:** 5 hotels, 1 hotel/motel, 21 motels, 3 B&B, 6 cara./camp. parks. MAP REF. 226 A5, 287 I13

Murray Bridge
Pop. 12 725

Murray Bridge is South Australia's largest river town. The South Eastern Freeway provides access to Adelaide, 80 km away. First settled in the 1850s, the city overlooks a broad sweep of the Murray and still retains some of the feeling of the time when it was a centre for the bustling riverboat traders. Water sports, river cruises and excellent accommodation make Murray Bridge a perfect holiday spot. **Of interest:** Captain's Cottage Museum, Thomas St. Butterfly House, Jervois Rd. Puzzle Park, also in Jervois Rd, a funpark for adults as well as children. Rock Rose Farm, Doyle Rd, herb garden and small animals. Cottage Box chocolate factory, Wharf Rd; open daily. Sturt Reserve, on banks of the river, fishing, swimming, picnic and playground facilities. Jan.: State Championship swimming. Nov.: Big River Challenge Festival, incorporates speedboat racing, water-skiing events and land-based sporting challenges. **In the area:** Monarto Zoological Park, 10 km W off old Princes Hwy; open-range zoo with many endangered species; open Sun. Charter and regular cruises on MV *Barrangul* and MV *Zane Grey*; houseboats for hire. Willow Glen Wines, 10 km S on Jervois Rd. Riverglen Marina, 11 km S; houseboats and mooring. Earthworks Pottery, 9 km NE, on Karoonda Rd. Talyala Emu Farm, 6 km N on Mannum Rd; open daily. Mypolonga, 14 km N, centre of beautiful citrus and stone-fruit orchards and rich dairying country. Cruises of 2, 3 or 5 days on PS *Proud Mary* and PS *River Queen*.

The Coorong

The Coorong National Park curves along the southern coast of South Australia for 145 kilometres, extending from the mouth of the Murray in the north almost to the township of Kingston S.E. in the south. A unique area, it has an eerie isolation, a silence broken only by the sounds of any of the 280 species of native birds wheeling low over the scrub and dunes and the thunder of the Southern Ocean.

The Coorong proper is a shallow lagoon, a complex system of low-lying saltpans and claypans. Never more than 3 kilometres wide, the lagoon is divided from the sea by the towering white sandhills of Younghusband Peninsula, known locally as the Hummocks. One of the best natural bird sanctuaries in Australia, the Coorong is home for giant pelicans, cormorants, ibis, swans and terns.

Access to the Park is gained by leaving the Princes Highway at **Salt Creek** and following the old road along the shore. Noonameena, Mark Point and Long Point in the northern section can be accessed from the turnoff at Meningie. Explore the unspoiled stretches of beach where the rolling surf washes up gnarled driftwood and beautiful shells. Year-round beach access is from a point further south known as 'the 42 mile'; the final 1.3 kilometres is suitable for 4WD or walking. The coastal scenery is magnificent.

For those who wish to explore in comfort, **Meningie** in the north and the fishing port of **Kingston S.E.** have a range of accommodation and can be used as touring bases. Camping is permitted in the Coorong National Park; however, in the Younghusband Peninsula section it is allowed in designated areas only. Permits may be obtained from local commercial outlets (look for the pelican logo), from self-registration points in the Park or from the Coorong Shop in Meningie. The area is rich in history as well as being a naturalists' haven; pick up the *Coorong Tattler* for details. Fishing, boating and walking are popular.

For further information, contact the Department of Environment and Natural Resources office, Meningie; (085) 75 1200. **See also:** Entries for Kingston S.E. and Meningie in A–Z listing.

The Fleurieu Peninsula

Starting 22 kilometres south of Adelaide, the Fleurieu Peninsula region stretches from O'Halloran Hill for about 90 km to Cape Jervis on the west coast, and east around the vast fresh waters of Lake Alexandrina, where the Murray River meets the sea.

The ocean scenery varies from magnificent cliff faces and roaring surf to wide, sandy beaches and sheltered bays and coves. Maslin Beach is renowned as Australia's first nude bathing beach. Cape Jervis, at the tip of the Peninsula, commands a clear view across Backstairs Passage.

McLaren Vale, the centre of the Southern Vales wine-producing district, has over 50 wineries. Many are in historic buildings with attached restaurants.

Victor Harbor is one of South Australia's most popular beach resorts. Either walk or take the old horse tram along the causeway to Granite Island to see the colony of little (fairy) penguins. On the way to **Goolwa**, spend time in **Port Elliot** to take in its history and perhaps take a ride to Goolwa on the Cockle Train, a steam train restored from the original line opened in 1854; for operating times enquire at the Tourist Information Centre.

There is superb fishing at Goolwa. Once a busy port, Goolwa is now the starting point for leisurely paddle-steamer cruises up the Murray, and cruises to Hindmarsh Island and the Barrages.

For further information on the area, contact the Victor Harbor Tourist Information Centre, Railway Tce, Victor Harbor; (085) 52 5821. **See also:** Individual entries in A–Z listing. **Note** detailed map of Southern Vales on page 284.

Yankalilla Bay on the Fleurieu Peninsula

Naracoorte Caves

Avoca Dell, 5 km upstream, boating, water-skiing, mini-golf and picnic facilities. Thiele Reserve, east of river, good water-skiing. Other riverside reserves incl. Hume, Long Island, Swanport and White Sands. Lookouts, incl. White Hill, west on Princes Hwy, and east at new Swanport Bridge. **Tourist information:** Community Information and Tourist Centre, 3 South Tce; (085) 32 6660. **Accommodation:** 2 hotels, 4 motels, 1 B&B, 1 hostel, 5 cara./camp. parks. MAP REF. 283 P9, 287 D3, 289 N9

Naracoorte   Pop. 4711

Situated 390 km SE of Adelaide, Naracoorte dates from the 1840s. The area is world-renowned for its limestone caves. Beef cattle, sheep and wheat are the local primary industries. **Of interest:** Sheep's Back Wool Museum, in former flour mill (1860), MacDonnell St; incorporates National Trust Museum, Art Gallery and Tourist Information. Naracoorte Museum and Snake Pit, Jenkins Tce, 100 collections, incl. gemstones, candles, coins, antiques and snakes (closed mid-July–end August). Mini Jumbuk Factory, Smith St, woollen products. Restored locomotive on display in Pioneer Park. Regional Art Gallery, Smith St. Jubilee Park and Swimming Lake, off Park Tce. For anglers, trout and redfin abound in local streams and creeks. Oct.: Agricultural Show. Dec.: Street Traders Party and Carols by Candlelight. **In the area:** Tiny Train Park, 3 km S; trains, mini-golf. Naracoorte Caves, 12 km SE, in Conservation Park: Victoria Fossil Cave, has unique

fossilised specimens of Ice Age animals; Blanche Cave and Alexandra Cave have spectacular stalagmites and stalactites; tours daily, and beginners' and advanced adventure tours (bookings required). Bool Lagoon Game Reserve 17 km S, sanctuary for ibis and diverse waterbirds; guided boardwalks and bird hide. Coonawarra wine region, 40 km S. Padthaway and Keppoch wine districts, about 40 km NW. **Tourist information:** The Sheep's Back, MacDonnell St; (087) 62 1518. **Accommodation:** 2 hotels, 1 hotel/motel, 4 motels, 1 B&B, 2 cara./ camp. parks. **See also:** National Parks. MAP REF. 228 A11, 287 H9

Nuriootpa   Pop. 3321

The Para River runs through the town of Nuriootpa, its course marked by fine parks and picnic spots, incl. Coulthard Reserve off Penrice Rd. The town is the commercial centre of the Barossa Valley. **Of interest:** Coulthard House, Murray St, pioneer settler's home; not open to the public. St Petri Church, First St. **In the area:** Wineries, incl. Gnadenfrei Estate, Seppelts, Greenock Creek, Heritage Wines, Elderton, Kaesler, Penfolds, Stockwell Wines, The Willows (at Light Pass) and Wolf Blass. Also Tarac Distillers. Day tours of Barossa Valley available. May: Hot Air Balloon Regatta at Seppeltsfield, 6 km W. **Tourist information:** Barossa Valley Visitors Centre, 68 Murray St, Tanunda; 1800 81 2662 or (085) 63 0600. **Accommodation:** 1 hotel, 1 motel, 1 cara./camp. park. **See also:** Vineyards and Wineries. MAP REF. 283 N4, 286 G3, 289 M6

Old Noarlunga   Pop. 2000

A small village in the Southern Vales winegrowing region, Old Noarlunga is 32 km S of Adelaide on the Fleurieu Peninsula. **Of interest:** Horseshoe Mill (1844); Church of St Philip and St James (1850), Church Hill Rd; Uniting Church, Malpas St; old Jolly Miller Hotel (1850), now Noarlunga Hotel, Patapinda Rd; and Market Square, site of first public market 1841. Aug.: Cobb & Co. re-enactment. **In the area:** Port Noarlunga and Christies Beach, 10 km NW, and Moana and Maslin Beaches, 3 km and 6 km S, all offer good swimming and fishing. About 8 km N of Port Noarlunga, Hallett Cove has tracks left by glaciers millions of years ago. Lakeside Leisure Park at Hackham, 4 km N. At McLaren Vale, 5 km S, some 50 vineyards and wineries. At Myponga, 27 km S: Myponga Reservoir, barbecue/picnic facilities; several historic buildings. **Tourist information:** Noarlunga Hotel, Patapinda Rd; (08) 386 2061. **Accommodation:** 1 hotel, 1 motel, 1 cara./camp. park. MAP REF. 283 K9

Oodnadatta   Pop. 180

A tiny but famous outback town 1050 km NW of Adelaide, Oodnadatta is an old railway town with a well-preserved sandstone station (1890), now a museum. It is thought the name Oodnadatta originated from an Aboriginal term meaning 'yellow blossom of the mulga'. Fuel and supplies available. **In the area:** Witjira National Park, gateway to Simpson Desert, 180 km N; hot thermal ponds in Dalhousie Springs. Camping and accommodation at Mt Dare Homestead, within park, or at Springs. The Oodnadatta Track runs from Marree through Oodnadatta and joins Stuart Hwy at Marla, 200 km W. Painted Desert, 100 km SW, scenic drive. **Tourist information:** Pink Roadhouse, Ikaturka Tce; (086) 70 7822 or 1800 80 2074. **Accommodation:** 1 hotel, 1 cara./camp. park. MAP REF. 292 B7

Paringa   Pop. 588

Paringa, 4 km from Renmark, is the eastern gateway to the Riverland region. **Of interest:** Paringa Suspension Bridge (1927). Bert Dix Memorial Park, adjacent to Paringa Bridge. On Murtho Rd: the Black Stump, root system of river red gum estimated to be about 500–600 years old. Houseboat marina, Lock 5 Rd;

houseboat hire. **In the area:** Off Murtho Rd: Headings Lookout tower, 12 km N, excellent views of surrounding irrigated farmland and river cliffs; Murtho Forest Reserve, 15 km N, picnic and limited camping facilities. On Lock 5 Rd: E & WS Lock 5 and Weir, 2 km SW, Margaret Dowling National Trust Park, 3 km SW, area of natural bushland. Dunlop Big Tyre spans Sturt Hwy at Yamba, 12 km SE; also fruit fly inspection point (no fruit allowed into SA). Scenic drive, 36 km E into Vic., to see blossoms at Lindsay Point Almond Park in early spring. **Tourist information:** Council Offices, Murtho Rd; (085) 95 5102. **Accommodation:** 1 hotel/motel, 1 cara./camp. park.
MAP REF. 126 A7, 230 A4, 289 R5

Penola   Pop. 1147
The oldest town in the south-east of SA, Penola, 50 km N of Mount Gambier, has fine examples of slab and hewn-timber cottages erected in the 1850s. Several famous names are associated with Penola. Poets Adam Lindsay Gordon, John Shaw Neilson and Will Ogilvie all spent time here. The first school in Australia catering for children regardless of income or social class was established here in 1866 by Mother Mary McKillop, recently beatified. The stone classroom in which she taught is on the corner of Portland St and Petticoat Lane. **Of interest:** John Riddoch Interpretive Centre, Arthur St, in former Mechanics Institute, audiovisual, poetry recitals. In Petticoat Lane: heritage buildings, arts and crafts. Self-guide heritage walk; details from Tourist Information. **In the area:** Yallum Park Homestead (1880), 8 km W, historic two-storeyed homestead built by John Riddoch, founder of Coonawarra wine industry. Picnic areas and signposted walk at Penola Conservation Park, 10 km W. Coonawarra vineyards, 10 km N, magnificent table wines from 15 wineries. **Tourist information:** Arthur St; (087) 37 2855, (018) 84 9909. **Accommodation:** 2 hotels, 1 hotel/motel, 1 cara./camp. park.
MAP REF. 226 A3, 287 I11

Peterborough   Pop. 2138
Peterborough is a railway town 250 km N of Adelaide, surrounded by grain-growing and pastoral country. It is the principal town on the Port Pirie to Broken Hill railway line. **Of interest:** The Steamtown Peterborough Railway Preservation Society runs limited historic narrow-gauge steam-train journeys to Orroroo or Eurelia; check times. Rann's Museum, 144 Moscow St, exhibits of historic railway equipment and farm implements. The Gold Battery, end Tripney Ave, an ore-crushing machine; open by appt. Saint Cecilia, Callary St, gracious home (with splendid stained glass) once a bishop's residence; accommodation, dining, murder-mystery nights. Ley's Museum, Queen St, exhibition of antiques. Victoria Park, Grove St, picnic facilities, children's playground. **In the area:** Terowie, 24 km SE, old railway town with historic buildings. At Orroroo, 37 km NW: historic buildings, Yesteryear Costume Gallery with display of fashion from 1850; nearby, scenic walk among Aboriginal carvings along Pekina Ck; panoramic views from Black Rock Peak, east. At Magnetic Hill, 8 km W of Black Rock, a vehicle with the engine turned off rolls uphill! **Tourist information:** Main St; (086) 51 2708. **Accommodation:** 2 hotels, 2 hotel/motels, 1 motel, 1 hostel, 1 cara./camp. park.
MAP REF. 289 L1, 291 L13

Pinnaroo   Pop. 645
This little township on the Mallee Hwy is only 6 km from the Victorian border. **Of interest:** Australia's largest cereal collection (1300 varieties), Pinnaroo Institute, Railway Tce South. Historical Museum in railway station, Railway Tce Sth. Working printing museum, South Tce; animal park and aviary with native birds. Farm-machinery museum at showgrounds, Homburg Tce. **In the area:** Walking trail in Karte Conservation Park, 30 km NW, on Karte Rd. Gum Family Collection, 25 km N at Kombali; stationary engine museum. Peebinga Conservation Park, 42 km N, on Loxton Rd. Scorpion Springs Conservation Park, 28 km S; walking trail at Pine Hut Soak. Ngarkat Conservation Park, 48 km S. Pertendi Walking Trail, 49 km S. **Tourist information:** Council Offices, Day St; (085) 77 8002. **Accommodation:** 2 hotels, 1 motel, 1 B&B, 1 cara./camp. park.
MAP REF. 126 A11, 230 A11, 287 I3, 289 R9

Port Augusta   Pop. 14 595
A thriving industrial city at the head of Spencer Gulf and in the shadow of the Flinders Ranges, Port Augusta is the most northerly port in SA. It is 317 km from Adelaide and is a vital supply centre for the outback areas of the State and the large sheep stations of the district. Port Augusta is an important link on the Indian–Pacific railway and a stopover for the famous *Ghan* train to Alice Springs, which departs from Adelaide. The city has played an intrinsic role in SA's development since the State Electricity Trust built a series of major power stations here. Fuelled by coal from the huge open-cut mines at Leigh Creek, the stations generate more than a third of the State's electricity. **Of interest:** Award-winning Wadlata Outback Centre, Flinders Tce, introduction to the sights and sounds of the outback. Homestead Park Pioneer Museum, Elsie St, large photographic collection, picnic areas, blacksmith's shop, old steam train and crane, and rebuilt 130-year-old pine-log Yudnappinna Homestead. Royal Flying Doctor Service Base, Vincent St; open weekdays. School of the Air, Power Cres.; tours during term time. Curdnatta Art and Pottery Gallery in town's original railway station, Commercial Rd; check opening times. Self-guide Heritage Walks (2 hrs) incl.: town hall (1887), Commercial Rd; courthouse (1884) cnr Jervios St and Beauchamp's Lane, cells built of Kapunda marble; and St Augustine's Church (1882), Church St, magnificent stained glass. McLellan Lookout, Whiting Pde, site of Matthew Flinders landing in 1802, and Water Tower Lookout (1882), Mitchell Tce; scenic views, picnic facilities in adjacent parks. Matthew Flinders Lookout, end of McSporran Cres., excellent view of Gulf and Flinders Ranges; adjacent, site for Australian Arid Lands Botanic Gardens. **In the area:** Tours of Northern power station, 4 km E, weekdays. Scenic drive 23 km NE to splendid Pichi Richi Pass, where Railways Preservation Society runs old steam engines (school holidays), to historic Quorn, 39 km NE, and Warren and Buckaringa Gorges, 21 km and 37 km further N, respectively. Winninowie Conservation Park, 30 km SE. Hancocks Lookout, 38 km SE towards Wilmington: excellent views of surrounding country, Port Augusta and Whyalla; turnoff road dangerous when wet. Mt Remarkable National Park, 63 km SE, rugged mountain terrain, magnificent gorges and abundant wildlife. Historic Melrose, 65 km SE, oldest town in Flinders Ranges.

Tourist information: Wadlata Outback Centre, Flinders Tce; (086) 41 0793. **Accommodation:** 7 hotels, 9 motels, 3 cara./camp. parks.
MAP REF. 285 A12, 290 I11

Port Broughton
Pop. 681

A small port on the extreme north-west coast of Yorke Peninsula, Port Broughton is 169 km from Adelaide. On a protected inlet, the town is a major port for fishing boats and is renowned for its deep-sea prawns. **Of interest:** Safe swimming beach along foreshore. Charter boats and dinghies. Historical Museum, Harvey St (old school building) and Cottage Museum, Kadina Rd, contain much of town's history. Historic walking trail. In Harvey St, Shandelé porcelain dolls made and on display. **In the area:** Fisherman's Bay, 10 km N, popular fishing, boating and holiday spot. Heritage copper-mining towns of Moonta, Wallaroo and Kadina, 47 km S. Clare Valley and surrounding wine districts 100 km E. **Tourist information:** Yorke Peninsula Visitor Information Centre, 51 Taylor St, Kadina; (08) 8821 2093. **Accommodation:** 1 hotel, 1 hotel/motel, 2 cara./camp. parks.
MAP REF. 289 J3

Port Elliot
Pop. 1203

Only 5 km NE of Victor Harbor, Port Elliot is a charming, historic coastal town with the main focus on scenic Horseshoe Bay, the town's beach. The town was established in 1854, the same year Australia's first public iron railway operated between Goolwa and Port Elliot. **Of interest:** Along The Strand: National Trust historical display in Port Elliot railway station (1911); council chamber (1879); police station (1853); St Jude's Church (1854); guided walks available, (085) 54 2024. Spectacular views from Freeman's Knob, end of The Strand. Port Elliot Art Pottery, Main Rd. **In the area:** Middleton Winery, 11 km NE via Middleton. **Tourist information:** Dodd & Page Land Agents, 51 The Strand; (085) 54 2029 **Accommodation:** 2 hotels, 1 motel, 1 cara./camp. park.
MAP REF. 283 L12, 284 E12, 287 C4, 289 L10

Port Lincoln
Pop. 11 345

Port Lincoln, originally chosen as the State's capital, is attractively sited on the clear waters of Boston Bay, which is three times the size of Sydney Harbour. The port, 250 km due west of Adelaide across St Vincent and Spencer Gulfs, was reached by Matthew Flinders in 1802 and settled by Europeans in 1839. With its sheltered waters, Mediterranean climate, scenic coastal roads and attractive farming hinterland, Port Lincoln is a tourist resort growing in popularity. It is also the base for Australia's largest tuna fleet and also an important export centre for wheat, wool, fat lambs, live sheep, frozen fish, lobster, prawns and abalone. The coastline is deeply indented, offering magnificent scenery: sheltered coves, steep cliff faces and impressive surf beaches. **Of interest:** Boston Bay; swimming, water-skiing, yachting and excellent fishing. Mill Cottage Museum (1867) and Settler's Cottage Museum; both in picturesque Flinders Park. Old Mill lookout, Dorset Place, views of town and bay. Lincoln Hotel (1840), Tasman Tce, oldest hotel on Eyre Peninsula. Axel Stenross Maritime Museum, north end of town; First Landing site nearby. Rose–Wal Memorial Shell Museum in grounds of Eyre Peninsula Old Folks Home. Arteyrea Gallery, Washington St, community art centre. Barbed Wire and Fencing Equipment Museum; open by appt, (086) 82 1162. M.B. Kotz Collection of Stationary Engines, Baltimore St. Lincoln Cove, off St Andrews Tce, marina and holiday charter boats. *Dangerous Reef Explorer* ferries visitors to reef, home for large sea lion colony, and a commercial tuna farm. Apex Wheelhouse, original wheelhouse from tuna boat *Boston Bay,* adjacent to Kirton Point Caravan Park, Hindmarsh St. Jan.: Tunarama Festival, (Australia Day holiday) celebrates opening of tuna season. Feb.: Lincoln Week Regatta; Adelaide–Lincoln Yacht Race. **In the area:** Boat charter available for game fishing, diving, day fishing and island cruises. Yacht charters available. Regular launch cruises of Boston Bay and Boston Island. Several pleasant parks close to town, and vast natural reserves abounding in wildlife, within a day's outing. Winter Hill Lookout, 5 km NW on Flinders Hwy. Greenpatch Farm, 15 km NW, native animals, bird-feeding, open Wed.–Sun. At Koppio, 38 km N: Koppio Smithy Museum; Kurrabi Lodge, local crafts; Tod Reservoir, museum with heritage display and picnic area. Coffin Bay, 49 km NW: lookout; Coffin Bay Oyster Farm for fresh oysters and other seafood; Oyster Trail; boat hire; nearby Coffin Bay National Park. Boston Bay Wines, 6 km N on Lincoln Hwy, sales on weekends or by appt, (086) 84 3600. Tiny Tots Gnome Village, Lincoln Hwy. Karlinda Collection, adjacent to post office at North Shields, 16 km N, shells, marine life and Deepwater Trawl Fish Exhibit. At Poonindie, 20 km N, church (1850) with two chimneys. Award-winning Quandong Farm, 45 km N, orchids, quandong seedlings and trees. Tumby Bay, 48 km N, small beach resort. Lincoln National Park, 20 km S, wildlife, cliff-top walk to impressive coastal scenery; permit required. Whalers Way, southernmost tip of Eyre Peninsula, stunning coastal scenery; permit required, contact tourism information. On road to Whalers Way: Constantia Designer Craftsmen, world-class furniture factory and showroom (guided tours available); historic Mikkira sheep station, open winter. Offshore islands for boating enthusiasts: Boston and Thistle Islands offer accommodation for getaway holidays; Thistle and Wedge Islands (both privately owned), popular with bluewater sailors and fishermen. **Tourist information:** Eyre Travel, Civic Centre, Tasman Tce; (086) 82 4577. **Accommodation:** 5 hotels, 7 motels, 2 cara./camp. parks. **See also:** Festival Fun; The Eyre Peninsula.
MAP REF. 288 D7

Port MacDonnell
Pop. 677

Port MacDonnell is 28 km S of Mount Gambier. It is a quiet, well-planned fishing town that was once a thriving port. The rock-lobster fishing fleet here is the largest in SA. **Of interest:** Old Customs House (1860), National Trust classified. Maritime Museum, Meylin St, display includes salvaged artefacts from shipwrecks, photographic history of town. **In the area:** 'Dingley Dell' (1862, but restored), home of poet Adam Lindsay Gordon, now a museum, 2 km W. Cape Northumberland Lighthouse, on dramatic coastline west of town. Devonshire teas at Ye Olde Post Office Tea Rooms at Allendale East, 6 km N. For keen walkers, track to summit of Mt Schank, 10 km N; crater of extinct volcano, picnic facilities available. Mt Schank Fish Farm, fresh fish, yabbies for sale. Heading east, good surf fishing at Orwell Rocks. Sinkholes for experienced cave divers at Ewens Ponds and Picaninnie Ponds Conservation Parks, 7 km and 20 km E. **Tourist information:** Council

The Outback

Motorists contemplating travel in the outback should prepare their vehicles well and familiarise themselves with expected conditions before setting out.

The outback of South Australia covers almost 60 million hectares and is one of the most remote areas of the world; conditions are harsh, the climate extreme and distances are daunting.

The countryside is usually dry, barren and dusty, but freak rains and heavy floods can transform the land. Dry creek beds and waterholes fill, wildflowers bloom and birdlife flocks to the area. The enormous salt **Lake Eyre** has rarely been filled since Europeans first saw the desert.

The main road to the Northern Territory, the Stuart Highway, is a sealed road. From **Port Augusta** to **Alice Springs** the road covers a distance of 1243 kilometres. Turn off the highway to visit **Woomera**, the new mining town of **Roxby Downs** and the opal-mining town of **Andamooka.**

Petrol, food and supplies are available at Port Augusta, **Pimba**, **Glendambo**, **Coober Pedy**, **Cadney Park Roadhouse**, **Marla**, and **Kulgera** just over the Northern Territory border.

The notorious Birdsville Track starts at **Marree**, once a supply outpost for Afghan camel traders, and follows the route originally used to drove cattle from southwest Queensland to the railhead at Marree. The track skirts the fringes of the Simpson Desert, with its giant sand dunes, and the desolate Sturt's Stony Desert. Artesian bores line the route, pouring out 64 million litres of salty boiling water every day. The road is fair; however, sometimes it is washed out by heavy rains and travellers can be left stranded for weeks. Sandstorms are another problem. Petrol and supplies are available at Marree and **Mungerannie**, and at **Birdsville** over the Queensland border.

The Oodnadatta Track runs from Marree to Oodnadatta and continues to join the Stuart Highway at Marla, 200 kilometres west. Check track conditions with Marree police before departing. Fuel available only at Marree and William Creek.

The Strzelecki Track begins at **Lyndhurst**; a harsh, dusty road, it stretches 494 kilometres to the almost deserted outpost of **Innamincka**, with no stops for petrol or supplies.

Only experienced and well-equipped outback motorists should consider driving along the Birdsville, Strzelecki and Oodnadatta Tracks.

For further information on the area, contact Flinders Ranges and Outback of South Australia Regional Tourism, PO Box 666, Adelaide 5001, (08) 373 3430. **See also:** Individual entries in A–Z listing.

Remote outback scene

Offices, 7 Charles St; (087) 38 2207.
Accommodation: 1 hotel, 1 motel, 2
cara./camp. parks.
MAP REF. 287 H13

Port Pirie   Pop. 14 110

Huge grain silos and smelters' chimneys
dominate the skyline of Port Pirie, 227
km N of Adelaide on Spencer Gulf. Situated on the tidal Port Pirie River, the city
is a major industrial and commercial
centre. The first European settlers came
in 1845; wheat farms and market gardens
were established around the sheep industry in the region. Broken Hill Associated
Smelters began smelting lead in 1889
and today the largest lead smelters in the
world treat thousands of tonnes of con-
centrates annually from the silver, lead
and zinc deposits at Broken Hill, NSW.
Wheat and barley from the mid-north of
the State are exported and there is a thriving fishing industry. Port Pirie is also a
vital link in the road and rail routes to
Alice Springs, Darwin, Port Augusta and
Perth. Wheat farms, rolling hills and the
ocean are all close by. Swimming, water-
skiing, fishing and yachting are popular
sports on the river. **Of interest:** Regional
Tourism and Arts Centre, Mary Elie St,
local and touring exhibitions and craft
shop. National Trust Museum Buildings,
Ellen St, incl. Victorian pavilion-style
railway station; open daily. Historic
residence 'Carn Brae', Florence St, antique exhibits and a collection of over
2500 dolls; open daily. On waterfront:
loading and discharging of Australian and
overseas vessels. Tours of Pasminco Me-
tals BHAS smelting works; details from
Tourism Centre. Northern Festival Centre
in Memorial Park, Gertrude St, cultural
heart of the State's north, venue for local
and national performances. Oct.: Festival
of Country Music. Sept.: Blessing of the
Fleet and associated festivals, reminder of
role of Italians at turn of century in establishing local fishing industry. May: Street
Go-Kart Grand Prix. **In the area:** Weeroona Island, 13 km N. Port Germein,
beach resort 24 km N; wooden jetty said
to be longest in southern hemisphere.
Southern reaches of beautiful Flinders
Ranges are within 50 km; further east,
ruggedly beautiful Telowie Gorge, lined
with giant red river gums. **Tourist information:** Regional Tourism and Arts
Centre, Mary Elie St; (086) 33 0439.
Accommodation: 2 hotels, 1 hotel/
motel, 4 motels, 3 cara./camp. parks.
MAP REF. 289 J2

Port Victoria   Pop. 313

A tiny township on the west coast of the
Yorke Peninsula, Port Victoria was once
the main port for sailing ships carrying
grain from the area. **Of interest:** Port
Victoria Geology trail; booklet available
from Tourist Office. Swimming and jetty
fishing, from original 1888 jetty, end of
Main St. National Trust Maritime Museum on jetty; check opening times.
Wardang Island, Aboriginal reserve, 10
km off coast, permission required from
Point Pearce Community Council. Eas-
ter: Fishing Competition. **In the area:**
Conservation Islands are breeding areas
for several bird species. Underwater He-
ritage Trail in waters around Wardang
Island, for scuba divers visits to 8
wrecks; self-guide leaflet available.
Tourist information: Yorke Peninsula
Visitor Information Centre, 51 Taylor St,
Kadina; (08) 8821 2093. **Accommoda-
tion:** 1 hotel/motel, 2 cara./camp. parks.
See also: The Yorke Peninsula.
MAP REF. 282 E4, 288 I7

Quorn   Pop. 1056

Nestled in a valley in the Flinders
Ranges, 331 km N of Adelaide, Quorn
was established as a railway town, on the
Great Northern Railway, in 1878. Built
by Chinese and British workmen, the line
was closed in 1957. Part of the line
through Pichi Richi has been restored; a
steam locomotive operates Easter, taking
passengers on the 33-km round trip. **Of
interest:** Many historic buildings; Historic Walk leaflet available. Quorn Mill
(1878), Railway Tce, originally a flour
mill, now motel and restaurant. Quornu-
copia Galley, Railway Tce. Nairana Craft
Centre, First St. **In the area:** Colourful
rocky outcrops of Dutchman's Stern, 6
km W; walking trails. Junction Gallery, 16 km N on Yarrah Vale Rd. Warren
Gorge, 22 km N, popular with climbers.

Popular Pichi Richi railway, Quorn

Buckaringa Gorge, 32 km N, picnic and camping areas. Kanyaka Homestead, 42 km NE, ruins of sheep station that supported 70 families from 1850s to 1870s. Kanyaka Death Rock, also 42 km N, overlooks permanent waterhole, once an Aboriginal ceremonial ground. Scenic drive 50 km S to Devil's Peak, Pichi Richi Pass, Mt Brown, Mt Brown Conservation Park and picturesque Waukarie Creek, 16 km away; walking trails. Towns of Bruce and Hammond, 22 km and 38 km SE respectively; 1870s architecture. Hammond has unusual museum and restaurant in original bank building. **Tourist information:** 3 Seventh St; (086) 48 6419. **Accommodation:** 2 hotels, 2 hotel/motels, 1 motel, 7 B&B, 1 cara./camp. park.
MAP REF. 285 B12, 291 J11

Renmark   Pop. 4256
Renmark is at the heart of the oldest irrigation area in Australia, 260 km NE of Adelaide on the Sturt Hwy. In 1887 the Chaffey brothers from Canada were granted 250 000 acres to test their irrigation scheme. Today lush orchards and vineyards thrive with the water piped from the Murray. There are canneries, wineries and fruit-juice factories. Wheat, sheep and dairy cattle are other local industries. **Of interest:** Historic Renmark Hotel, community-owned and run. National Trust Museum 'Olivewood', cnr Renmark Ave (Sturt Hwy) and 21st St, former Chaffey homestead. Display of old hand-operated wine-press, in Renmark Ave, and one of the Chaffeys' original wood-burning irrigation pumps, on display outside Renmark Irrigation Trust Office, Murray St, original Chaffey Bros. office. *PS Industry* (1911), now floating museum moored behind Tourist Centre. Rivergrowers Ark packing shed, Renmark Ave, near 19th St; sales of local products; group tours available. Zenith Art Gallery, Murtho St; Ozone Art Gallery, Murray Ave. Houseboats for hire. Oct.: Agricultural Show. **In the area:** Renmano Winery, 5 km SW on Sturt Hwy. Unique collection of fauna, particularly reptiles, at Bredl's Wonder World of Wildlife, 7 km SW on Sturt Hwy; open daily. Ruston's Roses, 3000 varieties, 7 km SW, off Sturt Hwy; open Oct.–May. Angove's winery and distillery, Bookmark Ave, 5 km SW. Danggali Conservation Park, 60 km N, vast area of mallee scrub, bluebush and black oak woodland, wildlife; permit required.

Tourist information: Tourist and Heritage Centre, Murray Ave; (085) 86 6704. **Accommodation:** 1 hotel/motel, 4 motels, 1 B&B, 1 hostel, 3 cara./camp. parks. **See also:** Festival Fun.
MAP REF. 126 A7, 289 R5

Robe   Pop. 730
A small, historic town on Guichen Bay, 336 km S of Adelaide, Robe is a fishing port and holiday centre. The rugged, windswept coast has many beautiful and secluded beaches, including Long Beach, 17 km north of town. Lagoons and salt lakes are all round the area and wildlife abounds; penguins appear on the beach in the evening in summer. In the 1850s, Robe was a major wool port. From 1857, 16 500 Chinese disembarked there and travelled overland to the goldfields to avoid the Victorian Poll Tax. **Of interest:** National Trust buildings, art and craft galleries; especially Smillie and Victoria Sts. Robe Historic Interpretation Centre in Library building, Victoria St; displays and tourist information; leaflets on self-guide Heritage walks and drives. Old Customs House Museum, (1863), Royal Circus. Karatta House, off Christine Dr, summer residence of Governor Sir James Fergusson in 1860s; not open to the public. Caledonian Inn (1858), Victoria St; accommodation and meals. Jan.: Beer Can Regatta. Sept.: Blessing of the Fleet. **In the area:** Lakeside (1884), Main Rd, 2 km SE, historic home, accommodation, caravan park. Waterskiing on adjacent Lake Fellmongery. Narraburra Woolshed, 14 km SE, sheep and wool activities. Beacon Hill, 2 km S; panoramic views. Little Dip Conservation Park, 13 km S, complex moving sand-dune system, salt lakes and freshwater lakes, abundant wildlife. The Obelisk at Cape Dombey, 3 km W, northern vantage point for views. Crayfish fleet anchors in Lake Butler (Robe's harbour), fresh crays and fish Oct.–Apr. **Tourist information:** Robe Library, Victoria St; (087) 68 2465. **Accommodation:** 2 hotels, 6 motels, 8 B&B, 3 cara./camp. parks.
MAP REF. 287 F10

Roxby Downs   Pop. 1999
A modern, newly established township built to accommodate the employees of the Olympic Dam Mining Project, Roxby Downs is 85 km N of Pimba, which is just off Stuart Hwy, 555 km N

of Adelaide. A road from Roxby Downs joins the Oodnadatta Track just south of Lake Eyre South, 125 km N of Roxby. **In the area:** Olympic Dam Mining Complex, 15 km N, tours of mining operations available. Heritage Centre and Missile Park, 90 km S at Woomera. **Tourist information:** Council Offices, Richardson Place; (086) 71 0010. **Accommodation:** 1 motel, 1 cara./camp. park.
MAP REF. 290 F4

Stansbury   Pop. 513
Situated on the lower east coast of Yorke Peninsula, Stansbury was originally known as Oyster Bay because it was once one of the best oyster beds in South Australian waters. In days gone by, ketches shipped grain across the gulf from Stansbury to Port Adelaide. A popular holiday resort, the town has scenic views of Gulf St Vincent. The bay is excellent for water sports, including diving and water-skiing. May: Sheepdog trials. **Of interest:** Museum, North Tce, in first Stansbury School (1878) and residence. Jetty fishing. **In the area:** Lake Sundown, 15 km NW, one of many salt lakes in area; photographer's delight at sunset. **Tourist information:** Yorke Peninsula Visitor Information Centre, 51 Taylor St, Kadina; (08) 8821 2093. **Accommodation:** 1 hotel, 2 motels, 2 cara./camp. parks.
MAP REF. 282 G8, 288 I8

Strathalbyn   Pop. 2623
An inland town with a Scottish heritage, on the Angas River, Strathalbyn is 58 km S of Adelaide and a designated heritage township. The picturesque Soldiers Memorial Gardens follow the river through the town, offering shaded picnic grounds. **Of interest:** National Trust Museum, Rankine St; in old police station and courthouse. St Andrew's Church (1848), Alfred Pl. Old Provincial Gas Company (1868), South Tce, now Gasworks Restaurant. Antique and craft shops. March: Penny Farthing Race. Aug.: Collectors, Hobbies and Antique Fair. Oct.: Glenbarr Scottish Festival. **In the area:** Lakeside resort of Milang, 20 km SE; museum, Langhorne Creek, 15 km E; winegrowing district. Pottery at Paris Creek, near Meadows, 15 km NW. Iris gardens 2 km W of Meadows; open Oct.–Mar. **Tourist information:** Old Railway Station, South Tce; (085) 36 3212. **Accommodation:** 3 hotels, 1

cara./camp. park.
MAP REF. 283 N10, 284 I7, 287 C3, 289 M9

Streaky Bay   Pop. 957
Streaky Bay, 727 km NW of Adelaide, is an excellent holiday resort, fishing port and agricultural centre for the cereal-growing hinterland. Matthew Flinders, the explorer, named the bay for the streaking effect caused by seaweed in its waters. The town is almost surrounded by small bays and coves, pleasant sandy beaches and spectacular towering cliffs. Crayfish and many species of fish abound, and fishing from boat or jetty is good. **Of interest:** At Tourist Centre: fishing information and interesting shark replica. Restored Engine Centre, Alfred Tce, exterior historic murals. Old School House Museum, Montgomery Tce. Hospital Cottage (1864), first building in Streaky Bay. Jan.: Mardi Gras.; Perlubie Beach Sports and Race Day. Nov.–Jan.: Snapper Fishing Contest. **In the area:** Magnificent coastal scenery and rugged cliffs. Point Labatt Conservation Park, 55 km S, has only permanent colony of sea lions on Australian mainland. On half-day tourist drive (map available): diving and snorkelling; sea lions; and Murphy's Haystacks, 2 sculptural groups of ancient pink granite rocks, 40 km SE off Flinders Hwy. Port Kenny, 62 km S on Venus Bay; excellent fishing. Further 12 km S, fishing village of Venus Bay; nearby, breathtaking views from Needle Eye Lookout. Spectacular limestone caves at Talia, 88 km S. **Tourist information:** 13–15 Alfred Tce; (086) 26 1126. **Accommodation:** 1 hotel/motel, 1 motel, 1 B&B, 1 hostel, 1 cara./camp. park. **See also:** The Eyre Peninsula.
MAP REF. 297 P12

Swan Reach   Pop. 230
Swan Reach is a quiet little township on the Murray River, about 100 km E of Gawler. Picturesque river scenery and excellent fishing make it an increasingly popular holiday resort. **In the area:** Swan Reach (11 km W) and Ridley (5 km S) Conservation Parks. Punyelroo, 7 km S, fishing, boating and water-skiing. Yookamurra Sanctuary, 21 km NW; conservation project, incl. eradication of feral animals and restocking with native animals. Guided walks for pre-European atmosphere, overnight accommodation; booking essential, (085) 62 5011 or (08) 370 9422. The Murray Plains Museum,

45 km NW, open by appt. At Nildottie, 14 km S, and junction of Rivers Marne and Murray, 15 km S; picnic facilities. Water sports at Walker Flat, 26 km S. **Tourist information:** Swan Reach Supermarket, Anzac Ave; (085) 70 2036. **Accommodation:** 1 hotel, 1 cara./camp. park.
MAP REF. 283 R5, 287 E1, 289 N7

Tailem Bend   Pop. 1502
Once a railway-workshop town, now a service centre situated at the junction of the Dukes, Mallee and Princes Hwys, 107 km SE of Adelaide, Tailem Bend has excellent views across the Murray as the river bends sharply towards Wellington. **Of interest:** Picnic/barbecue facilities, children's playground. Feb.: Gumi Racing Festival. **In the area:** Scenic drive via vehicular ferry across river to Jervois, cheese factory here; then 11 km S to Wellington, where river meets lake. At Wellington, restored courthouse complex (1864); incl. cells, stables, post and telegraph office, courtyard and kiosk. Historic buildings, SE on Dukes Hwy: old woolshed on left, approaching Cooke Plains; Braeside Homestead on left after town. Old Tailem Town Pioneer Village, 5 km N of Tailem Bend; open daily. **Tourist information:** 87–89 Railway Tce; (085) 72 3537. **Accommodation:** 2 hotels, 1 motel, 2 cara./camp. parks.
MAP REF. 283 Q10, 287 E3, 289 N9

Tanunda   Pop. 3087
The town of Tanunda is the heart of the Barossa Valley. It was the focal point for early German settlement, growing out of the village of Langmeil, established in 1843, part of which can be seen in the western areas of town. The National Trust has classified Goat Square, site of the old market square and surrounded by century-old cottages. **Of interest:** Fine examples of Lutheran churches. Historical museum, Murray St; former 1865 post and telegraph office houses collections specialising in German heritage. Award-winning Kev Rohrlach Technology and Heritage Centre, Barossa Valley Way, Tanunda Nth; open daily. Barossa Kiddypark, Magnolia St, family funpark with rides. Jan.: Oom-Pah Fest. March: Essenfest. **In the area:** Local wineries incl. St Hallett Wines, Rockford Wines, Charles Melton Wines, Bethany Wines, High Wycombe Wines, Basedow Wines, Old Barn Wines (also has local crafts), Veritas Winery, Kroemer Estate Wines,

Richmond Grove Barossa Winery, Tarchalace Winery, Turkey Flat Vineyard, Tolley Pedare Wines, Lanzerac Estate Winery, Grant Burge Wines, Chateau Dorrien, Peter Lehmann Wines and Krondorf Wines. Story Book Cottage and Whacky Wood, Oak St, for children. Norm's Coolie Sheep Dogs, south off Barossa Valley Way; 3 performances weekly. The Keg Factory, St Hallett Rd; makers of kegs, barrel furniture, wine racks. Bethany, 4 km S, first German settlement in Barossa, pretty village with creekside picnic area, pioneer cemetery, attractive streetscapes, two wineries. At Kersbrook, 40 km S, historic building; trout farm. **Tourist information:** Barossa Valley Visitors Centre, 68 Murray Street; 1800 81 2662 or (085) 63 0600. **Accommodation:** 1 hotel, 1 hotel/motel, 2 motels, 2 B&B, 1 cara./camp. park. **See also:** Festival Fun; Vineyards and Wineries.
MAP REF. 283 N4, 286 F5, 287 D1, 289 M7

Tintinara   Pop. 316
A quiet little town 206 km SE of Adelaide in the Coonalpyn Downs. **Of interest:** Post office (1865), Becker Tce. **In the area:** Historic buildings at Tintinara Homestead, 9 km W. Mt Boothby Conservation Park, 20 km W. Access to Mt Rescue Conservation Park, 15 km E; sandplains with heath, native fauna, Aboriginal campsites and burial grounds. **Tourist information:** Heart of the Park Tourist and Craft Shop, Becker Tce; (087) 57 2220. **Accommodation:** 1 hotel, 1 motel, 1 cara./camp. park.
MAP REF. 287 G5, 289 P11

Tumby Bay   Pop. 1147
Tumby Bay is a pretty coastal resort 49 km N of Port Lincoln on the east coast of Eyre Peninsula. The town is well-known for its long crescent beach and white sand. Lawns and picnic/barbecue facilities along the foreshore. **Of interest:** C. L. Alexander National Trust Museum, in old wooden schoolroom; open Fri. and Sat. p.m. Police station (1871). Two jetties, one more than 100 years old. Jan.: Fishing competition. **In the area:** Rock and surf fishing. Island Lookout for spectacular views. Rugged, beautiful scenery and fishing at Poonta and Cowley's Beaches; catches incl. snapper, whiting and bream. Koppio, about 40 km SW, through attractive fertile countryside; National Trust-classified Smithy Museum.

Tod Reservoir Museum in Koppio hills. At Port Neill, 42 km NE: grassed foreshore for picnics; safe swimming beach; Vic and Jill Fauser's Museum (open daily); 1 km N, Port Neill Lookout for spectacular views. At Wanilla, 60 km SW, wildflowers in spring. At Thuruna, excellent fishing. At Lipson Cove visitors can walk across to Lipson Island at low tide. Fishing, sea lions, dolphins and birdlife at Sir Joseph Banks Group of islands; charter tours available. Trinity Haven Scenic Drive. **Tourist information:** Hales Minimart, 1 Bratten Way; (086) 88 2584. **Accommodation**: Tumby Bay, 2 hotels, 1 motel, 1 cara./ camp. park; Port Neill, 1 hotel, 2 cara./camp. parks. **See also:** The Eyre Peninsula.
MAP REF. 288 E6

Victor Harbor   Pop. 5930

A popular coastal resort town and unofficial capital of the Fleurieu Peninsula, Victor Harbor is 84 km S of Adelaide. Established in the early days of whaling and sealing (1830s), 'Victor' overlooks historic Encounter Bay, protected by Granite Island. **Of interest:** Historic buildings: Newland Memorial Congregational Church (1869), Mount Breckan (1879), Adare (1860s), The Drive; Renown Ave; Victoria St; St Augustine's Church (1869), Burke St. Telegraph Station Art Gallery, Coral St, in former telegraph station (1866). Golfing. Whale-watching; SA Whale Centre, Railway Tce, aims to assist conservation of the 25 species of whale and dolphin in southern Australian waters. Oct.: Folk Festival. **In the area:** Granite Island: joined to mainland by 0.6-km causeway; walk or take horse-drawn tram; chairlift (operates SA school holidays and weekends) offers magnificent views of land and sea; penguin rookeries and seals. Greenhills Adventure Park, 3.5 km N on banks of Hindmarsh River. Urimbirra Wildlife Park, 5 km N. Opposite, Nangawooka Flora Reserve with over 1000 named trees and plants. At Mt Compass, 24 km N: pottery, strawberry and blueberry farms, begonia farm, nursery, Tooperang Trout Farm. The Steam Ranger, a railway service, operates between Victor Harbor and Goolwa, via Port Elliot. To north: Hindmarsh and Inman Rivers, good fishing and peaceful picnic spots. Spring Mount Conservation Park, 14 km NW. Glacier Rock at Inman Valley, 19 km NW, shows effect of glacial erosion. Hindmarsh Valley Falls, 15 km

Horse-drawn tram, Victor Harbor

NE, pleasant walks, spectacular waterfalls. The Bluff (Rosetta Head), 5 km S, worth 100-m climb for views. Waitpinga Beach, 17 km SW. Deep Creek Conservation Park, 50 km SW, Heysen Trail for walking, spectacular flora and fauna; park is well known for rugged cliffs, orchids and ferns in gullies. Talisker Conservation Park (next to Deep Creek Conservation Park) is site of historic silver–lead mine, old mine buildings, diggings. At tip of Fleurieu Peninsula is Cape Jervis, 70 km SW, panoramic views. **Tourist information:** 10 Railway Tce; (085) 52 5821. **Accommodation:** 2 hotels, 10 motels, 10 B&B, 1 hostel, 3 cara./camp. parks. **See also:** The Fleurieu Peninsula.
MAP REF. 283 L12, 284 D13, 287 C4, 289 L10

Waikerie   Pop. 1748

Waikerie, the citrus centre of Australia, is surrounded by an oasis of irrigated vegetables, orchards and vineyards in mallee-scrub country in the Riverland. Situated 170 km NE of Adelaide, the town has beautiful views of the river gums and magnificent sandstone cliffs along the Murray. The name means 'anything that flies': the river and lagoons teem with birdlife, and the mallee scrub is a haven for parrots and other native birds. **Of interest:** Co-op Fruit-packing House, Sturt Hwy, largest in Australia. Lions Park, on riverfront, children's playground, picnic/barbecue facilities. Harts Lagoon, Ramco Rd, bird wetlands. Houseboat hire. Feb.: International Food Fair. Easter: Horse and Pony Club Gymkhana. **In the area:** Orange Tree kiosk, Sturt Hwy, 2 km E, fruit products and river-viewing platform. Gliding

Club, 4 km E, off Sturt Hwy, internationally acclaimed as a glider's paradise; joy rides and courses available. On northern side of river near Lock 2, close to Taylorville: one of few areas in Australia where crystallised gypsum fossils are found in abundance. Devlin's ghost sighted, 11 km E. Holder Bend Reserve and Maize Island Conservation Park, 6 km NE. At Blanchetown, 42 km W: first of Murray's 6 SA locks; lookout at Blanchetown Bridge; floating restaurant. Brookfield Conservation Park, 11 km W, home of southern hairy-nosed wombat. **Tourist information:** Waikerie Travel Centre, 20 McCoy St; (085) 41 2188. **Accommodation:** 1 motel, 1 hotel/motel, 1 cara./ camp. park.
MAP REF. 289 P5

Wallaroo   Pop. 2465

Situated 154 km NW of Adelaide, Wallaroo is a key shipping port for the Yorke Peninsula, exporting barley and wheat. Processing of rock phosphate is another major industry here. The safe beaches and excellent fishing in this historical area make it a popular tourist resort. In 1859 vast copper-ore deposits were discovered. A smelter was built, thousands of Cornish miners arrived and Wallaroo and surrounding areas boomed until the 1920s, when copper prices dropped and the industry gradually died out. The nearby towns of Moonta and Kadina form part of the trio known as 'Little Cornwall', and the area still has many reminders of its colourful past. **Of interest:** Several charming old Cornish-style cottages in district. Cemetery, Moonta Rd, grave of Caroline Carleton, author of 'Song of Australia'. National Trust Wallaroo Heritage and Nautical Museum, in

town's original post office (1865) in Jetty Rd, maritime exhibits. Wallaroo Historical Walks brochure available at museum or town hall, Irwin St; guided tours on Sun. Historic buildings incl.: old railway station, Owen Tce; in Jetty Rd, customs house (1862), and Hughes chimney stack (1865), which contains over 300 000 bricks and is more than 7 m square at its base. Jan.: Wallaroo Regatta. May: Prize-winning Kernewek Lowender, Cornish Festival, held in conjunction with Moonta and Kadina (odd-numbered years). **In the area:** Wallaroo Mines site in Kadina, 10 km E; open for signposted self-guide walking tour. Towns of Moonta and Kadina. Bird Island, 10 km S, good crabbing. **Tourist information:** Yorke Peninsula Visitor Information Centre, 51 Taylor St, Kadina; (08) 8821 2093. **Accommodation:** 1 hotel, 1 hotel/motel, 2 motels, 3 cara./camp. parks. **See also:** Festival Fun; The Yorke Peninsula.
MAP REF. 288 I4

Whyalla   Pop. 25 526

In 90 years Whyalla, northern gateway to Eyre Peninsula, has grown from a small settlement known as Hummock Hill to the largest provincial city in the State and an important industrial centre based on steel. It is famous for its heavy industry, particularly the enormous BHP iron and steel works and ore mining at Iron Knob and Iron Monarch in the Middleback Ranges. A shipyard operated from 1939–78, and the largest ship ever built in Australia was launched here in 1972. Whyalla is a modern, well-planned city with a good shopping centre, safe beaches, fishing, boating and excellent recreational facilities. The area enjoys a sunny, Mediterranean-type climate. **Of interest:** At Whyalla Maritime Museum Complex, Lincoln Hwy: 650-tonne corvette *Whyalla;* and Tanderra Building, housing collection of models, incl. what is believed to be largest OO gauge model railway in Australia; open daily 10–4. Mount Laura Homestead Museum (National Trust), Ekblom St; check opening times. Whyalla Art Gallery, Darling Tce; open daily. Foreshore redevelopment incl. attractive beach, jetty for recreational fishing, landscaped picnic/barbecue area, and marina with boat-launching facilities. Hummock Hill lookout from Queen Elizabeth Dr, spectacular · iews. Flinders Lookout, Farrel St; Ada Ryan Gardens, Cudmore Tce; mini-zoo and

picnic facilities under shady trees. Guided tours of BHP steel works Mon. and Wed.; bookings at Tourist Centre (for safety reasons, visitors must wear closed footwear). Large arid area wildlife and reptile sanctuary, south-east on Lincoln Hwy, near airport, offers Nocturnal Walk Guided Tour; open daily, bookings essential. Whyalla Tourist Drive; brochure from Tourist Centre. Jan.: National Jet Ski Titles. Oct.: Australian Amateur Snapper Fishing Championship. **In the area:** Port Bonython, 20 km E, and Point Lowly, 34 km E: Point Lowly Lighthouse (1882), oldest building in area (not open for inspection); and scenic coastal drive through Fitzgerald Bay to Point Douglas. Whyalla Conservation Park, 10 km N off Lincoln Hwy, near Port Bonython turn-off. At Iron Knob, 53 km NW: iron ore quarries (tours available); Mining Museum and Iron Knob Mineral and Shell Display. **Tourist information:** Lincoln Hwy; (086) 45 7900, 1800 08 8589. **Accommodation:** 5 hotels, 1 hotel/motel, 5 motels, 2 cara./camp. parks. **See also:** The Eyre Peninsula.
MAP REF. 288 I1, 290 H13

Willunga   Pop. 1164

An historic town surveyed in 1839, Willunga was named from the Aboriginal word *willa-unga*, meaning 'the place of green trees'. The town is just south of the Southern Vales winegrowing region and is Australia's major almond-growing centre. **Of interest**: Historic pug cottages and fine examples of colonial architecture. National Trust police station and courthouse (1855), Main St. Anglican church, St Andrews Tce, Elizabethan bronze bell. On Main Rd: Bush Inn (1889) and Vanessa's Restaurant. Delabole Quarry (1842), operated for 60 years, now National Trust site. July: Almond Blossom Festival. **In the area:** Cowshed Gallery at Yundi, 9 km E. Mt Magnificent Conservation Park, 12 km SE; western grey kangaroos in bushland, scenic walks, picnic areas. Kyeema Conservation Park, 14 km NE. Strawberry farm, 4 km N. **Tourist information:** The Cottage, Main Rd, McLaren Vale; (08) 323 8537. **Accommodation:** 1 hotel, 2 B&B.
MAP REF. 283 L10, 284 C7, 287 B3, 289 L9

Wilmington   Pop. 250

A tiny settlement formerly known as Beautiful Valley, Wilmington is 290 km

N of Adelaide in the Flinders Ranges. **Of interest:** Police station (1880), now a private residence, and old coaching stables (1880) at rear of Wilmington Hotel, both Main St. Early 20th century billiard rooms, Main St, open by appt. Butter Factory (1898), adjacent to school, off Main St. Beautiful Valley Aussie Relics Museum, Main North Rd; check opening times. **In the area:** Many scenic drives. Hancock's Lookout, 7 km W, at top of Horrocks Pass, off road to Port Augusta, for views of Spencer Gulf. Mount Remarkable National Park, 13 km S, crystal-clear mountain pools, dense vegetation, abundant wildlife. Mambray Creek and spectacular Alligator Gorge in park, access 2 km S near Beautiful Valley Caravan Park. Historic Melrose, 24 km S, oldest town in the Flinders. Booleroo Steam and Traction Preservation Society's Museum (open by appt), Booleroo Centre, 48 km SE. Hammond, 26 km NE, historic railway town and Molly Brown's restaurant. At Carrieton, 56 km NE: historic buildings; Aboriginal carvings, 5 km along Belton Rd; scenic drive to deserted Johnberg. **Tourist information:** Wilmington Deli, Main St; (086) 67 5117. **Accommodation:** 1 hotel, 2 cara./camp. parks.
MAP REF. 285 B13, 291 J12

Wilpena   Pop. 20

Wilpena, 429 km N of Adelaide, consists of a motel and caravan park outside Wilpena Pound. The Pound, part of the Flinders Ranges National Park, is a vast natural amphitheatre surrounded by colossal peaks that change colour as the light falls on them through the day. The only entrance is through a narrow gorge and across Sliding Rock. In 1900 a wheat farmer built a homestead inside the Pound, but a flood destroyed the log road and the farm was abandoned. **In the area:** Bushwalking and mountain climbing in surrounding countryside. Numerous walking trails into Wilpena Pound, including one to St Mary's Peak, the highest point (1188 m). Aboriginal rock carvings and paintings at Arkaroo Rock on slopes of Rawnsley Bluff, south, and at Sacred Canyon, south-east. Rawnsley Park Station, 20 km S on Hawker Rd; demonstrations of sheep-drafting and shearing Sept.–Oct. Appealinna Homestead (1851), 16 km N, off Blinman Rd, ruins of house built of flat rock from creek bed. Scenic drives: most of area within Flinders Ranges National Park

Vineyards and Wineries

South Australia provides about 65 per cent of the wines and 83 per cent of the brandy made in Australia. In the equable dry climate of the southern and eastern regions of the State, kilometres of vineyards stretch over valleys, plains and hillsides. The State has eight distinct grape-growing regions: the Barossa Valley, the Southern Vales region of the Fleurieu Peninsula, the Clare Valley, Murraylands, Riverland, the Adelaide Hills, the Coonawarra area, and Boston Bay on Eyre Peninsula.

The **Barossa Valley**, Australia's most famous wine-producing area, is located about 55 kilometres north-east of Adelaide. It is a warm and intimate place of charming old towns, with vineyards spreading across undulating hills in well-tended, precise rows. Visitors can view the valley from a hot-air balloon and afterwards enjoy a champagne breakfast (bookings at Kersbrook)

The Barossa Valley was named in 1837 by Colonel Light in memory of Barrosa in Spain, where he fought a decisive battle in 1811. The recorded spelling 'Barossa' was an error that was never rectified. The district was settled in 1839 by English and German settlers. Today the Barossa has a distinctive culture and atmosphere that derives from this German concentration in the mid-nineteenth century and is evidenced in the vineyards, the stone buildings, the restaurants, the bakeries and the Lutheran churches that dot the valley.

The Barossa produces brandy, dry and sweet table wines, and fortified styles of wine. Some of the most famous wineries

of the Barossa are Yalumba, Orlando, Penfolds and Seppelts. A number of these wineries are still run by members of the same families that established them last century. Others have been taken over by big international companies, but the distinctive qualities of the wine remain. There are many medium-size wineries making excellent wines, such as Wolf Blass, Basedows and Krondorf, and many boutique wineries specialising in producing a small number of quality wines, including Barossa Settlers, Henschke, Grant Burge and Elderton.

The **Southern Vales** region, which is particularly suitable for red wines, is on the Fleurieu Peninsula, just south of Adelaide. Nestled in the gentle folds of the Mount Lofty Ranges with a westerly view to the sea lies McLaren Vale, the centre of this winegrowing area. There are more than fifty wineries in the region, among them Chapel Hill, Hardy's Reynella, James Haselgrove, Seaview and Wirra Wirra, and they range from very large to very small. In most of the wineries, the person at the cellar door is the person who makes the wine, so meet your maker at McLaren Vale!

The vineyards of the **Clare Valley** are about 130 kilometres north of Adelaide and produce fine table wines, riesling, chablis and some terrific reds. Two of the better known of the twenty-odd wineries in this district are Eaglehawk Estate and Leasingham Wines.

The **Murraylands** region extends from Middleton Estate Wines at Middleton, north-east to Willowglen Wines near Murray Bridge. Another wine region that

includes a stretch of the Murray River near the Victorian border is **Riverland**. Famous for a wide range of products from top-quality table wines to ouzo and brandy, the region is represented by such wineries as Kingston Estate at Kingston-on-Murray and Angove's near Renmark.

There are vineyards scattered throughout the **Adelaide Hills**. Wineries to the north (south-east of the Barossa Valley) include Hamiltons, Craneford and Grand Cru Estate; this area is noted especially for its riesling. Closer to Adelaide are Petaluma and Stonyfell Wineries.

Many vineyards at **Coonawarra** in the far south-east produce red wines from a small area of unique rich, volcanic soil; examples are Ladbroke Grove, Mildara and Rouge Homme. Further vineyards have been established in the south-east at Keppoch and Padthaway.

Boston Bay, perched on the southern tip of the spectacular Eyre Peninsula, is one of Australia's newest wine regions. Its reputation as the 'home of the great white shark' is fast changing to 'home of great white wines', with national award recognition for the region's first major vintage.

Most of the South Australian wineries are open for inspection, tastings and cellar-door sales.

For further information about hours of inspection and winery tours, contact the South Australian Tourism Commission Travel Centre, 1 King William Street, Adelaide; (08) 212 1505. **See also:** Individual entries in A–Z listing. **Note** detailed maps of Southern Vales and Barossa Valley on pages 284 and 286 respectively.

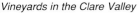
Vineyards in the Clare Valley

(ranger station at Wilpena) and to Stokes Hill Lookout, 2 km NE; Bunyeroo and Brachina Gorges, Aroona Valley, 5 km NW; Moralana Scenic Drive, 25 km S. Organised tours, 4WD tours and scenic flights available. **Tourist information:** Wilpena Pound Motel; (086) 48 0004. Accommodation: 1 motel, 2 cara./camp. parks. **See also:** The Flinders Ranges. MAP REF. 285 D8, 291 K8

Woomera   Pop. 1600

Established in 1947 as a site for launching British experimental rockets, Woomera was, until 1982, a prohibited area to visitors. The town, 490 km NW of Adelaide, is still administered by the Defence Department. **Of interest:** Missile Park and Heritage Centre, displays of rockets, aircraft and weapons. Guided tours of old rocket launch area. Old Guard Gate, Old Pimba Rd. Breen Park picnic area. **In the area:** Roxby Downs, 78 km N, service centre for Olympic Dam mining operations; tours of mining operations. Andamooka opal field, 107 km NE; tours available. **Tourist information:** Wadlata Outback Centre, Flinders Tce, Port Augusta; (086) 41 0793. **Accommodation:** 1 hotel, 1 cara./camp. park. MAP REF. 290 F7

Wudinna   Pop. 573

Wudinna is a small settlement on the Eyre Hwy, 571 km NW of Adelaide. The township is the gateway to the timeless Gawler Ranges and has become an important service point for Eyre Peninsula. **In the area:** Wilderness Safaris, 3–11 days; (086) 80 2020. Mt Wudinna, 10 km NE, second largest granite outcrop in Southern Hemisphere; summit (261 m) offers scenic views of countryside; recreation area at base. Nearby, Turtle Rock, turtle-shaped ancient granite rock. Signposted tourist drives to all major rock formations. Prolific wildlife and wildflowers in spring. At Minnipa, 37 km NW: Grain Research centre; Pildappa Rock (wave rock); recreation area at Tcharkuldu Hill. **Tourist information:** District Council of Lehunte, Burton Tce; (086) 80 2002. **Accommodation:** 1 hotel/motel, 1 motel, 1 cara./camp. park. MAP REF. 288 C1, 290 B13

Yankalilla   Pop. 408

A growing settlement just inland from the west coast of the Fleurieu Peninsula, Yankalilla is 35 km W of Victor Harbor. **Of interest:** In Main St: Uniting Church (1878); Bungala House, gifts and pottery; leatherwork, woodwork and gumnut creations at craft shops; Yankalilla Hotel, country-style counter meals; historical museum; tearooms. **In the area:** Seaside town of Normanville, 4 km W. Bay Tree Farm, Cape Jervis Rd, Second Valley, 14 km SW; herbs, flowers, afternoon teas. Glacier Rock, 22 km E; 500 million year old Cambrian Kanmantoo quartzite. Steep hillsides and gullies at Myponga Conservation Park, 14 km NE; home of western grey kangaroo. At Myponga, 14 km NE: begonia farm; Myponga Reservoir for barbecues or picnics. **Tourist information:** Council Offices, Main St; (085) 58 2048. **Accommodation:** Yankalilla, 1 hotel. Normanville, 1 motel, 2 cara./ camp. parks. MAP REF. 283 J11, 287 B4, 289 K10

Yorketown   Pop. 738

The principal town at the southern end of the Yorke Peninsula, Yorketown's shopping centre services the surrounding cereal-growing district. Yorketown is surrounded by extensive inland salt lakes (some are pink), which are still worked. Oct.: Picnic races and gymkhana. **In the area:** Toy Factory, 5 km NE; locally crafted wooden toys. Rugged coastal scenery and peaceful hinterland at tip of Peninsula, incl. Innes National Park, 77 km SW. Inneston, historic mining town in park, managed as historic site by the Dept of Environment and Natural Resources. Surfing at Daly Head, 50 km W. At Corny Point, on north-western tip of Peninsula, 55 km NW: lighthouse; lookout; camping; fishing. **Tourist information:** Yorke Peninsula Visitor Information Centre, 51 Taylor St, Kadina; (08) 8821 2093. **Accommodation:** 1 hotel, 1 hotel/ motel, 1 cara./camp. park. **See also:** Yorke Peninsula. MAP REF. 282 F8, 288 I8

Wudinna, gateway to the Gawler Ranges
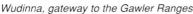

South Australia

Location Map

Other Map Coverage

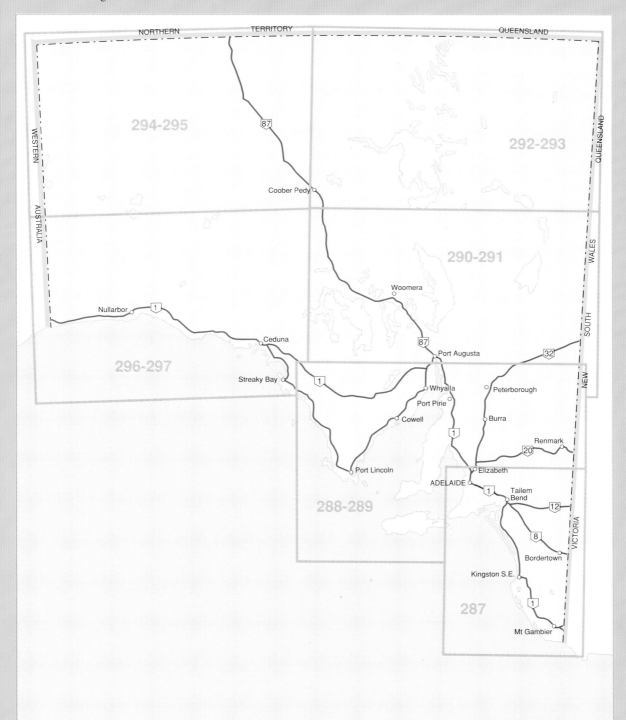

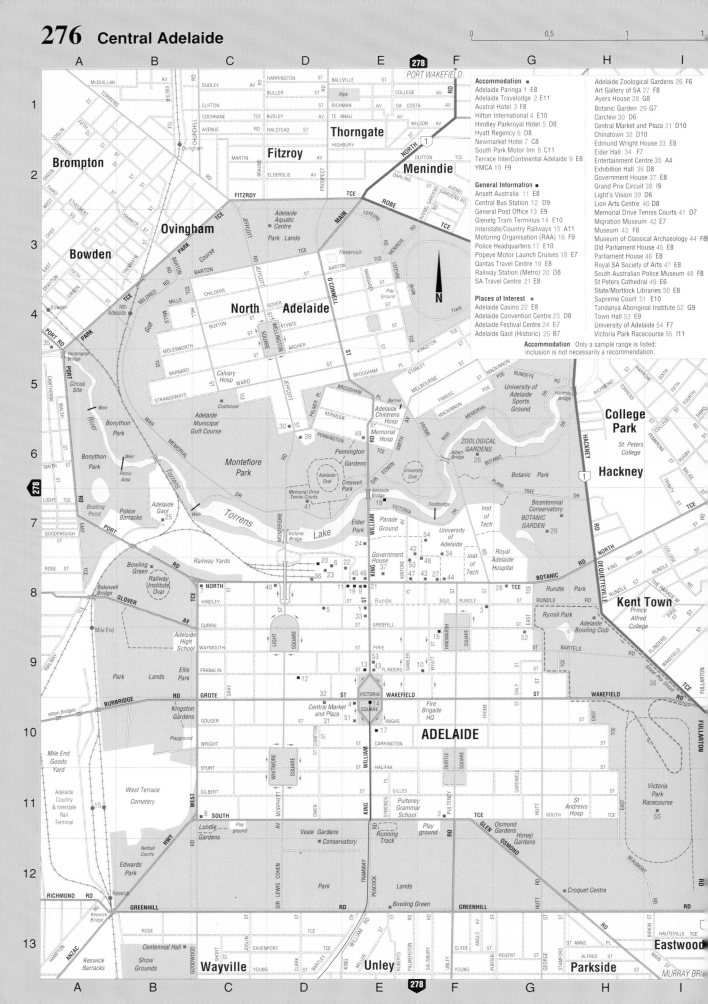

276 Central Adelaide

Accommodation ■
Adelaide Paringa 1 E8
Adelaide Travelodge 2 E11
Austral Hotel 3 F8
Hilton International 4 E10
Hindley Parkroyal Hotel 5 D8
Hyatt Regency 6 D8
Newmarket Hotel 7 C8
South Park Motor Inn 8 C11
Terrace InterContinental Adelaide 9 E8
YMCA 10 F9

General Information ■
Ansett Australia 11 E8
Central Bus Station 12 D9
General Post Office 13 E9
Glenelg Tram Terminus 14 E10
Interstate/Country Railways 15 A11
Motoring Organisation (RAA) 16 F9
Police Headquarters 17 E10
Popeye Motor Launch Cruises 18 E7
Qantas Travel Centre 19 E8
Railway Station (Metro) 20 D8
SA Travel Centre 21 E8

Places of Interest ■
Adelaide Casino 22 E8
Adelaide Convention Centre 23 D8
Adelaide Festival Centre 24 E7
Adelaide Gaol (Historic) 25 B7

Adelaide Zoological Gardens 26 F6
Art Gallery of SA 27 F8
Ayers House 28 G8
Botanic Garden 29 G7
Carclew 30 D6
Central Market and Plaza 31 D10
Chinatown 32 D10
Edmund Wright House 33 E8
Elder Hall 34 F7
Entertainment Centre 35 A4
Exhibition Hall 36 D8
Government House 37 E8
Grand Prix Circuit 38 I9
Light's Vision 39 D6
Lion Arts Centre 40 D8
Memorial Drive Tennis Courts 41 D7
Migration Museum 42 E7
Museum 43 F8
Museum of Classical Archaeology 44 F8
Old Parliament House 45 E8
Parliament House 46 E8
Royal SA Society of Arts 47 E8
South Australian Police Museum 48 F8
St Peters Cathedral 49 E6
State/Mortlock Libraries 50 E8
Supreme Court 51 E10
Tandanya Aboriginal Institute 52 G9
Town Hall 53 E9
University of Adelaide 54 F7
Victoria Park Racecourse 55 I11

Accommodation Only a sample range is listed;
inclusion is not necessarily a recommendation.

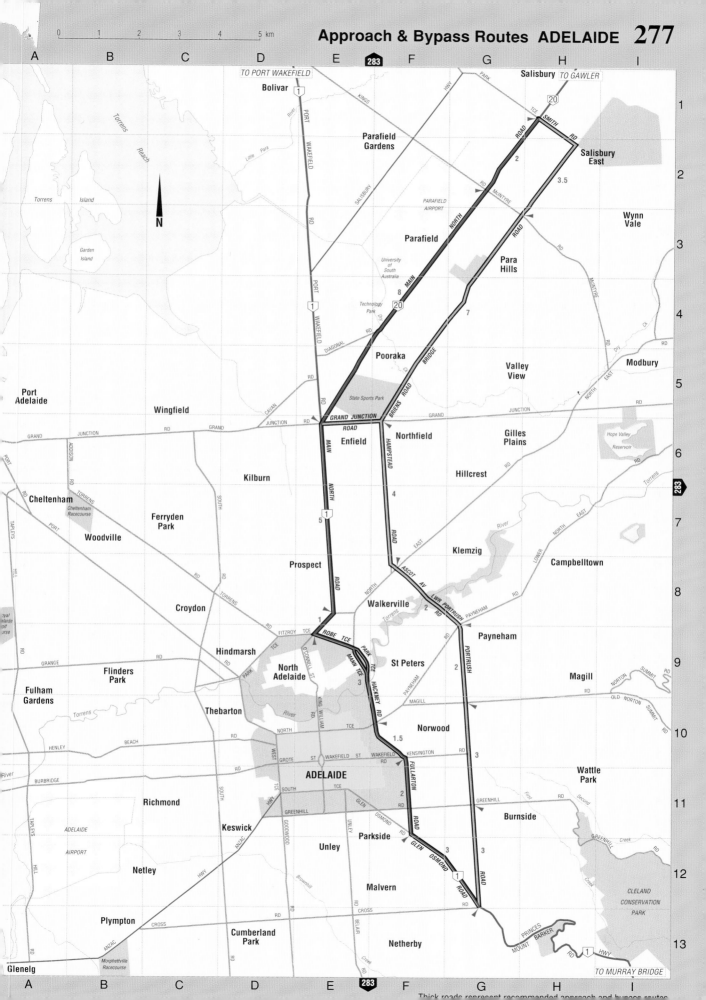

0 1 2 3 4 5 km

A B C D E F G H I

283

TO PORT WAKEFIELD

Bolivar

Salisbury *TO GAWLER*

20

Parafield
Gardens

Salisbury
East

SMITH RD

2

ROAD

TCE

NORTH

3.5

McINTYRE

ROAD

Wynn
Vale

PARAFIELD
AIRPORT

Parafield

Para
Hills

University
of South
Australia

8 MAIN

20

7

Modbury

Technology
Park

DIAGONAL

Pooraka

BRIENS ROAD

BRIDGE

Valley
View

McINTYRE

Port
Adelaide

Wingfield

CAVAN

JUNCTION

GRAND JUNCTION
ROAD

Northfield

GRAND JUNCTION

Gilles
Plains

Hope Valley
Reservoir

GRAND   JUNCTION   RD   GRAND

MAIN

Enfield

HAMPSTEAD

Hillcrest

Cheltenham

TORRENS
Cheltenham
Racecourse

Kilburn

NORTH

4

Torrens

Ferryden
Park

SOUTH

1

5

ROAD

Klemzig

EAST   NORTH

River

Campbelltown

Woodville

RD

Prospect

Walkerville

ASCOT AV

LWR PORTRUSH

RD

2

PAYNEHAM

Croydon

TORRENS

NORTH

Torrens

Payneham

Royal
Adelaide
Golf
Course

GRANGE

Flinders
Park

RD

FITZROY TCE

1

ROBE TCE

PARK TCE

O'CONNELL ST

MANN TCE

3

HACKNEY RD

PORTRUSH

St Peters

2

Magill

Hindmarsh

RD

North
Adelaide

PAYNEHAM

MAGILL

OLD NORTON

Fulham
Gardens

Thebarton

River

KING WILLIAM RD

TCE

Norwood

MAGILL

NORTON SUMMIT

Torrens

NORTH

TCE

1.5

KENSINGTON

3

NORTON SUMMIT

HENLEY   BEACH   RD

WEST TCE

GROTE ST

WAKEFIELD ST

WAKEFIELD RD

Wattle
Park

River

BURBRIDGE

Richmond

SOUTH

TCE

ADELAIDE

GREENHILL

Burnside

Keswick

GOODWOOD RD

GREENHILL RD

2 FULLARTON ROAD

GREENHILL RD

Fish

Second

GREENHILL

Creek

ADELAIDE
AIRPORT

ANZAC HWY

UNLEY RD

Parkside

GLEN OSMOND RD

3

ROAD

3

CLELAND
CONSERVATION
PARK

Netley

Malvern

GLEN OSMOND

1

ROAD

Plympton

CROSS

ANZAC

Cumberland
Park

CROSS

BELAIR

Netherby

PRINCES

MOUNT BARKER RD

1 HWY

Glenelg

TO MURRAY BRIDGE

A B C D E F G H I

283

1 2 3 4 5 6 7 8 9 10 11 12 13

Thick roads represent recommended approach and bypass routes

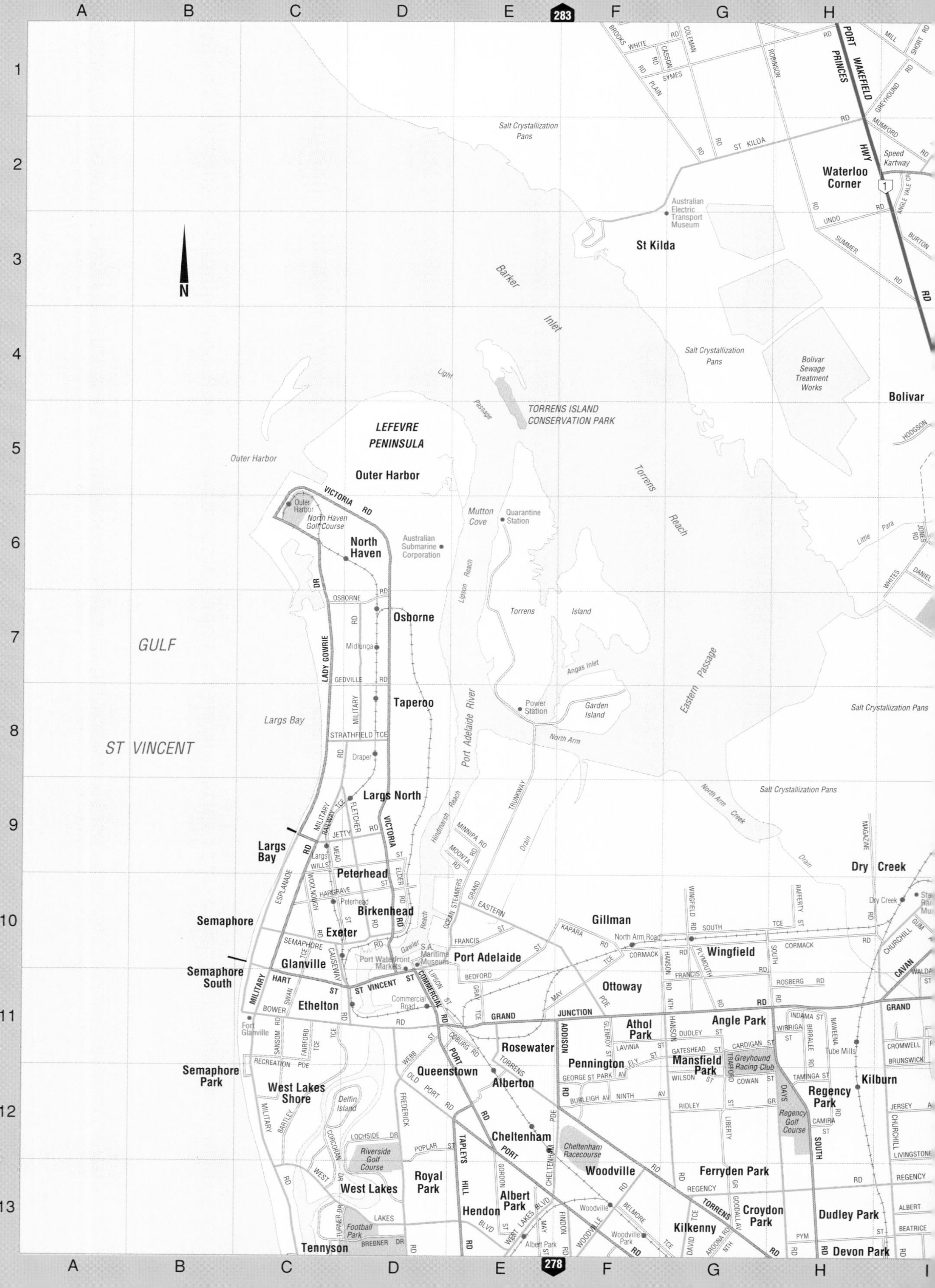

A B C D E 283 F G H

1
2
3

N

Salt Crystallization Pans

ST KILDA

Australian Electric Transport Museum

St Kilda

Waterloo Corner

Barker Inlet

Torrens Island Conservation Park

Bolivar Sewage Treatment Works

Bolivar

LEFEVRE PENINSULA

Outer Harbor

Outer Harbor

Light Passage

Mutton Cove

Quarantine Station

Torrens Reach

North Haven Golf Course

North Haven

Australian Submarine Corporation

Lipson Reach

Torrens Island

GULF

Osborne

Midlunga

Angas Inlet

Eastern Passage

Salt Crystallization Pans

Taperoo

ST VINCENT

Largs Bay

Power Station

Garden Island

North Arm

Strathfield TCE

Draper

Port Adelaide River

North Arm Creek

Salt Crystallization Pans

Largs North

Hindmarsh Reach

Minnipa Rd

Moonta

Drain

Dry Creek

Largs Bay

Jetty

Victoria

Peterhead

Hargrave

Birkenhead

Ocean Steamers

Eastern

Gillman

Wingfield

Semaphore

Exeter

Semaphore

Port Waterfront Markets

S.A. Maritime Museum

Port Adelaide

Kapara

North Arm Road

Cormack

Ottoway

Semaphore South

Glanville

Causeway

Gawler

Bedford

Gray

St Vincent

Commercial

Ethelton

Commercial Road

Grand

Junction

Athol Park

Angle Park

Dry Creek

Kilburn

Fort Glanville

Bower

Rosewater

Pennington

Mansfield Park

Semaphore Park

West Lakes Shore

Delfin Island

Queenstown

Alberton

Cheltenham

Cheltenham Racecourse

Woodville

Ferryden Park

Regency Park

Regency Golf Course

Riverside Golf Course

Royal Park

West Lakes

Hendon

Albert Park

Woodville

Kilkenny

Croydon Park

Dudley Park

Tennyson

Football Park

Woodville Park

Devon Park

A B C D E 278 F G H

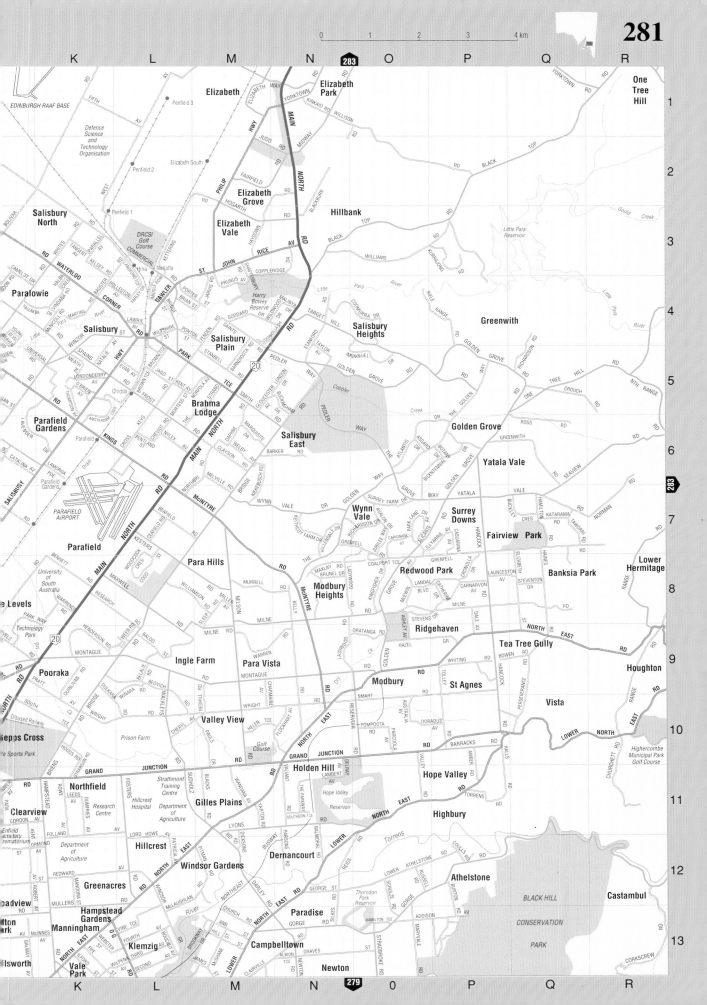

0 1 2 3 4 km

K L M N O P Q R

EDINBURGH RAAF BASE

Defence Science and Technology Organisation

Penfield 3
Elizabeth South
Penfield 2
Penfield 1

Elizabeth
Elizabeth Park

Yorktown

One Tree Hill

Hillbank

Salisbury North

DRCSI Golf Course

Paralowie

Elizabeth Grove
Elizabeth Vale

Little Para Reservoir

Gould Creek

Salisbury

Salisbury Plain

Harry Bowey Reserve

Salisbury Heights

Greenwith

Parafield Gardens

Brahma Lodge

Cobbler Creek

Salisbury East

Golden Grove

Yatala Vale

PARAFIELD AIRPORT

Parafield

Wynn Vale

Surrey Downs

Fairview Park

Banksia Park

Lower Hermitage

Para Hills

Modbury Heights

Redwood Park

Levels

University of South Australia

Technology Park

Ingle Farm

Para Vista

Ridgehaven

Tea Tree Gully

Houghton

Pooraka

Modbury

St Agnes

Vista

Valley View

Golf Course

Prison Farm

Grand Junction

Holden Hill

Hope Valley

Highercombe Municipal Park Golf Course

eps Cross

Sports Park

Northfield

Strathmont Training Centre

Hillcrest Hospital

Department of Agriculture

Gilles Plains

Hope Valley Reservoir

Highbury

Clearview

Enfield Cemetery Crematorium

Research Centre

Department of Agriculture

Hillcrest

Windsor Gardens

Dernancourt

Torrens

Athelstone

Castambul

adview

Greenacres

Hampstead Gardens

Manningham

Klemzig

Paradise

Thorndon Park Reservoir

BLACK HILL CONSERVATION PARK

ton rk

Vale Park

Campbelltown

Newton

1
2
3
4
5
6
7
8
9
10
11
12
13

K L M N O P Q R

A B C D E **289** F G H

1
2
3
4
5
6
7
8
9
10
11
12
13

TO PO

Moonta Bay
Moonta Bay
Port Hughes
Moonta
Tiparra Bay
Mining Ruins
Yelta
15
Cunliffe
Paskeville
13
Kulpara
Melton
14
10
Port Arthur
49
Port Wakef
18
Kainton
17
18
Agery
Sunnyvale
21
Clinton Centre
Clinton
CON PARK
Cape Elizabeth
16
7
5
Port Clinton
Sandy Po
35
50
Weetulta
23
Price
Mangrove Point
Tiparra West
Arthurton
Winulta
14
15

Balgowan
Dowlingville
24
Petersville
Macs Beach
Chinamen Wells
Reef Point
Maitland
13
24
Cunningham
Pt Pierce Mission
South Kilkerran
11
Ardrossan
Island Point
9
8
GOOSE ISLAND CON PARK
Green Island
Port Victoria
Point Pearce
16
Yorke Valley
13
Underwater Maritime Heritage Trail
Bird Point
Wardang Island
Port Victoria
Sandilands
18
Point Gawler
Urania
11
Muloowurtie Point
Cliff Point
Renowden Rocks

SPENCER

GULF

18
12
Pine Point
Port Alfred
Wauraltee
13
Black Point
YORKE
48
42
MT BAT
Koolywurtie
Port Julia
PENINSULA
44
14
Port Rickaby
16
Curramulka
6
Mulbura Park Flora Res
16
Barker Rocks
18
11
Ramsay Park Fauna Res
Bluff Beach
Minlaton
Port Vincent
Butler Memorial
11
Surveyor Point

ST VI

G

Hardwicke Bay
Port Minlacowie
14
26
Brentwood
18
LEVEN BEACH CON PARK
Galway Bay
Hardwicke Bay
Stansbury
Burners Beach
Point Souttar
ROGERS CORNER
Stansbury "School House" Museum
Corny Point
Dany Beach
31
Oyster Point
West Beach
Greig Lookout
3
Point Turton
18
873
37
Berry Bay
Corny Point
24
Weaver Lagoon
Kleins Point
Point Annie
16
8
CARRIBIE CON PARK
18
Warooka
7
Oaklands
21
Wool Bay
Gleesons Landing
9
21
Daly Head Blowhole
20
Yorketown
Formby Bay
16
Coobowie
15
Giles Point
Constance Bay
Point Margaret
41
18
Lake Fowler
15
Salt Creek Bay
Edithburgh
District Maritime Museum
Gym Beach
MOOROWIE
Sultana Point
Browns Beach
Diamond Lake
Wattle Point
TROUBRIDGE ISLAND CONSERVATION PARK
Royston Head
Chain of Lakes
10
2
Sheoak Beach
Royston Island
Spider Lake
31
Point Yorke
Goldsmiths Beach
Middle Island
Marion Bay
Lookout
Lookout
HONITON
Troubridge Point
Pondalowie Bay
Snow Lake
Hillock Point
Point Davenport
INNES NATIONAL PARK
Deep Lake
Inneston Historic Site
6
Penguin Point
Marion Bay
Sturt Bay
Point Gilbert
West Cape
Rhino Head
POINT DAVENPORT CONSERVATION PARK
Pondalowie Bay
Stenhouse Bay
Waterloo Bay
The Ethel (Shipwreck)
Cable Hut Bay
Chinamans Hat Island
Foul Bay
Reef Head
Cape Spencer
Haystack Island
ALTHORPE ISLANDS CONSERVATION PARK
Seal Island

INVESTIGATOR   **STRAIT**

KANGAROO

ISLAND

Cape Jervis Lighthouse
Mt Marsden 182m
Point Marsden
Cape Jervis
Daswood Bay
Smith Bay
Cape D'Estaing
Emu Bay
Cape Rouge
Kangaroo Island Ferries
Cape Cassini
Emu Bay
Bay Of Shoals
19
Knob Point
BACKSTAIRS
Stokes Bay
7
Stokes Bay
27
17
Kingscote
Cape Dutton
LATHAMI CP
Cygnet River
12
Kangaroo Head
AMEN CORNER
Cygnet River
Penneshaw
Nepean Bay

Vehicular Ferry Port Adelaide to Kingscote
Passenger Ferry Glenelg to Kingscote

A B C D E **288** F G H

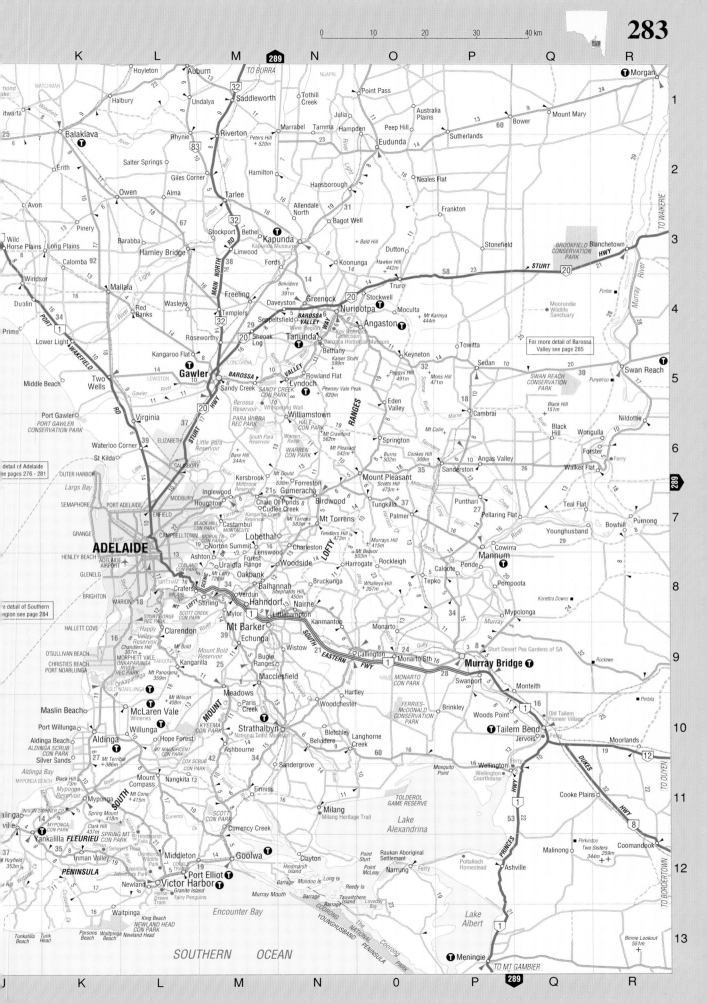

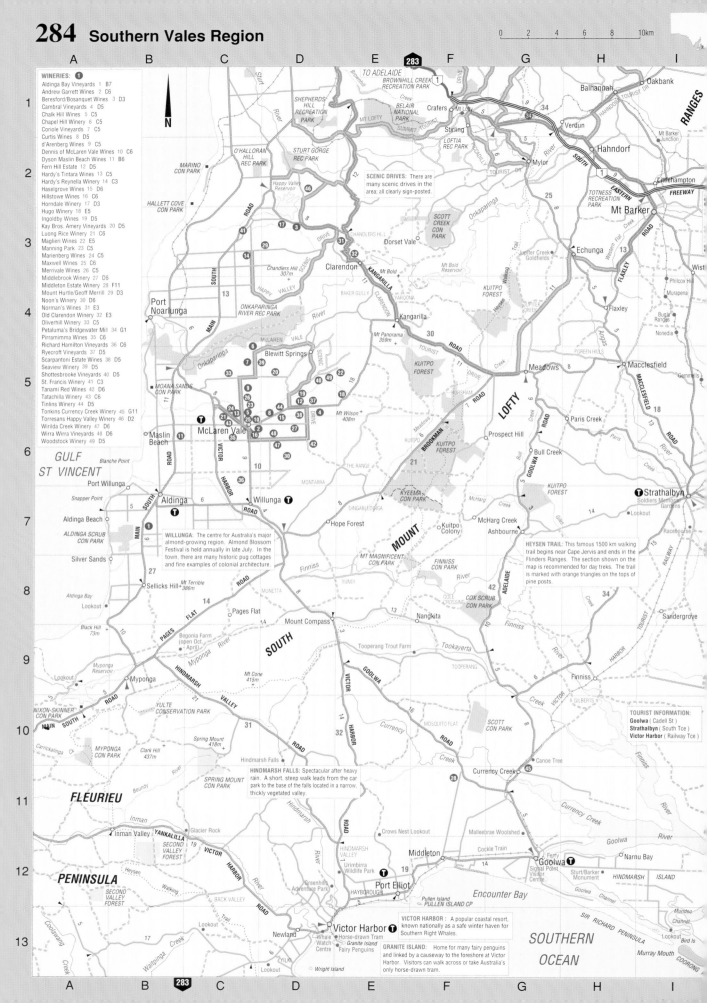

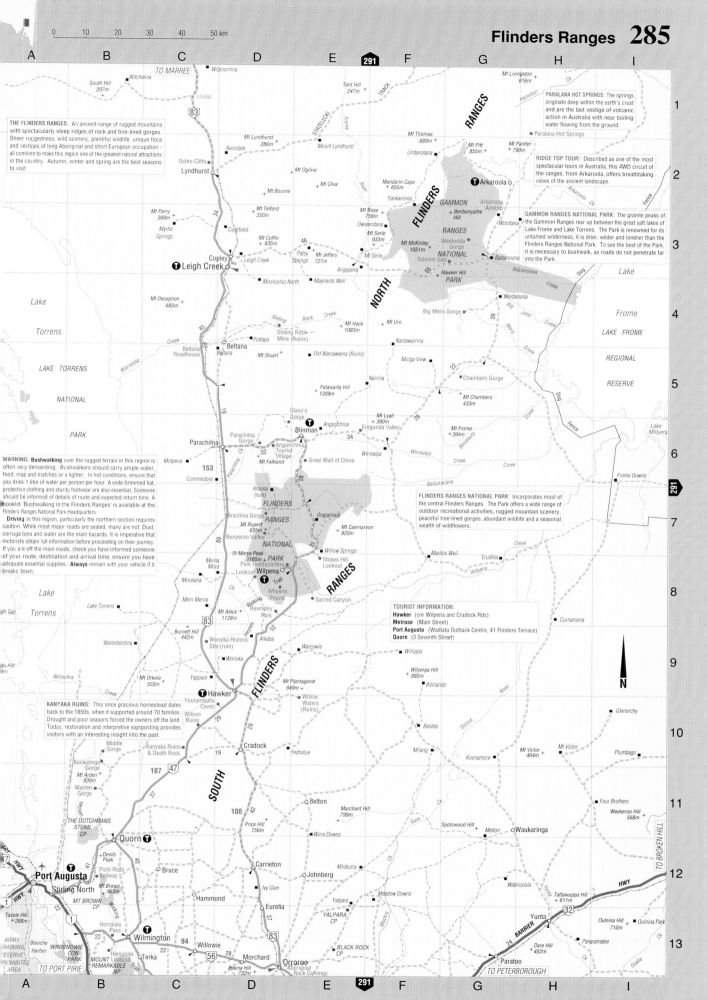

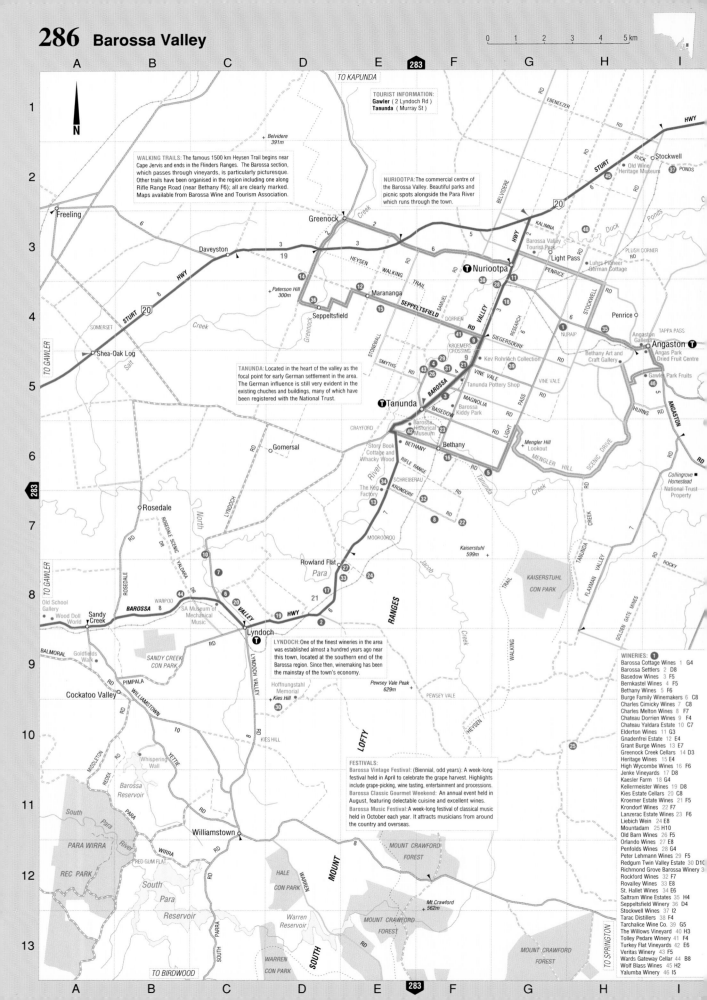

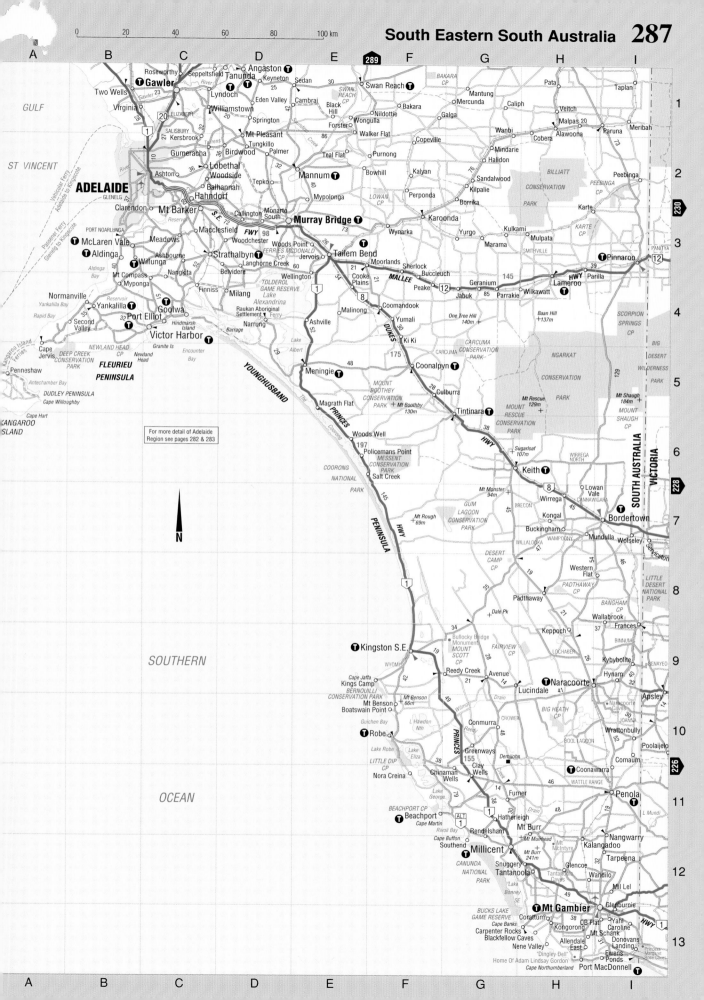

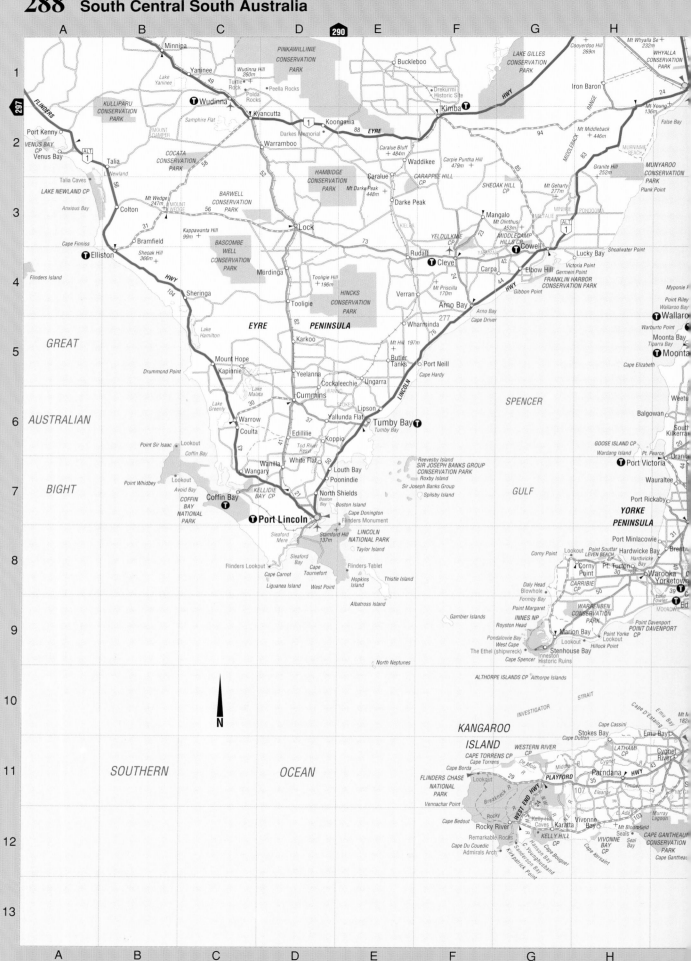

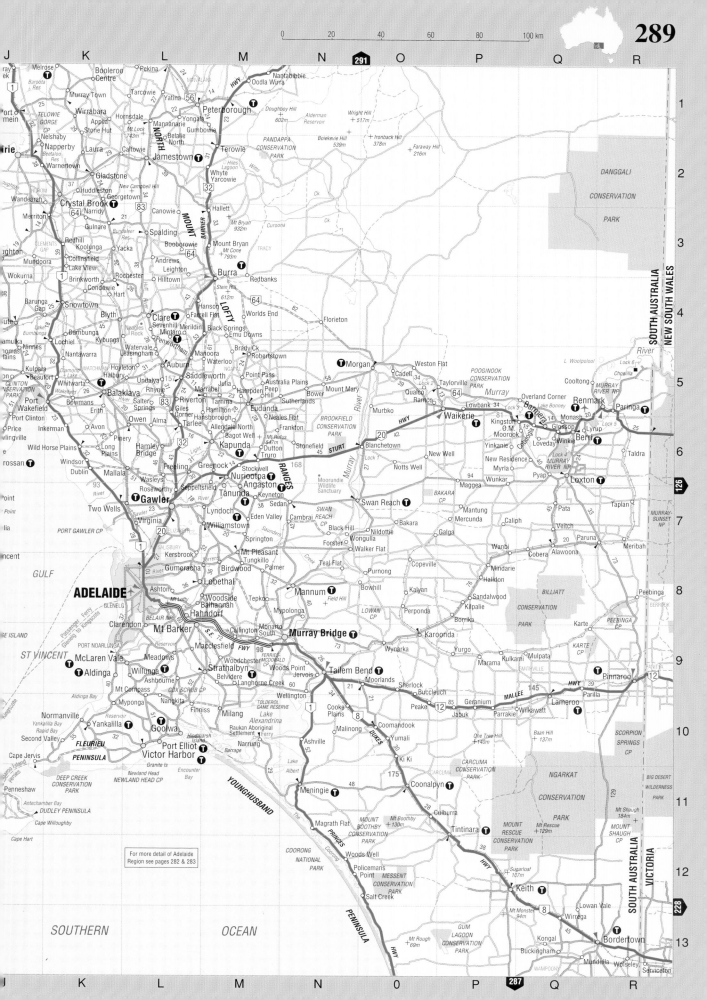

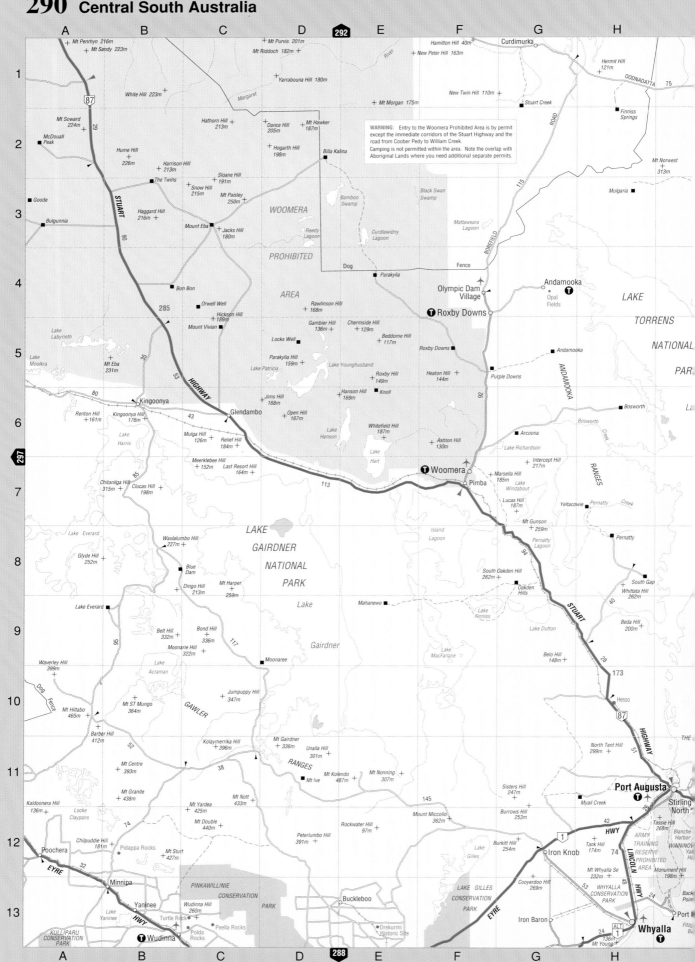

WARNING: Entry to the Woomera Prohibited Area is by permit except the immediate corridors of the Stuart Highway and the road from Coober Pedy to William Creek.
Camping is not permitted within the area. Note the overlap with Aboriginal Lands where you need additional separate permits.

0 20 40 60 80 100 km

J K L M N 293 O P Q R

WARNING: In outback Australia, long distances separate some towns. Travellers should familiarise themselves with prevailing conditions before departure, and take care to ensure their vehicle is roadworthy and that they carry adequate supplies of petrol, water and food.

In northern Australia, rainfall during the 'wet' season (Oct-March) can make some roads impassable. Full information on road conditions should be obtained before departure.

If visitors intend diverting off public roads within Aboriginal Land areas, a permit is required from the relevant Aboriginal authority.

STRZELECKI REGIONAL RESERVE

Mount Hopeless

Lake Callabonna

1

indowdna

195

Macdonnell

Creek

Prospect Hill
+ 218m

Winnathee

2

83

Wilpoorinna

Farina (ruin)

79

Dog

Creek

Fence

Mt Gardiner
+ 374m

Mt Babbage
+ 369m

Mt Livingston
616m

Moolawatana

Creek

Boolkaree

Yandama

Creek

Hawker Gate House

Mount Freeling

Tent Hill
247m +

Mt Fitton

Mt Neil
+ 571m

Smithville House

3

Hill

Lyndhurst

Mt Lyndhurst
286m +

Avondale

Mount Lyndhurst

STRZELECKI TRACK

FLINDERS RANGES

Paralana Hot Springs

Mt Ritt
855m +

Mt Painter
790m

Dog

Fence

Wallace Ck

39

Mt Coffin
835m +

Mandarin Caps
655m +

GAMMON

Mt Mckinlay
1051m +

Mt Serle
933m +

Arkaroola

Wooltana

Westootla Gorge

Turleys Gate

Starvation Lake

4

Copley

Leigh Creek

Mt Jeffery
727m +

RANGES

NATIONAL

Balcanoona

LAKE FROME REGIONAL RESERVE

Packsaddle Ck

272

Leigh Creek

Maynards Well

NORTH

PARK

Pine View

5

Mt Deception
+ 685m

Beltana Roadhouse

Beltana

Beltana

Sliding Rock Mine (Ruins)

Mt Hack
+ 1083m

Old Warraween A (Ruins)

Lake Frome

Lake Culberta

Boughams Gate

65

Patawarta Hill
1009m +

Narrina

Chambers Gorge

Mt Chambers
+ 433m

Lake Karpi

Lake Carnanto

Teilta

6

Parachilna

32

Blinman

Angorichina Tourist Village

Great Wall of China

Wirrealpa

For more detail of Flinders Ranges see page 285

Lake Tarkarooloo

Lake Millyera

Dog

Fence

Eurinilla Ck

124

tpena

Commodore

59

FLINDERS RANGES

Oraparinna

Frome Downs

Lake Moko

Lake Namba

Lake Yentaawena

Morphens Ck

SOUTH AUSTRALIA

NEW SOUTH WALES

7

Mt Rupert
655m +

Mt Caernarvon
920m +

Reaphook Hill
388m +

Creek

Benagerie

8

Moralana

Wilpena

NATIONAL PARK

RANGES

Lookout

Martins Well

Wilpena

Erudina

Curnamona

Mooleulooloo

Mulyungarie

Creek

MUNDI MUNDI PLAIN

Wilpena Pound

Rawnsley Park

83

Burnett Hill
442m +

Mt Aleck
1128m

52

Arkaba

Wonoka Historic Site (ruin)

FLINDERS

Mt Plantagenet
949m +

Willippa

Wilyerpa Hill
880m +

Bibliando

Killawarra

Old Telechie

Umberumberka Reservoir

Ghost Town

9

Hawker

Yourambulla Caves

RANGES

Willow Waters (Ruins)

Baratta

River

Siccus

Mt Victor
+ 464m

Bimbowrie

Donatra Creek

Wompinie

10

Hut Hill
618m

107

47

Cradock

Mt Plumbago

Outalpa Hill
496m +

Outalpa

HIGHWAY

32

68

Tepco

Mingary

Cockburn

SOUTH

71

Belton

Marchant Hill
799m +

Wirra Downs

Spotswood Hill

Waukaringa

Weekeroo Hill
568m +

Weekeroo

Wiawera Ck

223

Olary

81

Aroona

Ballara

11

Carrieton

Johnberg

Ivy Glen

37

Eurelia

Meadow Downs

Yalpara

Mannahill

Tattawuppa Hill
+ 611m

Yunta

Oulnina

Wadnaminga

Maldorky Hill
428m +

Browns Hill
152m

Mutooroo

Burta

12

Hammond

56

Willowie

50

Morchard

Price Hill
756m +

83

Orroroo

Pekina Hill
732m

72

BARRIER

74

Paratoo

Dare Hill
452m

Oulnina Hill
710m +

Oulnina Park

Oulnina Ck

BENDA RANGE

Ocalta Ck

West Ck

126

ton

Melrose

Booleroo

Pekina

Black Rock

24

Dawson

Nackara Hill
661m +

Nantabibbie

Nackara

MINVALARA

Oodla Wirra

13

Booleroo Centre

Tarcowie

Yatina

56

14

UCOLTA

Peterborough

Doughboy Hill
602m +

Alderman Reservoir

Wright Hill
517m

DANGGALI CONSERVATION PARK

Murray Town

Wirrabara

Appila

Stone Hut

Hornsdale

23

Yongala

Mannanarie

Mt Lock
743m +

Gumbowie

Belalie North

Boiekevie Hill
539m +

Ironback Hill
+ 378m

K L M 289 N O P Q R

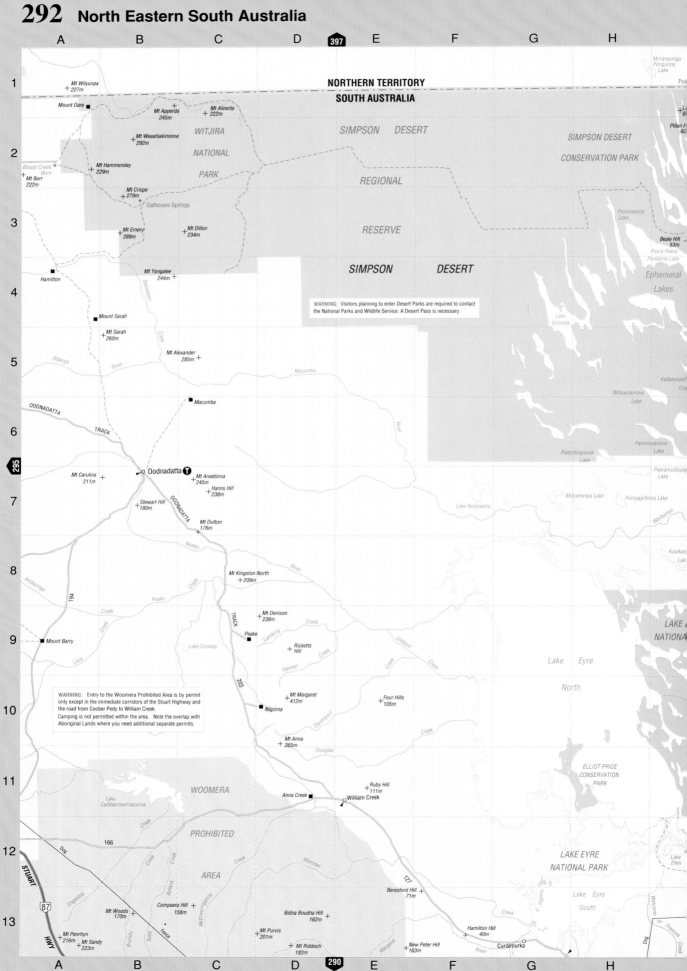

A B C D **397** E F G H

NORTHERN TERRITORY
SOUTH AUSTRALIA

Mirranponga
Pongunna
Lake

1
Mt Wilyunpa
+ 227m
Po

Mount Dare ■
Mt Apperda
+ 245m
Mt Alinerta
+ 222m
Pillan H
60

SIMPSON DESERT

WITJIRA
Mt Weeahiakiminne
+ 292m

SIMPSON DESERT

2
Blood Creek
Bore
Mt Hammersley
+ 229m
NATIONAL
CONSERVATION PARK

Mt Barr
222m

PARK
REGIONAL
Poolowanna
Lake

Mt Crispe
+ 279m

Dalhousie Springs
Beale Hill
53m

3
RESERVE
Peera Peera
Poolanna Lake

Mt Emery
+ 289m
Mt Dillon
+ 234m

SIMPSON
DESERT
Ephemeral

Lakes

Mt Yangalee
+ 244m

4
Hamilton ■
Lake
Griselda

WARNING: Visitors planning to enter Desert Parks are required to contact
the National Parks and Wildlife Service. A Desert Pass is necessary.

Mount Sarah ■

Kallakoopa
Cre

Mt Sarah
+ 260m

5
Mt Alexander
+ 285m
Macumba
Willawlianina
Lake

Alberga
River

Oodnadatta
Macumba ■
River
Pantoowarinna
Lake

6
TRACK
Pialpotingoona
Lake
Peeramudiaye
Lake

295
Mt Carulina
+ 211m
Oodnadatta T
Mt Areebinna
+ 245m
Milryeewilpa Lake
Pompapillina Lake

7
Hanns Hill
+ 238m
Lake Noolyeana

Stewart Hill
+ 180m
OODNADATTA
Warburton

Mt Dutton
+ 176m

8
Neales
Mt Kingston North
+ 209m
River
Koolkoe
Lak

Arckaringa
Creek
Peake

194
Creek
TRACK
Mt Denison
+ 238m
Creek
LAKE
NATIONA

9
Lora
Creek
Peake ■
Ricketts
+ Hill
Creek
Umbum
Creek
Lake Eyre

Lake Conway
Lambing
Creek

Mount Barry ■
Hawker
North

203

10
WARNING: Entry to the Woomera Prohibited Area is by permit
only except in the immediate corridors of the Stuart Highway and
the road from Coober Pedy to William Creek.
Camping is not permitted within the area. Note the overlap with
Aboriginal Lands where you need additional separate permits.
Nilpinna ■
Mt Margaret
+ 412m
Four Hills
+ 105m
Davenport

Mt Anna
+ 265m
Douglas
Creek

11
WOOMERA
ELLIOT PRICE
CONSERVATION
PARK

Lake
Cadibarrawirracanna
Ruby Hill
+ 111m

Anna Creek ■
William Creek

Creek

PROHIBITED

12
166
Lake Eyre
Lake
Ellen

Dog
Creek
Warriner
Creek
LAKE EYRE

STUART
AREA
NATIONAL PARK

Ballaria
Creek
127

13
Beresford Hill
+ 71m
Lake Eyre

87
Compeera Hill
+ 158m
South

HWY
Mt Woods
+ 170m
Bidna Boudna Hill
+ 162m
Hamilton Hill
+ 40m
Welcome

Mt Penrhyn
+ 216m Mt Sandy
+ 223m
Mt Purvis
+ 201m
New Peter Hill
+ 163m
Curdimurka
or Frances

Engenina
Fence
Mt Riddoch
+ 182m
Margaret
River

A B C D **290** E F G H

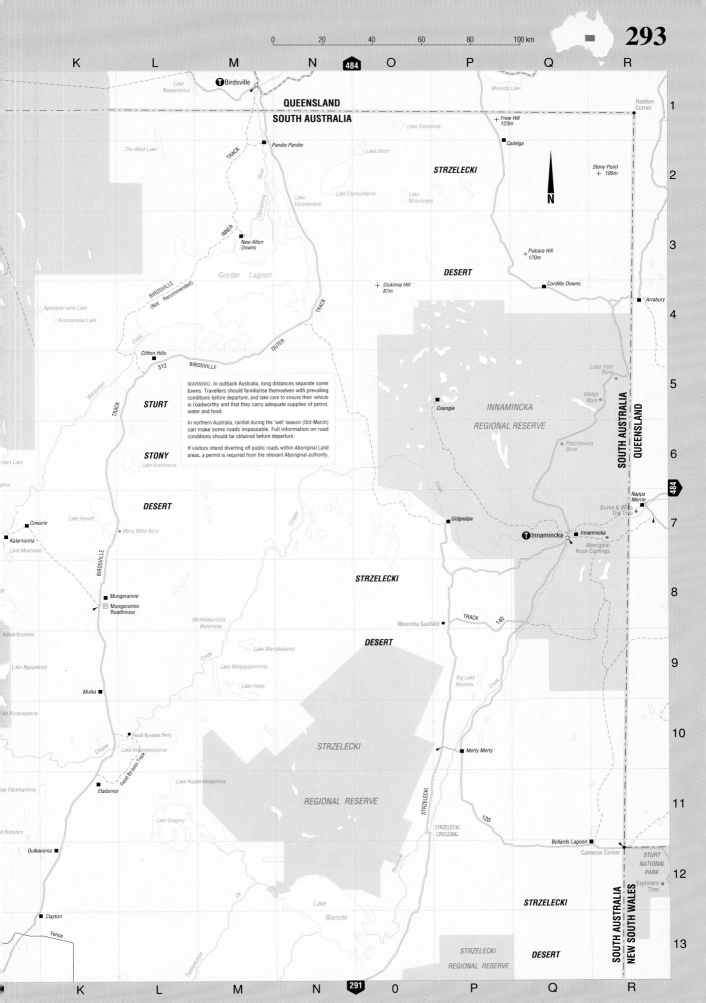

0   20   40   60   80   100 km

QUEENSLAND
SOUTH AUSTRALIA

T Birdsville
Lake Nappanerica

The West Lake

Pandie Pandie

Lake Coolnnie

Lake Short

STRZELECKI

Frew Hill
123m

Cadelga

Haddon
Corner

Stony Point
195m

N

Lake Etamunbanie

Lake Moorayepe

Lake Uloowaranie

INNER

New Alton
Downs

DESERT

Pulcara Hill
170m

Goyder   Lagoon

Dickinna Hill
87m

Cordillo Downs

Arrabury

BIRDSVILLE
(Not Recommended)

OUTER

Apawyilarranie Lake

Koomarinna Lake

Clifton Hills

312

BIRDSVILLE

Leap Year
Bore

Mulga
Bore

WARNING: In outback Australia, long distances separate some
towns. Travellers should familiarise themselves with prevailing
conditions before departure, and take care to ensure their vehicle
is roadworthy and that they carry adequate supplies of petrol,
water and food.

In northern Australia, rainfall during the "wet" season (Oct-March)
can make some roads impassable. Full information on road
conditions should be obtained before departure.

If visitors intend diverting off public roads within Aboriginal Land
areas, a permit is required from the relevant Aboriginal authority.

STURT

STONY

Lake Koodnanie

Coongie

INNAMINCKA

REGIONAL RESERVE

Patchawara
Bore

SOUTH AUSTRALIA
QUEENSLAND

484

DESERT

Lake Howitt

Mirra Mitta Bore

Cowarie

Kalamurina

Lake Miamiana

Gidgealpa

Nappa
Merrie

Burke & Wills
Dig Tree

T Innamincka
Innamincka
Aboriginal
Rock Carvings

BIRDSVILLE

STRZELECKI

Mungerannie
Mungerannie
Roadhouse

Winthekarrinna
Waterhole

Moomba Gasfield

TRACK   140

DESERT

Lake Warrakalanna

Lake Walpayapeninna

Lake Hope

Big Lake
Moomba

Lake Ngapakaldi

Mulka

Flood By-pass Ferry
Lake Kilamperpunna

STRZELECKI

Merty Merty

Flood By-pass Track

Lake Palankarinna

Etadunna

Lake Kopperekoppinna

REGIONAL   RESERVE

STRZELECKI

Lake Gregory

120

STRZELECKI
CROSSING

Bollards Lagoon

Cameron Corner

SOUTH AUSTRALIA
NEW SOUTH WALES

Dulkaninna

STURT
NATIONAL
PARK

Explorers
Tree

Clayton

Fence

STRZELECKI

Lake
Blanche

DESERT

STRZELECKI
REGIONAL RESERVE

1 2 3 4 5 6 7 8 9 10 11 12 13

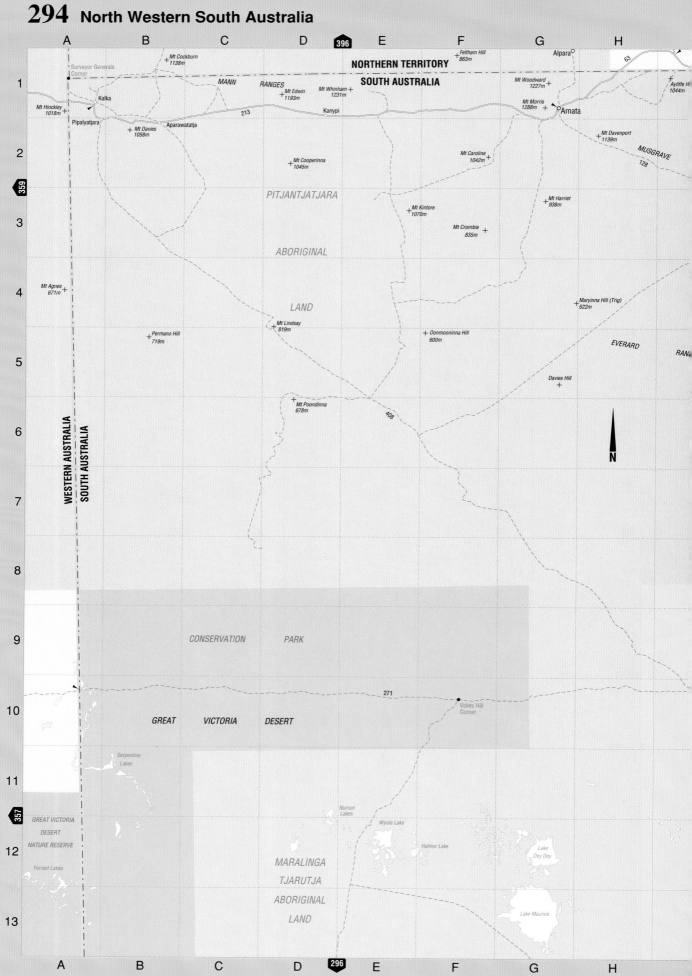

A B C D 396 E F G H

63

Surveyor Generals
Corner

NORTHERN TERRITORY
SOUTH AUSTRALIA

+ Mt Cockburn
1138m

Feltham Hill
863m

Alpara

1

+ Mt Hinckley
1018m

Kalka

MANN RANGES

+ Mt Edwin
1193m

+ Mt Whinham
1231m

Mt Woodward
1227m

Ayliffe H
1044m

Pipalyatjara

+ Mt Davies
1058m

Aparawatatja

213

Kanypi

Mt Morris
1288m

Amata

2

+ Mt Cooperinna
1045m

Mt Caroline
1042m

+ Mt Davenport
1139m

MUSGRAVE

128

359

PITJANTJATJARA

Mt Kintore
1070m

Mt Harriet
938m

3

ABORIGINAL

Mt Crombie
835m

4

+ Mt Agnes
671m

LAND

Mt Lindsay
819m

Oonmooninna Hill
600m

Maryinna Hill (Trig)
622m

EVERARD

RAN

5

+ Permano Hill
719m

Davies Hill

6

+ Mt Poondinna
678m

408

N

7

8

9

CONSERVATION PARK

271

Vokes Hill
Corner

10

GREAT VICTORIA DESERT

11

Serpentine
Lakes

357

GREAT VICTORIA
DESERT
NATURE RESERVE

Nurrari
Lakes

Wyola Lake

Halinor Lake

Lake
Dey Dey

12

Forrest Lakes

MARALINGA
TJARUTJA
ABORIGINAL

Lake Maurice

13

LAND

A B C D 296 E F G H

NORTHERN TERRITORY

SOUTH AUSTRALIA

J K L M N O P Q R

396 **397**

Victory Downs
Sentinel Hill 910m
24 Mount Cavenagh
Victory Downs

Mt Cecil 551m

Mt Darling 544m
Mt Parlue 478m
Mt Mead 376m
Mt Hearne 306m

Tieyon

Mt Howe 519m

Mt Warrabillinna 1125m

PITJANTJATJARA

ABORIGINAL

LAND

Echo Hill 604m

Eringa
Mt Barr 222m

Marryat

Creek

117

STUART

Mt Britton 334m

Hamilton

Creek

Marble Hill 523m

143

Mimili

Mt Illbillee 917m

Chandler
Mt Chandler 551m

Alberga

Lambina (ruin)

River

EVERARD RANGE

44

HIGHWAY

Todmorden

192

OODNADATTA

TRACK

Marla

Mintabie

Welbourn Hill

87

CENTRAL

Neales

River

Ammaroodinna Hill 359m

83

Wintinna

Arckaringa

AUSTRALIAN

292

Mt Arckaringa 243m

172

Cadney Homestead

Mount Willoughby

Arckaringa

Creek

Evelyn

MARALINGA

TJARUTJA

ABORIGINAL

LAND

RAILWAY

Evelyn Downs

Mount Barry

Creek

Lora

Creek

Pootnoura

Pootnoura

Creek

153

Algebullcullia

Woorong

JUNCTION

TALLARINGA

CONSERVATION

PARK

Dog

Fence

STUART

Giddi-giddinna

Creek

Oolgelima

Ck

265

Manguri

Creek

Long

WOOMERA

Coober Pedy

PROHIBITED

HIGHWAY

Mabel

Creek

WARNING: Entry to the Woomera Prohibited Area is by permit only except in the immediate corridors of the Stuart Highway and the road from Coober Pedy to William Creek.
Camping is not permitted within the area. Note the overlap with Aboriginal Lands where you need additional separate permits.

AREA

Dog

Fence

Wilkinson Lakes

Lake Phillipson

Wirrida

87

Mt Penrhyn 216m

1
2
3
4
5
6
7
8
9
10
11
12
13

0 20 40 60 80 100 km

K L M N O P Q R

297

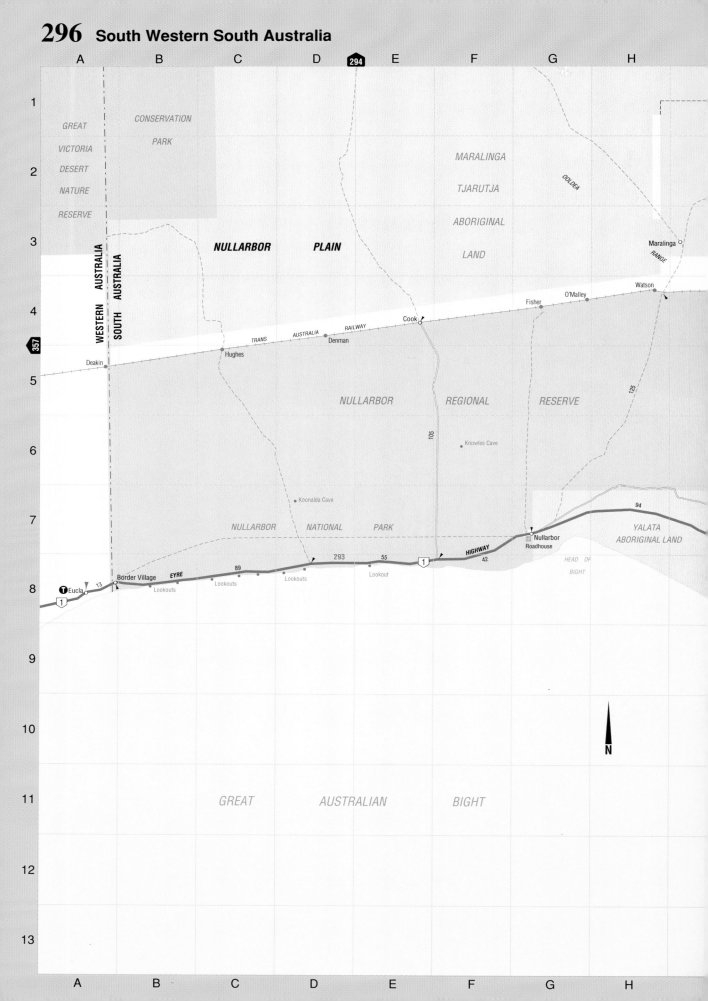

A B C **294** E F G H

1

GREAT

CONSERVATION
VICTORIA

PARK
DESERT

MARALINGA
2
NATURE

TJARUTJA
OOLDEA
RESERVE

ABORIGINAL

3 **NULLARBOR PLAIN** LAND
Maralinga
RANGE

Watson
O'Malley
4 Fisher
WESTERN AUSTRALIA
SOUTH AUSTRALIA
Cook

357 Denman
TRANS AUSTRALIA RAILWAY
Hughes
Deakin
5
125
NULLARBOR REGIONAL RESERVE

105
6 Knowles Cave

Koonalda Cave
7
94
NULLARBOR NATIONAL PARK YALATA
Nullarbor ABORIGINAL LAND
HIGHWAY Roadhouse
293 HEAD OF
55
89 **1** 42 BIGHT
8 Eucla 13 Border Village EYRE Lookout
Lookouts Lookouts Lookouts
1

9

10
N

11 GREAT AUSTRALIAN BIGHT

12

13

A B C D E F G H

Western Australia

The Golden West

Even a casual glance at a map of Australia will quickly reveal that a motor touring holiday in Western Australia requires a great deal of thought and advance planning. For one thing, just getting there from the eastern States involves travelling huge distances, so fly/drive or MotoRail facilities are well worth investigation; and, given that it is almost one-third the size of the whole of Australia, unless you have unlimited time and energy, touring by road will only get you to certain sections. The south-west region is relatively easily and pleasantly covered by car, but to travel the unique north and north-east requires more time and careful planning.

The vast distances to be covered are such that it is worth considering some touring by air when planning your itinerary and budget. The major airlines operate tours, varying in length, to all the spectacular remote regions. There is a network of almost 100 heritage trails across the State, each designed by the local community. Once you have settled your method of travel, you will find an amazing State waiting to be explored.

Despite the fact that the Dutch had mapped the western coastline of Australia as early as the sixteenth century, it was not until 1826 that a British party from Sydney landed at King George Sound (Albany) and then only for fear of possible French colonisation. Three years later Perth, the first non-convict settlement in the country, was founded by Captain James Stirling. Due mainly to the ruggedness and sheer size of the land, the West remained pretty much as it had always been until 1892, when gold was discovered at Coolgardie and the first economic boom for the region began. Today it is an immensely rich mineral State, its thriving economy still growing.

The beautiful city of Perth has the best climate of any Australian capital: midwinter average maximum temperature of 18°C, a year-round average of 23°C and an average of almost eight hours of sunshine a day. The climate in the north of the State is tropical, and as you travel south it becomes subtropical and then temperate.

It is easy to assume from the map that Perth is a coastal city, though it is 19 kilometres inland, up the broad and beautiful Swan River, home of the black swan. A city of over one million people, Perth is large enough to offer excitement and variety, yet compact enough to be seen quite easily. King's Park, 404 hectares of natural bushland, is only a short drive from the city centre, and nearby ocean beaches provide year-round swimming and surfing.

Once you start touring, the Swan Valley is a must, whether or not you are interested in wine. Up in the Darling Range the valley is fertile and beautiful and the vineyards flourish on the rich loam that is perfect for grape-growing. At the end of a day's drive you can sample some notable results of these conditions.

Nearby Rottnest Island is low, small, sandy and only 20 kilometres off the coast from Fremantle. Regular air and ferry services from Perth will take you to this popular holiday island, where even the surrounding sea has been declared a sanctuary. Conditions for skindiving could not be better.

The southern corner of this State, ablaze every spring with wildflowers, is aptly described as the garden of Western Australia. Hardwood forests of massive karri and jarrah trees soar above the hundreds of different species of wildflowers that bloom from September to November. Great surfing beaches and coastal panoramic views add to the attractions of the south-west region, with such popular locations as Margaret River, Busselton and Yallingup.

North-east of this well-vegetated corner, and 596 kilometres from Perth, is the one-time gold-boom area around Kalgoorlie–Boulder, surrounded by ghost towns such as Coolgardie and Broad Arrow. South of Kalgoorlie–Boulder the modern town of Kambalda owes its prosperity to nickel. Further east you reach the Nullarbor Plain; further north are the Great Victoria and Gibson Deserts.

Along the Brand Highway, 424 kilometres north of Perth, is Geraldton, situated between Western Australia's agricultural heartland and the beautiful coastline. Here you can sample freshly caught crays, and a little farther north you can see a range of flora and fauna in the Kalbarri National Park and explore the spectacular coastal gorges and cliffs.

The Pilbara region has some of the country's most spectacular gorges in Karijini (Hamersley Range) National Park. This is where Western Australia's second economic boom began, with the exploitation of the dramatic Hamersley Range, which is literally a mountain of iron. The Range stretches for 320 kilometres, yet from the air seems dwarfed by endless stretches of red sand. At the State's very top is the Kimberley region, with the spectacular King Leopold Range in the west and Purnululu (Bungle Bungle) National Park in the east. The region's economy is based on diamond mining, as well as the more traditional cattle industry, supported by the Ord River irrigation scheme. A visit to this remote, dramatic region with its gorges and rivers is a unique experience—in keeping with many areas of Australia's largest State.

Kangaroo paw, the floral emblem of Western Australia

Perth

A Friendly City

With a Mediterranean-type climate and a river setting, Perth is made for an outdoor lifestyle. Within easy reach of the city lie clean surf beaches, rolling hills, tranquil forests and well-kept parklands. The **Swan River** winds through Perth and suburbs, widening to lake size at Perth and Melville Waters; and the Canning River provides another attractive waterway through the southern suburbs.

The city centre, 19 kilometres upstream from the port of Fremantle, is on the Swan River and ringed by a series of gardens, parks and reserves, including the magnificent 404-hectare **Kings Park**. The green slopes of Mount Eliza in Kings Park contrast dramatically with Perth's skyline, and the serene blue hills of the Darling Range can be seen in the distance.

Perth was founded by Captain James Stirling in 1829, but the progress of the isolated Swan River Settlement, made up entirely of free settlers, was slow; it was not until the first shipment of convicts arrived in 1850 that the colony found its feet. The convicts were soon set to work building roads, bridges and fine public buildings, and in 1856 Perth was proclaimed a city. Gold discoveries in the State in the 1880s gave Perth another boost and the recent diamond finds in the Kimberley and the reopening of goldmines in the Kalgoorlie–Boulder region have stimulated new growth.

The capital has a population of just over 1.2 milion, many of whom live in the pleasant suburbs that stretch north and south. Perth is cosmopolitan, home to significant numbers of people born in Britain, New Zealand, Italy, the Netherlands, Malaysia, Vietnam and the Philippines, and there is a substantial Greek community. In addition, of a total Aboriginal population of 42 000 in the State, almost 12 000 live in the capital.

The city centre is compact, and easy to explore. Travel by bus or train within the city's **Free Transit Zone** (FTZ), day or night, seven days a week. A free ten-minute bus service, the City Clipper, circles the city during the day; other **Clipper** services connect the city with East and West Perth, and Northbridge.

Most of Perth's shops and arcades are in the blocks bounded by St Georges Terrace and William, Wellington and Barrack Streets, centring around **Hay Street Mall**, **Raine Square Shopping Plaza**, and **Murray Street Mall** and **Forrest Chase**. Perth's shopping and business area is linked by pedestrian malls, overpasses and underground walkways, enabling access unhampered by motor vehicles. Perth's unique **London Court**, an Elizabethan-style arcade, runs from Hay Street Mall to St Georges Terrace. At the Hay Street entrance, four knights on horseback joust above a replica of Big Ben every fifteen minutes, while St George and the Dragon do battle above the clock over the St Georges Terrace entrance. Perth's decorative **Town Hall** on the corner of Hay and Barrack Streets was built by convicts between 1869 and 1879.

Stately **St Georges Terrace**, Perth's financial and professional heart, is worth strolling down for its historic buildings, cheek by jowl with towering modern glass giants. Start at the western end, where you will see the mellow brickwork of **Barracks Arch** (all that remains of the Tudor-style Pensioner Barracks built in 1863) in front of **Parliament House**.

City view from Kings Park

Perth's historic Old Mill

When Parliament is not sitting, there are guided tours Monday to Friday.

Continuing along St Georges Terrace you reach the charming **Cloisters** (1858), a former boys' school that has been integrated with the modern complex behind. The ecclesiastical-looking building nearby is another former boys' school and now the National Trust headquarters. The **Palace Hotel**, a grand old Victorian iron-lace balconied hotel, has been modified as a banking chamber and forms an impressive exterior facade for Perth's second largest building, the Bankwest Tower. Further along the terrace is an ornate Victorian church—**Trinity Church Chapel**—and the arched entrance to London Court. The handsome **Treasury Building** on the corner of Barrack Street overlooks **Stirling Gardens**, part of the **Supreme Court Gardens** and a popular picnic spot for shoppers and city workers. **St George's Cathedral** and the **Deanery** are another two interesting old buildings at this end of St Georges Terrace. Tucked behind the imposing modern **Council House** on the opposite side is one of Perth's oldest buildings, the **Old Courthouse** (1836), and the turrets of the Gothic-style **Government House** in its lush private gardens.

Further along is the modern **Perth Concert Hall**, which seats 1900 and is used for everything from hard rock to opera. Inside, a restaurant, a tavern and a cocktail bar cater for music lovers.

Just north of the city centre in Northbridge is the attractive **Perth Cultural Centre** complex. Nationally and internationally renowned artworks are on display in the **Art Gallery of Western Australia**. Nearby is the **Alexander Library**, and the original Perth Gaol (1856) within the modern complex of the **Western Australian Museum**. A blue whale skeleton, Aboriginal artefacts and veteran and vintage cars are among the exhibits.

A visit to the Cultural Centre could be combined with a meal at one of the many reasonably priced restaurants in this area, as **Northbridge** is also the centre of the city's nightlife. Numerous hotels, nightclubs and piano bars offer live entertainment and dancing until dawn.

At the City West shopping complex in **West Perth** are the **Omni Theatre** and the award-winning **Scitech Discovery Centre**. The specially constructed theatre presents visitors with real adventure

Hotels
Burswood Resort Hotel
Great Eastern Hwy, Victoria Park
(09) 362 7777
Hilton Parmelia
14 Mill St, Perth
(09) 322 3622
Hyatt Regency
99 Adelaide Tce, Perth
(09) 225 1234
Sheraton
207 Adelaide Tce, Perth
(09) 325 0501

Family and Budget
All Seasons Freeway
55 Mill Point Rd, South Perth
(09) 367 7811

Jewell House Private Hotel (YMCA)
180 Goderich St, Perth
(09) 325 8488

Motel Groups: Bookings
Flag 13 2400
Best Western (008) 22 2166
Hospitality Inns (008) 99 8228
Quality Pacific (008) 09 0600
Travelodge (008) 22 2446

This list is for information only; inclusion is not necessarily a recommendation.

experiences, and the centre has a hands-on science and technology display.

Kings Park, just west of the city centre, is one of Perth's major attractions. Within this huge natural bushland reserve there are landscaped gardens and walkways, lakes, children's playgrounds, lookouts and the **Botanic Garden** on **Mount Eliza Bluff**, where a blaze of Western Australian wildflowers is to be seen in spring. You can drive by car through the park or hire a bicycle, stopping at the many scenic lookouts over the city and river; or you can wander on foot along the many walking trails right to the top of Mount Eliza.

Other city parks include **Hyde Park**, with its waterbirds, ornamental lake and English trees, and the beautiful **Queens Gardens**, with a replica of London's Peter Pan statue. Just outside the city centre is **Lake Monger**, a favourite picnic spot that is also the home of black swans, ducks and other varieties of birds. **Matilda Bay** offers grassed areas and ample shade, with stunning views of the Swan River and Perth city skyline. The **Swan River Estuary Marine Park** includes three areas at Alfred Cove, Pelican Point and Milyu, about halfway between the Narrows and Canning Bridges.

A pleasant way to visit **Perth's Zoo**, with its magnificent garden environment and nocturnal house, is to catch a ferry from the Barrack Street Jetty. The trip can be combined with a visit to the **Old Mill**, on the South Perth foreshore. This picturesque whitewashed windmill (1838) now houses an interesting collection of early colonial relics.

Further north along the coast at **Sorrento** is **Hillarys Boat Harbour**. A day can easily be spent here, enjoying the atmosphere and variety of Sorrento Quay or experiencing the thrill of **Underwater World**, where you are transported through a submerged acrylic tunnel on moving walkways to see the enormous variety of underwater life. From September to November, charter boats offer visits to see whales basking between Perth and **Rottnest Island**. **Carnac Island**, a nature reserve 15 kilometres off the coast near Perth, has a colony of sea lions and its main beach is accessible in daylight hours by private boat.

Swimming and surfing are part of the joy of Perth and several beautiful **Indian Ocean beaches**—including Cottesloe, Swanbourne (a nude bathing beach), Port, City, Scarborough and Trigg Island—are within easy reach of the city, and the sheltered **Swan River beaches** along Perth's riverside suburbs are even closer.

There are many other places of interest around Perth, including the historic port of **Fremantle**, which underwent a complete facelift in preparation for the America's Cup challenge. In Fremantle you can relive the past by strolling along the streets of terraced houses, or visiting the city's magnificent historic buildings and the many galleries, museums and craft workshops. **Cottesloe Civic Centre**, in Broome Street, Cottesloe, is one of Perth's showplaces and the magnificent grounds of this beautiful Spanish-style mansion are open during office hours. The **University of Western Australia**, with its Mediterranean-style

buildings and landscaped gardens in the riverside suburb of **Crawley**, is also worth seeing. The university's new **Fortune Theatre** has been built as a replica of Shakespeare's Fortune Theatre in Elizabethan London.

At nearby **Subiaco**, a popular shopping and market area an easy train ride from the city, you will find the Aboriginal art gallery **Indiginart**; there is another, the **Creative Native Gallery**, in King Street in the city. **Adventure World** in the southern suburb of **Bibra Lake** offers among its attractions a wildlife park, animal circus, rides and Australia's largest swimming-pool, and is open from October to April.

Perth's sporting facilities are excellent, with two racecourses, **Ascot** and **Belmont Park**; night pacing at **Gloucester Park** (the famous WACA cricket ground is near here); greyhound racing at **Cannington**; and speedcar and motorcycle racing at the **Claremont Showgrounds**. Major athletics meetings, rugby and soccer matches are held at **Perry Lakes Stadium** (built for the 1962 British Empire and Commonwealth Games), and Australian Rules football finals at **Subiaco Oval**. Hockey is played at the **Commonwealth Hockey Stadium**, the first Astroturf stadium in Australia. The **Superdrome** hosts many international sporting events.

By night, Perth offers a wide range of entertainment: the modern **Perth Entertainment Centre** (home of the Perth Wildcats basketball team), in Wellington Street, seats 8000. At the **Burswood Casino**, across the river at Rivervale, you can try your luck at the tables, or enjoy the five-star splendour of the hotel. Another resort complex is **Raddison Observation City Resort Hotel** on the coast at **Scarborough**. Perth offers an excellent range of accommodation to suit all requirements—from the many five-star hotels to convenient self-contained family accommodation and dozens of quality hotels and motels.

During February and March, the **Festival of Perth** combines the visual arts, theatre, music and film.

Kings Park

For further information on Perth and Western Australia, contact the Western Australian Tourist Centre, Albert Facey House, cnr Forrest Place and Wellington St, Perth; (09) 483 1111 or (008) 81 2808.

Tours from Perth

With the sparkling Indian Ocean surf beaches beckoning from the west, the peaceful Darling Range on the east and the Swan River meandering through Perth from Fremantle to the Swan Valley vineyards, there are many enjoyable trips within easy reach of Perth.

A delightful way to visit the vineyards is by river. Cruisers operate wine-tasting tours; the *Lady Houghton* and the *Miss Sandalford* leave Barrack Street Jetty. Refreshments are served on board, and lunch is served at Mulberry Farm. At Houghtons Winery you can tour the vineyard and sample a variety of wines.

Other cruises will take you to the historic riverside home Tranby. From Wednesday to Saturday nights, in season, you can have dinner aboard a vessel that leaves the Barrack Street Jetty in the early evening and returns at midnight.

There is a daily ferry service from the Barrack Street Jetty to Rottnest Island, Perth's popular hideaway and once the site of the infamous Rottnest Native Prison. **See**: Rottnest Island.

Travel to Adventure World on Transperth Route 600; buses depart Perth central bus station daily. Adventure World is open most weekends, and daily except Christmas Day and Good Friday, between October 1 and April 30. For more information contact the Western Australian Tourist Centre, Albert Facey House, cnr Forrest Place and Wellington St, Perth; (09) 483 1111 or (008) 81 2808.

Fremantle, 19 km from Perth via the Stirling or Canning Highways

A visit to this fascinating old port can make an interesting round trip by car if you return via the opposite side of the river. Fremantle is also easily accessible by bus, train and boat. **See also:** Entry in A–Z listing.

Historic Guildford in the Swan Valley, 18 km from Perth via Guildford Road or the Great Eastern Highway

This tour takes you near the vineyards of the Swan Valley, noted for their high-quality wines, to Guildford, one of the earliest settlements in the State. Many reminders of the colony's early days remain, including Woodbridge, a gracious, towered, two-storey mansion overlooking the river, beautifully restored and furnished by the National Trust. The Mechanics Hall in Meadow Street houses a folk museum, and a rail museum in the nearby suburb of Bassendean is also of interest. The Vines Resort, 15 km north of Guildford, has a world-class golf course and sporting and fitness facilities for guests. Whiteman Park, 7 km north of Guildford, has train and tram rides, a picnic area and the Trade Village, where trades people ply traditional skills.

Walyunga National Park, 35 km from Perth via Guildford Road and the Great Northern Highway

The Avon River flows swiftly through a narrow gorge of the Darling Range in this beautiful bushland park.

John Forrest National Park, 28 km from Perth on the Great Eastern Highway

This huge bushland park in the Darling Range is popular with tourists. Walking trails, streams, waterfalls and a safe swimming pool for children are among its attractions. At weekends enjoy a Devonshire tea at the old Mahogany Inn, built in 1837 and now the oldest licensed inn in Western Australia.

Mundaring Weir, 42 km from Perth via the Great Eastern Highway

This water catchment area, which provides water for the goldfields over 500 kilometres away, is surrounded by picnic areas. A visit to the O'Connor Museum will help you to understand the construction and operation of this complex water scheme. Kalamunda History Village is nearby.

Serpentine Dam, 54 km from Perth via the South Western Highway

The picnic grounds here overlook the Serpentine Dam, which is set among peaceful hills and beautiful landscaped gardens of wildflowers.

Pioneer World, Armadale, 29 km from Perth via the Albany Highway

Pioneer World is a reconstruction of the days of the gold rush when every town boasted a blacksmith and a coaching-house. Nearby is Araluen Botanic Park, a refreshing oasis of beautiful gardens and waterfalls. Close to Armadale, Tumbulgum Farm features a farm show, an Aboriginal culture show and Mundijong's Showcase WA, offering a superb range of WA-made products for purchase. At nearby Gosnells, the Cohuna Koala Park has an abundance of Australian fauna, including a koala sanctuary.

Pinjarra, 84 km from Perth on the South Western Highway

This picturesque old town on the Murray River, only 19 km east of Mandurah, is becoming a popular base for exploring the area. Several historic buildings in the town include Old Blythewood (c. 1860), a former coaching inn, family home and post office; check times with the National Trust, (09) 321 6088. A novel way of seeing the surrounding country is on board a steam train that occasionally runs from Pinjarra to Dwellingup, a quiet little timber town in the foothills of the Darling Range. **See also:** Entry in A–Z listing.

Rottnest Island

Commodore Willem de Vlamingh referred to Rottnest Island as a 'terrestrial paradise' when he landed there in 1696, and holidaymakers still flock to the island to enjoy its peace, beauty and unique holiday atmosphere. A low, sandy island, just 20 kilometres north-west of Fremantle, Rottnest is a public reserve. Only 11 kilometres long and about 5 kilometres wide, it has an attractive coastline, with many small bays and coves, sparkling white beaches and turquoise waters. Vlamingh named it Rottnest, or Rat's Nest, for the island's marsupial resident, the quokka, which he believed to be a type of rat.

Quokka

The Rottnest Hotel, completed in 1864, was originally the summer residence of the governors of Western Australia. Now commonly known as the **Quokka Arms**, it is a good place to stay, or just to enjoy a relaxing drink in the beer garden. **Rottnest Lodge Resort** has modern convention facilities in an informal setting. Other accommodation includes chalets, cabins, hostels and a camping area.

There is no lack of things to do on Rottnest. Cars are not permitted (which contributes to the wonderful sense of peace), but you can hire a bicycle and explore the island. You may even catch a glimpse of peacocks and pheasants, which were introduced at the turn of the century. Special 2-hour coach tours of the island are conducted three times daily. A tramway operates several times daily except Christmas Day, on a 7 kilometre route from the historic settlement area to the Oliver Hill Battery. There are tennis courts, a 9-hole golf course and bowling facilities. You can hire a boat, dinghy or canoe, play mini-golf or go trampolining; or you can just laze on the beach in the sunshine. Scuba diving is available; contact the Dive, Surf and Ski Shop.

The *Underwater Explorer*, a glass-bottomed pleasure cruiser, leaves regularly from Main Jetty, giving glimpses of shipwrecks, reefs and a startling array of fish. Ferries operate daily services to Rottnest from Barrack Street Jetty in Perth and also from Fremantle and Hillarys Boat Harbour. There are daily flights from Perth. As all wildlife on Rottnest is protected, no pets and no guns of any description, including spear guns, are allowed on the island. In the interests of their health and survival, please do not feed the quokkas.

For further information, contact the Rottnest Island Authority; (09) 372 9729 or the Rottnest Visitor Centre; (09) 372 9752.

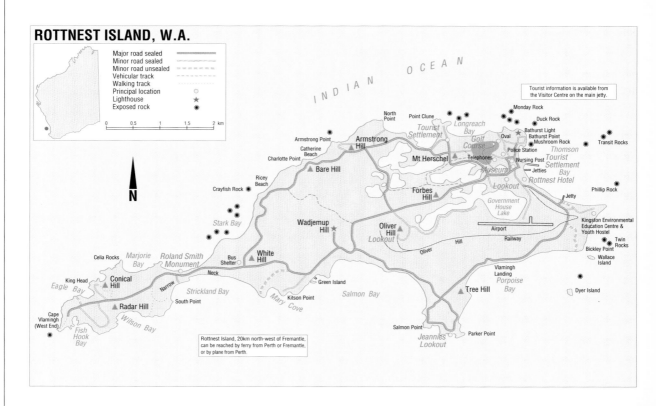

Western Australia from A to Z

Albany   Pop. 18 826
Picturesque Albany is WA's oldest town. On the edge of King George Sound and the magnificent Princess Royal Harbour, the town is 406 km S of Perth. Albany dates back to 1826, when a military post was established to give the English a foothold in the West. Whaling was important in the 1840s; in the 1850s Albany became a coaling station for steamers bound from England. As WA's most important holiday centre, it offers visitors a wealth of history and a variety of coastal, rural and mountain scenery. Its harbours, weirs and estuaries provide excellent fishing. **Of interest:** Colonial Buildings Historic Walk; self-guide brochure from Tourist Information. Old Post Office–Intercolonial Communications Museum, opp. cnr Stirling Tce and Spencer St. Victorian shopfronts in Stirling Tce. Albany Residency Museum (1850s), Residency Rd, originally home of Resident Magistrates, historical and environmental exhibits; open daily. Old Gaol and Museum (1851), Residency Rd, two gaols in one. Vancouver Arts Centre, Vancouver St. House of Gems, Frenchman Bay Rd. Old Farm (1836), Middleton Rd, Strawberry Hill, site of first Government farm in WA, begun 1872. Patrick Taylor Cottage (1832), Duke St, faithfully restored, extensive collection of period costume and household goods. Extravaganza Gallery, next to Esplanade Hotel, Middleton Beach; vintage and veteran cars, art and craft. Princess Royal Fortress (commissioned 1893) on Mt Adelaide, Albany's first federal fortress, restored. Mt Adelaide Forts Heritage Trails, starting cnr Apex Dr and Forts Rd; self-guide leaflets from Tourist Information. The *Amity*, Princess Royal Dr, full-scale replica of brig that brought Major Lockyer and convicts to establish Albany in 1826. On Princess Royal Dr, Amity Crafts, local art, craft. Anzac Light Horse Memorial statue, near top of Mt Clarence, off Marine Dr. Spectacular view from here and from John Barnesby Memorial Lookout at Mt Melville. Feb.: Great Southern Wine Festival. Nov.: Perth–Albany Ocean Yacht Race. **In the area:** Swimming and fishing: Jimmy Newhill's Harbour, 20 km S; Frenchman Bay, 25 km S; Emu Point, 8 km NE; Oyster Harbour, 15 km NE. Jolly Barnyard family farm, 3 km N. 'O'Dome deer farm, 6 km N. To north: Porongurup National Park, 37 km, huge granite peaks; Stirling Range National Park, 80 km, climbing, bushwalks, breathtaking scenery. Brilliant wildflowers in spring, some unique to area. West towards Denmark: Cosy Corner, 20 km; West Cape Howe National Park, 30 km, one of south coast's most popular parks, walking, fishing, swimming, hang-gliding, one of best lookouts on coast. Torbay Head in park is southernmost point in WA. Care should be taken when exploring coast, king waves can be dangerous and have been known to rush in unexpectedly, causing death. At Camp Quaranup, site of old quarantine station, south on Geake Point, historical walk. Torndirrup National Park, 17 km S, coastal views. To south: The Gap and Natural Bridge, 18 km; The Blow Holes and The Gorge, 19 km, sheer drop to sea. Cheyne's Beach Whaling Station, 25 km SE, ceased operation 1978, now Albany Whaleworld; in its heyday, the Station's chasers took up to 850 whales per season. Locomotion, tourist railway, 15 km E, train rides, historic trams, art, craft, tearooms, accommodation. Willowie Game Park, 30 km E. To east: Nanarup, 20 km, and Little Beach, 40 km have sheltered waters. Two Peoples Bay Nature Reserve, 40 km E. **Tourist information:** Old Railway Station, Proudlove Pde; (098) 41 1088. **Accommodation:** 5 hotels, 9 motels, 15 B&B, 2 hostels, 10 cara./camp. parks. **See also:** The Great Southern.
MAP REF. 351 N12, 354 G13

Augusta   Pop. 838
Set on the slopes of the Hardy Inlet, the town of Augusta overlooks the mouth of the Blackwood River, the waters of Flinders Bay and rolling, heavily wooded countryside. Augusta is one of the oldest settlements in WA and a popular holiday resort. Jarrah, karri and pine forests supply the district's 100-year-old timber industry. **Of interest:** In Blackwood Ave: Historical Museum, Lumen Christi Catholic Church. Crafters Croft, Ellis St, art, craft. March: Dragon Boat Racing. Sept.–Oct.: Spring Flower Show **In the area:** Both 8 km NW: Jewel Cave, famous for colourful limestone formations; Moondyne Cave, guided adventure tours. Alexandra Bridge, 10 km N, charming picnic spot, towering jarrah trees, beautiful wildflowers. Both 30 km N: Lake Cave, Mammoth Cave. Hillview Lookout, 6 km W. Cape Leeuwin, 8 km SW, most south-westerly point of Australia, where Indian and Southern Oceans meet; 1895 lighthouse and water wheel. Picturesque coastline, swimming, surfing. Good fishing in river and ocean. Marron (freshwater lobster) caught in season. Marron Fishing Licences required; from Post Office, Blackwood Ave. Augusta–Busselton Heritage Trail; details from Tourist Information. **Tourist information:** Leeuwin Souvenirs, Blackwood Ave; (097) 58 1695, or Augusta–Margaret River Tourist Bureau, cnr Tunbridge Rd and Bussell Hwy, Margaret River; (097) 57 2911. **Accommodation:** 1 hotel/motel, 1 motel, 1 hostel, 4 cara./camp. parks.
MAP REF. 349 D12, 354 D11

The Goldfields

The land that boasted the first goldmining boom in Western Australia is almost as forbidding as that of the far north-west. This is the vast region to the east of Perth that contains the famous towns of Kalgoorlie–Boulder, Coolgardie, Norseman, Kambalda, Leonora, Gwalia and Laverton. Although some towns, like Gwalia, are colourful but nearly deserted reminders of the great rush days, all are once again active goldmining areas, with Kalgoorlie–Boulder the main centre.

The western gold rush began in 1892 with strikes around **Coolgardie**. The town sprang up from nowhere and enjoyed a boisterous but short life. With great optimism diggers flocked to the area. In 1900 there were 15 000 people, today Coolgardie has a population of 1063. The grand old courthouse, built at the height of the boom, is used as a museum and has a record of life on the fields as it once was.

In 1893 Irishman Paddy Hannan made a bigger strike of gold at **Kalgoorlie**. The area became known as the Golden Mile, reputedly the richest square mile in the world. Kalgoorlie and its twin town Boulder boasted a population of 30 000 in 1902.

The modern **Kalgoorlie–Boulder** is a prosperous goldmining centre, producing 70 per cent of the gold mined in Australia. At Hannans North Historical Mining Complex visitors can don a hard hat and cap lamp and go below the surface, where guides explain the hardships endured by the miners in their search for gold. To the south is **Kambalda**, a new boom town, founded on rich nickel deposits.

Most of the towns north of Kalgoorlie are alive again as a result of the current gold-mining operations. Deep underground mines are being replaced by massive open-cuts, which create their own adjacent table top mountains of overburden. The little town of **Menzies** is a shadow of its former self. The renovated, stately old Gwalia Hotel just outside **Leonora** is one of the few buildings left in what was once one of the State's most prosperous gold-mining centres.

Kanowna once boasted a population of 12 000. Now all that remains is old and new mine workings, and historic markers describing what used to be. Siberia, Broad Arrow, Niagara and Bulong are the exotic names of some of the towns that flourished and died in a few short years. Nevertheless, mining is once again active in most of these areas.

See also: Individual town entries in A–Z listing.

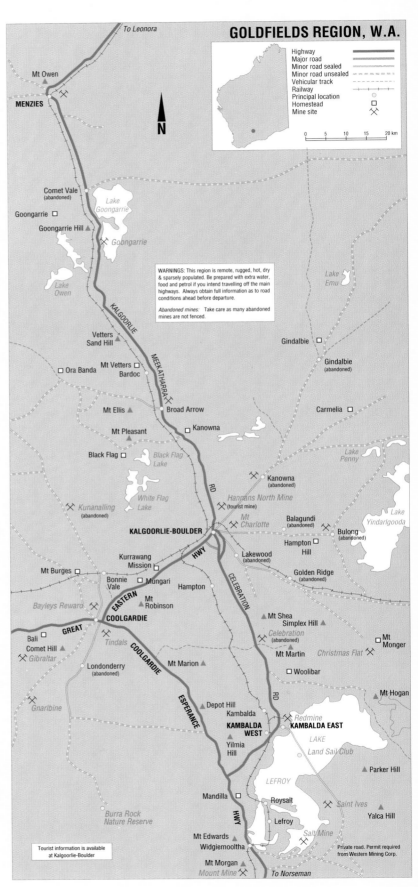

Australind
Pop. 4407

The popular holiday resort of Australind is located 11 km NE of Bunbury on the Leschenault Estuary. Fishing, crabbing, swimming and boating on the estuary and the Collie River are the main attractions. **Of interest:** Henton Cottage (1841), Paris Rd, two early buildings; open daily. Church of St Nicholas (1842), Paris Rd, restored, thought to be smallest church in WA. Rock and Gem Museum, Old Coast Rd, Bunbury agate; check times. **In the area:** Pioneer Cemetery, 2 km N, pioneer graves, wildflowers. To north, pleasant beach towns of Binningup, 26 km, and Myalup, 30 km. Kemerton Industrial Park (SCM Chemicals), 15 km N, guided tours. **Tourist information:** Harvey Tourist and Interpretative Centre, South West Hwy, Harvey; (097) 29 1122. **Accommodation:** 3 cara./camp. parks.
MAP REF. 346 C13, 354 D10

Balladonia

Pop. 10

Balladonia is on the Eyre Hwy, 191 km E of Norseman. At this point, the road crosses gently undulating dryland forest surrounding the Fraser Range. Visitors can see claypans typical of the region and old stone fences built by pioneer farmers in the 1800s. In July 1979, debris from the US Skylab fell to earth near the town. **In the area:** Balladonia Station Homestead, (1886), off north side of highway, behind old telegraph station, 22 km E of Balladonia, museum; by appt. In hotel complex, gallery of paintings depicting history of Balladonia and Eyre Hwy. Newmans Rocks, 50 km w on Eyre Hwy; signposted. Wildflowers in spring. **Tourist information:** Balladonia Hotel/Motel; (090) 39 3453. **Accommodation:** 1 hotel/motel, 1 cara./camp. park (limited facilities). **See also:** Crossing the Nullarbor.
MAP REF. 357 K9

Beverley
Pop. 818

On the Avon River, 130 km E of Perth, is the town of Beverley. **Of interest:** Delightful picnic spots beside Avon River. Aeronautical Museum, Vincent St: shows development of aviation in WA; incl. biplane built in 1929 by local aircraft designer Selby Ford; 9–4 daily. Dead Finish (1872), Hunt Rd, one of oldest buildings in town; once a hotel in town centre but with the coming of the railway in 1886 the town centre moved nearer the station. Barry Ferguson's Garage, Hunt Rd, display of old hand-operated machinery; open normal trading hours. Jan: Cross-country Gliding Regatta. Aug.: Agricultural Show. **In the area:** The Avon Ascent, self-guide drive tour of the Avon Valley; leaflet from Tourist Information. Restored St Paul's Church (consecrated 1862), opp. original town site, 5 km NW. Magnificent view from top of nearby Seaton Ross Hill. Avondale Discovery Farm, 6 km W, 10–4 daily. Restored church, St John's in the Wilderness (consecrated 1895), 27 km SW. Farm Fresh Yabby Company 8 km SE, check times. County Peak (362 m), 35 km SE, bushwalking, picnic area, spectacular views from summit. Yenyening Lakes, 36 km S, water-skiing, motorboating, yachting, swimming. **Tourist information:** Aeronautical Museum, Vincent St; (096) 46 1555. **Accommodation:** 2 hotels, 1 cara. park.
MAP REF. 346 I5, 354 F7, 356 B9

Boyup Brook
Pop. 584

A small town near the junction of Boyup Creek and the Blackwood River, Boyup Brook is a centre for the district's sheep, dairy-farming and timber industries. Blackboys, huge granite boulders, shaded pools, charming cottages and farms are scenic features. **Of interest:** Pioneers Museum, Jayes Rd. Sandy Chambers Art Studio, Gibbs St artworks, aviaries, camels. Stagline Woollen Clothing, Henderson St. Flax Mill, on Blackwood River, off Barron St. Haddleton Flora Reserve, Arthur River Rd. Pioneer Garden, Kojonup Rd, picnic/barbecue facilities. Carnaby Collection, at Tourist Information, beetles and butterflies. Bicentennial Walk Trail; details at Tourist Information. Sept.: Country Music Weekend. Oct.: Blackwood River Marathon Relay; running, canoeing, horseriding, cycling, swimming, to Bridgetown. **In the area:** Glacier Hill, 18 km S, glacial rock formations. Wineries: Scotts Brook, 18 km SE, open by appt; Blackwood Crest, Kulikup, 40 km NE. Harvey Dickson Country Music Centre, 5 km NE. School and teacher's house (1900), Dinninup, 21 km NE. At Wilga, 22 km N, vintage engines, old timber-mill. Stormboy Jumpers, 20 km W on Jayes Rd, locally produced woollen goods; appt at Tourist Information. Visits to farms (wheat, sheep, pig, goat, deer, angora) and Early Pioneer Homestead, Norlup; appts at Tourist Information. Boyup Brook Flora Drive; details at Tourist Information. **Tourist information:** Cnr Bridge and Able Sts; (097) 65 1444. **Accommodation:** 1 hotel, 1 B&B, 1 hostel, 1 cara./camp. park. **See also:** The Great Southern.
MAP REF. 350 E2, 354 F10, 356 A12

Bremer Bay
Pop. 250

Bremer Bay, a popular holiday destination 181 km NE of Albany, was named in 1849 by Surveyor-General John Septimus Roe in honour of the captain of HMS *Tamar*, Sir Gordon Bremer. The town was built around the Old Telegraph Station at the mouth of Wellstead Estuary (named after John Wellstead, who settled in the area in the 1850s). **Of interest:** Fishing, boating, scuba diving, water-skiing. Rammed-earth buildings, hotel/motel, Franton Way; church in John St, overlooking estuary. **In the area:** Fitzgerald River National Park, 17 km N. Military museum at Jerramungup, 90 km NW. **Tourist information:** Roadhouse, Gnombup Tce; (098) 37 4093. **Accommodation:** 1 hotel, 1 B&B, 1 cara./camp. park. **See also:** The Great Southern.
MAP REF. 356 E13

Bridgetown
Pop. 2017

Bridgetown is a quiet spot in undulating country in the south-west corner of WA. Here the Blackwood River, well stocked with marron and trout, curves through some of the prettiest country in the State. The first European settlers arrived 1857 and the first apple trees were planted soon after. **Of interest:** In Hampton St: Bridgetown Pottery; Brierley Jigsaw Gallery (at Tourist Information); Gentle Era craft shop; Orchard Studio; St Paul's Church (1911), paintings by local artists; Memorial Park, peaceful picnic location. Geegelup Pottery, Mount St. Elizabeth Endisch Studio, Steere St. Bridgedale (1862), on South West Hwy, near bridge and overlooking river, constructed of local clay and timber by John Blechynden, first European settler, restored by National Trust; check times. Kalara Park Stud, Doust St; by appt. Wildflower season and apple blossom begin Oct. Apple-orchard packing sheds worth a visit. Oct.: Blackwood Classic, 3-day 250-km power-boat event; Blackwood Marathon Relay, international and local competitors, 58.3-km course, running, canoeing, swimming, horseriding, cycling. **In the area:** Fine views: Sutton's

Lookout, off Phillip St, Hester's Hill, 5 km N. Greenbushes Historical Park, 18 km N, displays of tin-mining industry. Bridgetown Jarrah Park, 20 km SW, bush-walking and picnics. Donnelly Whippole Well, 15 km S on South West Hwy, pioneer well. Geegelup Heritage Trail (52 km): history of agriculture, mining and timber; details from Tourist Information. Scenic drives through rolling green hills, orchards and valleys, into noted karri and jarrah timber country. **Tourist information:** Hampton St; (097) 61 1740. **Accommodation:** 2 hotels, 1 hotel/motel, 1 cara./camp. park. **See also:** The South-west.
MAP REF. 350 C3, 354 E11, 356 A12

Brookton   Pop. 576

An attractive town 137 km SE of Perth, near the Avon River in the heart of fertile farming country, Brookton was founded in 1884 when the Great Southern Railway line was opened. **Of interest:** In Robinson Rd: Old Police Station Museum; St Mark's Anglican Church (1895); Old Railway Station, houses tourist centre, art and craft shop. Lions Picnic Park, off Corrigin Rd, at eastern entrance to town. March: Old Time Motor Show (even-numbered years). Sept.: Wildflower Display. **In the area:** Nine Acre Rock, Brookton–Kweda Rd, 12 km E, one of the largest natural granite outcrops in the area, unusual home of pioneer Jack Hansen. Yenyening Lakes nature reserve, 35 km NE, picnic/barbecue facilities. Boyagin Rock, 18 km SW, reserve, picnic ground. Brookton Pioneer Heritage Trail; details from Tourist Information. **Tourist information:** Old Railway Station, Robinson Rd; (096) 42 1316. **Accommodation:** 2 hotels, 1 cara./camp. park.
MAP REF. 346 I7, 354 F8, 356 B9

Broome   Pop. 8906

Situated on the coast at the southern tip of the Kimberley, Broome enjoys wide beaches, turquoise water and a warm climate with plenty of sunshine. Closer to Bali than to Perth, and with an international airport, the town is lively and cosmopolitan. The discovery of pearling grounds off the coast in the 1880s led to the foundation of Broome township in 1883. By 1910 Broome was the world's leading pearling centre. However, the industry began to suffer when world markets collapsed in 1914. With increasing tourism, Broome is again rapidly

expanding. **Of interest:** Many old buildings; self-guide Broome Heritage Trail (2 km) introduces buildings and places of interest. Chinatown, including Pearl Emporiums, reminder of Broome's early multicultural mix. Historical Society Museum, in Old Customs House, Saville St. Library, Haas St. Captain Gregory's House, Carnarvon St; not open to public. Several art galleries, incl. Kimberley art. Bedford Park, Hamersley St, relics of Broome's history. Courthouse (former Cable House), Hamersley St, gardens and markets open Sat. Broome Crocodile Park, Cable Beach Rd. Shell House, Guy St; one of largest shell collections in Australia. Sun Pictures, Carnarvon St; opened 1916, believed to be oldest operating outdoor theatre in world. On Port Dr: Chinese Cemetery, Japanese Cemetery (graves of early Japanese pearl divers). Pioneer Cemetery in Apex Park. Aug.–Sept.: Shinju Matsuri, (Festival of the Pearl), recalls Broome's heyday. June: Fringe Arts Festival. **In the area:** Beaches, ideal swimming spots, prized by collectors for beautiful shells. Cable Beach, 3 km NW, 22 km long; named after underwater cable that links Broome to Java. Gantheaume Point, 5 km SW, giant dinosaur tracks, believed to be 130 million years old, can be seen when tide is out. Staircase to the Moon: natural phenomenon, visible at most full moons during dry season (April–Oct.); caused by moonlight reflecting off exposed mudflats at extreme low tides; best seen from southern end of Dampier Tce (dates and times from Tourist Information). Hovercraft *Spirit of Broome* visits local beaches. Good fishing all year. Broome Bird Observatory, Roebuck Bay, 18 km E. Safaris, cruises, scenic flights, short tours. Charter boats: 6- to 10-day Kimberley expeditions to coral reefs, Roley Shoals, Prince Regent River, waterfalls at Kings Cascades. Day tours: Lombardina Mission, 200 km NE; Cape Leveque, 220 km NE. Willie Creek Pearl Farm, 35 km N, tours incl. pearl farm, history of pearling industry. **Tourist information:** Cnr Bagot St and Great Northern Hwy; (091) 92 2222. **Accommodation:** 5 hotels, 1 hotel/motel, 1 hostel, 4 cara./ camp. parks. **See also:** The Kimberley.
MAP REF. 360 H8

Bunbury   Pop. 24 003

Bunbury, 'Harbour City', is the second largest urban area in WA and serves as the

major port, commercial and regional centre for the south-west. Situated 185 km S of Perth on the Leschenault Estuary, at the junction of the Preston and Collie Rivers, it is one of the State's most popular tourist resorts, with a warm temperate climate, beautiful beaches, and the Darling Range in the distance. Originally called Port Leschenault, Bunbury was settled by Europeans in 1838, and the whalers who anchored in Koombana Bay provided a market for the pioneer farmers. Today the port is the main outlet for the thriving timber industry, mineral sands and the produce of the fertile hinterland. **Of interest:** Drive along breakwater, to Koombana Bay, modern harbour facilities. King Cottage (1880), Forrest Ave, historical museum, open Sun. Tree-lined pathways lead to Boulter's Lookout, Haig Cres; views of city, suburbs, hills, farmland. Bunbury Lighthouse, Ocean Dr, notable landmark, painted in black and white checks, lookout at base. Marlston Hill Lookout, Apex Dr. Art Gallery, cnr Victoria and Carey Sts. Centenary Gardens, cnr Wittenoom and Prinsep Sts, in city centre; peaceful picnic spot, kiosk. Grassed foreshore of estuary, picnic/barbecue facilities, playground, boat ramp. Excellent beaches, surf club at Ocean Beach. Koombana Bay, Koombana Dr., water-skiing, yachting; Dolphin Discovery Centre, chance to stand among dolphins or swim with them under ranger guidance. Good fishing: bream, flounder, tailor and whiting in bay, deep-sea fishing. Succulent blue manna crabs in season in estuary. Great variety of birdlife in bush near waters of inlet. Big Swamp Wildlife Park, Prince Phillip Dr. Historic wooden jetty in outer harbour; popular for fishing, crabbing. Miniature railway, Forrest Park, Blair St. March: Show, Aqua Spectacular. Nov.: Bunbury Fest. **In the area:** Gelorup Museum, 12 km S. Cockelup Gardens and Anns Farmyard, Stratham, 17 km S. St Mark's (1842), Picton, 5 km SE, oldest church in WA; restored, retains some of original timber structure. Boyanup Transport Museum, 20 km SE. Church of St Nicholas (1842), Australind, 11 km N, thought to be smallest church in WA. Spring Hill Homestead (1855), 26 km N, off Old Coast Road; not open to public. Scenic drive off Old Coast Road, good crabbing, picnic spots. Bunbury Heritage Trails; details from Tourist Information. **Tourist information:** Old Railway Station,

Carmody St; (097) 21 7922. **Accommodation:** 8 hotels, 10 motels, 3 B&B, 2 hostels, 6 cara./camp. parks. **See also:** The South-west.
MAP REF. 346 C13, 354 D10

Busselton
Pop. 8936

First settled by Europeans in the 1830s, and one of the oldest towns in WA, Busselton is a pleasant seaside town at the centre of a large rural district. Situated 228 km S of Perth, on the shores of Geographe Bay and the picturesque Vasse River, the town is a popular holiday resort. Inland are jarrah forests for the local timber industry, and dairy and beef cattle and vineyards. Fishing is important, with crayfish and salmon in season. **Of interest:** Prospect Villa (1855), Pries Ave, two-storey colonial building (now motel), antiques. Opposite, first steam locomotive in WA. St Mary's (1844), Peel Tce, oldest stone church in State. Villa Carlotta (1897), Adelaide St, boarding school for 50 years, now guest house. Near jetty on beachfront, Oceanarium, Nautical Lady Entertainment Centre. Old Courthouse Arts Centre, Queen St. Old Butter Factory Museum, Peel Tce, on riverbank, old butter- and cheese-making equipment. Wonnerup House (1859), Layman Rd: National Trust Museum; fine example of colonial Australian architecture; furnished in period style.

Old school and teacher's house, Layman Rd, restored, built of local timber. Busselton Jetty, on beachfront near Queen St, longest timber jetty (2 km) in Australia; partially destroyed by Cyclone Alby in 1978, still popular with fishermen. Vasse River Parkland, Peel Tce, barbecue/picnic facilities. Archery Park and Minigolf, Bussell Hwy. Bay has good sheltered beaches for swimming. Western coast ideal for surfing. Jan.: Festival of Busselton. Oct.: 4-wk Cape to Cape Festival. **In the area:** Woodcrafts, locally produced gourmet items. Several protea nurseries. Many scenic drives; to north west, excellent views of rugged coast at Eagle Bay, 30 km, Sugar Loaf Rock, 35 km, and Cape Naturaliste, 39 km. Wildflower, scenic and 4WD tours. Augusta–Busselton Heritage Trail; details from Tourist Information. Orchid farm, Vasse, 9 km w. Wildwood Pottery, 16 km w. Quindalup Fauna Park, 20 km w, birds, fish, tropical butterflies, native mammals. Both 26 km w: Bannamah Wildlife Park; Country Life Farm: hayrides, boat rides, children's farm. Yallingup, 32 km w, surfing, sheltered rock pool. Yallingup Caves; open daily. Over 20 wineries in Willyabrup Valley, 30 km SW, and around town of Margaret River, 47 km SW. Whistle Stop, miniature railway, on Vasse Hwy, 11 km SE. Bunyip Craft Centre, 7 km E. **Tourist information:**

Southern Drive; (097) 52 1288. **Accommodation:** 4 hotels, 7 motels, 13 B&B, 1 hostel, 12 cara./camp. parks. **See also:** The South-west.
MAP REF. 349 F3, 354 D10

Caiguna
Pop. 10

This is the first stop for petrol and food after the long drive from Balladonia, 181 km w. This section of Eyre Highway is one of the longest straight stretches of sealed road in the world. **In the area:** Afghan Rocks, 14 km E, natural freshwater dams, used as resting place by camel drivers in 1890s. **Tourist information:** John Eyre Motel; (090) 39 3459. **Accommodation:** 1 motel, 1 cara./camp. park. **See also:** Crossing the Nullarbor.
MAP REF. 357 M9

Carnamah
Pop. 367

Carnamah is a small, typically Australian country town, 290 km N of Perth. Wheat and sheep are the local industries. **Of interest:** Historical Society Museum, McPherson St, old farm machinery reflecting agricultural heritage. Sept.: Agricultural show. **In the area:** MacPherson Homestead (1880), 1 km E, grounds open to the public, house by appt. Several old goldmining and ghost towns 40–50 km E; area rich in minerals, popular with gemstone enthusiasts. Yarra

Camel riding on Cable Beach, Broome

Coastline near Carnarvon

Yarra Lakes, 2 km W, waters range in colour from red to green to blue; many varieties of migratory birds; wildflowers in season. Lake Indoon, 61 km SW, water-skiing. Perenjori area, 58 km NE, and Tathra National Park, 50 km SW, variety of wildflowers in spring. **Tourist information:** Shire Offices, McPherson St; (099) 51 1055. **Accommodation:** 1 hotel/motel, 1 cara./camp. park.
MAP REF. 354 E3

Carnarvon   Pop. 6901
Carnarvon, at the mouth of the Gascoyne River, 904 km N of Perth, is the commercial centre of the productive Gascoyne region. The district was seen 1616 by Dirk Hartog. Another explorer, Willem de Vlamingh, landed at Shark Bay in 1697. Pioneers arrived in 1876; by the 1880s there were a number of European settlers in the region. Today most of the land is used for pastoral activities, with sheep and beef cattle. The Gascoyne River has been tapped for irrigation. The Overseas Telecommunications Commission earth station (no longer operating) and Radio Australia base are at nearby Browns Range. The USA National Aeronautics and Space Administration (NASA) operated here 1964–1974. Carnarvon has warm winters and takes on a tropical appearance when the bougainvilleas and hibiscus bloom. The main street, c.1880s is 40 m wide, to enable camel trains to turn. **Of interest:** Museum, Correia Arcade. Jubilee Hall (1887),

Francis St. Pioneer Park, Olivia Tce. Rotary Park, North West Coastal Hwy. Fishing: snapper or groper; game fishing for marlin or sailfish; charter boats available. May: Mirari Tropical Festival; Fremantle–Carnarvon Yachting Classic. **In the area:** On Babbage Island, 5 km off Carnarvon, museum at lighthouse keeper's cottage. Prawning factory, 6 km off Binning Rd; tours in season, usually mid-April to late Oct; contact Tourist Information. One Mile Jetty, 5 km NW, almost 1500 m long; Pelican Point, 8 kn NW, picnics, swimming. OTC earth station, Browns Range, 8 km E, mammoth 157-m diameter reflector ('the Big Dish'); views of area from platform of disc. Rocky Pool, deep freshwater billabong, swimming and picnics. 55 km E, along Gascoyne Rd. Munro's Banana Plantation, 10 km N via hwy and South River Rd, fresh-picked bananas, melons, other fruit and vegetables, for sale in season. Department of Agriculture Research Station, 3 km from South River Rd turnoff, experimental farming; book at Tourist Information. Bibbawarra artesian bore, 16 km N, hot water surfaces at 70°C; picnic area. Miaboolya Beach, 22 km N, has good fishing, crabbing and swimming. Blowholes 70 km N, water dramatically forced 20 m into air; about 1 km S, superb sheltered beach, oysters on rocks, but beware of king waves and tides. Excellent fishing at Cape Cuvier, 30 km N of blowholes. **Tourist information:** Robinson St; (099) 41 1146.

Accommodation: 5 hotel/motels, 7 cara./camp. parks.
MAP REF. 355 B8

Cocklebiddy   Pop. 11
The ruins of an Aboriginal mission station can be seen on the coast 30 km S of this tiny settlement on the Eyre Hwy, between Madura and Caiguna, 310 km from the SA border. **In the area:** Cocklebiddy Cave, for experienced speleologists only (directions at Wedgetail Inn). Bird observatory and Post Office Historical Society Museum at Eyre on coast, 47 km S (4WD only); guided tours, 24 hrs notice, contact Tourist Information. **Tourist information:** Wedgetail Inn; (090) 39 3462. **Accommodation:** 1 hotel/motel, 1 cara./camp. park (limited facilities). **See also:** Crossing the Nullarbor.
MAP REF. 357 N8

Collie   Pop. 7684
Collie, the centre of WA's only coal-producing region, plays an integral part in the State's development. Set in dense jarrah forest, 202 km S of Perth near the winding Collie River, the town has an abundance of attractive parks and gardens. Fine views on the drive into Collie from the South West Hwy. **Of interest:** In Throssell St: tourist coal mine, guided tours daily; Historical and Mining Museum in old Roads Board buildings, history of area and of coal industry; Steam Locomotive Museum; old police station (1926); post office (1898); art gallery at Shire Office, collection of local art. Old courthouse cnr Wittenoon and Pendleton Sts. Impressive All Saints' Anglican Church, Venn St, built in Norman· style. Soldiers Park, Steer St, on banks of Collie River; shady trees and lawns, ideal for picnics. Minninup Pool off Mungalup Rd, bushland, wildflowers in season. **In the area:** Harris Dam, 10 km N. Trout and freshwater marron crayfish, abound in dam Dec.–April. (Inland Fishing Licence required; from post office or Tourist Information). Scenic drive to Collie River, 5 km W. Wellington Dam, 27 km W, in heart of Collie River Irrigation Scheme, major tourist attraction, fishing, bushwalking, grassy picnic spots. Muja open-cut mines and Muja Power Station, 15 km E. ('*Muja*', Aboriginal word for bright yellow Christmas tree that grows in area.) **Tourist information:** Tourist Bureau, Throssell St;

(097) 34 2051. **Accommodation:** 5 hotels, 1 hotel/motel, 2 motels, 1 cara./camp. park.
MAP REF. 346 E13, 354 E10, 356 A11

Coolgardie
Pop. 1063

The old goldmining town of Coolgardie is one of the best-known ghost towns in Australia. After Arthur Bayley and William Ford found alluvial gold at Fly Flat in 1892, Coolgardie grew to a boom town of 15 000 people, 23 hotels, 6 banks and 2 stock exchanges in just 10 years. The main street was wide enough for camel trains to turn, splendid public buildings were erected and ambitious plans were made. Sadly, the gold soon petered out. By 1985 there were only 700 people in the town; however, with an increase in tourism the population of this pleasant town is increasing. **Of interest:** Historic buildings in Bayley St incl. Goldfields Exhibition building (1898), most comprehensive prospecting museum in WA; Post Office (1898); Old Gaol; Denver City Hotel (1898), handsome verandahs; Ben Prior's Open-air Museum, wagons, horse- and camel-drawn vehicles; Railway Lodge, wonderfully preserved building providing ghost town atmosphere. Railway station (1896), Woodward St, transport exhibition, display of famous Varischetti mine rescue. Warden Finnerty's house (1895), McKenzie St, striking example of early Australian architecture and furnishings. St Anthony's Convent, Lindsay St, now boarding school for Aboriginal Self Help Group Concerned Parents Society (CAPS). Goal Tree, Hunt St. Lions Bicentennial Lookout, near southern end of Hunt St. Lindsay's Pit Mine Lookout, Ford St. Sept.: Coolgardie Day, Camel Races. **In the area:** Cemetery, 1 km w, evokes harsh early days of gold rush. Camel farm, 4 km w. Kurrawang Emu Farm, 20 km E. Eastern Goldfields Heritage Trail; details from Tourist Information. **Tourist information:** Bayley St; (090) 26 6090. **Accommodation:** 1 hotel, 3 motels, 2 hostels, 2 cara./camp. parks. **See also:** The Goldfields.
MAP REF. 356 G7

Coral Bay
Pop. 726

The Ningaloo Coral Reef system approaches the shore at Coral Bay, 150 km s of Exmouth. Unspoilt expanses of white beaches offer good swimming, snorkelling, boating and fishing. **In the area:** Ningaloo Marine Park, just off beach. Views of reef from glass-bottomed boats. Diving equipment hire. Numerous shipwreck sites at Pt Cloates, 8 km N, and ruins of Norwegian Bay whaling station (1915). **Tourist information:** Bayview Caravan Park; (099) 42 5932. **Accommodation:** 1 hotel/motel, 2 cara./camp. parks.
MAP REF. 355 C5

Corrigin
Pop. 725

Rich farming country surrounds Corrigin, 230 km SE of Perth. **Of interest:** In Kunjin St, folk museum: historical exhibits, photographs; miniature railway, steam train. RSL monument, Gayfer St, Turkish mountain gun from Gallipoli. Art and craft shop, Walton St. Sept.: Agricultural Show. Nov.: Creative Arts Exhibition. **In the area:** Dog Cemetery, 5 km w. Good views from observation tower, 3 km w, on Wildflower Scenic Drive, Trott Dr (well signposted). Gorge Rock, 20 km SE, picnics. **Tourist information:** Shire Offices, Lynch St; (090) 63 2203. **Accommodation:** 1 hotel, 1 motel, 1 cara./camp. park.
MAP REF. 347 N7, 354 G8, 356 C9

Cossack
Pop. 1 & 1 dog

Cossack, once called Tien Tsin, has had a chequered history. It was the first port in the north-west and serviced the nearby town of Roebourne, as well as being the centre of a gold rush and the location for a turtle-product factory. Pearling in WA began at Cossack before moving to Broome in the 1890s. Cossack was also a centre for the Pilbara's developing pastoral and mining industries. Today it is a ghost town, but almost completely restored. **Of interest:** Historic buildings, all open April–Christmas: in Pearl St, courthouse (now museum), bond store (now tearoom), post and telegraph office; in Perseverance St, police quarters (budget accommodation all year). Cemetery, off Perseverance St, headstones reflect town's colourful past. At mouth of Harding River, Cossack is ideal for picnics, fishing, crabbing, swimming. Boat hire. June: Fair and Yachting Regatta. Sept.: Art Awards, Art Ball. **In the area:** To north-west, Wickham, 8 km, a modern company town; Point Samson, 18 km, popular seaside resort. **Tourist information:** Roebourne Tourist Bureau, Queen St, Roebourne; (091) 82 1060. **Accommodation:** 1 hostel. **See also:** The Pilbara.
MAP REF. 358 A2

Cranbrook
Pop. 306

In the 1800s sandalwood was exported from Cranbrook to China, where it was used as incense. Today this attractive town, near the foothills of the Stirling Range, 320 km SE of Perth, is a sheep and wheat centre. **Of interest:** Sept.: Wildflower Show. **In the area:** Gateway to Stirling Arch, Salt River Rd, picnic area, native garden, tourist information. Stirling Range National Park, 15 km SE. Sukey Hill Lookout, 5 km E, off Salt River Rd. High-quality table wines produced in Frankland district, 50 km w. Lake Poorrarecup, 55 km SW, swimming, water skiing, picnic facilities, playground, camping. Frankland Heritage Trail; details from Tourist Information. **Tourist information:** Shire Offices, Gathorne St; (098) 26 1008. **Accommodation:** 1 hotel, 1 B&B, 1 cara./camp. park.
MAP REF. 351 L6, 354 G11, 356 B13

Cue
Pop. 394

Cue, 640 km NE of Perth on the Great Northern Hwy, grew up as a boom town, an important centre for the Murchison goldfields. Today its well-kept stone buildings are a testimony to those frenzied days. **Of interest:** National Trust-classified buildings in Austin Street incl. bandstand built over well, water from which was said to have started typhoid epidemic; impressive government offices. Masonic Lodge (1899), Dowley St, built largely of corrugated iron. **In the area:** Day Dawn, 5 km w, where town was established on site of gold reef; town disappeared when reef died out in 1930s. Big Bell, 30 km w, large mine opened in 1989 (access restricted). Walga Rock, 50 km w, monolith, 1.5 km long, 5 km around base, second largest in Australia; largest gallery of Aboriginal rock paintings in WA. Details from Tourist Information. Wilgie Mia Red Ochre Mine, 64 km NW; mined by Aborigines 30,000 years ago; gemstone fossicking; Cue Heritage Trail; a number of other Aboriginal sites. **Tourist information:** Tourist Information Centre, Robinson St; (099) 63 1291. **Accommodation:** 1 hotel, 1 cara./camp. park.
MAP REF. 355 I12, 356 C1, 358 B13

Dampier
Pop. 1810

A model town with modern facilities, Dampier lies on King Bay, facing the

unique islands of the Dampier Archipelago. Hamersley Iron Pty Ltd established the town as a port for ore mined from two of the world's richest iron-ore deposits, Tom Price and Paraburdoo. The town's deepwater port with its export facilities loads over 400 million tonnes of ore loaded yearly. Salt is harvested from ponds near the port. **Of interest:** Jurat Park, Haig Close, picnic/barbecue facilities, children's playground. Tours of the Hamersley Iron port facility, Mon.–Fri.; bookings (091) 44 4600. Boating, sailing, fishing, diving, windsurfing, swimming. Game fishing; charter boat hire. Aug.: 2-day FeNaCLNG Festival (Fe: iron; NaCl: salt; LNG: liquefied natural gas), Dampier Game Fishing Classic. **In the area:** North West Shelf Gas Project on Burrup Peninsula 8 km NW; Visitors Centre open weekdays, except public holidays. Nearby Hearsons Cove, popular tidal swimming beach and picnic area. Aboriginal rock carvings on Burrup Peninsula; details from Tourist Information. Pilbara Railway Historical Society Museum, 10 km W, home of *Pendennis Castle* steam locomotive; open Sun. **Tourist information:** King Bay Holiday Village, The Esplanade; (091) 83 1440. **Accommodation:** 2 motels, 1 cara./camp. park. **See also:** The Hamersley Range; The Pilbara.
MAP REF. 355 G1

Denham–Shark Bay
Pop. 943
Two peninsulas form the geographical feature of Shark Bay, 833 km from Perth. Denham is the most westerly town in Australia and the main centre of the Shark Bay region. Dirk Hartog, the Dutch navigator, landed on an island at the entrance to Shark Bay in 1616. Pearling developed as the main industry and the population was a mixture of Malays, Chinese and Europeans. Until recently Shark Bay was known only for its excellent fishing, but today its most spectacular tourist attraction is the wild dolphins of Monkey Mia, which come to be fed. **In the area:** Francois Peron National Park, 7 km N. Eagle Bluff, 20 km S, habitat of sea eagle, good fishing. Catamaran MV *Explorer* variety of cruises. Safaris and coach tours. Nanga Station, 50 km S, half-million-acre sheep station; motel units, restaurant, tourist facilities, sailboards, dinghy hire on beach, charter fishing. Zuytdorp Cliffs,

160 km S and extending further south to Kalbarri, striking scenery, 4WD only. Shell Beach, 50 km S, 110-km stretch of unique Australian coastline comprising countless tiny shells. Hamelin Pool, 100 km SE: historic displays in Flint Cliff Telegraph Station and Post Office Museum (1894); stromatolites ('living rocks' communities) in nature reserve. **Tourist information:** Shark Bay Visitor and Travel Centre, 83 Knight Tce, Denham; (099) 48 1253. **Accommodation:** 1 hotel/motel, 1 motel, 2 hostels, 4 cara./camp. parks.
MAP REF. 355 B10

Denmark
Pop. 1586
The attractive 100-yr-old coastal town of Denmark, 54 km W of Albany, is at the foot of Mt Shadforth, overlooking the tranquil Denmark River. The town offers good fishing, sandy white beaches and scenic drives through farming country and karri forests. The dense hardwood forests supply timber for local mills. **Of interest:** Kurrabup Aboriginal Art Gallery, South Coast Hwy. Mitchell St: Historical Museum, Cottage Industries Shop. Strickland St: Denmark Gallery, Sutra Gifts. Alpaca stud and tourist farm, Scotsdale Rd. Jassi Skincraft, Glenrowan Rd, off Mt Shadforth Scenic Drive, local craft, wines. Rambling Rose Crafts, Holling Rd. Esplanade Parkland, along riverbank, shaded picnic areas, recreation and sports facilities. Winery and Craft Centre, Old Butter Factory, North St. Mt Shadforth Lookout, top of Illsley Dr, magnificent views. Jan.: Rainbow Festiival. July: Winter Festival. **In the area:** Knoll Drive, 3 km E. Twelve wineries in Denmark–Mount Barker–Albany region, 15 km E. Meelia Strawberry Farm, 25 km E. Scotsdale Rd–McLeod Rd Tourist Drive and Denmark Timber, Mokare and Wilson Inlet Heritage Trail; details from Tourist Information. Picturesque Albany, 54 km E, rich history, beautiful beaches. Jonathan Hook Ceramic Studio. Wynella Living Museum, 15 km W. Spiral Studio Pottery, 25 km W. Parry's Beach, 25 km W, fishing, salmon in season. Majestic Merino Wool Farm, 38 km W. Musty Creek Marron Farm, 40 km W. Drive through Valley of the Giants, 45 km W, massive karri and tingle trees. Boating, fishing, bushwalking and scenic drives around Nornalup, 50 km W, and Walpole, 66 km W, adj. to Walpole–Nornalup National Park. Greens Pool–William Bay National

Park, 17 km SW. William Bay, 18 km SW, sheltered swimming. Ocean Beach, 8 km S, surfing. **Tourist information:** Strickland St; (098) 48 2055. **Accommodation:** 1 hotel, 2 motels, 3 B&B, 5 cara./camp. parks. **See also:** The Great Southern.
MAP REF. 351 K12, 354 G12

Derby
Pop. 3022
Derby is an administrative centre for several Aboriginal communities and a hinterland rich in pastoral and mineral wealth. On King Sound, 220 km NE of Broome, the town is an ideal base for exploring the outback regions of the Kimberley. Roads have been greatly improved, incl. the Gibb River road, spanning the 667 km from Derby to the junction of the Great Northern Hwy between Wyndham and Kununurra. However, as rain usually closes the road Nov.– March, check local conditions before setting out. **Of interest:** In Loch St: Botanic Gardens; Old Derby Gaol; Wharfinger House museum, incl. photographic display. In Clarendon St: Raintree Craft Shop; Royal Flying Doctor Service. In Stanley St, Ngunga Craft Shop. July: Country Music Festival; Boab Festival (rodeo, mardi gras, mud football). Boxing Day: Kimberley Sports. **In the area:** Prison Tree, 7 km S, boab (or baobab) tree reputedly used as prison in early days. Close by, Myall's Bore, 120-m-long cattle trough. Fitzroy River empties into King Sound, 48 km S. Tours: spectacular Windjana Gorge, 145 km E; remarkable Tunnel Creek, 184 km E, colonies of flying foxes, wade through with torch; also Pigeon's Cave, hideout of Aboriginal outlaw active in 1890s. Pigeon Heritage Trail, from Derby to Windjana Gorge and Tunnel Creek National Park; details from Tourist Information. King Leopold Ranges, 200 km E. Mitchell Plateau, 580 km NE, via Gibb River Rd and Kalumburu Rd; incl. spectacular Mitchell Falls, King Edward River, Surveyor's Pool; in this remote region, visitors must be entirely self-sufficient. Motor yacht charter to Buccaneer Archipelago and Walcott Inlet. Charter flights over Kimberley coast and Cockatoo and Koolan Islands. **Tourist information:** 1 Clarendon St; (091) 91 1426. **Accommodation:** 2 hotels, 1 B&B, 1 hostel, 1 cara./camp. park. **See also:** The Kimberley.
MAP REF. 352 B9, 361 J7

Dongara–Port Denison
Pop. 1677

These quiet towns are on the coast 359 km N of Perth. Dongara has beaches, reef-enclosed bays and an abundance of delicious rock lobster. There is good fishing in the waters around Port Denison, which also has swimming and golf. **Of interest:** Fisherman's Lookout, near Leander Point, Port Denison, gives panoramic views of harbour. Historic buildings incl. in Waldeck St: Anglican rectory and church, old police station; on Brand Hwy, Royal Steam Flour Mill (1894), Russ Cottage (1870), St Dominicks Rd. Dongara's main street, Moreton Tce, shaded by huge 85-year-old Moreton Bay fig trees. Dongara Cemetery, Dodd St, headstones date from 1874. Heritage Trail from Old Mill to Priory Lodge; details from Tourist Information. Nov.: Blessing of the Fleet. **In the area:** South of Dongara: Western Flora Caravan Park, 60 km, wildflowers in river and bushland setting; Eneabba, 81 km, mineral sand mining, with large concentrations of rutile. Holiday towns south west of Eneabba: Leeman, 38 km, and Green Head, 50 km. Greenough, historic hamlet, 40 km N. **Tourist information:** Old Police Station Building, 5 Waldeck St; (099) 27 1404. **Accommodation:** 1 hotel/motel, 1 motel, 1 B&B, 1 hostel, 5 cara./camp. parks.
MAP REF. 354 C3

Donnybrook
Pop. 1570

The township of Donnybrook, the home of the Granny Smith apple, is at the heart of the oldest apple-growing area in WA, 210 km S of Perth. Gold was found here in 1897, but mined for only 4 years. Donnybrook stone has been used in construction State-wide. **Of interest:** On South West Hwy, Anchor and Hope Inn (1865), once staging post for mail coaches. Rotary Lookout, Trigwell St East. Arboretum, junction Irishtown Rd and South West Hwy. Trigwell Place, near river at southern end of town, picnic/barbecue facilities, playground. Easter: Apple Festival (odd-numbered years). Oct.: Apple Blossom Festival. **In the area:** Glen Mervyn Dam, 30 km NE, picnic/barbecue facilities. At Balingup, 30 km S: Old Cheese Factory, now art and craft centre; Tinderbox, herbs, herbal remedies; further 2 km, Golden Valley Tree Park. Scenic drives; details from Tourist Information. **Tourist information:** 'Old' Railway Station, South West Hwy; (097) 31 1720. **Accommodation:** 2 hotels, 1 motel, 2 B&B, 2 hostels, 1 cara./camp. park. **See also:** The Southwest.
MAP REF. 354 E10

Dumbleyung
Pop. 292

Dumbleyung lies in the central south of WA, 217 km E of Bunbury and 224 km N of Albany. **Of interest:** Craft and Tourist Shop, Absolon St. **In the area:** Lake Dumbleyung, 10 km W, via Rollands–Lake King Hwy: where Donald Campbell established new world water-speed record in 1964; swimming, boating, birdwatching, picnics. Wheatbelt Wildflower Drive, beginning at Kukerin, 39 km E; includes Tarin Rock Nature Reserve. Sept.–Oct.: Kukerin Tracmach Vintage Fair. Historic Schools Heritage Trails, 4 scenic drives; details from Tourist Information. **Tourist information:** Shire Offices, Harvey St; (098) 63 4012. **Accommodation:** 1 hotel, 1 cara./camp. park.
MAP REF. 347 M13, 354 G10, 356 C11

Dunsborough
Pop. 656

Dunsborough is a quiet town on Geographe Bay, west of Busselton, popular because of its beaches. **Of interest:** Greenacres Shell Museum, off Naturaliste Tce. Hutchings Museum, Newbury Rd. Bush Cottage Markets, Commonage Rd. Moonshine Brewery and Rivendell Gardens, both in Wildwood Rd. Nov.: Down South Dive Classic. **In the area:** Bannamah Wildlife Park, 2 km W.

Torpedo Rock, 10 km W. Yallingup Caves and surfing beach, 8 km SW. Canal Rocks, 15 km SW. Shearing Shed, Wildwood Rd, 15 km SW: shearing demonstrations, wool craft; check times. Several wineries situated in the south west. Gunyulgup Galleries, 4 km S of Yallingup. Sugarloaf Rock, 12 km NW. Cape Naturaliste Lighthouse, 13 km NW, daily except Wed; several walking tracks in area. Good beaches: Meelup, 5 km N; Eagle Bay, 8 km N; Bunker Bay, 12 km NW. Scuba diving, snorkelling, canoeing. Tours: 4WD, wildflowers, winery, craft, day trips to Pemberton; details from Tourist Information. **Tourist information:** Shop 3 Naturaliste Tce; (097) 55 3299. **Accommodation:** 1 hotel, 5 B&B, 1 hostel, 2 cara./camp. parks.
MAP REF. 349 C2, 354 D10

Dwellingup
Pop. 383

This quiet little town is 24 km SE of Pinjarra and 109 km from Perth. The road into Dwellingup offers panoramic views of the Indian Ocean and Peel Inlet. The impressive jarrah forests nearby supply the local timber mill. Bauxite is mined in the area. **Of interest:** Country-style meals in Dwellingup Community Hotel, Marrinup St. Hotham Valley Tourist Railway runs old-style steam train from Dwellingup into jarrah forest; check times. **Tourist information:** Tourist Information Centre, Marrinup St; (09) 538 1108. **Accommodation:** 1 hotel, 1 B&B.
MAP REF. 346 E9, 354 E9

Dolphins at Monkey Mia, near Denham

Western Wildflowers

The sandplains, swamps, flats, scrub and woodlands of south-western Australia light up with colour in spring as the 'wildflower State' puts on its brilliant display. The plains can become carpeted, almost overnight, with the gold of everlastings or feather flowers or the red and pinks of boronia and leschenaultia. The banksia bushes throw up their red and yellow cylinders along the coast and in the woodlands, grevilleas spill their flowers down to the ground and orchids proliferate. Flowering gums become a mass of red and the felty kangaroo paws invade the plains. Lilies, banksias, parrot bush, flame peas, feather flowers and native foxgloves—all are displayed in a magnificent abundance.

There are over 8000 named species and 2000 unnamed species of wildflowers in Western Australia, giving the State one of the richest floras in the world. Around 75 per cent of them are unique to the region, although they may have family connections with other plants of northern or eastern Australia. Isolation by the barrier of plain and desert that separates the west from the eastern States has caused plants on both sides to pursue their own evolution; some families of plants are unique to the west.

On even a short trip to Perth, visitors can see a wide variety of Western Australian wildflowers. At **King's Park** close to the city, wildflower species give a brilliant display between August and October. Visitors in any part of the south-west at that time will see wildflowers all around them. Often, however, it is in the State's national parks that the full beauty of massed wildflowers is best seen. Only 25 kilometres east of Perth on the Great Eastern Highway is the **John Forrest National Park**, on the edge of the Darling Range escarpment. On these undulating hills and valleys the undergrowth of the jarrah forest is rich in flowering plants; red and green kangaroo paw, swamp river myrtle, blue leschenaultia and pink calytrix are the most common. Fifty kilometres north of Perth is the **Yanchep National Park**, a place of coastal limestone and sandy plains, covered with wildflowers. There are many places farther north that are worth visiting; one such is the **Kalbarri National Park**, 670 kilometres north of Perth, at the mouth of the Murchison River. The park contains magnificent flowering trees and shrubs of banksia, grevillea and melaleuca, while the ground beneath is covered with many species, such as leschenaultia, twine rushes and sedges.

Display of wildflowers

Prolific displays of wildflowers can also be found throughout the wheat belt, forests and sandplains of the south-west. The **Dryandra State Forest**, a few kilometres from Narrogin in the south-west, has magnificent woodlands of wandoo and powderbark, with brown mallet and bush thickets. An important sanctuary for mallee fowl and numbat, this forest contains a number of species of dryandra.

Another interesting area of Western Australia is the **Stirling Range National Park**, 450 kilometres south of Perth and near the Porongurup Range. The Stirlings are very jagged peaks that rise above flat farmlands. The scenery is magnificent and wildflowers abound, many unique to the region. There are banksias here, as well as dryandra, cone bushes, cats paws, and a number of mountain bells, which have red or pink flower heads. The bare granite domes and the boulders of the Porongurup Range tower over slopes of flowering trees such as *Banksia grandis* and creepers such as the native clematis.

There are many coastal parks around Albany. The **Torndirrup National Park** is an area of coastal hills and cliffs and such scenic features as the Gap, the Blowhole and the Natural Bridge. In the stunted, windswept coastal vegetation there are many wildflowers, including the endemic giant-coned *Banksia praemorsa* and the Western Australian Christmas tree with its brilliant orange flowers.

Twenty-five kilometres east of Albany is the peaceful and beautiful **Two Peoples Bay** flora and fauna reserve, which has thickets of mallee, banksia and peppermint, together with many flowering shrubs and plants. Along the coast west of Albany is the **Walpole–Nornalup National Park**, where dense karri forest mingles with red tingle, jarrah, marri, casuarina and banksia, and many wildflowers including the tree kangaroo paw, the babe-in-cradle orchid and the potato orchid.

Although most wildflowers occur in the south-west of the State, northern areas also have displays peculiar to climatic changes and times of rainfall. While enjoying Western Australia's brilliant native flora, visitors should remember that wildflowers are protected under the State's *Native Flora Protection Act*.

For further information on national parks and wildflower display areas, contact the Western Australian Tourist Centre or the Department of Conservation and Land Management, 50 Hayman Rd (GPO Box 104), Como WA 6152; (09) 334 0333.

Esperance
Pop. 7066

Wide sandy beaches, scenic coastline and the offshore islands of the Recherche Archipelago are all attractions of Esperance, on the south coast of WA. The town, 720 km from Perth via Wagin, is the port and service centre for the productive agricultural and pastoral hinterland. The first permanent European settlers came in 1863. The town boomed during the 1890s as port for the goldfields. From the 1950s, when scientists realised that the heath plains could become fertile pasture and farming country, the town's development began in earnest. **Of interest:** Municipal Museum, James St: old machinery, furniture and farm equipment; display of Skylab, which fell to earth over Esperance in 1979. Public Library, Windich St, collection of books on history of Esperance. On the Esplanade: art and craft centre at Old Cannery; Esperance Diving Academy. Tanker Jetty, fishing, seal watching. Boat charters for deepsea fishing. Motorcycle tours and horseriding. Dec.–Jan.: Turf Racing. Oct.: Agricultural Show. **In the area:** Windfarms at Ten Mile Beach Lagoon, 16 km SW on tourist loop, supplies 14% of town's electricity; SECWA research programme. Salmon Beach, 5 km W. Rotary Lookout, or Wireless Hill, 2 km W, panoramic views of bay, town, farmlands. Pink Lake, 5 km W, dense pink saltwater lake. Twilight Bay, 12 km W, on tourist loop, swimming, fishing. Nearby Picnic Cove, sheltered swimming beach. Views of bay and islands from Observatory Point and Lookout, 17 km W. Dalyup River Wines, 42 km W, open 10–4 weekends. Recherche Archipelago (Bay of Isles), off Esperance, 105 small unspoiled islands, haven for native fauna. Launch cruises, 2- and 3-hr around Gull, Button, Charlie and other islands; landing not permitted. Regular cruises Oct.–March to Woody Island, SE of Esperance (50 min. by boat); developed as tourist attraction, overnight camping facilities. Cape Le Grand National Park, 56 km E, spectacular coastline, attractive beaches, scenic walks, beautiful wildflowers for which the region is famous. Magnificent view from Frenchmans Peak, in park. Cape Arid National Park, 120 km E, fishing, camping, 4WD routes. Telegraph Farm, 21 km N on South Coast Hwy, proteas, deer, buffalo, native animals, farm tours. **Tourist information:** Tourist Bureau, Museum Village, Dempster St; (090) 71 2330. **Accommodation:** 3 hotels, 8 motels, 2 hostels, 6 cara./camp. parks. **See also:** Crossing the Nullarbor; National Parks.
MAP REF. 356 H12

Eucla
Pop. 30

Eucla is just 12 km from the WA–SA border, on the Eyre Hwy. Oct.: Eucla Shoot. May: Golf Day. **In the area:** Cross on escarpment overlooking ocean and sand-covered ruins of old telegraph station and former town site, 5 km S, dedicated to all Eyre Hwy travellers, illuminated at night. Highway westward from Eucla descends to coastal plain via Eucla Pass. Midway down Pass (about 200 m), track to left leads to old town site and ruins among sand dunes. Nine-hole golf course, 7 km N. Weebubby Cave, 12 km N, experienced cavers only. **Tourist information:** Motor Hotel; (090) 39 3468. **Accommodation:** 1 hotel/motel, 1 cara./camp. park. **See also:** Crossing the Nullarbor.
MAP REF. 296 A8, 357 R8

Exmouth
Pop. 3128

Exmouth is one of the newest towns in Australia and was founded in 1967 as a support town for the US Naval Communications station, which is the main source of employment in the area. The town has modern sporting and community facilities. Excellent year-round fishing and its beaches has made Exmouth a main tourist destination. The town is situated on the north-eastern side of North West Cape, which is the nearest point in Australia to the continental shelf, so there is an abundance of fish and other marine life in the surrounding waters. Turtle-nesting Nov.–Jan.; coral-spawning March; whale sharks March–May; humpback whales and manta rays July–Nov. **Of interest:** Exmouth House of Dolls, Craft St. Ocean Exhibits Museum, Pellew St. July: Gala Week, Arts and Crafts Show. Nov.: Gamex (world-class game fishing). **In the area:** Swimming, snorkelling, fishing. To south, Shothole Canyon Rd: easy access to one of many spectacular gorges in Cape Range National Park; park's Milyering Visitor Centre, 52 km SW. Yardie Creek Gorge, in park, deep blue waters, multi-coloured rock, abundant wildlife. Charles Knife Canyon Rd, to south, picnic spots, scenic lookouts, walking trail. Prawn fishery, 23 km S; open in season, May–Oct. Learmonth RAAF base, 34 km S. Charter fishing at Bundegi Beach jetty, 14 km N. Panoramic views from Vlaming Head Lighthouse, 17 km N; guided tours. Wreck of SS *Mildura* nearby. Ningaloo Marine Park, 14 km W of Cape, largest coral reef in WA, 500 fish species, 220 reef-building coral species. Daily coral-viewing trips from Exmouth and Coral Bay. Safari tours of Cape. Dive courses, dive trips. Lightfoot Heritage Trail; details from Tourist Information. **Tourist information:** Thew St; (099) 49 1176. **Accommodation:** 2 motels, 2 hostels, 5 cara./camp. parks.
MAP REF. 355 C3

Fitzroy Crossing
Pop. 1119

In the Kimberley, where the road north crosses the Fitzroy River, is the settlement of Fitzroy Crossing, 260 km inland from Derby. Once a sleepy little hamlet, the last few years have seen unprecedented growth of the town as a result of Aboriginal settlement, mining by BHP at Cadjebut, 50 km E, and an increase in the number of visitors to the nearby Geikie Gorge National Park. July: Rodeo. Nov.: Barra Bash (barramundi fishing competition). **In the area:** Picturesque waterholes, which support abundance of fish and other wildlife. Magnificent Geikie Gorge, 20 km NE, plentiful sawfish and stingrays, adapted to fresh water, and barramundi and freshwater crocodiles; twice-daily boat trips May–Nov. Fitzroy River Lodge tourist complex, on Great Northern Hwy. Between Dec. and March check road conditions, as area is prone to flooding. **Tourist information:** Fitzroy River Lodge; (091) 91 5141. **Accommodation:** 1 hotel, 1 motel, 3 cara./camp. parks. **See also:** National Parks.
MAP REF. 352 H11, 361 M9

Fremantle
Pop. 27 000

The largest port in the State and western gateway to Australia, Fremantle is a bustling city 19 km S of Perth. It is a city of contrasts, with galleries and museums, beautiful sandy white beaches and many historic buildings as a reminder of the city's heritage. Captain Charles Fremantle arrived in May 1829 to 'take possession' of 'the whole of the west coast of New Holland', and was followed one month later by Captain James Stirling, who brought a small group to found the first Australian colony made up entirely of European free settlers. The engineer C. Y. O'Connor, who began

The Kimberley

Until relatively recently the Kimberley region in the far north of Western Australia was only for hardened pioneers and prospectors. Now the National Highway puts it on Australia's travel map and it can offer both excitement and adventure. In addition, the 40 tonne, 18 metre ketch-rigged motor yacht *Opal Shell* cruises along the Kimberley coast out of Derby.

There are two seasons in the Kimberley. The long dry period in winter brings delightful weather, while the green season brings higher temperatures, with monsoonal rains usually falling between December and March.

On the west side, the gateway to the Kimberley is the old pearling town of Broome. In the boisterous days of the early 1900s the pearling fleet numbered some 400 luggers with 3000 crewmen. Today cosmopolitan Broome is rapidly expanding into one of Western Australia's most popular tourist destinations. There are many points of interest, including a set of dinosaur tracks believed to have been embedded in limestone 130 million years ago, and Buccaneer Rock, reputed to be the place where Dampier was wrecked in the *Roebuck* in 1699.

Further north-east is **Derby**, on King Sound near the mouth of the Fitzroy River, a centre for the beef cattle industry of the Fitzroy Valley and the King Leopold Ranges. Just 7 kilometres south of the town is a centuries-old boab tree. Shaped like an inverted wineglass and 14 metres in diameter, it is hollow and is reputed to have been used as a cell for prisoners.

Derby is a useful base for excursions to Windjana Gorge and Tunnel Creek in the Napier Range, and Geikie Gorge near the town of **Fitzroy Crossing**, which is a centre for local Aboriginal communities and also has excellent accommodation and camping facilities. The river gorges here are among the most colourful and spectacular in northern Australia.

The old gold settlement of **Halls Creek**, 16 kilometres from the site of the present town, was the scene of the first gold rush in Western Australia in 1885. Scores of diggers perished of hunger and thirst and very little gold was found. Nearby is the meteorite crater at Wolfe Creek, the second largest in the world, with an average depth of 50 metres. The meteorite is believed to have struck the earth about one million years ago. Also near Halls Creek is the China Wall, a natural white stone wall above a placid creek.

The most northerly town and safe port harbour in Western Australia is **Wyndham**, the terminus of the Great Northern Highway and now also the port for the Ord River irrigation area as well as for the east Kimberley cattle stations. A 100 kilometre route from Wyndham to **Kununurra** winds through spectacular ancient gorge country. Kununurra, a lively town with excellent facilities, is the base for Lake Argyle, Hidden Valley National Park and Purnululu (Bungle Bungle) National Park. South of Lake Argyle is the Argyle diamond mine, the world's largest. Kununurra is then linked to **Darwin** by the National Highway, which is often used by travellers making a round trip of Australia.

For further information contact the Kununurra Tourist Bureau, Coolibah Drive, Kununurra; (091) 68 1177. **See also:** Individual town entries in A–Z listing. **Note** detailed map of Kimberley Region on page 352.

The Ord River

The development of the Ord River Scheme was a far-sighted move to develop the tropical north of Western Australia. During the rainy season, the rivers of the Kimberley become raging torrents and at times the waters of the Ord River empty more than 50 million litres a second into Cambridge Gulf. With the end of the monsoon rain, the rich seasonal pastures die and the land becomes dry again. The Ord River Dam was built to harness this tremendous wealth of water for agriculture.

The Kimberley Research Station was established in 1945 to investigate the likelihood of producing crops on the black alluvial soil of the plains. The land was found to be suitable for a variety of tropical crops. Between 1963 and 1972 the Diversion Dam at Kununurra was built to divert water from the river into supply channels. **Lake Argyle**, 72 kilometres south of the Carr Boyd Range, is the main storage reservoir. It is the largest constructed lake in Australia, its normal capacity being 5674 million cubic metres. This vast expanse of water is dotted with islands that were once peaks rising above the surrounding valleys. The water of the Ord is now capable of irrigating 72 000 hectares of land. A third of the projected irrigation area will be along the Keep River Plain in the Northern Territory.

The area is becoming increasingly attractive to tourists. Surrounding Lake Argyle are rugged red slopes, a haven for native animals such as the bungarra lizard, the brush-tailed wallaby and the euro. Looking out over the lake is a tourist village with a hotel/motel, caravan and camping facilities and areas of shaded lawns. There are lake cruises, fishing trips, bushwalks, tennis and a picnic area.

The original Durack homestead from **Argyle Downs Station** is also to be found here; once the residence of the cattle-pioneer Durack family, the homestead was moved to its present site to prevent it being covered by the waters of the lake as it filled. A fascinating memorial to the early settlers of the district, it recreates life as it once was in the Kimberley.

The town of **Kununurra**—the name means 'big water'—was established in the 1960s as the residential and administrative centre of the Ord River Scheme.

For further information contact the Kununurra Tourist Bureau, Coolibah Drive, Kununurra; (091) 68 1177. **See also:** Individual town entries in A–Z listing; The Kimberley.

Round House, Fremantle, Western Australia's oldest building

the Goldfields Water Scheme, was responsible for building the harbour that turned Fremantle into an important port. The city has become home to many more recent immigrants. With its old-world charm and colourful cosmopolitan culture, Fremantle is one of the most fascinating port cities in the world. **Of interest:** Many coffee shops and restaurants in South Terrace–Cappucino Strip. In Cliff St: Maritime Museum (1860s), fine example of colonial Gothic architecture; Port Authority Building, Fremantle's tallest building, panoramic views from roof viewing area. Old Customs House (1853), Georgian style; Fremantle Museum and Arts Centre, Finnerty St, musical performances in courtyard during summer. Boat Museum, on Victoria Quay, not far from Maritime Museum. Energy Museum, Parry St. Film and Television Institute, Adelaide St. Round House (1830), end of High St, oldest building in WA; 12-sided structure, constructed as gaol. Joan Campbell's Pottery Workshop, near The Round House, in converted boatshed. Magnificent Samson House (1900), cnr Ellen and Ord Sts; guided tours. Shell Museum, Beach St. Spare Parts Puppet Theatre, Short St, permanent puppet display, regular performances. Fremantle

Crocodile Park, at Fishing Boat Harbour, off Mews Rd, both saltwater and smaller freshwater species. Former Fremantle Gaol (1851–59) The Tce, via Fairbairn St, forbidding building of local stone; open to visitors. Fremantle Prison Museum, displays recording penal system in WA, adj. to prison. In Henderson St: award-winning Warders' Quarters, Georgian terrace; Fremantle Markets, incl. seafoods, crafts, antiques, clothing, souvenirs, Fri.–Sun. St John's Church and Square (1882). Town Hall in Kings Square, cnr William and Adelaide Sts; opened 1887. Quaint old building, 5 Mouat St, originally housed German Consulate and shipping offices. Adjacent to Marine Tce and the Esplanade, modern Challenger Harbour marina facilities, developed for first Australian defence of the America's Cup, yachting's most prestigious trophy. Fremantle's large fishing fleet, which works Australia's most valuable fishing grounds (mainly lobster), and its considerable Italian community, give city a Mediterranean flavour. Sail & Anchor Hotel, South Tce, Australia's first pub brewery, serves specialty beers. Pavement cafes and excellent restaurants. May: Fremantle–Exmouth Yachting Classic. Nov.: Fremantle Festival. **In the area:**

Swimming: Port, Leighton and South Beaches. Ferries to Rottnest Island, 20 km W, from wharf daily; charter boats to Rottnest also available. Daily tram tours; details from Tourist Information. **Tourist information:** Town Hall Shop, King Sq., High St; (09) 430 2346. **Accommodation:** 10 hotels, 2 hotel/motels, 1 motel, 10 B&B, 1 hostel, 3 caravan parks. MAP REF. 342 B11, 346 C5, 348, 354 D7

Gascoyne Junction   Pop. 34

Located 178 km E of Carnarvon, at the junction of the Gascoyne and Lyons Rivers, this town is the administration centre for the Shire of Upper Gascoyne. The old-fashioned pub is a good rest stop before the many scenic attractions of the Kennedy Ranges National Park, 60 km N. **Tourist information:** Carnarvon District Tourist Bureau, Robinson St, Carnarvon; (099) 41 1146. **Accommodation:** 1 hotel.
MAP REF. 355 E8

Geraldton   Pop. 24 361

The key port and administration centre for the Midwest region, Geraldton is 424 km N of Perth on Champion Bay. A year-round sunny climate and a mild winter, make it one of the State's most popular holiday resorts. The flourishing city has a modern shopping centre, interesting museums, excellent accommodation, white, sandy beaches and good fishing. Rich agricultural land surrounds Geraldton and the district is noted for beautiful spring wildflowers and picturesque countryside. The Houtman Abrolhos Islands, so named in the sixteenth century, lie 64 km off the coast and are used mainly as a base for rock-lobster fishermen. **Of interest:** In Cathedral Ave: Queens Park Theatre (1922), surrounded by gardens; St Francis Xavier Cathedral, designed by Mons. John C. Hawes, architect of some fine buildings in and around Geraldton. On Marine Tce: Sir John Forrest Memorial; Geraldton Museum (incl. Maritime Display building and Old Railway building), earthenware pots and wine vessels, bronze cannon, coins, other relics from shipwrecks off coast. Art Gallery, cnr Durlacher St and Chapman Rd. Old Gaol Craft Centre, Bill Sewell Complex, Chapman Rd. Tourist Lookout and Wishing Well on Waverley Heights, Brede St, views. Point Moore Lighthouse (1878), Willcock Dr. Fishing is popular; many varieties can be caught, town's breakwater is good location. At Fisherman's Wharf in season Nov.–June, watch huge hauls of lobster being unloaded. Jan.: Windsurfing Blast. Oct.: Festival of Geraldton. Water sports, ten-pin bowling, archery, Indy Kart racing, golf. **In the area:** Sunset Beach, 6 km N, good fishing. Fishing and surfing: Drummond Cove, 10 km N; mouth of Greenough River, 10 km S. Greenough River also favourite place for picnics, safe swimming for children. Greenough hamlet, 24 km S, National Trust-restored village, preserved to look as it did in 1880s; guided tours. Ellendale Bluffs and Pool, 45 km SE, permanent waterhole at base of steep rock face. Mill's Park Lookout, on Waggrakine Cutting, 15 km NE; views over Moresby Range and coastal plain towards Geraldton. Chapman Valley, 35 km NE, farming district, brilliant wildflowers in spring. At Kalbarri, 164 km N, sheer coastal rock faces and deep gorges of Murchison River, stunningly beautiful. Kalbarri National Park, 170 km N. Geraldton Heritage Trail; details from Tourist Information. **Tourist information:** Bill Sewell Complex, cnr Bayley St and Chapman Rd; (099) 21 3999. **Accommodation:** 14 hotel/motels, 2 hostels, 7 cara./camp. parks. MAP REF. 354 C2

Gingin   Pop. 473

Situated 83 km N of Perth and 30 km from the coast, Gingin is mainly a centre for sheep, cattle, mixed farming and horticulture. An interesting day trip from Perth, it offers alternative return trips touring coastal centres or inland via the scenic Chittering Valley. The town is built around a loop of Gingin Brook, which rises from springs not far from town and flows strongly all year. **Of interest:** Gingin has style of English village. Fine examples of traditional Australian architecture: in Weld St, St Luke's Anglican Church (1860s), Granville (1871), Uniting Church (1868), Dewar's House (1886); Philbey's Cottage (1906), Brockman St. May: British Car Day. **In the area:** At Bullsbrook, 30 km S: The Maze; Bullsbrook Antiques and Cottage Crafts. At Lower Chittering, 30 km SE, Golden Grove Citrus Orchard. At Bindoon, 24 km E, Neroni Wines, Chittering Valley Estate, Kay Road Art and Craft Gallery. Sewell Leisure Park, 44 km NE, golf, rides, flora, fauna, picnic/barbecue facilities. **Tourist information:** Shire Offices, 7 Brockman St; (09) 575 2211. **Accommodation:** 1 hotel/motel, 1 cara./camp. park. MAP REF. 354 E6

Guilderton   Pop. 385

At the mouth of the Moore River, 94 km from Perth, Guilderton is a popular day trip and holiday destination. There is excellent fishing in both river and sea, and safe swimming for children. Many Dutch relics have been found here, possibly from the wreck of the *Vergulde Draeck* (the Gilt Dragon) in 1656. Easter: King of the River. Jan.: Lancelin Ocean Classic. **In the area:** Seabird, 20 km N, small but growing fishing village offering tranquillity with safe beach, ample recreational options. Ledge Point, 28 km N, centre built around fishing industry; activities for all ages; sporting facilities, swimming and boating, picnic facilities. **Tourist information:** Shire Offices, 7 Brockman St, Gingin; (09) 575 2211. **Accommodation:** 1 cara./camp. park. MAP REF. 354 D6

Halls Creek   Pop. 1305

In the heart of the Kimberley, 2832 km from Perth, at the edge of the Great Sandy Desert, is Halls Creek, site of WA's first gold find in 1885. In 1885–7, 10 000 men came to the Kimberley fields in search of gold then gradually drifted away, leaving 2000 on the diggings. Today mineral exploration is still carried out and the pastoral industry is supported by steady beef prices. **Of interest:** Arts Centre, Great Northern Hwy, Aboriginal art and artefacts, jewellery made from Halls Creek gold. Russian Jack Memorial, Thomas St, honours early European settlers. July: Agricultural Show. Aug.: Races. **In the area:** China Wall, 16 km SE, natural quartz formation, picnic spot above creek. Fishing, swimming, picnicking: Ruby Queen Mine, Sawpit Gorge, both 40 km SE. Old Halls Creek, 16 km E, prospecting, mud-brick ruins of original settlement. Caroline Pool, off Duncan Rd, near old town site, picnic spot, swimming Oct.–May. Purnululu (Bungle Bungle) National Park, 165 km NE. Aerial tours and 4WD safaris. Town is base for visiting Wolfe Creek Meteorite Crater, (almost 1 km wide, 49 m deep and second largest meteorite crater in world),148 km S. **Tourist information:** Memorial Park, Great Northern Hwy; (091) 68 6262. **Accommodation:** 1 hotel, 1 motel, 1 cara./camp. park. **See also:** The Kimberley. MAP REF. 353 N11, 361 P9

Harvey   Pop. 2597

The thriving town of Harvey is set in some of the finest agricultural country in Australia, 139 km S of Perth. Bordered by the Darling Range and the Indian Ocean, the fertile plains make perfect dairying country. The town's irrigation storage dams, with their recreation areas, have become a popular tourist attraction. **Of interest:** Historical Society Museum, in old railway station (1914), Harvey St. Tourist and Interpretative Centre, South West Hwy, industry displays, incl. dairy industry in Moo Shoppe; craft. Stirling Cottage, behind Tourist Centre: 1880s home of May Gibbs (author of Snugglepot and Cuddlepie); museum rooms; teas, light lunches; open daily. Internment Camp Memorial Shrine, South Coast Hwy, built by prisoners of war in 1940s; key from Tourist Information. Jan.: Australia Day Breakfast. Oct.: Agricultural Show. **In the area:** Weir, 3 km E, off Weir Rd. Scenic drive (7 km) around north west side of Stirling Dam, 19 km E, leads to Harvey Falls and Trout Ladder; fishing spot. Hoffmans Mill, 25 km NE, picnic facilities, camping. Logue Brook Dam, 15 km N, bushwalking, swimming, water-skiing, trout fishing. Workshops Museum, Yarloop, 15 km N;

The Pinnacles, Nambung National Park

working exhibit, closed Tues. Yarloop Heritage Trail; details from museum. Yalgorup National Park, 35 km NW. Myalup and Binningup beaches, 25 km W, off Old Coast Rd, wide and sandy, ideal for swimming, fishing, boating. Emu Tech Farm, Old Coast Rd, Myalup; restaurant, picnic area. Kemerton Industrial Park (SCM Chemicals), 20 km S; group tours. **Tourist information:** South West Hwy; (097) 29 1122. **Accommodation:** 1 hotel, 1 motel, 2 cara./camp. parks. **See also:** The South-west.
MAP REF. 346 D11, 354 E9

Hopetoun   Pop. 206

Hopetoun is a peaceful holiday resort overlooking the Southern Ocean. The town is 59 km S of Ravensthorpe and offers rugged but beautiful coastal scenery and year-round wildflowers. Once called Mary Anne Harbour, the town has a colourful history. **Of interest:** White-sand beaches, sheltered bays, excellent fishing. Chatterbox Craft, Veal St, local art, craft. **In the area:** Dunn's Swamp, 5 km N, picnics, bushwalking, birdwatching. Fitzgerald River National Park, 10 km W: the Barrens, a series of rugged mountains, undulating sandplains and steep narrow gorges; Hamersley Inlet, in park, scenic picnic and camping spot. Take care fishing from rocks—king waves can roll in unexpectedly and take lives. **Tourist information:** Hardware and Tackle Store, Veal St; (098) 38 3088. **Accommodation:** 1 hotel, 1 motel, 1 cara./camp. park.
MAP REF. 356 F12

Hyden   Pop. 150

Hyden is in the Shire of Kondinin, 351 km east of Perth, in the semi-arid eastern wheat area of WA. **In the area:** Fascinating rock formations, the most famous of which is Wave Rock, 4 km E of Hyden: 2700 million-yr-old granite outcrop rising 15 m, like a giant wave about to break. At Wave Rock: wildlife park; coffee shop; caravan park with chalets; Pioneer Town, collection of Australiana; lace collection (from 1600) at Visitors Centre. Award-winning Wave Rock Experience. Other rock formations within walking distance of Wave Rock: Hippo's Yawn, The Falls, The Breakers. Aboriginal rock paintings at Mulka's Cave, 18 km N of Wave Rock. Nearby, The Humps, another unusual granite formation. **Tourist information:** Wave Rock Visitors Centre, Wave Rock Rd, 4 km E of town; (098) 80 5182. **Accommodation:** 1 hotel/motel, 1 B&B, 1 cara./camp. park.
MAP REF. 354 I8, 356 D9

Jurien   Pop. 603

On the shores of an attractive, sheltered bay between Perth and Geraldton, Jurien is a lobster-fishing centre. The town is also a growing holiday destination because of its magnificent safe swimming beaches, excellent climate and reputation as a fisherman's paradise. Jurien boat harbour, a 17-ha inland marina, excellent facilities for boating enthusiasts. **Of interest:** Tours of rock-lobster processing factory, Roberts Rd, in fishing season. Nov.: Expo and Blessing of the Fleet. Dec.: Slalom Carnival (windsurfing in Cervantes). **In the area:** Cockleshell Gully, 31 km N, great diversity of flora and fauna. Stockyard Gully National Park, 50 km N (4WD only): walk through 300-m Stockyard Gully Tunnel along winding underground creek; torch necessary. Spectacular sand dunes along coast. Nambung National Park, boundary 55 km S: check road conditions before leaving Jurien if taking coastal track; main, signposted route further inland recommended. The Pinnacles, further 17 km into park: thousands of spectacular calcified spires, around 30 000 years old, scattered over 400 ha of multi-coloured sand; guided coach tours daily. Waddi Farms, Koonah Rd, off Brand Hwy, Badgingarra, 60 km SE, wildflowers, emu farm, native gardens, shop, restaurant. **Tourist information:** Shire Offices, Bashford St; (096) 52 1020. **Accommodation:** 1 hotel/motel, 4 B&B, 1 cara./camp. park.
MAP REF. 354 C4

Kalbarri   Pop. 1521

This popular holiday resort is between Geraldton and Carnarvon, 661 km N of Perth. The town's picturesque setting on the Murchison River estuary, its year-round sunny climate and the spectacular gorges of the river running through the Kalbarri National Park attract a growing number of tourists. Kalbarri is also noted for excellent fishing and the brilliance of more than 500 wildflower species. **Of interest:** Kalflora, off Ajana Rd, wide range of Kalbarri wildflowers. In Grey St: Doll and Marine Museum, Fantasy Land, Gemstone Mine. In Porter St: Echoes Restaurant, overlooking river, fully licensed, fresh seafood; Kalbarri Entertainment Centre, bicycle hire. March: Sport Fishing Classic. Nov.: Blessing of the Fleet. **In the area:** Book at Tourist Information: horsedrawn wagon tour of town; *River Queen* ferry cruise; sunset or wildflower camel safari, 1/2 hr, Red Bluff, 4 km S. Kalbarri National Park, large area of magnificent virgin bushland surrounding town, picnic/barbecue facilities, no camping. Inside park: Kalbarri Big River Ranch, 3 km E, horseriding; spectacular Murchison River gorges, 11 km E, abundance of wildlife and native flora. Coach tours of park, joy flights over gorges, canoe safaris, abseiling adventure tours. All 4 km S: Red Bluff, swimming, fishing, rock

National Parks

The national parks of Western Australia are tourist attractions in themselves: their spectacular displays of wildflowers create a paradise for photographers and a wonderland for bushwalkers and campers.

Western Australia has more than 8000 named species and 2000 unnamed species of wildflowers, growing undisturbed in their natural surroundings. One quarter of these species cannot be found anywhere else and they lure admirers from all over the world. The best months to see them are from August to October. This is also the best time for camping trips and bushwalking.

Within a 100 kilometre radius of Perth there are ten national parks well worth a visit. **Yanchep National Park**, about 50 kilometres north on a belt of coastal limestone, has forests of massive tuart trees. Islands on Loch Ness, within the park, are waterfowl sanctuaries. Yanchep is also famed for its underground limestone caves and spring wildflowers.

Some 80 kilometres north-east of Perth is the **Avon Valley National Park;** its most popular attractions are upland forests and river valleys, as well as the beautiful wildflowers in season. The highest point in the park is Bald Hill, which gives panoramic views of the Avon River. After winter rains, a tributary of the Avon, Emu Spring Brook, spills 30 metres down in a spectacular waterfall.

A cluster of national parks to the east of Perth includes **John Forrest National Park**, which was Western Australia's first proclaimed national park. With the Darling Escarpment within its boundaries, the park features granite outcrops, dams and waterfalls, creeks and rock pools.

Other nearby national parks are **Kalamunda**, **Greenmount**, **Gooseberry Hill** and **Lesmurdie Falls**, all within 20–25 kilometres of Perth. The Bibbulmun Track, once an Aboriginal walking trail, begins its 650 kilometre route in Kalamunda National Park.

Proclaimed as the State's first flora and fauna reserve in 1894, **Serpentine National Park** is about 60 kilometres south of Perth and a firm favourite of day picnickers to the falls area in the park. Jarrah and marri forests, and wildflowers in spring, are some of the park's attractions.

Stirling Range National Park, 450 kilometres south-east of Perth, is one of Australia's outstanding reserves. Surrounded by a flat, sandy plain, the Stirling Range rises abruptly to over 1000 metres, its jagged peaks veiled in swirling mists. The cool, humid environment created by these low clouds contributes to the survival of more than 1000 flowering plant species, some of which, like the mountain bells, are found nowhere else in the world.

Brilliant displays of wildflowers are also a feature of the nearby **Porongurup National Park**, where the granite domes of the Porongurup Ranges are clothed in a forest of karri trees. The South Western Highway bisects the **Shannon National Park,** 358 kilometres south of Perth. A base from which to explore the park is at the former timber-milling town site of Shannon. The remainder of the park consists of towering karri and jarrah forests, surrounding the Shannon River.

Spectacular coastal scenery is the main attraction of the **Torndirrup National Park** on the Flinders Peninsula, 460 kilometres south of Perth. Also on the south coast are other outstanding parks, including **Cape Le Grand National Park,** with its wide beaches and magnificent bays, protected by granite headlands, located 40 kilometres east of Esperance.

Two other parks are near Esperance, both to the west of the town. **Stokes National Park** hugs the coastline around Stokes Inlet and features long sandy beaches and rocky headlands backed by sand dunes and low hills. Stokes Inlet and its associated lakes support a rich variety of wildlife. Inland from Stokes about 100 kilometres, lies **Peak Charles National Park**. A walk to the ridge of this ancient granite peak allows sweeping views of its companion, Peak Eleanora, and over the dry sandplain heaths and salt-lake systems of the surrounding country.

One of the loveliest sections of the south coast of Western Australia is **Fitzgerald River National Park**, through which the rugged Barren Range (named

Millstream–Chichester National Park

Purnululu (Bungle Bungle) National Park

by Matthew Flinders) stretches from west to east. The park's 330 000 hectares comprise gently undulating sandplains, river valleys, precipitous cliff edges, narrow gorges, and beaches for swimming and rock fishing. The park contains many rare species of flora and fauna, including unique species of flowering plants; one, the exotic royal hakea, resembles a flame shooting from the earth.

Along the lower south-west coast is **Walpole–Nornalup National Park,** 18 166 hectares of wilderness in which creeks gurgle under tall eucalypts, rivers meander between forested hills and inlets rich in fish create a haven for anglers and boating enthusiasts. A network of roads and walking tracks, through forests of karri and tingle, attracts bushwalkers and birdwatchers to enjoy the variety of animal and bird life.

About 100 kilometres east is **West Cape Howe National Park**, the spectacular coastline of which includes the gabbro cliffs of West Cape Howe and the granite of Torbay Heads, fronting the cold waters of the Southern Ocean. Extensive coastal heath, swamps, lakes and karri forest cover the inland, and the park is popular with anglers, bushwalkers, rock climbers and hang-gliding enthusiasts.

Unusual rock formations are to be found at **Nambung National Park**, 230 kilometres north of Perth on the coast. Here a moonscape of coloured quartz is studded with fantastic limestone pillars ranging in size from stony 'twigs' to columns more than 2 metres tall. This is the unique Pinnacle Desert, a favourite subject for photographers.

Keeping to the coast but travelling further north, the visitor will discover the wild beauty of ancient landscapes, unsurpassed at **Kalbarri National Park**. Its 186 050 hectares encompass the lower reaches of the Murchison River, which winds its way through spectacular gorges to the Indian Ocean. Sea cliffs in layers of multi-coloured sandstone loom over the crashing white foam at Red Bluff.

In the Pilbara, 1400 kilometres north of Perth, is **Karijini (Hamersley Range) National Park**, part of a massive block of weathered rock over 450 kilometres long. Within this huge, spectacular park are many well-known gorges, including Dales Gorge, its strata in horizontal stripes of blue, mauve, red and brown dating back almost 2000 million years. Further north, still in the Pilbara, **Millstream–Chichester National Park** encompasses almost 20 000 hectares of clay tablelands and sediment-capped basalt ranges. At Millstream, on the Fortescue River, natural freshwater springs have created an oasis in arid country. In contrast, there are the Chichester Ranges: rolling hills, hummocks of spinifex, white-barked snappy gums on the uplands, and pale coolibahs along the usually dry watercourses.

In the far north of Western Australia are the national parks of the Kimberley region—mountain ranges formed millions of years ago. The largest of these parks, **Geikie Gorge**, has an area of 3136 hectares and is 20 kilometres north-east of Fitzroy Crossing. The multi-coloured cliffs are reflected in the placid waters of the Fitzroy River, which flows through the gorge. The area is too rugged for extensive walking, but organised boat trips go up the river through the gorge, enabling visitors to see one of Australia's most beautiful waterways.

Other nearby national parks are **Windjana Gorge** and **Tunnel Creek**, both north-west of Geikie Gorge. Tunnel Creek, a permanent watercourse, flows underground for 750 metres. It is possible to walk through the high, wide tunnel to a small river beach beyond; some deep wading may be necessary, and carry a torch.

South of Lake Argyle is the spectacular **Purnululu (Bungle Bungle) National Park**, with its tiger-striped, beehive-shaped domes, sheer walls, deep gullies and unique palms. Because of the fragility of internal roads in wet conditions, this park is closed from approximately 1 January to 1 April.

Hidden Valley National Park, only 2.5 kilometres east of Kununurra, has features typical of the Kimberley: banded sandstone outcrops similar to those of the Bungle Bungle massif, boab trees, red soil dotted with eucalpyts, and black kites circling overhead. Aboriginal rock paintings are also a feature of the park.

For further information on Western Australia's national parks, contact the Department of Conservation and Land Management, 50 Hayman Rd (GPO Box 104), Como, WA 6152; (09) 334 0333.

climbing; Rainbow Jungle and Tropical Bird Park; Cairn at Wittecarra Creek, marks what is believed to be site of first permanent landing of Europeans in Australia, two Dutchmen sent ashore for their part in *Batavia* mutiny in 1629. Meanarra Lookout, 7 km SE. The Loop and Z Bend lookouts, 30 km NE. Majestic coastal gorges, precipitous red cliffs dropping to Indian Ocean below; coach tours and joy flights. **Tourist information:** Allen Community Centre, Grey St; (099) 37 1104. **Accommodation:** 1 hotel/motel, 2 motels, 1 hostel, 4 cara./camp. parks. MAP REF. 355 C13

Kalgoorlie–Boulder
Pop. 25 016
At the heart of WA's largest goldmining area is the city of Kalgoorlie–Boulder, 597 km E of Perth and centred on the famous Golden Mile, reputed to be the richest square mile in the world. Over 1300 tonnes of gold have been mined from this small area. Paddy Hannan found gold in 1893; by 1902 the population was 30 000, with 93 hotels operating. Fortunes were made overnight; the impressive stone buildings and magnificent wide streets recall the town's boom past. Miners set up their tents on the Golden Mile near the Great Boulder Mine, and this camp became the town of Boulder. One of the greatest difficulties facing the miners in this semi-desert area was lack of water. Determination and the brilliant scheme of engineer C. Y. O'Connor saved the day. A pipeline was completed in 1903, carrying water an incredible 563 km from a reservoir near Perth. Goldmining continues with renewed vigour now that gold prices have risen. The Kalgoorlie–Boulder region is also an important pastoral district for high-quality wool. **Of interest:** Fine examples of early Australian architecture: in Hannan St, Exchange and Palace Hotels, Australia Hotel, Government Buildings, Kalgoorlie Post Office. Distinctive Kalgoorlie Town Hall (1908), impressive staircase, paintings by local artists. Also in Hannan St: Museum of the Goldfields and British Arms Hotel (1899), display recalling heyday of gold-rush boom; statue of Paddy Hannan. Goldfields Aboriginal Art Gallery, next to museum. Paddy Hannan's Tree, Outridge Tce, marks site of first gold find in Kalgoorlie. School of Mines Museum, Egan St, world-class display, incl. most minerals found in WA.

Hannans North Historical Mining Complex, Broad Arrow Rd, underground and surface tours, gold-pouring demonstrations. Super Pit Lookout, off Eastern Bypass Rd; open daily. In Burt St: Boulder Town Hall (1908), regular art exhibits; Eastern Goldfields Historical Museum, in Boulder railway station. Picturesque Cornwall Hotel (1898), Chesapeake St. Royal Flying Doctor Base, Killarney St, serves one of largest areas in Australia; tours weekdays. Hammond Park, Lyall St, wildlife sanctuary, small lake, scale model of Bavarian castle. Mt Charlotte Reservoir and Lookout, off Sutherland St: storage for Kalgoorlie's vital fresh-water supply. The Loop Line, tourist railway line around the Golden Mile. Sept.: Kalgoorlie Cup, Spring Festival. Nov.: Goldfields Mining Expo. **In the area:** WA's only two-up school, 7 km N of Kalgoorlie, on eastern side of road to Menzies. Kurrawang Emu Farm, 18 km W, Aboriginal artefacts, tours; closed Sun. Kalgoorlie–Boulder is an ideal base for visiting old goldmining towns, some now ghost towns, in district. All within a day's drive and all active again: Coolgardie, 37 km SW; Broad Arrow, 38 km N; Ora Banda, 54 km N; Kookynie, 200 km N; Leonora–Gwalia, 235 km N. Eastern Goldfields Heritage Trail; details from Tourist Information. **Tourist information:** 250 Hannan St, Kalgoorlie; (090) 21 1966. **Accommodation:** Kalgoorlie; 13 hotels, 9 motels, 4 cara./camp. parks. Boulder, 8 hotels, 2 motels, 2 cara./camp. parks. **See also:** Crossing the Nullarbor; The Goldfields. MAP REF. 356 H6

Kambalda
Pop. 4259
Kambalda's goldmining history lasted from 1897 to 1906, during which time 30 000 ounces of gold were produced. When the gold petered out, so did the town. In 1966, however, rich nickel deposits were discovered and the town has since boomed. Today Kambalda, 634 km E of Perth, consists of two well-planned centres (Kambalda and Kambalda West), 6 km apart, and is noted for its environmental protection policy. **Of interest:** Several pleasant picnic areas in centre of town. Red Hill Lookout, off Gordon Adams Rd; excellent views of area, incl. vast Lake Lefroy (510 sq. km). June: Sky Diving Gathering. Nov.: Raft Regatta. **In the area:** Land yachting on salt bed of lake. Defiance Open Cut Gold Mine

Lookout, 20 km S; obtain entry permit, from town's Western Mining office. **Tourist information:** Emu Rocks Rd, Kambalda West; (090) 27 1446. **Accommodation:** 1 hotel, 1 cara./camp. park. **See also:** The Goldfields. MAP REF. 356 H7

Karratha
Pop. 11 325
Karratha was established on Nickel Bay in 1968 as a result of the continuing development of the Hamersley Iron Project, when there was a lack of suitable land for expansion at Dampier and a need for a regional centre. The town grew even faster when Woodside Petroleum developed the immense offshore gas reserve on the North West Shelf, and Karratha now has the best facilities in the north-west. Karratha's warm winter temperatures make it a good place to escape the southern cold in a clean, modern town. **Of interest:** Largest shopping centre outside Perth. Swimming, boating, golf, bowls. Excellent views from TV Hill Lookout, Millstream Rd. Easter: Pilbara Pursuit Jetboat Classic. Aug.: FeNaCLING Festival. **In the area:** Scenic flights, day tours and safari tours of Pilbara outback. Details at Tourist Information. Jaburara Heritage Trail, 3.5 km W on Main Rd, incl. Aboriginal rock carvings; Chichester Range Camel Trail. **Tourist information:** 4548 Karratha Rd; (091) 44 4600. **Accommodation:** 2 motels, 3 cara./ camp. parks. **See also:** The Hamersley Range; The Pilbara. MAP REF. 355 G1

Katanning
Pop. 4139
A thriving town 186 km N of Albany, Katanning's well-planned streets have some impressive Federation buildings. The countryside is given over to grain-growing and pastoral activities, and is noted for its fine merino sheep. **Of interest:** Old Mill Museum (1889), cnr Clive St and Austral Tce, outstanding display of vintage roller flour-milling process. Majestic Kobeelya mansion (1902), Brownie St, country retreat now owned by Baptist Church; by appt. All Ages Playground, Clive St, miniature steam railway, 600 m of track. Old Winery ruins, Andrews Rd, being restored. In Dore St: largest country-based sheep-selling facility in WA; regular sales on Thurs. throughout year, ram sale in Aug. Meatworks, Wagin Rd; guided tours by appt, contact meatworks or Tourist

The South-West

The south-west corner of Western Australia is a lush green land. Its gently rolling hills are crossed by rivers winding through deep-sided valleys. The soils are fertile and the farms prosperous. Along the coast there are beautiful bays, and inland, majestic towering karri and jarrah forests. The countryside is dotted with orchards and many wildflowers; Western Australia is one of the richest areas of flora in the world.

Pinjarra, 84 kilometres south of Perth, is one of the State's oldest districts. It has interesting historic buildings and makes a good base for touring the area.

Near **Harvey** there is fine agricultural land and the undulating farms stretch to the foothills of the Darling Range. Northwest of Harvey is **Yalgorup National Park** (one of only three sites in Western Australia with stromatolites), where the lakes attract a wide variety of birdlife. The Old Coast Road, which edges down the coast to Bunbury, is a perfect choice if you want to go off the beaten track.

The coast of the south-west is fascinating: an unusual mixture of craggy outcrops and promontories, sheltered bays with calm waters and beaches pounded by rolling surf. In the course of a day at **Cape Leeuwin** it is possible to see the sun rising over one ocean and setting over another. The length of the coast, together with the many rivers and estuaries, makes the south-west an angler's paradise. The Murray, Harvey and Brunswick rivers and their tributaries are only some of the streams annually stocked with trout.

The main port for the south-west, **Bunbury** rests on Geographe Bay looking out over the Indian Ocean. It is a perfect holiday town. One of the oldest towns in the State, **Busselton**, sited on the Vasse River, has a wealth of pioneer houses, many restored and open to the public.

Margaret River on the river of the same name, offers beaches, caves, magnificent scenery, and world-class wineries. **Leeuwin–Naturaliste National Park** combines a scenic coast with magnificent wildflowers and the tall timbers of karri and jarrah forests.

Yallingup is known for its excellent surf and spectacular limestone caves. Dripping water has created strange shapes in the limestone, with magic colours reflected in the glittering underground water.

Bridgetown, Donnybrook and Greenbushes are small townships tucked away in green, hilly country and pretty apple orchards. Goldmining flourished briefly here at the turn of the century. **Manjimup** and Pemberton are world famous for the source of their timber, the karri and jarrah trees. Here some of the world's tallest trees reach straight up, often 80 and 90 metres. The **Pemberton**, **Scott**, **Warren** and **Brockman** national parks are nearby, introduced to protect the unique environment.

For further information contact the Bunbury Tourist Bureau, Carmody Place, Bunbury; (097) 21 7922.**See also:** Individual town entries in A–Z listing. **Note** detailed map of Margaret River Region on page 349.

The Great Southern

The Great Southern, also known as the Rainbow Coast, is bounded by a rugged coastline and the roaring Southern Ocean. During the winter months spectacular rainbows regularly occur. The coast gives way to an amazingly beautiful hinterland with rivers winding through forests, ancient mountain ranges and gentle valleys.

The district has an important historical heritage. **Albany** was the first town in Western Australia, established two and a half years before the Swan River colony. Major Edmund Lockyer landed here in 1826 to claim the western half of the continent as British territory.

Albany is the unofficial capital of the area, and retains a charming English atmosphere from the colonial days. The town looks out over the magnificent blue waters of Princess Royal Harbour in King George Sound. Albany has a number of fine old homesteads, museums and galleries. There are numerous scenic drives around the coast, to the Gap, the Natural Bridge and the Blowholes. There are also stretches of golden sand and secluded bays. The fishing is superb. **Denmark**, a holiday resort, lies on the banks of the tranquil Denmark River, and the little village of **Nornalup** nestles near the Frankland River. Near Nornalup is the awe-inspiring Valley of the Giants

The Great Southern has a thriving new viticulture industry, with the vineyards around **Mt Barker** producing award-winning wines. Mt Barker itself is the gateway to the Stirling and Porongurup mountain ranges, both within the confines of national parks. The Porongurup Range has granite peaks dominating giant hardwood trees and a maze of wildflowers and creepers. There are many easy climbs, rewarded by splendid views: Castle Rock, Howard's Peak and Devil's Slide are three of the most popular.

The high, jagged peaks of the Stirling Range (the highest is Bluff Knoll at 1037 metres) tower over virgin bushland. From a distance, with the changing light, the vegetation varies from heathery shades to blues and reds. The peaks can sometimes be seen shrouded in mist, and on occasions even tipped with snow.

There are more than 100 bird species in the park and native animals are plentiful. Look also for the beautiful wild orchids, Stirling banksia and mountain bells.

The inland area of the Great Southern is dotted with small towns including **Tambellup** with its colonial buildings. The thriving towns of **Katanning**, **Kojonup**, **Gnowangerup** and **Jerramungup**, are all surrounded by peaceful rural farmland.

For further information contact the Albany Tourist Bureau, Railway Station, Proudlove Pde, Albany; (098) 41 1088. **See also:** Individual town entries in A–Z listing. **Note** detailed map of Albany Region on page 350.

Lake Argyle, south of Kununurra

Information. Feb.: Katanning Triathlon. Dec.: Katanning Caboodle. **In the area:** Lakes surrounding town: excellent swimming, boating, water-skiing. Stirling Range National Park, 80 km S. At Gnowangerup, 60 km SE, work of local woodcarver John Davis; subjects incl. native birds. Katanning–Piesse Heritage Trail; details from Tourist Information. **Tourist information:** Flour Mill, cnr Austral Tce and Clive St; (098) 21 2634. **Accommodation:** 3 hotels, 2 motels, 2 cara./camp. parks. **See also:** The Great Southern.
MAP REF. 351 L1, 354 G10, 356 B11

Kojonup   Pop. 1023
Situated on the Albany Hwy, 154 km NW of Albany, Kojonup takes its name from the Aboriginal word kodja, meaning 'stone axe'. In 1837, when surveying the road from Albany to the newly established Swan River settlement, Alfred Hillman was guided to the Kojonup Spring by local Aborigines. Later a military outpost was set up on the site, and this marked the beginning of the town. **Of interest:** Kojonup Spring and picnic area, Spring St. Military Barracks Museum (1845), Barracks Pl. Elverd's Cottage (1850s), Soldier Rd, display of pioneers' tools and implements. Sundial in Hillman Park, Albany Hwy. Walsh's Cattle Complex, Broomehill Rd, regular cattle sales. Sept.: Wildflower and Country Festival. **In the area:** Variety of flora (incl. more than 60 orchid species) and fauna (especially birds). Yeedabirrup

Rock, 10 km E, one of many granite monoliths in area. Locally made jarrah furniture, hand-turned blackboy articles, woollen jumpers. Tours and farmstay at Kalpara Farm; details from Tourist Information. **Tourist information:** Benn Pde; (098) 31 1686. **Accommodation:** 1 hotel, 1 hotel/motel, 1 motel, 1 cara./camp. park. **See also:** The Great Southern.
MAP REF. 351 J2, 354 F10, 356 B12

Kondinin   Pop. 312
The small settlement of Kondinin is 278 km SE of Perth. There are sheep studfarms nearby. Kondinin Craft Shop, Gordon St, local craft. **In the area:** Kondinin Lake, 8 km W, water-skiing and yachting after a rainy winter. **Tourist information:** Kondinin Craft Shop, Gordon St; (098) 89 1130. **Accommodation:** 1 hotel, 1 motel, 1 cara./camp. park.
MAP REF. 347 P8, 354 H8, 356 C9

Kulin   Pop. 321
A centre for the sheep and grain farms of the district, Kulin lies 283 km SE of Perth. **Of interest:** *Eucalyptus macrocarpa*, spectacular feature of local flora. **In the area:** Several species of native orchids. Jilakin Rock and Lake, 18 km E salt lake, salt plants. Buckley's Breakaway (pit caused by granite decomposing to kaolin), 58 km E, unusual coloured rock formations, wildflowers. Hopkins Nature Reserve, 20 km NE, important flora conservation area. **Tourist information:** Wally's Woolshed, Johnston St; (098) 80

1275. **Accommodation:** 1 hotel/motel, 1 cara./camp. park.
MAP REF. 347 O9, 354 H8, 356 C10

Kununurra   Pop. 4061
Kununurra is situated along Lake Kununurra on the Ord River. Adjoining is the magnificent Hidden Valley National Park. The town supports several industries, incl. agriculture and mining, and is the major centre for the Argyle Diamond Mine (the largest diamond mine in the world) and the Ord River Irrigation area. **Of interest:** April: Dam to Dam Regatta. April–Sept.: Ord River Festival (float parade, rodeo, mardi gras, art and craft exhibitions, famous Ord Tiki Race, water-ski display). **In the area:** Kununurra is major starting point for flights and ground tours: remarkably coloured and shaped Bungle Bungles in the south; Mitchell Plateau and Kalumburu in the north west wilderness of lower Ord River. Three-hr minibus tours of local attractions; details at Tourist Information. Hidden Valley National Park, 2 km E. Both 2 km N: Warringarri Aboriginal Arts; Kelly's Knob Lookout, views of surrounding irrigated land. Melon Farm, Ivanhoe Rd, 8 km N and Banana Farm, River Farm Rd, 9 km N, tasting and sales, daily May–Oct. Top Rockz Gallery, 10 km N. Ivanhoe Crossing, 13 km N, fishing. Kimberley Research Station, 16 km N. Middle Springs, 30 km N, and Black Rock Falls, 32 km N, wet-season attractions. Pump Station, 6 km W. Cruises on Lake Kununurra: from Pump Station and upstream past the Everglades and rugged gorges; teeming birdlife. Good fishing, barramundi a prized catch. El Questro Station 100 km W, Aboriginal rock art, rugged scenery, hot springs, fishing, boating, camping, accommodation. Sleeping Buddha (Elephant Rock), 10 km S. All 16 km S: Pandanus Wildlife Park, Nimberlee Art Gallery, Zebra Rock Gallery. Durack Homestead, 70 km S, reconstructed homestead of Durack family, now pioneer museum and memorial to settlers of district. Scenic Lake Argyle, 72 km S in Carr Boyd Range: one of largest constructed lakes in southern hemisphere; created by Ord River Dam, transforming mountain peaks into rugged islands; tourist village with hotel, caravan park, camping area. Visits to Argyle Diamond Mine, charter flights, bush camping holidays. **Tourist information:** Coolibah Dr; (091) 68 1177.

Accommodation: Kununurra, 2 hotels, 2 motels, 5 cara./camp. parks. Lake Argyle, 1 hotel motel, 1 cara./camp. park. **See also:** The Kimberley; The Ord River.
MAP REF. 361 R5, 392 B13, 394 B2

Kwinana   Pop. 13 517
Kwinana, 20 km S of the port of Fremantle, is a major industrial centre, containing the BP Oil Refinery and Alcoa's Alumina Works. Kwinana Industrial Complex, built on Cockburn Sound, one of the world's finest natural harbours, was begun in 1951. The town is surrounded by pockets of bush and wetland, providing numerous opportunities for recreation. **Of interest:** Group tours of local industries. Hull of the wrecked SS *Kwinana*, at Kwinana Beach. Jet ski and go-kart hire, horseriding. **In the area:** Spectacles Wetlands, on McLachlan Hwy, 5 km NE. Seaside resort city of Rockingham, 10 km S; cruises to offshore islands, Point Peron (7 km W) and Penguin Island (10 km SW). **Tourist information:** Town Council, cnr Gilmore Ave and Sulphur Rd; (09) 419 2222. **Accommodation:** 1 motel.
MAP REF. 346 C6, 353 Q2, 354 D8

Lake Grace   Pop. 596
A pleasant country town with first-class service facilities, situated 252 km N of Albany in the peaceful rural countryside of the central south wheat belt, Lake Grace derives its name from the shallow lake just west of the settlement. **Of interest:** Wildlife sanctuary, South Rd. Restored Inland Mission hospital, Stubbs St, last in WA. Old railway buildings under restoration. **In the area:** Lookout, 5 km W. Roe Heritage Trail; details from Tourist Information. **Tourist information:** Lake Grace Newsagency; (098) 65 1029. **Accommodation:** 1 hotel, 3 motels, 1 cara./camp. park.
MAP REF. 347 Q11, 354 H9, 356 D10

Lake King   Pop. 29
A crossroads centre with a tavern and store, Lake King is a stopping place for visitors travelling across arid country and through Frank Hann National Park to Norseman. **Of interest:** Interdenominational community church. **In the area:** Lake King, 5 km W, and Lake Pallarup, 15 km S. Pioneer well at Pallarup, 18 km S. Mt Madden cairn and lookout, 25 km SE; picnic area. Frank Hann National Park, 35 km E, cross-section of heath

flora of inland sandplain east of wheat belt; park is traversed by Lake King–Norseman Rd, a formed gravel all-weather road. (No visitor facilities or supplies available between Lake King and Norseman.) Wildflowers in season. Hollands Track, early goldfields access route. **Tourist information:** Morgane St, Ravensthorpe; (098) 38 1163. **Accommodation:** 1 hotel/motel, 1 caravan park.
MAP REF. 356 E10

Lancelin   Pop. 531
This quiet little fishing town on the shores of Lancelin Bay is 127 km N of Perth. A natural breakwater extends from Edward Island to Lancelin Island, providing a safe harbour and a perfect breeding ground for fish. There are rock lobsters to be caught on the offshore reefs outside the bay. Long stretches of white sandy beach provide an ideal swimming area for children. Lancelin is becoming known as the sailboard mecca of WA and affords a colourful spectacle each Dec. with large numbers of international and interstate windsurfers taking part in the Ledge Point Ocean Race. **Of interest:** Large off-road area for dune buggies. Easter: National Beach Buggy Championships **In the area:** Track (4WD only) leads 55 km N to Nambung National Park; check road conditions before setting out. **Tourist information:** 102 Gingin Rd; (096) 55 1100. **Accommodation:** 1 hotel motel, 2B&B, 1 hostel, 2 cara./camp. parks.
MAP REF. 354 D6

Laverton   Pop. 1197
Laverton, situated 360 km NE of Kalgoorlie, is a modern satellite town. The nickel mine at Windarra, 28 km W, and goldmining ceased at the end of 1994. With an annual rainfall of around 200 mm, summers are hot and dry; April–Oct. is recommended time to travel. From Laverton to Ayers Rock (1200 km), all roads are unsealed, and the following points should be noted:
- Permit required to divert from the Laverton–Yulara Road. Obtained from Aboriginal Planning Authority in Perth or Alice Springs.
- Water is scarce.
- Supplies at Laverton. Fuel and accommodation at Warburton and Giles. Petrol and supplies at Papulankutja Aboriginal Community, 312 km N of Laverton.

- Check on road conditions at the Laverton Police Station or at Shire Offices. Roads can be hazardous when wet.
Tourist information: Shire Offices, MacPherson Pl; (090) 31 1202. **Accommodation:** 1 hotel, 1 cara./camp. park. **See also:** The Goldfields.
MAP REF. 356 I3

Leonora   Pop. 1194
A busy mining centre 243 km N of Kalgoorlie, Leonora has a typical Australian country-town appearance, with wide streets and verandahed shopfronts. The town is the centrepoint of and railhead for the north-eastern goldfields, with mining of gold, copper and nickel at Laverton, 120 km NE, and Leinster, 134 km NW. Oct.: Art Prize Inc. and Ball. **In the area:** Three major gold producers, incl. famous Sons of Gwalia. Town of Gwalia, 2 km S, museum capturing miners' lifestyle; 1 km Heritage Trail. Small goldmining town of Menzies, 110 km S, most of country is flat mulga scrub, but brilliant wildflowers Aug. and early Sept. after good rains. Kookynie, 92 km SE, ghost town, old mine workings, Grand Hotel offers warm welcome. Malcolm, 20 km NE, good picnic spot, Malcolm Dam. **Tourist information:** Shire Offices, Tower St; (090) 37 6044. **Accommodation:** 2 hotels, 1 motel, 1 cara./camp. park. **See also:** The Goldfields.
MAP REF. 356 G3

Madura   Pop. 15
The Hampton Tablelands form a backdrop to Madura, 195 km from the WA–SA border, on the Eyre Hwy. The settlement dates back to 1876 when horses for the Indian Army were bred here. Now it is surrounded by private sheep stations. **In the area:** The Pass, 1.5 km N, blowholes. **Tourist information:** Madura Pass Oasis Motel; (090) 39 3464. **Accommodation:** 1 motel, 1 cara./camp. park. **See also:** Crossing the Nullarbor.
MAP REF. 357 O8

Mandurah   Pop. 23 343
The popular holiday resort of Mandurah is on the coast, 72 km S of Perth. The Murray, Serpentine and Harvey Rivers meet here, forming the vast inland waterway of Peel Inlet and the Harvey Estuary. The river waters and the Indian Ocean offer excellent conditions for yachting,

boating, swimming, water-skiing and fishing, and the town becomes a mecca for tourists in holiday periods. **Of interest:** Hall's Cottage, Leighton Rd, small whitewashed cottage, built in 1845 by two of the colony's earliest European settlers. Christ Church (1870), cnr Pinjarra Rd and Sholl St, hand-carved furniture. Mandurah Farm World, Fremantle Rd; group bookings only. Kerryelle's Collectors Museum, Gordon Rd. Boat hire and cruises on inlet and river. Dolphins sometimes seen in estuary. Waters attract abundance of birdlife. Mandurah Estuary Bridge, good fishing spot. King Carnival Amusement Park, in Hall Park. At Halls Head, just over old traffic bridge: beaches, Peel Pottery. Jan.: Mandurah Festival. **In the area:** Pleasant picnic areas near numerous storage dams in nearby Darling Range. Boating and swimming: Waroona and Logue Brook Dams. Bavarian Castle Fun Park, Old Coast Rd, 2 km s. Ten km s: Threlfall Galleries; Dawes Channel (being dug between inland waterways and ocean) fishing, boating. Cape Bouvard Studios, Henry Rd, Melros, 15 km s. Lakes Clifton and Preston, 45 km s, two long, narrow lakes running parallel to coast. Wineries: Cape Bouvard, Mt John Rd, 22 km s (weekends only); Peel Estate, Fletcher Rd, Baldivis, 20 km N. Hamel Forestry Department Nursery, 42 km SE. Durnago Gallery, Amarillo Dr, Karnup, 14 km N. Western Rosella Bird Park, 5 km E. Houseboat hire. **Tourist information:** 5 Pinjarra Rd; (09) 535 1155. **Accommodation:** 2 hotels, 5 motels, 11 cara./camp. parks.
MAP REF. 346 C8, 354 D8

Manjimup   Pop. 4353

Fertile agricultural country and magnificent karri forests surround Manjimup, 307 km s of Perth. This is the regional centre of the State's south-west, and one of its most diversified horticultural regions: there is a flourishing timber industry, quality fresh fruit and vegetables are grown for the State and Asian markets, and wine, wool and dairying also contribute to the local economy. **Of interest:** Manjimup Regional Timber Park, Rose St, major tourist attraction, incl. Visitors Centre, Blacksmith's Shop; Timber Museum, display on development of timber industry in WA; original sawmill steam loco; Age of Steam Museum; Historical Hamlet; Fire

Tower Lookout; gallery and tearooms, picnic/barbecue facilities; timber tours. WA Chip and Pulp (Paper Wood Co.) mill, Eastbourne Rd; guided tours. Yallambee Gem Museum, Chopping St. June: 15 000 Motocross. **In the area:** Diamond Tree Fire Tower, 9 km s, in use 1941–74, may not be climbed, picnic/barbecue area. Piano Gully Wines, 10 km s. Diamond Woodchip Mill, 12 km s; guided tours. Southern Wildflowers farm, Quininup, 33 km SE. King Jarrah, 4 km E, 47-m-high tree estimated to be 600 years old. The 19-km round trip to Dingup, north-east of Manjimup: through farmland and forest; Dingup Church (1896); historic Dingup House (1870). Constable Wines, Graphite Rd, 8 km w. One Tree Bridge, 21 km w, pleasant walk along river edge to Four Aces, four magnificent karri trees, 300–400 years old. Donnelly River Holiday Village, 28 km w, abundant wildlife; horseriding. Fonty's Pool, 10 km SW, originally dammed for irrigation; swimming, picnic area, lawns, gardens. Warren National Park, 40 km SW, bushwalking, picnics. Details from Tourist Information: King Jarrah Heritage Trail; abseiling, rockclimbing, bushcraft, horse-drawn picnic excursions, safari tours. **Tourist information:** Cnr Rose and Edward Sts; (097) 71 1831. **Accommodation:** 2 hotels, 4 motels, 3 cara./camp. parks. **See also:** The Southwest.
MAP REF. 350 D6, 354 E11, 356 A13

Marble Bar   Pop. 383

Widely known as the hottest town in Australia because of its consistently high temperatures, Marble Bar lies 200 km SE of Port Hedland (last 90 km is unsealed). The town takes its name from the unique bar of red jasper that crosses the Coongan River, 4 km w of town. Alluvial gold was discovered at Marble Bar in 1891, and in 1931 at Comet Mine (now open to public). Today the major industries are gold mining and pastoral production. Marble Bar is a typical WA outback town. **Of interest:** Government buildings (1895), General St, locally quarried stone still in use. State Battery site (1910), Newman–Tabba Rd; not open to public. June: Cup Race Weekend, Gymkhana. **In the area:** Jasper deposit at Marble Bar Pool, 4 km w. Nearby Chinaman's Pool, ideal picnic spot. Flying Fox Lookout, 6 km SW, spectacular when river is running. Beautiful

scenery, especially in winter and after rain, when spinifex is transformed into flowering plants; rugged ranges, rolling plains, steep gorges, deep rock pools, many natural scenic spots. Nullagine, 111 km s, in mineral-rich area, old goldmines. Corunna World War II RAAF Base, 40 km SE, functioning airstrip, worth a visit. Scenic gorges, picnic grounds. Good swimming: Coppin's Gap, 68 km NE; Kitty's Gap, further 6 km. **Tourist information:** BP Garage, 1 Francis St; (091) 76 1041. **Accommodation:** 1 hotel/motel, 1 motel, 1 cara./camp. park. **See also:** The Pilbara.
MAP REF. 358 E2

Margaret River   Pop. 1725

Margaret River is a pretty township nestled on the side of the Margaret River near the coast 280 km from Perth. The area is noted for its world-class wines, magnificent coastal scenery, excellent surfing beaches and spectacular cave formations. **Of interest:** Rotary Park, Bussell Hwy, heritage walks start from park; details from Tourist Information. On Bussell Hwy: Old Settlement Craft Village; Margaret River Gallery; Margaret River Pottery. On Boodjidup Rd: Melting Pot Glass Studio; Eagles Heritage, large collection of birds of prey. Inn and restaurant, Farrelly St; formerly 1885 homestead. Feb.: Award-winning Leeuwin Estate Concert; Wine and Food Festival. **In the area:** Over 30 wineries: at Cowaramup, 10 km N; Willyabrup, 10 km N, and Margaret River; incl. Leeuwin Estate Winery, 8 km s, function room with Australian paintings, picnic/barbecue facilities. Bellview Shell Museum, Witchcliffe, 6 km s. Marron Farm, 11 km s. Boranup Gallery, Caves Rd, Boranup, 20 km s. Berry Farm, 13 km SE. Cheese outlets on Bussell Hwy: Fonti's and Margaret River Cheese Factory, 4 km N; Adinfern Farm, 5 k N. At Cowaramup, 10 km N: Antique-a-Brac: Excentrix; Cowaramup Pottery; Silverthread Silversmith. Gunyulgup Gallery, Caves Rd, Yallingup, 45 km N. Ellensbrook Homestead (1853–5), National Trust property, 15 km NW. Prevelly, on coast, 8 km w. Greek Chapel at Prevelly Park. Mammoth Cave, 21 km SW, fossil remains of prehistoric animals; 4 km on is Lake Cave. Other coastal areas: Gracetown, 15 km NW; Redgate, 10 km s; Hamelin Bay, 34 km s. Augusta–Busselton, Margaret River and Hamelin Bay Heritage Trails; details from Tourist Information. **Tourist**

information: Cnr Tunbridge Rd and Bussell Hwy; (097) 57 2911. **Accommodation:** 1 hotel, 4 motels, 10 B&B, 2 hostels, 4 cara./camp. parks. MAP REF. 349 C7, 354 D11

Meekatharra   Pop. 1414
Meekatharra lies 768 km NE of Perth on the Great Northern Hwy. Gold, copper and other minerals are mined, and there are huge sheep and cattle stations in the area. Meekatharra was once important as the railhead for cattle that had travelled overland from the Northern Territory or the East Kimberley. **Of interest:** In Main St: Royal Flying Doctor Service base; State Battery relics. School of the Air, High St; open to public during school term. Old Courthouse, Darlot St. **In the area:** Old goldmining towns, relics of mining equipment, mine shafts. Several mines, incl. Peak Hill and Nannine, have reopened. Peace Gorge (The Granites), 5 km W. Mt Gould, 15 km W, restored police station. Mt Yagahong, 40 km SE. Bilyuin Pool, 88 km NW, swimming. **Tourist information:** Shire Offices, Main St; (099) 81 1101. **Accommodation:** Meekatharra, 2 hotels, 2 motels, 1 cara./camp. park. Sandstone (to SE), 1 hotel, 1 caravan park. MAP REF. 358 C12

Merredin   Pop. 3068
A main junction on the important Kalgoorlie–Perth railway line, this important wheat centre is situated 259 km E from Perth. During the late 1800s, Merredin grew up as a shanty town as miners stopped on their way to the goldfields. The town has excellent parks and recreation facilities. **Of interest:** Wildlife Park, Cummings St. Cummins Theatre (1926), Bates St, oldest theatre outside Perth. Harling Memorial Library, Queen St. Military Museum, East Barrack St, World War II collection. Old Railway Station Museum, Gt Eastern Hwy. CBH wheat storage and transfer depot, Gamenya Ave, built 1966, additions 1978; largest horizontal storage in southern hemisphere, capacity of 220 000 tonnes. **In the area:** Pumping Station No. 4 (1902), 3 km W, designed by C. Y. O'Connor, fine example of early industrial architecture; station closed 1960 to make way for electrically driven stations. Folk Museum, Kellerberrin, 55 km W. Durakoppin Wildlife Sanctuary, 27 km N of Kellerberrin, and Gardner Flora Reserve, 35 km SW. Totadgin Dam

Boranup Beach, south of Margaret River

Reserve, 16 km SW. Totadgin Rock has wave formation similar to Wave Rock. Bruce Rock, 50 km SW, museum, craft centre, Australia's smallest bank. Hunts Dam, 5 km N, picnics, bushwalking. Lake Chandler, 45 km N. Mangowine Homestead, Nungarin, 56 km N National Trust property. At Koorda, 140 km NW, museum, several wildlife reserves in vicinity. Merredin Peak Heritage Trail wildflowers in season; to east, a number of sites of historical and geological interest, and picnic and camping areas details from Tourist Information. **Tourist information:** Barrack St; (090) 41 1668, or (090) 41 1666. **Accommodation:** 2 hotels, 4 motels, 2 cara./camp. parks. **See also:** Crossing the Nullarbor. MAP REF. 347 P1, 354 H6, 356 C8

Mingenew   Pop. 357
The little town of Mingenew is in the wheat district of the mid-west, 378 km N of Perth. **Of interest:** Mingenew Museum, Victoria St, in small, original school building; pioneer relics. Mingenew Hill Lookout and Pioneer Memorial, off Mingenew–Mullewa Rd, views. Sept.: Mingenew Rural Expo, Wildflower Display. **In the area:** Depot Hill, 15 km W, picnic spots. Dongara, 53 km W, superb beaches, excellent fishing. Irwin Gorge, at Coalseam Park, 32 km NE: WA's first coal shafts; rock-hunting in riverbed; wildflowers in spring. **Tourist information:** Post Office building;

(099) 28 1060. **Accommodation:** 1 hotel, 1 cara./camp. park. MAP REF. 354 D2

Morawa   Pop. 624
Renowned for its grain harvests, Morawa is in the mid-west, 394 km N of Perth. Wildflowers are in brilliant bloom in spring. **Of interest:** In Prater St: Historical Museum; St David's Anglican Church. Holy Cross Catholic Church, Davis St. Jo's Taxidermy, Winfield St; open daily. Oct.: Music Spectacular. **In the area:** Koolanooka Springs reserve and Koolanooka Hills mine site, 24 km E, picnics. Bilya Rock Reserve, 4 km W, 20-min walk around rock. **Tourist information:** Shire Offices; (099) 71 1004. **Accommodation:** 1 hotel/motel, 1 cara./camp. park. MAP REF. 354 E3

Mount Barker   Pop. 1520
Mount Barker is a quiet, friendly town in the Great Southern district of WA. It is 360 km from Perth, with the Stirling Ranges to the north and the Porongurups to the east. Mt Barker was discovered by Europeans in 1829 and settlers arrived in the 1830s. Vineyards in the area, though relatively new, are producing some top-quality wines. **Of interest:** Historic police station and gaol (1868), Albany Hwy, now museum. March: Field Day Wine Festival. Nov.:

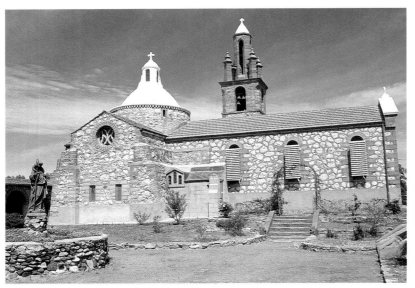

Monsignor John C. Hawes Priesthouse Museum, Mullewa

Vintage Motorbike Hill Climb. **In the area:** Lookout on summit of Mt Barker, 5 km SW, pinpointed by 168-m-high television tower: excellent views, worth the drive. Narrikup Country Store, 16 km S, craft. Porongurup National Park, 24 km E, granite peaks, brilliant seasonal wildflowers. Stirling Range National Park, 80 km NE, tall peaks, picturesque plains, native flora and fauna. Kendenup, 16 km N, historic town, WA's first gold find here. Lake Poorrarecup, 50 km NW; area also noted for orchids and brown and red boronia, which bloom Sept.–Nov. St Werburgh's Chapel (1872), 12 km W, small mud-walled chapel, privately owned, overlooking Hay River Valley. Details from Tourist Information: Mt Barker Heritage Trail; 12 wineries in surrounding area. **Tourist information:** 57 Lowood Rd; (098) 51 1163. **Accommodation:** 1 hotel, 1 hotel/motel, 1 motel, 1 cara./camp. park. **See also:** The Great Southern.
MAP REF. 351 M9, 354 G12, 356 C13

Mount Magnet　Pop. 1076

The former goldmining town of Mount Magnet, 562 km from Perth on the Great Northern Hwy, is now a popular stopping-place for motorists driving north to Port Hedland. The surrounding land is used for pastoral farming. Spectacular wildflowers in spring. Sept.: Fun Day. **In the area:** Tourist drive, 37 km, working open-cut goldmine, granites, ghost towns; map from Tourist Information. The Granites, 7 km N, picnic spot with some Aboriginal rock art. Fossick for gemstones, but take care as there are dangerous old mine shafts. Ghost town, Lennonville, 11 km N. **Tourist information:** Hepburn St; (099) 63 4172. **Accommodation:** 2 hotels, 1 motel, 1 cara./camp. park.
MAP REF. 354 G1, 355 I13, 356 B2

Mullewa　Pop. 739

Gateway to the Murchison goldfields, Mullewa is 99 km from Geraldton. **Of interest:** Kembla Zoo, Stock Rd. In Maitland Rd: Our Lady of Mount Carmel Church, Monsignor John C. Hawes Priesthouse Museum. Water Supply Reserve, Lovers Lane, native plants. Aug.–Sept.: Wildflower Show. Sept.: Agricultural Show. **In the area:** Waterfalls after heavy rain, 5 km N, near airport. Tallering Peak and Gorge, 58 km N, spectacular wildflowers. Bindoo Hill Glacier Bed, 40 km NW; scenic drive incl. Coalseam National Park. Tenindewa Pioneer Well, 18 km W, stone-lined well, early 1900s. Butterabby grave site, 18 km S, burial-place of Aborigines hanged there after clash with European settlers. Near Tardun, 40 km SE, St Mary's Agricultural School, Pallotine Mission. The Woolly Baa Baa, Tallering Station, 40 km NE, gallery, sheepskin and wool products; accommodation, camping; open April–Oct. Mons. Hawes Heritage Trail; details from Tourist Information. **Tourist information:** Shire Offices; (099) 61 1007, or Jose St. **Accommodation:** 1 hotel, 1 hotel/motel, 1 caravan park.
MAP REF. 354 D1

Mundaring　Pop. 1542

Mundaring is situated on the Great Eastern Hwy, 34 km E of Perth. The picturesque Mundaring Weir, 8 km S of town, is the source of water for the eastern goldfields. The original dam was opened in 1903, and the pumping station was used until 1955. The attractive hilly bush setting makes the weir a popular picnic spot in summer. **Of interest:** Sculpture Park, Jacoby St, sculptures by WA artists. **In the area:** Lake Leschenaultia, 10 km NW, camping, swimming, canoeing, walking, picnic/barbecue facilities; miniature scenic railway, open daily. Old Mahogany Inn (1837), 7 km W, served as military outpost to offer protection to travellers from hostile Aborigines. John Forrest National Park, on high point of Darling Range, 26 km W; picnic spot, natural pool at Rocky Pool. The C. Y. O'Connor Museum (1880s), 8 km S, former summer residence of Justice Parker, first WA judge; models of Eastern Goldfields water supply. **Tourist information:** Shire Offices, 7000 Great Eastern Hwy; (09) 295 1400. **Accommodation:** 1 hotel, 1 hotel/motel, 1 hostel, 1 cara/camp. park.
MAP REF. 346 E4, 354 E7

Mundrabilla　Pop. 11

A tiny settlement on the Eyre Hwy where travellers can break the journey across the continent. There is a bird and animal sanctuary behind the motel. **Tourist information:** Roadhouse; (090) 39 3465. **Accommodation:** 1 motel, 1 cara./camp. park.
MAP REF. 357 Q8

Nannup　Pop. 472

Nannup is a quiet, friendly town in the Blackwood Valley, 290 km S of Perth. The surrounding countryside is lush, gently rolling pasture alongside jarrah and pine forests. **Of interest:** In Brockman St: old police station (1922); Arboretum. In Warren Rd: art and craft centre; Bunnings Timber Mill, largest jarrah sawmill in State; Robz Art Gallery, Nannup Temptations and Crafty Creations, local art and craft incl. jarrah goods. Gemstone Museum. Easter: Music Festival. Sept.: Discovery Weekend. **In the area:** Walking trails and Nannup Heritage Trail; details from Tourist Information. Scenic drives: jarrah forest and pine plantations. Blackwood River, canoeing. Barrabup Pool, 10 km W. Tathra Wines, 14 km NE.

Tourist information: 4 Brockman St; (097) 56 1211. **Accommodation:** 1 hotel/motel, 1 B&B, 1 hostel, 2 cara./ camp. parks.
MAP REF. 350 A4, 354 D11

Narrogin   Pop. 4638
The centre of prosperous agricultural country, Narrogin is also a major railway junction. Sheep, pigs and cereal farms are the main primary industries. Largest in the Central South region, the town is 189 km SE of Perth on the Great Southern Hwy. Its name is derived from an Aboriginal word meaning waterhole. **Of interest:** Old Butter Factory, at exit to Wagin, memorabilia. Courthouse Museum (1894), Egerton St, originally school, later district courthouse. Foxes Lair, Williams Rd; 5 ha of natural bushland. Lions Lookout, Kipling St; panoramic views. Restoration Group Museum, Federal St, restored cars, stationary engines, other machinery. Centenary Park, picnic/barbecue facilities; pathway marked with 100 commemorative tiles designed by local artists. Jan.: State Gliding Championships. Oct.: Spring Festival. **In the area:** South Central Wheatbelt Heritage Trail; details from Tourist Information. Yilliminning and Birdwhistle Rocks, 11 km E, unusual rock formations. Albert Facey's homestead, 40 km NE, mini-zoo, local crafts; open daily. Dryandra Forest, 30 km NW, numbats, mallee fowl. **Tourist information:** 23 Egerton St; (098) 81 2064. **Accommodation:** 3 hotels, 2 motels, 1 cara./camp. park.
MAP REF. 347 J10, 354 F9, 356 B10

New Norcia   Pop. 73
In 1846 Spanish Benedictine monks established a mission at New Norcia, 132 km N of Perth to help the Australian Aborigines. The handsome Spanish-inspired buildings come as a surprise, surrounded by paddocks and distant bushland. The settlement is in the secluded Moore Valley, and wheat, wool and other farm products are grown. **Of interest:** Heritage Trail (2 km) incl. inspection of oldest operating flour mill in WA (1879), abbey church, cemetery, 19th-century blacksmith's forge, historic olive press; details from Tourist Information. Benedictine Community's Museum and art gallery, Great Northern Hwy: priceless collection, incl. gifts sent by Queen Isabella of Spain, fine paintings and Roman, Egyp-

tian and Spanish artefacts; shop sells local products, souvenirs. Group accommodation for up to 250 (advance bookings required). Tours: monastery buildings; Wyening Mission and Cellars (April–Oct.); details from Tourist Information. **Tourist information:** Museum and art gallery, Great Northern Hwy; (096) 54 8056. **Accommodation:** 1 hotel, 1 guest house.
MAP REF. 354 E6

Newman   Pop. 5627
This town was built by Mt Newman Mining Co. for employees involved in the extraction of iron ore. Mt Newman ships its ore from Port Hedland, and the two towns are connected by a 426-km railroad. In 1981 responsibility for the town was handed over to the local shire. With the sealing of the National Hwy and improved tourist facilities in the town, Newman has become a popular stopping-place. **Of interest:** Tours of Mt Whaleback mine, Newman Dr, largest iron ore open-cut mine in world. New BHP Iron Ore Silver Jubilee Museum and Gallery, cnr Fortescue Ave and Newman Dr. Mining and pastoral museum, behind tourist centre. Radio Hill Lookout, off Newman Dr. Walking trail and climb from museum to Lookout. Aug.: Fortescue Festival. **In the area:** Ophthalmia Dam, 15 km N, swimming, picnic/barbecue facilities. Good views from Mt Newman, 20 km N. Kalgans

Sand goanna

Pool, 51 km NW; day trip, conventional vehicles with care. Eagle Rock Falls and pool, 69 km NW, permanent pools, picnic spots, falls may require 4WD. Aboriginal rock carvings, rock pools, waterholes: Wanna Munna, 70 km W, and Punda (4WD only), 75 km NW. **Tourist information:** Cnr Fortescue Ave and Newman Dr; (091) 75 2888. **Accommodation:** 1 motel, 1 hostel, 3 cara./camp. parks. **See also:** The Hamersley Range; The Pilbara.
MAP REF. 358 E6

Norseman   Pop. 1398
Norseman, 200 km S of Kalgoorlie, is the last large town on the Eyre Hwy for travellers heading east towards SA. Gold put Norseman on the map in the early 1890s, and the richest quartz reef in Australia is still being mined today. The town is steeped in goldmining history, with colossal tailings dumps a reminder. The area is popular with amateur prospectors and gemstone collectors; gemstone fossicking permits are available from Norseman Tourist Bureau. There is a quarantine checkpoint for westbound travellers at Norseman, so visitors should make sure they are not carrying fruit, vegetables, honey, used fruit and produce containers, plants or seeds. **Of interest:** Historical Collection, Battery Rd, mining tools, household items. Post Office (1896), cnr Prinsep and Ra Sts. Heritage Trail (33 km), following original Cobb & Co. route, incl. descent into a 'decline'; details from Tourist Information. In Roberts St: statue, commemorates horse called Norseman, who allegedly pawed the ground and unearthed a nugget of gold, thus starting a gold rush in area; Norseman Tourist Reception Centre, visitor facilities, day parking, barbecues. Mine tours of massive open-cut mine conducted weekdays. **In the area:** Dundas Rocks, 22 km S, 550 million years old; excellent picnic area, old Dundas town site nearby. Peak Charles, 50 km S, then 40 km off hwy, magnificent views, for energetic climbers. Gemstone leases on Eyre Hwy and off Kalgoorlie Hwy; details from Tourist Information. Beacon Hill (also called Mararoa or Lookout Hill), 2 km E, good views of surrounding salt lakes (spectacular at sunrise and sunset), old mines and Jimberlana Dyke, reputedly one of oldest geological areas in world. Mt Jimberlana, 7 km E, good views, walking trail to summit. To south-west, Frank Hahn National Park, 50 km E of Lake King

township, traversed by Lake King–Norseman Rd. Twice-daily bus tours of town, the 'decline', Beacon Hill and part of Heritage Trail. **Tourist information:** 68 Roberts St; (090) 39 1071. **Accommodation:** 2 hotels, 2 motels, 1 hostel, 1 cara./camp. park. **See also:** Crossing the Nullarbor; The Goldfields.
MAP REF. 356 H9

Northam
Pop. 6560

The regional centre of the fertile Avon Valley at the junction of the Avon and Mortlock Rivers, Northam is an attractive rural town. On the Great Eastern Hwy, 99 km E of Perth, it is an important supply point for the farms of the eastern wheat belt. Northam is also a major railway centre and the main depot for the Goldfields Water Scheme, which takes water as far east as Kalgoorlie. WA's largest military training camp is on the outskirts of town. **Of interest:** In Wellington St: Old Police Station (1866), Courthouse (1896), Town Hall (1897), Avon Valley Arts Society art and craft shop. Flour Mill (1871), Newcastle St. In Fitzgerald St: Old Railway Station Museum; Shamrock Hotel (1886), fully renovated. Weir across Avon River, near Peel Tce bridge, forms lake that has a colony of white swans and many other species of native birdlife. Morby Cottage (1836), Old York Rd, built by pioneer family, the Morrells. Sir James Mitchell House (1905), Duke St, National Trust-classified. Aug.: Avon Descent (white-water raft race), Festival. Nov.: Avon Valley Country Music Festival. **In the area:** Hot-air ballooning (in cooler months), horseriding, canoeing. Blue Gum Camel Farm, near Spencer Brook Rd, at Clackline, 19 km SW, camel- and trail-riding in picturesque bushland surroundings. Muresk Agricultural College, 10 km S, former early farming property. At Dowerin, 58 km NE, museum, craft centre, Hagbooms Lake. In spring, wildflowers abound near Wubin, 190 km N. Northam–Katrine Heritage Trail and Farming Heritage Trail; details from Tourist Information. **Tourist information:** Fitzgerald St; (096) 22 2100. **Accommodation:** 4 hotels, 1 motel, 1 cara./camp. park.
MAP REF. 346 H2, 354 F7, 356 A8

Northampton
Pop. 786

Northampton nestles among gentle hills in the valley of Nokarena Brook, 48 km N of Geraldton. Inland there is picturesque country with vivid wildflowers in spring. The drive west leads to the coast, with beaches for swimming and fishing. **Of interest:** Chiverton House Folk Museum, Hampton Rd. Gwalla church site and cemetery, Gwalla St. St Mary's Convent and Church, Main St, designed by Mons. Hawes. Miners' cottages (1860s), Brook St. **In the area:** Alma Schoolhouse, disused Ghurka lead mine, 12 km N. Near coast at Port Gregory, 47 km NW, labour-hiring depot for convicts, dating from 1800s; this squat building with slits for windows was probably erected as protection from hostile Aborigines. Hutt Lagoon, near Port Gregory, turns pink in light of midday sun. At Horrocks Beach, 20 km W, pleasant bays, sandy beaches, good fishing. **Tourist information:** Nagle Centre, Main St; (099) 34 1488. **Accommodation:** 2 hotel/motels, 1 hostel, 1 cara./camp. park.
MAP REF. 354 C1

Northcliffe
Pop. 190

Magnificent virgin karri forests surround the little township of Northcliffe, 32 km S of Pemberton in the extreme south-west corner of the State. Unique flora and fauna is to be found in this area. **Of interest:** In Wheatley Coast Rd: Pioneer Museum, historical relics and photographs; at Tourist Information, rock and mineral collection, Aboriginal Interpretation Room, photographic folio of native flora and birds; Northcliffe Art and Craft. Earthworm Farm, North St; 10–4 daily. Off Wheatley Coast Rd: South West Timber Trekking Company; horseriding on forest tracks. Forest Park, Hollow Butt Karri, Twin Karri walking trails, picnic areas. Warren River; fishing. Easter: Forest Festival. Sept.: Mountain Bike Carnival. **In the area:** Mt Chudalup, 20 km S, giant granite outcrop, walking trail to summit for views. Point D'Entrecasteaux, 27 km S, cliffs popular with climbers. Windy Harbour and Salmon Beach, 29 km S. Sandy beaches: fishing, swimming. National Parks: D'Entrecasteaux, 5 km S; Warren, 20 km NW; Shannon, 30 km E; Bibbulmun Track links all three. Boorara Tree (once used as fire lookout) and Lane–Poole Falls, 18 km SE. **Tourist information:** Adjacent to Pioneer Museum, Wheatley Coast Rd; (097) 76 7203. **Accommodation:** 1 hotel, 1 cara./camp. park.
MAP REF. 350 C9, 354 E12, 356 A13

Onslow
Pop. 881

Onslow, on the NW coast of the State, is important as the base for the gas and oil fields off the coast. The town was originally at the mouth of the Ashburton River, but was moved to Beadon Bay after constant cyclones. The remains of the old town site can still be seen. Onslow was a bustling pearling centre and in the 1890s gold was discovered. US submarines refuelled here during World War II, and the town was bombed by the Japanese. In 1952 it was the mainland base for Britain's nuclear experiments at Monte Bello Islands. July: Bouganvillea Festival. **In the area:** Excellent fishing. Native fauna incl. emus, red kangaroos, sand goannas, bustards, variety of birdlife. Wildflowers in spring after rain; incl. the Sturt desert pea, Ashburton pea. **Tourist information:** Shire Offices; (091) 84 6001. **Accommodation:** 1 hotel, 2 cara./camp. parks.
MAP REF. 355 E2

Pemberton
Pop. 934

The town of Pemberton, 335 km S of Perth, is nestled in a quiet valley, surrounded by towering karri forests. This lush forest area has some of the tallest hardwood trees in the world, and, in spring, brilliant flowering bush plants. **Of interest:** Pemberton is known as a centre for high-quality woodcraft, and there are a number of craft outlets: Pemberton Arts and Craft, Broadway Ave; Old Picture Theatre Gallery, Ellis St; in Jamieson St: Warren River Arts and Craft, Woodcraftsman's Studio, Fine Woodcraft, Dickinson St. In Brockman St: Museum, collection of historic photographs and authentic forestry equipment, incl. tourist centre; Pemberton Sawmill, guided tours Mon.–Fri. Trout and Marron Hatchery, supplies for WA rivers and dams; daily tours. Fishing in local rivers; Inland Fishing Licence required for trout and marron. Wineries incl: Warren Vineyard, Dickinson St; Gloucester Ridge, Burma Rd; Mountford Wines, Bamess Rd. March: King Karri Karnival. **In the area:** Gloucester Tree, signposted off Brockman St, tallest fire lookout in world; over 60 m high, 150 rungs spiralling upwards; open for climbing during daylight hours. Further south, picturesque Lane Poole Falls; at Northcliffe, pioneer museum. The Cascades, 8 km S, picnics, bushwalking, fishing. King Trout Farm, 9 km S. Brockman Sawpit, 13 km S, restored to show

how timber was sawn in 1860s. Moon's Crossing, 18 km S, picnics; 4WD in winter. Piano Gully Vineyard, 24 km NE, off South West Hwy. Marron and dairy farm, 1 km N. Big Brook Dam and Arboretum, 7 km NW. Donnelly River Wines, 35 km NW. Kangaroo Creek Studio, Channybearup Rd, 16 km W, woodcarving, pottery, tearoom. Eagle Springs marron farm, 18 km W. At Windy Harbour: sandy beaches, rugged coast, good fishing. National Parks close by: Warren, 9 km S; Brockman, 13 km S; Beedelup, 18 km W. Some of best accessible virgin karri forest in Warren National Park, where tallest of karri trees (89 m) can be found. Swamp Willow Farm on Hawke Rd near park, 12 km S, local wood craft. Details from Tourist Information: Tramcars based on 1907 Fremantle trams operate daily through tall-forest country between Pemberton and Northcliffe. Forest Industry tours into logging and regrowth areas Mon.–Fri., scenic bus tours daily; 4WD adventure tours, 2 hrs to overnight, and horseriding, incl. pub crawl. **Tourist information:** Brockman St; (097) 76 1133. **Accommodation:** 1 hotel/motel, 2 motels, 1 cara./camp. park. **See also:** The South-west.
MAP REF. 350 C7, 354 E12, 356 A13

Perenjori   Pop. 250

On the Northam–Mullewa Hwy (known as 'Wildflower Way'), 352 km NE of Perth, Perenjori lies on the fringes of the Murchison goldfields and the great sheep stations of the west. **Of interest:** Historical Museum behind tourist centre, Fowler St. Arts and Crafts Centre, Russell St. **In the area:** Wildflower season July–Sept.; many scenic drives. Salt lakes: variety of waterbirds. Perenjori–Rothsay Heritage Trail (180 km), recalls early goldmining days; details from Tourist Information. For fossickers, many gemstones in this mineral-rich region. Old goldmining and ghost towns: Rothsay, 67 km E (working mine, not open to public); Nows Nest, 176 km E. Care should be taken, as unfenced pits make the area dangerous. Mongers Lake Lookout, 35 km E. Camel Soak, 47 km E, picnic spot. Aboriginal Stones at Damperwah Soak, 40 km NE. Warriedar, 107 km NE. **Tourist information:** Fowler Street; (099)73 1105. **Accommodation:** 1 hotel, 1 cara./camp. park.
MAP REF. 354 E3

Karri forest near Pemberton

Pingelly   Pop. 763

On the Great Southern Hwy, 154 km SE of Perth, Pingelly is part of the central southern farming district. The cutting of sandalwood was once a local industry, but today the land is given over to sheep and wheat. **Of interest:** In Parade St: Community Craft Centre; Courthouse Museum. Apex Lookout, Stone St, fine views of town and country. **In the area:** Moorumbine Heritage Trail; details from Tourist Information. Historic St Patrick's Church (1873), Mourambine, 10 km E. Tuttanning Flora and Fauna Reserve, 21 km E. Yealering Lake and picnic ground, 58 km E. Boyagin Rock Picnic Ground and Reserve, 26 km NW. Dryandra Reserve, 40 km SW, unique flora; fauna incl. the numbat, WA's fauna emblem; timber also produced; reserve has been called an ecological oasis. **Tourist information:** Shire Offices, 17 Queen St; (098) 87 1066. **Accommodation:** 1 hotel, 1 motel, 1 cara./camp. park.
MAP REF. 347 J8, 354 F8, 356 B10

Pinjarra   Pop. 1779

Pinjarra is a pleasant drive 84 km S of Perth, along the shaded South Western Hwy or the scenic Old Coast Road. The town has a picturesque setting on the banks of the Murray River in one of the earliest established districts in WA. The Alcoa Refinery, 4 km NE of town on South West Hwy, is the largest alumina refinery in Australia. Pinjarra is a good base for exploring the area. Bus tours from Tour Reception Centre at the Pinjarra Refinery. **Of interest:** In Henry St: St John's Church (1845); Heritage Rose Garden; Liveringa (1880); Old School (1896), Teacher's House. Edenvale (1888), George St. **In the area:** Pinjarra Heritage Trail; details from Tourist Information. Hotham Valley Tourist Railway runs old-style steam train from Pinjarra to forest (Sun., May–Oct.). Scarp Pool, 20 km SE, picnics, swimming. Marrinup Falls, 3-km walk from Scarp Rd, Dwellingup, 24 km SE. Alcoa Scarp Lookout, 14 km E. Athlone Angora Stud and Goat Farm, 16 km E. Fairbridge Village, 5 km NE. At North Dandalup, 10 km NE: Whittakers Mill, bushwalking, camping, barbecues; Dandalup Studio (art and craft). Award-winning Tumbulgum Farm, at Mundijong, 38 km N, Australian experience, native and farm animals, daily Aboriginal culture and farm shows.

Crossing the Nullarbor

The trip from Adelaide to Perth along the Eyre Highway is one of Australia's great touring experiences. It is far from monotonous, with breathtaking views of the Great Australian Bight only a few hundred metres from the road in many places. There is nothing quite like a long straight road stretching as far as the eye can see ahead and in the rear-vision mirror.

If you are planning a return journey, it is well worth considering driving one way and putting the car on the train for the return. As there is a limited amount of space for cars, train bookings need to be made well in advance, even at off-peak times. (**See:** Planning Ahead.)

The Eyre Highway is bitumen for its entire length. The highway is well signposted, with indications of the distance to the next town with petrol and other services.

If the journey is undertaken at a sensible pace, it can be surprisingly relaxing, especially during the quieter times of year. The standard of accommodation is good and reasonably priced, with a friendly atmosphere in the bars and dining rooms of the large motel/roadhouses that are strategically situated along the highway. Many friendships have been made during the trip across the Eyre Highway as the same carloads of travellers meet at stopping-places each night.

Although the highway is bitumen, there are certain hazards. The road can have breakaways on the shoulders in places, requiring caution when drivers are overtaking. And it can be difficult to overtake the big semitrailers as they thunder along the highway, particularly when they tailgate to save fuel. Overtaking also can be hazardous in damp conditions when the spray from the vehicle in front completely cuts visibility ahead. On the other hand, the semitrailer drivers are usually courteous and signal when it is safe to overtake. Kangaroos also can be a hazard, especially at dusk or after rain.

The setting sun can make driving somewhat unpleasant for drivers travelling in a westerly direction. Also, do not forget the time changes you will encounter on the way! (**See also:** Time Zones.)

Above all, it is most important to have a safe, reliable car. The settlements along the highway are mainly motels with garage and roadhouse; you could have a long wait for mechanical or medical help.

The journey proper begins at **Port**

Eyre Highway

Augusta, 330 kilometres north-east of Adelaide, at the head of Spencer Gulf. Port Augusta is a provincial city that services a vast area of semi-arid grazing and wheat-growing country to the north and west. As you head out of the city on the Eyre Highway, you see the red peaks of the Flinders Ranges soaring above the sombre bluebush plains; these are the last hills of any size for 2500 kilometres. Through the little towns of **Kimba** and **Kyancutta** the scenery can vary from mallee scrub to wide paddocks of wheat. This area was once called Heartbreak Plains, a reminder of the time when farmers walked off their land in despair, leaving behind them the crumbling stone homesteads that today dot the plains.

The highway meets the sea at **Ceduna**, a small town of white stone buildings and limestone streets set against a background of blue-green sea. The waters of the Great Australian Bight here are shallow and unpredictable, but they yield Australia's best catches of its most commercially prized fish, whiting. On the outskirts of Ceduna is a warning sign about the last reliable water. This marks the end of cultivated country and the beginning of the deserted, almost treeless land that creeps towards the Nullarbor Plain. The highway stays close to the coast and there is always a little scrub and other vegetation on the plains, or on the sand dunes that lie between the highway and the ocean.

Further north the Nullarbor Plain covers an area greater than the State of Victoria. The name 'Nullarbor' is a corruption of the Latin words meaning 'no trees' and the name is apt. Geologists believe that the completely flat plain was once the bed of a prehistoric sea, which was raised to dry land by a great upheaval of the earth.

West of Ceduna the traveller will find **Penong**, a town of 100 windmills, and the breathtaking coastal beauty around Point

Sinclair and Cactus Beach. Then on to **Nundroo** and south to the abandoned settlement of **Fowlers Bay**, once an exploration depot for Edward John Eyre and now a charming ghost town best known for its fishing. At the **Yalata Roadhouse**, run by the Yalata Aboriginal Community, there are genuine artefacts for sale at reasonable prices. Between **Nullarbor** and **Border Village** are five of Australia's most spectacular coastal lookouts, where giant ocean swells pound the towering limestone cliffs that make up this part of the Great Australian Bight. From June to October an added bonus is the chance of spotting the majestic southern right whale on its annual migration along the southern part of the continent. Fuel, refreshments and accommodation are all available at Penong, Nundroo, Nullarbor and Border Village.

The stone ruins of an Aboriginal mission remain at **Cocklebiddy**. The road continues until it reaches the first real town in opver 1200 kilometres, **Norseman**, an ideal stopping-place.

From here you turn north to **Kalgoorlie** or south to **Esperance** on the coast. At **Kalgoorlie–Boulder** you will see one of the longest-established and most prosperous goldmining centres in Western Australia. After a working life of more than 100 years, the mines around Kalgoorlie still produce more than 70 per cent of Australia's gold. Set in vast dryland eucalypt forest, the town is picturesque in frontier style. Esperance, on the other hand, offers coastal scenery including long, empty beaches. Nearby, wildflowers spread across the countryside in spring.

As you travel west from Kalgoorlie–Boulder, the undulating forest and wildflower scrub continue for a further 250 kilometres until the road reaches the wheat- and wool-growing lands surrounding the towns of **Southern Cross** and **Merredin**. The farmland becomes increasingly rich as it rises into the Darling Range, the beautiful, wooded mountain country that overlooks Perth. At the end of this long journey Perth glitters like a jewel on the Indian Ocean—a place of civilisation and style, of beaches, waterways and greenery.

For further information on the Eyre Highway, see South Australian entries for **Ceduna, Kimba, Penong** and **Wudinna** and Western Australian entries for **Balladonia, Caiguna, Cocklebiddy, Eucla, Mundrabilla** and **Madura**. See also: Individual town entries in A–Z listing.

Yalgorup National Park on coast, 48 km SW of Waroona. Old Blythewood (1860s), 4 km S, former post office, coaching inn, family home; check times. Lake Navarino Forest Resort and Waroona Dam, 33 km S, watersports, fishing, walking, horseriding, tours. **Tourist information:** Murray Tourist Centre (in Edenvale stately home), George St; (09) 531 1438. **Accommodation:** 4 hotels, 1 motel, 7 cara./camp. parks. **See also:** The Southwest.
MAP REF. 346 D9, 354 E8

Point Samson   Pop. 180

Point Samson was named in honour of Michael Samson, who accompanied the district's first settler, Walter Padbury, on his 1863 journey. The town was established in 1910 as the major port for the Roebourne district, replacing Cossack, where the harbour had silted up after a cyclone. The port was very active for many years, but today Point Samson supports a small fishing industry and its extremely attractive setting has made it a popular beach resort. **Of interest:** Point Samson's sandy beach is protected by a coral reef; good swimming, fishing, skindiving. Tidal rivers: immense variety of marine life, from barramundi to mud crabs. Offshore waters: some of the best game fishing along coast. Honeymoon Cove, Johns Creek Rd, swimming, picnicking. Nearby at John's Harbour, jetty, boat ramp. Trawlers Tavern, local seafood. **In the area:** Emma Withnell Heritage Trail; details from Tourist Information. Sam's Creek, 1 km N, fishing boat harbour. Samson Reef can be explored at low tide. **Tourist information:** Point Samson Fisheries, Point Samson Rd; (091) 87 1414. **Accommodation:** 1 caravan park.
MAP REF. 355 H1, 358 A1

Port Hedland   Pop. 11 344

Port Hedland's remarkable growth has been due to the iron-ore boom, which started in the early 1960s. The town was named after Captain Peter Hedland, who reached the harbour in 1829. Today Port Hedland handles the largest tonnage of any Australian port. Iron ore from some of the world's biggest mines is loaded on to the world's biggest ore carriers. Gathering of salt is another major industry, with about 2 million tonnes exported per annum. The Aboriginal

population represents several language groups. International airport, also serves north-west region of the State. **Of interest:** Stairway to the Moon, natural wonder, seen at Cooke Point at certain times; details from Tourist Information. Observation Tower, at Tourist Information, Wedge St. Lions Park, Hunt St, pioneer relics. Royal Flying Doctor Base, Richardson St; visitors 11.15 a.m. Mon.–Fri. Visitors welcome at wharf, where ore is loaded onto giant ships. BHP mine tours; booked at Tourist Information. Don Rhodes Mining Museum, Wilson St. At Two Mile Ridge, opp. fire brigade in Wilson St, Aboriginal carvings in limestone ridge (no public access). Old St Matthew's Church (1917), Edgar St, historic building, art gallery and exhibition centre. Olympic pool, McGregor St, next to Civic Centre. The 2-km-long trains operated by BHP Iron Ore arrive 6 times daily. Heritage trails incl. Port Hedland cemetery; graves of early gold prospectors, and Japanese pearl divers. Aug.: Spinifex Spree. Sept.: All Can Regatta. **In the area:** Picnic, fish and swim safely at Pretty Pool, next to Cooke Point caravan park. (Poisonous fish frequent coast, especially Nov.–March: make local enquiries before swimming in sea.) At Cargill Salt, 8 km S, giant cone-shaped mounds of salt awaiting export. Stone carvings, Woodstock, 300 km SE. Tour of bauxite mine and alumina refinery, 8 km E; Wed. and Sun. Port Hedland Heritage Trail; details from Tourist Information. Whale-watching trips June–Oct. Excellent fishing; charter boat hire. Birdlife is abundant in district, watch for bustards, eagles, cockatoos, galahs, ibises, pelicans, parrots. **Tourist information:** 13 Wedge St; (091) 73 1650. **Accommodation:** 6 hotel/motels, 3 cara./camp. parks. **See also:** The Pilbara.
MAP REF. 358 C1, 360 B13

Ravensthorpe   Pop. 392

Ravensthorpe, situated 533 km SE of Perth, is the centre of the old Phillips River goldfield. Copper mining was also important here, reaching a peak in the late 1960s. Many old mine shafts can be seen around the district. Wheat and sheep are the local industries. **Of interest:** Historical Society Museum, Morgan St. Historic buildings: Anglican Church, Dunn St; old mine manager's house, Carlisle St; in Morgan St, Dance

Cottage (museum), Palace Hotel, restored Commercial Hotel (now Community Centre). Sept.: Wildflower Display, features over 600 species from Fitzgerald River National Park. **In the area:** Catlin Creek Heritage Trail and short scenic drives; details from Tourist Information. Ravensthorpe Range, 3 km N, and Mt Desmond, 10 km SE, views. WA Time Meridian at first rest bay west of town. Fitzgerald River National Park, 46 km S, now Biosphere Reserve for UNESCO. Old copper smelter, 2 km E. Rock-collecting: check locally to avoid trespass. **Tourist information:** Community Centre, Morgan St; (098) 38 1277. **Accommodation:** 1 hotel/motel, 1 motel, 1 cara./camp. park.
MAP REF. 356 F11

Rockingham   Pop. 36 675

At the southern end of Cockburn Sound, 45 km S of Perth, Rockingham is a coastal city and seaside resort. Begun in 1872 as a port, the harbour fell into disuse with the opening of the Fremantle inner harbour in 1897. Today its magnificent golden beaches and protected waters are Rockingham's main attraction. **Of interest:** Museum, Kent St. Lookout at Point Peron, Peron Rd. WA Waterski Park, St Albans Rd. Sunday markets, Flinders Lake. Jan.: Cockburn Yachting Regatta. **In the area:** Old Rockingham Heritage Trail and Rockingham–Jarrahdale Heritage Trail; details from Tourist Information. Penguin Island, with a colony of little (fairy) penguins. Garden Island, home to HMAS *Stirling*, naval base; normally closed to public, but accessed by bus tour from Perth weekly; causeway link to mainland closed to public. Kwinana Industrial Complex, 10 km N. Shoalwater Bay Islands Marine Park, 6 km NW, extends from just south of Garden Island to Becher Point in Warnbro; cruises, incl. swimming with the dolphins. Lake Richmond, 4 km S, walks, freshwater flora and fauna, domed stromalites. Seal Island cruises from Safety Bay, 10 km S. Marapana Deer Park, 16 km S. Wineries: Baldivis Estate, 15 km SE, Peel Estate, 17 km SE. Scenic drive 48 km SE to Serpentine Dam, WA's major water conservation area; brilliant wildflowers, gardens, bushland; nearby, Serpentine Falls. **Tourist information:** 43 Kent St; (09) 592 3464. **Accommodation:** 2 hotels, 2 motels, 5 cara./camp. parks.
MAP REF. 346 C6, 354 D8

Roebourne   Pop. 1213

Named after John Septimus Roe, the State's first surveyor-general, Roebourne was established in 1864 and is the oldest town on the north-west coast. It was developed as the capital of the North-West and was at one time the administrative centre for the whole area north of the Murchison River. As the centre for the early mining and pastoral industries in the Pilbara it was connected to the pearling port of Cossack, and later to Point Samson, by tramway for the transport of passengers and goods. Although now overshadowed by the iron-ore and other industries, Roebourne has retained its special character. **Of interest:** Old stone buildings (some National Trust-classified): police station, Queen St; Post Office (1887), Shell St; in Hampton St, hospital (1887), courthouse; Holy Trinity Church (1894), Withnell St; in Roe St, Union Bank (1889, now Shire library), Victoria Hotel, last of town's five original pubs. Old Roebourne Gaol (1886), Queen St, art and craft centre. Good views from Mt Welcome, Fisher Dr. July: Royal Show; Roebourne Cup and Ball. **In the area:** Emma Withnell Heritage Trail, 52 km, incl. towns of Wickham (15 km), Cossack (17 km, restored buildings, archaeological project, art gallery), ending at Point Samson. Fishing at Cleaverville, 25 km N. **Tourist information**: Old Goal, Queen St; (091) 82 1060. **Accommodation:** 1 hotel motel, 1 cara./camp. park. **See also:** The Pilbara. MAP REF. 355 H1, 358 A2

Southern Cross   Pop. 982

A small but flourishing town on the Great Eastern Hwy, 368 km E of Perth, Southern Cross is the centre of a prosperous agricultural and pastoral area and a significant gold-producing area. **Of interest:** First courthouse in eastern goldfields (1893), Antares St, now history museum; open daily. Other historic buildings incl.: Post Office (1891), Antares St; Railway Tavern (1890s), Spica St. Restored Palace Hotel, Orion St. Town and its wide streets, originally designed to allow camel trains to turn around, named after stars and constellations. Goldmining activities around Southern Cross: Marvel Loch, 35 km S; Bullfinch, 36 km N. Sept.: Agricultural Show. **In the area:** Wildflowers on sandplains in spring. Hunt's Soak, 7 km N, picnic area. Koolyanobbing, 56 km N, built for miners extracting iron ore, now virtually a ghost town since closure in 1983; recently mining of rich iron ore has recommenced. Several interesting rock formations; adj. areas ideal for picnics. **Tourist information:** Yilgarn Shire Offices, Antares St; (090) 49 1001. **Accommodation:** 2 hotels, 1 motel, 1 cara./camp. park. **See also:** Crossing the Nullarbor. MAP REF. 356 E7

Three Springs

Pop. 473

Sir John Forrest named Three Springs, which is 170 km SE of Geraldton. WA's finest talc, exported for use in the ceramics industry, is mined here from an open-cut mine 13 km E. **Of interest:** At town entrance, information bay and path through living display of stunning wildflowers. Heritage Walk, incl. wildflowers; details from Tourist Information. Oct.: White Rock Stakes Wheelbarrow Race. **In the area:** Cockatoo Canyon, 6 km W. Emu Farm, 14 km W on Eneabba Rd; open daily. Eneabba, 56 km SW, major mineral sands mining centre. Yarra Yarra Lake system, 5 km S, attracts many migratory birds. Wildflower Drives (best Aug.–Nov.); details from Tourist Information. Wildflower farm adjacent. Pink Lakes, 6 km E. Old copper-mine ruins, 7 km NW. Blue Waters, near Arrino, 18 km NW, picnic area amid river gums. **Tourist information:** Thomas Street; (099) 54 1041. **Accommodation:** 1 hotel/motel. MAP REF. 354 D3

Tom Price   Pop. 3634

The huge iron ore deposit now known as Mt Tom Price was discovered in 1962, after which the Hamersley Iron Project was established. The construction of a mine, two towns (Dampier and Tom Price) and a railway between the mine followed, all of which was achieved in a remarkably short period of time. **Of interest:** Aug.: Nameless Festival. **In the area:** Proximity of Tom Price to spectacular Karijini (Hamersley Range) National Park, 38 km E, and chance to tour open-cut mining operation, make town a popular stopping-place. Kings Lake, 2 km W, constructed lake, park, picnic/barbecue facilities. Views of remarkable scenery around Tom Price from Mt Nameless lookout, 6 km W, via walking trail. Aboriginal carvings, 10 km S; details from Tourist Information. **Tourist information:** Central Rd; (091) 88 1112. **Accommodation:** 1 hotel, 1 motel, 1 cara./camp. park. **See also:** The Hamersley Range; The Pilbara. MAP REF. 355 I4, 358 B5

Toodyay   Pop. 604

The historic town of Toodyay, nestled in the Avon Valley, has many charming old buildings recalling its pioneering days. Situated 85 km NE of Perth, Toodyay is surrounded by picturesque farming country and, to the west, virgin bushland. **Of interest:** Classified by the National Trust as an historic town, Toodyay has many buildings of historic significance in or near Stirling Tce. Connor's Flour Mill (1870s), imposing structure now housing tourist centre; displays; steam engine in working order. Old Newcastle Gaol Museum (1865), Clinton St, and police stables (1870), opposite, built by convicts with random rubble stone. May: Moondyne (colonial and convict) Festival. Sept.: Folk Festival. **In the area:** Hoddywell Archery Park, 8 km S. Northam, 27 km SE. Nearby Avon River Weir, sanctuary for swans, grassy riverbank is delightful picnic spot. On Perth road, 4 km SW, Coorinja Winery, begun 1870. White Gum Flower Farm, 9 km SW, just off road to Perth, native and exotic flowers under cultivation. Trout farm, 12 km SW, fishing, sales. Blinkbonny Cottage Tea Shop, 14 km SW, crafts, tearoom. Emu farm, 15 km SW, 10–4 daily. Avon Valley National Park, 25 km SW, spectacular scenery, seasonal wildflowers. **Tourist information:** Connor's Mill, Stirling Tce; (09) 574 2435. **Accommodation:** 2 hotels, 2 cara./camp. parks. MAP REF. 346 G2, 354 E7, 356 A8

Wagin   Pop. 1293

The prosperous rural countryside surrounding Wagin supports grain crops and pastures for livestock, especially sheep. Wagin's development has been tied to its important location as a railway-junction town, 177 km E of Bunbury. **Of interest:** Wagin Historical Village, Ballagin Rd, collection of early pioneer artefacts, set in 20 authentic old buildings. Fine Victorian buildings and shopfronts in Tudhoe and Tudor Sts. Giant Ram (7 m high), Arthur Rd. Adjacent park, ponds, waterfalls. Great Southern Gamebirds, Ware St, many native bird varieties. March: 2-day Woolorama, atended by sheep farmers Australia-wide, attracts crowds of over 25 000. June: Foundation Day. **In**

The Hamersley Range

Stretching over 300 kilometres through the heart of the mineral-rich Pilbara, the Hamersley Range forms a wild and magnificent panorama. The mountains slope gently up from the south to the flat-topped outcrops and Western Australia's highest peak, **Mt Meharry**. In the north they rise majestically from golden spinifex plains.

Although the main activity in the area is centred on mining towns like **Tom Price**, **Paraburdoo** and **Newman**, visitors will find many other areas of interest.

Spectacular gorges have been carved by watercourses. Precipitous walls of rock are layered in colours from reddish brown to green and blue to pink in the changing light. The gorges are up to 50 metres deep, and at their base are sometimes only one metre wide. Others have wide, crystal-clear pools. Lush green vegetation thrives and the gorges are cool oases in the harsh climate.

Tom Price is a good base from which to explore the beauty of the Hamersley Ranges. The **Wittenoom Gorge** is a popular spot because it is so easily accessible (camping is not permitted). At Yampire Gorge there is a well once used by Afghani camel-drivers in the 1800s. The breathtaking **Dales Gorge**, approached through Yampire Gorge, is 45 kilometres long. Here are found crystal-clear pools and the splendid Fortescue Falls. The small but intriguing **Rio Tinto Gorge,** and **Hamersley Gorge** with its folded bands of coloured rock, are also quite beautiful.

One particularly enchanting oasis in the Hamersley Range area is the tropical paradise of **Millstream–Chichester National Park**, on the Fortescue River, inland from Roebourne. Thousands of birds flock to this delightful spot, where ferns, lilies, palms and rushes grow in abundance. There are two long, deep, natural pools. The springs produce over 36 million litres of water a day from an underground basin, which is piped to Roebourne, Dampier, Karratha, Wickham and Cape Lambert. In contrast to the **Karijini** (Hamersley Range) **National Park**, the scenery in the Millstream–Chichester National Park varies from magnificent views over the coastal plain to the deep permanent river pools of tropical Millstream. This attractive spot offers excellent swimming conditions and pleasant camping areas.

The Hamersley Range is rugged, exciting country, and is enticing and often beautiful. Keep in mind, however, that you are travelling in remote areas. Old roads are being improved and new ones constructed in an effort to open up one of the oldest areas in the world.

For further information contact the Tom Price Tourist Bureau, Central Rd, Tom Price; (091) 88 1112. **See also:** Individual town entries in A–Z listing.

The Pilbara

In the Pilbara there are over 3000 speakers of 28 Aboriginal languages belonging to one language 'family'. It is still common among Aboriginal people in the area to speak two or three languages, with some people able to use more. In the Port Hedland area the traditional language was Kariyarra; today you will also hear Ngarla, Nyarual Martuwangka and Nyangurnarta being spoken.

The iron ore boom has created employment opportunities in this land of sand spinifex, mulga scrub and massive red mountains, and model mining-company towns have sprung up. Gardens, swimming pools, golf courses and communal activities help compensate for the isolation and harsh climate.

Dampier, on King Bay, is a modern iron ore company town, with a major salt industry nearby. Offshore is the Woodside North West Shelf Gas Project, the largest single resource development undertaken in Australia; it includes a 1500-kilometre pipeline. Another side to the town is the Dampier Archipelago, comprising 42 islands of which 25 are incorporated into flora and fauna reserves. Fishing, diving, swimming, boating, camping and bushwalking allowed around and on several of these outcrops.

Roebourne, the oldest town in the north-west, has been a centre for the pastoral, copper and pearling industries. The old pearling port of **Cossack** is nearby. Inland on the Fortescue River, lush ferns, palms and lilies grow near the deep pools at **Millstream**, the source of water for many Pilbara towns. The **Millstream–Chichester National Park** is also well worth a visit. To the south, the fishing village of Onslow and its offshore islands is the perfect holiday retreat.

Karratha is a modern town and regional centre, as is **Wickham**. Wickham's port at Cape Lambert has the tallest and second-longest jetty in Australia, standing 18.5 metres above water and 3 kilometres long. At **Port Hedland**, streamlined port facilities cope with more tonnage than any other port in the country. Ore mined inland at **Tom Price**, **Newman**, **Paraburdoo** and other centres is railed on giant trains to the ports for export.

The fishing in the Port Hedland area is good, with many world records being set. Swimming in the sea can be dangerous, because sharks, sea snakes and poisonous fish frequent the waters; always make local enquiries before you swim. Port Hedland also offers the visitor historical sites, exhibition centres, interesting flora and fauna, and sporting facilities. **Tom Price** affords easy access to the magnificent gorges in the **Karijini (Hamersley Range) National Park**, with their many-coloured walls, deep cool waters and lush green growth. And, of course, there is **Marble Bar**, the hottest place in Australia and keeping alive the tradition of the great Australian outback.

Despite great improvements to the main roads–many are sealed—they are still liable to deterioration, and can have long stretches of rough and dangerous surface. It is wise to check local conditions before setting out.

For further information contact the Pilbara Regional Tourism Assn, Central Rd, Tom Price; (091) 88 1112. **See also:** Individual town entries in A–Z listing; Outback Motoring.

the area: Wagin Heritage Trail; details from Tourist Information. Corralyn Emu Farm, 4 km N. Granite Mt Latham, 6 km W, views, bushwalking. Puntapin, 6 km SE, rock formation used as water-catchment area; wildflowers abound in spring. Lakes Norring, 13 km SE, picnics, swimming, sailing, water-skiing. Dumbleyung, 30 km E, sightseeing. **Tourist information:** Shire Offices, Arthur Rd; (098) 61 1177; Wagin Historical Village, Showgrounds, Ballagin Rd; (098) 61 1232. **Accommodation:** 3 hotels, 2 motels, 1 cara./camp. park. **See also:** The Great Southern.
MAP REF. 347 K13, 354 G10, 356 B11

Walpole   Pop. 290

Walpole is literally where the forest meets the sea. Surrounded by the Walpole–Nornalup National Park where a variety of trees grow, incl. karri, jarrah, and the giant red tingle (*Eucalyptus jacksouii*), unique to the area. The area is known for its wildflowers in season as well as its wildlife. **Of interest:** Pioneer Cottage, Pioneer Park: opened 1987 to commemorate district pioneers, cottage follows design of early pioneer homes, but not intended as a replica. Bibbulmun Track (530 km), leading south from Kalamunda, 30 km E of Perth, ends at Walpole. **In the area:** Coalmine Beach Heritage Trail; details from Tourist Information. Knoll Drive, 3 km E. Valley of the Giants, 16 km E, huge tingles and karris, canopy walk under construction. Circular Pool, on Frankland River, 11 km NE. Tingle trees on Hilltop Rd, near Circular Pool. Mt Frankland, 29 km N. Fernhook Falls, 32 km NW. For bushwalkers, Nuyts Wilderness area, 7 km W, and other walking trails. Ocean, river and inlet for anglers. Peaceful Bay, 28 km SE. **Tourist information:** Pioneer Cottage, Pioneer Park; (098) 40 1111. **Accommodation:** 1 hotel/motel, 1 B&B, 1 hostel, 3 cara./camp. parks.
MAP REF. 354 F12

Wanneroo   Pop. 6745

Just a short drive from Perth, the district around Wanneroo stretches along 50 km of constantly changing coastline. **Of interest:** Botanic Golf, Burns Beach Rd. Dizzy Lamb Park, cnr Karoborup Rd and Wanneroo Rd. At junction of Whitfords Ave, Hepburn Ave and West Coast Dr: Hillarys Boat Harbour, Sorrento Quay and Underwater World. Mindarie Keys

Original town site, Wyndham

Resort, Ocean Falls Bvd. In Prindiville Dr, Wangara: Gumnut Factory, Wanneroo Weekend Markets. In Wanneroo Rd: Conti Estate Wine Cellars and Restaurant; Magic Wildflowers. International competitors are attracted to regular meetings at Wanneroo Motor Racing Circuit. **In the area:** Kristen Leigh Creations, Dellamarta Rd, Wangara, Australian wildflowers made into jewellery. Nearby lakes: Joondalup, 1 km W; Jandabup, 4 km E; Gnangara, 7 km SE. Vineyards: Faranda, 2 km S; Conti Estate, 4 km S; Hartridge, 10 km NW. Wildflower Cottage, 10 km N. Yanchep National Park, 27 km NW. Gloucester Lodge Museum in park. **Tourist information:** Joondalup Railway Station; (09) 300 0155 or WA Coach Service 3–6 Dellamarta Rd, Wangara; (09) 309 1680. **Accommodation:** 1 B&B, 3 cara./camp. parks.
MAP REF. 346 C3, 354 D7

Wickepin   Pop. 245

Wickepin dates back to the 1890s, when the first European settlers came to the district. The town is 214 km SE of Perth in farming country. **Of interest:** Good examples of Edwardian architecture in Wogolin Rd. **In the area:** Town has become well known following the publication of Albert Facey's autobiography *A Fortunate Life*; the house he built is 15 km S of Wickepin. Albert Facey Heritage Trail; details from Tourist Information. Toolibin Lake reserve, 20 km S, wide variety of waterfowl. Sewell's Rock Nature Reserve, 14 km E of Yealering, ideal

for picnics and nature walks. Tiny town of Yealering, and Yealering Lake, 30 km NE. **Tourist information:** Wickepin Newsagency and Milkbar, 56 Wogolin Rd; (098) 88 1070. **Accommodation:** 1 hotel, 1 cara./camp. park.
MAP REF. 347 L9, 354 G9, 356 B10

Wickham   Pop. 1973

Construction of Wickham, 49 km N of Karratha, was begun in 1970 by the Cliff's Robe River Iron Associates. Today the town is still company-owned and -operated, now by Robe River Iron Associates. Wickham is the sister town to Pannawonica; iron ore mined out of Pannawonica is processed here before being exported from nearby Cape Lambert. **Of interest:** Tours of processing plant and port operations; from Robe River Visitors Centre, Wickham Dr, Mon.–Fri. Boat Beach off Walcott Dr. Lookout at Tank Hill, views of town. July: Cossack–Wickham Fun Run. **In the area:** At Cape Lambert, 10 km NW, tallest and second-longest open-ocean wharf in Australia. Point Samson, 9 km W, popular beach resort, game fishing. Roebourne, 10 km S, oldest town in north-west; old gaol, government buildings. Cossack, 8 km SE, restored town, once pearling port. **Tourist information:** Roebourne Tourist Bureau, Queen St, Roebourne; (091) 82 1060. **Accommodation:** Limited budget accommodation. **See also:** The Hamersley Range; The Pilbara.
MAP REF. 355 H1, 358 A2

Williams
Pop. 371

This historical town enjoys a picturesque setting on the banks of the Williams River, 161 km SE of Perth. **In the area:** Dryandra State Forest, 25 km N. **Tourist information:** Williams Hotel, Albany Hwy; (098) 85 1016. **Accommodation:** 1 hotel, 1 motel, 1 cara./camp. park. MAP REF. 346 I11, 354 F9, 356 B10

Wittenoom
Pop. 50

Wittenoom is situated at the mouth of Wittenoom Gorge on the northern face of the magnificent Hamersley Range. The town lies 289 km from Roebourne, 300 km from Port Hedland, 240 km from Newman and 130 km from Tom Price. Wittenoom was established in 1947 as a service centre for the workers of the blue asbestos mining industry, but world demand had declined by 1966 and mining ceased. **In the area:** Gem Shop, 1 km E; gemstones, museum, photograph collection, paintings, picnic area. Karijini (Hamersley Range) National Park, surrounding and south of town, renowned for its spectacular gorges. Mt Meharray (1245 m), WA's highest peak, just inside eastern boundary of park. Wittenoom Gorge extends southward; 12-km scenic drive. Yampire Gorge, 52 km SE; turnoff 24 km E gives access to other gorges. Dales Gorge, 60 km SE, permanent waterfalls, Fortescue Falls, Fern Pool. Kalamina Gorge and pool, 35 km W of Dales Gorge; the most accessible gorge in the National Park. Joffre, Hancock, Weano and Red Gorges, joining below Oxer Lookout, begin 97 km S by road, 30–45 m deep at junction; Weano Gorge, section 1 m wide and 30 m deep, the most accessible of this group. Oxer Lookout has breathtaking view. Hamersley Gorge, 53 km W, permanent pools for swimming, coloured folds in rock. Warning: Although the asbestos mine at Wittenoom was closed in 1966, there is still a significant health risk from microscopic asbestos fibres created by the milling process; these fibres are present in tailing dumps near the Wittenoom mine site and in landfill used in and around the town site. While the risk from airborne asbestos fibres to short-term visitors in the town is considered to be significantly low, **warning is given that inhaling asbestos fibres may cause cancer.** Any activity that disturbs asbestos tailings and generates airborne fibres should be avoided. Visitors travelling through Wittenoom are advised to take the following precautions:

- Keep to main roads in the town and gorge areas.
- When driving in windy or dusty conditions, keep car windows closed.
- Avoid parking on or adjacent to asbestos tailings.
- Prevent children playing in asbestos tailings in the town or at mine site.
- Camp only in designated camping areas. Camping is not allowed in the Wittenoom Gorge.

Tourist information: Wittenoom Gem Shop and Information Centre, Sixth Ave; (091) 89 7096. **Accommodation:** 2 hostels, 1 cara./camp. park. MAP REF. 355 I3, 358 C4

Wyndham
Pop. 860

Wyndham is the most northerly town and safe port harbour in WA. The town consists of two main areas: the original town site of Wyndham port, situated on Cambridge Gulf, and Wyndham East ('Three Mile'), on the Great Northern Hwy, the residential and shopping area. In 1985 the meatworks, representing Wyndham's main industry, closed. Today Wyndham is a service town for the pastoral industry, mining exploration, tourism and nearby Aboriginal communities. Port now handles live cattle shipment to SE Asia. **Of interest:** Historic buildings in main street (Great Northern Hwy): Port Post Office (now tourist information centre); Durack's Wool Store; courthouse; Anthon's Landing. Warriu Park Aboriginal Monument in town centre. Port display

Wittenoom Gorge

next to Marine and Harbours Offices, near wharf. Crocodile-spotting from wharf. Crocodile Farm, Priority Rd, Wyndham Port; daily feeding. Three Mile Caravan Park, huge boab tree, 1500–2000 yrs old. Aug.: 4-week Top of the West Festival. Nov.: Hang Gliding Competition. **In the area:** To south-east on King River Rd: Aboriginal rock paintings, 18 km; prison tree 2000–4000 years old, 22 km. Afghan cemetery, 1 km E. Marlgu Billabong, 12 km E, abundant birdlife. The Grotto, 36 km E (2 km off road), rock-edged waterhole, at base of volcanic hole estimated to be 100 m deep; cool, shaded oasis, safe year-round swimming. Five Rivers Lookout, 5 km N, atop Bastion Range, spectacular views of Kimberley landscape, mountain ranges, Cambridge Gulf, Wyndham port, rivers. The 100-km sealed road leading to Wyndham passes through splendid gorge country. Alligator Airways Resort, Drysdale River, 80 km NW. El Questro Station, 100 km S: vast cattle station, accommodation, touring options; details from Tourist Information. **Tourist information:** Old Post Office building, O'Donnell St, Wyndham Port; (091) 61 1054. **Accommodation:** 1 hotel, 1 hotel/motel, 1 B&B, 1 cara./camp. park. **See also:** The Kimberley. MAP REF. 353 O1, 361 Q4, 392 A12, 394 A2

Yalgoo
Pop. 80

Yalgoo lies 216 km E of Geraldton along an excellent road in real Australian outback country. Alluvial gold was discovered in the 1890s. Small traces of gold are still found in the district, which encourages fossicking by locals and visitors. **Of interest:** Courthouse Museum, Gibbons St. Restored Dominican Convent Chapel, Henty St. **In the area:** Joker's Tunnel, 10 km S on Paynes Find Rd, carved through solid rock by early prospectors, named after Joker mining syndicate. Golden Grove zinc mine, 300 employees, 50 km S; by appt, contact Tourist Information. Area harbours abundant native wildlife. Prolific wildflowers in season (July–Sept.). **Tourist information:** Shire Offices; (099) 62 8042. **Accommodation:** 1 hotel/motel, 2 caravan parks. MAP REF. 354 F1, 356 A2

Yallingup
Pop. 150

Yallingup is known for its excellent surf, with the Australian Surf Championships

held in the area. Its caves were a well-known attraction before the turn of the century. **Of interest:** Caves House Hotel, off Caves Rd, built by government as holiday hotel in 1903. Early visitors arrived from Busselton via horse and buggy along dirt road, a journey of 2½ hours. Hotel was rebuilt in 1938 after fire, using locally milled timber; now has award-winning accommodation and restaurant. Oct.: October Festival. Dec.: Malibu Competition. **In the area:** Gunyulgup Gallery, 2 km S. Goanna Galley and Bush Cottage Market, 8 km SE, local art, craft. Shearing Shed, Wildwood Rd, 10 km SE, shearing demonstrations, woolshop; check times. Rivendell Gardens, 10 km SE, Devonshire teas, pick-your-own strawberries in season. Yallingup Caves, 2 km E, open daily. Canal Rocks and Smith's Beach, 5 km SW, good fishing, surfing, swimming, spectacular scenery. Wineries: Hunts Foxhaven Estate, 3 km S, by appt; Wildwood, 5 km S; Cape Clairault Wines, 10 km S; Willyabrup Valley district, 20 km S; Margaret River area, 40 km S; Happ's Vineyard and Pottery, 8 km SE; Moonshine Brewery and Abbey Vale Vineyards, 11 km SE. **Tourist information:** Busselton Tourist Bureau, Southern Dr, Busselton; (097) 52 1288. **Accommodation:** 1 hotel, 4 B&B, 3 cara./camp. parks. **See also:** The Southwest.
MAP REF. 354 C10

Yanchep   Pop. 1577

Within easy driving distance from Perth is the resort of Yanchep, 51 km to the north. **In the area:** Yanchep National Park, 15 km E, covering 2799 ha of natural bushland. In park: Gloucester Lodge Museum; Crystal Cave, startling limestone formations; launch cruises on freshwater Loch McNess (Sun.). Wild Kingdom, 3 km NE, halfway between Yanchep and Two Rocks, wildlife park and zoo. Two Rocks, 6 km NW, marina. Wreck of *Alkimos,* south of Yanchep, said to be guarded by ghost. Picturesque Gnangara Lake, 30 km SE, location with picnic facilities. **Tourist information:** Information Office, Yanchep National Park; (09) 561 1004 and 935 Wanneroo Rd, Wanneroo; (09) 405 4678. **Accommodation:** 1 hotel/motel.
MAP REF. 346 C2, 354 D7

York   Pop. 1562

Founded in 1830, York is the oldest inland town in WA, set on the banks of the Avon River in the fertile Avon Valley, 97 km from Perth. The town has a wealth of historic buildings, carefully preserved. Many festivals and events held annually, including the York Jazz Festival Sept–Oct. **Of interest:** All in Avon Tce: Old Gaol, Courthouse, Police Station, all built of local stone 1895; Settlers' House (1850), restored two-storey mud-brick building, old-world accommodation; Castle Hotel and Imperial Inn, fine examples of early coaching inns; Romanesque Town Hall (1911), impressive dimensions; Art Gallery, York Pottery, Loder Antiques; Motor Museum, Australia's best collection of veteran, classic and racing cars (and some bicycles and motorcycles); historic Balladong Farm, old buildings and equipment, domestic animals. Old railway station (1886), Railway Rd, railway museum. In Brook St: old hospital, original shingle roof, group accommodation; Residency Museum (1843), colonial furniture, early photographs. Fine churches: Holy Trinity (consecrated 1858), Suburban Rd; St Patrick's (1886), South St; Uniting Church (1888), Grey St. De Ladera Alpaca Farm, North Rd; alpacas, other animals, picnic/barbecue facilities. Suspension Bridge (originally 1906) across river in Low St. Lookout: follow signs from Castle Hotel to Pioneer Drive and then to Mt Brown. Picnic/barbecue facilities at Avon Park in Low St, and Railway Park, Railway Rd. Sept.: Jazz Festival. **In the area:** Near Quairading, 64 km E, Toapin Weir and Mt Stirling, panoramic views. Several Heritage Trails; details from Tourist Information. **Tourist information:** 105 Avon Tce; (096) 41 1301. **Accommodation:** 1 hotel, 3 hotel/motels, 1 motel, 4 B&B, 1 cara./camp. park.
MAP REF. 346 H4, 354 F7, 356 A8

Yallingup Caves

Western Australia

Location Map

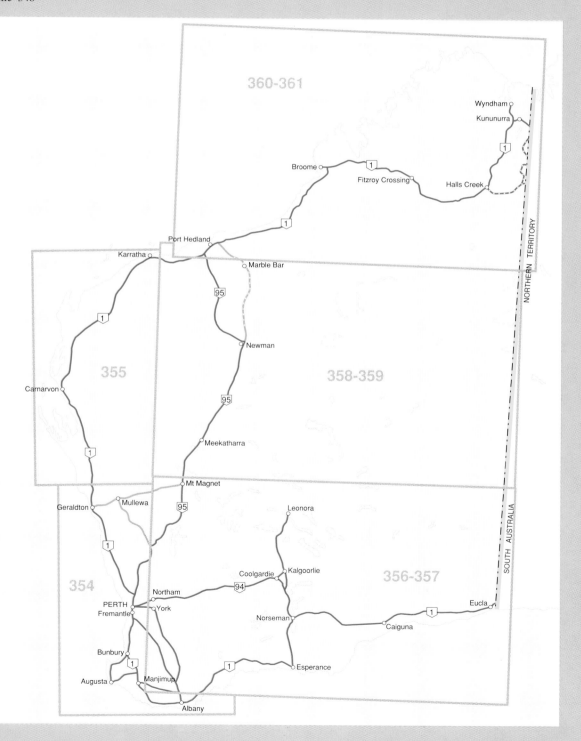

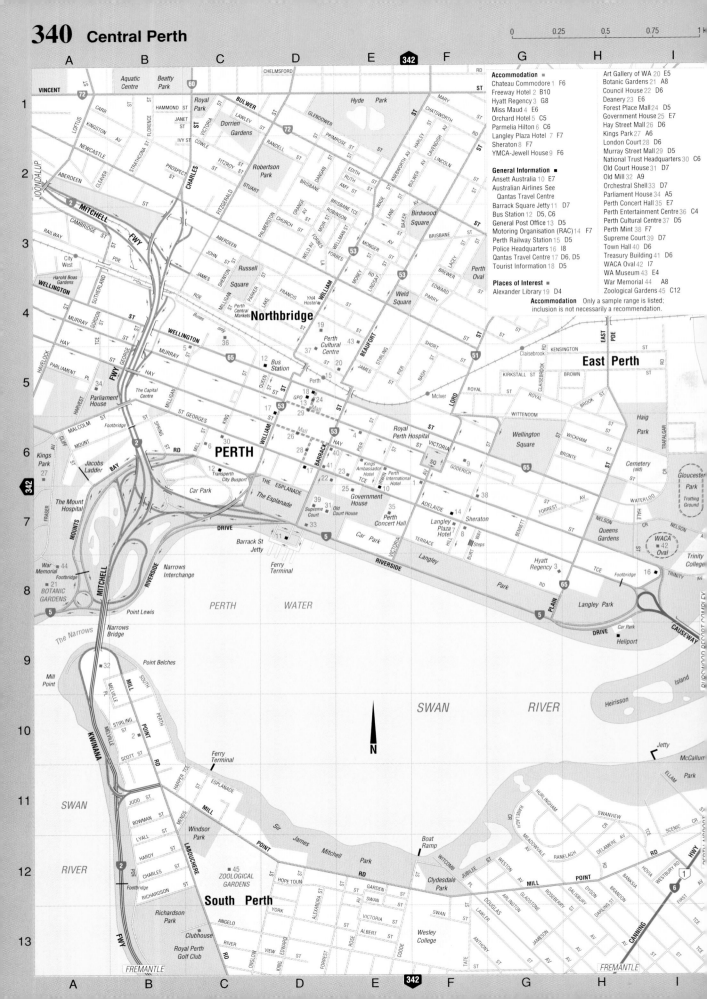

0   0.25   0.5   0.75   1 K

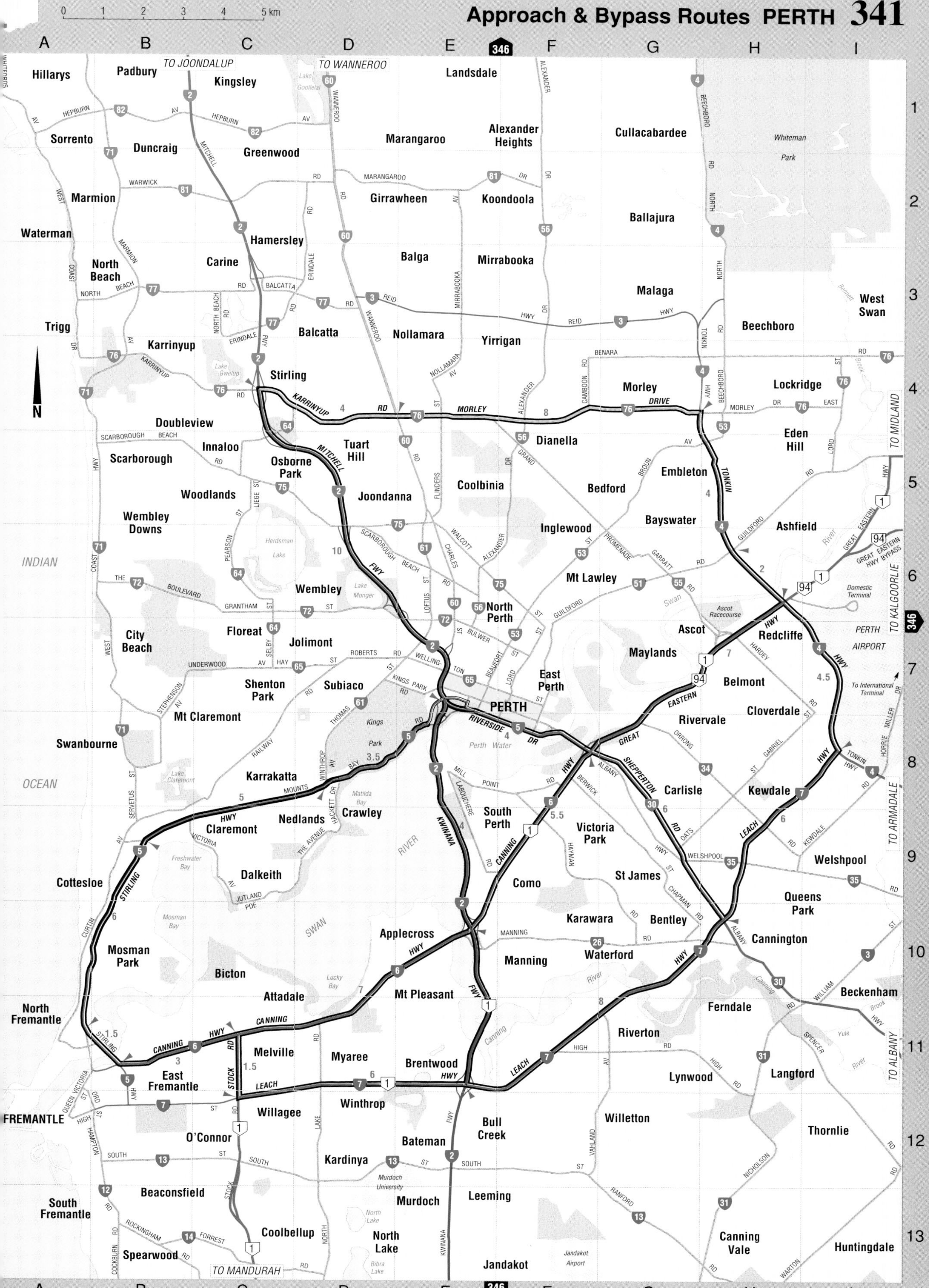

0 1 2 3 4 5 km

N

TO JOONDALUP

TO WANNEROO

Hillarys
Padbury
Kingsley
Landsdale
Sorrento
Duncraig
Greenwood
Marangaroo
Alexander Heights
Cullacabardee
Whiteman Park
Marmion
North Beach
Carine
Hamersley
Girrawheen
Koondoola
Ballajura
Waterman
Balga
Mirrabooka
Malaga
Beechboro
West Swan
Trigg
Karrinyup
Balcatta
Nollamara
Yirrigan
Morley
Lockridge
Doubleview
Stirling
Tuart Hill
Dianella
Eden Hill
Scarborough
Innaloo
Osborne Park
Joondanna
Coolbinia
Embleton
Ashfield
Woodlands
Wembley Downs
Herdsman Lake
Lake Monger
North Perth
Inglewood
Bedford
Bayswater
Mt Lawley
City Beach
Floreat
Jolimont
Wembley
Mt Claremont
Shenton Park
Subiaco
PERTH
East Perth
Ascot
Maylands
Redcliffe
Belmont
PERTH AIRPORT
Swanbourne
Karrakatta
Nedlands
Crawley
Kings Park
Perth Water
Rivervale
Cloverdale
To International Terminal
Cottesloe
Claremont
Dalkeith
SWAN RIVER
South Perth
Victoria Park
St James
Carlisle
Kewdale
Welshpool
Mosman Park
Bicton
Attadale
Applecross
Como
Karawara
Bentley
Cannington
Queens Park
North Fremantle
Melville
Myaree
Mt Pleasant
Manning
Waterford
Riverton
Ferndale
Beckenham
East Fremantle
Willagee
Winthrop
Brentwood
Bull Creek
Lynwood
Langford
FREMANTLE
O'Connor
Kardinya
Bateman
Leeming
Willetton
Thornlie
South Fremantle
Beaconsfield
Murdoch
Murdoch University
Jandakot Airport
Canning Vale
Huntingdale
Spearwood
Coolbellup
North Lake
Bibra Lake
Jandakot

TO MANDURAH

TO MIDLAND

TO KALGOORLIE

TO ARMADALE

TO ALBANY

Thick roads represent recommended approach and bypass routes

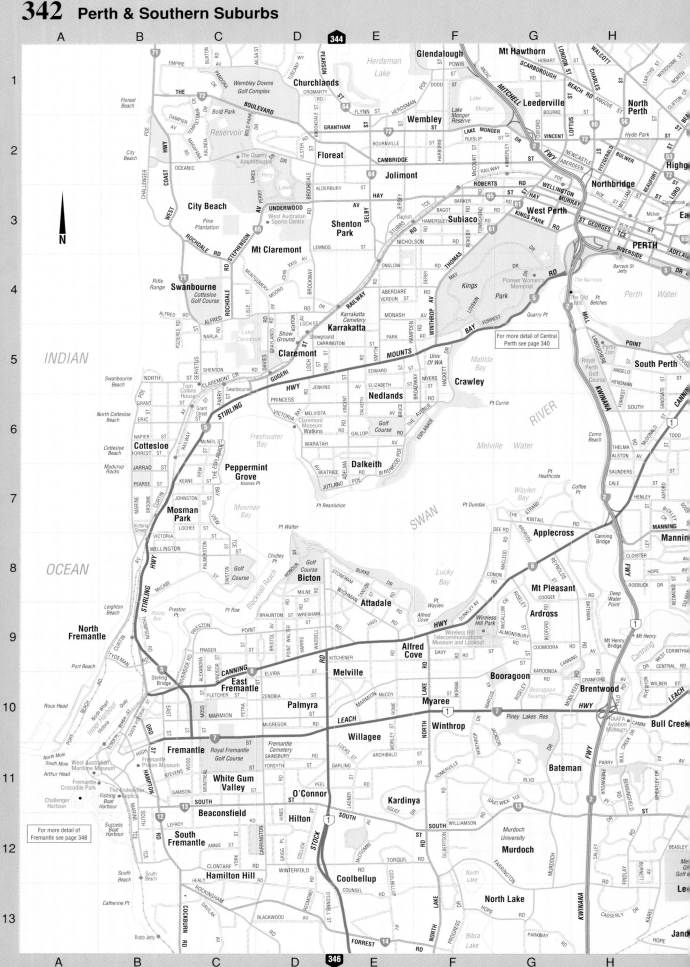

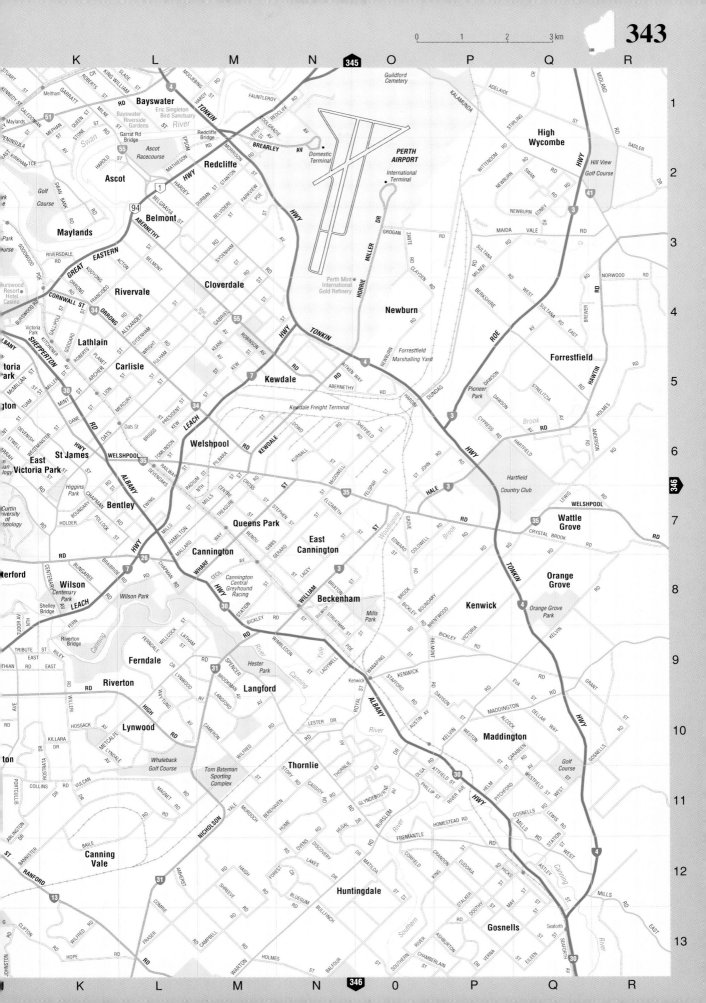

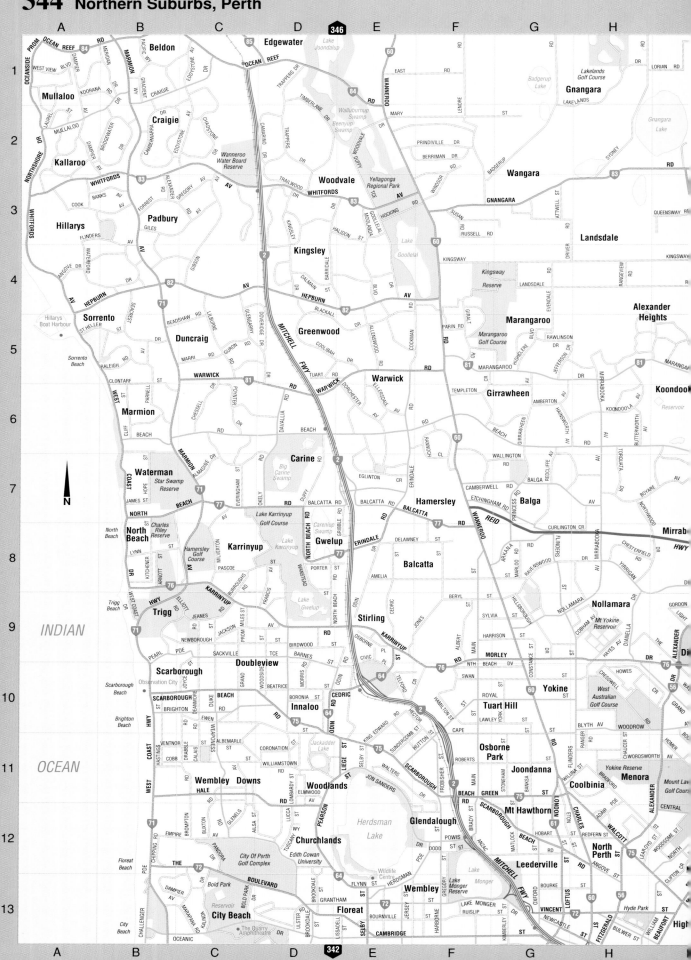

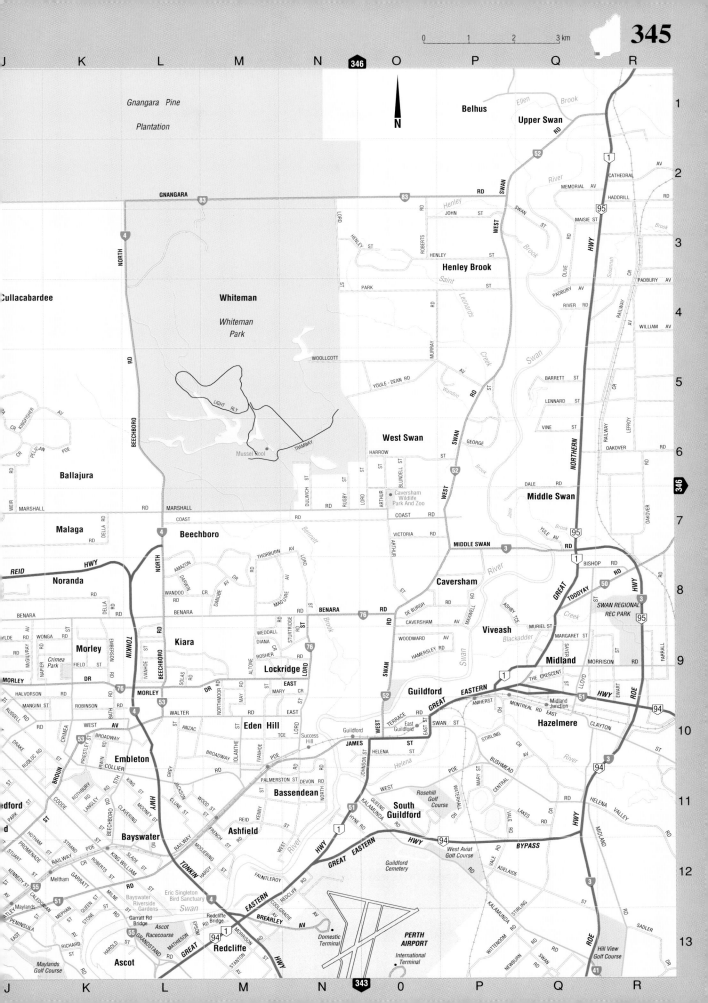

354

TO GERALDTON

Bindoon
TO MOUNT MAGNET

BRAND HWY
NORTHERN HWY
GREAT

Lake Chittering
SOUTH BINDOON

Jennacubbine

Dewars Pool

CHITTERING
CHITTERING VALLEY

Two Rocks

Wreck Point

YANCHEP NATIONAL PARK

Caves

Toodyay

YARRAMONY

Yanchep Beach
Eglinton Rock

Yanchep

Lake Pinjar

Muchea

KYOTMUNGA

RINGA

Avon River

NOGGOJERRING

MEENAR

Quinns Rock

AVON VALLEY NATIONAL PARK

Archery Park

Northam

QUELLINGTON

Bullsbrook

Peace RAAF Station

Swan R.

WALYUNGA NP

Clackline

EASTERN

MOKINE

Camel Farm

NEERABUP NATIONAL PARK

Burns Beach

MULLALOO

Whitfords Beach

Wanneroo

UPPER SWAN

Gidgegannup

Wundowie

GREAT

Bakers Hill

Historical Balladong Farm

Hillarys Boat Harbour & Underwater World
NORTH BEACH
SCARBOROUGH

WHITEMAN PARK

MIDLAND
GUILDFORD

JOHN FORREST NATIONAL PARK

Mount Helena

Chidlow

GREAT

DYOTT RANGE

York

York Motor Museum

For more detail of Perth Suburbs see pages 342 - 345

PERTH

PERTH AIRPORT

Mundaring

KALAMUNDA NATIONAL PARK
O'Connor Museum

Helena Reservoir

Helena R.

Mt Talbot 398m

SOUTHERN

COTTESLOE

KALAMUNDA

CANNINGTON

Rottnest Island

Passenger Ferry

Fremantle

SPEARWOOD

KELMSCOTT
JANDAKOT

KARRAGULLEN

Coburn Wildlife Sanctuary
Kelmscott Museum

Mt Dale 548m

Darkin R.

TALBOT BROOK

Aeronautical Museum

Carnac Island

Garden Island

Armadale

The Elizabethan Village
Mt Paradise Water Gardens

BROOKTON

Christmas Tree Well

INDIAN

Byford

SOUTH

Canning Dam

Mt Randall 525m

Kwinana
Rockingham

Cape Peron

Safety Bay

Penguin Island

Waikiki
Warnbro Beach
Becher Point

Mundijong
Mardella
Serpentine

Tumblegum Farm

SERPENTINE NATIONAL PARK

Serpentine Dam

ALBANY

DARLING

WESTDALE

HIGHWAY

OCEAN

Peelhurst
Singleton
Madora

Keysbrook

Mt Solus 574m

Boyagin Rock

Halls Head
Miami

Mandurah

North Dandalup

Boonerring Hill 529m

RANGE

Peel Inlet

Nth Yunderup

Fairbridge Farm School

Wandering

Florida
Melros
Cape Bouvard

Dawesville

Sth Yunderup

Pinjarra

Hotham Valley Tourist Railway

South Dandalup Dam

Bannister

DWARDA

CAERNARVON HILLS

YALGORUP NATIONAL PARK

Harvey Estuary

Meelon

Marrinup

Dwellingup

Lane Pool Reserve

AMPHION

Boddington

Crossman

Hotham R.

Coolup

Murray River

NANGA

Mt Keats 474m

Marradong

Lake Clifton

Lake Clifton

WAGERUP

Waroona

Waroona Dam

Samson Bk Dam

Mt Saddleback 75m

Williams R.

Preston Beach

YALGORUP NATIONAL PARK

Hamel

HWY

Quindanning

Williams

Lake Preston

Yarloop

Logue Bk Dam

JOSBURY

Myalup

Harvey

Harvey R.

WARAWARRUP

Harvey Weir

Mt Tallanalla

BORANING

Wild Horse Hill 395m

Binningup

Benger

Stirling Dam

Leschenault Inlet

BEELA

Worsley Aluminium Refinery

Harris R.

Bingham R.

Hillman R.

DARDADINE

Brunswick Junction

Australind
Eaton

Koombana Bay

Bunbury

Roelands
Burekup

Waterloo

Worsley

Allanson

Collie

Wellington Dam

Boolading

Darkan

Dardanup

TO BUSSELTON

Collie R.

Collieburn
Buckingham

Shotts

Bowelling

354

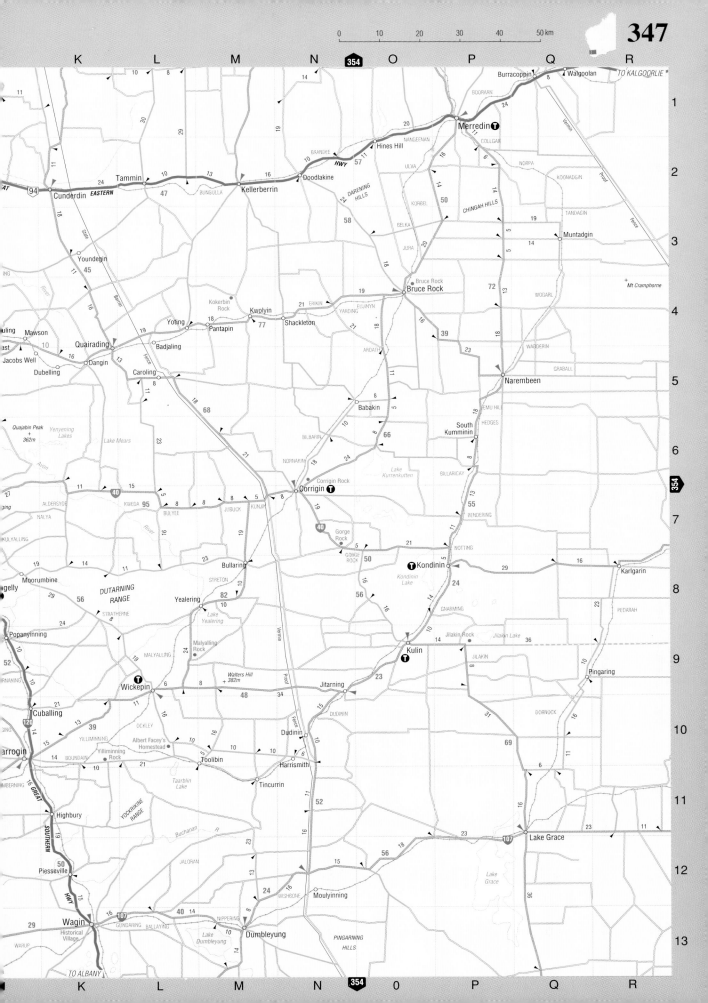

348 Fremantle

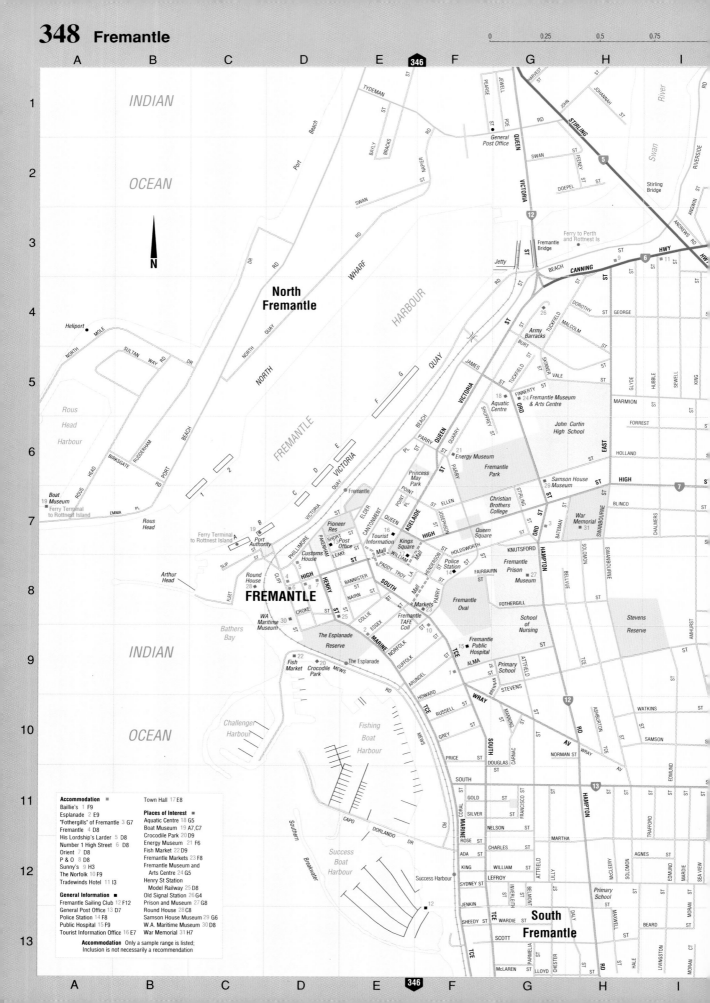

INDIAN

OCEAN

North
Fremantle

Rous
Head
Harbour

Heliport

Boat
Museum
Ferry Terminal
to Rottnest Island

Arthur
Head

INDIAN

OCEAN

Bathers
Bay

FREMANTLE

WA
Maritime
Museum

Round
House

Customs
House

Port
Authority

Ferry Terminal
to Rottnest Island

Challenger
Harbour

Fishing
Boat
Harbour

Fish
Market

Crocodile
Park

The Esplanade
Reserve

The Esplanade

Fremantle
TAFE Coll

Fremantle
Markets

Fremantle
Oval

Fremantle
Public
Hospital

Primary
School

School
of
Nursing

Fremantle
Prison
Museum

Knutsford

Fremantle
Park

John Curtin
High School

Fremantle Museum
& Arts Centre

Army
Barracks

Samson House
Museum

War
Memorial

Christian
Brothers
College

Queen
Square

Princess
May
Park

Energy Museum

Aquatic
Centre

Fremantle
Bridge

Ferry to Perth
and Rottnest Is

General
Post Office

Stirling
Bridge

Swan
River

Success
Boat
Harbour

Southern
Breakwater

South
Fremantle

Stevens
Reserve

Success Harbour

Old Signal
Station

Pioneer
Res

Tourist
Information

Kings
Square

Police
Station

Fairbairn

Town Hall

Ferry
Terminal

Jetty

Primary
School

Legend

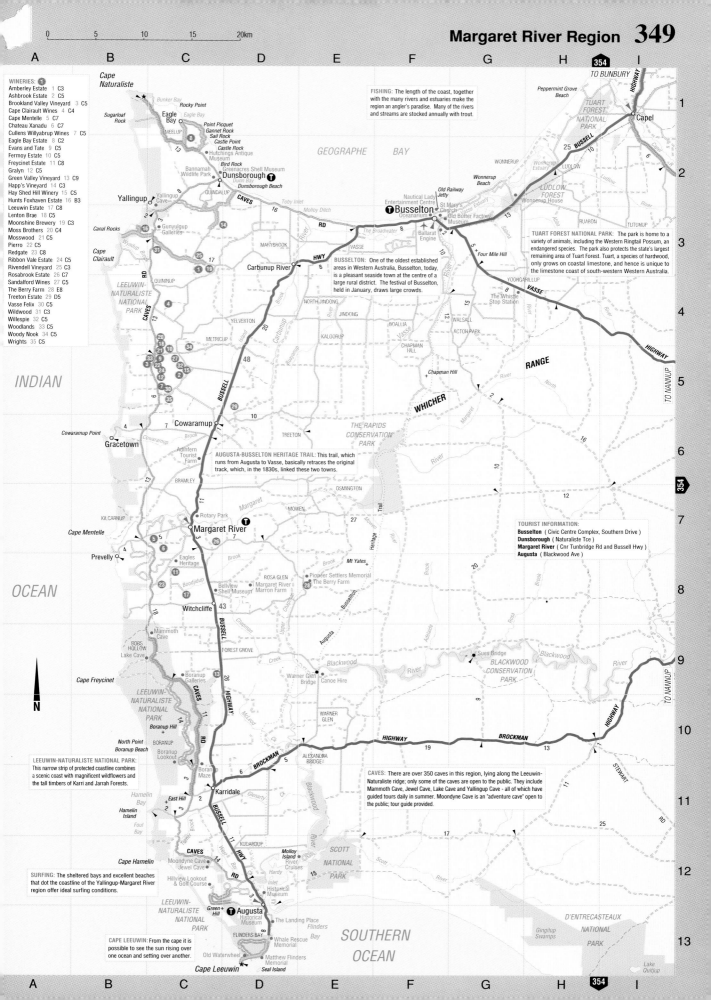

354

TO BUNBURY

HIGHWAY

WINERIES: 1

Amberley Estate 1 C3
Ashbrook Estate 2 C5
Brookland Valley Vineyard 3 C5
Cape Clairault Wines 4 C4
Cape Mentelle 5 C7
Chateau Xanadu 6 C7
Cullens Willyabrup Wines 7 C5
Eagle Bay Estate 8 C2
Evans and Tate 9 C5
Fermoy Estate 10 C5
Freycinet Estate 11 C8
Gralyn 12 C5
Green Valley Vineyard 13 C9
Happ's Vineyard 14 C3
Hay Shed Hill Winery 15 C5
Hunts Foxhaven Estate 16 B3
Leeuwin Estate 17 C8
Lenton Brae 18 C5
Moonshine Brewery 19 C3
Moss Brothers 20 C4
Mosswood 21 C5
Pierro 22 C5
Redgate 23 C8
Ribbon Vale Estate 24 C5
Rivendell Vineyard 25 C3
Rosabrook Estate 26 C7
Sandalford Wines 27 C5
The Berry Farm 28 E8
Treeton Estate 29 D5
Vasse Felix 30 C5
Wildwood 31 C3
Willespie 32 C5
Woodlands 33 C5
Woody Nook 34 C5
Wrights 35 C5

INDIAN

OCEAN

FISHING: The length of the coast, together with the many rivers and estuaries make the region an angler's paradise. Many of the rivers and streams are stocked annually with trout.

GEOGRAPHE BAY

BUSSELTON: One of the oldest established areas in Western Australia, Busselton, today, is a pleasant seaside town at the centre of a large rural district. The festival of Busselton, held in January, draws large crowds.

TUART FOREST NATIONAL PARK: The park is home to a variety of animals, including the Western Ringtail Possum, an endangered species. The park also protects the state's largest remaining area of Tuart Forest. Tuart, a species of hardwood, only grows on coastal limestone, and hence is unique to the limestone coast of south-western Western Australia.

TO NANNUP

HIGHWAY

AUGUSTA-BUSSELTON HERITAGE TRAIL: This trail, which runs from Augusta to Vasse, basically retraces the original track, which, in the 1830s, linked these two towns.

TOURIST INFORMATION:
Busselton (Civic Centre Complex, Southern Drive)
Dunsborough (Naturaliste Tce)
Margaret River (Cnr Tunbridge Rd and Bussell Hwy)
Augusta (Blackwood Ave)

354

OCEAN

LEEUWIN-NATURALISTE NATIONAL PARK: This narrow strip of protected coastline combines a scenic coast with magnificent wildflowers and the tall timbers of Karri and Jarrah Forests.

TO NANNUP

HIGHWAY

CAVES: There are over 350 caves in this region, lying along the Leeuwin-Naturaliste ridge; only some of the caves are open to the public. They include Mammoth Cave, Jewel Cave, Lake Cave and Yallingup Cave - all of which have guided tours daily in summer. Moondyne Cave is an 'adventure cave' open to the public; tour guide provided.

SURFING: The sheltered bays and excellent beaches that dot the coastline of the Yallingup-Margaret River region offer ideal surfing conditions.

CAPE LEEUWIN: From the cape it is possible to see the sun rising over one ocean and setting over another.

SOUTHERN OCEAN

N

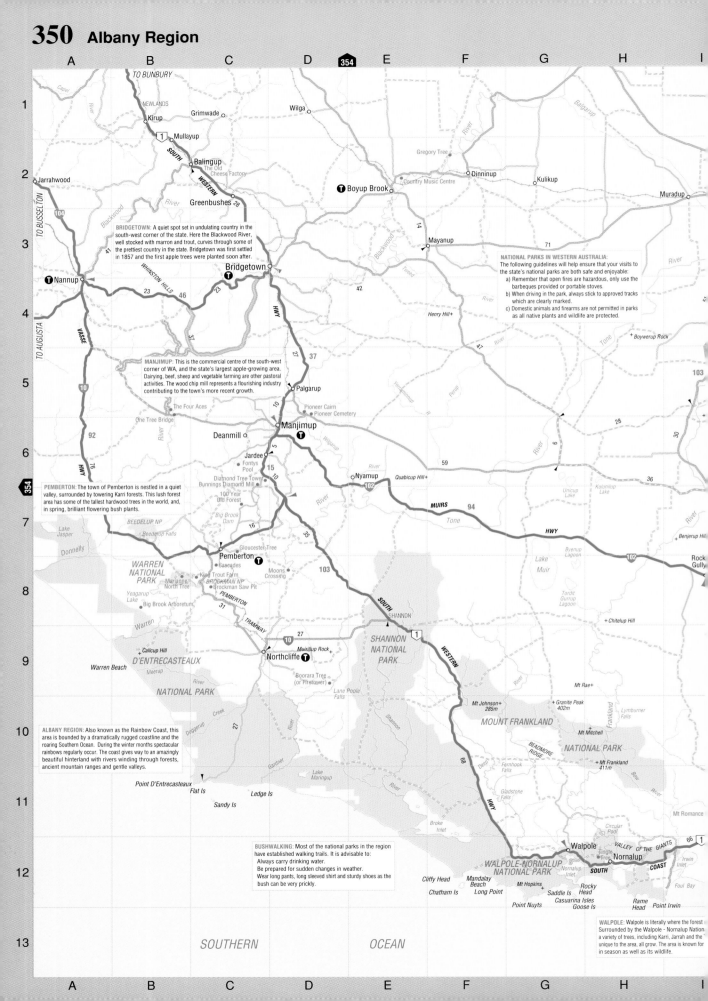

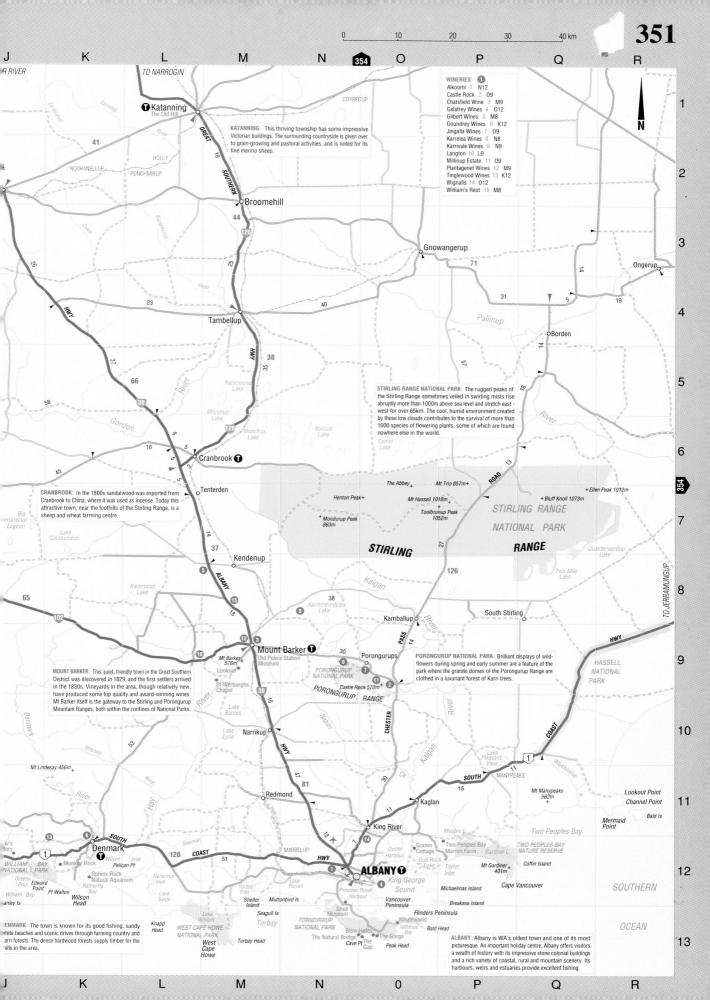

0 10 20 30 40 km

TO NARROGIN

J K L M N O P Q R

WINERIES:
Alkoomi 1   N12
Castle Rock 2   O9
Chatsfield Wine 3   M9
Galafrey Wines 4   O12
Gilbert Wines 5   M8
Goundrey Wines 6   K12
Jingalla Wines 7   O9
Karrelea Wines 8   N8
Karrivale Wines 9   N9
Langton 10   L9
Millinup Estate 11   O9
Plantagenet Wines 12   M9
Tinglewood Wines 13   K12
Wignalls 14   O12
William's Rest 15   M8

Katanning
The Old Hill

KATANNING: This thriving township has some impressive Victorian buildings. The surrounding countryside is given over to grain-growing and pastoral activities, and is noted for its fine merino sheep.

Broomehill

Gnowangerup

Ongerup

41

44

120

25

23

40

71

31

14

5

19

Tambellup

Borden

38

35

57

14

26

27

66

30

120

8

58

Milyunup Lake

Racecourse Lake

Munnrilup Lake

Balicup Lake

Camel Lake

Pallinup

River

STIRLING RANGE NATIONAL PARK: The rugged peaks of the Stirling Range sometimes veiled in swirling mists rise abruptly more than 1000m above sea level and stretch east - west for over 65km. The cool, humid environment created by these low clouds contributes to the survival of more than 1000 species of flowering plants, some of which are found nowhere else in the world.

16

45

5

3

Cranbrook

The Abbey +   Mt Trio 857m+   + Ellen Peak 1012m

Henton Peak+   Mt Hassell 1018m +   + Bluff Knoll 1073m

ROAD

13

STIRLING RANGE

+ Mondurup Peak 863m   + Toolbrunup Peak 1052m

NATIONAL PARK

Tenterden

CRANBROOK: In the 1800s sandalwood was exported from Cranbrook to China, where it was used as incense. Today this attractive town, near the foothills of the Stirling Range, is a sheep and wheat farming centre.

STIRLING   **RANGE**

Quarderwardup Lake

14

37

Kendenup

27

126

Two Mile Lake

65

5

18

Kalgan

38

Kairnmerndyiip Lake

102

15

8

HASSELL

NATIONAL PARK

HWY

Kwornicup Lake

Kamballup

South Stirling

12

3

Mount Barker

Old Police Station Museum

Porongurups

PORONGURUP NATIONAL PARK: Brilliant displays of wild-flowers during spring and early summer are a feature of the park where the granite domes of the Porongurup Range are clothed in a luxuriant forest of Karri trees.

10

Mt Barker 576m+   Lookout

30

7

PORONGURUP   **RANGE**

Castle Rock 570m+   11   2

St Werburghs Chapel

MOUNT BARKER: This quiet, friendly town in the Great Southern District was discovered in 1829, and the first settlers arrived in the 1830s. Vineyards in the area, though relatively new, have produced some top quality and award-winning wines. Mt Barker itself is the gateway to the Stirling and Porongurup Mountain Ranges, both within the confines of National Parks.

30

16

Lake Barnes

CHESTER

PASS

14

River

53

Mt Lindesay 456m +

Lake Eyrie

Narrikup

HWY

47

81

Lake Pleasant View

11

SOUTH

1

MANYPEAKS

Lookout Point
Channel Point

Mitchell

River

30   Ck

16   **COAST**

Mt Manypeaks 562m +

Redmond

11   Kaglan

Mermaid Point

Bald Is

13   6

Denmark

SOUTH   **COAST**

120   51

15

7   14

King River

Two Peoples Bay

WILLIAM
NATIONAL

1   **BAY PARK**

Monkey Rock

Pelican Pt

Sphinx Rock Natural Aquarium

Nenamup Inlet

MARBELUP

HWY

1   2

ALBANY

Gomm Cottage

Two Peoples Bay
Marron Farm

TWO PEOPLES BAY
NATURE RESERVE

Gardner L

Greens Pool

Edward Point

Pt Walton

Wilson Head

Lake Saide

Lake Powell

Lake William

Shelter Island

Muttonbird Is

Seagull Is

Torbay

Oyster Harbour

Gull Rock Pt

Taylor Inlet

4

King George
Sound

Mt Gardner 401m +

Coffin Island

Michaelmas Island

Cape Vancouver

SOUTHERN

William Stanley Is

Knapp Head

WEST CAPE HOWE
NATIONAL PARK

West Cape Howe

Torbay Head

TORNDIRRUP
NATIONAL PARK

The Natural Bridge
Cave Pt

Shell Museum

Princess Royal
Harbour

Vancouver Peninsula

Flinders Peninsula

Whaleworld

Blow Holes

The Gap   The Gorge

Peak Head   Bald Head

Breaksea Island

Isthmus Bay

OCEAN

DENMARK: The town is known for its good fishing, sandy white beaches and scenic drives through farming country and karri forests. The dense hardwood forests supply timber for the mills in the area.

ALBANY: Albany is WA's oldest town and one of its most picturesque. An important holiday centre, Albany offers visitors a wealth of history with its impressive stone colonial buildings and a rich variety of coastal, rural and mountain scenery. Its harbours, weirs and estuaries provide excellent fishing.

J K L M N O P Q R

1 2 3 4 5 6 7 8 9 10 11 12 13

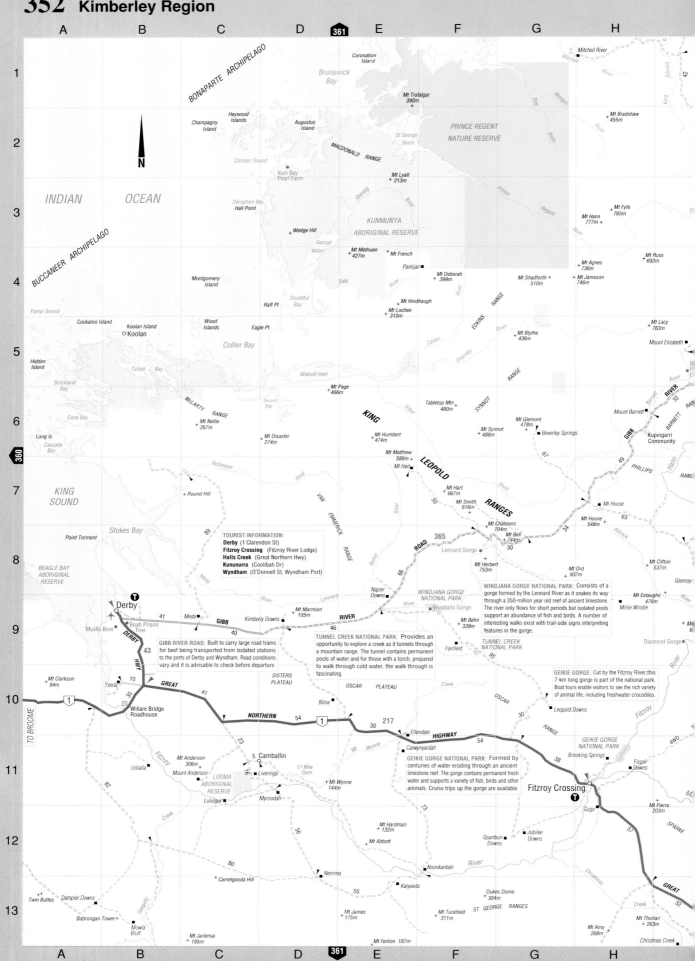

A   B   C   D   E   F   G   H

1

2

3

4

5

360

6

7

8

9

10

11

12

13

BONAPARTE ARCHIPELAGO

Coronation
Island

Brunswick
Bay

Mitchell River

Champagny
Island

Heywood
Islands

Augustus
Island

Mt Trafalgar
390m +

Mt Bradshaw
+ 455m

INDIAN   OCEAN

BUCCANEER ARCHIPELAGO

Camden Sound

MACDONALD   RANGE

St George
Basin

PRINCE REGENT
NATURE RESERVE

Kuri Bay
Pearl Farm

Mt Lyall
+ 213m

Mt Fyfe
+ 765m

Deception Bay
Hall Point

Wedge Hill +

KUNMUNYA
ABORIGINAL RESERVE

Mt Hann
777m +

Mt Russ
+ 692m

Montgomery
Island

George
Water

Mt Methuen
+ 427m

Mt French +

Pantijan

Mt Deborah
+ 399m

Mt Agnes
736m +

Mt Jameson
746m +

Yampi Sound

Raft Pt

Doubtful
Bay

Sale

Mt Hindhaugh +

Mt Shadforth +
510m

Mt Lochee
310m

EDKINS   RANGE

Mt Blythe
436m

Mt Lacy
+ 763m

Hidden
Island

Cockatoo Island

Koolan Island
○ Koolan

Wood
Islands

Eagle Pt

Collier Bay

Walcott Inlet

Calder   River

Charnley   River   RANGE

Mount Elizabeth

Strickland
Bay

Talbot Bay

Secure
Bay

Mt Page
+ 466m

Tabletop Mtn +
480m

SYNNOT

Mt Glemont
478m

BARNETT   RIVER

Cone Bay

McLARTY   RANGE

Mt Nellie
+ 267m

KING

Mt Humbert
+ 474m

Mt Synnot
+ 488m

Beverley Springs

Mount Barnett

GIBB

Kupingarri
Community

Long Is
Cascade
Bay

Mt Disaster
+ 274m

Mt Matthew
586m +

LEOPOLD

Mt Hart

67

49

PHILLIPS

RANG

KING
SOUND

Robinson   River

+ Round Hill

VAN

EMMERICK   RANGE

Mt Hart
+ 667m

Mt Smith
616m +

RANGES

Mt Chalmers
704m +

Mt Bell
+ 744m

50

34

Mt House
548m +

Mt House

63

Adcock

Point Torment

Stokes Bay

89

ROAD   365

Lennard Gorge ○

30

Mt Herbert
753m +

Mt Ord
+ 937m

Mt Clifton
537m +

BEAGLE BAY
ABORIGINAL
RESERVE

TOURIST INFORMATION:
Derby (1 Clarendon St)
Fitzroy Crossing (Fitzroy River Lodge)
Halls Creek (Great Northern Hwy)
Kununurra (Coolibah Dr)
Wyndham (O'Donnell St, Wyndham Port)

Meda   River

Lennard   River

Napier
Downs

Barker

66

WINDJANA GORGE
NATIONAL PARK

Windjana Gorge

Mt Estaughs
476m +

Millie Windie

Glenror

Glenelg

River

Gleneig River

Isdell

Mt Behn
+ 339m

TUNNEL CREEK
NATIONAL PARK

WINDJANA GORGE NATIONAL PARK: Consists of a
gorge formed by the Lennard River as it snakes its way
through a 350-million year old reef of ancient limestone.
The river only flows for short periods but isolated pools
support an abundance of fish and birds. A number of
interesting walks exist with trail-side signs interpreting
features in the gorge.

Derby T

Boab Prison
Tree

Myalls Bore

DERBY   HWY

43

Meda

GIBB

41

Kimberly Downs

RIVER

Mt Marmion
105m

46

95

Diamond Gorge

TUNNEL CREEK NATIONAL PARK: Provides an
opportunity to explore a creek as it tunnels through
a mountain range. The tunnel contains permanent
pools of water and for those with a torch, prepared
to walk through cold water, the walk through is
fascinating.

Fairfield

GEIKIE GORGE: Cut by the Fitzroy River, this
7-km long gorge is part of the national park.
Boat tours enable visitors to see the rich variety
of animal life, including freshwater crocodiles.

+ Mt Clarkson
94m

Yeeda

10

GREAT

GIBB RIVER ROAD: Built to carry large road trains
for beef being transported from isolated stations
to the ports of Derby and Wyndham. Road conditions
vary and it is advisable to check before departure.

SISTERS
PLATEAU

OSCAR   PLATEAU

Creek

OSCAR

Leopold Downs

GEIKIE GORGE
NATIONAL PARK

4WD

TO BROOME

1

Willare Bridge
Roadhouse

30

41

NORTHERN   54   1

Blina

30   217

Ellendale

HIGHWAY   54

RANGE

30

Fitzroy

23

Mt   Wynne

Calwynyardah

38

Brooking Springs

Fossil
Downs

Udialla

Fitzroy

Mt Anderson
306m +

Mount Anderson

5 Camballin

16

Liveringa

17 Mile
Dam

LOOMA
ABORIGINAL
RESERVE

GEIKIE GORGE NATIONAL PARK: Formed by
centuries of water eroding through an ancient
limestone reef. The gorge contains permanent fresh
water and supports a variety of fish, birds and other
animals. Cruise trips up the gorge are available.

Fitzroy Crossing
T

Mt Pierre
203m +

82

Lulugui

Myroodah

+ Mt Wynne
144m

73

Gogo

57

SPARKE

Creek

56

Mt Hardman
+ 132m

Quanbun
Downs

Jubilee
Downs

80

+ Camelgooda Hill

Nerrima

Mt Abbott +

Noonkanbah   River

Christmas

GREAT

Twin Buttes

Dampier Downs

55

Kalyeeda

Dukes Dome
+ 304m

ST   GEORGE   RANGES

32

Babrongan Tower+

Mowla
Bluff

Mt Jarlemai
+ 195m

Mt James
+ 175m

Mt Fenton 187m +

Mt Tuckfield
+ 311m

Mt Amy
268m +

Mt Thorlan
+ 263m

Christmas Creek

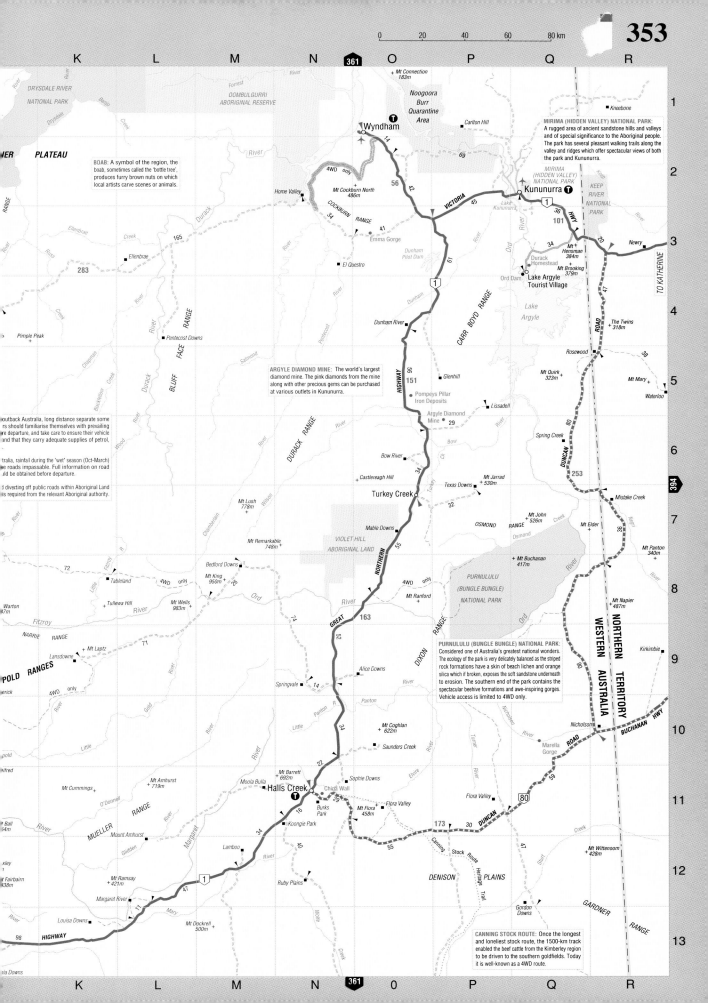

0   20   40   60   80 km

K   L   M   N   O   P   Q   R

DRYSDALE RIVER
NATIONAL PARK

Forrest
OOMBULGURRI
ABORIGINAL RESERVE

Noogoora
Burr
Quarantine
Area

Mt Connection
183m

Kneebone

ER PLATEAU

Carlton Hill

MIRIMA (HIDDEN VALLEY) NATIONAL PARK:
A rugged area of ancient sandstone hills and valleys
and of special significance to the Aboriginal people.
The park has several pleasant walking trails along the
valley and ridges which offer spectacular views of both
the park and Kununurra.

BOAB: A symbol of the region, the
boab, sometimes called the 'bottle tree',
produces furry brown nuts on which
local artists carve scenes or animals.

Wyndham

4WD
only

Home Valley

MIRIMA
(HIDDEN VALLEY)
NATIONAL PARK

KEEP
RIVER
NATIONAL
PARK

Kununurra

14

56

42

69

VICTORIA

45

36

101

HWY

TO KATHERINE

RANGE

Ellenbrae

165

Ellenbrae

283

Mt Cockburn North
486m

COCKBURN

RANGE

34

Emma Gorge

41

El Questro

Dunham
Pilot Dam

61

1

Mt
Hensman
384m

34

Durack
Homestead

Mt Brooking
379m

Ord Dam

Lake Argyle
Tourist Village

Newry

20

47

The Twins
318m

Rosewood

38

Mt Mary

Waterloo

Pimple Peak

BLUFF

FACE

RANGE

Pentecost Downs

Dunham River

CARR

BOYD

RANGE

56
151

HIGHWAY

Glenhill

Pompeys Pillar
Iron Deposits

Lake
Argyle

Mt Quirk
323m

ARGYLE DIAMOND MINE: The world's largest
diamond mine. The pink diamonds from the mine
along with other precious gems can be purchased
at various outlets in Kununurra.

DURACK

RANGE

Lissadell

Argyle Diamond
Mine

29

Bow

Ck

Spring Creek

80

DUNCAN

253

outback Australia, long distance separate some
rs should familiarise themselves with prevailing
re departure, and take care to ensure their vehicle
and that they carry adequate supplies of petrol,

Bow River

Castlereagh Hill

34

Mt Jarrad
530m

Texas Downs

Mistake Creek

36

Mt Panton
340m

ralia, rainfall during the 'wet' season (Oct-March)
e roads impassable. Full information on road
ld be obtained before departure.

Turkey Creek

Mt Lush
778m

32

Mt John
526m

RANGE

Mt Elder

d diverting off public roads within Aboriginal Land
is required from the relevant Aboriginal authority.

VIOLET HILL
ABORIGINAL LAND

Mable Downs

55

OSMOND

Osmond

Mt Remarkable
748m

NORTHERN

Mt Ranford

4WD
only

PURNULULU
(BUNGLE BUNGLE)
NATIONAL PARK

Mt Buchanan
417m

River

Mt Napier
487m

Kirkimbie

72

Bedford Downs

4WD only

Tableland

Mt King
950m

26

Tullewa Hill

Mt Wells
983m

Ord

74

GREAT

163

52

DIXON

RANGE

PURNULULU (BUNGLE BUNGLE) NATIONAL PARK:
Considered one of Australia's greatest national wonders.
The ecology of the park is very delicately balanced as the striped
rock formations have a skin of beach lichen and orange
silica which if broken, exposes the soft sandstone underneath
to erosion. The southern end of the park contains the
spectacular beehive formations and awe-inspiring gorges.
Vehicle access is limited to 4WD only.

90

NORTHERN

WESTERN
AUSTRALIA

TERRITORY

Fitzroy

NARRIE

RANGE

71

Mt Laptz

Lansdowne

OLD RANGES

erick

4WD only

Alice Downs

Springvale

14

Mt Coghlan
622m

Saunders Creek

Panton

Nicholsons

Marella
Gorge

ROAD

BUCHANAN HWY

34

River

Little

Gold

22

Mt Barrett
692m

Moola Bulla

Halls Creek

China Wall

Sophie Downs

Elvire

Flora Valley

59

Mt Cummings

O'Donnell

Mt Amhurst
719m

RANGE

16

Burks
Park

29

Mt Flora
458m

Flora Valley

80

DUNCAN

Mt Wittenoom
428m

Ball
64m

MUELLER

Mount Amhurst

Glidden

Koongie Park

Lamboo

34

40

173

30

55

Canning

Stock

Route

Heritage

Trail

47

DENISON
PLAINS

Fairbairn
38m

Mt Ramsay
421m

Margaret River

1

11

Mary

Ruby Plains

Gordon
Downs

GARDNER

RANGE

Louisa Downs

98 HIGHWAY

Mt Dockrell
500m

Creek

CANNING STOCK ROUTE: Once the longest
and loneliest stock route, the 1500-km track
enabled the beef cattle from the Kimberley region
to be driven to the southern goldfields. Today
it is well-known as a 4WD route.

K   L   M   N   O   P   Q   R

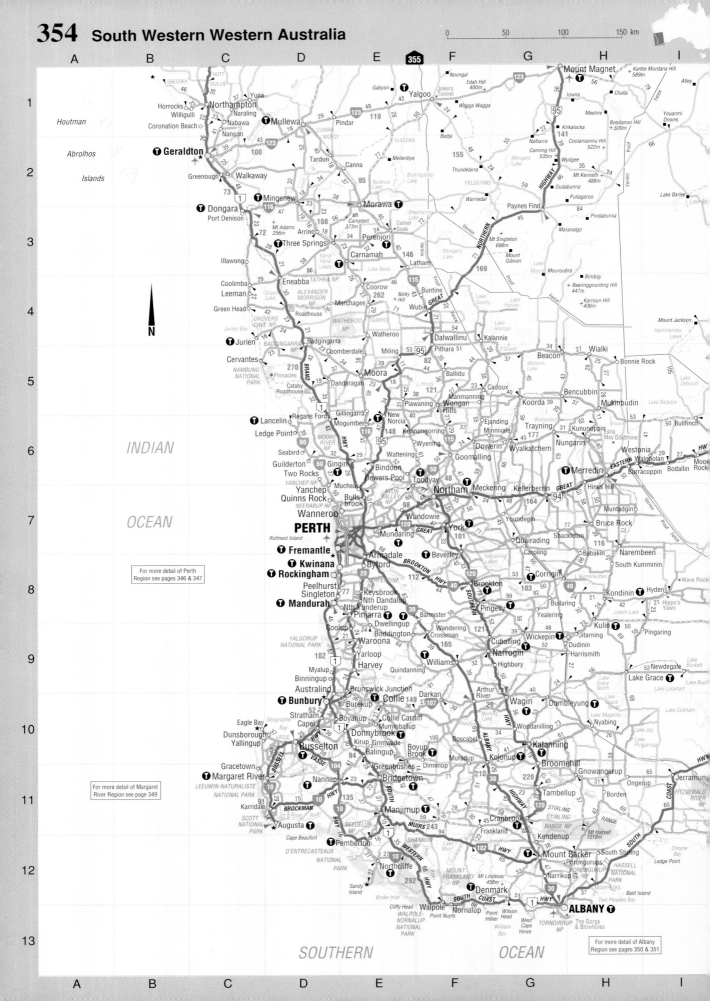

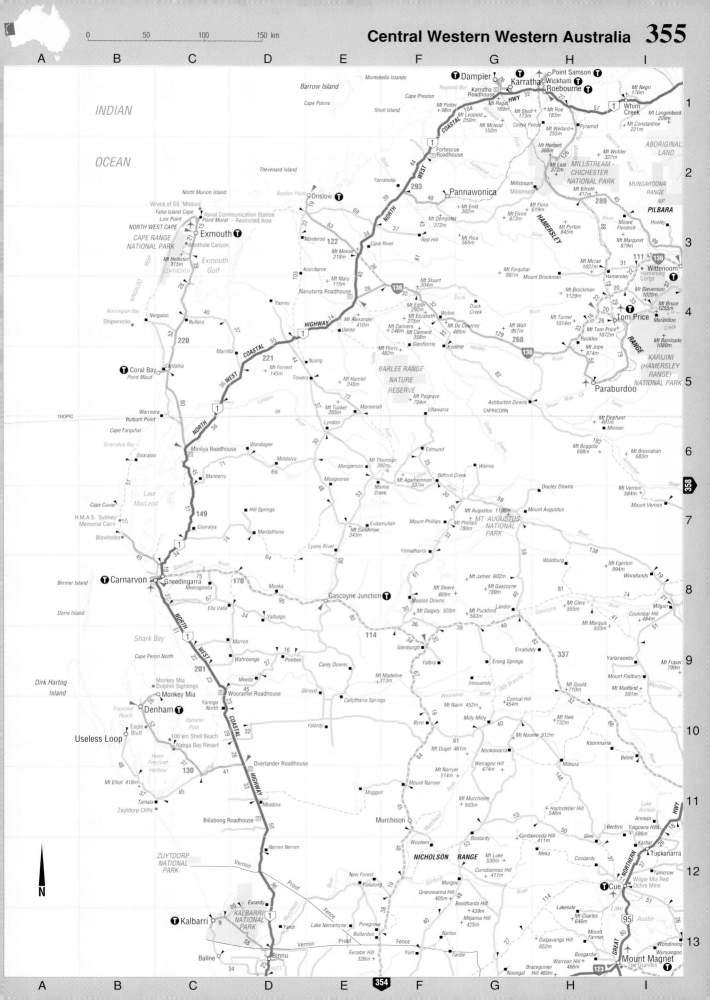

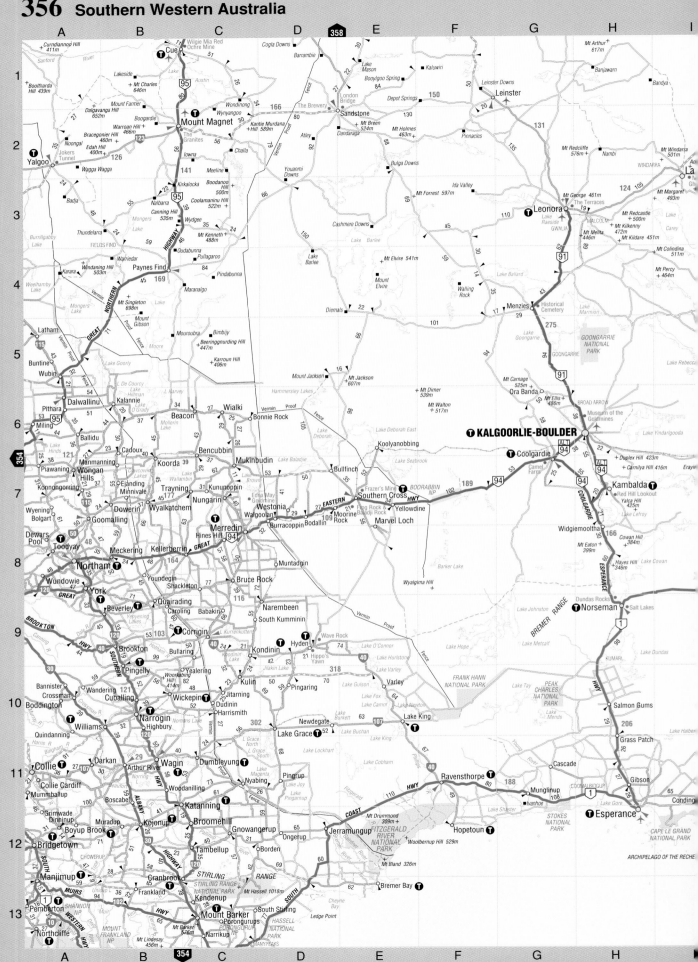

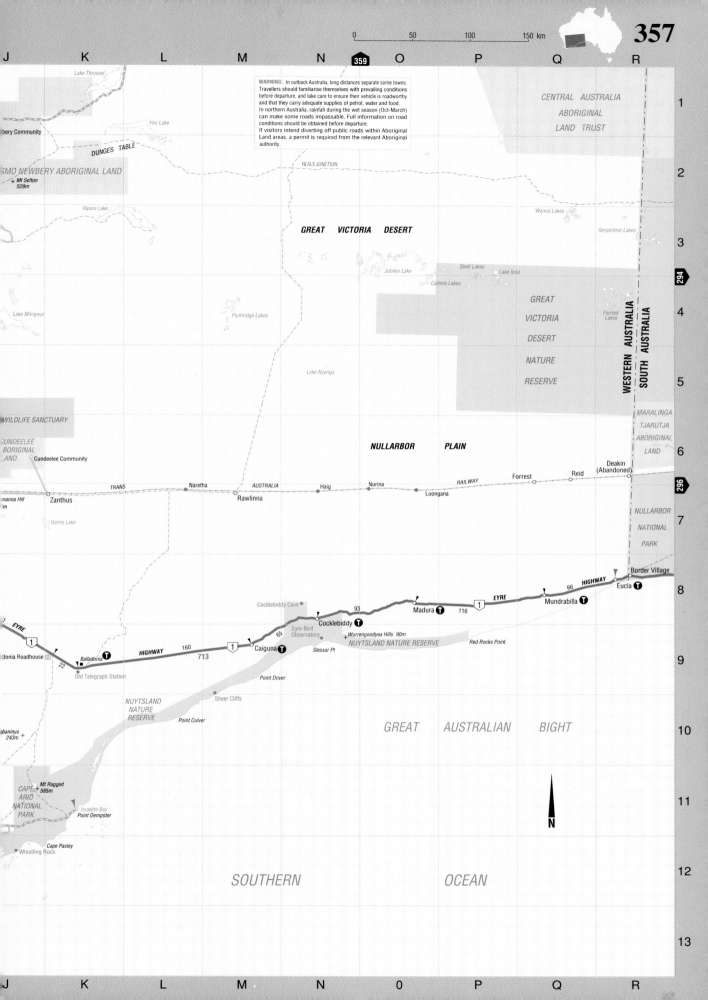

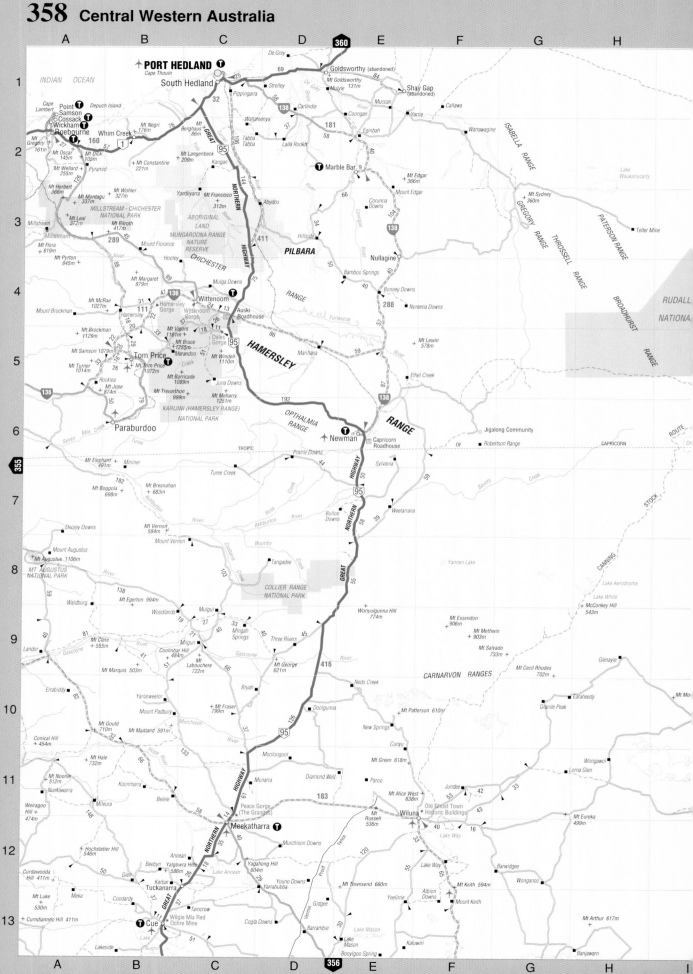

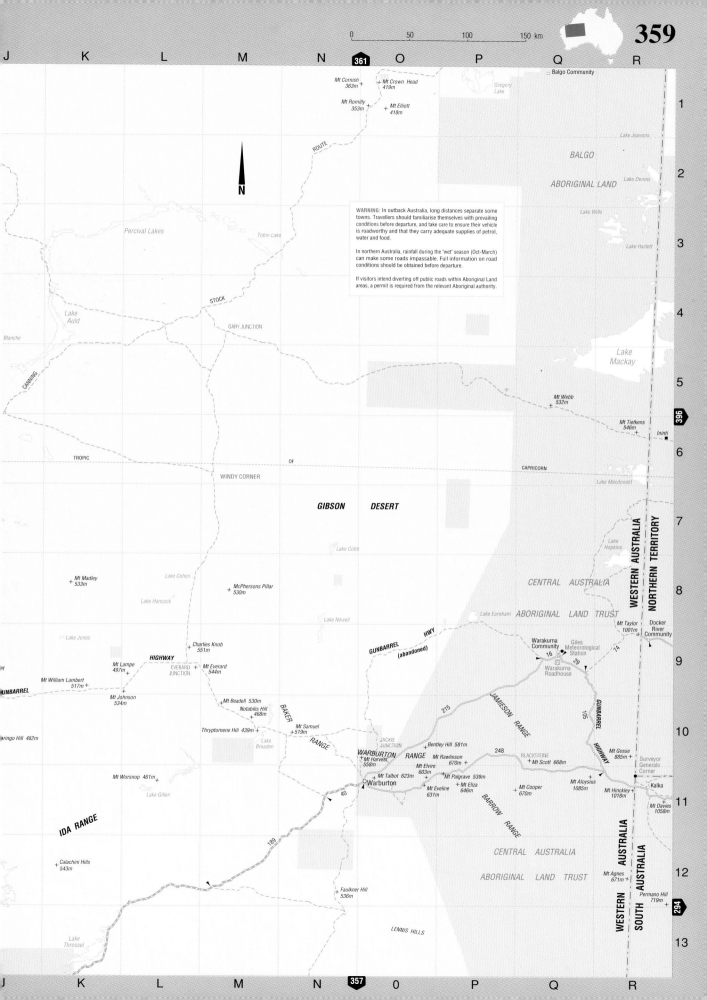

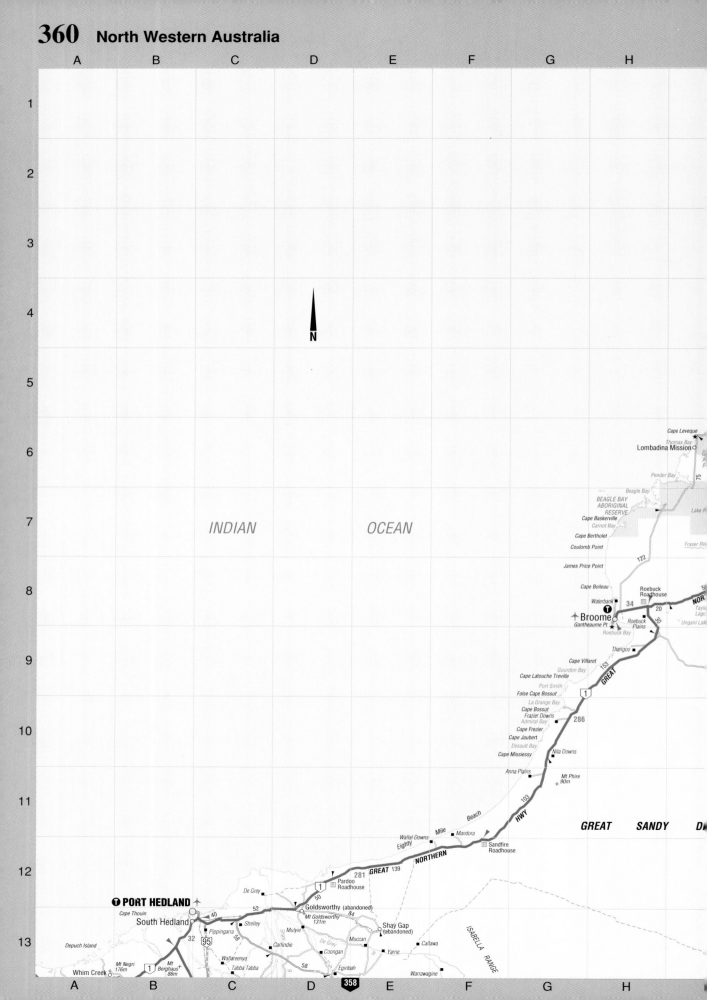

INDIAN   OCEAN

N

Cape Leveque
Thomas Bay
Lombadina Mission

Pender Bay

Beagle Bay
BEAGLE BAY
ABORIGINAL
RESERVE
Cape Baskerville
Carnot Bay
Cape Bertholet
Coulomb Point

James Price Point

Cape Boileau
Roebuck
Roadhouse
Waterbank   NOR
34   20
Broome   Taylo
Gantheaume Pt   30   Lagu
Roebuck
Plains   Ungani Lake
Roebuck Bay

Thangoo
Cape Villaret
Gourdon Bay   153
Cape Latouche Treville   GREAT
Port Smith
False Cape Bossut   1
La Grange Bay
Cape Bossut   286
Frazier Downs
Admiral Bay
Cape Frezier
Cape Jaubert
Desault Bay   Nita Downs
Cape Missiessy
Anna Plains   Mt Phire
+ 90m

GREAT   SANDY   D

103
HWY
Beach
Wallal Downs   Mile
Eighty   Mandora   NORTHERN
Sandfire
Roadhouse

281   139
GREAT
Pardoo
Roadhouse
De Grey   1

PORT HEDLAND
Cape Thouin   Goldsworthy (abandoned)
52   84
South Hedland   Mt Goldsworthy
40   131m
Strelley
Pippingarra   Shay Gap
32   95   Mulyie   (abandoned)   ISABELLA RANGE
58   De Grey   Muccan
Carlindie   Coongan   Yarrie   Callawa
Wallareenya
Depuch Island   Tabba Tabba   58   Eginbah
Mt Negri
176m   Mt   Warrawagine
Whim Creek   Berghaus
86m   1   358

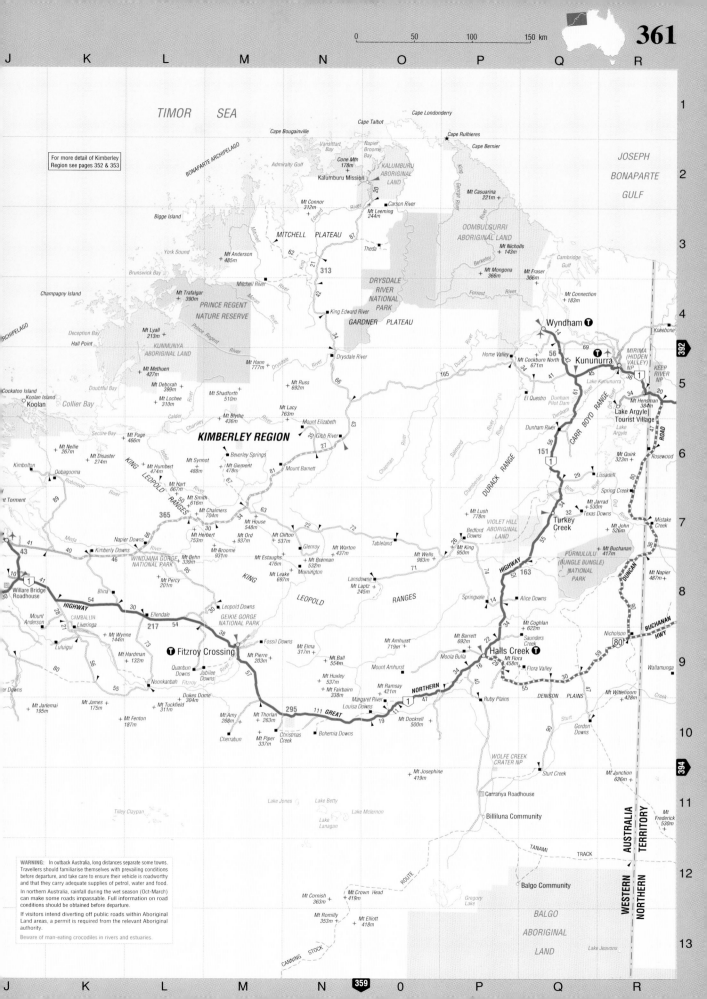

Northern Territory

Outback Australia

There are only three main highways that take motorists into the Northern Territory: the Barkly Highway from Mount Isa in Queensland; the Stuart Highway from South Australia; and the Victoria Highway from the extreme north-east of Western Australia. Given the enormous distances involved, you may well decide to fly, either to Darwin or to Alice Springs, and then hire a car. Alternatively, airlines, coach companies and tour operators offer day and extended coach tours, coach camping tours and adventure and safari trek tours, all of which allow you to discover this unique, relatively uninhabited and exciting Territory in experienced hands.

Six times the size of Great Britain, the Northern Territory has a population similar to that of Newcastle in New South Wales. Among numerous places of interest it boasts the famous Red Centre, the world's largest monolith Uluru (Ayers Rock), and many of the best Aboriginal rock art sites in the continent.

The first, unsuccessful, attempt to settle this huge, forbidding region was not on the mainland at all, but on Melville Island in 1824. It was not until 1869 that a town called Palmerston, later to become Darwin, was established. Originally the Territory was part of New South Wales, when that State's western boundary extended to the 129th east meridian; later it was annexed to South Australia and it did not come under Commonwealth control until 1911. In July 1978 the Territory attained self-government.

In terms of monetary value, the Territory's main industry is mining. Gold, bauxite, manganese ore, copper, silver, iron ore and uranium all contribute to this industry. The tourist industry ranks second, but beef cattle farming is significant, even though sixteen hectares or more are often required to support one animal.

Poor soil, winter droughts and huge distances from markets all combine to render commercial crop-growing virtually impossible.

The dry season, between May and October, is a good time to visit; and 'dry' *means* dry—during the wet season Darwin has an average annual rainfall of 1500 millimetres, while only 25 millimetres falls in the dry season. In the wet season the rain falls mainly in the afternoon and overnight. July is the Territory's coolest month when temperatures in Darwin range between 20° and 30° C. In 'the Alice' (as Alice Springs is affectionately known) the average maximum in August is 22.5° C, cooling at night to around zero.

The Northern Territory's two main centres are more than 1500 kilometres apart. Darwin, at the 'Top End', with a population of about 78 000, was largely rebuilt after Cyclone Tracy in 1974. It is known for its relaxed lifestyle and beautiful beaches, and makes a perfect jumping-off spot for exploring the Top End region.

If, however, you are going it alone by car, you should research your trip before setting out; read the section on Outback Motoring and bear in mind that the dry season is definitely the most pleasant weather for touring. Always make full enquiries about conditions before leaving sealed roads. The Stuart, Victoria and Barkly Highways are now all-weather roads, sealed for their entire length. Even so, any driving at night should be undertaken with care because of the danger from wildlife and wandering cattle.

East of Darwin is the spectacular Kakadu National Park. Further east is Arnhem Land, which can be explored by extended coach tour or adventure tour. Many Aboriginal lands require entry permission from an Aboriginal Land Council. These lands belong to the Aborigines; their land is sacred to them and should be respected by visitors.

South of Darwin is Katherine with its spectacular gorge, on the southern fringe of Arnhem Land. Freshwater crocodiles are common in the Katherine River, so its beauty is best viewed from either bank. From Katherine, the Stuart Highway continues south to Alice Springs. The major town along the way is Tennant Creek, which is 104 kilometres north of Devil's Marbles. The marbles are a random pile of granite boulders, some of which are almost perfect spheres. An Aboriginal legend says that they are eggs laid by the mythical Rainbow Serpent.

Many people outside Australia think of Alice Springs as one of the most important towns in Australia. Certainly it has been immortalised on film and in snapshots countless times. No other town, or even tiny settlement, is nearer to the geographic centre of the country. In 1872 Alice Springs was simply a repeater station for the Overland Telegraph Service; today it is not only the centre for the outback cattle industry but also a lively tourist centre with a population of approximately 25 000.

Uluru (Ayers Rock), 450 kilometres to the south-west in Uluru–Kata Tjuta National Park, is the world's biggest monolith: one huge rock, nine kilometres in circumference and rising 348 metres above the plain on which it stands. Traditionally the Aborigines made the rock part of their sacred rituals. The mythology of the cave paintings at its base is explained on tours conducted by park guides.

The magnificent Kata Tjuta (The Olgas) and, closer to the Alice, the prehistoric palms at Palm Valley, the dramatic Kings Canyon, Standley Chasm and Ormiston Gorge, all add their own character to the wonders of the Northern Territory.

Sunset over the Olgas

Darwin

A Relaxed City

The first coastal town established in the Northern Territory was Palmerston in 1869. Located at the mouth of the Adelaide River, it was quickly abandoned after a disastrous wet season in 1865.

Another expedition, led by Surveyor-General George Goyder, established a base at Adam Bay about 50 kilometres east of present-day Darwin. After surveying the area, he recommended that Port Darwin, which had been discovered in 1839 and named after Charles Darwin, would be the best place for a settlement. The town was also officially called Palmerston, but the locals referred to it as Port Darwin to distinguish it from the original settlement. The name was officially changed to Darwin in 1911 when the Federal Government took control of the Territory.

At first Darwin's development was hampered by its isolation. During World War II, however, the Stuart Highway was completed, linking Darwin with the railhead at Alice Springs; but even when the town had recovered from the bomb damage of the war, growth was still slow.

The modern Darwin's prosperity is based largely on tourism and the mineral wealth of the Territory. Over the last 20 years the city has developed as a thriving capital that is Australia's gateway to Asia and a strategic defence location for the whole continent.

Life for the early citizens was hard and changed very little until World War II. Graziers and agriculturalists struggled to cope with the violent climatic changes. Gradual development saw the population grow to 45 000 by 1974, when Cyclone Tracy destroyed most of the city. Now the figure has pushed past 78 000, which says something for either the hardiness of its people or the desirability of the rebuilt city as a place to live, or perhaps a bit of both. With Broome, in Western Australia, Darwin is one of Australia's most multicultural settlements, embracing people of 70 racial and cultural backgrounds. Chinese people have always formed a major part of the city's population and, in more recent years, Timorese and Southeast Asian refugees have arrived in Darwin and many have stayed. Quite large contingents of armed-forces personnel are also stationed at bases around Darwin.

In the city there is very little or no rain between May and October, when the average Top End maximum temperature is 32°C. From November to April, maximum Top End temperatures average 33°C with high relative humidity; make sure you take light summer clothing on your holiday! However, Darwin is always good for sailing, swimming, water-skiing or enjoying the sunshine.

The city's business district is much like any other similar-sized city, but with a relaxed and tropical atmosphere all its own. Modern air-conditioned shopping centres serve Darwin's suburbs, which

Tropical palms line the entrance to Government House

Sunset over Mindil Beach

are in two main sections, divided by the international airport.

City sightseeing is conveniently done from air-conditioned motor coaches that make regular tours. The main features are the splendidly tropical 34-hectare **Darwin Botanic Gardens**, the surviving historic buildings, churches, and memorials, the **Reserve Bank**, the **Supreme Court**, the new **Parliament House**, Darwin's busy **harbour** area and, on the Esplanade overlooking the harbour, the **Beaufort Darwin Centre**, including a world-class hotel and the **Performing Arts Centre**. A lookout on the Esplanade commemorates the fiftieth anniversary of the bombing of Darwin in 1942. Day, half-day and one-hour cruises around the harbour are available.

On the Historic Walk around the city you will see 14 old buildings and sites, including the elegant colonial architecture of **Government House** (near the southern end of the Esplanade) and **Old Admiralty House** (on the Esplanade).

Christ Church Cathedral was completed and consecrated in March 1977. It incorporates the porch from its predecessor, which was a garrison church during World War II and came under fire from Japanese bombers, but was eventually destroyed by Cyclone Tracy. The new cathedral, built at a cost of $800 000, features a stained glass window in memory of the trawlermen lost at sea during the cyclone. The altar, weighing 2.5 tonnes, was hewn from a jarrah log believed to be more than 400 years old. At the **Civic Centre**, not far from the cathedral, is the 'Tree of Knowledge', an ancient, spreading banyan tree. There are several other interesting places of worship in Darwin, particularly the **Chinese Temple**. Visitors are welcome to inspect the interior.

One of Darwin's most historic hotels, the **Old Victoria** in the Smith Street Mall, has been converted to a modern shopping complex, at the same time retaining its colonial character with punkahs to cool the Balcony Bar.

For those with cultural interests the city boasts a theatre group that welcomes visitors' participation in its workshops held in **Brown's Mart**, another historic building. The **Beaufort Centre** includes a 1000-seat theatre for the performing arts. Cinemas are located in Mitchell Street, at Casuarina, and the new Deckchair Cinema has opened at the Darwin Wharf Precinct.

Hotels
Beaufort
The Esplanade, Darwin
(089) 82 9911
Diamond Beach Hotel Casino
Gilruth Ave, Mindil Beach
(089) 46 2666
The Plaza Hotel, Darwin
32 Mitchell St, Darwin
(089) 82 0000

Family and Budget
Hotel Darwin
10 Herbert St, Darwin
(089) 81 9211
Poinciana Inn
84 Mitchell St, Darwin
(089) 81 8111

Top End
Cnr Daly and Mitchell Sts, Darwin
(089) 81 6511
YWCA, Banyan View Lodge
119 Mitchell St, Darwin
(089) 81 8644

Motel Groups: Bookings
Best Western (008) 22 2166
Flag 13 2400
Travelodge (008) 22 2446

This list is for information only: inclusion is not necessarily a recommendation.

Several art galleries, including some which feature the work of the Aboriginal people, can be visited in the city area. The **Museum of Arts and Art Gallery of the Northern Territory** at Bullocky Point houses important collections of Aboriginal, Balinese and New Guinean artefacts, as well as works by Australia's most famous painters.

At the end of the Esplanade, at Doctors Gully off Mitchell Street, **Aquascene** provides the opportunity at feeding times to hand-feed the ocean fish, which come in to the jetty. For feeding times, call 81 7837. At the entrance to the Darwin Wharf Precinct is a marine complex housing the **Australian Pearling Exhibition**, which features static, audiovisual and live displays on pearl farming. At Temira Crescent on the outskirts of the city centre is the **Myilly Point** Heritage Precinct, headquarters for the National Trust. The Trust building houses an information centre and gift shop.

The **East Point Military Museum** at **East Point Reserve** displays artillery, war planes and other militaria close to the gun turrets that were constructed during World War II. Nearby **Fannie Bay** is the site where Ross and Keith Smith landed their Vickers Vimy aircraft in 1919, completing the first flight from the UK to Australia. One of the most beautiful spots in the world to have had a prison, Fannie Bay also has some fine beaches. The former gaol, now the **Fannie Bay Gaol Museum**, features various displays including one on Cyclone Tracy. Darwin boasts of its beautiful sunsets and **East Point Reserve** is one of the best viewing places.

Darwin's best-known annual event is probably the Beer Can Regatta, held each September. The competing boats and other floating craft are constructed out of cans, and it's a day with lots of family fun.

Darwin's restaurants offer an excellent choice of cuisine, all the way from the fare of simple steak houses to French, Italian and Indonesian menus. There are also wine bars that offer varied menus and pleasant settings for lunch and dinner.

To the north of the city area, Darwin's suburbs have been virtually rebuilt since 1974. The tropical climate has encouraged a lush regrowth and the gardens are a feast of beautiful bougainvilleas, hibiscus and alamanders.

Sporting interests are well served. There is a golf course, a speedway track, a racecourse at Fannie Bay, and the usual facilities for tennis, squash, bowls (lawn and tenpin) and football (Aussie Rules, Rugby and soccer). **Olympic Pools** are located on Ross Smith Avenue and at Casuarina and Nightcliffe. Box jellyfish are common in the waters off Darwin, so swimming in the sea for much of the year is not recommended.

Darwin is the natural jumping-off point for touring the Top End. The pressure on luxury hotels and motels is often great and a range of alternative, less luxurious accommodation has developed, offering affordable alternatives. Many caravan parks in Darwin have permanent residents, so it is worth booking ahead.

The **Diamond Beach Casino** in Darwin is a few metres from the shores of **Mindil Beach**. This large complex offers luxury accommodation, restaurants and discos, sporting, gambling and convention facilities. The **Mindil Beach Sunset Market** operates on the foreshore from May to September; watch the setting sun while browsing through the food, art and craft stalls.

For further information on Darwin, contact the Darwin Region Tourism Association, 33 Smith St Mall (PO Box 4392, Darwin 0801); (089) 81 4300.

Botanic Gardens, Darwin

Tours from Darwin

The 9.4 million hectares of Arnhem Land, one of Australia's most fascinating wilderness areas, lie to the east of Kakadu. It is an ancient land that changes from broken mountains to vast plains, irrigated by constantly flowing rivers. An entry permit is required, which tourist agencies arrange through Aboriginal Land Councils. In the 'dry', many tours of places of interest in and around the city are available, by bus or hire car. Safaris by air and 4WD take sporting enthusiasts to less accessible areas for sightseeing, shooting and fishing.

The best time to go bush is May–September. On a clear night the stars seem to get in your eyes and you would not swap your cutlet of barramundi, grilled in the traditional manner on a shovel over an open fire, for the finest dish in the world. But any time in the Top End is suitable for getting back to nature. When you do, busy cities seem a long way off.

Fogg Dam, 65 km from Darwin via the Arnhem Highway
A sunrise or sunset tour of this area offers an excellent opportunity to view animals and birds on the move between their feeding grounds and where they sleep.

Not only is Fogg Dam a likely spot to see Top End birdlife, but you will also see many wallabies. The nearby swamps are the haunt of the elegant jabiru. Other birds in abundance are the pelican, egret, galah, cockatoo and kitehawk. The tour route then goes on to the Marrakai Plains where many species of birds can be seen. Millions of dollars were lost in this area when the rice irrigation scheme at Humpty Doo failed. Stop at Reptile World at Humpty Doo, which has the largest range of snakes in Australia (250 species), as well as many lizards.

Kakadu National Park, 250 km from Darwin via the Arnhem Highway
Recently placed on the World Heritage List, Kakadu is rich in natural and cultural heritage. Apart from abundant wildlife, the scenery here is dramatic and there are many fine examples of ancient Aboriginal rock art at sites throughout the park. The drive is fascinating, and can be topped off by a cruise on the South Alligator River. You would be unlucky not to see crocodiles, as well as wallabies, and the birdlife is prolific; however, sightings of buffalo are becoming rare. The Arnhem Highway is sealed all the way to Jabiru, and you could do

Tourist boat on the South Alligator River

the trip in your own car or a hired vehicle. Approximately 100 kilometres south of Jabiru are the Jim Jim Falls, accessible only by 4WD. There are many good camping spots on Jim Jim Creek and other billabongs. The deep and clear stretches of water on Nourlangie Creek, west of the Kakadu Highway, afford excellent opportunities for fishing. The safari guides have local knowledge and can show you far more than if you explore on your own. **See also**: Aboriginal Art; The Top End.

Howard Springs Nature Park, 31 km from Darwin via the Stuart Highway

There is safe swimming here in a spring-fed pool surrounded by monsoon forest. Avid birdwatchers can spot 50 or more species in a few hours; varieties of reptiles abound. Picnic areas and a kiosk are provided.

Territory Wildlife Park at Berry Springs, 56 km from Darwin via the Stuart Highway

A wildlife park of international standard, located in more than 400 ha of bushland at Berry Springs, the Territory Wildlife Park is designed to display only animals native and feral to the Northern Territory. The exhibits are all connected by a 4-km link road and include open-moated enclosures with kangaroos, wallabies, dingoes, bustards, buffalo and banteng; a naturally occurring lagoon where native birds can be viewed from a hide; an aquarium that features an acrylic walk- through tunnel for underwater viewing of large freshwater fish; a series of aviaries that display birds in natural habitats; a walk-through rainforest aviary; and the second largest nocturnal house in the world, artificially moonlit, where visitors can see about 50 species of mammal, bird and reptile. The park is a project of the Conservation Commission of the Northern Territory. Adjacent to the Territory Wildlife Park is the Berry Springs Nature Park, which features a spring-fed swimming area. The park is ideal for a picnic.

Crocodile Farm, 40 km from Darwin via the Stuart Highway

Australia's first and largest commercial crocodile farm has over 7000 stock, ranging in length from a few centimetres to four metres. There are feeding displays and tours daily. Be adventurous and try some farm-raised crocodile delicacies.

Ferry trips to the Mandorah and Harbour Cruises

Daily trips depart from the wharf in Darwin Harbour to Mandorah on the Cox Peninsula, an ideal place for a relaxed day on the beach, swimming or fishing. Cruises on the harbour provide a delightful way to see the city shores; sunset cruises are popular. There is also a wide range of fishing tours available around various locations in Darwin Harbour.

Cruises on the Adelaide River, 64 km from Darwin via the Arnhem Highway

For a look at nature as you've never seen it, take a river cruise on which you will see jumping crocodiles from the safety of an air-conditioned vessel.

Air tours

Several tours by air from Darwin are available, including day or weekend excursions and fishing and shooting trips. A three-day air tour into Western Australia, including a jungle cruise at Lake Kununurra, the Hidden Valley, the Carr Boyd Ranges, Lake Argyle and the Ord River, makes a most enjoyable trip if you can spare the time.

Crocodile farm, near Darwin

Northern Territory from A to Z

Adelaide River
Pop. 356

A small settlement set in pleasant country 112 km SE of Darwin on Stuart Hwy, Adelaide River was the location for 30,000 Australian soldiers during World War II. **Of interest:** War memorial and Australian War Graves. Adelaide River is the starting point for visits to: Litchfield Park, 30 km W, clear pools, spectacular waterfalls; the Daly River district, 110 km SW, the Batchelor and Tipperary experimental farming areas, 40 km N and 90 km S. June: Bush Race Meeting. **In the area:** Majestic Orchids, 7 km SW of Berry Springs Nature Park and near Litchfield Park entrance: part of Hydro Majestic, 48-ha horticultural and recreational development, also 16-ha orchid-growing area. **Accommodation:** 1 hotel/motel, 1 cara./camp. park. MAP REF. 388 E8, 392 F7

Aileron
Pop. 50

A rest stop on Stuart Hwy, 139 km N of Alice Springs. **Of interest:** At Roadhouse: Aboriginal art, native wildlife, Sunday roast lunch. Playground, picnic/barbecue facilities. **Accommodation:** 1 hotel/motel, 1 hostel. MAP REF. 397 J6

Alice Springs
Pop. 20 448

Alice Springs is at the heart of the Red Centre, almost 1500 km from the nearest capital city, and is a base for many tourist attractions, including Uluru (Ayers Rock). Some 350 000 visitors a year pass through this modern and well-maintained town in the heart of the MacDonnell Ranges. 'The Alice' offers a variety of restaurants, an international casino, sports grounds, an Olympic swimming pool and an 18-hole golf course. There is a wide variety of shops and a number of art galleries specialising in Aboriginal art. The Todd River, which runs through the town, is dry except after flash floods; for the annual Henley-on-Todd Regatta in Oct. the boats are carried or fitted with wheels. Between May and September days are warm and nights can be cold. For the rest of the year daytime temperatures rise into the high 30s but

View over Alice Springs

The Red Centre

First priority for most tourists in the Red Centre is **Uluru (Ayers Rock)**. About 450 kilometres south-west of the Alice, the world's greatest monolith rises majestically 348 metres above a wide, sandy floodplain covered in spinifex and desert oak. The rock is 9 kilometres in circumference and, with the movement of the sun during the day, it changes colour through shades of fiery red, delicate mauve, blues, pinks and browns. When rain falls it veils the rock in a torrent of silver.

Yulara, about 20 minutes' drive north of Uluru, is a self-contained township; it has accommodation, a supermarket, and other shops and services.

Ayers Rock Resort at Yulara offers a range of accommodation—the top-class Sails in the Desert Hotel, the Outback Pioneer Hotel and Lodge, the Desert Gardens four-star resort, Spinifex Lodge, Emu Walk self-contained serviced apartments, and well-equipped camping grounds.

With its prize-winning design, Yulara does not intrude into the landscape but blends into the ochre colours of the desert. If you can, allow for a stay of at least three days, this will give you time to explore Uluru and see a sunrise and a sunset there, and to visit Kata Tjuta (The Olgas).

An excellent way to familiarise yourself with the region is to spend an hour or so at the Yulara Visitors Centre. Displays depict the geology, history, flora and fauna of the region and there is a spectacular collection of photographs. Audiovisual shows are held regularly.

According to Aboriginal legends, Uluru and Kata Tjuta were created and given their distinctive forms during the Tjukurpa or creation period. At the base of Uluru there are cave paintings and carvings made thousands of years ago by members of the Loritja and Pitjanjatjara tribes. It is not difficult to appreciate that this is a sacred place of ancient times.

Do not attempt the 1.6-kilometre climb of Uluru unless you are fit and well and have a good head for heights, or if the weather is hot: the track is exposed and steep, and casualties are common. The climb follows a religious track, and the Anangu (the traditional owners) prefer visitors to take some of the other discovery walks in the park and near the rock itself.

Taking the 9-kilometre circuit walk around the base of Uluru, you will see rock art, the Mutitjulu (Sound Shell), a cavity as smooth as if formed by the sea, and the Taputji (Kangaroo Tail), a 160-metre strip of stone. Tours include the Mala Walk, the Edible Desert Walk (Aboriginal bush tucker) and the Liru Walk, conducted by Aboriginal guides.

Some 50 kilometres to the west are **Kata Tjuta (The Olgas)**, a cluster of rounded, massive rocks equally mysterious. They too are dramatic and vividly coloured. The tallest dome of Kata Tjuta, Mount Olga, is 546 metres above the oasis-like Valley of the Winds that runs through the rock system. Ernest Giles, who first saw Mount Olga named it after the Queen of Spain.

Curtin Springs cattle station and roadside inn is on the Lasseter Highway, 82 kilometres east of Yulara. Accommodation, meals, and tours from Yulara to the unusual flat-topped Mount Conner are available; bookings at Yulara.

A good way to see many of the tourist attractions in the Red Centre is to start from Alice Springs. You can take advantage of the coach tours that operate from there, or take your own vehicle. A few tourist destinations require 4WD, check before you set out.

The Alice Springs **Telegraph Station Historical Reserve** is only three kilometres north of town. The original Alice Springs settlement's stone buildings have been restored by the Conservation Commission of the Northern Territory and furnished with artefacts from early this century. There is also an historic display. Guided tours are available half-hourly. The 570 hectare Reserve offers bushwalking, picnicking and wildlife observation. A small waterhole, the original water source for the settlement, from which Alice Springs obtained its name, is nearby.

The telegraph station was built to link Port Augusta to Darwin, the link continuing by submarine cable to Java. Completed in 1872, the line was used until 1932, when operations were transferred to the site at the corner of Parsons Street and Railway Terrace in Alice Springs. The telegraph station site then housed an Aboriginal Mission, **The Bungalow** which closed in 1963.

An interesting day tour from Alice Springs, 50 kilometres west, is the beautiful **Standley Chasm**, managed by the Angkerle Aboriginal Corporation. This colourful cleft in the West MacDonnells is only five metres wide. At midday when the sunlight reaches the floor of the chasm, turning the walls a blazing red, it is a memorable sight. **Simpsons Gap**, 18 kilometres west of Alice Springs, can be visited at the same time and has walking access.

Further west, about 133 kilometres from Alice Springs on the Finke River, are Glen Helen and Ormiston Gorges. Their colours were captured by Aboriginal artist Albert Namatjira; they also lend themselves to photography, as does the sunrise on Mount Sonder to the west. Glen Helen Lodge is an accommodation base for the West MacDonnells, or a day tour is available from Alice Springs.

A day tour from Alice Springs will also take you to **Palm Valley** and the **Finke River Gorge,** 155 kilometres south-west. The Finke River is one of the oldest watercourses in the world and to walk along its bed is an unforgettable experience.

Palm Valley, with its rock pools, cycad palms and *Livistona* palms unique to the area, is yet another of the wonders of the Centre. The plant life has such a prehistoric appearance that to enter the valley is like taking a trip back in time.

These two attractions can also be visited by taking a two-day tour from Alice Springs, staying overnight at Glen Helen. Also well worth a visit is the restored **Hermannsburg Mission**, 125 kilometres west of Alice Springs, on the way to Palm Valley—arrive for their splendid morning tea, lunch or afternoon tea.

East of Alice Springs are the scenic **Trephina Gorge** and **John Hayes Rockhole**; **N'Dhala Gorge**, which has a variety of flora and ancient rock engravings; **Corroboree Rock**, which is of significance to the Eastern Arrernte Aborigines; and historic **Ruby Gap**, a picturesque area accessible to high-clearance 4WD.

The **Arltunga Historical Reserve**, 110 kilometres east of Alice Springs, beyond Trephina Gorge, preserves memorabilia of the goldmining era in the region. Little evidence remains of the shanty town that grew up after 1887 when alluvial gold was found. You can explore the stone ruins, scattered workings, gravestones and go down a mine. At the Ranger Station there are historical exhibits, with a gaol and restored police station two kilometres away. There is a private camping ground next to the reserve. Fossicking in the area is good.

Ross River Homestead, 88 kilometres east of Alice Springs, offers a range of outback experiences and comfortable accommodation. The historic pub bar has an display of antiques.

Thirty-five kilometres south of Alice Springs are the ancient **Ewaninga Rock Carvings** or petroglyphs. Signs along a short walk explain Aboriginal use of this area.

A turning off the Stuart Highway about 140 kilometres south-west of Alice Springs leads to the **Henbury meteorite craters** and, some 200 kilometres further west, the spectacular beauty of **Kings Canyon** in Watarrka National Park. The **Kings Canyon Frontier Lodge** and **Kings Creek Campground** are good accommodation bases from which to see these attractions.

The Henbury craters are believed to have been formed several thousand years ago when a falling meteor broke into pieces and hit the earth. The largest of the twelve craters is 180 metres wide and 15 metres deep. The smallest is six metres wide and only a few centimetres deep.

Kings Canyon, 330 kilometres south-west of Alice Springs, is one of the most interesting and scenic areas of the Centre. The climb to the rim of the canyon is fairly arduous, but well worth the effort. Even more spectacular views can be obtained by crossing via the small, railed Cotterills Bridge, near the old, nerve-racking tree-trunk bridge. The Lost City and the Garden of Eden are superb sights here.

For further information about the attractions of the Red Centre, contact Central Australian Tourism Industry Association, Centrepoint Building, cnr Gregory Tce and Hartley St, Alice Springs; (089) 52 5199. **Note** detailed map of Red Centre on page 390.

Uluru (Ayers Rock) with wildflowers

nights are milder. Rains, usually brief, can come at any time of year. Small irrigated areas support dairy and fruit-growing enterprises, but the main produce is beef cattle from huge runs. The town site was seen by William Whitfield Mills in 1871, when he was surveying a route for the Overland Telegraph Line. He named the Todd River after the SA Superintendent of Telegraphs, Sir Charles Todd, and a nearby waterhole Alice Springs after Lady Todd. The first settlement was at the repeater station, built for transmitting messages across the continent. In 1860 John McDouall Stuart had passed about 50 km w of the site. He named Central Mt Sturt after Captain Sturt, who had commanded an earlier expedition, but the South Australian Government renamed the mountain in Stuart's honour. Pastoralist John Ross also helped look for a route for the telegraph line. Until 1880 the repeater station was the only reason for the existence of a handful of people in this remote area, then the Government sent surveys north seeking suitable sites for railheads. The township of Stuart, 3.2 km from the telegraph station, was gazetted in 1880, but the railway remained unbuilt. Regular supply was maintained by the expensive and slow camel train from Port Augusta. Even the discovery of gold at Arltunga, 96 km E of the settlement, did little to develop Stuart. The Federal Government took control of NT from SA in 1911, from that time the township developed slowly. The Australian Inland Mission stationed Sister Jane Finlayson there in 1916 and the growing needs of the area led to the establishment of Adelaide House nursing hostel in 1926. The railway was completed in 1929. The service became known as *The Ghan*, after the Afghan camel drivers it had replaced. As the township grew there was too much confusion between Stuart and Alice Springs, only 3 km apart, so the name Stuart was dropped. **Of interest:** Royal Flying Doctor Service base, Stuart Tce, tours daily. School of the Air, Head St, open weekdays a.m.. Araluen Arts Centre, Larapinta Dr, focal point for performing and visual arts, art galleries. Strehlow Research Centre, collection of artefacts of Arunta people. Panorama 'Guth', Hartley St, 360° landscape painting of Central Australia. Aboriginal Art and Culture Centre, Todd St. Flynn Memorial Church, Todd Mall, in memory of founder of RFDS. Old Stuart Gaol, Parsons St. Lasseter's Casino, Barrett Dr. Technology, Transport and Communications Museum, Memorial Dr. Olive Pink Flora Reserve, cnr Barrett Dr and Causeway, Australia's only arid-zone botanic garden. A number of Aboriginal-owned outlets for Aboriginal art and artefacts. April: Country Music Festival. May: Food and Wine Festival. June: Finke Desert Race, World Paddymelon Bowls Championship. July: Bangtail Muster, Agricultural Show, Camel Cup. Aug.: Yuendyumu Aboriginal Sports Carnival. Sept.: Rodeo. Nov.: Corkwood Festival (Central Australian art, craft, music and dance). **In the area:** Anzac Hill at north end of town, views. Old telegraph station, 3 km N, off Stuart Hwy, historic reserve, original stone buildings and equipment. Pitchi Richi Sanctuary, 3 km SW, William Ricketts clay sculptures, open-air museum. Old Timers' Museum, 5 km S, exhibits of 1890s era. The *Old Ghan*, runs on 23.5 km of private line between MacDonnell Siding and Ewaninga (trip includes meal at siding stop), train is feature of Ghan Preservation Society rail museum at MacDonnell Siding, 10 km S. Frontier Camel Farm, 7 km SE, off Ross Hwy, reptile house, camel rides, museum displays highlight importance of camels and their Afghan masters in the area. Nearby, Mecca Date Gardens, Australia's first commercial date farm. To north: Ryan Well and Central Mt Stuart Historical Reserves (126 and 216 km), Barrow Creek Telegraph Station (284 km), Wycliffe Well and Bonney Well (392 and 422 km), and Devils Marbles (420 km). To west, several scenic reserves: Simpsons Gap, Ormiston Gorge and Pound National Parks (18 and 132 km), Standley Chasm (50 km), Ellery Creek Big Hole, Serpentine Gorge, Glen Helen Gorge and Redbank Gorge Nature Parks (93, 104, 133 and 170 km). Also west: Hermannsburg Mission (125 km), and Gosse Bluff meteor crater (210 km). To south-west: Henbury Meteorites Conservation Park (147 km); Palm Valley in Finke Gorge National Park (155 km), unique *Livistona* palms; Kings Canyon in Watarrka National Park (323 km), spectacular scenery; and Uluru–Katja Tjutu National Park (450 km), Uluru (Ayers Rock) and Kata Tjutu (the Olgas). To south: Ewaninga Rock Carvings Conservation Reserve (39 km), Aboriginal cultural site, rock engravings, and Chambers Pillar Historical Reserve (149 km).

To east: Chateau Hornsby, NT's only commercial winery, (11 km); Emily Gap, Jessie Gap and Ruby Gap Nature Parks (13, 18 and 141 km); Corroboree Rock Conservation Park (48 km), rocks significant to Eastern Arrernte people, signposted walk; Trephina Gorge Nature Park (80 km); N'Dhala Gorge Nature Parks (98 km), ancient Aboriginal Rock engravings, flora; Ross River Homestead (88 km), bush experiences, accommodation; Arltunga Historical Reserve (110 km), former goldmine, historic sites, restored buildings. To north-east: Gemtree, fossicking for garnet or zircon (140 km). Great variety of tours of varying duration covering scenic attractions, Aboriginal culture and specialist interests, many 'off beaten track'. Experience these by bus or coach, limousine, 4WD safari, Harley Davidson motorcycle, camel, horse, aircraft, helicopter or balloon. **Tourist information:** Centrepoint Building, cnr Gregory Tce and Hartley St; (089) 52 5800. **Accommodation:** 2 hotels, 16 motels, 6 cara./camp. parks. **See also:** Aboriginal Art; The Red Centre.
MAP REF. 391 K3, 397 J9

Barkly Homestead   Pop. 20
On the junction of Barkly Hwy, 185 km from the junction of Stuart and Barkly Hwys. **Accommodation:** 1 motel, 1 cara./camp. park.
MAP REF. 395 N11, 397 N1

Barrow Creek   Pop. 30
On Stuart Hwy, 283 km N of Alice Springs. Originally a water stop for cattle-droving. **Of interest:** Old Telegraph Station (1872). **Tourist information:** Barrow Creek Hotel; (089) 56 9753. **Accommodation:** 1 hotel/motel, 1 cara./camp. park.
MAP REF. 397 J4

Batchelor   Pop. 635
In the heart of the Coomalie area. Former town for Rum Jungle Uranium Mine, now a major education centre for the training of Aboriginal teachers at Batchelor College. Of interest: Mini-replica of Karlstein Castle of Bohemia. Parachuting and gliding. June–Aug.: International Skydiving and Parachuting Championships. **In the area:** Rum Jungle Lake, 10 km w, swimming. Litchfield Park, 40 km w, spectacular waterfalls (Wangi, Sandy Creek, Florence and Tolmer), pockets of scenic

The Top End

With improved roads and the vast increase in tourism in Australia, Darwin has become a major tourist destination. There is accommodation to suit all budgets. With its warm weather, excellent beaches and abundance of fish, Darwin itself is a winter haven, but its real attraction is as a base for exploring the wild and fascinating country at the 'Top End'. Here you see wide billabongs covered with lilies, clouds of geese wheeling above the trees, crocodiles sunning themselves on waterside rocks, plunging waterfalls, rows of pillar-like termite mounds, spectacular cliff and rock features, and caves and cliffs carrying the Aboriginal rock art of the past.

The Northern Territory Government has created a number of reserves to preserve the features of the region and to make them accessible to travellers. The most spectacular of these, in an area fast becoming one of the top natural tourist attractions in Australia, is **Kakadu National Park**, in the dense and wild country along the East Alligator River, bordering Arnhem Land.

Kakadu has World Heritage status; it is considered to be of outstanding worth for both its natural features and its cultural significance. Situated 250 kilometres from Darwin, it encompasses an area of 1 307 300 ha (approximately 20 000 square kilometres). Owned by the Aboriginal people, the park is leased to the Australian Nature Conservation Agency (ANCA) to manage for all visitors to enjoy.

Kakadu contains a wealth of archaeological and rock-art sites that provide insights into Aboriginal culture. The park's traditional owners are willing to share their knowledge and understanding of their land so that visitors will appreciate the importance of Kakadu and share responsibility for its protection.

Kakadu is unique in that it encompasses an entire river catchment, the black-soil floodplains and paperbark lagoons of the South Alligator River system, and within it are found all the major habitat types of the Top End. The park is rich in vegetation, ranging from pockets of rainforest through dwarf shrubland to open forest and swamps. The abundant wildlife includes several animals unique to the area, such as the banded pigeon, the rock possum and a species of rock wallaby.

Jim Jim Falls, Kakadu National Park

Features in the park include Yellow Waters, a spectacular wetlands area with prolific birdlife, particularly in the dry season, and Nourlangie Rock, where there is Aboriginal rock art. A spectacular point in the park is the Jim Jim Falls, 215 metres high and with a sheer drop of 152 metres of water pouring (in the wet season) over a rugged escarpment.

North of the Jim Jim Falls is the East Alligator River, a well-known fishing ground where barramundi can be caught and where the river reaches wind through spectacularly beautiful country. Visits to some isolated locations in the park are subject to a permit system and limited visitor numbers, because of the sensitive nature of those areas.

As crocodiles are present in park, swimming is not recommended and those who fish from the banks of rivers or from boats should take care.

Accommodation in the park consists of hotels, caravan parks, a youth hostel and private camping grounds. Facilities are available for the disabled. Fuel, food and provisions may be obtained at Jabiru township and at Border Store.

Visitors over sixteen years of age pay a park use fee (valid for fourteen days).

Small parks close to Darwin are **Berry Springs**, 65 kilometres south, and **Howard Springs**, 35 kilometres south-east. Berry Springs is noted for its warm water, pleasant and safe swimming, and its birdlife. More than 120 species of birds have been recorded. Adjacent to Berry Springs is the new **Territory Wildlife Park**, where visitors can see animals and birds of the area in a bush setting; shuttle trains and guided tours are available. At Howard Springs the pool is surrounded by rainforest, including pandanus palms, milkwood, red ash, white cedar, wild nutmeg and camphorwood trees. Again, the park abounds in birds and other wildlife.

Along the Stuart Highway, known as 'the track', 354 kilometres south-east of Darwin are the town of **Katherine** and the spectacular **Nitmiluk (Katherine Gorge) National Park**. Here the clear river flows between the brilliantly coloured walls of the gorge, which reach a height of 60 metres. A boat tour through the gorge is guaranteed to be a highlight of any holiday.

A further 110 kilometres south-east of Katherine is **Elsey National Park**, which includes the **Mataranka Pool Reserve**, near the Mataranka Homestead, where thermal springs are surrounded by lush tropical forest and the water is permanently at body temperature. Four-wheel-drive wildlife safaris can be arranged in Darwin; an ideal way to see the country and experience something of life in the Top End.

There are major roads to all these Top End attractions. However, if you are contemplating an unguided tour of the region, it is vital to recognise that, should you stray into unknown areas, you may experience difficulties; so plan carefully. **See also:** Outback Motoring.

For further information on Kakadu contact Park Manager, Kakadu National Park, PO Box 71, Jabiru NT 0886; (089) 79 9101. *Visitor Guides* to the park are available from the ANCA: GPO Box 636, Canberra ACT 2601; and GPO Box 1260, Darwin NT 0800; or from Park Headquarters. For further information on the Top End contact the Darwin Region Tourism Association, 33 Smith St Mall (PO Box 4392, Darwin 0801); (089) 81 4300. **Note** detailed map of Kakadu National Park on page 387.

National Parks

There are over 90 parks, reserves and protected areas in the Northern Territory. The major ones are grouped in three sections. One group is at the Top End, close to Darwin, the second around Katherine, and the third at the southern end, around Alice Springs in central Australia.

Best-known of all the parks in the Centre is **Uluru–Kata Tjuta National Park**, which contains the monolith Uluru (Ayers Rock) and Kata Tjuta (The Olgas) rising abruptly from the surrounding plains. The area is of vital cultural and religious significance to the Anangu (the traditional owners), whose ancestors have lived in the area for at least 30 000 years.

An easy way to explore Uluru's attractions is either by undertaking the Circuit Walk or joining a guided coach tour around the nine-kilometre rock base to see significant traditional sites, such as the Mutitjulu Cave containing elaborate Aboriginal paintings, and Kantju Gorge.

The climb to the 348-metre summit is strictly for those with a good head for heights. It should not be attempted by anyone who is unfit or unwell, or in hot weather; casualties are common. Traditional owners encourage visitors to seek alternatives to the climb.

Further west, the great domes of Kata Tjuta are separated by deep clefts, many of which hold sweet water and support abundant wildlife. The name Kata Tjuta means 'many heads'. There are several walks—Lookout, Valley of the Winds, Olga Gorge—which take from one to two hours to complete. Please keep to these marked tracks and consult a ranger before attempting any unmarked walks.

In the **West MacDonnell National Park** lie the MacDonnell Ranges, the land of the Arrernte Aboriginal people and a paradise for photographers and artists. Cutting through the ranges are spectacular gorges offering some of the finest scenery in Australia: crimson and ochre rock walls bordering deep blue pools, and slopes covered with spring wildflowers.

In this Park are a number of highlights. Close to Alice Springs is **Simpsons Gap**, only eighteen kilometres west and best seen on foot. There are several walking tracks as well as guided ranger tours, through rocky gaps and along steep-sided ridges overlooking huge gums and timbered creek flats. A new bicycle path linking Alice Springs to Simpsons Gap provides a different way to see this part of the MacDonnell Ranges. Other well-known scenic spots include Ormiston Gorge and Pound, where fish bury themselves in the mud as a string of waterholes shrink to puddles, then wait for the rains to fill them again. The deepest part of Ormiston Creek is a magnificent permanent pool the Arrernte believe to be inhabited by a great watersnake. At the far end of the gorge, the walls are curtained by a variety of ferns and plants, including the lovely Sturt's desert rose and the relic *Macrozamia*.

Ubirr Rock, Kakadu National Park

The MacDonnell Ranges near Alice Springs

Finke Gorge National Park, a scenic wilderness straddling the Finke River, includes the picturesque Palm Valley. This valley is a refuge for cycad palms and the ancient Livistona mariae, estimated to be about 5000 years old. The park is particularly rugged and visitors who do not join tours are advised to use 4WD.

Between Finke and Uluru lies **Watarrka National Park**, its main attraction being the beautiful Kings Canyon. Waterholes, rock formations, and abundant wildlife provide excellent photographic and bushwalking opportunities.

At the Top End of the Territory are several impressive national parks, including the splendid **Kakadu National Park**, leased by the traditional Aboriginal owners to the Australian Nature Conservation Agency. Here the visitor can see Aboriginal rock-art and the magnificent scenery of Arnhem Land, go bushwalking or take a boat cruise through wetlands. On the way to this park, don't miss the new Territory Wildlife Park, where you can see native fauna in a bush setting.

Litchfield National Park, 100 kilometres south of Darwin, features four spectacular waterfalls that flow throughout the year. Tjaynera Creek Falls and the Lost City with its fascinating sandstone formation, are on 4WD tracks. Swimming, photography, wildlife observation and bushwalking are all popular activities. Located 348 kilometres south of Darwin is **Nitmiluk (Katherine Gorge) National Park**. This fascinating river canyon, with its abundant wildlife and Aboriginal rock paintings, can be seen from a walking track, canoe or tour boat. When the river flows peacefully in the dry season (May-October), anglers make good catches of barramundi and other fish in the gorge's deep pools. **Elsey National Park**, 100 kilometres south of Katherine, includes Mataranka Hot Springs, a refreshing swimming area.

On the Victoria Highway to the west of Katherine lie **Keep National Park** and one of the largest parks in the Territory, **Gregory National Park**. Both feature tropical and semi-arid plant life and spectacular range and gorge scenery. Significant Aboriginal sites and evidence of early European settlement and pastoral history are also features. Boat tours are available at Timber Creek on Victoria River.

Gurig National Park, on the Cobourg Peninsula, can be reached by 4WD but a permit is necessary for this Aboriginal land. A wilderness lodge, Seven Spirit Bay (not in the park), overlooks Coral Bay and can only be reached from Darwin by air. The complex offers a true wilderness experience. Fishing, sailing, a trip to historic ruins at Victoria Settlement, and exploration of the area's natural environment can all be arranged.

Note: In national parks and reserves and other areas, it is essential to heed local advice on the dangers of swimming. The saltwater crocodile (found mainly in river estuaries) is highly dangerous. The freshwater or Johnstone's crocodile (found in billabongs and rivers) is regarded as harmless though it has been known to attack humans.

For more information about the Territory's parks and reserves, contact the Conservation Commission of the Northern Territory, PO Box 496, Palmerston NT 0830, (089) 99 5511. For Kakadu and Uluru, contact the Australian Nature Conservation Agency (ANCA), GPO Box 636, Canberra ACT 2601, (06) 250 0200, or PO Box 1260, Darwin NT 0801, (089) 81 5299. **See also:** The Top End. **Note** detailed map of Kakadu National Park on page 387.

rainforest. On Daly River, 70 km SW (4WD), barramundi fishing. Nearby at Nauuiyu Nambiyu (Daly River), June Merrepen Arts Festival, Aboriginal art and craft. **Tourist information:** Rum Jungle Motor Inn, Rum Jungle Rd; (089) 76 0123. **Accommodation:** 1 motel, 1 cara./camp. park.
MAP REF. 388 D7, 392 E6

Borroloola   Pop. 594
Small settlement on the McArthur River. Once one of the north's larger and more colourful frontier towns, it is now very popular with fishing enthusiasts. Local Aboriginal basket-weaving. **Of interest:** Off Robinson Rd: museum in old police station (1886); from airstrip, scenic flights over town and Sir Edward Pellew Islands. Easter: Fishing Classic. Aug.: Agricultural Show, Rodeo. **In the area:** McArthur River Mine, new silver–lead mine 60 km SW. Cape Crawford, 110 km SW; gateway to the Gulf area. **Tourist information:** McArthur River Caravan Park, Robinson Rd; (089) 75 8734. **Accommodation:** 1 hotel, 1 cara./camp. park.
MAP REF. 393 N13, 395 O3

Daly Waters   Pop. 298
Situated 4 km N of the junction of Stuart and Carpentaria Hwys, during World War II Daly Waters became the first international refuelling stop for Qantas. **Of interest:** Historic pub (1930), Stuart St. Sept.: Rodeo. **In the area:** Airport museum. Tree, 1 km N, reputedly marked with the letter S by explorer John McDouall Stuart. **Tourist information:** Daly Waters Pub, Stuart St; (089) 75 9927. **Accommodation:** 1 hotel, 1 motel, 1 cara./camp. park.
MAP REF. 395 J3

Dunmarra   Pop. 30
This stopping-place on Stuart Hwy is 8 km S of the Stuart–Buchanan Hwy junction, and 363 km N of Tennant Creek. **Of interest:** At Wayside Inn, historic photograph collection. **Tourist information:** Wayside Inn; (089) 75 9922. **Accommodation:** 1 motel, 1 cara./camp. park.
MAP REF. 395 J4

Elliott   Pop. 423
On Stuart Hwy, 254 km N of Tennant Creek. Go-kart racing twice yearly. **In the area:** Lake Woods, 13 km SW, NT's largest lake; gum leaves make water a curious milky white. **Accommodation:**

1 hotel, 1 motel, 1 hostel, 2 cara./camp. parks.
MAP REF. 395 J6

Glen Helen   Pop. 20
On Namatjira Drive, 132 km W of Alice Springs, Glen Helen is an excellent base for exploring the superb scenery of Ormiston Gorge, 12 km NE, the 'jewel of the MacDonnell Ranges'. **Of interest:** At Glen Helen Gorge, 300 m E, walk along Finke River bed, between towering cliffs. Helicopter flights to surrounding areas, incl. Mt. Sonder. Award-winning Glen Helen Lodge, Yapalpa Restaurant. **In the area:** Redbank Gorge, 24 km NW, deep, narrow cleft, spectacular pool. Hermannsburg, 25 km SE, restored Aboriginal mission, birthplace of artist Albert Namatjira, lunches, morning and afternoon teas. Finke River Gorge, 37 km SE, amazing rock formations: 'amphitheatre', 'sphinx', 'battleship'. Red cabbage palms (*Livistona mariae*) in nearby Palm Valley, found nowhere else in the world. **Tourist information:** Glen Helen Lodge, Namatjira Dr; (089) 56 7489. **Accommodation:** 1 hotel/motel, 1 hostel.
MAP REF. 390 E3, 396 H9

Jabiru   Pop. 1731
A mining town within the Kakadu National Park, 280 km from Darwin on Arnhem Hwy, Jabiru's services are designed to limit the effect of the town on the surrounding World Heritage National Park. **Of interest:** Gagudju Crocodile Hotel, Flinders St, 250-m crocodile shaped building; design was approved by the Gagudju people, to whom the crocodile is a totem. Kakadu Frontier Lodge and Caravan Park, Jabiru Dr, laid out in traditional Aboriginal circular motif. Jabiru Olympic Swimming Pool, Civic Dr, largest in NT; also 9-hole golf course. Aug.: Arts Council Wind Festival. **In the area:** Ranger Uranium Mine, 6 km E, daily tours May–Oct. (information from Kakadu Air Services at Jabiru Air Terminal). Scenic flights over unique Kakadu territory—virtually inaccessible sandstone formations standing 400 m above vast floodplains, seasonal waterfalls, wetland wilderness, remote beaches. Daily tours to Arnhem Land. Boat, and safari tours. **Tourist information:** 6 Tasman Plaza; (089) 79 2548. **Accommodation:** 1 hotel, 1 cara./ camp. park. **See also:** The Top End.
MAP REF. 387 H5, 389 Q4, 392 I5

Katherine   Pop. 7064
The multicultural town of Katherine is 320 km SE of Darwin, by a ruler-straight stretch of bitumen. Katherine's economic mainstays are the Mt Todd goldmine, tourism and the Tindal RAAF airbase, 27 km SE, but this neat township, sited in some of NT's most promising agricultural and grazing country, is still the centre of scientific experiments designed to improve the beef cattle industry. The town is on the southern side of the Katherine River and has several churches, parks, sporting clubs, a golf course, a bowling green and showground. **Of interest:** Katherine Museum, Gorge Rd. Railway Station Museum, Railway Tce. School of the Air, Giles St. O'Keefe House, Riverbank Dr, one of oldest houses in town. June: Burunga Sport and Cultural Festival, Katherine Cup, Canoe Marathon. July: Agricultural Show. **In the area:** Katherine River was named after a daughter of one of the sponsors of John McDouall Stuart, who first saw it in 1862. The gorge, named Nitmiluk by the Aboriginal people, towers above the water in the dry season. The ancient rock walls are dotted with caves. Aboriginal paintings, thousands of years old, from miniatures to huge murals, decorate both faces above floodline. In the wet, the water level often rises 18 m, caves are swamped and a bigger flood than average may wash away another ancient piece of an irreplaceable art form. Fifty-eight reptile and amphibian species, incl. burrowing frog, freshwater crocodile, long-necked tortoise, three kinds of tree-climbing frogs, legless lizard, 2-m pythons and many poisonous snakes have been identified in the area. In higher reaches of gorge, kangaroos and wallabies in hundreds crowd in to drink. The best way to see the gorge is by flat-bottomed boat. You can hire a canoe and camp in the gorge overnight, or take a guided tour; cruises run daily. Three easily-reached pools in the gorge. No motorboats allowed in gorge May–Oct. The weather is hot Nov.–March, but there is little humidity for the remaining months of the year, when it is warm during the day and cool at night. Historic Springvale Homestead (1879), 8 km W on Shadforth Rd, oldest remaining homestead in NT, built by Alfred Giles; Aboriginal Corroboree performed here three times a week. Rowlands Dairy, 12 km W on Florina Rd, 600-1200 cows milked daily, tours weekdays. At Timber

Creek, 285 km w, in Gregory National Park: boat tours on Victoria River; fishing, bushwalking. Rock art: Land of the Lightning Brothers, 140 km sw and Muniyung, 170 km se. Cutta Cutta Caves, 26 km se, guided tours. Heli tours, scenic flights, 4WD safaris, barramundi fishing tours, horse trail rides. Manyallaluk (formerly Eva Valley Station), 100 km se, experience of Aboriginal culture combined with magnificent scenery of wilderness park. Mataranka Homestead, 115 km se, thermal pool believed to have therapeutic powers, tourist resort. Old Gallon Licensed Store Gallery (1847), 2 km e on Giles St: original site of township, National Trust-classified, work of local artists. Edith Falls, 62 km n, picnics, swimming, camping. **Tourist information:** Cnr Stuart Hwy and Lindsay St; (089) 72 2650. **Accommodation:** 2 hotel/motels, 7 motels, 3 hostels, 8 cara./camp. parks. **See also:** Aboriginal Art; The Top End.
MAP REF. 392 H10

Kulgera   Pop. 25
A rest stop about 20 km from SA border on Stuart Hwy. **Of interest:** Town's name is Aboriginal for 'place of weeping eye', named for 45 m-high rocks with a continuous trickle of water down the sides. Kulgera Homestead museum and animal centre. **Tourist information:** Kulgera Hotel, Stuart Hwy; (089) 56

0973. **Accommodation:** 1 hotel/motel, 1 hostel, 1 cara./camp. park.
MAP REF. 396 I13

Larrimah   Pop. 20
On Stuart Hwy, 90 km n of Daly Waters. **Of interest:** Historical museum, Mahoney St. Green Park, Stuart Hwy, crocodiles, buffalo. **Tourist information:** Green Park Tourist Complex, Stuart Hwy; (089) 75 9937. **Accommodation:** 1 hotel, 1 hostel, 2 cara./camp. parks.
MAP REF. 392 I12, 394 I2

Mataranka   Pop. 180
This small settlement, is 110 km se of Katherine. **Of interest:** On Stuart Hwy: Stockyard Museum, Territory Manor Wildlife Park. Aug.: Rodeo. **In the area:** At Mataranka Homestead Tourist Resort, 10 km s, camping, horse-trail riding, scenic flights, river cruises, barramundi fishing, canoe hire; thermal pool, replica of Elsey Homestead. Elsey Cemetery, 25 km s, graves of outback pioneers immortalised by Mrs Aeneas Gunn (who lived at Elsey Station Homestead 1902-3) in *We of the Never Never.* Elsey National Park, 5 km e, swimming, fishing, camping, canoeing, walking. **Accommodation:** 1 hotel, 2 motels, 1 hostel, 3 cara./camp. parks. **See also:** The Top End.
MAP REF. 392 I11, 394 I1

Noonamah   Pop. 8
On Stuart Hwy, 38 km s of Darwin. **Accommodation:** 1 hotel/motel.
MAP REF. 388 D4, 392 F5

Pine Creek   Pop. 437
On Stuart Hwy, 90 km nw of Katherine, Pine Creek experienced a brief gold rush in the 1870s; today the town is experiencing a resurgence following the reopening of goldmining operations. **Of interest:** Numerous historic buildings. Miners Park, Main Tce, historic mining machinery, photographs. Railway Station Museum, off Main Tce. National Trust Museum, Railway Tce. Mine Lookout, off Moule St. Restored steam crusher at Back O' Beyond Tours (signposted in town). **In the area:** Gold fossicking (licence required). Goldmine tours, scenic drive, hunting safaris. Douglas Hot Springs Nature Park, 64 km nw, off Stuart Hwy (52 km w). Umbrawarra Gorge, 22 km sw, swimming, walking. Butterfly Gorge Nature Park, 14 km ne of Hot Springs (4WD) only, bushwalking. **Accommodation:** 1 hotel/motel, 1 cara./camp. park.
MAP REF. 387 A13, 389 J13, 392 G8

Renner Springs   Pop. 19
A roadside stop on Stuart Hwy, 161 km n of Tennant Creek. Picnic/barbecue

The spectacular Katherine Gorge

Aboriginal Art

Art is one of the essential element in Aboriginal culture, often using symbols to communicate ideas that cannot be expressed in any other way. Traditional art serves this purpose throughout the Australian continent, but the form of expression varies considerably from region to region.

Much of the rock art at Uluru (Ayers Rock), for example, is symbolic and may appear to be quite abstract. Aboriginal artists in Central Australia also traditionally used the ground as their 'canvas'; large sand paintings are made with coloured earths, feathers and other natural objects to represent the travels of the 'Dreaming' ancestors, the ancient beings that created the landforms on the vast plains. These paintings are intricate patterns of circles, lines, dots and tracks.

The designs found at the Top End, particularly at the spectacular rock-art sites in Kakadu National Park, are quite different: here there is 'X-ray' art, which gives great attention to internal detail. This style has been practised in other civilisations, but is believed to have reached its highest level in Western Arnhem Land.

Some of the places where Aboriginal rock art can be seen, or paintings and artefacts viewed or purchased, are as follows.

Alice Springs
In the Alice Springs area there are a number of Aboriginal-owned art and craft outlets. They include: Aputula Arts, (089) 56 0976; Ernabella Arts (089) 56 2954; Hermannsburg Potters, (089) 567414; Jukurrpa Artists, (089) 53 1052; Kaltjiti Crafts, (089) 56 7720; Keringke Arts, (089) 56 0956; Maruku Arts and Crafts, (089) 56 2153; Papunya Tula Artists, (089) 52 4731; Pertame, (089) 53 0617; Utju Arts, (089) 56 7311; Warlukurlangu Artists, (089) 56 4031; Warumpi Arts and Crafts, (089) 52 9066.

The **Alice Springs Aboriginal Art and Culture Centre**, 86–88 Todd Street, features works by Central Australian and Western Desert artists and craftspeople. Stock includes paintings and artefacts, books and cassettes. Worldwide mail-order and delivery.

The **Ewaninga rock carvings**, or petroglyphs, 39 kilometres south of Alice Springs, are considered to be the work of an ancient culture, since present-day Aborigines do not understand their meaning. The rock carvings form a part of the Ewaninga Rock Carvings Conservation Reserve. **N'Dhala Gorge Nature Park**, 93 km east of Alice Springs (the last 11 km is 4WD) has 6000 Eastern Arrernte petroglyphs, some over 5000 years old. There are also several galleries of Aboriginal rock art at **Kuyunba Conservation Reserve**, 15 kilometres south-west of Alice Springs.

Uluru Region
The **Maruku Arts and Crafts** complex next to the Ranger Station inside Uluru National Park, specialises in works of more than 800 artists and craftspeople from the tribal groups in the area—Pitjantjatjara, Yankunytjatjara, Matuntjara and Luritja.

Anangu cave art sites around Uluru and Kata Tjuta (the Olgas), 50 kilometres west of Uluru, are extremely vulnerable. Protective measures are given high priority by the Anangu, the traditional owners. Unlike some other cave art in Australia, the painting pigments are water-based and very susceptible to moisture, such as sweat from human hands.

Darwin
The **Museum of Arts and Sciences**, Bullocky Point, houses a fine permanent collection of Aboriginal art. Each September it brings together the finest traditional and contemporary Aboriginal art from around Australia for the National Aboriginal Art Award, which coincides with the Danggalaba Festival of Aboriginal Art and Life. The award provides an opportunity to see and buy some of the best paintings, carvings and fabric prints in Australia.

Kakadu's 'X-ray' art can be viewed at Nourlangie Rock

Raintree Gallery, 18 Knuckey Street has northern Australian Aboriginal artwork for both collectors and gift buyers. Stock includes paintings, artefacts, garments, books, musical instruments and cassettes. A gift shop is just off Smith Street Mall. Worldwide packing and mailing facilities.

Kakadu National Park
The rock art in Kakadu National Park is among the world's finest, and represents a close personal and spiritual relationship between the Aboriginal people and the environment. The richness of Kakadu's Aboriginal rock art can be viewed at **Nourlangie Rock** and **Ubirr**, both accessible by road. There are four main periods of rock art here. Some of the occupation sites have been carbon-dated at 23 000 years, and others go back even earlier.

The main subject of the *pre-estuarine* period (which ended with the rise of sea-level 7000–9000 years ago) was the hunter, with stone axes, simple spears and boomerangs. The *estuarine* period is marked by the introduction of paintings representing estuarine species, especially the barramundi fish. This was also the era of 'X-ray' art, with its depiction of the internal organs and skeletons of animals. Between 2000 and 4000 years ago freshwater systems began to replace estuarine conditions. This is reflected in the depiction of freshwater species such as the long-necked tortoise and the magpie goose. The *contact* period began when Aboriginal people were subject to intense contact with outsiders. Europeans' activities and their possessions, particularly rifles and steel axes, are graphically portrayed in the main rock-art gallery at Ubirr.

Katherine
The town of Katherine has developed historically as the regional centre for diverse Aboriginal communities. The paintings and artefacts at **Mimi Arts and Crafts Gallery**, Lindsay Street, reflect this, from the desert communities of the west to the coastal communities in the east. Stock includes contemporary music. Fabrics are also available from the Pearce Street shop.

Tennant Creek
Anyinginyi Art and Crafts, 2/139 Paterson Street, specialises in the artwork of the four groups that share this part of the country: the Warlpiri (renowned for their sand paintings), and the Warumungu, Kaytetye and Alyawarr, whose paintings and carvings depict aspects of life from the Tanami and Barkly regions.

Arnhem Land
A group of ancient rock paintings, ranging from simple stick figures and handprints to more intricate and heavily symbolic paintings, was discovered in 1988 in caves deep in escarpment country at **Umorrduk,** near Mount Borradaile, 225 kilometres east of Darwin. Tours from Darwin, travelling through Kakadu National Park and Arnhem Land, go to these 20 000-year-old sites in Gummulkbin tribal lands.

Further details of outlets that specialise in Aboriginal arts and crafts are available from the Darwin Region Tourism Association, 33 Smith St Mall; (089) 81 4300.

Aboriginal-operated Tours

For over 60 000 years the Aboriginal people have developed a unique understanding of the relationship between the physical and spiritual world. Today many Aborigines work professionally to share their knowledge with visitors.

There is a wide range of Aboriginal-operated tours available throughout the Northern Territory, each offering an insight into the Aboriginal culture of that area.

The Northern Territory Tourist Commission has produced an excellent brochure Come Share our Culture which includes specific details of the tours available. To obtain a copy, contact the Northern Territory Holiday Information HELPLINE; 1800 62 1336.

Aboriginal corroboree

Aboriginal Lands

In the Northern Territory, Commonwealth and Northern Territory laws do not permit people to enter Aboriginal Land unless they have been issued with a permit.

It should be noted that as a general rule, Land Councils have been asked by traditional owners not to issue entry permits for unaccompanied tourist travel. This does not affect visitors travelling on organised tours on to Aboriginal Land where tour bookings include the necessary permit.

When making an application for entry to any Aboriginal Land, applicants must state the reason for entry, dates and duration of intended stay, names of persons travelling, and itinerary and routes to be used while on these lands. Permits can be issued only after consultation and approval of the traditional owners and relevant Aboriginal communities. Processing permit applications can take four to six weeks. It is the right of tradi-

tional owners of Aboriginal Land to refuse entry permits.

All public roads that cross Aboriginal Lands are exempt from the permit requirements; the exemption covers the immediate road corridor only. If travellers are unsure about the status of roads on which they are driving, they should seek advice from the Land Councils before departure. If there is a likelihood of a need to enter Aboriginal Land for any reason, including fuel, travellers should seek permits from the relevant Land Councils. Some towns within Aboriginal Land are also exempt from the provisions.

A pass for the spectacular new Mereenie Loop Road, which links Glen Helen and Kings Canyon and passes through Aboriginal homeland, may be picked up from the CATIA office in Alice Springs, or from Hermannsburg, Glen Helen or Kings Canyon. Intending travellers also receive an information brochure.

A number of tourist ventures operate on Aboriginal Land; they include tourist camps and outlets for artworks and artefacts. For details contact Northern Territory Tourist Commission, 67 Stuart Hwy, Alice Springs; (089) 51 8555.

The relevant land councils to whom applications for permits and any inquiries must be directed in writing, are:

Alice Springs and Tennant Creek Regions:
Central Land Council
33 Stuart Hwy
PO Box 3321
Alice Springs NT 0871
(089) 52 3800

Darwin, Nhulunbuy and Katherine Regions:
Northern Land Council
9 Rowling St
PO Box 42921
Casuarina NT 0811
(089) 20 5100

Melville and Bathurst Islands:
Tiwi Land Council
PO Box 38545
Winnellie NT 0821
(089) 47 1838

Nguiu Community Council
Bathurst Island (via Darwin)
NT 0822
(089) 78 3966

Pirlangimpi Community Council
Bathurst Island NT 0822
(089) 78 3988

Aboriginal Land

Gove

The Gove Peninsula, named after W.H.J. Gove, an Australian airman killed in the area during World War II, is situated at the far northeast point of Arnhem Land.

The whole of the peninsula is set aside as Aboriginal Land and the main centres are **Yirrkala** and **Nhulunbuy**. Gove Resort, and Hideaway Safari Lodge near Nhulunbuy's airport, offer

visitors long white beaches and good fishing. Nine kilometres west of Nhulunbuy, near Dundas Point, is **Melville Bay**, which the explorer Matthew Flinders described as the best natural harbour on the Gulf of Carpentaria. Accommodation is limited.

The **Yirrkala Mission**, near Mount Dundas, provides a residential base for many of the Aborigines in the area. Its name became familiar during the struggle by its people to win title to their land. The *Aboriginal Land Rights (Northern Territory) Act* was finally assented to on 16 December 1976. It represents to the

people of Yirrkala the culmination of years of struggle to win recognition for their claims to land on which their people have lived for many thousands of years. The Yirrkala area is noted for Aboriginal carvings of birds and fish.

The easiest way to visit Nhulunbuy is by air. If you plan to explore by 4WD and without a tour guide, a permit is required from the Northern Land Council.

For further information contact the Darwin Region Tourism Association, 33 Smith St Mall, Darwin; (089) 81 4300.

facilities. **Accommodation:** 1 hotel/
motel, 1 cara./camp. park.
MAP REF. 395 J8

Ross River   Pop. 30
Settlement 85 km E of Alice Springs. **Of
interest:** Ross River Homestead: ranch-
style outback resort; overnight horse and
camel safaris; horse, camel and wagon
rides; guided walks; whipcracking,
boomerang-throwing; billy tea, damper.
Nov.: Ross River Cup (horseracing). **In
the area:** Trephina Gorge, 17 km NW,
scenic walking tracks. N'Dhala Gorge,
11 km SW, Aboriginal rock engravings,
ancient fossil deposits. Arltunga Historical Reserve, 25 km E, old goldmining
town, restored sites, tours, Visitor Centre.
Tourist information: Ross River Homestead, Ross Hwy; (089) 56 9711.
Accommodation: 1 hostel, 1 cara./camp
park.
MAP REF. 391 O3, 397 K8

Tennant Creek   Pop. 3480
According to legend, the town of Tennant Creek was founded when a beer
wagon carrying building supplies broke
down at the site. The town is 507 km N
of Alice Springs, on the Stuart Hwy.
Gold and copper deposits account for its
development today. The town is a thriving centre for the Barkly Tablelands. **Of
interest:** Civic Centre, Peko Rd, art,
gem and mineral collection. Travellers
Rest Area, Purkiss Reserve, Ambrose St,
picnic area, adj. swimming pool. Vintage cars and horse-drawn tours around
town; bookings at Tourist Information.
May: Cup Day (horseracing), Go Kart
Grand Prix. July: Agricultural Show.
Aug.: Goldrush Folk Festival. Sept.: 7-
day Desert Harmony Festival, local
artists, craftspeople, musicians and per-
formers. **In the area:** Gold Stamp
Battery and Museum, 1 km E, one of very
few batteries still operational. Juno Horse
Centre, 10 km E, cattle drives, horseriding. Nobles Nob, 16 km E, once richest
open-cut goldmine of its size in world.
Mary Ann Dam, 4 km NE, swimming,
canoeing, windsurfing, cycling, bushwalking. Telegraph Station, 12 km N,
tours. Three Ways Roadhouse, junction of
Stuart and Barkly Hwys, 25 km N, nearby,
John Flynn Memorial. Attack Creek Historical Reserve, 73 km N, site of encounter
between John McDouall Stuart and local
Aborigines. The Dot Mine, 5 km W, 1930s
goldmine, night tours. Devil's Marbles,
103 km S, huge 'balancing rocks'.

Trephina Gorge near Ross River

Equally impressive, Devils Pebbles, 16
km NW. **Tourist information:** New
Coach Transit Centre, Paterson St; (089)
62 3388. **Accommodation:** 1 hotel/
motel, 3 motels, 1 hostel, 2 cara./camp.
parks. **See also:** Aboriginal Art.
MAP REF. 395 K11

Ti Tree   Pop. 50
A rest stop on Stuart Hwy, 194 km N of
Alice Springs. **Of interest:** Aakki Gallery, Aboriginal art. Ti Tree Park, picnic
area, playground. **Accommodation:** 1
motel, 1 cara./camp. park.
MAP REF. 397 J6

Timber Creek   Pop. 100
Located 290 km SW of Katherine on Victoria Hwy. **Of interest:** National Trust
Museum, off Hwy, historical artefacts.
Boat tours, cruises, fishing tours, scenic
flights. Sept.: Timber Creek Races
(horseracing). **In the area:** Gregory National Park, 15 km W, boab trees. Keep
River National Park, 175 km W, rugged
scenery, Aboriginal rock art, wildlife,
Aboriginal and European heritage sites,
4WD tracks, check with Tourist Information for access. **Tourist information:**
Timber Creek Hotel, (089) 75 0722. **Accommodation:** 2 hotels/motels, 2 cara./
camp. parks. **See also:** National Parks.
MAP REF. 392 E12, 394 E2

Victoria River   Pop. 6
Rest stop located where the Victoria Hwy
crosses the mighty Victoria River, between Timber Creek and the junction
with Delamere Road. Scenic bushwalks.
Tourist information: Victoria River
Wayside Inn, Victoria Hwy; (089) 75
0744. **Accommodation:** 1 hotel/ motel,
1 cara./camp. park.
MAP REF. 392 F12, 394 F2

Victory Downs   Pop. 15
A station situated on the border with SA,
just off the Stuart Hwy, 316 km from
Alice Springs.
MAP REF. 295 M1, 396 I13

Wauchope   Pop. 7
On the Stuart Hwy, 113 km S of Tennant
Creek. April: Outback Go Kart Classic.
Sept.: 2-day Wimbledon at Wauchope.
In the area: Devil's Marbles, 8 km N.
Wycliffe Well, 18 km S, well-known for
large selection of international beers. Old
Wolfram Mines, 15 km E (4WD only).
Tourist information: Wauchope Well
Hotel, Stuart Hwy; (089) 64 1963. **Ac-
commodation:** 1 hotel/motel, 1 hostel, 1
cara./camp. park.
MAP REF. 395 K13, 397 K2

Yulara   Pop. 2169
Situated on outskirts of Uluru–Kata Tjua
National Park, this town is the location
for the world-class Ayers Rock Resort,
offering full visitor facilities and comfortable air-conditioned accommodation
in all price brackets (advance bookings
are essential). **Of interest:** Visitors
Centre, displays and information on national park; open 8 a.m. to 9 p.m. Tours
include Aboriginal Desert Culture Tour,
Uluru Experience Night Sky Show,
which offers night sky viewing and nar-
ration of Aboriginal and European
legends relating to the night sky. **In the
area:** Uluru (Ayers Rock), 20 km SE,
Australia's famous sandstone monolith,
Aboriginal rock art, walks, spectacular
sunrise and sunset. Kata Tjuta (The
Olgas), 50 km W, splendid rock formations, Valley of Winds walk, lookout,
flora and fauna. Book tours at Tourist
Information or reception in accommodation areas. **Tourist information:** Visitors
Centre; (089) 56 2240. **Accommodation:** 3 hotels, hostel units, apartments,
cara./camp. ground. **See also:** The Red
Centre.
MAP REF. 396 F12

Touring the Territory

Many people will not want to embark alone on a tour of the Northern Territory's outback areas. Fortunately, an enormous variety of accompanied tours leave from all capital cities, enabling even the least intrepid visitor to see Australia's magnificent centre. These tours range from quite basic holidays under canvas, travelling by coach or 4WD between overnight stops, to air-conditioned coaches (for those who prefer a few home comforts), choosing a route served by motel, hotel or caravan park accommodation.

The main tourist season operates from approximately April to September, but intending visitors are now exhorted to see the tropical summer, and excellent reductions are being offered on travel and accommodation costs during the offseason months between October and March. This is the hot season, and if you do not like intense heat it may be better to pay the higher in-season prices.

On a camping tour it is usual for campers to help put up the tents, prepare, serve and wash up after meals, and generally clean up, but all this makes the holiday a truly different experience. It does also mean, however, that adaptability is an advantage, since you cannot choose the people who accompany you.

Another way to tackle the outback is to join a convoy expedition, where you drive your own vehicle but are guided by experts. Motoring organisations arrange such tours, but departure times are limited and you will not be able to join the tour unless your vehicle is in an acceptable condition.

If you do decide to travel alone on roads that are off the beaten track, it is wise to take a few security precautions. It is not advisable to pick up hitch-hikers or to camp, other than in a lockable caravan, outside organised sites. **See also:** Outback Motoring.

The Ghan, the famous train which runs between Adelaide and Alice Springs, is another way of avoiding the long stretches of car travel. To travel one way by train and return by air is a time-saving way of seeing the Centre. Operating from Alice Springs are organised tours that will enable you to see the main tourist attractions of the region. Coach operators also combine a one-way rail trip (approximately 22 hours) with a return coach journey.

Overnight stop, Devil's Marbles

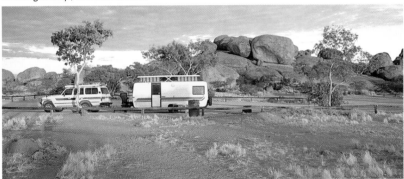

Sportsman's Territory

Even though the Northern Territory has an area of 135 million hectares—there are few places where you can legally shoot game. Even fishing is restricted in some areas.

Every kind of firearm must be registered. The possession of pistols and some semi-automatic high-powered rifles (military-pattern weapons) is tightly controlled. Visitors with a high-powered weapon properly licensed in their home State or country may be allowed to carry it in the Territory if a valid certificate or licence is produced at a police station. The police must be satisfied that the weapon is safe. Visitors carrying firearms must report to police within three days of entering the Territory. The booklet Before You Shoot, available at any NT police station, outlines licensing requirements for shooters and firearms.

Firearms are prohibited in the Territory's main sanctuaries and protected areas. Sanctuaries include: Cobourg Peninsula, Tanami Desert, Woolwonga Aboriginal Land, Daly River Aboriginal Land, Murgenella River and the Arnhem Land Aboriginal Land. All Aboriginal Lands are protected. It is an offence to take firearms, nets, snares or traps into protected areas. Penalties range from fines of up to $400 to imprisonment for up to twelve months. Maps showing existing protected areas can be seen at police stations. Firearms and shooting are prohibited in NT parks, except for the hunting reserves—Howard Swamp, Lambell's Lagoon, Harrison Dam and Marrakai (all in the Top End). Further information about these reserves, and the permits that must be obtained before arrival, is available from the Northern Territory Conservation Commission, Frances Mall, Palmerston; (089) 99 5511. On entering Kakadu National Park, visitors must lodge all firearms, nets, snares and traps with the Ranger; receipts issued.

Property owners rarely give permission for strangers to shoot on their land. Trigger-happy tourists are known to have caused stock losses in the Territory and those who shoot on private property without permission from the owner are liable to find themselves under fire, or being prosecuted in the courts. In general, fishing is unrestricted both inland and in the sea, but because some fish are protected in some areas, check first. Visitors who want to mount a hunting, shooting and fishing expedition in the Territory could well save themselves heavy fines and confiscation of weapons and gear by booking into an organised safari through a hometown travel agency.

Northern Territory

Location Map

Other Map Coverage
Central Darwin 384
Darwin & Northern Suburbs 385
North Eastern Suburbs, Darwin 386
Kakadu National Park 387
Darwin Region 388
The Red Centre 390

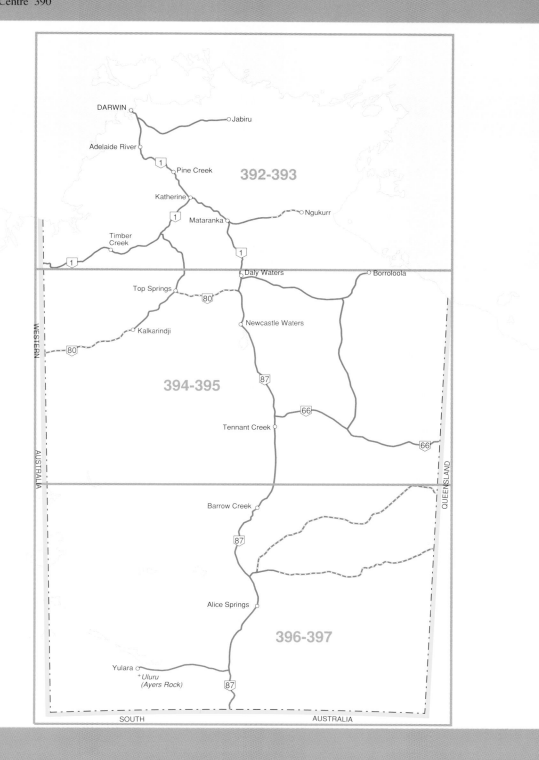

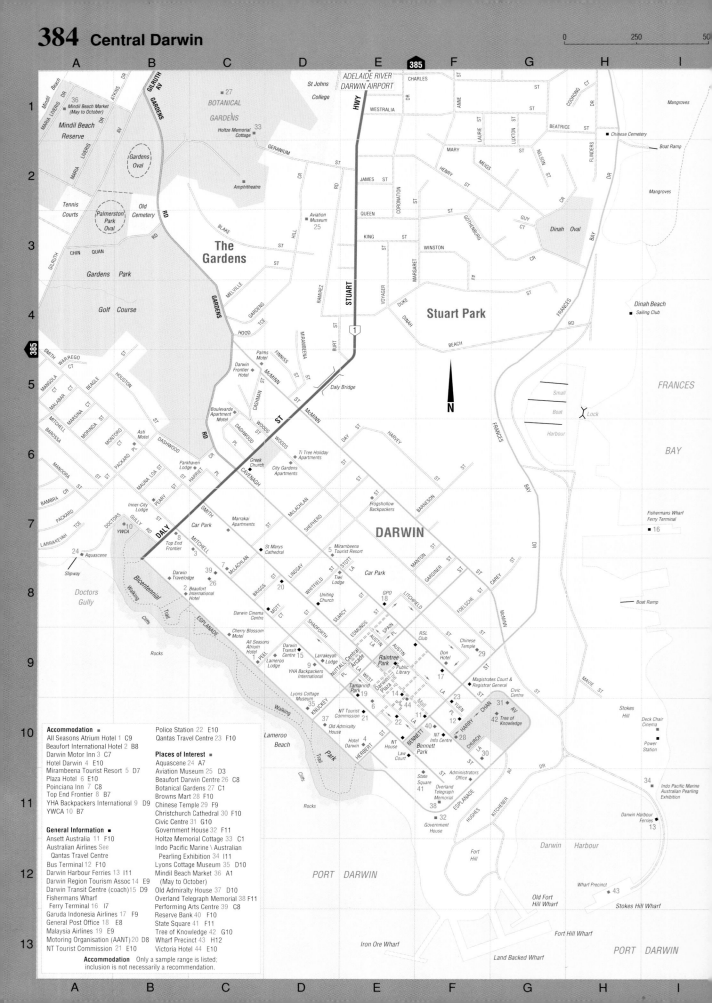

384 Central Darwin

0   250   50

Accommodation ■
All Seasons Atrium Hotel 1 C9
Beaufort International Hotel 2 B8
Darwin Motor Inn 3 C7
Hotel Darwin 4 E10
Mirambeena Tourist Resort 5 D7
Plaza Hotel 6 E10
Poinciana Inn 7 C8
Top End Frontier 8 B7
YHA Backpackers International 9 D9
YWCA 10 B7

General Information ■
Ansett Australia 11 F10
Australian Airlines See
  Qantas Travel Centre
Bus Terminal 12 F10
Darwin Harbour Ferries 13 I11
Darwin Region Tourism Assoc 14 E9
Darwin Transit Centre (coach) 15 D9
Fishermans Wharf
  Ferry Terminal 16 I7
Garuda Indonesia Airlines 17 F9
General Post Office 18 E8
Malaysia Airlines 19 E9
Motoring Organisation (AANT) 20 D8
NT Tourist Commission 21 E10

Police Station 22 E10
Qantas Travel Centre 23 F10

Places of Interest ■
Aquascene 24 A7
Aviation Museum 25 D3
Beaufort Darwin Centre 26 C8
Botanical Gardens 27 C1
Browns Mart 28 F10
Chinese Temple 29 F9
Christchurch Cathedral 30 F10
Civic Centre 31 G10
Government House 32 F11
Holtze Memorial Cottage 33 C1
Indo Pacific Marine \ Australian
  Pearling Exhibition 34 I11
Lyons Cottage Museum 35 D10
Mindil Beach Market 36 A1
  (May to October)
Old Admiralty House 37 D10
Overland Telegraph Memorial 38 F11
Performing Arts Centre 39 C8
Reserve Bank 40 F10
State Square 41 F11
Tree of Knowledge 42 G10
Wharf Precinct 43 H12
Victoria Hotel 44 E10

Accommodation Only a sample range is listed;
  inclusion is not necessarily a recommendation.

0 0.25 0.5 0.75 1km

A B C D E F G H I

386

1 2 3 4 5 6 7 8 9 10 11 12 13

DARWIN AIRPORT

East Point
Rocks
East Point
Rocks
Artillery War Museum
East Point Reserve
Mangroves
Lake Alexander
Dudley Point
Boat Ramp
Mangroves
Mangroves
Creek

Ludmilla
Bagot Aboriginal Reserve
RAAF Base
The Narrows
Benwerrin ST
Camara ST
Carryong ST
Bukatilla ST
Careela ST
Collendina
Curringa ST
Coorabin
Damala
Damala ST
Coorajull
Bellara
Narrows
Dwyer Park
Wilmot
Reichardt

Waratah Sports Club
Bayview ST
George ST
Phillip CR
Hinkler CR
Kurringal CT
Warata CT
Banyan
Nettis
Ross Smith Memorial
Fannie Bay Gaol Museum
Ross ST
Smith ST
Christie
Holtze
Giles
Conigrave
Lampe ST
Brown
Playford
Clancy
Freer
Edwards ST
Porter ST
Wells ST
Hudson
Urquhart ST
Parap PL
Gordon ST
Stretton ST
Fysh ST

Fannie Bay Racecourse
Richardson Park
Gilbert
Bremer
Ludmilla
TCE
Douglas

Trailer Boat Club
Boat Ramp
Sailing Club
Vesteys Beach
Ski-ing and Yachting Area
Boat Ramp
Water Ski Club
Boat Ramp
Bullocky Point
Rocks

FANNIE BAY

Fannie Bay
Darwin Bowling Club
CONACHER Museum and Art Gallery
Darwin High School
Parap
McKinlay
Charlotte
Weddell ST
Mackillop
Parap
Drysdale
Somerville GDNS
Railway
Bishop
Jolly
Winnellie
Bishop ST
HWY
Brennan
Tiger
DR

Sacred Heart College
St Johns College
Botanical Gardens
Armidale ST
Stuart
Iliffe
Woolner
Goyder RD
Lander
Nudl
Quarry CR
Verburg
Primary School

The Gardens
Mindil Beach
Mindil Beach Reserve
Diamond Beach Hotel Casino
Gardens Oval NTFL
Amphitheatre
Geranium ST
Ashley ST
Eden DR
Charles ST
Westralia ST
Mary ST
Henry ST
Meigs ST
Nelson ST
Beatrice
Coronation DR
Anne ST
Gothenburg
Dinah
Stuart Park
Dinah Oval
Dinah Beach

Myilly Point
Cullen Bay
Marina Mandorah Ferries
Indo Pacific Museum
Larrakeyah
Military Area
Emery Point
Elliott Point
Patrol Boat Harbour

Chin Quan Gardens Park
Golf Course
Kahlin
Smith
Mitchell
Malabar
Beagle
Houston
Melville
Gardens
Blake
Hill
Ramirez
Queen ST
King ST
Voyager
Winston
Duke
Beach
Bay DR

Whittle AV
Stevens
Allen
Herring RD
Nurses Walk
Kirkland
Schultze
Barossa
Marella
Packard
Dashwood PL
Larrakeyah TCE
Slipway
Aquascene
Doctors Gully

Daly Bridge
Daly
Mitchell
Cavenagh
Smith
Woods
Shepherd
Lindsay
Whitfield
Edmunds
Shadforth
Mall
West LA
Knuckey
Herbert
Peel
Bennett
Harry Chan AV
Esplanade
Hughes AV
Kitchener DR

DARWIN
Harvey
Day
McMinn
Barneson
Carey ST
Frances ST
Litchfield
Austin
Mavie ST
Chinese Temple
Stokes Hill
Old Power Station

Lyons Cottage
Old Admiralty House
Lameroo Beach
Overland Telegraph Memorial
Government House
Fort Hill
Bicentennial Park

PORT DARWIN

FRANCES BAY
Sadgroves Creek
Mangroves
Small Boat Harbour
Lock
Boat Ramp
Darwin Harbour
Stokes Hill Wharf
Fort Hill Wharf
Iron Ore Wharf
Land Backed Wharf

For more detail of Central Darwin see page 384

388

HWY
Dick Ward DR
Bagot RD
De Latour RD
Totem
Fitzer
Harney ST
Tudawali ST
Nadpur ST
Mosec
Cardo CT
Nemarluk
Fleming ST
Billeroy
Amaroo RD
Gandarra
CIR

KAKADU

NATIONAL

PARK

KAKADU HWY

WARNINGS: Freshwater and saltwater (estuarine) crocodiles are present in the Park. Both species can be dangerous, particularly the saltwater crocodile which may be found in both saltwater and freshwater.

Do not swim or paddle in natural waterways.
Do not allow children to play near the water's edge.

BOATING: Boat tours available; details provided at Park Headquarters. Boat ramps provided throughout the Park.

When boating:
Take safety equipment including life jackets, safety light and oars.
Do not overload boat.
Carry extra fuel in tidal areas as making way against tidal flow can double fuel consumption.
Beware of mudbanks, snags and shifting sandbanks.
If stranded, stay with your boat until help arrives; remember, crocodiles inhabit the waters.
When planning a long trip, advise ranger of your destination, estimated return time and number of people on board.

CAMPING: Camping grounds are provided throughout the Park. Permits are required for camping outside designated camping grounds and can be obtained at Park Headquarters.

FISHING: Fishing is permitted using lures. Northern Territory bag limits apply. Cast nets, traps, live bait, spear guns and crab pots are not permitted. East of the Kakadu Highway, fishing is permitted only in specific areas.

ART SITES: Kakadu contains a wealth of archaeological and rock art sites which provide insights into Aboriginal culture and the environmental changes witnessed through generations.

The various styles of rock art that can be seen include the stick-like mimi figures (believed to be the oldest), x-ray style paintings which show the internal structure of animals and contact art which began with the arrival of non-Aboriginal people. The principle sites are at Ubirr and Nourlangie Rock.

Do not touch the paintings.
Keep to walking tracks and behind fences.

WALKING TRACKS: Numerous marked tracks of various lengths and degrees of difficulty have been constructed enabling visitors to view both the natural wonders of the Park and the richness of Aboriginal art.
Rangers conduct guided walks in the dry season; details are available at Park Headquarters.
Wear comfortable shoes and a hat.
Walk in the cooler hours of the day.
Carry a litre of water for every hour you intend to walk.
Keep to the marked tracks.
Do not walk alone.
If you get lost, do not wander, sit in the shade and wait for help.
Obtain a camping permit if bushwalking for more than one day.

PROTECTING THE PARK:
Drive carefully and keep to roads and carparks.
Pets are prohibited.
Fires to be lit only in fireplaces provided.
Use litter bins for rubbish.
All animals and plants in the Park are protected.
Avoid damage to rock paintings and other sacred sites.

FURTHER INFORMATION: Park Headquarters, P.O. Box 71, Jabiru NT 0886; (089)79 9101. The Park Headquarters, open daily, has displays providing interesting information about the Park; brochures and leaflets are available.

WARNINGS: In outback Australia, long distances separate some towns. Travellers should familiarise themselves with prevailing conditions before departure, and take care to ensure their vehicle is roadworthy, and that they carry adequate supplies of petrol, water and food.
In northern Australia, rainfall during the 'wet' season (October to March) can make some roads impassable. Full information on road conditions should be obtained before departure.
If visitors intend diverting off public roads within Aboriginal Land areas, a permit is required from the relevant Aboriginal authority.

Van Diemen Gulf
Finke Bay
Point Stuart (Gurnaynjarr)
Pococks Beach
West Alligator Head
Field Island (Gardangarl)
Point Farewell (Gularri)
Barron Island (Djidbordu)
Midnight Point (Mandola)
Cunningham Channel
CAIRNCURRY PLAIN
POINT STUART COASTAL RESERVE
CARMOR PLAIN
SWIM CREEK RAINFOREST RESERVE
Cashew Plantation
CSIRO Kapalga Field Research Station
CULALY PLAIN
Mt Hooper (Mayambanjdju)
BOGGY PLAIN (NANJBAGU)
Four Mile Hole Camping area
Two Mile Hole Camping area
Kakadu Holiday Village
Gungarre Monsoon Rainforest Walk
Mamukala Wetlands Walk
Munmarlary (Manmularri)
Chirracarwoo Lagoon
Nourlangie Billabongs
MAGELA PLAIN (MARNANJ)
Mamurdi Hill
Turkey Dreaming (Imagirrk)
Oenpelli Hill (Injalak)
Cannon Hill (Ngamarr-karangka)
Ubirr (Obiri Rock)
Ubirr Art Site Walk
Meri (Mel) Camping area
Cahills Crossing
Border Store
Boat ramp
East Alligator Ranger Station
Oenpelli (Gunbalanya)
Djaburluku (Jabiluka) Camping area
Ja Ja
Djawumba Hill
JABILUKA MINERAL LEASE
Road impassable in wet
Gadjuduba Camping area
MUDGINBERRI
RANGER MINERAL LEASE
Bowali Visitor Centre Park Headquarters
Jabiru
Jabiru East
Gagudju Crocodile Hotel
Ranger Uranium Mine
Mt Brockman
ARNHEM
Northern Park Entrance Station
TO DARWIN
POINT STUART RD
ARNHEM HWY
STUART HWY
Malabanjbanjdju Camping area
Lligadjarr Wetlands Walk
Burdulba (Baroalba) Camping area
Muirella Park Camping area
Boat ramp
Baboalba Springs (Gubara)
Nourlangie Rock
Nourlangie Art Site Walk
Koongarra
KOONGARRA MINERAL LEASE
ARNHEM LAND
Red Lilly Billabong
Yellow Waters
Yellow Water Walk
Cooinda
Gagudju Vista Lodge
Mardugal Billabong Walk
Camping area
Boat ramp
Mt Cahill 154m
Mt Cahill Lookout
Camping area
Gnarl-ah-rogie Hill
Jim Jim Billabong
Spring Peak
Mt Basedow 220m
Sandy Billabong
Table Top
Deaf Adder Gorge
Kunkamoula Billabong (Gunkumulu)
Black Jungle Spring (Giyamungkurr)
Camping area
Mundogie Hill
Dird Djahdjam Hill
COIRWONG GORGE
Mount Harris Mine (abandoned)
Long Billabong Camping area
Maguk (Barramundie Gorge) Camping area
Maguk Plunge Pool Walk
Jim Jim Falls Plunge Pool Walk
Camping area
Jim Jim Falls (Barrkmalam)
Twin Falls (Gungkurdul)
Goodparla
Waterfall Creek Falls
Gunlom (Waterfall Creek) Camping area
Gunlom Lookout Walk
Mt George 275m
Old Goodparla (Aband)
Bukbukluk Lookout
Southern Entrance Ranger Station
Ikoymarrwa Lookout
Kambolgie Camping area
Road impassable in wet
CONSERVATION ZONE
Gimbat
Mt Evelyn 365m
Coronation Hill (Guratba) 300m
Mary River Roadhouse
Moline Goldmine
Walter Spring
Eva Spring
Wells Springs
Big Sunday (Nilyanjurrung) 338m
Coronet Hill 320m
Bloomfield Springs
Frances Creek (ruins)
Union Hill 275m
Esmeralda Farm
Cullen Hill 216m
McCarthy Hill
Aston Hill
Ranford Hill
Pine Creek
TO KATHERINE
Ngartluk Billabongs
ARNHEM LAND
ARNHEM LAND ABORIGINAL LAND TRUST
PLATEAU

For more detail of Darwin
Suburbs see pages 385 & 386

A B C D E F G H

1

CAPE HOTHAM FORESTRY RESERVE
CAPE HOTHAM CONSERVATION RESERVE
Chambers Bay
Shoal Bay
BEAGLE GULF

MARY RIVER CONSERVATION RESERVE

2

Charles Point
Radio Australia Transmitter Station
Mandorah
CASUARINA
NIGHTCLIFF
SANDERSON
Lee Point
Hope Inlet
HUNTING RESERVE
Howard Springs
Koolpinyah
Lake Finniss Woolner
Lake Finniss Farm
SHADY CAMP RESERVE
Tapa Bay
Magnetic Anthills
DARWIN AIRPORT
WINNELLIE
BERRIMAH
PALMERSTON
24
49
55
Adelaide River

3

DARWIN
Point Margaret
IDA BAY
COX PENINSULA
Belyuen
Mica Beach
Kings Table
Flagstaff Hill
Port Darwin
East Arm
Peak Hill
Howard Springs
HOWARD SPRINGS NP
ARNHEM
Magnetic Anthills
FOGG DAM CONSERVATION RESERVE
Fogg Dam
Tommy Policeman Lagoon
Coastal Research Station
MIDDLEPOINT
MARRAKAI
Opium Creek Station
Point Stuart Wilderness Lodge
DELISSAVILLE WAGAIT LARRAKIA ABORIGINAL LAND TRUST
34
10
1
5

4

Turnbull Bay
COX PENINSULA
Haycock Hill
Crocodile Farm
Noonamah
Humpty Doo
Gows Reptile Park
Humpty Doo (Wariuk)
Window on the Wetlands Interpretation Centre
BEATRICE HILL
Bird Sanctuary
CONSERVATION RESERVE
Helens Creek
Wildman Wilderness Lodge
WILDMAN RESERVE
Corroborree Billabong
Rockhole
Couzens Lookout
Bynoe Harbour
Observation Hill
TERRITORY WILDLIFE PARK
Berry Springs
Mantons Hill
Roaming Buffaloes
LEANING TREE LAGOON NATURE PARK
Mt Daly
Dennys Hill
11
21
25
18
12

5

Charlotte
Tidy Hill
Magnetic Anthills
Tumbling Waters
Arthurs Hill
Southport Ruins Historic Town
Lagoon Hill
Acacia Store
DELISSAVILLE WAGAIT LARRAKIA ABORIGINAL LAND TRUST
Corroboree Park Tavern
Old Mount Bundy Outstation
Mt Gol +105m
Bark Hut Inn
PENINSULA
RANGE
ROAD
STUART
HIGHWAY
36
11
24
14
7
19
12
21
5

6

Finniss River
Sweets Lookout
Mt Bennett
Mt Finniss
FINNISS PARK
Darwin River Dam
Giants Reef
MANTON DAM PARK
Manton Reservoir
Lake Bennett
Buffalo Rise +43m
Luckie Hill
Mt Gunn
MARY RIVER CROSSING RESERVE
Annaburroo
11
8
9
7

7

DELISSAVILLE WAGAIT LARRAKIA ABORIGINAL LAND TRUST
Two Sisters Hills +84m
LITCHFIELD
Bamboo Creek Tin Mine Ruins
Rum Jungle
Mt Charles
Meneling
Batchelor
Wild Horse Hill
Johns Hill
RINGWOOD RANGE
84
10
13
11
16
19

8

Woolaning
Fenwicks Rain Forest
Florence Falls
Buley Waterhole
Magnetic Anthills
Ladelle Downs Outstation
Wangi Falls
Wangi
Banyan
Cameron Downs
Heaton Hill
Predictor Hill
Sargents
Stapleton
Finniss
Bobs Hill
Mount Ringwood
Lost Hill
Mt Ringwood +195m
Mt Do
HIGHWAY
17
18
12

9

Welltree
Keri
Tolmer Falls
The Lost City
Blyth (aband)
Tjaynera Falls (Sandy Creek Falls)
TABLE TOP RANGE
LITCHFIELD NATIONAL PARK
Adelaide River War Cemetery
Adelaide River
Robin Falls
Mt Foelsche +113m
Mt Tymn
Mt Paqualin +195m
Mt Ellison 205m
Ban Ban Springs
Julie Peak
DORAT
STUART
West
15
12
1

10

Reynolds
Prospect Hill
Neds Knob
Litchfield
Mt Litchfield 203m
Mt Wells 263m
The Banyans
112
43
24
21
18
51
27
14

11

MALAK MALAK ABORIGINAL LAND TRUST
Mt Thomas
Mt Pleasant 255m
Mt Smith
Mt Shoobridge
Douglas
Hayes Creek Roadhouse
Emerald Springs Roadhouse
HIGHWAY
ROAD
RIVER
29
5
6
30
33
27
1

12

Elizabeth Downs
Marion Hill
Mt Hayward 178m
DALY
Tipperary
Kumbyechants
Ceres Downs
Douglas
BUTTERFLY GORGE NATURE PARK
DOUGLAS HOT SPRINGS NATURE PARK
22
18
24

13

Mt Green
Hermit Hill 95m
Daly River
ROCK CANDY RANGE
Douglas Daly Experimental Station
Mt Muriel
Mt Briggs
Ooloo
Quartz Knob
Mt Boulder 244m
27
17

392

A B C D E F G H

0   10   20   30   40 km

J   K   L   M   N   392   O   P   Q   R

STUARTS CREEK
HISTORICAL
RESERVE
Finke Bay

CARMOR PLAIN

N

CULALY PLAIN

CAIRNCURRY PLAIN

Mt Hooper
86m

+ Balkanini Hill

+ Turkey Dreaming (Imakirrk)

Oenpelli Hill (Injalak) +
Oenpelli
Gunbalanya

Cannon Hill +
(Ngamarr-kanangka)

Ubirr
Rock Paintings +

Cahills Crossing
Border Store

4WD

West

Wildman

Alligator

Alligator

Creek

Bunga Ck

Cattle Creek

Four Mile
Hole

track

River

Alligator

Nardaba
Munmarlary (Manmularri)

MAGELA PLAIN

Jowmbu Hill

Djawumba Hill

Djarrdjarr +
Njimbardi +

Ja Ja

Mayaamarleprard
Waterhole

Alligator River

BOGGY PLAIN

33

For more detail of Kakadu
National Park see page 387

Road impassable
in wet

MUDGINBERRI

28

Two Mile Hole

River

Alligator

Kakadu Holiday Village

20

HIGHWAY

20

11

Jabiru East

Park Headquarters
Bowali Visitor Centre

Jabiru

Ranger
Uranium Mine

ARNHEM

16

215

55

Ck

Fox

37

ARNHEM

Flying

River

Chirrcarwoo Lagoon

21

21

+ Mt Brockman
289m

Creek

Nourlangie
Billabongs

+ Djalandjal Hill

58

KAKADU

Alligator Billabong

7

12

Baralaba Creek

KOONGARRA

ARNHEM

Alligator

Yellow Waters

Cooinda

10

11

Gnari-ah-rogie Hill +

JIM JIM

West

Spring Peak +

9

Jim Jim Billabong

+ Mt Cahill
154m

6

Nourlangie Rock
Cave Paintings

Namarrgon

LAND

ROAD

101

Kunkamoula Billabong

Alligator

South

NATIONAL

+ Mt Basedow
220m +

+ Table Knob

Table Top
+ 490m

392

LAND

Deaf

Adder Creek

Mundogie Hill +

Barramundie

Dird Djahdjam Hill +
+ Mt Partridge
240m

Jim

Jim

4WD track

Nourlangie

Creek

ABORIGINAL

Craig Creek

Coirwong

COIRWONG GORGE

+ Bokawh

Konbolu Hill +

PARK

Koolpin

Creek

Jim Jim Falls

LAND

TRUST

Long Billabong

KAKADU

55

Coirwong

151

Masson
m

Goodparla

14

South

Twin Falls

Mt George
275m

27

Waterfall Creek
Falls

13

Road impassable
in wet

Halfway Peak
217m +

Mary River

23

Old Goodparla (Aband)

27

18

Alligator

Fisher

River

Mt Evelyn
365m

s Creek
Ruins)

Mt Saunders
+ 304m

Mt Daniels
141m

HIGHWAY

Mt Callanan
318m

Gimbat

Coronation Hill (Guratba) +
300m

13

Mary River
Roadhouse

21

47

Big Sunday
338m +

KAKADU

smeralda
Farm

28

Cullen

Creek

Bonrook

e Creek

+ Cullen Hill
216m

+ McCarthy Hill

Mt Gardiner
264m +

+ Coronet Hill
320m

+ Aston Hill

Ranford Hill +

Two Sisters
260m +

River

Wandie

Creek

WARNING: In outback Australia, long distances separate some
towns. Travellers should familiarise themselves with prevailing
conditions before departure, and take care to ensure their vehicle
is roadworthy and that they carry adequate supplies of petrol,
water and food.

In northern Australia, rainfall during the "wet" season (Oct–March)
can make some roads impassable. Full information on road
conditions should be obtained before departure.

If visitors intend diverting off public roads within Aboriginal Land
areas, a permit is required from the relevant Aboriginal authority.

Beware of man-eating crocodiles in rivers and estuaries.

+ Ngartluk Hill
364m

Katherine

Fergusson

River

Birdie

Creek

TO KATHERINE

J   K   L   M   N   392   O   P   Q   R

1

2

3

4

5

6

7

8

9

10

11

12

13

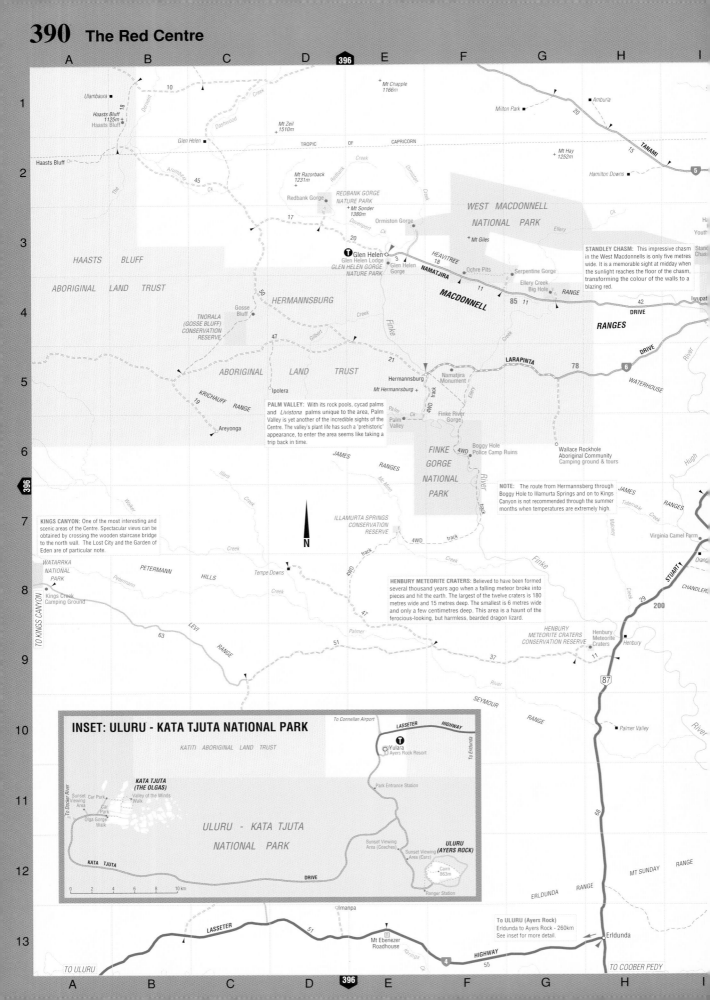

STANDLEY CHASM: This impressive chasm in the West Macdonnells is only five metres wide. It is a memorable sight at midday when the sunlight reaches the floor of the chasm, transforming the colour of the walls to a blazing red.

PALM VALLEY: With its rock pools, cycad palms and *Livistona* palms unique to the area, Palm Valley is yet another of the incredible sights of the Centre. The valley's plant life has such a "prehistoric" appearance, to enter the area seems like taking a trip back in time.

KINGS CANYON: One of the most interesting and scenic areas of the Centre. Spectacular views can be obtained by crossing the wooden staircase bridge to the north wall. The Lost City and the Garden of Eden are of particular note.

NOTE: The route from Hermannsberg through Boggy Hole to Illamurta Springs and on to Kings Canyon is not recommended through the summer months when temperatures are extremely high.

HENBURY METEORITE CRATERS: Believed to have been formed several thousand years ago when a falling meteor broke into pieces and hit the earth. The largest of the twelve craters is 180 metres wide and 15 metres deep. The smallest is 6 metres wide and only a few centimetres deep. This area is a haunt of the ferocious-looking, but harmless, bearded dragon lizard.

INSET: ULURU - KATA TJUTA NATIONAL PARK

To ULURU (Ayers Rock)
Erldunda to Ayers Rock - 260km
See inset for more detail.

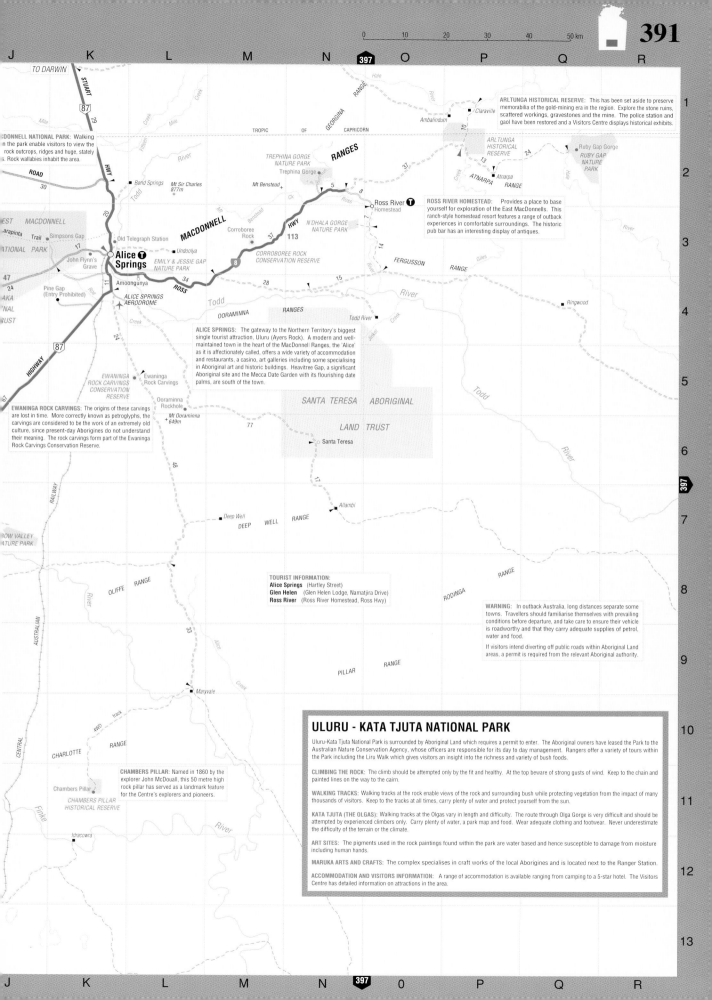

0   10   20   30   40   50 km

ARLTUNGA HISTORICAL RESERVE: This has been set aside to preserve memorabilia of the gold-mining era in the region. Explore the stone ruins, scattered workings, gravestones and the mine. The police station and gaol have been restored and a Visitors Centre displays historical exhibits.

ROSS RIVER HOMESTEAD: Provides a place to base yourself for exploration of the East MacDonnells. This ranch-style homestead resort features a range of outback experiences in comfortable surroundings. The historic pub bar has an interesting display of antiques.

MACDONNELL NATIONAL PARK: Walking in the park enable visitors to view the rock outcrops, ridges and huge, stately s. Rock wallabies inhabit the area.

ALICE SPRINGS: The gateway to the Northern Territory's biggest single tourist attraction, Uluru (Ayers Rock). A modern and well-maintained town in the heart of the MacDonnell Ranges, the 'Alice' as it is affectionately called, offers a wide variety of accommodation and restaurants, a casino, art galleries including some specialising in Aboriginal art and historic buildings. Heavitree Gap, a significant Aboriginal site and the Mecca Date Garden with its flourishing date palms, are south of the town.

EWANINGA ROCK CARVINGS: The origins of these carvings are lost in time. More correctly known as petroglyphs, the carvings are considered to be the work of an extremely old culture, since present-day Aborigines do not understand their meaning. The rock carvings form part of the Ewaninga Rock Carvings Conservation Reserve.

TOURIST INFORMATION:
Alice Springs (Hartley Street)
Glen Helen (Glen Helen Lodge, Namatjira Drive)
Ross River (Ross River Homestead, Ross Hwy)

WARNING: In outback Australia, long distances separate some towns. Travellers should familiarise themselves with prevailing conditions before departure, and take care to ensure their vehicle is roadworthy and that they carry adequate supplies of petrol, water and food.

If visitors intend diverting off public roads within Aboriginal Land areas, a permit is required from the relevant Aboriginal authority.

CHAMBERS PILLAR: Named in 1860 by the explorer John McDouall, this 50 metre high rock pillar has served as a landmark feature for the Centre's explorers and pioneers.

ULURU - KATA TJUTA NATIONAL PARK

Uluru-Kata Tjuta National Park is surrounded by Aboriginal Land which requires a permit to enter. The Aboriginal owners have leased the Park to the Australian Nature Conservation Agency, whose officers are responsible for its day to day management. Rangers offer a variety of tours within the Park including the Liru Walk which gives visitors an insight into the richness and variety of bush foods.

CLIMBING THE ROCK: The climb should be attempted only by the fit and healthy. At the top beware of strong gusts of wind. Keep to the chain and painted lines on the way to the cairn.

WALKING TRACKS: Walking tracks at the rock enable views of the rock and surrounding bush while protecting vegetation from the impact of many thousands of visitors. Keep to the tracks at all times, carry plenty of water and protect yourself from the sun.

KATA TJUTA (THE OLGAS): Walking tracks at the Olgas vary in length and difficulty. The route through Olga Gorge is very difficult and should be attempted by experienced climbers only. Carry plenty of water, a park map and food. Wear adequate clothing and footwear. Never underestimate the difficulty of the terrain or the climate.

ART SITES: The pigments used in the rock paintings found within the park are water based and hence susceptible to damage from moisture including human hands.

MARUKA ARTS AND CRAFTS: The complex specialises in craft works of the local Aborigines and is located next to the Ranger Station.

ACCOMMODATION AND VISITORS INFORMATION: A range of accommodation is available ranging from camping to a 5-star hotel. The Visitors Centre has detailed information on attractions in the area.

A B C D E F G H I

1

2

TIMOR

SEA

Cape Van Diemen

MELVILLE
ISLAND

Deception Point

Pularumpi
Milikapiti

BATHURST
ISLAND

TIWI
ABORIGINAL LAND

TRUST

Nguiu
Paru

Pickertaramoor

Cape Keith

Conder Point

3

Point Jahleel

Vashon Head
Lingi Pt

COBOURG
PENINSULA

Danger Pt
Minjilang

CROKER
ISLAND

Cape Croker

McClue
Grant Island

Cape Cockbur

GURIG NATIONAL PARK

Port Essington

COBOURG
Greenhill
Island
MARINE PARK

Morsel
Island

Murgenella

Endyalgout
Island

Cape Gambier

Beagle
Gulf

Clarence Strait

Dundas
Strait

Van Diemen

Gulf

Mt Perm
220m

Cooper

East

Oenpelli
Gunbalán

4

CAPE HOTHAM
FORESTRY RES

Cape Hotham

CAPE HOTHAM
CONSERVATION RES

Field Island

Point Stuart

Ubirr
Rock Paintings

Cahills C
Border

5

For more detail of Darwin
Region see pages 388 & 389

Gunn Point

Radio Australia
Transmitter Station

DARWIN

Mandorah
Belyuen

Noonamah
Berry
Springs

Howard
Springs

Koolpinyah

Fogg
Dam

ARNHEM

Humpty
Doo

Humpty Doo
(Wariuk)

Acacia Store

Woolner

MARY RIVER
CONSERVATION
RESERVE

MARRAKAI
CONSERVATION
RESERVE

Point Stuart
Melaleuca

Helens Creek

Swim Creek
Plains

Kakadu Holiday Village

HIGHWAY

Munmarlary (Manmularri)

Ja Ja

Jabiru

Mt Brockm
289m

Mt Cahill
152m

KAKADU

6

Finniss
River

Fog Bay

Point Blaze

Finniss
River

DELISSAVILLE
WAGAIT LARRAKIA
ABORIGINAL
LAND TRUST

Darwin
River
Dam

Rum Jungle

Batchelor

Banyan

Mary
River

Mary

Four Mile
Hole

Yellow Waters

Cooinda

NATIONAL

Nourlangie Ro

Adder

7

North Peron
Island

Wangi
Falls

Welltree
Keri

Reynolds
River

Wangi

LITCHFIELD
NATIONAL
PARK

Litchfield

Robin Falls

Tortilla Flats
War Cemetery

Adelaide River

Mount Ringwood

Ban Ban
Spring

Mt Masson

Mt Douglas
250m

Goodparla

Mt George
274m

Mary River
Station

HWY

Gunlom

Jim Jim Falls

Twin Falls

South Peron
Island

Anson Bay

8

Cape Ford

Daly

River

Elizabeth Downs

MALAK MALAK
ABORIGINAL
LAND TRUST

Daly River

Tipperary

STUART

Hayes Creek
Roadhouse

DOUGLAS
HOT SPRINGS
NATURE
PARK
Hot
Springs

Douglas Daly
Experimental Station

Oolloo

Middle

Tha Banyans

Emerald Springs
Roadhouse

BUTTERFLY
GORGE

Esmeralda Farm

Setay Valley

Bonrook

Pine Creek

Esmerald

River

Creek

Mt Evelyn
366m

Gimbat

9

Joseph

Bonaparte

Gulf

Cape Dombey

DALY   RIVER

PORT KEATS

ABORIGINAL

LAND TRUST

Moyle

River

Fish

River

Wadeye
Community

WINGATE MOUNTAINS

Bonalbo

Jindare

Claravale Station

Umbrawarra
Gorge

Claravale

Morrisons
Mariliyum

Fergusson

Mt Lambell 317m

Edith Falls

NITMILUK
Katherine
Gorge
NP

Mt Felix 332m

O'Sullivans
House

HIGHWAY

BESWICK
ABORIGINAL
LAND
TRUST

Eva Valley

Birdie

10

Pearce Point

Treachery Bay

Swamp Point

MACADAM   RANGE

FISH RIVER
FORESTRY
RESERVE

Dorisvale

Florina

Kintore Caves

Katherine

Mt Shepherd
232m

Maranboy

Barunga

Tindal

Manbulloo

RAAF
Base

Cutta
Cutta
Caves

Ropen

Creek

11

Cambridge
Gulf

Turtle Point

YAMBARRAN   RANGE

Fitzmaurice
River

Wombungi

Mt Thymanan 304m

Katherine
River

King

O'Brien

HIGHWAY

Dry River

Mataranka

We Of The Never Never
Graves

12

Mt Connection
183m

Legune

Bradshaw

Angalarri

Victoria

River

GREGORY
NATIONAL
PARK

Innesvale

Willeroo

DELAMERE

Old Delamere

Gorrie

Larrin

13

Wyndham

361

56

Mt Cockburn
North
671m

Kununurra

VICTORIA

WESTERN

NORTHERN   TERRITORY

AUSTRALIA

MIRIMA
(HIDDEN
VALLEY) NP

KEEP
RIVER
NP

PINKERTON

RANGE

Kneebone

Bulla

Sandy

Baines

Auvergne

Bulla

GREGORY
NATIONAL
PARK

Newry

Timber
Creek

Timber Creek
Police Station
& Store

VICTORIA

Jasper Gorge

Victoria
River

Cookibah

Fitzroy

Victoria

Delamere

ROAD

Western Creek

Gilnockie

Sunday Creek

NOTE: The towns of Borroloola an
Creek, while located on Aboriginal
open towns.
No entry permit is required.

Dunham
Pilot Dam

HIGHWAY

394

Dunham

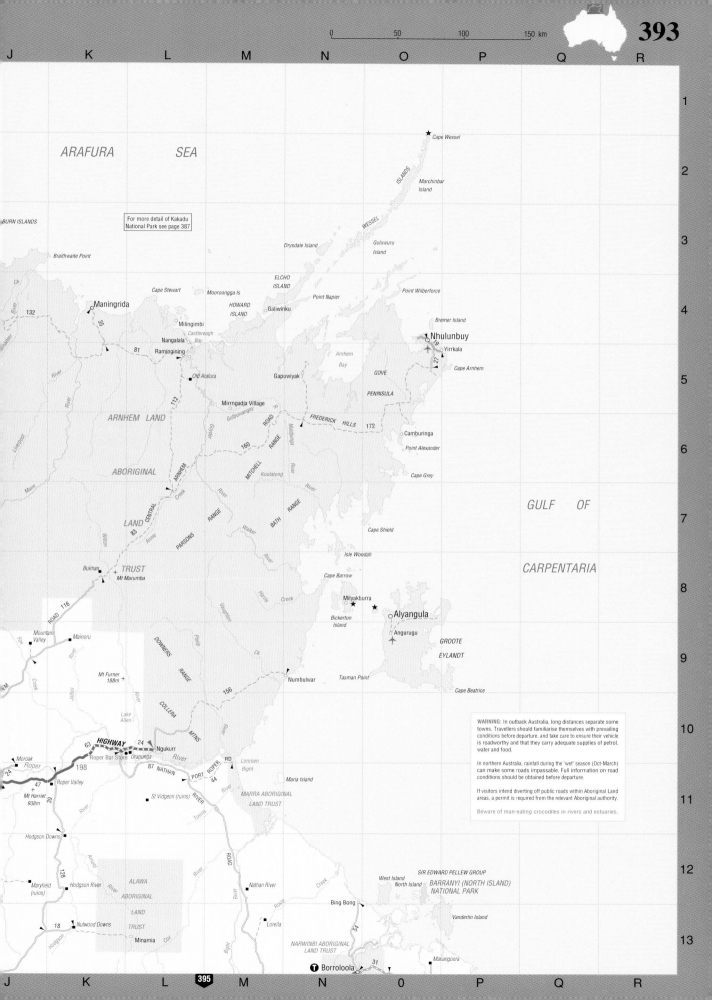

0   50   100   150 km

ARAFURA   SEA

BURN ISLANDS

Braithwaite Point

Ck

River

132

35

Maningrida

Cape Stewart

Mooroongga Is

Milingimbi

Nangalala

Castlereagh
Bay

Ramingining

81

Old Arafura

112

ARNHEM   LAND

ABORIGINAL

Goyder

River

160

MITCHELL

Koolatong

LAND   CENTRAL

ARNHEM

Creek

Arnie

River

83

TRUST

RANGE

PARSONS

River

Walker

River

Bulman

Mt Marumba

ROAD

116

River

Mountain
Valley

Mainoru

Fox

Jalboi

Creek

River

Mt Furner
188m +

DOWNERS

RANGE

Phelp

Ck

156

River

COLLERA

MTNS

Lake
Allen

CM

Creek

HIGHWAY   24

63

Ngukurr

Moroak

Roper

Roper Bar Store

Urapunga

198

87

NATHAN

River

24

47

Roper Valley

PORT   ROPER   RD

RD

Limmen

Bight

Mt Harriet
938m +

39

Arnolt

River

St Vidgeon (ruins)

Towns

RIVER

River

44

Maria Island

MARRA ABORIGINAL

LAND TRUST

Hodgson Downs

Maryfield
(ruins)

128

Hodgson River

River

ALAWA

ABORIGINAL

LAND

TRUST

ROAD

River

Nathan River

Rosie

Creek

Bight

River

SIR EDWARD PELLEW GROUP

West Island

North Island

BARRANYI (NORTH ISLAND)
NATIONAL PARK

18

Nutwood Downs

Hodgson

Minamia

Cox

River

Bing Bong

Lorella

54

NARWINBI ABORIGINAL
LAND TRUST

Borroloola

31

Manangoora

Vanderlin Island

Drysdale Island

ELCHO
ISLAND

HOWARD
ISLAND

Galiwinku

Point Napier

WESSEL

Guluwuru
Island

Marchinbar
Island

Cape Wessel

Point Wilberforce

Bremer Island

Nhulunbuy

19

Yirrkala

27

Cape Arnhem

Gapuwiyak

Arnhem
Bay

GOVE

PENINSULA

Mirrngadja Village

Gulbuwangay

Maldjunga

FREDERICK   HILLS   172

Camburinga

Point Alexander

RANGE

RANGE

Cape Grey

Cape Shield

BATH

Maltunga

Isle Woodah

Harris

Creek

Vaughton

Cape Barrow

Milyakburra

Bickerton
Island

Alyangula

Angurugu

GROOTE

EYLANDT

Tasman Point

Cape Beatrice

Numbulwar

GULF   OF

CARPENTARIA

WARNING: In outback Australia, long distances separate some
towns. Travellers should familiarise themselves with prevailing
conditions before departure, and take care to ensure their vehicle
is roadworthy and that they carry adequate supplies of petrol,
water and food.

In northern Australia, rainfall during the 'wet' season (Oct-March)
can make some roads impassable. Full information on road
conditions should be obtained before departure.

If visitors intend diverting off public roads within Aboriginal Land
areas, a permit is required from the relevant Aboriginal authority.

Beware of man-eating crocodiles in rivers and estuaries.

A B C D 392 E F G H I

1 2 3 4 5 6 7 8 9 10 11 12 13

Cambridge Gulf
Mt Connection +183m
Legune
Kneebone
YAMBARRAN RANGE
Bradshaw
Mt Thymanan 304m
Dry River
Matarnaka
We Of The Never Never Graves
86

Wyndham
14
69
Victoria
Bulla
RANGE
Avergne
58
Timber Creek Police Station & Store
Coplibah
Fitzroy
Victoria River
Innesvale
Willeroo
HIGHWAY 1
24 28
38
GREGORY NATIONAL PARK
Delamere
14
131
Old Delamere
23
Gregory Creek
Western Creek
Gorrie
Larr

56
Kununurra
45
42
36
1
MIRIMA (HIDDEN VALLEY) NP
KEEP RIVER NP
Newry
40
Bulla
Baines
VICTORIA 1
21
Jasper Gorge
VICTORIA
80
113
RIVER
96
164 44
41
33
ROAD
Killarney
Mt Sullivan 267m
DELAMERE
Gilnockie
Sunday Cr

El Questro
41
Dunham Pilot Dam
61
34
Mt Brooking 379m
47
27
Newry
73
ROAD
306
69
GREGORY NATIONAL PARK
213
DOWNS
Yarralin
Victoria River Downs
100
Mt Sullivan
35
Birrimba
Hidden
16
HIGHW

Dunham River
NORTHERN
1
56
Lake Argyle Tourist Village
CARR BOYD RANGE
Lake Argyle
Rosewood
38
Kildurk
Humbert River
30
River
ROAD
Top Springs
14
Montejinni
BUCHANAN
180
80
127

151
Lissadell
29
Spring Creek
80
West
Mt Mary
Waterloo
Mt Stevens 194m
HIGHWAY
75
Mt Northcote 225m

Bow
34
32
Texas Downs
Mt Jarrad 530m
Mistake Creek
Wickham
Mount Sanford
Camfield
170
N

VIOLET HILL ABORIGINAL LAND
GREAT
55
Turkey Creek
Mt John 526m
36
Nelson Springs
Limbunya
DAGARAGU ABORIGINAL LAND TRUST
Dagaragu
BUCHANAN
81
Wave Hill
TANAMI DESERT

361
Mt Buchanan 417m
PURNULULU (BUNGLE BUNGLE) NATIONAL PARK
DUNCAN
Mt Panton 340m
116
Mt Copley 439m
50
96
Kalkarindji
Camfield
Cattle Creek
KARLANTIJPA

Ord River
Panton River
90
Kirkimbie
Mt Napier 487m
56
Riveren
Mt Gordon 135m
ROAD
NORTH

Mt Coghlan 622m
Saunders Creek
80
HIGHWAY
Nicholson
Inverway
Creek
Mt Farquharson 446m
Mt Barton 388m
121
HOOKER CREEK ABORIGINAL
ABORIGINAL

59
Mt Archie 478m
Nongra Lake
LAND
Mt Browne
Lajamanu
LAND

Flora Valley
BUCHANAN
30
47
Creek
Wallamunga
Birrindudu
TRUST
TRUST

WESTERN AUSTRALIA
NORTHERN TERRITORY
Sturt
Winnecke
Creek
LAJAMANU
245

Sturt
Gordon Downs
90
CENTRAL DESERT

Sturt Creek
Suplejack
ABORIGINAL
TANAMI DESERT
KARLANTIJPA

Mt Frederick 530m
LAND
SOUTH

TANAMI TRACK
79
Mt Tanami 499m
Tanami
TRUST
ABORIGINAL

Balgo Community
45
Rabbit Flat Roadhouse
TANAMI
Lake Surprise
Mt Davidson 461m
Mt Solitaire 458m
LAND

54
57
The Granites
ROAD
Tanami Downs
BALGO ABORIGINAL LAND
Fiddlers Lake
TRUST
Landor

NOTE: The towns of Borroloola, Kalkarindji and Timber Creek, while located on Aboriginal Land, are open towns. No entry permit is required.

WARNING: In outback Australia, long distances separate some towns. Travellers should familiarise themselves with prevailing conditions before departure, and take care to ensure their vehicle is roadworthy and that they carry adequate supplies of petrol, water and food.

In northern Australia, rainfall during the 'wet' season (Oct-March) can make some roads impassable. Full information on road conditions should be obtained before departure.

If visitors intend diverting off public roads within Aboriginal Land areas, a permit is required from the relevant Aboriginal authority.

Beware of man-eating crocodiles in rivers and estuaries.

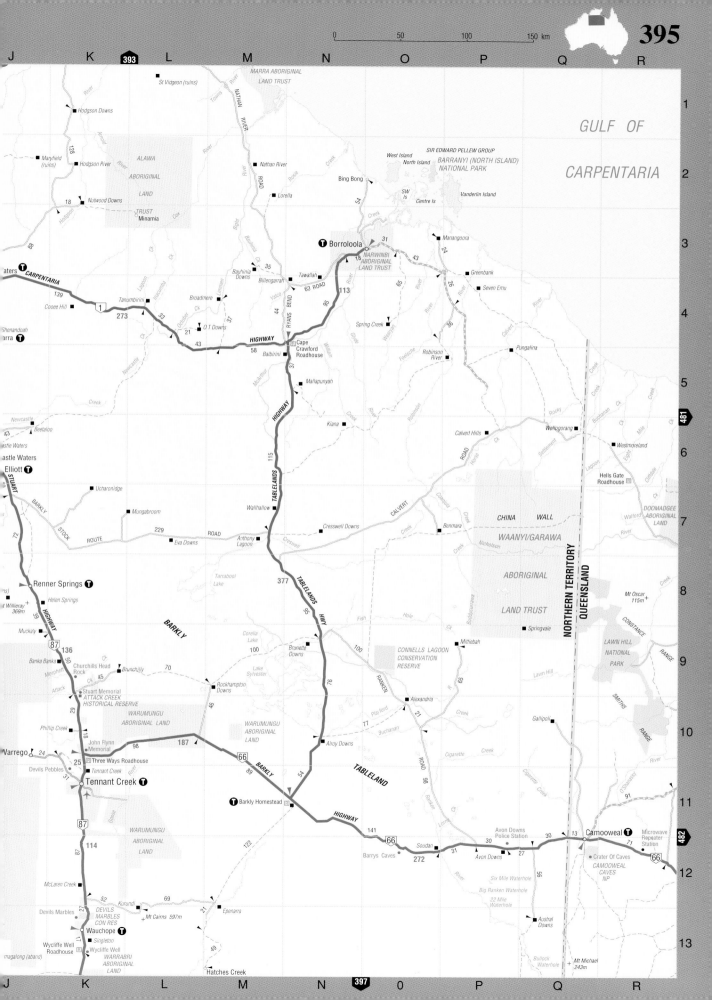

A **B** **C** **D** 394 **E** **F** **G** **H** **I**

1
TANAMI
TRACK
79
Mt Tanami 499m
45

CENTRAL DESERT
ABORIGINAL
LAND
TRUST

TANAMI   DESERT

Balgo Community

Rabbit Flat Roadhouse
51
TANAMI
57

Lake Surprise

2
BALGO
ABORIGINAL
LAND

Tanami Downs
The Granites

3
Lake Dennis

YININGARRA
ABORIGINAL
LAND
TRUST

Fiddlers Lake

Lander River

Willowra

Lake White

4
Lake Willis

LAKE MACKAY
ABORIGINAL
LAND
TRUST

Mt Patricia 577m

189
ROAD

PAWA
ABORIGINAL
LAND
TRUST

Mount Barkly

Old
85

5
Mt Farewell 603m
Mt Singleton 808m
Mount Doreen
Mt Hardy 840m
31
28
MOUNT
38
DENISON
Mount Denison
Mt Campbell 628m
Yuelamu
Mt Leichhardt 1139m
Mt Stafford 1049m
Coniston
Coniston (ruins)
Mt Gardiner 999m
178
ROAD
Annin

6
Lake Mackay
Mt Nicker 632m
Vaughan Springs
77
Yuendumu
26
TANAMI
61
YUNKANJINI ABORIGINAL LAND TRUST
YALPIRAKINU ABORIGINAL LAND TRUST
Napperby

359

7
Mt Webb 532m
Mt Tietkens 546m
Nyirripi
Mt Cockburn 846m
Lake Bennett
Newhaven
118
Central Mount Wedge
Mount Wedge
29
Lake Lewis
288
Mt Hammond 750m
64
ROAD
Mt 72

8
TROPIC
Ininti
Pinpirnga
Kintore
Mt Leisler 901m
Tinki
Ilpilla
OF
273
Warren Creek Bore
Mt Liebig 1524m
Mt Liebig
CAPRICORN
HAASTS BLUFF
Papunya
Ulambaura
Derwent
Nanwietooma
Haast Bluff 1125m
HAASTS BLUFF
Glen Helen
Redbank Gorge & Nature Park
51
31
23
Mt Chapple 1166m
Mt Zeil 1510m
44
47
Mt Sonder 1380m
Milton Park
Mt Ha 1252m
Hami
WE
MA

Lake Macdonald
Ualki

9
Mt Forbes 762m
HAASTS BLUFF ABORIGINAL LAND TRUST
Gosse Bluff
TNORALA (GOSSE BLUFF) CONSERVATION RES
Ipolera
Areyonga
19
MACDONNELL
20
46
Glen Helen
HERMANNSBURG
NAMATJIRA
Ormiston Gorge
29
29
LARAPINTA
24
RANGES
Hermanns
ABORIGINAL LAND TRUST
Palm Valley
FINKE GORGE NP
Ser
Aborigin

10
CENTRAL
AUSTRALIA
Mt Murray
Lake Neale
WATARRKA NP
Ulpanyali
Lila
Kings Canyon
35
Mt Lewis 100m
ERNEST
63
GILES
ILLAMURTA SPRINGS CONSERVATION RES
Tempe Downs
47
51
47
He Me
ROAD
Palme
Kings Creek Camping Ground
50

Mt Harris 1067m

PETERMANN
ABORIGINAL
LAND
TRUST

11
Warakurna Community
Giles Meteorological Station
16
29
Warakurna Roadhouse
ABORIGINAL
Mt Taylor 1001m
74
Docker River Community
PETERMANN
183
231
RANGES
Lake Amadeus
LASSETER
Curtin Springs
41
18
244
Angas Downs
52
Mt Ebenezer
HWY
Erl
56

12
JAMIESON RANGE
LAND
105
Mt Olga 1069m
Yulara
84
Kata Tjuta (The Olgas)
40
8
8
Uluru (Ayers Rock)
ULURU - KATA TJUTA NATIONAL PARK
Mygoora Lake
11
68
Mt Conner 863m
Mt Conner (ruins)

Stevensons Pk 1319m
Butlers Dome 1111m

13
TRUST
Mt Gosse 885m
Surveyor Generals Corner
Mt Cockburn 1138m
Kalka
Alpara
Mulga Park
141
Victory Downs
Mt Elliott 573m
Mt Scott 668m
Mt Aloysius 1085m
Mt Hinckley 1018m
NORTHERN TERRITORY
SOUTH AUSTRALIA
Aparawatatja
MANN
RANGES
Mt Morris 1288m
Amata
Mt Davenport 1139m
Mt Cuthbert 1035m
Vi

A **B** 294 **C** **D** **E** **F** **G** 295 **H**

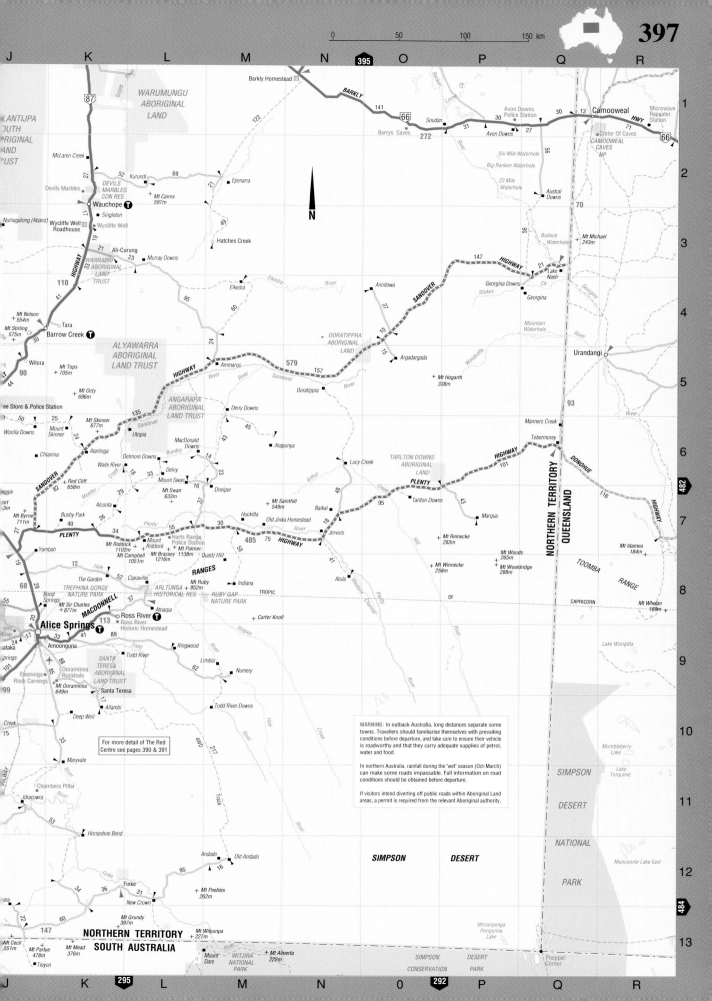

Queensland Sunshine State

To visitors from other States, as well as to many Queenslanders, the Sunshine State is holiday country, evoking dreams of long, golden days, tropical islands set in jewel-blue seas and the chance to relax outdoors. The first settlers in the tropical north, however, were there for grimly practical reasons.

In 1821 Sir Thomas Brisbane, Governor of New South Wales, sent John Oxley, his Surveyor-General, to explore the almost unknown country north of the Liverpool Plains. Oxley's task was to find a suitable site for a penal settlement and he decided on Moreton Bay. In 1824 troops and convicts arrived at Redcliffe, but a lack of fresh water and the hostility of the Aborigines persuaded them to move south and they settled at the present site of Brisbane. By 1859 the settlement was well established and the free settlers were urging separation from New South Wales; and so, on 10 December, the state of Queensland was proclaimed.

Having gained legislative independence, the population of just 23 000 then set about achieving economic independence. Fortunately the new State was well endowed with excellent farming land, and wool and beef production were soon established on the western plains and tablelands. It was not long before sugar production, worked by 'kanaka' labour from the Pacific Islands, became much more important, and it is still very significant.

As well as being blessed with fertile land that produces grain, sugar, dairy produce, wool, mutton, beef, cotton, peanuts and timber, Queensland has immensely rich mineral deposits, and the vast Mount Isa mining complex in the west produces copper, lead and zinc in enormous quantities.

Over the years, Queensland has been developing another, very different, form of industry—tourism. Its attraction as a holiday destination is very much due to its climate.

In the west, the climate is similar to that of the arid Red Centre, with fierce daytime heat, but on the coast the temperature rarely exceeds 38°C and for seven months or so of the year the weather is extremely pleasant. If you are unused to high humidity, however, the period from December to April can be uncomfortably damp.

Four geographic and climatic regions run north to south, neatly dividing the State. In the west is the Great Artesian Basin, flat and hot. Parched and bare during drought, it becomes grassy after rain, thanks to a complex system of boreholes that distribute water through channels and allow grazing. The tablelands to the east are undulating and sparsely timbered, broken up by slow, meandering rivers. The backbone of Queensland is the Great Dividing Range—most spectacular in its extreme north and south, where it comes closest to the coast. Although the coastal region is the area most popular with visitors, Queensland's hinterland is lushly beautiful and its national parks, with many species of bird, animal and plant life unique to the State, total more than one million hectares. The State's highway and road system is good in the south-east and in areas close to the larger northern towns, but elsewhere roads tend to be narrow and poorly graded and conditions deteriorate during drought or heavy rain.

The two main towns of the tropical northern region are Townsville and Cairns. The more northerly Cairns is fast becoming a fashionable holiday centre and makes an excellent base for deep-sea fishing and for exploring the region, with its lush sugar-lands, mountainous jungle country and the wilds of the Cape York Peninsula. The Atherton Tableland is a rich volcanic area west of Cairns, with superb lakes, waterfalls and fern valleys. Stretching along this coastline are Queensland's famed islands: Lizard, north of Cooktown, Green Island, Dunk, Hinchinbrook, Magnetic, the beautiful Whitsundays, Great Keppel, Heron, Fraser and Lady Musgrave. If you are planning an island holiday, make sure your choice fits in with your idea of a tropical paradise. Many islands are extensively developed for tourism; others are quiet and offer simple accommodation. Beyond, and protecting them from the South Pacific, is the outer Great Barrier Reef, the world's largest and most famous coral formation.

South of the Reef is the Sunshine Coast. This scenic coastal region, with its leisurely pace and its wide variety of natural attractions and sporting facilities, offers an alternative to the more commercialised Gold Coast. Bribie Island, the weird and wonderful shapes of the Glass House Mountains and the beautiful Lakes District are nearby.

Brisbane, Australia's third-largest capital city, is a far-spread capital, built on both sides of the Brisbane River. An easygoing, friendly city, its parks and gardens lush with subtropical plants, Brisbane has a year-round average of $7\frac{1}{2}$ hours of sunshine a day. The Gold Coast, 75 kilometres to the south, is the heart of holiday country. Luxuriously developed, it offers a wide range of accommodation, glittering nightlife, seemingly endless golden beaches and constant sun. Inland is rich and rolling wheat and dairy farming country, its setting a sharp contrast with the tropical north or the mining areas of Mount Isa. The Sunshine State is a diverse place indeed.

Eastern edge of Cape Tribulation National Park

Brisbane

A Subtropical City

The best place from which to see the layout of Brisbane is the lookout on **Mount Coot-tha**, 8 kilometres southwest of the city centre and easily distinguished by its television towers. Brisbane sprawls over the series of small hills below, with the Brisbane River wandering lazily through the suburbs and city and out into **Moreton Bay**, 32 kilometres downstream. Surprisingly little use is made of the river for public transport, and most riverside houses back on to rather than face it.

Moreton and Stradbroke Islands look like a protective mountain range against the Pacific Ocean, far to the east. On a good day you can see the rugged mountains behind the Gold Coast to the south, and northward the strange **Glass House Mountains** just south of the Sunshine Coast. Tangalooma Moreton Island Resort offers visitors the opportunity to hand-feed wild dolphins and try sand tobogganing, fishing, water sports and bushwalking. From July to October whale-watching can be enjoyed off both Moreton and Stradbroke Islands.

Brisbane's best-known building, the **City Hall**, is now lost among the cluster of high-rise office buildings that dominate the skyline.

Although it has developed into an international tourist destination following its hosting of the Commonwealth Games in 1982 and World Expo in 1988, Brisbane still does not bustle like the larger southern capitals, and the suburban architecture, except for the newer, western areas, is predominantly the traditional galvanised iron-roofed timber houses on stumps that residents think sensible and visitors find quaint. What is occasionally lacking in paint is more than made up for by colourful subtropical trees and shrubbery.

The city started inauspiciously as a convict settlement as far removed from Britain, and even from Sydney, as possible. In 1799 Matthew Flinders sailed into Moreton Bay on the sloop *Norfolk*. In 1823 John Oxley, then Surveyor-General, on board the cutter *Mermaid* sailed up the river that flowed into the bay and called it the Brisbane, after the Governor of New South Wales, Sir Thomas Brisbane.

The first troops and convicts arrived in 1824 on the brig *Amity*. The original settlement at Redcliffe was soon abandoned, mainly because of a lack of fresh water, and barracks were built on the present site of the city centre, previously investigated by Oxley. The penal settlement was closed in 1839 and the region was opened for free settlement in 1842.

Today Brisbane is a busy city with a modern and extensive public transport system, a wide selection of restaurants, entertainment and nightlife, parks and gardens which thrive in the subtropical climate, and a population of over 1.3 million.

Among several interesting historic buildings is the **Observatory** or **Old Windmill** on Wickham Terrace, overlooking the city. Built in 1828, the mill proved unworkable, so convicts were pressed into service to crush the grain on a treadmill. In 1934 a picture of the mill was the first television image transmitted in Australia, sent to Ipswich, 33 kilometres away.

The restored **Commissariat Stores**, at North Quay below the old **State Library** building, were built by convicts in 1829. The nearby **Treasury Building** at the top of Queen Street, an impressive Italian Renaissance structure built of local grey sandstone, was commenced in 1888. (The nearby *Lands Administration Building* is undergoing a transformation into a boutique hotel for Brisbane's first casino, both opening in 1995.) **Newstead House**, a charming building overlooking the river at Breakfast Creek, was built in 1846 by Patrick Leslie, the first settler on the Darling Downs. He sold it to his brother-in-law Captain John Wickham, RN, resident of the Moreton Bay colony, and it was the centre of official and social life in Brisbane until the first Government House was built in 1862. Newstead

City skyline

Hotels

Chancellor on the Park
Cnr Leichhardt St and Wickham Tce,
Spring Hill
(07) 3831 4055

The Beaufort Heritage
Cnr Edward and Margaret Sts, Brisbane
(07) 3221 1999

Brisbane Hilton
190 Elizabeth St, Brisbane
(07) 3231 3131

Sheraton Brisbane Hotel and Towers
249 Turbot St, Brisbane
(07) 3835 3535

Family and Budget

Kingsford Hall Private Hotel
114 Kingsford Smith Dr, Hamilton
(07) 3862 1317

Queensland Countrywomen's Association Club
89–95 Gregory Tce, Spring Hill
(07) 3831 8188

Story Bridge Motor Inn
321 Main St, Kangaroo Point
(07) 3393 1433

Wickham Terrace Motel
491 Wickham Tce, Spring Hill
(07) 3839 9611

Motel Groups: Bookings

Best Western (008) 22 2166
Flag 13 2400
Travelodge (008) 22 2446

This list is for information only; inclusion is not necessarily a recommendation.

House is Brisbane's oldest house and has been restored to illustrate a bygone past. **Old Government House**, a classic colonial building with additions made between 1882 and 1895, was also the original University. It is now part of the **Queensland University of Technology** complex at the bottom of George Street and is the home of the National Trust of Queensland. Nearby **Parliament House** designed by Charles Tiffin in a 'tropical Renaissance' style was opened in 1868. The **Parliament House Annexe** (irreverently called the Taj Mahal) is a modern tower block behind Parliament House overlooking the river. The exclusive **Queensland Club** is diagonally opposite Parliament House and was built during the 1880s.

The **General Post Office** in Queen Street was built between 1871 and 1879 on the site of the female convict barracks. The small church behind the Post Office in Elizabeth Street and beside **St Stephen's Catholic Cathedral** is the third oldest building in Brisbane, having been dedicated in 1850. The **Customs House** at Petrie Bight at the bottom of Queen Street was built in 1884. The **Deanery**, built in 1849, behind **St John's Anglican Cathedral** in Ann Street, became a temporary residence for the first Governor of Queensland, Sir George Bowen. The proclamation announcing Queensland as a separate colony was read from its balcony in 1859. It became the residence of

the Dean of Brisbane in 1910. Further south along Ann Street is **All Saints' Church**, which dates from 1861.

Earlystreet Historical Village is a particularly fine collection of Queensland buildings and architecture at 75 McIlwraith Avenue, Norman Park, east of the city centre. Among the buildings are reconstructions of Stromness, one of the first houses at Kangaroo Point, and the ballroom and billiard-room of Auchenflower House. The village is open daily and afternoon teas are served on Sundays.

To the north of the city another building open to the public is **Miegunyah**, a traditional Queensland house with verandahs and ironwork at Jordan Terrace, Bowen Hills. This is home to the Queensland Women's Historical Society.

There are very few terrace houses in Brisbane, but a row at the **Normanby Junction** has been lovingly restored and incorporates two restaurants. A similar development has occurred on **Coronation Drive**. Brisbane's more impressive houses, including the famous old 'Queenslanders', are scattered throughout the inner-city suburbs. Many small cottages in the **Spring Hill**, **Paddington** and **Red Hill** areas are being restored. The **Regatta Hotel** on the river at Coronation Drive is worth a visit, and the famous **Breakfast Creek Hotel** has a popular beer garden serving excellent steaks.

The main city department stores are located in Queen Street, which, between Edward and George Streets, is now a mall containing three large shopping complexes, boutiques, entertainment centres, major department stores, restaurants and taverns. Two of the city's most popular markets are the kilometre-long stretch of Sunday craft markets at the **Riverside Centre** in Eagle St, and the **South Bank Markets**, held on Friday nights, Saturdays and Sundays.

For the sports enthusiast, Brisbane's famous 'Gabba' ground at Woolloongabba hosts cricket matches and greyhound racing. There are four horse-racing venues at Albion Park, Doomben, Eagle Farm and Bundamba. The **ANZ Stadium** at Nathan and the Chandler aquatic centre, indoor sports hall and velodrome were all built for the 1982 Commonwealth Games. The ANZ Stadium is now the home of the rugby league premiers, the Brisbane Broncos.

The **King George Square** facing the **City Hall** is a popular spot for watching the world go by. The **Anzac Memorial and Eternal Flame** is opposite **Central Railway Station** with its towering backdrop, the **Sheraton Brisbane Hotel and Towers**.

Across Victoria Bridge lies **South Bank Parklands**, 16 hectares of redeveloped and landscaped parklands with walking and bicycle paths, a constructed beach, a series of canals where the South Ships cruise, and several restaurants. The Gondwana Rainforest Sanctuary, the Butterfly and Insect House and Our World Environment Display are special features attracting visitors to Brisbane's newest open space.

For the art lover, the **Queensland Art Gallery**, part of the **Queensland Cultural Centre**, is on the southside riverbank. This impressive gallery includes significant Australian, British and European collections. The Cultural Centre also houses an auditorium, the award-winning **Queensland Performing Arts Complex** with three theatres, the **State Library of Queensland** and **Queensland Museum**. The **Civic Art Museum** in the City Hall, the **Museum of Contemporary Art** at South Brisbane and the **University of Queensland Art Museum** at St Lucia are excellent. Private galleries include the Philip Bacon Gallery at New Farm, the Ray Hughes Gallery at Red Hill, the Victor Mace Gallery at Para Galleries at South Brisbane, which specialises in

Mt Coot-tha

Only 8 kilometres from Brisbane's city centre, Mt Coot-tha offers city dwellers an attractive breathing space. Here the Brisbane City Council has plans for an ambitious development scheme that will make the best recreational use of the area.

Brisbane's newest Botanic Gardens are in the foothills of Mt Coot-tha. The tropical display house, in the form of a futuristic-looking dome, has a superb display of tropical plants and is open daily. The arid-zone garden and cactus house are nearby. The gardens also include a lagoon and pond, a demonstration garden, ornamental trees and shrubs, areas of Australian and tropical rainforest, and a large collection of Australian native plants.

Situated in the Botanic Gardens is the Sir Thomas Brisbane Planetarium. The largest planetarium in Australia, it accommodates 144 people and was named after the 'founder of organised science in Australia'. When Sir Thomas was Governor of New South Wales, in 1821 he set up an astronomical observatory at Parramatta. His observations resulted in the publication of *The Brisbane Catalog of Stars*.

Various programmes are shown at the Planetarium's Star Theatre. A representation of the night sky is projected on to the interior of the dome and the movements of sun, moon and stars are described as they occur. Special effects can also be obtained by additional projectors to demonstrate more unusual phenomena in the sky.

Programmes are shown in both the afternoon and evening, Wednesday to Sunday, with an additional afternoon show at weekends. Children under six are not admitted.

The planetarium complex also contains an observatory that is used by members of the public, by prior arrangement, to view the day or night sky.

Outside again, there are many picnic and barbecue areas at Mt Coot-tha, including a particularly attractive spot for walks at the J.C. Slaughter Falls. The Mount Coot-tha Summit Restaurant on Sir Samuel Griffith Drive is open daily for lunches and morning and afternoon teas, and visitors can dine at the Mount Coot-tha Lookout. The view from the summit is superb, across the city and Moreton Bay, and sometimes as far as the Lamington Plateau in the south and the Glass House Mountains in the north.

Perhaps the best view of all from Mt Coot-tha is at night when the lights of the city of Brisbane are spread out before you—a breathtaking sight. Even if you have only one evening in Brisbane, it is worth making the short trip to the lookout to take in this memorable scene.

Botanic Gardens

Queensland artists, and the New Central Galleries, the Town Gallery, the Don McInnes Galleries, Barry's Gallery and two Aboriginal galleries in the city proper. The Potter's Gallery in Fortitude Valley has pottery by local artists for sale. The **Leichhardt Street** area of Spring Hill has developed as a centre for arts and crafts enthusiasts.

Brisbane's annual Warana Festival, a feast of art, craft and cultural activities, occurs in September. Also held annually are the Royal National Exhibition (in August) at Herston and the Spring Hill Fair (usually on the second weekend in September) in the streets of Spring Hill. The Biennial International Festival of Music begins in late May in odd-numbered years. The Brisbane International Film Festival is held Aug.–Sept and the Queensland Winter Racing Carnival—sport, racing, and visual and performing arts—spans May and June.

Queensland University is on a superb site on the river at St Lucia. It is built mainly from Helidon freestone. A second university, **Griffith**, is in beautiful bush country in the southern suburb of Nathan. **Queensland University of Technology** is on several campuses throughout Brisbane. The present **Government House** at Bardon was built in 1865 for Johann Heussler, who brought German farm-workers to the State, and it became the official residence in 1920.

The old **Queensland Museum** is an ornate building on the corner of Bowen Bridge Road and Gregory Terrace. The main **Post Office** in Queen Street has a museum of telegraphic material. The **Queensland Maritime Museum** in Stanley Street, South Brisbane, incorporates the old South Brisbane dry dock. Nearby are the newly developed **Riverside Esplanade** walking and bicycle paths leading to Kangaroo Point, with access to picnic areas.

The city **Botanic Gardens** next to Parliament House are magnificent. New Farm Park, which is close to the city via the Valley, has 12 000 rose bushes, jacaranda trees that blossom in October and November, and poinciana trees flowering in November and December.

Self-guide leaflets outlining details of **Heritage Trails** within the city and suburbs, and a booklet listing a wide choice of attractions and eating-places are available from the **Brisbane Visitors and Convention Bureau** on the ground floor of the City Hall in King George

Story Bridge

Square, or the Queen St Mall Information Booth.

Brisbane is famous for its seafood, and several good restaurants allow you the opportunity to come to grips with the awesome Queensland mudcrab, Moreton Bay bugs, tiger prawns and delicious reef fish and barramundi. Popular venues are Pier Nine Oyster Bar and Restaurant at Eagle Street Pier; Michael's Riverside Restaurant at the Riverside Centre in Eagle Street; Rumpoles in Turbot Street; Muddie's in Edward Street; the Milano Italian Restaurant in the Queen Street Mall; Oxley's Wharf Restaurant on the river at **Milton**; and the exotic Cat's Tango in St Lucia. Chinatown in **Fortitude Valley** offers distinctive shopping and dining.

Because of its vast size (the Brisbane City Council controls an area of 12 200 hectares), the city's public transport network is extensive. Council buses take most of the load, while modern electric air-conditioned trains run to many areas. An excellent pocket map is produced by the Metropolitan Transit Authority. Small ferries operate from the city to **Kangaroo Point**, **East Brisbane** and **New Farm Park**. Golden Mile operates river and bay cruises from North Quay, and Mirimar Cruises offer cruises to **Lone Pine Koala Sanctuary**. The City Ferry Cruise, operated by the Brisbane City Council, leaves the Edward Street ferry terminal near the Botanic Gardens, travelling downstream to **Breakfast Creek** and upstream to Queensland University. The paddlewheeler *Kookaburra Queen* cruises the river daily and is a good place to dine.

There is plenty of accommodation in and near Brisbane, together with a number of caravan parks within easy reach of

the central city area.

Several of Brisbane's attractions lie just outside the city area. Views from the surrounding hills are good, particularly from Bartley's Hill Lookout at **Hamilton**. The Historical Observation Tower at the Boardwalk in **Newstead**, a 33-metre tower, affords outstanding city views. The *Southern Cross*, Sir Charles Kingsford Smith's Fokker tri-motor aircraft, is on display at **Brisbane Airport** in Airport Drive. Just across the river is **Fort Lytton**, a garrison built in 1880 and opened to visitors in 1989. Brisbane's famous Lone Pine Koala Sanctuary, with its koalas and other fauna, is 11 kilometres away at **Fig Tree Pocket**. Samford Alpine Adventureland at **Samford**, 21 kilometres from the city, offers grass-skiing, a 700-metre bobsled, and swimming and picnic areas. Amazons Aquatic Adventureland at **Jindalee**, 12 kilometres from the city, has family water-slide entertainment and picnic areas. Bunya Wildlife Sanctuary Park, 14 kilometres north at **Cash's Crossing**, has a wildlife sanctuary, World Koala Research Station and picnic and barbecue facilities. Brisbane Forest Park at **The Gap**, 12 kilometres from the city, provides 'bushranger' and wildlife tours in its 25 000 hectares of bushland. Tours of the Castlemaine Perkins brewery are available.

The **Australian Woolshed**, fourteen kilometres north-west of the city, features trained rams, sheep-shearing demonstrations and tame koalas and kangaroos.

For further information on Brisbane, contact the Brisbane Visitors and Convention Bureau, City Hall, King George Square; (07) 3221 8411, or visit the BVCB Information Booth in the Queen Street Mall.

Tours from Brisbane

There is a variety of things to see and do around Brisbane. Most tours can be done in one day, but some are more suited to an overnight stop.

The Brisbane forest parks concept is being developed as breathing space for the city, and many new national parks have been declared in the surrounding area. As well as visiting the beaches, take advantage of these parks—they are well worth a visit.

Redcliffe, 34 km from Brisbane via Gympie Road
Drive to Redcliffe via Petrie and a detour to the North Pine Dam. The Redcliffe Peninsula is almost completely surrounded by the waters of Moreton Bay. The sandy beaches are safe for swimming and the fishing is good. High on the volcanic red cliffs there are spectacular views far across Moreton Bay to Moreton and Stradbroke Islands, famous for their natural surroundings and mountainous sand dunes. The Redcliffe jetty is a favourite spot for local anglers. **See also:** Entry in A–Z listing.

Bribie Island, 47 km from Brisbane via Bruce Hwy
See: Other Islands

Wynnum–Manly and Redland Bay, 35 km from Brisbane via Routes 23, 30 and 44
You will not have to drive far to enjoy the bayside suburbs of Wynnum and Manly, south-east of Brisbane on the shores of Moreton Bay. Manly has five marinas and is the headquarters of the Royal Queensland Yacht Squadron. There is a golf course at Wynnum, and other sporting facilities. Continue on to Redland Bay, a peaceful tourist resort. The area is famed for its market gardens and the Strawberry Festival (on the first Saturday of each September). Wayside stalls sell fruit and flowers at weekends. Boats can be hired all along this coast, so that you can do your own exploring, go fishing or visit the islands of Moreton Bay. **See also:** Entry in A–Z listing.

The Gold Coast, 70 km from Brisbane via the Pacific and Gold Coast Highways
See: City of the Gold Coast.

Gold Coast Hinterland, about 100 km from Brisbane via the Pacific Highway and Nerang
If possibly you are bored by the Gold Coast, simply drive west. The nearby McPherson Ranges have some of Australia's finest scenery: rainforest, deep ravines, waterfalls, and a spectacular view of the coast.

Mount Tamborine, 70 km from Brisbane via the Pacific Highway
Mount Tamborine, some 30 kilometres from Oxenford, is a retreat from the bustle of Brisbane. Here walking tracks lead through the rainforest, where palms, staghorns, elkhorns, ferns and orchids grow in profusion, to waterfalls and lookouts. There are picnic and barbecue facilities here and in the nearby Joalah, Knoll and Palm Grove National Parks. **See also:** National Parks.

O'Reilly's Guest House, Lamington National Park, 112 km from Brisbane via the Mt Lindesay or Pacific Highways and Canungra
Lamington National Park is one of the wildest and finest in Queensland. On a plateau at the top is O'Reilly's Guest House, and it is worth making this a full weekend's trip, though an advance booking should be made. A maze of walking tracks and an elevated treetop walkway allow you to see the area's many attractions. But if walking is not for you, you can just sit in the sun, breathe in the refreshing mountain air and admire the superb scenery or feed the birds. The subtropical rainforest has an abundance of wildlife, which has been protected for many years. Information on the area is available at the tourist information centre in Canungra or from the ranger at O'Reilly's. **See also:** National Parks.

Binna Burra, Lamington National Park, 108 km from Brisbane via the Mt Lindesay or Pacific Highways and Canungra
If you choose to walk from O'Reilly's to Binna Burra Lodge it is a distance of some 22 kilometres. It is a much longer trip by road. Binna Burra Lodge is a good centre from which to enjoy the great variety of walks in the area, but a sensible pair of shoes is a must. Bring a jumper too—it can get cold even in summer. If you plan to spend a weekend wilderness camping in the mountains, a permit is necessary and can be obtained from the Chief Ranger at Binna Burra. Information is available in Canungra about the many walks and places of interest on the way. Those who prefer more comforts can stay overnight at the Binna Burra Lodge, but book in advance. **See also:** National Parks.

Toowoomba, 127 km from Brisbane via the Warrego Highway
A comfortable distance from Brisbane for a day trip, this drive takes you past some small towns and old farmhouses. Stop at Marburg on the way to admire the old timber pub with its latticed verandah. Toowoomba's most popular tourist attraction is its parks and gardens, with a touch of England in the magnificent oaks, elms, plane trees and poplars. The gardens are best seen during September

when the city has its Carnival of Flowers. The carnival is usually held during the last week of September, and includes a procession, dancing and entertainment in the streets. The Blue Arrow Drive around the city, laid out by the city council, is a must for the visitors. You could return to Brisbane via the New England and Cunningham Highways. **See also:** Entry in A–Z listing.

The Jondaryan Woolshed Historical Museum and Park, 176 km from Brisbane via the Warrego Highway

The Jondaryan Woolshed, between Oakey and Bowenville, was built in 1859, with space for eighty-eight blade shearers to handle some 200 000 sheep a season. Now an ideal outing for all the family, it has been developed as a working memorial to the early pastoral pioneers. As well as the Woolshed, see the blacksmith's shop, the one-roomed schoolhouse, and the dairy. There is also a fascinating collection of old agricultural machinery. Open every day except Good Friday and Christmas Day; conducted tours operate daily.

The Bunya Mountains, 250 km from Brisbane via the Warrego and Brisbane Valley Highways

This three-hour drive is often spectacular, but hairpin bends make the journey unsuitable for cars towing caravans or trailers. Because there is so much to see along the way, it would be wise to stay overnight either camping or at a hotel. On the way, Savages Crossing is a good place for a picnic, and Bellevue Homestead at Coominya is worth a detour. A major National Trust project, the homestead has been moved from its original site and rebuilding and restoration is continuing. Further on, stop to see the Koomba Falls and King House at Maidenwell. There are many more places to visit on the way to the mountains and all are fully signposted. Most of the area is set aside as the Bunya Mountains National Park; there are two major camping sites in the park. Bushwalkers will enjoy the excellent graded tracks. If you have time and do not want to camp, continue on to Kingaroy, the peanut-growing area, where there is plenty of accommodation. **See also:** National Parks.

Mt Glorious, 40 km from Brisbane via Waterworks Road

One of the more interesting short drives from Brisbane through mountainous country due west of the city is to Mt Glorious, via Mt Nebo, and then back via Samford. From Mt Glorious it is possible to extend this drive to take in the delights of Lake Wivenhoe, only 15 kilometres further on. Spectacular views of the mountainous Brisbane Forest Park. Stop at McPhee's and Jolly's Lookouts before arriving at the pretty town of Mount Nebo. Hear bellbirds and whipbirds in the Manorina National Park. In the Maiala National Park at Mt Glorious there are many well-documented short and long walks through the lush rainforest. At the information centre for the Brisbane Forest Park (60 Mt Nebo Rd, The Gap; (07) 3300 4855), you can see exhibits of Queensland's native freshwater fish at the Walkabout Creek aquatic study centre, and then dine in the restaurant upstairs.

The Sunshine Coast, 100 km from Brisbane to its nearest point via the Bruce Highway

See: Sunshine Coast.

Beerwah and Buderim past the Glass House Mountains, 100 km from Brisbane via the Bruce Highway and the Glass House Mountains Tourist Road

Travelling past the Glass House Mountains, you will see the ten spectacular trachyte peaks named by Captain Cook as he sailed up the coast in 1770. The sun shining on the rockfaces reminded him of glasshouses in his native Yorkshire. Further north from Beerwah is the Queensland Reptile and Fauna Park, reputed to be one of the best such parks in Australia. Here venomous snakes,

Gold Coast hinterland

including taipans, and lizards of all sizes, can be seen. A recent addition is the 2-hectare Crocodile Environment Park, where guided tours allow visitors to see crocodiles and alligators in their natural surroundings. Continue on through Landsborough to Buderim. Visit the Pioneer Cottage, one of Buderim's earliest houses, which retains much of its original furnishings from last century, and the art galleries and the Festive Markets. **See also:** Entries in A–Z listing.

The Big Pineapple and Sunshine Plantation, 115 kilometres from Brisbane via the Bruce Highway

Seven kilometres south of Nambour, the Sunshine Plantation is the largest and most popular tourist attraction on the Sunshine Coast. On the pleasant drive up the Bruce Highway you will pass colourful roadside stalls offering tropical fruit at prices that amaze the southern visitor.

The Big Pineapple itself is a 16-metre replica of a pineapple, with a top-floor observation deck that looks out on the plantation of tropical fruit below. Two floors of audiovisual displays tell the story of the pineapple and there is a Polynesian-style restaurant and tropical market. Ride on a sugarcane train through more than 40 hectares of pineapples, mangoes, avocados, sugar cane, and nuts and spices. The attractive animal farm is fun for children. The Nutmobile will take you to the Magic Macadamia, a giant nut replica. Here the complete process, from cracking the nut to the final product, is revealed. Admission to the Big Pineapple and the industry display is free.

Miva Station, 202 km from Brisbane, and Susan River Homestead, 284 km from Brisbane, both via the Bruce Highway

At Miva Station via Gympie you can camp in your own tent, or hire one already erected on site. Trail-riding and hayrides are popular, or go canoeing or fishing. If you are very quiet you may see a lungfish or platypus in the creek. The area is a bird and animal sanctuary. At the Susan River property, 15 km past Maryborough on the Hervey Bay road, a stay at the homestead includes full board. Here you can join in the mustering, swim in the pool, or simply feed the emus and wallabies. For further information about Station and Farm Holidays, contact the Queensland Government Travel Centre; (07) 3221 6111.

City of the Gold Coast

The Gold Coast, Australia's premier holiday destination, boasts 42 kilometres of golden, unpolluted beaches stretching from Southport in the north to Coolangatta in the south, with a lush subtropical backdrop in the Gold Coast hinterland—the 'green behind the gold'.

Only one hour's drive south of Brisbane, this international resort city offers a multitude of constructed and natural attractions, and, of course, superb surfing beaches—Main Beach, Southport, Surfers Paradise, Broadbeach, Mermaid Beach, Miami, Burleigh Heads, Tallebudgera, Palm Beach, Currumbin, Tugun, Kirra and Coolangatta.

With almost 300 days of sunshine each year—an average winter maximum of 22°C and average summer maximum of 28°C—it is no wonder the region is the country's holiday playground, attracting three million visitors annually.

Accommodation caters for all budgets, ranging from international five-star-plus hotels and resorts to hotels, motels, apartments, guest houses, caravan parks, camping grounds and backpackers' hostels. It is estimated there are more than 15 000 rooms with more than 50 000 beds available on the Gold Coast.

Sporting facilities, restaurants, shops, nightlife and entertainment, guarantee to satisfy all tastes. The Gold Coast is said to have the largest number of restaurants per square kilometre in Australia.

With its towering skyline, beachfront esplanade, glitz and glamour, Surfers Paradise is the hub of the Gold Coast, while the Gold Coast hinterland is a subtropical hideaway with seven national parks complete with massive trees, spectacular views, cascading waterfalls and bush walks only thirty minutes from the hustle and bustle of the city.

Moving west from the coastline into the hinterland, the terrain climbs steadily to 1000 metres to breathtaking scenery in the Numinbah Valley and at Springbrook. Highlights here include the 190-metre Purlingbrook Falls, and Winburra Lookout and the Hinze Dam.

In the Numinbah Valley on the southern Queensland border is the Natural Arch, a spectacular waterfall which plummets through a stone archway into a rock pool below. This is an excellent spot for picnics, barbecues and bush walks.

Mount Tamborine rainforests and Lamington National Park provide the backdrop to Beaudesert Shire. The more adventurous are easily tempted into tackling the rugged ranges and gorges of Lamington National Park, the largest preserved natural subtropical rainforest in Australia, with 160 kilometres of graded walking tracks.

The 'old-time' flavour of the hinterland has been preserved in the design of the area's buildings, some of which date back to the early 1900s.

At the southern end of the Gold Coast the bustling twin towns of Coolangatta–Tweed Heads sit on opposite headlands at the mouth of the Tweed River. Both towns are thriving holiday centres with a range of top accommodation, shopping resorts, restaurants, entertainment and tourist facilities.

At **Oxenford:** Award-winning Warner Bros Movie World, based on the famous Hollywood movie set, is a theme park and part of a fully operational movie set. Close by is Wet 'n' Wild, Australia's largest aquatic fun park.

At **Coomera:** To the north is Dreamworld, an Australiana theme park with fun rides for all the family. Nearby is the exclusive Sanctuary Cove residential resort, which incorporates the Hyatt Hotel, two golf courses and a marina. The links-style Hope Island Golf Club is one of the Gold Coast's newest international golf courses. Just south is Cable Ski World at Coombabah.

Marina Mirage resort, Southport

Beach at Coolangatta

At **Southport:** Sea World, on The Spit at Main Beach, is the largest marine park in the southern hemisphere. Its world-class attractions include performing dolphins, false killer whales, a monorail, a skyway, water-ski ballet, helicopter rides, a replica of the *Endeavour* and the Old Fort. It adjoins the Sea World Nara Resort. Also on The Spit overlooking the Broad-water is Fisherman's Wharf, a complex of specialty shops, outdoor cafes and res-taurants. The Gold Coast's major cruise boats operate from its jetties. Also along the Broadwater is Mariner's Cove with marina, shopping and restaurants and Marina Mirage, an upmarket shopping and boating complex opposite the Shera-ton Mirage Hotel. Visitors can enjoy a variety of water sports on the Broadwater, including jetskiing, sailing, windsurfing, parasailing, hovercraft rides and bungy jumping.

At **Surfers Paradise:** Attractions in-clude: Ripleys Believe It or Not Museum; Hoyts cinema complex; resort shopping; restaurants; many international hotels, among them the Gold Coast's newest five-star hotel the Marriott Surfers Paradise Resort; numerous nightclubs; and the sport of 'people watching'. Near Surfers at Bundall, the Gold Coast Arts Centre has

an art gallery, cinema and a performing arts complex. Five kilometres inland from Surfers is the award-winning Royal Pines Resort. The complex includes a 5-star hotel, convention facilities, a 27-hole golf course and a marina.

At **Broadbeach:** The Pacific Fair Shop-ping Resort is on the Nerang River, which has recently had a major facelift. Conrad Jupiters, Australia's largest casino, is linked by monorail to the Oasis Shopping Resort and the Pan Pacific Hotel. Cas-cade Park and Gardens on the Nerang River has constructed waterfalls and still-water pools, ideal for picnicking. One way to view the area is by an open-cockpit flight in a Tiger Moth plane.

At **Mermaid Beach:** A huge cinema complex is close to family restaurants and a variety of specialty restaurants.

At **Miami:** The Miami Hotel features live music and dancing, food and beer.

At **Burleigh Heads:** Burleigh Knoll En-vironmental Park, Burleigh Heads National Park and Fleay's Fauna Centre are all worth a visit.

Inland at **Mudgeeraba** are the Gold Coast War Museum, Skirmish, Movie Mili-taria and the Boomerang Farm.

At **Tallebudgera:** The Camp Eden Health Resort, Tally Valley art and craft

markets and the Playroom rock venue.

At **Currumbin:** Feed the thousands of lorikeets that flock to the Currumbin Sanc-tuary daily. The Chocolate Expo Factory is opposite. Visit Olson's Bird Gardens, Mount Cougal National Park and the Cur-rumbin Rock Pool.

At **Coolangatta:** Foyster Mall links the main street with the beachfront. The Land of Legend, a fairytale and fable exhibition, delights children. Captain Cook Memorial and Lighthouse at Point Danger.

At **Tweed Heads:** Across the border from Coolangatta, try your luck on the pokies at Twin Towns Services Club and Seagulls Rugby League Club.

For further information on the Gold Coast, contact the Gold Coast Tourism Bureau, 5th Floor, 105 Upton St, Bundall; (07) 5574 0999. There are information centres at Cavill Mall, Surfers Paradise, (075) 5538 4419, and Beach House, Marine Pde, Coolangatta, (075) 5536 7765. **See also:** Entries in A–Z listing. **Note** detailed map of the Gold Coast on page 469.

Queensland from A to Z

Airlie Beach   Pop. 2524
Since 1987 Airlie Beach has been part of
the town of Whitsunday. Centre of the
thriving Whitsunday coast, Airlie Beach
offers many eating-places, several major
resorts with all facilities, top-grade holiday accommodation and a large range
of activities and services for visitors.
Twenty kilometres from the Bruce Hwy
at Proserpine, Airlie overlooks the Whitsunday Passage and islands, and has its
own beach and marina. From Airlie and
Shute Harbour passengers can travel to
the outer reef and reef-fringed islands.
Of interest: Sept.: Fun Race. **In the
area:** Neighbouring Shute Harbour and
islands of Whitsunday Passage. Conway
National Park, 5 km SE: renowned for its
natural beauty; habitat of the rock wallaby and many species of butterfly.
Tourist information: Beach Plaza, The
Esplanade, (079) 46 6673. **Accommodation:** 1 hotel, 4 motels, 7 hostels, 6 cara./
camp. parks.
MAP REF. 476 I2

Allora   Pop. 950
North of Warwick on the Toowoomba
road, Allora is in a prime agricultural
area. **Of interest:** Historical museum,
Drayton St. April: 500 Endurance Motor
Race. **In the area:** Historic National
Trust-classified Talgai Homestead (c.
1860) 6 km W, meals, accommodation.
Goomburra State Forest and Valley, 35
km E. Main Range National Park, 50 km
E, camping and picnic areas; extensive
walking tracks through dense rainforest.
Tourist information: 49 Albion St (New
England Hwy), Warwick; (076) 61 3686.
Accommodation: Limited.
MAP REF. 466 E12, 475 L7

Aramac   Pop. 326
This small pastoral town is 67 km N of
Barcaldine. Originally called Marathon,

it was renamed by explorer William
Landsborough as an acronym of Sir Robert Ramsay Mackenzie, Colonial
Secretary in 1866 and Premier of Qld
1867–8. **Of interest:** Tramway Museum
housing old engines and rolling stock. **In
the area:** Lake Dunn, 68 km NE, swimming, fishing, birdwatching. **Tourist
information:** Shire Offices, Gordon St;
(076) 51 3311. **Accommodation:** 1 hotel,
1 cara./camp. park.
MAP REF. 476 B8, 483 P8

Atherton   Pop. 5206
Atherton is the agricultural hub of the
Atherton Tableland. This farming town is
100 km SW of Cairns on the Kennedy
Hwy and is surrounded by a patchwork
of dense rainforest that abounds in varied
birdlife and tropical vegetation. The fertile and gently undulating basalt soil and
abundant rainfall have made it the centre
of the dairy and grain-growing industries
that are still the major income-earners.
The area bounded by Atherton, Kairi and
Tolga is particularly suited to growing
tomatoes, avocados, potatoes, peanuts,

maize and other grains. **Of interest:**
Chinese Joss House and Old Post Office
Gallery, Herberton Rd. Mineralogical
Museum, Main St: constructed underground attraction comprising tunnels and
chambers and displaying minerals, gemstones, agate. June: Pro-Rodeo. **In the
area:** Atherton Tableland (surrounding
area), one of oldest land masses in Australia, provides picturesque alternative to
coast route; rainforest-fringed volcanic
crater lakes, spectacular waterfalls, fertile farmlands. Bushwalking at Halloran
Hill, 3 km E, Baldy Mountain, 10 km SW,
and Wongabel State Forest, 8 km SE. At
Tolga, 5 km N, woodworks, peanut factory, craft. Mareeba, 32 km N, tobacco
and rice area. At Herberton, 19 km SW,
Foster's Winery, Historical Village with
more than 30 restored buildings. Mt
Hypipamee National Park, 26 km S,
sheer-sided explosion crater 124 m deep.
At Malanda, 25 km SE, Malanda Falls
Environmental Park: signposted rainforest walk at edge of town. McHugh
Road Lookout, 20 km S of Malanda, panoramic views. Cruises on crater lakes,

Airlie Beach

Lakes Eacham and Barrine, in national parks 25 km E, through historic Yungaburra: crystal-clear waters, picturesque beauty, steeped in Aboriginal legend. The Curtain Fig Tree, 2.5 km S of Yungaburra, spectacular aerial roots in curtain formation. Lake Tinaroo, 15 km NE, swimming, fishing, water-skiing, sailing, houseboats. **Tourist information:** Cnr Mabel and Vernon Sts; (070) 91 4222. **Accommodation:** 5 motels, 4 cara./camp. parks. **See also:** Atherton Tableland; The Far North.
MAP REF. 473 C13, 479 K7

Ayr   Pop. 8637
This busy sugar town on the north side of the Burdekin delta is surrounded by intensively irrigated sugarcane fields, the most productive in Australia. Visitors are welcome at the Inkerman Sugar Mills during the crushing season, June–Dec. Townsville, 82 km NW, is the outlet for the bulk sugar. **Of interest:** Ayr Nature Display, Wilmington St, fine collection of butterflies and beetles. Burdekin Cultural Complex, 530-seat theatre, library, activities centre. The beautiful Cooktown orchid blooms March–Aug. Oct.: Water Festival. **In the area:** Home Hill, Ayr's sister town, on opposite side of the Burdekin River. Alva Beach, 18 km N, beach walks, birdwatching, swimming, fishing. Mt Kelly Orchids, 16 km SW, orchid displays, sales, Devonshire teas; by appt. **Tourist information:** Community Information Centre, Queen St; (077) 83 2888. **Accommodation:** 6 hotels, 6 motels, 4 caravan parks.
MAP REF. 479 O13

Babinda   Pop. 1268
A swimming-hole and picnic area known as The Boulders is a feature of interest 10 km W of this small sugar town, which is 57 km S of Cairns in the Bellenden Ker National Park. In the park are Qld's two highest mountains, Mt Bartle Frere (1611 m) and Mt Bellenden Ker (1591 m), and the Josephine Falls. **Of interest:** Deeral Cooperative, Nelson Rd, makes footwear and Aboriginal artefacts. **In the area:** Deeral, 14 km N, departure point for cruises through rainforest and the saltwater-crocodile haunts of the Mulgrave and Russell Rivers. **Tourist information:** Far North Qld Promotion Bureau, cnr Grafton and Hartley Sts, Cairns; (070) 51 3588. **Accommodation:** Limited.
MAP REF. 479 L8

Barcaldine   Pop. 1530
A pastoral and rail town, Barcaldine is 108 km E of Longreach. All the streets are named after trees. **Of interest:** Beta Farm Outback and Wildlife Centre, cnr Pine and Bauhinia Sts: mud mix slab hut, restoration of early settler's hut; old shearing sheds, incl. plant and press. Folk Museum, cnr Gidyes and Beech Sts. 'Tree of Knowledge', ghost gum in main street, meeting-place for 1891 shearers' strike, which resulted in the formation of the Australian Labor Party. Australian Workers' Heritage Centre, Ash St, landscaped area around Burnsy's Billabong, flowing bore, parkland. **In the area:** Marraroo Gallery, 1 km W, unique Qld colonial and Aboriginal contemporary works. Wondae Deer Farm, 1 km W, 10 acres of walk-through park, Kiddies Corner, reptile compound. Botanical Walk, 9 km S, through variety of bushland. North Delta Station, 32 km E, outback station at work, accommodation. Red Mountain scenic drive, 55 km E, on Richmond Hills Station; by appt. **Tourist information:** Oak St; (076) 51 1724. **Accommodation:** 6 hotels, 4 motels, 2 cara./camp. parks.
MAP REF. 476 B9, 483 P9

Bargara   Pop. 2703
This popular surf beach, 13 km E of Bundaberg, is patrolled by one of Qld's top surf clubs. Nearby beaches include Nielson Park and Kelly's. **Of interest:** Professional and amateur competitions at 18-hole golf course. **In the area:** Mon

Millaa Millaa Falls, near Atherton

Repos Environmental Park, 3 km N, largest and most accessible mainland turtle rookery in Australia; giant sea turtles come ashore to lay their eggs Nov.–Feb. In 1912 Bert Hinkler, engineering apprentice, flew to a height of 9 m in his home-made glider off Mon Repos beach, marking the start of his distinguished aviation career. **Tourist information:** Cnr Bourbong and Mulgrave Sts, Bundaberg; (071) 52 2333. **Accommodation:** 1 hotel/motel, 5 motels, 3 cara./camp. parks.
MAP REF. 477 P12

Beaudesert   Pop. 4028
Beaudesert is a major market town on the Mount Lindesay Hwy, 66 km SW of Brisbane, near the NSW border. A road west leads to the Cunningham Hwy, and the road east leads to the Gold Coast via Tamborine. The district is noted for dairying, agriculture and beef cattle. **Of interest:** Historical Museum, Brisbane St. Popular Beaudesert race meetings. Nov.–Jan.: Australian Rodeo Championships. **In the area:** Woollahra Farmworld, Gleneagle, 5 km N. Bigriggen Park, 30 km SW, and Dartington Park, 12 km S; recreation areas, picnic/barbecue facilities. Lamington National Park, 40 km S. Mt Barney National Park, 55 km SW. **Tourist information:** Historical Museum, 54 Brisbane St; (075) 41 1284. **Accommodation:** 3 hotels, 3 motels, 1 caravan park.
MAP REF. 467 L12, 475 N7

Beenleigh   Pop. 16 388
Midway between Brisbane and the Gold Coast, Beenleigh is now almost a satellite town of Brisbane. The Beenleigh Distillery on the Albert River has been producing rum from local sugar since 1884. Rocky Point Sugar Mill, 20 km E, is Australia's only privately owned mill. Easter: Brisbane to Gladstone Yacht Race. **In the area:** Coomera, 20 km S: several family attractions incl. Dreamworld family fun park, Movie World theme park, Wet 'n' Wild Water Park. **Tourist information:** Visitors and Convention Bureau, City Hall, King George Square, Brisbane, Brisbane; (07) 221 8411 **Accommodation:** 2 motels, 3 cara./camp. parks.
MAP REF. 465 P13, 467 N10, 475 N6

Biggenden   Pop. 686
This agricultural centre is set in the shadow of Mt Walsh National Park and The

Aerial view of Birdsville

Bluff, 100 km SE of Bundaberg. Sept.: Rose Festival (odd-numbered years). **In the area:** Magnetite mine, 5 km S; tours. Mt Walsh National Park, 8 km S, wilderness park popular with experienced bushwalkers. Silver Bell Novelty Farm, 2 km N on Old Coach Rd: varied buildings and collections; open by appt. Coalstoun Lakes National Park, 3 km N, protects two volcanic crater lakes. Mt Woowoonga, 20 km N, forestry reserve, bushwalking, picnic/barbecue facilities. Chowey Bridge (1905), 20 km NW, concrete arch railway bridge (1 of 2 surviving in Aust.), picnic facilities nearby. **Tourist information:** Cnr Mulgrave and Bourgong Sts, Bundaberg; (071) 52 2333. **Accommodation:** 1 hotel, 1 hotel/motel, 1 cara./camp. park. MAP REF. 475 L1

Biloela
Pop. 6200

This modern, thriving town in the fertile Callide Valley is at the crossroads of the Burnett and Dawson Hwys, 142 km S of Rockhampton. The name is Aboriginal for 'white cockatoo'. Underground water provides irrigation for lucerne, cotton and sunflower crops. **Of interest:** Greycliffe Homestead, Gladstone Rd; open by appt. Primary Industries Exhibition, Dawson Hwy, theme park, combines display of hi-tech farming techniques with scenes of rural life. Sept.: Thangool Arts Festival. **In the area:** Callide Dam, 5 km E, boating, swimming. Callide open-cut coal mine and power station, lookout 15 km E. Cotton Ginnery, 2 km N, tours March–July, video offseason. Lyle Semgreen Gems at Jambin, 32 km N, open by appt. Bindiggin, 47 km W at Banana, displays of dolls, bottles, rocks. Mt Scoria, 14 km S, solidified volcano core. **Tourist information:** Callide St; (079) 92 2405. **Accommodation:** 2 hotels, 6 motels, 4 cara./camp. parks. **See also:** Capricorn Region. MAP REF. 477 L11

Birdsville
Pop. 102

The well-known Birdsville Track starts here on its long path into and across SA. In the 1870s the first settlers arrived in Birdsville, nearly 2000 km by road west of Brisbane, and at the turn of the century it was a thriving settlement with 3 hotels, 3 stores, several offices and a doctor. When the toll on cattle crossing the border near the town was abolished after Federation in 1901, prosperity declined and the population diminished. **Of interest:** Museum, McDonald St, Australiana, domestic artefacts, working farm equipment. Ruins of Royal Hotel, Adelaide St, reminder of Birdsville's boom days. Birdsville Pub, also Adelaide St, comes into its own on first weekend in Sept. when Birdsville Races are held; population then swells to about 3000 and have been known to consume about 50 000 cans of beer over period of race meeting! Hotel is an important overnight stop for tourists travelling down the Track, west across the Simpson Desert (4WD country), north to Mount Isa or east to Brisbane. **Travel in this area can be hazardous, especially in wet season (approx. Oct.–March). Supplies of food and water should always be carried, as well as petrol, oil and spare parts. Check noticeboard at police station, which details local conditions, before setting out. See also: Outback Motoring.** The famous Flynn of the Inland founded the first Australian Inland Mission at Birdsville and there is still a well-equipped medical outpost, run by Frontier Services, in the town. Birdsville's water comes from a 1219 m-deep artesian bore, one of the hottest in Qld. The water comes from the ground almost at boiling point and four cooling ponds bring it to a safe temperature. Electricity is supplied by two diesel-run generators. **In the area:** Big Red, 40 km W, biggest sand dune in the Western Desert. **Tourist information:** Brooklands Store, Arthur St; (076) 56 3241. **Accommodation:** 1 hotel/motel, 1 cara./camp. park. **See also:** The Channel Country. MAP REF. 293 M1, 484 D2

Blackall
Pop. 1578

Centre of some of the most productive sheep and cattle country in central Qld, Blackall has many cattle studs in its vicinity. In 1892 the legendary Jackie Howe set the almost unbelievable record of shearing 321 sheep with blade shears in less than 8 hours, at Alice Downs Station, 25 km N. Blackall sank the first artesian bore in Qld in 1885. **Of interest:** Jackie Howe statue, junct. Short and Shamrock Sts. Petrified tree stump, millions of years old. June: Race meeting. **In the area:** Steam-driven Blackall Wool Scour (1906), 4 km N, on Clematis St; under restoration. Idalia National Park, 100 km SW; habitat of rare yellow-footed rock wallaby. **Tourist information:** Short St; (076) 57 4637. **Accommodation:** 4 hotels, 2 motels, 1 cara./camp. park. MAP REF. 476 C11, 483 P11

Blackwater
Pop. 6760

This major mining town is 190 km W of Rockhampton on the Capricorn Hwy. The name comes from the discolouration of the local waterholes caused by ti-trees. Coal mined in the area is railed to Gladstone for use at the power station before export. The town's population is made up of workers of many nationalities and it displays what is claimed to be the most

Sunshine Coast

A chain of sundrenched beaches bathed by the cobalt-blue Pacific stretches from Rainbow Beach southward to Bribie Island to form Queensland's Sunshine Coast. This scenic coastal region, with its average winter temperature of 25°C, its leisurely pace and its wide variety of natural attractions and sporting facilities, offers an alternative to the more commercialised Gold Coast.

While huge waves thunder on to white sand beaches to provide year-round surfing, the calmer waters of protected beaches ensure safe swimming, boating and water-skiing. Rivers and streams alive with fish lure the angler, and forest-fringed lakes become perfect picnic spots for the family.

The Sunshine Coast is blessed with many wonders of nature. The coloured sands of Teewah in **Cooloola National Park**, between Tewantin and Rainbow Beach, rise in multi-coloured cliffs to over 200 metres. Geologists say that these sandcliffs are over 40 000 years old and claim the main colouring is either the result of oxidisation or the dye of vegetation decay. However, an Aboriginal legend relates that the colours come from a rainbow serpent killed by a boomerang when it came to the rescue of a young woman.

Another marvel of nature is the **Glass House Mountains**, formed by giant cores of long-extinct volcanoes.

The **Noosa** area, at the northern end of the region, has facilities for fishing, boating and golf. Poised on the edge of Laguna Bay is the resort area of **Noosa Heads**, with its 430-hectare national park. This coastal park contains a network of walking tracks that wind through rainforests, giving spectacular ocean views of such unusual rock formations as Hell's Gates, Paradise Caves, Lion's Rock, Devil's Kitchen and Witches' Cauldron. The park also houses an animal sanctuary and there are coastal lakes inhabited by elegant black swans, pelicans, ducks and cranes.

The southernmost town of the Sunshine Coast is **Caloundra**, 'the beautiful place', where Aborigines once came down from the hills to feast on seafood.

The hinterland of the Sunshine Coast is like a huge cultivated garden, covered with pineapples, sugarcane, ginger and citrus, dotted with dairy farms and enclosing within its folds cascading waterfalls, lush rainforests and bubbling streams. Looming majestically behind this garden of plenty is the **Blackall Range**, a world apart with art and craft galleries, Devonshire tea places, comfortable pubs and a feeling of 'olde England'. The scenic drive through the towns of Mapleton, Flaxton, Montville and Maleny is one of the best in south-east Queensland. The **Kondalilla National Park** and **Mapleton Falls National Park** are a must for nature lovers. Kondalilla, an Aboriginal word meaning 'rushing waters', is apt, as the park has an 80-metre waterfall that drops into a valley of rainforest. The Mapleton Hotel offers authentic country-pub hospitality with panoramas from the traditional Queensland verandah. Visit the miniature English village with its castles, churches, thatched cottages and inns. A number of art and craft cottages surround Montville's Village Green. Take in the view from the picture window at the De'Lisle Gallery while being surrounded by works of art from the Sunshine Coast's best artists. Mary Cairncross Park, at the southern end of the range, gives breathtaking views of the coast and the Glass House Mountains. **Nambour** is conveniently located, just off the Bruce Highway, for trips to the mountains of the Blackall Range or to the beach.

The Sunshine Coast has accommodation to suit all tastes and budgets, from beachfront caravan parks through to luxury 5-star international motels. And if you enjoy dining out, there are dozens of fine restaurants where you can indulge your tastebuds.

For more information on the Sunshine Coast, contact Tourism Sunshine Coast Ltd, 126 Alexandra Pde, Alexandra Headland; (008) 07 2041. **See also:** Individual town entries in A–Z listing. **Note** detailed map of Sunshine Coast on page 470.

Glass House Mountains

Lake Moogerah, near Boonah

varied collection of national flags this side of the United Nations. Cattle is the traditional industry. **Of interest:** Tours of Utah coal mine, bookings necessary. **In the area:** Expedition Range (732 m), at Springsure, 139 km SW, discovered by Ludwig Leichhardt. Blackdown Tableland National Park, 50 km SE, picnic/barbecue facilities at Horseshoe Lookout and Mimosa Creek camping area. **Tourist information:** Clermont St, Emerald; (079) 82 4142. **Accommodation:** 3 motels, 2 cara./camp. parks. **See also:** The Capricorn Region.
MAP REF. 476 I9

Boonah   Pop. 2100

Eighty-six km SW of Brisbane between Warwick and Ipswich, Boonah is the main town in the Fassifern district, a highly productive agricultural and pastoral area. Its location was noted as a 'beautiful vale' by the colonial administrator and explorer Captain Logan in 1827, and by the explorer Allan Cunningham in 1828. **Of interest:** Sept.: Fassifern German Festival. **In the area:** Templin Historical Village, 5 km N; Sun.–Thurs. 9.30–3.30. Fassifern Valley National Park, 12 km W. Lake Moogerah, 20 km SW, for water sports. The Scenic Rim, ring of mountains bordering shire: scenic drives, bushwalking, trail-riding, rock-climbing, skydiving, water sports, picnic spots, recreation facilities, camping, accommodation. Coochin Coochin, historic homestead, 14 km S; not open to public. **Tourist information:** Shire Offices, High St; (074) 63 1599. **Accommodation:** 2 hotels, 1 motel, 1 cara./camp. park.
MAP REF. 467 J12, 475 M7

Boulia   Pop. 281

Situated on the Burke River, 365 km W of Winton, 305 km S of Mt Isa and 200 km E of the NT border, Boulia is the capital of the Channel Country. **Of interest:** Stone Cottage Museum (1880s), Pituri St, town's oldest house, Aboriginal artefacts, historic relics of region. The Red Stump in main street warns travellers of dangers of Simpson Desert. Artificial 'Min Min' light, Herbert St. Koree Yuppiree Tree, near Boulia State School, thought to be last known corroboree tree of Pitta Pitta tribe. Varied birdlife around river. Golf, swimming. Aug.: Boulia Rodeo and Gymkhana. **In the area:** Mysterious Min Min light, first reportedly sighted near ruins of Min Min Hotel (130 km E), has been seen within 24 km of town. Wills Creek, to north, another reminder in area of ill-fated explorers Burke and Wills. **Travel by road in wet season not possible. See:** Outback Motoring. **Tourist information:** Shire Offices, Herbert St; (077) 46 3188. **Accommodation:** 1 hotel/motel, 1 cara./camp park. **See also:** The Channel Country.
MAP REF. 482 F8

Bowen   Pop. 8312

A relaxed town exactly halfway between Mackay and Townsville, Bowen was named after Qld's first Governor. The town was established in 1861 on the shores of Port Denison and was the first settlement in North Qld. It boasts an excellent climate with an average of 8 hours' sunshine daily. Bowen is famous for its tomatoes, and particularly for its mangoes (in season Nov.–Jan.). **Of interest:** Signposted Golden Arrow tourist route starts at Salt Works, Don St. Historical murals in Powell, Herbert and George Sts. Historical Museum, Gordon St. Aug.: Art, Craft and Orchid Expo. Oct.: Coral Coast Festival. **In the area:** Excellent small bays within 7 km of town; fishing, snorkelling, swimming. At Delta, 7 km N, coffee plantation. Collinsville coal mines, 92 km SW. Day trips to resort on Stone Island. Boat racing, charter fishing, diving. **Tourist information:** Council Offices, 67 Herbert St; (077) 86 1866. **Accommodation:** 3 hotels, 5 motels, 7 cara./camp. parks.
MAP REF. 476 H1

Buderim   Pop. 7499

Buderim is a delightful town just inland from the Sunshine Coast, high on the fertile red soil of Buderim Mountain, between the Bruce Hwy and Mooloolaba on the coast. It is a popular residential and retirement area. **Of interest:** Blue Marble and Fine Art Images galleries, Burnett St. Pioneer timber cottage (1876), Ballinger Rd, one of Buderim's earliest houses; faithfully restored and retaining many original furnishings. Buderim Festive Markets, in Old Ginger Factory, Burnett St; open daily. Buderim Forest Park, Quorn Close, waterfalls, walking tracks. **In the area:** Self-guide Forest Glen–Tenawha Tourist Drive, incl. Super Bee honey factory; Forest Glen Sanctuary; and Moonshine Valley Winery, wines made from local tropical fruits. **Tourist information:** Cnr Aerodrome Rd and Sixth Ave, Maroochydore; (074) 79 1566. **Accommodation:** 2 motels, 2 cara./camp. parks.
MAP REF. 467 N1, 470 G9, 475 N4

Bundaberg   Pop. 38 074

Bundaberg, 368 km N of Brisbane, is the southernmost access point to the Great Barrier Reef and an important provincial city in the centre of the fertile Burnett River plains. The district is known for its sugar (the area's main crop), timber, beef production and, in more recent years, tomatoes, avocados and small crops. Bundaberg is a city of parks and botanical gardens; its wide streets lined with poincianas provide a brilliant display in spring. Several famous Australians have called Bundy home: aviator Bert Hinkler, in 1928 the first man to fly solo from England to Australia; singer Gladys Moncrieff; cricketer Don Tallon; and rugby league star Mal Meninga. Sugar has been grown in the area since 1866. Raw sugar is exported from an extensive storage and bulk terminal facility at Port Bundaberg, 16 km NE. Industry sidelines include the distilling of the world famous Bundaberg Rum, refined sugar production, and the manufacture and export of advanced Austoft cane-harvester equipment. **Of interest:** Alexandra Park and Zoo, Quay St, on Burnett River, cacti garden, children's playground. Bundaberg Rum Distillery, Avenue St, East Bundaberg; guided tours daily to see Famous Aussie Spirit being made. Whaling Wall, Bourbong St, whale mural. Boyd's Antiquatorium, Bourbong St, boasts best Edison Gramophone collection in Australia. Schmeider's Cooperage and Craft Centre, Alexandra St, East Bundaberg, demonstrates ancient art of barrel-making. Hinkler House Memorial Museum, Botanical Gardens, Mt Perry Rd, Nth Bundaberg, repository of aviation history. Also in Botanical Gardens: steam-train rides around lakes; Bundaberg Historical Museum. Tropical Wines and Sunny Soft Drinks, Mt Perry Rd, Nth Bundaberg, unique tropical-fruit wine. Banio's Horseriding Centre, Patterson's Rd, Nth Bundaberg, 300 acres of picturesque riverside country. Easter: Country Music Roundup. **In the area:** Unexplained

mystery, 25 km N: 35 strange craters said to be 25 million years old. Pennyroyal Herb Farm, 6 km S, snacks at Culinary Corner. Dreamtime Reptile Reserve, 8 km S on Childers Rd, educational tours. Avocado Grove, 10 km S, subtropical gardens. Bauers Gerbera Nursery, 61 km SW, near Gin Gin. Hummock Lookout, 7 km E, excellent views over city, 'patchwork quilt' of canefields and coast. Surfing beaches at Bargara–Nielson Park and Kelly's Beach (15 km E), Moore Park (21 km N) and Elliott Heads (18 km SE). Turtles at Mon Repos Environmental Park, 14 km E, Nov.–Feb. Tours to see migrating humpback whales, mid-Aug.–mid-Oct. Fishing at Burnett Heads, Elliott Heads, Bargara and Moore Park. House of Rare Bits, The Esplanade, Burnett Heads: local craft, Devonshire teas. Poseidon Seashells, Rickets Rd, Burnett Heads, coral, seashells, local shellcraft. Cruises to Lady Musgrave Island, uninhabited coral cay, on either MV *Lady Musgrave* (departs Bundaberg Port) or by seaplane with Bundaberg Seaplane Tours. Flights available to Lady Elliot Island resort, day and overnight stays. **Tourist information:** Cnr Mulgrave and Bourbong Sts; (071) 52 2333. **Accommodation:** Many hotels, 33 motels, 8 cara./camp. parks.
MAP REF. 477 P12

Burketown   Pop. 200

The centre of rich beef country, Burketown is 230 km W of Normanton. The Gulf is accessible by boat from Burketown, which is on the Albert River and on the east–west dividing line between

the wetlands to the north and the beginning of the Gulf Savannah grass plains to the south. In September and October visitors can see the meteorological phenomenon locally known as Morning Glory: a tubelike cloud formation that rolls across the sky. **Of interest:** 100-year-old bore, which issues boiling water. Burketown Pub (1860s), original customs house; oldest building in the Gulf. Burketown to Normanton telegraph line, post office and cemetery offer insights into town's historic past. Easter: World Barramundi Handline-Rod Fishing Championships. **In the area:** Original Gulf meatworks just north of town. Nicholson River wetlands, 17 km W, breeding grounds for crocodiles and variety of fish and birdlife. Escott Lodge, 17 km W, operating cattle station, camping and accommodation available. **Tourist information:** Burke Shire Council; (077) 45 5100 or Old Post Office and Museum; (077) 45 5177. **Accommodation:** 1 hotel/motel, 1 cara./camp. park. **See also:** Gulf Savannah.
MAP REF. 481 E9

Burrum Heads   Pop. 770

This pleasant holiday resort on Hervey Bay, 45 km N of Maryborough off Bruce Hwy, offers excellent fishing. **In the area:** Burrum River Wilderness National Park, near town. Woodgate National Park, 5 km N by boat, picnic spots, walking, camping. **Tourist information:** Phillips Travel, 45 Burrum St; (071) 29 5211. **Accommodation:** 1 hotel/motel, 2 cara./camp. parks.
MAP REF. 477 P13

Horseshoe Bay, near Bowen

Caboolture   Pop. 12 716

A major dairying centre just off the Bruce Hwy, 46 km N of Brisbane, Caboolture is noted for its butter, yoghurt and cheese. The area is also rich in Aboriginal history and relics. June: Agricultural Show. **In the area:** Caboolture Historical Village, 2 km N on Beeburum Rd, faithfully restored. Distinctive landmark of Glass House Mountains, 22 km N. Popular fishing resorts Donnybrook and Toorbul (20 and 22 km NE), and Beachmere on Deception Bay (13 km SE). Abbey Museum, 9 km E on road to Bribie Island, traces growth of Western civilisation. Bribie Island, 23 km E, family day trips, picnic areas, fishing, safe swimming. **Tourist information:** Shire Offices, Hasking St; (074) 95 3122. **Accommodation:** 3 hotels, 3 motels, 2 cara./camp. parks.
MAP REF. 467 M4, 475 N5

Cairns   Pop. 64 463

A modern, colourful city and capital of the tropical Far North. The cosmopolitan esplanade traces the bay foreshore and parks and gardens abound with colour and tropical trees and plants. Cairns' location is superb: the Great Barrier Reef to the east, the mountain rainforests and plains of the Atherton Tableland to the west, and palm-fringed beaches to the north and south. Cairns is one of the great black marlin fishing locations and offers easy access to the Great Barrier Reef for snorkelling enthusiasts, scuba divers and visitors wishing to see the coral from glass-bottomed boats. **Of interest:** Cairns Red Explorer bus from Lake St, 9 stops and attractions in and around city. Cairns Museum, cnr Lake and Shields Sts. Big-game fishing boats moor at Marlin Marina, end of Spence St. Trinity Wharf and The Pier shopping and entertainment complex. Historical complex Freshwater Connection, also departure point for 100-year-old Kuranda Scenic Railway trip through Barron Gorge to rainforest village of Kuranda, 34 km NW. Wetland areas, incl. the Esplanade, provide opportunities for birdwatching. Flecker Botanic Gardens, Collins Ave: plants used by Aborigines; exotic trees and shrubs; 200 varieties of palms. Walking track links gardens to Centenary Lakes Parkland. Jack Barnes Bicentennial Mangrove Boardwalk, Airport St, 2 educational walks through mangroves, viewing platforms. Rusty's Bazaar, Grafton and Sheridan Sts, markets with local craft, home-made produce, plants, new and secondhand goods; open Fri. and Sat. Royal Flying Doctor Service Visitor Centre, Junction St, Edge Hill. Doll and Bear Museum, Mayers St, Manunda. July: Agricultural Show. Oct.: Fun in the Sun Festival. **In the area:** Bulk sugar terminal, Cook St, Portsmith, south of city centre, guided tours during crushing season. Sugarworld Gardens, Edmonton, 8 km S. Marlin Coast, extending from Machans Beach (10 km N) to Ellis Beach, 26 km of spectacular coastline. Holloways Beach, 11 km N, popular seaside spot. Wild World and Outback Opal Mine, 22 km N. Hartley's Creek Crocodile Farm, 40 km N. Delightful rural settings of Barron and Freshwater Valleys, north and south of Cairns; attractions include the Crystal Cascades, Barron Gorge hydro-electric power station and Copperlode Dam (Lake Morris); bushwalking, hiking, whitewater rafting, camping. Reef and islands can be explored by private charters, daily cruises and air (seaplane and helicopter). Longer cruises to resort islands and reef on catamarans *Coral Princess* and *Reef Escape*. Access to nearby Green, Fitzroy and Frankland Islands on cruise vessels. Cairns also offers easy access to wilderness areas of Cape York, Daintree and Atherton Tableland. Off-road safaris (4WD) to Cape York and Gulf Savannah. Panjinka Wilderness Lodge at Injinoo, Cape York: fishing, sailing, walking, wildlife; 4WD; contact Dept of Environment and Heritage, (070) 52 3096. **Tourist information:** Cnr Grafton and Hartley Sts; (070) 51 3588. **Accommodation:** 60 hotels, numerous motels from 5-star, international-standard hotels to family and budget; 12 cara./camp. parks. **See also:** The Far North; Cape York.
MAP REF. 472, 473 G9, 479 L6

Caloundra   Pop. 22 094

This popular holiday spot on the Sunshine Coast is 96 km N of Brisbane via a turnoff from the Bruce Hwy. The main beaches are Kings, Shelly, Moffat, Dicky, Golden and Bulcock. The main shipping channel to Brisbane is just offshore. Pumicestone Passage (State marine park) to the south, between Bribie Island and the mainland, has sheltered waters for fishing, boating, water-skiing and sailboarding. **Of interest:** Queensland Air Museum at aerodrome, Pathfinder Dr. Teddy Bear World, Bowman Rd, museum, water-slide, mini-golf. Jan.: Kabi Cook, Aboriginal cultural festival on anniversary of Captain Cook's landing. Sept.: Art and Craft Show. **In the area:** Glass House Mts, 29 km SW. Old Lighthouse, Golden Beach, 4 km S. Landborough Historical Museum, 17 km S. Queensland Reptile Park at Beerwah, 23 km S. Wreck of SS *Dicky* (1893), Dicky Beach, 4 km N. Lake and Seaside Environment Park, Currimundi, 4 km N. Opals Down Under and House of Herbs,

Rafting on Barron River, near Cairns

Bruce Hwy, 9 km N. Suncoast Crayfish Farm, off Glenview Rd, 9 km N. Aussie World and Ettamogah Pub, Bruce Hwy, 10 km N; pure *Australasian Post*. Pt Cartwright Lookout, 12 km N. **Tourist information:** Caloundra Rd; (074) 91 0202. **Accommodation:** 2 hotels, 13 motels, 12 cara./camp. parks. **See also:** Sunshine Coast.
MAP REF. 467 N2, 470 I13, 475 N4

Camooweal   Pop. 234

On the Barkly Hwy, 188 km NW of Mount Isa, Camooweal is the last Qld town before crossing the NT border, 13 km W. **Of interest:** Shire Hall (1922–3) and Freckleton's Store, both National Trust-classified. Ellen Finlay Park, picnic/barbecue areas. Cemetery; headstones tell local history. **In the area:** Camooweal Caves, in national park, 25 km S; challenge to experienced potholers. **Tourist information:** Tourism Precinct, Marian St, Mount Isa; (077) 43 7966 (Council Offices). **Accommodation:** 1 hotel, 1 motel, 1 caravan park.
MAP REF. 395 Q12, 397 Q1, 482 B1

Cannonvale   Pop. 2402

Cannonvale is the first of the three seaside resorts along the Shute Harbour road from the Proserpine turnoff, and is a suburb of the town of Whitsunday. Located 3 km from Airlie Beach, Cannonvale is fast becoming a vital centre for service and manufacturing businesses in the region. **Of interest:** Wildlife Park, Shute Harbour Rd. **In the area:** Airlie Beach and Shute Harbour, neighbouring resorts to south. Conway National Park, 10 km S. Tours to Whitsunday Islands. **Tourist information:** Beach Plaza, The Esplanade, Airlie Beach; (079) 46 6673. **Accommodation:** 1 hotel, 1 motel, 1 hostel, 3 cara./camp. park.
MAP REF. 476 I2

Cardwell   Pop. 1294

From Cardwell, 58 km N of Ingham, there are beautiful views of Rockingham Bay and many islands, incl. the well known Hinchinbrook, all of which may be visited by boat from Cardwell. Departure point for 4-day walk on Hinchinbrook Is. Local fishing and snorkelling is excellent. Channel is sheltered area for houseboats (4 for hire). Cruises daily. **Of interest:** Museum (part of library), Victoria St. National Parks Office, Victoria St, information about local national parks and Great Barrier Reef Marine Park. May:

Gold panning statue, Charters Towers

Country and Western Music Festival. June: Coral Sea Memorial. **In the area:** Scenic drives in Cardwell Forest, with spectacular coastal scenery, and Kirrama Range, 9–10 km N, on Kennedy Rd. Murray Falls in State Forest Park, 20 km NW; camping, picnic area. Dalrymple walking track, 20 km S. Houseboat and yacht hire. **Tourist information:** Hinchinbrook Travel, 13 Victoria St; (070) 66 8539. **Accommodation:** 1 hotel, 6 motels, 5 cara./camp. parks.
MAP REF. 479 L10

Charleville   Pop. 3513

Charleville marks the terminus of the Westlander rail service and is at the centre of a rich pastoral district carrying some 800 000 sheep and 100 000 cattle. Charleville's river, the Warrego, was explored by Edmund Bourke in 1847, and in 1862 William Landsborough camped nearby when searching for Burke and Wills. By the 1890s Charleville was a frontier town with its own brewery, 10 pubs and 500 registered bullock teams. Cobb & Co. had a coach-building factory here in 1893. The last coach on Australian roads ran to Surat in 1923. A monument 19 km N of the town marks the spot where Ross and Keith Smith landed with engine trouble on the first flight from London to Sydney in 1919. Amy Johnson also landed here in 1920. Qantas started flights from Charleville in

1922. The town is the heart of the Mulga Country; the mulga ('the life-giving trees') provide welcome shade and in drought are cut down for sheep fodder. **Of interest:** Historic House Museum in restored Qld National Bank building (1880), Alfred St: amazing 5-m-long 'vortex gun' used in unsuccessful rain-making experiments in 1902; Cobb & Co coach. Skywatch at Meteorological Bureau at airport: powerful telescopes outside; guided 'Adventure Through the Night Sky' in evenings. 'Weary Willie' swagman statue in main street. National Parks and Wildlife Service Research Centre, Park St. Sept.: Booga Woongaroo (mulga tree) Festival. **In the area:** Tree blazed by Landsborough in 1862, 16 km S; guide required. **Tourist information:** Town Hall Building, Wills St; (076) 54 3057. **Accommodation:** 4 hotels, 3 motels, 2 cara./camp. parks.
MAP REF. 474 A3, 485 Q3

Charters Towers   Pop. 9016

This peaceful and historic city once had a gold rush population of some 30 000. Between 1872 and 1916, Charters Towers produced ore worth 25 million pounds ($50m). On 25 December 1871 an Aboriginal boy named Jupiter made the first strike while looking for horses that had bolted during a thunderstorm. He brought some quartz back to his employer, Hugh Mosman, who rode to Ravenswood to register his claim, and the gold rush was on. The Government rewarded Mosman, who adopted and educated Jupiter. Charters Towers is 135 km inland from Townsville in hot, dry country, on the road and rail line to Mount Isa. Cattle-raising is the main industry in the Dalrymple Shire, together with citrus and grapes and another gold boom—there are 4 large goldmines open in the area. **Of interest:** Much classic Australian architecture with verandahs and lacework still remains, particularly facades in Mosman and Gill Sts. Historic homes: Ay-Ot-Lookout(1890s), Hodgkinson St, and Pffither House (1890s), Paul St. Zara Clark Museum, Mosman St, local history; open Sat. and Sun. Souvenir centre in restored Stock Exchange, Mosman St. Buckland's Hill lookout, Fraser St. May: Country Music Festival. June: Annual Vintage Car Restorers Swap Meet. **In the area:** Mount Leyshon goldmine, 24 km S. Burdekin Falls Dam, 150 km SE, camping, accommodation. Old Venus gold treatment

Gladstone Region

Gladstone is only 6 hours drive north of Brisbane and offers the closest major southern access to the Great Barrier Reef. Reef trips depart daily from Gladstone's marina and regularly from the Town of Seventeen Seventy.

With its gracious palm-studded city centre, Gladstone faces the harbour and offers accommodation ranging from international hotels to caravan parks, as well as restaurants serving the region's famous mud crabs. Gladstone, the outlet for Central Queensland's mineral and agricultural wealth, is a world-class port and one of Australia's busiest.

The hinterland west of Gladstone features national parks, rainforests and an historical village, and is ideal for trail riding, camping, walking and fishing.

South of the city and nestled in the delta of the picturesque Boyne River, **Boyne Island**, noted for its beautiful foreshore parks, is linked by a bridge to its twin beachside community, **Tannum Sands**. In an easy blend of scenery and industry, a major smelter on the island produces a quarter of Australia's aluminium output.

Further south, the **Agnes Water–Town of Seventeen Seventy** area is well-known for its natural springs, palm groves, pockets of wilderness, and rare birds, animals and plants. The beaches with their crystal-clear waters are virtually unaltered since Captain Cook landed here in 1770.

Heron Island, a world-famous coral cay resort, is on the Barrier Reef just off Gladstone. **Wilson Island**, another beautiful coral cay, offers camping holidays in comfortable seclusion. Locally based helicopters, and a host of vessels moored in the Gladstone marina, enable visits to this tropical paradise. Most of the islands are national parks and offer diverse flora, birdlife, and fish and marine life. A large charter-boat fleet departs regularly for fishing and diving trips or to take campers to the reef islands.

For further information contact Gladstone Area Promotion and Development Ltd, 56 Goondoon St, Gladstone; (079) 72 9922. **See also:** Individual town entries in A–Z listing.

Heron Island, offshore from Gladstone

battery, 5 km E; 2 guided tours daily. Ravenswood, 88 km E, small mining town. **Tourist information:** Downstairs Post Office, 15–17 Gill St; (077) 87 1280. **Accommodation:** 5 hotels, 3 hotel/motels, 6 motels,1 hostel, 3 cara./camp. parks. **See also:** The Far North. MAP REF. 476 D1, 483 R1

Childers
Pop. 1473

Childers is a picturesque sugar town, 53 km S of Bundaberg. Much of it was destroyed by fire in 1902; today it is a National Trust Town. **Of interest:** Historic Childers, self-guide town walk taking in many historic buildings: Old Butcher's Shop (1896), North St; Grand Hotel and Federal Hotel, Churchill St; Royal Hotel, Randall St; Gaydon's Building (1894), Churchill St, now Pharmaceutical Museum, art gallery and tourist centre; and Historic Complex, Taylor St, incl. school, cottage, locomotive. May: Agricultural Show. **In the area:** Woodgate National Park, 45 km E, accommodation. Cane Cutters' Cottage, Apple Tree Creek, 5 km N, craft, Devonshire teas. Isis Central Sugar Mill, Cordalba, 10 km N; tours July–Nov. **Tourist information:** Pharmaceutical Museum, Churchill St; (071) 26 1994. **Accommodation:** 4 hotels, 4 motels, 1 hostel, 2 cara./camp. parks. MAP REF. 475 M1, 477 P13

Chillagoe
Pop. 502

Chillagoe, once a thriving town where copper, silver, lead, gold and wolfram were mined, is now a small outback town where the recent development of tourism, international-standard marble mines and the Red Dome goldmine have returned the town to some of its former glory. **Of interest:** Local museum gives glimpse of history of town, with relics of old mining days on display. **In the area:** Rugged limestone outcrops in Chillagoe Mungana National Park, 8 km S, contain many magnificent caves; guided tours. **Tourist information:** Atherton Tableland Promotion Bureau, cnr Mabel & Vernon Sts, Atherton; (070) 91 4222. **Accommodation:** 1 hotel, 1 motel, 1 cara./camp. park. MAP REF. 478 I7

Chinchilla
Pop. 3152

Chinchilla is a prosperous town in the western Darling Downs, 354 km NW of Brisbane on the Warrego Hwy. Ludwig Leichhardt named the area in 1844 from

Display at the Historical Museum, Chinchilla

Jinchilla, the local Aboriginal name for cypress pines. Grain-growing is the traditional industry, as well as cattle, sheep, pigs, timber and, more recently, grapes and watermelons. **Of interest:** Chinchilla Historical Museum, Villiers St; working steam engines and 1880s slab cottage. Newman's Collection of Petrified Wood, Boyd St. Fishing on Charley's Creek and Condamine River. July: Polocrosse Carnival. **In the area:** Barakula State Forest, 40 km N, Qld's largest commercial forest. Petrified wood, fossils and gemstones fossicking near Eddington, 20 km SW, and also closer to town. Cactoblastis Hall at Boonarga, 8 km E. **Tourist information:** Tourist Centre, Warrago Hwy; (076) 68 9564. **Accommodation:** 1 hotel/motel, 3 motels, 2 cara./camp. parks. MAP REF. 474 I4

Clermont
Pop. 2727

Centre of a fertile region which breeds cattle and sheep and grows wheat, sorghum, safflower and sunflower as well as hardwood timber, Clermont is 350 km SW of Mackay, just off the Gregory Hwy. Nearby is the Blair Athol open-cut mine, the largest seam of steaming coal in the world. About 170 houses were built in 1982 in Clermont for coal workers. The town, which takes its name from Clermont in France, was established over 120 years ago (the first inland settlement in the tropics) after the discovery of gold. At first the settlement was at Copperfield, but was moved to the present site when gold was discovered. Remnants of

the gold rushes can still be seen. Jan.: Beef 'n' Beer festival. Sept.: Rodeo. **In the area:** Clermont and District Historical Museum, 4 km NW on Charters Towers Rd. Copperfield Store, 5 km S, original shop from copper-mining era, now a museum. Copperfield Chimney, 8 km SW, last remaining chimneys from copper-mining days. Theresa Creek Dam, 17 km SW, picnics, bush walks. **Tourist information:** Shire Offices, cnr Carmoo and Daintree Sts; (079) 83 1133. **Accommodation:** 4 hotel/motels, 2 motels, 1 caravan park. MAP REF. 476 G7

Cleveland
Pop. 9270

Centre of the Redland Shire, 35 km SE of Brisbane, Cleveland was nearly the capital for the new colony of Qld; however, when Governor Gipps and his official party arrived for an inspection, the tide was out and the trudge over the mudflats created a less than favourable impression. **Of interest:** Ye Olde Court House (1853), built by Francis Bigge for timber-getters; later first police station and courthouse, now restaurant. The Old Lighthouse (1864), wooden structure restored and relocated; held Australian record for length of tenancy by one attendant, fifty years by James Froy. Restored Grand View Hotel (1849), built by Francis Bigge in anticipation of influx of holidaymakers when Cleveland was named capital of Qld, later known as Bigge's Folly; main bar exhibits murals depicting historic events. Cleveland is departure point for barges and water taxis

Lakefield National Park, near Cooktown

to Nth Stradbroke and other Moreton Bay islands. July: Flinders Day. **In the area:** Ormiston House (1862), overlooking bay at Ormiston, 5 km N; its builder, Captain Louis Hope, pioneered Qld's sugar industry at this location; open Sun. 1–4, March–Nov. Whepstead Manor (1874), at Wellington Point, 7 km N, historic Queenslander; beautifully landscaped grounds; now restaurant and function centre. **Tourist information:** 152 Shore St, Cleveland; (07) 821 0057. **Accommodation:** 2 motels. MAP REF. 467 N8

Clifton   Pop. 805

Located between Toowoomba and Warwick, Clifton is the centre of a rich grain-growing and dairying area. **Of interest:** Historic buildings, incl.: Club Hotel (1889), King St; Church of St James and St John (1890s), cnr Tooth St and Mears Pl. **In the area:** Tours of peanut factory, 5 km E. Arthur Hoey Davis (Steele Rudd), author of *On Our Selection*, grew up at East Greenmount, 10 km N. Sister Kenny, remembered for her method of treating poliomyelitis, is buried at Nobby, 8 km N. Also at Nobby, Rudd's Pub (1893); has museum in part of dining room. **Tourist information:** Shire Offices, King St; (076) 97 3299. **Accommodation:** 4 hotels, 1 cara. park. MAP REF. 466 E11, 475 L7

Cloncurry   Pop. 2309

An important mining town, 124 km E of Mount Isa, Cloncurry has an interesting history. In 1861, John McKinlay of Adelaide, leading an expedition to search for Burke and Wills, reported distinctive traces of copper in the area. Six years later, pioneer pastoralist Ernest Henry discovered the first copper lodes. A rail link to Townsville was built in 1908. During World War I, Cloncurry was the centre of a copper boom and in 1916 it was the largest source of copper in Australia, with four smelters operating. After copper prices slumped following the war, pastoral industry took its place. In 1920 a new Qantas air service linked Cloncurry to Winton and in 1928 the town became the base for the famous Royal Flying Doctor Service. In 1974 a rare type of pure 22-carat gold, resembling crystallised straw, was discovered, and is now used for jewellery-making. The Cloncurry Shire is mainly cattle country, and Cloncurry is a main railhead for transporting stock. **Of interest:** John Flynn Place, Daintree St, incl. Fred McKay Art Gallery and RFDS Museum, cultural centre, outdoor theatre and Cloncurry Gardens. Cloncurry–Mary Kathleen Memorial Park, McIlwraith St: 4 buildings from abandoned town of Mary Kathleen, re-erected and used to display items of historic interest; rock, mineral and gem collection. Cloister of Plaques (RFDS memorial), Uhr St. Courthouse (1884), Shaeffe St. Afghan Cemetery, Henry St. Chinese Cemetery, Flinders Hwy. Old Qantas hangar at aerodrome, Sir Hudson Fyshe Dr. Saleyards in Sir Hudson Fyshe Dr. June: Agricultural Show. Aug.: Merry Muster Rodeo. **In the area:** Ruins of Great Australia Copper Mine, 2 km S. Alluvial gold workings at Soldiers Cap, 48 km SW. Kuridala ghost town, 88 km SE; amethyst fossicking a further 8 km, signposted. Walkabout Creek Hotel at McKinlay, 105 km SE, location for film *Crocodile Dundee*. Ruins of old goldmining town of Mount Cuthbert, 10 km from Kajabbi (77 km NW). Rotary Lookout, near Normanton Rd turnoff, Mt Isa Hwy, 2 km W. Burke and Wills cairn on Corella River, 50 km W. **Tourist information:** Cloncurry–Mary Kathleen Memorial Park, McIlwraith St; (077) 42 1361. **Accommodation:** 2 hotels, 2 motels, 1 caravan park. **See also:** Gulf Savannah. MAP REF. 482 G3

Cooktown   Pop. 1342

Captain James Cook beached the *Endeavour* here in 1770 to repair damage after running aground on a coral reef. Gold was discovered at the Palmer River in 1872 and by 1877 Cooktown was a booming, brawling gold rush port with 37 busy pubs and a transient population of some 18 000 people a year, incl. 6000 Chinese. Cooktown now has only three hotels left and the town's main industry is tourism. Located 240 km NW of Cairns, it is the departure point for Cape York Peninsula. The surrounding district has good agricultural potential and the town is also supported by prawning, fishing and tin mining. **Of interest:** Cooktown Cemetery, with graves of tutor, early immigrant and heroine Mrs Mary Watson, and the nearby Chinese Shrine to the many who died on the goldfields. Grassy Hill offers views across the reef, township and hinterland. James Cook Historical Museum (est. 1945) with collection tracing Cooktown's 2 centuries of history, incl. an anchor from the *Endeavour*. Cooktown Museum, featuring maritime history of area; also shell collection. June: Discovery Festival (long weekend), featuring re-enactment of Cook's landing. July: Laura–Cape York Aboriginal Dance Festival. **In the area:** Bicentennial National Trail (5000 km) for walkers and horse riders runs from Cooktown to Healesville in Vic. Lakefield National Park, 58 km NE: rivers, lagoons and swamps provide habitat for great variety of wildlife and are crucial area for crocodile conservation. Lizard Island, 90 km NE, resort, national park, secluded beaches. Quinkan Aboriginal Reserve near Laura, 145 km W: 100 000 hectares; guided tours of hundreds of

cave paintings, perhaps the largest Aboriginal art site in Australia, best seen May–Nov; beautiful sandstone escarpments. **Tourist information:** Far North Qld Promotion Bureau, cnr Grafton and Hartley Sts, Cairns; (070) 51 3588. **Accommodation:** 3 hotels, 6 motels, 3 cara./camp. parks. **See also:** Atherton Tableland.
MAP REF. 479 K3

Coolangatta
Pop. part of Gold Coast
Coolangatta is the most southerly of Qld's coastal towns, with its twin town of Tweed Heads across the border in NSW. Six major clubs offer international shows, poker machines, dining. At Point Danger is the Captain Cook Memorial and Lighthouse. June: Wintersun. **In the area:** Coolangatta Airport, Bilinga, services Gold Coast for domestic flights, charters, joy flights, tandem skydiving. Tom Beaston Outlook (Razorback Lookout), behind Tweed Heads, excellent views. **Tourist information:** Beach House, Marine Pde; (075) 36 7765. **Accommodation:** 3 hotels, 4 motels. **See also:** City of the Gold Coast.
MAP REF. 469 I10, 475 O7

Crows Nest
Pop. 1154
This small town, 45 km N of Toowoomba, acquired its name from Jim Crow, an Aborigine from the Kabi-Kabi tribe who once made his home in a hollow tree near what is now the police station. A memorial in Centenary Park

commemorates this. **Of interest:** Salts Antiques, Thallon St; open weekends. John French VC Memorial Library, William St. Carbethon Folk Museum and Pioneer Village, Thallon St. Oct.: Crows Nest Day; Worm Races. **In the area:** Authentic split-timber and shingle pioneer's hut north on Crows Nest–Cooyar Rd. Crows Nest Falls National Park, 6 km E (look for sign to Valley of Diamonds), walking tracks to falls, picnic and camping facilities. Ravensbourne National Park, 25 km SE. **Tourist information:** Toowoomba and Golden West Tourist Association, 541 Ruthven St, Toowoomba; (076) 39 3797. **Accommodation:** 1 motel, 1 cara./camp. park.
MAP REF. 466 F5, 475 L5

Croydon
Pop. 220
This Gulf town is 561 km SW from Cairns. Many original buildings (1887–97) have been restored to their former splendour and are a reminder of bygone days. **Of interest:** Old gaol, butcher shop, general store, hospital. Gaslights still stand on footpaths, and old courthouse and mining warden's office still have their original furnishings. Outdoor Museum, featuring a display of mining machinery from age of steam. Guided walking tours of town. Terminus of Normanton to Croydon railway. June: Rodeo. **Tourist information:** Shire Offices; (077) 45 6185. **Accommodation:** 1 hotel, 1 roadhouse, 1 cara./camp. park. **See also:** Gulf Savannah.
MAP REF. 478 E9

Cunnamulla
Pop. 1683
A western sheep town known for its friendliness and hospitality, Cunnamulla is on the Warrego River, 122 km N of the NSW border. It is the biggest wool-loading station on the Qld railway network, with some 2 million sheep in the area, plus beef cattle and Angora goats. Explorers Sir Thomas Mitchell and Edmund Kennedy were the first white visitors in 1846 and 1847, and by 1879 it had become a town with regular Cobb & Co. services. **Of interest:** In 1880 a daring but disorganised villain, Joseph Wells, held up the local bank and tried to escape with the loot, but could not find his horse. Irate locals bailed him up in a tree, demanding justice and their money back. The tree, in Stockyard St, is still a landmark. Historical Society display in Bicentennial Museum, John St; history of wool-growing district. Yupunga Tree in Centennial Park, Jane St; picnic/barbecue facilities. Aug.: Opal Festival. **In the area:** Wildflowers in spring. Varied birdlife, incl. black swans, brolgas, pelicans, eagles. Visits to shearing sheds in season. Yowah opal fields, on Paroo River, 190 km W via Eulo. **Tourist information:** Cor-dale Enterprises, 49 Jane St; (076) 55 1416. **Accommodation:** 4 hotels, 3 hotel/motels, 1 motel, 1 cara./camp. park.
MAP REF. 485 P7

Currumbin
Pop. part of Gold Coast
Situated at the mouth of the Currumbin

Rainbow lorikeets at Currumbin Sanctuary

The Great Barrier Reef

The Great Barrier Reef is a living phenomenon. Its coloured coral branches sit upon banks of limestone polyps that have been built up slowly over thousands of years from the seabed. The banks of coral are separated by channels of water, shading from the delicate green of the shallows to the deepest blue. The reef area is over 1200 kilometres long, stretching from near the coast of western Papua New Guinea to Breaksea Spit, east of Gladstone on the central Queensland coast. It is only between 15 and 20 kilometres wide in the north, but south of Cairns the reef area can extend up to 325 kilometres out to sea. The Great Barrier Reef was proclaimed a marine park in 1979 and a management programme was undertaken to balance the interests of scientists, tourists and fishing enthusiasts, and to preserve the reef for future generations. With over 700 islands scattered through the tropical sea, and the banks of reefs darkening the water, this sun-drenched, tropical paradise attracts thousands of visitors each year.

The coral presents an incredibly beautiful picture. Visitors can see it from semi-submersible vessels, which allow occupants to go underwater without getting wet, or from glass-bottomed boats; or, even better, they can swim around using snorkels or diving gear. The colours of purple, pink, yellow, white and red are intermixed and made more startling by the spectacular shapes of the coral. There are more than 340 varieties of identified coral, the most common being the staghorns, brain corals, mushroom corals, organ pipes and blue corals. Spread among these are waving fields of soft coral, colourful anemones, sea urchins and sea slugs. Shellfish of all kinds, ranging from great clams to tiny cowries, cling to the reef while shoals of brightly coloured tropical fish—among them red emperors, coral trout, sweetlip, angel-fish, parrot-fish and demoiselles—glide and dart through the coral gardens. Multitudes of seabirds nest on the islands of the reef through spring and summer.

Four island resorts, Green Island, Heron Island, Lizard Island and Lady Elliot Island, are coral cays—actually part of the reef—and at low tide it is possible to walk on the coral ledges that surround them. Other resort islands are continental islands, having once been part of the mainland, and are generally more wooded and mountainous.

The Barrier Reef is Australia's most beautiful tourist attraction, and the best way to see it is by boat. If you do not have your own yacht, and the holiday budget will not stretch to chartering one, there are many excellent cruises available through the reef and its islands. Charter boats, scuba diving and fishing trips are also available.

The resort islands off the reef and the Queensland coast offer different styles of living to suit various tastes in holidays and entertainment. Their common denominator is their beautiful setting and a consistency of climate, broken only by the sudden and short-lived downpours of the monsoonal period from December to February.

Southern Reef Islands

The Southern Reef extends offshore from Bundaberg to Rockhampton. One of the uninhabited islands, North West Island, is the largest coral cay in the Great Barrier Reef. It is the major breeding site for two species of bird—the white-capped noddy and the wedgetailed shearwater—and is also a major nesting site for the green turtle. A catamaran service to the island operates from Yeppoon.

Great Keppel Island, 48 kilometres north-east of Rockhampton, offers 30 kilometres of white, sandy beaches and unspoiled tropical island scenery. Great Keppel Island is for everyone, from families and couples to young singles.

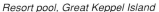

Resort pool, Great Keppel Island

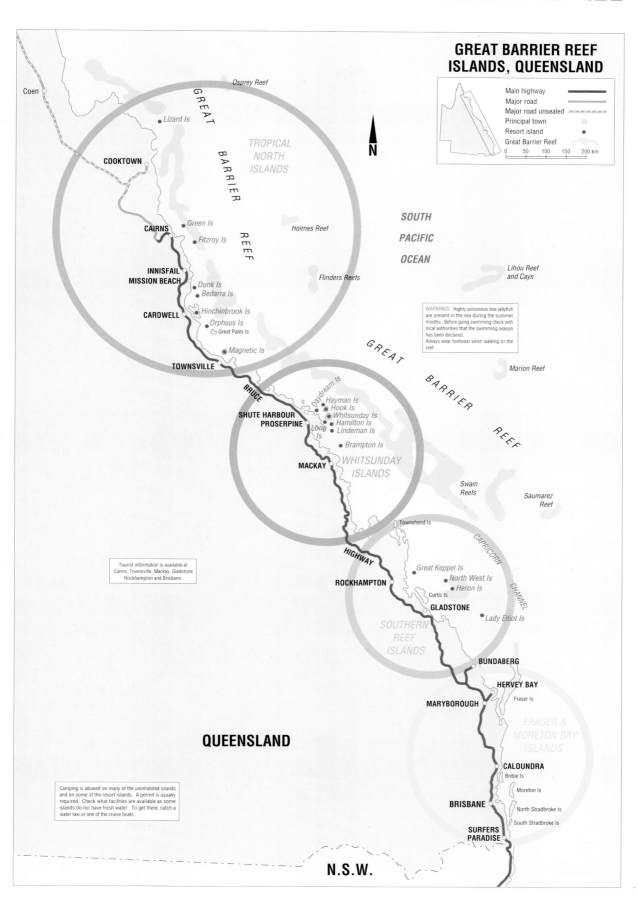

GREAT BARRIER REEF
ISLANDS, QUEENSLAND

Main highway
Major road
Major road unsealed
Principal town
Resort island
Great Barrier Reef

0   50   100   150   200 km

Coen

GREAT BARRIER REEF

Osprey Reef

Lizard Is

TROPICAL
NORTH
ISLANDS

N

COOKTOWN

CAIRNS

Green Is
Fitzroy Is

Holmes Reef

SOUTH

PACIFIC

OCEAN

Lihou Reef
and Cays

INNISFAIL
MISSION BEACH

CARDWELL

Dunk Is
Bedarra Is
Hinchinbrook Is
Orpheus Is
Great Palm Is

Flinders Reefs

WARNINGS: Highly poisonous box jellyfish
are present in the sea during the summer
months. Before going swimming check with
local authorities that the swimming season
has been declared.
Always wear footwear when walking on the
reef.

Magnetic Is

TOWNSVILLE

GREAT BARRIER REEF

Marion Reef

BRUCE

Daydream Is
Hayman Is
Hook Is
Whitsunday Is
Hamilton Is
Lindeman Is

SHUTE HARBOUR
PROSERPINE

Long
Is

Brampton Is

WHITSUNDAY
ISLANDS

MACKAY

Swain
Reefs

Saumarez
Reef

Townshend Is

HIGHWAY

Tourist information is available at
Cairns, Townsville, Mackay, Gladstone
Rockhampton and Brisbane.

ROCKHAMPTON

Great Keppel Is
North West Is
Heron Is

CAPRICORN CHANNEL

Curtis Is

GLADSTONE

Lady Elliot Is

SOUTHERN
REEF
ISLANDS

BUNDABERG

HERVEY BAY
Fraser Is

MARYBOROUGH

FRASER &
MORETON BAY
ISLANDS

QUEENSLAND

CALOUNDRA
Bribie Is

Moreton Is

Camping is allowed on many of the uninhabited islands
and on some of the resort islands. A permit is usually
required. Check what facilities are available as some
islands do not have fresh water. To get there, catch a
water taxi or one of the cruise boats.

BRISBANE

North Stradbroke Is

South Stradbroke Is

SURFERS
PARADISE

N.S.W.

The resort has accommodation for about 500 people and offers many well-organised activities: tennis, water-skiing, island safari trips, skindiving, parasailing and coral viewing. During school holidays the Keppel Kids' Klub organises games and activities. **Getting there:** Light plane from Rockhampton, or a launch from Rosslyn Bay near Yeppoon.

Heron Island is a very small, genuine coral island, 72 kilometres offshore from Gladstone. Heron is only about 1 kilometre across, with a continuous white sand beach and coral reef. It is a true coral cay with part of the reef emerging at low tide. The island has palms, pandanus, pisonia, tournefortia and she-oaks, and is world famous for its birdlife, including sea eagles, noddy terns, muttonbirds and of course herons. Over 1150 types of fish have been recorded in the lagoon. The island and reefs are a national park and wildlife sanctuary, and there is a Marine Biological Research Station. It is a mecca for divers, and scuba gear may be hired. Turtles come ashore to lay their eggs from October to March, and hatching can be seen from late December to May. The resort overlooks the island's boat harbour and accommodates about 280 people. **Getting there:** Catamaran or helicopter from Gladstone (daily services).

Lady Musgrave Island, 2¼ hours by catamaran north-north-east of Bundaberg, is a superb coral cay with a navigable lagoon 13 kilometres in circumference. An underwater observatory and tours in a glass-bottomed boat enable day trippers to see the coral and prolific sealife. The island hosts a myriad of bird-life in its gigantic pisonia trees. Turtles nest on the beaches from November to February. The island is uninhabited, but permits are available from the Marine Parks Authority for camping; numbers are limited to 50 at any one time. **Getting there:** Seaplane from Bundaberg, or by catamaran aboard MV *Lady Musgrave* from Bundaberg Port.

Lady Elliot Island, 80 kilometres northeast of Bundaberg at the southern end of the Great Barrier Reef, is a small, sand-covered coral cay. Lady Elliot is extremely popular with snorkellers and divers. Surrounded by 40 metres of deep water and yet right on the reef, the island has 10 major dive areas. As it is a coral cay, divers and snorkellers can simply walk into the water and be among the spectacular reefs in a few moments. The island is surrounded by beautiful coral gardens built by hundreds of different varieties of coral. The aquamarine depths are rich with marine life. Sighting exotic fish, giant velvety clams, green turtles, starfish and huge manta rays is normal during an underwater venture. On land, the island is becoming known as one of the most significant bird rookeries off the Australian coast, with up to 56 species of birds nesting on the island. In the summer months it is possible to see green turtles laying their eggs. The resort is low-key, with simple but comfortable accommodation for a small number of people. **Getting there:** Fixed-wing aircraft from Bundaberg Airport (25-minute flight).

Whitsunday Islands

These magnificent islands in the Whitsunday Passage include Lindeman, South Molle, Daydream, Hayman, Hook, Hamilton and Long Island. These are only the resort islands; there are over 73 uninhabited islands. Hamilton and Hayman Islands have marinas and excellent service facilities. All islands have anchorage and their own individual attractions and sporting activities.

Brampton Island is a mountainous island of 800 hectares in the Cumberland Group, 32 kilometres from Mackay and south of the major group of the Whitsundays. It is a national park and wildlife sanctuary with lush forests, palm trees and fine white beaches. The island is surrounded by coral reefs, particularly in the passage between Brampton and Carlisle Islands. The resort's world-class facilities include a golf course. The island has a beautiful resort beach overlooking neighbouring Carlisle Island. Daily activities vary from cruises to the Great Barrier Reef to water sports, weaving palm fronds, archery, snorkelling and bushwalking. **Getting there:** Light plane or launch from Mackay.

Lindeman Island, 67 kilometres north of Mackay, is another beautiful national park island. It is some 700 hectares in area and 73 other islands in the Whitsunday Group can be seen from the peak of its Mt Old-field. The island, noted for its birds and butterflies, is covered by extensive walking tracks and has seven secluded sandy beaches. The island's Club Med resort has all the benefits and services associated with that group. The island will appeal to young professionals, sporty types, nature lovers and families at every stage. The island's golf course is one of the most picturesque in Australia. **Getting there:**

Underwater Observatory, Hook Island

From Proserpine, light plane; from Hamilton Island, light plane or launch; from Shute Harbour, light plane or launch; from Mackay, light plane or launch.

Hamilton Island is 16 kilometres from Shute Harbour. The island's grazing land was transformed in the early 1980s into one of the most complex island resorts in Australia. Extensive facilities have made Hamilton almost a town on its own, with a school, banks and post office. Its 200-berth marina hosts the nation's most famous yachts, particularly during Hamilton Race Week in May each year. The resort has the largest hotel of any type in Australia, accommodating over 2000 people, and features a wide range of activities and entertainment, including facilities for windsurfing, sailing, fishing, scuba diving, parasailing, tennis and squash. There are also hot spas, a gymnasium, a fauna park and a waterside village. The catamaran *Southern Spirit* offers 7-night cruises around the Whitsundays. **Getting there:** Plane from Melbourne, Sydney, Brisbane, Cairns, Proserpine, Shute Harbour and Mackay, or launch from Shute Harbour.

Long Island is a mountainous, bushy island in the Whitsunday Group, 9 kilometres from Shute Harbour and 43 kilometres from Proserpine. Excellent walking tracks climb through the rainforest to give postcard views of the other islands. Scrub turkeys are friendly and common. Oysters are plentiful. The island is part of the Conway National Park system, one of the most beautiful waterways in the world. Long Island has three resorts. The Island Resort is a fun-filled location with an exciting range of activities in a beautiful setting. Palm Bay Hideaway Resort, the nature-lover's favourite, is 2 kilometres down the island's coast and offers peaceful, relaxed family and group accommodation as well as catering for the single visitor. Paradise Bay is ideal for the keen fisherman or families who want to get away from it all. **Getting there:** Launch or helicopter from Shute Harbour or Hamilton Island.

South Molle Island is situated in the heart of the Whitsunday Passage, 8 kilometres from Shute Harbour. The island is only 4 kilometres by 2.4 kilometres in area, lightly timbered, with numerous inlets, quiet bays, coral gardens and reefs. Walking tracks lead to the island's peaks for uninterrupted views of the Whitsunday Passage. The well-known resort accommodates about 500 people and offers a wide range of entertainment and facilities,

View from South Molle Island

including a golf course and gymnasium as well as a reef pontoon with a fish observation chamber and a platform for swimmers, snorkellers and scuba divers. **Getting there:** Launch, helicopter or seaplane from Shute Harbour.

Daydream Island, 5 kilometres from Shute Harbour, is a small island (1.2 kilometres by half a kilometre) of volcanic rock and coral. Foliage is dense and tropical, while the beaches end in spectacular coral gardens offshore. The luxurious resort, totally rebuilt in 1990, has a beautifully appointed 303-room hotel at the northern end of the island. Trips to the outer reef and other islands are available. **Getting there:** Launch or helicopter from Shute Harbour or Hamilton Island.

Hook Island is renowned for its breathtaking Underwater Observatory, a must for the visitor, where coral and other reef marine life can be seen in their natural habitat. Accommodation is in 12 bunk-style units, and there is a walking track with splendid views. The island is 90 minutes by launch from Shute Harbour and most cruises visit Hook Island. It is a perfect retreat from the hustle and bustle of city life. **Getting there:** Launch from Shute Harbour.

Hayman Island is the most northerly of the Whitsunday Group and the closest to the outer reef. There are some 80 varieties of bird in the island's tropical bushland. Hayman is a luxury resort offering lush gardens, culinary delights in six

restaurants, enjoyment and relaxation; its hotel is a member of the leading Hotels of the World group. Fishing, sightseeing trips, scenic flights or diving adventures are among the sporting and leisure activities that can be arranged. **Getting there:** Launch from Abel Point Marina, Airlie Beach or plane from Airlie Beach, Townsville, Mackay or Cairns, or direct flights from most major Australian cities; but accommodation bookings must be made first with the island.

Tropical North Islands
This group of islands is located off the north coast of Queensland between Townsville and Cooktown. Generally speaking, the Reef in this section is closer to the mainland than it is further south. The resort islands include Magnetic, Orpheus, Hinchinbrook, Bedarra, Dunk, Fitzroy, Green and Lizard.

Magnetic Island is only a 20-minute catamaran ride across Cleveland Bay from Townsville. The island is a seaside 'suburb' of Townsville, with some 2000 permanent residents. Over 2709 hectares of this 5184-hectare mountainous island is a national park and bird sanctuary, with 22 bays and excellent walking tracks. Trees are mostly pine, with she-oaks, pandanus, poincianas and banyans giving variety. Hotels and accommodation range from economy to resort. Buses and taxis operate on the island. Attractions include horseriding, Harley tours, snorkelling, parasailing, beautiful beaches and excellent fishing. **Getting there:** Vehicular ferry, catamaran or water taxi from Townsville.

Orpheus Island, a small, volcanic island surrounded by coral reefs, is 80 kilometres north of Townsville and 16 kilometres off Lucinda Point. The island is a densely wooded national park, and some 50 varieties of birds have been seen there. Turtles regularly nest on the beaches and it is the base for a giant-clam farm. There is a 5-star exclusive resort on the island. Camping permits can be obtained from National Parks and Wildlife Service, Townsville; (077) 74 1588. **Getting there:** Plane from Townsville or Cairns or charter boats from Lucinda.

Hinchinbrook Island is the largest island national park in the world; all of its 642 square kilometres are totally protected, and even insecticides are banned. There are rugged mountain ranges with thick tropical vegetation and waterfalls, which contrast with long sandy beaches and secluded coves on the eastern side. A marine research station has been set up at Cape Ferguson to study the ecology of mangroves. Permits to camp on the island may be obtained from the National Parks and Wildlife Service in Townsville or Cardwell. A small, pleasant resort at Cape Richards accommodating a maximum of 30 people offers natural, unsophisticated holidays. **Getting there:** Resort's launch collects visitors from Cardwell; includes day trips from Cardwell to mangrove areas and other points.

Bedarra Island is a very small, heavily wooded island, 6 kilometres from the mouth of the Hull River near Tully. The island is an oasis of untouched tropical beauty. There is one exclusive resort. No day visitors are permitted on the island. **Getting there:** Plane from Townsville or Cairns to Dunk Island and launch from Dunk Island.

Dunk Island, a national park 5 kilometres off the coast at Mission Beach, is one of the most popular of the resort islands. The island's resort is owned by Qantas and can accommodate 200 guests in various degrees of luxury. There are extensive walking tracks through the island's superb rainforest. More than 90 bird varieties have been identified. Butterflies and wild orchids complete the tropical picture. The writer E.J. Banfield (Beachcomber) lived on the island from 1897 to 1913, and the film *Age of Consent* was made here. **Getting there:** Plane from Townsville or Cairns, or launch from Clump Point near Mission Beach, or water taxi from South Mission Beach.

Fitzroy Island, 30 kilometres from Cairns, covers 324 hectares. The island offers magnificent native flora and fauna, secluded sandy beaches and giant clams being bred to restock the Reef. Visitors to the lighthouse are rewarded with breathtaking 360-degree panoramas. The island, once a well-kept secret of divers and boat and fish enthusiasts, now has accommodation ranging from villa-style, to bunkhouse with communal amenities. **Getting there:** Catamaran from Cairns.

Green Island, 27 kilometres from Cairns, is a coral cay surrounded by beautiful patches of reef and crested with thick tropical vegetation. The resort, rebuilt in 1994, is best known as the daily host to visitors from Cairns, who can see the reef through glass-bottomed boats and at the underwater observatory. There is a theatrette showing colour films of the reef and a display of coral and other marine and animal life. **Getting there:** Catamaran from Cairns.

Lizard Island, 95 kilometres north-east of Cooktown, caters for a small number of guests in a resort built in homestead style, facing a beautiful lagoon. The reefs around this national park are magnificent, with excellent fishing, including the famous black marlin. Big-game fishing enthusiasts descend on Lizard Island during the marlin season (September to November). The first 'tourist' was Captain James Cook in August 1770. He landed and climbed Cook's Look (359 metres) to spy out a safe passage through the reefs to the open sea. The island takes its name from the large but harmless monitor lizards he found. **Getting there:** Plane from Cairns.

For further information on the islands of the Great Barrier Reef, contact the Queensland Tourist and Travel Corporation, 36th Floor, Riverside Centre, 123 Eagle Street, Brisbane; (07) 833 5400; or any Queensland Government Travel Centre.

Arthur Bay, Magnetic Island

Other Islands

Fraser Island If you like sand, sea, sailing, fishing and plenty of peace and quiet, Fraser Island is your ideal holiday place. Fraser is the largest sand island in the world, 123 km long, and the largest island on Australia's east coast. It acts as a breakwater, protecting the coast from Bundaberg to well south of Maryborough, and forms the eastern shores of Hervey Bay. Ideal for sailing, it attracts hundreds of fishermen each year for the tailor season.

Fraser's remote and abundant sand dunes are particularly attractive to those with 4WD or beach buggies, but the island is large enough to accommodate them without upsetting the peace and quiet. Apart from its long stretches of beautiful beach, Fraser Island has a unique area of freshwater lakes and tangled rainforests. There are over 40 lakes on the island, all of them above sea level, and the dense forests surrounding them attract a wide range of bird and animal life.

An odd feature of the island is its ever-shifting creeks, which may run parallel to the ocean for several kilometres, then spill through a dune, carving a new course through the sand to the sea.

The island is accessible by air from Brisbane, Maroochydore, Maryborough, Hervey Bay or Toowoomba, or by barge from Inskip Point (Rainbow Beach) and Hervey Bay. Visitors to the island must have permits.

Kingfisher Bay Resort Village is at North White Cliffs, on the western side of the island opposite Mary River Heads.

There are 5 areas of accommodation on the ocean side of Fraser Island: at Kingfisher Bay Resort, Happy Valley, Eurong, Dilli Village and Cathedral Beach Camping Park. Korawinga Lodge at Eurong has time-share units.

Orchid Beach is at the northern end of the island, overlooking the 32-kilometre sweep of Marloo Bay and the main surf beach—a rarity on Queensland islands,

as those further north are sheltered from the surf by the Barrier Reef. All these holiday centres offer family accommodation. Day tours leave daily from Hervey Bay and Rainbow Beach.

Moreton Bay Islands

Bribie Island is a largely undeveloped island, 69 kilometres north of Brisbane, reached via a turnoff on the Bruce Highway and a 1 kilometre bridge across Pumicestone Passage. Bribie is about 31 kilometres long, the northern tip being opposite Caloundra on the Sunshine Coast. Matthew Flinders landed on the southern tip in 1799. Apart from the townships of **Bongaree** on the mainland side and **Woorim** on the surf side, little has changed. Bribie is a wildlife sanctuary, with excellent fishing, boating and crabbing. **Accommodation:** 4 motels, 6 cara./camp. parks.

Moreton Island, predominantly national park, is a remarkable wilderness island only 35 kilometres east of Brisbane. Apart from rocky headlands, the island is mostly huge sandhills, native scrub, banksias and freshwater lakes, which attract over 125 species of birds. A lighthouse at the northern tip, built in 1857, still guides shipping into Brisbane. There are few roads on the island, but cars (mostly 4WD) use the tracks and the magnificent 40 kilometre beach. Mt Tempest (280 m) is probably the highest permanent sandhill in the world. The resort of **Tangalooma** is on the leeward side and its latest attraction are the wild dolphins which come to be fed each night as soon as the tide is high enough. Other activities include sand tobogganing, water sports and bushwalking. There are several campsites in the park. Transport is by launch (1¼ hours) or air (15 minutes) from Brisbane.

North Stradbroke Island, or 'Straddie', is a 32-kilometre-long unspoiled island east of Brisbane across Moreton Bay, and noted for being the home of the Aboriginal poet and activist Oodgeroo Noonuccal (Kath Walker), who died in 1993. It is popular for fishing, patrolled surfing and weekend stays. The small settlements of **Dunwich** and **Amity Point** are on the leeward side, and **Point Lookout** is the vantage-point for watching the annual migration of whales, beginning in June, and has the only hotel on the island. Dunwich started as a quarantine station for Brisbane in 1828, and from a typhoid plague in 1850 there are some historic gravestones. Straddie is a sanctuary for many unique species of flora and fauna. The 500-hectare **Blue Lake National Park** offers walks through coastal woodland, and a variety of wildlife. Vehicular ferries sail regularly from Redland Bay and Cleveland to Dunwich; the journey takes an hour, while a taxi boat from Cleveland takes 20 minutes. **Accommodation:** 4 resorts/hotels, 4 hostels, 10 cara./camp. parks.

South Stradbroke Island was separated from North Stradbroke Island by a cyclone in 1896, and the channel between them is called Jumpinpin. South Stradbroke stretches down to Southport on the Gold Coast, the protected Broadwater being a well-used boating playground. The island is almost uninhabited. Day cruises operate from Southport. **Accommodation:** 1 resort.

For further information, contact the Queensland Tourist and Travel Corporation, 36th Floor, Riverside Centre, 123 Eagle Street, Brisbane; (07) 833 5400; or any Queensland Government Travel Centre.

Maheno *wreck, a well known landmark of Fraser Island*

Railway station, Emerald

Creek, this part of the Gold Coast has many attractions for visitors. **Of interest:** Currumbin Sanctuary, 20 ha reserve, owned by National Trust: free-ranging animals in open areas; twice-daily lorikeet feeding; walk-through rainforest aviary with pools and waterfalls; rides through sanctuary on miniature railway. Opposite: Chocolate Expo Factory; convention centre. **In the area:** Olson's Bird Gardens, Currumbin Valley, 9 km W, large landscaped aviaries in subtropical setting. Mt Cougal National Park, 22 km SW, at end of Currumbin Creek Rd, rainforest area for bushwalking, picnicking. The Land of Legend, 3 km S, thousands of dolls in fairytale settings. **Tourist information:** Beach House, Marine Pde, Coolangatta; (075) 36 7765. **Accommodation:** 1 hotel, 8 motels. **See also:** City of the Gold Coast.
MAP REF. 469 G10

Daintree   Pop. 200
This unspoilt township lies in the heart of the Daintree River catchment basin surrounded by the McDowall Ranges, 115 km NW of Cairns. The area has abundant native plant life, birds and tropical butterflies. Australia's prehistoric reptile, the estuarine crocodile, can be seen in the mangrove-lined creeks and tributaries of the Daintree River. **Of interest:** Daintree Timber Museum. Local art and craft, restaurants, a truly old-time local store. River cruises. **In the area:** Daintree Butterfly Farm, 2 km S. Wonga-Belle Orchid Garden, 17 km S, 3.5 ha of lush gardens. Daintree Rainforest Environmental

Centre, 11 km N via ferry, boardwalk through rainforest. Cape Tribulation, 35 km N, where rainforest meets reef: crystal-clear creeks and forests festooned with creepers and vines; palm trees and orchids; butterflies and cassowaries; bushwalking. Bloomfield Falls, 85 km N, via Cape Tribulation. **Tourist information:** Port Douglas and Cooktown Tourist Information Centre, 27 Macrossan St, Port Douglas; (070) 99 5599. (Also at Shop 18, Marina Mirage, Wharf St, Port Douglas.) **Accommodation:** 1 B&B, 1 cara./camp. park.
MAP REF. 473 B1, 479 K5

Dalby   Pop. 9385
Dalby is a pleasant, well planned country town at the crossroads of the Warrego, Bunya and Moonie Hwys, 84 km NW of Toowoomba on the Darling Downs. It is the centre of Australia's richest grain-growing area. Cattle, pigs and sheep add wealth to the district. **Of interest:** Dalby Pioneer Park Museum, Black St, early buildings, household and agricultural items, craft shop. Obelisk at crossing in Edward St marks spot where explorer Henry Dennis camped in 1841. Memorial cairn in Myall Creek picnic area pays homage to the cactoblastis, the Argentinian caterpillar that eradicated the dreaded prickly pear cactus in the 1920s. Dalby Cultural and Administration Centre, Drayton St, theatre, cinema, art gallery, restaurant. Oct.: Harvest Festival. **In the area:** Lake Broadwater, 29 km SW, boating and water-skiing when full. Lake Broadwater Environmental

Park, 3 km walk, birdwatch tower, picnic/barbecue facilities, camping. Bunya Mountains National Park, 60 km NE. Heritage-listed Jimbour House, 27 km N, grounds open daily except in wet weather. **Tourist information:** Thomas Jack Park, cnr Drayton and Condamine Sts; (076) 62 1066. **Accommodation:** 3 hotels, 1 hotel/motel, 5 motels, 2 cara./camp. parks. **See also:** Darling Downs.
MAP REF. 466 A4, 475 K5

Dirranbandi   Pop. 460
A small pastoral township and railhead on the Balonne River, Dirranbandi is south-west of St George, close to the NSW border. **Tourist information:** Balonne Shire Council, Victoria St, St George; (076) 25 3222. **Accommodation:** 1 motel.
MAP REF. 122 C2, 474 E8

Eidsvold   Pop. 587
The Eidsvold goldfield was extremely productive for 12 years from 1888 and remains attractive to fossickers. The district is the State's best producer of quality beef cattle. **Of interest:** Historical Museum, incl.: Knockbreak Homestead (1850s); George Schafer and Eric Schultz Collection of rocks and minerals; Noel Duncan Bottle Collection; local history section, especially goldmining. **In the area:** Waruma Dam, 48 km N via Burnett Hwy, swimming, sailing, waterskiing. **Tourist information:** Historical Museum, Mt Rose St; (071) 65 1277. **Accommodation:** 1 hotel/motel, 1 motel, 1 cara./camp. park.
MAP REF. 475 J1, 477 M13

Emerald   Pop. 6557
An attractive town, 263 km W of Rockhampton at the junction of the Capricorn and Gregory Hwys, Emerald is the hub of the Central Highlands. As well as the cattle industry, grain, oilseeds, soybeans and cotton are important. **Of interest:** Shady Moreton Bay fig trees line Clermont and Egerton Sts. National Trust-classified Railway station (1901), Clermont St. Pioneer Cottage complex, Harris St. Pastoral College, Capricorn Hwy. March: Sunflower Festival. **In the area:** Fairbairn Dam, 19 km S, picnics, water sports. Gregory coalfields, 60 km N. **Tourist information:** Clermont St, Emerald; (079) 82 4142. **Accommodation:** 3 hotels, 6 motels, 6 cara./camp. parks. **See also:** The Capricorn Region.
MAP REF. 476 H9

Emu Park
Pop. 1919

On the way to this seaside resort, 45 km NE of Rockhampton, is St Christopher's Chapel. Built by the US Army in 1943, the chapel is on the Rockhampton–Emu Park Rd, 25 km SW of the resort. Emu Park has excellent picnic spots and a safe beach. **Of interest:** Historical Museum, Hill St: King O'Malley Memorial; unusual 'singing ship' memorial to Captain Cook, who discovered the bay on voyage up east coast in May 1770; hidden organ pipes create music with sea breezes. Bell Park, on beach, picnic/barbecue facilities; markets every 4th Sun. Great Keppel Island and underwater observatory; tours daily. July: Service of Remembrance, memorial to American troops. Oct.: Octoberfest. **In the area:** Coral Life Marineland, 3 km NE at Kinka Beach. Koorana Crocodile Farm, Emu Park–Rockhampton Rd, 20 km W; boardwalk guided tours. **Tourist information:** Historical Museum, Hill St; (079) 39 6080. **Accommodation:** 2 motels, 1 cara./camp. park.
MAP REF. 477 M8

Eromanga
Pop. 90

A centre for extensive oil exploration, 103 km W of Quilpie, the refinery at Eromanga produces around 1.5 million barrels of oil a year. Named from an Aboriginal word meaning 'hot windy plain', Eromanga is reputedly the furthest town from the sea in Australia. **Of interest:** Royal Hotel, once Cobb & Co. staging post, some original 19th-century buildings. May: Race Day. **Tourist information:** Quilpie Shire Council, Brolga St, Quilpie; (076) 56 1133. **Accommodation:** 1 cara./camp. park.
MAP REF. 485 K4

Esk
Pop. 882

Esk, in the Upper Brisbane Valley, is one of the largest towns in the Esk Shire and known for its lakes and dams. **Of interest:** Numerous antique and local craft shops. July: Picnic Races. **In the area:** Somerset Dam and Lake Wivenhoe, source of Brisbane's main water supply, and Atkinson Dam—all popular swimming, fishing and boating spots. Lake Wivenhoe, 70 km NW of Brisbane, picnic/barbecue facilities, restaurant, State's main centre for championship rowing. At Cominya, 22 km SE of Esk, historic Bellevue Homestead; camel races Sept. Further north in shire, some of finest grazing country in Brisbane Valley; this is deer country, where progeny of small herd of deer presented to Qld by Queen Victoria in 1873 still roam. **Tourist information:** Shire Offices, 2 Redbank St; (074) 24 1200. **Accommodation:** 2 hotels, 3 motels, 1 cara./camp. park.
MAP REF. 466 I5, 475 M5

Eulo
Pop. 42

Once the centre for opal mining in the area, Eulo lies near the Paroo River, 64 km W of Cunnamulla. **Of interest:** Eulo Queen Hotel; owes its name to Isobel Robinson (nee Richardson), who ran the hotel and virtually reigned over the opal fields at turn of century. Eulo Date Farm, west of town; enquire at caravan park for appt. Aug.: World Lizard Racing Championships, at Paroo Lizard Race Track, next to the hotel. Destructo Cockroach Monument commemorates death of racing cockroach. **In the area:** Currawinya National Park, 100 km SW, birdwatching, fishing. **Tourist information:** Paroo Shire Hall, James St; (076) 55 2121. **Accommodation:** 1 hotel, 1 hotel/motel, 1 cara./camp. park.
MAP REF. 485 O7

Gatton
Pop. 5098

First settled in the 1840s, this agricultural town in the Lockyer Valley is midway between Ipswich and Toowoomba and 96 km W of Brisbane on the Warrego Hwy. Sawmilling, dairy cattle, small-crop farming and raising of beef cattle,

Lake Wivenhoe, near Esk

pigs and calves, are the main activities of the area, which also incl. the towns of Grantham, Helidon and Withcott. May: Heavy Horse Day. **In the area:** University of Qld Gatton Agricultural College, 5 km E, opened 1897. Helidon, 14 km W, noted for its spa water and for Helidon freestone, used in many Brisbane buildings. Grantham, 7 km SW, known for fresh fruit and vegetables; many roadside stalls offer local produce. **Tourist information:** Gatton Tourist Information Centre and Lakeside Diner, Apex Lake Dr; (074) 62 3430. **Accommodation:** 3 hotels, 1 hotel/motel, 1 motel, 3 cara./camp. parks. **See also:** Darling Downs.
MAP REF. 466 H8, 475 L9

Gayndah
Pop. 1750

Gayndah claims to be Qld's oldest town, having been founded in 1848. It is on the Burnett River and the Burnett Hwy, just over 100 km W of Maryborough. **Of interest:** Original school (1863), still in use. Several homesteads in district built in 1850s. Capper St, location for film *The Mango Tree*. Historical Museum, Simon St, includes Ban Ban Springs homestead. June: Orange Festival (odd-numbered years). **In the area:** Claude Warton Weir Recreation Area, 3 km W, fishing, picnics. Ban Ban Springs, 26 km S, natural spring, popular picnic area. **Tourist information:** Cnr Mulgrave and Bourbong Sts, Bundaberg; (071) 52 2333. **Accommodation:** 1 motel, 1 cara./camp. park.
MAP REF. 475 K1

Georgetown
Pop. 310

A town on the Gulf Developmental Road to Croydon and Normanton. Once one of many small goldmining towns on the Etheridge Goldfield. The area is now noted for its gemstones, especially agate and onyx. Georgetown is also a trans-shipping centre for beef road-trains. New Year's Day, June, Oct. and Nov.: Race meetings. **In the area:** Gemfields at Agate Creek, 95 km S, and O'Briens Creek, 129 km NE. Tallaroo hot springs, 55 km E. Undara Volcanic National Park, 129 km E. **Tourist information:** Etheridge Shire Council, St George St; (070) 62 1233. **Accommodation:** 1 hotel, 1 motel, 2 cara./camp. parks. **See also:** Gulf Savannah.
MAP REF. 478 H10

Gin Gin
Pop. 907

Some of Qld's oldest cattle properties are in the area of this pastoral town on the

Bruce Hwy, 52 km SW of Bundaberg. The district is known as Wild Scotsman Country, after James McPherson, Qld's only authentic bushranger. **Of interest:** The Residence, Mulgrave St, former police sergeant's house with district's pioneering memorabilia. **In the area:** Mystery Craters, 17 km NE, curious formation of 35 craters, about 25 million years old. Lake Monduran, 24 km NW, held back by Fred Haigh Dam, Qld's second largest: boating, picnic facilities. Currajong Gardens, 9 km S, indoor and outdoor plants incl. exotic and rare cacti. Moonara Craft Spinning, 25 km W, demonstrations from fibre to product, daily. **Tourist information:** Cnr Mulgrave and Bourbong Sts, Bundaberg; (071) 52 2333. **Accommodation:** 2 motels, 1 cara./camp. park.
MAP REF. 477 O12

Gladstone   Pop. 23 462
Matthew Flinders discovered Port Curtis, Gladstone's impressive deep-water harbour, in 1802, but it was not until the 1960s that its potential began to be utilised. As an outlet for Central Qld's mineral and agricultural wealth, Gladstone, 550 km NW of Brisbane, is now one of Australia's most prosperous seaboard cities. Its harbour is one of Australia's busiest, handling more shipping tonnage per annum than Sydney. One reason for this growth is the opening up of the almost inexhaustible coal supplies in the hinterland. Another is that the world's largest single alumina plant is at Parsons Point, operated by the multinational-backed Queensland Alumina

Limited. Millions of tonnes of bauxite from Weipa on the Gulf of Carpentaria are processed annually into millions of tonnes of alumina, the halfway stage of aluminium. Comalco has built an aluminium smelter at Boyne Island. A large power station has been built in Gladstone to supply power to the refinery and smelter, as well as feeding into the State's electricity grid. Chemical processing is a new regional industry. Gladstone's most important tourist advantage is its proximity to the southern section of the Great Barrier Reef. The city is known for its mud crabs and prawns, and has won the State Tidy Towns Competition 7 times. **Of interest:** Self-guide Gladstone Visitor Circuit, drive or walk. Historic Kullaroo House (1911), Goondoon St. Gladstone Regional Art Gallery and Museum, cnr Goondoon and Bramston Sts. Potter's Place, Dawson Hwy, art gallery, craft. Tondoon Botanic Gardens, end Glenlyon St. Barney Point Beach and Friend Park, Barney St, picnic/barbecue facilities. Reg Tanna Park, Glenlyon St, Railway Dam, picnic/barbecue facilities. Waterfall at bottom of Auckland Hill, end Auckland St; floodlit at night. Views of harbour and islands from Auckland Hill Lookout. Radar Hill Lookout, Goondoon St. Round Hill Lookout, West Gladstone. Auckland Inlet: anchorage alongside James Cook Park; finishing-line for annual Brisbane to Gladstone yacht race, highlight of 10-day Harbour Festival held Easter. **In the area:** Tours of Gladstone Power Station, north of town. Curtis Island, also north, in Gladstone Harbour, family recreation area. Port

Curtis Historical Village, 26 km SW at Calliope River. Lake Awoonga, 30 km S, picnic and camping areas, water-based recreation, walking trail, varied wildlife. Quoin Island Resort, 20 min. by ferry: fishing, swimming, live entertainment; day trippers welcome. Ferry harbour cruise, incl. lunch on Quoin Is. **Tourist information:** 56 Goondoon St; (079) 72 9922. **Accommodation:** 19 motels, 5 hotel/motels, 10 cara./camp. parks. **See also:** Gladstone Region.
MAP REF. 477 N10

Goondiwindi   Pop. 4331
This modern country town at the junction of the five highways is on the picturesque MacIntyre River, which was discovered by explorer Allan Cunningham in 1827 and forms the State border. The Aboriginal word *goonawinna* means 'resting place of the birds'. The district's thriving economy is based on cotton, wheat, beef and wool and a growing manufacturing sector. Oct.: Spring Festival; coincides with flowering of jacarandas and silky oaks. **Of interest:** Botanic Gardens of Western Woodlands (25 ha), access from Brennans Rd, 1 km NW. Statue of famous racehorse Gunsynd, the 'Goondiwindi Grey', in Apex Park, MacIntyre St. Customs House Museum, opposite park. Historic Victoria Hotel, Marshall St. Univ. of Qld Pastoral Veterinary Centre, Leichhardt Hwy (N). Tours of Bulk Grains depot and cotton gin; by appt, in season. **In the area:** Boobera Lagoon, 20 km SW into NSW, wildlife sanctuary. **Tourist information:** Watertower, McLean St; (076) 71 2653. **Accommodation:** 2 hotels, 2 hotel/motels, 7 motels, 3 cara./camp. parks. **See also:** Darling Downs.
MAP REF. 122 H2, 474 I8

Gordonvale   Pop. 2658
This town is 24 km S of Cairns. **In the area:** Gillies Hwy, with 295 bends, leads west to Atherton. Goldsborough Valley State Forest, 6 km W (15 km off Gillies Hwy), walking, swimming, canoeing, picnicking. Bellenden Ker National Park, 10 km S, spectacular views from summit of Walsh's Pyramid. The Mulgrave Rambler, 15 km steam-train ride along cane railway system through canefields and rainforest; incl. visit to spectacular orchid nursery (charter only). Hambledon Sugar Mill at Edmonton, 16 km N. **Tourist information:** Far North Queensland Promotion Bureau,

Boyne River, Gladstone

Rainbow Beach, near Gympie

cnr Grafton & Hartley Sts, Cairns; (070) 51 3588. **Accommodation:** 4 hotels, 1 cara./camp. park.
MAP REF. 473 G11, 479 L7

Gympie
Pop. 10 791
The city of Gympie started with the 'Great Australian Gold Rush' in 1867, following the discovery of gold by James Nash. The field proved extremely rich, and some 4 million ounces had been found by the time the gold petered out in the 1920s. By then dairying and agriculture were well established and Gympie continued to prosper. On the Mary River and 70 km N of Brisbane via the Bruce Hwy, Gympie is the major provincial city servicing the Cooloola region. It is an attractive city, with jacarandas, flowering silky oaks, cassias, poincianas and flame trees. **Of interest:** Woodworks Museum, Frazer Rd. Sept.: Kilkiwan Great Horse Ride. Oct.: Gold Rush Festival. **In the area:** Goldmining Museum, Brisbane Rd, 5 km S; nearby, cottage of Andrew Fisher, first Queenslander to become Prime Minister (1908). Rock pools and views at Mothar Mountain 20 km SE. Cooloola National Park, 50 km E. Peaceful fishing resort of Tin Can Bay (55 km NE), and small resort of Rainbow Beach with its coloured sands, 77 km NE, through vast pine forests. Ferry to Fraser Island operates from Inskip Point north of Rainbow Beach. Part of the Bicentennial National Trail runs through Kilkivan, 50 km NW. Goomeri, 25 km further W; known as 'clock town' because of unique memorial clock in town centre. Lake Borumba, picnics, water sports, 50 km SW in picturesque Mary Valley. Nearby Imbil Forest Drive, through pine-forest plantations. Mary Valley Scenic Way runs south between Gympie and Maleny via Kenilworth. **Tourist information:** Bruce Hwy, Lake Alford; (074) 82 5444. **Accommodation:** 12 hotels, 7 motels, 4 cara./camp. parks.
MAP REF. 475 M3

Hervey Bay
Pop. 22 205
Hervey (pronounced Harvey) Bay is the large area of water between Maryborough and Bundaberg that is protected by Fraser Island. It is a thriving city that comprises the pleasant strip of seaside resorts along its southern shore, some 34 km NE of Maryborough, incl. Gatakers Bay, Pialba, Scarness, Torquay, Urangan, Burrum Heads, Toogoom, Howard and Torbanlea. An ideal climate makes the area popular, and during the winter months there is an influx of visitors from the south. Hervey Bay is actively promoted as 'Australia's family aquatic playground'. As there is no surf, swimming is safe even for children. Fishing is the main recreation. Boats may be hired and yabbies caught for bait. **Of interest:** Hervey Bay Historical Society Museum, Zephyr St, Scarness, recalls pioneer days. In Pialba: Village Pottery, Old Maryborough Rd, open for tour of manufacturing process; Hervey Bay Tourist and Visitors Centre, Old Maryborough Rd, model village and ships, woodwork; Wide Bay Gallery, Main St, paintings; Nature World Wildlife Park, koalas, other marsupials, lorikeets, crocodiles, and other reptiles. Golf 'n' Games, Cypress St Torquay, 18-hole mini-golf, 120 m water-slide. At Urangan: cairn at Dayman Point commemorates landing by Matthew Flinders in 1799 and the 2-Force commandoes who trained there on the *Krait* in World War II; pier 1 km long, used by fishermen; Neptune's Aquarium, performing seals and sharks; Vic Hislop's Shark Show. Humpback whales visit Hervey Bay early Aug.–mid-Oct. on annual migration; viewing cruises. Day trips to Fraser Island. Sun. markets at Urangan and Nikenbar. Aug.: Whale Festival. Oct.: Hervey Bay to Fraser Island Sailboard Marathon. **In the area:** Hervey Bay Marine Park. Quiet seaside resorts at Toogoom and Burrum Heads, 15 km N. Historic Brooklyn House at Howard, 25 km W. Go-kart track, 2 km W. **Tourist information:** 63 Old Maryborough Rd, Pialba; (071) 24 4050. **Accommodation:** 4 hotel/motels, 18 motels, 20 caravan parks.
MAP REF. 475 N1, 477 Q13

Home Hill
Pop. 3197
Sister town to Ayr, Home Hill is on the south side of the Burdekin River, 84 km SE of Townsville. The towns are joined by a high-level bridge as the river is liable to flood. **Of interest:** Tours of Inkerman Sugar Mill during each crushing season (June-Dec.). Ashworth's Rock Shop and Museum; also art and craft. Nov.: Harvest Festival. **In the area:** Groper Creek, 16 km W, fishing and giant mud crabs; camping, caravan, picnic areas. **Tourist information:** Community Information Centre, Queen St, Ayr; (077) 83 2888.

430

The Far North

Sitting in a tropical garden through dusk and into lush evening, dining superbly on king prawns and Queensland mud crabs you will find it hard to believe you are at 'the end of the line'—**Port Douglas** is the most northerly of the easily accessible coastal towns of Queensland.

This is part of the continuing joy of travelling in the north, a region larger than most European countries and considered by many to be the most diversely beautiful and exciting part of Australia.

This Port Douglas scene typifies the beauty of coastal Queensland; the restaurant looks down from a forest-covered hill that looms over the small town and the 7 kilometres of ocean beach. By day the dense tropical forest is revealed in showers of coloured flowers against the intense green. The lavish rainforest and the rush of sparkling mountain streams are lasting impressions for the traveller in the north.

Cairns, 1766 kilometres from Brisbane, is the stepping-stone to a variety of sightseeing excursions. A major city for tourism, Cairns is often known as the 'capital of Far North Queensland'. Nestling beside Trinity Bay, this scenic city is an ideal base for visiting the surrounding tourist attractions. From Cairns you can relax on a launch cruise that takes you to see the wonders of the Great Barrier Reef or to explore uninhabited islands. Aerial tours from Cairns take you over the Great Plateau, with its lush tablelands and spectacular waterfalls.

Four-wheel drive tours of the region with an Aboriginal guide are available. Visitors are educated on the local Aboriginal sites, Dreamtime legends and native flora. Details are available at Port Douglas Dive Centre. Near Mission Beach, members of the Giramay Aboriginal Tribe share with visitors the beauty of the Murray Falls area, as well as their knowledge of the environment, in the Giramay Walkabout.

The pleasant climate in winter and early spring is one of the main attractions of this city. Visitors can enjoy snorkelling or other water sports, while fishermen flock to Cairns from September to December to catch the big black marlin. Cairns itself is a picturesque city. Delicate ferns, tropical shrubs and fragrant flowers thrive in the Botanical Gardens, where a walking track joins the Centenary Lakes Parkland, created in 1976 to mark the city's hundredth anniversary. Two lakes, one saltwater and the other freshwater, provide a haven for wildlife among native trees and shrubs. You can also see orchids growing to perfection in orchid nurseries, which form the basis of one of Cairns' important export industries.

There are dozens of places around Cairns, all within easy driving distance on good roads, that will claim the traveller's attention. Port Douglas is only one of them. The 60-kilometre journey from Cairns passes through a magnificent stretch of coastal scenery as the Cook Highway winds past white coral beaches, through archways of tropical forest and past the islands that dot the blue northern waters. Despite its increasing popularity with tourists, Port Douglas still retains some of its fishing-village atmosphere. The motels and holiday units are all set back from the beachfront. Just out of town is the Sheraton Mirage Resort, with 300 rooms but only 3 storeys high.

Just north of Port Douglas (and remember to stop at the cemetery that contains the graves of many pioneer settlers who were lured north by the Palmer River gold rush) is the sugar town of **Mossman**, where the cane-crushing plant can be visited from July to October. During these months sugarcane farmers once created raging fires to prepare the cane for harvesting; nowadays, however, cane is more often harvested green. These days the cane cutter is seldom seen, having exchanged his machete for a seat on an ingenious machine that cuts the cane and throws it, in a shower of short sticks, into

Bally Hooley Steam Express, Mossman

Turtle Bay, near Cairns

the hopper that trails behind. Sugar-growing is a major industry of the north, and the waving fields of cane wind through the mountains for hundreds of kilometres down the lush coastal plain.

Near Mossman is one of those perfect places that seem so plentiful in the north, the Mossman River Gorge. A short walk under the dense green canopy of the rainforest leads to the boulder-strewn river, which rushes in a series of cascades through the jungle-sided gorge. It is a place to picnic, to swim or simply to bask in the rays of the North Queensland sun.

There are many such places, particularly on the edge of the Atherton Tableland, where the mountains have thrown up fascinating geological oddities and where waterfalls spill. For example, near **Atherton** township there are two volcanic lakes, Barrine and Eacham, where walking tracks through the rainforest give beautiful water views and a chance to see the abundant wildlife—parrots, waterfowl, turtles, platypuses, goannas and many marsupials.

South-west of **Malanda** is Mt Hypipamee National Park, where visitors can walk beneath huge rainforest trees, past staghorn ferns and orchids, along Dinner Creek to the falls and up to the crater, a funnel of sheer granite walls that fall away into dark and forbidding water.

Ten kilometres away from the Malanda

Falls, where water cascades over a fern-swathed precipice into a delightful swimming pool, is the huge Curtain Fig Tree, which has resulted from a strangling fig taking over its host tree, climbing higher and higher and throwing down showers of roots to support its massive structure. There are dozens of other waterfalls in this area. Near **Millaa Millaa** is Falls Circuit, where the Millaa Millaa, Zillie, Mungalli and Elinjaa waterfalls are sited amid a magnificent panorama of rainforest mountains and plains.

There are four main highways linking the tablelands with the coast; all are magnificent scenic routes. Undoubtedly, however, the most novel and popular way of getting up to the tableland is by the scenic railway to **Kuranda**, built to serve the Herberton tin mine in the 1890s and now regarded as one of the most difficult feats of engineering in Queensland. The track climbs 300 metres in 20 kilometres to traverse the Barron Gorge, and part of it runs over a viaduct along the edge of a 200-metre precipice. The lovely old carriages of the train have rear platforms with decorative iron railings where travellers can stand and take in the superb uninterrupted view. The Kuranda railway station, festooned in tropical plants, ferns and orchids, is a much-photographed stop before the descent to Cairns.

The Atherton and Evelyn Tablelands

are areas of volcanic land at altitudes between 600 and 1000 metres, mild in climate and supporting dairying, maize and tobacco-farming. Gradually the tablelands change to dry, rough country, where tin, copper, lead and zinc was once mined. Beyond the main tableland settlement of Atherton is the fascinating mining town of **Herberton**, with its Historical Village and old houses proclaiming its boom days of the late nineteenth century.

Southward from Cairns the plain is flanked by the Walter Hill Range on the seaward side and the Bellenden Ker Range, with its superb rainforest. A turn off the highway beyond the town of Innisfail leads into the tropical holiday resort area, where many small towns nestle in the encroaching forest and peep through palms across the sand to the Barrier Reef islands. Further south is the Hinchinbrook Channel, opposite the large continental island of Hinchinbrook.

For further information on the Far North, contact the Far North Qld Promotion Bureau Ltd, cnr Grafton & Hartley Sts, Cairns; (070) 51 3588. **See also:** Individual town entries in A–Z listing. **Note** detailed map of Cairns Region on page 473.

Accommodation: 2 hotels, 1 motel, 2 cara./camp. parks.
MAP REF. 479 O13

Hughenden
Pop. 1592

An expedition led by Frederick Walker was the first to pass by this spot on the Flinders River, while searching for the Burke and Wills expedition, in 1861. Two years later a cattle station was established by Ernest Henry, and Hughenden came into existence. The town is on the Townsville–Mount Isa rail line and the Flinders Hwy, 250 km SW of Charters Towers, and is a major centre for wool and cattle produced in the Flinders Shire. **Of interest:** Explorers' Tree, Stansfield St E, on east bank of Station Creek: coolibah tree blazed by Walker, and again by William Landsborough in 1862 when he passed through the area on a second Burke and Wills expedition. Dinosaur Display Centre, Gray St, houses 14 m replica of Muttaburrasaurus, most complete dinosaur fossil found in Australia. July: Dinosaur Festival (even-numbered years). **In the area:** At Prairie, 40 km E, on Flinders Hwy: mini-museum; historical relics at Cobb & Co. Yards. Porcupine Gorge National Park, 62 km N, 'mini-Grand Canyon'. Gemstone fossicking at Cheviot Hills, 200 km N. **Tourist information:** Hughenden Shire Offices, 34 Gray St; (077) 41 1288. **Accommodation:** 1 hotel, 2 hotel/motels, 2 motels, 2 cara./camp. parks.
MAP REF. 483 N3

Ilfracombe
Pop. 350

This town, 28 km E of Longreach on the Landsborough Hwy, was developed in 1891 as a transport nucleus for Wellshot Station, the largest sheep station in the world, in terms of stock numbers, at that time; the head station was itself the size of a town. The first Qld motorised mail service departed from Ilfracombe in 1910. **Of interest:** Folk Museum. **Tourist information:** Shire, Council Office, Devon St; (076) 58 2233. **Accommodation:** 1 hotel, 1 cara./camp. park.
MAP REF. 476 A9, 483 N9

Ingham
Pop. 5075

A major sugar and sightseeing town near the waterways of the Hinchinbrook Channel, Ingham is on the Bruce Hwy, 111 km NW of Townsville. The town has a strong Italian and Spanish Basque cultural background. **Of interest:** Macknade Mill, Halifax Rd, oldest sugar

mill still operating on original site. Victoria Sugar Mill, Forrest Beach Rd largest in southern hemisphere; guided tours in crushing season, June–Nov. May: Australian-Italian Festival. Oct.: Maraka Festival. **In the area:** Herbert River Gorge National Park, 100 km NW. Wallaman Falls National Park, 51 km W, spectacular scenery, excellent camping, swimming and picnic spots, 305 m Wallaman Falls. Jourama Falls National Park, 25 km S. Mt Fox, extinct volcano, 65 km SW. Cemetery, 5 km E, interesting Italian mausoleums. Forrest Beach, 20 km E, 16 km of sandy beaches overlooking Palm Group of islands, stinger net swimming enclosures installed in summer. Taylor's Beach, 24 km NE, popular family seaside spot. Hinchinbrook and Orpheus resort islands offshore. Lucinda, 27 km NE on banks of Herbert River, base for fishing holidays. **Tourist information:** Bruce Hwy; (077) 76 5211. **Accommodation:** 7 hotels, 2 motels, 3 B&B, 1 hostel, 2 cara./camp. parks.
MAP REF. 479 M10

Inglewood
Pop. 1007

An early hostelry called Brown's Inn grew into the town of Inglewood, in the south-western corner of the Darling Downs, 108 km SW of Warwick. Beef cattle and sheep are raised, and lucerne, grain and fodder crops are irrigated from Coolmunda Dam, 20 km E, which attracts boating enthusiasts as well as many pelicans and swans. **Tourist information:** 40 High St, Texas; (076) 52 1444. **Accommodation:** 2 motels, 3 cara./camp. parks.
MAP REF. 123 J1, 475 J8

Injune
Pop. 394

This small cattle and timber town, 89 km N of Roma, is the southern gateway to the Carnarvon National Park. Explorer Ludwig Leichhardt called the region 'ruined Castle Valley'. **In the area:** Carnarvon National Park, 154 km N: major Aboriginal art sites, Art Gallery and Cathedral Cave. Spectacular sandstone scenery with gorges and escarpments. Carnarvon Gorge Oasis Lodge adjacent to park. **Tourist information:** Kookas Travel, Bowen St, Roma; (076) 22 1333. **Accommodation:** 1 hotel, 1 motel.
MAP REF. 474 F2

Innisfail
Pop. 8520

Innisfail is a prosperous, colourful town on the banks of the North and South

Johnstone Rivers, 92 km SE of Cairns. Sugar has been grown here since the early 1880s and its contribution to the area is celebrated with 9-day gala Harvest Festival held early Oct. Besides the growing of sugarcane, bananas, pawpaws and other tropical and rare fruit, beef cattle are raised, and the town has a prawn and reef fishing fleet. **Of interest:** Local history museum, Edith St. Chinese Joss House, Owen St. Cane Cutter Monument, Fitzgerald Esplanade. Warrina Lakes and Botanical Gardens, Charles St. Several lovely parks with riverside picnic facilities. July: Agricultural Show. **In the area:** Flying Fish Point and Ella Bay, 5 km N, swimming, camping. Bramston Beach, palm-fringed shoreline, 23 km N. Johnstone River Crocodile Farm, 8 km NE. Mt Bartle Frere (1611 m), 25 km NW, Qld's highest peak, track to summit. Johnstone River Gorge, via Palmerston Hwy, 18 km W, walking tracks to several waterfalls. Palmerston National Park, 30 km W; from here road leads to Atherton Tableland. Australian Sugar Museum at Mourilyan, 7 km S. Etty Bay, 15 km S, fine beach, picnic area. Innisfail is excellent base for exploration of quieter lagoons and islands (including Dunk) of Great Barrier Reef. **Tourist information:** Cassowary Coast Development Bureau, Australian Sugar Museum, Bruce Hwy, Mourilyan; (070) 63 2306. **Accommodation:** 2 hotels, 7 motels, 1 hostel, 4 cara./camp. parks.
MAP REF. 479 L8

Ipswich
Pop. 65 346

In 1827 a convict settlement was established on the Bremer River to quarry limestone and convey it down river to Brisbane for building. In 1842 the settlement, called Limestone, opened to free settlers and in 1843 it was renamed Ipswich. The town is a major industrial centre, with coalmining, earthenware works, sawmills, abattoirs and foundries. **Of interest:** 1774 heritage buildings, incl. St. Pauls Anglican Church (1859), Brisbane St; Claremont (1858), Milford St, open 1st Sun. in month; Gooloowan (1864), Quarry St; Ginn Cottage, Ginn St; and Ipswich Grammar School (1863), Burnett St. Markets, 1st Sun. in month. April: Heritage Week. July: Medieval Fair and Markets. **In the area:** Northeast: College's Crossing (7 km), Mt Crosby (12 km) and Lake Manchester (22 km), popular swimming and picnic spots. Outback Emu Farm, 6 km N. St

Atherton Tableland

The tropical Atherton Tablelands is a peaceful and productive area where small towns and farmlands merge with the rainforests and timber forests, rivers, waterfalls and lakes. It has rich volcanic soil and a perfect climate 600–1000 metres above sea level (10°C in winter to 30°C in summer).

The Tablelands offers World Heritage-listed rainforests, with primitive ferns and giant kauri pines growing much as their ancestors did hundreds of millions of years ago, clear mountain streams, and misty waterfalls. Wildlife is plentiful: tree-climbing kangaroos live in the upland rainforests, platypus in the rivers, and sugar-gliders, possums and other mammal species in the forest and woodland. Bird-watchers can see magpie geese, sarus cranes and cassowaries; Bromfield Swamp is recommended.

A century ago the Tableland was unknown to Europeans until an aptly named prospector, James Venture Mulligan, led several expeditions south-west from **Cooktown** between 1874 and 1876, having previously discovered the spectacular Palmer River goldfields in 1873. The northern Aboriginal tribes bitterly resented the miners' intrusion, and during the 1860s and 1870s there were many skirmishes between new settlers and Aborigines, and several massacres.

In 1874 Mulligan named the Hodgkinson and St George Rivers and Mt Mulligan, north of the tobacco town of **Dimbulah**. He returned in 1875 and found a beautiful river flowing north. This was the Barron River, which eventually flows east to the Pacific coast. Mulligan travelled up the Barron and camped at Granite Creek, where **Mareeba** now stands. He travelled over rich basaltic plains, now the tobacco fields on the Kuranda road, until stopped by dense, impenetrable forest near what is now **Tolga**. He marvelled at huge cedar and kauri trees, but skirted the forest and camped near the site of **Atherton**. Nearby he discovered the Wild River and traces of tin. However, as the nearest ports were Cooktown and Cardwell, some 500 kilometres away, Mulligan considered the area too isolated for tin mining.

Mulligan later found extensive gold strikes as he prospected the valley. The Hodgkinson gold rush started as soon as he reported his find, most of the diggers

coming from Cooktown and the Palmer River. The towns of **Kingsborough** and **Thornborough** quickly sprang up in 1876 between Mt Mulligan and Mareeba, and in two years the population was approximately 10 000.

This caused an unusual situation, the interior being opened up before a direct route to the coast had been discovered and a port founded. During 1876 several difficult tracks were cut down the steep, densely jungled coastal ranges towards Port Douglas and Trinity Bay. The latter eventually became **Cairns**. Some epic hauls up the range were recorded: in 1881, 80 bullocks hauled up the complete battery for the Great Northern tin mine at **Herberton**. An impressive monument at the foot of the Cairns–Kuranda road, the Kennedy Highway commemorates the trailblazers.

The railway line from Cairns to **Kuranda**, on the edge of the Tableland, is only 34 kilometres long but took four years to build, cost 20 workers their lives, and has 15 tunnels. It was completed in 1888, and the prosperity of the Atherton Tableland, and Cairns, was assured.

In April 1877 John Atherton settled at the junction of Emerald Creek and the Barron River and formed Emerald End station. When he found alluvial tin in the headwaters of the creek, he reputedly yelled 'Tin-hurroo' to his mate: hence the name of the area, **Tinaroo**. Atherton led others to major tin lodes on the Wild River, discovered by Mulligan four years earlier. Mining commenced and the town of Herberton came into existence. The Tate River field was also an important find, and tin proved to be more influential in the development of the area than the short-term excitement of gold.

In 1880 Atherton built a wide-verandahed shanty at Granite Creek, a popular camping spot halfway between Port Douglas and Herberton and used by men

flocking to the new field. This became Mareeba. Eventually the railway linked Herberton and Ravenshoe with Cairns. Today, Herberton is an interesting historic town that holds an annual Tin Festival in September. The local museum, called the Tin Pannikin, is in a classic old (unlicensed) pub, and is a tourist 'must'.

Ravenshoe (pronounced Ravens-ho) is on the Palmerston Highway, 93 kilometres west of Innisfail, and is 30 kilometres south of Atherton on the Kennedy Highway. It is noted for its gemstones and the fine cabinet timbers grown and milled in the area. The Torimba Forest Festival shows off the district's products every October.

Mount Garnet, 47 kilometres west of Ravenshoe, is an old copper-mining town where tourists can pan the tailings to find alluvial tin.

The rich dairy country around **Malanda**, 14 kilometres south-east of Atherton, supplies milk for what is known as the longest milk run in the world: to Weipa, Mount Isa, Darwin, and into Western Australia. The Malanda Dairy Festival is held every August.

Millaa Millaa, 24 kilometres south of Malanda, has a cheese factory, and the Millaa Millaa, Zillie and Elinjaa waterfalls are nearby. McHugh Lookout gives an excellent view of the southern Tableland.

Tinaburra is a popular tourist settlement on Tinaroo Dam. Nearby on the Malanda–Yungaburra road is the amazing and much-photographed Curtain Fig Tree.

For more information on the Atherton Tableland, contact the Atherton Tableland Promotion Bureau, Cnr Mabel and Grafton Sts, Atherton; (070) 91 4222. **See also:** Individual town entries in A–Z listing. **Note** detailed map of Cairns Region on page 473.

Elinjaa Falls, near Millaa Millaa

Brigid's Church, Rosewood, 20 km SW, largest wooden church in South Pacific. Swanbank Power Station, 12 km SE, steam trains run by Qld Pioneer Steam Railway Co-op, April–Dec; check times. Restored historic homestead Wolston House at Wacol, 16 km E. **Tourist information:** Regional Tourist Information Centre, cnr Brisbane St and d'Arcy Doyle Pl.; (07) 281 0555. **Accommodation:** 3 hotel/motels, 6 motels, 3 B&B, 1 hostel, 5 cara./camp. parks.
MAP REF. 467 K9, 475 M6

Isisford
Pop. 150
Established in 1877 by travelling hawkers William and James Whitman, Isisford is 117 km S of Longreach. First called Wittown, the town was renamed in 1880 to recall the ford in the nearby Barcoo River and the proximity of Isis Downs Station homestead. **Of interest:** Bicentennial Museum, Centenary Dr. **In the area:** Huge, semicircular prefabricated shearing shed, erected 1913, at Isis Downs Station, 20 km E; largest in Australia. Visits by appt; (076) 58 8203. Oma Waterhole, 16 km W; popular spot for fishing and water sports. **Tourist information:** Shire Offices, St Marys St; (076) 58 8277. **Accommodation:** 2 hotels, 1 cara./camp. park.
MAP REF. 476 A11, 483 N11

Julia Creek
Pop. 572
A small cattle and rail township on the Flinders Hwy, Julia Creek is 134 km E of Cloncurry. A sealed road runs north to Normanton in the Gulf Savannah. The town is an important cattle-trucking centre. **Of interest:** McIntyre Museum, Burke St. May: Campdraft. **Tourist information:** Shire Offices, Julia St; (077) 46 7166. **Accommodation:** 2 hotels, 1 motel, 1 cara./camp. park. **See also:** Gulf Savannah.
MAP REF. 482 I3

Jundah
Population 100
Jundah (an Aboriginal word for 'women'), 219 km SW of Longreach, was gazetted as a town in 1880. For about 20 years the area was important for opal mining, but lack of water eventually caused the mines to close. **Of interest:** Barcoo Historical Museum. Oct.: 2-day Race Carnival. **In the area:** Jundah Opal Fields, 27 km NW. **Tourist information:** Barcoo Shire Council, Dickson St, Jundah; (076) 58 6133. **Accommodation:** 1 hotel, 1 cara./camp. park.
MAP REF. 483 L12

Karumba
Pop. 708
Karumba, 69 km NW of Normanton, is at the mouth of the Norman River and is the centre of the prawning industry in the Gulf of Carpentaria. A barramundi fishing industry also operates from the town. **Of interest:** Slipway once used by the Sydney-to-England Empire Flying Boats Service. Boat hire and accommodation at Karumba Pt. Old cemetery on road to Karumba Point. July: Karumba Kapers. Dec.: Fishermen's Ball. **In the area:** Town is surrounded by flat wetlands extending 30 km inland, habitat of salt-water crocodiles and many species of bird, incl. brolgas and cranes. Karumba is easiest point of access to the Gulf. Charter vessels for fishing and exploration of the Gulf and Norman River. *The Ferryman*, cruises on Norman River. **Tourist information:** Carpentaria Shire Council, Haig St, Normanton; (077) 45 1166. **Accommodation:** 1 hotel/motel, 4 cara./camp. parks. **See also:** Gulf Savannah.
MAP REF. 478 B8, 481 H8

Kenilworth
Pop. 257
West of the Blackall Range, through the Obi Obi Valley, is Kenilworth. The town is famous for its Kenilworth Country Foods hand-crafted cheeses. This enterprise began as the Kraft cheese factory closed and 6 employees mortgaged their homes to start the venture. **Of interest:** Kev Franzi's Photo Workshop and Movie Museum, Eumundi Rd; 2 hr shows. **In the area:** Little Yabba Creek, 8 km S, good picnic spot, bellbirds. At Lake Borumba 32 km NW, sailing, water-skiing. From Lake Borumba, 39 km N, Imbil Forest Drive, through scenic forests and farmlands to Gympie. **Tourist information:** Cnr Sixth Ave and Aerodrome Rd, Maroochydore; (074) 79 1566. **Accommodation:** 1 hotel, 1 motel, camping facilities.
MAP REF. 475 M4

Killarney
Pop. 827
This attractive small town is on the Condamine River, 34 km SE of Warwick, and very close to the NSW border. Feb.: 2-day Agricultural Show. **In the area:** Noteworthy mountain scenery. Dagg's and Brown's waterfalls, 1–2 km S. Cherrabah Homestead Resort, 7 km S, horseriding, golf, sailing, bushwalking. Queen Mary Falls National Park, 7 km E, native birds feed daily at kiosk. **Tourist information:** 49 Albion St (New England Hwy), Warwick; (076) 61 3122. **Accommodation:** 1 cara./camp. park, 1 resort.
MAP REF. 123 M1, 475 L8

Kingaroy
Pop. 6672
This prosperous agricultural town is known for its peanuts and is the home of Sir Johannes (Joh) Bjelke-Petersen, former Premier of Qld. Peanuts, maize, wheat, soy and navy beans are grown, and specialised agricultural equipment is manufactured. Kingaroy is 233 km NW of Brisbane and its giant peanut silos are a

Peanut silos behind original Council Chambers, Kingaroy

distinctive landmark. Kingaroy claims the title 'Peanut Capital of Australia', and also 'Baked Bean Capital of Australia', with 75% of Australia's navy beans grown in the district. **Of interest:** In Haly St: Kingaroy Bicentennial Heritage Museum; at Tourist Information Centre, videos on peanut and navy bean industries; at Garden of Rocks, landscaping with semi-precious stones and petrified wood. April: Peanut Festival (odd-numbered years). **In the area:** Mt Wooroolin scenic lookout, 3 km W. Bunya Mountains National Park, 56 km S. **Tourist information:** Haly St (opp. silos); (071) 62 3199. **Accommodation:** 5 hotels, 6 motels, 2 cara./camp. parks.
MAP REF. 475 L3

Kuranda   Pop. 616

This village in the rainforest at the top of the Macalister Range is best known to tourists who have taken the 34-km trip from Cairns on the 100-year-old scenic railway. **Of interest:** Railway station with platforms adorned by lush ferns and orchids. Wildlife Noctarium, rainforest animals normally active only at night. World's largest Butterfly Sanctuary, over 2000 butterflies in aviary; static museum display. Award-winning Tjapukai Aboriginal Dance Theatre; 2–3 performances daily. Kuranda Rainforestation, Pamagirri Aboriginal dancers, army-duck rides in rainforest. Markets Wed.–Fri., Sun. May: Folk Festival. **In the area:** Guided tours of river and rainforest. Paradise in the Rainforest, scenic rides on tractor train. Barron Falls, spectacular after heavy rain. **Tourist information:** Far North Queensland Promotion Bureau, cnr Grafton and Hartley Sts, Cairns; (070) 51 3588. **Accommodation:** 2 hotels, 3 motels, 1 cara./camp. park. **See also:** Atherton Tableland; The Far North.
MAP REF. 479 L6

Kynuna   Pop. 18

On the Matilda Hwy, 161 km NW of Winton, Kynuna was established in the 1860s and was a staging point for Cobb & Co. coaches. **Of interest:** Kynuna's only hotel is the famous Blue Heeler. Waltzing Matilda Exhibition, CWA Hall, Matilda Hwy. Sept.: 'Surf' Carnival. Nov.: Rodeo. **In the area:** Combo Waterhole, scene of the events described in 'Waltzing Matilda', 24 km SE on western side of old Winton–Kynuna road. **Tourist information:** Blue Heeler Hotel,

Matilda Hwy; (077) 46 8650. **Accommodation:** 1 hotel/motel, 2 cara./camp. parks.
MAP REF. 482 I5

Laidley   Pop. 2315

Laidley, 75 km from Brisbane, is between Ipswich and Gatton, in the Lockyer Valley. It is the principal town for the Laidley Shire, a rural area of the Greater Brisbane Region regarded as 'Queensland's country garden'. **Of interest:** Das Neumann Haus (1893), William St, historic house, tourist centre, art gallery. Country Market, last Sat.–Sun. in month. Sept.: Chelsea Festival Week. Oct.: Festival of Performing Arts. **In the area:** Laidley Pioneer Village, 1 km S, original buildings from old township. Adj., Narda Lagoon, flora and fauna sanctuary. Lake Clarendon, 17 km NW. Scenic drives; leaflets from Tourist Information. Lake Dyer, 1 km W, picnic/barbecue facilities. **Tourist information:** Cnr William and Patrick Sts; (074) 65 3241. **Accommodation:** 4 hotels, 1 motel, 1 B&B.
MAP REF. 466 H9, 475 M6

Landsborough   Pop. 1150

Just off Glass House Mountains Tourist Drive, Landsborough is 9 km S of the Caloundra turnoff. **Of interest:** In Maleny St: Historical Museum, De Maine Pottery. Bottle, gemstone and shell museum, Glass House Mountains Tourist Dr. June: William Landsborough Day. **In the area:** Queensland Reptile and Fauna Park, 4 km S. Big Kart Track, 5 km N. **Tourist information:** Landsborough

Scenic railway, Kuranda

Museum, Maleny St; (074) 941 755. **Accommodation:** 1 motel, 2 cara./camp. parks.
MAP REF. 467 M2, 470 E13

Logan City   Pop. 132 000

Captain Patrick Logan, one of the founders and first Commandant of the Moreton Bay Penal Settlement, first discovered the area now known as Logan City. On 21 August 1862 he reported sighting a 'very considerable river which empties itself into the Moreton Bay . . . I have named it the Darling'. This river later became the Logan River, an acknowledgment by Governor Darling of Logan's 'zeal and efficient service'. The region was named after Logan when it was declared a shire in 1978; it became a city in 1981. Midway between Brisbane and the Gold Coast, Logan is Qld's fastest growing city. Enjoying close proximity to both Brisbane and the Gold Coast (a little more than half an hour from each), it has a strong economic base. **Of interest:** Mayes Cottage (1871), Mawarra St, National Trust Building, once home of early pioneers. Daisy Hill Forest Park (430 ha), Daisy Hill Rd, picnics, bushwalking, horseriding, koalas, other wildlife. Kingston Butter Factory Community Art Centre, Milky Way, off Kingston Rd. Logan Hyperdome, off Pacific Hwy, largest shopping complex under one roof in Australia. Oct.: Street Parade. Nov.: River Festival, Raft Race. **Tourist information:** 4195 Pacific Hwy, Loganholme; (07) 801 3400. **Accommodation:** 4 motels, 11 cara./camp. parks.
MAP REF. 467 M9

Longreach
Pop. 3607

Longreach has a relatively small human population, but if you count the 800 000 sheep and 20 000 beef cattle in the area, it becomes the most important and prosperous town in the Central West. On the Thomson River, it is a friendly, modern town some 700 km by road or rail west of Rockhampton. It was here in 1870 that Harry Redford, better known as Captain Starlight, with four mates rounded up 1000 head of cattle and drove them 2400 km into SA over wild unmapped country that only 10 years before had been the downfall of Burke and Wills. There Starlight sold the cattle. Since they did not belong to him, he was arrested in Adelaide and brought back to Qld to be put on trial at Roma. Despite the evidence, the jury found him not guilty, probably because of the pioneer philosophy that if you are daring enough to carry out that sort of deed you deserve to get away with it! The events were the basis for Rolf Boldrewood's novel *Robbery Under Arms*. Although Qantas (**Q**ueensland **A**nd **N**orthern **T**erritory **A**ir **S**ervices) actually started in Winton, it soon moved its base to Longreach and then began regular operations. The same hangar used then became Australia's first aircraft factory and the first of 6 DH-50 biplanes was assembled there in 1926. The world's first Flying Surgeon Service started from Longreach in 1959. **Of interest:** Broad streets and several historic buildings: Uniting Church (1892), Galah St, built for Grazier's Association; courthouse (1892), Eagle St; post office (1902), cnr Duck and Galah Sts. Stockman's Hall of Fame and Outback Heritage Centre, Capricorn Hwy: exhibition hall; theatre with audiovisuals; library and resource centre. School of Distance Education, Capricorn Hwy; tours during term. Preview Centre for proposed Qantas Founders' Museum in Qantas Park, Eagle St. Longreach Pastoral College, Capricorn Hwy. Jackson's Weapon Museum, Cassowary St. Pamela's Doll Display and Syd's Outback Collection Corner, Quail St. Cruises on Thomson River: *Yellowbelly Express* and Billabong Boat Cruises. June: Hall of Fame Race Meeting. Sept.: Starlight Stampede (even-numbered years). **In the area:** Folk Museum at Ilfracombe, 27 km E. **Tourist information:** Qantas Park; (076) 58 3555. **Accommodation:** 5 hotels, 5 motels, 2 cara./camp. parks.
MAP REF. 483 N9

Main street, Mackay

Lucinda–Dungeness
Pop. 784

Lucinda, the port for Ingham's sugar has the world's longest offshore sugar-loading jetty. The conveyor belt, 5.76 km long, loads 2000 tonnes of sugar an hour. Charter boats leave the Dungeness harbour for fishing, cruising and trips to the islands, incl. popular Hinchinbrook. **In the area:** Unique Italian cemetery, 3 km N, mausoleums and architecture. Wallaman Falls, 80 km S; 305-m-high single fall, highest in Qld. **Tourist information:** Tourist Centre, Bruce Hwy, Ingham; (077) 76 5211. **Accommodation:** 1 hotel/motel, 1 cara./camp. park.
MAP REF. 479 M10

Mackay
Pop. 40 250

Mackay is often called the sugar capital of Australia, producing one-third of the nation's sugar crop. Five mills operate in the area, and the bulk-sugar loading terminal is the world's largest. Sugar was first grown in 1866, a mill was built and in the same year Mackay became a town. It became a major port in 1939 when an breakwater was built, making it one of Australia's largest artificial harbours. The nearby Hay Point coal loading terminals handle the output from the Central Qld coalfields. Gazetted in 1918, Mackay is now a progressive tropical city. Besides sugar and coal, the town's economy depends on beef cattle, dairying, timber, grain, seafood and the

growing of tropical fruit. Tourism is a growth industry, with cruises to Brampton, Lindeman, Hamilton, the Great Barrier Reef and the Whitsunday Islands. **Of interest:** Self-guide heritage walk of historic buildings, incl. Commonwealth and National Banks, town hall, courthouse, police station and customs house. Queens Park and Orchid House, Goldsmith St. Mackay Entertainment Centre, Gordon St. Tourism Mackay, Nebo Rd; building is replica of old Richmond sugar mill. Just north of town: Mt Bassett Weather Station and lookout; Mt Pleasant Reservoir and lookout. Numerous beaches: Harbour, Town, Blacks, Bucasia, Illawong, Lamberts and Shoal Point. Illawong Fauna Park at Illawong Beach. July: Festival of the Arts. Sept.: Sugartime Festival. **In the area:** Farleigh sugar mill, 15 km N. Cape Hillsborough National Park, 40 km N. Eungella National Park, 84 km NW. Polstone Sugar Cane Farm 15 km W. Historic Greenmount Homestead, 20 km W, near Walkeston. Kinchant Dam, 20 km W of Walkerston. At Mirani, 30 km W Juipera Walkabout; contact Mirani museum, Victoria St. Orchidways, on Homebush Rd, 25 km S of Mackay: orchid farm. At Homebush, craft and art gallery. Hay Point coal loading terminal lookout, 30 km S. Cape Palmerston National Park, 80 km S; 4WD access only. Cruises to Great Barrier Reef and Whitsunday Islands. **Tourist information:** The Mill, Nebo Rd; (079) 52 2677. **Accommodation:** 19 hotels, 29 motels, 10 cara./camp. parks.
MAP REF. 477 J4

Maleny
Pop. 789

A steep road climbs west to Maleny, 50 km SW of Maroochydore on the Blackall Range. This is excellent dairy country. From Mary Cairncross Park, an area of thick rainforest, there is a fine view of the Glass House Mountains to the south. These 10 spectacular trachyte peaks were named by Captain Cook as he sailed up the coast in 1770, for the sun shining on the rockfaces reminded him of glasshouses in his native Yorkshire. **Of interest:** Art and craft galleries. **In the area:** 28 km scenic drive north-east from Maleny through Montville and Flaxton to Mapleton, one of best in south-east Qld. Most of Sunshine Coast can be seen: views of Moreton Island, and closer, pineapple and sugarcane fields. Montville, 17 km NE, excellent potteries, art and craft galleries. Museums, antique

shops, fruit stalls, tea rooms and tourist attractions along the way. Flaxton, 3 km further N, miniature English village, clock museum. Kondalilla and Mapleton Falls National Parks, 7 km W of Montville. **Tourist information:** Maroochy Tourist Information Centre, cnr Sixth Ave and Aerodrome Rd, Maroochydore; (074) 79 1566. **Accommodation:** 1 hotel, 3 motels, 1 cara./camp. park. **See also:** Sunshine Coast.
MAP REF. 467 L2, 470 B11

Mareeba   Pop. 6795
This town is at the centre of the main tobacco-growing region of Australia. Farms in the Mareeba–Dimbulah area are irrigated from Lake Tinaroo. Mining and cattle are also important industries. **Of interest:** In Mason St: Bicentennial Lakes, park with plantings to encourage wildlife, picnic facilities, children's playground. May: Dimbulah Festival. July: Rodeo. **In the area:** Pinevale Ranch, 10 km E, day horseriding. Granite Gorge, 12 km W, off Chewko Rd. Dirt and sealed road via Dimbulah crosses Great Dividing Range to Chillagoe (145 km W), old mining town with fine limestone caves. Aerodrome 11 km S on Kennedy Hwy. Mareeba Coffee Estates, 7 km W on Mareeba–Dimbulah Rd. **Tourist information:** Shire Offices; (070) 92 1222. **Accommodation:** 4 hotels, 2 motels, 4 cara./camp. parks. **See also:** Atherton Tableland; Cape York.
MAP REF. 473 C10, 479 K7

Maroochydore   Pop. 28 509
A well-established and popular beach resort, Maroochydore is the business centre of the Sunshine Coast, 112 km N of Brisbane. **Of interest:** Famous surfing beaches and Maroochy River, with pelicans and swans, offers safe swimming. Cotton Tree, at river mouth, popular camping area. Oct.: Mapleton Yarn Festival. **In the area:** Yacht Harbour, beach and Pilot Station at Mooloolaba, 5 km S. Mooloolah River National Park, 10 km S (access difficult). Sunshine Coast Airport has daily flights to and from Sydney. River cruises up Maroochy River to Dunethin Rock through sugarcane fields. Fairytale Castle, 10 km N. Nostalgia Town, 11 km N via Bli Bli; emphasises humour in history. **Tourist information:** Cnr Sixth Ave and Aerodrome Rd; (074) 79 1566. **Accommodation:** 2 hotels, 11 motels, 4 cara./camp. parks.
MAP REF. 467 N1, 470 H9, 475 N4

Maryborough   Pop. 20 790
Maryborough is a well-planned, attractive provincial city, 3 hours' drive north of Brisbane and situated on the banks of the Mary River, which was discovered in 1842. In 1847 a wool store was established near the original town site. A village and port soon grew to handle wool being grown inland. The settlement was officially proclaimed a port in 1859 and a municipality in 1861. Maryborough is promoted as the Heritage City and visitors are encouraged to take the Heritage Walk and drive through the suburbs to see the excellent architecture of a bygone era. The climate is dry subtropical with warm moist summers and mild winters, and several seaside resorts are nearby. **Of interest:** Some fine examples of early Qld colonial architecture incl. Baddow House, Queen St, furnished in period style; St Paul's bell tower (1887), with one of the last sets of pealing bells in Qld; Brennan & Geraghty's Store, Lennox St, property of National Trust. Fruit Salad Cottage Heritage Museum, Banana St. Pioneer gravesites and original township site in Alice St, Baddow, and historic time gun outside city hall; signposted walk. Several parks: Queen's Park, unusual domed fernery and waterfall; Elizabeth Park, rose gardens; Anzac Park; and Ululah Lagoon, near the golf links, scenic waterbird sanctuary, black swans, wild geese, ducks, waterhens may be hand-fed. Heritage City Market Thurs. May: Best of Brass. Sept.: Heritage Festival. **In the area:** Hervey Bay, Rainbow Beach, Tin Can Bay, Burrum

The Herb Garden, Montville, near Maleny

Heads and Woodgate seaside resorts; all offer fishing. Also at Hervey Bay, tours to see humpback whale migration. Fraser Island, just off coast, World Heritage-listed sand island. Pioneer museum at Brooweena, 49 km W on Biggenden Rd. Teddington Weir, 15 km S. Tuan Forest, 24 km SE. Houseboat hire. **Tourist information:** 30 Ferry St; (071) 21 4111. **Accommodation:** 5 hotel/motels, 8 motels, 6 cara./camp. parks.
MAP REF. 475 M1

Mary Kathleen   Pop. Nil
Well known to many Australians because of the controversial issue of uranium mining, Mary Kathleen was once a small mining town on the Barkly Hwy between Mount Isa and Cloncurry. The area has now been returned to its natural state, leaving no trace of the former inhabitants. In late 1982 the mine was shut down and by the end of 1983 the houses were sold and removed to new areas. Four buildings have been re-erected in the Mary Kathleen Memorial Park at Cloncurry. **In the area:** Mount Frosty, off Mt Isa Rd, popular swimming-hole, fossicking area for minerals and gemstones. **Note: Not recommended for children; hole is some 9 metres deep with no shallow areas. Tourist information:** Tourism Precinct, Marian St, Mt Isa; (077) 43 7966 (Council).
MAP REF. 482 F3

Miles   Pop. 1260
Ludwig Leichhardt passed through the Miles district (340 km W of Brisbane) on

Cape York

The Cape York Peninsula is a vast area as large as Victoria. There are more than 10 000 people living on the Cape. About half live in Weipa, and the rest in Aboriginal and Islander communities, isolated townships and scattered pastoral stations. Many of these are on the telegraph line to the northern tip.

The first European exploration of Cape York was in the 1840s and the 1860s, by the Jardine brothers, John Bradford, Robert Jack, and the ill-fated Edmund Kennedy and his famous Aboriginal guide Jacky Jacky. Little has changed since then. Vegetation varies from gums and anthills in the south to swamps and rainforests in the north. Many areas of the Cape are national parks and a sanctuary for much of Australia's unique wildlife, including crocodiles, orchids and insect-eating pitcher plants. Further information and permits may be obtained from the Dept of Environment and Heritage, McLeod St, Cairns; (070) 52 3096.

There are two distinct seasons: the wet and the dry. During the wet virtually all road transport stops and the only movement is by regular flights with Flight West and Sunstate airlines; both run scheduled daily flights into Cape York Airport. Some 50 kilometres on a dirt track brings the comfortable Pajinka Wilderness Lodge, managed by the Injinoo Aboriginal Community, for those who don't want to rough it. **There are almost no sealed roads or bridges in the area.**

All Aboriginal communities are self-sufficient and may be visited, but **it is essential that a permit be obtained in writing beforehand.** The main communities are **Lockhart River** and **Portland Roads** on the east coast; **Bamaga** at the tip; and **Edward River**, **Weipa South**, and **Aurukun** on the Gulf. The Ang-Gnarra Aboriginal Corporations at Laura offer a guide and ranger service to visitors. Details at the caravan park.

The Cape is the ideal place to go exploring. A reliable and well-equipped 4WD vehicle, preferably with a winch, is essential for this area. It is possible to drive north from Cairns or Mareeba to Bamaga through Laura and Coen. The Royal Automobile Club of Queensland provides an excellent map and information sheet and it is essential reading before an expedition north is planned. **Conditions on the track are unpredictable and the RACQ or police at Cairns should be contacted before heading north.**

June to November are the recommended travel months. At the peak of the season over one hundred vehicles travel northern Cape roads daily. The narrow, rough and blind roads are difficult, and a motorist travelling fast has no chance of avoiding an oncoming car. There are many accidents in this area each year. Drivers are advised to travel slowly and exercise particular care.

The Laura, Kennedy, Stewart, Archer, Wenlock, Dulhunty and Jardine Rivers must be forded. There is a vehicular ferry across the Jardine and it is recommended that motorists use this instead of risking vehicle damage in the dangerous ford crossing. During good dry conditions it is possible to take a conventional car, with care, north to Coen and west to Weipa.

Weipa, on the Gulf of Carpentaria, has the world's largest deposits of bauxite, the raw material for aluminium. Comalco offers conducted tours of the bauxite mining operation. Once mined the bauxite is shipped to the huge alumina plant at Gladstone on the central Queensland coast. The first European to see the red bauxite cliffs was the Dutch explorer Captain Willem Jansz in 1606. Direct access to Weipa is by regular Ansett flights from Cairns.

Permits are required to enter the Injinoo area north of the Dulhunty River; these can be obtained from the Jardine River ferry on your way, or by contacting Injinoo; (070) 69 3253.

For further information on Cape York, contact the Far North Qld Promotion Bureau Ltd, cnr Grafton & Hartley Sts, Cairns; (070) 51 3588. **See also:** Individual town entries in A–Z listing.

Thursday Island

Situated 35 kilometres north-west off the tip of Cape York Peninsula in the Torres Strait, Thursday Island is a colourful outpost. Its population of around 2900 is made up of islanders, a minority of Europeans, and Malays, Polynesians, Chinese and Japanese. At Rosie's Shop, at the corner of Douglas and Blackall Streets, a range of Torres Strait Islander and Aboriginal artefacts are available for purchase. The Harbours and Marine Department's Torres Strait Pilot Service operates from its harbour, once the base for 150 pearling luggers. Ferry and day cruises depart from the harbour and operate between Bamaga, Horn Island, Punsand Bay and Pajinka Lodge Cape York. A Cultural Festival is held each May. For further information on Thursday Island, contact the Far North Qld Promotion Bureau Ltd, cnr Grafton & Hartley Sts, Cairns; (070) 51 3588.

Fishing boats, Thursday Island

three separate expeditions. He named the place Dogwood Crossing, after the shrub that grows on the banks of the creek. In 1878 the western railway line reached Dogwood Crossing, and Cobb & Co. continued the journey to Roma. The town was renamed Miles after a local member of parliament. The area has always been good sheep country, but today the emphasis is on cattle, mainly Herefords, and wheat; tall silos dominate the surrounding plains. After the spring rains the wildflowers are magnificent. Gorges, walks, wildlife and fishing. **Of interest:** Historical village, Warrego Hwy, 'pioneer settlement' with all types of early buildings, war museum, vehicles and implements on display. Easter: Museum Display. Sept.: Wildflower Festival. **In the area:** Possum Park, 21 km N: historical display; caravans and camping; ex-airforce ammunition store with underground bunkers converted for accommodation. Myall Park Botanical Gardens at Glenmorgan, 100 km SW. **Tourist information:** Miles and District Historical Village, Warrego Hwy; (076) 27 1492. **Accommodation:** 3 hotels, 3 motels, 2 cara./camp. parks.
MAP REF. 474 I4

Millaa Millaa Pop. 325
Located 75 km inland from Innisfail, Millaa Millaa is noted for the many spectacular waterfalls in the area. The town's main industry is dairying. **Of interest:** Eacham Historical Society Museum. **In the area:** Millaa Millaa Falls, Zillie Falls and Elinjaa Falls, all seen from 15 km gravel road that leaves and rejoins Palmerston Hwy east of town. Lookout to west of town, excellent views of district. **Tourist information:** Atherton Tableland Promotion Bureau, cnr Mabel and Vernon Sts, Atherton; (070) 91 4222. **Accommodation:** 1 hotel, 1 cara./camp. park. **See also:** Atherton Tableland; The Far North.
MAP REF. 479 L8

Millmerran Pop. 1159
This town on the Condamine River produces eggs, cotton, grain, vegetables, cattle and wool. **Of interest:** Ned's Corner: camp oven meals, Australiana, yarns and poetry, bullock team; by appt. Historical Society Museum, Charlotte St. Bottle and Brick Museum, Mary St. **Tourist information:** Toowoomba and Golden West Tourist Association, 541 Ruthven St, Toowoomba; (076) 39 3797.

Hotel and bottle tree, Mitchell

Accommodation: 1 hotel, 1 motel, 1 cara./camp. park.
MAP REF. 466 A10, 475 K6

Miriam Vale Pop. 447
Situated on the Bruce Hwy, 150 km N of Bundaberg, this town is renowned for its mud crab sandwiches. Watch for the Giant Crab. The twin towns of Town of Seventeen Seventy and Agnes Water lie 25 km E. Captain Cook, while on his voyage of discovery in Australian waters, made his second landing here. Estuary and beaches provide ideal spots to get away from it all. Fishing is excellent. **Tourist information:** Discovery Coast Information Centre, Roe St; (079) 74 5428. **Accommodation** (incl. Agnes Water and Town of Seventeen Seventy): 1 hotel, 1 motel, 1 B&B, 1 cara./camp. park.
MAP REF. 477 N11

Mission Beach Pop. 814
This quiet tropical 14-km-long beach of magnificent golden sand, close to Tully, is fringed by coconut palms and unique heritage rainforest. The Great Barrier Reef is close to shore. Day trips to Dunk and the surrounding Family Group of islands (excluding Bedarra) can be taken from the jetty at Clump Point. At the southern end of the beach a cairn at Tam O'Shanter Point commemorates the ill-fated 1848 Cape York expedition of Edmund Kennedy. Horse and camel rides on beach. July: Cassowary Festival. Oct.: Aquatic Festival. **In the area:** Giramay Walkabouts, Dunlop St, Wongaling Beach, Aboriginal cultural

experience, full-day adventure trek. Art and craft galleries. Horseriding, boat and jetski hire, game fishing, water taxis. Whitewater rafting and kayaking on Tully River, 10 km inland; superb scenery and swimming in the top reaches. Tully Railway Station, tropical plants. Tully Sugar Mill; tours weekdays in crushing season. **Tourist information:** Porters Promenade; (070) 68 7099. **Accommodation:** 1 hotel, 6 motels, 1 B&B, 3 hostels, 3 cara./camp. parks.
MAP REF. 479 M9

Mitchell Pop. 1101
This typical western country town, on the banks of the Maranoa River, lies on the Warrego Hwy between Roma and Charleville and was named after Sir Thomas Mitchell, explorer and Surveyor-General of NSW, who visited the region in 1845. **Of interest:** Old Courthouse, Cambridge St, courtroom display, local craft. **In the area:** Unsealed tourist road leads north into Great Dividing Range and former stronghold of local turn-of-century bushrangers, the Kenniff brothers. Region behind Carnarvon National Park, 256 km N, is little known; sufficient petrol and supplies must be carried for return trip. Neil Turner Weir, 3.5 km NW. **Tourist information:** Booringa Shire Council; (076) 23 1133. **Accommodation:** 5 hotels, 2 motels, 2 cara./camp. parks.
MAP REF. 474 D3

Monto Pop. 1339
Monto, on the Burnett Hwy, 250 km inland from Bundaberg, is the centre of a

Aerial view of Mount Isa

rich dairying, beef cattle and agricultural district. June: Dairy Festival (even-numbered years). **In the area:** Cania Gorge National Park, 25 km N, spectacular sandstone formations. **Tourist information:** Cnr Mulgrave and Bourbong Sts, Bundaberg; (071) 52 2333. **Accommodation:** 2 motels, 1 cara./camp. park. MAP REF. 477 M12

Mooloolaba – Alexandra Headland

Pop. part of Maroochydore

Because of its excellent clean, sandy beach and variety of restaurants and nightlife, Mooloolaba is equally in demand for family and young people's holidays. The Mooloolaba Esplanade, offering beachside resort shopping, rises to the bluff at Alexandra Headland. Alexandra Headland beach is a popular board-riding location. Few visitors forget the sweeping panoramic views up the beach to the Maroochy River and Mudjimba Island, with Mt Coolum creating an impressive backdrop. One of the safest anchorages on the eastern coast is at Mooloolaba Harbour. It is the finishing point for the annual Sydney-to-Mooloolaba Yacht Race and the starting point for the Mooloolaba-to-Gladstone Race. **Of interest:** Wharf complex, The Spit, Mooloolaba, dozens of specialty shops. Underwater World oceanarium, cnr River Esplanade and Parkyn Pde, 80-m transparent tunnel for seeing 3 separate marine environments; freshwater section; seal pool. Harbour is also base for Sunshine Coast's main prawning and fishing fleet; yachting and game-fishing trips to near offshore reefs; and pilot vessels guiding ships into Port of Brisbane. Paraflying off Mooloolaba Beach. **Tourist information:** Cnr Aerodrome Rd and Sixth Ave, Maroochydore; (074) 79 1566. **Accommodation:** 2 hotels, 10 motels, 3 cara./camp. parks. MAP REF. 470 I9

Moranbah   Pop. 6525

Just off the Peak Downs Hwy, 200 km SW of Mackay, this town services the huge open-cut coal mines of Goonyella/Riverside and Peak Downs, managed by BHP Australia Coal Ltd. Coking coal is railed to the Hay Point export terminal just south of Mackay. **Of interest:** Tours to Peak Downs leave town Thurs. 10 a.m. **Tourist information:** Shire Offices, Goonyella Rd; (079) 41 7254. **Accommodation:** 2 hotel/motels, 1 motel, 2 cara./camp. parks. MAP REF. 476 H6

Mossman   Pop. 1771

Mossman, the sugar town of the north, situated 78 km NW of Cairns on the Captain Cook Hwy, is surrounded by green mountains and fields of green sugarcane. **Of interest:** Mt Demi (1159 m) towers over town. Tours of Mossman Central Mill during cane-crushing season (July–Oct.). Bally Hooley Steam Express, genuine steam train; trip incl. Port Douglas (20 km SE), canefields, tour of mill. June: Bavarian Festival. **In the area:** Popular beaches Cooya, Newell and Wonga; latter two provide public facilities. Silky Oaks Wilderness Lodge, backing on to Daintree National Park, 10 km W. Mossman Gorge, 9 km S, short walk through rainforest to picturesque cascades. Karnak Playhouse Theatre, 12 km N. High Falls Farm at Miallo, 15 km N. Wonga Belle Orchid Garden, 20 km N. Exotic jungle river cruises on Daintree River, 25 km N. Cape Tribulation National Park, 64 km NE, largest tract of tropical rainforest in Australia. **Tourist information:** Cnr Grafton & Hartley Sts, Cairns; (070) 51 3588. **Accommodation:** 2 hotels, 2 motels, 1 cara./camp. park. **See also:** The Far North. MAP REF. 473 B3, 479 K6

Mount Isa   Pop. 23 667

In 1923, John Campbell Miles discovered a rich silver-lead deposit on the western edge of the Cloncurry field. Today the progressive city of Mount Isa is the most important industrial, commercial and administrative centre in north-west Qld. The city is a company town, with Mount Isa Mines operating one of the largest silver-lead mines in the world. Copper and zinc are also mined and processed. Ore trains run 900 km E to Townsville for shipment. The city is an oasis of civilisation with excellent amenities and facilities in the otherwise hot and monotonous spinifex and cattle country surrounding it. **Of interest:** Surface and underground mine tours, advance bookings essential. Lead smelter stack, Australia's tallest free-standing structure (265 m). In Church St: John Middlin Mining Display and Visitors Centre; Frank Aston Underground Museum, opp. KMart. National Trust Tent House, Fourth Ave. Kalkadoon Tribal Centre and Cultural Keeping Place, Marian St. Riversleigh Fossil Display, Civic Centre, West St. Mt Isa Potters Gallery, Alma St. Flying Doctor Service base, Barkly Hwy. School of Distance Education, Kalkadoon High School, Abel Smith Pde. City Lookout, Hilary St. Donaldson Memorial Lookout and Walking Track, off Marian St. April: Country Music Festival. Aug.: Art Society Exhibition; Rodeo, attracts rough-riders from all over Qld and almost doubles the population of Mount Isa. **In the area:** Artificial Lake Moondarra, 15 km N, swimming, water sports, picnic/barbecue facilities. Lake Julius, 100 km NE, Aboriginal cave paintings, fishing, water-skiing, nature trails, abandoned goldmine. Air charter companies provide

flights to excellent barramundi fishing grounds near Birri Fishing Lodge at Birri Beach on Mornington Island and Sweers Island, in Gulf of Carpentaria. Gunpowder Resort, 140 km NW, activities range from bull-catching to water-skiing. Tours of Riversleigh Fossil Site, 200 km NW, and Lawn Hill National Park, 500 km NW. Campbell's Travel; full-day bush and mine-surface tours. Camooweal, 188 km NW on Barkly Hwy, last Qld town before crossing NT border. Mount Frosty, 53 km E, old limestone mine and swimming-hole, popular area for fossickers. Lake Corella, 90 km E, Burke and Wills memorial cairn. **Tourist information:** Tourism Precinct, Marian St; (077) 43 7966 (Council). **Accommodation:** 4 hotels, 13 motels, 2 hostels, 8 caravan parks.
MAP REF. 482 E3

Mount Morgan Pop. 2782
Found only 32 km SW of Rockhampton, the crater of the Mount Morgan open-cut gold, silver and copper mine is one of the world's largest man-made holes, measuring some 800 m across and 185 m deep. In the golden heyday of the mine, the town had 14 000 people. Mine tours leave town 1 p.m. daily. **Of interest:** Museum, Morgan St. Courthouse and other historic buildings have National Trust classifications. May: Golden Mount Festival. **In the area:** The Big Dam, 2.7 km N via William St, boating, picnics. **Tourist information:** Mount Morgan Railway Station, Burnett Hwy; (079) 38 2312. **Accommodation:** 3 hotels, 1 hotel/motel, 2 cara./camp. parks. **See also:** The Capricorn Region.
MAP REF. 477 L9

Mourilyan Pop. 446
Located 7 km S of Innisfail, Mourilyan is the bulk-sugar outlet for sugar produced in the Innisfail area. **Of interest:** Australian Sugar Museum, Bruce Hwy. **In the area:** On Old Bruce Hwy, south-west: tours of South Johnstone Sugar Mill (8 km) in season, July–Oct.; National Trust-classified Paronella Park (15 km), ruins of Spanish castle set in rainforest; suspension bridge; waterfall; picnic and camping areas. Etty Bay, 8 km E, quiet tropical beach, cara./camp. park. **Tourist information:** Australian Sugar Museum, Bruce Hwy; (070) 63 2306. **Accommodation:** 1 hotel.
MAP REF. 479 L8

Mundubbera Pop. 1118
The citrus capital of Queensland, Mundubbera is on the Burnett Hwy, 410 km NW of Brisbane. **Of interest:** The Big Mandarin Information Centre, local art and craft. **In the area:** Golden Mile Orchard, 13 km W, open when operating; check times. Rare Neoceratodus (lungfish) found in Burnett River. Jones Weir, Auburn River National Park, 40 km SW. Gurgeena and Binjour Plateaus; peanut, maize and bean areas to north-east. **Tourist information:** The Big Mandarin Information Centre, Dalby–Durong Hwy; (071) 65 4188. **Accommodation:** 2 motels, 1 cara./camp. park.
MAP REF. 475 K1

Murgon Pop. 2210
Murgon, known as the beef capital of the Burnett, is one of the most attractive towns in southern Qld. Settlement dates back to 1843 and the name comes from an Aboriginal word meaning 'lily pond'. Beef, dairying and mixed crops are the main industries. The town is 101 km inland from Gympie and 46 km N of Kingaroy. **Of interest:** Vic Rewald's Lapidary Display, Nutt St, semi-precious gemstone collection. Queensland Dairy Museum, Gayndah Rd. Adjacent, relocated Trinity Homestead, one of district's original buildings. Murgon Cheese Factory, Macalister St. Goschnick's Farm Machinery Museum, Bunya Hwy. **In the area:** Cherbourg Emu Farm at Cherbourg Aboriginal Community, 5 km SW, walk-through enclosures; educational displays; sales of emu products and Aboriginal artefacts. Bjelke-Petersen Dam, 15 km SE, water sports, fishing, picnic facilities, camping, accommodation. Jack Smith's Scrub Environment Park, 15 km NE, nature walk, views. Adjacent, Boat Mountain Environment Park. **Tourist information:** 118b Lamb St; (071) 68 1984. **Accommodation:** 1 hotel/motel, 1 motel, 2 caravan parks.
MAP REF. 475 L3

Muttaburra Pop. 195
Muttaburra, 114 km N of Longreach, was developed as a town in the late 1870s, the name being derived from an Aboriginal word meaning 'meeting of the waters'. **Of interest:** Joe Amatta Memorial Museum, in old hospital; tours by appt with

Australian Sugar Museum, Mourilyan

National Parks

The diverse landscapes of Queensland's national parks lure visitors by the million each year. They are drawn not only to the endless stretches of sandy beaches and the magnificent Great Barrier Reef cays and islands off the coast, but also to the cooler mountains of the southern ranges, the inland plains and semi-arid areas, and the wilderness of Cape York.

Many parks and reserves are accessible by conventional vehicle, some by 4WD only. Their major attraction is the climate—beautiful one day, glorious the next! Certainly, daytime temperatures in the north and west can reach a searing 40°C or more, and the monsoonal period (November to March) brings the occasional cyclone and rainfall that can be measured in metres, but other than these extremes the climate makes for pleasant visits and extended bushwalking, camping and other recreation-based activities.

Today Cape York Peninsula is like a magnet to tourists, even though the only aim of thousands of visitors may be simply to stand at its tip. The peninsula's vast and monotonous country is interspersed with surprising pockets of forest, broad vegetation-fringed rivers and occasional waterfalls, all the home of a wide variety of wildlife. **Jardine River/Heathlands, Rokeby** and **Iron Range** national parks are destinations for keen and experienced wilderness explorers. However, a growing number of visitors divert to **Lakefield**, the State's second largest national park, encompassing 537 000 hectares. Its fringing rainforest, paperbark woodland, open grassy plains, swamps and coastal mudflats leading to mangroves along Princess Charlotte Bay, all offer a variety of attractions for the most demanding visitor. Basic campsites are located along many watercourses.

Within a several-hundred-kilometre radius of Cairns are scores of national parks catering for all tastes. **Chillagoe–Mungana Caves** National Parks, three hours' drive from Cairns, are dominated by weird limestone outcrops, castle-like pinnacles that house a wonderland of colourful caves. Guided tours are conducted daily. Once Queensland's leading mineral producing area, it is popular with fossickers.

About 50 kilometres from Cairns is the **Atherton Tableland**, on which lie several national parks. Here visitors can follow walking tracks through rainforest at **Mt Hypipamee**, or visit the 65-metre-wide **Millstream Falls**, or the crater lakes of **Eacham** and **Barrine**.

A north Queensland visit would not be complete without a train trip to Kuranda via **Barron Gorge National Park**, or a visit to the **Bellenden Ker**, **Lumholz**, **Cape Tribulation** and **Daintree** national parks. This undeveloped mountainous country, with its scenic waterfalls and lush rainforest, should not be missed.

One of the most breathtakingly beautiful scenic reserves in Australia is **Carnarvon National Park**, 720 kilometres by road north-west of Brisbane. The Carnarvon Gorge section of this 298 000 hectare park, a dramatic, twisting chasm of soft sandstone gouged from vertical white cliffs, is a popular destination for campers. Graded tracks lead through forests of eucalypt, she-oaks, tall cabbage palms and relic macrozamia palms. Two major Aboriginal art sites, the Art Gallery and Cathedral Cave, contain rock paintings of great significance. Year-round limits on visitor numbers protect the ecology of the park.

Some 300 kilometres east of Carnarvon National Park and north-west of Monto is **Cania Gorge National Park**, featuring prominent sandstone cliffs up to 70 metres high, cave formations, dry rainforest on sheltered slopes and open eucalypt forest. Though not as extensive as Carnarvon Gorge, this park protects a valuable scenic resource and provides an important wildlife habitat. **Auburn River National Park**, south-west of Mundubbera, protects an area of open eucalypt forest and dry scrub. The Auburn River flows through this 389-hectare park over a jumbled mass of pink granitic boulders. Over time, water erosion has sculptured the river's rock pools and cataracts. Vegetation along the river banks includes stunted figs, and bottle trees are common.

Cape Tribulation National Park

Daintree National Park

Rainforest species occur in some areas and small lizards can be seen sunbaking on rocks near the water.

Queensland's coastal islands range from large, steep continental types to coral cays, many of them lying between the mainland and the outer Great Barrier Reef. Several national park islands have been developed for tourism; these include Hinchinbrook, one of the world's largest national park islands, 39 900 hectares of wilderness and quiet beaches. More than 90 per cent of the 100 islands in the Whitsunday–Cumberland Group (including **Conway National Park**) are national parks and 6 of these islands have resorts. Sail-yourself yachts are a novel way to visit some of the more isolated spots.

Eungella National Park, 83 kilometres west of Mackay, is the Aboriginal 'Land of the Clouds'. It is one of Queensland's wildest and most majestic parks, and the freshness under the canopy of rainforest makes it a perfect destination for a day trip. Many visitors, however, choose to camp by the Broken River, where the normally shy platypus can be seen swimming casually in the creek waters.

Cape Hillsborough National Park, 50 kilometres north of Mackay, is often referred to as 'the island you can drive to', because it combines the beauty of an island with the accessibility of the mainland. A wide variety of wildlife includes kangaroos, wallabies, possums, echidnas and 100 bird species.

Launches and charter vessels from Gladstone will take visitors to Heron, Masthead North West and Tryon Islands, all rich in coral and marine life and a paradise for snorkellers and scuba divers. The Capricorn–Bunker islands are outstanding rookeries of the loggerhead and green turtles and the summer nesting-grounds for thousands of wedgetailed shearwaters and white-capped noddies.

Eurimbula National Park is south east of Gladstone, near the twin communities of Agnes Water–Town of Seventeen Seventy. Over 200 years ago Captain Cook and his crew chose this picturesque stretch of coast, with its broad sandy beaches between small rocky headlands, for their first landing in what is now Queensland. Botanically this is a key coastal area, preserving a complex array of vegetation, including some plants common in southern areas and others found in northern forests.

Lady Musgrave Island is a charming coral cay reached from Bundaberg and Town of 1770. Around the cay's edge, exposed to wind and salt spray, grows a vegetation fringe of casuarina and pandanus, which protects the shady pisonia forest on the inner part of the island. The sheltered lagoon is used by many yachties, and by day trippers for snorkelling and reef-viewing in glass-bottomed boats.

Situated only 3 kilometres east of Bundaberg and covering 40 hectares is the Baldwin Wetlands, containing the **Baldwin Swamp Environmental Park**. Walking tracks and a boardwalk allow observation of the park's wildlife. **Mon Repos Environmental Park**, 14 kilometres east of Bundaberg, is eastern Australia's largest mainland turtle rookery. The turtle season extends from November to March. Visitors to the information centre get some basic knowledge of sea turtles and acceptable human interaction with them. This ensures that a visit to the rookery is an enlightening and enjoyable experience.

Woodgate National Park, south of Bundaberg, is at the mouth of the Burrum River near Woodgate township. This coastal park of 5490 hectares provides an essential habitat for wildlife; plant communities in the park include mangroves lining the Gregory and Burrum Rivers, wallum heathland, eucalypt and angophora forests, ti-tree swamps and small pockets of palm forest. Roads within the park are gravel or sand, and 4WD vehicles are recommended, although at times conventional vehicle access is possible.

Off Hervey Bay is the world's largest sand island, Fraser Island. The northern third of the island is **Great Sandy National Park**. This and two parks further south, **Moreton Island** and **Cooloola National Parks**, require 4WD vehicles for access; the latter offers excellent boating opportunities, particularly on the Noosa River.

Noosa National Park, 160 kilometres north of Brisbane, offers the visitor a wide variety of coastal scenery. Walking tracks lead to lookouts from which can be seen such unusual rock formations as Hell's Gates, Boiling Pot and Fairy Pool.

Further south towards Brisbane lie the **Glass House Mountains**, eroded volcanic plugs that rise suddenly from the landscape. First sighted by Captain Cook in 1770, four of these mountains are national parks—**Coonoorwin**, **Tibrogargan Ngungun**, and **Beerwah**.

Bunya Mountains National Park, 250 kilometres north-west of Brisbane, was established to preserve the last remaining community of bunya pine forest. It was here that Aborigines used to gather about every third year to feast on bunya nuts.

The crescent of national parks, or Scenic Rim, around Brisbane, includes **Main Range**, **Mount Barney**, **Lamington** and **Springbrook** national parks. These offer Brisbane residents and visitors panoramic views, extensive walking tracks, picnic facilities and a range of recreational opportunities. Lamington attracts visitors by the thousands to its cool rainforest, rich in elkhorn and staghorn ferns and over 700 plant species, including orchids.

Nine small national park areas at **Mt Tamborine** also attract many day visitors to their varied rainforests, waterfalls and lookouts.

Girraween National Park, 'Place of Flowers', lies south of Stanthorpe and close to the New South Wales border, and offers visitors the best floral displays in the State. This is a photographer's paradise, while the park's massive granite outcrops provide a challenge for the rock climber.

For more information about Queensland's national parks, including the requirement for camping permits, contact the Naturally Queensland Information Centre, 160 Ann St, Brisbane (PO Box 155, Brisbane Albert St 4002); (07) 227 8185. **See also:** Individual town entries in A–Z listing.

Lawn Hill National Park, close to the NT border

Tourist Information. Behind Museum, site of Shearers' Strike 1891. June: Landsborough Flock Ewe Show. **In the area:** Formerly part of an inland sea, the area has many fossil remains. The name Muttaburrasaurus was given to a previously unknown dinosaur, the fossilised bones of which were discovered here; full-sized replica of dinosaur in Edkins St. Fishing, water-skiing, agate fossicking. **Tourist information:** Muttaburra Motors and Cafe, Edkins St; (076) 58 7140. **Accommodation:** 1 hotel, 1 cara./camp. park.
MAP REF. 476 A7, 483 N7

Nambour
Pop. 10 355
Nambour is a busy provincial town, 106 km N of Brisbane, just off the Bruce Hwy. The district was settled in the 1860s, mainly by disappointed miners from the Gympie goldfields, and sugar has been the main crop since the 1890s. Small locomotives pulling trucks of sugarcane trundle across the main street to Moreton Central Mill during the crushing season. Pineapples and tropical fruit are grown extensively. Nambour is the Aboriginal name for the red-flowering ti-tree that grows locally. **In the area:** Spectacular Glass House Mountains to south, and scenic Blackall Ranges to west. Sunshine Plantation, home of the Big Pineapple, and CSR Macadamia Nut Factory, both 7 km S. Moonshine Valley Winery, Forest Glen deer sanctuary and Super Bee honey factory, 10 km further S on Forest Glen–Tanawha Tourist Drive. Beach resorts of Maroochydore and Mooloolaba, 20 km E at mouth of Maroochy and Mooloolah Rivers. **Tourist information:** Sunshine Plantation, Bruce Hwy, Woombye; (071) 42 1333. **Accommodation:** 12 hotels, 8 motels, 2 cara./camp. parks. **See also:** Sunshine Coast.
MAP REF. 467 M1, 470 E8, 475 N4

Nanango
Pop. 2571
Gold was mined here from 1850 to 1900, but the area, 24 km SE of Kingaroy, now relies on beef cattle, beans and grain. The 1400-megawatt Tarong Power Station and Meandu Coal Mine, 18 km SW, also are of economic importance to the area. **Of interest:** Astronomical Observatory, Faulkners Rd. Oct.: Pioneer Festival. **In the area:** Bunya Mountains National Park, 84 km W. Berlin's Gem and Historical Museum, 17 km SW; open daily. Coomba Falls, near Maidenwell, 28 km SW. Forest drive from Benarkin, 40 km

Noosa

SE. **Tourist information:** Shire Offices, 48 Drayton St; (071) 63 1307. **Accommodation:** 3 hotels, 3 motels, 2 cara./camp. parks.
MAP REF. 475 L4

Nebo
Pop. 160
Nebo is situated 100 km SW of Mackay on the Peak Down Hwy. Beef cattle and grain-farming are the major industries. **Of interest:** Nebo Museum, Reynolds St. July: Rodeo. **Tourist information:** Shire Offices, 10 Reynolds St; (079) 50 5133. **Accommodation:** 1 hotel, 1 motel, 1 cara./camp. park.
MAP REF. 476 I5

Nerang
Pop. 10 174
This town in the Gold Coast hinterland is 10 km from Southport. **In the area:** At Carrara, 5 km S, weekend Hinterland Country Market. Hinze Dam on Advancetown Lake, 8 km S; swimming and sailing, picnic/barbecue facilities. Spectacular scenery in Numinbah Valley area 15 km SW, near Beechmont. Natural Arch National Park, 38 km S, popular picnic spot, walking tracks through scenic rainforest, lookout nearby. Glow-worms in cave under arch. Towards Springbrook, 42 km S: Wunburra Lookout on Springbrook Plateau; Best of All View, off Repeater Station Rd; Purlingbrook Falls in Springbrook National Park. **Tourist information:** Albert Shire Council, Nerang–Southport Rd; (075) 78 0211. **Accommodation:** 2 hotels, 3 motels, 1 cara./camp. park.
MAP REF. 467 N12, 469 C5, 475 N7

Noosa
Pop. 17 776
Noosa extends from Tewantin to Sunshine Beach and includes Noosa Heads and the commercial area Noosa Junction. The most northerly of the Sunshine Coast resorts, it is noted for its natural scenery. A combination of the Noosa National Park, a protected main beach facing north, the Noosa River and lakes system, and Qld sunshine, has made a fashionable, relaxed resort with temperate weather and safe year-round swimming. Wildlife abounds in the area. There are excellent restaurants and accommodation, but without Gold Coast-style high-rise development. Tewantin, 6 km up river, was first settled in the 1870s as a base for timber-cutters. Noosaville, on the river between Tewantin and Noosa Heads, is a family-style resort. **Of interest:** At Tewantin: Noosa Regional Gallery, Pelican St; Big Shell, Gympie St; House of Bottles, Myles St. Selina Antiques, Sunshine Beach Rd, at Noosa Junction. Noosa National Park, between Noosa Heads and Sunshine Beach: walking, surfing, rocky headlands, sandy coves, patches of rainforest, views of river and lakes from Laguna Lookout. Sept.: Jazz Party. Oct.: Beach Car Classic, Triathlon. **In the area:** Camel rides on Noosa's north shore beach. Horse-riding through the bush. All 20–40 km N: Teewah coloured sands, stranded freighter *Cherry Venture* (both 4WD); Noosa River Everglades (part accessible by car, all by boat tours from Noosaville); Cooloola National Park (accessible by 4WD). Noosa Lakes system, navigable for 50 km into Cooloola National Park, boating, sailing, windsurfing; houseboat hire. Boreen Point, quiet holiday and sailing centre on Lake Cootharaba, 21 km N of Tewantin. At Eumundi, 16 km SW, markets Sat. **Tourist information:** Noosa Information Centre, Hastings St roundabout, Noosa Heads; (074) 47 4988, or Noosa Central Booking Service, Shop 5, Oasis Centre, 20 Sunshine Beach Rd, Noosa Heads; (074) 47 3755. **Accommodation:** 47 hotels/motels, 3 cara./camp. parks. **See also:** Sunshine Coast.
MAP REF. 470 H1, 475 N3

Normanton
Pop. 1189
Normanton, 151 km from Croydon, is the central town of the Gulf Savannah and is situated on a high gravel ridge on the edge of the savannah grasslands that extend to the west and the wetlands that extend to the north. The town is also the

Darling Downs

The 72 500 square kilometres of black volcanic soil on the Darling Downs produce 90 per cent of the State's wheat, 50 per cent of its maize, 90 per cent of its oilseeds, two-thirds of its fruit and one-third of its tobacco, as well as oats, sorghum, millet, cotton, soybeans and navy beans. It is a major sheep, cattle and dairying area and the home of several famous bloodstock studs.

Allan Cunningham was the first white man to ride across these fertile plains in 1827. The Darling Downs is rural Australia at its best, with a touch of England in the magnificent oaks, elms, plane trees and poplars of **Toowoomba's** parks, and the colourful rose gardens of **Warwick** in the south. The climate is cooler and more bracing than in the rest of the State.

Driving across the Downs with its neat strips of grainfields, lush pastures, patches of forest and national parks, and well-established homesteads, gives the visitor an impression of beauty and quiet prosperity.

The Warrego Highway leads north-west from Toowoomba to the wheatfields and silos of **Dalby**, the hub of the Downs. Gowrie Mountain is a popular lookout. At **Jimbour**, 27 kilometres north of Dalby, stands the stately two-storey Jimbour House. On an elevated site with panoramic views of the Jimbour Plains, this historic home in landscaped gardens was constructed between 1874 and 1876, mainly from local materials, including cedar from the Bunya Mountains. Part of an earlier (1870) bluestone building still stands at the rear of the house.

The New England Highway, the main Sydney to Brisbane route, turns into the Cunningham Highway at Warwick, and descends from the Downs towards the coast through Cunninghams Gap, discovered in 1827. Main Range National Park has lovely rainforest, palms and native wildlife. An alternative inland route between Brisbane and Melbourne is the Newell Highway, which runs west from Warwick to **Goondiwindi** and then south through **Moree** and **Narrabri**. A less-used but scenic route is the Heifer Creek Way through the Lockyer Valley from near **Greenmount East** to **Gatton**.

For further information on the Darling Downs, contact the Southern Downs Tourist Association, 49 Albion St (New England Hwy), Warwick; (076) 61 3122. **See also:** Individual town entries in A–Z listing.

Scene near Cunninghams Gap

terminus of the historic Normanton to Croydon railway, and the Normanton railway station is the home of the award-winning *Gulflander* tourist train. **Of interest:** Penitentiary, Haig St. Restored Bank of NSW building, Little Brown St. Town well, Landsborough St; no longer in use. June: Show, Rodeo and Gymkhana. **In the area:** Fishing and camping at Walkers Creek, 32 km NW, and Norman River at Glenore, 23 km S. Lakes on outskirts of Normanton, jabirus, brolgas, herons and other birds. At Shady Lagoons, 18 km E, bush camping, bird watching, wildlife. Dorunda Station, 170 km NE, working cattle station, barramundi and saratoga fishing in lake and rivers, accommodation. Karumba, 69 km NW, prawn-fishing centre for Gulf region. **Tourist information:** Carpentaria Shire Council, Haig St; (077) 45 1166. **Accommodation:** 3 hotel/motels, 1 motel, 1 cara./camp. park. **See also:** Cape York; Gulf Savannah.
MAP REF. 478 C8, 481 H9

Railway station, Normanton

Oakey   Pop. 3425
On the Warrego Hwy, 29 km NW from Toowoomba, this town is the base for Australian Army Aviation. **Of interest:** Tourist Centre, Campbell St, memorabilia, bronze statue of racehorse Bernborough. Oakey Historical Museum, Warrego Hwy. Flypast, Museum of Australian Army Flying, at army base, via Kelvanugh St; large collection of original and replica aircraft (some in flying condition), aviation memorabilia. **In the area:** Acland Coal Mine Museum, 18 km N. Jondaryan Woolshed (1859), off Warrego Hwy, 22 km NW: space for 88 blade shearers; shearing demonstrations; billy tea and damper; sales of goods at wool store. Aug.: Jondaryan Australian Heritage Festival, at Woolshed. **Tourist information:** 68 Campbell St; (076) 91 1595. **Accommodation:** 4 hotels, 3 motels, 2 cara./camp. parks.
MAP REF. 466 D6, 475 K5

Palm Cove   Pop. 2800
Part of the Marlin Coast, serene Palm Cove, 27 km NW of Cairns, offers visitors an inviting selection of world-class accommodation with an equally splendid range of boutiques, art galleries and souvenir shops—all set on a tropical beach. Dive and tour bookings to the Barrier Reef are available, as are pick-up services for a host of day tours to the Atherton Tableland and surrounding

areas. There is also convenient access to Mossman and Port Douglas. **In the area:** On Captain Cook Hwy at Clifton Beach, 7 km S: Wild World, Australian Wildlife Showpark, exotic range of flora and fauna; Outback Opal Mine, simulated mine with displays of Australia's most famous stone. Bungy tower in rainforest, McGregor Rd, Smithfield; 14 km S. **Tourist information:** Cnr Hartley and Grafton Sts, Cairns; (070) 51 3588. **Accommodation:** 12 motels, 3 resorts, 2 cara./camp. parks.
MAP REF. 473 F7

Pittsworth   Pop. 2110
Pittsworth is a typical Darling Downs town, situated 40 km SW of Toowoomba on the road to Millmerran. It is the centre of a rich grain and dairying district. Cotton is grown with the help of irrigation. **Of interest:** Some buildings listed by National Trust. Folk Museum, Pioneer Way; pioneer cottage, blacksmith's shop, early school. Dec.: Great Australian Team Truck Pull. **Tourist information:** Sunkist Cafe, Yandilla St; (076) 93 1246. **Accommodation:** 1 hotel/motel, 1 motel, 1 cara./camp. park.
MAP REF. 466 C9, 475 K6

Pomona   Pop. 885
This small farming centre is in the northern hinterland of the Sunshine Coast, 33 km S of Gympie. Mt Cooroora (439 m) dominates the town. July: King of the Mountain, race and festival, tests skill of mountain runners world-wide. **Of interest:** Majestic Theatre, cinema museum,

annual film festival. **In the area:** Lake Cootharaba, 18 km NE, large, shallow saltwater lake on Noosa River where Mrs Eliza Fraser spent time with Aborigines after wreck of *Stirling Castle* on Fraser Island in 1836. **Tourist information:** Noosa Information Centre, Hastings St roundabout, Noosa Heads; (074) 47 4988. **Accommodation:** 1 hotel.
MAP REF. 470 B1

Port Douglas   Pop. 3660
Just 65 km NW of Cairns, along one of the most scenic coastal drives in Australia, Port Douglas offers the contrast of cosmopolitanism in a tropical, tree-covered mountain setting. Once a small village, Port Douglas has become an international tourist destination, particularly since the opening of the Sheraton Mirage Hotel, a resort complex with golf course and marina, just out of town. The town, off the main highway, is surrounded by lush vegetation and pristine rainforests. This setting, along with its proximity to the Great Barrier Reef, makes it an ideal holiday destination. **Of interest:** Ben Cropp's Shipwreck Museum, end of Macrossan St, in Anzac Park. Market in park Sun. Rainforest Habitat, Port Douglas Rd, flora and fauna in natural setting. Tours from town include: horse trail-riding, rainforest hiking, Native Guide rainforest tours, 4WD safaris, coach tours, reef tours to Outer Barrier Reef and Low Isles, the Lady Douglas paddlewheel cruise, and tours to Wetherby cattle station. Sept.: Regatta. **In the area:** Flagstaff Hill, end Murphy St, commands excellent views

Old goldmining equipment, Ravenswood

of Four Mile Beach and Low Isles. Sugar town of Mossman, 15 km N: picturesque Mossman Gorge; sugar mill; Balley Hooley steam train tour. Daintree River rainforest cruises begin further 40 km NW. **Tourist information:** Port Douglas and Cooktown Tourist Information Centre, 27 Macrossan St and Shop 18, Marina Mirage, Wharf St; (070) 99 5599. **Accommodation:** 3 resorts, 47 motels, 4 cara./camp. parks. **See also:** The Far North.
MAP REF. 473 C4, 479 K6

Proserpine   Pop. 3034
A sugar town, Proserpine is close to Airlie Beach, Shute Harbour and the islands of Whitsunday Passage. **Of interest:** Bulk sugar mill, Hinschen St; tours during crushing season. **In the area:** Conway National Park, 10 km SE, views across islands of Whitsunday Passage. Lake Proserpine at Peter Faust Dam, 20 km W, boat hire, water-skiing, fishing, swimming, picnic/barbecue facilities. **Tourist information:** Beach Plaza, The Esplanade, Airlie Beach; (079) 46 6673. **Accommodation:** 5 hotels, 5 motels, 3 cara./camp. parks.
MAP REF. 476 I2

Quilpie   Pop. 624
Quilpie, 217 km W of Charleville, was established as a centre for the large sheep

and cattle properties in the area, but is better known as a boulder opal town. It takes its name from the Aboriginal word *quilpeta*, meaning 'stone curlew'. **Of interest:** Opal sales in town and opal workings outside town. Altar, font and lectern of St Finbarr's Catholic Church, Buln Buln St, made from opal-bearing rock. Sept.: Agricultural Show. **In the area**: Duck Creek Opal Mine at Cheepie, 75 km E. Lake Houdrahan, 6 km N on river road to Adavale, water sports, popular recreation area. **Tourist information:** Shire Offices, Brolga St; (076) 56 1133. **Accommodation:** 1 hotel/motel, 1 motel, 1 cara./camp. park. **See also:** The Channel Country.
MAP REF. 485 M4

Ravenswood   Pop. 120
Ravenswood, friendly and 'not quite a ghost town', is 88 km E of Charters Towers via Mingela. One hundred years ago it was the classic gold-rush town. Visitors will find interesting old workings and perhaps a little gold along with the nostalgia. **Of interest:** Several restored historic buildings in town, incl. courthouse, shops, present ambulance centre. Oct.: Halloween Ball. **In the area:** Burdekin Dam, 80 km SE, popular recreational area. **Tourist information:** Railway Hotel, Barton St; (077) 70 2144. **Accommodation:** 2 hotels, 1

motel/camping park, camping in showgrounds.
MAP REF. 476 E1

Redcliffe   Pop. 39 073
Redcliffe was the first European settlement in Qld. Matthew Flinders landed here in 1799 while exploring Moreton Bay and the spot was named for what he found: red cliffs. In 1824 John Oxley and Commandant Miller arrived with convicts and troops to set up the Moreton Bay penal colony, which was abandoned the following year in favour of Brisbane. The Aborigines called the place Humpybong, meaning 'dead houses', and the name is still used for the Redcliffe Peninsula, which comprises the towns of Woody Point, Margate, Clontarf, Scarborough and Redcliffe. The City of Redcliffe, 35 km N of Brisbane, was proclaimed in 1959 and is a fast-growing separate-but-satellite area of Brisbane. The 2.6-km bridge, which links the two cities, is known as the Houghton Hwy, which in 1979 replaced the old Hornibrook Hwy. Fishing and boating are popular pastimes. **Of interest:** Historical museum, Marine Pde. Self-guide heritage walk. Seawater lagoon at Redcliffe Point. Craft markets on beach, Sun. Jan.: Blessing of the Fleet. **In the area:** Redcliffe is departure point for vehicular ferry to Moreton Island, where sand dunes are reputed to be highest in world. Popular Tangalooma resort on western side of island. **Tourist information:** Jetty Building, Redcliffe Pde; (07) 284 5595. **Accommodation:** 6 hotels, 3 motels, 11 cara./camp. parks. **See also:** Tours from Brisbane.
MAP REF. 467 N6, 475 N5

Redland Bay   Pop. 2576
Some 30 km SE of Brisbane on the shores of Moreton Bay, the famous red soil of this area grows excellent vegetables and strawberries, mainly for the Brisbane market. It is a popular Sunday afternoon drive from the city. Cleveland is the main centre of the Redland area, and beaches at Wellington Point, Victoria Point and Redland Bay offer safe swimming and boating. **Of interest:** Heritage Trail incl.: Grand View Hotel (1851), Qld's first licensed hotel, restored; Ormiston House (1862); The Old Lighthouse (1864); Ye Old Courthouse (1853). Bayside Markets, Bloomfield St, Sun. Sept.: Strawberry Festival. **In the area:** Venman Environmental Park, Mt Cotton, 12 km SW, fauna sanctuary, walking tracks,

The Capricorn Region

This rich and varied slice of Queensland stretches inland from Rockhampton and the Capricorn Coast out to Jericho, and straddles the Tropic of Capricorn. The area includes the Capricorn Coast, Rockhampton City and surrounds, the Central Highlands and the Rural Hinterlands, and is drained by the Fitzroy, Mackenzie, Comet, Nogoa and Dawson Rivers. The district was first opened up by gold- and copper-mining around **Emerald** in the 1860s, and the discovery of sapphires around **Anakie**. The original owners of the land have left their heritage in superb and mysterious rock paintings on the silent stone walls of the Carnarvon Ranges to the south. Cattle have been the economic mainstay since European settlement, but vast tracts of brigalow scrub were cleared after World War II to grow wheat, maize, sorghum and safflower. These days coal has become king, with mainly American companies gouging out enormous deposits for local and Japanese markets. On a smaller scale, professional and amateur fossickers are still finding gems with a great deal of enjoyment.

For a pleasurable tour of the region, drive west from **Rockhampton**, the commercial and manufacturing capital, along the Capricorn Highway. Detour to Blackdown Tableland National Park where there are waterfalls, rock pools and camping areas; the turnoff is between **Blackwater** and **Dingo**. (You will need a permit from the Queensland National Parks office in Rockhampton to enter the park.) At Emerald turn south to Springsure, then east to **Biloela** on the Dawson Highway. Continue north on the Burnett Highway via **Mount Morgan** back to Rockhampton.

Mount Hay Gemstone Tourist Park, 41 kilometres from Rockhampton, allows visitors to fossick for thunder-eggs and rhyolite, which may be cut and polished at the factory in the park. Utah's Blackwater coalmine produces 4 million tonnes of coking coal and almost 3 million tonnes of steaming coal annually. Tours can be arranged.

Emerald is the main town in the Central Highlands region, with the central-western railway continuing much further west to Longreach and the Channel Country. Clermont and the Blair Athol coalfields are 106 kilometres to the north-west. The

gemfields of Anakie, **Rubyvale**, **Sapphire**, **The Willows** and **Tomahawk Creek** are west of Emerald, and are popular with tourists seeking a different holiday. (A fossicker's licence is necessary.)

Springsure, 66 kilometres south of Emerald, is one of Queensland's oldest towns, having been surveyed in 1854. It produces beef and grain. Nearby is the Old Rainworth Fort at **Burnside**, a fascinating piece of Australiana, where early farm equipment, wool presses and the like are on display. It was built in 1853 from local stone.

Rolleston, 70 kilometres to the southeast, is the turnoff to the magnificent Carnarvon National Park, 103 kilometres further south. The park covers 28 000 hectares of rugged mountains, forests, caves and deep gorges, some of which are Australia's earliest art galleries; there are countless Aboriginal paintings and

engravings, which in places extend in a colourful frieze for more than 50 metres.

The Callide open-cut mine is situated near **Biloela**, the principal town in the Callide Valley. The nearby Callide Power Station supplies the Rockhampton, Moura and Blackwater districts as well as Biloela.

What are known as the 'Snowy Mounts' are actually huge piles of salt in the Fitzroy River delta between **Bajool** and **Port Alma**. Underground salty water is pumped to the surface into pools called crystallisers, and the salt is harvested during October–November after solar evaporation.

For further information on the Capricorn Region, contact the Capricorn Information Centre, The Spire, Gladstone Rd, Rockhampton; (079) 27 2055. **See also:** Individual town entries in A–Z listing.

Botanic Gardens, Rockhampton

picnic/barbecue area. Roseworld, 2 km S, exhibition gardens showing most varieties of roses. King Country Nursery at Thornlands, 10 km N, rainforest setting, picnic facilities. At Cleveland, 15 km N, bayside markets on Sun. Cleveland is departure point for boats to Stradbroke Island, while Redland Bay is departure point for Russell, Lamb, Macleay and Karragarra Islands. Off Victoria Point, 6 km N, Coochiemudlo Island, quiet but popular. Islands are all excellent places to picnic, swim and explore; full range of facilities and services. **Tourist information:** Redlands Tourism, 152 Shore St, Cleveland; (07) 821 0057. **Accommodation:** 3 hotel/motels, 4 motels, 4 cara./camp. parks. **See also:** Tours from Brisbane.
MAP REF. 467 O9, 475 N6

Richmond   Pop. 631
This small town on the Flinders Hwy, 500 km SW from Townsville, serves the surrounding sheep and cattle properties. **Of interest:** In Goldring St: Restored Cobb & Co. coach; Marine Fossil Museum, Old Strand Theatre; in Lions Park, display of moon rocks (spherical fossil rocks of various sizes, feature of local landscape). Aug.: Rodeo. **In the area:** The area is rich in fossils. **Tourist information:** Shire Offices, Goldring St; (077) 41 3277. **Accommodation:** 1 hotel, 1 hotel/ motel, 2 motels, 1 caravan park.
MAP REF. 483 L3

Rockhampton   Pop. 55 768
Rockhampton is called the beef capital of Australia, with some 2.5 million cattle in the region. Gold was discovered at Canoona, 60 km NW of Rockhampton, in 1858; however, cattle became the major industry, with Herefords the main breed, since cross-bred with more exotic breeds to produce disease-resistant herds. Rockhampton straddles the Tropic of Capricorn. It is a prosperous city on the Fitzroy River and has considerable architectural charm. Many of the original stone buildings and churches remain, set off by flowering bauhinia and brilliant bougainvilleas. The city has several well-established secondary industries, including two of Australia's largest meat processing and exporting factories. **Of interest:** Quay St, alongside river, National Trust-classified buildings incl. ANZ Bank (1864), Customs House (1901). Botanic Gardens on Athelstane Range, via Spencer St, fine tropical

Cotton fields, St George

display, orchid and fern house, Japanese-style garden, monkeys, koala park, walk-in aviary. Old Queensland houses carefully preserved. Cliff Kershaw Gardens, Bruce Hwy features Braille Trail. Fitzroy River Barrage, Savage St, provides 63 700 million litres of water and separates tidal salt water from upstream fresh water. The Capricorn Spire (14 m) at Curtis Park, Gladstone Rd, marks exact line of Tropic of Capricorn. April: Good Earth Expo. July: Bauhinia Arts Festival. **In the area:** Dreamtime Cultural Centre, Bruce Hwy, North Rockhampton; largest Aboriginal and Torres Strait Islander cultural centre in Australia: incl. culture of Aborigines in Carnarvon Gorge area. Old Glenmore historic homestead, 5 km N, has displays and historic buildings. Rockhampton Heritage Village, Gangalook, 20 km N, heritage buildings, hall of clocks, pioneering tools, steam engine; tours daily, special events last Sun. in month. St Christopher's Chapel, Emu Park Rd, 20 km N; built by American servicemen. Olsen's Capricorn Caverns and Cammoo caves, both limestone cave systems, 32 km N; guided tours. Thunder-eggs fossicking at Mt Hay Gemstone Tourist Park, 41 km W on Capricorn Hwy. Great Keppel Island Resort, 13 km off Capricorn Coast. Underwater Observatory off Middle Island. Mt Morgan Mine and Museum, 38 km SW, rail-motor rides Sat. p.m. Pleasant drive to top of Mt Archer, 6 km E. Yeppoon and Emu Park beaches, 25–30 km NE. **Tourist information:** The Spire, Gladstone Rd; (079) 27 2055. **Accommodation:** 18 hotels, 8 hotel/ motels, 32 motels, 9 cara./camp. parks. **See also:** The Capricorn Region.
MAP REF. 477 L9

Roma   Pop. 5669
Roma is 261 km W of Dalby at the junction of the Warrego and the Carnarvon Hwys. It was named after the wife of Sir George Bowen, Qld's first Governor. In 1859 it became the first gazetted settlement after the separation from NSW. The Mt Abundance cattle station was established in 1857 and sheep and cattle have been the area's economic mainstay ever since. The famous trial of Harry Redford, alias Captain Starlight, was held in Roma in 1872. In 1863 the SS Bassett brought vine cuttings to Roma and Qld's first wine-making enterprise got under way. Australia's first natural gas strike was made at Hospital Hill in 1900, and the gas from this source was used, briefly, to light the town. Further deposits were found periodically, and 'oil' (actually gas and condensate) caused excitement in the area in the early 1960s. Roma now supplies Brisbane with gas via a 450-km pipeline. **Of interest:** Oil rig, named Big Rig by locals, erected as landmark at eastern entrance to town on Warrego Hwy. Romavilla Winery, Injune Rd. Cultural Centre, cnr Bungil and Injune Rds, mural by local artists. Park adj. to Cultural Centre, picnic facilities. Largest inland cattle market in Australia, on Warrego Hwy. Easter: Easter in the Country. **In the area:** Carnarvon National Park, 251 km NW, Aboriginal cave paintings, varied scenery, guided tours, walks, accommodation. Meadowbank Museum, 15 km W on Warrego Hwy. **Tourist information:** Kookas Travel, Bowen St; (076) 22 1333. **Accommodation:** 10 hotels, 8 motels, 4 cara./camp. parks.
MAP REF. 474 F4

St George
Pop. 2512

Situated at a major road junction, St George is in the centre of a rich cotton-growing district. It is on the Balonne River, 118 km NW of Mungindi on the Carnarvon Hwy, and 292 km SW of Dalby on the Moonie Hwy. As St George has a rainfall of only 500 mm a year, extensive irrigation is carried out by means of a dam and three weirs. Cotton-growing and harvesting is completely mechanised; planting is Oct. to Nov., harvesting April to June. Wheat, barley, oats and sunflowers are also irrigated, and sheep and cattle are raised. **Of interest:** Balonne Creative Arts Group, Klinge Lane, local craft. Riversands Winery, Lower Alfred St; open daily. **In the area:** Rosehill Aviaries, 64 km W, one of Australia's largest private collections of Australian parrots. St George Cotton Ginnery, 20 km S; open by appt, harvesting months. Moon's Geraldton Wax Flower Farm, 26 km S; flower tours Aug.–Oct; watch rockmelons being prepared and packed Nov.–March. Fishing for Murray cod, yellow-belly and freshwater jew on Balonne River. Pig-hunting by arrangement with property owners. **Tourist information:** Balonne Shire Council, Victoria St; (076) 25 3222; or Merino Motor Inn; (076) 25 3333. **Accommodation:** 1 hotel, 3 hotel/motels, 2 motels, 3 cara./camp. parks
MAP REF. 474 F7

Sarina
Pop. 3094

In the sugar belt, Sarina lies 37 km S of Mackay on the Bruce Hwy. The area has many fine beaches, including Sarina, Armstrong, Campwin, Grasstree, Halftide and Salonika. Sarina produces molasses and ethyl alcohol as byproducts of the sugar industry. **Of interest:** Plane Creek Central Sugar Mill. CSR Distillery, Bruce Hwy, also produces Dundah, fertiliser for local sugarcane crops. Flea market, Broad St, last Thurs. in month. July: Visual Arts Festival. Aug.: Agricultural Show. **In the area:** To north: Tours of Campwin Beach Prawn Farm (8.5 km) and Prawn and Crab Hatchery, Grasstree Beach (13 km). Viewing gallery at Hay Point and Dalrymple Bay coal terminal complex, 12 km N. **Tourist information:** Shire Council, 65 Broad St; (079) 56 1444. **Accommodation:** 4 hotels, 3 motels, 1 hostel, 3 cara./camp. parks.
MAP REF. 477 J4

Shute Harbour
Pop. 200

Shute Harbour, 36 km NE of Proserpine, is a suburb of the town of Whitsunday. It is also one of the largest marine passenger terminals in Australia, second only to Sydney's Circular Quay. Shute Harbour's first marina is a 400-berth project. The jetty at Shute Harbour is the best place to start exploring the 80 or so tropical islands in the beautiful Whitsunday waters; Hayman, Daydream, South Molle and Lindeman Islands are the best known. Every morning a variety of cruise boats take tourists for a memorable day out. Booking offices, souvenir and food outlets are on the main jetty, fuel available nearby. Try boom-net riding on one of the 3-island tours available daily, or fly by seaplane to Hardy's Lagoon on the outer Barrier Reef for snorkelling among the coral. Ex-America's Cup challenger *Gretel* takes day trips through the Whitsunday Islands. There are also day trips to the pontoon at Hardy Reef for swimming, scuba diving and snorkelling. The brigantine *Romance* offers 5-night cruises off the islands and the Reef. Sail and power vessels, varying sizes and classes, can be hired. **Of interest:** Lions Lookout, spectacular views. Heritage Doll Museum, Shute Harbour Rd, adj. to Whitsunday Airport. **In the area:** Airlie Beach, 5 km N. Conway National Park, 15 km S. Great Barrier Reef (30 min. by air, 90 min. by boat) and Whitsunday Islands. **Tourist information:** Beach Plaza, The Esplanade, Airlie Beach; (079) 46 6673. **Accommodation:** 4 motels, 3 cara./camp. parks.
MAP REF. 476 I2

Southport
Pop. part of Gold Coast

At the northern end of the Gold Coast strip, Southport is packed with attractions. It also serves as the commercial and administrative centre for the Gold Coast. **Of interest:** Sea World, The Spit: marine park; dolphins, sea lions, false killer whales; replica of the *Endeavour*; Johnson Water Ski Show; monorail. Also on The Spit: Marina Mirage, Mariner's Cove and Fisherman's Wharf (tourist complexes with speciality shops, restaurants, outdoor cafes and weekend entertainment); Southport Yacht Club. **In the area:** Attractions of the Gold Coast and its hinterland. **Tourist information:** Cavill Mall, Surfers Paradise; (075) 38 4419. **Accommodation:** Low and high-rise hotels and motels, self-contained apartments, cara./camp. parks. **See also:** City of the Gold Coast.
MAP REF. 469 E5

Stanthorpe
Pop. 4187

The main town in the Granite Belt, 225 km SW of Brisbane and in the mountain ranges along the border between Qld and NSW, Stanthorpe came into being after the discovery of tin at Quartpot Creek in 1872. Silver and lead were discovered in 1880, but the minerals boom did not last. The area has produced excellent wool for more than a century, but is best known for large-scale growing of apples, pears, plums, peaches and grapes. Stanthorpe is 915 m above sea level and is often the coolest part of the

Shute Harbour

State. Spring is particularly beautiful with fruit trees and wattles in bloom. There are 90 varieties of wild orchids found in the area. **Of interest:** Museum, High St. Art Gallery and Library Complex, Weeroona Park, Marsh St. March: Rodeo. April: Opera at Sunset. **In the area:** Granite Belt wineries: Old Caves, just north of Stanthorpe; Granite Cellars Stone Ridge, Felsberg, Mountview and Kominos, near Glen Alpin; Heritage at Cottonvale, 12 km NW; Mt Magnus at Pozieres, 14 km NW; Inigo at Glen Aplin, 10 km S. Rumbalara at Fletcher, 14 km S; Golden Grove, Winewood, Bungawarna and Robinson's Family Winery, near Ballandean, 19 km S; Bald Mountain at Wallangarra, 30 km S. Girraween National Park, 32 km S, camping, bushwalking, rock climbing, spectacular wildflowers. Sundown National Park, 79 km S, wilderness area; camping on Severn River in south-west of park. Sunworld Park at Eukey, 13 km SE, displays of sun and wind-powered instruments. Storm King Dam, 26 km SE, canoeing, water-skiing. Mt Marlay, 2 km E, for excellent views. **Tourist information:** 61 Marsh St; (076) 81 2057. **Accommodation:** 5 hotels, 6 motels, 1 B&B, 1 hostel, 3 cara./camp. parks. MAP REF. 123 L2, 475 L8

Strathpine   Pop. 10 108

Immediately behind Brisbane and to the north is the Pine Rivers Shire, a peaceful rural district that includes the forested areas and national parks closest to Brisbane. Taking advantage of this rural setting so close to the city are a number of art and craft industries. Each Sunday the oldest and largest country market is held at North Pine Country Park, Whiteside, 6 km NW of Strathpine. Local artworks, food and produce are sold while buskers entertain and craft demonstrations are given. June: Pine Rivers Heritage Festival. **In the area:** Alma Park Zoo at Dakabin, 14 km N, Australian native animals; grizzly bears, camels; other animals; birds; Friendship Farm for children, features baby animals. Bunya Park Wildlife Sanctuary, Eatons Hill, 8 km SW, native animals in bush setting. Australian Woolshed at Ferny Hills, 16 km SW, shearing, spinning, trained rams, working sheepdogs; bush dances with bush band; traditional Australian food. Brisbane Forest Park, via Ferny Hills, and a number of national parks. **Tourist information:** Shire Offices, 220 Gympie

Girraween National Park, near Stanthorpe

Rd; (07) 205 0555. **Accommodation:** 2 hotels, 2 motels, 3 hostels, 1 cara./camp. park, 1 overnight camp. ground. MAP REF. 462 C3, 467 M6

Tambo   Pop. 351

Tambo, 101 km SE of Blackall on the Matilda Hwy, was established in the mid-1860s. From a point where the town now stands, explorer Thomas Mitchell first saw the Barcoo River. **Of interest:** Old Post Office Museum, Arthur St; also produces Tambo Teddies, all-wool teddy bears. Sept.: Spring Flower Festival, Ram Racing. **In the area:** Salvator Rosa section of Carnarvon National Park, 120 km E; area named by Major Mitchell, who was reminded of landscapes painted by 17th-century artist. Access to park via Dawson Development Rd and Cungelella Station; 4WD recommended. Permission to camp must be obtained from Qld NPWS. **Tourist information:** Tambo News and Gear, Arthur St (Matilda Hwy); (076) 54 6288. **Accommodation:** 1 hotel, 1 hotel/motel, 1 motel, 1 cara./camp. park. MAP REF. 476 D12, 483 R12

Taroom   Pop. 705

Taroom is almost 300 km due W of Maryborough, on the Dawson River and Leichhardt Hwy. Cattle-raising is the main industry. **Of interest:** Coolibah tree in main street, marked 'L.L.' by Ludwig Leichhardt on his 1844 trip from Jimbour

House near Dalby to Port Essington (Darwin). Museum, Kelman St; old telephone exchange equipment, farm machinery, local history. May: 2-day Agricultural Show. Sept.: Leichhardt Festival. **In the area:** Rare Livistona palms near Leichhardt Hwy, 15 km N. Isla Gorge National Park, 55 km N. Robinson Gorge, 108 km NW. Reedy Creek Homestead, 115 km NW; working cattle station, holidays. **Tourist information:** Shire Offices, Yaldwyn St; (076) 27 3211. **Accommodation:** 1 hotel, 1 hotel/motel, 1 motel, 1 cara./camp. park. MAP REF. 474 H1

Texas   Pop. 816

Quite the opposite in size to its US namesake, Texas lies on the Dumaresque River and the Qld-NSW border, 55 km SE of Inglewood. **Of interest:** Historical Museum in old police station (1893). July: Agricultural show. **In the area:** Glenlyon Dam, 51 km SE, good fishing. **Tourist information:** 40 High St; (076) 52 1444. **Accommodation:** 1 motel, 1 cara./camp. park. MAP REF. 123 J3, 475 J9

Theodore   Pop. 502

Grain and cotton are the main crops around this town on the Leichhardt Hwy, 220 km N of Miles. Theodore was named after Edward Theodore, a Premier of Qld, and designed by Burley Griffin. **Of interest:** Theodore Hotel, The Boulevard; only cooperative hotel in Qld. Dawson Folk Museum, Second Ave. Fishing on Glebe Weir. **In the area:** Isla Gorge National Park, 35 km SW. Cracow, 52 km SE, where gold was produced from famous Golden Plateau mine 1932–76. **Tourist information:** Callide St, Biloela; (079) 92 2405. **Accommodation:** 1 hotel, 1 cara./camp. park. MAP REF. 477 K12

Thuringowa   Pop. 36 000

Thuringowa is a growing city surrounding the city of Townsville. It depends not only on its established grazing and sugar industries but on such diversification as tropical fruit plantations, including mango and pineapple, extensive mixed vegetable farming, the Qld Nickel Refinery at Yabulu and, increasingly, tourism. Some of north Qld's best beaches, stretching along more than 120 km of coastline, provide visitors with surfing and fishing. **In the area:** Tropical Agriculture Research Station at Lansdowne

The Channel Country

The remote Channel Country is an endless horizon of sweeping plains in Queensland's far west and south-west corner. It seldom rains in the Channel Country itself, but after the northern monsoons the Georgina, Hamilton and Diamantina Rivers and Cooper Creek completely take over the country as they flood through hundreds of channels in their valiant efforts to reach Lake Eyre. There is scarcely any gradient. After the 'wet without rain', the enormous quantities of water carried by these rivers usually vanish into waterholes, saltpans and desert sands; lush grass, wildflowers and bird and animal life miraculously appear, and cattle are moved in for fattening.

The region is sparsely populated except for large pastoral holdings and scattered settlements linked by essential beef-roads. The Diamantina Development Road runs south from Mount Isa through Dajarra and Boulia to Bedourie, then swings east across the many channels of the Diamantina River and Cooper Creek through Windorah to the railhead at Quilpie, then on to Charleville, a journey of some 1335 kilometres.

Boulia, proclaimed the capital of the Channel Country, was first settled by Europeans in 1877. It is 305 kilometres south of Mount Isa and 365 kilometres west of Winton. A friendly, relaxed town on the Burke River, its name comes from an Aboriginal word meaning 'clear water'. Burke and Wills filled their water-bags here. The first mail service was by horse from Cloncurry, and a telegraph station was established in 1884.

Bedourie, 198 kilometres further south, is the administrative centre for the Diamantina Shire, and has a store, school, police station and Flying Doctor medical clinic. It has ample artesian water, without the usual pungent smell, and swimming is popular. The hotel serves petrol as well as beer.

South of Bedourie the Diamantina Road swings east for the partly sealed drive to **Windorah**, on Cooper Creek. The name means 'place of large fish'. During drought the area is a dustbowl, during the monsoonal period, a lake. There is a good pub in town and sheep-raising is the only industry.

A good but narrow sealed road leads 237 kilometres east to **Quilpie**, the eastern gateway to the Channel Country. Cattle, sheep and wool are transported by rail to the coast from here. The name derives from the Aboriginal word for the stone curlew, and all but one of the streets have birds' names. Opals have been found here since 1880. Although it is on the Bulloo River, the town's water supply is obtained from a near-boiling artesian bore.

The Kennedy Developmental Road from Winton to Boulia is sealed for most of its 256 kilometres. A welcome stop is the bush pub at Middleton. Visitors are sure to be told about the Min Min light, a totally unexplained phenomenon that often appears at night near the old Min Min pub, some 130 kilometres from Boulia. One theory says it is an earthbound UFO that chases cars and then disappears.

Betoota has one building (a pub) that basks in the centre of a very large, virtually featureless gibber plain. It is the only stop on the lonely 394-kilometre drive from Windorah to Birdsville, and Betoota can be truly welcome. The pub is open every day and sells fuel.

Birdsville, the most isolated settlement in Queensland, is 11 kilometres from the South Australian border, with the Simpson Desert to the west. It is at the top end of the Birdsville Track to Marree in South Australia.

Thargomindah is a small settlement on the eastern fringe of the Channel Country, 187 kilometres from Cunnamulla. Around the turn of the century Cobb & Co. was operating regularly to Cunnamulla, Hungerford, Charleville, Noccundra and Eromanga.

Noccundra, 142 kilometres even further west, has a permanent population of 3, but they can put you up at the pub and sell you fuel (leaded, unleaded and diesel). Waterholes on the nearby Wilson River are the places for yellow-belly and catfish, brolgas, pelicans, emus and red kangaroos.

Visitors should realise that summer in the Channel Country can become unbearably hot. The best time to go is between April and October, and particularly for the wildflowers, which usually bloom in late August or early September.

For further information on the Channel Country, contact the Outback Qld Tourism Authority, Library Building, Shamrock St, Blackall; (076) 57 4255. **See also:** Individual town entries in A–Z listing.

Channel country

Station. Woodstock, 33 km SW. Australian farm display at Alligator Creek, 18 km SE; also Billabong Sanctuary, Muntalunga Dr., wildlife park. Haughton River Company's Invicta Sugar Mill at Giru, 27 km SE. Internationally recognised Australian Institute of Marine Science at Turtle Bay on Cape Bowling Green, 97 km SE. **Tourist information:** Bruce Hwy, Townsville; (077) 78 3555. **Accommodation:** 3 hotels, 2 hotel/motels, 1 motel, 5 cara./camp. parks.
MAP REF. 479 N12

Tin Can Bay–Rainbow Beach

Pop. 1355
Half an hour's drive north-east of Gympie takes travellers to Tin Can Bay and Rainbow Beach. These two hamlets are popular fishing, prawning and crabbing areas; the quiet waters of Tin Can Bay are ideal for boating and fishing, while Rainbow Beach has good surfing. **Of interest:** Easter: Festival. Dec.: Robert Pryde Memorial Surf Classic. **In the area:** Road south from Rainbow Beach (4WD) leads to coloured sands and beaches of Cooloola National Park. North, at Inskip Point, ferry to Fraser Island. Boats for hire at Carlo Point for cruising, fishing, swimming. **Tourist information:** 8 Rainbow Beach Rd, Rainbow Beach; (074) 86 3227, or 6 Gympie Rd, Tin Can Bay; (074) 86 4333. **Accommodation:** Rainbow Beach, 1 hotel, 4 motels, 2 cara./camp. parks; Tin Can Bay, 1 hotel, 3 motels, 4 cara./camp. parks.
MAP REF. 475 N2

Tin Can Bay

Toowoomba   Pop. 75 990
The garden city of Toowoomba has a distinctive charm and graciousness in its wide, tree-lined streets, colonial architecture and many fine parks and gardens. It is at its best in Sept. for the Carnival of Flowers. Toowoomba is 127 km W of Brisbane, on the rim of the Great Dividing Range. It began in 1849 as a village near an important staging post for teamsters and travellers, and was known as The Swamp. Aborigines pronounced the name 'T'wamp-bah'; this became 'Toowoomba'. Today it is the commercial centre for the fertile Darling Downs, with butter and cheese factories, sawmills, flour mills, tanneries, engineering and railway workshops, a modern iron foundry, clothing and shoe factories. It has an active cultural and artistic life. **Of interest:** Self-guide Russell St heritage walk. Cobb & Co. Museum, Lindsay St, traces history of horse-drawn vehicles. St Patrick's Cathedral (1880s), James St. St Luke's Anglican Church (1897), cnr Herries and Ruthven St. Parks incl. Lake Annand, MacKenzie St, for birdlovers; Laurel Bank, scented gardens; Botanic Gardens and adjacent Queens Park, Lindsay St; Waterbird Habitat, MacKenzie St. Ascot House (1870s), Newmarket St, teas, lunches. Royal Bull's Head Inn (1847), Brisbane St, fully restored by National Trust. Toowoomba Art Gallery, Linton Gallery and Gould Gallery, all Ruthven St; Downs Gallery, Margaret St. Willow Springs Adventure Park, Spring St. Antique and craft shops. **In the area:** Self-guide scenic drives of varying lengths: many picnic spots on 48 km circuit to Spring Bluff and Murphy's Creek; old railway station at Spring Bluff has superb gardens; 100 km circuit to Heifer Creek, known as Valley of the Sun, provides spectacular scenery; 255 km circuit takes in Bernborough Centre, Jondaryan Woolshed, Cecil Plains Cotton Ginnery, Millmerran Museum and Pittsworth Folk Museum. Picnic Point, 5 km E, mountain views and Carnival Falls. At Highfields, 15 km N: Balyarta Fragrant Gardens; Highfields Orchid Park; Danish Flower Art; Pioneer Museum. At Cabarlah, 20 km N: Telopea Gallery, Black Forest Hill Cuckoo Clock Centre. Acland Coal Mine Museum, near Oakey, 25 km NW. **Tourist information:** 541 Ruthven St; (076) 39 3797. **Accommodation:** 35 motels, 2 B&B, 1 hostel, 5 cara./camp. parks. **See also:** Tours from Brisbane; Darling Downs.
MAP REF. 466 F8, 475 L6

Townsville   Pop. 75 990
In 1864 a sea captain named Robert Towns commissioned James Melton Black to build a wharf and establish a settlement on Cleveland Bay to service the new cattle industry inland. Townsville was gazetted in 1865 and declared a city in 1903. Today Australia's largest tropical city, Townsville has an international airport and its rapid expansion includes the Sheraton Breakwater Island Casino-Hotel, The Breakwater Entertainment Centre and the Great Barrier Reef Wonderland, as well as the Victoria Bridge Complex and the Lakes Project.

There are also many handsome historic buildings, particularly in the waterfront park area around Cleveland Bay. The city's busy port handles minerals from Mount Isa and Cloncurry; beef and wool from the western plains; sugar and timber from the rich coastal region; and its own manufacturing and processing industries. Townsville is the administrative, commercial, education and manufacturing capital of northern Qld. Among its impressive new public buildings is the James Cook University, which offers Australia's first tourism degree and is involved in a number of tropical research programmes. A 20 min. catamaran trip across the bay takes you to Magnetic Island National Park and resort, or you may walk the length of the Strand with its tropical parks, waterfall and over-hanging bougainvillea gardens. At the end of the Strand is the Rockpool, which allows year-round swimming. Flinders Mall in the heart of the city has the Cotters Market every Sun. morning. Townsville is becoming a renowned centre for research into marine life and is the headquarters for the Great Barrier Reef Marine Park Authority. **Of interest:** Sheraton Breakwater Casino, Western Breakwater, end Flinders St. Great Barrier Reef Wonderland, Flinders St East: aquarium with touch-tank and walk-through transparent underwater viewing-tunnel; Omnimax theatre. Billabong Sanctuary, entry from Muntalunga Dr, koala feeding, crocodile shows. Museum of Tropical Queensland, Flinders St, adj. to Wonderland. Perc Tucker Regional Art Gallery, Flinders Mall. Jezzine Military Museum, end The Strand. Copper refinery at Stuart; conducted tours. Queen's Gardens, cnr Paxton and Gregory Sts. Botanic Gardens, Anderson Park, Kings Rd. Historic Flinders Street East. Castle Hill Lookout, off Burke St. Town Common Environmental Park, Pallarenda Rd, coastline park. Maritime Museum, Palmer St, South Townsville. July: Australian Festival of Chamber Music. Aug.: Festival of Peace. **In the area:** 4-day cruises to Cairns via resort islands and Reef on catamaran *Coral Princess*. Reef day trips and dive cruises. Day sailing around Magnetic Island. Daily connections to resort islands: Magnetic, Orpheus, Hinchinbrook, Dunk and Bedarra. Day outback tours, rainforest and whitewater rafting tours. Mt Spec, Crystal Creek National Park, Hidden Valley and Paluma, all 80–100 km NW.

Busy port of Townsville

Mt Elliott National Park (25 km S), on Bruce Hwy, and Pangola Park (32 km S) at Spring Creek, Giru: waterfalls, bush walks, swimming, picnic and camping facilities. Australian Institute of Marine Science at Cape Bowling Green, 47 km SE. **Tourist information:** Bruce Hwy; (077) 78 3555. **Accommodation:** 40 hotel/motels, 1 hostel, 11 cara./camp. parks. **See also:** The Far North. MAP REF. 471, 479 N12

Tully   Pop. 2715

Situated at the foot of Mt Tyson, Tully receives the highest annual rainfall in Australia, averaging around 4200 mm. Major industries are sugarcane, bananas, tropical fruit, cattle and timber. **Of interest:** Beautiful railway station, Booth Hwy, profusion of tropical plants. **In the area:** Whitewater rafting, canoeing and reef and island cruising. Popular picnic spot on Tully River near Cardstone, 44 km W. Fishing at Cardwell, 45 km S. Spectacular rainforests at Mission Beach and Clump Point (9 km NE), Bingil Bay (25 km NE), and Tully River Gorge (44 km W) and Murray Falls (40 km SW). **Tourist information:** Bruce Hwy; (070) 68 2288. **Accommodation:** 2 hotels, 1 motel, 1 hostel, 1 cara./camp. park. MAP REF. 479 L9

Warwick   Pop. 10393

An attractive city on the Darling Downs, Warwick is 162 km SW of Brisbane on the Cunningham Hwy, and 82 km S of Toowoomba on the New England Hwy. The area was first explored by Allan Cunningham in 1827; in 1840 the Leslie brothers arrived from the south and established a sheep station at Canning Downs, and other pastoralists followed. The NSW government asked Patrick Leslie to select a site for a township, and in 1849 Warwick was surveyed and established. It was the first town, after Brisbane, in what became Qld. The railway line from Ipswich was opened in 1871 and Warwick became a city in 1936. In what seemed to be a minor incident in 1917, Prime Minister Billy Hughes was hit by an egg while addressing a crowd on the controversial conscription issue of the day. He asked a local policeman to arrest the man responsible but the policeman refused. The result was the formation of the Commonwealth Police Force. Warwick is on the willow-shaded Condamine River, 453 m above sea level, and calls itself 'the Rose and Rodeo city'. The surrounding rich pastures support famous horse and cattle studs, and produce some of Australia's finest wool and grain. Fruit, vegetables and timber grow well, and the area is noted for its dairy products and bacon. **Of interest:** Pringle Cottage (1870), Dragon St, housing large photo collection, vehicles and machinery. Leslie Park in Palmerin St. Jubilee Gardens, cnr Alice and

Whitsunday Passage

Helene Sts, displays of roses. Warwick Regional Art Gallery, Albion St. Feb.: Antique and Collectables Fair. Oct.: Rose-Rodeo Festival. **In the area:** Leslie Dam, 15 km W, water sports and picnics. Queen Mary Falls National Park, 45 km E via Killarney, and Carr's Lookout, a further 14 km. Main Range National Park, 50 km NE. Goomburra State Forest Park, east of Allora, 26 km N: Scenic Rim; Sylvester's Lookout; Mt Castle; the Hole in the Wall; picnic/barbecue facilities, camping. **Tourist information:** 49 Albion St (New England Hwy); (076) 61 3122. **Accommodation:** 13 hotels, 10 motels, 1 hostel, 3 cara./camp. parks. **See also:** Darling Downs.
MAP REF. 123 M1, 466 F13, 475 L7

Weipa   Pop. 2510
Located on the west coast of Cape York, the township of Weipa is the home of the world's largest bauxite mine, operated by Comalco. This small mining town provides a comprehensive range of services and facilities for travellers just visiting, or calling in for urgently needed repairs or supplies. **Of interest:** Guided tours of bauxite mine provide comprehensive coverage of whole mining process at Weipa. **In the area:** Tours of local areas such as Rocky Point, Trunding, Nanum and Evans Landing give insight into town's development and lifestyle. Number of fishing and camping areas near the town developed for well-equipped tourist. **Tourist information:** Cnr Grafton & Hartley Sts, Cairns; (070)

51 3588. **Accommodation:** Limited. **See also:** Cape York.
MAP REF. 480 B7

Whitsunday   Pop. 6093
Named by Captain Cook in 1770, Whitsunday Island (uninhabited) is the largest in the group. The mainland town of Whitsunday is one of Australia's fastest-growing tourist destinations. Whitsunday (incl. the suburbs of Airlie Beach, Cannonvale and Shute Harbour) depends on the tourism industry and offers a large range of activities for 500 000 visitors each year. Stretching along 15 km of the coastline, Whitsunday town was gazetted in 1987. **Of interest:** Scenic and bush walks through areas behind town in Conway National Park. June and Dec.: Festival of Sail. Nov.: Whitsunday Passage and Outer Reef Gamefishing Championships. **In the area:** Coral-viewing and tours of Great Barrier Reef and Whitsunday Islands. Extensive half- and full-day mainland tours, taking in Cedar Creek Falls, rainforests and other major attractions. **Tourist information:** Beach Plaza, The Esplanade, Airlie Beach; (079) 46 6673. **Accommodation:** 7 hotels, 14 motels, 9 hostels, 15 caravan parks, 5 resorts.
MAP REF. 477 J2

Winton   Pop. 1156
Banjo Paterson wrote Australia's most famous song, 'Waltzing Matilda', on Dagworth Station near Winton in 1895. Combo Waterhole was then part of

Dagworth, and the ballad had its first public airing in Winton on 6 April, 1895. The town is 173 km NW of Longreach on the Matilda Hwy. A major sheep area, Winton is also a large trucking centre for the giant road trains bringing cattle from the Channel Country to the railhead. In 1920 the first office of a company called Qantas was registered in Winton. The town's water supply comes out of deep artesian bores at a temperature of 83°C. **Of interest:** In Elderslie St: Historic Royal Theatre, open-air, one of oldest still operating in Australia, films Wed. and Sat.; swagman statue near swimming-pool; Gift and Gem Shop, 'Opal Walk' set up in shop; Qantilda Pioneer Place, complex of 5 buildings, incl. relocated Dagworth Station lounge room, Qantas Room, old telephone exchange, radio display, Aboriginal artefacts, steam locomotive, vintage vehicles, collection of 8000 bottles. Sept.: Outback Festival (odd-numbered years). **In the area:** Aboriginal paintings and bora ceremonial grounds at Skull Hole, 40 km S. Opalton, 115 km S, historic ghost town, gemfields. Lorraine Station, 60 km SE, day tours, accommodation. Combo Waterhole, 141 km NW via Matilda Hwy. Outback tours. Carisbrooke Station, 85 km SW: working sheep station, Aboriginal cave paintings, scenic drives; day tours, accommodation. Lark Quarry Environmental Park, 110 km SW, preserved tracks of dinosaur 'stampede'. **Tourist information:** Qantilda Pioneer Place, Elderslie St; (076) 57 1618.

Gulf Savannah

The Gulf Savannah is a vast, remote, thinly populated region stretching east to the Undara Volcanic National Park, north from **Mount Isa** and **Cloncurry** to the mangrove-covered shores of the Gulf of Carpentaria, and west to the Queensland–Northern Territory border. The unfortunate Burke and Wills were the first white visitors, although the waters of the Gulf itself were first charted by Dutch navigators almost 400 years ago. The country is flat and open and has more rivers than roads. April to October is the recommended time to see the Gulf country. During the monsoon period, generally November–March, rain may close the dirt roads and on rare occasions may flood the sealed roads from Cloncurry and **Julia Creek**. However, bird-migration patterns make this the best time for observing the spectacular bird life. Motorists should realise that this is not 'Sunday-driving' country, although main roads have been upgraded, and should plan accordingly. The safest way to travel in the monsoon period is by air out of Cairns, Mount Isa or Karumba. The Gulf Savannah is, however, an ideal corner of Australia if you want to get away from it all, and the people are exceptionally friendly and helpful.

The wide expanses of the Gulf Savannah region divide themselves into separate areas. The **Eastern Savannah** is easily reached via the Great Top Road (Gulf Development Road), which winds up the eastern face of the Dividing Range, passing above Cairns. As an alternative route to Georgetown, or for travellers with limited time to explore the outback, the Undara Loop is a leisurely 3-day round trip from Cairns through the Lynd Junction, Einasleigh and Forsayth to Georgetown. **Georgetown**, 411 kilometres from Cairns, is the centre of the Etheridge Goldfield, where nuggets can still be found. Completing the loop back to Cairns takes the traveller to Tallaroo Hot Springs, Mt Surprise and Undara Volcanic National Park, where visitors can see the lava tubes, a geological phenomenon.

From Georgetown the traveller can head west 150 kilometres to Croydon, terminus of the railway from Normanton, an historic link established to service Croydon, a rich goldmining town of the last century.

Normanton is the central town of the whole Gulf Savannah, with a population of 1189, although in the gold days of 1891 it counted some 3000 people. The former goldmining town of **Croydon** is 151 kilometres to the east. The railway between the two towns is not connected to any other system. It is used once a week by the *Gulflander*, the award-winning tourist train, which leaves Normanton every Wednesday and Croydon every Thursday. Many of Croydon's buildings have been classified by the National Trust and the Australian Heritage Commission.

Karumba, 69 kilometres north of Normanton on the mouth of the Norman River, is the centre of the Gulf prawning industry and home to the barramundi fishing industry. Keen fishermen from all over Australia come to Karumba to try their skills in what is described as the best light-tackle gear fishing in Australia. Grunter, king salmon and blue salmon are plentiful, and northern Australia's top table and sporting fish, the barramundi, is to be found in estuaries, rivers and foreshore waters. Experts consider barramundi one of Australia's finest fish, and eaten fresh they are superb.

The **Western Savannah** has endless flat grassed plains stretching as far as the eye can see, while the wetlands around Karumba stretch across the top of the Western Savannah above Burketown and beyond to the border. Here rivers some 8 kilometres apart overflow their banks during the monsoons and form an unbroken sheet of water.

The town of **Burketown**, close to the Gulf, usually makes the headlines during round-Australia car trials or when it is

Lawn Hill National Park

flooded. It can be isolated for long periods during the wet. Explorer John Stokes termed the surrounding area the 'Plains of Promise', and today, like most of the Gulf region, it is cattle country. Barramundi fishing and birdwatching attract adventurers; a well-equipped 4WD vehicle is advisable in some areas, but is not essential for the majority of locations.

Lawn Hill National Park, 262 000 hectares of rare vegetation, incorporates the Riversleigh Fossil Field Section. The park is to the west of the **Gregory Downs Hotel**, a welcome watering-hole for the traveller. Here, 60-metre sheer sandstone walls form Lawn Hill Gorge with emerald green water at their base. The National Parks Service has established 20 kilometres of walking tracks to enable visitors to see this beautiful country safely.

When travelling on the sealed beef-road from Cloncurry to Normanton, motorists notice the Bang Bang Jump-up, a change in terrain height, 29 kilometres north of the Donors Hill Station turnoff.

Flight West operate regular flights from both Cairns and Mt Isa, and this is probably the best way to appreciate the vast beauty of the Gulf Savannah and its many sleepy, winding rivers.

Although towns in this area are fully serviced, motorists are advised to carry basic supplies of food and water in case of breakdown. Check local road conditions before departure from service points and, if possible, notify someone of your destination and expected time of arrival. ABC Radio also issues reliable road reports.

The Gulf Savannah is a new frontier in Australia that is opening up to those in search of interesting but authentic educational and adventure experiences. To assist visitors, an organisation of Savannah Guides has been formed. These guides are professional interpreters who have lived in the Gulf Savannah for many years and are able to offer a wide range of knowledge concerning the wilderness environment. There are guide stations at: Tallaroo (at Tallaroo Station); Hells Gate (at Hell's Gate Roadhouse); Undara Volcanic National Park (at Lava Lodge, Undara); Borroloola, NT (at McArthur River Caravan Park); Lawn Hill National Park (at Adels Grove); and Cape Crawford, NT (at Heartbreak Hotel).

For further information on the area, contact Savannah Guide Headquarters, 57 McLeod St, Cairns; (070) 31 7933. **See also:** Individual town entries in A–Z listing.

Accommodation: 4 hotels, 2 motels, 2 cara./camp. parks.
MAP REF. 483 L7

Wondai   Pop. 1156
This typical small country town in the South Burnett is 23 km S of Murgon and 31 km N of Kingaroy. The surrounding area produces peanuts and a variety of grains; other industries include dairying, beef and pork production, timber milling and dolomite mining. **Of interest:** Museum, Mackenzie St. **In the area:** Gem-fossicking areas surround district. Boondooma Dam, 50 km NW near Proston, recreation area, water sports. **Tourist information:** Shire Offices, Scott St; (071) 68 5155. **Accommodation:** 2 hotels, 1 hotel/motel, 1 motel, 1 cara./camp. park.
MAP REF. 475 L3

Yandina   Pop. 707
Yandina lies 10 km N of Nambour on the Bruce Hwy and is the home of the world-famous Ginger Factory and Gingertown, where visitors may enjoy ginger goodies. The processing of the crop can be observed from the tower platform at the factory and the Ginger Bell paddle-steamer offers river cruises from the factory to a working ginger farm. **Of interest:** Carinya, historic homestead on Bruce Hwy at northern edge of town. The Queenslander, antiques, bric-a-brac. Wappa Dam, nearby, pleasant picnic spot. Oct.: Spring Flower and Ginger Festival. **In the area:** At Eumundi, 8 km N, markets Sat. a.m.; goods range from locally grown fruit and vegetables to art and craft. Old and impressive Imperial Hotel, near markets. **Tourist information:** Cnr Aerodrome Rd and Sixth Ave, Maroochydore; (074) 79 1566. **Accommodation:** 1 hotel, 1 cara./camp. park.
MAP REF. 470 E6

Yeppoon   Pop. 7542
This popular coastal resort, 40 km NE of Rockhampton, lies on the shores of Keppel Bay. Yeppoon and the strip of beaches to its south—Cooee Bay, Rosslyn Bay, Causeway Lake, Emu Park and Keppel Sands—are known as the Capricorn Coast. Great Keppel Island Resort is 13 km offshore. **Of interest:** Feb.: Surf Lifesaving Championships. Sept.: Pineapple Festival. **In the area:** Cooberrie Park, 15 km N, noted flora and fauna reserve, picnic facilities. Byfield State Forest, 17 km further N: home of extremely rare Byfield fern; picnic facilities. Nearby at Waterpark Creek, Upper Stony and Red Rock. Coral Life Marineland, Kinka Beach, 13 km S, unique living displays of coral and marine life. Catamaran service daily to Great Keppel Is., twice weekly to Barren Island. **Tourist information:** Ross Creek Roundabout; (079) 39 4888. **Accommodation:** 3 hotels, 1 hotel/motel, 8 motels, 9 cara./camp. parks.
MAP REF. 477 M8

Yungaburra   Pop. 807
On the edge of the Atherton Tableland, 13 km from Atherton and inland from Cairns, the town is known for its National Trust Historic Precinct listing. **Of interest:** Self-guide Historic Precinct Buildings Walk. Lake Eacham Hotel, Cedar St, Gem Gallery, Eacham Rd, mineral display, gem-fossicking information. Artists Galleries, Gillies Hwy and Cedar St. produce and craft markets, 4th Sat. of month on Gillies Hwy. **In the area:** Curtain Fig Tree, 2.5 km SW, spectacular example of strangler fig. Nearby, Tinaburra, on the shores of Lake Tinaroo. Lakes Eacham (5 km E) and Barrine (10 km E), volcanic crater lakes. **Tourist information:** Atherton Tableland Promotion Bureau, cnr Mabel and Vernon Sts, Atherton; (070) 91 4222. **Accommodation:** 1 hotel, 3 motels.
MAP REF. 473 E13

Rosslyn Harbour, Yeppoon

Queensland

Other Map Coverage
Central Brisbane 460
Brisbane Approach & Bypass Routes 461
Brisbane & Northern Suburbs 462
Southern Suburbs, Brisbane 464
Brisbane Region 466
Gold Coast Approach & Bypass Routes 468

The Gold Coast 469
The Sunshine Coast 470
Townsville 471
Cairns 472
Cairns Region 473

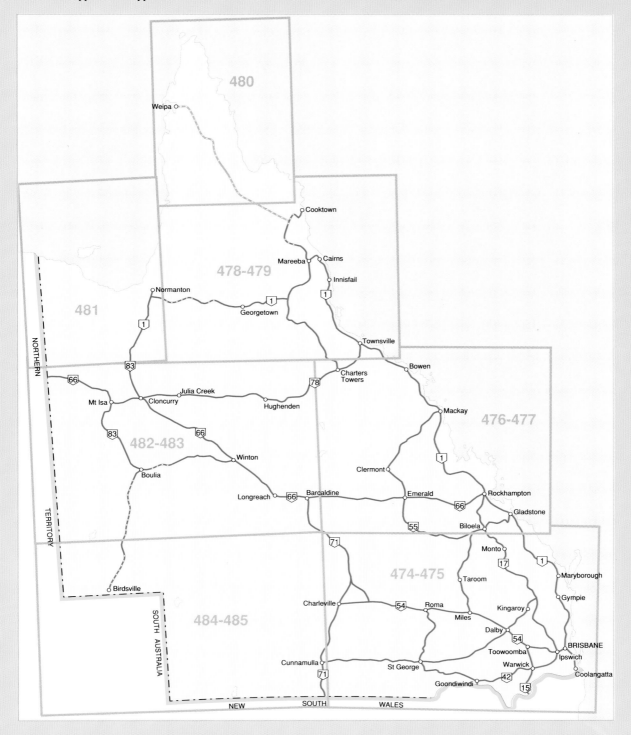

0   0.25   0.5   0.75   1 km

Spring Hill

Petrie Terrace

Albert Park

Brisbane Boys Grammar School

Albert Park Motor Inn

St. Andrews War Memorial Hospital

St. James Christian Brothers

St. James Christian Brothers School

All Hallows Convent & School

Centenary Place

Victoria Barracks

Roma St

Brisbane Transit Centre

King Edward Park

Observatory

Jacobs Ladder

Anzac Square

Post Office

King George Square

Rowes Arcade

Brisbane Arcade

GPO

RACQ

City Hall

Tourist Information

Pedestrian Overpass

Tourist Information

Mall

Pedestrian Underpass

Bus Underground

Brisbane Casino (under construction)

Treasury Building

Queens Gardens

Victoria Bridge

River Cruises

BRISBANE

Admiralty Wharf Development

Customs House

Deanery

River Cruises

Riverside Centre

Central Plaza

Ferry Terminal

Ferry Terminal

Waterfront Place

Ferry Terminal

Edward Street Ferry Terminal

Ferry Terminal

RIVER

Petrie Bight

Kangaroo Point

Capt John Burke Park

James Warner Park

CT White Park

Kangaroo Point

Mt Olivet Hospital

St. Marys Anglican Church

Kangaroo Point College of TAFE

Pedestrian Underpass

Dockside

Story Bridge

Raymond Park

State Library of Queensland

Queensland Art Gallery

Museum

Cultural Centre

Performing Arts Centre

South Brisbane

Brisbane Convention & Exhibition Centre (under construction)

South Brisbane

Brisbane State High School

South Brisbane College of TAFE

Musgrave Park

Entertainment Piazza

South Bank Ferry Terminal

Stanley Street Plaza

Parklands

Heliport

Gardens Point Ferry Terminal

Parliament House

QUT

BOTANIC GARDENS

Information Pavilion

Queensland University of Technology

Griffith University Conservatorium of Music

Kiosk

Domain

Brisbane River Stage

Gardens Point

Kangaroo Point Cliffs Lookout

Kangaroo Point

Woolloongabba

Brisbane Cricket Ground (The Gabba)

Queensland Maritime Museum

Dry Dock

River Plaza Hotel Ferry Terminal

Memorial Park

Sommerville House Girls School

St Laurences School

Mater Misericordiae Hospital

N

Accommodation

Bellevue Hotel 1 E7
Chancellor on the Park 2 C2
Gateway 3 C5
Gazebo Terrace 4 C3
Heritage 5 G6
Hilton International 6 E5
Lennons Plaza Hotel 7 D6
Parkroyal 8 F7
Radisson 9 A4
Ridge Hotel 10 E2
Sheraton Brisbane Hotel 11 E3
Story Bridge Motor Inn 12 I6
Travel Lodge 13 B4

General Information

Ansett Australia 14 D6
Australian Airlines See
   Qantas Travel Centre
Brisbane Transit Centre 15 B4
Central Railway Station 16 E3
General Post Office 17 F4
Motoring Organisation (RACQ) 18 F4
Police Headquarters 19 B4

Qantas Travel Centre 20 F4
River Cruises 21 D7/H2
Roma Street Station 22 B3
Tourist Information 23 E5/D5

Places of Interest

Anzac War Memorial 24 E4
Brisbane Cricket Ground 25 I13
City Botanic Gardens 26 G8
City Hall 27 D5
City Plaza 28 D5
Commissariat Stores 29 D7
Customs House 30 G3
Deanery 31 G3
Observatory (Old Windmill) 32 D3
Old Government House 33 F9
Parliament House 34 E8
Qld Art Gallery 35 B7
Qld Cultural Centre 36 B7
Qld Maritime Museum 37 E11
Qld Museum 38 B7
Qld University of Technology 39 F9
State Library of Qld 40 B6
Treasury Building 41 D6

Accommodation Only a sample range is listed; inclusion is not necessarily a recommendation.

CABOOLTURE
GOLD COAST
IPSWICH

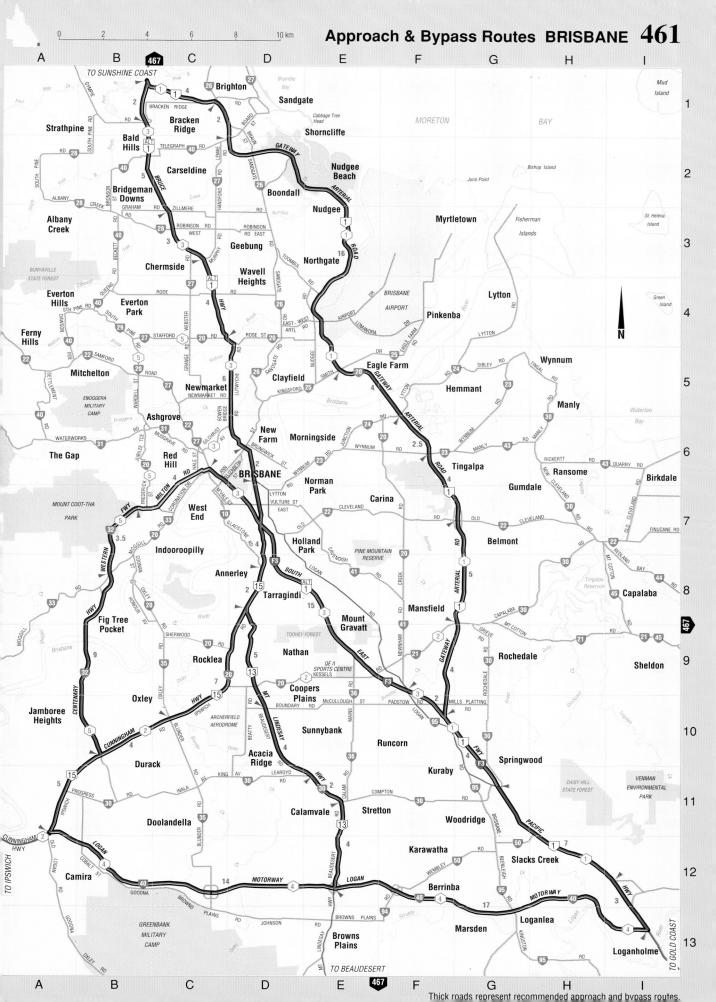

Thick roads represent recommended approach and bypass routes.

0 1 2 3 4 5 km

J K L M N O P Q R

1

2

*Mud
Island*

MORETON   *BAY*   3

N   4

For more detail of Central
Brisbane see page 460

*Bishop
Island*

Juno Point

Fisherman Point   5

Jubilee Ck   *CHANNEL*   *DR*
*Luggage
Point*   *Port
of
Brisbane*   *St. Helena
Island*

MAIN SHIPPING   *Fisherman
Islands*   *ST HELENA
ISLAND
NATIONAL
PARK*   6

Myrtletown

MAIN BEACH
BANCROFT
PRIORS   *Oil Refinery*
RD   *Bulwer Island*   *Boat*   *Passage*   7
*Whyte
Island*   *(Private*
Crab Ck   *Road)*

*Green
Island*

BRISBANE   *Fort Lytton
National Park*   8
AIRPORT   *Quarantine
Station*   **Lytton**

Pinkenba   *Oil Refinery*

*International
Terminal*   *PRITCHARD*
ST
Meeandah   *Pinkenba*   *Elanora
Park*   *Oyster Point*   9
SMITH *DR* *Wall*   *WYNNUM NORTH RD* *TINGAL RD*
Eagle Farm   *Gibson Island* *Wynnum
North*   **Wynnum**   *Darling Point*

GATEWAY   *Aquarium* *GOSPORT RD* **SIBLEY RD**   *PINE ST* *King Island* *ENVIRONMENTAL
PARK*
24   *30* **Lindum** *Wynnum Golf Course* *MOUNTJOY TCE*   10
20 Toll   *CRAWFORDS*   *NEW
LINDUM RD* *Memorial
Park* **Manly** *Manly
Boat Harbour*
Hemmant   *KIANAWAH RD* *PRESTON* *30*
Queensport *Doboy* *Hemmant
Park* **Wynnum
West**   *Waterloo
Bay*   **Erobin**

24 RD *GARRETT ST* *Cemetery* *FLEMING* *23* **Manly
West** *WHITES RD* *Fig Tree Point* *Wellington Point*   11
WYNNUM *QUEENSPORT RD* *Carmichael
Park* *Villanova
College
Sports
Ground* **Lota** *Mooroondu Point* *DOURO RD* *Geoff Skinner
Reserve*
Murarrie   *Murarrie
Recreation
Reserve*   *WONDALL RD* *WHITES* *43* *THORNESIDE* *BATH ST* *BLIGH ST*
23 *Kianawah
Park* *BELMONT* *MANLY
NEW RD* *GREEN CAMP RD* *43* **Thorneside** *MAKAHA* *43* **Wellington
Point**
**Cannon
Hill** **Tingalpa** *EVERSHOLT
ST* *THURSTON
ST* *CLEVELAND* **Wakerley** *RICKERTT* *QUARRY RD* **Birkdale** *MARLBOROUGH RD*   12
20 *Reserve* *1* *DAIRY SWAMP RD* *TILLEY* *30* **Ransome** *MOLLE* *Howeston
Golf Course* *PITT* *NELSON* *DUNCAN RD*
Bullimba Ck *FORMOSA* *NEW CLEVELAND RD* *The
Plantation* *CLEVELAND* *ROAD* *EAST*
Carina *MEADOWLANDS RD* **Gumdale** *Tingalpa
Creek
Reserve* **Ormiston** *STURGEON
RD*
22 *Clem
Jones
Centre* **Carindale** *LONDON RD* *TILLEY RD* *22* *Chelsea* *NORTHERN
ARTERIAL*
*Belmont
Hospital* *Carindale
Shopping
Centre* *OLD* *CLEVELAND* **Chandler** *30* *John Frederick
Park* *FINUCANE RD* *SHORE ST* *WEST*   13
WINSTANLEY ST *Belmont
Rifle
Range* *Cannon
Hill
Rifle Range* *Chandler
Sports
Complex* *22*

J K L M N O P Q R

N

BRISBANE FOREST PARK

Gap Creek Reserve

The Pinnacle

MOUNT COOT-THA PARK

Constitution Hill 258m

Mt Coot-tha 244m

One Tree Hill Lookout

Kenmore Hills

Brookfield

Chapel Hill

Kenmore

Pullenvale

Pinjarra Hills

Anstead

Bellbowrie

Moggill

Redbank

Goodna

Camira

Priors Pocket

Wacol

Carole Park

Ellen Grove

Forest Lake

Fig Tree Pocket

Jindalee

Westlake

Mt Ommaney

Middle Park

Jamboree Heights

Sumner

Riverhills

Darra

Sinnamon Park

Seventeen Mile Rocks

Cubberla Creek Reserve

Chelmer

Sherwood

Corinda

Oxley

Graceville

Toowong

Taringa

Indooroopilly

Chelmer

West End

South Brisbane

Highgate Hill

St Lucia

Ironside

Auchenflower

Fairfield

Annerley

Greenslopes

Stones Corner

Dutton Park

Woolloongabba

East Brisbane

Yeronga

Yeerongpilly

Tennyson

Tarragindi

Moorooka

Rocklea

Salisbury

Archerfield

Coopers Plains

Acacia Ridge

Durack

Inala

Richlands

Doolandella

Willawong

Pallara

Forestdale

Larapinta

Heathwood

Algester

GREENBANK MILITARY CAMP

Botanic Gardens

Griffith University

Queensland University

Indooroopilly Golf Course

St Lucia Golf Course

Brisbane Golf Course

Oxley Golf Course

Gailes Golf Course

McLeod Country Golf Course

Jindalee Golf Course

Moggill Country Club

Wolston Park Hospital

Department of Primary Industries

Wacol Prison

Steam Locomotive Museum

ARCHERFIELD AERODROME

Archerfield International Astrodome

Sherwood Forest Park

Lone Pine Koala Sanctuary

Amazons Aquatic Adventureland

Toohey Mountain Reserve

Toohey Forest Park

War Veterans Home

Kenmore Repatriation Hospital

BRISBANE RIVER

CUNNINGHAM HWY

LOGAN MOTORWAY

IPSWICH MOTORWAY

CENTENARY HWY

MOGGILL RD

WESTERN FREEWAY

IPSWICH ROAD

BLUNDER RD

BEAUDESERT RD

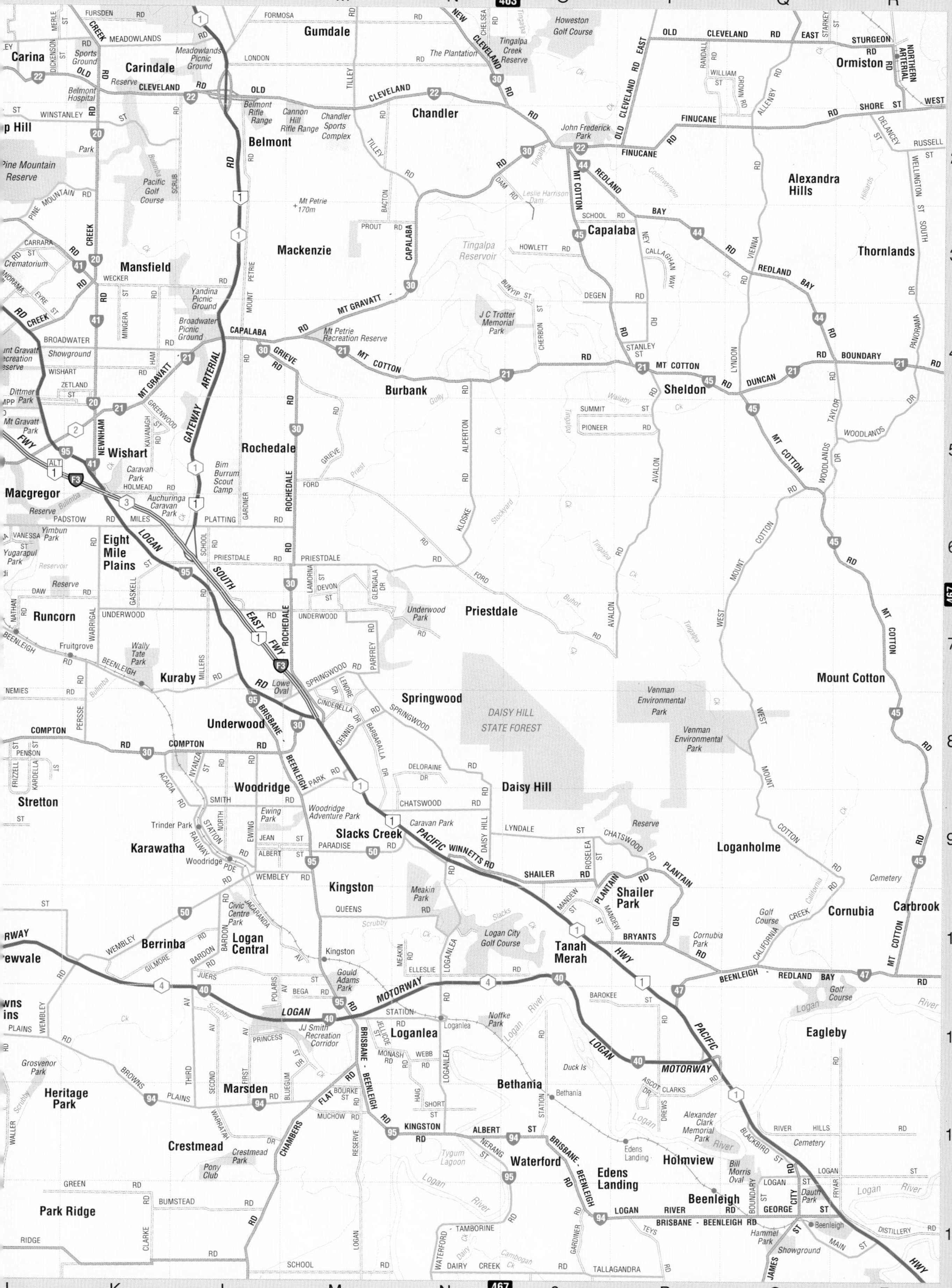

0 1 2 3 4 5 km

Carina
Carindale
Gumdale
Meadowlands
Meadowlands Picnic Ground
Belmont Rifle Range
Cannon Hill Rifle Range
Chandler Sports Complex
Belmont
Chandler
The Plantation
Howeston Golf Course
Tingalpa Creek Reserve
Old Cleveland Rd
Cleveland Rd
Ormiston
East
Sturgeon Rd
Shore St
Finucane
John Frederick Park
Leslie Harrison Dam
Mt Cotton
Redland Bay Rd
Alexandra Hills
Thornlands
Capalaba
Mackenzie
Mt Petrie 170m
Tingalpa Reservoir
J C Trotter Memorial Park
Mansfield
Belmont Hospital
Pacific Golf Course
Yandina Picnic Ground
Broadwater Picnic Ground
Mt Gravatt
Capalaba
Grieve Rd
Mt Petrie Recreation Reserve
Mt Cotton Rd
Burbank
Sheldon
Duncan Rd
Redland Bay Rd
Gateway Arterial
Wishart
Rochedale
Bim Burrum Scout Camp
Macgregor
Caravan Park
Auchuringa Caravan Park
Eight Mile Plains
Priestdale
Underwood
Priestdale
Mount Cotton
Runcorn
Wally Tate Park
Kuraby
Underwood Park
Springwood
Daisy Hill State Forest
Venman Environmental Park
Stretton
Woodridge
Ewing Park
Slacks Creek
Springwood
Daisy Hill
Chatswood
Caravan Park
Loganholme
Karawatha
Kingston
Meakin Park
Shailer
Shailer Park
Reserve
Cornubia
Carbrook
Berrinba
Logan Central
Civic Centre Park
Gould Adams Park
Logan City Golf Course
Tanah Merah
Cornubia Park
Golf Course
Logan Motorway
Pacific Motorway
Heritage Park
Marsden
Loganlea
JJ Smith Recreation Corridor
Bethania
Eagleby
Alexander Clark Memorial Park
Bill Morris Oval
Holmview
Crestmead
Crestmead Park Pony Club
Waterford
Kingston
Edens Landing
Beenleigh
Park Ridge
Brisbane - Beenleigh Hwy

0   10   20   30 km

J   K   L   M   475   N   O   P   Q   R

N

BRISBANE

IPSWICH

LOGAN CITY

BEENLEIGH

Nambour
Bli Bli
Maroochydore
Buderim
Mons
Woombye
Palmwoods
Forest Glen
Montville
Eudlo
Maleny
Mooloolah
Landsborough
Caloundra
Peachester
Coochin
Beerwah
Glass House Mountains
Beerburrum
Woodford
Elimbah
Wamuran
Donnybrook
Toorbul
White Patch
Bellara
Woorim
Caboolture
Morayfield
Bongaree
Beachmere
Burpengary
Narangba
Deception Bay
Dakabin
Kallangur
Redcliffe
Margate
Scarborough
Petrie
Lawnton
Strathpine
Mt Samson
Closeburn
YugaR
Samford
Highvale
Chermside
Brisbane Airport
Sandgate
Newmarket
Indooroopilly
Morningside
Capalaba
Cleveland
Peel Island
Dunwich
Point Lookout
Victoria Point
Redland Bay
Sunnybank
Loganholme
Eagleby
Alberton
Woongoolba
Steiglitz
Jacobs Well
Logan City
Waterford
Bethania
Yatala
North Maclean
Wolfdene
Ormeau
Norwell
Cedar Grove
Jimboomba
Tamborine
Upper Coomera
Oxenford
Woodhill
Veresdale
Gleneagle
North Tamborine
Eagle Heights
Maudsland
Nerang
Beaudesert
Boys Town
Mt Tamborine
Advancetown
Worongary
Mudgeeraba
Canungra
Laravale
Kerry
Tabooba
Kooralbyn
Tamrookum
Boonah
Milford
Roadvale
Harrisville
Limestone Ridge
Peak Crossing
Flinders
Purga
Ripley
Loamside
Rosewood
Walloon
Wanora
Borallon
Fernvale
Kilcoy
Glenfern
Neurum
Durundur
Villeneuve
Mount Mee
Campbells Pocket
Mount Pleasant
Dayboro
Upper Laceys Creek
Somerset Dam
Lake Somerset
Crossdale
Bryden
Dundas
Cambroon Bridge
Obi Obi
Dulong
Flaxton
Hunchy
Witta
Reesville
Wootha
Booroobin
Crohamhurst
Bald Knob
Bellthorpe
Stanmore
Commissioners Flat
Diamond Valley
Mooloolah
Didillibah
Maleny
Mount Kilcoy
Mount Mee

MORETON ISLAND NATIONAL PARK
Cape Moreton
North Point
Bulwer
Tangalooma
Moreton Island
Cowan Cowan Point

NORTH STRADBROKE ISLAND
Amity Point
Rocky Point
Point Lookout
Dunwich
BLUE LAKE NATIONAL PARK
Kooringal

SOUTH STRADBROKE ISLAND

MORETON BAY
PACIFIC OCEAN
SOUTH PACIFIC

Bribie Island
Banksia Beach
PUMICESTONE NATIONAL PARK

Sea World
Main Beach
Surfers Paradise
Southport
Broadbeach
Burleigh Heads
GOLD COAST

TO NOOSA HEADS
TO WOODENBONG
TO TWEED HEADS

CONONDALE NP
CONONDALE RANGE
D'AGUILAR RANGE
BRISBANE FOREST PARK
GLASSHOUSE MOUNTAINS
CABBAGE TREE RANGE

For more detail of Sunshine Coast see page 470
For more detail of Brisbane Suburbs see pages 462-465
For more detail of Gold Coast see page 469

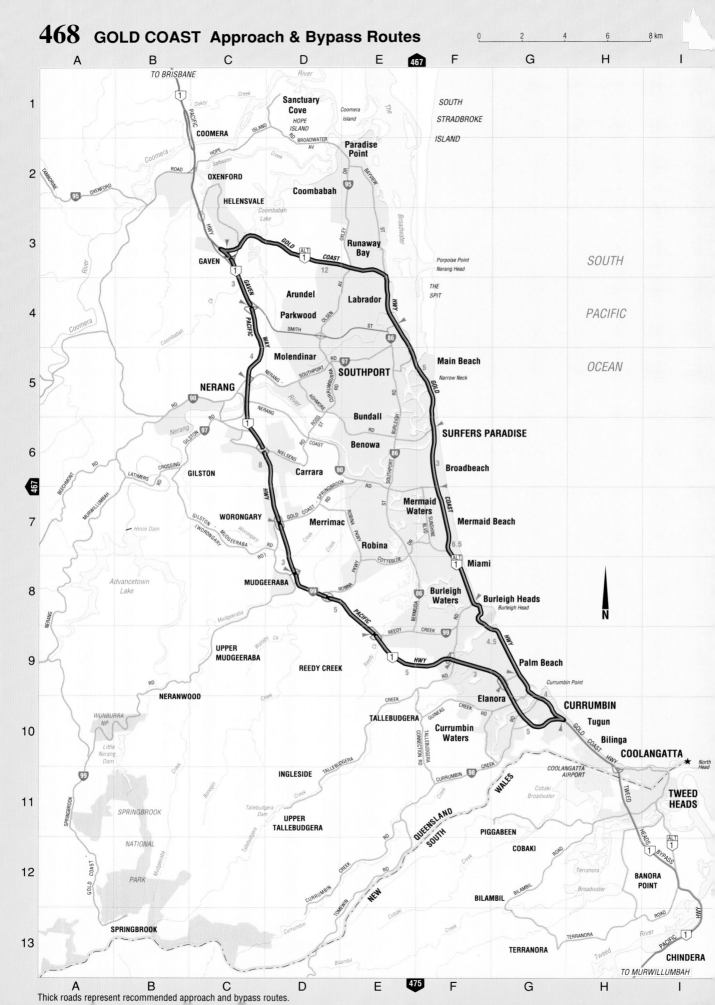

468 GOLD COAST Approach & Bypass Routes

0   2   4   6   8 km

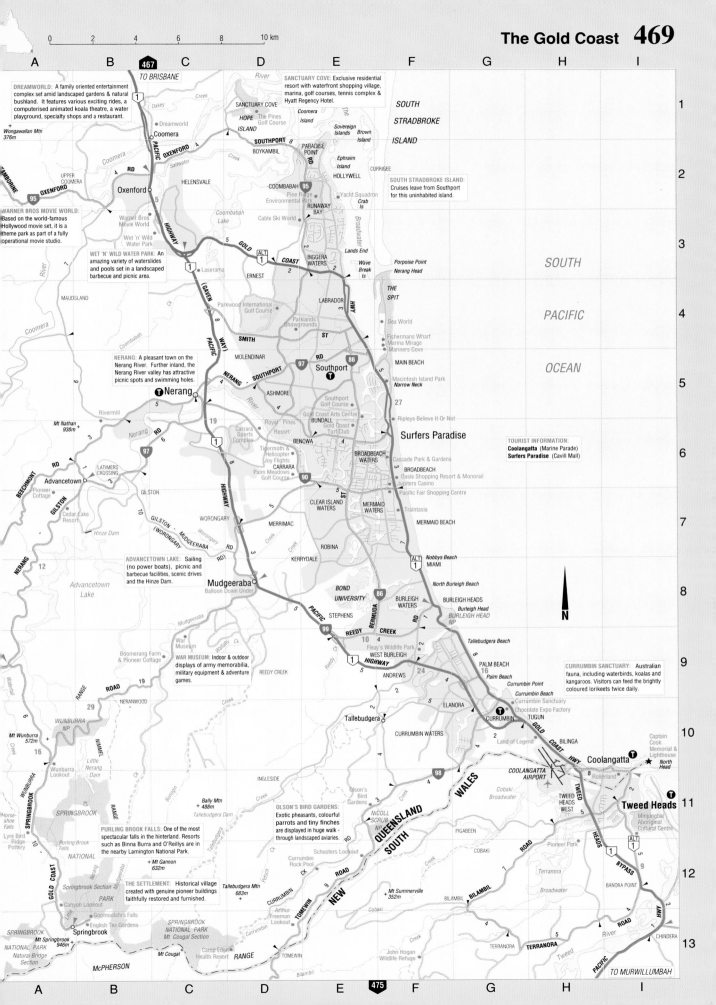

0   2   4   6   8   10 km

A   B   467   C   D   E   F   G   H   I

TO BRISBANE

DREAMWORLD: A family oriented entertainment complex set amid landscaped gardens & natural bushland. It features various exciting rides, a computerised animated koala theatre, a water playground, specialty shops and a restaurant.

Wongawallan Mtn 380m

UPPER COOMERA

TAMBORINE

95 OXENFORD

WARNER BROS MOVIE WORLD: Based on the world-famous Hollywood movie set, it is a theme park as part of a fully operational movie studio.

WET 'N' WILD WATER PARK: An amazing variety of waterslides and pools set in a landscaped barbecue and picnic area.

Oakey
Dreamworld
Coomera
Oxenford
PACIFIC OXENFORD RD
Saltwater
Warner Bros Movie World
Wet 'n' Wild Water Park
HIGHWAY
Laserama
1

MAUDSLAND

Coomera

Coombabah Lake

Coombabah

NERANG: A pleasant town on the Nerang River. Further inland, the Nerang River valley has attractive picnic spots and swimming holes.

Mt Nathan 938m
Rivermill
Nerang
97
Nerang RD
PACIFIC (GAVEN) WAY
SMITH
NERANG - SOUTHPORT
19
1

SANCTUARY COVE
HOPE ISLAND
The Pines Golf Course
SOUTHPORT
BOYKAMBIL
COOMBAH
Pine Ridge Environmental Park
Cable Ski World
Parkwood International Golf Course
Parklands Showgrounds
MOLENDINAR
97
RD
Southport
ASHMORE
Southport Golf Course
River
Royal Pines Resort
Carrara Sports Complex
BUNDALL
Gold Coast Arts Centre
Gold Coast Turf Club
BENOWA

SANCTUARY COVE: Exclusive residential resort with waterfront shopping village, marina, golf courses, tennis complex & Hyatt Regency Hotel.

Coomera Island
SANCTUARY COVE
Sovereign Islands
Brown Island
PARADISE POINT
Ephraim Island
HOLLYWELL
RUNAWAY BAY
Yacht Squadron
Crab Is
BIGGERA WATERS
ERNEST
Lands End
Wave Break Is
Porpoise Point
Nerang Head
THE SPIT
Sea World
Fishermans Wharf
Marina Mirage
Mariners Cove
MAIN BEACH
Macintosh Island Park
Narrow Neck
Ripleys Believe It Or Not
27
86
ALT 1
GOLD COAST
HWY

SOUTH STRADBROKE ISLAND

SOUTH STRADBROKE ISLAND: Cruises leave from Southport for this uninhabited island.

SOUTH

PACIFIC

OCEAN

Surfers Paradise

TOURIST INFORMATION:
Coolangatta (Marine Parade)
Surfers Paradise (Cavill Mall)

BEECHMONT
Pioneer Cottage
Advancetown
GILSTON
Cedar Lake Resort
Hinze Dam
LATIMERS CROSSING
GILSTON
97
Nerang RD
WORONGARY
GILSTON - MUDGEERABA (WORONGARY) RD
MERRIMAC
CLEAR ISLAND WATERS
KERRYDALE
ROBINA
BROADBEACH WATERS
Cascade Park & Gardens
BROADBEACH
Oasis Shopping Resort & Monorail
Jupiters Casino
Pacific Fair Shopping Centre
MERMAID WATERS
Traintasia
MERMAID BEACH

ADVANCETOWN LAKE: Sailing (no power boats), picnic and barbecue facilities, scenic drives and the Hinze Dam.

Advancetown Lake
NERANG

Mudgeeraba
Balloon Down Under
PACIFIC HIGHWAY
99
BERMUDA
REEDY CREEK
10
86
BOND UNIVERSITY
STEPHENS
Fleay's Wildlife Park
WEST BURLEIGH
24
ANDREWS
HIGHWAY
NOBBYS BEACH
MIAMI
North Burleigh Beach
BURLEIGH WATERS
BURLEIGH HEADS
Burleigh Head
BURLEIGH HEAD NP
ALT 1

WAR MUSEUM: Indoor & outdoor displays of army memorabilia, military equipment & adventure games.

War Museum
Boomerang Farm & Pioneer Cottage
NERANWOOD
29
RANGE ROAD
19

Waterfall

WUNBURRA NP
Mt Wunburra 572m
16
Wunburra Lookout
Little Nerang Dam
NIMMEL

SPRINGBROOK
Horseshoe Falls
Lyre Bird Ridge Pottery
10
GOLD COAST
SPRINGBROOK NATIONAL PARK
Mt Springbrook 946m
Natural Bridge Section
Springbrook Section

PURLING BROOK FALLS: One of the most spectacular falls in the hinterland. Resorts such as Binna Burra and O'Reillys are in the nearby Lamington National Park.

Purling Brook Falls
Mt Gannon 632m
Canyon Lookout
Goomoolahra Falls
English Tea Gardens
Springbrook
Mt Cougal
SPRINGBROOK NATIONAL PARK Mt Cougal Section

THE SETTLEMENT: Historical village created with genuine pioneer buildings faithfully restored and furnished.

McPHERSON
RANGE

Bally Mtn 488m
Tallebudgera Dam
INGLESIDE
Tallebudgera Mtn 683m
Camp Eden Health Resort
Mt Cougal

OLSON'S BIRD GARDENS: Exotic pheasants, colourful parrots and tiny finches are displayed in huge walk - through landscaped aviaries.

Olson's Bird Gardens
NICOLL SCRUB NP
Currumbin Rock Pool
Schusters Lookout
Arthur Freeman Lookout
CURRUMBIN
TOMEWIN ROAD
NEW
Mt Summerville 352m
John Hogan Wildlife Refuge
TOMEWIN

QUEENSLAND
SOUTH WALES

Tallebudgera
Tallebudgera Beach
Palm Meadows Golf Course
90
CARRARA
Tigermoth & Helicopter Joy Flights

CURRUMBIN SANCTUARY: Australian fauna, including waterbirds, koalas and kangaroos. Visitors can feed the brightly coloured lorikeets twice daily.

ELANORA
TUGUN
Currumbin
Chocolate Expo Factory
Currumbin Sanctuary
Currumbin Point
Currumbin Beach
CURRUMBIN WATERS
PALM BEACH
16
Palm Beach
Land of Legend
BILINGA
COOLANGATTA AIRPORT
GOLD COAST HWY
98
Cobaki Broadwater
Cobaki
TWEED HEADS WEST
Rollerland
Coolangatta
Captain Cook Memorial & Lighthouse
North Head
PIGABEEN
BILAMBIL
Terranora
Broadwater
TWEED HEADS
Minjungbal Aboriginal Cultural Centre
Banora Point
TWEED HEADS
BYPASS
9
ALT 1
Pioneer Park
ROAD
CHINDERA
PACIFIC HWY
TERRANORA
Tweed River
TO MURWILLUMBAH

A   B   475   C   D   E   F   G   H   I

0 2 4 6 8 10 km

A B C D E F G H I

NOOSA-TEWANTIN: A highly developed tourist infrastructure of restaurants, boutiques, apartment-style accommodation & resorts have not impacted on the area's great natural beauty. Drive up Viewland Drive to Laguna Lookout for a spectacular view of the area.

NOOSA NATIONAL PARK: This 430 hectare coastal park contains a network of walking tracks that wind through rainforest, giving spectacular views of the ocean and several unusual rock formations.

TOURIST INFORMATION:
Alexandra Headland (Alexandra Pde)
Caloundra (Caloundra Rd)
Maroochydore (Cnr Aerodrome Rd & Sixth Ave)
Noosa Heads (Hastings St)
Woombye (Sunshine Plantation, Bruce Hwy)

YANDINA: The home of the world-famous ginger factory and Gingertown, where visitors may partake of ginger "goodies". The processing of the crop can be observed from the tower platform at the factory and the Ginger Bell Paddlesteamer offers river cruises from the factory to a working ginger farm.

NAMBOUR: The centre of the sugar industry on the Sunshine Coast. The sugar mill is open for public tours (July - Nov.) and cane trains can be seen during harvest time rattling through the town carrying their loads to the mill.

HINTERLAND: The inland towns including Mapleton, Flaxton, Montville, Maleny and Palmwoods are renowned for their galleries, antique shops, craft shops, inns, guest-houses and tea shops. The surrounding area is particularly scenic and ideal for bushwalking and picnicking. Note that the road linking Palmwoods and Montville is steep and winding.

THE BIG PINEAPPLE: This 16 m high fibreglass replica of a pineapple is one of the best-known landmarks on the Sunshine Coast and is situated on an 112-hectare subtropical plantation. Other attractions include train rides, Nutmobile rides to the Macadamia Nut Factory, boat tours, restaurants and a tropical fruit market.

BUDERIM: Fertile red soil and a warm climate combine to establish the prize-winning gardens evident throughout this delightful village. Nearby Buderim Forest Park and Foote Sanctuary have bushwalking tracks through the rainforest.

MARY CAIRNCROSS PARK: Considered the best vantage point in the Blackall Range for spectacular views that extend back to the coast. The park also features walking tracks through the rainforest.

GLASS HOUSE MOUNTAINS: A group of 13 volcanic peaks that dominate the landscape ten km south of Landsborough. Formed by giant cores of long-extinct volcanoes they were first sighted by Captain Cook in 1770. Four of them - Mounts Coonoowrin, Beerwah, Tibrogargan and Ngungun - are national parks.

CALOUNDRA: A popular holiday destination, renowned for its relaxed lifestyle and beaches. Pumicestone Passage is a haven for all types of water sports, famous for its fishing, and harbours Bulcock Beach and Golden Beach, two of the safest beaches on the Sunshine Coast.

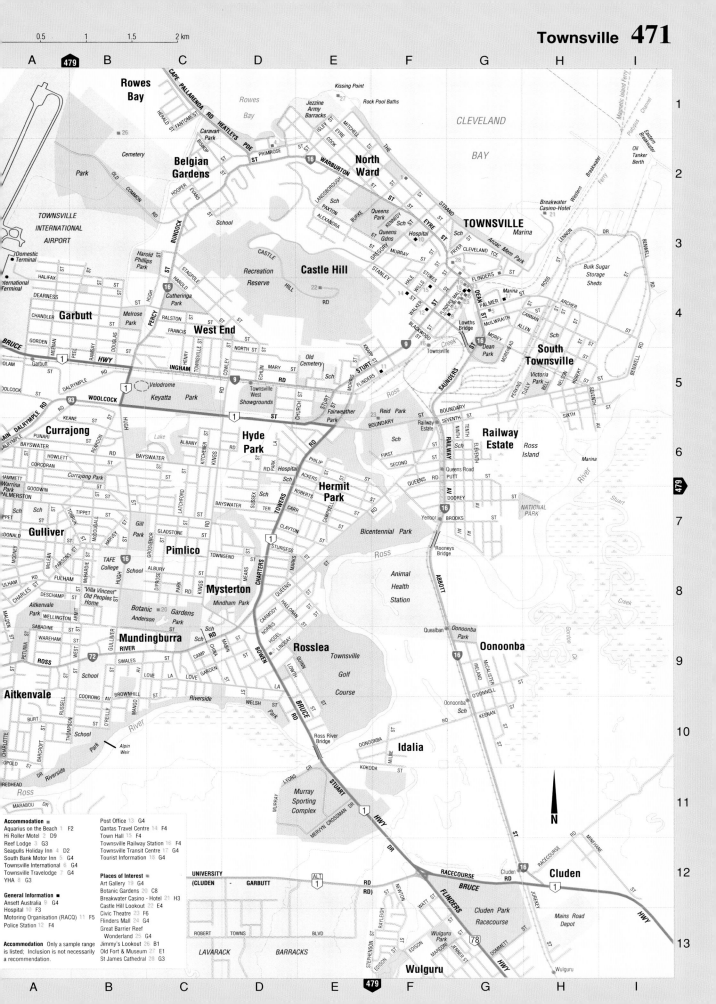

0.5 1 1.5 2 km

A B C D E F G H I

Rowes Bay

Rowes Bay

Kissing Point
Jezzine Army Barracks
Rock Pool Baths

CLEVELAND BAY

Belgian Gardens

WARBURTON

North Ward

TOWNSVILLE

Breakwater Casino-Hotel

TOWNSVILLE INTERNATIONAL AIRPORT

Domestic Terminal

International Terminal

Harold Phillips Park

CASTLE HILL

Recreation Reserve

Castle Hill

Queens Park
Queens Gdns
Hospital

Marina

Bulk Sugar Storage Sheds

Garbutt

Melrose Park

Cutheringa Park

West End

Old Cemetery

South Townsville

Victoria Park

BRUCE HWY

Garbutt

INGHAM

Townsville West Showgrounds

Fairweather Park

Reid Park

Railway Estate

Ross Island

Marina

WOOLCOCK

Velodrome Keyatta Park

Railway Estate

Currajong

Currajong Park

Lake

Hyde Park

Hermit Park

Bicentennial Park

NATIONAL PARK

River

Gulliver

TAFE College

Pimlico

Ross

Animal Health Station

Mysterton

Mindham Park

Botanic Anderson Gardens Park

CHARTERS

Rooneys Bridge

Mundingburra

RIVER

Rosslea

Townsville Golf Course

Oonoonba Park

Oonoonba

Aitkenvale

River

Alpin Weir

Riverside

Ross River Bridge

Idalia

Ross

Murray Sporting Complex

UNIVERSITY (CLUDEN – GARBUTT)

BRUCE HWY

RACECOURSE

Cluden

Cluden Park Racecourse

Mains Road Depot

LAVARACK BARRACKS

Wulguru

Scale: 0   0.5   1   1.5   2

Accommodation ≡
All Seasons Sunshine Tower   1   G8
City Caravan Park   2   F8
Hilton Hotel   3   I9
Holiday Inn   4   H8
Pacific Coast Guest House   5   H10
Pacific International   6   I9
Radisson Plaza   7   I9
Tuna Towers   8   H8
Youth Hostels   9   H9, H10

General Information ■
Ansett Australia   10   H9
Bus Station   11   I10
Cairns and Far North
  Environment Centre   12   E7
Cairns Railway Station   13   H10
Hospital   14   G8
Motoring Organisation (RACQ)   15   H9
Police   16   I9
Post Office   17   I9
Qantas Travel Centre   18   H9
Tourist Information   19   H9

Places of Interest ●
Flecker Botanic Gardens   20   D6
Hides of Cairns Hotel   21   H9
Museum   22   H9
Marlin Jetty   23   I9
Royal Flying Doctor Service   24   C6
The Pier   25   I9

Accommodation Only a sample range is listed; inclusion is not necessarily a recommendation.

Major labels:

Stratford
Aeroglen
Whitfield
Edge Hill
Mt Whitfield Environmental Park
Mount Whitfield
CAIRNS INTERNATIONAL AIRPORT
International Terminal
Domestic Terminal
Cairns North
Manoora
Manunda
Parramatta Park
Westcourt
Bungalow
Mooroobool
Earlville
Portsmith
CAIRNS
CAIRNS HARBOUR
PORT OF CAIRNS
TRINITY INLET
Admiralty Island
Flecker Botanic Gardens
Centenary Lakes
Cemetery
Cannon Park Racecourse
HMAS Cairns Naval Patrol Boat Base
The Pier
Marlin Marina
Marlin Jetty
Stafford Point

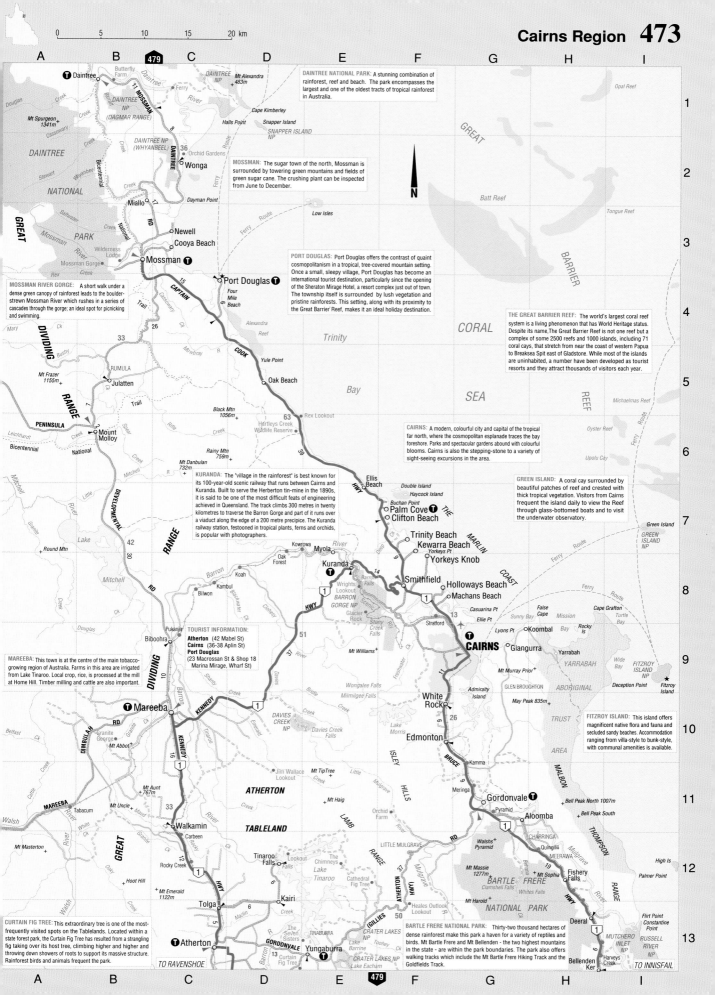

0   5   10   15   20 km

DAINTREE NATIONAL PARK: A stunning combination of rainforest, reef and beach. The park encompasses the largest and one of the oldest tracts of tropical rainforest in Australia.

MOSSMAN: The sugar town of the north, Mossman is surrounded by towering green mountains and fields of green sugar cane. The crushing plant can be inspected from June to December.

PORT DOUGLAS: Port Douglas offers the contrast of quaint cosmopolitanism in a tropical, tree-covered mountain setting. Once a small, sleepy village, Port Douglas has become an international tourist destination, particularly since the opening of the Sheraton Mirage Hotel, a resort complex just out of town. The township itself is surrounded by lush vegetation and pristine rainforests. This setting, along with its proximity to the Great Barrier Reef, makes it an ideal holiday destination.

MOSSMAN RIVER GORGE: A short walk under a dense green canopy of rainforest leads to the boulder-strewn Mossman River which rushes in a series of cascades through the gorge; an ideal spot for picnicking and swimming.

THE GREAT BARRIER REEF: The world's largest coral reef system is a living phenomenon that has World Heritage status. Despite its name, The Great Barrier Reef is not one reef but a complex of some 2500 reefs and 1000 islands, including 71 coral cays, that stretch from near the coast of western Papua to Breaksea Spit east of Gladstone. While most of the islands are uninhabited, a number have been developed as tourist resorts and they attract thousands of visitors each year.

CAIRNS: A modern, colourful city and capital of the tropical far north, where the cosmopolitan esplanade traces the bay foreshore. Parks and spectacular gardens abound with colourful blooms. Cairns is also the stepping-stone to a variety of sight-seeing excursions in the area.

KURANDA: The "village in the rainforest" is best known for its 100-year-old scenic railway that runs between Cairns and Kuranda. Built to serve the Herberton tin-mine in the 1890s, it is said to be one of the most difficult feats of engineering achieved in Queensland. The track climbs 300 metres in twenty kilometres to traverse the Barron Gorge and part of it runs over a viaduct along the edge of a 200 metre precipice. The Kuranda railway station, festooned in tropical plants, ferns and orchids, is popular with photographers.

GREEN ISLAND: A coral cay surrounded by beautiful patches of reef and crested with thick tropical vegetation. Visitors from Cairns frequent the island daily to view the Reef through glass-bottomed boats and to visit the underwater observatory.

TOURIST INFORMATION:
Atherton (42 Mabel St)
Cairns (36-38 Aplin St)
Port Douglas
(23 Macrossan St & Shop 18 Marina Mirage, Wharf St)

MAREEBA: This town is at the centre of the main tobacco-growing region of Australia. Farms in this area are irrigated from Lake Tinaroo. Local crop, rice, is processed at the mill at Home Hill. Timber milling and cattle are also important.

FITZROY ISLAND: This island offers magnificent native flora and fauna and secluded sandy beaches. Accommodation ranging from villa-style to bunk-style, with communal amenities is available.

CURTAIN FIG TREE: This extraordinary tree is one of the most-frequently visited spots on the Tablelands. Located within a state forest park, the Curtain Fig Tree has resulted from a strangling fig taking over its host tree, climbing higher and higher and throwing down showers of roots to support its massive structure. Rainforest birds and animals frequent the park.

BARTLE FRERE NATIONAL PARK: Thirty-two thousand hectares of dense rainforest make this park a haven for a variety of reptiles and birds. Mt Bartle Frere and Mt Bellenden - the two highest mountains in the state - are within the park boundaries. The park also offers walking tracks which include the Mt Bartle Frere Hiking Track and the Goldfields Track.

0 20 40 60 80 100 km

J K L M N O P Q R

1

Eidsvold
35 44
Binjour
Mundubbera
Dallarnil
Childers
Buxton Toogoom
Howard 33 Torbanlea
Hervey Bay
FRASER
ISLAND
GREAT SANDY
NATIONAL PARK

2

Gayndah
109
Biggenden
Brooweena 55
Mungar
Maryborough
Eurong
BURNETT
102
Coalstoun Lakes
Owanyilla Tuan
Maaroom
AUBURN RIVER NP
Proston 40
Tansey Woolooga
Cloyna Goomeri
Tiaro
Bauple
Gundiah
Miva
Neerdie
Gunalda
Tin Can Bay
Wide Bay Military Training Area
Rainbow Beach
Double Island Point
COOLOOLA NATIONAL PARK
Lake Cootharaba

3

Murgon
Wondai
Kilkivan
Gympie
Cooran
Tewantin
Noosa Heads
Peregian Beach
Coolum Beach
COOLOOLA COAST
Kingaroy
Tingoora
Memerambi
Cooroy
Imbil
Eumundi
Bli Bli
SUNSHINE COAST

4

Kumbia
Nanango
Kenilworth
Gallangowan
Borumba Resvr
Nambour
Witta
Maroochydore
Buderim
Caloundra
For more detail of Sunshine Coast see page 470
Bell
Yarraman
Linville
Beerwah
Glass House Mountains

5

Dalby
Blackbutt
Moore
Harlin
Kilcoy
Woodford
Wamuran
Elimbah
Bongaree
Caboolture
Burpengary
Deception Bay
Redcliffe
MORETON ISLAND NP
MORETON ISLAND
SOUTH

6

TOOWOOMBA
Crows Nest
Esk
STRATHPINE
Samford
BRISBANE
Point Lookout
Dunwich
Victoria Point
Redland Bay
NORTH STRADBROKE ISLAND
Moreton Bay
For more detail of Brisbane Suburbs see pages 462-465

7

IPSWICH
Rosewood
Peak Crossing
Jimboomba
Tamborine Village
Oxenford
Southport
SURFERS PARADISE
Burleigh Heads
CURRUMBIN
PACIFIC
SOUTH STRADBROKE ISLAND
Beenleigh

8

QUEENSLAND
Warwick
Boonah
Beaudesert
Nerang
Mudgeeraba
Coolangatta
Tweed Heads
Banora Point
Kingscliff
Bogangar
Pottsville Beach
Murwillumbah
GOLD COAST
For more detail of Gold Coast see page 469
Ocean Shores
Brunswick Heads

9

Stanthorpe
Kyogle
Nimbin
Bangalow
Clunes
Byron Bay
Newrybar
Lennox Head
Ballina
Tenterfield
Casino
Coraki
Lismore
Alstonville
Wardell
Broadwater
Evans Head
OCEAN

10

NEW SOUTH WALES
Baryulgil
Chatsworth
Iluka
Yamba
BUNDJALUNG NP
Deepwater
GIBRALTAR RANGE NP
Copmanhurst
Lawrence
Brooms Head

11

Inverell
Glen Innes
Carrs Creek Junction
Grafton
YURAYGIR NP
Minnie Water
Wooli
Coutts Crossing
Nymboida
Red Rock
Arrawarra
Woolgoolga
Emerald Beach

12

Armidale
Dorrigo
Bellingen
Coramba
Moonee Beach
Coffs Harbour
Sawtell
Mylestom
Urunga
Valla Beach
Nambucca Heads

13

Bowraville
Macksville
Scotts Head
Stuarts Point
South West Rocks

J K L M N O P Q R

0 20 40 60 80 100 km

1

J K L M N O P Q R

THE WHITSUNDAYS

N

y Island
TSUNDAY ISLANDS GROUP
ATIONAL PARK
nd

2

n Island

Island
WHITSUNDAY ISLANDS GROUP
NATIONAL PARK

3

Brampton Island

ooal Point
Bucasia
lenella
Mackay
ston

4

akers Creek
Half Tide
Grasstree
Sarina Beach
Armstrong Beach

GREAT

Koumala
Ilbilbie

5

CAPE PALMERSTON NATIONAL PARK
Middle Island
NORTHUMBERLAND
South Island
SOUTH ISLAND NATIONAL PARK

NDORS RANGE
1
100
Carmila
Flaggy Rock

SOUTH

6

White Bluff Mtn 522m
334
Broad Sound
Quail Island
BARRIER
Mt Edward +171m
Mt Price 164m
St Lawrence

ISLES

7

PACIFIC

Mt Joss 421m
Mt Phillip 393m
Shoalwater Bay
Mt Westall 550m
Mt Buffalo 518m
Mt Wellington 528m
Pine Mtn 375m
Double Mtn 747m
Military Training Area
Mt Bora 350m
Mt Magog 575m
Mt Mulgrave 655m
Mt Atherton 438m
BRUCE
82
Marlborough

8

REEF

OCEAN

Mt Gardiner 450m
Clifton
Apis Creek
Kunwarara
BYFIELD NATIONAL PARK
Arizona
Glen Geddes
Capricorn
Fitzroy River
1
Yaamba
The Caves
South Yaamba
Yeppoon
Round Mtn 146m
Ridgelands
Mulambin
Great Keppel Island
River
32
Kinka
Emu Park
FOLEYVALE ABORIGINAL COMMUNITY
Parkhurst
Keppel Sands

9

ROCKHAMPTON
Tungamull
Heron Island
OF
CAPRICORN
Gracemere
Joskeleigh
Warren
50
Broadmount
TROPIC
263
Westwood
Stanwell
Midgee
405m
Mt Barker 161m
CURTIS ISLAND NATIONAL PARK
Dingo
Bouldercombe
17
CURTIS ISLAND
Duaringa
66
Gogango
Mount Morgan
Wallaroo
Mt Battery 486m
Marmor
Raglan
107
Scrubby Mtn 333m
Mt Hope 458m
Southend

10

DAWSON RANGE
Mt Wheal 606m
Dululu
Mount Larcom
Ambrose
33
Wowan
145
Yarwun
Gladstone
Cedric Mtn 699m
34
Boyne Island
Tannum Sands
19
RODDS PENINSULA NP
Lady Musgrave Island
Rannes
108
Calliope
DAWSON
Mt Dawson 317m
Mt Redshirt 597m
66
HWY
1
Bustard Bay
WOORABINDA ABORIGINAL COMMUNITY
Goovigen
Specimen Hill 671m
EURIMBULA NP
Town of Seventeen Seventy
Lady Elliott Island
Baralaba
Jambin
Callide Coal Mine & Power Station
BRUCE
Bororen
Agnes Water
Mt Ramsay 445m
Argoon
Callide Dam
KROOMBIT TOPS NP
Nagoorin
Miriam Vale
Mt Dromedary 477m
DEEPWATER NP

11

Biloela
Thangool
Ubobo
HWY
Banana
Bruno Hill
17
Blue Mtn 640m
Many Peaks
Lowmead
Baffle Creek
Moura
Lake Cania
Builyan
215
Rosedale
Bauhinia Downs
19
HWY
54
Mt Booroomen 330m
CANIA GORGE NP
Mt Molangul 769m
25
Yandaran
Moore Park
Kalpawor
Bucca
Burnett Heads
PALM GROVE NP
Mt Shaw 449m
Moonford
Mungungo
Bancroft
60
Lake Monduran
Avondale
Bargara
257
Monto
Mt Gaeta 542m
37
Bundaberg

12

ISLA GORGE NP
Theodore
Mt Kandoonan 561m
Mulgildie
River
38
14
Gin Gin
53
Elliott Heads
Coonarr
Sandy Cape
GREAT
Rooney Point
SANDY
Orchid Beach
Mt Mungungal 568m
Abercorn
20
55
Wallaville
Cordalba
Goodwood
37
Woodgate
Hervey Bay
Platypus Bay
PRECIPICE NP
RANGE
34
26
Mount Perry
27
Booyal
Buxton
Burrum Heads
NP
FRASER
Mt Round 460m
Cracow
37
35
33
Childers
Toogoom
Mt Kandoonan
Eidsvold
AUBURN RANGE
9
Dallarnil
Sandy
35
Howard
33
Torbanlea
Hervey Bay
ISLAND

13

Quaggy Mtn 493m
17
Broadmere

J K L M N O P Q R

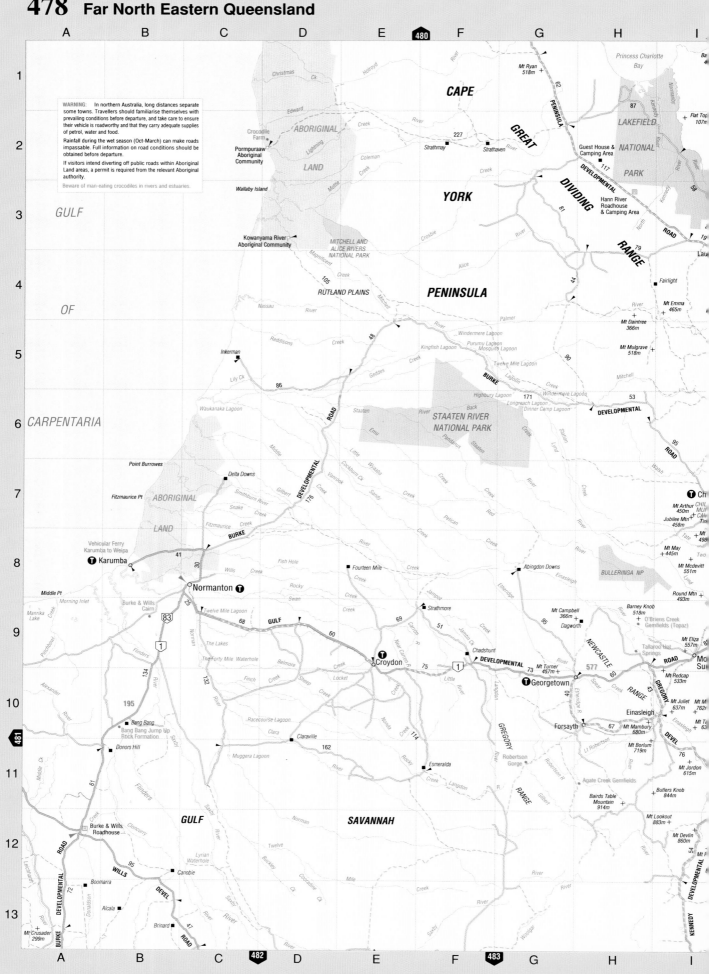

CAPE

GREAT

YORK

PENINSULA

DIVIDING

RANGE

LAKEFIELD NATIONAL PARK

ABORIGINAL LAND

GULF

OF

CARPENTARIA

ABORIGINAL LAND

GULF

SAVANNAH

STAATEN RIVER NATIONAL PARK

BURKE DEVELOPMENTAL ROAD

BULLERINGA NP

NEWCASTLE RANGE

GREGORY RANGE

Pormpuraaw Aboriginal Community

Crocodile Farm

Kowanyama River Aboriginal Community

Wallaby Island

MITCHELL AND ALICE RIVERS NATIONAL PARK

RUTLAND PLAINS

Inkerman

Point Burrowes

Fitzmaurice Pt

Delta Downs

Karumba

Normanton

Middle Pt

Mannika Lake

Burke & Wills Cairn

Bang Bang
Bang Bang Jump Up
Rock Formation

Donors Hill

Burke & Wills Roadhouse

Boomarra

Alcala

Brinard

Canobie

Mt Crusader 299m

Twelve Mile Lagoon

Croydon

Georgetown

Strathmore

Chadshunt

Mt Turner 457m

Forsayth

Einasleigh

Claraville

Esmeralda

Racecourse Lagoon

Muggera Lagoon

Lyrian Waterhole

Strathmay

Strathaven

Mt Ryan 518m

Guest House & Camping Area

Hann River Roadhouse & Camping Area

Fairlight

Mt Emma 465m

Mt Daintree 366m

Mt Mulgrave 518m

Windermere Lagoon
Purumu Lagoon
Mosquito Lagoon
Twelve Mile Lagoon

Kingfish Lagoon

Highbury Lagoon
Longreach Lagoon
Dinner Camp Lagoon

Windermere Lagoon

Abingdon Downs

Mt Campbell 366m
Dagworth

Mt Arthur 450m
Jubilee Mtn 458m

Mt May 445m

Mt Mcdevitt 551m

Round Mtn 493m

Barney Knob 518m
O'Briens Creek Gemfields (Topaz)

Tallaroo Hot Springs

Mt Eliza 557m

Mt Redcap 533m

Mt Juliet 637m

Mt Mambury 680m

Mt Borlum 719m

Mt Jordon 615m

Bairds Table Mountain 914m

Agate Creek Gemfields

Butlers Knob 844m

Mt Lookout 883m

Mt Devlin 860m

Princess Charlotte Bay

Flat Top 107m

Lau

Mo Su

J K L M N O P Q R

0 20 40 60 80 100 km

1

2

Howick Island

LIZARD ISLAND NP

Lizard Island

Hope Vale Aboriginal Community
Cape Bedford

Mt Piebald 117m
ENDEAVOUR RIVER NATIONAL PARK

3

Cape Flattery

CORAL

Mt Mccormack 518m Cooktown

Mt Byerley 445m Black Mtn 475m
Helenvale
Rossville

Mt Finnigan 1148m CEDAR BAY NP

4

Mt Misery 869m Ayton
Mt Boolbun South 999m
Mt Amy 869m Wujal Wujal
Mt Eykin 595m Mt Halycon 874m
Mt Mcdowall 548m CAPE TRIBULATION NP
Mt Hemmant 1092m

Cape Tribulation

DAINTREE NATIONAL PARK

Mt Alexandra 483m

5

For more detail of Cairns Region see page 473

Palmer River Roadhouse

Daintree

Mt Elephant 1046m Mt Spurgeon 1341m Miallo
Trinity Bay
Cooya Beach
Mossman

CORAL

Mount Carbine Mt Frazer 1155m
Maryfarms Julatten
PEBBLY BEACH
Port Douglas

Mount Molloy
Ellis Beach
Clifton Beach
Smithfield

6

Kuranda CAIRNS

GREEN ISLAND NP
Green Island

Biboohra New Northcote
Mareeba
Edmonton

BARRON GORGE NP
FITZROY ISLAND NP
Fitzroy Island

SEA

Gordonvale Aloomba
Tinaroo Falls Fishery Falls
High Island

7

Dimbulah
Tolga Kairi
Atherton
Deeral

BARTLE FRERE NP

Herberton
Babinda
Bramston Beach

Malanda Miriwinni
Topaz
RUSSELL RIVER NP

Millaa Millaa
Flying Fish Point
EUBENAGEE SWAMP NP

8

Tumoulin
Innisfail
Mourilyan

Ravenshoe
Mena Creek
Inarlinga

Innot Hot Springs Mt Koolmoon 1117m
Silkwood
Kurrimine Beach

Mount Garnet
El Arish
Bingil Bay

Mission Beach
Dunk Island
DUNK ISLAND NP

9

Tully
Euramo
Tully Heads

HULL RIVER NP

EDMUND KENNEDY NP
Rockingham Bay

Cardwell
HINCHINBROOK ISLAND

10

For more detail of Townsville see page 471

REEF

Lucinda-Dungeness
Halifax
Cassady Beach
Ingham
Trebonne Toobanna
Allingham

Great Palm Island Aboriginal Community
Great Palm Island

11

GREGORY

Bagal Beach
Rollingstone

Magnetic Island
MAGNETIC ISLAND NP
Nelly Bay

Clarke River
Blue Water Springs Roadhouse
Bluewater Jalloonda
Pallarenda

12

Jalloonda
TOWNSVILLE
Cape Bowling Green
BOWLING GREEN BAY NP

Cungulla
Alligator Creek Alva
Giru
Brandon Seaforth

13

Mingela
Ayr Home Hill
Clare
CAPE UPSTART NP

Sellheim
Millaroo
Gumlu Guthalungra
Abbot Point

J K L M N O P Q R

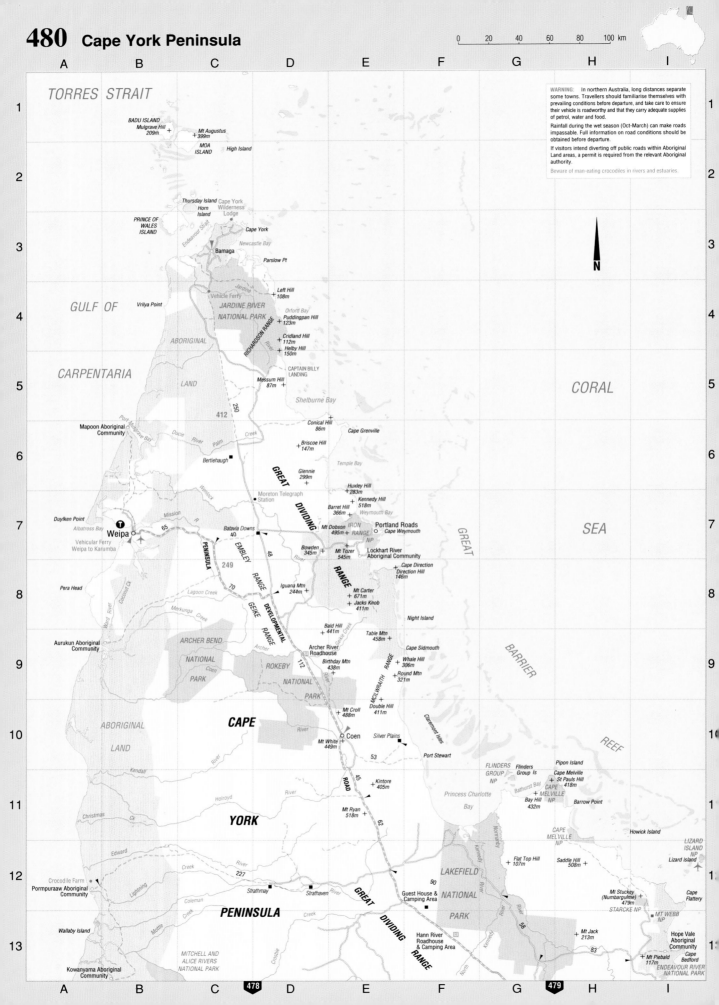

480 Cape York Peninsula

0   20   40   60   80   100 km

TORRES STRAIT

N

BADU ISLAND
Mulgrave Hill
209m

Mt Augustus
399m

MOA ISLAND

High Island

Thursday Island
Horn Island
Cape York Wilderness Lodge

PRINCE OF WALES ISLAND

Endeavour Strait

Cape York

Newcastle Bay

Bamaga

Parslow Pt

GULF OF

Vrilya Point

Vehicle Ferry

Jardine

Left Hill
108m

JARDINE RIVER NATIONAL PARK

RICHARDSON RANGE

Orford Bay
Puddingpan Hill
123m

Cridland Hill
112m
Helby Hill
150m

CARPENTARIA

ABORIGINAL

LAND

River

CAPTAIN BILLY LANDING

Messum Hill
87m

Shelburne Bay

CORAL

250

412

Mapoon Aboriginal Community

Port Musgrave Bay

Ducie   River   Palm   Creek

Conical Hill
86m

Cape Grenville

Briscoe Hill
147m

Bertiehaugh

Temple Bay

GREAT

Glennie
299m

Wenlock

DIVIDING

Moreton Telegraph Station

Huxley Hill
283m

Kennedy Hill
518m

Barret Hill
366m

Weymouth Bay

Duyfken Point
Albatross Bay
Weipa

Mission

65

R

Batavia Downs
40

48

Mt Dobson
495m

IRON RANGE NP

Portland Roads
Cape Weymouth

SEA

GREAT

Vehicular Ferry
Weipa to Karumba

PENINSULA

EMBLEY

249

Bowden
345m

Mt Tozer
545m

Lockhart River Aboriginal Community

Pera Head

Coconut Ck

70

GEIKE

RANGE

River

Lagoon Creek

Iguana Mtn
244m

RANGE

Cape Direction
Direction Hill
146m

Merkunga   Creek

DEVELOPMENTAL

Mt Carter
671m

Jacks Knob
411m

Night Island

Aurukun Aboriginal Community

Ward River

Archer

Bald Hill
441m

Table Mtn
458m

Cape Sidmouth

BARRIER

ARCHER BEND

NATIONAL

Coen

Archer River Roadhouse

Birthday Mtn
438m

McILWRAITH RANGE

Whale Hill
306m

Round Mtn
321m

PARK

ROKEBY

NATIONAL

PARK

112

River

Double Hill
411m

Claremont Isles

REEF

ABORIGINAL

CAPE

Mt Croll
488m

Mt White
449m

Coen

Silver Plains

Port Stewart

Pipon Island

LAND

Kendall

River

53

FLINDERS GROUP NP

Flinders Group Is

Cape Melville
St Pauls Hill
418m

CAPE MELVILLE NP

Barrow Point

YORK

Holroyd

River

45

Kintore
405m

63

Bay Hill
432m

Princess Charlotte Bay

Bathurst Bay

CAPE MELVILLE NP

Howick Island

LIZARD ISLAND NP

Christmas   Ck

Mt Ryan
518m

Lizard Island

Edward

River

227

Coleman

River

Strathmay

Strathaven

Creek

ROAD

GREAT

Normanby

Flat Top Hill
107m

Saddle Hill
508m

Mt Stuckey
(Numbargulme)
479m

STARCKE NP

MT WEBB NP

Cape Flattery

Crocodile Farm
Pormpuraaw Aboriginal Community

Lightning

PENINSULA

Creek

Mt White
90

Guest House & Camping Area

LAKEFIELD

NATIONAL

Kennedy

River

58

River

Mt Jack
213m

Hope Vale Aboriginal Community

Cape Bedford

Wallaby Island

Mottle

Crosbie

DIVIDING

Hann River Roadhouse & Camping Area

PARK

Kennedy

North

RANGE

83

Mt Piebald
117m

ENDEAVOUR RIVER NATIONAL PARK

Kowanyama Aboriginal Community

MITCHELL AND ALICE RIVERS NATIONAL PARK

478

479

0 20 40 60 80 100 km

A B C D E F G H I

1

2

GULF OF CARPENTARIA

3

4

5

N

Reddisons Ck

Inkerman

6

Mornington Island

ABORIGINAL LAND

WELLESLEY ISLANDS

Bountiful Islands

Point Burrowes

Waukanaka Lagoon

478

7

Forsyth Islands

SOUTH WELLESLEY ISLANDS

Bentinck Island

Sweers Island

ABORIGINAL

Delta Downs

Smithburn River

Fitzmaurice

8

Gold
Creek
Redbank

Settlement Ck

Buchanan Ck

Eight Mile Creek

Cliffdale Creek

Beryl Creek

Westmoreland

Hells Gate Roadhouse

Buck Hill 258m

Creek

Lily Creek

Creek

Beard Pt

Vehicular Ferry Karumba to Weipa

Karumba

LAND

Snake Ck

BURKE DEVEL RD

41

30

Fish Hole Ck

Wills Creek

9

CHINA WALL

WAANYI/GARAWA

Nicholson

Doomadgee Aboriginal Community

Walford River

Albert River

Escott

Burketown

Tirranna Roadhouse

71

Timor Lagoon
The Lake
Dingo Dam

Rocky Lake

Morning Inlet

Manrika Lake

Burke & Wills Cairn

160

231

Normanton

83

GULF DEVEL RD

Twelve Mile Lagoon

The Lakes

10

Bullock Ck

ABORIGINAL

Southern Nicholson R

Megan Ck

LAND TRUST

QUEENSLAND

NORTHERN TERRITORY

CONSTANCE RANGE

Musselbrook Creek

Mt Oscar 115m

Hells Creek

117

WILLS

Creek

Twelve Mile Creek

Almora

Millot Creek

Creek

65

Augustus Downs

NARDOO

BURKETOWN

Leichhardt Falls

Alexander

ROAD

Single Or Quimerine Creek

Punchbowl

Flinders

River

134

195

1

The Forty Mile Waterhole

Bang Bang

Bang Bang Jump Up Rock Formation

Donors Hill

Finch Creek

Racecourse Lagoon

Clara River

132

10

LAWN HILL NP

Archie Creek

ROAD

126

Little Horse Ck

Little Cartridge Ck

Sandy

Cartridge

68

DEVELOPMENTAL

Creek

Leichhardt

Creek

Muggera Lagoon

11

SMITHS RANGE

Lawn Hill

Gregory

River

CAMOOWEAL

River

Thornton

Mintgudi

145

61

Cloncurry

River

GULF SAVANNAH

12

Gallipoli

Cigarette Creek

O'Shannassy Creek

BURKETOWN

River

Mammoth Mines

Gunpowder

ROAD

Burke & Wills Roadhouse

95

Boomarra

ROAD

Donaldson

Alcala

Lyrian Waterhole

Canobie

Brinard

13

482

A B C D E F G H I

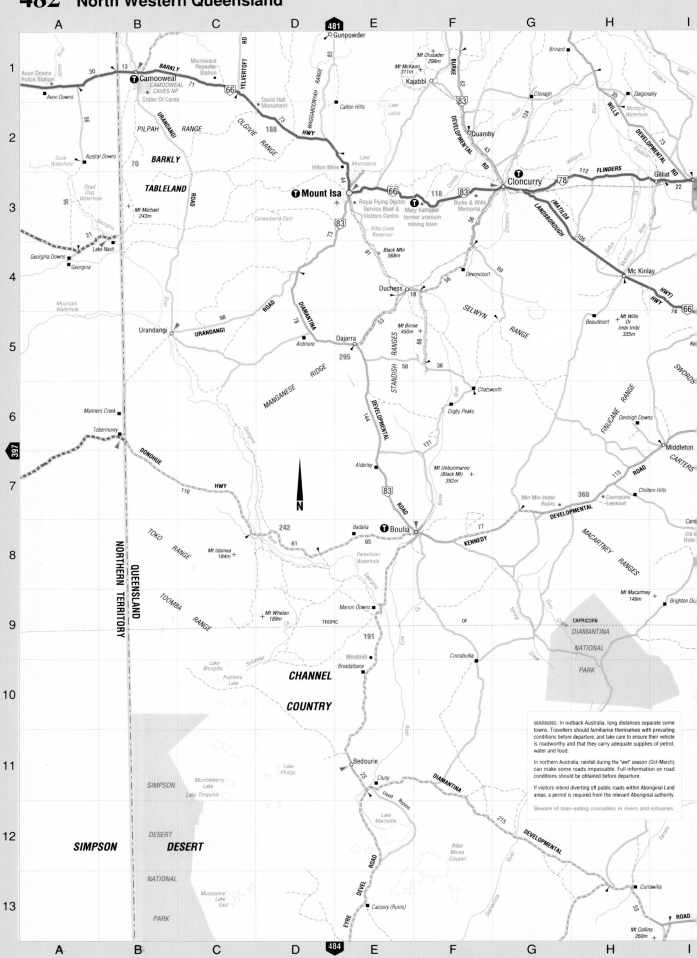

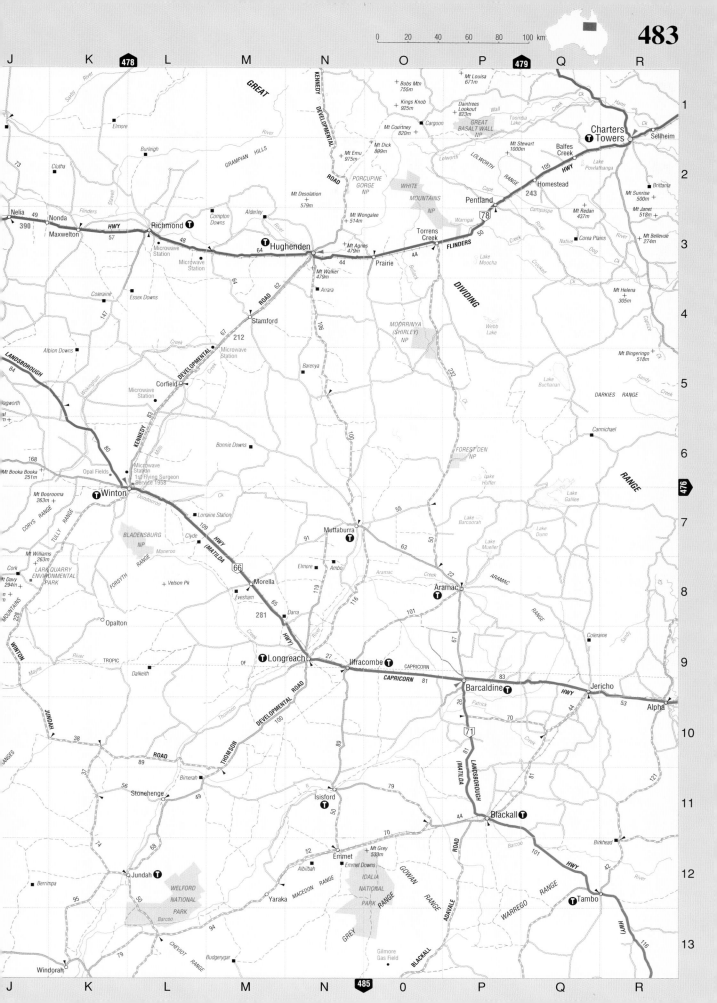

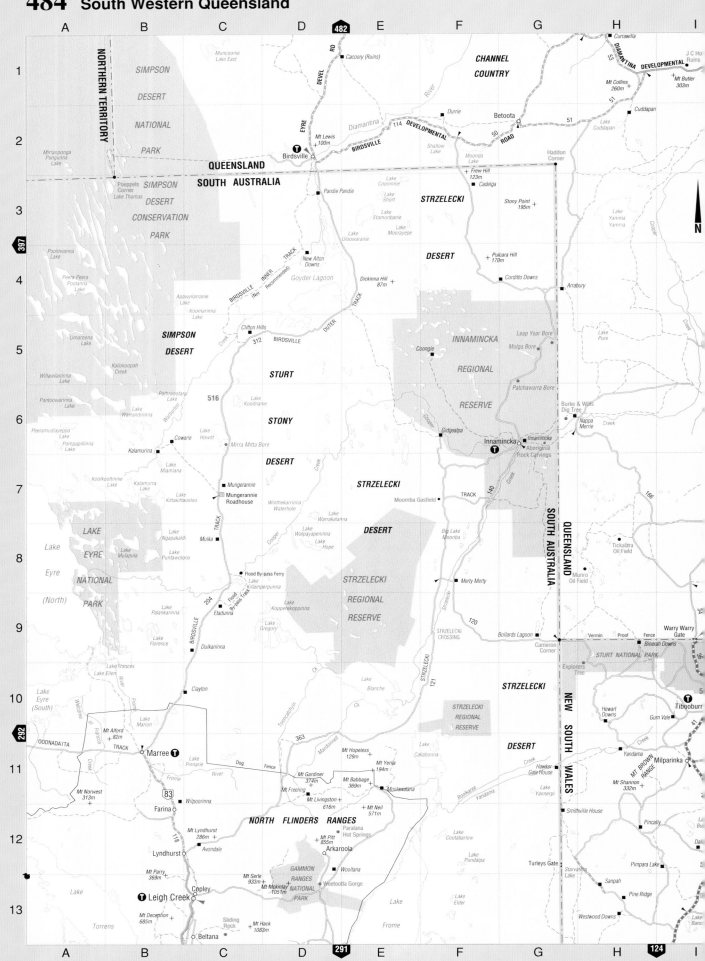

0 20 40 60 80 100 km

J K L M N 483 O P Q R

Warrego / Landsborough region map

Windorah
JUNDAH QUILPIE RD
79
57
50
Budgerygar
CHEVIOT RANGE
HELL HOLE GORGE NP
GREY RANGE
GOWAN RANGE
Gilmore Gas Field
LANDSBOROUGH
71

38
Clifton
134
BLACKALL
ADAVALE
87
Augathella
71

DIAMANTINA
103
Cornwall
Earlstoun
Bull Creek Opal Field
97
Adavale
ADAVALE
Ambathala
MARIALA NP
Lake Dartmouth
179
CHARLEVILLE ROAD
84
71
HWY

COLEMAN RANGE
Kyabra
Kyabra Ck
Oil Fields
Mt Bellalie 216m
Numerous Opal Fields
DEVELOPMENTAL ROAD
Quilpie
Paroo
Boothulla
Charleville
Royal Flying Doctor Base & Visitors Centre
54

MCGREGOR RANGE
Eromanga
Congie
36
Cheepie
210
Cooladdi
HWY
99
73
Boatman Bore

234
Oil Fields
RANGE
Mt Prara +309m
49

QUILPIE RD
79
GREY RANGE
NORLEY RANGE
Toompine
THARGOMINDAH
35
Opal Mines
Wyandra
199
MATILDA
46
Clifton
87

occundra
122
Lake Bullawarra
Kulthy Ck
Bullo
82
127
LAKE BINDEGOLLY NP
Coongoola
MITCHELL
54
474

Repeater Station
Thargomindah
BULLOO
Lake Bindegolly
130
Blackgate Opal Field
Yowah Opal Field
198
68
Cunnamulla
BALONNE
Charlotte Plains
134
49 HWY

DEVELOPMENTAL
Mud Springs
Eulo
ROAD
71
118

WARNING: In outback Australia, long distances separate some towns. Travellers should familiarise themselves with prevailing conditions before departure, and take care to ensure their vehicle is roadworthy and that they carry adequate supplies of petrol, water and food.

In northern Australia, rainfall during the "wet" season (Oct-March) can make some roads impassable. Full information on road conditions should be obtained before departure.

If visitors intend diverting off public roads within Aboriginal Land areas, a permit is required from the relevant Aboriginal authority.

146
122
Lake Wyara
Lake Numalla
CURRAWINYA NP
Kungie Lake
MITCHELL
Noorama Sports Centre

Adelaide Gate
Lake Caliamulcha
Vermin Proof Fence
QUEENSLAND
Hamilton Gate
Waverley Gate
Hungerford
Paragundy Gate
Barringun
NEW SOUTH WALES
Jobs Gate
Sharoon
38

Teurika
Berawinnia Downs
Ourimbah
128
Maureen Joy
145
Enngonia
Beulah
42
142
River

Pindera Downs
Owen Downs
101
213
52
71
Bullaroon

Clifton Downs
86
226
Colane
Koridina
87
Wanaaring
57
Fords Bridge
68
97

Whyjonta
Barrona Downs
191
Murphys Lake
Brewarrina
Bogan

Allandy
138
Bundara
Petita
The Range
134
85
+Mt Bendemeer 149m

Gumpopla
Questa Park
Glendara
Nantilla
Noonamah
163
Utah Lake
Bourke
OXLEYS TABLELAND
MITCHELL
41
28

Quichra
Purnanga
Cawnalmurtee
Tonga Lake
Polocara
Mt Mulyah 162m
Louth
Ben Lomond
101
Mulga
76
HWY
62
32

Oak Vale
74
Goodwood
Lake Poloka Yantabangee
Peery Lake
Jinki Lake
MT DEERIMA RANGE
Darling River
Mt Wammiga 380m
Wilga Downs
Byrock
43

White Cliffs
Opal Mines
32
THOOLABOOL RANGE
124
125

J K L M N O P Q R

Tasmania Heritage Island

Tasmania has certainly won many more hearts than it can claim square kilometres. It has only 68 000 of the latter, but it crams into them its rugged west, a central plateau broken by steep mountains and narrow river valleys, and an eastern coastal region offering a soft 'English' pastoral beauty. Its diverse charms have made it a popular tourist attraction for Australians from 'the mainland' for many years.

This dramatically beautiful island, however, has a far from beautiful early history. The first European to sight the island was Abel Tasman in 1642; it was later claimed by Captain Cook for the English and the British settlement dates from 1803. For the next fifty years it was maintained primarily as a penal colony, although prosperous settlements developed around Hobart and New Norfolk. The convicts did the hard labour and lived in brutal conditions at Port Arthur. The Tasmanian Aborigines, who resisted the takeover of their land, were treated even more harshly than the convicts. Political separation from New South Wales was granted in 1825 and transportation of convicts ceased in 1853. Today the ruins of Port Arthur have taken on a mellow charm and Tasmania is an infinitely more hospitable place.

Tasmania was first called Van Diemen's Land; these days it is known as the 'heritage island', 'treasure island' or the 'apple isle'. Its economy is basically agricultural with the major growth area being in quality specialised food products. The Tasmanian hydro-electric system has a greater output than that of the Snowy Mountains Scheme; Tasmania's high rainfall helps this. The climate offers mild summers and cool winters, with much of the mountain regions receiving heavy winter snowfall. Mid-December to late January is very popular with tourists; late spring or autumn are also pleasant. Even the winter months offer good touring.

When planning a trip to Tasmania note the heavy booking for the *Spirit of Tasmania* ferry service between Melbourne and Devonport from December to March. Either book well in advance or consider a fly/drive holiday, which can be a relaxing and economic alternative.

Tasmania's roads are well suited to relaxed meandering, many of them being winding and narrow. In a fortnight, however, you can happily complete what is virtually a round tour of the island.

Built on either side of the Derwent River, Hobart, the capital of Tasmania, is dominated by Mount Wellington. The Wrest Point Hotel-Casino, Australia's first casino, with its lavish entertainment and International Convention Centre, is now competing for first place as the city's best-known landmark, towering over Hobart's many colonial buildings. All within easy reach are Port Arthur, Richmond with its beautiful bridge (the oldest in Australia) and the settlements of Bothwell and New Norfolk.

The Derwent Valley with its hopfields and apple orchards, lovely in blossom-time and in autumn, lies to the west. Further west is Lake Pedder; the flooding of this country was a source of great controversy when it was made part of the hydro-electric scheme. The surrounding country makes up the Southwest National Park, Tasmania's largest and one which has been given World Heritage status. The Lyell Highway leads to the Cradle Mountain Lake St Clair National Park. Queenstown, surrounded by eerie white mountains, is the largest settlement in this wild, forested region. Nearby coastal Strahan was once a mining boom-town and is the starting-point of the Gordon River cruises. North of Queenstown, the town of Zeehan is currently enjoying a mining revival with the reopening of the Renison Bell Tin Mine.

The north coast is yet another contrasting area. Burnie is one of the larger towns and Stanley is a classified historic town situated beneath the Nut, an unusual peninsula. East of Burnie, the Bass Highway hugs the coast as far as Devonport, the terminal of the Bass Strait passenger/vehicle ferry *Spirit of Tasmania* and the centre of an apple-growing area. Inland is Launceston, Tasmania's second largest city. Situated on the Tamar River, Launceston has many old buildings. Only minutes from the city centre is the beautiful Cataract Gorge. The nearby colonial villages of Evandale, Hagley, Westbury, Carrick, Perth, Longford and Hadspen are well worth a visit.

A mild climate, good surfing beaches and sheltered seaside resorts add to the attraction of the east-coast region. St Helens, 160 kilometres east of Launceston, is the principal resort town. Try not to miss Bicheno, a picturesque old port and one-time whaling town. Further south, the Hazards, a red granite mountain range, towers up behind Coles Bay, at the entrance to the Freycinet National Park. Nearby Swansea offers top-class ocean and freshwater fishing.

A sense of Tasmania's history can be gained from studying graveyards and headstones: in St David's Park in the centre of Hobart; on Maria Island, on the Isle of the Dead off Port Arthur, King Island, Flinders Island, and Sarah Island in Macquarie Harbour; at National Trust properties; and in towns like Stanley, Richmond, Ross, Evandale and Corinna.

Whether you complete a round trip or only explore parts of this island State, it is very likely that, by the time you come to leave, Tasmania will have won yet another heart.

Hobart

An Historic City

Hobart is an enchanting city built around a beautiful harbour and under the spell of nearby majestic Mount Wellington. A strong seafaring flavour and sense of the past give Hobart an almost European air. This feeling is heightened in winter when Mount Wellington is snow-capped and temperatures drop to a crisp 5°C. The rest of the year Hobart has plenty of days with sparkling blue skies, but temperatures rarely exceed 25°C.

Many of Hobart's beautiful colonial sandstone buildings were erected by the unfortunate convicts who formed the majority of the European settlers in 1803.

Hobart's deepwater harbour on the broad estuary of the Derwent River soon became a thriving seaport and by 1842 Hobart was proclaimed a city. The harbour is still Hobart's lifeblood and the port is always busy with yachts. The suburbs nestle right up to the lower slopes of **Mount Wellington** and the city's population of 172 500 spreads both sides of the graceful **Tasman Bridge**, which made tragic world headlines in January 1975 when it was rammed by the bulk-carrier *Lake Illawarra*.

From the bridge you will see **Government House** and the **Royal Tasmanian Botanical Gardens** set in the Queen's Domain, a large parkland with sporting facilities and an adventure playground. In the lovely old Botanical Gardens are a playground, a Japanese garden and a restaurant that serves lunch and teas.

In a matter of minutes from the Botanical Gardens you are in the heart of Hobart, which has escaped the usual pressures of modern city life. Parking is no problem. Visitors should note that most of the city streets are one-way.

Hobart's waterfront retains much of its early character and it is not hard to imagine it in the early whaling days when Hobart Town was a lusty, brawling seaport known to sailors all round the world. Foreign ships tie up almost in the centre of town, battered whalers now replaced by fishing-trawlers. Wander around to **Constitution Dock**, the haven for the

Hobart skyline viewed from Mt Nelson

yachts in the annual Sydney to Hobart Yacht Race; here you can buy live seafood from the local fishermen.

Just round the corner in Argyle Street is the **Tasmanian Museum and Art Gallery**, which has a fine collection of Aboriginal artefacts, early prints and paintings, and convict relics. From here it is only a short stroll to the **Theatre Royal**, which was built in 1837 and is the oldest theatre in Australia. It is worth going inside to glimpse its charming dolls'-house-scale Georgian interior. Dame Sybil Thorndike rated it as the finest theatre she had played in outside of London. Not far from the Theatre Royal are the **Criminal Courts** and **Penitentiary Chapel**, operated by the National Trust; guided tours are conducted daily.

Heading back towards the centre of the city, you will see Hobart's sandstone old **Town Hall**, built on the site of the original **Government House**, on the corner of Macquarie and Elizabeth Streets.

Australia's second oldest capital, Hobart has a wealth of beautiful Georgian buildings, mostly concentrated in **Macquarie and Davey Streets**. More than ninety of them have a National Trust classification and the **Anglesea Barracks**, in Davey Street, is the oldest military establishment in Australia still used by the army. The Cascade Brewery in **South Hobart**, over a century and a half old, offers conducted tours.

Several modern complexes blend in with the older buildings without destroying the overall scale and atmosphere. The largest landmark is the tower of Australia's first hotel-casino, **Wrest Point**, built on a promontory in the suburb of **Sandy Bay**, just out of town. Back towards the waterfront is the famous **Salamanca Place**, which displays the finest row of early merchant warehouses in Australia. Dating back to the whaling days of the 1830s, the whole area has been sympathetically restored and the warehouses are now used as art and craft galleries, restaurants and a puppet theatre. A colourful open-air craft market, where almost anything is sold for almost any price, is held here each Saturday. Children will particularly enjoy the nearby **Post Office Museum**, in Castray Esplanade, where they can see old telephones, letter-boxes and a small post office.

The steep **Kelly's Steps**, wedged between two old warehouses in Salamanca Place, lead to the heart of unique **Battery Point**, a former mariners' village, which has retained its nineteenth-century character. Battery Point has several quaint cottage tearooms and many excellent restaurants offering a variety of different cuisines.

The area is also Hobart's mecca for antique-hunters. Just round the corner is the **Van Diemen Folk Museum**, with its interesting collection of colonial relics housed in Narryna, a gracious old town house, complete with a shady garden and an ornamental fountain. A short walk from here is the graceful old **St George's Anglican Church**, which was built between 1836 and 1847 and designed by two of Tasmania's most prominent colonial architects, John Lee Archer and James Blackburn. The **Tasmanian Maritime Museum** has a collection of old seafaring relics and documents.

Back towards the city, **St David's Park**, with its beautiful old trees, is an ideal place for a rest. One side of this park was Hobart Town's first colonial burial ground; the pioneer gravestones, which date from 1804, make fascinating reading. Across the road, in Murray Street, is **Parliament House**, one of the oldest buildings in Hobart. Originally used as the Customs House, it was built by convicts between 1835 and 1841. Visitors may ask to see the tiny **Legislative Council Chamber**, which is exactly as it was when it was inaugurated. The ceiling has been painstakingly repainted in its original ornate pastel patterns and the benches refurbished in plush red velvet. The building was designed by John Lee Archer.

The **Allport Library and Museum of Fine Arts**, a library of rare books and a collection of antique furniture, china and silver, is also in Murray Street, in the **State Library**.

The main shopping area of Hobart is centred round the **Elizabeth Street Mall**, between Collins and Liverpool Streets. The **Cat and Fiddle Arcade and Square** is located between the Mall and Murray Street. Shoppers can relax in the modern square with its fountain and an animated mural which 'performs' on the hour. In the Mall, in addition to the hourly antics of the Cat and Fiddle Clock, entertainment is provided by strolling buskers. Further along Elizabeth Street, in **Franklin Square**, you can play giant chess.

Hobart offers a sophisticated nightlife with the Wrest Point Hotel-Casino, cabaret and revolving restaurant, and a range of licensed restaurants—from Japanese and Mexican to colonial-style. For a touch of old-world class you can sip cocktails in the drawing-room of **Lenna**, an Italianate former mansion (now a distinctive hotel-motel) in Battery Point, before dining in the lavishly decorated restaurant. Fresh seafood is a specialty of many of the city's restaurants. **Mures Fish Centre**, at Victoria Dock, offers a range of fish delights from takeaway to fisherman's basket (brimming with such delicacies as crayfish, mussels, squid and scallops). Hobart also has several interesting old pubs with a nautical flavour; a good example is the **Customs House Hotel** on the corner of Murray and Morrison Streets.

The suburbs of Hobart have much to offer the visitor. Nearby **Sandy Bay** is the site of both the **University of Tasmania** and the **Model Tudor Village**. Beyond this, just out of **Taroona**, is the convict-built **Shot Tower**, from which you can get a superb view of the Derwent Estuary. As well as the original owner's house, built in 1835, the Shot Tower

Hotels
Lenna of Hobart
20 Runnymede St, Battery Point
(002) 23 2911
Sheraton Hobart
1 Davey St, Hobart
(002) 35 4535
Wrest Point Hotel-Casino
410 Sandy Bay Rd, Sandy Bay
(002) 25 0112

Family and Budget
Hobart Pacific Motor Inn
Kirby Crt, West Hobart
(002) 34 6733
Hobart Tower Motel
300 Park St, New Town
(002) 28 0166
Taroona
178 Channel Hwy, Taroona
(002) 27 8748

Motel Groups: Bookings
Best Western 1800 22 2166
Flag 13 2400
Innkeepers 1800 03 0111

The above list is for information only; inclusion is not necessarily a recommendation.

Battery Point

A most delightful part of Hobart is the former maritime village **Battery Point**, perched between the city docks and Sandy Bay. Battery Point dates back to the early days of Hobart Town, when it became a lively mariners' village with fishermen's cottages, shops, churches, a village green and a riot of pubs with such evocative names as the Whalers' Return and the Neptune Inn. Miraculously, it has hardly changed since those days. To anyone strolling through its narrow, hilly streets—with enchanting glimpses of the harbour, yachts and mountains at every turn—it looks almost like a Cornish fishing village.

Quaint **Arthurs Circus** is built around the former village green, now a children's playground. A profusion of old-fashioned flowers—sweet william, honeysuckle, daisies and geraniums—grow in pocket-sized gardens.

Pubs such as the Knopwood's Retreat and the Shipwright's Arms add to the feeling that time has stood still. Knopwood Street and Kelly's Steps are reminders of two pioneer settlers: the Reverend Bobby Knopwood, Battery Point's first landowner, and the adventurer James Kelly, who owned a whaling fleet and undertook a daring voyage around Van Diemen's Land.

Battery Point gets its name from a battery of guns set up on the promontory in front of a small guardhouse in 1818. This soon became a signalling station and is now the oldest building in Battery Point.

Today the Point has many inviting restaurants and tearooms, and several antique shops to explore, but it is still mainly a residential area. Most of the houses are tiny dormer-windowed fishermen's cottages, with a few grander houses such as Secheron, Stowell, Narryna and Lenna. An attractive leaflet with a detailed map, *Let's Talk About Battery Point*, is available from the Tasmanian Travel Centre, and the National Trust organises walking tours of the area, departing from the Wishing Well, Franklin Square, each Saturday morning.

Arthurs Circus

complex includes a small museum and tearooms, both housed in an 1855 building. **North Hobart**, only a few minutes from the centre of the city, is the gourmet's suburb, where a concentration of excellent restaurants and delicatessens have proliferated to the delight of residents and visitors alike. Slightly further north, in the suburb of **New Town** is **Runnymede**, a National Trust homestead. Beautifully restored, it commands an attractive view over New Town Bay and **Risdon**, where Hobart's first European settlement began. Further north, in the suburb of **Goodwood**, the **Derwent Entertainment Centre** stands beside the river and **Elwick Racecourse**. **Bellerive**, the ruins of an old fort at **Kangaroo Bluff**, was built to guard Hobart against a feared Russian invasion late last century. Some of Hobart's best beaches, including **Lauderdale**, **Cremorne** and **Seven Mile Beach**, are in this area. For surfers there is a wild ocean beach at **Clifton**, where the Australian surfing championships have been held.

There are dozens of scenic drives and lookouts around Hobart, with spectacular views from the pinnacle of **Mount Wellington** and from the old **Signal Station** on top of **Mount Nelson**. The **Waterworks Reserve** is an attractive picnic area only a few minutes' drive from town.

The hundreds of yachts moored near the prestigious **Royal Yacht Club** in Sandy Bay are evidence of one of Hobart's most popular sports. Other sports are well catered for with a public golf course at **Rosny Park**, racing and trotting at **Glenorchy**, and public squash courts at **Sandy Bay**, **New Town** and **Bellerive**. The Southern Tasmanian Tennis Association Courts and an Olympic swimming pool are in **Queen's Domain**. Tasmania's cricket headquarters is at Bellerive.

Hobart offers a complete range of accommodation, from the modern Sheraton Hobart Hotel and Wrest Point Hotel-Casino, with superb views from its 17-storey tower, to tiny Georgian cottage guest houses at Battery Point. Between these two extremes there are many modern hotels and motels and numerous guest houses, as well as caravan parks and holiday flats and cottages. Campercraft, small houseboats like floating caravans, can be hired throughout the State.

For further information, contact the Tasmanian Information Centre, 20 Davey St; (002) 30 8233.

Tours from Hobart

A marvellous range of tourist attractions is within easy reach of Hobart. To appreciate its superb natural setting it is worth going on a scenic flight over the city and its surroundings, taking in the beautiful Derwent estuary, the patchwork fields of the Midlands, the Tasman Peninsula and the spectacular lakes and mountains of central and south-western Tasmania. Flight bookings can be made at the Tasmanian Information Centre, Hobart, which also can arrange half-day and full-day coach tours.

Mt Wellington, 22 km from Hobart via the Huon Road

The most popular short trip from Hobart is to the pinnacle of Mt Wellington, 1271 metres above the city, which commands panoramic views of both the D'Entrecasteaux Channel to the south and the Derwent Valley to the north. A novel way to see the views is the half-day tour Mt Wellington Downhill: transport to the summit and a thrilling bike ride back down.

Cadbury's Factory, Claremont, 14 km from Hobart on the Lyell Highway

A visit to this beautifully sited model factory, the biggest chocolate and cocoa factory in Australia, is another popular short trip. Privately run coach tours leave daily and self-drive tours may be made Tuesday–Thursday. Information and bookings at Travel Centre. The factory is usually closed for two weeks in September and from the end of December to mid-January.

Richmond, 26 km from Hobart via the Eastern Outlet Road

Tasmania's oldest and most famous historic village, Richmond has the oldest bridge in Australia, and a wealth of mellow old colonial buildings, including Tasmania's oldest gaol and two historic churches. Prospect House, built in the 1830s, another historic building, is now a licensed restaurant and colonial accommodation property. **See also:** Entry in A–Z listing.

New Norfolk, 32 km from Hobart on the Lyell Highway

This historic town, in the centre of Tasmania's hop-growing country, is delightful in autumn when the leaves on the many English trees planted here last century turn to beautiful golden tones. Quaint old oast houses are a feature of the landscape and the town's attractions include the historic Old Colony Inn, now a museum and tearooms set in charming

Mt Wellington

grounds, and the famous Salmon Ponds, 11 km north-west at Plenty, the first successful trout hatchery in Australia. **See also:** Entry in A–Z listing.

Mt Field National Park and Russell Falls, 72 km from Hobart via the Lyell Highway and Gordon River Road

The road from New Norfolk to Mt Field passes through some of the loveliest parts of the Derwent Valley. A nature walk leads to the magnificent Russell Falls, cascades that drop 32 metres into a gorge of rainforest and tree ferns, from near the park entrance. This large scenic wildlife reserve shelters many native birds and animals, including the elusive Tasmanian devil. **See also:** National Parks.

Lake Pedder and Lake Gordon, 170 km from Hobart via the Lyell Highway and Gordon River Road

In clear weather, the road from Mt Field National Park to the township of Strathgordon is probably the most spectacular stretch of mountain highway in Australia. Unfortunately (from the visitor's point of view), there is very high rainfall in the area, which of course results in its unique natural topography. Motorists are advised to cancel trips on overcast days. Constructed Lakes Pedder and Gordon, part of the Hydro-Electric Commission's giant Gordon River power development, are liberally stocked with trout. The underground power station at the Gordon Dam can be inspected on regular tours. You can hire boats and fishing tackle, and charter scenic cruises from Strathgordon, where a chalet is available for overnight accommodation. Enquiries should be directed to the Tasmanian Information Centre in Hobart. **See also:** National Parks; Dams for Power.

Tasman Peninsula and Port Arthur, 100 km from Hobart via the Arthur Highway

There is so much to see on this fascinating trip that it would be well worth staying overnight at the narrow isthmus of Eaglehawk Neck or at Port Arthur. Once guarded by a line of tethered dogs to prevent convicts escaping, Eaglehawk Neck is now a base for game fishing charter boats. There are four unique coastal formations in the area: the spectacular Devil's Kitchen, the Blowhole, Tasman's Arch and the Tessellated Pavement. The old penal settlement of Port Arthur is Tasmania's number one tourist attraction. Other attractions in the area include Bush Hill, Remarkable Cave and Safety Cove. **See also:** Entries in A–Z listing; A Convict Past.

Huonville, 37 km from Hobart via Huon Road and the Huon Highway

You can make a scenic trip to Huonville, the centre of Tasmania's picturesque apple-growing district, via the shoulder of Mt Wellington on the Huon Highway, returning via the coastal town of Cygnet and along the Channel Highway, which commands spectacular vistas of the coastline and rugged Bruny Island. **See also:** Entry in A–Z listing.

Hastings Caves, 110 km from Hobart via the Huon Road and Huon Highway

These caves, 13 km from the small township of Hastings, are another popular attraction. There are regular guided tours of the only illuminated cave, Newdegate Cave, regarded as one of the most beautiful limestone caves in Australia. A natural thermal swimming-pool with an average temperature of 27°C is nearby. Motorists are warned that Dover is the last place to buy petrol en route to Recherche Bay. The Ida Bay Scenic Railway is another popular tourist attraction near Hastings. **See also:** Entry in A–Z listing.

Lake Pedder, South West National Park

Tasmania from A to Z

Avoca
Pop. 207

This small town with a mining background, on the Esk Main Road, also serves the small communities of Rossarden and Storys Creek, in the foothills of Ben Lomond, the highest mountain in north-east Tasmania. **Of interest:** Historic buildings incl. St Thomas's Church and Parish Hall, Falmough St. **In the area:** Bona Vista (1848), 1 km NW on Storys Creek Rd, once one of Tasmania's most attractive historic houses; restored, private property; by appt. **Tourist information:** Fingal Valley Neighbourhood House, Talbot St, Fingal; (003) 74 2344. **Accommodation:** Limited.
MAP REF. 527 O9

Beaconsfield
Pop. 1088

The ruins of several impressive brick buildings with Romanesque arches dominate this quiet town on the West Tamar Hwy, 46 km NW of Launceston. Formerly a thriving gold township (called Cabbage Tree Hill), the ruins are the remains of several buildings erected at the pithead of the Tasmanian Gold Mine in 1904. When the mine closed 10 years later after water seepage, more than 6 million dollars' worth of ore had been won from the reef. In 1804 a party of officers established a settlement north of the town, called York Town. **Of interest:** Grubb Shaft Museum, West St, in one of old mine buildings; restored miner's cottage and original Flowery Gully School alongside museum. **In the area:** York Town monument, 9 km N on Kelso–Greens Beach Rd. Batman Bridge, 7 km SE, near Sidmouth; A-frame reaches 100 m above Tamar River. Auld Kirk (1843) at Sidmouth, 9 km SE. **Tourist information:** Tamar Visitor Centre, Main Rd, Exeter; (003) 94 4454. **Accommodation:** None.
MAP REF. 523 J5, 527 K5

Beauty Point
Pop. 1137

This popular fishing and yachting centre on the West Tamar Hwy, 48 km NE of Launceston, is the oldest deepwater port in the area and was constructed to serve the Beaconsfield goldmine. Today cargo is loaded at Bell Bay on the eastern shore of the River Tamar. **Of interest:** Nearby Sandy Beach for safe swimming. **In the area:** Two northern resorts: Kelso, 15 km N, dates back to early York Town settlement; Greens Beach, 20 km N, at mouth of Tamar River. Marion's Vineyard, Deviot, 12 km SE. Holm Oak Vineyard, at Rowella, 15 km SE. **Tourist information:** Tamar Visitor Centre, Main Rd, Exeter; (003) 94 4454. **Accommodation:** 1 hotel, 2 motels, 1 cara./camp. park.
MAP REF. 523 K5, 527 K5

Bicheno
Pop. 705

A fishing port and holiday resort on the east coast, 195 km from Hobart, Bicheno offers surf, rock, sea and estuary fishing. The town's mild climate, outstanding fishing, nearby fine sandy beaches and its

Old mine building, Beaconsfield

picturesque setting make it one of Tasmania's most popular holiday resorts. Licensed seafood restaurants and a range of accommodation add to its appeal. Originally a sealing and whaling town from about 1803, it later became a coal-mining port in 1854. Today crayfishing is the main local industry. **Of interest:** On Tasman Hwy: Sea Life Centre, aquarium, seafood restaurant; Bicheno Dive Centre, diving school, charters. Foreshore walkway, from Redbill Point north of town to Blowhole to south. Lookouts at top of town's twin hills. Little (fairy) Penguin Rookery, nightly tours in season, contact Tourist Information. Grave of Aboriginal heroine Waubedebar, Lions Park, Burgess St. Adventure tours, incl. scuba diving, water-skiing and mountain-bike-riding. **In the area:** East Coast Bird Life and Animal Park, 8 km N, Tasmanian devils, other native fauna. Douglas Apsley National Park, 14 km NW. Freycinet National Park, 40 km S. Freycinet Vineyard, 18 km SW, all on Tasman Hwy. **Tourist information:** Bicheno Penguin Adventure Tours, Foster St; (003) 75 1333. **Accommodation:** 2 hotel/motels, 2 hostels, 2 cara./camp. parks.
MAP REF. 527 Q10

Boat Harbour
Pop. 109

The clear water and rocky points of this attractive resort make it an ideal spot for skindiving and spear fishing. Situated on the north-west coast, 31 km W of Burnie, it adjoins one of the richest agricultural areas in the State. **Of interest:** Shannondoah Cottage, Bass Hwy, local craft, lunches, Devonshire teas. **In the area:** Boat Harbour Beach, 3 km N, safe swimming, marine life in pools at low tide, fishing, water-skiing, bushwalking. Sisters Beach, 5 km NW, good fishing, swimming. Rocky Cape National Park, 19 km NW. Birdland Native Gardens

nearby, in park. **Tourist information:** Civic Centre Precinct, Burnie; (004) 32 1999. **Accommodation:** 2 motels, 1 hostel, 1 cara./camp. park.
MAP REF. 526 F4

Bothwell   Pop. 396

This peaceful old country town in the beautiful Clyde River valley, 74 km NW of Hobart, has been proclaimed an historic village. It has 52 buildings either classified or recorded by the National Trust. Surveyed in 1824 and named by Lieut.-Governor Arthur after the Scottish town, it is now the centre of sheep and cattle country. It is possible that the first golf in Australia was played at the nearby homestead of Ratho in the 1830s. This course still exists and is open to visitors with golf-club membership elsewhere. **Of interest:** Bothwell Grange (c. 1836), Alexander St, guest house, tearooms, art gallery. Lamont Weaving Studio, Patrick St, demonstrations, sales, tearoom. Peter Muere Woodturning, Queens St. St Luke's Church (1830), Dennistoun St. Georgian brick Slate Cottage (1836), High St, restored and furnished in style of day. **In the area:** Restored and operational Thorpe Water Mill, 2 km N on Interlaken Rd; tours by appt. Excellent fishing at Arthurs Lake, 51 km N, Penstock Lagoon, 45 km NW, Great Lake, 56 km N, and Lake Echo, 48 km NW; all via Lakes Hwy. **Tourist information:** Council Offices, Alexander St; (002) 59 5503. **Accommodation:** 1 camp./cara. park. **See also:** Scenic Island State.
MAP REF. 525 K3, 527 L12

Branxholm   Pop. 262

This small, former tin-mining town on the Tasman Hwy, 90 km NE of Launceston, now serves the surrounding rich vegetable-growing and dairying district. **Of interest:** Pine plantations and Firth Memorial Grove, Mt Horror Rd, Mt Horror. Old tin-mine workings and lapidary. **In the area:** Milk-processing plant at Legerwood, 10 km S. **Tourist information:** Rose's Travel, 11 Alfred St, Scottsdale; (003) 52 2186. **Accommodation:** 1 hotel, 1 cara./camp. park.
MAP REF. 527 O5

Bridgewater   Pop. 8684

This town, only 19 km N of Hobart, is situated on the bank of the main northern crossing of the Derwent River. The causeway was built in the early 1830s by 200 convicts, who barrowed 2 million tonnes of stone and clay from the site. The original bridge was opened in 1849; the present one dates from 1946. **In the area:** At Granton, 1 km S across bridge: Old Watch House (1838, now petrol station), built by convicts to guard causeway, has smallest cell in Australia (50 cm square, 2 m high); Black Snake Inn (1833), also convict-built. **Tourist information:** Council Offices, Tivoli Rd, Gagebrook; (002) 63 0333. **Accommodation:** Limited.
MAP REF. 520 H4, 525 L5

Bridport   Pop. 1165

Bridport is a popular holiday resort and fishing town on the north-east coast, 85 km from Launceston. Of interest: Fine beaches, excellent river, sea and lake fishing. 'Towards 2000' Information Centre, Main St. **In the area:** Bowood (1839), 8 km W historic homestead near town; not open to public. Views from Waterhouse Point and Ranson's Beach. Winegrowing at Piper's Brook, 18 km SW. **Tourist information:** Rose's Travel, 11 Alfred St, Scottsdale; (003) 52 2186.

Accommodation: 1 hotel, 1 hotel/motel, 1 hostel, 1 cara./camp. park.
MAP REF. 527 M4

Brighton   Pop. 1472

This town, near Hobart on the Midland Hwy, has always been an important military post. It was first established in 1826 and today the Brighton Army Camp is the main military base in Tasmania. The town was named after the English resort by Governor Macquarie in 1821. **Of interest:** Nov.: Agricultural Show. **In the area:** Bonorong Park Wildlife Sanctuary, 2 km SE. Historic village of Pontville, 2 km N. **Tourist information:** Council Offices, Tivoli Rd, Gagebrook; (002) 63 0333. **Accommodation:** 1 hotel/motel. **See also:** Rural Landscapes.
MAP REF. 520 H3, 525 L5

Bruny Island   Pop. 520

Almost two islands, separated by a narrow isthmus, Bruny was named after the French Admiral Bruni D'Entrecasteaux, who surveyed the channel between the island and the mainland of Tasmania in 1792; the Aboriginal name for the island was Lunawannaaloona. Abel Tasman saw the island in 1642 but did not land. Other European visitors in the 18th century incl. Furneaux (1773), James Cook (1777) and William Bligh (1788, 1792). The first apple trees in Tasmania are said to have been planted here by a botanist with the Bligh expedition. Bruny Island ferry departs from Kettering, on the mainland, several times daily. **Of interest:** On isthmus between North and South Bruny, memorial to Truganini, Tasmania's last full-blood Aborigine, died 1876. On South Bruny: both at Adventure Bay, Bligh Museum, exhibits island's recorded history, and Mavista Falls, scenic reserve; lookouts at Adventure and Cloudy Bays; lighthouse (1836) at Cape Bruny, second oldest in Australia; walking tracks to Mt Mangana and Mt Bruny. On North Bruny: memorials to early navigators; Dennes Point beach, D'Entrecasteaux Channel, picnic/barbecue facilities; at Variety Bay, remains of convict-built church on private property near airstrip, conducted tours; at Barnes Bay, vault of William Lawrence (1839). Fishing. Camel Tours. **Tourist information:** Bruny D'Entrecasteaux Visitor Centre, Ferry Rd, Kettering; (002) 67 4494. **Accommodation:** 1 hotel, 2 cara./camp. parks.
MAP REF. 525 L9

Colonial Accommodation

As a result of the popularity of this type of accommodation over the last few years, there are now over 150 properties, including host farms and colonial cottages, available for visitors.

Host farms provide a wide variety of standard and type of service, and offer guests the opportunity to observe farm life or become involved in it.

Colonial accommodation is provided in buildings or cottages established on their present sites before 1901. Although concessions are made to allow modern facilities to be incorporated, interiors are presented in colonial style by the use of genuine or reproduction furniture and other decoration.

For further information, contact the nearest Tasmanian Travel Centre.

Buckland
Pop. 228

A stained glass window depicting the life of John the Baptist and dating back to the 14th century is in the church in this tiny township, 64 km NE of Hobart. History links the window with Battle Abbey, England. The abbey was sacked by Oliver Cromwell in the 17th century, but the window was hidden before it could be destroyed. Two centuries later it was given to Rev. T.H. Fox, Buckland's first rector, by the Marquis of Salisbury. It is now set into the east wall of the Church of St John the Baptist, built 1846. Although the window has been damaged and restored several times in its long life, the original figure-work is intact. Also of interest is Ye Olde Buckland Inn, a 19th-century tavern and restaurant. **Tourist information:** Council Offices, cnr Vicary and Henry Sts, Triabunna; (002) 57 3113. **Accommodation:** 1 hotel. MAP REF. 521 M2, 525 N4

The Hazards, Freycinet National Park, near Coles Bay

Burnie
Pop. 20 505

The rapid expansion of Burnie, now Tasmania's 4th largest city, is based on one of the State's largest industrial enterprises, Australian Paper. Situated on Emu Bay, 148 km NW of Launceston, Burnie has a busy deepwater port, which serves the west coast mining centres. Other important industries incl. plants for the manufacture of titanium oxide pigments, dried milk, chocolate products and cheese. **Of interest:** Lactos cheese factory, Old Surrey Rd. Tours of Amcor, Marine Tce. Pioneer Village Museum, High St, reconstruction of Burnie's small tradesmen's shops c. 1900. Restored Burnie Inn, town's oldest remaining building, re-erected in Burnie Park; meals. Glen Osborne, Aileen Cres, historic building, B&B. New Year's Day: Athletic Carnival. Oct.: Rhododendron Festival. **In the area:** Round Hill, 5 km E, views. Fern Glade, off Old Surrey Rd, 5 km W, riverside walks, picnics. Emu Valley Rhododendron Gardens, off Cascade Rd, 6 km S. Annsleigh Gardens, 9 km S on Mount Rd, tearooms. Guide Falls, Ridgley, 17 km S. Upper Natone Forest Reserve, 20 km S, picnics. Day tours to: Cradle Mountain, Gunns Plains, Leven Canyon, Fossil Cliffs. Pieman River cruises. **Tourist information:** Civic Centre Precinct; (004) 32 1999. **Accommodation:** 4 hotels, 2 hotel/motels, 5 motels, 2 B&B, 2 cara./camp. parks. **See also:** Scenic Island State. MAP REF. 526 G4

Campbell Town
Pop. 820

Campbell Town, on the Midlands Hwy, 66 km SW of Launceston, is a national centre for selling stud sheep. The area's links with the wool industry go back to the early 1820s, when Saxon merinos were introduced to the Macquarie Valley, west of the town. Timber and stud beef are also important primary industries. The town and the Elizabeth River were named by Governor Macquarie for his wife, the former Elizabeth Campbell. **Of interest:** Wesleyan Chapel (1846), King St; National Trust owned. National Trust-classified buildings incl. St Michael's Church (1857), King St; Balmoral Cottage (1840s), Bridge St; St Luke's Church (1839), The Grange (1840), Campbell Town Inn (1840) and convict-built Red Bridge (1837), all High St. Memorial to Harold Gatty, first round-the-world flight navigator, High St. Nov.: Country Music Muster. **In the area:** Trout fishing in local rivers and lakes, particularly Lake Leake, 30 km SE. Evansville Game Park, 30 km E. **Tourist information:** 75 High St; (003) 81 1388. **Accommodation:** 2 hotels. **See also:** Scenic Island State. MAP REF. 527 N10

Coles Bay
Pop. 120

This beautiful unspoiled bay, 39 km S of Bicheno on the Freycinet Peninsula, is a good base for visitors to the 70 000-ha Freycinet National Park. **Of interest:** In park: pleasant beaches, clear waters and heathland make it ideal for swimming, fishing, bushwalking; abundant birdlife; variety of wildflowers, incl. 60 varieties of small ground orchid; rock climbing on 'The Hazards' and nearby cliffs; waterskiing, skindiving, canoeing, sailing. Charter boat trips to Schouten Island. Tours by arrangement. **Tourist information:** Park Ranger; (002) 57 0107. **Accommodation:** Freycinet National Park, 1 motel, 5 cara./camp. parks. **See also:** National Parks. MAP REF. 525 Q2, 527 Q11

Cygnet
Pop. 924

The centre of a fruit-growing district, 52 km from Hobart, the town was originally named Port de Cygne Noir (meaning Black Swan Port) by the French Admiral Bruni D'Entrecasteaux because of the number of swans in the bay. **Of interest:** Good beaches and boat-launching facilities at nearby Verona Sands, Randalls Bay, Egg and Bacon Bay. Jan.: Huon Folk Festival. March: Port Cygnet Fishing Carnival. **In the area:** Boating, fishing, bushwalks, gem fossicking. Pelvereta Falls, 10 km N on Sandfly Rd. Deepings Woodturning, Nicholls Rivulet, 10 km W. Unique Lymington lace agate sometimes found at Drip Beach, Lymington, 12 km SW. Talune Wildlife Park and Koala Gardens, Gardners Bay, 6 km SE: good picnic/barbecue facilities, cabin accommodation for hire. Harts View and Winter Wood wineries, 10 km SE. **Tourist information:** Talune

National Parks

Tasmania packs an incredible variety into a remarkably compact area. Even in a few days you can experience a surprising cross-section of the natural and cultural heritage that help make Tasmania unique. But the best of the island State, from wild rivers and deep forests to grand mountains and ancient cave shelters, is to be found in its national parks. The island's landscape is shaped by ice as much as by isolation. In the national parks you can find mountains, tarns and lakes carved out during the last ice age, and a unique flora and fauna that survives from ancient times. The rainforests are clothed in trees that trace their origins back to the supercontinent of Gondwana. Nowhere else in Australia is there such rich and unusual flora and fauna.

The Parks and Wildlife Service of Tasmania manages not only the State's 14 national parks but also many State reserves with their Aboriginal sites, caves, gorges, waterfalls, rivers, and historic sites that date back as far as 1803, when Europeans first arrived.

All parks are accessible year round, but some tourists believe the highland parks are best seen in summer and autumn, when the climate is more reliable, and when wildflowers bloom in profusion and flowering trees and shrubs attract birdlife. The two areas to be declared the first national parks of Tasmania were Mount Field, just 80 kilometres north-west of Hobart, and Freycinet, on the central east coast. **Mount Field** is a popular tourist venue, offering such activities as climbing and bushwalking. It has the only developed skiing area in southern Tasmania. There are several waterfalls in the park, the best-known being Russell Falls, first seen by Europeans in 1856. Here the cascading water plunges in two stages into deep gorges shaded by tree ferns that filter sunlight and create a mosaic effect. The forest, includes large myrtles, giant 250-year-old gum trees, sassafras, huge tree ferns, the unique horizontal scrub and a variety of mosses, ferns, lichens and fungi. There is a wide range of walks from leisurely to strenuous, including the famed Lyrebird Walk, where you may see the black currawong, native to Tasmania, and hear the noisy yellow wattlebird or perhaps the lyrebird's mimicry.

Freycinet National Park offers wide stretches of white sands, rocky headlands, granite peaks, quiet beaches and small coves, with windswept eucalypt forests on its slopes and excellent short and long walking tracks. Just north of the park is Moulting Lagoon, the breeding ground of the lovely black swan and a refuge for other waterfowl. Freycinet National Park also includes Schouten Island, separated from the Freycinet Peninsula by-a kilometre-wide passage, and reached only by boat. Near the park is Coles Bay, a fishing and swimming resort with delightful coastal scenery.

A short distance north of Freycinet National Park is Tasmania's newest national park, **Douglas–Apsley** (16 080 hectares). Proclaimed in 1990, this park contains the State's last large dry sclerophyll forest and can be traversed along a 3-day north–south walking track. Here forest-clad ridges contrast with patches of rainforest and river gorges. Waterfalls and spectacular coastal views add to the grandeur of the area. Facilities are basic.

Many of Tasmania's national parks are important wildlife reserves. One such park, the 13 899-hectare **Mount William National Park** in north-east Tasmania, is a sanctuary for native animals, including the Forester kangaroo (Tasmania's only kangaroo), echidna, wombat, pademelon, Bennetts wallaby and Tasmanian devil. Spring brings a carpet of wildflowers to this park: red and white heaths, golden wattle and guinea flower. At Lookout Point, thousands of rock orchids cover the granite rocks. Sheltered bays and beaches complete this little-known but beautiful park.

Fifty kilometres south-east of Launceston is **Ben Lomond National Park**, one of Tasmania's two main ski fields, with an alpine village, ski-tows, ski hire, a tavern with accommodation, and a public shelter.

Steep, jagged mountains create a natural amphitheatre at the **Walls of Jerusalem National Park** (51 800 hectares) in the State's north central zone. Ancient forests of pencil pines ring tiny glacially formed lakes, making the park very popular with bushwalkers.

The central north coastal strip of **Asbestos Range National Park** is an important refuge for the rare ground parrot and the rufous wallaby. Its islands off Port Sorell provide an important breeding area for little (fairy) penguins and the tidal and mud flats are ideal feeding grounds for a variety of migratory seabirds. On the

Dove Lake, Cradle Mountain Lake St Clair National Park

Wineglass Bay, Freycinet National Park

unspoiled beaches, white sands come to life with thousands of soldier crabs.

Further west along the coast, **Rocky Cape National Park** (3064 hectares) encompasses rugged coastline with small sheltered beaches backed by heath-covered hills. It is known for its rock shelters used for over 800 years by Tasmanian Aborigines.

Covering some of Tasmania's highest country is **Cradle Mountain Lake St Clair National Park**. There is a visitors centre near the park entrance at Cradle Mountain, and a nature walk into the nearby rainforest incorporates a suspended walkway. Cradle Mountain has a variety of fine bushwalks, including one of Australia's best-known walking routes, the 85-kilometre Overland Track, through forests of deciduous beech, Tasmanian 'myrtle', pandanus, King Billy pine and a wealth of wildflowers. At the other end of the park, the tranquil Lake St Clair, with a depth of over 200 metres, occupies a basin gouged out by two glaciers more than 20 000 years ago; cruises operate daily, and 6-day treks take in Mt Ossa (Tasmania's highest mountain) and the Pine Valley region. Lake St Clair was discovered by Europeans as early as 1826 and is now popular for boating. There are several campsites. Cradle Mountain Wilderness Lodge lies on the northern boundary of the national park.

Maria Island, off the east coast, is well worth a visit. You can get there either by light aircraft or by passenger ferry from Louisville Point. On arrival, it seems as if you have stepped into another world, for on Maria Island no tourist vehicles are permitted. This island national park embraces magnificently coloured sandstone cliffs and is a refuge for over 80 species of birds. Forester kangaroos, emus and Cape Barren geese roam freely in this unspoiled landscape. Its intriguing history and historic buildings date back to the convict era of 1825.

Tasmania's largest national park is **Southwest National Park**, which has 605 213 hectares of mainly remote wilderness country. Here there are dolerite- and quartzite-capped mountains, sharp ridges and steep valleys left by glaciers; the dense forests are made up of eucalypts, ancient Huon pines and limbs of the Antarctic beech, all covered with mosses, ferns and lichens and tangled with pink-flowered climbing heath and bauera. Climbers will find a challenge in Federation Peak, Mount Anne and Precipitous Bluff, while anglers will be kept busy with trout fishing at Lakes Pedder and Gordon. A new bird hide at Melaleuca can be used in summer to observe the extremely rare orange-bellied parrot.

The 440 000-hectare **Franklin–Gordon Wild Rivers National Park** forms the central portion of Tasmania's World Heritage Area. The Franklin attracts wilderness adventurers from around the world to test its challenging rapids. Along the slightly more placid Gordon River are stands of 2000-year-old Huon pine. Unusual buttongrass vegetation, growing right to the edge of the water, stains it the colour of tea. The Lyell Highway, the road link between Hobart and the west coast, runs through the park. A number of excellent short walks lead off the highway to rainforests and spectacular lookouts.

A 2-hour drive from Hobart, through Geeveston to the south-west, brings visitors to the **Hartz Mountains National Park**. Most of the area is over 600 metres in altitude with Hartz Peak being 1255 metres high. There are basic facilities for the day visitor and no camping facilities, although camping is permitted. Bushwalking is popular; however, all visitors are warned that the area is subject to sudden storms, even in summer.

At the southern end of Flinders Island in Bass Strait is **Strzelecki National Park** (4215 hectares). Famed for its exhilarating views from Mt Strzelecki's granite summit, the park also boasts beaches and camping among she-oaks at Trousers Point.

In some of the many State reserves, limestone caves are a popular attraction. The cave interiors are dramatically lit to enhance the wonderland of limestone-derived calcite formations. The Hastings Caves, located 110 kilometres from Hobart, include a nearby thermal swimming pool with a year-round warm temperature. Lawns and picnic areas surround the pool and incorporate a sensory trail designed for wheelchair access and the visually impaired. In the north central region, King Solomon and Marakoopa Caves are popular destinations.

For further information on Tasmania's national parks, contact the Parks and Wildlife Service, 134 Macquarie Street, Hobart (GPO Box 44A, Hobart 7001); (002) 33 6191.

Wildlife Park, Gardners Bay; (002) 95 1775. **Accommodation:** 3 hotels, 2 hostels, 1 cara./camp. park.
MAP REF. 520 F10, 525 L8

Deddington   Pop. 50
In 1830 artist John Glover arrived from England and bought land on the site of this little town, 37 km SE of Launceston. He named his property Deddington after the village in the English Lake District where he had lived. **Of interest:** Deddington Chapel (1840), possibly designed by Glover, National Trust-classified. Glover's grave beside chapel. **Tourist information:** Council Offices, Smith St, Longford; (003) 91 1303. **Accommodation:** None.
MAP REF. 527 M8

Deloraine   Pop. 2098
Scenic Deloraine, with Bass Strait to the north and the Great Western Tiers to the south, is an ideal base for exploring the many attractions of northern Tasmania. The surrounding rich countryside is used mainly for dairying and mixed farming. **Of interest:** Self-guide Heritage Walk. Deloraine Folk Museum, Emu Bay Rd; in Plough Inn, National Trust-classified, Gallery 9, West Barrack St. Nov.: Tasmanian Cottage Industry Exhibition and Craft Fair. **In the area:** Ashgrove Farm, Elizabeth Town, 6 km NW, English-style cheeses. Trowanna Wildlife Park, on Mole Creek Rd, 18 km W; specially designed noctarium for displaying nocturnal animals. Scenic drives south to forest reserves and falls: Quamby Bluff; Liffey; Meander; Drys Bluff; Montana. Also south to Central Highlands, through Golden Valley, to Great Lake, one of the largest high-water lakes in Australia. Excellent trout fishing on lake and in Mersey and Meander Rivers. Heidi Cheese Factory, Exton, 6 km E, Swiss-style cheeses. **Tourist information:** 29 Westchurch St; (003) 62 2046. **Accommodation:** 1 motel, 6 B&B, 2 hostels,1 cara./camp. park. **See also:** Stately Homes.
MAP REF. 522 I11, 527 J7

Derby   Pop. 200
Derby is a former mining town on the Tasman Hwy, 34 km E from Scottsdale in the north-east. In its heyday, tin mining was a flourishing industry, but there has been a gradual swing to rural production, although tin is still worked. **Of interest:** Derby Tin Mine Museum, in old school

(1890s), local history, gemstone and mineral displays, tin panning, tearooms. Reconstructed Shanty Town surrounding museum, has original buildings from area: miner's cottage, newspaper office, mining assay office, butcher's shop, general store, blacksmith's shop, two cells from old Derby gaol. In Main St: Wallaby's Woodcraft, woodturning; Taylor Made Crafts, in old bank, local craft. Oct.: River Derby. **Tourist information:** Tin Mine Museum, Main St; (003) 54 2262. **Accommodation:** 1 hotel, 1 camping area.
MAP REF. 527 O5

Devonport   Pop. 22 660
As the terminal for a vehicular ferry from Melbourne, Devonport has become a busy industrial and agricultural-export town, as well as a major tourist centre. Devonport has its own airport, and is ideally suited as a visitor base for seeing scenic northern Tasmania. **Of interest:** Tiagarra, Tasmanian Aboriginal Culture and Art Centre, Bluff Rd, Mersey Bluff, open daily; parklands and beach resort promontory at river mouth; Tasmanian Aboriginal rock carvings outside display area. Maritime Museum, Victoria Pde, The Bluff. Home Hill, Middle Rd, home of former Prime Minister Joseph Lyons and Dame Enid Lyons, National Trust-classified; tours. Feb.: Food and Wine Festival. March: Harbours Festival. **In the area:** Walking track (12 km) from The Bluff to Don River Railway and Museum, at Don, 6 km W. Forth, 13 km W, spring of pure water claimed to have medicinal qualities. Braddon's Lookout, near Forth, panoramic view of coastline.

Lighthouse on the Bluff, near Devonport

Tasmanian Aboretum (45 ha), Eugenana, 10 km S, picnic area, walking tracks. **Tourist information:** Tasmanian Travel and Information, Devonport Showcase, 5 Best St; (004) 24 4466. **Accommodation:** 4 hotels, 2 hotel/motels, 2 motels, 3 B&B, 2 hostels, 3 cara./camp. parks. **See also:** Scenic Island State.
MAP REF. 522 E5, 526 I5

Dover   Pop. 521
This attractive fishing port, south west of Hobart, was once a convict station. The original Commandant's Office still stands, but the cells, which are underground just up from the wharf, can no longer be seen. From the late 1850s several large sawmills were built, with a big output of first-class timber. The main industries today are fruit-growing, fishing, and Atlantic salmon fish-farming. Quaint old cottages and English trees give the town an old-world atmosphere. The 3 islands in the bay are called Faith, Hope and Charity. **Of interest:** Chartered fishing trips. Several old graves on Faith Island. Attractive scenery and unspoiled beaches, ideal for bushwalking, swimming. Casey's Steam Museum, Main St, working steam engines. **In the area:** South and west via Huon Hwy, Esperance River Picnic Area on Esperance Self Drive Tour; picnic/barbecue facilities. Southport, 21 km S, originally fishing port established in days of sealers and whalers; good fishing, swimming, surfing and bushwalking. Cockle Creek, further 41 km S, is start of extended South Coast Walking Track. **Tourist information:** Church St, Geeveston; (002) 97 1836. **Accommodation:** 1 hotel, 1 motel, 1 hostel, 1 cara./camp. park.
MAP REF. 520 E12, 525 K9

Dunalley   Pop. 306
This prosperous fishing village stands on the narrow isthmus connecting the Forestier Peninsula to the rest of Tasmania. The Denison Canal, spanned by a swing bridge, provides access to the east coast for small vessels. **Of interest:** Tasman Memorial, Imlay St, marks first landing by Europeans on 2 Dec. 1642, to northeast, near Cape Paul Lamanon. **In the area:** Bangor Farm, on Arthur Hwy, conservation farm, home of Oyster Bay Aborigines, site of Abel Tasman's landing; tours of farm, middens, artefacts and nature reserves incl. lunch; bookings essential; (002) 53 5233. **Tourist information:** Tasmanian South Regional

Tourism Association, 20 Davey St, Hobart; (002) 65 2201. **Accommodation:** 1 motel.
MAP REF. 521 M6, 525 O6

Eaglehawk Neck
Pop. 150
In convict days this narrow isthmus, which separates the Tasman from the Forestier Peninsula, was guarded by a line of ferocious tethered dogs. Soldiers and constables also stood guard, to ensure that no convicts escaped from the notorious convict settlement at Port Arthur. The only prisoners to escape did so by swimming. The town today, in complete contrast, is a pleasant fishing resort. A charter tuna fishing fleet operates from Pirate's Bay. **Of interest:** Historic officers' quarters, next to Officers Mess, off Arthur Hwy; restored. Dec.: Port Arthur Chopping Carnival. **In the area:** Four unusual natural features 4 km E, in Tasman Arch State Reserve, off Arthur Hwy: Tasman's Arch, Devil's Kitchen, Blowhole, Tessellated Pavement. Dive centres, near Blowhole, below Lookout; groups for diving and lessons. Fortescue Forest Reserve south, along coast from Waterfall Bay to Munro Bight: water sports, picnic facilities; coastal walking track from Waterfall Bay to Fortescue Bay. Good sailing in Eaglehawk Neck Bay. Port Arthur convict settlement, 21 km SW. **Tourist information:** Officers Mess, off Arthur Hwy; (002) 50 3635. **Accommodation:** 1 hotel, 1 motel, 1 B&B. **See also:** A Convict Past; Tours from Hobart.
MAP REF. 521 N8, 525 O7

Evandale
Pop. 772
This little township, 19 km from Launceston, has been proclaimed an historic village. Founded in 1829, some of its buildings date from 1809. Originally it was named Collins Hill, but was renamed in 1836 in honour of Tasmania's first Surveyor-General, G. W. Evans. Streetscapes remain unspoiled by progress and there are many buildings of historical and architectural significance. **Of interest:** Self-guide Heritage Walk from Tourism and History Centre, High St. Also in High St: Solomon House (1836), Devonshire teas, accommodation; St Andrew's (1871) and Uniting (1839) churches; Blenheim (1840s), stained glass sales, workshop. Strickland's Gallery, Russell St, bronze castings, foundry. Clarendon Arms Hotel, Russell St, mural depicting early history of area. Market, Falls Park, Russell St, Sun. Feb.: Village Fair and National Penny Farthing Championships. **In the area:** Clarendon (1836), 8 km S near Nile: Georgian mansion designed in grand manner, in extensive formal gardens. Also at Nile, historic inn. **Tourist information:** High St; (003) 91 8128. **Accommodation:** 2 motels. **See also:** Stately Homes.
MAP REF. 523 P12, 527 M8

Exeter
Pop. 394
Exeter serves a large fruit-growing area 24 km NW of Launceston. **In the area:** To north-east, former river resorts of Gravelly Beach and Paper Beach. Walking track (5 km return) from Paper Beach to Supply River. Near mouth of Supply River, 10 km N off Gravelly Beach Rd, ruins of first water-driven flour mill in Tasmania, built 1825. Five wineries in West Tamar area; Wine Centre in Main Rd. Notley Fern Gorge, Notley Hills, 11 km S, 10-ha rainforest reserve, picnic/barbecue areas. Brady's Lookout, rocky outcrop used by notorious bushranger Matthew Brady, in State Reserve, 5 km SE. At Rosevears, 6 km SE, monument to John Batman's ship *Rebecca*, in which he crossed Bass Strait to Yarra River; ship was built at the once busy shipyards. On Rosevears Dr: historic Rosevears Hotel, first licensed 1831; Waterbird Haven, wetlands habitat, treetop hide. **Tourist information:** Tamar Visitor Centre, Main Rd; (003) 94 4454. **Accommodation:** Limited.
MAP REF. 523 L7, 527 L6

Fingal
Pop. 428
Situated in the Esk Valley, 21 km inland from St Marys on the South Esk River, Fingal is the headquarters of the State's coal industry. The first payable gold in Tasmania was found in 1852 at The Nook, near Fingal. **Of interest:** Historic buildings incl.: St Joseph's Church, Grey St, Masonic Lodge, Brown St. In Talbot St: St Peter's Church; Holder Bros. General Store; Fingal Hotel, collection of over 280 brands of Scotch whisky. Feb.: Fingal Valley Festival, incorporating World Coal Shovelling Championships and Roof Bolting Championships. **In the area:** Mathinna, 27 km N, extensive forestry development area, waterfalls nearby. White Gum Forest Reserve, Evercreech, further 3 km, 89-m white gum, picnic/barbecue areas, rainforest walking tracks. **Tourist information:** Fingal Valley Neighbourhood House, Talbot St; (003) 74 2344. **Accommodation:** 1 hotel. **See also:** Stately Homes.
MAP REF. 527 P8

St Andrew's Church, Evandale

Scenic Island State

Wherever your holiday journey in Tasmania takes you, you will be sure to see magnificent scenery and to have many fascinating experiences along the way. Most travellers start their Tasmanian holiday in the north, where they have either taken their car off the ferry or have hired a car or mobile home for the journey south.

Probably the best way to see what Tasmania has to offer is to take the 'circle route', with as many diversions along the way as time permits to see and explore scenic or historic highlights. Such a tour of the island, will take you through some of the most fascinating country that Australia has to offer. The incomparable wilderness of the west coast, the towering mountains of the central district, the gentle pastoral landscapes of the Midlands, the lavish orchard country around Launceston and the Huon Valley, the snug beaches, bays and villages of the east coast, are all relatively accessible on good roads.

You will soon find that not everything about Tasmania is small. Nurtured by the temperate climate, the trees are taller here than on the mainland (Tasmania has the world's tallest hardwood trees, some exceeding 90 metres); mountains vault to the skies from wild forest land. The great inland lakes in the mountains feed savage rivers, some of which harness the State's hydro-electric schemes. The hills and valleys are harshly carved by the weather and become gentle only in the rolling pastoral lands of the Midlands and the north.

In this romantic landscape, more reminiscent of Scotland than Australia, are set the remnants of a rich past of convict and colonial life—the prisons, churches, cottages and courthouses, the barracks, mansions and homesteads from the earliest days of European settlement.

From **Devonport** the coast road to the west runs with the northern railway along the sea's edge. Along this road are the thriving towns of **Ulverstone**, **Burnie**, **Wynyard** and **Stanley**, and the striking headlands of Table Cape, Rocky Cape and the Nut. They are worth a special trip, as is a detour down the side road from **Penguin** to the peaceful mountain farmland of Gunns Plains and the Gunns Plains caves. The road from **Forth** into the vast wilderness areas of the magnificent Cradle Mountain Lake St Clair National Park is also well worth a visit, but the turnoff to follow the circle route is at **Somerset**, and from there you head south down the Murchison Highway through the rich farmlands towards the increasingly mountainous country of the west coast. An interesting diversion leads to **Corinna**, once a thriving town but now virtually abandoned, on the beautiful Pieman River, not far from its mouth. A launch trip from Corinna travels through deeply-cut river gorges west to the Indian Ocean.

Back on the main road, the mountain scenery is unique and quite spectacular. The towns here developed as a result of their mineral wealth. **Zeehan** now has only a small population, but at the turn of the century there were more than 10 000 inhabitants when silver, lead and zinc mining was at its height. Many buildings of those days still stand. The larger town of **Queenstown** has grown up around the Mount Lyell copper mine, in a valley beneath bare, bleached hills, streaked and stained with the hues of minerals—chrome, purple, grey and pink. Nearby is **Strahan** on Macquarie Harbour, the only coastal town in the west. The harbour can be reached only by shallow-draught vessels through the notorious passage called Hell's Gates. Visitors can cruise through wilderness country along the Gordon River, past the ruins of the remote convict settlement on Sarah Island.

The road turns inland from these towns, avoiding the almost inaccessible southwest, and travels through the Franklin–Gordon Wild Rivers National Park, across the Central Highlands past Lake St Clair and down the Derwent River valley through the town of **New Norfolk**, centre of the Tasmanian hop-growing industry. This valley, brilliantly coloured with foliage in autumn, is of both scenic and historical interest. It was settled by Europeans in 1808, the site having been chosen by Governor Macquarie.

A detour from the Hobart road leads to the lovely old town of Richmond, one of the many historic towns the visitor bypasses if the circle route is followed. (Some of the others are **Ross, Oatlands, Campbell Town, Bothwell** and **Longford**, all set in the charming rolling countryside of the Midlands with their English trees framing or hiding the landowners' mansions.) Richmond is

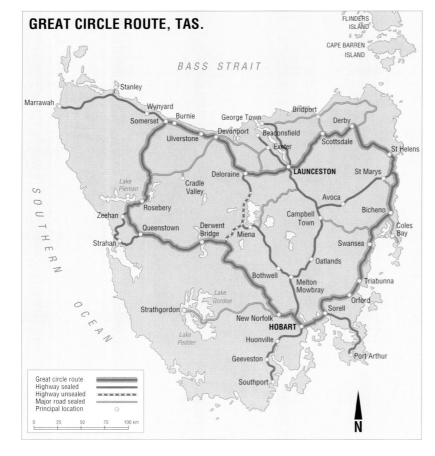

GREAT CIRCLE ROUTE, TAS.

probably the best example of an historic town, its old Georgian houses and cottages clustered together with its bridge, convict-built and the oldest freestone bridge still in use in Australia. The gaol pre-dates Port Arthur as a penal settlement: two churches, a courthouse, a schoolhouse, a rectory, the hotel granary, a general store and a flour mill were all built in the 1820s and 1830s.

Hobart, Australia's second oldest and most southerly city, is attractively sited on the Derwent River, with Mount Wellington looming above it. The port area at Salamanca Place, where the old bond stores and warehouses are sited, is a reminder of the days when the whaling fleet and the timber ships tied up at the wharf and sailors went out on the town. Battery Point with its barracks, workers' cottages and Arthur's Circus—its Georgian-style houses built around a circular green—is part of Hobart's beginnings.

There is modern-day fun in Hobart, too, since the Wrest Point Hotel–Casino developed as Hobart's best-known entertainment complex.

In complete contrast, the grim but beautiful penal settlement of **Port Arthur** is not far from Hobart, on the Tasman Peninsula. Here, within the forbidding sandstone walls, visitors will feel some of the hopelessness and isolation of the thousands of convicts who passed

Scenery near Strahan

through this settlement during its 47 years of existence.

South of Hobart is the scenic Huon Valley, particularly spectacular when the apple trees are in blossom. At the southern end of the route is Cockle Creek on Recherche Bay, where the South Coast walking track begins.

North on the circle route from Hobart the Tasman Highway traverses the east coast, a region enjoying a mild and equable climate throughout most of the year and with a number of attractive seaside resorts. Most are on sheltered inlets but within easy

reach of surf beaches and fishing grounds: towns like **Orford, Triabunna**, **Swansea**, **Bicheno**, **Scamander** and **St Helens**.

Off the Tasman Highway near Bicheno is the Freycinet National Park on the Freycinet Peninsula. There are many walking tracks through this park, which is dominated by the Hazards, a red-granite mountain range.

The road cuts across the less developed farming country of the north and goes west to **Launceston**, the northern capital of Tasmania, 64 kilometres from the north coast at the junction of the North Esk, South Esk and Tamar Rivers. It is a smaller, more provincial city than Hobart, set in hilly countryside, and makes an excellent base from which to explore the rich coastal plain of the Tamar Valley and the mountain country to the north. Cataract Gorge, historic Franklin House and Entally House, and the hydro-electric station at Duck Reach, built in 1895, are all within easy reach of Launceston.

On to Devonport, where this description of the circle route began. Many of Tasmania's magnificent national parks are not far from the circle route highway.

For further information, contact the Tasmanian Information Centre, 20 Davey St, Hobart; (002) 30 8233. **See also:** Individual town entries in A–Z listing; National Parks.

Dams for Power

Tasmania is the only State in Australia to rely almost entirely on water to generate electricity. Clean, renewable water power provides the energy for Tasmania's homes and industries.

Rainfall in the highland catchments and rivers not only provides water for drinking and other uses, but is also the source of fuel for the State's hydro-electric system. Several rivers around Tasmania have been harnessed for power production, with dams, canals, and penstocks directing the water through 28 power stations.

Perhaps the best known power development—and the largest in Tasmania—is the Gordon River scheme in the southwest wilderness area. The scheme includes two inter-connected lakes, Gordon and Pedder, and an underground power station capable of generating 432 megawatts of power.

The most spectacular feature is the 140-metre high Gordon Dam, a twin curvature arch dam, constructed in a narrow

gorge in the Gordon River. Both the dam and the power station are open to the public, with a visitor centre overlooking the dam site. Stocked with trout, the lakes are tourist attractions in themselves.

The west coast of Tasmania has power developments on the King, Pieman, and Anthony rivers. The most recent—the 84MSw Anthony scheme—was opened in May 1994, completing 80 years of hydro-electric power construction in Tasmania.

Visitors have easy access to most of the major dams on the west coast, including the mighty Reece Dam at the head of a 50-kilometre-long lake on the lower reaches of the Pieman River.

From the Lyell Highway, the visitor can see parts of the Derwent power scheme. Rising in Lake St Clair, 738 metres above sea level, the Derwent River provides most of the energy for 10 power stations in a run-of-river system, with all but the last 44 metres of the river's fall utilised. There are public viewing galleries at Tungatinah,

Tarraleah, and Liapootha power stations.

In the north of the State the Mersey Forth scheme, although smaller than the derwent, is quite spectacular as the river system lies in a very steep valley. The scheme includes seven power stations and rises at Lake Mackenzie, 1121 metres above sea level. One of the features is Lake Barrington, a world-class rowing venue and site of national and world rowing champions.

Right in the centre of Tasmania is the State's oldest power station, Waddamana. Now a museum, it is open from 10–4 every day except Good Friday and Christmas Day.

For further information on HEC public viewing areas, roads open to the public, environmental issues, guided tours and accommodation, contact the Hydro-Electric Commission, 4–16 Elizabeth St, Hobart 7000; (002) 30 5553.

Franklin
Pop. 462

This timber milling town, 45 km SW of Hobart, was the site of the first European settlement in the Huon district in 1804. It was named after Governor Sir John Franklin, who took up 259 ha on the banks of the Huon River. Timber milling has been an important local industry since the very early years. Orcharding and dairy farming are the other main industries. **Tourist information:** Huon River Jet Boats, Esplanade, Huonville; (002) 64 1838. **Accommodation:** Limited. **See also:** Rural Landscapes.
MAP REF. 520 E9, 525 K7

Geeveston
Pop. 826

This important timber town is the gateway to Tasmania's south-west World Heritage Area. **Of interest:** Esperance Forest and Heritage Centre, Church St, tourist complex incorporating Gateway to South-West (Huon Hwy), Hartz Gallery (wilderness art and craft) and 5 forest walks. **In the area:** Arve and Weld valleys west of town contain world's tallest (87 m) hardwood trees. Hartz Mountains National Park, 23 km SW, off Arve Rd. Arve Road Forest Drive, incl. Arve River Picnic area and Tahune Forest Reserve, 27 km NW; camping and recreation area. Cruises on Huon River. **Tourist information:** Church St; (002) 97 1836. **Accommodation:** Limited.
MAP REF. 520 D10, 525 K8

George Town
Pop. 5026

Situated at the mouth of the Tamar River, George Town was settled by Europeans in 1811, when it was named for King George III. Today it is a commercial centre, mainly as a result of the Comalco plant at Bell Bay and other industrial developments. **Of interest:** Self-guide walk. Monument on Esplanade commemorates unintentional landing in 1804, when Lieut.–Col. William Paterson and his crew in HMS Buffalo ran aground during storm. The Grove (c. 1838), cnr Elizabeth and Cimitiere Sts, Devonshire teas, lunches. **In the area:** Comalco plant, Bell Bay, 6 km S; tours. At Hillwood, 24 km SE, pick-your-own strawberry farm. Ghost town of goldmining settlement, Lefroy, 10 km E, ruins, old diggings, cemetery. Several wineries at Pipers Brook, 33 km E. Low Head, 5 km N: surf beach and river beach; Maritime Museum in Australia's oldest continuously used pilot station, opened

1803. Day and weekend cruises to Bass Strait islands on SS *Furneaux Explorer*. **Tourist information:** Main Rd; (003) 82 1700. **Accommodation:** 2 hotels, 1 hotel/motel, 1 motel, 3 B&B, 1 hostel, 1 cara./camp. park. **See also:** Stately Homes.
MAP REF. 523 K4, 527 K5

Gladstone
Pop. 200

The small town of Gladstone is one of the few communities in the far north-east that still relies on tin mining. The district was once a thriving tin and goldmining area, with a colourful early history. Now many of these once-substantial townships are ghost towns or nearly so. **In the area:** Gladstone and South Mt Cameron area, geological formations. Boobyalla, 20 km NW, old mining town. Gemstone fossicking park on Tasman Hwy at Moorinna, 30 km W. Moorina, 30 km SW, cemetery has graves of Chinese miners. Weldborough, former tin mining town, 37 km SW, once headquarters for 900 Chinese miners. Mt William National Park, 25 km E, prolific flora and fauna, excellent beaches. Eddystone Point, 35 km E, historic lighthouse. **Tourist information:** Rose's Travel, 11 Alfred St, Scottsdale; (003) 52 2186. **Accommodation:** 1 hotel.
MAP REF. 527 P4

Hadspen
Pop. 1334

The township of Hadspen, which was first settled in the early 1820s, has many historic buildings some of which offer accommodation or meals. **Of interest:** Row of Georgian buildings, Main Rd: incl. Red Feather Inn (c. 1844); old coaching station; Hadspen Gaol (c. 1840); Church of the Good Shepherd. Building of church commenced in 1858, funded by Thomas Reibey, who withdrew his support after a dispute with the bishop. Church was completed in 1961, almost 50 years after Reibey's death. **In the area:** Entally House (1819), one of Tasmania's most famous historic homes, 1 km W on banks of South Esk River; magnificent collection of Regency furniture and fine silverware. **Tourist information:** Tasmaian Travel and Information Centre, cnr St John and Paterson Sts, Launceston; (003) 36 3133 **Accommodation:** 1 hotel/motel, 1 cara./camp. park. **See also:** Stately Homes.
MAP REF. 523 N11, 527 L7

Hamilton
Pop. 150

A classified historic town in a rural setting, Hamilton has retained many of its colonial buildings. **Of interest:** Glen Clyde House (c. 1840), Grace St, craft gallery, tearooms. **In the area:** Meadowbank Lake, 10 km NW, popular venue for picnics, boating, water-skiing, trout fishing. **Tourist information:** Council Offices, Tarleton St; (002) 86 3202. **Accommodation:** 1 hotel.
MAP REF. 520 D1, 525 K4, 527 K13

Hastings
Pop. 20

This small centre, about 100 km from Hobart on the Huon Hwy, attracts many tourists to its famous limestone caves, local gemstones and nearby scenic railway. **In the area:** Esperance Self Drive Tour begins off Hastings Rd; to Esperance River, north-west; picnic/barbecue facilities. Hastings Caves, 13 km NW, tours of illuminated Newgate Cave, swimming in thermal pool, streamside walks, picnic/barbecue facilities. Lune River, 2 km S, haven for gem collectors. Beyond river, 2 km further S, Ida Bay Scenic Railway, originally built to carry dolomite, now carries passengers 7 km to Deep Hole and back; picnic facilities at both ends of track. **Tourist information:** Church St, Geeveston; (002) 97 1836. **Accommodation:** Limited. **See also:** Tours from Hobart.
MAP REF. 520 D13, 525 K9

Hawley Beach
Pop. 1000

This popular seaside area near Port Sorell is well known for its good fishing, excellent beaches and safe swimming. **Of interest:** Historic Hawley House (1878), Main Rd, meals, accommodation. **Tourist information:** Tasmanian Travel and Information, Devonport Showcase, 5 Best St, Devonport; (004) 24 4466. **Accommodation:** Limited.
MAP REF. 527 J5

Huonville
Pop. 1524

Huonville is an commercial centre serving the surrounding townships, and is the largest apple-producing centre in the area. The valuable softwood now known as Huon pine was discovered in this district. **Of interest:** Daily river cruises, over rapids, to Glen Huon. Model Train World, Main Rd. Horseback Wilderness Tours, Sale St. Pedal boat and aqua bike hire, Esplanade. **In the area:** Apple and Heritage Museum just out of Grove, 6 km

NE. Susans Country Cupboard, Huon Hwy, 4 km N, craft. Snowy Range Trout Fishery, Little Dennison River, 25 km NW. Scenic drives west to Glen Huon, Judbury and Ranelagh, south east to Cygnet. Antique Motor Museum near Ranelagh, 5 km NW. Model Miniature Village at Glen Huon, 8 km W. At Port Huon, 10 km SW, indoor sports centre, river cruises in estuary. **Tourist information:** Huon River Jet Boats, Esplanade; (002) 64 1838. **Accommo- dation:** 1 hotel. **See also:** Tours from Hobart. MAP REF. 520 F8, 525 K7

Kettering   Pop. 295
This town on the Channel Hwy serves a large fruit-growing district. The Bruny Island ferry leaves several times daily from the terminal at Kettering, extra services during holidays. Oyster Cove Inn and marina, Ferry Rd. Variety of boats for hire; skippered cruises available. In the area: Bruny Island. Pleasant walks in Snug Falls Track area, near township of Snug, 8 km N. Also at Snug: Mother's Favourites, seafood. Nearby Coningham Beach, good swimming, boating. Monument to French explorer Admiral Bruni D'Entrecasteaux, Gordon, 21 km S. **Tourist information:** Bruny D'Entrecasteaux Visitor Centre, Ferry Rd, Kettering; (002) 67 4494. **Accommodation:** 1 hotel/motel, 1 cara./camp. park. MAP REF. 520 H9, 525 L8

Kingston–Blackmans Bay
Pop. 12 907
Kingston Beach, 12 km S of Hobart, was discovered by Scottish botanist Robert Brown in 1804. **Of interest:** Display at Federal Government's Antarctic research headquarters, Channel Hwy. March: Kingborough festival (incl. road cycle race). Oct.: Kingston Oliebollen Festival. **In the area:** Scenic drives south through Blackmans Bay, Tinderbox and Howden; magnificent views of Droughty Point and Bruny Island from Piersons Point. Small blowhole at Blackmans Bay, at reserve on Blowhole Rd; spectacular in stormy weather. **Tourist information:** Council Chambers, Channel Hwy; (002) 29 555. **Accommodation:** 2 hotel/motels. MAP REF. 520 H7, 520 H8, 525 M7

Latrobe   Pop. 2551
Situated on the Mersey River, 9 km SE of Devonport, the Latrobe area was once the home of the 4 main Aboriginal groups together known as the North Tribe. After European settlement Latrobe became a busy town with its own shipyards. Today it is the site of one of the biggest cycling carnivals in Australia, the Latrobe Wheel Race and Latrobe Gift, held at Christmas. **Of interest:** Many early buildings and shopfronts dating from 1840s, incl. some National Trust-classified. Self-guide leaflet. Court House Museum, Gilbert St, local history. Bell's Parade, along riverbank, picturesque reserve, picnic areas. **In the area:** Frogmore, historic homestead, host farm, 1 km SW. **Tourist information:** Visitor Information, Gilbert St; (004) 26 1041. **Accommodation:** 1 hotel, 1 motel. MAP REF. 522 E6, 526 I6

Launceston   Pop. 66 747
Although it is Tasmania's second-largest city and a busy tourist centre, Launceston manages to retain a relaxed, friendly atmosphere. Nestling in hilly country where the Tamar, North Esk and South Esk rivers meet, Launceston is also at the junction of 3 main highways and has direct air links with Melbourne and Hobart. It is sometimes known as the Garden City because of its beautiful parks and gardens. **Of interest:** Yorktown Square, The Avenue, Quadrant Mall, Civic Square, and Prince's Square with its magnificent baroque fountain and fine surrounding buildings. Main shopping area around the Mall. Old Umbrella Shop, George St, unique 1860s shop preserved by National Trust. Penny Royal World, Paterson St: collection of buildings originally sited at Barton, near Cressy, and moved stone by stone to Launceston; incl. accommodation, restaurants, tavern, museum, working water mill, corn mill, graceful windmill; linked by restored tramway to Penny Royal Gunpowder Mill at old Cataract quarry site; boat trips on artificial lake. Parks incl. 5 ha City Park with Monkey Island and conservatory (Design Centre of Tasmania nearby displays contemporary art and craft); Royal Park, formal civic park on South Esk River; Zig Zag Reserve, leading to Cataract Gorge area. Queen Victoria Museum and Art Gallery, in Royal Park, with displays of Aboriginal and convict relics, Tasmania's mineral wealth, flora and fauna, early china and glassware, colonial and

Kings Bridge, Launceston

Marakoopa Cave, near Mole Creek

modern art. *Lady Stelfox*: cruises on lower reaches of Tamar, departs from Ritchie's Mill Arts Centre, Bridge Rd. Boags Brewery, William St; guided tours. Walking tours: self-guide (leaflets from Tourist Information) and guided. Oct.: Garden festival, Royal National Show, Tasmanian Poetry festival. **In the area:** One of Launceston's outstanding natural attractions, spectacular Cataract Gorge, 2 km W of city centre. Cataract Cliff Grounds Reserve, on north side of gorge, formal park with lawns, European trees, peacocks, licensed restaurant. Area linked to south side (swimming pool, kiosk) by scenic chairlift and suspension bridge. Delightful walks on both sides of gorge. Trevallyn Dam, 6 km W, landscaping, attractive picnic spot. Nearby, Australia's only hang-gliding simulator. Waverley Woollen Mills, 5 km E, tours incl. historic collection of plant machinery, creating industry for which Launceston earned national reputation. Launceston Federal Country Club Casino, 7 km SW. Punchbowl Reserve and Rhododendron Gardens, 5 km SW, native and European fauna in natural surroundings. Grindelwald Holiday Resort, near Legana, 12 km N: Swiss-style village on edge of Lake Louise; shops, restaurant, chalet accommodation. St Matthias' Church, Windermere, 15 km N. Tamar Valley wineries, 50 km N/NE, incl. St Matthias, Marions, Heemskerk, Rochecombe, Pipers Brook. Guided tours throughout northern Tasmania; details from Tourist Information. Three National Trust historic houses: Entally House, 13 km SW at Hadspen; Franklin House, 6 km S; Clarendon, near Nile, 28 km SE. **Tourist information:** Cnr St John and Paterson Sts; (003) 36 3133. **Accommodation:** 17 hotels, 12 motels, 1 cara./camp. park. **See also:** Fisherman's Paradise; Scenic Island State; Stately Homes.
MAP REF. 523 N10, 527 L7

Lilydale   Pop. 333

At the foot of Mt Arthur, 27 km from Launceston, the town of Lilydale has many nearby bush tracks and picnic spots. **In the area:** Lilydale Falls Reserve, 3 km N, two oak trees grown from acorns from Windsor Great Park, planted here on coronation day of British King George IV, 12 May 1937. Scenic walks to top of Mt Arthur (1187 m). At Lalla, 4 km W: Walker Rhododendron Gardens; Appleshed, local art and craft. Brown Mountain School of Bonsai, Brown Mountain Rd, Underwood, 11 km SW, by appt. Hollybank Forest Reserve, Underwood, 5 km S; picnic/barbecue areas. Bridestowe Lavender Farm, near Nabowla, 26 km NE, sales of lavender products, tours in flowering season, Dec.–Jan. **Tourist Information:** Tasmanian Travel and Tourist Information Centre, cnr St John and Paterson Sts, Launceston; (003) 36 3133. **Accommodation:** 1 hotel.
MAP REF. 527 M6

Longford   Pop. 2601

This quiet country town, 22 km S of Launceston, was established in 1813 when former settlers of Norfolk Island were given land grants in the area. Since then it has had 3 name changes, having previously been known as Norfolk Plains and Latour. Now classified as an historic town, it serves a rich agricultural district. **Of interest:** Self-guide leaflet on town and area. Many historic buildings, some convict-built. In Wellington St: Christ Church (1839), outstanding stained glass window, pioneer gravestones. Country Club Hotel, 'car in window'. March: Targa Tasmania motor racing, classic and veteran car displays. **In the area:** Brickendon (1824), 2 km S, homestead built by William Archer, still owned by descendants; tours by appt. At Cressy, 10 km S, Connorville sheep station, established by Roderic O'Connor, whose descendants still produce superfine wool there. At Perth, 5 km NE, historic buildings incl. Eskleigh, Jolly Farmer Inn, Old Crown Inn, Leather Bottell Inn. Longford Wildlife Park, 5 km N, conservation area for fallow deer and Australian fauna and flora, picnic/barbecue areas and constructed lake. **Tourist information:** Council Offices, Smith St; (003) 91 1303. **Accommodation:** 1 hotel, 1 cara./camp. park. **See also:** Scenic Island State; Stately Homes.
MAP REF. 523 N13, 527 L8

Mole Creek   Pop. 249

This town, 74 km S of Devonport, serves an important farming and forestry district. The unique Tasmanian leatherwood honey from the blossom of the leatherwood tree, which grows only in the rainforests of the west coast of Tasmania, is processed here. Each summer, apiarists transport hives to the nearby leatherwood forests. **In the area:** Guided tours of fine limestone caves in State reserves: Marakoopa, 8 km W, glow worm display; and smaller but still spectacular, King Solomon Cave, further 7 km W. **Tourist information:** 29 Westchurch St; (003) 62 2046. **Accommodation:** 1 hotel, 1 B&B, 1 hostel, 1 cara./camp. park.
MAP REF. 522 E12, 526 I7

New Norfolk   Pop. 5822

Colonial buildings set among English trees and hop fields dotted with oast houses give this classified historic town a decidedly English look; the countryside has often been compared with that of Kent in England. On the Derwent River, 33 km NW of Hobart, the town owes its name to the fact that displaced European settlers from the abandoned Norfolk Island settlement were granted land in this area. Although the New Norfolk district produces a majority of the hops used by

Australian breweries, the chief industry today is paper manufacture. **Of interest:** At Historical Centre in Council Chambers, Circle St: self-guide historic walk leaflet; genealogical and other records. Scenic lookouts: Peppermint Hill, off Blair Rd; Pulpit Rock and Four Winds Display Gardens, off Rocks Rd. Old Colony Inn (c. 1835), Montague St, museum, tearooms. Oast House, Tynwald Park, Lyell Hwy, hop museum, art gallery, tearooms. St Matthew's Church (1823), Bathurst St, reputedly oldest church still standing in Tasmania; craft centre in adjoining Close. Bush Inn (1815), Lyell Hwy; claims oldest licence in Commonwealth, although contested by Launceston Hotel. Jet boat rides on Derwent River rapids leave from Bush Inn. March: Hop Festival. Aug.: Winter Challenge. **In the area:** Tours of Australian Newsprint Mills, Boyer, 5 km E; 24 hrs notice required. Famous Salmon Ponds, Plenty, 11 km NW: hatchery where first brown and rainbow trout in southern hemisphere were bred in 1864; restaurant, museum. Mt Field National Park, 40 km NW, impressive Russell Falls. **Tourist information:** Council Chambers, Circle St; (002) 61 2777. **Accommodation:** 3 hotels, 1 motel, 3 B&B, 1 cara./camp. park. **See also:** Rural Landscapes; Scenic Island State; Stately Homes; Tours from Hobart.
MAP REF. 520 F4, 525 K6

Oatlands   Pop. 522
This classified historic town on the shores of Lake Dulverton, 84 km N of Hobart, attracts both anglers and lovers of history. It was designated as a garrison town by Governor Macquarie in 1821 and surveyed in 1832. Many of the town's unique sandstone buildings were constructed in the 1830s and it is said that almost everyone lives in an historic house. **Of interest:** Convict-built courthouse (1829), Campbell St. Holyrood House (1840), High St, historic gardens. St Peter's Church (c. 1838), William St. Callington Flour Mill (1836), Mill Lane. Lake Dulverton Wildlife Sanctuary, Esplanade. Feb.: Rodeo. **In the area:** Trout fishing on Lake Sorell, 29 km NW, and adjoining Lake Crescent. **Tourist information:** Southern Midlands Council Offices, 71 High St; (002) 54 0011. **Accommodation:** 1 hotel, 4 B&B. **See also:** Rural Landscapes; Scenic Island State.
MAP REF. 525 M3, 527 M12

Orford   Pop. 502
Views from this popular holiday resort at the estuary of the Prosser River, on the Tasman Hwy, are dominated by Maria Island National Park, 20 km offshore. **Of interest:** Bushwalks, golf, river and sea fishing, scuba diving. **In the area:** The Thumbs Lookout, 2 km S, overlooks Maria Island. Daily ferry service from Eastcoaster Resort, 4 km NE on Louisville Rd, to Maria Island. Church of St John the Baptist, Buckland, 18 km SW, beautiful 14th-century stained glass window. **Tourist information:** Council Offices, cnr Vicary and Henry Sts, Triabunna; (002) 57 3113. **Accommodation:** 1 hotel/motel, 1 motel, 1 cara./camp. park. **See also:** Scenic Island State.
MAP REF. 521 N2, 525 O4

Penguin   Pop. 2876
The Dial Range rises over this quiet town, named after little (fairy) penguins still found in rookeries nearby. **Of interest:** In Main St: National Trust-classified St Stephen's Church and Uniting Church. Hiscutt Park, off Crescent St, working Dutch windmill, tulips in season. Tours of penguin rookeries, Dec.–early March. Old School Market, King Edward St, 2nd and 4th Sun. in month. **In the area:** Pindari Deer Farm Riana, 15 km SW, deer-handling demonstrations. Mt Montgomery, 5 km S, magnificent view from summit. Mason's Fuschia Fantasy, 6 km S on West Pine Rd, 750 varieties; open p.m. and Sat. Ferndean Wildlife Reserve, 6 km S, picnic spot, walking tracks. Pioneer Park, Riana, 10 km S, gardens, walks,

Callington Flour Mill, Oatlands

picnic facilities. Beyond South Riana (20 km S), Gunns Plains, caves, hopfields. Scenic drive south-east to Ulverstone via coast road. **Tourist information:** Penguin Tourist Information Centre, Main St; (004) 37 1421. **Accommodation:** 1 hotel, 2 B&B, 1 caravan park. **See also:** Scenic Island State.
MAP REF. 522 A4, 526 H5

Poatina   Pop. 20
Fifty-five kilometres south-west of Launceston and no longer in operation, the plateau village of Poatina (an Aboriginal word for 'cavern') was built to house the construction team working on the hydro-electric power station. **In the area:** Poatina underground power station, 5 km W; guided tours. **Tourist information:** Council Offices, Smith St, Longford; (003) 91 1303. **Accommodation:** None. **See also:** Dams for Power.
MAP REF. 527 K9

Pontville   Pop. 1125
Much of the freestone used in Tasmania's old buildings was quarried near this classified historic town. On the Midland Hwy, 27 km N of Hobart, Pontville was founded in 1830 and many of its early buildings remain. **Of interest:** Historic buildings on or adj. to Midland Hwy incl.: St Mark's Church (1841); The Sheiling (built 1819, restored 1953), behind church; old post office; Crown Inn; and 'The Row', thought to have been built in 1824 as soldiers' quarters, now restored. **In the area:** Towns nearby with interesting historic buildings: Bagdad, 8

Rural Landscapes

Tasmania's homesick European settlers were amazingly successful in their attempts to tame their strange new antipodean home. They set about systematically clearing the more accessible lowlands of all traces of native bush, replacing it with neatly tilled fields fringed by hedgerows and the exotic trees familiar to them. Georgian farmhouses set in gardens with flower beds and borders completed the picture.

Tasmania's main pastoral district is the beautiful Midlands area between **Brighton** and **Perth**, noted for stock-raising and high-quality merino wool. This was one of the first farming areas established in Tasmania and its gently undulating plains are offset by mellow farmhouses, historic villages and a wealth of huge old English trees. The historic township of New Norfolk is the centre of Tasmania's long-established hop-growing district, which is a main supplier of hops for Australian beer. This enchanting countryside is enhanced by quaint old oast houses, or hop-drying kilns. Apples and dairy products are produced in the **Derwent Valley**, which is also an important beef-raising and wool-growing district.

The **Huon Valley**, south of Hobart, is the centre of Tasmania's famous apple-growing industry, which dates back to the early nineteenth century when Lady Franklin, wife of Governor Sir John Franklin, established a farm at **Franklin.**

Tasmania's richest and most highly productive farmland lies on the north-west coast, where the main industries are potato-growing and the raising of prime beef and dairy cattle.

See also: Individual town entries in A–Z listing.

Stately Homes

One of Tasmania's attractions is its wealth of beautiful stately homes with a distinctly English air. You can dine in style in some, such as Prospect House in the historic town of **Richmond**, and stay in others.

Several of Tasmania's grand old mansions, such as Malahide and Killymoon, both on the Esk Highway near **Fingal**, are privately owned and cannot be inspected, but many of the State's finest homesteads are open daily to the public.

Clarendon House, via Evandale, 27 kilometres from Launceston, is probably Australia's grandest Georgian mansion. Completed in 1838 for woolgrower James Cox and given to the National Trust in 1962, it has been meticulously restored.

Three other stately homesteads within reach of **Launceston** are Franklin House, just 6 kilometres south; Entally House at **Hadspen**, 18 kilometres from Launceston; and Brickendon in **Longford**.

Prospect House, Richmond

Franklin House, another elegant Georgian mansion now owned by the National Trust, was built in 1838 for Mr Britton Jones, a Launceston brewer and innkeeper. In 1842 it became the W.K. Hawkes School for Boys.

Charming Entally House, the most historic of the Trust houses, was built in 1819. Set in superb grounds, Entally has a greenhouse, chapel and coach-house. It was opened to the public in 1950.

Two-storeyed, shuttered Brickendon, with its graceful metal front porch, looks French, but long stretches of hawthorn hedges and many old chestnuts, oaks, ash and junipers make it seem part of an English landscape.

The Grove in **George Town**, north of Launceston, is another privately owned historic house open to visitors. Built in the 1820s, it has been painstakingly restored by the present owners, who dress in period costume to serve lunch and teas.

Home Hill in Middle Road, **Devonport**, the home of former Prime Minister Joseph Lyons and Dame Enid Lyons, was built by them in 1916. Now open to the public, the house and grounds are owned by the City of Devonport. The contents of the house are owned by the National Trust.

Privately owned but operated by the Trust, the White House, in **Westbury**, near **Deloraine**, was built c. 1841 as a corner shop and residence. It stands on a corner of the town's Village Green and displays a collection of Staffordshire china.

Hobart has two historic houses open for inspection: the National Trust property Runnymede, in the suburb of **New Town**, and Narryna in **Battery Point**. Graceful Runnymede, built c. 1836, has been restored and furnished by the Trust. Narryna, a Georgian sandstone and brick townhouse with a walled courtyard, is set in an old-world garden shaded by elm trees. Also known as the Van Diemen's Land Memorial Folk Museum, it houses a significant collection of colonial artefacts.

The misleadingly named Old Colony Inn in **New Norfolk** serves lunches (with fresh trout as a specialty) and Devonshire teas. This beautiful old building, set in delightful grounds, has become one of Tasmania's most photographed tourist attractions. Despite its name, it was never used as an inn.

For further information, contact the National Trust of Australia (Tasmania), 413 Hobart Rd, Franklin Village 7249; (003) 44 6233. **See also:** Individual town entries in A–Z listing.

km N; Kempton, 15 km N, beyond Bag-dad; Broadmarsh, 10 km W; Tea Tree, 5 km E. **Tourist information:** Council Offices, Tivoli Rd, Gagebrook; (002) 63 0333. **Accommodation:** Limited. MAP REF: 520 H3, 525 L5

Port Sorell
Pop. 1494

Sheltered by hills, this well-established holiday resort at the estuary of the Rubicon River near Devonport has a mild climate. Named after Governor Sorell and established in 1822, it is the oldest township on the north-west coast. Unfortunately many of its old buildings were destroyed by bushfires early this century, after it had been almost deserted for the thriving new port of Devonport. **Of interest:** Swimming, fishing, boating, bushwalking. Views from Watch House Hill, off Meredith St, once site of old gaol, now bowling green. Asbestos Range National Park across estuary. **In the area:** At neighbouring Shearwater, 3 km NW, resort with 9-hole golf course. **Tourist information:** Tasmania Travel and Information, Devonport Showcase, 5 Best St, Devonport; (004) 24 4466. **Accommodation:** 2 cara./camp. parks. **See also:** National Parks. MAP REF. 522 G5, 527 J5

Queenstown
Pop. 3368

The discovery of gold and mineral resources in the Mt Lyell field last century led to the almost overnight emergence of Queenstown. It is a town carved out of the mountains that tower starkly around it. Mining has been continuous in Queenstown since 1888, and the field has so far produced more than 670 000 tonnes of copper, 510 000 kg of silver and 20 000 kg of gold. The Mt Lyell Company, which employed most of the town's inhabitants, ceased operation at the end of 1994; tours of mine continue. The town has modern shops and facilities, but its wide streets, remaining historic buildings, and unique setting give it an old mining-town flavour. In certain lights, multi-coloured boulders on the bare hillsides surrounding the town reflect the sun's rays and turn to amazing shades of pink and gold. **Of interest:** Guided tours of Mt Lyell Mine from Farmers Store, Driffield St, incl. Mining Museum. Galley Museum, cnr Sticht and Driffield Sts, history of west coast, photographs, memorabilia. **In the area:** Spectacular views from Lyell Hwy as it climbs steeply out of town. Original (1833) Iron Blow

Antique shop, Richmond

goldmine, off Lyell Hwy at Gormanston, 6 km E. Ghost town of Linda, 9 km E. Mt Jukes Rd lookout, 7 km SW, road leads to old mining settlement of Lynchford, and Crotty Dam. Rafting on Franklin River, to the east and south. Mt Mullens and Franklin River scenic nature walk along old mining railway line between Queenstown and Zeehan, 37 km N. Lyell Tours, 4WD day or half-day tours south to Bird River rainforest area. **Tourist information:** RACT, 18 Orr St; (004) 71 1974. **Accommodation:** 2 hotels, 2 hotel/motels, 3 motels, 1 cara./camp. park. **See also:** Scenic Island State; The West Coast; Dams for Power. MAP REF. 524 E1, 526 F11

Railton
Pop. 996

This substantial country town south east of Devonport owes its existence to the Goliath Portland Cement Company, representing one of Tasmania's major industries. Raw materials are taken from a quarry on the site and carried by an overhead conveyor to the crusher. **In the area:** Scenic drive through area known as Sunnyside to Stoodley Forest Reserve, 14 km S, walking tracks, picnic/barbecue areas. **Tourist information:** Kentish Museum, 93 Main St, Sheffield; (004) 91 1861. **Accommodation:** 1 hotel. MAP REF. 522 F8, 526 I6

Richmond
Pop. 754

Charming Richmond, 26 km from Hobart, is one of the oldest and most important historic towns in Australia.

The much-photographed Richmond Bridge is the oldest bridge in Australia (1823–5) and many of the town's buildings were constructed in the 1830s or even earlier. Some of these structures, incl. the bridge, were built by convicts under appallingly harsh conditions. Legend has it that the ghost of an overseer who was murdered by convicts still haunts the bridge. **Of interest:** Self-guide leaflet of town and area. Old Richmond Gaol (1825), Bathurst St, one of Australia's best preserved convict prisons; guided tours. St John's (1837), St John's Circle, oldest Catholic church in Australia still in use. St Luke's Church (1834–36), Torrens St, fine timber ceiling. General store and former post office (1832), Bridge St, oldest postal building in Australia. Also in Bridge St: galleries featuring local art and craft, incl. Saddler's Court (c. 1848) and Peppercorn Gallery (c. 1850); restored Bridge Inn, one of town's oldest buildings, housing complex of shops; Old Hobart Town, model of Hobart in early 1800s; Toy Museum; The Maze. Village Store (1836), one of oldest general stores still operating in Tasmania. Georgian mansion Prospect House (1830s) off Hobart Rd, haunted by ghost of Mrs Buscombe; meals, colonial accommodation. Feb.: Country Music Festival. Oct.: Village Fair. **In the area:** Scenic drive north through Campania (7 km) and Colebrook (19 km). Colonial Cottage. **Tourist information:** Saddler's Court Gallery, 48 Bridge St; (002) 60 2132. **Accommodation:** 1 hotel, 1 cara./camp park. **See also:** Scenic Island State; Stately Homes; Tours from Hobart. MAP REF. 521 J4, 525 M5

Ringarooma
Pop. 235

Dairy farming and timber milling support this north-eastern town, which dates back to the 1860s. Oct.: Agricultural Show. **In the area:** Views of Ringarooma and surrounding towns from Mathinna Hill and Mt Victoria. Pleasant drives on New River Rd and Alberton Rd. Old Tin Mining Rd to Branxholm, 16 km NE, gives glimpses of area as it was in days of early pioneers. **Tourist information:** Rose's Travel, 11 Alfred St, Scottsdale; (003) 52 2186. **Accommodation:** Limited. MAP REF. 527 O6

Rokeby
Pop. 3495

This old town on the eastern shore of the Derwent River was first settled in 1809.

Township of Ross

The first apples to be exported from Tasmania were grown here, as was the first wheat ever produced in Tasmania. Rokeby's rural character is now rapidly changing with the expansion of the Clarence Municipality. **Of interest:** Historic cemetery, the Mall (main road), contains graves of many First Fleeters. Historic buildings include Rokeby Court, Rokeby House, Hawthorn Pl, and St Matthew's Church (1843), North Pde. Some chairs in church's chancel were carved from wood from ship in Nelson's fleet; organ, brought from England in 1825 and first installed in what is now St David's Cathedral, Hobart, is still in use. **In the area:** Historic buildings at Bellerive, 8 km NW. New Historic Centre at Rosny, 10 km NW. To south, excellent surfing at Clifton Beach; boating and swimming at South Arm. **Tourist information:** Council Offices, 38 Bligh St, Rosny Park; (002) 44 0600. **Accommodation:** Limited.
MAP REF. 519 O10, 521 J6, 525 M6

Rosebery   Pop. 1637
Gold was discovered at Rosebery in 1893 in what is now called Rosebery Creek. Huge deposits of lead and zinc were also discovered in the area. Goldmining has long since been abandoned and the town now owes its existence to the zinc mining company Pasminco-EZ. **In the area:** Montezuma Falls, highest waterfall in State, 5 km SW, accessible by 4WD or walking track. Tullah, 12 km N: picturesque lake; accomodation; 10-km route on historical Wee Georgie Wood Railway, check times. **Tourist information:** West Coast Pioneers Museum, Main St, Zeehan; (004) 71 6225. **Accommodation:** 2 hotels, 1 cara./camp. park. **See also:** The West Coast.
MAP REF. 526 F9

Ross   Pop. 282
One of the oldest and most beautiful bridges in Australia spans the Macquarie River at this classified historic township. The bridge was designed by colonial architect John Lee Archer and built by convicts in 1836. The convict stonemason Daniel Herbert received a free pardon in recognition for his 186 fine carvings on the bridge. Ross was established in 1812 as a military post for the protection of travellers who once stopped there to change coaches. Today it is still an important stopping-place on the Midland Hwy between Launceston and Hobart. The district is famous for its superfine wool. **Of interest:** Self-guide leaflet on town and area. Ruins of women's prison, off Bond St. Tasmanian Wool Centre, Church St, highlights area's links with wool industry. Avenue of English elms in Church St complements historic buildings: Scotch Thistle Inn and Coach House, former coaching stop, now licensed restaurant; old Ross General Store and Tea Room, Tasmanian crafts, Devonshire teas. In Bridge St, old barracks building, restored by local National Trust. Street leads to Ross Bridge (floodlit at night). Nov.: Rodeo. **In the area:** Fishing in Macquarie River. Some of State's best trout-fishing lakes—Sorell, Crescent, Tooms and Leake—are within hour's drive of town. **Tourist information:** 75 High St, Campbell Town; (003) 81 1388. **Accommo- dation:** 1 hotel, 1 B&B, 1 cara./camp. park. **See also:** Scenic Island State.
MAP REF. 525 M1, 527 N10

St Helens   Pop. 1145
This popular resort on the shores of Georges Bay is renowned for its crayfish and scalefish. The largest east coast town, it has 3 fish-processing plants in or near the settlement to handle the catch of the fishing fleet based in its harbour. **Of interest:** Bayside beaches ideal for swimming, coastal beaches for surfing. Charter boats for deep-sea fishing. Excellent fishing for bream and trout on Scamander River. Many local restaurants specialise in fish dishes. St Helens History Room, Cecilia St; guided tours of town and district. Premier Tourist Town in Tasmania, 1994. March: Tasmanian Sport and Game Fishing Festival. June: Suncoast Jazz Festival. **In the area:** Bushwalks to view birdlife and wildflowers. Scamander, 19 km S; swimming and fishing. Binalong Bay, 11 km NE; surf and rock fishing. At Pyengana, 28 km NW: Columba Falls; Healey's Cheese Factory. Several coastal reserves in Bay of Fires district: camping, good beach fishing. **Tourist information:** St Helens Secretariat, 20 Cecilia St; (003) 76 1329. **Accommodation:** 1 hotel, 1 hotel/motel, 1 motel, 2 cara./camp. parks. **See also:** Scenic Island State.
MAP REF. 527 Q6

St Marys   Pop. 629
The position of this small town, at the junction of the Tasman Hwy and the Esk Main Rd, makes it a busy thoroughfare. At the headwaters of the South Esk River system, St Marys is about 10 km inland from the attractive east coast. **In the area:** Small coastal township of Falmouth, 14 km NE: early settlement of

The West Coast

The beautiful but inhospitable west coast, with its wild mountain ranges, lakes, rivers, eerie valleys and dense rainforests, is one of Tasmania's most fascinating regions. The majestic, untamed beauty of this coast is in complete contrast to the State's pretty pastures. The whole area has vast mineral wealth and a colourful mining history, reflected in its towns. The discovery of tin and copper in 1871 and 1883 started a rush to the west coast, booming at the turn of the century. **Queenstown**, the largest town, and the other main towns—Zeehan, Rosebery and Strahan—largely owe their existence to mining.

It was not until 1932 that a rough road was pushed through the mountainous country between Queenstown and Hobart. Fortunately, modern road-making techniques have improved the situation and today west coast towns are linked by the Murchison, Zeehan and Waratah Highways, and the Lyell Highway (the original road to Hobart) has been brought up to modern standards. In fact, the flooding of lake burbury has resulted in the re-routing of the highway, which now takes motorists across the lake itself, enhancing the spectacular entry to Queenstown. Driving round the west coast road circuit and seeing the superb mountain scenery and colourful towns of the area is an unforgettable experience. The only drawback is the area's exceptionally heavy rainfall, even in summer and autumn.

The little township of **Zeehan**, southwest of Rosebery, typifies the changing fortunes of mining towns. Following the rich silver-lead ore discoveries in 1882 its population swelled to 10 000 and the town boasted 26 hotels and the Gaiety Theatre, with seating for over 10 000, where Dame Nellie Melba sang. Many of these fine buildings from the boom period can still be seen, including the Gaiety Theatre at the Grand Hotel. Zeehan's West Coast Pioneers Memorial Museum, housed in the former School of Mines, is a popular tourist attraction.

One of the most spectacular views on any highway in Australia can be seen as you drive into Queenstown. As the narrow road winds down the steep slopes of Mt Owen, you can see the amazingly bare hills—tinged with pale pinks, purples, golds and greys—that surround the town. At the turn of the century, the trees from these hills were cut down to provide fuel for the copper smelters, and heavy rains eroded their topsoil, revealing the strangely hued rocks beneath.

The first European settlement of the west coast was established in 1821, when the most unruly convicts from Hobart were dispatched to establish a penitentiary on **Sarah Island** (Settlement Island) in Macquarie Harbour and to work the valuable Huon pine forests around the Gordon and King Rivers. Sarah Island soon became a notorious prison and most of the unfortunate convicts who managed to escape died in the magnificent but unyielding surrounding bush. The horrors of that time are echoed in the name of the entrance to the harbour—Hell's Gates. Today the port of **Strahan** on Macquarie Harbour has thousands of visitors each year, many attracted to the spectacular Gordon River, one of Tasmania's largest and most remote wild rivers. Cruise boats make regular trips to Heritage Landing at the mouth of the river. On the return trip they stop along the way to allow visitors to see the old convict ruins on Sarah Island. Scenic flights departing from Strahan enable visitors to take in the beauty of more inaccessible areas. Another interesting trip from Strahan is to Ocean Beach, 6 kilometres from the town. This long, lonely stretch of beach, lashed by spectacular breakers, somehow typifies the magnificent wild west coast.

The magnificent scenic wilderness of Melaleuca in Tasmania's remote south west can be reached only by plane or boat. Flights with Par Avion leave Cambridge Airport near Hobart daily. Fishing, hiking and sailing are offered in this incredibly rugged area of Tasmania; also, sightings of the almost extinct orange-bellied parrot are becoming more frequent.

See also: Individual town entries in A–Z listing.

Landscape around Queenstown

historical interest, several convict-built structures; fine beaches, attractive rocky headlands, good fishing. Spectacular mountain and coast views to south through Elephant Pass. **Tourist information:** St Helens Secretariat, 20 Cecilia St, St Helens; (003) 76 1329. **Accommodation:** 1 hotel.
MAP REF. 527 Q8

Savage River
Pop. 540
This town in the rugged west coast region serves the workers on the major Savage River iron-ore project, which has been financed by a consortium of American, Japanese and Australian interests. Ore deposits are formed into a slurry and pumped through an 85-km pipeline north to Port Latta on the coast, where they are pelletised and shipped to Japan. **Of interest:** Mine complex, Mine Rd; tours. **In the area:** Former gold-rush town of Corinna, 28 km SW, good fishing, spectacular scenery, regular launch excursions on *Arcadia II* to Pieman Head. Old graves with Huon pine headstones are reminders of past. **Tourist information:** Council Offices, Smith St, Waratah; (004) 39 1231. **Accommodation:** 1 hotel/motel.
MAP REF. 526 D7

Scamander
Pop. 407
This well-developed resort town, midway between St Marys and St Helens, offers excellent sea and river fishing, and has good swimming beaches. **Of interest:** Scenic walks and drives via forestry roads through plantations. Scamander River, noted for bream fishing, trout in upper reaches. **In the area:** Beaches and lagoons at Beaumaris, 5 km N. Trout Creek Reserve, 10 km W, fishing landing stage, picnic/barbecue facilities. **Tourist information:** St Helens Secretariat, 20 Cecilia St, St Helens; (003) 76 1329. **Accommodation:** 1 hotel/motel, 1 cara./camp. park. **See also:** Scenic Island State.
MAP REF. 527 Q7

Scottsdale
Pop. 2020
Scottsdale is the major town in Tasmania's north-east and serves some of the richest agricultural and forestry country on the island. A large food-processing factory specialises in the deep-freezing of vegetables grown in the district. Feb.: Golconda: Tasmanian Circus Festival. Nov.: Agricultural Show. **In the area:** Bridport, 23 km NW, beach resort. Bridestowe Lavender Farm

near Nabowla, 13 km W, sales of lavender products, tours in flowering season, Dec.–Jan. Sideling Lookout, 16 km W. To the south via South Springfield, Springfield Picnic Area and Mt Maurice Forest Reserve. **Tourist information:** Rose's Travel, 11 Alfred St; (003) 52 2186. **Accommodation:** 2 hotels, 1 motel, 1 cara./camp. park.
MAP REF. 527 N5

Sheffield
Pop. 992
This town, 30 km S of Devonport, stands at the foothills Mt Roland, in one of the most scenically attractive areas of the State. The town's economy is based on farming. **Of interest:** 28 murals on various buildings depict area's history. Kentish Museum, Main St, local history, hydro-electric exhibits. Steam Museum, cnr Main and Spring Sts. Red Water Creek and Heritage Society runs steam train 1st weekend of month, daily in summer. Sept.: Daffodil Festival. **In the area:** Lakes and dams of Mersey–Forth Power Development Scheme, 10 km W. Lake Barrington: created by scheme; major recreation area; international rowing venue. Devil's Gate Dam, 13 km W, unique circular dam, spectacular scenery from viewing areas. Cradle Mountain Lake St Clair National Park, 61 km SW, bushwalking, spectacular rainforest and mountain scenery, flora and fauna. **Tourist information:** Kentish Museum, 93 Main St; (004) 91 1861. **Accommodation:** 1 hotel, 2 motels, 1 B&B, 1 cara./camp. park. **See also:** National Parks.
MAP REF. 522 D9, 526 I6

Smithton
Pop. 3495
This substantial township is the administrative centre of Circular Head in the far north-west. It serves the most productive dairying and vegetable-growing area in the State, and is also the centre of one of Tasmania's most important forestry areas, with several large sawmills. Fishing is another important industry. **Of interest:** Duck River and Duck Bay, fishing, boating. Lookout tower, Tier Hill, end of Massey St. **In the area:** Forestry Commission reserves throughout district for wide range of recreational activities. Lacrum Dairy Farm, Mella, 6 km W, milking demonstrations, afternoon teas, cheese tastings, sales. Nearby Wombat Tarn, picnic/barbecue area, lookout, bushwalks, playground. Graveyard at ghost town of Balfour, 40 km SW. At Marrawah, 50 km SW, excellent surfing.

Allendale Gardens, Edith Creek, 13 km S, rainforest walks, Devonshire teas. Seasonal scenic cruises on Arthur River, 70 km S. Rocky Cape National Park, 45 km E; Aboriginal caves, walks. **Tourist information:** Council Offices, Goldie St; (004) 52 1265. **Accommodation:** 1 hotel, 1 motel.
MAP REF. 526 D3

Somerset
Pop. 3257
At the junction of the Bass and Waratah Hwys, Somerset has become a satellite town for Burnie, 6 km E. **In the area:** Scenic drive from town, south through Elliott to small rural settlement of Yolla, which serves surrounding rich pastoral country. **Tourist information:** Civic Centre Precinct, Burnie; (004) 32 1999. **Accommodation:** 1 hotel, 1 hotel/motel, 1 motel, 1 cara./camp. park. **See also:** Scenic Island State.
MAP REF. 526 G4

Sorell
Pop. 3199
Named after Governor Sorell, this town is 23 km NE of Hobart. Founded in 1821, it played an important part in early colonial history by providing most of the grain for the State from 1816 to 1860. It also provided grain for NSW for more than 20 years. The area is still an important agricultural district, specialising in fat lambs. **Of interest:** In Somerville St: Historic Blue Bell Inn; picnic/barbecue facilities in park. **In the area:** Saddletramp Horseback Tours near Woodsdale 37 N, 1-hr to 7-day rides, bushman's meals, hostel accommodation. Many holiday homes in extensive and popular beach area around Dodges Ferry and Carlton, 18 km S. **Tourist information:** Tasmania South Regional Tourism Association, 20 Davey St, Hobart; (002) 30 8233. **Accommodation:** 1 hotel.
MAP REF. 521 K5, 525 N6

Stanley
Pop. 576
This quaint little village, nestling under a huge rocky outcrop called the Nut, is steeped in history. It was the site for the headquarters of the Van Diemen's Land Company, set up in 1825 to establish a high-quality merino wool industry. Then its wharf handled whalers and sailing ships. Today these are replaced by a strong fleet of cray and other fishing boats, but little else has changed. The birthplace of Australia's only Tasmanian prime minister, the Hon. J. A. (Joe) Lyons, Stanley has been declared an historic

town and for 5 of the last 7 years has won the State's Premier Tourist Town award. **Of interest:** Chairlift to top of the Nut (152 m). Historic buildings in wharf area: bluestone bond store, Wharf Rd; former VDL Co. store, in Marine Park, designed by colonial architect John Lee Archer, who lived in township. Archer's own home, now Poet's Cottage, Alexander Tce, at base of the Nut; not open to public. Also in Alexander Tce, Lyons Cottage, birthplace of J. A. Lyons. Other historic buildings in Church St incl.: still-licensed Union Hotel (1849), nest of cellars, narrow stairways; Commercial Hotel (1842), now private residence; multi-award-winning Plough Inn (1850s), authentic 19th century house museum, fine Tasmanian craft, tourist information. Next door, Discovery Centre Folk Museum. Graves in burial ground on Browns Rd, dating from 1828, incl. those of John Lee Archer and explorer Henry Hellyer. Small colonies of little (fairy) penguins near wharf and cemetery, and on Scenic Drive. Nov.: Tasmania Day. Dec.: Agricultural Show. **In the area:** Highfield Historic Site (1835), headquarters of VDL Co., on Scenic Drive, 2 km N: homestead, chapel, schoolhouse, barn, stables, workers' cottages and remains of barracks nearby; two arched gates remain of former deer park. Dip Falls, off hwy, 40 km SE, via Mawbanna, Big Tree (giant eucalypt), picnic area. Pelletising plant of Savage River Mines, Port Latta, 20 km SE, where ore is moved by conveyor to jetty for loading onto bulk ore ships. **Tourist information:** Plough Inn, 35 Church St; (004) 58 1226. **Accommodation:** 1 hotel, 1 motel, 1 hostel, 1 cara./camp. park. **See also:** Scenic Island State. MAP REF. 526 E3

Strahan
Pop. 597

This pretty little port on Macquarie Harbour is the only town on Tasmania's forbidding west coast. Originally a Huon pine timber-milling town, its growth was boosted by the copper boom at the Mt Lyell mine. When the Strahan–Zeehan railway opened in 1892 it became a busy port. Today it handles freight to and from Queenstown and is used by crayfish, abalone and shark fishermen, but the use of the harbour is limited because of the formidable bar at Hell's Gates, the mouth of the harbour. Seaplane flights over Gordon River and Frenchmans Cap, landing at Sir John's Falls. **Of interest:** Award-winning Wharf Centre, Esplanade; historical display of Tasmania's South West, from Aboriginal times to present. Adjacent, Morrison's Mill, one of few remaining Huon pine sawmills. Excellent views of township and harbour from Water Tower Hill. NPWS World Heritage display at Customs House. Franklin Manor, Esplanade: built late last century; colonial accommodation. Mineral and gemstone museum, Innes St. Strahan Trail Rides. **In the area:** Botanical Creek Peoples Park and Hogarth Falls on outskirts of town, picnic/barbecue areas. At Ocean Beach, 6 km W, surfing, trail rides, mutton-bird rookery. Teepookana Forest Reserve, 6 km S, Huon pines, walking tracks, viewing platform, historic bridge. At Henty Dunes, 12 km N on Strahan–Zeehan Hwy, spectacular, vast sand dunes, picnic/barbecue areas. Cruises: up Gordon River to Heritage Landing and infamous Sarah (or Settlement) Island, Tasmania's first and most brutal penal establishment; across Macquarie Harbour to Hell's Gates. Strahan Wilderness 4WD tours, follow Old Abt Railway from Strahan towards Queenstown. **Tourist information:** Wharf Centre, The Esplanade; (004) 71 7488. **Accommodation:** 2 hotels, 1 motel, 9 B&B, 1 hostel, 1 cara./camp. park. **See also:** Scenic Island State; The West Coast. MAP REF. 524 D2, 526 E11

Swansea
Pop. 418

Swansea is a small town of historical interest on scenic Great Oyster Bay, in the centre of Tasmania's east coast. It is the administrative centre of Glamorgan, the oldest rural municipality in Australia. The original council chambers (c. 1860), Noyes St, are still in use. **Of interest:** Self-guide leaflet on town and area. On Tasman Hwy: Bark Mill and Yesteryear Museum (c. 1885); restored mill machinery; tearooms. In Franklin St: Morris' General Store (1838), run by Morris family for over 100 years; Community Centre (c. 1860), museum with unusually large slate billiard table made for 1880 World Exhibition. Schouten House (c. 1841), Bridge St, once Swansea Inn, now

The Nut, Stanley

A Convict Past

The infamous Port Arthur settlement ruins are the greatest historic tourist attraction in Tasmania. The fact that they were a place of incarceration for more than 12 000 prisoners has been blurred by time but it is still possible, particularly in bleak weather, for the ruins to create something of the atmosphere of hopelessness and misery that existed there about 150 years ago.

Port Arthur is on the Tasman Peninsula, which extends from the Forestier Peninsula south-east of Hobart, screening Pitt Water and the Derwent estuary from the Tasman Sea. Both peninsulas are very beautiful, with sweeping pasture, timbered areas and sheltered bays and towering cliffs. Accommodation includes a motor inn, self-contained villas and log cabins, guest house, colonial accommodation, a caravan park and youth hostel.

Eaglehawk Neck is the isthmus between the two peninsulas. In the days of the penal colony, dogs were tethered in a tight line across the Neck to prevent escapes. The line was continually patrolled and guard posts were established in the nearby hills. No prisoner ever broke through this fearful barrier, although some did swim to freedom.

A major Port Arthur conservation project was completed in 1986. Among the ruins still standing are the church, penitentiary, guard tower, hospital and model prison. Buildings that have been restored include Exile Cottage, home of exiled Irish rebel William Smith O'Brien, the Commandant's House and the Junior Medical Officer's House. The restored former lunatic asylum is a museum and gift shop. Introductory walking tours of the site are conducted all year round, 9.30–4. The settlement was established by Governor Arthur in 1830 and, although transportation ceased in 1853, it was not abandoned until 1877. Many buildings were demolished by contractors and others were badly damaged by bushfires in 1895 and 1897. Today, nocturnal historical 'ghost tours' through the settlement are an unforgettable experience; they begin at 8.30 p.m. in winter and 9.30 p.m. during daylight saving. The site is open daily; an entrance fee allows visitors access to over 40 hectares of ruins and sites. An alternative way to experience Port Arthur is an audio tour, with 'Frank the Poet' recounting his experiences as a Port Arthur convict.

Every year on the Saturday closest to Australia Day, Port Arthur presents Beating Retreat, an impressive military display, with band music, staged among the ruins.

In Port Arthur Bay stands the **Island of the Dead**, with its 1769 unnamed convict graves; 180 additional named graves mark the resting places of free settlers, prison staff and the military. As well as harbour cruises, the ferry *Bundeena* makes regular trips to this unique island cemetery.

For further information, contact Port Arthur Historic Site, Clougha, Port Arthur 7182; (002) 50 2363. **See also:** Individual town entries in A–Z listing.

Ruins at Port Arthur

restaurant and colonial accommodation. Meredith House (c. 1853), 2-storeyed Georgian house, colonial accommodation. **In the area:** Splendid views from Duncombes Lookout, 3 km s. Spikey Beach, 7 km s, picnic area, excellent rock fishing. Mayfield Beach, 14 km s, safe swimming, popular fishing area, walking track from camping area to Three Arch Bridge. **Tourist information:** Panache at Swansea, 3 Franklin St; (002) 57 8488. **Accommodation:** 1 hotel/motel, 2 cara./camp. parks. **See also:** Scenic Island State.
MAP REF. 525 P2, 527 P11

Triabunna Pop. 831
When Maria Island was a penal settlement, Triabunna, 86 km NE of Hobart, was a garrison town and whaling base. Today it is a centre for the scallop and abalone industries, with an important export wood-chipping mill just south of the town. **Of interest:** On The Esplanade: Bicentennial Park, picnic/barbecue areas; National Trust-run Pioneer Park, machinery exhibits. Working Horse Museum, Vicary St. Daily ferry to historic settlement of Darlington, Maria Island National Park. Charter fishing boats for hire. Local beaches for swimming, waterskiing, fishing. Jan. Spring Bay Crayfish Derby. Dec.: Tandara Woodchoppers Classic. **Tourist information:** Council Offices, cnr Vicary and Henry Sts; (002) 57 3113. **Accommodation:** 1 hotel, 1 hotel/motel, 1 cara./camp. park. **See also:** National Parks; Scenic Island State.
MAP REF. 521 O1, 525 O4, 527 O13

Ulverstone Pop. 9923
Situated 19 km w of Devonport, near the mouth of the Leven River, Ulverstone is a well-equipped tourist centre that was established as a town in 1852. Dairying, furniture making and poultry and vegetable farming are the main industries of the area. **Of interest:** Shrine of Remembrance Clock Tower (1953), On Beach Rd: Riverside Anzac Park, children's playground, picnic/barbecue areas; Fairway Park, wildfowl reserve, giant water-slide. Weeda Copperware, Eastland Dr, hand-made local copperware. Oct.: Ulverstone Show. Dec.: Christmas Mardi Gras. **In the area:** Extensive beaches east and west of town, safe swimming for children. Good beach, river and estuary fishing. Tours of hop fields. Scenic views at Preston Falls, 19 km s. Goat Island Sanctuary, 5 km w;

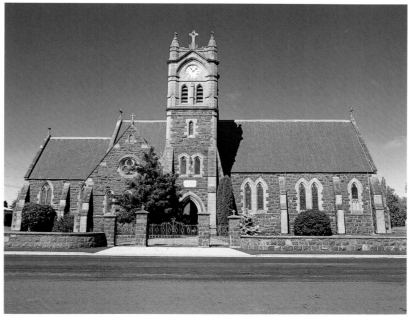
Holy Trinity Church, Westbury

walking access to island, low tide only. Guided tours of Gunns Plains Caves, 24 km sw. Walking tracks to viewing platform at Leven Canyon, 41 km sw; beyond, near South Nietta, Winterbrook Rainforest Walk and Falls. **Tourist information:** Visitor Information Centre, Car Park Lane, (behind PO); (004) 25 2839. **Accommodation:** 2 hotels, 3 motels, 1 B&B, 2 cara./camp. parks. **See also:** Scenic Island State.
MAP REF. 522 B5, 526 H5

Waratah Pop. 360
This picturesque little settlement, set in mountain heathland 100 km N of Queenstown, was the site of the first mining boom in Tasmania. In 1900 it had a population of 2000 and Mount Bischoff was the richest tin mine in the world. The deposits were discovered in 1871 by James 'Philosopher' Smith, a colourful local character, and the mine closed in 1947, with dividends totalling 200 pounds for every one pound of original investment. Today the town is experiencing a revival of mining activity at nearby Hellyer Mine, operated by Aberfoyle. **Of interest:** Self-drive tour of town. In Smith St: Waratah Museum and Gift Shop; adj. Philosopher Smith's Hut, replica of miner's hut, audio historical commentary; Atheneum Hall (c. 1887), portrait of Smith; St James' Anglican Church (1880), first church in Tasmania to be lit by hydro power. **In the area:**

River and lake trout fishing. Mining townships: Savage River, 38 km w; Corinna, 66 km sw, fascinating former goldmining town. At Corinna, cruises on Pieman River. **Tourist information:** Fossey River Information Bay, 8 km s on Murchison Hwy, or Council Offices, Smith St; (004) 39 1231. **Accommodation:** 1 hotel, 1 cara./camp. park. **See also:** The West Coast.
MAP REF. 526 F7

Westbury Pop. 1292
A village green, said to be unique in Australia, gives this town, 35 km w of Launceston, a decidedly English air. Situated on the Bass Hwy, Westbury was first surveyed in 1823, laid out in 1828 and has several fine old colonial buildings. **Of interest:** Self-guide leaflet on town and area. White House (c. 1841), Village Green, King St: house, bakehouse, coachhouse, courtyard, vintage cars, bicycles, wagons; dolls and toys in stable complex. On Bass Hwy: Hedge maze; Gemstone and Mineral Display; Pearn's Steam World, display of old tractors, farm machinery, motor vehicles. March: Maypole Festival incl. Morris dancing on Village Green. **In the area:** At Hagley, 5 km E, St Mary's Anglican Church, noted for fine east window donated by Lady Dry, wife of Sir Richard Dry, first Tasmanian-born premier. At Carrick, 10 km E, fine examples of Georgian and Victorian buildings. At Four

The Bass Strait Islands

King Island and Flinders Island, Tasmania's two main Bass Strait islands, are ideal holiday spots for the adventurous. You can fish, swim, go bushwalking or skindive among the wrecks of the many ships that foundered off their shores last century. Each spring millions of muttonbirds make a spectacular sight as they fly in to nest in coastal rookeries.

King Island, at the western end of the strait, is a picturesque, rugged island with an unspoiled coastline of beautiful sandy beaches on the east and north coasts, contrasting with the forbidding cliffs of Seal Rocks and the lonely coast to the south. The lighthouse at Cape Wickham is the largest in Australia. There is a penguin colony on the breakwater at Grassy Harbour. Once famous for its seal population and now almost extinct sea lions, the island's main industries today are scheelite mining and farming. King Island dairy products have earned a reputation for their high quality. The unofficial capital is **Currie**, which has a kelp factory. Accommodation includes a hotel, 2 motels, numerous guest houses, several holiday flats and a caravan/camping park.

Flinders Island is renowned for its excellent fishing, its magnificent granite mountains and its gemstones, including the Killiecrankie 'diamonds', actually a kind of topaz. Strzelecki National Park, near the civic centre, **Whitemark**, provides challenging rock climbing. From Whitemark 4WD tours are available to hills and remote beaches. The island is also popular with scuba divers, naturalists and photographers. Accommodation on the island includes 2 hotels, 2 guest houses and several holiday flats. Flinders is one of more than 50 islands in the Furneaux Group that were once part of the land bridge linking Tasmania with the mainland.

In the 1830s the few surviving Tasmanian Aborigines were settled near **Emita** in an attempt to save them from extinction. All that remains of the settlement today is the graveyard and the chapel, Wybalenna, which has been restored by the National Trust.

Fishing is the main industry of the tiny community of **Lady Barron** to the south, a port village overlooking Franklin Sound and **Cape Barren Island**, the home of the protected Cape Barren goose.

For further information contact: King Island Shoppe, Edward St, King Island; (004) 62 1666; and Council Offices, Davey St, Flinders Island; (003) 59 2131.

Fisherman's Paradise

Fish are biting all year round in Tasmania, which is a fisherman's paradise by any standards. Tasmania is famous for three species of fish: trout in fresh water, bream in the estuaries, and tuna off the coast.

One area alone contains hundreds of lakes and lagoons stocked with trout of world-class size. This is the undeveloped 'Land of Three Thousand Lakes'. You are more likely, however, to choose from the huge range of developed areas brimming with trout in the central highlands region, among them Great Lake, Bronte Lagoon, Lake Sorell and Arthurs Lake. Brumby Creek, just 25 kilometres from **Launceston** between **Cressy** and **Poatina**, is rapidly gaining a reputation as one of the great trout waters of Australia.

As the trout season closes in May, game fish begin to move down the mild east coast and fishermen start hauling in the big ones: bluefin tuna, often weighing over 45 kilograms. Then, as the bluefin leave in the midwinter months, schools of barracouta arrive in their thousands, and large Australian salmon schools return to the estuaries and along the shoreline.

In spring, one of the great sport fish of Tasmania, the tasty silver bream, arrives in the river estuaries. Anglers regard this as one of the best fighting fish for its size.

Of course, in late spring and early summer the whole island is an angler's dream. January and February are peak inland trout-fishing months, and from February to March schools of Australian salmon swim close to the shoreline of Tasmania's many river estuaries, providing exciting fishing for the angler from the beach or rocks.

For further information on licence requirements, fees, bag limits, seasons and regulations for freshwater fishing contact the Inland Fisheries Commission, 127 Davey St, Hobart 7000; (002) 23 6622. For sea fishing enquiries, contact the department of Primary Industries and Fisheries, Sea Fisheries Division, 23 Old Wharf, Hobart 7000; (002) 33 6280. **See also:** Individual town entries in A–Z listing.

Trout fishing near Cressy

View of Wynyard from Table Cape Lookout

Springs, 15 km NE, and Brushy Lagoon: trout fishing, recreation 15 km N. Liffey Falls, 25 km S, picnic/barbecue area, walking tracks. **Tourist information:** Old Bakehouse, 52 William St; (003) 93 1140. **Accommodation:** 1 hotel. **See also:** Stately Homes.
MAP REF. 523 K11, 527 K7

Wynyard   Pop. 4679

Situated within a short driving distance of many varied attractions, this small centre at the mouth of the Inglis River, west of Burnie, has become a well-developed tourist centre, offering a range of accommodation and sporting facilities. There are daily flights between nearby Burnie airport and Melbourne. The Waratah–Wynyard municipality is a prosperous dairying and mixed-farming district and the town has a large, modern dairy factory. **Of interest:** Excellent trout, fly and sea fishing. Table Cape Tulip Farm; open in season. Oct.: Tulip Festival. **In the area:** Table Cape Lookout, 5 km N, views. Oldest marsupial fossil in Australia found at Fossil Bluff, 7 km N. Mallavale Farm, Boat Harbour, 11 km NW, local craft, teas.

Excellent beach at Boat Harbour. Good swimming and fishing at Sisters Beach, 5 km NW beyond Boat Harbour, in Rocky Cape National Park, 30 km NW. Also at Sisters Beach, adjoining National Park: Birdland Native Gardens, nature trail, aviaries, camellias, rhododendrons, displays, craft shop. Scenic flights, walks. **Tourist information:** Visitor Information Centre, cnr Hogg and Goldie St; (004) 42 4143. **Accommodation:** 2 hotels, 1 hotel/motel, 1 motel, 1 B&B, 1 hostel, 2 cara./camp. parks. **See also:** Scenic Island State; National Parks.
MAP REF. 526 F4

Zeehan   Pop. 1132

Named after one of Abel Tasman's ships, this former mining town, situated 36 km NW of Queenstown, has had a chequered history and is now a National Trust-classified historic town. Silver-lead deposits were discovered here in 1882. By 1901, Zeehan had 26 hotels and a population of 10 000, making it Tasmania's third largest town. Just 7 years later mining began to decline and Zeehan became almost a ghost town. In the boom period between 1893 and 1908, 8 million

dollars' worth of ore had been recovered. Now the town is again on an upward swing with the reopening of the Renison Bell tin mine. **Of interest:** Many 'boom' buildings in Main St: Gaiety Theatre at the Grand Hotel, ANZ Bank, St Luke's Church, post office and courthouse (now art gallery). West Coast Pioneers Memorial Museum, Main St; mineral, historical, geological and biological collections. Beside museum, unique display of steam locomotives and rail carriages used on west coast. Scenic drive, 7.5 km round trip; incl. Spray Tunnel, old train tunnel. Oct.: Octoberfest. Nov.: King of the Mountain Fun Run. **In the area:** Old mine workings at Dundas, 13 km E. Trial Harbour, 20 km W; popular fishing area. Unsealed roads to both areas often in poor condition; check before departure. Fishing and boating on Lake Pieman, 50 km NW. Trout fishing on Henty River, 25 km S. **Tourist information:** West Coast Pioneers Memorial Museum, Main St; (004) 71 6225. **Accommodation:** 1 hotel, 1 hotel/motel, 1 motel, 1 hostel, 1 cara./camp. park. **See also:** Scenic Island State; The West Coast.
MAP REF. 526 E9

Tasmania

Location Map

Other Map Coverage
Central Hobart 517
Hobart & Suburbs 518
Hobart Region 520
Launceston Region 522

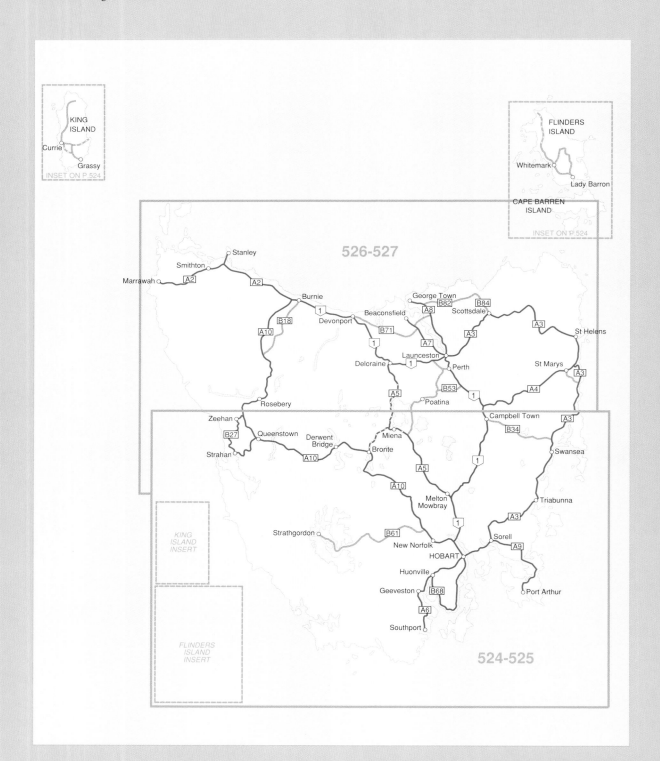

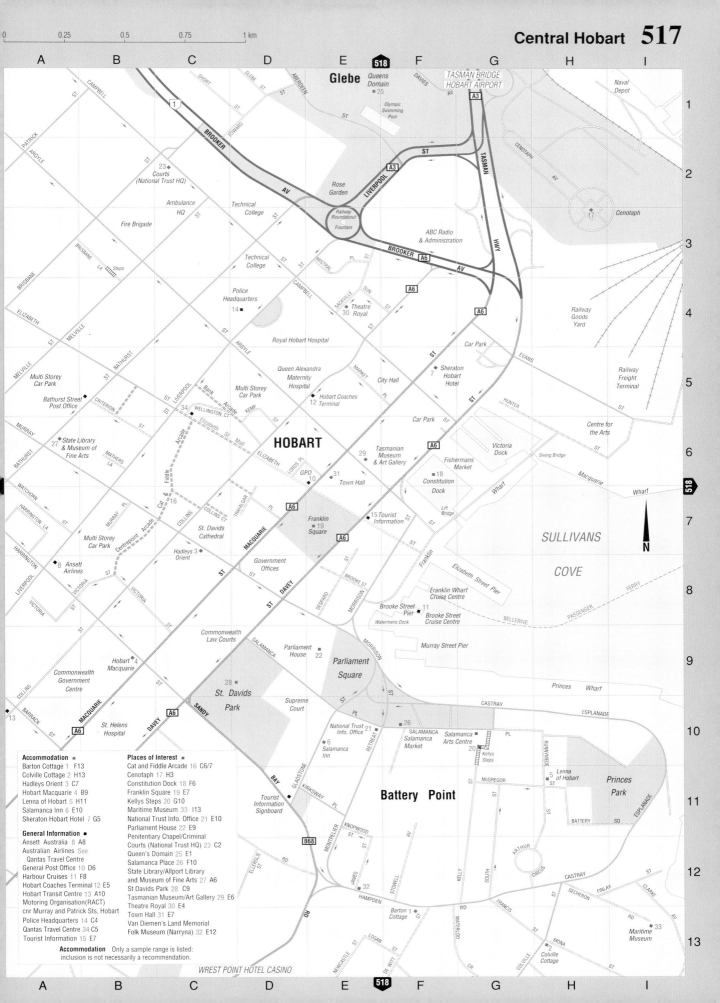

Scale: 0   0.25   0.5   0.75   1 km

Glebe

HOBART

SULLIVANS COVE

Battery Point

Princes Park

WREST POINT HOTEL CASINO

518

Accommodation ▪
Barton Cottage 1 F13
Colville Cottage 2 H13
Hadleys Orient 3 C7
Hobart Macquarie 4 B9
Lenna of Hobart 5 H11
Salamanca Inn 6 E10
Sheraton Hobart Hotel 7 G5

General Information ▪
Ansett Australia 8 A8
Australian Airlines See
Qantas Travel Centre
General Post Office 10 D6
Harbour Cruises 11 F8
Hobart Coaches Terminal 12 E5
Hobart Transit Centre 13 A10
Motoring Organisation(RACT)
cnr Murray and Patrick Sts, Hobart
Police Headquarters 14 C4
Qantas Travel Centre 34 C5
Tourist Information 15 E7

Places of Interest ▪
Cat and Fiddle Arcade 16 C6/7
Cenotaph 17 H3
Constitution Dock 18 F6
Franklin Square 19 E7
Kellys Steps 20 G10
Maritime Museum 33 I13
National Trust Info. Office 21 E10
Parliament House 22 E9
Penitentiary Chapel/Criminal
Courts (National Trust HQ) 23 C2
Queen's Domain 25 E1
Salamanca Place 26 F10
State Library/Allport Library
and Museum of Fine Arts 27 A6
St Davids Park 28 C9
Tasmanian Museum/Art Gallery 29 E6
Theatre Royal 30 E4
Town Hall 31 E7
Van Diemen's Land Memorial
Folk Museum (Narryna) 32 E12

Accommodation Only a sample range is listed;
inclusion is not necessarily a recommendation.

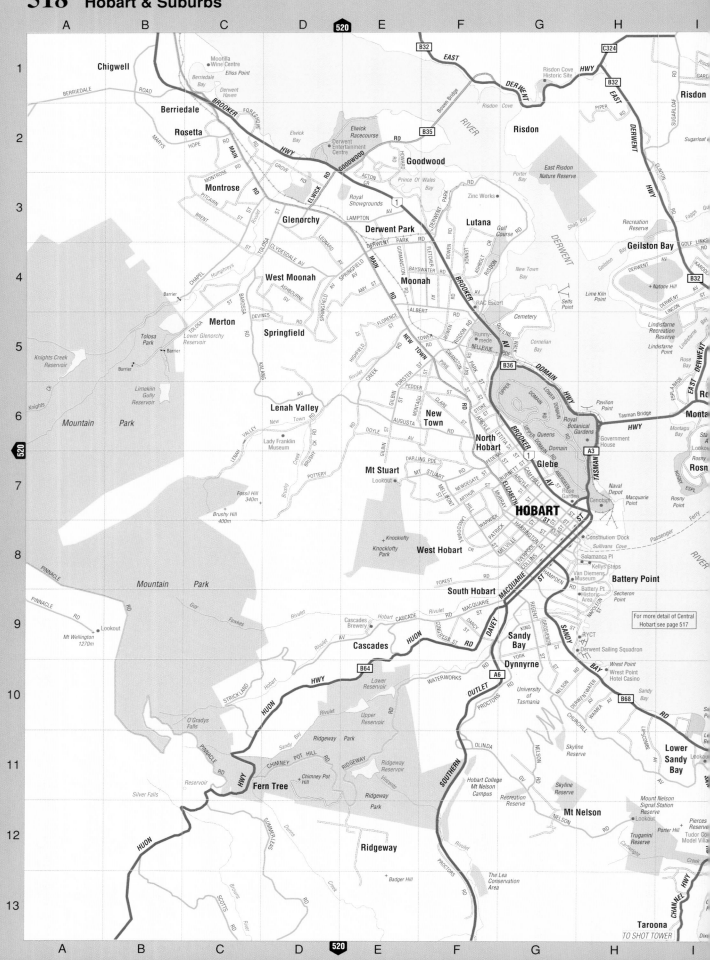

0 0.5 1 1.5 2 2.5 3 km

J K L M N 521 O P Q R

1

MEEHAN RANGE STATE RECREATIONAL AREA

Creek

Pitt Water

Railway Point

COLEBROOK RD

HANSLOW RD

Richmond Golf Course

Barilla Bay

Mile Beach

2

MEEHAN

RANGE

COLEBROOK RD

CAMBRIDGE AERODROME

DR

KENNEDY

TASMAN HWY

A3

HOBART AIRPORT

HOLYMAN AV

3

MEEHAN RANGE STATE RECREATIONAL AREA

Flagstaff Gully Reservoir

RD

B31

A3

CAMBRIDGE

C330

Cambridge

ACTON RD

4

farne

Flagstaff Gully

GORDONS HILL RD

S HILL ST

HELENS ST

FLAGSTAFF GULLY LINK

FLAGSTAFF GULLY RD

RD

TASMAN HWY

Canopus Hill

Observatory

Tunnel Hill

C329

C328 MT RUMNEY RD

5

Rosny Park

BLIGH ST

A3

C329

Mornington

CAMBRIDGE

PASS

RD

Lookout
Mt Rumney 378m

BEACH RD

C330 RD

SEVEN MILE

Seven Mile Beach

6

Warrane

BINALONG

BLIGH ST

Bay

RD

B33

SOUTH

Waverley Park

Mornington Hill

Knopwood Hill

KNOPWOOD HILL STATE RECREATION AREA

C329

Knopwood Hill

Clarence Plains RD

MEEHAN

RANGE

ACTON

DR

521

7

sny Park

QUEEN ST

CLARENCE ST

DERWENT ST

Bellerive

WAVERLEY ST

HILL ST

ST

WENTWORTH ST

TILANBI ST

NINABAH ST

NORMA ST

ARM HWY

Howrah

PASS

Rivulet RD

TARA DR

TARA DR

Roches Beach

ROCHES BEACH

8

Kangaroo Bluff Historic Site

Bellerive Beach

Second Bluff

Wentworth Park

Howrah Beach

HOWRAH RD

ST

Glebe Hill

ROKEBY RD

GOODWINS RD

RD

MOCKRIDGE DR

ROCKINGHAM DR

Clarendon Vale

MARSTON ST

ACTON DR

ST

NOWRA RD

ROCHES BEACH

Roches Beach

DU

9

Howrah Point

MINERVA ST

OCEANA DV

TRANMERE RD

CARELLA ST

Tranmere

TOLLARD DR

DUNTROON

DR

Clarence Plains Rivulet

B33

RD

SOUTH

Rokeby

ARM

Tasmania Police Academy

RD

C330

B33

SOUTH

Lauderdale

BANGALEE ST

Frederick Henry Bay

ARM

BAYVIEW RD

Roches Beach

10

DERWENT

N

ROKEBY HILLS

DROUGHTY POINT RD

Rokeby Beach

Mill Point

RALPHS BAY COASTAL RESERVE

11

Droughty Hill 153m

Gibsons Point

Mt Mather 175m

RD

12

RALPHS BAY

Sandford

13

Trywork Point

Droughty Point

J K L M N 521 O P Q R

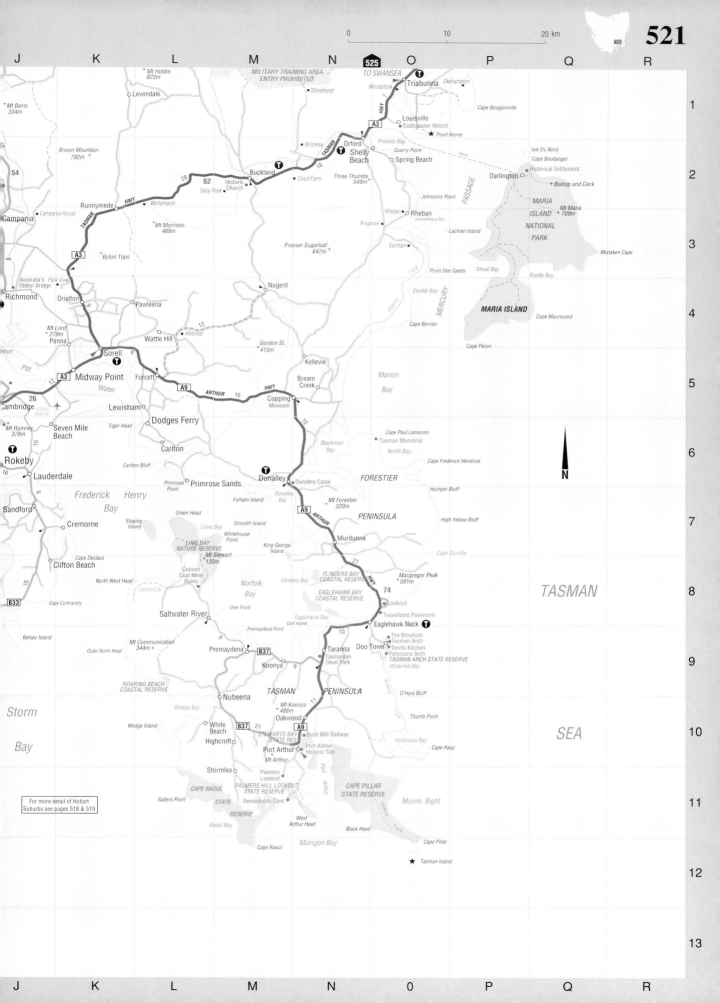

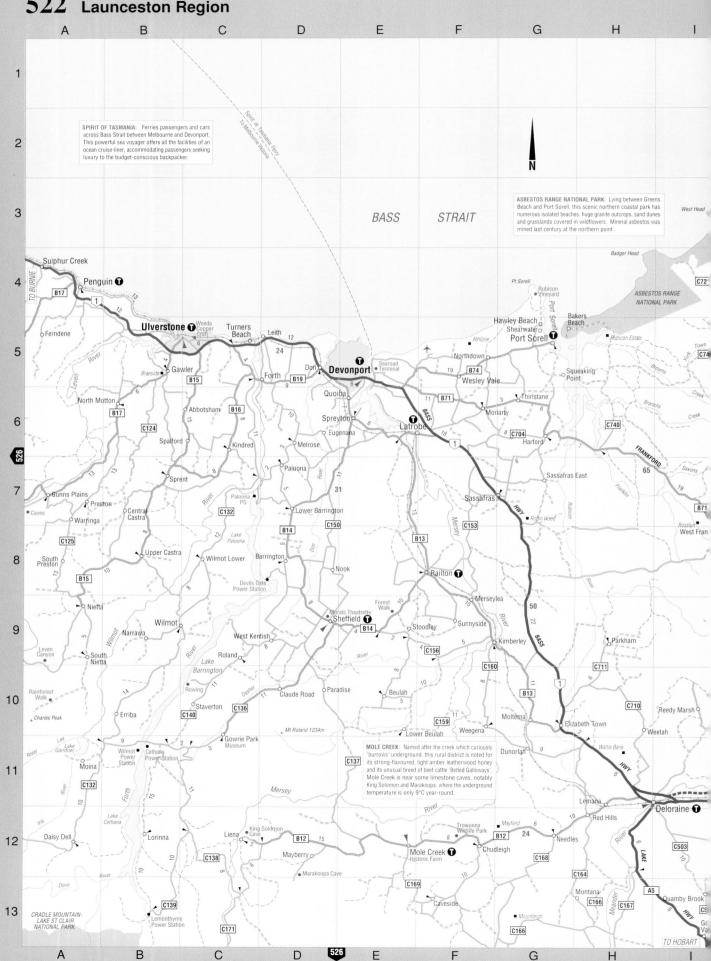

1

2

3

BASS   STRAIT

SPIRIT OF TASMANIA: Ferries passengers and cars across Bass Strait between Melbourne and Devonport. This powerful sea voyage offers all the facilities of an ocean cruise-liner, accommodating passengers seeking luxury to the budget-conscious backpacker.

Spirit of Tasmania Ferry — To Melbourne Victoria

ASBESTOS RANGE NATIONAL PARK: Lying between Greens Beach and Port Sorell, this scenic northern coastal park has numerous isolated beaches, huge granite outcrops, sand dunes and grasslands covered in wildflowers. Mineral asbestos was mined last century at the northern point.

West Head

Badger Head

4

Sulphur Creek
Penguin
TO BURNIE
B17
Ferndene
1
13
12
Ulverstone
Weeda Copper Craft
Turners Beach
Leith
Don
12
ASBESTOS RANGE NATIONAL PARK
C72
Pt Sorell
Rubicon Vineyard
Hawley Beach
Shearwater
Port Sorell
Bakers Beach
Rubicon Estate
C74
York Town

5

Braeside
Gawler
B15
Forth
24
Devonport
Searoad Terminal
Northdown
Athlone
Squeaking Point
Leven River
Ferndene

North Motton
B17
Abbotsham
B16
Quoiba
Spreyton
Eugenana
Latrobe
Wesley Vale
B74
B71
Moriarty
Thirlstane
C704
Harford
C740
Browns Creek
Branchs Creek
FRANKFORD
65
Saxons

6

C124
Spalford
Kindred
Melrose
10
18
1
8
Sassafras East
19

7

Gunns Plains
Preston
Sprent
Paloona
River
31
Sassafras
C153
HWY
Robin Hood
Franklin River
B71
Rosslyn
West Fran

Caves
Warringa
Central Castra
C132
Paloona PS
Lower Barrington
Mersey River
13

8

C125
Upper Castra
Wilmot Lower
Barrington
B14
C150
Nook
B13
Railton
Merseylea
River

South Preston
B15
Nietta
10
Devils Gate Power Station
Don River
8

9

Wilmot
Narrawa
West Kentish
Murals Theatrette
Sheffield
B14
Forest Walk
Stoodley
Sunnyside
Kimberley
50
22
BASS
Parkham
C711

Leven Canyon
South Nietta
Roland
Lake Barrington
8
C156
C160
1
B13

10

Rainforest Walk
Charles Peak
Staverton
C136
Rowing
Dasher River
Claude Road
Paradise
Beulah
C159
Weegena
Moltema
Elizabeth Town
C710
Reedy Marsh
Weetah

Lea River
Lake Gairdner
C140
Erriba
Gowrie Park Museum
Mt Roland 1234m
Lower Beulah
C137
Dunorlan
Wattle Bank
HWY

11

Moina
Wilmot Power Station
Cethana Power Station
C132
MOLE CREEK: Named after the creek which curiously 'burrows' underground, this rural district is noted for its strong-flavoured, light amber leatherwood honey and its unusual breed of beef cattle 'Belted Galloways'. Mole Creek is near some limestone caves, notably King Solomon and Marakoopa, where the underground temperature is only 9°C year-round.
Lemana
Red Hills

12

Daisy Dell
Lorinna
Liena
King Solomon Cave
Mayberry
B12
15
Mersey River
Trowunna Wildlife Park
Mayfield
Chudleigh
B12
24
Needles
C168
Deloraine
River
LAKE
C503
Montana
C164
C167
A5
Quamby Brook
C5

Lake Cethana
Forth River
C138
Marakoopa Cave
Mole Creek
Historic Farm
Caveside
C169
C166
Mountleigh
C166
TO HOBART

13

CRADLE MOUNTAIN-LAKE ST CLAIR NATIONAL PARK
Lemonthyme Power Station
C139
C171
Dove River

526

J K L M N O P Q R

0   5   10   15   20 km

1

West Sandy Cape   East Sandy Cape

Anderson Bay

Stony Head

Lulworth

Noland Bay

Weymouth   Bellingham

2

Bridport T
Trout Farm

Beechford

Turquoise Bluff +167m

Weymouth Farm

Little

B82 12

Micks Creek

Little

B84

Five Mile Bluff

Leura

C816

Delamere Winery

Pipers Brook Winery

Heemskerk Winery

Pipers

Creek

3

C827

Low Head ★

Low Head

Port Dalrymple

s Beach

Dam

C807

Lefroy

Pipers River

Rochecombe Winery

Idlewilde

Pipers Brook

Pipers Brook

Brook

C818

Forester

Lavender Farm

C826

4

WINERIES: Pipers Brook is referred to as the centre of northern Tasmania's grape-growing area. Vineyards in the district are open to visitors for tours and tastings.

Kelso

George Town T
Museum

Mt George +242m

B82 8

EAST

Clarence Point

Bell Bay

A7

Ilfraville

Bell Bay

14 A8

C809

B83

Retreat

C819

Glen

Fairbanks

Vermont 3

Blumont

B81

Golconda

Nabowla

5

Beauty Point T

Rowella

Teddy Bear Park

B73

TAMAR

The Glen

River

Lebrina

Wyena

Denison Gorge

Beaconsfield T
Museum

Kayena

Tamar

4

8

Lower Turners Marsh

C812 13

Bangor

Tunnel

B81 9

Lilydale Falls

Lilydale North

Lisle

C827

TO SCOTTSDALE

6

C715

Sidmouth

Batman Bridge

Marion's Winery

Devoit

Mt Direction +367m

Mount Direction

DISMAL

Karoola

Lilydale T

LILYDALE: Lilydale is Tasmania's 'country garden' with an expansive Rhododendron Reserve and rows of ash trees originally planted for an unsuccessful tennis racquet and cricket bat manufacturing firm. Numerous pathways provide excellent bushwalking through forest parks and to the Lilydale Falls.

Sideling

527

The

7

Flowery Gully

Hillwood

C811

Lalla Gardens

La Provence Winery

Myrtle Bank

River

C717

WEST 25

Robigana

Paper Beach

Leam

Swan Bay

A8

RANGE

Turners Marsh

Patricks

Myrtle Grove

olwell

Stewarts Hill +419m

Exeter T

Lanena

Gravelly Beach

Blackwall

53

HWY

Underwood

Hollybank Forest

Targa

St Patricks River

St

8

Frankford

Winkleigh

Loira

Rosevears

Windermere

Dilston

B83

B81

Patersonia

C404 16

Glengarry

St Matthias Winery

Grindelwald Swiss Village

A7

A8

C824

HWY 70

Mt Barrow +1413m

B71

FRANKFORD

Notley Hills

Notley Gorge

C731

Legana

Rocherlea

Nunamara

9

C714

Bridgenorth

C732

24

NEWNHAM

TASMAN

A3

Frankford

Birralee

C732

HWY

MOWBRAY

INVERMAY

WAVERLEY

23

TOURIST INFORMATION:
Deloraine (29 Westchurch St)
Devonport (5 Best St)
Evandale (7 High St)
Exeter (Tamar Visitors Centre, Main Rd)
George Town (Main Rd)
Latrobe (Council Offices, Gilbert St)
Launceston (cnr St John and Paterson Sts)
Longford (Council Offices, Smith St)
Scottsdale (11 Alfred St)
Ulverstone (Roelf Vos carpark)
Westbury (52 William St)

10

B72

Glenburn

Rosevale

C734

RIVERSIDE

Penny Royal World
Cataract Gorge

TAMAR RIVER: This magnificent broad river was the passageway of the first European settlement and exploration in northern Tasmania. Batman Bridge, one of the world's first cable-stayed truss bridges, is 30km from Launceston and links the east and west banks.

Lake Trevallyn

TREVALLYN

LAUNCESTON T
SUMMERHILL

NEWSTEAD

ST LEONARDS
Illarg

Selbourne

C735

PROSPECT

KINGS MEADOWS

North

Esk

River

Corra Linn

10

C401

11

Glenvista

Westwood

C738

River

Hadspen T
Entally House

Longford Wildlife Park

Country Club Casino

1

10

YOUNGTOWN
Franklin House

16

Relbia

White Hills

C401 2

Violet Banks

BASS

Hagley

44

C531

Strathroy

MIDLAND

Breadalbane

C402

11

1

10

B54

Mt Arnon +314m

19 13

C401

C505

Westbury T

Carrick

B52

South

Mount Irch

Esk

1

B41

LAUNCESTON AIRPORT

Western Junction

Evandale T
Historic Town

C413 15

12

C501

C506

C507

1

C513

Pateena

Perth

B52

C416

Deddington

C505

Glenore

C511

Oaks

West Lagoon

River

Newry

Bra

Nile

River

13

Whitemore

5

East Lagoon

Woodstock

Longford T

C519

Rosebank

HWY 34

C419

Bishopsbourne

Toiberry

B51

C520

C521

Brickendon

Clarendon House

Symmons Plains Raceway

Hampden

Cluan

Woolmers

TO HOBART

527

J K L M N 527 O P Q R

526

Lake Margaret

Mt Gould 1491m

Layatinna Hill 1219m

South Eldon R

Mt Ida 1158m

A10

Henty River

Mt Lyell Mine

Linda

LYELL HWY

Gormanston

Lake Burbury

Alma River

Mt Olympus 1447m

Lake St Clair

Ski

Nive R

B27

Queenstown

Mt Owen 1146m

Collingwood R

Mt Hugel 1307m

Mt Rufus 1402m

A10

LYELL

Bronte

Ocean Beach

LYELL

B24

Lynchford

King River PS

A10

Mt Gell 1439m

Derwent Bridge

LYELL HWY

26

Strahan

36

Point Hibbs

Regatta Point

King River

Mt Jukes 1168m

81

Mt Arrowsmith 981m

Mt King William I 1324m

Butlers Gorge

Tarraleah

A

Cape Sorel

Mt Darwin 1031m

Darwin Dam

Franklin R

Lyddon R

Mt King William II 1372m

Clark Dam

Butlers Gorge PS

26

HWY

Mt Sorell 1144m

Frenchmans Cap 1443m

KING WILLIAM RANGE

Gordon R

Derwent R

A

Sloop Point

PILLINGER

Mt Seal 878m

Mt King William III 1158m

Liapootah PS

SOUTHERN

Gorge Point

Sarah Island Convict Ruins

FRANKLIN-GORDON WILD RIVERS NATIONAL PARK

Jane R

PRINCE OF WALES RANGE

Wayatinah

Wayatinah

Birthday Bay

Moddler R

Birch Inlet

Part of World Heritage Area

Mt Humboldt 1079m

Mt Curly 1039m

MOUN NATIONA

OCEAN

Hibbs Bay

Hibbs R

Mt Discovery 680m

Gordon R

Maxwell R

Mt Wright 1119m

Clear Hill 1198m

Point Hibbs

Spero Bay

Spero R

Mt Lee 734m

Denison R

Franklin R

Endeavour Bay

Wanderer R

Gordon PS Dam

Lake Gordon

ADAMSFIELD

Old Mine

High Rocky Point

Welcome R

Strathgordon

B61

GORDON

SCOTTS PEAK RD

ROAD

Mt Mueller 1234m

Frederick Hill 518m

Serpentine Dam

Lookout

84

Lookout Forest Walk

Lewis R

Serpentine Dam

Mt Sprent 1058m

Mt Wedge 1146m

Lookout

Mt Bowes 957m

Mainwaring R

Mt Osmund 369m

Lewis R

FRANKLAND RANGE

Serpentine R

Lake Pedder

Mt Anne 1425m

Low Rocky Point

Elliott Hill 209m

Elliott Bay

Mt Giblin 878m

Lookout

Scotts Peak Dam

Edgar Dam

Gibb R

Nye Bay

SOUTHWEST NATIONAL PARK

Mt Gaffney 588m

Davey R

Crossing R

Mt Orion 1119m

ARTHUR RANGE

Walking River

Mulcahy Bay

Mt Hean 747m

Mt Braddon 729m

KING ISLAND

Cape Wickham

Cape Farewell

Wreck Bay

Kelly Basin

Payne Bay

Part of World Heritage Area

Mt Norold 978m

Phoques Bay

Lavinia Point

37

Egg Lagoon

Yambacoona

New Year I Christmas I Whistler Point

BASS STRAIT

Reekara

B25

Loorana

Dairy Factory

Sea Elephant Bay

Naracoopa

Point St Vincent

Port Davey

Mt Rugby 771m

Bathurst Harbour

Mt Counsel 800m

SOUTHWEST NATIONAL PAR

Fitzmaurice Bay

Currie

29

Parenna

Pegarah

Yarra Creek

King Island

Flinders Island

Stephens Bay

Island Bay

Mt Melaleuca

Roy R

Soho R

Cataraqui Point

Lymwood

Grassy

Bold Head

Launceston

Window Pane Bay

Mt Melaleuca 595m

Walls R

SOUTHERN

Surprise Point

Surprise Bay

Pearshape

Seal Point

HOBART

Cox Bight

Louisa Bay

Ile Du Go

Seal Bay

Stokes Point

South West Cape

Karama Bay

New Harbour

De Witt Island

FLINDERS ISLAND

Inner Sister Island

Stanley Point

Flat Witch Island

MAATSUYKER GROUP

Blyth Pt

Palana

Killiecrankie Bay

FURNEAUX

Maatsuyker Island

Killiecrankie

Cape Frankland

Leeka

29

Babel I

Lughrata

Marshall Bay

Emita Museum

B85

Memana

Sellars Lagoon

72

Prime Seal Island

Arthur Bay

19

Whitemark

Cameron Inlet

GROUP

Long Point

21

Ranga

15

Loccota

Lady Barron

Parry's Bay

Trousers Pt

STRZELECKI NP

Great Dog I

Vansittart I

Puncheon Pt

Mt Chappell I

Anderson I

FRANKLIN SOUND

SOUTHERN

Badger I

Long I

Mt Munro 716m

Cape Barren Island

Cape Barren

BASS STRAIT

Preservation I

CAPE BARREN ISLAND

Sloping Pt

Kent Bay

Mt Kerford 499m

Clarke Island

Passage I

Forsyth I

BANKS STRAIT

Lookout Heads

Moriarty Point

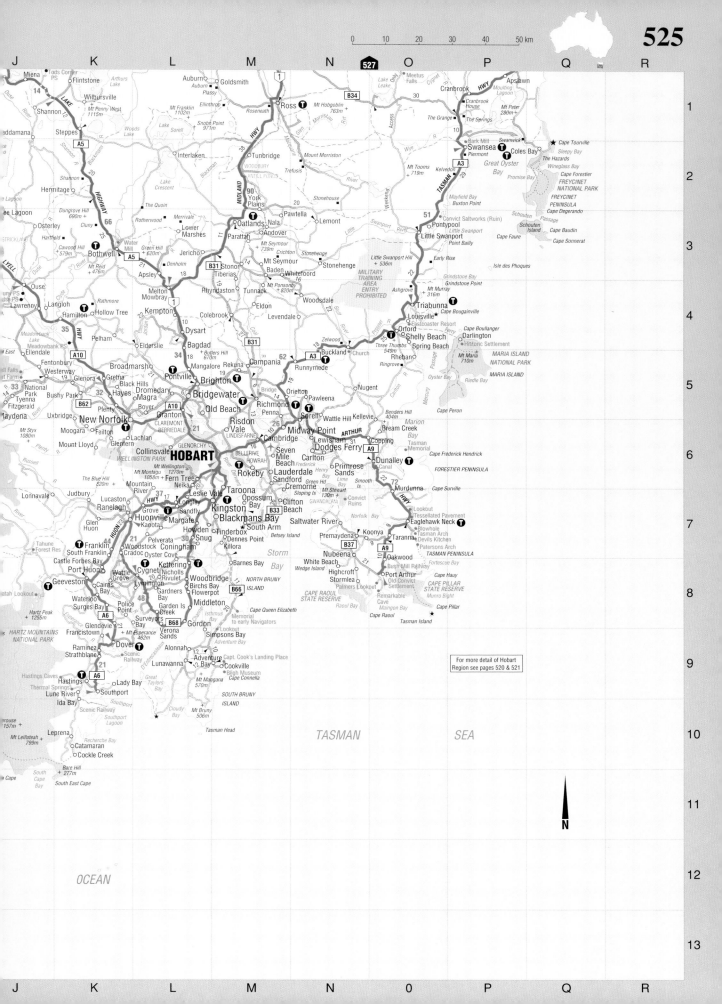

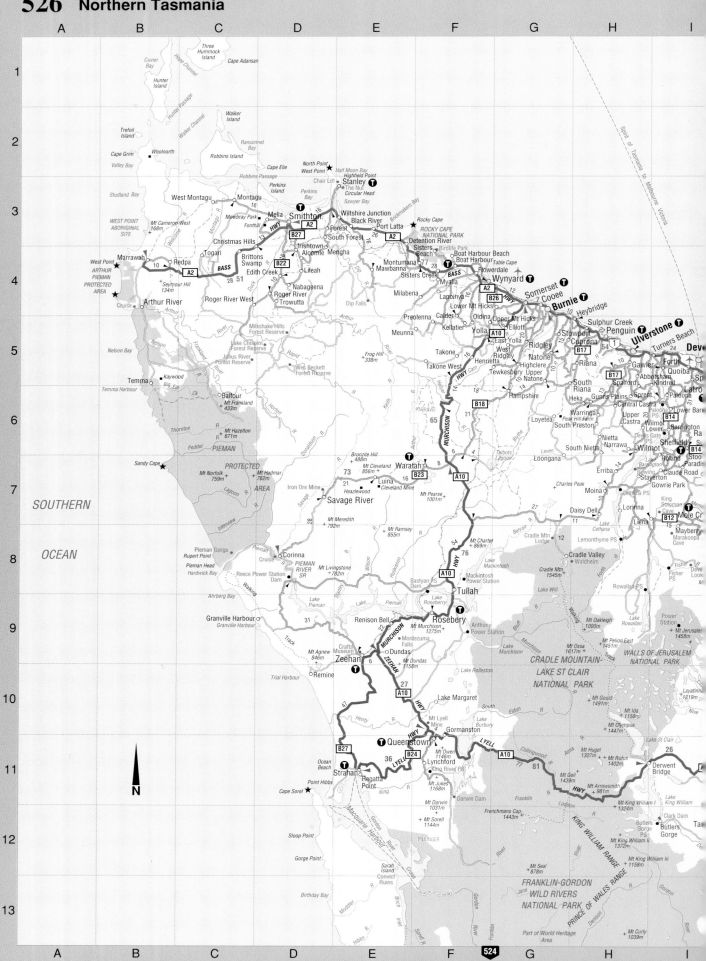

Grid columns: J K L M N O P Q R
Grid rows: 1 2 3 4 5 6 7 8 9 10 11 12 13

Scale: 0 10 20 30 40 50 km

BASS STRAIT · Banks Strait

CAPE BARREN ISLAND · Mt Kerford 499m · Kent Bay · Sloping Pt · Forsyth I · Passage I · Preservation I · Clarke Island

Look Out Heads · Moriarty Point

Cape Portland · Swan Island · Vinegar Hill 52m · Great Mussel Roe Bay · Poole · Cape Naturaliste · Rushy Lagoon · Icena

Mt William 216m · MOUNT WILLIAM NATIONAL PARK · Eddystone Point · Ansons Bay · The Gardens · Bay Of Fires · Henderson Lagoon

Waterhouse Island · Waterhouse Point · Waterhouse · Croppies Point · West Sandy Cape · East Sandy Cape · Anderson Bay · Noland Bay · Stony Head · Five Mile Bluff

Tomahawk · Booyalla · Mt Cameron 551m · South Mt Cameron · Gladstone · B82 · Anson Park · Pioneer · Mt Horror 686m · Winnaleah · Herrick · Moorina · Derby · A3 · Weldborough · 99 · Lotta · Goulds Country · Goshen · Priory · Mt Pearson 373m · Binalong Bay · St Helens Point · Akaroa · Stieglitz · Parnella · St Helens Island · Dianas Basin

Weymouth · Back Creek · Bellingham · Bridport · Trout Farm · B82 · Pipers River · Pipers Brook · B84 · Lavender Farm · North Scottsdale · Forester · Scottsdale · Mt Stronach 497m · West Scottsdale · Springfield · A3 · Tonganah · Tulendeena · Legerwood · Cuckoo Hill 732m · Talawah · Ringarooma · St Columba Falls · Pyengana · Goshen

Lulworth · Beechford · Low Head · George Town · Kelso · Leura · Bell Bay · Sidmouth · The Glen · Lower Turners Marsh · Turners Marsh · Golconda · Lietinna · Nabowla · Lisle · Karoola · Lilydale · Myrtle Bank · Mt Arthur 1187m · Targa · Myrtle Grove · Didlenna Plains · Mt Maurice 1120m · Trenah · Alberton · Mt Victoria 1208m · Mt Young 903m · St Helens · Parkside · Beaumaris · Scamander · Upper Scamander

Greens Beach · Clarence Point · Low Head · ASBESTOS RANGE NATIONAL PARK · Port Sorell · Beauty Point · Beaconsfield · B73 · Rowella · Devonport · Robigana · Gravelly Beach · Exeter · Windermere · Dilston · Legana · Rocherlea · Waverley · LAUNCESTON · Hadspen · RIVERSIDE NORTH · Relbia · White Hills · Breadalbane · Western Junction · Evandale · Clarendon · Deddington · Nile · Powranna · Epping Forest · Cleveland · Conara · Campbell Town · B34 · Ross

Flowery Gully · Holwell · Winkleigh · Lanena · Glengarry · Notley Hills · Bridgenorth · Birralee · Rosevale · Selbourne · Reedy Marsh · Westwood · Hagley · Carrick · Perth · Longford · Bishopsbourne · Cressy · Kilrea · B53 · Esk Vale · Kelvin Grove · Ellerslie · Brambletye · Woodford · Front Rocky Hill 574m

Port Sorell · Sassafras East · Frankford · West Frankford · Frankford · B71 · B72 · Parkham · Weetah · Elizabeth Town · Deloraine · Osmaston · Quamby Brook · Glenore · Whitemore · Toiberry · Cluan · Bracknell · Liffey · Blackwood Creek · Breona

Lemana · Needles · A5 · Golden Valley · Meander · Jackeys Marsh · Liffey Falls · GREAT · WESTERN · TIERS · Cramps · Poatina PS · Pisa · Parknook · The Glen · The Bend · Rokeby · Lake · Macquarie

Miena · Shannon · Wilburville · Penny West · St Patricks Plains · Flintstone · Tods Corner PS · Arthurs Lake · Steppes · Waddamana · Interlaken · Woodbury House · Tunbridge · Trefusis · Auburn · Goldsmith · Ross · Mt Franklin 1102m · Snops Point 971m · Mount Morriston

Shannon · Hermitage · Dungrove Hill 690m · Forest Green · Cluny · The Quoin · Rotherwood · York Plains · Nala · Pawtella · Lemont · Oatlands · Lower Marshes · Andover · Mt Seymour 739m · Crichton · Stonehouse · The Gables · Hillcrest

Dee Lagoon · Glengowan · Lake Echo PS · Sunny Banks · Osterley · Hartford · Ousedale · Glen Dhu · Cawood Hill 579m · Bothwell · Apsley · Jericho · Parattah · Tedworth · Denholm · Tunnack · Mt Seymour · Whitefoord · Stonehenge · Mt Tooms 719m · Pontypool · Little Swanport · Point Bailly

Black Bobs · Victoria Valley Falls · Montacute · Mt Reid 476m · Stonor · Tiberias · Rhyndaston · Baden · Mt Ponsonby 820m · Woodsdale · Early Rise Hermitage · MILITARY TRAINING AREA · ENTRY PROHIBITED

Ouse · Cluny PS · Lawrenny · Repulse PS · Langloh · Hamilton · Hollow Tree · Melton Mowbray · Kempton · Windsor Park · Bonnie Vue · Colebrook · Eldon · Levendale · Woodstock · Rostrevor House · Stonehurst · Triabunna · Cape Bougainville · Louisville · Eastcoaster Resort

St Marys · A4 · MAIN ROAD · Fingal · Mangana · Storys Creek · Rossarden · Ormley · B42 · Avoca · Llewellyn Siding · Royal George · Mt St John 777m · Cornwall · Four Mile Creek · Gray · Chain Of Lagoons · Seymour · Long Point · DOUGLAS APSLEY NATIONAL PARK · Lookout Hill · Mt Nicholas 869m · B43 · B42 · A4 · ESK · FINGAL VALLEY · 74 · Mt Saddleback 1277m · Upper Esk · Mathinna · ALPINE VILLAGE · BEN LOMOND NATIONAL PARK · Legges Tor 1575m · Roses Tier · Mt Barrow 1413m

Falmouth · Henderson Lagoon · A3 · Lookout · Birdlife Park · Waubs Harbour · Sealife Park · Bicheno · Cape Lodi · Ferndale · Greenlawn · Apslawn · Llandaff · Cranbrook · Mt Peter 280m · Swansea · Bark Mill · Coles Bay · Cape Tourville · The Hazards · FREYCINET NP · Sleepy Bay · Wineglass Bay · Cape Forestier · FREYCINET NATIONAL PARK · FREYCINET PENINSULA · Cape Degerando · Promise Bay · Great Oyster Bay · Schouten Passage · Cape Baudin · Cape Faure · Cape Sonnerat · Schouten Island · Grindstone Bay · Grindstone Point · Mt Murray 316m · Ashgrove · Isle des Phoques · Buxton Point · Mayfield Bay · Moulting Lagoon · Maclean Bay · Convict Saltworks (Ruin)

525

Index of Place Names

To enable the ready location of the place names that appear in this gazetteer, each is followed by a map page number and grid reference, and/or the text page number on which that place name occurs. A page number set in bold type indicates the main text entry for that place name.

Sale Vic. 225 M6, 179, 190, **194**

Sale — Place name

Vic. — State

225 M6 — Sale appears on this map page

179, 190 — Sale is mentioned on these pages

194 — Main entry for Sale

The alphabetical order followed in the index is that of 'word-by-word', where all entries under one word are grouped together. Where a place name consists of more than one word, the order is governed by the first and then the second word. For example:

Green Bay

Green River

Greenbank

Greens Beach

Greenwood Forest

Greg Greg

Gregafell

Names beginning with Mc are indexed as Mac and those beginning with St, as Saint.

The following abbreviations and contractions are used in the index:

ACT — Australian Capital Territory

NSW — New South Wales

NT — Northern Territory

Qld — Queensland

SA — South Australia

St — Saint

Tas. — Tasmania

Vic. — Victoria

WA — Western Australia

Helidon Qld 466 G8
Hell Hole Gorge National Park Qld 485 M1
Hells Gate Roadhouse Qld 395 R6, 481 C8
Hemmant Qld 463 L10
Henbury Meteorite Craters Con. Park NT 390 G9, 372
Hendon SA 278 D1, 280 E13
Hendra Qld 462 I9
Henley NSW 99 J8
Henley Beach SA 278 B4, 283 K8
Henley Brook WA 345 P3
Henrietta Tas. 526 F5
Henty NSW 127 P11, 233 P1, **72**
Hepburn Springs Vic. 210 E2, 221 P9, 227 Q2, 229 Q13, 232 B12, 171
Herbert River National Park Qld 479 L10
Herberton Qld 479 K8, 408, 409, 431, 433
Heritage Park Qld 465 J12
Hermannsburg NT 390 E5, 396 I9
Hermit Park Qld 471 E7
Hermitage Tas. 525 K2, 527 K12
Herne Hill Vic. 216 A4
Heron Island Qld 477 O9, 416, 420, **422**
Herons Creek NSW 109 F9
Herrick Tas. 527 O5
Herston Qld 462 G11
Hervey Bay Qld 475 N1, 477 Q13, 425, **429**, 437
Hexham Vic. 227 J7
Heybridge Tas. 526 H5
Heyfield Vic. 225 L5, **185**, 194
Heywood Vic. 226 E7, 191
Hiawatha Vic. 202
Hidden Vale Qld 466 I9
Hidden Valley Nat. Park WA *see* Mirima Nat. Park
Hideaway Bay Tas. 520 E11
Higgins ACT 138 B6
High Wycombe WA 343 Q1
Highbury SA 281 P11
Highbury WA 347 K11, 354 G9, 356 B10
Highclere Tas. 526 G5
Highcroft Tas. 521 M10, 525 N8
Highett Vic. 209 B3
Highfields Qld 466 F7
Highgate SA 279 J7
Highgate WA 342 I2, 344 I13
Highgate Hill Qld 462 G13, 464 G1
Highton Vic. 216 A10, 217 E7
Highvale Qld 467 L7
Hill End NSW 120 F5, 56
Hill End Vic. 211 R8, 224 I5
Hillarys WA 344 A3
Hillbank SA 281 N3
Hillcrest SA 281 L12
Hillgrove NSW 123 L8, 475 L13, 51
Hillsdale NSW 103 P5
Hillside Vic. 225 O4, 234 E13
Hillston NSW 127 M5
Hilltop NSW 116 C5, 119 H2, 120 I10
Hilltown SA 289 L4
Hillview Qld 123 O1, 475 N7
Hillwood Tas. 523 M6, 527 L5, 502
Hilton SA 278 F5
Hilton WA 342 D12
Hinchinbrook Island Qld 479 M10, **423–4**
Hinchinbrook Island Nat. Park Qld 479 M10
Hincks Conservation Park SA 288 E4
Hindmarsh SA 278 F3
Hindmarsh Island SA 243, 256, 263
Hindmarsh Valley SA 271
Hines Hill WA 347 O2, 354 H6, 356 C8
Hinnomunjie Vic. 234 E8
Hinton NSW 112 D6
Hirstglen Qld 466 F10
Hobart Tas. 517, 518 G7, 520 H6, 525 L6, 487, **488–90**, 491–2, 501, 506, 507
Hobbys Yards NSW 120 F8
Holbrook NSW 127 Q12, 233 Q2, **72**

Holden Hill SA 281 N11
Holder ACT 138 C13, 139 A4
Holey Plains State Park Vic. 225 L7, 194
Holgate NSW 105 O5, 108 G5
Holland Park Qld 464 I3
Hollow Tree Tas. 525 K4, 527 K13
Holloways Beach Qld 473 F8, 414
Hollydeen NSW 120 I3
Hollywell Qld 469 E2
Holmview Qld 465 P12
Holsworthy Village NSW 102 B6
Holt ACT 138 A5
Holwell Tas. 523 J7, 527 K6
Home Hill Qld 479 O13, 409, **429**, **432**
Homebush NSW 98 G10
Homebush Bay NSW 98 F9
Homestead Qld 476 C2, 483 Q2
Hook Island Qld 476 I1, **423**
Hook Island National Park Qld 476 I1
Hope Forest SA 283 L10, 284 D7
Hope Vale Aboriginal Comm. Qld 479 K3
Hope Valley SA 281 O11
Hopetoun Vic. 126 E12, 228 H3, **178**
Hopetoun WA 356 F12, **319**
Hoppers Crossing Vic. 206 C11, 210 I7, 217 I3
Hornsby NSW 100 F9, 105 L7, 121 J8
Hornsby Heights NSW 100 F7
Hornsdale SA 289 L1, 291 K13
Horrocks WA 354 B1
Horsham Vic. 228 G9, **178**, 197
Horsley Park NSW 105 J9
Hotham Heights Vic. 233 P10, 234 C8, 179
Houghton SA 281 R9, 283 M7
Hove SA 278 D11
Howard Qld 475 M1, 477 P13, 429
Howard Island NT 393 M4
Howard Springs NT 388 D3, 392 F5, 368, 373
Howden Tas. 520 H8, 525 L7, 503
Howlong NSW 233 N3
Howqua Vic. 211 R3, 222 C12, 233 L11
Howrah Tas. 519 M7, 520 I6, 525 M6
Hoyleton SA 283 L1, 289 L5
Huddleston SA 289 K2
Hughenden Qld 483 N3, **432**
Hughes ACT 138 F13, 139 D3
Hughes SA 272
Hull River National Park Qld 479 M9
Hume ACT 139 H7
Humevale Vic. 211 L4
Humpty Doo NT 388 E3, 392 F5, 367
Hunchy Qld 467 M1
Hungerford Qld 125 J2, 485 M9, 453
Hungerford Hill NSW 73
Hunter Island Tas. 526 B1
Hunter Valley NSW 113, 37, 49, 54, 73, 82, 86
Hunters Hill NSW 99 J7
Huntingdale WA 343 N12
Huntly Vic. 229 R9, 232 C8
Huonville Tas. 520 F8, 525 K7, 492, **502–3**
Hurlstone Park NSW 98 I13, 99 J13, 103 K3
Hurstbridge Vic. 208 B1, 211 L5, 224 D3
Hurstville NSW 103 J6, 105 L10
Huskisson NSW 119 H5, 120 I12, 141 R1, 72, **74**
Hyams Beach NSW 141 R1
Hyde Park Qld 471 D6
Hyde Park SA 278 H7
Hyden WA 354 I8, 356 D9, **319**
Hynam SA 228 A11, 287 I9

Ida Bay Tas. 525 K10
Idalia Qld 471 F10, 476 A12
Idalia Nat. Park Qld 476 A12, 483 N12, 410
Ilbilbie Qld 477 I3
Ilford NSW 120 G5
Ilfracombe Qld 476 A9, 483 N9, **432**, 436
Ilfraville Tas. 523 J4
Illabarook Vic. 210 B6, 227 N5

Illabo NSW 119 A4, 120 B11, 127 R9
Illamurta Springs Con. Res. NT 390 D7, 396 H10
Illawarra Coast, The NSW 37, **54**
Illawong NSW 102 G9
Illawong WA 354 C3
Iluka NSW 123 P4, 475 N10, 70, **74**, 78, 94
Imbil Qld 475 M3, 429, 434
Inala Qld 464 F8
Inarlinga Qld 479 M8
Indented Head Vic. 210 I9, 212 B1, 217 I7, 224 B6
Indooroopilly Qld 464 E2, 467 L8
Ingham Qld 479 M10, **432**
Ingle Farm SA 281 L9
Ingleside NSW 101 O7
Inglewood Qld 123 J1, 475 J8, **432**
Inglewood SA 283 M7
Inglewood Vic. 229 O9, 232 A7, **180**, 194
Inglewood WA 345 J11
Injune Qld 474 F2, **432**
Inkerman SA 283 J2, 289 K6
Inman Valley SA 283 K12, 284 B11, 271
Innaloo WA 344 D10
Innamincka SA 293 Q7, 484 G6, 250, 251, **256**, 267
Innes Nat. Park SA 282 A10, 288 G9, 247, **251**, 274
Inneston SA 288 G9, 247, 251, 274
Innisfail Qld 479 L8, 431, **432**
Innot Hot Springs Qld 479 K8
Interlaken Tas. 525 L2, 527 L11
Inverell NSW 123 J6, 475 J11, 68, **74**
Inverleigh Vic. 210 D9, 217 B6, 227 P7, **180**
Inverloch Vic. 224 G9, 153, **180**, 201
Invermay Vic. 219 E1
Invermay Tas. 523 O10
Ipolera NT 390 D5, 396 H9
Ipswich Qld 467 K9, 475 M6, 400, **432**, **434**
Irishtown Tas. 526 D4
Iron Baron SA 288 H1, 290 G13
Iron Knob SA 290 G12, 272
Iron Range National Park Qld 480 E7, **442**
Ironbark SA 279 N13
Ironside Qld 464 F2
Irrewillipe Vic. 215 E8, 227 M9
Irvinebank Qld 479 K8
Irymple Vic. 126 D7, 230 G4
Isaacs ACT 139 E6
Isabella Plains ACT 139 D10
Isisford Qld 476 A11, 483 N11, 434
Isla Gorge National Park Qld 477 K13, 452
Island of the Dead Tas. **512**
Isles of St Francis Con. Park SA 297 M11
Islington NSW 110 B5
Ivanhoe NSW 127 J3
Ivanhoe Vic. 207 N6, 145
Ivory Creek Qld 466 I3
Iwupataka NT 397 J9, 390 I4

Ja Ja NT 387 H4, 389 Q3, 392 I5
Jabiru NT 387 H5, 389 Q4, 392 I5, 367, 373, **376**
Jabiru East NT 387 H5, 389 Q4
Jabuk SA 287 G4, 289 P10
Jackeys Marsh Tas. 527 J8
Jackson Qld 474 H4
Jacobs Well Qld 467 O11
Jacobs Well WA 347 J5
Jalloonda Qld 479 N12
Jamberoo NSW 116 F9, 119 I3, 120 I11, **74**
Jambin Qld 477 L11
Jamboree Heights Qld 464 C6
Jamestown SA 289 L2, **256**
Jamieson Vic. 211 R3, 222 C13, 224 I1, 233 L12, 185–7, 198
Jandakot WA 342 I13, 346 D5
Jandowae Qld 475 J4
Jannali NSW 102 I10

Mount Gambier SA 226 A5, 287 I13, 237, **262**
Mount Garnet Qld 479 K8, 433
Mount Gravatt Qld 465 J4
Mount Greville National Park Qld 466 I12
Mount Hallen Qld 466 I6
Mount Hawthorn WA 342 G1, 344 G12
Mount Helen Vic. 210 C5, 221 M13, 227 O4
Mount Helena WA 346 E4
Mount Hope SA 288 C5, 252
Mount Hotham Vic. 223 N9, 173
Mount Hunter NSW 104 I11, 116 E1
Mount Imlay National Park NSW 117 D12, 119 F12, 235 O9
Mount Isa Qld 482 E3, 399, **440–1**
Mount Kaputar National Park NSW 122 H7, 474 I12, **59**, 81
Mount Keira NSW 114 A9
Mount Kembla NSW 116 G6
Mount Kosciusko NSW 140 A13, 62
Mount Kilcoy Qld 467 J2
Mount Kuring-gai NSW 100 G6
Mount Lambie NSW 104 D4
Mount Larcom Qld 477 M10
Mount Lawley WA 343 J1, 344 I12
Mount Lewis Vic. 98 E13, 102 H3
Mount Liebig NT 396 F8
Mount Lloyd Tas. 520 E5, 525 K6
Mount Lofty SA 237, 238, 241, 243, 251
Mount Macedon Vic. 210 H3, 224 A2, 232 D13, 177, 184
Mount Magnet WA 354 G1, 355 I13, 356 B2, **328**
Mount Magnificent Con. Park SA 283 L10, 284 E8
Mount Martha Vic. 212 I5, 155
Mount Mary SA 283 Q1, 289 N5
Mount Mee Qld 467 K4
Mount Mistake Nat. Park Qld 466 H11, **444**
Mount Molloy Qld 473 B6, 479 K6
Mount Morgan Qld 477 L9, **441**
Mount Moriac Vic. 210 E9, 217 C7, 227 Q8
Mount Mulligan Qld 479 J6
Mount Nebo Qld 405
Mount Nelson Tas. 518 G12
Mount Olga NT 396 E12, 370, 374
Mount Ommaney Qld 464 C6
Mount Osmond SA 279 L8
Mount Ousley NSW 114 C6
Mount Perry Qld 477 N13
Mount Pleasant NSW 114 A6
Mount Pleasant Qld 467 K5
Mount Pleasant SA 283 O6, 287 D2, 289 M7
Mount Pleasant Vic. 219 E10
Mount Pleasant WA 342 G8
Mount Pritchard NSW 102 A2
Mount Remarkable Nat. Park SA 285 B13, 291 J12, 260, 272
Mount Rescue Con. Park SA 287 G5, 289 P11, 258
Mount Richmond National Park Vic. 226 D8
Mount St Thomas NSW 114 C13
Mount Samson Qld 467 L6
Mount Schank SA 226 A6, 287 H13, 262
Mount Scott Conservation Park SA 287 G9
Mount Seaview NSW 123 M11
Mount Selwyn NSW 118 D4, 119 C8, 140 C8, 234 I1
Mount Seymour Tas. 525 M3, 527 N13
Mount Shaugh Con. Park SA 126 A13, 228 A4, 287 I5, 289 R11
Mount Skillion NSW 109 E2
Mount Sonder NT 370
Mount Spec/Crystal Creek Nat. Park Qld 479 M11
Mount Stirling Vic. 173
Mount Stuart Tas. 518 E7
Mount Surprise Qld 478 I9
Mount Sylvia Qld 466 G9

Mount Tamborine Qld 467 N12, 406
Mount Tarampa Qld 466 I7
Mount Taylor Vic. 119 A13, 225 P4, 234 E12
Mount Torrens SA 283 N7, 243
Mount Tyson Qld 466 C7
Mount Victoria NSW 104 F6, 106 B3, 120 H7, 75
Mount Walsh National Park Qld 475 L1, 410
Mount Warning Nat. Park NSW 123 O1, 475 N8, 80
Mount Waverley Vic. 207 Q11
Mount Webb National Park Qld 480 I13
Mount Wellington Tas. 487, 488, 490, 501
Mount White NSW 105 N5, 108 C9, 121 J7
Mount Whitestone Qld 466 G9
Mount William Nat. Park Tas. 527 Q4, **496**
Mount Wilson NSW 104 G5
Mountain River Tas. 520 G7, 525 L6
Moura Qld 477 K11
Mourilyan Qld 479 L8, 432, **441**
Mowbray Tas. 523 O9
Mowbray Park NSW 104 H12
Moyhu Vic. 222 F3, 233 M7, 199
Moyreisk Vic. 220 I3, 229 M11
Moyston Vic. 220 B8, 227 J2, 229 J13
Muchea WA 346 D2, 354 E7
Muckadilla Qld 474 E4
Mudgee NSW 120 F4, 73, **80**
Mudgegonga Vic. 223 K1, 233 O7, 234 A5
Mudgeeraba Qld 467 O13, 469 D8, 475 N7, 407
Mudjimba Qld 470 H8, 440
Mukinbudin WA 354 H5, 356 C7
Mulambin Qld 477 M8
Mulbring NSW 112 D10
Mulgildie Qld 477 M12
Mulgoa NSW 104 I9, 119 H1, 120 I8
Mulgrave NSW 105 K7
Mulgrave Vic. 208 B13, 209 H2
Mullaley NSW 122 G10
Mullaloo WA 344 A1, 346 C3
Mullayup WA 350 B2
Mullewa WA 354 D1, **328**, 331
Mulli Mulli NSW 475 M8
Mullumbimby NSW 123 P2, 475 N8, 61, **80**
Mulpata SA 287 H3, 289 Q9
Mulwala NSW 127 N13, 233 K3, **80**, 143, 193, **202**
Mumbil NSW 120 E4
Mummballup WA 354 E10, 356 A11
Mummulgum NSW 123 O3, 475 M9
Munbilla Qld 467 J11, 475 M7
Mundalla SA 249
Mundaring WA 346 E4, 354 E7, **328**
Mundaring Weir WA 328
Mundijong WA 346 D6, 331
Mundingburra Qld 471 B9
Mundoora SA 289 J3
Mundrabilla WA 357 Q8, **328**, 332
Mundubbera Qld 475 K1, **441**
Mundulla SA 287 H7, 289 Q13
Mungallala Qld 474 D3
Mungar Qld 475 M1
Mungaroona Range Nat. Park WA 355 I2
Mungerannie SA 267
Mungerannie Roadhouse SA 293 K8, 484 C7
Mungindi NSW 122 E3, 474 F9
Munglinup WA 356 G11
Mungo Nat. Park NSW 126 G5, 231 L1, 51, **59**, 92
Mungungo Qld 477 M12
Muntadgin WA 347 Q3, 354 H7, 356 D8
Munyaroo Conservation Park SA 288 H2
Muogamurra NSW 108 C11
Muradup WA 350 I2, 354 F10, 356 B12
Murarrie Qld 463 K11
Murbko SA 289 O5
Murchison Vic. 232 G7, 188, 194

Murchison WA 355 F11
Murdinga SA 288 D4
Murdoch WA 342 G12
Murdunna Tas. 521 N7, 525 O7
Murgenella River NT 382
Murgenella Settlement NT 392 I3
Murgon Qld 475 L3, **441**, 445
Murphys Creek Qld 466 F7, 475 L6
Murrabit Vic. 126 I11, 229 P2, 232 A1, 181
Murramarang Nat. Park NSW 119 H6, 141 P6
Murray Bridge SA 283 P9, 287 D3, 289 N9, 253, **262**, 264
Murray-Kulkyne Nat. Park Vic. 126 E8, 230 I6
Murray River NSW 126 C7, 127 O3, 283 P8, 289 N6, 37, 50, 51, 53, 65, 68, 72, 79, 80, 86, 89
Murray River SA 243, 251, 263, 273
Murray River Vic. 167, 189, 192, **193**, 196, 202
Murray-Sunset Nat. Park Vic. 126 B9, 230 C8, 289 R7, **168**, 190
Murray Town SA 289 K1, 291 J13, 260
Murrayville Vic. 126 B11, 230 C11
Murrindal Vic. 119 B12, 225 R2, 234 H10
Murrindindi Vic. 211 N3, 224 F1, 232 I12
Murringo NSW 94
Murrumba Qld 466 I5
Murrumbateman NSW 119 D4, 120 E12, 94
Murrumbeena Vic. 207 O12
Murrumburrah NSW 119 B3, 120 C10, **71–2**
Murrurundi NSW 120 I1, 122 I12, **80**
Murtoa Vic. 228 I9, **188**
Murwillumbah NSW 123 P1, 475 N8, **80**
Musk Vic. 221 P9, 171
Musk Vale Vic. 210 E3, 221 O9
Musselboro Tas. 527 N7
Muswellbrook NSW 121 J3, 122 I13, **80**, 86
Mutchero Inlet National Park Qld 473 I13
Mutdapilly Qld 467 J10
Muttaburra Qld 476 A7, 483 N7, **445**
Myall Lakes Nat. Park NSW 121 M4, 54, **59**, 61, 69
Myalla Tas. 526 F4
Myalup WA 346 C11, 354 D9, 307, 319
Myamyn Vic. 226 E6
Myaree WA 342 F10
Myers Flat Vic. 163
Mylestom NSW 123 O8, 475 N12
Mylor SA 279 Q12, 283 M8, 284 G2, 243
Myola Qld 473 E7
Mypolonga SA 283 P8, 287 E2, 289 N8, 262
Myponga SA 283 K11, 284 B9, 287 B4, 289 K10, 264, 274
Myponga Con. Park SA 283 K11, 284 A10, 243, 274
Myrla SA 289 P6
Myrniong Vic. 210 F5, 221 Q13, 227 Q4, 160
Myrrhee Vic. 222 E5
Myrtle Bank SA 279 J7
Myrtle Bank Tas. 523 Q7, 527 M6
Myrtleford Vic. 223 J2, 233 N7, 234 A5, **188**
Myrtletown Qld 463 L6
Mysia Vic. 229 O6
Mysterton Qld 471 C8
Mystic Park Vic. 126 H12, 229 O2, 231 O12, 196

Nabageena Tas. 526 D4
Nabawa WA 354 C1
Nabiac NSW 121 M2, 123 M13
Nabowla Tas. 523 R5, 527 M5, 504, 510
Nackara SA 291 M12
Nadda SA 126 A9, 230 A7
Nagambie Vic. 232 G9, 183, **188**, 194
Nagoorin Qld 477 N11
Nailsworth SA 278 I1, 281 J13
Nairne SA 283 N8, 243
Nakara NT 386 G2
Nala Tas. 525 M3, 527 N12

Richmond Tas. 521 J4, 525 M5, 487, 491, 500, 501, 506, **507**
Richmond Vic. 207 L9, 148, 149
Riddells Creek Vic. 210 I4, 224 B2, 232 E13
Ridgehaven SA 281 O9
Ridgelands Qld 477 L8
Ridgeway Tas. 518 E12, 520 H6
Ridgley Tas. 526 G5
Ridleyton SA 278 G2
Ringarooma Tas. 527 O6, **507**
Ringwood Vic. 208 C9, 211 L7
Ripley Qld 467 K9
Risdon Tas. 518 G2, 490
Risdon Vale Tas. 518 I1, 520 I5, 525 M6
Riverhills Qld 464 C7
Riverside Tas. 523 N9
Riverside North Tas. 527 L7
Riverstone NSW 105 K7
Riverton SA 283 M2, 289 L5, 254, 258
Riverton WA 343 K9
Rivervale WA 343 L4, 302
Riverview NSW 99 K7
Riverwood NSW 102 H5
Rivett ACT 138 B13, 139 A4
Roadvale Qld 467 J11, 475 M7
Rob Roy Vic. 208 E1
Robbins Island Tas. 526 C2
Robe SA 287 F10, **269**
Robertson NSW 116 D8, 119 H3, 120 I10, 52, **86**
Robertson Qld 464 I5
Robertstown SA 289 M5
Robigana Tas. 523 L6, 527 L6
Robina Qld 469 E7
Robinvale Vic. 126 F8, 231 J6, **192**
Rochedale Qld 465 L5
Rocherlea Tas. 523 O9, 527 L6
Roches Beach Tas. 519 R7
Rochester SA 289 K4
Rochester Vic. 232 E6, **192**
Rockbank Vic. 206 A5, 210 H6, 224 B4
Rockdale NSW 103 L5
Rockhampton Qld 477 L9, 420, **450**
Rockingham WA 346 C6, 354 D8, **333**
Rocklands Reservoir Vic. 170, 174, 180
Rocklea Qld 464 G5
Rockleigh SA 283 O8
Rockley NSW 104 A6, 120 F8, 56
Rocksberg Qld 467 L5
Rocky Cape Nat. Park Tas. 526 F3, 493, **497**, 510, 515
Rocky Gully WA 350 I8
Rodd Point NSW 99 J10
Rodds Peninsula National Park Qld. 477 O10
Roebourne WA 355 H1, 358 A2, 311, 333, **334**, 335, 336
Roebuck Roadhouse WA 360 H8
Roelands WA 346 D13
Rogans Hill NSW 98 D1, 100 B11
Roger River Tas. 526 D4
Roger River West Tas. 526 C4
Rokeby Tas. 519 O10, 521 J6, 525 M6, **507–8**
Rokeby Vic. 211 P9, 224 H6
Rokeby National Park Qld 480 D9, **442**
Rokewood Vic. 210 B7, 215 H1, 227 O6
Roland Tas. 522 C9, 526 I7
Rolleston Qld 476 I11, 449
Rollingstone Qld 479 M11
Roma Qld 474 F4, **450**
Romsey Vic. 210 I3, 224 B1, 232 E12, 184, **192**
Rookwood NSW 98 F11, 102 G1
Rooty Hill NSW 105 K8
Ropeley Qld 466 H9
Rosanna Vic. 207 O5
Rose Bay NSW 99 P9
Rose Bay Tas. 518 I6
Rose Park SA 279 J5
Rosebery NSW 99 M13, 103 O3

Rosebery Tas. 526 F9, **508**, 509
Rosebrook Vic. 226 H9
Rosebud Vic. 211 J11, 212 G8, 224 C8, 155
Rosebud West Vic. 212 F8
Rosedale Qld 477 O12
Rosedale SA 286 B7
Rosedale Vic. 225 L6
Rosegarland Tas. 520 E3
Rosehill NSW 98 D7
Roselands NSW 102 H4
Roseneath Vic. 166
Rosetta Tas. 518 B2
Rosevale Qld 466 I11, 475 M7
Rosevale Tas. 523 L9, 527 K7
Rosevears Tas. 523 M8, 499
Roseville NSW 99 K5
Rosewater SA 280 E11
Rosewhite Vic. 223 K3, 233 O7, 234 B5
Rosewood Qld 467 J9, 475 M6, 434
Roseworthy SA 283 M4, 287 C1, 289 L7
Roslyn NSW 65
Rosny Tas. 518 I7, 508
Rosny Park Tas. 519 J6
Ross Tas. 525 M1, 527 N10, 487, 500, **508**
Ross River NT 391 O3, 397 K8, 370, 372, **381**
Rossarden Tas. 527 O8, 493
Rossbridge Vic. 220 C10, 227 J3
Rosslea Qld 471 E9
Rosslyn Park SA 279 L4
Rossmore NSW 105 J10
Rossville Qld 479 K4
Rostrevor SA 279 M2, 241
Rothsay WA 331
Rottnest Island WA 354 D7, 299, 302, 303, **304**, 317
Round Corner NSW 100 B9
Rowella Tas. 523 L5, 527 K5, 493
Rowena NSW 122 D6, 474 F11
Rowes Bay Qld 471 B1
Rowland Flat SA 283 N5, 286 D8, 259
Rowsley Vic. 210 F5, 224 A4, 227 R5
Rowville Vic. 208 D13
Roxby Downs SA 290 F4, 246, 267, **269**, 274
Royal George Tas. 527 P9
Royal Nat. Park NSW 105 L12, 116 I1, 121 J9, 47, **58**
Royal Park SA 278 C1, 280 D13
Royston Park SA 279 J2
Rozelle NSW 99 K9
Rubyvale Qld 476 G9, 449
Rudall SA 288 E4
Rudall River National Park WA 358 I4
Ruffy Vic. 211 N1, 232 I10
Rugby NSW 119 D3, 120 E10
Rum Jungle NT 388 D7, 392 E6, 369, 376
Runaway Bay Qld 469 E2
Runcorn Qld 465 J7
Runnymede Tas. 521 K3, 525 N5
Rupanyup Vic. 228 I9, 188
Rushcutters Bay NSW 99 O10, 46
Rushworth Vic. 232 F7, **192**
Russell ACT 136 H8, 138 I10, 139 G1
Russell Lea NSW 99 J3
Russell River Nat. Park Qld 473 I13, 479 I7
Rutherglen Vic. 127 O13, 233 M4, 183, **192**, 193, **194**
Rydal NSW 104 E4, 120 H7
Rydalmere NSW 98 D6
Ryde NSW 98 H6
Rye Vic. 210 I11, 212 E8, 153, 155
Rye Park NSW 119 D3, 120 E10
Rylstone NSW 120 G5, **86**

Sackville North NSW 105 K5
Saddleworth SA 283 M1, 289 L5
Safety Bay WA 346 C6, 333
St Agnes SA 281 P9
St Albans NSW 105 L3l, 121 J6

St Albans Vic. 206 F5, 210 I6
St Andrews Vic. 211 L5, 224 E3, 153, 183
St Arnaud Vic. 229 L9, **194**, 195
St George Qld 474 F7, **450–1**
St Georges SA 279 K7
St Georges Basin NSW 119 H5, 120 I12, 141 Q1
St Helena Island Nat. Park Qld 463 P6, 467 N7
St Helens Tas. 527 Q6, 487, 501, **508**
St Ives NSW 99 K1, 100 I11
St Ives Chase NSW 101 J10
St James Vic. 233 J5
St James WA 343 K6
St Johns Park NSW 102 A1
St Kilda SA 280 F3, 283 K6, 241
St Kilda Vic. 207 K10, 148
St Kilda East Vic. 207 M10
St Lawrence Qld 477 J6
St Leonards NSW 99 L7
St Leonards Tas. 523 O10
St Leonards Vic. 210 I9, 212 B2, 217 I7, 224 B6, **194**
St Lucia Qld 464 F2, 401, 403
St Marys SA 278 G10
St Marys Tas. 527 Q8, **508**, **510**
St Morris SA 279 K3
St Patricks River Tas. 523 Q8, 527 M6
St Peter Island SA 252
St Peters NSW 99 L12, 103 N2
St Peters SA 279 J3, 240
Sale Vic. 225 M6, 179, 190, **194**
Salisbury Qld 464 H5
Salisbury SA 281 K4, 283 L6, 287 C1, 289 L8
Salisbury East SA 281 N6
Salisbury Heights SA 281 O4
Salisbury North SA 281 K3
Salisbury Plain SA 281 M4
Salmon Gums WA 356 H10
Salt Creek SA 287 E6, 289 O12, 263
Salter Springs SA 283 L2, 289 L5
Saltwater River Tas. 521 L8, 525 N7
Samford Qld 467 L7, 475 N5, 403
San Remo Vic. 211 M13, 213 R13, 224 E9, 165, 170
Sanctuary Cove Qld 469 D1
Sanctuary Point NSW 141 R1, 119 H5
Sandalwood SA 287 G2, 289 P8
Sanderson NT 388 C2
Sanderston SA 283 P6
Sandfire Roadhouse WA 360 F12
Sandfly Tas. 520 G7, 525 L7
Sandford Tas. 519 R13, 521 J7, 525 M6
Sandford Vic. 226 D4
Sandgate Qld 462 H3, 467 M6
Sandilands SA 282 G4, 288 I7
Sandringham NSW 103 L8
Sandringham Vic. 209 A3, 211 K8
Sandstone WA 356 E2
Sandy Bay Tas. 518 G9, 490
Sandy Creek SA 283 M5, 286 A8
Sandy Creek Con. Park SA 283 M5, 286 B9
Sandy Hollow NSW 120 I3
Sandy Island WA 354 E12
Sandy Point NSW 102 E7
Sandy Point Vic. 224 I11, 176
Sans Souci NSW 103 L8
Santa Teresa NT 391 N6, 397 K9
Sapphire Qld 476 G9, 449
Sapphiretown SA 288 I11
Sarah Island Tas. 487, 500, 509
Sarina Qld 477 J4, **451**
Sarina Beach Qld 477 J4
Sarsfield Vic. 225 P4, 234 F13
Sassafras Tas. 522 G7, 527 J6
Sassafras Vic. 208 G11, 174
Sassafras East Tas. 522 G7, 527 J6

Suggestion Form

This 14th edition of *Explore Australia* is updated from information supplied by consultants, tourist organisations and the general public. We would welcome suggestions from you. Please use the form below to supply us with any information you feel is relevant.

Suggestions for improvement

Text: ....

....

....

Maps: ....

....

....

Suggested amendment or addition

Text

Town Name	Amendment/Addition

Maps

Page no.	Grid	Amendment/Addition

Have you purchased a copy of *Explore Australia* before? ....

If so, what edition? ....

Optional

Name: ....

Address: ....

Please cut out and send to:
   Editorial Manager
   Penguin Cartographic
   A division of Penguin Books Australia Ltd
   487 Maroondah Hwy
   Ringwood Vic. 3134

Accident Action

Those vital first moments

Treating an unconscious person

1. CLEAR AIRWAY
Lie victim on side and tilt head back.

2. CLEAR MOUTH
Quickly clear mouth, using fingers if necessary. If breathing, leave on side.

3. TILT
IF NOT BREATHING, place victim on back. Tilt head back. Support the jaw, keeping fingers away from neck.

4. BLOW
Kneel beside victim's head. Place your widely open mouth over victim's slightly open mouth, sealing nostrils with your cheek. Blow until victim's chest rises.

5. LOOK, LISTEN
Watch chest fall. Listen for air escaping from mouth. Repeat steps 4 and 5, 15 times per minute.

6. RECOVERY POSITION
When breathing begins, place victim on side, head back, jaw supported, face pointing slightly towards ground.

NOTE: For an injured child, cover mouth and nose with your mouth. Blow until chest rises (20 times per minute).

7. IF UNCONSCIOUS
If victim is unconscious and trapped in the car, still tilt head back and support the jaw.

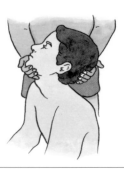

SEND SOMEONE FOR AN AMBULANCE.

DO NOT LEAVE AN UNCONSCIOUS PERSON.